COLLEGES IN THE MIDWEST

2004

19th edition

THOMSON
PETERSON'S™

Australia • Canada • Mexico • Singapore • Spain • United Kingdom • United States

About The Thomson Corporation and Peterson's

The Thomson Corporation, with 2002 revenues of US$7.8 billion, is a global leader in providing integrated information solutions to business and professional customers. The Corporation's common shares are listed on the Toronto and New York stock exchanges (TSX: TOC; NYSE: TOC). Its learning businesses and brands serve the needs of individuals, learning institutions, corporations, and government agencies with products and services for both traditional and distributed learning. Peterson's (www.petersons.com) is a leading provider of education information and advice, with books and online resources focusing on education search, test preparation, and financial aid. Its Web site offers searchable databases and interactive tools for contacting educational institutions, online practice tests and instruction, and planning tools for securing financial aid. Peterson's serves 110 million education consumers annually.

For more information, contact Peterson's, 2000 Lenox Drive, Lawrenceville, NJ 08648; 800-338-3282; or find us on the World Wide Web at www.petersons.com/about.

ISSN 1525-3813
ISBN 0-7689-1136-2

Printed in the United States of America

10 9 8 7 6 5 4 3 2 1 05 04 03

Nineteenth Edition

CONTENTS

A Note from Peterson's Editors

Welcome to the world of college decision making. This guide can be an invaluable tool as you think about college and where to apply. You are probably considering at least one college that is relatively near your home. It may surprise you to learn that the majority of all students go to college within a 300-mile radius of where they live. Because of that factor, we publish this series of college guides that focuses on the colleges in each of six regions of the country so that students can easily compare the colleges in their own area. (Two-year public and proprietary colleges are not included because their admission patterns are significantly different from other colleges).

For advice and guidance in the college search and selection process, just turn the page. "Surviving Standardized Tests" describes the most frequently used test and lists test dates for 2003–04. Of course, part of the college selections process involves visiting the schools themselves and "The Whys and Whats of College Visits" is just the planner you need to make those trips well worth your while. Next, "Applying 101" provides advice on how best to approach the application phase of the process. If you've got questions about transferring, "Successful Transfer" has got the answers you need. "Who's Paying for This? Financial Aid Basics" and the "State Financial Aid Programs" articles provide you with the essential information on how to meet your educational expenses. Lastly, you'll want to read through the "How to Use This Guide" and learn how to use all the information presented in this volume.

Following these articles is the ***College Profiles and Special Messages*** section. The college profiles are easy to read and should give you a good sense of whether a college meets your basic needs and should be considered further. This consistently formatted collection of data can provide a reference balance to the individual mailings you are likely to receive from colleges. The profiles appear in geographical order by state.

In a number of the profiles (those marked with a U.S. map icon), you will find helpful information about social life, academic life, campus visits, and interviews. This extra material was written in each case by a college admissions office staff member. You will find valuable insights into what each writer considers special about his or her institution (both socially and academically), what is expected of you during your interview at that college, and how important the interview is there. You will also be alerted to outstanding attractions on campus or nearby so you can plan a productive visit. In many cases travel information (nearest commercial airport and nearest interstate highway) is included that will be of help on your campus visit.

And if you still thirst for even more information, look for the two-page narrative descriptions appearing in the ***In-Depth Descriptions of Colleges*** sections of the book. These descriptions are written by admissions deans and provide great detail about each college. They are edited to provide a consistent format across entries for your ease of comparison.

The ***Indexes*** at the back of the book (***Majors and Degrees, Athletic Programs and Scholarships,*** and ***ROTC Programs***) enable you to pinpoint colleges listed in the profiles according to their specific offerings. Additionally, there is an ***Alphabetical Listing of Colleges and Universities*** to enable you to quickly find a school that you may have already determined meets your criteria.

We hope you will find this information helpful. Try to remember that admission directors are as interested in you and the possibility of your attending their college as you are in the possibility of applying. They spend most of their time reaching out to students, explaining their colleges' programs and policies, and easing the application process whenever they can. If you think of them as people who like students and if you can picture them taking the time to carefully provide the information in this book for you, it might help to lessen any anxiety you are feeling right now about applying.

Our advice is to relax, enjoy high school, and do as well as you can in your courses. Give yourself enough time during the early stages of your search to think about what kind of person you are and what you want to become so you can choose colleges for the right reasons. Read all college materials with an open mind, and visit as many campuses as you can. Plan ahead so you do not rush through your applications. If you can keep yourself in balance during this process, it need not become the panic period you may have seen some friends go through. We urge you to contact admission staff members at any college in which you are interested. They are all willing to help you. In fact, the admission people whose names you will find in this book hope to hear from you. We at Peterson's wish you success and happiness wherever you enroll.

Surviving Standardized Tests

Don't Forget To . . .

- Take the SAT or ACT Assessment before application deadlines
- Note that test registration deadlines precede test dates by about six weeks
- Register to take the TOEFL test if English is not your native language and you are planning on studying at a North American college.
- Practice your test-taking skills with Peterson's *SAT Success*, *ACT Assessment Success*, and *TOEFL CBT Success*
- Contact the College Board or American College Testing, Inc., in advance if you need special accommodations when taking tests

What Are Standardized Tests?

Colleges and universities in the United States use tests to help evaluate applicants' readiness for admission or to place them in appropriate courses. The tests that are most frequently used by colleges are the ACT Assessment of American College Testing, Inc., and the College Board's SAT. In addition, the Educational Testing Service (ETS) offers the TOEFL test, which evaluates the English-language proficiency of nonnative speakers. The tests are offered at designated testing centers located at high schools and colleges throughout the United States and U.S. territories and at testing centers in various countries throughout the world. The ACT Assessment test and the SAT tests are each taken by more than a million students each year. The TOEFL test is taken by more than 300,000 students each year.

Upon request, special accommodations for students with documented visual, hearing, physical, or learning disabilities are available. Examples of special accommodations include tests in Braille or large print and such aids as a reader, recorder, magnifying glass, or sign language interpreter. Additional testing time may be allowed in some instances. Contact the appropriate testing program or your guidance counselor for details on how to request special accommodations.

College Board SAT Program

The SAT Program consists of the SAT I Reasoning Test and the SAT II Subject Tests. The SAT I is a 3-hour test made up of seven sections, primarily multiple-choice, that measures verbal and mathematical abilities. The three verbal sections test vocabulary, verbal reasoning, and critical reading skills. Emphasis is placed on reading passages, which are 400–850 words in length. Some reading passages are paired; the second opposes, supports, or in some way complements the point of view expressed in the first. The three mathematics sections test a student's ability to solve problems involving arithmetic, algebra, and geometry. They include questions that require students to produce their own responses, in addition to questions that students can choose from four or five answer choices. Calculators may be used on the SAT I mathematics sections.

The SAT II Subject Tests are 1-hour tests, primarily multiple-choice, in specific subjects that measure students' knowledge of these subjects and their ability to apply that knowledge. Some colleges may require or recommend these tests for placement, or even admission. The Subject Tests measure a student's academic achievement in high school and may indicate readiness for certain college programs. Tests offered include Writing, Literature, U.S. History, World History, Mathematics Level IC, Mathematics Level IIC, Biology E/M (Ecological/Molecular), Chemistry, Physics, French, German, Modern Hebrew, Italian, Latin, and Spanish, as well as Foreign Language Tests with Listening in Chinese, French, German, Japanese, Korean, Spanish, and English Language Proficiency (ELPT). The Mathematics Level IC and IIC tests require the use of a scientific calculator.

SAT scores are automatically sent to each student who has taken the test. On average, they are mailed about three weeks after the test. Students may request that the scores be reported to their high schools or to the colleges to which they are applying.

ACT Assessment Program

The ACT Assessment Program is a comprehensive data collection, processing, and reporting service designed to assist in educational and career planning. The ACT Assessment instrument consists of four academic tests, taken under timed conditions, and a Student Profile Section and Interest Inventory, completed when students register for the ACT Assessment.

The academic tests cover four areas—English, mathematics, reading, and science reasoning. The ACT Assessment consists of 215 multiple-choice questions and takes approximately 3 hours and 30 minutes to complete with breaks (testing time is actually 2 hours and 55 minutes). They are designed to assess the student's educational development and readiness to handle college-level work. The minimum standard score is 1, the maximum is 36, and the national average is 21.

The Student Profile Section requests information about each student's admission and enrollment plans, academic and out-of-class high school achievements and aspirations, and high school course work. The student is also asked to supply biographical data and self-reported high school grades in the four subject-matter areas covered by the academic tests.

The ACT Assessment has a number of career planning services, including the ACT Assessment Interest Inventory, which is designed to measure six major dimensions of student interests—administrative and sales, business operations, social service, technical, arts, and science and technology. Results are used to compare the student's interests with those of college-bound students who later majored in each of a wide variety of areas. Inventory results are also used to help students compare their work-activity preferences with work activities that characterize twenty-three "job families."

Because the information resulting from the ACT Assessment Program is used in a variety of educational settings, American College Testing, Inc., prepares three reports for each student: the Student Report, the High School Report, and the College Report. The Student Report normally is sent to the student's high school, except after the June test date, when it is sent directly to the student's home address. The College Report is sent to the colleges the student designates.

Early in the school year, American College Testing, Inc., sends registration packets to high schools across the country that contain all the information a student needs to register for the ACT Assessment. High school guidance offices also receive a supply of *Preparing for the ACT Assessment*, a booklet that contains a complete practice test, an answer key, and general information about preparing for the test.

2003–04 ACT ASSESSMENT AND SAT TEST DATES

ACT Assessment

September 27, 2003*
October 25, 2003
December 13, 2003
February 7, 2004**
April 13, 2004
June 12, 2004

All test dates fall on a Saturday. Tests are also given on the Sundays following the Saturday test dates for students who cannot take the test on Saturday because of religious reasons. The basic ACT Assessment registration fee for 2002–03 was $25 ($28 in Florida and $41 outside of the U.S.).

*The September test is available only in Arizona, California, Florida, Georgia, Illinois, Indiana, Maryland, Nevada, North Carolina, Pennsylvania, South Carolina, Texas, and Washington.

**The February test date is not available in New York.

SAT

October 11, 2003 (SAT I and SAT II)
November 1, 2003 (SAT I, SAT II, and Language Tests with Listening, including ELPT*)
December 6, 2003 (SAT I and SAT II)
January 24, 2004 (SAT I, SAT II, and ELPT)
March 27, 2004 (SAT I only)**
May 1, 2004 (SAT I and SAT II)
June 5, 2004 (SAT I and SAT II)

For the 2002–03 academic year, the basic fee for the SAT I Reasoning Test was $26, which included the $14 basic registration and reporting fee. The basic fee for the SAT II Subject Tests was $12 for the Writing Test, $9 for the Language Tests with Listening, and $7 each for all other Subject Tests. Students can take up to three SAT II Subject Tests on a single date, and a $14 basic registration and reporting fee should be added for each test date. Tests are also given on the Sundays following the Saturday test dates for students who cannot take the test on Saturday because of religious reasons. Fee waivers are available to juniors and seniors who cannot afford test fees.

*Language Tests with Listening (including the English Language Proficiency Test, or ELPT) are only offered on November 1; the ELPT is offered on November 1 and January 24 at some test centers. See the Registration Bulletin for details.

**The March 27 test date is only available in the U.S. and its territories.

Test of English as a Foreign Language (TOEFL)

The TOEFL test is used by various organizations, such as colleges and universities, to determine English proficiency. The test is mainly offered in a computer-based format (TOEFL CBT), although the paper-based test is still offered in some areas. Eventually, the TOEFL will be completely computer-based.

The TOEFL tests students in the areas of listening, structure, reading comprehension, and writing. Score requirements are set by individual institutions. For more information on TOEFL, and to obtain a copy of the Information Bulletin, contact Educational Testing Service.

Peterson's *TOEFL CBT Success* can help you prepare for the exam. The CD version of the book includes a TOEFL practice test and adaptive English skill building exercise. An online CBT test can also be taken for a small fee at Petersons.com.

Contact your secondary school counselor for full information about the SAT and ACT Assessment programs and the TOEFL test.

The Whys and Whats of College Visits

Dawn B. Sova, Ph.D.

The campus visit should not be a passive activity for you and your parents, and you will have to take the initiative and use all of your senses to gather information beyond that provided in the official tour. You will see many important indicators during your visit that will tell you more about the true character of a college and its students than the tour guide will reveal. Know what to look for and how to assess the importance of such indicators.

What Should You Ask and What Should You Look For?

Your first stop on a campus visit is the visitor center or admissions office, where you will probably have to wait to meet with a counselor and undergo the interview. Colleges usually plan to greet visitors later than the appointed time in order to give them the opportunity to review some of the campus information that is liberally scattered throughout the visitor waiting room. Take advantage of the time to become even more familiar with the college by arriving 15 to 30 minutes before your appointment to observe the behavior of staff members and to browse through the yearbooks and student newspapers that will be available.

If you prepare in advance, you will have already reviewed the college catalog and map of the campus. These materials familiarize you with the academic offerings and the physical layout of the campus, but the true character of the college and its students emerges in other ways.

Begin your investigation with the visitor center staff members. As a student's first official contact with the college, they should make every effort to welcome prospective students and to project a friendly image.

- How do they treat you and other prospective students who are waiting? Are they friendly and willing to speak with you, or do they try their hardest to avoid eye contact and conversation?
- Are they friendly with each other and with students who enter the office, or are they curt and unwilling to help?
- Does the waiting room have a friendly feeling or is it cold and sterile?

If the visitor center staff members seem indifferent to *prospective* students, there is little reason to believe that they will be warm and welcoming to current students. View such behavior as a warning to watch very carefully the interaction of others with you during the tour. An indifferent or unfriendly reception in the admissions office may be simply the first of many signs that attending this college will not be a pleasant experience.

Look through several yearbooks and see the types of activities that are actually photographed, as opposed to the activities that colleges promise in their promotional literature. Some questions are impossible to answer if the college is very large, but for small and moderately sized colleges the yearbook is a good indicator of campus activity.

- Has the number of clubs and organizations increased or decreased in the past five years?
- Do the same students appear repeatedly in activities?
- Do sororities and fraternities dominate campus activities?
- Are participants limited to one sex or one ethnic group or are the participants diverse?
- Are all activities limited to the campus, or are students involved in activities in the community?

Use what you observe in the yearbooks as a means of forming a more complete understanding of the college, but don't base your entire impression on just one facet. If time permits, look through several copies of the school newspaper, which should reflect the major concerns and interests of the students. The paper is also a good way to learn about the campus social life.

- Does the paper contain a mix of national and local news?
- What products or services are advertised?
- How assertive are the editorials?
- With what topics are the columnists concerned?
- Are movies and concerts that meet your tastes advertised or reviewed?
- What types of ads appear in the classified section?

The newspaper should be a public forum for students, and, as such, should reflect the character of the campus and of the student body. A paper that deals only with seemingly safe and well-edited topics on the editorial page and in regular feature columns might indicate administrative censorship. A lack of ads for restaurants might indicate either a lack of good places to eat or that area restaurants do not welcome student business. A limited mention of movies, concerts, or other entertainment might reveal a severely limited campus social life. Even if ads and reviews are included, you can also learn a lot about how such activities reflect your tastes.

You will have only a limited amount of time to ask questions during your initial meeting with the admissions counselor, for very few schools include a formal interview in the initial campus visit or tour. Instead, this brief meeting is often just a social nicety that allows the admissions office to begin a file for the student and to record some initial impressions. Save your questions for the tour guide and for campus members that you meet along the way.

How Can You Assess the True Character of a College and Its Students?

Colleges do not train their tour guides to deceive prospective students, but they do caution guides to avoid unflattering topics and campus sites. Does this mean that you are condemned to see only a sugarcoated version of life on a particular college campus? Not at all, especially not if you are observant.

Most organized campus visits include such campus facilities as dormitories, dining halls, libraries, student activity and recreation centers, and the health and student services centers. Some may only be pointed out, while you will walk through others. Either way, you will find that many signs of the true character of the college emerge if you are observant.

Bulletin boards in dormitories and student centers contain a wealth of information about campus activities, student concerns, and campus groups. Read the posters, notices, and messages to learn what *really* interests students. Unlike ads in the school newspaper, posters put up by students advertise both on- and off-campus events, so they will give you an idea of what is also available in the surrounding community.

Review the notices, which may cover either campuswide events or events that concern only small groups of students. The catalog may not mention a performance group, but an individual dormitory with its own small theater may offer regular productions. Poetry readings, jam sessions, writers' groups, and other activities may be announced and show diversity of student interests on that campus.

Even the brief bulletin board messages offering objects for sale and noting objects that people want to purchase reveal a lot about a campus. Are most of the items computer related? Or do the messages specify compact discs, audio equipment, or musical instruments? Are offers to barter goods or services posted? Don't ignore the "ride wanted" messages. Students who want to share rides home during a break may specify widely diverse geographical locations. If so, then you know that the student body is not limited to only the immediate area or one locale. Other messages can also enhance your knowledge of the true character of the campus and its students.

As you walk through various buildings, examine their condition carefully.

- Is the paint peeling, and do the exteriors look worn?
- Are the exteriors and interiors of the building clean?
- Do they look well maintained?
- Is the equipment in the classrooms up-to-date or outdated?

Pay particular attention to the dormitories, especially to factors that might affect your safety. Observe the appearance of the structure, and ask about the security measures in and around the dormitories.

- Are the dormitories noisy or quiet?
- Do they seem crowded?
- How good is the lighting around each dormitory?
- Are the dormitories spread throughout the campus or are they clustered in one main area?
- Who has access to the dormitories in addition to students?
- How secure are the means by which students enter and leave the dormitory?

While you are on the subject of dormitory safety, you should also ask about campus safety. Don't expect that the guide will rattle off a list of crimes that have been committed in the past year. To obtain that information, access the recent year of issues of *The Chronicle of Higher Education* and locate its yearly report on campus crime. Also ask the guide about safety measures that the campus police take and those that students have initiated.

- Can students request escorts to their residences late at night?
- Do campus shuttle buses run at frequent intervals all night?
- Are "blue-light" telephones liberally placed throughout the campus for students to use to call for help?
- Do the campus police patrol the campus regularly?

If the guide does not answer your questions satisfactorily, wait until after the tour to contact the campus police or traffic office for answers.

Campus tours usually just point out the health services center without taking the time to walk through. Even if you don't see the inside of the building, you should take a close look at the location of the health services center and ask the guide questions about services.

- How far is the health center from the dormitories?
- Is a doctor always on call?
- Does the campus transport sick students from their dormitories or must they walk?
- What are the operating hours of the health center?
- Does the health center refer students to the town hospital?

If the guide can't answer your questions, visit the health center later and ask someone there.

Most campus tours seem to take pride in showing students their activities centers, which may contain snack bars, game rooms, workout facilities, and other means of entertainment. Should you scrutinize this building as carefully as the rest? Of course. Outdated and poorly maintained activity equipment contributes to your total impression of the college. You should also ask about the hours, availability, and cost (no, the activities are usually *not* free) of using the bowling alleys, pool tables, air hockey tables, and other items.

As you walk through campus with the tour, also look carefully at the appearance of the students who pass. The way in which both men and women groom themselves, the way they dress, and even their physical bearing communicate a lot more than any guidebook can. If everyone seems to conform to the same look, you might feel that you would be uncomfortable at the college, however nonconformist that look might be. On the other hand, you might not feel comfortable on a campus that stresses diversity of dress and behavior, and your observations now can save you discomfort later.

- Does every student seem to wear a sorority or fraternity t-shirt or jacket?
- Is everyone of your sex sporting the latest fad haircut?
- Do all of the men or the women seem to be wearing expensive name-brand clothes?
- Do most of the students seem to be working hard to look outrageous in regard to clothing, hair color, and body art?
- Would you feel uncomfortable in a room full of these students?

Is appearance important to you? If it is, then you should consider very seriously if you answer *yes* to any of the above questions. You don't have to be the same as everyone else on campus, but standing out too rigorously may make you unhappy.

As you observe the physical appearance of the students, also listen to their conversations as you pass them? What are they talking about? How are they speaking? Are their voices and accents all the same, or do you hear diversity in their speech? Are you offended by their language? Think how you will feel if surrounded by the same speech habits and patterns for four years.

Where Should You Visit on Your Own?

Your campus visit is not over when the tour ends because you will probably have many questions yet to be answered and many places to still be seen. Where you go depends upon the extent to which the organized tour covers the campus. Your tour should take you to view residential halls, health and student services centers, the gymnasium or field house, dining halls, the library, and recreational centers. If any of the facilities on this list have been omitted, visit them on your own and ask questions of the students and staff members you meet. In addition, you should step off campus and gain an impression of the surrounding community. You will probably become bored with life on campus and spend at least some time off campus. Make certain that you know what the surrounding area is like.

The campus tour leaves little time to ask impromptu questions of current students, but you can do so after the tour. Eat lunch in one of the dining halls. Most will allow visitors to pay cash to experience a typical student meal. Food may not be important to you now while you are living at home and can simply take anything you want from the refrigerator at any time, but it will be when you are away at college with only a meal ticket to feed you.

- How clean is the dining hall? Consider serving tables, floors, and seating.
- What is the quality of the food?
- How big are the portions?
- How much variety do students have at each meal?
- How healthy are the food choices?

While you are eating, try to strike up a conversation with students and tell them that you are considering attending their college. Their reactions and advice can be eye-opening. Ask them questions about the academic atmosphere and the professors.

- Are the classes large or small?

- Do the majority of the professors only lecture or are tutorials and seminars common?
- Is the emphasis of the faculty career-oriented or abstract?
- Do they find the teaching methods innovative and stimulating or boring and dull?
- Is the academic atmosphere pressured, lax, or somewhere in between?
- Which are the strong majors? The weak majors?
- Is the emphasis on grades or social life or a mix of both at the college?
- How hard do students have to work to receive high grades?

Current students can also give you the inside line on the true nature of the college social life. You may gain some idea through looking in the yearbook, in the newspaper, and on the bulletin boards, but students will reveal the true highs and lows of campus life. Ask them about drug use, partying, dating rituals, drinking, and anything else that may affect your life as a student.

- Which are the most popular club activities?
- What do students do on weekends? Do most go home?
- How frequently do concerts occur on campus? Ask them to name groups that have recently performed.
- How can you become involved in specific activities (name them)?
- How strictly are campus rules enforced and how severe are penalties?
- What counseling services are available?
- Are academic tutoring services available?
- Do they feel that the faculty really cares about students, especially freshmen?

You will receive the most valuable information from current students, but you will only be able to speak with them after the tour is over. And you might have to risk rejection as you try to initiate conversations with students who might not want to reveal how they feel about the campus. Still, the value of this information in making the right decision is worth the chance.

If you have the time, you should also visit the library to see just how accessible research materials are and to observe the physical layout. The catalog usually specifies the days and hours of operation, as well as the number of volumes contained in the library and the number of periodicals to which it subscribes. A library also requires accessibility, good lighting, an adequate number of study carrels, and lounge areas for students. Many colleges have created 24-hour study lounges for students who find the residence halls too noisy for studying, although most colleges claim that they designate areas of the residences as "quiet study" areas. You may not be interested in any of this information, but when you are a student you will have to make frequent use of the campus library so you should know what is available. You should at least ask how extensive their holdings are in your proposed major area. If they have virtually nothing, you will have to spend a lot of time ordering items via interlibrary loan or making copies, which can become expensive. The ready answer of students that they will obtain their information from the Internet is unpleasantly countered by professors who demand journal articles with documentation.

Make a point of at least driving through the community surrounding the college, because you will be spending time there shopping, dining, working in a part-time job, or attending events. Even the largest and best-stocked campus will not meet all of your social and personal needs. If you can spare the time, stop in several stores to see if they welcome college students.

- Is the surrounding community suburban, urban, or rural?
- Does the community offer stores of interest, such as bookstores, craft shops, boutiques?
- Do the businesses employ college students?
- Does the community have a movie or stage theater?
- Are there several types of interesting restaurants?
- Do there seem to be any clubs that court a college clientele?
- Is the center of activity easy to walk to, or do you need a car or other transportation?

You might feel that a day is not enough to answer all of your questions, but even answering some questions will provide you with a stronger basis for choosing a college. Many students visit a college campus several times before making their decision, as you also should. Keep in mind that for the rest of your life you will be associated with the college that you attend. You will spend four years of your life at this college. The effort of spending several days to obtain the information to make your decision is worthwhile.

Dawn B. Sova, Ph.D., is a former newspaper reporter and columnist, as well as the author of more than eight books and numerous magazine articles. She teaches creative and research writing, as well as scientific and technical writing, newswriting, and journalism.

Applying 101

The words "applying yourself" have several important meanings in the college application process. One meaning refers to the fact that you need to keep focused during this important time in your life, keep your priorities straight, and know the dates that your applications are due so you can apply on time. The phrase might also refer to the person who is really responsible for your application—you.

You are the only person who should compile your college application. You need to take ownership of this process. The intervention of others should be for advisement only. The guidance counselor is not responsible for completing your applications, and your parents shouldn't be typing them. College applications must be completed in addition to your normal workload at school, college visits, and SAT, ACT Assessment, or possibly, TOEFL testing.

Standardized Tests

In all likelihood, you will take the SAT I, the ACT Assessment, or both tests sometime during your junior year of high school and, perhaps, again in your senior year if you are trying to improve your scores. If your native language is not English, you may also have to take the TOEFL test.

The Application

The application is your way of introducing yourself to a college admissions office. As with any introduction, you should try to make a good first impression. The first thing you should do in presenting your application is to find out what the college or university needs from you. Read the application carefully to find out the application fee and deadline, required standardized tests, number of essays, interview requirements, and anything else you can do or submit to help improve your chances for acceptance.

Completing college applications yourself helps you learn more about the schools to which you are applying. The information a college asks for in its application can tell you much about the school. State university applications often tell you how they are going to view their applicants. Usually, they select students based on GPAs and test scores. Colleges that request an interview, ask you to respond to a few open-ended questions, or require an essay are interested in a more personal approach to the application process and may be looking for different types of students than those sought by a state school.

In addition to submitting the actual application, there are several other items that are commonly required. You will be responsible for ensuring that your standardized test scores and your high school transcript arrive at the colleges to which you apply. Most colleges will ask that you submit teacher recommendations as well. Select teachers who know you and your abilities well and allow them plenty of time to complete the recommendations. When all portions of the application have been completed and sent in, whether electronically or by mail, make sure you follow up with the college to ensure their receipt.

The Application Essay

Some colleges may request one essay or a combination of essays and short-answer topics to learn more about who you are and how well you can communicate your thoughts. Common essay topics cover such simple themes as writing about yourself and your experiences or why you want to attend that particular school. Other colleges will ask that you show your imaginative or creative side by writing about a favorite author, for instance, or commenting on a hypothetical situation. In such cases, they will be looking at your thought processes and your level of creativity.

Whereas the other portions of your application—your transcript, test scores, and involvement in extracurricular activities—are a reflection of what you've accomplished up to this point, your application essay is an opportunity to present yourself in the here and now. The essay shows your originality and verbal skills and is very important. Test scores and grades may represent your academic results, but your essay shows how you approach a topic or problem and express your opinion.

Admissions officers, particularly those at small or midsize colleges, use the essay to determine how you, as a student, will fit into life at that college. The essay, therefore, is a critical component of the application process. Here are some tips for writing a winning essay:

- Colleges are looking for an honest representation of who you are and what you think. Make sure that the

FOLLOW THESE TIPS WHEN FILLING OUT YOUR APPLICATION:

- **Follow the directions to the letter.** You don't want to be in a position to ask an admissions officer for exceptions due to your inattentiveness.
- **Make a photocopy** of the application and work through a rough draft before you actually fill out the application copy to be submitted.
- **Proofread all parts of your application,** including your essay. Again, the final product indicates to the admissions staff how meticulous and careful you are in your work.
- **Submit your application as early as possible,** provided all of the pieces are available. If there is a problem with your application, this will allow you to work through it with the admissions staff in plenty of time. If you wait until the last minute, it not only takes away that cushion but also reflects poorly on your sense of priorities.

tone of the essay reflects enthusiasm, maturity, creativity, the ability to communicate, talent, and your leadership skills.

- Be sure you set aside enough time to write the essay, revise it, and revise it *again.* Running the "spell check" feature on your computer will only detect a fraction of the errors you probably made on your first pass at writing it. Take a break and then come back to it and reread it. You will probably notice other style, content, and grammar problems—and ways that you can improve the essay overall.
- Always answer the question that is being asked, making sure that you are specific, clear, and true to your personality.
- Enlist the help of reviewers who know you well—friends, parents, teachers—since they are likely to be the most honest and will keep you on track in the presentation of your true self.

The Personal Interview

Although it is relatively rare that a personal interview is required, many colleges recommend that you take this opportunity for a face-to-face discussion with a member of the admissions staff. Read through the application materials to determine whether or not a college places great emphasis on the interview. If they strongly recommend that you have one, it may work against you to forego it.

In contrast to a group interview and some alumni interviews, which are intended to provide information about a college, the personal interview is viewed both as an information session and as further evaluation of your skills and strengths. You will meet with a member of the admissions staff who will be assessing your personal qualities, high school preparation, and your capacity to contribute to undergraduate life at the institution. On average, these meetings last about 45 minutes—a relatively short amount of time in which to gather information and leave the desired impression—so here are some suggestions on how to make the most of it.

Scheduling Your Visit. Generally, students choose to visit campuses in the summer or fall of their senior year. Both times have their advantages. A summer visit, when the campus is not in session, generally allows for a less hectic visit and interview. Visiting in the fall, on the other hand, provides the opportunity to see what campus life is like in full swing. If you choose the fall, consider arranging an overnight trip so that you can stay in one of the college dormitories. At the very least, you should make your way around campus to take part in classes, athletic events, and social activities. Always make an appointment and avoid scheduling more than two college interviews on any given day. Multiple interviews in a single day hinder your chances of making a good impression, and your impressions of the colleges will blur into each other as you hurriedly make your way from place to place.

Preparation. Know the basics about the college before going for your interview. Read the college viewbook or catalog in addition to this guide. You will be better prepared to ask questions that are not answered in the literature and that will give you a better understanding of what the college has to offer. You should also spend some time thinking about your strengths and weaknesses and, in particular, what you are looking for in a college education. You will find that as you get a few interviews under your belt, they will get easier. You might consider starting with a college that is not a top contender on your list, where the stakes are not as high.

Asking Questions. Inevitably, your interviewer will ask you, "Do you have any questions?" Not having one may suggest that you're unprepared or, even worse, not interested. When you do ask questions, make sure that they are ones that matter to you and that have a bearing on your decision about whether or not to attend. The questions that you ask will give the interviewer some insight into your personality and priorities. Avoid asking questions that can be answered in the college literature—again, a sign of unpreparedness.

Although the interviewer will undoubtedly pose questions to you, the interview should not be viewed merely as a question-and-answer session. If a conversation evolves out of a particular question, so much the better. Your interviewer can learn a great deal about you from how you sustain a conversation. Similarly, you will be able to learn a great deal about the college in a conversational format.

Separate the Interview from the Interviewer. Many students base their feelings about a college solely on their impressions of the interviewer. Try not to characterize a college based only on your personal reaction, however, since your impressions can be skewed by whether you and your interviewer hit it off. Pay lots of attention to everything else that you see, hear, and learn about a college. Once on campus, you may never see your interviewer again.

In the end, remember to relax and be yourself. Don't drink jitters-producing caffeinated beverages prior to the interview, and suppress nervous fidgets like leg-wagging, finger-drumming, or bracelet-jangling. Your interviewer will expect you to be somewhat nervous, which will relieve some of the pressure. Consider this an opportunity to put forth your best effort and to enhance everything that the college knows about you up to this point.

The Final Decision

Once you have received your acceptance letters, it is time to go back and look at the whole picture. Provided you received more than one acceptance, you are now in a position to compare your options. The best way to do this is to compare your original list of important college-ranking criteria with what you've discovered about each college along the way. In addition, you and your family will need to factor in the financial aid component. You will need to look beyond these cost issues and the quantifiable pros and cons of each college, however, and know that you have a good feeling about your final choice. Before sending off your acceptance letter, you need to feel confident that the college will feel like home for the next four years. Once the choice is made, the only hard part will be waiting for an entire summer before heading off to college!

Successful Transfer

Adrienne Aaron Rulnick

Transfer students need and deserve detailed and accurate information but often lack direction as to where it can be obtained. Few general college guides offer information about transfer deadlines and required minimum grade point averages for transfer admission. College catalogs are not always clear about the specific requirements and procedures for transfer students who may be confused about whether they need to present high school records, SAT I or ACT Assessment scores, or a guidance counselor's recommendation, particularly if they have been out of high school for several years. Transfer advisers are not available to those enrolled at a baccalaureate institution; at community and junior colleges, the transfer advising function may be performed by a designated transfer counselor or by a variety of college advisers who are less clearly identified.

The challenge for transfer students is to determine what they need to know in order to make good, informed decisions and identify the individuals and resources that can provide that information. An organized research process is very much at the heart of a successful transfer.

How to Begin

Perhaps the most important first step in this process is one of self-analysis. Adopting a consumer approach is appropriate—higher education is a formidable purchase, no matter how it is financed. The reputation of the college from which you obtain your degree may open doors to future jobs and careers; friendships and contacts you make at college can provide a significant network for lifelong social and professional relationships. The environment of a transfer school may be the perfect opportunity for you to test out urban living or the joys of country life, explore a different area of the country, experience college residential living for the first time, or move out of the family nest into your first apartment. Like any major purchase in your life, there are costs and benefits to be weighed. Trade-offs include cost, distance, rigor of academic work, extra time in school required by a cooperative education program, and specific requirements, such as foreign language competence at a liberal arts institution or courses in religion at an institution with a denominational affiliation.

Use Experience as a Guide

The wise consumer reflects on his or her own experience with a product (i.e., your initial college or colleges) and then seeks out people who have firsthand experience with the new product being considered. Talk to friends and family members who have attended the colleges you are considering; ask college faculty members you know to tell you about the colleges they attended and how they view these schools. Talk to people engaged in the careers you are considering: what are their impressions of the best programs and schools in their field? Make sure you sample a variety of opinions, but beware of dated experiences. An engineering department considered top-notch when Uncle Joe attended college twenty years ago might be very different today!

The Nitty-Gritty

Once your list is reduced to a manageable number of schools, usually fewer than ten, it is important to identify academic requirements, requisite grade point averages for admission, and deadline dates. Most schools admit for both the fall and spring semesters; those on a trimester system may have winter and summer admissions as well. Some schools have rolling admission policies and will process applications as they are received; others, particularly the more selective colleges, have firm deadlines because their admission process involves a committee review, and decisions are made on a competitive basis. It is helpful to know how many transfer students are typically accepted for the semester you wish to begin, whether the minimum grade point average is indicative of the actual average of accepted students (this can vary widely), and whether the major you are seeking has special prerequisites and admission procedures. For example, fine arts programs usually require portfolios or auditions. For engineering, computer science, and some business majors, there are specific requirements in mathematics that must be met before a student is considered for admission. Many specialized health-care programs, including nursing, may only admit once a year. Some schools have different standards for sophomore and junior transfers or for in-state and out-of-state students.

Other criteria that you should identify include whether college housing and financial aid are available for transfer students. Some colleges have special transfer scholarships that require separate applications and references, while others simply award aid based on applications that indicate a high grade point average or membership in a nationally recognized junior and community college honor society, such as Phi Theta Kappa. There are also scholarships for transfer students who demonstrate accomplishment in specified academic and performance areas; the latter may be based on talent competitions or accomplishment evidenced in a portfolio or audition.

Nontraditional Students

For the nontraditional student, usually defined as anyone beyond the traditional college age of 18 to 23, there may be additional aspects to investigate. Some colleges award credit based on demonstrated life experience; many colleges grant credit for qualifying scores on the CLEP exams or for participation in the DANTES program. Experience in industry may yield college credit as well. If you are ready and able to pursue further college work but are not in a position to attend regular classes at a senior college, there are a variety of distance learning options at fully accredited colleges. Other colleges provide specialized support services for nontraditional students and may allow students the opportunity to attend part-time if they have family and work responsibilities. In some cases, usually at large universities, there may be married student housing or family housing available. More and more schools have established daycare facilities, although the waiting lists are often very long.

Applying

Once you have identified the schools that meet the needs you have established as priorities, it is time to begin the application process. Make sure you observe all the indicated deadlines: it never hurts to have everything in early, as there are consequences, such as closed-out majors and the loss of housing and financial aid, if you submit your application late. Make appointments with faculty members and others who are providing references; make sure they understand what is required of them and when and where their references must be sent. It is your responsibility to follow through to make sure all of your credentials are received, including transcripts from all colleges previously attended, even if you only took one summer course or attended for less than a semester. If you have not yet had the opportunity to visit the schools to which you are applying, now is the time to do so. Arrange interviews wherever possible, and make sure to include a tour of the campus and visits to the department and career offices to gain a picture of the facilities and future opportunities. If you have questions about financial aid, schedule an appointment in the financial aid office, and make sure you are aware of all the deadlines and requirements and any scholarship opportunities for which you are eligible.

Making Your Choice

Congratulations! You have been accepted at the colleges of your choice. Now what? Carefully review the acceptance of your previous college credit and how it has been applied. You are entitled to know how many transfer credits you have received and your expected date of graduation. Compare financial aid packages and housing options. The best choice should emerge from this review process. Then, send a note to the schools you will not be attending. Acknowledge your acceptance, but indicate that you have chosen to attend elsewhere. Carefully read everything you have received from the college of your choice. Return required deposits within the deadline, reserve time to attend transfer orientation, arrange to have your final transcript sent from the college you currently attend, and review the financial picture. This is the time to finalize college loan applications and make sure you are in a position to meet all the costs entailed at this college. Don't forget to include the costs of travel and housing.

You've done it! While many transfer students reflect on how much work was involved in the transfer admission process, those who took the time to follow all of the steps outlined above report a sense of satisfaction with their choices and increased confidence in themselves. We wish you an equally rewarding experience.

Adrienne Aaron Rulnick is a Transfer Counselor at Berkshire Community College.

Who's Paying for This? Financial Aid Basics

A college education can be expensive—costing more than $100,000 for four years at some of the higher-priced private colleges and universities. Even at the lower-cost state colleges and universities, the cost of a four-year education can approach $50,000. Determining how you and your family will come up with the necessary funds to pay for your education requires planning, perseverance, and learning as much as you can about the options that are available to you.

Paying for college should not be looked on as a four-year financial commitment. For most families, paying the total cost of a student's college education out of current savings is usually not realistic. For families that have planned ahead and have financial savings established for higher education, the burden is a lot easier. But for most, meeting the cost of college requires the pooling of current income and assets and investing in longer-term loan options. These family resources, together with possible financial assistance from the state, federal, and institutional resources enable millions of students each year to attend the institution of their choice.

How Need-Based Financial Aid Is Awarded

When you apply for aid, your family's financial situation is analyzed using a government-approved formula called the Federal Methodology. This formula looks at five items:

1. Demographic information of the family.
2. Income of the parents.
3. Assets of the parents.
4. Income of the student.
5. Assets of the student.

This analysis determines the amount you and your family are expected to contribute toward your college expenses, called your Expected Family Contribution or EFC. If the EFC is equal to or more than the cost at a particular college, then you do not demonstrate financial need. However, even if you don't have financial need, you may still qualify for aid, as there are grants, scholarships, and loan programs that are not need-based.

If the cost of your education is greater than your EFC, then you do demonstrate financial need and qualify for assistance. The amount of your financial need that can be met varies from school to school. Some are able to meet your full need, while others can only cover a certain percentage of need. Here's the formula:

Cost of Attendance
– Expected Family Contribution
= Financial Need

The EFC remains constant, but your need will vary according to the costs of attendance at a particular college. In general, the higher the tuition and fees at a particular college, the higher the cost of attendance will be. Expenses for books and supplies, room and board, and other miscellaneous costs are included in the overall cost of attendance. It is important to remember that you do not have to be "needy" to qualify for financial aid. Many middle- and upper-middle-income families qualify for need-based financial aid.

Sources of Financial Aid

The largest single source of aid is the federal government, which awards almost $74 billion to more than 8½ million students each year.

The next largest source of financial aid is found in the college and university community. Institutions award an estimated $8 billion to students each year. Most of this aid is awarded to students who have a demonstrated need based on the Federal Methodology. Some institutions use a different formula, the Institutional Methodology, to award their own funds in conjunction with other forms of aid. Institutional aid may be either need-based or non-need-based. Aid that is not based on need is usually awarded for a student's academic performance (merit awards), specific talents or abilities, or to attract the type of students a college seeks to enroll.

Another source of financial aid is state government. All states offer grant and/or scholarship aid, most of which is need-based. However, more and more states are offering substantial merit-based aid programs. Most state programs award aid only to students attending college in their home state.

Other sources of financial aid include:

- Private agencies
- Foundations
- Corporations
- Clubs
- Fraternal and service organizations
- Civic associations
- Unions
- Religious groups that award grants, scholarships, and low-interest loans
- Employers that provide tuition reimbursement benefits for employees and their children

More information about these different sources of aid is available from high school guidance offices, public libraries, college financial aid offices, and directly from the sponsoring organizations.

Applying for Financial Aid

Every student must complete the Free Application for Federal Student Aid (FAFSA) to be considered for financial aid. The FAFSA is available from your high school guidance office, many public libraries, colleges in your area, or directly from the U.S. Department of Education.

Students also can apply for federal student aid over the Internet using the interactive FAFSA on the Web. FAFSA on the Web can be accessed at www.fafsa.ed.gov. Both the student and at least one parent must apply for a federal pin number at www.pin.ed.gov. The pin number serves as your electronic signature when applying for aid on the Web.

To award their own funds, some colleges require an additional application, the Financial Aid PROFILE® form. The PROFILE® asks additional questions that some colleges and awarding agencies feel provide a more accurate assessment of the family's ability to pay for college. It is up to the college to decide whether it will use only the FAFSA or both the FAFSA and the PROFILE®. PROFILE® applications are available from the high school guidance office and on the Web. Both the paper application and the Web site list those colleges and programs that require the PROFILE® application.

If Every College You're Applying to for Fall 2004 Requires Just the FAFSA

. . . then it's pretty simple: Complete the FAFSA after January 1, 2004, being certain to send it in before any college-imposed deadlines. (You are not permitted to send in the 2004-05 FAFSA before January 1, 2004.) Most college FAFSA application deadlines are in February or early March. It is easier if you have all your financial records for the previous year available, but if that is not possible, you are strongly encouraged to use estimated numbers.

After you send in your FAFSA, either with the paper application or electronically, you'll receive a Student Aid Report (SAR) in the mail that includes all of the information you reported and shows your EFC. Be sure to review the SAR, checking to see if the information you reported is accurate. If you used estimated numbers to complete the FAFSA, you may have to resubmit the SAR with any corrections to the data. The college(s) you have designated on the FAFSA will receive the information you reported and will use that data to make their decision. In many instances, the colleges you've applied to will ask you to send copies of your and your parents' income tax returns for 2003, plus any other documents needed to verify the information you reported. The SAR will be sent electronically if you used FAFSA on the Web; otherwise, you will receive a paper copy in the mail.

If a College Requires the PROFILE®

Step 1: Register for the Financial Aid PROFILE® in the fall of your senior year in high school.

Registering for the Financial Aid PROFILE® begins the financial aid process. You can register by calling the College Scholarship Service at 1-800-778-6888 and providing basic demographic information, a list of colleges to which you are applying, and your credit card number to pay for the service. You can also apply for the PROFILE® online at http://profileonline.collegeboard.com/index.jsp. Registration packets with a list of the colleges that require the PROFILE® are available in most high school guidance offices. There is a fee for using the Financial Aid PROFILE® application ($22 for the first college and $16 for each additional college). You must pay for the service by credit card when you register. If you do not have a credit card, you will be billed.

Step 2: Fill out your customized Financial Aid PROFILE®.

A few weeks after you register, you'll receive in the mail a customized financial aid application that you can use to apply for institutional aid at the colleges you've designated as well as from some private scholarship programs, like the National Merit Scholarship. (Note: If you've waited until winter and a college's financial aid application deadline is approaching, you can get overnight delivery by paying an extra fee.) The PROFILE® contains all the questions necessary to calculate your "institutional" EFC, plus the questions that the colleges and organizations you've designated require you to answer. Your individualized packet will also contain a customized cover letter instructing you what to do and informing you about deadlines and requirements for the colleges and programs you designated when you registered for the PROFILE®, codes that indicate which colleges wanted which additional questions, and supplemental forms (if any of the colleges to which you are applying require them—e.g., the Business/Farm Supplement for students whose parents own a business or farm or the Divorced/Separated Parents' Statement).

Make sure you submit your PROFILE® by the earliest deadline listed. Two to four weeks after you do so, you will receive an acknowledgment and a report estimating your "institutional" EFC based on the data elements you provided in your PROFILE®. Remember, this is a different formula from the federal system that uses the FAFSA.

Financial Aid Programs

There are three types of financial aid:

1. Gift-aid (including scholarships and grants)—Scholarships and grants are funds that do not have to be repaid.
2. Loans—Loans must be repaid, usually after graduation; the amount you have to pay back is the total you've borrowed plus any accrued interest. This is considered a source of self-help aid.
3. Student employment—Student employment is a job arranged for you by the financial aid office. This is another source of self-help aid.

The federal government has two major grant programs—the Federal Pell Grant and the Federal Supplemental Educational Opportunity Grant. These grants are targeted to low- to moderate-income families with significant financial need. The federal government also sponsors a student employment program called Federal Work-Study, which offers jobs both on and off campus; and several loan programs, including those for students and for parents of undergraduate students.

There are two types of student loan programs, subsidized and unsubsidized. The Subsidized Stafford Loan and the Federal Perkins Loan are need-based, government-subsidized loans. Students who borrow through these programs do not have to pay interest on the loan until after they graduate or leave school. The Unsubsidized Stafford Loan and the parent loan programs are not based on need, and borrowers are responsible for the interest while the student is in school. There are different methods on how these loans are administered. Once you choose your college, the financial aid office will guide you through this process.

After you've submitted your financial aid application and you've been accepted for admission, each college will send you a letter describing your financial aid award. Most award letters show estimated college costs, how much you and your family are expected to contribute, and the amount and types of aid you have been awarded. Most students are awarded aid from a combination of sources and programs. Hence, your award is often called a financial aid "package."

If You Don't Qualify for Need-Based Aid

If you are not eligible for need-based aid, you can still find ways to lessen the burden on your parents.

Here are some suggestions:

- Search for merit scholarships. You can start at the initial stages of your application process. College merit awards are becoming increasingly important as more and more colleges award these grants to students they especially want to attract. As a result, applying to a college at which your qualifications put you at the top of the entering class may give you a larger merit award. Another source of aid to look for is private scholarships that are given for special skills and talents. Additional information can be found at www.petersons.com and at www.finaid.com.
- Seek employment during the summer and the academic year. The student employment office at your college can help you locate a school-year job. Many colleges and local businesses have vacancies remaining after they have hired students who are receiving federal work-study financial aid.
- Borrow through the Unsubsidized Stafford Loan programs. These are open to all students. The terms and conditions are similar to the subsidized loans. The biggest difference is that the borrower is responsible for the interest while still in college, although most lenders permit students to delay paying the interest right away and add the accrued interest to the total amount owed. You must file the FAFSA to be considered.
- After you've contributed what you can through scholarships, working, and borrowing, your parents will be expected to meet their share of the college bill (the Expected Family Contribution). Many colleges offer monthly payment plans that spread the cost over the academic year. If the monthly payments are too high, parents can borrow through the Federal Parent Loan for Undergraduate Students (PLUS), through one of the many private education loan programs available, or through home equity loans and lines of credit. Families seeking assistance in financing college expenses should inquire at the financial aid office about what programs are available at the college. Some families seek the advice of professional financial advisers and tax consultants.

How Is Your Family Contribution Calculated?

The chart below makes the following assumptions:

- two-parent family where age of older parent is 45
- lower-income families will file the 1040A or 1040EZ tax form
- student income is less than $2300
- there are no student assets
- there is only one family member in college

All figures are estimates and may vary when the complete FAFSA or PROFILE® application is submitted.

Approximate Expected Family Contribution

ASSETS	FAMILY SIZE	INCOME BEFORE TAXES $ 20,000	30,000	40,000	50,000	60,000	70,000	80,000	90,000	100,000
$ 20,000										
	3	$ 0	950	2,550	4,500	7,300	10,100	12,800	18,300	21,300
	4	0	160	1,750	3,450	5,800	8,600	11,350	16,800	19,800
	5	0	0	1,000	2,600	4,600	7,200	10,000	15,400	18,500
	6	0	0	200	1,800	3,500	5,700	8,400	13,800	16,900
$ 30,000										
	3	$ 0	950	2,550	4,500	7,300	10,100	12,800	18,300	21,300
	4	0	160	1,750	3,450	5,800	8,600	11,350	16,800	19,800
	5	0	0	1,000	2,600	4,600	7,200	10,000	15,400	18,500
	6	0	0	200	1,800	3,500	5,700	8,400	13,800	16,900
$ 40,000										
	3	$ 0	950	2,550	4,500	7,300	10,100	12,800	18,300	21,300
	4	0	160	1,750	3,450	5,800	8,600	11,350	16,800	19,800
	5	0	0	1,000	2,600	4,600	7,200	10,000	15,400	18,500
	6	0	0	200	1,800	3,500	5,700	8,400	13,800	16,900
$ 50,000										
	3	$ 0	950	2,550	4,800	7,700	10,500	13,300	18,700	21,800
	4	0	160	1,750	3,700	6,200	9,000	11,800	17,200	20,300
	5	0	0	1,000	2,800	4,900	7,600	10,400	15,800	18,900
	6	0	0	200	2,000	3,800	6,100	8,800	14,200	17,300
$ 60,000										
	3	$ 0	950	2,550	5,200	8,300	11,100	13,800	19,300	22,300
	4	0	160	1,750	4,100	6,700	9,600	12,400	17,800	20,900
	5	0	0	1,000	3,100	5,400	8,200	11,000	16,400	19,500
	6	0	0	200	2,300	4,100	6,600	9,400	14,800	17,900
$ 80,000										
	3	$ 0	950	2,550	6,200	9,400	12,200	15,000	20,400	23,500
	4	0	160	1,750	4,800	7,800	10,700	13,500	18,900	22,000
	5	0	0	1,000	3,800	6,300	9,300	12,100	17,500	20,600
	6	0	0	200	2,800	4,900	7,700	10,500	15,900	19,000
$100,000										
	3	$ 0	950	2,550	7,200	10,500	13,300	16,100	21,500	24,600
	4	0	160	1,750	5,700	9,000	11,800	14,600	20,000	23,100
	5	0	0	1,000	4,500	7,400	10,500	13,200	18,600	21,700
	6	0	0	200	3,400	5,800	8,800	11,600	17,000	20,100

		INCOME BEFORE TAXES								
	ASSETS	$ 20,000	30,000	40,000	50,000	60,000	70,000	80,000	90,000	100,000
	$120,000									
FAMILY SIZE	3	$ 0	950	2,550	8,300	11,600	14,400	17,200	22,600	25,700
	4	0	160	1,750	6,700	10,100	12,900	15,700	21,100	24,200
	5	0	0	1,000	5,400	8,500	11,600	14,300	19,800	22,800
	6	0	0	200	4,100	6,800	10,000	12,800	18,200	21,300
	$140,000									
FAMILY SIZE	3	$ 0	950	2,550	9,500	12,800	15,600	18,400	23,800	26,800
	4	0	160	1,750	7,800	11,200	14,100	16,900	22,300	25,400
	5	0	0	1,000	6,300	9,700	12,700	15,500	20,900	24,000
	6	0	0	200	4,900	7,900	11,100	13,900	19,300	22,400

State Financial Aid Programs

Each state government has established one or more state-administered financial aid programs for qualified students. The state programs may be restricted to legal residents of the state, or they also may be available to out-of-state students who are attending public or private colleges or universities within the state. In addition, other qualifications may apply.

The programs are described below in alphabetical order, along with information about how to determine eligibility and how to apply. The information refers to awards for 2002–03, unless otherwise stated. Students should write to the address given for each program to request that award details for 2003–04 be sent to them as soon as they are available.

ILLINOIS

Golden Apple Scholars of Illinois. Between 75 and 100 forgivable loans are given to undergraduate students. Loans are $7,000 a year for 4 years. Applicants must be between 17 and 21 and carry a minimum GPA of 2.5. Eligible applicants will be residents of Illinois who are studying in Illinois. The deadline is December 1. Recipients must agree to teach in high-need Illinois schools. *Academic/Career Areas:* Education. *Award:* Forgivable loan for use in freshman, sophomore, junior, or senior year; renewable. *Award amount:* $7000. *Number of awards:* 75–100. *Eligibility Requirements:* Applicant must be age 17-21; enrolled or expecting to enroll full-time at a four-year institution or university; resident of Illinois and studying in Illinois. Applicant must have 2.5 GPA or higher. Available to U.S. citizens. *Application Requirements:* Application, autobiography, essay, interview, photo, references, test scores, transcript. *Deadline:* December 1. *Contact:* Pat Kilduff, Director of Recruitment and Placement, Golden Apple Foundation, 8 South Michigan Avenue, Suite 700, Chicago, IL 60603-3318. *E-mail:* patnk@goldenapple.org. *Phone:* 312-407-0006 Ext. 105. *Fax:* 312-407-0344. *Web site:* www.goldenapple.org.

Grant Program for Dependents of Police, Fire, or Correctional Officers. Award for dependents of police, fire, and corrections officers killed or disabled in line of duty. Provides for tuition and fees at approved Illinois institutions. Must be resident of Illinois. Continuous deadline. Provide proof of status. *Award:* Grant for use in freshman, sophomore, junior, senior, graduate, or postgraduate years; renewable. *Award amount:* $3000–$4000. *Number of awards:* 50–55. *Eligibility Requirements:* Applicant must be enrolled or expecting to enroll at a two-year, four-year, or technical institution or university; resident of Illinois and studying in Illinois. Applicant or parent of applicant must have employment or volunteer experience in police/firefighting. Available to U.S. and non-U.S. citizens. *Application Requirements:* Application, proof of status. *Deadline:* continuous. *Contact:* David Barinholtz, Client Information, Illinois Student Assistance Commission (ISAC), 1755 Lake Cook Road, Deerfield, IL 60015-5209. *E-mail:* cssupport@isac.org. *Phone:* 847-948-8500 Ext. 2385. *Web site:* www.isac-online.org.

Higher Education License Plate Program—HELP. Need-based grants for students at institutions participating in program whose funds are raised by sale of special license plates commemorating the institutions. Deadline: June 30. Must be Illinois resident. *Award:* Grant for use in freshman, sophomore, junior, or senior year; not renewable. *Award amount:* up to $2000. *Number of awards:* 175–200. *Eligibility Requirements:* Applicant must be enrolled or expecting to enroll full- or part-time at a two-year or four-year institution or university; resident of Illinois and studying in Illinois. Available to U.S. and non-U.S. citizens. *Application Requirements:* Financial need analysis. *Deadline:* June 30. *Contact:* David Barinholtz, Client Information, Illinois Student Assistance Commission (ISAC), 1755 Lake Cook Road, Deerfield, IL 60015-5209. *E-mail:* cssupport@isac.org. *Phone:* 847-948-8500 Ext. 2385. *Web site:* www.isac-online.org.

Illinois College Savings Bond Bonus Incentive Grant Program. Program offers holders of Illinois College Savings Bonds a $20 grant for each year of bond maturity payable upon bond redemption if at least 70% of proceeds are used to attend college in Illinois. May not be used by students attending religious or divinity schools. *Award:* Grant for use in freshman, sophomore, junior, senior, graduate, or postgraduate years; not renewable. *Award amount:* $40–$220. *Number of awards:* 1200–1400. *Eligibility Requirements:* Applicant must be enrolled or expecting to enroll full- or part-time at a two-year, four-year, or technical institution or university and studying in Illinois. Available to U.S. and non-U.S. citizens. *Application Requirements:* Application. *Deadline:* continuous. *Contact:* David Barinholtz, Client Information, Illinois Student Assistance Commission (ISAC), 1755 Lake Cook Road, Deerfield, IL 60015-5209. *E-mail:* cssupport@isac.org. *Phone:* 847-948-8500 Ext. 2385. *Web site:* www.isac-online.org.

Illinois Incentive for Access Program. Award for eligible first-time freshmen enrolling in approved Illinois institutions. One-time grant of up to $500 may be used for any educational expense. Deadline: October 1. *Award:* Grant for use in freshman year; not renewable. *Award amount:* $300–$500. *Number of awards:* 19,000–22,000. *Eligibility Requirements:* Applicant must be enrolled or expecting to enroll full- or part-time at a two-year, four-year, or technical institution or university; resident of Illinois and studying in Illinois. Available to U.S. and non-U.S. citizens. *Application Requirements:* Financial need analysis. *Deadline:* October 1. *Contact:* David Barinholtz, Client Information, Illinois Student Assistance Commission (ISAC), 1755 Lake Cook Road, Deerfield, IL 60015-5209. *E-mail:* cssupport@isac.org. *Phone:* 847-948-8500 Ext. 2385. *Web site:* www.isac-online.org.

Illinois Monetary Award Program. Award for eligible students attending Illinois public universities, private colleges and universities, community colleges, and some proprietary institutions. Applicable only to tuition and fees. Based on financial need.

Deadline: October 1. *Award:* Grant for use in freshman, sophomore, junior, or senior year; not renewable. *Award amount:* $300–$4320. *Number of awards:* 135,000–145,000. *Eligibility Requirements:* Applicant must be enrolled or expecting to enroll full- or part-time at a two-year, four-year, or technical institution or university; resident of Illinois and studying in Illinois. Available to U.S. and non-U.S. citizens. *Application Requirements:* Financial need analysis. *Deadline:* October 1. *Contact:* David Barinholtz, Client Information, Illinois Student Assistance Commission (ISAC), 1755 Lake Cook Road, Deerfield, IL 60015-5209. *E-mail:* cssupport@isac.org. *Phone:* 847-948-8500 Ext. 2385. *Web site:* www.isac-online.org.

Illinois National Guard Grant Program. Award for qualified National Guard personnel which pays tuition and fees at Illinois public universities and community colleges. Must provide documentation of service. Deadline: September 15. *Award:* Grant for use in freshman, sophomore, junior, or senior year; renewable. *Award amount:* $1300–$1700. *Number of awards:* 2000–3000. *Eligibility Requirements:* Applicant must be enrolled or expecting to enroll full- or part-time at a two-year or four-year institution or university; resident of Illinois and studying in Illinois. Available to U.S. and non-U.S. citizens. Applicant must have served in the Air Force National Guard or Army National Guard. *Application Requirements:* Application, documentation of service. *Deadline:* September 15. *Contact:* David Barinholtz, Client Information, Illinois Student Assistance Commission (ISAC), 1755 Lake Cook Road, Deerfield, IL 60015-5209. *E-mail:* cssupport@isac.org. *Phone:* 847-948-8500 Ext. 2385. *Web site:* www.isac-online.org.

Illinois Student-to-Student Program of Matching Grants. Award provides matching funds for need-based grants at participating Illinois public universities and community colleges. Deadline: October 1. *Award:* Grant for use in freshman, sophomore, junior, or senior year; not renewable. *Award amount:* $300–$500. *Number of awards:* 2000–4000. *Eligibility Requirements:* Applicant must be enrolled or expecting to enroll full- or part-time at a two-year or four-year institution or university; resident of Illinois and studying in Illinois. Available to U.S. and non-U.S. citizens. *Application Requirements:* Financial need analysis. *Deadline:* October 1. *Contact:* David Barinholtz, Client Information, Illinois Student Assistance Commission (ISAC), 1755 Lake Cook Road, Deerfield, IL 60015-5209. *E-mail:* cssupport@isac.org. *Phone:* 847-948-8500 Ext. 2385. *Web site:* www.isac-online.org.

Illinois Veteran Grant Program—IVG. Award for qualified veterans for tuition and fees at Illinois public universities and community colleges. Must provide documentation of service (DD214). Deadline is continuous. *Award:* Grant for use in freshman, sophomore, junior, or senior year; renewable. *Award amount:* $1400–$1600. *Number of awards:* 11,000–13,000. *Eligibility Requirements:* Applicant must be enrolled or expecting to enroll full- or part-time at a two-year or four-year institution or university; resident of Illinois and studying in Illinois. Available to U.S. and non-U.S. citizens. Applicant must have general military experience. *Application Requirements:* Application, documentation of service. *Deadline:* continuous. *Contact:* David Barinholtz, Client Information, Illinois Student Assistance Commission (ISAC), 1755 Lake Cook Road, Deerfield, IL 60015-5209. *E-mail:* cssupport@isac.org. *Phone:* 847-948-8500 Ext. 2385. *Web site:* www.isac-online.org.

ITEACH Teacher Shortage Scholarship Program. Award to assist Illinois students planning to teach at an Illinois pre-school, elementary school, or high school in a teacher shortage discipline. Must agree to teach one year in teacher shortage area for each year of award assistance received. Deadline: May 1. *Academic/Career Areas:* Education; Special Education. *Award:* Forgivable loan for use in freshman, sophomore, junior, senior, or graduate year; not renewable. *Award amount:* $4000–$5000. *Number of awards:* 500–600. *Eligibility Requirements:* Applicant must be enrolled or expecting to enroll full- or part-time at a two-year or four-year institution or university; resident of Illinois and studying in Illinois. Applicant must have 2.5 GPA or higher. Available to U.S. and non-U.S. citizens. *Application Requirements:* Application, transcript. *Deadline:* May 1. *Contact:* Dave Barinholtz, Client Information, Illinois Student Assistance Commission (ISAC), 1755 Lake Cook Road, Deerfield, IL 60015-5209. *E-mail:* cssupport@isac.org. *Phone:* 847-948-8500 Ext. 2385. *Web site:* www.isac-online.org.

Merit Recognition Scholarship (MRS) Program. Award for Illinois high school seniors graduating in the top 5% of their class and attending Illinois postsecondary institution. Deadline: June 15. Contact for application procedures. *Award:* Scholarship for use in freshman year; not renewable. *Award amount:* $900–$1000. *Number of awards:* 5000–6000. *Eligibility Requirements:* Applicant must be high school student; planning to enroll or expecting to enroll full- or part-time at a two-year or four-year institution or university; resident of Illinois and studying in Illinois. Applicant must have 3.5 GPA or higher. Available to U.S. and non-U.S. citizens. *Application Requirements:* Application. *Deadline:* June 15. *Contact:* David Barinholtz, Client Information, Illinois Student Assistance Commission (ISAC), 1755 Lake Cook Road, Deerfield, IL 60015-5209. *E-mail:* cssupport@isac.org. *Phone:* 847-948-8500 Ext. 2385. *Web site:* www.isac-online.org.

MIA/POW Scholarships. One-time award for spouse, child, or step-child of veterans who are missing in action or were a prisoner of war. Must be enrolled at a state-supported school in Illinois. Candidate must be U.S. citizen. Must apply and be accepted before beginning of school. Also for children and spouses of veterans who are determined to be 100% disabled as established by the Veterans Administration. *Award:* Scholarship for use in freshman, sophomore, junior, senior, or graduate year; renewable. *Eligibility Requirements:* Applicant must be enrolled or expecting to enroll full- or part-time at a two-year or four-year institution or university; resident of Illinois and studying in Illinois. Available to U.S. citizens. Applicant or parent must meet one or more of the following requirements: general military experience; retired from active duty; disabled or killed as a result of military service; prisoner of war; or missing in action. *Application Requirements:* Application. *Deadline:* continuous. *Contact:* Ms. Tracy Mahan, Grants Section, Illinois Department of Veterans' Affairs, 833 South Spring Street, Springfield, IL 62794-9432. *Phone:* 217-782-3564. *Fax:* 217-782-4161.

Minority Teachers of Illinois Scholarship Program. Award for minority students planning to teach at an approved Illinois preschool, elementary, or secondary school. Deadline: May 1. Must be Illinois resident. *Academic/Career Areas:* Education; Special Education. *Award:* Forgivable loan for use in freshman, sophomore, junior, senior, graduate, or postgraduate years; renewable. *Award amount:* $4000–$5000. *Number of awards:* 450–550. *Eligibility Requirements:* Applicant must be American Indian/Alaska Native, Asian/Pacific Islander, Black (non-Hispanic), or Hispanic; enrolled or expecting to enroll full-time at a two-year or four-year institution or university; resident of Illinois and studying in Illinois. Applicant must have 2.5 GPA or higher. Available to U.S. and non-U.S. citizens. *Application Requirements:* Application. *Deadline:*

May 1. *Contact:* David Barinholtz, Client Information, Illinois Student Assistance Commission (ISAC), 1755 Lake Cook Road, Deerfield, IL 60015-5209. *E-mail:* cssupport@isac.org. *Phone:* 847-948-8500 Ext. 2385. *Web site:* www.isac-online.org.

Veterans' Children Educational Opportunities. Award is provided to each child age 18 or younger of a veteran who died or became totally disabled as a result of service during World War I, World War II, Korean, or Vietnam War. Must be an Illinois resident and studying in Illinois. Death must be service-connected. Disability must be rated 100% for two or more years. *Award:* Grant for use in freshman year; not renewable. *Award amount:* up to $250. *Eligibility Requirements:* Applicant must be age 10-18; enrolled or expecting to enroll at an institution or university; resident of Illinois and studying in Illinois. Available to U.S. citizens. Applicant or parent must meet one or more of the following requirements: general military experience; retired from active duty; disabled or killed as a result of military service; prisoner of war; or missing in action. *Application Requirements:* Application. *Deadline:* June 30. *Contact:* Ms. Tracy Mahan, Grants Section, Illinois Department of Veterans' Affairs, 833 South Spring Street, Springfield, IL 62794-9432. *Phone:* 217-782-3564. *Fax:* 217-782-4161.

INDIANA

Child of Disabled Veteran Grant or Purple Heart Recipient Grant. Free tuition at Indiana state-supported colleges or universities for children of disabled veterans or Purple Heart recipients. Must submit Form DD214 or service record. *Award:* Grant for use in freshman, sophomore, junior, or senior year; renewable. *Eligibility Requirements:* Applicant must be enrolled or expecting to enroll full- or part-time at a two-year or four-year institution or university; resident of Indiana and studying in Indiana. Available to U.S. citizens. Applicant or parent must meet one or more of the following requirements: general military experience; retired from active duty; disabled or killed as a result of military service; prisoner of war; or missing in action. *Application Requirements:* Application. *Deadline:* continuous. *Contact:* Jon Brinkley, State Service Officer, Indiana Department of Veterans' Affairs, 302 West Washington Street, Room E-120, Indianapolis, IN 46204-2738. *E-mail:* jbrinkley@dva.state.in.us. *Phone:* 317-232-3910. *Fax:* 317-232-7721. *Web site:* www.ai.org/veteran/index.html.

Department of Veterans Affairs Free Tuition for Children of POW/MIA's in Vietnam. Renewable award for residents of Indiana who are the children of veterans declared missing in action or prisoner-of-war after January 1, 1960. Provides tuition at Indiana state-supported institutions for undergraduate study. *Award:* Grant for use in freshman, sophomore, junior, or senior year; renewable. *Eligibility Requirements:* Applicant must be enrolled or expecting to enroll at a two-year or four-year institution or university; resident of Indiana and studying in Indiana. Available to U.S. citizens. Applicant or parent must meet one or more of the following requirements: general military experience; retired from active duty; disabled or killed as a result of military service; prisoner of war; or missing in action. *Application Requirements:* Application. *Deadline:* continuous. *Contact:* Jon Brinkley, State Service Officer, Indiana Department of Veterans' Affairs, 302 West Washington Street, Room E-120, Indianapolis, IN 46204-2738. *E-mail:* jbrinkley@dva.state.in.us. *Phone:* 317-232-3910. *Fax:* 317-232-7721. *Web site:* www.ai.org/veteran/index.html.

Hoosier Scholar Award. The Hoosier Scholar Award is a $500 nonrenewable award. Based on the size of the senior class, one to three scholars are selected by the guidance counselor(s). The award is based on academic merit and may be used for any educational expense at an eligible Indiana institution of higher education. *Award:* Scholarship for use in freshman year; not renewable. *Award amount:* $500. *Number of awards:* 790–840. *Eligibility Requirements:* Applicant must be high school student; planning to enroll or expecting to enroll full-time at a two-year or four-year institution or university; resident of Indiana and studying in Indiana. Applicant must have 3.5 GPA or higher. Available to U.S. citizens. *Application Requirements: Deadline:* March 1. *Contact:* Ms. Ada Sparkman, Program Coordinator, State Student Assistance Commission of Indiana (SSACI), 150 West Market Street, Suite 500, Indianapolis, IN 46204-2805. *Phone:* 317-232-2350. *Fax:* 317-232-3260. *Web site:* www.ssaci.in.gov.

Indiana Freedom of Choice Grant. The Freedom of Choice Grant is a need-based, tuition-restricted program for students attending Indiana private institutions seeking a first undergraduate degree. It is awarded in addition to the Higher Education Award. Students (and parents of dependent students) who are U.S. citizens and Indiana residents must file the FAFSA yearly by the March 10 deadline. *Award:* Grant for use in freshman, sophomore, junior, or senior year; not renewable. *Award amount:* $200–$3906. *Number of awards:* 10,000–11,830. *Eligibility Requirements:* Applicant must be enrolled or expecting to enroll full-time at a four-year institution or university; resident of Indiana and studying in Indiana. Available to U.S. citizens. *Application Requirements:* Application, financial need analysis, FAFSA. *Deadline:* March 10. *Contact:* Grant Counselor, State Student Assistance Commission of Indiana (SSACI), 150 West Market Street, Suite 500, Indianapolis, IN 46204-2805. *E-mail:* grants@ssaci.state.in.us. *Phone:* 317-232-2350. *Fax:* 317-232-3260. *Web site:* www.ssaci.in.gov.

Indiana Higher Education Award. The Higher Education Award is a need-based, tuition-restricted program for students attending Indiana public, private or proprietary institutions seeking a first undergraduate degree. Students (and parents of dependent students) who are U.S. citizens and Indiana residents must file the FAFSA yearly by the March 10 deadline. *Award:* Grant for use in freshman, sophomore, junior, or senior year; not renewable. *Award amount:* $200–$4734. *Number of awards:* 38,000–43,660. *Eligibility Requirements:* Applicant must be enrolled or expecting to enroll full-time at a two-year, four-year, or technical institution or university; resident of Indiana and studying in Indiana. Available to U.S. citizens. *Application Requirements:* Application, financial need analysis, FAFSA. *Deadline:* March 10. *Contact:* Grant Counselors, State Student Assistance Commission of Indiana (SSACI), 150 West Market Street, Suite 500, Indianapolis, IN 46204-2805. *E-mail:* grants@ssaci.state.in.us. *Phone:* 317-232-2350. *Fax:* 317-232-3260. *Web site:* www.ssaci.in.gov.

Indiana Minority Teacher and Special Education Services Scholarship Program. For Black or Hispanic students seeking teaching certification or for students seeking special education teaching certification or occupational or physical therapy certification. Must be a U.S. citizen and Indiana resident enrolled full-time at an eligible Indiana institution. Must teach in an Indiana-accredited elementary or secondary school after graduation. Contact institution for application and deadline. Minimum 2.0 GPA required. *Academic/Career Areas:* Education; Special Education; Therapy/Rehabilitation. *Award:* Scholarship for use in freshman, sophomore, junior, or senior year; not renewable. *Award amount:* $1000–$4000. *Number of awards:* 330–370. *Eligibility Requirements:* Applicant must be Black (non-Hispanic) or Hispanic; enrolled or expecting to enroll full-time at a four-year institution or university; resident of Indiana and studying in Indiana. Available to U.S. citizens. *Application Requirements:* Application, financial need analysis. *Deadline:* continuous. *Contact:* Ms. Yvonne Heflin, Director, Special Programs, State Student Assistance Commission of Indiana (SSACI), 150 West Market Street, Suite 500, Indianapolis, IN 46204-2805. *E-mail:* grants@ssaci.state.un.is. *Phone:* 317-232-2350. *Fax:* 317-232-3260. *Web site:* www.ssaci.in.gov.

Indiana National Guard Supplemental Grant. One-time award, which is a supplement to the Indiana Higher Education Grant program. Applicants must be members of the Indiana National Guard. All Guard paperwork must be completed prior to the start of each semester. The FAFSA must be received by March 10. Award covers tuition and fees at select public colleges. *Award:* Grant for use in freshman, sophomore, junior, or senior year; not renewable. *Award amount:* \$200–\$5314. *Number of awards:* 350–870. *Eligibility Requirements:* Applicant must be enrolled or expecting to enroll full- or part-time at a two-year or four-year institution or university; resident of Indiana and studying in Indiana. Available to U.S. citizens. Applicant must have served in the Air Force National Guard or Army National Guard. *Application Requirements:* Application, financial need analysis. *Deadline:* March 10. *Contact:* Grants Counselor, State Student Assistance Commission of Indiana (SSACI), 150 West Market Street, Suite 500, Indianapolis, IN 46204-2805. *E-mail:* grants@ssaci.state.in.us. *Phone:* 317-232-2350. *Fax:* 317-232-2360. *Web site:* www.ssaci.in.gov.

Indiana Nursing Scholarship Fund. Need-based tuition funding for nursing students enrolled full- or part-time at an eligible Indiana institution. Must be an Indiana resident and have a minimum 2.0 GPA or meet the minimum requirements for the nursing program. Upon graduation, recipients must practice as a nurse in an Indiana health care setting for two years. *Academic/Career Areas:* Nursing. *Award:* Scholarship for use in freshman, sophomore, junior, or senior year; not renewable. *Award amount:* \$200–\$5000. *Number of awards:* 510–690. *Eligibility Requirements:* Applicant must be enrolled or expecting to enroll full- or part-time at a two-year or four-year institution or university; resident of Indiana and studying in Indiana. Available to U.S. citizens. *Application Requirements:* Application, financial need analysis. *Deadline:* continuous. *Contact:* Ms. Yvonne Heflin, Director, Special Programs, State Student Assistance Commission of Indiana (SSACI), 150 West Market Street, Suite 500, Indianapolis, IN 46204-2805. *Phone:* 317-232-2350. *Fax:* 317-232-3260. *Web site:* www.ssaci.in.gov.

Indiana Wildlife Federation Scholarship. A \$1000 scholarship will be awarded to an Indiana resident accepted for the study or already enrolled for the study of resource conservation or environmental education at the undergraduate level. For more details see Web site: www.indianawildlife.org. *Academic/Career Areas:* Natural Resources. *Award:* Scholarship for use in sophomore, junior, or senior year; not renewable. *Award amount:* \$1000. *Eligibility Requirements:* Applicant must be enrolled or expecting to enroll at an institution or university and resident of Indiana. Available to U.S. citizens. *Application Requirements:* Application. *Deadline:* April 30. *Contact:* application available at Web site, Indiana Wildlife Federation Endowment. *Web site:* indianawildlife.org.

Part-time Grant Program. Program is designed to encourage part-time undergraduates to start and complete their associate or baccalaureate degrees or certificates by subsidizing part-time tuition costs. It is a term-based award that is based on need. State residency requirements must be met and a FAFSA must be filed. Eligibility is determined at the institutional level subject to approval by SSACI. *Award:* Grant for use in freshman, sophomore, junior, or senior year; not renewable. *Award amount:* \$50–\$4000. *Number of awards:* 4000–6366. *Eligibility Requirements:* Applicant must be enrolled or expecting to enroll part-time at a two-year, four-year, or technical institution or university; resident of Indiana and studying in Indiana. Available to U.S. citizens. *Application Requirements:* Application, financial need analysis. *Deadline:* continuous. *Contact:* Grant Division, State Student Assistance Commission of Indiana (SSACI), 150 West Market Street, Suite 500, Indianapolis, IN 46204-2805. *E-mail:* grants@ssaci.state.in.us. *Phone:* 317-232-2350. *Fax:* 317-232-3260. *Web site:* www.ssaci.in.gov.

Police Corps Incentive Scholarship. Forgivable loans are available to highly qualified men and women entering the Police Corps. Up to \$7500 a year can be used to cover the expenses of study toward a baccalaureate or graduate degree. For more details and an application see Web site: www.in.gov/cji.policecorps. *Academic/Career Areas:* Criminal Justice/Criminology. *Award:* Forgivable loan for use in freshman, sophomore, junior, senior, or graduate year; renewable. *Award amount:* up to \$7500. *Eligibility Requirements:* Applicant must be enrolled or expecting to enroll at an institution or university. Available to U.S. citizens. *Application Requirements:* Application, driver's license, references, transcript. *Deadline:* continuous. *Contact:* application available at Web site, Indiana Police Corps. *Web site:* www.state.in.us/cji/policecorps.

Scholarships for Dependents of Fallen Officers. Scholarships are available to the dependents of officers who have been killed in the line of duty. For more details and an application see Web site: www.in.gov/cji/policecorps. *Award:* Scholarship for use in freshman, sophomore, junior, or senior year; renewable. *Award amount:* up to \$30,000. *Eligibility Requirements:* Applicant must be enrolled or expecting to enroll at an institution or university. Applicant or parent of applicant must have employment or volunteer experience in police/firefighting. Available to U.S. citizens. *Application Requirements:* Application. *Deadline:* continuous. *Contact:* application available at Web site, Indiana Police Corps. *Web site:* www.state.in.us/cji/policecorps.

Twenty-first Century Scholars Award. Income-eligible 7th graders who enroll in the program fulfill a pledge of good citizenship and complete the Affirmation Form are guaranteed tuition for four years at any participating public institution. If the student attends a private institution, the state will award an amount comparable to that of a public institution. If the student attends a participating proprietary school, the state will award a tuition scholarship equal to that of Ivy Tech State College. FAFSA and affirmation form must be filed yearly by March 10. Applicant must be resident of Indiana. *Award:* Scholarship for use in freshman, sophomore, junior, or senior year; not renewable. *Award amount:* \$1000–\$5314. *Number of awards:* 2800–8100. *Eligibility Requirements:* Applicant must be enrolled or expecting to enroll full-time at a two-year, four-year, or technical institution or university; resident of Indiana and studying in Indiana. Applicant must have 2.5 GPA or higher. Available to U.S. citizens. *Application Requirements:* Application, financial need analysis, affirmation form. *Deadline:* March 10. *Contact:* Twenty-first Century Scholars Program Counselors, State Student Assistance Commission of Indiana (SSACI), 150 West Market Street, Suite 500, Indianapolis, IN 46204-2805. *Phone:* 317-233-2100. *Fax:* 317-232-3260. *Web site:* www.ssaci.in.gov.

IOWA

Governor Terry E. Branstad Iowa State Fair Scholarship. Up to four scholarships ranging from $500 to $1000 will be awarded to students graduating from an Iowa high school. Must actively participate at the Iowa State Fair. For more details see Web site: www.iowacollegeaid.org. *Award:* Scholarship for use in freshman year; not renewable. *Award amount:* $500–$1000. *Number of awards:* up to 4. *Eligibility Requirements:* Applicant must be high school student; planning to enroll or expecting to enroll at an institution or university; resident of Iowa and studying in Iowa. Available to U.S. citizens. *Application Requirements:* Application, essay, financial need analysis, references, transcript. *Deadline:* May 1. *Contact:* Julie Leeper, Director, State Student Aid Programs, Iowa College Student Aid Commission, 200 10th Street, 4th Floor, Des Moines, IA 50309-3609. *E-mail:* icsac@max.state.ia.us. *Phone:* 515-242-3370. *Fax:* 515-242-3388. *Web site:* www.iowacollegeaid.org.

Iowa Foster Child Grants. Grants renewable up to four years will be awarded to students graduating from an Iowa high school who are in Iowa foster care under the care and custody of the Iowa Department of Human Service. Must have a minimum GPA of 2.25 and have applied to an accredited Iowa college or university. For more details see Web site: www.iowacollegeaid.org. *Award:* Grant for use in freshman year; renewable. *Award amount:* $2000–$4200. *Eligibility Requirements:* Applicant must be high school student; planning to enroll or expecting to enroll at a two-year or four-year institution or university; resident of Iowa and studying in Iowa. Available to U.S. citizens. *Application Requirements:* Application. *Deadline:* April 15. *Contact:* Julie Leeper, Director, State Student Aid Programs, Iowa College Student Aid Commission, 200 10th Street, 4th Floor, Des Moines, IA 50309-3609. *E-mail:* icsac@max.state.ia.us. *Phone:* 515-242-3370. *Fax:* 515-242-3388. *Web site:* www.iowacollegeaid.org.

Iowa Grants. Statewide need-based program to assist high-need Iowa residents. Recipients must demonstrate a high level of financial need to receive awards ranging from $100 to $1,000. Awards are prorated for students enrolled for less than full-time. Awards must be used at Iowa postsecondary institutions. *Award:* Grant for use in freshman, sophomore, junior, or senior year; not renewable. *Award amount:* $100–$1000. *Eligibility Requirements:* Applicant must be enrolled or expecting to enroll full- or part-time at a two-year, four-year, or technical institution or university; resident of Iowa and studying in Iowa. Available to U.S. citizens. *Application Requirements:* Application, financial need analysis. *Deadline:* continuous. *Contact:* Julie Leeper, Director, State Student Aid Programs, Iowa College Student Aid Commission, 200 10th Street, 4th Floor, Des Moines, IA 50309-3609. *E-mail:* icsac@max.state.ia.us. *Phone:* 515-242-3370. *Fax:* 515-242-3388. *Web site:* www.iowacollegeaid.org.

Iowa National Guard Education Assistance Program. Program provides postsecondary tuition assistance to members of Iowa National Guard Units. Must study at a postsecondary institution in Iowa. Contact for additional information. *Award:* Grant for use in freshman, sophomore, junior, or senior year; not renewable. *Award amount:* up to $1200. *Eligibility Requirements:* Applicant must be enrolled or expecting to enroll full- or part-time at a two-year, four-year, or technical institution or university; resident of Iowa and studying in Iowa. Available to U.S. citizens. Applicant must have served in the Air Force National Guard or Army National Guard. *Application Requirements:* Application. *Deadline:* continuous. *Contact:* Julie Leeper, Director, State Student Aid Programs, Iowa College Student Aid Commission, 200 10th Street, 4th Floor, Des Moines, IA 50309-3609. *E-mail:* icsac@max.state.ia.us. *Phone:* 515-242-3370. *Fax:* 515-242-3388. *Web site:* www.iowacollegeaid.org.

Iowa Teacher Forgivable Loan Program. Forgivable loan assists students who will teach in Iowa secondary schools. Must be an Iowa resident attending an Iowa postsecondary institution. Contact for additional information. *Academic/Career Areas:* Education. *Award:* Forgivable loan for use in freshman, sophomore, junior, or senior year; not renewable. *Award amount:* $2686. *Eligibility Requirements:* Applicant must be enrolled or expecting to enroll full- or part-time at a four-year institution or university; resident of Iowa and studying in Iowa. Applicant or parent of applicant must have employment or volunteer experience in teaching. Available to U.S. citizens. *Application Requirements:* Application, financial need analysis. *Deadline:* continuous. *Contact:* Brenda Easter, Special Programs Administrator, Iowa College Student Aid Commission, 200 10th Street, 4th Floor, Des Moines, IA 50309-3609. *E-mail:* icsac@max.state.ia.us. *Phone:* 515-242-3380. *Fax:* 515-242-3388. *Web site:* www.iowacollegeaid.org.

Iowa Tuition Grant Program. Program assists students who attend independent postsecondary institutions in Iowa. Iowa residents currently enrolled, or planning to enroll, for at least three semester hours at one of the eligible Iowa postsecondary institutions may apply. Awards currently range from $100 to $4000. Grants may not exceed the difference between independent college and university tuition and fees and the average tuition and fees at the three public Regent universities. *Award:* Grant for use in freshman, sophomore, junior, or senior year; not renewable. *Award amount:* $100–$4000. *Eligibility Requirements:* Applicant must be enrolled or expecting to enroll full- or part-time at a two-year or four-year institution; resident of Iowa and studying in Iowa. Available to U.S. citizens. *Application Requirements:* Application, financial need analysis. *Deadline:* July 1. *Contact:* Julie Leeper, Director, State Student Aid Programs, Iowa College Student Aid Commission, 200 10th Street, 4th Floor, Des Moines, IA 50309-3609. *E-mail:* icsac@max.state.ia.us. *Phone:* 515-242-3370. *Fax:* 515-242-3388. *Web site:* www.iowacollegeaid.org.

Iowa Vocational Rehabilitation. Provides vocational rehabilitation services to individuals with disabilities who need these services in order to maintain, retain, or obtain employment compatible with their disabilities. Must be Iowa resident. *Award:* Grant for use in freshman, sophomore, junior, senior, graduate, or postgraduate years; renewable. *Award amount:* $500–$4000. *Number of awards:* up to 5000. *Eligibility Requirements:* Applicant must be enrolled or expecting to enroll full- or part-time at a two-year, four-year, or technical institution or university and resident of Iowa. Applicant must be hearing impaired, learning disabled, physically disabled, or visually impaired. Available to U.S. and non-U.S. citizens. *Application Requirements:* Application, interview. *Deadline:* continuous. *Contact:* Ralph Childers, Policy and Workforce Initiatives Coordinator, Iowa Division of Vocational Rehabilitation Services, Division of Vocational Rehabilitation Services, 510 East 12th Street, Des Moines, IA 50319. *E-mail:* rchilders@dvrs.state.ia.us. *Phone:* 515-281-4151. *Fax:* 515-281-4703. *Web site:* www.dvrs.state.ia.us.

Iowa Vocational-Technical Tuition Grant Program. Program provides need-based financial assistance to Iowa residents enrolled in career education (vocational-technical), and career option programs at Iowa area community colleges. Grants range from $150 to $650, depending on the length of program, financial need, and available funds. *Award:* Grant for use in freshman or sophomore year; not renewable. *Award amount:* $150–$650. *Eligibility Requirements:* Applicant must be enrolled or expecting to enroll full- or part-time at a technical institution; resident of Iowa and studying in Iowa. Available to U.S. citizens. *Application Requirements:* Application, financial need analysis. *Deadline:* July 1. *Contact:* Julie Leeper, Director, State Student Aid Programs, Iowa College Student Aid Commission, 200 10th Street, 4th Floor, Des Moines, IA 50309-3609. *E-mail:* icsac@max.state.ia.us. *Phone:* 515-242-3370. *Fax:* 515-242-3388. *Web site:* www.iowacollegeaid.org.

State of Iowa Scholarship Program. Program provides recognition and financial honorarium to Iowa's academically talented high school seniors. Honorary scholarships are presented to all qualified candidates. Approximately 1700 top-ranking candidates are designated State of Iowa Scholars every March, from an applicant pool of nearly 5000 high school seniors. Must be used at an Iowa postsecondary institution. Minimum 3.5 GPA required. *Award:* Scholarship for use in freshman year; not renewable. *Award amount:* up to $400. *Number of awards:* up to 1700. *Eligibility Requirements:* Applicant must be high school student; planning to enroll or expecting to enroll full-time at a two-year, four-year, or technical institution or university; resident of Iowa and studying in Iowa. Applicant must have 3.5 GPA or higher. Available to U.S. citizens. *Application Requirements:* Application, test scores. *Deadline:* November 1. *Contact:* Julie Leeper, Director, State Student Aid Programs, Iowa College Student Aid Commission, 200 10th Street, 4th Floor, Des Moines, IA 50309-3609. *E-mail:* icsac@max.state.ia.us. *Phone:* 515-242-3370. *Fax:* 515-242-3388. *Web site:* www.iowacollegeaid.org.

KANSAS

Ethnic Minority Scholarship Program. This program is designed to assist financially needy, academically competitive students who are identified as members of the following ethnic/racial groups: African-American; American-Indian or Alaskan Native; Asian or Pacific Islander; or Hispanic. Must be resident of Kansas and attend college in Kansas. Application fee is $10. Deadline: May 1. Minimum 3.0 GPA required. Must be U.S. citizen. *Award:* Scholarship for use in freshman, sophomore, junior, or senior year; renewable. *Award amount:* $1850. *Number of awards:* 200–250. *Eligibility Requirements:* Applicant must be American Indian/Alaska Native, Asian/Pacific Islander, Black (non-Hispanic), or Hispanic; enrolled or expecting to enroll full-time at a two-year or four-year institution or university; resident of Kansas and studying in Kansas. Applicant must have 3.0 GPA or higher. Available to U.S. citizens. *Application Requirements:* Application, financial need analysis, test scores, transcript. *Fee:* $10. *Deadline:* May 1. *Contact:* Diane Lindeman, Director of Student Financial Assistance, Kansas Board of Regents, 1000 Southwest Jackson, Suite 520, Topeka, KS 66612-1368. *E-mail:* dlindeman@ksbor.org. *Phone:* 785-296-3517. *Fax:* 785-296-0983. *Web site:* www.kansasregents.org.

Kansas Comprehensive Grant Program. Grants available for Kansas residents attending public or private baccalaureate colleges or universities in Kansas. Based on financial need. Must file Free Application for Federal Student Aid to apply. Renewable award based on continuing eligibility. Up to $3000 for undergraduate use. Deadline: April 1. *Award:* Grant for use in freshman, sophomore, junior, or senior year; renewable. *Award amount:* $1100–$3000. *Number of awards:* 7000–8200. *Eligibility Requirements:* Applicant must be enrolled or expecting to enroll full-time at a four-year institution or university; resident of Kansas and studying in Kansas. Available to U.S. citizens. *Application Requirements:* Financial need analysis. *Deadline:* April 1. *Contact:* Diane Lindeman, Director of Student Financial Assistance, Kansas Board of Regents, 1000 Southwest Jackson, Suite 520, Topeka, KS 66612-1368. *E-mail:* dlindeman@ksbor.org. *Phone:* 785-296-3517. *Fax:* 785-296-0983. *Web site:* www.kansasregents.org.

Kansas Educational Benefits for Children of MIA, POW, and Deceased Veterans of the Vietnam War. Full-tuition scholarship awarded to students who are children of veterans. Must show proof of parent's status as missing in action, prisoner of war, or killed in action in the Vietnam War. Kansas residence required of veteran at time of entry to service. Must attend a state-supported postsecondary school. *Award:* Scholarship for use in freshman, sophomore, junior, or senior year; not renewable. *Eligibility Requirements:* Applicant must be enrolled or expecting to enroll at a two-year, four-year, or technical institution or university and studying in Kansas. Available to U.S. citizens. Applicant or parent must meet one or more of the following requirements: general military experience; retired from active duty; disabled or killed as a result of military service; prisoner of war; or missing in action. *Application Requirements:* Application, report of casualty, birth certificate, school acceptance letter. *Deadline:* continuous. *Contact:* Dave DePue, Program Director, Kansas Commission on Veterans Affairs, 700 Southwest Jackson, Jayhawk Tower, #701, Topeka, KS 66603. *E-mail:* kcva004@ink.org. *Phone:* 785-291-3422. *Fax:* 785-296-1462. *Web site:* www.kcva.org.

Kansas National Guard Educational Assistance Award Program. Service scholarship for enlisted soldiers in the Kansas National Guard. Pays up to 100% of tuition and fees based on funding. Must attend a state-supported institution. Recipients will be required to serve in the KNG for four years after the last payment of state tuition assistance. Must not have over 15 years of service at time of application. Deadlines are January 15 and August 20. Contact KNG Education Services Specialist for further information. Must be Kansas resident. *Award:* Scholarship for use in freshman, sophomore, junior, or senior year; not renewable. *Award amount:* $250–$3500. *Number of awards:* up to 400. *Eligibility Requirements:* Applicant must be enrolled or expecting to enroll full- or part-time at a two-year, four-year, or technical institution or university; resident of Kansas and studying in Kansas. Available to U.S. citizens. Applicant must have served in the Air Force National Guard or Army National Guard. *Application Requirements:* Application. *Contact:* Steve Finch, Education Services Specialist, Kansas National Guard Educational Assistance Program, Attn: AGKS-DOP-ESO, The Adjutant General of Kansas, 2800 South West Topeka Boulevard, Topeka, KS 66611-1287. *E-mail:* steve.finch@ks.ngb.army.mil. *Phone:* 785-274-1060. *Fax:* 785-274-1617.

Kansas Nursing Service Scholarship Program. This program is designed to encourage Kansans to enroll in nursing programs and commit to practicing in Kansas. Recipients sign agreements to practice nursing at specific facilities one year for each year of support. Application fee is $10. Deadline: May 1. *Academic/Career Areas:* Nursing. *Award:* Forgivable loan for use in freshman, sophomore, junior, or senior year; renewable. *Award amount:* $2500–$3500. *Number of awards:* 100–200. *Eligibility Requirements:* Applicant must be enrolled or expecting to enroll full-time at a two-year or four-year institution or university; resident of Kansas and studying in Kansas. Available to U.S. citizens. *Application Requirements:* Application, financial need analysis, sponsor agreement form. *Fee:* $10. *Deadline:* May 1. *Contact:* Diane Lindeman, Director of Student Financial Assistance, Kansas Board of Regents, 1000 Southwest

Jackson, Suite 520, Topeka, KS 66612-1368. *E-mail:* dlindeman@ksbor.org. *Phone:* 785-296-3517. *Fax:* 785-296-0983. *Web site:* www.kansasregents.org.

Kansas State Scholarship Program. The Kansas State Scholarship Program provides assistance to financially needy, academically outstanding students who attend Kansas postsecondary institutions. Must be Kansas resident. Minimum 3.0 GPA required for renewal. Application fee is $10. Deadline: May 1. *Award:* Scholarship for use in freshman, sophomore, junior, or senior year; renewable. *Award amount:* $1000. *Number of awards:* 1000–1500. *Eligibility Requirements:* Applicant must be enrolled or expecting to enroll full-time at a two-year or four-year institution or university; resident of Kansas and studying in Kansas. Applicant must have 3.0 GPA or higher. Available to U.S. citizens. *Application Requirements:* Application, financial need analysis, test scores, transcript. *Fee:* $10. *Deadline:* May 1. *Contact:* Diane Lindeman, Director of Student Financial Assistance, Kansas Board of Regents, 1000 Southwest Jackson, Suite 520, Topeka, KS 66612-1368. *E-mail:* dlindeman@ksbor.org. *Phone:* 785-296-3517. *Fax:* 785-296-0983. *Web site:* www.kansasregents.org.

Kansas Teacher Service Scholarship. Several scholarships for Kansas residents pursuing teaching careers. Must teach in a hard-to-fill discipline or underserved area of the state of Kansas for one year for each award received. Renewable award of $5000. Application fee is $10. Deadline: May 1. Must be U.S. citizen. *Academic/Career Areas:* Education. *Award:* Forgivable loan for use in freshman, sophomore, junior, or senior year; renewable. *Award amount:* $5000. *Number of awards:* 60–80. *Eligibility Requirements:* Applicant must be enrolled or expecting to enroll full-time at a two-year or four-year institution or university; resident of Kansas and studying in Kansas. Applicant must have 3.0 GPA or higher. Available to U.S. citizens. *Application Requirements:* Application, references, test scores, transcript. *Fee:* $10. *Deadline:* May 1. *Contact:* Diane Lindeman, Director of Student Financial Assistance, Kansas Board of Regents, 1000 Southwest Jackson, Suite 520, Topeka, KS 66612-1368. *E-mail:* dlindeman@ksbor.org. *Phone:* 785-296-3517. *Fax:* 785-296-0983. *Web site:* www.kansasregents.org.

Vocational Education Scholarship Program—Kansas. Several scholarships for Kansas residents who graduated from a Kansas accredited high school. Must be enrolled in a vocational education program at an eligible Kansas institution. Based on ability and aptitude. Deadline is July 1. Renewable award of $500. Must be U.S. citizen. *Academic/Career Areas:* Trade/Technical Specialties. *Award:* Scholarship for use in freshman or sophomore year; renewable. *Award amount:* $500. *Number of awards:* 100–200. *Eligibility Requirements:* Applicant must be enrolled or expecting to enroll full-time at a two-year or technical institution; resident of Kansas and studying in Kansas. Available to U.S. citizens. *Application Requirements:* Application, test scores. *Deadline:* July 1. *Contact:* Diane Lindeman, Director of Student Financial Assistance, Kansas Board of Regents, 1000 Southwest Jackson, Suite 520, Topeka, KS 66612-1368. *E-mail:* dlindeman@ksbor.org. *Phone:* 785-296-3517. *Fax:* 785-296-0983. *Web site:* www.kansasregents.org.

MICHIGAN

Michigan Adult Part-time Grant. Grant for part-time, needy, independent undergraduates at an approved, degree-granting Michigan college or university. Eligibility is limited to two years. Must be Michigan resident. Deadlines determined by college. *Award:* Grant for use in freshman, sophomore, junior, or senior year; not renewable. *Award amount:* up to $600. *Eligibility Requirements:* Applicant must be enrolled or expecting to enroll part-time at a two-year or four-year institution or university; resident of Michigan and studying in Michigan. Available to U.S. citizens. *Application Requirements:* Application, financial need analysis. *Contact:* Program Director, Michigan Bureau of Student Financial Assistance, PO Box 30466, Lansing, MI 48909-7966. *Web site:* www.michigan.gov/mistudentaid.

Michigan Competitive Scholarship. Awards limited to tuition. Must maintain a C average and meet the college's academic progress requirements. Must file Free Application for Federal Student Aid. Deadlines: February 21 and March 21. Must be Michigan resident. Renewable award of $1300 for undergraduate study at a Michigan institution. *Award:* Scholarship for use in freshman, sophomore, junior, or senior year; renewable. *Award amount:* $100–$1300. *Eligibility Requirements:* Applicant must be enrolled or expecting to enroll at a two-year or four-year institution or university; resident of Michigan and studying in Michigan. Available to U.S. citizens. *Application Requirements:* Application, financial need analysis, test scores, FAFSA. *Contact:* Scholarship and Grant Director, Michigan Bureau of Student Financial Assistance, PO Box 30466, Lansing, MI 48909. *Web site:* www.michigan.gov/mistudentaid.

Michigan Educational Opportunity Grant. Need-based program for Michigan residents who are at least half-time undergraduates attending public Michigan colleges. Must maintain good academic standing. Deadline determined by college. Award of up to $1000. *Award:* Grant for use in freshman, sophomore, junior, or senior year; not renewable. *Award amount:* up to $1000. *Eligibility Requirements:* Applicant must be enrolled or expecting to enroll full- or part-time at a two-year or four-year institution or university; resident of Michigan and studying in Michigan. Available to U.S. citizens. *Application Requirements:* Application, financial need analysis. *Contact:* Program Director, Michigan Bureau of Student Financial Assistance, PO Box 30466, Lansing, MI 48909-7966. *Web site:* www.michigan.gov/mistudentaid.

Michigan Indian Tuition Waiver. Renewable award provides free tuition for Native-Americans of one-quarter or more blood degree who attend a Michigan public college or university. Must be a Michigan resident for at least one year. For more details and deadlines contact college financial aid office. *Award:* Scholarship for use in freshman, sophomore, junior, senior, graduate, or postgraduate years; renewable. *Eligibility Requirements:* Applicant must be American Indian/Alaska Native; enrolled or expecting to enroll full- or part-time at a two-year or four-year institution or university; resident of Michigan and studying in Michigan. Available to U.S. and Canadian citizens. *Application Requirements:* Application, driver's license. *Contact:* Harriet Moran, Executive Assistant to Programs, Inter-Tribal Council of Michigan, Inc., 405 East Easterday Avenue, Sault Ste. Marie, MI 49783. *E-mail:* itchmm@yahoo.com. *Phone:* 906-632-6896. *Fax:* 906-632-1810. *Web site:* www.itcmi.org.

Michigan Tuition Grants. Need-based program. Students must attend a Michigan private, nonprofit, degree-granting college. Must file the Free Application for Federal Student Aid and meet the college's academic progress requirements. Deadlines: February 21 and March 21. Must be Michigan resident. Renewable award of $2750. *Award:* Grant for use in freshman, sophomore, junior, or senior year; renewable. *Award amount:* $100–$2750. *Eligibility Requirements:* Applicant must be enrolled or expecting to enroll at a two-year or four-year institution or university; resident of Michigan and studying in Michigan. Available to U.S. citizens. *Application Requirements:* Application, financial need analysis, FAFSA.

Contact: Scholarship and Grant Director, Michigan Bureau of Student Financial Assistance, PO Box 30466, Lansing, MI 48909-7966. *Web site:* www.michigan.gov/mistudentaid.

Michigan Veterans Trust Fund Tuition Grant Program. Tuition grant of $2800 for children of Michigan veterans who died on active duty or subsequently declared 100% disabled as the result of service-connected illness or injury. Must be 17 to 25 years old, be a Michigan resident, and attend a private or public institution in Michigan. *Award:* Grant for use in freshman, sophomore, junior, or senior year; renewable. *Award amount:* up to $2800. *Eligibility Requirements:* Applicant must be age 17-25; enrolled or expecting to enroll full-time at a two-year, four-year, or technical institution or university; resident of Michigan and studying in Michigan. Applicant or parent must meet one or more of the following requirements: general military experience; retired from active duty; disabled or killed as a result of military service; prisoner of war; or missing in action. *Application Requirements:* Application. *Deadline:* continuous. *Contact:* Phyllis Ochis, Department of Military and Veterans Affairs, Michigan Veterans Trust Fund, 2500 South Washington Avenue, Lansing, MI 48913. *Phone:* 517-483-5469. *Web site:* www.michigan.gov/dmva.

Tuition Incentive Program (TIP)-Michigan. Award for Michigan residents who receive or have received Medicaid for required period of time through the Family Independence Agency. Scholarship provides two years tuition towards an associate's degree at a Michigan college or university. Apply before graduating from high school or earning General Education Development diploma. *Award:* Scholarship for use in freshman or sophomore year; renewable. *Eligibility Requirements:* Applicant must be high school student; planning to enroll or expecting to enroll full- or part-time at a two-year or four-year institution or university; resident of Michigan and studying in Michigan. Available to U.S. citizens. *Application Requirements:* Application, financial need analysis. *Deadline:* continuous. *Contact:* Program Director, Michigan Bureau of Student Financial Assistance, PO Box 30466, Lansing, MI 48909. *Web site:* www.michigan.gov/mistudentaid.

MINNESOTA

Advanced Placement/International Baccalaureate Degree Program. A non-need-based grant available for incoming Freshman who had an average score of 3 or higher on five AP courses or an average score of 4 or higher on 5 IB courses. Must be a Minnesota resident and attend a college in Minnesota. *Award:* Grant for use in freshman or sophomore year; not renewable. *Award amount:* $300–$700. *Number of awards:* 300. *Eligibility Requirements:* Applicant must be high school student; planning to enroll or expecting to enroll full- or part-time at a two-year or four-year institution or university; resident of Minnesota and studying in Minnesota. Available to U.S. citizens. *Application Requirements:* Application, test scores. *Deadline:* continuous. *Contact:* Brenda Larter, Minnesota Higher Education Services Office, 1450 Energy Park Drive, Suite 350, St. Paul, MN 55108-5227. *E-mail:* larter@heso.state.mn.us. *Phone:* 651-642-0567 Ext. 3417. *Fax:* 651-642-0675. *Web site:* www.mheso.state.mn.us.

Leadership, Excellence and Dedicated Service Scholarship. Awarded to high school seniors who enlist in the Minnesota National Guard. The award recognizes demonstrated leadership, community services and potential for success in the Minnesota National Guard. *Award:* Scholarship for use in freshman year; not renewable. *Award amount:* $1000. *Number of awards:* 30. *Eligibility Requirements:* Applicant must be high school student and planning to enroll or expecting to enroll full- or part-time at a two-year, four-year, or technical institution or university. Applicant must have served in the Air Force National Guard or Army National Guard. *Application Requirements:* Application, essay, references, transcript. *Deadline:* March 15. *Contact:* Barbara O'Reilly, Education Services Officer, Minnesota Department of Military Affairs, Veterans Services Building, 20 West 12th Street, St. Paul, MN 55155-2098. *E-mail:* barbara.oreilly@mn.ngb.army.mil. *Phone:* 651-282-4508. *Web site:* www.dma.state.mn.us.

Minnesota Educational Assistance for War Orphans. War orphans may qualify for $750 per year. Must have lost parent through service-related death. Children of deceased veterans may qualify for free tuition at State university, college, or vocational or technical schools, but not at University of Minnesota. Must have been resident of Minnesota for at least two years. *Award:* Grant for use in freshman, sophomore, junior, or senior year; renewable. *Award amount:* $750. *Eligibility Requirements:* Applicant must be enrolled or expecting to enroll full- or part-time at a two-year, four-year, or technical institution or university; resident of Minnesota and studying in Minnesota. Available to U.S. citizens. Applicant or parent must meet one or more of the following requirements: general military experience; retired from active duty; disabled or killed as a result of military service; prisoner of war; or missing in action. *Application Requirements:* Application, financial need analysis. *Deadline:* continuous. *Contact:* Terrence Logan, Management Analyst IV, Minnesota Department of Veterans' Affairs, 20 West 12th Street, Second Floor, St. Paul, MN 55155-2079. *Phone:* 651-296-2652. *Fax:* 651-296-3954. *Web site:* www.state.mn.us/ebranch/mdva.

Minnesota Indian Scholarship Program. One time award for Minnesota Native-Americans Indian. Contact for deadline information. *Award:* Scholarship for use in freshman, sophomore, junior, or senior year; not renewable. *Eligibility Requirements:* Applicant must be American Indian/Alaska Native; enrolled or expecting to enroll full- or part-time at a two-year, four-year, or technical institution or university and resident of Minnesota. Available to U.S. citizens. *Application Requirements:* Application. *Contact:* Lea Perkins, Director, Minnesota Indian Scholarship Office, Minnesota Department of CFL 1500 Highway 36W, Roseville, MN 55113-4266. *Phone:* 800-657-3927.

Minnesota Nurses Loan Forgiveness Program. This program offers loan repayment to registered nurse and licensed practical nurse students who agree to practice in a Minnesota nursing home or an Intermediate Care Facility for persons with mental retardation for a minimum one-year service obligation after completion of training. Candidates must apply while still in school. Up to 10 selections per year contingent upon state funding. *Academic/Career Areas:* Health and Medical Sciences; Nursing. *Award:* Grant for use in senior or graduate year; not renewable. *Award amount:* up to $3000. *Number of awards:* up to 10. *Eligibility Requirements:* Applicant must be enrolled or expecting to enroll full- or part-time at a two-year, four-year, or technical institution or university. Available to U.S. citizens. *Application Requirements:* Application, essay. *Deadline:* December 1. *Contact:* Karen Welter, Minnesota Department of Health, 121 East Seventh Place, Suite 460, PO Box 64975, St. Paul, MN 55164-0975. *E-mail:* karen.welter@health.state.mn.us. *Phone:* 651-282-6302. *Web site:* www.health.state.mn.us.

Minnesota Reciprocal Agreement. Renewable tuition waiver for Minnesota residents. Waives all or part of non-resident tuition surcharge at public institutions in Iowa, Kansas, Michigan, Missouri, Nebraska, North Dakota, South Dakota, and Wisconsin. Deadline is last day of academic term. *Award:* Scholarship for use in freshman, sophomore, junior, senior, or graduate year; renewable. *Eligibility Requirements:* Applicant must be enrolled or expecting to enroll full- or part-time at a two-year or four-year institution or university; resident of Minnesota and studying in Iowa, Kansas, Michigan, Missouri, Nebraska, North Dakota, South Dakota, or Wisconsin. Available to U.S. citizens. *Application Requirements:* Application. *Contact:* Minnesota Higher Education Services Office, 1450 Energy Park Drive, Suite 350, St. Paul, MN 55108-5227. *Phone:* 651-642-0567 Ext. 1. *Web site:* www.mheso.state.mn.us.

Minnesota Safety Officers' Survivor Program. Grant for eligible survivors of Minnesota public safety officer killed in the line of duty. Safety officers who have been permanently or totally disabled in the line of duty are also eligible. Must be used at a Minnesota institution participating in State Grant Program. Write for details. Must submit proof of death or disability and Public Safety Officers Benefit Fund Certificate. Must apply each year. Can be renewed for four years. *Award:* Grant for use in freshman, sophomore, junior, or senior year; not renewable. *Award amount:* up to $7088. *Eligibility Requirements:* Applicant must be enrolled or expecting to enroll full- or part-time at a two-year, four-year, or technical institution or university and studying in Minnesota. Applicant or parent of applicant must have employment or volunteer experience in police/firefighting. Available to U.S. citizens. *Application Requirements:* Application, proof of death/disability. *Deadline:* continuous. *Contact:* Minnesota Higher Education Services Office, 1450 Energy Park Drive, Suite 350, St. Paul, MN 55108-5227. *Phone:* 651-642-0567 Ext. 1. *Web site:* www.mheso.state.mn.us.

Minnesota State Grant Program. Need-based grant program available for Minnesota residents attending Minnesota colleges. Student covers 46% of cost with remainder covered by Pell Grant, parent contribution and state grant. Students apply with FAFSA and college administers the program on campus. *Award:* Grant for use in freshman, sophomore, junior, or senior year; not renewable. *Award amount:* $100–$7770. *Number of awards:* 71,000. *Eligibility Requirements:* Applicant must be age 17; enrolled or expecting to enroll full- or part-time at a two-year, four-year, or technical institution or university; resident of Minnesota and studying in Minnesota. Available to U.S. citizens. *Application Requirements:* Application, financial need analysis. *Deadline:* June 30. *Contact:* Minnesota Higher Education Services Office, 1450 Energy Park Drive, Suite 350, St. Paul, MN 55108. *Phone:* 651-642-0567 Ext. 1. *Web site:* www.mheso.state.mn.us.

Minnesota State Veterans' Dependents Assistance Program. Tuition assistance to dependents of persons considered to be prisoner-of-war or missing in action after August 1, 1958. Must be Minnesota resident attending Minnesota two- or four-year school. *Award:* Scholarship for use in freshman, sophomore, junior, or senior year; renewable. *Eligibility Requirements:* Applicant must be enrolled or expecting to enroll at a two-year or four-year institution; resident of Minnesota and studying in Minnesota. Available to U.S. citizens. Applicant or parent must meet one or more of the following requirements: general military experience; retired from active duty; disabled or killed as a result of military service; prisoner of war; or missing in action. *Application Requirements:* Application. *Deadline:* continuous. *Contact:* Minnesota Higher Education Services Office, 1450 Energy Park Drive, Suite 350, St. Paul, MN 55108-5227. *Web site:* www.mheso.state.mn.us.

Minnesota VA Educational Assistance for Veterans. One-time $750 stipend given to veterans who have used up all other federal funds, yet have time remaining on their delimiting period. Applicant must be a Minnesota resident and must be attending a Minnesota college or university, but not the University of Minnesota. *Award:* Grant for use in freshman, sophomore, junior, or senior year; not renewable. *Award amount:* $750. *Eligibility Requirements:* Applicant must be enrolled or expecting to enroll full- or part-time at a two-year, four-year, or technical institution or university; resident of Minnesota and studying in Minnesota. Available to U.S. citizens. Applicant must have general military experience. *Application Requirements:* Application, financial need analysis. *Deadline:* continuous. *Contact:* Terrence Logan, Management Analyst IV, Minnesota Department of Veterans' Affairs, 20 West 12th Street, Second Floor, St. Paul, MN 55155-2079. *Phone:* 651-296-2652. *Fax:* 651-296-3954. *Web site:* www.state.mn.us/ebranch/mdva.

Postsecondary Child Care Grant Program—Minnesota. One-time grant available for students not receiving MFIP. Based on financial need. Cannot exceed actual child care costs or maximum award chart (based on income). Must be Minnesota resident. For use at Minnesota two- or four-year school. *Award:* Grant for use in freshman, sophomore, junior, or senior year; not renewable. *Award amount:* $300–$2600. *Eligibility Requirements:* Applicant must be enrolled or expecting to enroll full- or part-time at a two-year or four-year institution or university; resident of Minnesota and studying in Minnesota. Available to U.S. citizens. *Application Requirements:* Application, financial need analysis. *Deadline:* continuous. *Contact:* Minnesota Higher Education Services Office, 1450 Energy Park Drive, Suite 350, St. Paul, MN 55108-5227. *Phone:* 651-642-0567 Ext. 1. *Web site:* www.mheso.state.mn.us.

MISSOURI

Advantage Missouri Program. Applicant must be seeking a program of instruction in a designated high demand field. High demand fields are determined each year. Borrower must work in Missouri in the high-demand field for one year for every year the loan is received to be forgiven. For Missouri residents. Must attend a postsecondary institution in Missouri. *Award:* Forgivable loan for use in freshman, sophomore, junior, or senior year; not renewable. *Award amount:* $2500. *Eligibility Requirements:* Applicant must be enrolled or expecting to enroll full-time at a two-year, four-year, or technical institution or university; resident of Missouri and studying in Missouri. Available to U.S. citizens. *Application Requirements:* Application, financial need analysis. *Deadline:* April 1. *Contact:* MOSTARS Information Center, Missouri Coordinating Board for Higher Education, 3515 Amazonas Drive, Jefferson City, MO 65109. *E-mail:* icweb@mocbhe.gov. *Phone:* 800-473-6757 Ext. 1. *Fax:* 573-751-6635. *Web site:* www.mostars.com.

Charles Gallagher Student Assistance Program. Available to Missouri residents attending Missouri colleges or universities full-time. Must be undergraduates with financial need. May reapply for up to a maximum of ten semesters. Free Application for Federal Student Aid (FAFSA) or a renewal must be received by the central processor by April 1 to be considered. *Award:* Grant for use in freshman, sophomore, junior, or senior year; not renewable. *Award amount:* $100–$1500. *Eligibility Requirements:* Applicant must be enrolled or expecting to enroll full-time at a two-year, four-year, or technical institution or university; resident of Missouri and studying in Missouri. Available to U.S. citizens. *Application Requirements:* Financial need analysis. *Deadline:* April 1. *Contact:* MOSTARS Information Center, Missouri Coordinating Board for Higher Education, 3515 Amazonas Drive, Jefferson City, MO 65109. *E-mail:* icweb@mocbhe.gov. *Phone:* 800-473-6757 Ext. 1. *Fax:* 573-751-6635. *Web site:* www.mostars.com.

John Charles Wilson Scholarship. One-time award to members in good standing of IAAI or the immediate family of a member or must be sponsored by an IAAI member. Must enroll or plan to enroll full-time in an accredited college or university that offers courses in police or fire sciences. Application available at Web site. Deadline is February 15. *Academic/Career Areas:* Fire Sciences; Law Enforcement/Police Administration. *Award:* Scholarship for use in freshman or graduate year; not renewable. *Award amount:* \$500–\$1000. *Number of awards:* 5. *Eligibility Requirements:* Applicant must be enrolled or expecting to enroll full-time at a two-year or four-year institution or university. Available to U.S. and non-U.S. citizens. *Application Requirements:* Application, essay, references, transcript. *Deadline:* February 15. *Contact:* Marsha Sipes, Office Manager, International Association of Arson Investigators Educational Foundation, Inc., 12770 Boenker Road, Bridgeton, MO 63044. *E-mail:* iaai@firearson.com. *Phone:* 314-739-4224. *Fax:* 314-739-4219. *Web site:* www.fire-investigators.org/.

Marguerite Ross Barnett Memorial Scholarship. Applicant must be employed (at least 20 hours per week) and attending school part-time. Must be Missouri resident and enrolled at a participating Missouri postsecondary school. Awards not available during summer term. Minimum age is 18. *Award:* Scholarship for use in freshman, sophomore, junior, or senior year; not renewable. *Award amount:* \$849–\$1557. *Eligibility Requirements:* Applicant must be age 18; enrolled or expecting to enroll part-time at a two-year or four-year institution or university; resident of Missouri and studying in Missouri. Available to U.S. citizens. *Application Requirements:* Application, financial need analysis. *Deadline:* April 1. *Contact:* MOSTARS Information Center, Missouri Coordinating Board for Higher Education, 3515 Amazonas Drive, Jefferson City, MO 65109. *E-mail:* icweb@mocbhe.gov. *Phone:* 800-473-6757 Ext. 1. *Fax:* 573-751-6635. *Web site:* www.mostars.com.

Missouri College Guarantee Program. Available to Missouri residents attending Missouri colleges full-time. Minimum 2.5 GPA required. Must have participated in high school extracurricular activities. *Award:* Grant for use in freshman, sophomore, junior, or senior year; not renewable. *Award amount:* \$100–\$4600. *Eligibility Requirements:* Applicant must be enrolled or expecting to enroll full-time at a two-year or four-year institution or university; resident of Missouri and studying in Missouri. Applicant must have 2.5 GPA or higher. Available to U.S. citizens. *Application Requirements:* Financial need analysis, test scores. *Deadline:* April 1. *Contact:* MOSTARS Information Center, Missouri Coordinating Board for Higher Education, 3515 Amazonas Drive, Jefferson City, MO 65109. *E-mail:* icweb@mocbhe.gov. *Phone:* 800-473-6757 Ext. 1. *Fax:* 573-751-6635. *Web site:* www.mostars.com.

Missouri Higher Education Academic Scholarship (Bright Flight). Awards of \$2000 for Missouri high school seniors. Must be in top 3% of Missouri SAT or ACT scorers. Must attend Missouri institution as full-time undergraduate. May reapply for up to ten semesters. Must be Missouri resident and U.S. citizen. *Award:* Scholarship for use in freshman, sophomore, junior, or senior year; not renewable. *Award amount:* \$2000. *Eligibility Requirements:* Applicant must be high school student; planning to enroll or expecting to enroll full-time at a two-year, four-year, or technical institution or university; resident of Missouri and studying in Missouri. Available to U.S. citizens. *Application Requirements:* Test scores. *Deadline:* July 31. *Contact:* MOSTARS Information Center, Missouri Coordinating Board for Higher Education, 3515 Amazonas Drive, Jefferson City, MO 65109. *E-mail:* icweb@mocbhe.gov. *Phone:* 800-473-6757 Ext. 1. *Fax:* 573-751-6635. *Web site:* www.mostars.com.

Missouri Minority Teaching Scholarship. Award may be used any year up to four years at an approved, participating Missouri institution. Scholarship is for minority Missouri residents in teaching programs. Recipients must commit to teach for five years in a Missouri public elementary or secondary school. Graduate students must teach math or science. Otherwise, award must be repaid. *Academic/Career Areas:* Education. *Award:* Scholarship for use in freshman, sophomore, junior, senior, or graduate year; renewable. *Award amount:* \$3000. *Number of awards:* 100. *Eligibility Requirements:* Applicant must be of African, Chinese, Hispanic, Indian, or Japanese heritage; American Indian/Alaska Native, Asian/Pacific Islander, or Black (non-Hispanic); enrolled or expecting to enroll full-time at a two-year or four-year institution or university; resident of Missouri and studying in Missouri. Applicant must have 3.5 GPA or higher. Available to U.S. citizens. *Application Requirements:* Application, essay, financial need analysis, references, test scores, transcript. *Deadline:* February 15. *Contact:* Laura Harrison, Administrative Assistant II, Missouri Department of Elementary and Secondary Education, PO Box 480, Jefferson City, MO 65102-0480. *E-mail:* lharriso@mail.dese.state.mo.us. *Phone:* 573-751-1668. *Fax:* 573-526-3580. *Web site:* www.dese.state.mo.us.

Missouri Teacher Education Scholarship (General). Nonrenewable award for Missouri high school seniors or Missouri resident college students. Must attend approved teacher training program at Missouri institution. Nonrenewable. Must rank in top 15 % of high school class on ACT/SAT. Merit-based award. *Academic/Career Areas:* Education. *Award:* Scholarship for use in freshman, sophomore, junior, or senior year; not renewable. *Award amount:* \$2000. *Number of awards:* 200–240. *Eligibility Requirements:* Applicant must be enrolled or expecting to enroll full-time at a two-year or four-year institution or university; resident of Missouri and studying in Missouri. Applicant must have 3.5 GPA or higher. Available to U.S. citizens. *Application Requirements:* Application, essay, references, test scores, transcript. *Deadline:* February 15. *Contact:* Laura Harrison, Administrative Assistant II, Missouri Department of Elementary and Secondary Education, PO Box 480, Jefferson City, MO 65102-0480. *E-mail:* lharriso@mail.dese.state.mo.us. *Phone:* 573-751-1668. *Fax:* 573-526-3580. *Web site:* www.dese.state.mo.us.

NEBRASKA

Nebraska National Guard Tuition Credit. Renewable award for members of the Nebraska National Guard. Pays 75% of enlisted soldier's tuition until he or she has received a baccalaureate degree. *Award:* Scholarship for use in freshman, sophomore, junior, or senior year; renewable. *Number of awards:* up to 1200. *Eligibility Requirements:* Applicant must be enrolled or expecting to enroll full- or part-time at a two-year, four-year, or technical institution or university; resident of Nebraska and studying in Nebraska. Applicant must have served in the Air Force National Guard or Army National Guard. *Application Requirements:* Application. *Deadline:* continuous. *Contact:* Cindy York, Administrative Assistant, Nebraska National Guard, 1300 Military Road, Lincoln, NE 68508-1090. *Phone:* 402-309-7143. *Fax:* 402-309-7128. *Web site:* www.neguard.com.

Nebraska Scholarship Assistance Program. Available to undergraduates attending a participating postsecondary institution in Nebraska. Available to Pell Grant recipients only. Nebraska residency required. Awards determined by each participating institution. Contact financial aid office at respective institution for more information. *Award:* Scholarship for use in freshman, sophomore, junior, or senior year; not renewable. *Eligibility Requirements:* Applicant must be enrolled or expecting to enroll full- or part-time at a two-year, four-year, or technical institution or university; resident of Nebraska and studying in Nebraska. *Application Requirements:* Financial need analysis. *Deadline:* continuous. *Contact:* financial aid office at college or university, State of Nebraska Coordinating Commission for Postsecondary Education. *Web site:* www.ccpe.state.ne.us.

Nebraska State Scholarship Award Program. Available to undergraduates attending a participating postsecondary institution in Nebraska. Available to Pell Grant recipients only. Nebraska residency not required. Awards determined by each participating institution. Contact financial aid office at respective institution for more details. *Award:* Scholarship for use in freshman, sophomore, junior, or senior year; not renewable. *Eligibility Requirements:* Applicant must be enrolled or expecting to enroll full- or part-time at an institution or university and studying in Nebraska. *Application Requirements:* Financial need analysis. *Deadline:* continuous. *Contact:* financial aid office at college or university, State of Nebraska Coordinating Commission for Postsecondary Education. *Web site:* www.ccpe.state.ne.us.

Postsecondary Education Award Program—Nebraska. Available to undergraduates attending a participating private, nonprofit postsecondary institution in Nebraska. Available to Pell Grant recipients only. Nebraska residency required. Awards determined by each participating institution. Contact financial aid office at respective institution for more information. *Award:* Scholarship for use in freshman, sophomore, junior, or senior year; not renewable. *Eligibility Requirements:* Applicant must be enrolled or expecting to enroll full- or part-time at a two-year or four-year institution; resident of Nebraska and studying in Nebraska. Available to U.S. citizens. *Application Requirements:* Financial need analysis. *Deadline:* continuous. *Contact:* financial aid office at college or university, State of Nebraska Coordinating Commission for Postsecondary Education. *Web site:* www.ccpe.state.ne.us.

NORTH DAKOTA

North Dakota Department of Transportation Engineering Grant. Educational grants for civil or construction engineering, or civil engineering technology, are awarded to students who have completed one year of course study at an institution of higher learning in North Dakota. Recipients must agree to work for the Department for a period of time at least equal to the grant period or repay the grant at 6% interest. Minimum 2.0 GPA required. *Academic/Career Areas:* Civil Engineering; Engineering/Technology. *Award:* Grant for use in sophomore, junior, or senior year; renewable. *Award amount:* $2000. *Number of awards:* 1–10. *Eligibility Requirements:* Applicant must be enrolled or expecting to enroll full-time at a four-year, or technical institution and studying in North Dakota. Available to U.S. citizens. *Application Requirements:* Application, financial need analysis, interview, transcript. *Deadline:* continuous. *Contact:* Lorrie Pavlicek, Human Resources Manager, North Dakota Department of Transportation, 503, 38th Street South, Fargo, ND 58103. *E-mail:* lpavlice@state.nd.us. *Phone:* 701-239-8934. *Fax:* 701-239-8939. *Web site:* www.state.nd.us/dot/.

North Dakota Indian College Scholarship Program. Renewable award to Native-Americans residents of North Dakota. Priority given to full-time undergraduate students. Minimum 2.0 GPA required. *Award:* Scholarship for use in freshman, sophomore, junior, senior, or graduate year; renewable. *Award amount:* $700–$2000. *Number of awards:* up to 150. *Eligibility Requirements:* Applicant must be American Indian/Alaska Native; enrolled or expecting to enroll full-time at a two-year, four-year, or technical institution or university and resident of North Dakota. Available to U.S. citizens. *Application Requirements:* Application, financial need analysis, transcript, proof of tribal enrollment. *Deadline:* July 15. *Contact:* Rhonda Schauer, SAA Director, North Dakota University System, 600 East Boulevard Avenue, Department 215, Bismarck, ND 58505-0230. *Phone:* 701-328-9661. *Web site:* www.ndus.nodak.edu.

North Dakota Indian Scholarship Program. Assists Native-Americans North Dakota residents in obtaining a college education. Priority given to full-time undergraduate students and those having a 3.5 GPA or higher. Certification of tribal enrollment required. For use at North Dakota institution. *Award:* Scholarship for use in freshman, sophomore, junior, senior, or graduate year; renewable. *Award amount:* $700–$2000. *Number of awards:* 120–150. *Eligibility Requirements:* Applicant must be American Indian/Alaska Native; enrolled or expecting to enroll at a two-year or four-year institution or university; resident of North Dakota and studying in North Dakota. Applicant must have 3.5 GPA or higher. *Application Requirements:* Application, financial need analysis, transcript. *Deadline:* July 15. *Contact:* Rhonda Schauer, Coordinator of American Indian Higher Education, State of North Dakota, 600 East Boulevard, Department 215, Bismarck, ND 58505-0230. *Phone:* 701-328-2166. *Web site:* www.ndus.nodak.edu.

North Dakota Scholars Program. Provides scholarships equal to cost of tuition at the public colleges in North Dakota for North Dakota residents. Must score at or above the 95th percentile on ACT and rank in top twenty percent of high school graduation class. Must take ACT in fall. For high school seniors with a minimum 3.5 GPA. Application deadline is October ACT test date. *Award:* Scholarship for use in freshman, sophomore, junior, or senior year; renewable. *Number of awards:* 45–50. *Eligibility Requirements:* Applicant must be high school student; planning to enroll or expecting to enroll full-time at a two-year or four-year institution or university; resident of North Dakota and studying in North Dakota. Applicant must have 3.5 GPA or higher. Available to U.S. citizens. *Application Requirements:* Application, test scores. *Contact:* Peggy Wipf, Director of Financial Aid, State of North Dakota, 600 East Boulevard, Department 215, Bismarck, ND 58505-0230. *Phone:* 701-328-4114. *Web site:* www.ndus.nodak.edu.

North Dakota Student Financial Assistance Grants. Aids North Dakota residents attending an approved college or university in North Dakota. Must be enrolled in a program of at least nine months in length. *Award:* Grant for use in freshman, sophomore, junior, or senior year; not renewable. *Award amount:* up to $600. *Number of awards:* 2500–2600. *Eligibility Requirements:* Applicant must be enrolled or expecting to enroll full-time at a two-year or four-year institution or university; resident of North Dakota and studying in North Dakota. Available to U.S. citizens. *Application Requirements:* Application, financial need analysis. *Deadline:* April 15. *Contact:* Peggy Wipf, Director of Financial Aid, State of North Dakota, 600 East Boulevard, Department 215, Bismarck, ND 58505-0230. *Phone:* 701-328-4114. *Web site:* www.ndus.nodak.edu.

OHIO

Ohio Academic Scholarship Program. Award for academically outstanding Ohio residents planning to attend an approved Ohio college. Must be a high school senior intending to enroll full-time. Award is renewable for up to four years. Must rank in upper quarter of class or have a minimum GPA of 3.5. *Award:* Scholarship for use in freshman, sophomore, junior, or senior year; renewable. *Award amount:* $2000. *Number of awards:* 1000. *Eligibility Requirements:* Applicant must be high school student; planning to enroll or expecting to enroll full-time at a two-year or four-year institution; resident of Ohio and studying in Ohio. Applicant must have 3.5 GPA or higher. Available to U.S. citizens. *Application Requirements:* Application, test scores, transcript. *Deadline:* February 23. *Contact:* Sarina Wilks, Program Administrator, Ohio Board of Regents, PO Box 182452, Columbus, OH 43218-2452. *E-mail:* swilks@regents.state.oh.us. *Phone:* 614-752-9528. *Fax:* 614-752-5903. *Web site:* www.regents.state.oh.us.

Ohio Instructional Grant. Award for low- and middle-income Ohio residents attending an approved college or school in Ohio or Pennsylvania. Must be enrolled full-time and have financial need. Average award is $630. May be used for any course of study except theology. *Award:* Grant for use in freshman, sophomore, junior, or senior year; renewable. *Award amount:* $210–$3750. *Eligibility Requirements:* Applicant must be enrolled or expecting to enroll full-time at a two-year or four-year institution or university; resident of Ohio and studying in Ohio or Pennsylvania. Available to U.S. citizens. *Application Requirements:* Application, financial need analysis. *Deadline:* October 1. *Contact:* Charles Shahid, Assistant Director, Ohio Board of Regents, PO Box 182452, Columbus, OH 43218-2452. *E-mail:* cshahid@regents.state.oh.us. *Phone:* 614-644-9595. *Fax:* 614-752-5903. *Web site:* www.regents.state.oh.us.

Ohio Missing in Action and Prisoners of War Orphans Scholarship. Renewable award aids children of Vietnam conflict servicemen who have been classified as missing in action or prisoner of war. Must be an Ohio resident, be 16-21, and be enrolled full-time at an Ohio college. Full tuition awards. *Award:* Scholarship for use in freshman, sophomore, junior, or senior year; renewable. *Number of awards:* 1–5. *Eligibility Requirements:* Applicant must be age 16-21; enrolled or expecting to enroll full-time at a two-year or four-year institution; resident of Ohio and studying in Ohio. Available to U.S. citizens. Applicant or parent must meet one or more of the following requirements: general military experience; retired from active duty; disabled or killed as a result of military service; prisoner of war; or missing in action. *Application Requirements:* Application. *Deadline:* July 1. *Contact:* Sue Minturn, Program Administrator, Ohio Board of Regents, PO Box 182452, Columbus, OH 43218-2452. *E-mail:* sminturn@regents.state.oh.us. *Phone:* 614-752-9536. *Fax:* 614-752-5903. *Web site:* www.regents.state.oh.us.

Ohio National Guard Scholarship Program. Scholarships are for undergraduate studies at an approved Ohio postsecondary institution. Applicants must enlist for six years of Selective Service Reserve Duty in the Ohio National Guard. Scholarship pays 100% instructional and general fees for public institutions and an average of cost of public schools is available for private schools. Must be 18 years of age or older. Award is renewable. Deadlines: July 1, November 1, February 1, April 1. *Award:* Scholarship for use in freshman, sophomore, junior, or senior year; renewable. *Award amount:* up to $3000. *Number of awards:* 3500–10,000. *Eligibility Requirements:* Applicant must be age 18; enrolled or expecting to enroll full- or part-time at a two-year, four-year, or technical institution or university and studying in Ohio. Available to U.S. citizens. Applicant must have served in the Air Force National Guard or Army National Guard. *Application Requirements:* Application. *Contact:* Mrs. Toni Davis, Grants Administrator, Ohio National Guard, 2825 West Dublin Granville Road, Columbus, OH 43235-2789. *E-mail:* toni.davis@tagoh.org. *Phone:* 614-336-7032. *Fax:* 614-336-7318.

Ohio Safety Officers College Memorial Fund. Renewable award covering up to full tuition is available to children and surviving spouses of peace officers and fire fighters killed in the line of duty in any state. Children must be under 26 years of age. Must be an Ohio resident and enroll full-time or part-time at an Ohio college or university. *Award:* Scholarship for use in freshman, sophomore, junior, or senior year; renewable. *Number of awards:* 50–65. *Eligibility Requirements:* Applicant must be age 25 or under; enrolled or expecting to enroll full- or part-time at a two-year or four-year institution or university; resident of Ohio and studying in Ohio. Applicant or parent of applicant must have employment or volunteer experience in police/firefighting. Available to U.S. citizens. *Application Requirements: Deadline:* continuous. *Contact:* Barbara Metheney, Program Administrator, Ohio Board of Regents, PO Box 182452, Columbus, OH 43218-2452. *E-mail:* bmethene@regents.state.oh.us. *Phone:* 614-752-9535. *Fax:* 614-752-5903. *Web site:* www.regents.state.oh.us.

Ohio Student Choice Grant Program. Renewable award available to Ohio residents attending private colleges within the state. Must be enrolled full time in a bachelor's degree program. Do not apply to state. Check with financial aid office of college. *Award:* Grant for use in freshman, sophomore, junior, or senior year; renewable. *Award amount:* up to $1038. *Eligibility Requirements:* Applicant must be enrolled or expecting to enroll full-time at a four-year institution; resident of Ohio and studying in Ohio. Available to U.S. citizens. *Application Requirements: Deadline:* continuous. *Contact:* Barbara Metheney, Program Administrator, Ohio Board of Regents, PO Box 182452, Columbus, OH 43218-2452. *E-mail:* bmethene@regents.state.oh.us. *Phone:* 614-752-9535. *Fax:* 614-752-5903. *Web site:* www.regents.state.oh.us.

Ohio War Orphans Scholarship. Aids Ohio residents attending an eligible college in Ohio. Must be between the ages of 16-21, the child of a disabled or deceased veteran, and enrolled full-time. Renewable up to five years. Amount of award varies. Must include Form DD214. *Award:* Scholarship for use in freshman, sophomore, junior, or senior year; renewable. *Number of awards:* 300–450. *Eligibility Requirements:* Applicant must be age 16-21; enrolled or expecting to enroll full-time at a two-year or four-year institution; resident of Ohio and studying in Ohio. Available to U.S. citizens. Applicant or parent must meet one or more of the following requirements: general military experience; retired from active duty; disabled or killed as a result of military service; prisoner of war; or missing in action. *Application Requirements:* Application. *Deadline:* July 1. *Contact:* Sue Minturn, Program Administrator, Ohio Board of Regents, PO Box 182452, Columbus, OH 43218-2452. *E-mail:* sminturn@regents.state.oh.us. *Phone:* 614-752-9536. *Fax:* 614-752-5903. *Web site:* www.regents.state.oh.us.

Part-time Student Instructional Grant. Renewable grants for part-time undergraduates who are Ohio residents. Award amounts vary. Must attend an Ohio institution. *Award:* Grant for use in freshman, sophomore, or junior year; renewable. *Eligibility Requirements:* Applicant must be enrolled or expecting to enroll part-time at a two-year or four-year institution or university; resident of Ohio and studying in Ohio. Available to U.S. citizens.

Application Requirements: Application, financial need analysis. *Deadline:* continuous. *Contact:* Barbara Metheney, Program Administrator, Ohio Board of Regents, PO Box 182452, Columbus, OH 43218-2452. *E-mail:* bmethene@regents.state.oh.us. *Phone:* 614-752-9535. *Fax:* 614-752-5903. *Web site:* www.regents.state.oh.us.

Robert C. Byrd Honors Scholarship. Renewable award for graduating high school seniors who demonstrate outstanding academic achievement. Each Ohio high school receives applications by January of each year. School can submit one application for each 200 students in the senior class. *Award:* Scholarship for use in freshman, sophomore, junior, or senior year; renewable. *Award amount:* $1500. *Eligibility Requirements:* Applicant must be high school student; planning to enroll or expecting to enroll at a two-year or four-year institution or university and resident of Ohio. Applicant must have 3.5 GPA or higher. Available to U.S. citizens. *Application Requirements:* Application, test scores. *Deadline:* March 10. *Contact:* Charles Shahid, Program Coordinator, Ohio Board of Regents, PO Box 182452, Columbus, OH 43218-2452. *E-mail:* cshahid@regents.state.oh.us. *Phone:* 614-644-5959. *Fax:* 614-752-5903. *Web site:* www.regents.state.oh.us.

OKLAHOMA

Academic Scholars Program. Encourages students of high academic ability to attend institutions in Oklahoma. Renewable up to four years. ACT or SAT scores must fall between 99.5 and 100th percentiles, or be designated as a National Merit Scholar or finalist. *Award:* Scholarship for use in freshman, sophomore, junior, or senior year; renewable. *Award amount:* $3500–$5500. *Eligibility Requirements:* Applicant must be high school student; planning to enroll or expecting to enroll full-time at a two-year or four-year institution or university and studying in Oklahoma. Available to U.S. and non-U.S. citizens. *Application Requirements:* Application, test scores, transcript. *Deadline:* continuous. *Contact:* Oklahoma State Regents for Higher Education, PO Box 108850, Oklahoma City, OK 73101-8850. *E-mail:* studentinfo@osrhe.edu. *Phone:* 800-858-1840. *Fax:* 405-225-9230. *Web site:* www.okhighered.org.

Future Teacher Scholarship—Oklahoma. Open to outstanding Oklahoma high school graduates who agree to teach in shortage areas. Must rank in top 15% of graduating class or score above 85th percentile on ACT or similar test, or be accepted in an educational program. Students nominated by institution. Reapply to renew. Must attend college/university in Oklahoma. Contact institution's financial aid office for application deadline. *Academic/Career Areas:* Education. *Award:* Scholarship for use in freshman, sophomore, junior, senior, or graduate year; not renewable. *Award amount:* up to $1500. *Eligibility Requirements:* Applicant must be enrolled or expecting to enroll full- or part-time at a two-year or four-year institution or university; resident of Oklahoma and studying in Oklahoma. Available to U.S. and non-U.S. citizens. *Application Requirements:* Application, essay, test scores, transcript. *Contact:* Oklahoma State Regents for Higher Education, PO Box 108850, Oklahoma City, OK 73101-8850. *Phone:* 800-858-1840. *Fax:* 405-225-9230. *Web site:* www.okhighered.org.

Oklahoma Tuition Aid Grant. Award for Oklahoma residents enrolled at an Oklahoma institution at least part-time per semester in a degree program. May be enrolled in two- or four-year or approved vocational-technical institution. Award of up to $1000 per year. Application is made through FAFSA. *Award:* Grant for use in freshman, sophomore, junior, senior, or graduate year; renewable. *Award amount:* $200–$1000. *Number of awards:* 23,000. *Eligibility Requirements:* Applicant must be enrolled or expecting to enroll full- or part-time at a two-year, four-year, or technical institution or university; resident of Oklahoma and studying in Oklahoma. Available to U.S. citizens. *Application Requirements:* Application, financial need analysis, FAFSA. *Deadline:* April 30. *Contact:* Oklahoma State Regents for Higher Education, PO Box 3020, Oklahoma City, OK 73101-3020. *E-mail:* otaginfo@otag.org. *Phone:* 405-225-9456. *Fax:* 405-225-9392. *Web site:* www.okhighered.org.

Regional University Baccalaureate Scholarship. Renewable award for Oklahoma residents attending one of 11 participating Oklahoma public universities. Must have an ACT composite score of at least 30 or be a National Merit Semifinalist or commended student. In addition to the award amount, each recipient also will receive a resident tuition waiver from the institution. Must maintain a 3.25 GPA. Deadlines vary depending upon the institution attended. *Award:* Scholarship for use in freshman, sophomore, junior, or senior year; renewable. *Award amount:* $3000. *Eligibility Requirements:* Applicant must be enrolled or expecting to enroll full-time at an institution or university; resident of Oklahoma and studying in Oklahoma. *Application Requirements:* Application. *Contact:* Oklahoma State Regents for Higher Education, PO Box 108850, Oklahoma City, OK 73101-8850. *E-mail:* studentinfo@osrhe.edu. *Phone:* 800-858-1840. *Fax:* 405-225-9230. *Web site:* www.okhighered.org.

SOUTH DAKOTA

Education Benefits for Dependents of POWs and MIAs. Children and spouses of prisoners of war, or of persons listed as missing in action, are entitled to attend a state-supported school without the payment of tuition or mandatory fees provided they are not eligible for equal or greater federal benefits. File SDDVA for E-12 available at financial aid offices. Must be a South Dakota resident intending to study in South Dakota. *Award:* Scholarship for use in freshman, sophomore, junior, or senior year; not renewable. *Eligibility Requirements:* Applicant must be enrolled or expecting to enroll at an institution or university; resident of South Dakota and studying in South Dakota. Available to U.S. citizens. Applicant or parent must meet one or more of the following requirements: general military experience; retired from active duty; disabled or killed as a result of military service; prisoner of war; or missing in action. *Application Requirements:* Application. *Contact:* Dr. Lesta V. Turchen, Senior Administrator, South Dakota Board of Regents, 306 East Capitol Avenue, Suite 200, Pierre, SD 57501-3159. *Phone:* 605-773-3455. *Fax:* 605-773-2422. *Web site:* www.ris.sdbor.edu.

Haines Memorial Scholarship. One-time scholarship for South Dakota public university students who are sophomores, juniors, or seniors having at least a 2.5 GPA and majoring in a teacher education program. Include resume with application. Must be South Dakota resident. *Academic/Career Areas:* Education. *Award:* Scholarship for use in sophomore, junior, or senior year; not renewable. *Award amount:* $2150. *Number of awards:* 1. *Eligibility Requirements:* Applicant must be enrolled or expecting to enroll at an institution or university; resident of South Dakota and studying in South Dakota. Applicant must have 2.5 GPA or higher. *Application Requirements:* Application, autobiography, essay, resume. *Deadline:* February 25. *Contact:* South Dakota Board of Regents, 306 East Capitol Avenue, Suite 200, Pierre, SD 57501-3159. *Web site:* www.ris.sdbor.edu.

South Dakota Aid to Dependents of Deceased Veterans. Program provides free tuition for children of deceased veterans who are under the age of 25, are residents of South Dakota, and whose mother or father was killed in action or died of other causes while on active duty. ("Veteran" for this purpose is as defined by South Dakota Codified Laws.) Parent must have been a bona fide resident of SD for at least six months immediately preceding entry into active service. Eligibility is for state-supported schools only. Must use SDDVA form E-12 available at financial aid offices. *Award:* Scholarship for use in freshman, sophomore, junior, or senior year; not renewable. *Eligibility Requirements:* Applicant must be age 25 or under; enrolled or expecting to enroll at a two-year or four-year institution; resident of South Dakota and studying in South Dakota. Available to U.S. citizens. Applicant or parent must meet one or more of the following requirements: general military experience; retired from active duty; disabled or killed as a result of military service; prisoner of war; or missing in action. *Application Requirements:* Application. *Contact:* Dr. Lesta V. Turchen, Senior Administrator, South Dakota Board of Regents, 306 East Capitol Avenue, Suite 200, Pierre, SD 57501-3159. *Phone:* 605-773-3455. *Fax:* 605-773-2422. *Web site:* www.ris.sdbor.edu.

South Dakota Board of Regents Senior Citizens Tuition Assistance. Award for tuition assistance for any postsecondary academic year of study to senior citizens age 65 and older. Write for further details. Must be a South Dakota resident and attend a school in South Dakota. *Award:* Scholarship for use in freshman, sophomore, junior, or senior year; not renewable. *Eligibility Requirements:* Applicant must be age 65; enrolled or expecting to enroll at an institution or university; resident of South Dakota and studying in South Dakota. *Application Requirements:* Application. *Deadline:* continuous. *Contact:* South Dakota Board of Regents, 306 East Capitol Avenue, Suite 200, Pierre, SD 57501-3159. *Web site:* www.ris.sdbor.edu.

South Dakota Board of Regents State Employee Tuition Assistance. Award for South Dakota state employees for any postsecondary academic year of study in South Dakota institution. Must be U.S. citizen. Write for requirements and other details. *Award:* Scholarship for use in freshman, sophomore, junior, or senior year; not renewable. *Eligibility Requirements:* Applicant must be enrolled or expecting to enroll at an institution or university; resident of South Dakota and studying in South Dakota. Applicant or parent of applicant must have employment or volunteer experience in designated career field. Available to U.S. citizens. *Application Requirements: Deadline:* continuous. *Contact:* South Dakota Board of Regents, 306 East Capitol Avenue, Suite 200, Pierre, SD 57501-3159. *Web site:* www.ris.sdbor.edu.

South Dakota Education Benefits for National Guard Members. Guard members who meet the requirements for admission are eligible for a 50% reduction in undergraduate tuition charges at any state-supported school for up to a maximum of four academic years. Provision also covers one program of study, approved by the State Board of Education, at any state vocational school. Must be state resident and member of the SD Army or Air Guard throughout period for which benefits are sought. Must contact financial aid office for full details and forms at time of registration. *Award:* Scholarship for use in freshman, sophomore, junior, or senior year; not renewable. *Eligibility Requirements:* Applicant must be enrolled or expecting to enroll at a two-year, four-year, or technical institution or university; resident of South Dakota and studying in South Dakota. Available to U.S. citizens. Applicant must have served in the Air Force National Guard or Army National Guard. *Application Requirements:* Application. *Contact:* Dr. Lesta V. Turchen, Senior Administrator, South Dakota Board of Regents, 306 East Capitol Avenue, Suite 200, Pierre, SD 57501-3159. *Phone:* 605-773-3455. *Fax:* 605-773-2422. *Web site:* www.ris.sdbor.edu.

South Dakota Education Benefits for Veterans. Certain veterans are eligible for free undergraduate tuition assistance at state-supported schools provided they are not eligible for educational payments under the GI Bill or any other federal educational program. Contact financial aid office for full details and forms. May receive one month of free tuition for each month of qualifying service (minimum one year, maximum four years). Must be resident of South Dakota. *Award:* Scholarship for use in freshman, sophomore, junior, or senior year; not renewable. *Eligibility Requirements:* Applicant must be enrolled or expecting to enroll at an institution or university; resident of South Dakota and studying in South Dakota. Available to U.S. citizens. Applicant must have general military experience. *Application Requirements:* Application, DD Form 214. *Contact:* Dr. Lesta V. Turchen, Senior Administrator, South Dakota Board of Regents, 306 East Capitol Avenue, Suite 200, Pierre, SD 57501-3159. *Phone:* 605-773-3455. *Fax:* 605-773-2422. *Web site:* www.ris.sdbor.edu.

WISCONSIN

Handicapped Student Grant—Wisconsin. One-time awards available to residents of Wisconsin who have severe or profound hearing or visual impairment. Must be enrolled at least half-time at a nonprofit institution. If the handicap prevents the student from attending a Wisconsin school, the award may be used out-of-state in a specialized college. *Award:* Grant for use in freshman, sophomore, junior, or senior year; not renewable. *Award amount:* \$250–\$1800. *Eligibility Requirements:* Applicant must be enrolled or expecting to enroll full- or part-time at a two-year, four-year, or technical institution or university and resident of Wisconsin. Applicant must be hearing impaired or visually impaired. Available to U.S. and non-U.S. citizens. *Application Requirements:* Application, financial need analysis. *Deadline:* continuous. *Contact:* Sandra Thomas, Wisconsin Higher Educational Aid Board, PO Box 7885, Madison, WI 53707-7885. *E-mail:* sandy.thomas@heab.state.wi.us. *Phone:* 608-266-0888. *Fax:* 608-267-2808. *Web site:* www.heab.state.wi.us.

Minnesota-Wisconsin Reciprocity Program. Wisconsin residents may attend a Minnesota public institution and pay the reciprocity tuition charged by Minnesota institution. All programs are eligible except doctoral programs in medicine, dentistry, and veterinary medicine. *Award:* Scholarship for use in freshman, sophomore, junior, or senior year; renewable. *Eligibility Requirements:* Applicant must be enrolled or expecting to enroll full- or part-time at a two-year, four-year, or technical institution or university; resident of Wisconsin and studying in Minnesota. Available to U.S. citizens. *Application Requirements:* Application. *Deadline:* continuous. *Contact:* Cindy Lehrman, Wisconsin Higher Educational Aid Board, PO Box 7885, Madison, WI 53707-7885. *E-mail:* cindy.lehrman@heab.state.wi.us. *Phone:* 608-267-2209. *Fax:* 608-267-2808. *Web site:* www.heab.state.wi.us.

Minority Retention Grant-Wisconsin. Provides financial assistance to African-American, Native-Americans, Hispanic, and former citizens of Laos, Vietnam, and Cambodia, for study in Wisconsin. Must be Wisconsin resident, enrolled at least half-time in a two-year or four-year nonprofit college, and must show financial need. *Award:* Grant for use in sophomore, junior, senior, or graduate year; not renewable. *Award amount:* \$250–\$2500. *Eligibility Requirements:* Applicant must be American Indian/Alaska Native,

Asian/Pacific Islander, Black (non-Hispanic), or Hispanic; enrolled or expecting to enroll full- or part-time at a two-year, four-year, or technical institution; resident of Wisconsin and studying in Wisconsin. Available to U.S. and non-U.S. citizens. *Application Requirements:* Application, financial need analysis. *Deadline:* continuous. *Contact:* Mary Lou Kuzdas, Program Coordinator, Wisconsin Higher Educational Aid Board, PO Box 7885, Madison, WI 53707-7885. *E-mail:* mary.kuzdas@heab.state.wi.us. *Phone:* 608-267-2212. *Fax:* 608-267-2808. *Web site:* www.heab.state.wi.us.

Nursing Student Loan Program. Provides forgivable loans to students enrolled in a nursing program. Must be a Wisconsin resident studying in Wisconsin. Application deadline is May 3. *Academic/Career Areas:* Nursing. *Award:* Forgivable loan for use in freshman, sophomore, junior, or senior year; not renewable. *Award amount:* $250–$3000. *Eligibility Requirements:* Applicant must be enrolled or expecting to enroll full- or part-time at a two-year, four-year, or technical institution or university; resident of Wisconsin and studying in Wisconsin. Available to U.S. and non-U.S. citizens. *Application Requirements:* Application, financial need analysis. *Deadline:* May 3. *Contact:* Alice Winters, Program Coordinator, Wisconsin Higher Educational Aid Board, PO Box 7885, Madison, WI 53707-7885. *E-mail:* alice.winters@heab.state.wi.us. *Phone:* 608-267-2213. *Fax:* 608-267-2808. *Web site:* www.heab.state.wi.us.

Talent Incentive Program—Wisconsin. Assists residents of Wisconsin who are attending a nonprofit institution in Wisconsin and have substantial financial need. Must meet income criteria, be considered economically and educationally disadvantaged and be enrolled at least half-time. *Award:* Grant for use in freshman, sophomore, junior, or senior year; renewable. *Award amount:* $600–$1800. *Eligibility Requirements:* Applicant must be enrolled or expecting to enroll full- or part-time at a two-year, four-year, or technical institution or university; resident of Wisconsin and studying in Wisconsin. Available to U.S. and non-U.S. citizens. *Application Requirements:* Application, financial need analysis. *Deadline:* continuous. *Contact:* John Whitt, Program Coordinator, Wisconsin Higher Educational Aid Board, PO Box 7885, Madison, WI 53707-7885. *E-mail:* john.whitt@heab.state.wi.us. *Phone:* 608-266-1665. *Fax:* 608-267-2808. *Web site:* www.heab.state.wi.us.

Teacher of the Visually Impaired Loan Program. Provides forgivable loans to students who enroll in programs that lead to be certified as a teacher of the visually impaired or an orientation and mobility instructor. Must be a Wisconsin resident. For study in Wisconsin, Illinois, Iowa and Michigan. *Award:* Forgivable loan for use in freshman, sophomore, junior, senior, or postgraduate years; not renewable. *Award amount:* $250–$10,000. *Eligibility Requirements:* Applicant must be enrolled or expecting to enroll full- or part-time at a two-year, four-year, or technical institution or university; resident of Wisconsin and studying in Illinois, Iowa, Michigan, or Wisconsin. Available to U.S. and non-U.S. citizens. *Application Requirements:* Application, financial need analysis. *Deadline:* continuous. *Contact:* John Whitt, Program Coordinator, Wisconsin Higher Educational Aid Board, PO Box 7885, Madison, WI 53707-7885. *E-mail:* john.whitt@heab.state.wi.us. *Phone:* 608-266-0888. *Fax:* 608-267-2808. *Web site:* www.heab.state.wi.us.

Tuition and Fee Reimbursement Grants. Up to 85% tuition and fee reimbursement for Wisconsin veterans who were discharged from active duty within the last 10 years. Undergraduate courses must be completed at accredited Wisconsin schools. Those attending Minnesota public colleges, universities, and technical schools that have a tuition reciprocity agreement with Wisconsin also may qualify. Must meet military service requirements. Application must be received no later than 60 days after the completion of the course. *Award:* Grant for use in freshman, sophomore, junior, or senior year; renewable. *Eligibility Requirements:* Applicant must be enrolled or expecting to enroll full-time at a two-year, four-year, or technical institution or university; resident of Wisconsin and studying in Minnesota or Wisconsin. Available to U.S. citizens. Applicant must have general military experience. *Application Requirements:* Application. *Contact:* Mr. Steve Olson, Public Relations Officer, Wisconsin Department of Veterans Affairs, PO Box 7843, Madison, WI 53707-7843. *Phone:* 608-266-1311. *Web site:* dva.state.wi.us.

Wisconsin Academic Excellence Scholarship. Renewable award for high school seniors with the highest GPA in graduating class. Must be a Wisconsin resident. Award covers tuition for up to four years. Must maintain 3.5 GPA for renewal. Scholarships of up to $2250 each. Must attend a nonprofit Wisconsin institution full-time. *Award:* Scholarship for use in freshman, sophomore, junior, or senior year; renewable. *Award amount:* $250–$2250. *Eligibility Requirements:* Applicant must be high school student; planning to enroll or expecting to enroll full-time at a two-year, four-year, or technical institution or university; resident of Wisconsin and studying in Wisconsin. Applicant must have 3.5 GPA or higher. Available to U.S. and non-U.S. citizens. *Application Requirements:* Transcript. *Deadline:* continuous. *Contact:* Alice Winters, Program Coordinator, Wisconsin Higher Educational Aid Board, PO Box 7885, Madison, WI 53707-7885. *E-mail:* alice.winters@heab.state.wi.us. *Phone:* 608-267-2213. *Fax:* 608-267-2808. *Web site:* www.heab.state.wi.us.

Wisconsin Department of Veterans Affairs Retraining Grants. Renewable award for veterans, unmarried spouses of deceased veterans, or dependents of deceased veterans. Must be resident of Wisconsin and attend an institution in Wisconsin. Veteran must be recently unemployed and show financial need. Must enroll in a vocational or technical program that can reasonably be expected to lead to employment. Course work at four-year colleges or universities does not qualify as retraining. *Award:* Grant for use in freshman or sophomore year; renewable. *Award amount:* up to $3000. *Eligibility Requirements:* Applicant must be enrolled or expecting to enroll full- or part-time at a technical institution; resident of Wisconsin and studying in Wisconsin. Applicant or parent must meet one or more of the following requirements: general military experience; retired from active duty; disabled or killed as a result of military service; prisoner of war; or missing in action. *Application Requirements:* Application, financial need analysis. *Contact:* Mr. Steve Olson, Public Relations Officer, Wisconsin Department of Veterans Affairs, PO Box 7843, Madison, WI 53707-7843. *Phone:* 608-266-1311. *Web site:* dva.state.wi.us.

Wisconsin Higher Education Grants (WHEG). Grants for residents of Wisconsin attending a campus of the University of Wisconsin or Wisconsin Technical College. Must be enrolled at least half-time and show financial need. Renewable for up to five years. *Award:* Grant for use in freshman, sophomore, junior, or senior year; not renewable. *Award amount:* $250–$1800. *Eligibility Requirements:* Applicant must be enrolled or expecting to enroll full- or part-time at a two-year, four-year, or technical institution or university; resident of Wisconsin and studying in Wisconsin. Available to U.S. and non-U.S. citizens. *Application Requirements:* Application, financial need analysis. *Deadline:* continuous. *Contact:* Sandra Thomas, Program Coordinator, Wisconsin Higher

Educational Aid Board, PO Box 7885, Madison, WI 53707-7885. *E-mail:* sandy.thomas@heab.state.wi.us. *Phone:* 608-266-0888. *Fax:* 608-267-2808. *Web site:* www.heab.state.wi.us.

Wisconsin National Guard Tuition Grant. Renewable award for active members of the Wisconsin National Guard in good standing, who successfully complete a course of study at a qualifying school. Award covers full tuition, excluding fees, not to exceed undergraduate tuition charged by University of Wisconsin-Madison. Must have a minimum 2.0 GPA. *Award:* Grant for use in freshman, sophomore, junior, or senior year; renewable. *Award amount:* up to $1927. *Number of awards:* up to 4000. *Eligibility Requirements:* Applicant must be enrolled or expecting to enroll full- or part-time at a two-year, four-year, or technical institution or university and resident of Wisconsin. Applicant must have 2.5 GPA or higher. Available to U.S. citizens. Applicant must have served in the Air Force National Guard or Army National Guard. *Application Requirements:* Application. *Deadline:* continuous. *Contact:* Karen Behling, Tuition Grant Administrator, Department of Military Affairs, PO Box 14587, Madison, WI 53714-0587. *E-mail:* karen.behling@dma.state.wi.us. *Phone:* 608-242-3159. *Fax:* 608-242-3154. *Web site:* wisconsinguard.com.

Wisconsin Native American Student Grant. Grants for Wisconsin residents who are at least one-quarter American-Indian. Must be attending a college or university within the state. Renewable for up to five years. Several grants of up to $1100. *Award:* Grant for use in freshman, sophomore, junior, or senior year; renewable. *Award amount:* $250–$1100. *Eligibility Requirements:* Applicant must be American Indian/Alaska Native; enrolled or expecting to enroll full- or part-time at a two-year, four-year, or technical institution or university; resident of Wisconsin and studying in Wisconsin. Available to U.S. and non-U.S. citizens. *Application Requirements:* Application, financial need analysis. *Deadline:* continuous. *Contact:* Sandra Thomas, Program Coordinator, Wisconsin Higher Educational Aid Board, PO Box 7885, Madison, WI 53707-7885. *E-mail:* sandy.thomas@heab.state.wi.us. *Phone:* 608-266-0888. *Fax:* 608-267-2808. *Web site:* www.heab.state.wi.us.

Wisconsin Tuition Grant Program. Available to Wisconsin residents who are enrolled at least half-time in degree or certificate programs at independent, nonprofit colleges or universities in Wisconsin. Must show financial need. *Award:* Grant for use in freshman, sophomore, junior, or senior year; not renewable. *Award amount:* $250–$2350. *Eligibility Requirements:* Applicant must be enrolled or expecting to enroll full- or part-time at a four-year institution or university; resident of Wisconsin and studying in Wisconsin. Available to U.S. and non-U.S. citizens. *Application Requirements:* Application, financial need analysis. *Deadline:* continuous. *Contact:* Mary Lou Kuzdas, Program Coordinator, Wisconsin Higher Educational Aid Board, PO Box 7885, Madison, WI 53707-7885. *E-mail:* mary.kuzdas@heab.state.wi.us. *Phone:* 608-267-2212. *Fax:* 608-267-2808. *Web site:* www.heab.state.wi.us.

Wisconsin Veterans Part-time Study Reimbursement Grant. Open only to Wisconsin veterans and dependents of deceased Wisconsin veterans. Renewable for continuing study. Contact office for more details. Application deadline is no later than sixty days after the course completion. Veterans may be reimbursed up to 85% of tuition and fees. *Award:* Grant for use in freshman, sophomore, junior, or senior year; renewable. *Award amount:* $300–$1100. *Eligibility Requirements:* Applicant must be enrolled or expecting to enroll part-time at an institution or university; resident of Wisconsin and studying in Wisconsin. Available to U.S. citizens. Applicant or parent must meet one or more of the following requirements: general military experience; retired from active duty; disabled or killed as a result of military service; prisoner of war; or missing in action. *Application Requirements:* Application. *Contact:* Mr. Steve Olson, Public Relations Officer, Wisconsin Department of Veterans Affairs, PO Box 7843, Madison, WI 53707-7843. *Phone:* 608-266-1311. *Web site:* dva.state.wi.us.

How to Use This Guide

College Profiles and Special Messages

This section presents pertinent factual and statistical data for each college in a standard format for easy comparison. In addition, a number of college admissions office staff members, as part of a major information-dissemination effort described in "Special Message to Students," have supplemented the basic profile with special descriptive information on four topics of particular interest to students: social life on campus, special highlights of the college's academic program, the importance of individual interviews or admission counseling sessions, and what to look for on campus visits. The sample profile at the end of this article highlights some of the useful information that the profiles provide. This article provides an outline of the profile format, describing the items covered.

All college information presented was supplied to Peterson's by the colleges themselves. Any item that does not apply to a particular college or for which no information was supplied is omitted from that college's profile. Colleges that were unable to supply usable data in time for publication are listed by name and, if available, address.

General Information

The first paragraph gives a brief introduction to the college, covering the following elements.

Type of student body: The categories are *men's* (100 percent of the student body), *primarily men's*, *women's* (100 percent of the student body), *primarily women's*, and *coed*. A college may also be designated as coordinate with another institution, indicating that there are separate colleges or campuses for men and women, but facilities, courses, and institutional governance are shared.

Institutional control: A *public* college receives its funding wholly or primarily from the federal, state, and/or local government. The term *private* indicates an independent, nonprofit institution, that is, one whose funding comes primarily from private sources and tuition. This category includes independent, religious colleges, which may also specify a particular religious denomination or church affiliation. Profit-making institutions are designated as *proprietary*.

Institutional type: A *two-year college* awards associate degrees and/or offers the first two years of a bachelor's degree program. A *primarily two-year college* awards bachelor's degrees, but the vast majority of students are enrolled in two-year programs. A *four-year college* awards bachelor's degrees and may also award associate degrees, but it does not offer graduate (postbachelor's) degree programs. A *five-year college* offers a five-year bachelor's program in a professional field such as architecture or pharmacy but does not award graduate degrees. An *upper-level institution* awards bachelor's degrees, but entering students must have at least two years of previous college-level credit; it may also offer graduate degree programs. A *comprehensive institution* awards bachelor's degrees and may also award associate degrees; graduate degree programs are offered primarily at the master's, specialist's, or professional level, although one or two doctoral programs may also be offered. A *university* offers four years of undergraduate work plus graduate degrees through the doctorate in more than two academic and/or professional fields.

Founding date: This is the year the college came into existence or was chartered, reflecting the period during which it has existed as an educational institution, regardless of subsequent mergers or other organizational changes.

Degree levels: An *associate* degree program may consist of either a college-transfer program, equivalent to the first two years of a bachelor's degree, or a one- to three-year terminal program that provides training for a specific occupation. A *bachelor's* degree program represents a three- to five-year liberal arts, science, professional, or preprofessional program. A *master's* degree is the first graduate degree in the liberal arts and sciences and certain professional fields and usually requires one to two years of full-time study. A *doctoral* degree is the highest degree awarded in research-oriented academic disciplines and usually requires from three to six years of full-time graduate study; the *first professional* degrees in such fields as law and medicine are also at the doctoral level. For colleges that award degrees in one field only, such as art or music, the field of specialization is indicated.

Campus setting: This indicates the size of the campus in acres or hectares and its location.

Academic Information

This paragraph contains information on the following items.

Faculty: The number of full-time and part-time faculty members as of fall 2002 is given, followed by the percentage of the full-time faculty members who hold doctoral, first professional, or terminal degrees and the student-faculty ratio. (Not all colleges calculate the student-faculty ratio in the same way; Peterson's prints the ratio as provided by the college.)

Library holdings: The numbers of books, serials, and audiovisual materials in the college's collections are listed.

Special programs: *Academic remediation for entering students* consists of instructional courses designed for students deficient in the general competencies necessary for a regular postsecondary curriculum and educational setting. *Services for LD students* include special help for learning-disabled students with resolvable difficulties, such as dyslexia. *Honors programs* are any special programs for very able students offering the opportunity for educational enrichment, independent study, acceleration, or some combination of these. *Cooperative (co-op) education programs* are formal arrangements with off-campus employers allowing students to combine work and study in order to gain degree-related experience, usually extending the time required to complete a degree. *Study abroad* is an arrangement by which a student completes part of the academic program studying in another country. A college may operate a campus abroad or it may have a cooperative agreement with other U.S. institutions or institutions in other countries. *Advanced placement* gives credit toward a degree awarded for acceptable scores on College Board Advanced Placement tests. *Accelerated degree programs* allow students to earn a bachelor's degree in three academic years. *Freshmen honors college* is a separate academic program for talented freshmen. *Tutorials* allow undergraduates to arrange for special in-depth academic assignments (not for remediation) working with faculty members one-on-one or in small groups. *English as a second language (ESL)* is a course of study designed specifically for students whose native language is not English. *Double major* consists of a program of study in which a student concurrently completes the requirements of two majors. *Independent study* consists of academic work, usually undertaken outside the regular classroom structure, chosen or designed by the student with the departmental approval and instructor supervision. *Distance learning* consists of credit courses that can be accessed off campus via cable television, the Internet, satellite, videotapes, correspondence courses, or other media. *Self-designed major* is a program of study based on individual interests, designed by the student with the assistance of an adviser. *Summer session for credit* includes summer courses through which students may make up degree work or accelerate their program. *Part-time degree programs* offer students the ability to earn a degree through part-time enrollment in regular session (daytime) classes or evening, weekend, or summer classes. *External degree programs* are programs of study in which students earn credits toward a degree through a combination of independent study, college courses, proficiency examinations, and personal experience. External degree programs require minimal or no classroom attendance. *Adult/continuing education programs* are courses offered for nontraditional students who are currently working or are returning to formal education. *Internships* are any short-term, supervised work experience usually related to a student's major field, for which the student earns academic credit. The work can be full- or part-time, on or off campus, paid or unpaid. *Off-campus study* is a formal arrangement with one or more domestic institutions under which students may take courses at the other institution(s) for credit.

Most popular majors: The most popular field or fields of study at the college, in terms of the number of undergraduate degrees conferred in 2002, are listed.

Student Body Statistics

Enrollment: The total number of students, undergraduates, and freshmen (or entering students for an upper-level institution) enrolled in degree programs as of fall 2002 are given.

With reference to the undergraduate enrollment for fall 2002, the percentages of women and men and the number of states and countries from which students hail are listed. The following percentages are also provided: in-state students, international students, and the percentage of students who returned for their sophomore year.

Expenses

Costs are given, as indicated in the heading of this paragraph in each profile, in one of three ways according to the most up-to-date figures available from each college: (1) actual expenses for the 2002–03 academic year; (2) estimated expenses for 2002–03; or (3) actual expenses for 2001–02.

Annual expenses may be expressed as a comprehensive fee (includes full-time tuition, mandatory fees, and college room and board) or as separate figures for full-time tuition, fees, room and board, and/or room only. For public institutions where tuition differs according to residence, separate figures are given for area and/or state residents and for nonresidents. Part-time tuition and fees are expressed in terms of a per-unit rate (per credit, per semester hour, etc.) as specified by the college.

The tuition structure at some institutions is complex in that freshmen and sophomores may be charged a different rate from that for juniors and seniors, a professional or vocational division may have a different fee structure from the liberal arts division of the same institution, or part-time tuition may be prorated on a sliding scale according to the number of credit hours taken. In all of these cases, the average figures are given along with an explanation of the basis for the variable rate. For colleges that report that room and board costs vary according to the type of accommodation and meal plan, the average costs are given. The

Research Procedures

The data contained in the College Profiles and Indexes were researched between fall 2002 and spring 2003 through *Peterson's Annual Survey of Undergraduate Institutions.* Questionnaires were sent to the more than 2,000 colleges and universities that met the outlined inclusion criteria. All data included in this edition have been submitted by officials (usually admissions and financial aid officers, registrars, or institutional research personnel) at the colleges. In addition, many of the institutions that submitted data were contacted directly by the Peterson's research staff to verify unusual figures, resolve discrepancies, or obtain additional data. All usable information received in time for publication has been included. The omission of any particular item from an index or profile listing signifies that the information is either not applicable to that institution or not available. Because of Peterson's comprehensive editorial review and because all material comes directly from college officials, we believe that the information presented in this guide is accurate. You should check with a specific college or university at the time of application to verify such figures as tuition and fees, which may have changed since the publication of this volume.

phrase *no college housing* indicates that the college does not own or operate any housing facilities for its undergraduate students.

Financial Aid

This paragraph contains information on the following items.

Forms of financial aid: The categories of college-administered aid available to undergraduates are listed. College-administered means that the college itself determines the recipient and amount of each award. The types of aid covered are non-need scholarships, need-based scholarships, athletic grants, and part-time jobs.

Financial aid: This item pertains to undergraduates who enrolled full-time in a four-year college in 2001 or 2002. The figures given are the dollar amount of the average financial aid package, including scholarships, grants, loans, and part-time jobs, received by such undergraduates.

Financial aid application deadline: This deadline may be given as a specific date, as continuous processing up to a specific date or until all available aid has been awarded, or as a priority date rather than a strict deadline, meaning that students are encouraged to apply by that date in order to have the best chance of obtaining aid.

Freshman Admission

The supporting data that a student must submit when applying for freshman admission are grouped into three categories: required for all, recommended, and required for some. They may include an essay, a high school transcript, high school course requirements (e.g., three years of math), letters of recommendation, an interview on campus or with local alumni, standardized test scores, and, for certain types of schools or programs, special requirements such as a musical audition or an art portfolio.

The most commonly required standardized tests are the ACT Assessment and the College Board's SAT I and SAT II Subject Tests. TOEFL (Test of English as a Foreign Language) is for international students whose native language is not English.

The application deadline for admission is given as either a specific date or *rolling.* Rolling means that applications are processed as they are received, and qualified students are accepted as long as there are openings. The application deadline for out-of-state students is indicated if it differs from the date for state residents. *Early decision* and *early action* deadlines are also given when applicable. Early decision is a program whereby students may apply early, are notified of acceptance or rejection well in advance of the usual notification date, and agree to accept an offer of admission, the assumption being that only one early application has been made. Early action is the same as early decision except that applicants are not obligated to accept an offer of admission.

Transfer Admission

This paragraph gives the application requirements and application deadline for a student applying for admission as a transfer from another institution. In addition to the requirements for freshman applicants listed above, requirements for transfers may also include a college transcript and a minimum college grade point average (expressed as a number on a scale of 0 to 4.0, where 4.0 equals A, 3.0 equals B, etc.). The name of the person to contact for additional transfer information is also given if it is different from the person listed in **For Further Information.**

Transfer Associate Degree Program Admission

This paragraph may be substituted for the **Freshman Admission** paragraph for two-year colleges that offer a college transfer program. The categories and requirements are listed in the same way as in the **Freshman Admission** paragraph.

Terminal Associate Degree Program Admission

This paragraph may also be substituted for the **Freshman Admission** paragraph by two-year colleges. It contains the requirements for admission to a terminal program that provides specific occupational training. The format for this paragraph also follows that of the **Freshman Admission** paragraph.

Entrance Difficulty

This paragraph contains the college's own assessment of its *entrance difficulty level*, including notation of an *open admission policy* where applicable. Open admission means that virtually all applicants are accepted without regard to standardized test scores, grade average, or class rank. A college may indicate that open admission is limited to a certain category of applicants, such as state residents, or does not apply to certain selective programs, often those in the health professions.

The five levels of entrance difficulty are *most difficult*, *very difficult*, *moderately difficult*, *minimally difficult*, and *noncompetitive*.

The final item in this paragraph is the percentage of applicants accepted for the fall 2002 freshman (or entering) class.

For Further Information

The name, title, and mailing address of the person to contact for more information on application and admission procedures are given at the end of the profile. A telephone number, fax number, e-mail address, and Web site are also included in this paragraph for profiles that do not contain this information in the paragraph on interviews and campus visits.

Special Message to Students

This section appears only for those colleges that submitted supplementary information and covers the following topics:

Social Life: This paragraph conveys a feeling for life on campus by addressing such questions as: What are the most popular activities? Are there active fraternities and sororities? What is the role of student government? Do most students live on campus or commute? Does the college have a religious orientation?

Academic Highlights: This paragraph describes some of the special features and characteristics of the college's academic program, such as special degree programs and opportunities for study abroad or internships.

Interviews and Campus Visits: Colleges that conduct on-campus admission interviews describe the importance of an interview in their admission process and what they try to

Criteria for Inclusion in This Book

The term "four-year college" is the commonly used designation for institutions that grant the baccalaureate degree. Four years is the expected amount of time required to earn this degree, although some bachelor's degree programs may be completed in three years, others require five years, and part-time programs may take considerably longer. Upper-level institutions offer only the junior and senior years and accept only students with two years of college-level credit. Therefore, "four-year college" is a conventional term that accurately describes most of the institutions included in this guide, but should not be taken literally in all cases.

To be included in this guide, an institution must have full accreditation or be a candidate for accreditation (preaccreditation) status by an institutional or specialized accrediting body recognized by the U.S. Department of Education or the Council for Higher Education Accreditation (CHEA). Institutional accrediting bodies, which review each institution as a whole, include the six regional associations of schools and colleges (Middle States, New England, North Central, Northwest, Southern, and Western), each of which is responsible for a specified portion of the United States and its territories. Other institutional accrediting bodies are national in scope and accredit specific kinds of institutions (e.g., Bible colleges, independent colleges, and rabbinical and Talmudic schools). Program registration by the New York State Board of Regents is considered to be the equivalent of institutional accreditation, since the board requires that all programs offered by an institution meet its standards before recognition is granted. A Canadian institution must be chartered and authorized to grant degrees by the provincial government, affiliated with a chartered institution, or accredited by a recognized U.S. accrediting body. This guide also includes institutions outside the United States that are accredited by these U.S. accrediting bodies. There are recognized specialized or professional accrediting bodies in more than forty different fields, each of which is authorized to accredit institutions or specific programs in its particular field. For specialized institutions that offer programs in one field only, we designate this to be the equivalent of institutional accreditation. A full explanation of the accrediting process and complete information on recognized, institutional (regional and national) and specialized accrediting bodies can be found online at www.chea.org or at www.ed.gov/offices/OPE/accreditation/index.html.

learn about a student through the interview. For those colleges that do not interview applicants individually, there is information on how a student interested in the college can visit the campus to meet administrators, faculty members, and currently enrolled students as well as on what the prospective applicant should try to accomplish through such a visit. This paragraph may also include a list of the most noteworthy places or things to see during a campus visit and the location, telephone number (including toll-free numbers if available), and business hours of the office to contact for information about appointments and campus visits. Also included, when available, is travel information, specifically the nearest commercial airport and the nearest interstate highway, with the appropriate exit.

In-Depth Descriptions of Colleges in the Midwest and Other Colleges to Consider

Narrative descriptions appear in these sections. These descriptions are written by admissions deans and provide great detail about each college. They are edited to provide a consistent format across entries for your ease of comparison.

Indexes

Majors and Degrees: This index lists hundreds of undergraduate major fields of study that are currently offered most widely. The majors appear in alphabetical order, each followed by an alphabetical list of the colleges that report offering a program in that field and the degree levels (*A* for associate, *B* for bachelor's) available. The majors represented here are based on the National Center for Education Statistics (NCES) 2000 Classification of Instructional Programs (CIP). The CIP is a taxonomic coding scheme that contains titles and descriptions of instructional programs, primarily at the postsecondary level. CIP was originally developed to facilitate NCES's collection and reporting of postsecondary degree completions, by major field of study, using standard classifications that capture the majority of program activity. The CIP is now the accepted federal government statistical standard for classifying instructional programs. However, although the term "major" is used in this guide, some colleges may use other terms, such as "concentration," "program of study," or "field."

Athletic Programs and Scholarships: This index lists the colleges that report offering intercollegiate athletic programs, listed alphabetically. An *M* or *W* following the college name indicates that the sport is offered for menor women, respectively. An *s* in parentheses following an *M* or *W* indicates that athletic scholarships (or grants-in-aid) are offered by the college for men or women, respectively, in that sport.

ROTC Programs: This index lists the colleges that report offering Reserve Officers' Training Corps programs in one or more branches of the armed services, as indicated by letter codes following the college name: *A* for Army, *N* for Navy, and *AF* for Air Force. A *c* in parentheses following the branch letter code indicates that the program is offered through a cooperative arrangement on another college's campus.

Alphabetical Listing of Colleges and Universities: This index gives the page locations of various entries for all the colleges and universities in this book. The page numbers for the college profiles are printed in regular type, those for profiles with *Special Messages* in *italic* type, and those for **In-Depth Descriptions** in **boldface** type. When there is more than one number in **boldface** type, it indicates that the institution has more than one **In-Depth Description**.

College Profiles and Special Messages

Sample Profile

■ ALEXANDER UNIVERSITY

Anytown, USA

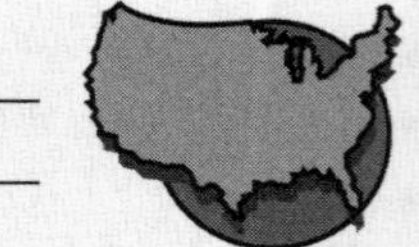

Alexander University is a coed, private comprehensive institution, founded in 1879, offering degrees at the bachelor's and master's levels. It has a 200-acre campus.

Academic Information The faculty has 79 full-time and 6 part-time members; 89 percent of full-time faculty members have doctoral/terminal/first professional degrees. The undergraduate student-faculty ratio is 16:1. The library holds 131,000 books and 28,300 serial subscriptions. Special programs include an honors program, off-campus study, and study abroad. There are Phi Beta Kappa and Sigma Xi chapters on campus. The most popular majors are business administration/commerce/management, computer science, and electrical engineering.

Student Body Statistics The student body totals 3,042, of whom 2,243 are undergraduates (549 freshmen). 59.1% are women and 40.9% are men. Students come from 36 states and territories and 62 other countries. 13.6% are international students. 3.4% are African American, 0.1% Native American, 4.3% Asian American, and 2.8% Hispanic American. 82% returned for their sophomore year.

Expenses for 2002–03 *Comprehensive fee:* $18,775 includes full-time tuition ($14,000), mandatory fees ($75), and college room and board ($4700).

Financial Aid Forms of aid include need-based scholarships and part-time jobs.

Freshman Admission Alexander University requires an essay, a high school transcript, 3 years of high school math, 1 recommendation, SAT I or ACT scores, and TOEFL scores for international students. 2 years of high school science, 2 years of high school foreign language, and an interview are recommended. The application deadline for regular admission is January 1 and for early decision it is November 15.

Transfer Admission Alexander University requires an essay, a high school transcript, 3 years of high school math, 1 recommendation, a college transcript, and a minimum 2.0 grade point average. 2 years of high school science, 2 years of high school foreign language, and an interview are recommended. The application deadline for admission is April 1. For additional transfer information, contact Mr. Eugene Roberts. Telephone: 800-555-1234.

Entrance Difficulty Alexander University assesses its entrance difficulty level as very difficult. For the fall 2002 freshman class, 39 percent of the applicants were accepted.

SPECIAL MESSAGE TO STUDENTS

Social Life Ski trips and Friday night mixers, as well as an intramural sports program, comprise the formal, sponsored activities on campus. Many students take advantage of the numerous social events offered by neighboring (and larger) colleges. Most students live in on-campus housing, and 20 percent of students are members of fraternities or sororities.

Academic Highlights Each Alexander University school adheres strongly to preparation for its profession and is committed to a problem-solving philosophy of education. A rigorous curriculum and group projects reinforce this distinct atmosphere in higher education and contribute to a strong sense of community and identity in each school. State-of-the-art computer facilities support the popular computer science program, and internships are available in almost every major field of study.

Interviews and Campus Visits While not a requirement, the interview is recommended as a way for the student to become more familiar with Alexander University and what it has to offer. Campus tours are available on a daily basis. Included on the tour are the business administration complex, computer science labs, and residence halls. For information about appointments and campus visits, call the Office of Admission at 800-555-3131, Monday through Friday, 9:30 a.m. to 4:30 p.m. The fax number is 800-555-3232. The office is located at 3001 Carnegie Point Avenue on campus.

For Further Information Write to Ms. Alice Kimmel, Director of Admission, Alexander University, Anytown, USA.

Margin annotations (left):

- **Indicates the inclusion of a Special Message to Students** —
- **What degrees are offered?** —
- **Are there special programs?** —
- **How much does it cost?** —
- **What is required for admission and when should I apply?** —
- **How difficult is it to be accepted?** —
- **What is special about this college academically?** —
- **What can I see on a campus visit?** —
- **Whom should I contact for further information?** —

Margin annotations (right):

- — **Is the college coed?**
- — **How big is this college?**
- — **What is the student-faculty ratio?**
- — **What are the enrollment statistics?**
- — **What kind of financial aid is available?**
- — **Whom should I contact for more transfer information?**
- — **What is social life like on campus?**
- — **Is an interview required?**
- — **How should I schedule an appointment or visit and are travel directions included?**

The Midwest

This map provides a general perspective on the Midwest and shows the major metropolitan areas and capital of each state.

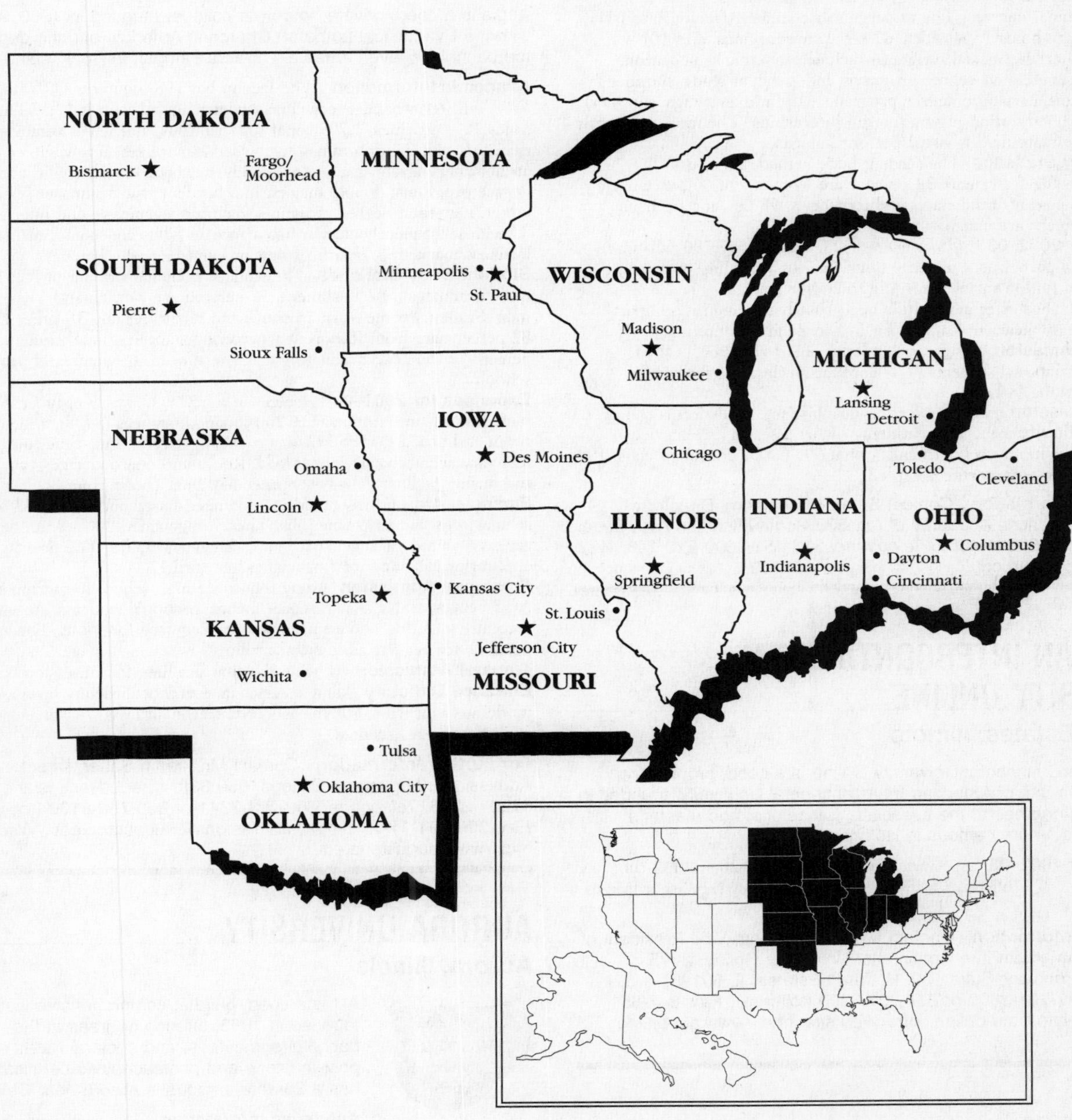

Illinois

AMERICAN ACADEMY OF ART

Chicago, Illinois

American Academy of Art is a coed, proprietary, comprehensive institution, founded in 1923, offering degrees at the bachelor's and master's levels in art.

Academic Information The faculty has 30 members (87% full-time), 73% with terminal degrees. The undergraduate student-faculty ratio is 13:1. The library holds 1,730 titles, 62 serial subscriptions, and 101 audiovisual materials. Special programs include academic remediation, study abroad, accelerated degree programs, independent study, summer session for credit, part-time degree programs (daytime, evenings, summer), adult/continuing education programs, and internships. The most frequently chosen baccalaureate field is visual/performing arts.
Student Body Statistics The student body is made up of 360 undergraduates (87 freshmen). 34 percent are women and 66 percent are men. Students come from 8 states and territories. 98 percent are from Illinois. 0.6 percent are international students.
Expenses for 2002–03 *Application fee:* $25. *Tuition:* $17,780 full-time, $4445 per term part-time. Full-time tuition varies according to course load. Part-time tuition varies according to course load.
Financial Aid Forms of aid include need-based scholarships and part-time jobs. The application deadline for financial aid is continuous.
Freshman Admission American Academy of Art requires TOEFL scores for international students. The application deadline for regular admission is rolling.
Transfer Admission The application deadline for admission is rolling.
Entrance Difficulty American Academy of Art assesses its entrance difficulty level as moderately difficult. For the fall 2002 freshman class, 100 percent of the applicants were accepted.

For Further Information Contact Stuart Rosenblom, Director of Admissions, American Academy of Art, 332 South Michigan Ave, Suite 300, Chicago, IL 60604-4302. *Telephone:* 312-461-0600 Ext. 143. *Web site:* http://www.aaart.edu/.

AMERICAN INTERCONTINENTAL UNIVERSITY ONLINE

Hoffman Estates, Illinois

American InterContinental University Online is a coed, proprietary, comprehensive unit of American InterContinental University, founded in 1970, offering degrees at the associate, bachelor's, and master's levels. It has a 1-acre campus in Hoffman Estates.

Expenses for 2002–03 *Application fee:* $50. *Tuition:* $20,400 full-time. *Mandatory fees:* $175 full-time. Full-time tuition and fees vary according to program.

For Further Information Contact Mr. Steve Fireng, Vice President of Admissions, American InterContinental University Online, 2895 Greenspoint Parkway, Suite 400, Hoffman Estates, IL 60195. *Telephone:* 877-701-3800 or 877-701-3800 (toll-free). *Fax:* 847-851-6002. *E-mail:* info@aiu-online.com. *Web site:* http://www.aiu-online.com/.

ARGOSY UNIVERSITY-CHICAGO

Chicago, Illinois

For Information Write to Argosy University-Chicago, Chicago, IL 60603.

ARGOSY UNIVERSITY-CHICAGO NORTHWEST

Rolling Meadows, Illinois

For Information Write to Argosy University-Chicago Northwest, Rolling Meadows, IL 60008.

AUGUSTANA COLLEGE

Rock Island, Illinois

Augie is a coed, private, four-year college, founded in 1860, affiliated with the Evangelical Lutheran Church in America, offering degrees at the bachelor's level. It has a 115-acre campus in Rock Island.

Academic Information The faculty has 198 members (72% full-time), 69% with terminal degrees. The student-faculty ratio is 12:1. The library holds 190,641 titles, 1,705 serial subscriptions, and 2,019 audiovisual materials. Special programs include services for learning-disabled students, an honors program, study abroad, advanced placement credit, accelerated degree programs, double majors, independent study, summer session for credit, part-time degree programs (daytime, evenings), and internships. The most frequently chosen baccalaureate fields are biological/life sciences, business/marketing, health professions and related sciences.
Student Body Statistics The student body is made up of 2,261 undergraduates (602 freshmen). 57 percent are women and 43 percent are men. Students come from 26 states and territories and 19 other countries. 87 percent are from Illinois. 1.1 percent are international students. 30 percent of the 2002 graduating class went on to graduate and professional schools.
Expenses for 2002–03 *Application fee:* $25. *Comprehensive fee:* $25,194 includes full-time tuition ($19,200), mandatory fees ($408), and college room and board ($5586). *College room only:* $2832. Full-time tuition and fees vary according to course load. Room and board charges vary according to housing facility. *Part-time tuition:* $800 per credit hour.
Financial Aid Forms of aid include need-based and non-need-based scholarships and part-time jobs. The average aided 2002–03 undergraduate received an aid package worth an estimated $15,068. The priority application deadline for financial aid is April 1.
Freshman Admission Augie requires a high school transcript, SAT I or ACT scores, and TOEFL scores for international students. An essay, 2 recommendations, and an interview are required for some. The application deadline for regular admission is rolling.
Transfer Admission The application deadline for admission is rolling.
Entrance Difficulty Augie assesses its entrance difficulty level as moderately difficult. For the fall 2002 freshman class, 74 percent of the applicants were accepted.

For Further Information Contact Mr. Martin Sauer, Director of Admissions, Augustana College, 639 38th Street, Rock Island, IL 61201-2296. *Telephone:* 309-794-7341 or 800-798-8100 (toll-free). *Fax:* 309-794-7422. *E-mail:* admissions@augustana.edu. *Web site:* http://www.augustana.edu/.

AURORA UNIVERSITY

Aurora, Illinois

AU is a coed, private, comprehensive institution, founded in 1893, offering degrees at the bachelor's, master's, and doctoral levels and post-master's and postbachelor's certificates. It has a 26-acre campus in Aurora near Chicago.

Academic Information The faculty has 110 members (75% full-time), 70% with terminal degrees. The undergraduate student-faculty ratio is 17:1. The library holds 115,642 titles, 749 serial subscriptions, and 6,015 audiovisual materials. Special programs include academic remediation, services for learning-disabled students, study abroad, advanced placement credit, double majors, independent study, distance learning, self-designed majors, summer session

for credit, part-time degree programs (daytime, evenings, weekends, summer), adult/continuing education programs, internships, and arrangement for off-campus study with 3 members of the Council of West Suburban Colleges. The most frequently chosen baccalaureate fields are business/marketing, education, protective services/public administration.
Student Body Statistics The student body totals 3,316, of whom 1,446 are undergraduates (294 freshmen). 65 percent are women and 35 percent are men. Students come from 14 states and territories. 98 percent are from Illinois. 15 percent of the 2002 graduating class went on to graduate and professional schools.
Expenses for 2003–04 *Application fee:* $25. *Comprehensive fee:* $19,764 includes full-time tuition ($14,250) and college room and board ($5514). *Part-time tuition:* $490 per semester hour.
Financial Aid Forms of aid include need-based and non-need-based scholarships and part-time jobs. The average aided 2002–03 undergraduate received an aid package worth an estimated $14,551. The priority application deadline for financial aid is April 15.
Freshman Admission AU requires a high school transcript, a minimum 2.0 high school GPA, and TOEFL scores for international students. An essay, an interview, and SAT I and SAT II or ACT scores are recommended. An essay, 2 recommendations, and an interview are required for some. The application deadline for regular admission is rolling.
Transfer Admission The application deadline for admission is rolling.
Entrance Difficulty AU assesses its entrance difficulty level as moderately difficult. For the fall 2002 freshman class, 57 percent of the applicants were accepted.

SPECIAL MESSAGE TO STUDENTS

Social Life Aurora University is a great place to get involved. Students may choose to participate in social clubs, student government, service activities, Campus Ministries, Greek organizations, and intramural sports. Students may also take advantage of the various social activities that are offered in Aurora—the third-largest city in Illinois—and Chicago, 40 miles to the east.

Academic Highlights The University comprises three colleges: the College of Arts and Sciences and the John and Judy Dunham School of Business; the College of Education; and the George Williams College of Aurora University, which includes the School of Social Work, the School of Nursing, and the School of Human Services. Aurora University offers the YMCA Senior Director Certificate program, indicative of its commitment to human service education.

Interviews and Campus Visits Aurora University encourages campus visits. Fall, winter, and spring open houses are held. Individual visits are always welcome. Students can meet with an admissions counselor, faculty members, a financial aid counselor, and coaches as well as take a tour of campus and visit with current students. Campus tours include academic buildings, such as Dunham and Stephens Halls, and four residence halls. Housed in Dunham Hall is the Schingoethe Museum of Native American Culture, which is open to the public. The University is accessible by train and local bus lines. For more information about appointments and campus visits, students should call the Office of Admission and Financial Aid at 630-844-5533 or 800-PICKAU-1 (toll-free).

For Further Information Write to the Office of Admission and Financial Aid, Aurora University, Aurora, IL 60506. *Web site:* http://www.aurora.edu.

See page 250 for a narrative description.

BARAT COLLEGE

See DePaul University

BENEDICTINE UNIVERSITY

Lisle, Illinois

Benedictine University is a coed, private, Roman Catholic, comprehensive institution, founded in 1887, offering degrees at the associate, bachelor's, master's, and doctoral levels. It has a 108-acre campus in Lisle near Chicago.

Academic Information The faculty has 220 members (42% full-time), 65% with terminal degrees. The undergraduate student-faculty ratio is 13:1. The library holds 166,341 titles, 8,900 serial subscriptions, and 9,349 audiovisual materials. Special programs include academic remediation, services for learning-disabled students, an honors program, study abroad, advanced placement credit, accelerated degree programs, ESL programs, double majors, independent study, distance learning, summer session for credit, part-time degree programs, adult/continuing education programs, internships, and arrangement for off-campus study with 3 members of the Council of West Suburban Colleges. The most frequently chosen baccalaureate fields are biological/life sciences, business/marketing, education.
Student Body Statistics The student body totals 2,809, of whom 2,044 are undergraduates (303 freshmen). 60 percent are women and 40 percent are men. Students come from 23 states and territories and 30 other countries. 97 percent are from Illinois. 2.3 percent are international students.
Expenses for 2002–03 *Application fee:* $40. *Comprehensive fee:* $22,460 includes full-time tuition ($16,150), mandatory fees ($510), and college room and board ($5800). Full-time tuition and fees vary according to class time and degree level. Room and board charges vary according to board plan and housing facility. *Part-time tuition:* $540 per credit hour. *Part-time mandatory fees:* $15 per credit hour. Part-time tuition and fees vary according to class time and degree level.
Financial Aid Forms of aid include need-based and non-need-based scholarships and part-time jobs. The average aided 2001–02 undergraduate received an aid package worth $10,984. The application deadline for financial aid is June 30 with a priority deadline of April 15.
Freshman Admission Benedictine University requires an essay, a high school transcript, recommendations, SAT I or ACT scores, and TOEFL scores for international students. An interview is required for some. The application deadline for regular admission is rolling.
Transfer Admission The application deadline for admission is rolling.
Entrance Difficulty Benedictine University assesses its entrance difficulty level as moderately difficult. For the fall 2002 freshman class, 74 percent of the applicants were accepted.

For Further Information Contact Ms. Kari Cranmer, Dean of Undergraduate Admissions, Benedictine University, 5700 College Road, Lisle, IL 60532-0900. *Telephone:* 630-829-6306 or 888-829-6363 (toll-free out-of-state). *Fax:* 630-960-1126. *E-mail:* admissions@ben.edu. *Web site:* http://www.ben.edu/.

See page 254 for a narrative description.

BLACKBURN COLLEGE

Carlinville, Illinois

Blackburn College is a coed, private, Presbyterian, four-year college, founded in 1837, offering degrees at the bachelor's level. It has an 80-acre campus in Carlinville near St. Louis.

Academic Information The faculty has 53 members (58% full-time), 45% with terminal degrees. The student-faculty ratio is 15:1. The library holds 87,175 titles, 17,000 serial subscriptions, and 1,940 audiovisual materials. Special programs include an honors program, cooperative (work-study) education, study abroad, advanced placement credit, double majors, independent study, self-designed majors, part-time degree programs (daytime), internships, and arrangement for off-campus study with American University. The most frequently chosen baccalaureate fields are business/marketing, biological/life sciences, education.
Student Body Statistics The student body is made up of 579 undergraduates (147 freshmen). 56 percent are women and 44 percent are

Blackburn College (continued)
men. Students come from 12 states and territories and 8 other countries. 3.1 percent are international students. 18 percent of the 2002 graduating class went on to graduate and professional schools.
Expenses for 2002–03 *Application fee:* $0. *Comprehensive fee:* $13,690 includes full-time tuition ($9200), mandatory fees ($220), and college room and board ($4270). Full-time tuition and fees vary according to program. *Part-time tuition:* $375 per semester hour.
Financial Aid Forms of aid include need-based and non-need-based scholarships and part-time jobs. The priority application deadline for financial aid is April 1.
Freshman Admission Blackburn College requires an essay, a high school transcript, a minimum 2.0 high school GPA, SAT I or ACT scores, and TOEFL scores for international students. 1 recommendation and an interview are required for some. The application deadline for regular admission is rolling.
Transfer Admission The application deadline for admission is rolling.
Entrance Difficulty Blackburn College assesses its entrance difficulty level as moderately difficult. For the fall 2002 freshman class, 52 percent of the applicants were accepted.

For Further Information Contact Mr. John Malin, Dean of Enrollment Management, Blackburn College, 700 College Avenue, Carlinville, IL 62626-1498. *Telephone:* 217-854-3231 Ext. 4252 or 800-233-3550 (toll-free). *Fax:* 217-854-3713. *E-mail:* admit@mail.blackburn.edu.

BLESSING-RIEMAN COLLEGE OF NURSING
Quincy, Illinois

Blessing-Rieman is a coed, primarily women's, private, four-year college, founded in 1985, offering degrees at the bachelor's level in nursing. It has a 1-acre campus in Quincy.

Academic Information The faculty has 13 members (100% full-time), 31% with terminal degrees. The student-faculty ratio is 10:1. The library holds 4,275 titles, 123 serial subscriptions, and 570 audiovisual materials. Special programs include academic remediation, an honors program, advanced placement credit, double majors, distance learning, summer session for credit, part-time degree programs (daytime, evenings), adult/continuing education programs, and internships. The most frequently chosen baccalaureate field is health professions and related sciences.
Student Body Statistics The student body is made up of 165 undergraduates (23 freshmen). 95 percent are women and 5 percent are men. Students come from 8 states and territories. 66 percent are from Illinois.
Expenses for 2003–04 *Application fee:* $0. *Comprehensive fee:* $18,200 includes full-time tuition ($12,400), mandatory fees ($350), and college room and board ($5450).
Financial Aid Forms of aid include need-based scholarships. The application deadline for financial aid is continuous.
Freshman Admission Blessing-Rieman requires a high school transcript, a minimum 3.0 high school GPA, SAT I or ACT scores, and TOEFL scores for international students. An essay and an interview are recommended. The application deadline for regular admission is rolling.
Transfer Admission The application deadline for admission is rolling.
Entrance Difficulty Blessing-Rieman assesses its entrance difficulty level as moderately difficult. For the fall 2002 freshman class, 62 percent of the applicants were accepted.

For Further Information Contact Heather Mutter or Kelli Collins, Admissions Counselor, Blessing-Rieman College of Nursing, PO Box 7005, Quincy, IL 62305-7005. *Telephone:* 217-228-5520 Ext. 6984 or 800-877-9140 Ext. 6964 (toll-free). *Fax:* 217-223-4661. *E-mail:* brenadmissions@blessinghospital.com. *Web site:* http://www.brcn.edu/.

BRADLEY UNIVERSITY
Peoria, Illinois

Bradley is a coed, private, comprehensive institution, founded in 1897, offering degrees at the bachelor's and master's levels. It has a 65-acre campus in Peoria.

Academic Information The faculty has 515 members (64% full-time), 52% with terminal degrees. The undergraduate student-faculty ratio is 14:1. The library holds 424,753 titles, 1,996 serial subscriptions, and 9,574 audiovisual materials. Special programs include academic remediation, an honors program, cooperative (work-study) education, study abroad, advanced placement credit, accelerated degree programs, double majors, independent study, distance learning, self-designed majors, summer session for credit, part-time degree programs (daytime, evenings, summer), adult/continuing education programs, internships, and arrangement for off-campus study with Georgetown University. The most frequently chosen baccalaureate fields are business/marketing, communications/communication technologies, engineering/engineering technologies.
Student Body Statistics The student body totals 6,098, of whom 5,190 are undergraduates (1,112 freshmen). 55 percent are women and 45 percent are men. Students come from 42 states and territories and 26 other countries. 86 percent are from Illinois. 1.6 percent are international students. 96 percent of the 2002 graduating class went on to graduate and professional schools.
Expenses for 2002–03 *Application fee:* $35. *Comprehensive fee:* $21,910 includes full-time tuition ($16,000), mandatory fees ($110), and college room and board ($5800). *College room only:* $3300. Full-time tuition and fees vary according to program. Room and board charges vary according to board plan. *Part-time tuition:* $435 per credit hour. *Part-time mandatory fees:* $20 per term. Part-time tuition and fees vary according to course load.
Financial Aid Forms of aid include need-based and non-need-based scholarships, athletic grants, and part-time jobs. The average aided 2001–02 undergraduate received an aid package worth $11,997. The priority application deadline for financial aid is March 1.
Freshman Admission Bradley requires a high school transcript, SAT I or ACT scores, and TOEFL scores for international students. An essay, a minimum 3.0 high school GPA, recommendations, and an interview are recommended. The application deadline for regular admission is rolling.
Entrance Difficulty Bradley assesses its entrance difficulty level as moderately difficult. For the fall 2002 freshman class, 67 percent of the applicants were accepted.

For Further Information Contact Ms. Nickie Roberson, Director of Admissions, Bradley University, 1501 West Bradley Avenue, 100 Swords Hall, Peoria, IL 61625-0002. *Telephone:* 309-677-3144 or 800-447-6460 (toll-free). *E-mail:* admissions@bradley.edu. *Web site:* http://www.bradley.edu/.

CHICAGO STATE UNIVERSITY
Chicago, Illinois

CSU is a coed, public, comprehensive institution, founded in 1867, offering degrees at the bachelor's and master's levels. It has a 161-acre campus in Chicago.

Academic Information The faculty has 438 members (74% full-time), 58% with terminal degrees. The undergraduate student-faculty ratio is 13:1. The library holds 320,000 titles and 1,539 serial subscriptions. Special programs include academic remediation, services for learning-disabled students, an honors program, cooperative (work-study) education, study abroad, advanced placement credit, accelerated degree programs, ESL programs, double majors, distance learning, self-designed majors, summer session for credit, part-time degree programs (daytime, evenings, weekends, summer), external degree programs, adult/continuing education programs, and internships. The most frequently chosen baccalaureate fields are business/marketing, education, liberal arts/general studies.
Student Body Statistics The student body totals 7,158, of whom 4,979 are undergraduates (474 freshmen). 74 percent are women and 26 percent are men. Students come from 12 states and territories and 8 other countries. 99 percent are from Illinois.

Expenses for 2003–04 *Application fee:* $20. *State resident tuition:* $4382 full-time, $132 per credit hour part-time. *Nonresident tuition:* $10,766 full-time, $398 per credit hour part-time. *Mandatory fees:* $1214 full-time, $203.50 per term part-time. *College room and board:* $5700.
Financial Aid Forms of aid include need-based and non-need-based scholarships and part-time jobs. The priority application deadline for financial aid is March 30.
Freshman Admission CSU requires a high school transcript, SAT I or ACT scores, and TOEFL scores for international students. The application deadline for regular admission is July 15.
Transfer Admission The application deadline for admission is July 15.
Entrance Difficulty CSU assesses its entrance difficulty level as moderately difficult. For the fall 2002 freshman class, 39 percent of the applicants were accepted.

For Further Information Contact Ms. Addie Epps, Director of Admissions, Chicago State University, 95th Street at King Drive, ADM 200, Chicago, IL 60628. *Telephone:* 773-995-2513. *E-mail:* ug-admissions@csu.edu. *Web site:* http://www.csu.edu/.

CHRISTIAN LIFE COLLEGE

Mount Prospect, Illinois

Christian Life College is a coed, private, four-year college, offering degrees at the associate and bachelor's levels.

Academic Information The faculty has 15 members (40% full-time), 27% with terminal degrees. The student-faculty ratio is 10:1. The most frequently chosen baccalaureate field is philosophy, religion, and theology.
Student Body Statistics The student body is made up of 80 undergraduates (8 freshmen). 44 percent are women and 56 percent are men. 9.4 percent are international students.
Expenses for 2002–03 *Tuition:* $5400 full-time, $225 per credit hour part-time. *Mandatory fees:* $600 full-time. *College room only:* $3300.
Financial Aid The average aided 2002–03 undergraduate received an aid package worth an estimated $5600. The priority application deadline for financial aid is June 1.
Freshman Admission Christian Life College requires TOEFL scores for international students.
Entrance Difficulty For the fall 2002 freshman class, 57 percent of the applicants were accepted.

For Further Information Contact Mr. Jim Spenner, Director of Admissions, Christian Life College, 400 East Gregory Street, Mount Prospect, IL 60056. *Telephone:* 847-259-1840 Ext. 17. *Web site:* http://www.christianlifecollege.edu/.

COLLEGE OF ST. FRANCIS

See University of St. Francis

COLUMBIA COLLEGE CHICAGO

Chicago, Illinois

Columbia is a coed, private, comprehensive institution, founded in 1890, offering degrees at the bachelor's and master's levels and postbachelor's certificates.

Academic Information The faculty has 1,439 members (20% full-time). The undergraduate student-faculty ratio is 13:1. The library holds 219,952 titles and 1,150 serial subscriptions. Special programs include academic remediation, services for learning-disabled students, study abroad, advanced placement credit, ESL programs, independent study, self-designed majors, summer session for credit, part-time degree programs (daytime, evenings, weekends, summer), internships, and arrangement for off-campus study with Adler Planetarium. The most frequently chosen baccalaureate fields are communications/communication technologies, liberal arts/general studies, visual/performing arts.
Student Body Statistics The student body totals 9,803, of whom 9,257 are undergraduates (1,699 freshmen). 51 percent are women and 49 percent are men. Students come from 50 states and territories and 73 other countries. 78 percent are from Illinois. 2.6 percent are international students. 9 percent of the 2002 graduating class went on to graduate and professional schools.
Expenses for 2002–03 *Application fee:* $25. *Comprehensive fee:* $20,409 includes full-time tuition ($13,714), mandatory fees ($390), and college room and board ($6305). *Part-time tuition:* $468 per semester hour. *Part-time mandatory fees:* $85 per term.
Financial Aid Forms of aid include need-based and non-need-based scholarships and part-time jobs. The priority application deadline for financial aid is August 15.
Freshman Admission Columbia requires an essay, a high school transcript, recommendations, and TOEFL scores for international students. A minimum 2.0 high school GPA, an interview, and SAT I or ACT scores are recommended. An interview is required for some. The application deadline for regular admission is August 15.
Transfer Admission The application deadline for admission is August 15.
Entrance Difficulty Columbia has an open admission policy.

For Further Information Contact Mr. Murphy Monroe, Director of Admissions and Recruitment, Columbia College Chicago, 600 South Michigan Avenue, Chicago, IL 60605-1996. *Telephone:* 312-663-1600 Ext. 7133. *E-mail:* admissions@mail.colum.edu. *Web site:* http://www.colum.edu/.

See page 270 for a narrative description.

CONCORDIA UNIVERSITY

River Forest, Illinois

Concordia is a coed, private, comprehensive unit of Concordia University System, founded in 1864, affiliated with the Lutheran Church–Missouri Synod, offering degrees at the bachelor's, master's, and doctoral levels and post-master's and postbachelor's certificates. It has a 40-acre campus in River Forest near Chicago.

Academic Information The faculty has 157 members (48% full-time), 41% with terminal degrees. The undergraduate student-faculty ratio is 11:1. The library holds 171,510 titles, 256 serial subscriptions, and 6,010 audiovisual materials. Special programs include academic remediation, services for learning-disabled students, an honors program, study abroad, advanced placement credit, accelerated degree programs, double majors, independent study, distance learning, summer session for credit, part-time degree programs (daytime, evenings, summer), adult/continuing education programs, internships, and arrangement for off-campus study with Chicago Consortium of Colleges and Universities, Dominican University. The most frequently chosen baccalaureate fields are business/marketing, education, health professions and related sciences.
Student Body Statistics The student body totals 1,802, of whom 1,285 are undergraduates (242 freshmen). 68 percent are women and 32 percent are men. Students come from 40 states and territories and 4 other countries. 68 percent are from Illinois. 0.4 percent are international students. 8 percent of the 2002 graduating class went on to graduate and professional schools.
Expenses for 2003–04 *Application fee:* $25. *Comprehensive fee:* $23,600 includes full-time tuition ($17,900), mandatory fees ($300), and college room and board ($5400). Full-time tuition and fees vary according to program. *Part-time tuition:* $530 per semester hour. *Part-time mandatory fees:* $10 per semester hour. Part-time tuition and fees vary according to program.
Financial Aid Forms of aid include need-based and non-need-based scholarships and part-time jobs. The average aided 2002–03 undergraduate received an aid package worth an estimated $13,650. The application deadline for financial aid is May 3 with a priority deadline of April 1.
Freshman Admission Concordia requires a high school transcript, a minimum 2.0 high school GPA, 1 recommendation, minimum ACT score of 20 or SAT I score of 930, SAT I or ACT scores, and TOEFL scores for international students. An essay and an interview are required for some. The application deadline for regular admission is rolling.
Transfer Admission The application deadline for admission is rolling.

Concordia University (continued)

Entrance Difficulty Concordia assesses its entrance difficulty level as moderately difficult. For the fall 2002 freshman class, 25 percent of the applicants were accepted.

For Further Information Contact Dr. Evelyn Burdick, Vice President for Enrollment Services, Concordia University, 7400 Augusta Street, River Forest, IL 60305. *Telephone:* 708-209-3100 or 800-285-2668 (toll-free). *Fax:* 708-209-3473. *E-mail:* crfadmis@curf.edu. *Web site:* http://www.curf.edu/.

DEPAUL UNIVERSITY

Chicago, Illinois

DePaul is a coed, private, Roman Catholic university, founded in 1898, offering degrees at the bachelor's, master's, doctoral, and first professional levels and post-master's and postbachelor's certificates. It has a 36-acre campus in Chicago.

Academic Information The faculty has 2,208 members (36% full-time). The undergraduate student-faculty ratio is 19:1. The library holds 1 million titles, 14,585 serial subscriptions, and 96,669 audiovisual materials. Special programs include academic remediation, services for learning-disabled students, an honors program, cooperative (work-study) education, study abroad, advanced placement credit, accelerated degree programs, Freshman Honors College, ESL programs, double majors, independent study, distance learning, summer session for credit, part-time degree programs, adult/continuing education programs, and internships. The most frequently chosen baccalaureate fields are business/marketing, computer/information sciences, liberal arts/general studies.
Student Body Statistics The student body totals 24,227, of whom 15,343 are undergraduates (2,256 freshmen). 58 percent are women and 42 percent are men. Students come from 50 states and territories and 44 other countries. 89 percent are from Illinois. 1.6 percent are international students.
Expenses for 2002–03 *Application fee:* $35. *Comprehensive fee:* $25,305 includes full-time tuition ($17,820), mandatory fees ($30), and college room and board ($7455). *College room only:* $5625. Full-time tuition and fees vary according to program. Room and board charges vary according to board plan and housing facility. *Part-time tuition:* $335 per quarter hour. *Part-time mandatory fees:* $10 per term. Part-time tuition and fees vary according to program.
Financial Aid Forms of aid include need-based and non-need-based scholarships, athletic grants, and part-time jobs. The average aided 2002–03 undergraduate received an aid package worth an estimated $14,106. The application deadline for financial aid is April 1 with a priority deadline of March 1.
Freshman Admission DePaul requires a high school transcript, a minimum 2.0 high school GPA, 1 recommendation, SAT I or ACT scores, and TOEFL scores for international students. A minimum 3.0 high school GPA is recommended. A minimum 3.0 high school GPA, an interview, and audition are required for some. The application deadline for regular admission is rolling and for early action it is December 15.
Transfer Admission The application deadline for admission is rolling.
Entrance Difficulty DePaul assesses its entrance difficulty level as moderately difficult. For the fall 2002 freshman class, 78 percent of the applicants were accepted.

For Further Information Contact Carlene Klaas, Undergraduate Admissions, DePaul University, 1 East Jackson Boulevard, Suite 9100, Chicago, IL 60604. *Telephone:* 312-362-8650 or 800-4DE-PAUL (toll-free out-of-state). *Fax:* 312-362-3322. *E-mail:* admitdpu@depaul.edu. *Web site:* http://www.depaul.edu/.

DEVRY UNIVERSITY

Addison, Illinois

DeVry is a coed, proprietary, four-year college of DeVry University, founded in 1982, offering degrees at the associate and bachelor's levels. It has a 14-acre campus in Addison near Chicago.

Academic Information The faculty has 162 members (43% full-time). The student-faculty ratio is 19:1. The library holds 18,500 titles, 4,000 serial subscriptions, and 1,000 audiovisual materials. Special programs include academic remediation, services for learning-disabled students, cooperative (work-study) education, advanced placement credit, accelerated degree programs, distance learning, summer session for credit, part-time degree programs (daytime, evenings, weekends, summer), and adult/continuing education programs. The most frequently chosen baccalaureate fields are business/marketing, computer/information sciences, engineering/engineering technologies.
Student Body Statistics The student body is made up of 3,028 undergraduates (597 freshmen). 23 percent are women and 77 percent are men. Students come from 30 states and territories and 23 other countries. 94 percent are from Illinois. 1.8 percent are international students.
Expenses for 2003–04 *Application fee:* $50. *Tuition:* $10,100 full-time, $360 per credit hour part-time. *Mandatory fees:* $165 full-time. Full-time tuition and fees vary according to course load. Part-time tuition varies according to course load.
Financial Aid Forms of aid include need-based and non-need-based scholarships and part-time jobs. The average aided 2001–02 undergraduate received an aid package worth $8374. The application deadline for financial aid is continuous.
Freshman Admission DeVry requires a high school transcript, an interview, CPT, TOEFL scores for international students, and CPT. SAT I or ACT scores are recommended. The application deadline for regular admission is rolling.
Transfer Admission The application deadline for admission is rolling.
Entrance Difficulty DeVry assesses its entrance difficulty level as minimally difficult; moderately difficult for electronics engineering technology program. For the fall 2002 freshman class, 70 percent of the applicants were accepted.

For Further Information Contact Ms. Jane Miritello, Assistant New Student Coordinator, DeVry University, 18624 W. Creek Drive, Tinley Park, IL 60477. *Telephone:* 708-342-3300 or 877-305-8184 (toll-free out-of-state). *Fax:* 708-342-3120. *Web site:* http://www.dpg.devry.edu/.

DEVRY UNIVERSITY

Chicago, Illinois

DeVry is a coed, proprietary, four-year college of DeVry University, founded in 1931, offering degrees at the associate and bachelor's levels. It has a 17-acre campus in Chicago.

Academic Information The faculty has 171 members (43% full-time). The student-faculty ratio is 21:1. The library holds 16,573 titles, 79 serial subscriptions, and 1,047 audiovisual materials. Special programs include academic remediation, services for learning-disabled students, cooperative (work-study) education, advanced placement credit, accelerated degree programs, ESL programs, distance learning, summer session for credit, part-time degree programs (daytime, evenings, weekends, summer), and adult/continuing education programs. The most frequently chosen baccalaureate fields are business/marketing, computer/information sciences, engineering/engineering technologies.
Student Body Statistics The student body is made up of 3,539 undergraduates (691 freshmen). 35 percent are women and 65 percent are men. Students come from 23 states and territories and 26 other countries. 98 percent are from Illinois. 2 percent are international students.
Expenses for 2003–04 *Application fee:* $50. *Tuition:* $10,100 full-time, $360 per credit hour part-time. *Mandatory fees:* $165 full-time. Full-time tuition and fees vary according to course load. Part-time tuition varies according to course load.
Financial Aid Forms of aid include need-based and non-need-based scholarships and part-time jobs. The average aided 2001–02 undergraduate received an aid package worth $10,268. The application deadline for financial aid is continuous.
Freshman Admission DeVry requires a high school transcript, an interview, CPT, TOEFL scores for international students, and CPT. SAT I or ACT scores are recommended. The application deadline for regular admission is rolling.
Transfer Admission The application deadline for admission is rolling.

Entrance Difficulty DeVry assesses its entrance difficulty level as minimally difficult; moderately difficult for electronics engineering technology program.

For Further Information Contact Ms. Christine Hierl, Director of Admissions, DeVry University, 3300 North Campbell Avenue, Chicago, IL 60618-5994. *Telephone:* 773-929-6550 or 800-383-3879 (toll-free out-of-state). *Fax:* 773-929-8093. *Web site:* http://www.chi.devry.edu/.

DEVRY UNIVERSITY

Tinley Park, Illinois

DeVry University is a coed, proprietary, four-year college of DeVry University, founded in 2000, offering degrees at the associate and bachelor's levels and postbachelor's certificates. It has a 12-acre campus in Tinley Park.

Academic Information The faculty has 103 members (35% full-time). The student-faculty ratio is 17:1. The library holds 17,500 titles, 82 serial subscriptions, and 476 audiovisual materials. Special programs include academic remediation, services for learning-disabled students, cooperative (work-study) education, advanced placement credit, accelerated degree programs, distance learning, summer session for credit, part-time degree programs (daytime, evenings, weekends, summer), and adult/continuing education programs.
Student Body Statistics The student body totals 1,928, of whom 1,701 are undergraduates (321 freshmen). 27 percent are women and 73 percent are men. Students come from 19 states and territories and 9 other countries. 92 percent are from Illinois. 0.8 percent are international students.
Expenses for 2003–04 *Application fee:* $50. *Tuition:* $10,100 full-time, $360 per credit hour part-time. *Mandatory fees:* $165 full-time. Full-time tuition and fees vary according to course load. Part-time tuition varies according to course load.
Financial Aid Forms of aid include need-based and non-need-based scholarships and part-time jobs. The average aided 2001–02 undergraduate received an aid package worth $8382. The application deadline for financial aid is continuous.
Freshman Admission DeVry University requires a high school transcript, an interview, CPT, TOEFL scores for international students, and CPT. SAT I or ACT scores are recommended. The application deadline for regular admission is rolling.
Transfer Admission The application deadline for admission is rolling.
Entrance Difficulty DeVry University assesses its entrance difficulty level as minimally difficult; moderately difficult for electronics engineering technology program. For the fall 2002 freshman class, 67 percent of the applicants were accepted.

For Further Information Contact Ms. Kerrie Flynn, Assistant New Student Coordinator, DeVry University, 18624 W. Creek Drive, Tinley Park, IL 60477. *Telephone:* 708-342-3300 or 877-305-8184 (toll-free out-of-state). *Web site:* http://www.tp.devry.edu/.

DOMINICAN UNIVERSITY

River Forest, Illinois

Dominican is a coed, private, Roman Catholic, comprehensive institution, founded in 1901, offering degrees at the bachelor's and master's levels and post-master's certificates. It has a 30-acre campus in River Forest near Chicago.

Academic Information The faculty has 204 members (44% full-time), 39% with terminal degrees. The undergraduate student-faculty ratio is 13:1. The library holds 280,475 titles, 4,422 serial subscriptions, and 7,000 audiovisual materials. Special programs include services for learning-disabled students, an honors program, study abroad, advanced placement credit, accelerated degree programs, ESL programs, double majors, independent study, distance learning, self-designed majors, summer session for credit, part-time degree programs (daytime, evenings, weekends, summer), adult/continuing education programs, internships, and arrangement for off-campus study with Concordia University (IL), Illinois Institute of Technology. The most frequently chosen baccalaureate fields are business/marketing, psychology, social sciences and history.
Student Body Statistics The student body totals 2,776, of whom 1,170 are undergraduates (192 freshmen). 69 percent are women and 31 percent are men. Students come from 23 states and territories and 19 other countries. 91 percent are from Illinois. 2.1 percent are international students. 15 percent of the 2002 graduating class went on to graduate and professional schools.
Expenses for 2003–04 *Application fee:* $20. *One-time mandatory fee:* $100. *Comprehensive fee:* $23,550 includes full-time tuition ($17,850), mandatory fees ($100), and college room and board ($5600). Room and board charges vary according to housing facility. *Part-time tuition:* $595 per semester hour. *Part-time mandatory fees:* $10 per course.
Financial Aid Forms of aid include need-based and non-need-based scholarships and part-time jobs. The average aided 2001–02 undergraduate received an aid package worth $11,208. The priority application deadline for financial aid is June 1.
Freshman Admission Dominican requires an essay, a high school transcript, a minimum 2.75 high school GPA, SAT I or ACT scores, and TOEFL scores for international students. Recommendations and an interview are recommended. 2 recommendations and an interview are required for some. The application deadline for regular admission is rolling.
Transfer Admission The application deadline for admission is rolling.
Entrance Difficulty Dominican assesses its entrance difficulty level as moderately difficult. For the fall 2002 freshman class, 81 percent of the applicants were accepted.

For Further Information Contact Ms. Hildegarde Schmidt, Dean of Admissions and Financial Aid, Dominican University, 7900 West Division Street, River Forest, IL 60305-1099. *Telephone:* 708-524-6800 or 800-828-8475 (toll-free). *Fax:* 708-366-5360. *E-mail:* domadmis@email.dom.edu. *Web site:* http://www.dom.edu/.

EASTERN ILLINOIS UNIVERSITY

Charleston, Illinois

Eastern is a coed, public, comprehensive institution, founded in 1895, offering degrees at the bachelor's and master's levels. It has a 320-acre campus in Charleston.

Academic Information The faculty has 659 members (89% full-time), 68% with terminal degrees. The undergraduate student-faculty ratio is 16:1. The library holds 955,245 titles, 3,510 serial subscriptions, and 33,460 audiovisual materials. Special programs include academic remediation, services for learning-disabled students, an honors program, study abroad, advanced placement credit, ESL programs, double majors, independent study, summer session for credit, part-time degree programs (daytime, evenings, summer), external degree programs, adult/continuing education programs, and internships. The most frequently chosen baccalaureate fields are business/marketing, education, English.
Student Body Statistics The student body totals 11,163, of whom 9,528 are undergraduates (2,003 freshmen). 57 percent are women and 43 percent are men. Students come from 35 states and territories and 36 other countries. 98 percent are from Illinois. 0.7 percent are international students. 31 percent of the 2002 graduating class went on to graduate and professional schools.
Expenses for 2002–03 *Application fee:* $30. *State resident tuition:* $3254 full-time, $108 per semester hour part-time. *Nonresident tuition:* $9761 full-time, $325 per semester hour part-time. *Mandatory fees:* $1394 full-time, $52.65 per semester hour part-time. Full-time tuition and fees vary according to course load. Part-time tuition and fees vary according to course load. *College room and board:* $6000. Room and board charges vary according to board plan.
Financial Aid Forms of aid include need-based and non-need-based scholarships, athletic grants, and part-time jobs. The average aided 2002–03 undergraduate received an aid package worth an estimated $8472. The priority application deadline for financial aid is April 15.
Freshman Admission Eastern requires a high school transcript, audition for music program, SAT I or ACT scores, and TOEFL scores for international students. An essay and 3 recommendations are required for some. The application deadline for regular admission is rolling.

Eastern Illinois University (continued)

Transfer Admission The application deadline for admission is rolling.
Entrance Difficulty Eastern assesses its entrance difficulty level as moderately difficult. For the fall 2002 freshman class, 78 percent of the applicants were accepted.

For Further Information Contact Mr. Dale W. Wolf, Director of Admissions, Eastern Illinois University, 600 Lincoln Avenue, Charleston, IL 61920-3099. *Telephone:* 217-581-2223 or 800-252-5711 (toll-free). *Fax:* 217-581-7060. *E-mail:* admissns@eiu.edu. *Web site:* http://www.eiu.edu/.

EAST-WEST UNIVERSITY

Chicago, Illinois

East-West University is a coed, private, four-year college, founded in 1978, offering degrees at the associate and bachelor's levels.

Academic Information The faculty has 79 members (18% full-time), 22% with terminal degrees. The student-faculty ratio is 20:1. The library holds 32,000 titles and 156 serial subscriptions. Special programs include academic remediation, double majors, independent study, summer session for credit, part-time degree programs (daytime, evenings, summer), and internships. The most frequently chosen baccalaureate fields are business/marketing, computer/information sciences, social sciences and history.
Student Body Statistics The student body is made up of 1,113 undergraduates (763 freshmen). 65 percent are women and 35 percent are men. Students come from 1 state or territory and 10 other countries. 13.6 percent are international students. 35 percent of the 2002 graduating class went on to graduate and professional schools.
Expenses for 2003–04 *Application fee:* $30. *Tuition:* $9900 full-time, $3300 per term part-time. *Mandatory fees:* $495 full-time, $465 per term part-time. Full-time tuition and fees vary according to course level.
Financial Aid Forms of aid include need-based and non-need-based scholarships and part-time jobs. The average aided 2001–02 undergraduate received an aid package worth $8720. The priority application deadline for financial aid is June 30.
Freshman Admission East-West University requires an essay, a high school transcript, and an interview. ACT scores and TOEFL scores for international students are recommended. 1 recommendation is required for some. The application deadline for regular admission is rolling.
Transfer Admission The application deadline for admission is rolling.
Entrance Difficulty East-West University assesses its entrance difficulty level as minimally difficult. For the fall 2002 freshman class, 90 percent of the applicants were accepted.

For Further Information Contact Mr. William Link, Director of Admissions, East-West University, 819 South Wabash Avenue, Chicago, IL 60605-2103. *Telephone:* 312-939-0111 Ext. 1830. *Fax:* 312-939-0083. *E-mail:* seeyou@eastwest.edu. *Web site:* http://www.eastwest.edu/.

ELMHURST COLLEGE

Elmhurst, Illinois

Elmhurst is a coed, private, comprehensive institution, founded in 1871, affiliated with the United Church of Christ, offering degrees at the bachelor's and master's levels. It has a 38-acre campus in Elmhurst near Chicago.

Academic Information The faculty has 263 members (43% full-time), 46% with terminal degrees. The undergraduate student-faculty ratio is 13:1. The library holds 222,441 titles, 2,010 serial subscriptions, and 7,537 audiovisual materials. Special programs include academic remediation, services for learning-disabled students, an honors program, cooperative (work-study) education, study abroad, advanced placement credit, accelerated degree programs, double majors, independent study, summer session for credit, part-time degree programs (daytime, evenings, weekends, summer), adult/continuing education programs, internships, and arrangement for off-campus study. The most frequently chosen baccalaureate fields are business/marketing, communications/communication technologies, education.
Student Body Statistics The student body totals 2,490, of whom 2,340 are undergraduates (310 freshmen). 65 percent are women and 35 percent are men. Students come from 26 states and territories and 29 other countries. 92 percent are from Illinois. 1.3 percent are international students. 22.4 percent of the 2002 graduating class went on to graduate and professional schools.
Expenses for 2002–03 *Application fee:* $25. *Comprehensive fee:* $23,296 includes full-time tuition ($17,500) and college room and board ($5796). *College room only:* $3296. Room and board charges vary according to board plan and housing facility. *Part-time tuition:* $498 per credit hour.
Financial Aid Forms of aid include need-based and non-need-based scholarships and part-time jobs. The average aided 2002–03 undergraduate received an aid package worth an estimated $15,715. The priority application deadline for financial aid is April 15.
Freshman Admission Elmhurst requires a high school transcript, SAT I or ACT scores, and TOEFL scores for international students. An essay and an interview are recommended. An essay, recommendations, and an interview are required for some. The application deadline for regular admission is July 15.
Transfer Admission The application deadline for admission is August 1.
Entrance Difficulty Elmhurst assesses its entrance difficulty level as moderately difficult. For the fall 2002 freshman class, 76 percent of the applicants were accepted.

For Further Information Contact Mr. Andrew B. Sison, Director of Admission, Elmhurst College, 190 Prospect Avenue, Elmhurst, IL 60126. *Telephone:* 630-617-3400 Ext. 3070 or 800-697-1871 (toll-free out-of-state). *Fax:* 630-617-5501. *E-mail:* admit@elmhurst.edu. *Web site:* http://www.elmhurst.edu/.

See page 278 for a narrative description.

EUREKA COLLEGE

Eureka, Illinois

Eureka is a coed, private, four-year college, founded in 1855, affiliated with the Christian Church (Disciples of Christ), offering degrees at the bachelor's level. It has a 112-acre campus in Eureka.

Academic Information The faculty has 69 members (61% full-time), 55% with terminal degrees. The student-faculty ratio is 13:1. The library holds 75,000 titles, 330 serial subscriptions, and 500 audiovisual materials. Special programs include an honors program, cooperative (work-study) education, study abroad, advanced placement credit, ESL programs, double majors, independent study, self-designed majors, summer session for credit, part-time degree programs (daytime, evenings, summer), and internships. The most frequently chosen baccalaureate fields are business/marketing, biological/life sciences, education.
Student Body Statistics The student body is made up of 516 undergraduates (138 freshmen). 56 percent are women and 44 percent are men. Students come from 15 states and territories and 2 other countries. 1.4 percent are international students. 11 percent of the 2002 graduating class went on to graduate and professional schools.
Expenses for 2003–04 *Application fee:* $25. *Comprehensive fee:* $24,580 includes full-time tuition ($18,300), mandatory fees ($400), and college room and board ($5880). *College room only:* $2820. Room and board charges vary according to housing facility. *Part-time tuition:* $550 per semester hour.
Financial Aid Forms of aid include need-based and non-need-based scholarships and part-time jobs. The average aided 2002–03 undergraduate received an aid package worth an estimated $13,802. The priority application deadline for financial aid is April 1.
Freshman Admission Eureka requires a high school transcript, a minimum 2.0 high school GPA, 1 recommendation, SAT I or ACT scores, and TOEFL scores for international students. An interview is recommended. An essay and 3 recommendations are required for some. The application deadline for regular admission is rolling.
Transfer Admission The application deadline for admission is rolling.

Entrance Difficulty Eureka assesses its entrance difficulty level as moderately difficult. For the fall 2002 freshman class, 75 percent of the applicants were accepted.

For Further Information Contact Mr. Richard R. Eber, Dean of Admissions and Financial Aid, Eureka College, 300 East College Avenue, Eureka, IL 61530-0128. *Telephone:* 309-467-6350 or 888-4-EUREKA (toll-free). *Fax:* 309-467-6576. *E-mail:* admissions@eureka.edu. *Web site:* http://www.eureka.edu/.

GOVERNORS STATE UNIVERSITY

University Park, Illinois

Governors State University is a coed, public, upper-level institution, founded in 1969, offering degrees at the bachelor's and master's levels. It has a 750-acre campus in University Park near Chicago.

Academic Information The faculty has 204 members (86% full-time), 71% with terminal degrees. The undergraduate student-faculty ratio is 16:1. The library holds 252,000 titles, 2,200 serial subscriptions, and 2,700 audiovisual materials. Special programs include academic remediation, services for learning-disabled students, an honors program, study abroad, advanced placement credit, independent study, distance learning, self-designed majors, summer session for credit, part-time degree programs (daytime, evenings, weekends, summer), external degree programs, adult/continuing education programs, internships, and arrangement for off-campus study with Chicago State University, Northeastern Illinois University, Western Illinois University, Eastern Illinois University.
Student Body Statistics The student body totals 5,855, of whom 2,980 are undergraduates. 69 percent are women and 31 percent are men. Students come from 9 states and territories and 21 other countries. 97 percent are from Illinois. 1.1 percent are international students. 26 percent of the 2002 graduating class went on to graduate and professional schools.
Expenses for 2002–03 *Application fee:* $0. *State resident tuition:* $2600 full-time, $108 per credit part-time. *Nonresident tuition:* $7800 full-time, $324 per credit part-time. *Mandatory fees:* $320 full-time, $180 per term part-time. Full-time tuition and fees vary according to location. Part-time tuition and fees vary according to course load and location.
Financial Aid Forms of aid include need-based and non-need-based scholarships and part-time jobs. The priority application deadline for financial aid is May 1.
Transfer Admission Governors State University requires a college transcript and a minimum 2.0 college GPA. Standardized test scores are required for some. The application deadline for admission is July 15.
Entrance Difficulty Governors State University assesses its entrance difficulty level as moderately difficult.

For Further Information Contact Mr. Larry Polselli, Executive Director of Enrollment Services, Governors State University, One University Parkway, University Park, IL 60466. *Telephone:* 708-534-3148. *Fax:* 708-534-1640. *Web site:* http://www.govst.edu/.

GREENVILLE COLLEGE

Greenville, Illinois

GC is a coed, private, Free Methodist, comprehensive institution, founded in 1892, offering degrees at the bachelor's and master's levels. It has a 12-acre campus in Greenville near St. Louis.

Academic Information The faculty has 104 members (66% full-time), 40% with terminal degrees. The undergraduate student-faculty ratio is 15:1. The library holds 126,210 titles, 490 serial subscriptions, and 4,377 audiovisual materials. Special programs include academic remediation, an honors program, cooperative (work-study) education, study abroad, advanced placement credit, accelerated degree programs, double majors, independent study, self-designed majors, summer session for credit, part-time degree programs (daytime, evenings, summer), adult/continuing education programs, internships, and arrangement for off-campus study with 13 members of the Christian College Consortium; 100 members of the Council for Christian Colleges and Universities. The most frequently chosen baccalaureate fields are business/marketing, biological/life sciences, education.
Student Body Statistics The student body totals 1,239, of whom 1,206 are undergraduates (244 freshmen). 51 percent are women and 49 percent are men. Students come from 40 states and territories and 11 other countries. 73 percent are from Illinois. 1.5 percent are international students.
Expenses for 2002–03 *Application fee:* $25. *Comprehensive fee:* $19,920 includes full-time tuition ($14,400), mandatory fees ($120), and college room and board ($5400). *College room only:* $2570. Room and board charges vary according to housing facility. *Part-time tuition:* $300 per credit hour.
Financial Aid Forms of aid include need-based and non-need-based scholarships and part-time jobs. The average aided 2002–03 undergraduate received an aid package worth an estimated $13,400. The application deadline for financial aid is continuous.
Freshman Admission GC requires an essay, a high school transcript, a minimum 2.25 high school GPA, 2 recommendations, agreement to code of conduct, SAT I or ACT scores, and TOEFL scores for international students. An interview is required for some. The application deadline for regular admission is rolling.
Transfer Admission The application deadline for admission is rolling.
Entrance Difficulty GC assesses its entrance difficulty level as moderately difficult. For the fall 2002 freshman class, 95 percent of the applicants were accepted.

For Further Information Contact Dr. R. Pepper Dill, Dean of Admissions, Greenville College, 315 East College Avenue, Greenville, IL 62246. *Telephone:* 618-664-7100, 800-248-2288 (toll-free in-state), or 800-345-4440 (toll-free out-of-state). *Fax:* 618-664-9841. *E-mail:* admissions@greenville.edu. *Web site:* http://www.greenville.edu/.

See page 282 for a narrative description.

HARRINGTON INSTITUTE OF INTERIOR DESIGN

Chicago, Illinois

Harrington Institute of Interior Design is a coed, primarily women's, proprietary, four-year college, founded in 1931, offering degrees at the associate and bachelor's levels in interior design.

Academic Information The faculty has 100 members. The student-faculty ratio is 15:1. The library holds 22,000 titles, 90 serial subscriptions, and 26,000 audiovisual materials. Special programs include study abroad, part-time degree programs (evenings), adult/continuing education programs, internships, and arrangement for off-campus study with Roosevelt University. The most frequently chosen baccalaureate field is visual/performing arts.
Student Body Statistics The student body is made up of 1,125 undergraduates.
Expenses for 2002–03 *Application fee:* $60. *One-time mandatory fee:* $600. *Tuition:* $12,000 full-time. *Mandatory fees:* $175 full-time.
Financial Aid Forms of aid include need-based and non-need-based scholarships. The average aided 2002–03 undergraduate received an aid package worth an estimated $3500. The application deadline for financial aid is continuous.
Freshman Admission Harrington Institute of Interior Design requires a high school transcript, an interview, and TOEFL scores for international students. The application deadline for regular admission is rolling.
Entrance Difficulty Harrington Institute of Interior Design has an open admission policy.

For Further Information Contact Ms. Wendi Franczyk, Director of Admissions, Harrington Institute of Interior Design, 410 South Michigan Avenue, Chicago, IL 60605-1496. *Telephone:* 877-939-4975 or 877-939-4975 (toll-free). *Fax:* 312-939-8005. *E-mail:* hiid@interiordesign.edu. *Web site:* http://www.interiordesign.edu/.

HEBREW THEOLOGICAL COLLEGE

Skokie, Illinois

For Information Write to Hebrew Theological College, Skokie, IL 60077-3263.

ILLINOIS COLLEGE

Jacksonville, Illinois

IC is a coed, private, interdenominational, four-year college, founded in 1829, offering degrees at the bachelor's level. It has a 62-acre campus in Jacksonville near St. Louis.

Academic Information The faculty has 93 members (71% full-time), 67% with terminal degrees. The student-faculty ratio is 14:1. The library holds 143,500 titles and 620 serial subscriptions. Special programs include study abroad, advanced placement credit, accelerated degree programs, double majors, independent study, summer session for credit, and internships. The most frequently chosen baccalaureate fields are business/marketing, education, social sciences and history.
Student Body Statistics The student body is made up of 963 undergraduates (306 freshmen). 56 percent are women and 44 percent are men. Students come from 12 states and territories and 6 other countries. 98 percent are from Illinois. 0.7 percent are international students. 27 percent of the 2002 graduating class went on to graduate and professional schools.
Expenses for 2002–03 *Application fee:* $25. *Comprehensive fee:* $17,110 includes full-time tuition ($11,850) and college room and board ($5260). *Part-time tuition:* $494 per credit hour.
Financial Aid Forms of aid include need-based and non-need-based scholarships and part-time jobs. The average aided 2002–03 undergraduate received an aid package worth an estimated $12,508. The priority application deadline for financial aid is March 15.
Freshman Admission IC requires a high school transcript, 1 recommendation, SAT I or ACT scores, and TOEFL scores for international students. An essay, a minimum 2.5 high school GPA, and an interview are recommended. An essay is required for some. The application deadline for regular admission is August 15.
Transfer Admission The application deadline for admission is December 15.
Entrance Difficulty IC assesses its entrance difficulty level as moderately difficult. For the fall 2002 freshman class, 77 percent of the applicants were accepted.

For Further Information Contact Mr. Rick Bystry, Associate Director of Admission, Illinois College, 1101 West College, Jacksonville, IL 62650. *Telephone:* 217-245-3030 or 866-464-5265 (toll-free). *Fax:* 217-245-3034. *E-mail:* admissions@ic.edu. *Web site:* http://www.ic.edu/.

THE ILLINOIS INSTITUTE OF ART

Chicago, Illinois

The Illinois Institute of Art is a coed, proprietary, four-year college of The Art Institutes, founded in 1916, offering degrees at the associate and bachelor's levels.

Academic Information The faculty has 160 members. The student-faculty ratio is 20:1. The library holds 11,324 titles, 264 serial subscriptions, and 502 audiovisual materials. Special programs include academic remediation, services for learning-disabled students, cooperative (work-study) education, advanced placement credit, accelerated degree programs, independent study, summer session for credit, part-time degree programs (daytime, evenings, weekends, summer), adult/continuing education programs, internships, and arrangement for off-campus study with members of the International Council of Design Schools.
Student Body Statistics The student body is made up of 1,950 undergraduates. Students come from 42 states and territories and 26 other countries. 70 percent are from Illinois. 3 percent of the 2002 graduating class went on to graduate and professional schools.
Expenses for 2002–03 *Application fee:* $50. *Tuition:* $15,189 full-time.
Financial Aid Forms of aid include need-based and non-need-based scholarships and part-time jobs. The application deadline for financial aid is continuous.
Freshman Admission The Illinois Institute of Art requires an essay, a high school transcript, an interview, and TOEFL scores for international students. A minimum 2.0 high school GPA and SAT I or ACT scores are recommended. Recommendations and a portfolio are required for some. The application deadline for regular admission is rolling.
Transfer Admission The application deadline for admission is rolling.
Entrance Difficulty The Illinois Institute of Art assesses its entrance difficulty level as minimally difficult. For the fall 2002 freshman class, 93 percent of the applicants were accepted.

For Further Information Contact Ms. Janis Anton, Director of Admissions, The Illinois Institute of Art, 350 North Orleans, Chicago, IL 60654. *Telephone:* 312-280-3500 Ext. 132 or 800-351-3450 (toll-free). *Fax:* 312-280-8562. *E-mail:* antonj@aii.edu. *Web site:* http://www.ilia.aii.edu/.

THE ILLINOIS INSTITUTE OF ART-SCHAUMBURG

Schaumburg, Illinois

The Illinois Institute of Art-Schaumburg is a coed, proprietary, four-year college of The Arts Institutes International, offering degrees at the bachelor's level.

Academic Information The faculty has 55 members (49% full-time), 18% with terminal degrees. The student-faculty ratio is 16:1. Special programs include services for learning-disabled students, advanced placement credit, accelerated degree programs, double majors, independent study, self-designed majors, summer session for credit, internships, and arrangement for off-campus study.
Student Body Statistics The student body is made up of 1,107 undergraduates (270 freshmen). 45 percent are women and 55 percent are men. Students come from 10 states and territories and 8 other countries. 90 percent are from Illinois. 1.1 percent are international students.
Expenses for 2002–03 *Application fee:* $50. *One-time mandatory fee:* $50. *Tuition:* $15,264 full-time, $318 per credit hour part-time. *Mandatory fees:* $100 full-time. *College room only:* $5500.
Financial Aid The average aided 2002–03 undergraduate received an aid package worth an estimated $9350. The priority application deadline for financial aid is May 1.
Freshman Admission The Illinois Institute of Art-Schaumburg requires an essay, a high school transcript, a minimum 2.0 high school GPA, and TOEFL scores for international students. SAT I or ACT scores and SAT I and SAT II or ACT scores are recommended. Recommendations and an interview are required for some. The application deadline for regular admission is rolling.
Transfer Admission The application deadline for admission is rolling.
Entrance Difficulty The Illinois Institute of Art-Schaumburg assesses its entrance difficulty level as minimally difficult. For the fall 2002 freshman class, 75 percent of the applicants were accepted.

For Further Information Contact Mr. Sam Hinojosa, Director of Admissions, The Illinois Institute of Art-Schaumburg, 1000 Plaza Drive, Schaumburg, IL 60173. *Telephone:* 847-619-3450 Ext. 4506 or 800-314-3450 (toll-free). *Fax:* 847-619-3064 Ext. 3064. *Web site:* http://www.ilis.artinstitutes.edu.

ILLINOIS INSTITUTE OF TECHNOLOGY

Chicago, Illinois

IIT is a coed, private university, founded in 1890, offering degrees at the bachelor's, master's, doctoral, and first professional levels and postbachelor's certificates. It has a 128-acre campus in Chicago.

Academic Information The faculty has 535 members (63% full-time). The undergraduate student-faculty ratio is 12:1. The library holds 854,771 titles, 773 serial subscriptions, and 52,368 audiovisual materials. Special programs include services for learning-disabled students, cooperative (work-study) education, study abroad, advanced placement credit, accelerated degree programs, double majors, independent study, distance learning, summer session for credit, part-time degree programs, and internships. The most frequently chosen baccalaureate fields are architecture, computer/information sciences, engineering/engineering technologies.

Student Body Statistics The student body totals 6,199, of whom 1,905 are undergraduates (365 freshmen). 24 percent are women and 76 percent are men. Students come from 50 states and territories and 61 other countries. 54 percent are from Illinois. 17.6 percent are international students. 30 percent of the 2002 graduating class went on to graduate and professional schools.

Expenses for 2002–03 *Application fee:* $40. *Comprehensive fee:* $25,700 includes full-time tuition ($19,200), mandatory fees ($556), and college room and board ($5944). Room and board charges vary according to board plan. *Part-time tuition:* $610 per credit hour. *Part-time mandatory fees:* $2.50 per credit hour.

Financial Aid Forms of aid include need-based and non-need-based scholarships, athletic grants, and part-time jobs. The average aided 2001–02 undergraduate received an aid package worth $18,232. The priority application deadline for financial aid is April 15.

Freshman Admission IIT requires an essay, a high school transcript, a minimum 3.0 high school GPA, 1 recommendation, SAT I or ACT scores, and TOEFL scores for international students. SAT II: Subject Test scores are recommended. An essay and an interview are required for some. The application deadline for regular admission is rolling.

Transfer Admission The application deadline for admission is rolling.

Entrance Difficulty IIT assesses its entrance difficulty level as very difficult. For the fall 2002 freshman class, 67 percent of the applicants were accepted.

For Further Information Contact Mr. Brent Benner, Director of Undergraduate Admission, Illinois Institute of Technology, 10 West 33rd Street PH101, Chicago, IL 60616-3793. *Telephone:* 312-567-3025 or 800-448-2329 (toll-free out-of-state). *Fax:* 312-567-6939. *E-mail:* admission@iit.edu. *Web site:* http://www.iit.edu/.

See page 288 for a narrative description.

ILLINOIS STATE UNIVERSITY

Normal, Illinois

Illinois State is a coed, public university, founded in 1857, offering degrees at the bachelor's, master's, and doctoral levels and post-master's and postbachelor's certificates. It has an 850-acre campus in Normal.

Academic Information The faculty has 1,101 members (77% full-time), 70% with terminal degrees. The undergraduate student-faculty ratio is 19:1. The library holds 2 million titles and 4,873 serial subscriptions. Special programs include academic remediation, services for learning-disabled students, an honors program, cooperative (work-study) education, study abroad, advanced placement credit, accelerated degree programs, ESL programs, double majors, independent study, distance learning, self-designed majors, summer session for credit, part-time degree programs (daytime, evenings, summer), adult/continuing education programs, internships, and arrangement for off-campus study with National Student Exchange. The most frequently chosen baccalaureate field is philosophy, religion, and theology.

Student Body Statistics The student body totals 21,183, of whom 18,353 are undergraduates (3,108 freshmen). 58 percent are women and 42 percent are men. Students come from 47 states and territories and 86 other countries. 98 percent are from Illinois. 0.8 percent are international students.

Expenses for 2002–03 *Application fee:* $30. *State resident tuition:* $3639 full-time, $121.33 per credit hour part-time. *Nonresident tuition:* $7830 full-time, $261 per credit hour part-time. *Mandatory fees:* $1397 full-time, $40.57 per credit hour part-time, $608.55 per term part-time. Full-time tuition and fees vary according to course load. Part-time tuition and fees vary according to course load. *College room and board:* $5062. *College room only:* $2508. Room and board charges vary according to board plan.

Financial Aid Forms of aid include need-based and non-need-based scholarships, athletic grants, and part-time jobs. The average aided 2002–03 undergraduate received an aid package worth an estimated $7675. The priority application deadline for financial aid is March 1.

Freshman Admission Illinois State requires an essay, a high school transcript, SAT I or ACT scores, and TOEFL scores for international students. ACT scores are recommended. The application deadline for regular admission is March 1.

Transfer Admission The application deadline for admission is rolling.

Entrance Difficulty Illinois State assesses its entrance difficulty level as moderately difficult. For the fall 2002 freshman class, 81 percent of the applicants were accepted.

For Further Information Contact Mr. Steve Adams, Director of Admissions, Illinois State University, Campus Box 2200, Normal, IL 61790-2200. *Telephone:* 309-438-2181 or 800-366-2478 (toll-free in-state). *Fax:* 309-438-3932. *E-mail:* ugradadm@ilstu.edu. *Web site:* http://www.ilstu.edu/.

ILLINOIS WESLEYAN UNIVERSITY

Bloomington, Illinois

IWU is a coed, private, four-year college, founded in 1850, offering degrees at the bachelor's level. It has a 70-acre campus in Bloomington.

Academic Information The faculty has 200 members (81% full-time), 95% with terminal degrees. The student-faculty ratio is 12:1. The library holds 307,861 titles, 14,264 serial subscriptions, and 13,833 audiovisual materials. Special programs include an honors program, cooperative (work-study) education, study abroad, advanced placement credit, double majors, independent study, self-designed majors, summer session for credit, internships, and arrangement for off-campus study with Case Western Reserve University, Northwestern University, Washington University, Dartmouth College. The most frequently chosen baccalaureate fields are business/marketing, social sciences and history, visual/performing arts.

Student Body Statistics The student body is made up of 2,107 undergraduates (566 freshmen). 57 percent are women and 43 percent are men. Students come from 32 states and territories and 22 other countries. 89 percent are from Illinois. 2.1 percent are international students. 25 percent of the 2002 graduating class went on to graduate and professional schools.

Expenses for 2003–04 *Comprehensive fee:* $30,380 includes full-time tuition ($24,390), mandatory fees ($150), and college room and board ($5840). *College room only:* $3470.

Financial Aid Forms of aid include need-based and non-need-based scholarships and part-time jobs. The average aided 2002–03 undergraduate received an aid package worth an estimated $16,671. The application deadline for financial aid is March 1.

Freshman Admission IWU requires an essay, a high school transcript, a minimum 2.0 high school GPA, SAT I or ACT scores, and TOEFL scores for international students. A minimum 3.0 high school GPA, 3 recommendations, and an interview are recommended. The application deadline for regular admission is March 1.

Transfer Admission The application deadline for admission is rolling.

Entrance Difficulty IWU assesses its entrance difficulty level as very difficult. For the fall 2002 freshman class, 48 percent of the applicants were accepted.

For Further Information Contact Mr. James R. Ruoti, Dean of Admissions, Illinois Wesleyan University, PO Box 2900, Bloomington, IL 61702-2900. *Telephone:* 309-556-3031 or 800-332-2498 (toll-free). *Fax:* 309-556-3411. *E-mail:* iwuadmit@titan.iwu.edu. *Web site:* http://www.iwu.edu/.

INTERNATIONAL ACADEMY OF DESIGN & TECHNOLOGY

Chicago, Illinois

International Academy is a coed, proprietary, four-year college of Career Education Corporation, founded in 1977, offering degrees at the associate and bachelor's levels. It has a 1-acre campus in Chicago.

Academic Information The faculty has 167 members (10% full-time), 1% with terminal degrees. The student-faculty ratio is 15:1. The library holds 5,000 titles, 90 serial subscriptions, and 500 audiovisual materials. Special programs include academic remediation, study abroad, advanced placement credit, independent study, summer session for credit, part-time degree programs (daytime, evenings, weekends, summer), adult/continuing education programs, and internships. The most frequently chosen baccalaureate fields are business/marketing, visual/performing arts.
Student Body Statistics The student body is made up of 2,309 undergraduates (559 freshmen). 65 percent are women and 35 percent are men. Students come from 28 states and territories and 10 other countries. 92 percent are from Illinois. 1 percent are international students.
Expenses for 2003–04 *Application fee:* $50. *Tuition:* $17,200 full-time, $1100 per course part-time. Full-time tuition varies according to program. Part-time tuition varies according to program.
Financial Aid Forms of aid include need-based scholarships and part-time jobs. The application deadline for financial aid is continuous.
Freshman Admission International Academy requires a high school transcript and an interview. An essay, a minimum 2.0 high school GPA, SAT I and SAT II or ACT scores, and SAT II: Writing Test scores are recommended. GED is required for some. The application deadline for regular admission is rolling.
Transfer Admission The application deadline for admission is rolling.
Entrance Difficulty International Academy assesses its entrance difficulty level as minimally difficult. For the fall 2002 freshman class, 58 percent of the applicants were accepted.

For Further Information Contact Ms. Dorothy Foley, Vice President of Student Management, International Academy of Design & Technology, One North State Street, Suite 400, Chicago, IL 60602. *Telephone:* 312-980-9200 or 877-ACADEMY (toll-free out-of-state). *Fax:* 312-541-3929. *E-mail:* academy@iadtchicago.com. *Web site:* http://www.iadtchicago.com/.

See page 290 for a narrative description.

ITT TECHNICAL INSTITUTE

Mount Prospect, Illinois

ITT Tech is a coed, proprietary, primarily two-year college of ITT Educational Services, Inc, founded in 1986, offering degrees at the associate and bachelor's levels. It has a 1-acre campus in Mount Prospect near Chicago.

Student Body Statistics The student body is made up of 499 undergraduates.
Expenses for 2002–03 *Application fee:* $100. *Tuition:* $347 per credit hour part-time.
Financial Aid Forms of aid include need-based scholarships and part-time jobs. The application deadline for financial aid is continuous.
Freshman Admission ITT Tech requires a high school transcript, an interview, and Wonderlic aptitude test. Recommendations and TOEFL scores for international students are recommended. The application deadline for regular admission is rolling.
Transfer Admission The application deadline for admission is rolling.
Entrance Difficulty ITT Tech assesses its entrance difficulty level as minimally difficult.

For Further Information Contact Mr. Ernest Lloyd, Director of Recruitment, ITT Technical Institute, 1401 Feehanville Drive, Mount Prospect, IL 60056. *Telephone:* 847-375-8800. *Fax:* 847-375-9022. *Web site:* http://www.itt-tech.edu/.

JUDSON COLLEGE

Elgin, Illinois

Judson is a coed, private, Baptist, four-year college, founded in 1963, offering degrees at the bachelor's and master's levels. It has an 80-acre campus in Elgin near Chicago.

Academic Information The faculty has 123 members (45% full-time), 41% with terminal degrees. The undergraduate student-faculty ratio is 15:1. The library holds 104,331 titles, 450 serial subscriptions, and 12,500 audiovisual materials. Special programs include academic remediation, an honors program, study abroad, advanced placement credit, accelerated degree programs, double majors, independent study, distance learning, self-designed majors, part-time degree programs (evenings, weekends), adult/continuing education programs, internships, and arrangement for off-campus study with Christian College Coalition. The most frequently chosen baccalaureate fields are business/marketing, education, personal/miscellaneous services.
Student Body Statistics The student body totals 1,172, of whom 1,167 are undergraduates (160 freshmen). 56 percent are women and 44 percent are men. Students come from 21 states and territories and 18 other countries. 70 percent are from Illinois. 3.8 percent are international students.
Expenses for 2003–04 *Application fee:* $30. *Comprehensive fee:* $22,050 includes full-time tuition ($15,800), mandatory fees ($250), and college room and board ($6000). Room and board charges vary according to board plan. *Part-time tuition:* $515 per term. *Part-time mandatory fees:* $56.25 per term. Part-time tuition and fees vary according to course load.
Financial Aid Forms of aid include need-based and non-need-based scholarships, athletic grants, and part-time jobs. The average aided 2001–02 undergraduate received an aid package worth $15,439. The application deadline for financial aid is continuous.
Freshman Admission Judson requires an essay, a high school transcript, a minimum 2.0 high school GPA, SAT I or ACT scores, and TOEFL scores for international students. ACT scores are recommended. 2 recommendations and an interview are required for some. The application deadline for regular admission is rolling.
Transfer Admission The application deadline for admission is rolling.
Entrance Difficulty Judson assesses its entrance difficulty level as moderately difficult. For the fall 2002 freshman class, 71 percent of the applicants were accepted.

For Further Information Contact Mr. Billy Dean, Director of Admissions, Judson College, 1151 North State Street, Elgin, IL 60123-1498. *Telephone:* 847-695-2500 Ext. 2315 or 800-879-5376 (toll-free). *Fax:* 847-695-0216. *E-mail:* admission@judson-il.edu. *Web site:* http://www.judsoncollege.edu/.

KENDALL COLLEGE

Evanston, Illinois

Kendall is a coed, private, United Methodist, four-year college, founded in 1934, offering degrees at the associate and bachelor's levels. It has a 1-acre campus in Evanston near Chicago.

Academic Information The faculty has 74 members, 41% with terminal degrees. The student-faculty ratio is 15:1. The library holds 37,000 titles, 215 serial subscriptions, and 150 audiovisual materials. Special programs include academic remediation, cooperative (work-study) education, study abroad, advanced placement credit, accelerated degree programs, ESL programs, independent study, self-designed majors, summer session for credit, part-time degree programs (daytime, evenings, weekends, summer), adult/continuing education programs, and internships.
Student Body Statistics The student body is made up of 550 undergraduates. Students come from 18 states and territories and 13 other countries. 3.1 percent are international students.
Expenses for 2003–04 *Application fee:* $30. *Comprehensive fee:* $21,664 includes full-time tuition ($14,445), mandatory fees ($391), and college room and board ($6828). Full-time tuition and fees vary according to program. Room and board charges vary according to housing facility. *Part-time tuition:* $436 per quarter hour. *Part-time mandatory fees:* $127 per term. Part-time tuition and fees vary according to program.

Financial Aid Forms of aid include need-based and non-need-based scholarships, athletic grants, and part-time jobs. The average aided 2002–03 undergraduate received an aid package worth an estimated $15,136. The priority application deadline for financial aid is May 1.
Freshman Admission Kendall requires an essay, a high school transcript, minimum ACT score of 18, SAT I or ACT scores, and TOEFL scores for international students. A minimum 2.0 high school GPA and an interview are recommended. Recommendations and an interview are required for some. The application deadline for regular admission is rolling.
Transfer Admission The application deadline for admission is rolling.
Entrance Difficulty Kendall assesses its entrance difficulty level as minimally difficult. For the fall 2002 freshman class, 72 percent of the applicants were accepted.

For Further Information Contact Carl Goodmonson, Assistant Director of Admissions, Kendall College, 2408 Orrington Avenue, Evanston, IL 60201-2899. *Telephone:* 847-448-2304 or 877-588-8860 (toll-free in-state). *Fax:* 847-448-2120. *E-mail:* admissions@kendall.edu. *Web site:* http://www.kendall.edu/.

See page 294 for a narrative description.

KNOX COLLEGE

Galesburg, Illinois

Knox is a coed, private, four-year college, founded in 1837, offering degrees at the bachelor's level. It has an 82-acre campus in Galesburg near Peoria.

Academic Information The faculty has 107 members (84% full-time), 85% with terminal degrees. The student-faculty ratio is 12:1. The library holds 185,923 titles, 1,037 serial subscriptions, and 6,336 audiovisual materials. Special programs include academic remediation, services for learning-disabled students, an honors program, study abroad, advanced placement credit, ESL programs, double majors, independent study, self-designed majors, part-time degree programs (daytime), internships, and arrangement for off-campus study with Associated Colleges of the Midwest, Great Lakes College Association. The most frequently chosen baccalaureate fields are biological/life sciences, English, social sciences and history.
Student Body Statistics The student body is made up of 1,121 undergraduates (300 freshmen). 53 percent are women and 47 percent are men. Students come from 45 states and territories and 42 other countries. 56 percent are from Illinois. 7.9 percent are international students. 35 percent of the 2002 graduating class went on to graduate and professional schools.
Expenses for 2002–03 *Application fee:* $35. *Comprehensive fee:* $29,259 includes full-time tuition ($23,235), mandatory fees ($264), and college room and board ($5760). *College room only:* $2550. Room and board charges vary according to board plan and housing facility. *Part-time tuition:* $860 per credit.
Financial Aid Forms of aid include need-based and non-need-based scholarships and part-time jobs. The average aided 2002–03 undergraduate received an aid package worth an estimated $20,356. The priority application deadline for financial aid is March 1.
Freshman Admission Knox requires an essay, a high school transcript, 2 recommendations, SAT I or ACT scores, and TOEFL scores for international students. An interview is recommended. The application deadline for regular admission is February 1 and for early action it is November 15.
Transfer Admission The application deadline for admission is April 1.
Entrance Difficulty Knox assesses its entrance difficulty level as very difficult. For the fall 2002 freshman class, 72 percent of the applicants were accepted.

For Further Information Contact Mr. Paul Steenis, Director of Admissions, Knox College, Box K-148, Galesburg, IL 61401. *Telephone:* 309-341-7100 or 800-678-KNOX (toll-free). *Fax:* 309-341-7070. *E-mail:* admission@knox.edu. *Web site:* http://www.knox.edu/.

See page 298 for a narrative description.

LAKE FOREST COLLEGE

Lake Forest, Illinois

Lake Forest is a coed, private, comprehensive institution, founded in 1857, offering degrees at the bachelor's and master's levels. It has a 110-acre campus in Lake Forest near Chicago.

Academic Information The faculty has 146 members (60% full-time), 77% with terminal degrees. The undergraduate student-faculty ratio is 12:1. The library holds 268,760 titles, 886 serial subscriptions, and 12,125 audiovisual materials. Special programs include services for learning-disabled students, an honors program, study abroad, advanced placement credit, accelerated degree programs, Freshman Honors College, double majors, independent study, self-designed majors, summer session for credit, part-time degree programs, adult/continuing education programs, internships, and arrangement for off-campus study with 14 members of the Associated Colleges of the Midwest. The most frequently chosen baccalaureate fields are business/marketing, psychology, social sciences and history.
Student Body Statistics The student body totals 1,341, of whom 1,319 are undergraduates (359 freshmen). 59 percent are women and 41 percent are men. Students come from 45 states and territories and 42 other countries. 48 percent are from Illinois. 8.3 percent are international students. 21 percent of the 2002 graduating class went on to graduate and professional schools.
Expenses for 2003–04 *Application fee:* $40. *Comprehensive fee:* $30,170 includes full-time tuition ($24,096), mandatory fees ($310), and college room and board ($5764). *College room only:* $3164. Room and board charges vary according to housing facility. *Part-time tuition:* $3012 per course. *Part-time mandatory fees:* $155 per term.
Financial Aid Forms of aid include need-based and non-need-based scholarships and part-time jobs. The average aided 2002–03 undergraduate received an aid package worth an estimated $20,020. The priority application deadline for financial aid is March 1.
Freshman Admission Lake Forest requires an essay, a high school transcript, 2 recommendations, graded paper, SAT I or ACT scores, and TOEFL scores for international students. An interview is recommended. The application deadline for regular admission is March 1; for early decision it is January 1; and for early action it is December 1.
Transfer Admission The application deadline for admission is rolling.
Entrance Difficulty Lake Forest assesses its entrance difficulty level as very difficult. For the fall 2002 freshman class, 66 percent of the applicants were accepted.

For Further Information Contact Mr. William G. Motzer Jr., Director of Admissions, Lake Forest College, 555 North Sheridan Road, Lake Forest, IL 60045-2399. *Telephone:* 847-735-5000 or 800-828-4751 (toll-free). *Fax:* 847-735-6271. *E-mail:* admissions@lakeforest.edu. *Web site:* http://www.lakeforest.edu/.

LAKEVIEW COLLEGE OF NURSING

Danville, Illinois

LCON is a coed, private, upper-level unit of Danville Area Community College, founded in 1987, offering degrees at the bachelor's level in nursing. It has a 1-acre campus in Danville.

Academic Information The faculty has 13 members (23% full-time), 8% with terminal degrees. The student-faculty ratio is 8:1. The library holds 1,500 titles, 60 serial subscriptions, and 450 audiovisual materials. Special programs include an honors program, independent study, distance learning, summer session for credit, part-time degree programs (daytime, evenings, weekends, summer), external degree programs, and arrangement for off-campus study with Eastern Illinois University-branch campus. The most frequently chosen baccalaureate field is health professions and related sciences.
Student Body Statistics The student body is made up of 83 undergraduates (9 in entering class). 94 percent are women and 6 percent are men. Students come from 3 states and territories. 95 percent are from Illinois.

Lakeview College of Nursing (continued)

Expenses for 2002–03 *Application fee:* $50. *Tuition:* $8000 full-time, $250 per credit hour part-time. Full-time tuition varies according to course load and location. Part-time tuition varies according to course load and location.
Financial Aid Forms of aid include need-based and non-need-based scholarships. The average aided 2002–03 undergraduate received an aid package worth an estimated $3200. The application deadline for financial aid is continuous.
Transfer Admission LCON requires a college transcript and a minimum 2.0 college GPA. Standardized test scores are recommended. The application deadline for admission is rolling.
Entrance Difficulty LCON assesses its entrance difficulty level as moderately difficult. For the fall 2002 entering class, 87 percent of the applicants were accepted.

For Further Information Contact Kelly M. Holden MS Ed, Registrar, Lakeview College of Nursing, 903 North Logan Avenue, Danville, IL 61832. *Telephone:* 217-443-5238 Ext. 5385, 217-443-5238 Ext. 5454 (toll-free in-state), or 217-443-5238 (toll-free out-of-state). *Fax:* 217-442-2279. *E-mail:* kholden@lakeviewcol.edu. *Web site:* http://www.lakeviewcol.edu/.

LEWIS UNIVERSITY

Romeoville, Illinois

Lewis is a coed, private, comprehensive institution, founded in 1932, affiliated with the Roman Catholic Church, offering degrees at the associate, bachelor's, and master's levels and postbachelor's certificates. It has a 600-acre campus in Romeoville near Chicago.

Academic Information The faculty has 152 members (93% full-time), 57% with terminal degrees. The undergraduate student-faculty ratio is 15:1. The library holds 149,870 titles, 1,990 serial subscriptions, and 2,281 audiovisual materials. Special programs include academic remediation, an honors program, study abroad, advanced placement credit, accelerated degree programs, ESL programs, double majors, independent study, distance learning, self-designed majors, summer session for credit, part-time degree programs (daytime, evenings, weekends, summer), adult/continuing education programs, and internships. The most frequently chosen baccalaureate fields are business/marketing, health professions and related sciences, protective services/public administration.
Student Body Statistics The student body totals 4,347, of whom 3,194 are undergraduates (373 freshmen). 56 percent are women and 44 percent are men. Students come from 24 states and territories and 31 other countries. 96 percent are from Illinois. 4.2 percent are international students. 10 percent of the 2002 graduating class went on to graduate and professional schools.
Expenses for 2002–03 *Application fee:* $35. *One-time mandatory fee:* $110. *Comprehensive fee:* $22,500 includes full-time tuition ($15,250) and college room and board ($7250). *College room only:* $3350. Full-time tuition varies according to course load and program. Room and board charges vary according to board plan and housing facility. *Part-time tuition:* $490 per credit hour. Part-time tuition varies according to course load and program.
Financial Aid Forms of aid include need-based and non-need-based scholarships, athletic grants, and part-time jobs. The average aided 2002–03 undergraduate received an aid package worth an estimated $13,422. The priority application deadline for financial aid is May 1.
Freshman Admission Lewis requires a high school transcript, a minimum 2.0 high school GPA, SAT I or ACT scores, and TOEFL scores for international students. An interview is required for some. The application deadline for regular admission is rolling.
Transfer Admission The application deadline for admission is rolling.
Entrance Difficulty Lewis assesses its entrance difficulty level as moderately difficult; noncompetitive for applicants 24 or over. For the fall 2002 freshman class, 68 percent of the applicants were accepted.

For Further Information Contact Mr. Ryan Cockerill, Admission Counselor, Lewis University, Box 297, One University Parkway, Romeoville, IL 60446. *Telephone:* 815-838-0500 Ext. 5684 or 800-897-9000 (toll-free). *Fax:* 815-836-5002. *E-mail:* admissions@lewisu.edu. *Web site:* http://www.lewisu.edu/.

LEXINGTON COLLEGE

Chicago, Illinois

Lexington College is a women's, private, primarily two-year college, founded in 1977, offering degrees at the associate and bachelor's levels.

Academic Information The faculty has 10 members (20% full-time), 20% with terminal degrees. The student-faculty ratio is 5:1. The library holds 2,000 titles and 40 serial subscriptions. Special programs include academic remediation, cooperative (work-study) education, part-time degree programs (daytime), adult/continuing education programs, and internships.
Student Body Statistics The student body is made up of 52 undergraduates (34 freshmen). Students come from 5 states and territories. 90 percent are from Illinois. 1.9 percent are international students.
Expenses for 2003–04 *Application fee:* $30. *Tuition:* $12,600 full-time, $450 per credit hour part-time. *Mandatory fees:* $750 full-time.
Financial Aid Forms of aid include need-based scholarships. The application deadline for financial aid is October 1.
Freshman Admission Lexington College requires an essay, a high school transcript, ACT or SATR, and SAT I or ACT scores. A minimum 2.0 high school GPA and an interview are recommended. 2 recommendations are required for some. The application deadline for regular admission is rolling.
Transfer Admission The application deadline for admission is rolling.
Entrance Difficulty Lexington College has an open admission policy. It assesses its entrance difficulty as minimally difficult for out-of-state applicants; minimally difficult for transfers.

For Further Information Contact Ms. Monica Hinchey, Director of Admissions, Lexington College, 310 South Peoria Street, Chicago, IL 60607-3534. *Telephone:* 312-226-6294 Ext. 225. *Fax:* 312-226-6405. *E-mail:* admissio@lexingtoncollege.edu. *Web site:* http://www.lexingtoncollege.edu/.

LINCOLN CHRISTIAN COLLEGE

Lincoln, Illinois

Lincoln Christian is a coed, private, four-year college, founded in 1944, affiliated with the Christian Churches and Churches of Christ, offering degrees at the associate and bachelor's levels. It has a 227-acre campus in Lincoln.

Academic Information The faculty has 59 members (49% full-time), 41% with terminal degrees. The student-faculty ratio is 16:1. The library holds 127,000 titles, 500 serial subscriptions, and 27,000 audiovisual materials. Special programs include academic remediation, services for learning-disabled students, an honors program, advanced placement credit, ESL programs, double majors, independent study, distance learning, summer session for credit, part-time degree programs (daytime, evenings, summer), external degree programs, adult/continuing education programs, internships, and arrangement for off-campus study with University of Illinois at Springfield, Illinois State University, Greenville College. The most frequently chosen baccalaureate field is philosophy, religion, and theology.
Student Body Statistics The student body is made up of 756 undergraduates (172 freshmen). 51 percent are women and 49 percent are men. Students come from 27 states and territories and 6 other countries. 70 percent are from Illinois. 1 percent are international students.
Expenses for 2003–04 *Application fee:* $20. *Comprehensive fee:* $13,558 includes full-time tuition ($7890), mandatory fees ($1200), and college room and board ($4468). *Part-time tuition:* $263 per semester hour. *Part-time mandatory fees:* $40 per semester hour. Part-time tuition and fees vary according to course load and program.
Financial Aid Forms of aid include need-based and non-need-based scholarships and part-time jobs. The average aided 2002–03 undergraduate received an aid package worth an estimated $8000. The application deadline for financial aid is continuous.
Freshman Admission Lincoln Christian requires an essay, a high school transcript, 3 recommendations, and SAT I or ACT scores. TOEFL scores

for international students are recommended. An interview is required for some. The application deadline for regular admission is rolling.
Transfer Admission The application deadline for admission is rolling.
Entrance Difficulty Lincoln Christian assesses its entrance difficulty level as moderately difficult. For the fall 2002 freshman class, 77 percent of the applicants were accepted.

For Further Information Contact Mrs. Mary K. Davis, Assistant Director of Admissions, Lincoln Christian College, 100 Campus View Drive, Lincoln, IL 62656. *Telephone:* 217-732-3168 Ext. 2367 or 888-522-5228 (toll-free). *Fax:* 217-732-4199. *E-mail:* coladmis@lccs.edu. *Web site:* http://www.lccs.edu/.

LINCOLN COLLEGE

Lincoln, Illinois

Lincoln College is a coed, private, two-year college, founded in 1865, offering degrees at the associate level. It has a 42-acre campus in Lincoln.

Academic Information The faculty has 53 members (64% full-time). The student-faculty ratio is 16:1. The library holds 42,500 titles and 380 serial subscriptions. Special programs include academic remediation, an honors program, accelerated degree programs, Freshman Honors College, independent study, summer session for credit, and part-time degree programs (daytime, evenings, summer).
Student Body Statistics The student body is made up of 758 undergraduates (380 freshmen). 46 percent are women and 54 percent are men. Students come from 15 states and territories. 91 percent are from Illinois. 89 percent of the 2002 graduating class went on to four-year colleges.
Expenses for 2003–04 *Application fee:* $25. *Comprehensive fee:* $18,535 includes full-time tuition ($12,400), mandatory fees ($935), and college room and board ($5200). *College room only:* $1900. Room and board charges vary according to housing facility.
Financial Aid Forms of aid include need-based scholarships and part-time jobs. The priority application deadline for financial aid is May 1.
Freshman Admission Lincoln College requires a high school transcript, SAT I or ACT scores, and TOEFL scores for international students. An interview is recommended. 1 recommendation is required for some. The application deadline for regular admission is rolling.
Transfer Admission The application deadline for admission is rolling.
Entrance Difficulty Lincoln College assesses its entrance difficulty level as minimally difficult. For the fall 2002 freshman class, 65 percent of the applicants were accepted.

For Further Information Contact Ms. Stacy Rachel, Director of Enrollment Management, Lincoln College, 300 Keokuk Street, Lincoln, IL 62656-1699. *Telephone:* 800-569-0556 or 800-569-0556 (toll-free). *Fax:* 217-732-7715. *E-mail:* information@lincolncollege.com. *Web site:* http://www.lincolncollege.edu/.

LINCOLN COLLEGE

Normal, Illinois

Lincoln College is a coed, private, primarily two-year college, founded in 1865, offering degrees at the associate and bachelor's levels. It has a 10-acre campus in Normal.

Academic Information The faculty has 50 members (18% full-time), 16% with terminal degrees. The student-faculty ratio is 14:1. The library holds 2 million titles and 25,000 audiovisual materials. Special programs include academic remediation, an honors program, cooperative (work-study) education, summer session for credit, part-time degree programs (daytime, evenings, weekends, summer), adult/continuing education programs, and internships.
Student Body Statistics The student body is made up of 520 undergraduates (225 freshmen). 62 percent are women and 38 percent are men. Students come from 6 states and territories and 3 other countries. 94 percent are from Illinois. 1 percent are international students. 89 percent of the 2002 graduating class went on to four-year colleges.
Expenses for 2003–04 *Application fee:* $25. *Comprehensive fee:* $18,470 includes full-time tuition ($12,400), mandatory fees ($570), and college room and board ($5500). *College room only:* $3700. Full-time tuition and fees vary according to program. Room and board charges vary according to board plan. *Part-time tuition:* $413 per credit hour. *Part-time mandatory fees:* $25 per term. Part-time tuition and fees vary according to course load.
Financial Aid Forms of aid include need-based scholarships and part-time jobs. The priority application deadline for financial aid is May 1.
Freshman Admission Lincoln College requires a high school transcript, an interview, and TOEFL scores for international students. 2 recommendations and SAT I or ACT scores are required for some. The application deadline for regular admission is rolling.
Transfer Admission The application deadline for admission is rolling.
Entrance Difficulty Lincoln College assesses its entrance difficulty level as minimally difficult.

For Further Information Contact Mr. Joe Hendrix, Director of Admissions, Lincoln College, 715 West Raab Road, Normal, IL 61761. *Telephone:* 800-569-0558 or 800-569-0558 (toll-free). *Fax:* 309-454-5652. *E-mail:* admissions@lincoln.mclean.il.us. *Web site:* http://www.lincoln.mclean.il.us/.

LOYOLA UNIVERSITY CHICAGO

Chicago, Illinois

Loyola is a coed, private, Roman Catholic (Jesuit) university, founded in 1870, offering degrees at the bachelor's, master's, doctoral, and first professional levels and post-master's and postbachelor's certificates (also offers adult part-time program with significant enrollment not reflected in profile). It has a 105-acre campus in Chicago.

Academic Information The faculty has 1,979 members (47% full-time). The undergraduate student-faculty ratio is 13:1. The library holds 1 million titles, 68,886 serial subscriptions, and 35,090 audiovisual materials. Special programs include academic remediation, services for learning-disabled students, an honors program, study abroad, advanced placement credit, accelerated degree programs, ESL programs, double majors, summer session for credit, part-time degree programs (evenings), adult/continuing education programs, internships, and arrangement for off-campus study with School of the Art Institute of Chicago. The most frequently chosen baccalaureate fields are business/marketing, psychology, social sciences and history.
Student Body Statistics The student body totals 13,061, of whom 7,533 are undergraduates (1,623 freshmen). 66 percent are women and 34 percent are men. Students come from 50 states and territories and 60 other countries. 68 percent are from Illinois. 1.7 percent are international students.
Expenses for 2003–04 *Application fee:* $25. *Comprehensive fee:* $28,954 includes full-time tuition ($20,544), mandatory fees ($510), and college room and board ($7900). Room and board charges vary according to board plan and housing facility. *Part-time tuition:* $405 per semester hour. *Part-time mandatory fees:* $66 per term. Part-time tuition and fees vary according to course load.
Financial Aid Forms of aid include need-based and non-need-based scholarships, athletic grants, and part-time jobs. The average aided 2002–03 undergraduate received an aid package worth an estimated $20,087. The priority application deadline for financial aid is March 1.
Freshman Admission Loyola requires an essay, a high school transcript, SAT I or ACT scores, and TOEFL scores for international students. An interview is recommended. The application deadline for regular admission is April 1.
Transfer Admission The application deadline for admission is July 9.
Entrance Difficulty Loyola assesses its entrance difficulty level as moderately difficult. For the fall 2002 freshman class, 84 percent of the applicants were accepted.

For Further Information Contact Ms. April Hansen, Director of Admissions, Loyola University Chicago, 820 North Michigan Avenue, Suite 613, Chicago, IL 60611. *Telephone:* 773-508-3080 or 800-262-2373 (toll-free). *Fax:* 312-915-7216. *E-mail:* admission@luc.edu. *Web site:* http://www.luc.edu/.

See page 300 for a narrative description.

MACCORMAC COLLEGE

Chicago, Illinois

MacCormac College is a coed, private, two-year college, founded in 1904, offering degrees at the associate level. It has an 8-acre campus in Chicago.

Expenses for 2002–03 *Application fee:* $20. *Tuition:* $4500 full-time, $195 per semester hour part-time.

For Further Information Contact Mr. Milton Kobus, Dean of Enrollment Management, MacCormac College, 506 South Wabash Avenue, Chicago, IL 60605-1667. *Telephone:* 312-922-1884 Ext. 210. *Fax:* 630-941-0937. *Web site:* http://www.maccormac.edu/.

MACMURRAY COLLEGE

Jacksonville, Illinois

MacMurray is a coed, private, United Methodist, four-year college, founded in 1846, offering degrees at the associate and bachelor's levels. It has a 60-acre campus in Jacksonville.

Academic Information The faculty has 69 members (67% full-time), 57% with terminal degrees. The student-faculty ratio is 12:1. The library holds 935,000 titles, 235 serial subscriptions, and 936 audiovisual materials. Special programs include academic remediation, services for learning-disabled students, an honors program, advanced placement credit, double majors, independent study, summer session for credit, part-time degree programs (daytime, evenings, summer), internships, and arrangement for off-campus study with 5 members of the Western Illinois Foreign Language Consortium. The most frequently chosen baccalaureate fields are education, protective services/public administration, psychology.
Student Body Statistics The student body is made up of 633 undergraduates (127 freshmen). 58 percent are women and 42 percent are men. Students come from 27 states and territories and 5 other countries. 85 percent are from Illinois. 1.6 percent are international students. 9 percent of the 2002 graduating class went on to graduate and professional schools.
Expenses for 2003–04 *Application fee:* $0. *Comprehensive fee:* $19,683 includes full-time tuition ($14,500) and college room and board ($5183). *College room only:* $2413. Room and board charges vary according to board plan and housing facility. *Part-time tuition:* $235 per credit hour.
Financial Aid Forms of aid include need-based and non-need-based scholarships and part-time jobs. The average aided 2002–03 undergraduate received an aid package worth an estimated $11,433. The priority application deadline for financial aid is May 31.
Freshman Admission MacMurray requires a high school transcript, SAT I or ACT scores, and TOEFL scores for international students. An essay, a minimum 2.5 high school GPA, recommendations, and an interview are required for some. The application deadline for regular admission is rolling.
Transfer Admission The application deadline for admission is rolling.
Entrance Difficulty MacMurray assesses its entrance difficulty level as moderately difficult. For the fall 2002 freshman class, 55 percent of the applicants were accepted.

For Further Information Contact Ms. Rhonda Cors, Dean of Enrollment, MacMurray College, 447 East College Avenue, Jacksonville, IL 62650. *Telephone:* 217-479-7056 or 800-252-7485 (toll-free in-state). *Fax:* 217-291-0702. *E-mail:* admiss@mac.edu. *Web site:* http://www.mac.edu/.

MCKENDREE COLLEGE

Lebanon, Illinois

McKendree is a coed, private, four-year college, founded in 1828, affiliated with the United Methodist Church, offering degrees at the bachelor's level. It has an 80-acre campus in Lebanon near St. Louis.

Academic Information The faculty has 197 members (35% full-time), 36% with terminal degrees. The student-faculty ratio is 15:1. The library holds 105,000 titles, 450 serial subscriptions, and 9,500 audiovisual materials. Special programs include academic remediation, services for learning-disabled students, an honors program, study abroad, advanced placement credit, accelerated degree programs, double majors, independent study, self-designed majors, summer session for credit, part-time degree programs (daytime, evenings, summer), internships, and arrangement for off-campus study with University of Evansville. The most frequently chosen baccalaureate fields are business/marketing, education, health professions and related sciences.
Student Body Statistics The student body is made up of 2,067 undergraduates (283 freshmen). 61 percent are women and 39 percent are men. Students come from 15 states and territories and 12 other countries. 71 percent are from Illinois. 1.2 percent are international students. 16 percent of the 2002 graduating class went on to graduate and professional schools.
Expenses for 2002–03 *Application fee:* $40. *Comprehensive fee:* $19,600 includes full-time tuition ($14,200) and college room and board ($5400). Full-time tuition varies according to class time, course load, and location. Room and board charges vary according to board plan and housing facility. *Part-time tuition:* $475 per credit. Part-time tuition varies according to class time, course load, and location.
Financial Aid Forms of aid include need-based and non-need-based scholarships, athletic grants, and part-time jobs. The average aided 2002–03 undergraduate received an aid package worth an estimated $11,368. The priority application deadline for financial aid is May 31.
Freshman Admission McKendree requires a high school transcript, a minimum 2.5 high school GPA, 1 recommendation, SAT I or ACT scores, and TOEFL scores for international students. An essay and an interview are required for some. The application deadline for regular admission is rolling.
Transfer Admission The application deadline for admission is rolling.
Entrance Difficulty McKendree assesses its entrance difficulty level as moderately difficult. For the fall 2002 freshman class, 68 percent of the applicants were accepted.

For Further Information Contact Mr. Mark Campbell, Vice President for Admissions and Financial Aid, McKendree College, 701 College Road, Lebanon, IL 62254. *Telephone:* 618-537-4481 Ext. 6835 or 800-232-7228 Ext. 6835 (toll-free). *Fax:* 618-537-6496. *E-mail:* mecampbell@mckendree.edu. *Web site:* http://www.mckendree.edu/.

MENNONITE COLLEGE OF NURSING

See Illinois State University

MIDSTATE COLLEGE

Peoria, Illinois

Midstate is a coed, primarily women's, proprietary, primarily two-year college, founded in 1888, offering degrees at the associate and bachelor's levels. It has a 1-acre campus in Peoria.

Academic Information The faculty has 45 members (22% full-time). The student-faculty ratio is 13:1. The library holds 8,724 titles and 104 serial subscriptions. Special programs include academic remediation, an honors program, cooperative (work-study) education, Freshman Honors College, summer session for credit, part-time degree programs (daytime, evenings, summer), and internships.
Student Body Statistics The student body is made up of 478 undergraduates (378 freshmen). 80 percent are women and 20 percent are men. Students come from 6 states and territories. 97 percent are from Illinois. 0.2 percent are international students.
Expenses for 2003–04 *Application fee:* $25. *Tuition:* $11,600 full-time, $775 per course part-time.
Financial Aid Forms of aid include need-based scholarships and part-time jobs. The application deadline for financial aid is continuous.
Freshman Admission Midstate requires a high school transcript, TOEFL scores for international students, and Wonderlic aptitude test. An interview is recommended. The application deadline for regular admission is rolling.
Transfer Admission The application deadline for admission is rolling.

Entrance Difficulty Midstate assesses its entrance difficulty level as moderately difficult; minimally difficult for transfers.

For Further Information Contact Ms. Jessica Auer, Director of Admissions, Midstate College, 411 West Northmoor Road, Peoria, IL 61614. *Telephone:* 309-692-4092. *Fax:* 309-692-3893. *Web site:* http://www.midstate.edu/.

MILLIKIN UNIVERSITY

Decatur, Illinois

Millikin is a coed, private, comprehensive institution, founded in 1901, affiliated with the Presbyterian Church (U.S.A.), offering degrees at the bachelor's and master's levels. It has a 70-acre campus in Decatur.

Academic Information The faculty has 260 members (58% full-time). The undergraduate student-faculty ratio is 13:1. The library holds 199,660 titles, 927 serial subscriptions, and 9,017 audiovisual materials. Special programs include services for learning-disabled students, an honors program, study abroad, advanced placement credit, double majors, independent study, self-designed majors, summer session for credit, part-time degree programs (daytime, evenings, summer), internships, and arrangement for off-campus study with Drew University, American University, Urban Life Center. The most frequently chosen baccalaureate fields are business/marketing, education, visual/performing arts.
Student Body Statistics The student body totals 2,496, of whom 2,468 are undergraduates (638 freshmen). 56 percent are women and 44 percent are men. Students come from 33 states and territories and 12 other countries. 84 percent are from Illinois. 0.5 percent are international students. 14 percent of the 2002 graduating class went on to graduate and professional schools.
Expenses for 2003–04 *Comprehensive fee:* $25,357 includes full-time tuition ($18,834), mandatory fees ($400), and college room and board ($6123). *College room only:* $3315. Full-time tuition and fees vary according to course load. Room and board charges vary according to board plan and housing facility. *Part-time tuition:* $554 per credit.
Financial Aid Forms of aid include need-based and non-need-based scholarships and part-time jobs. The average aided 2002–03 undergraduate received an aid package worth an estimated $15,641. The application deadline for financial aid is June 1 with a priority deadline of April 15.
Freshman Admission Millikin requires a high school transcript, a minimum 2.0 high school GPA, 2 recommendations, SAT I or ACT scores, and TOEFL scores for international students. An interview is recommended. Audition for school of music; portfolio review for art program is required for some. The application deadline for regular admission is rolling.
Transfer Admission The application deadline for admission is rolling.
Entrance Difficulty Millikin assesses its entrance difficulty level as moderately difficult; most difficult for James Millikin Scholars, Presidential Scholars programs. For the fall 2002 freshman class, 78 percent of the applicants were accepted.

For Further Information Contact Ms. Patricia Knox, Dean of Admission, Millikin University, 1184 West Main Street, Decatur, IL 62522-2084. *Telephone:* 217-424-6210 or 800-373-7733 Ext. # 5 (toll-free). *Fax:* 217-425-4669. *E-mail:* admis@mail.millikin.edu. *Web site:* http://www.millikin.edu/.

MONMOUTH COLLEGE

Monmouth, Illinois

Monmouth is a coed, private, four-year college, founded in 1853, affiliated with the Presbyterian Church, offering degrees at the bachelor's level. It has a 40-acre campus in Monmouth near Peoria.

Academic Information The faculty has 103 members (66% full-time), 64% with terminal degrees. The student-faculty ratio is 14:1. The library holds 176,470 titles, 514 serial subscriptions, and 3,975 audiovisual materials. Special programs include an honors program, study abroad, advanced placement credit, double majors, independent study, self-designed majors, part-time degree programs (daytime), internships, and arrangement for off-campus study with members of the Associated Colleges of the Midwest, Great Lakes Colleges Association. The most frequently chosen baccalaureate fields are business/marketing, education, social sciences and history.
Student Body Statistics The student body is made up of 1,089 undergraduates (291 freshmen). 53 percent are women and 47 percent are men. Students come from 19 states and territories and 20 other countries. 93 percent are from Illinois. 2.2 percent are international students. 20 percent of the 2002 graduating class went on to graduate and professional schools.
Expenses for 2003–04 *Application fee:* $0. *Comprehensive fee:* $23,600 includes full-time tuition ($18,600) and college room and board ($5000). *College room only:* $2800. Room and board charges vary according to board plan and housing facility. *Part-time tuition:* $775 per semester hour.
Financial Aid Forms of aid include need-based and non-need-based scholarships and part-time jobs. The average aided 2001–02 undergraduate received an aid package worth $15,376. The priority application deadline for financial aid is April 15.
Freshman Admission Monmouth requires a high school transcript, SAT I or ACT scores, and TOEFL scores for international students. An interview is recommended. An essay and 2 recommendations are required for some. The application deadline for regular admission is rolling.
Transfer Admission The application deadline for admission is rolling.
Entrance Difficulty Monmouth assesses its entrance difficulty level as moderately difficult. For the fall 2002 freshman class, 75 percent of the applicants were accepted.

For Further Information Contact Vice President for Enrollment, Monmouth College, 700 East Broadway, Monmouth, IL 61462-1998. *Telephone:* 309-457-2131 or 800-747-2687 (toll-free). *Fax:* 309-457-2141. *E-mail:* admit@monm.edu. *Web site:* http://www.monm.edu/.

MOODY BIBLE INSTITUTE

Chicago, Illinois

MBI is a coed, private, nondenominational, comprehensive institution, founded in 1886, offering degrees at the bachelor's, master's, and first professional levels. It has a 25-acre campus in Chicago.

Academic Information The faculty has 100 members (84% full-time), 73% with terminal degrees. The undergraduate student-faculty ratio is 20:1. The library holds 135,000 titles and 987 serial subscriptions. Special programs include study abroad, advanced placement credit, ESL programs, double majors, independent study, distance learning, summer session for credit, part-time degree programs (daytime, evenings, weekends, summer), external degree programs, adult/continuing education programs, internships, and arrangement for off-campus study with Roosevelt University, University of Illinois at Chicago, City Colleges of Chicago, Harold Washington College. The most frequently chosen baccalaureate fields are communications/communication technologies, philosophy, religion, and theology, trade and industry.
Student Body Statistics The student body totals 1,737, of whom 1,418 are undergraduates (408 freshmen). 43 percent are women and 57 percent are men. Students come from 48 states and territories and 41 other countries. 31 percent are from Illinois. 6.8 percent are international students.
Expenses for 2002–03 *Application fee:* $35. *Comprehensive fee:* $7606 includes full-time tuition ($0), mandatory fees ($1586), and college room and board ($6020). *College room only:* $3420. Room and board charges vary according to housing facility. All students are awarded full-tuition scholarships.
Financial Aid Forms of aid include need-based scholarships. The application deadline for financial aid is continuous.
Freshman Admission MBI requires an essay, a high school transcript, a minimum 2.3 high school GPA, 4 recommendations, Christian testimony, SAT I and SAT II or ACT scores, and TOEFL scores for international students. An interview is required for some. The application deadline for regular admission is March 1 and for early decision it is December 1.
Transfer Admission The application deadline for admission is March 1.

Moody Bible Institute (continued)

Entrance Difficulty MBI assesses its entrance difficulty level as moderately difficult. For the fall 2002 freshman class, 50 percent of the applicants were accepted.

For Further Information Contact Mrs. Marthe Campa, Application Coordinator, Moody Bible Institute, 820 North LaSalle Boulevard, Chicago, IL 60610. *Telephone:* 312-329-4267 or 800-967-4MBI (toll-free). *Fax:* 312-329-8987. *E-mail:* admissions@moody.edu. *Web site:* http://www.moody.edu/.

MORRISON INSTITUTE OF TECHNOLOGY

Morrison, Illinois

Morrison is a coed, primarily men's, private, two-year college, founded in 1973, offering degrees at the associate level in engineering technology. It has a 17-acre campus in Morrison.

Academic Information The faculty has 10 full-time members. The student-faculty ratio is 14:1. The library holds 7,946 titles and 39 serial subscriptions. Special programs include academic remediation, double majors, part-time degree programs (daytime), and internships.
Student Body Statistics The student body is made up of 155 undergraduates (74 freshmen). 17 percent are women and 83 percent are men. Students come from 5 states and territories. 94 percent are from Illinois.
Expenses for 2003–04 *Application fee:* $100. *Tuition:* $9990 full-time, $416 per credit part-time. *Mandatory fees:* $125 full-time, $125 per term part-time. *College room only:* $1800.
Financial Aid Forms of aid include need-based scholarships and part-time jobs. The priority application deadline for financial aid is June 1.
Freshman Admission Morrison requires a high school transcript and proof of immunization. SAT I or ACT scores are recommended. The application deadline for regular admission is rolling.
Entrance Difficulty Morrison has an open admission policy.

For Further Information Contact Mrs. Tammy Pruis, Admission Secretary, Morrison Institute of Technology, 701 Portland Avenue, Morrison, IL 61270. *Telephone:* 815-772-7218. *Fax:* 815-772-7584. *E-mail:* admissions@morrison.tec.il.us. *Web site:* http://www.morrison.tech.il.us/.

NAES COLLEGE

Chicago, Illinois

NAES College is a coed, private, four-year college, founded in 1974, offering degrees at the bachelor's level.

Expenses for 2002–03 *Tuition:* $5000 full-time. *Mandatory fees:* $140 full-time.

For Further Information Contact Ms. Christine Redcloud, Registrar, NAES College, 2838 West Peterson Avenue, Chicago, IL 60659-3813. *Telephone:* 773-761-5000. *Fax:* 773-761-3808.

NATIONAL-LOUIS UNIVERSITY

Chicago, Illinois

NLU is a coed, private university, founded in 1886, offering degrees at the bachelor's, master's, and doctoral levels and post-master's and postbachelor's certificates. It has a 12-acre campus in Chicago near Chicago.

Academic Information The faculty has 284 members (99% full-time), 17% with terminal degrees. The undergraduate student-faculty ratio is 19:1. The library holds 5,043 audiovisual materials. Special programs include academic remediation, services for learning-disabled students, an honors program, advanced placement credit, accelerated degree programs, ESL programs, independent study, summer session for credit, part-time degree programs (daytime, evenings, weekends, summer), external degree programs, adult/continuing education programs, and internships. The most frequently chosen baccalaureate fields are business/marketing, education, interdisciplinary studies.
Student Body Statistics The student body totals 7,904, of whom 3,043 are undergraduates (118 freshmen). 73 percent are women and 27 percent are men. Students come from 19 states and territories. 99 percent are from Illinois. 0.1 percent are international students.
Expenses for 2002–03 *Application fee:* $25. *Comprehensive fee:* $21,564 includes full-time tuition ($14,715), mandatory fees ($936), and college room and board ($5913). *Part-time tuition:* $327 per quarter hour.
Financial Aid Forms of aid include need-based and non-need-based scholarships and part-time jobs. The application deadline for financial aid is continuous.
Freshman Admission NLU requires a high school transcript and a minimum 2.0 high school GPA. An interview is recommended. 2 recommendations and SAT I or ACT scores are required for some. The application deadline for regular admission is rolling.
Transfer Admission The application deadline for admission is rolling.
Entrance Difficulty NLU assesses its entrance difficulty level as minimally difficult.

For Further Information Contact Ms. Pat Petillo, Director of Admissions, National-Louis University, 122 South Michigan Avenue, Chicago, IL 60603. *Telephone:* 888-NLU-TODAY, 888-NLU-TODAY (toll-free in-state), or 800-443-5522 (toll-free out-of-state). *Fax:* 312-261-3057. *Web site:* http://www.nl.edu/.

NORTH CENTRAL COLLEGE

Naperville, Illinois

North Central is a coed, private, United Methodist, comprehensive institution, founded in 1861, offering degrees at the bachelor's and master's levels. It has a 56-acre campus in Naperville near Chicago.

Academic Information The faculty has 196 members (64% full-time), 63% with terminal degrees. The undergraduate student-faculty ratio is 14:1. The library holds 145,707 titles, 707 serial subscriptions, and 3,367 audiovisual materials. Special programs include academic remediation, services for learning-disabled students, an honors program, cooperative (work-study) education, study abroad, advanced placement credit, accelerated degree programs, ESL programs, double majors, independent study, self-designed majors, summer session for credit, part-time degree programs, adult/continuing education programs, internships, and arrangement for off-campus study with Aurora University, Benedictine University. The most frequently chosen baccalaureate fields are business/marketing, education, social sciences and history.
Student Body Statistics The student body totals 2,533, of whom 2,116 are undergraduates (364 freshmen). 58 percent are women and 42 percent are men. Students come from 26 states and territories and 18 other countries. 91 percent are from Illinois. 1.7 percent are international students. 10 percent of the 2002 graduating class went on to graduate and professional schools.
Expenses for 2002–03 *Application fee:* $25. *Comprehensive fee:* $24,447 includes full-time tuition ($17,997), mandatory fees ($405), and college room and board ($6045). Room and board charges vary according to housing facility. *Part-time tuition:* $469 per semester hour. *Part-time mandatory fees:* $249 per year.
Financial Aid Forms of aid include need-based and non-need-based scholarships and part-time jobs. The average aided 2001–02 undergraduate received an aid package worth $16,323. The application deadline for financial aid is continuous.
Freshman Admission North Central requires a high school transcript, a minimum 2.0 high school GPA, and SAT I or ACT scores. An essay, 1 recommendation, and ACT scores are recommended. An interview is required for some. The application deadline for regular admission is rolling.
Transfer Admission The application deadline for admission is rolling.

Entrance Difficulty North Central assesses its entrance difficulty level as moderately difficult. For the fall 2002 freshman class, 74 percent of the applicants were accepted.

For Further Information Contact Mr. Stephen Potts, Coordinator of Freshman Admission, North Central College, 30 North Brainard Street, PO Box 3063, Naperville, IL 60566-7063. *Telephone:* 630-637-5802 or 800-411-1861 (toll-free). *Fax:* 630-637-5819. *E-mail:* ncadm@noctrl.edu. *Web site:* http://www.noctrl.edu/.

See page 316 for a narrative description.

NORTHEASTERN ILLINOIS UNIVERSITY

Chicago, Illinois

Northeastern Illinois University is a coed, public, comprehensive institution, founded in 1961, offering degrees at the bachelor's and master's levels. It has a 67-acre campus in Chicago.

Academic Information The faculty has 623 members (59% full-time), 54% with terminal degrees. The undergraduate student-faculty ratio is 17:1. The library holds 441,911 titles, 3,421 serial subscriptions, and 6,034 audiovisual materials. Special programs include academic remediation, services for learning-disabled students, an honors program, cooperative (work-study) education, study abroad, advanced placement credit, ESL programs, double majors, independent study, distance learning, summer session for credit, part-time degree programs (daytime, evenings, summer), external degree programs, adult/continuing education programs, internships, and arrangement for off-campus study with National Student Exchange. The most frequently chosen baccalaureate fields are education, business/marketing, liberal arts/general studies.
Student Body Statistics The student body totals 11,409, of whom 8,674 are undergraduates (1,059 freshmen). 62 percent are women and 38 percent are men. Students come from 18 states and territories and 45 other countries. 99 percent are from Illinois. 2.5 percent are international students. 32 percent of the 2002 graduating class went on to graduate and professional schools.
Expenses for 2002–03 *State resident tuition:* $2508 full-time, $125 per credit hour part-time. *Nonresident tuition:* $7524 full-time, $334 per credit hour part-time. *Mandatory fees:* $492 full-time, $20.50 per credit hour part-time.
Financial Aid Forms of aid include need-based and non-need-based scholarships and part-time jobs. The average aided 2002–03 undergraduate received an aid package worth an estimated $5426. The priority application deadline for financial aid is March 1.
Freshman Admission Northeastern Illinois University requires a high school transcript, ACT scores, and TOEFL scores for international students. The application deadline for regular admission is July 1.
Transfer Admission The application deadline for admission is July 1.
Entrance Difficulty Northeastern Illinois University assesses its entrance difficulty level as minimally difficult; moderately difficult for transfers. For the fall 2002 freshman class, 77 percent of the applicants were accepted.

For Further Information Contact Ms. Kay D. Gulli, Administrative Assistant, Northeastern Illinois University, 5500 North St. Louis Avenue, Chicago, IL 60625. *Telephone:* 773-442-4000. *Fax:* 773-794-6243. *E-mail:* admrec@neiu.edu. *Web site:* http://www.neiu.edu/.

NORTHERN ILLINOIS UNIVERSITY

De Kalb, Illinois

Northern Illinois University is a coed, public university, founded in 1895, offering degrees at the bachelor's, master's, doctoral, and first professional levels. It has a 589-acre campus in De Kalb near Chicago.

Academic Information The faculty has 1,201 members (80% full-time). The undergraduate student-faculty ratio is 17:1. The library holds 2 million titles, 17,000 serial subscriptions, and 50,182 audiovisual materials. Special programs include services for learning-disabled students, an honors program, cooperative (work-study) education, study abroad, advanced placement credit, accelerated degree programs, double majors, independent study, self-designed majors, summer session for credit, part-time degree programs, adult/continuing education programs, internships, and arrangement for off-campus study with Rockford Regional Academic Center, Quad-Cities Graduate Study Center, Hoffman Estate. The most frequently chosen baccalaureate fields are business/marketing, education, social sciences and history.
Student Body Statistics The student body totals 24,948, of whom 18,104 are undergraduates (3,040 freshmen). 53 percent are women and 47 percent are men. Students come from 50 states and territories and 105 other countries. 97 percent are from Illinois. 1.3 percent are international students. 10 percent of the 2002 graduating class went on to graduate and professional schools.
Expenses for 2002–03 *State resident tuition:* $3581 full-time, $132 per credit hour part-time. *Nonresident tuition:* $7161 full-time, $264 per credit hour part-time. *Mandatory fees:* $1221 full-time, $50.88 per credit hour part-time. Full-time tuition and fees vary according to course load. Part-time tuition and fees vary according to course load. *College room and board:* $5198. Room and board charges vary according to board plan and housing facility.
Financial Aid Forms of aid include need-based and non-need-based scholarships and part-time jobs. The average aided 2002–03 undergraduate received an aid package worth an estimated $8948. The priority application deadline for financial aid is March 1.
Freshman Admission Northern Illinois University requires a high school transcript, SAT I or ACT scores, and TOEFL scores for international students. The application deadline for regular admission is August 1.
Transfer Admission The application deadline for admission is August 1.
Entrance Difficulty Northern Illinois University assesses its entrance difficulty level as moderately difficult. For the fall 2002 freshman class, 64 percent of the applicants were accepted.

For Further Information Contact Dr. Robert Burk, Director of Admissions, Northern Illinois University, De Kalb, IL 60115-2854. *Telephone:* 815-753-0446 or 800-892-3050 (toll-free in-state). *E-mail:* admission-info@niu.edu. *Web site:* http://www.niu.edu/.

NORTH PARK UNIVERSITY

Chicago, Illinois

North Park is a coed, private, comprehensive institution, founded in 1891, affiliated with the Evangelical Covenant Church, offering degrees at the bachelor's, master's, doctoral, and first professional levels. It has a 30-acre campus in Chicago.

Academic Information The faculty has 121 members (73% full-time), 64% with terminal degrees. The undergraduate student-faculty ratio is 16:1. The library holds 260,685 titles and 1,178 serial subscriptions. Special programs include academic remediation, an honors program, study abroad, advanced placement credit, accelerated degree programs, Freshman Honors College, ESL programs, self-designed majors, summer session for credit, part-time degree programs, adult/continuing education programs, internships, and arrangement for off-campus study with Christian College Coalition. The most frequently chosen baccalaureate fields are biological/life sciences, education, philosophy, religion, and theology.
Student Body Statistics The student body totals 2,181, of whom 1,573 are undergraduates (320 freshmen). 62 percent are women and 38 percent are men. Students come from 38 states and territories and 32 other countries. 61 percent are from Illinois. 5 percent are international students. 20 percent of the 2002 graduating class went on to graduate and professional schools.
Expenses for 2002–03 *Application fee:* $20. *Comprehensive fee:* $25,230 includes full-time tuition ($18,680), mandatory fees ($30), and college room and board ($6520). *College room only:* $3440. Full-time tuition and fees vary according to program. Room and board charges vary according to board plan, housing facility, and student level. *Part-time tuition:* varies with program.
Financial Aid Forms of aid include need-based and non-need-based scholarships and part-time jobs. The priority application deadline for financial aid is May 1.
Freshman Admission North Park requires an essay, a high school transcript, a minimum 2.0 high school GPA, 1 recommendation, SAT I or

North Park University (continued)
ACT scores, and TOEFL scores for international students. A minimum 3.0 high school GPA is recommended. An interview is required for some. The application deadline for regular admission is rolling.
Transfer Admission The application deadline for admission is rolling.
Entrance Difficulty North Park assesses its entrance difficulty level as moderately difficult. For the fall 2002 freshman class, 74 percent of the applicants were accepted.

For Further Information Contact Office of Admissions, North Park University, 3225 West Foster Avenue, Chicago, IL 60625-4895. *Telephone:* 773-244-5504 or 800-888-NPC8 (toll-free). *Fax:* 773-583-0858. *E-mail:* afao@northpark.edu. *Web site:* http://www.northpark.edu/.

NORTHWESTERN UNIVERSITY

Evanston, Illinois

Northwestern is a coed, private university, founded in 1851, offering degrees at the bachelor's, master's, doctoral, and first professional levels and post-master's certificates. It has a 250-acre campus in Evanston near Chicago.

Academic Information The faculty has 1,142 members (81% full-time), 100% with terminal degrees. The undergraduate student-faculty ratio is 7:1. The library holds 4 million titles, 39,423 serial subscriptions, and 72,837 audiovisual materials. Special programs include services for learning-disabled students, an honors program, cooperative (work-study) education, study abroad, advanced placement credit, accelerated degree programs, double majors, independent study, self-designed majors, summer session for credit, part-time degree programs (daytime, evenings, summer), adult/continuing education programs, and internships. The most frequently chosen baccalaureate fields are engineering/engineering technologies, communications/communication technologies, social sciences and history.
Student Body Statistics The student body totals 16,032, of whom 7,946 are undergraduates (2,005 freshmen). 53 percent are women and 47 percent are men. Students come from 51 states and territories and 46 other countries. 26 percent are from Illinois. 4.7 percent are international students.
Expenses for 2003–04 *Application fee:* $60. *Comprehensive fee:* $37,491 includes full-time tuition ($28,404), mandatory fees ($120), and college room and board ($8967). *College room only:* $5152. *Part-time tuition:* $3371 per course.
Financial Aid Forms of aid include need-based scholarships, athletic grants, and part-time jobs. The average aided 2002–03 undergraduate received an aid package worth an estimated $23,382. The priority application deadline for financial aid is February 1.
Freshman Admission Northwestern requires an essay, a high school transcript, 1 recommendation, SAT I or ACT scores, and TOEFL scores for international students. SAT II: Subject Test scores and SAT II: Writing Test scores are recommended. Audition for music program, SAT II: Subject Test scores, and SAT II: Writing Test scores are required for some. The application deadline for regular admission is January 1 and for early decision it is November 1.
Transfer Admission The application deadline for admission is June 1.
Entrance Difficulty Northwestern assesses its entrance difficulty level as most difficult; very difficult for transfers. For the fall 2002 freshman class, 33 percent of the applicants were accepted.

For Further Information Contact Ms. Carol Lunkenheimer, Dean of Undergraduate Admission, Northwestern University, PO Box 3060, Evanston, IL 60204-3060. *Telephone:* 847-491-7271. *E-mail:* ug-admission@northwestern.edu. *Web site:* http://www.northwestern.edu/.

OLIVET NAZARENE UNIVERSITY

Bourbonnais, Illinois

Olivet is a coed, private, comprehensive institution, founded in 1907, affiliated with the Church of the Nazarene, offering degrees at the bachelor's and master's levels. It has a 168-acre campus in Bourbonnais near Chicago.

Academic Information The faculty has 123 members (70% full-time). The undergraduate student-faculty ratio is 20:1. The library holds 160,039 titles, 925 serial subscriptions, and 6,818 audiovisual materials. Special programs include academic remediation, study abroad, advanced placement credit, double majors, independent study, summer session for credit, part-time degree programs (daytime, evenings, summer), adult/continuing education programs, and internships. The most frequently chosen baccalaureate fields are education, business/marketing, health professions and related sciences.
Student Body Statistics The student body totals 3,863, of whom 2,229 are undergraduates (563 freshmen). 58 percent are women and 42 percent are men. Students come from 41 states and territories and 15 other countries. 49 percent are from Illinois. 1 percent are international students. 10 percent of the 2002 graduating class went on to graduate and professional schools.
Expenses for 2003–04 *Application fee:* $0. *Comprehensive fee:* $20,480 includes full-time tuition ($14,160), mandatory fees ($820), and college room and board ($5500). *College room only:* $2750. Full-time tuition and fees vary according to course load. Room and board charges vary according to board plan. *Part-time tuition:* $590 per hour. *Part-time mandatory fees:* $10 per term. Part-time tuition and fees vary according to course load.
Financial Aid Forms of aid include need-based and non-need-based scholarships, athletic grants, and part-time jobs. The average aided 2001–02 undergraduate received an aid package worth $12,470. The priority application deadline for financial aid is March 1.
Freshman Admission Olivet requires a high school transcript, a minimum 2.0 high school GPA, 2 recommendations, ACT scores, and TOEFL scores for international students. An essay and an interview are recommended. The application deadline for regular admission is rolling.
Transfer Admission The application deadline for admission is rolling.
Entrance Difficulty Olivet assesses its entrance difficulty level as minimally difficult. For the fall 2002 freshman class, 81 percent of the applicants were accepted.

For Further Information Contact Ms. Mary Cary, Applicant Coordinator, Olivet Nazarene University, One University Avenue, Bourbonnais, IL 60914. *Telephone:* 815-939-5203 or 800-648-1463 (toll-free). *Fax:* 815-935-4998. *E-mail:* admissions@olivet.edu. *Web site:* http://www.olivet.edu/.

See page 320 for a narrative description.

PRINCIPIA COLLEGE

Elsah, Illinois

Prin is a coed, private, Christian Science, four-year college, founded in 1910, offering degrees at the bachelor's level. It has a 2,600-acre campus in Elsah near St. Louis.

Academic Information The faculty has 76 members (68% full-time), 50% with terminal degrees. The student-faculty ratio is 9:1. The library holds 208,197 titles, 10,547 serial subscriptions, and 7,273 audiovisual materials. Special programs include an honors program, study abroad, advanced placement credit, accelerated degree programs, ESL programs, double majors, independent study, self-designed majors, and internships. The most frequently chosen baccalaureate fields are social sciences and history, biological/life sciences, visual/performing arts.
Student Body Statistics The student body is made up of 538 undergraduates (114 freshmen). 54 percent are women and 46 percent are men. Students come from 29 states and territories and 20 other countries. 9 percent are from Illinois. 12.3 percent are international students. 21 percent of the 2002 graduating class went on to graduate and professional schools.

Expenses for 2003–04 *Application fee:* $40. *Comprehensive fee:* $25,044 includes full-time tuition ($18,270), mandatory fees ($270), and college room and board ($6504). *College room only:* $3156. *Part-time tuition:* $403 per quarter hour.
Financial Aid Forms of aid include need-based and non-need-based scholarships and part-time jobs. The average aided 2001–02 undergraduate received an aid package worth $15,269. The application deadline for financial aid is continuous.
Freshman Admission Prin requires an essay, a high school transcript, a minimum 2.0 high school GPA, 4 recommendations, Christian Science commitment, SAT I or ACT scores, and TOEFL scores for international students. An interview is recommended. An interview is required for some. The application deadline for regular admission is March 1.
Transfer Admission The application deadline for admission is March 1.
Entrance Difficulty Prin assesses its entrance difficulty level as moderately difficult. For the fall 2002 freshman class, 83 percent of the applicants were accepted.

For Further Information Contact Mrs. Martha Green Quirk, Dean of Admissions, Principia College, One Maybeck Place, Elsah, IL 62028-9799. *Telephone:* 618-374-5180 or 800-277-4648 Ext. 2802 (toll-free). *Fax:* 618-374-4000. *E-mail:* collegeadmissions@prin.edu. *Web site:* http://www.prin.edu/college/.

QUINCY UNIVERSITY

Quincy, Illinois

Quincy University is a coed, private, Roman Catholic, comprehensive institution, founded in 1860, offering degrees at the associate, bachelor's, and master's levels. It has a 75-acre campus in Quincy.

Academic Information The faculty has 102 members (57% full-time), 58% with terminal degrees. The undergraduate student-faculty ratio is 14:1. The library holds 239,368 titles, 814 serial subscriptions, and 5,640 audiovisual materials. Special programs include academic remediation, an honors program, study abroad, advanced placement credit, accelerated degree programs, ESL programs, double majors, independent study, distance learning, self-designed majors, summer session for credit, part-time degree programs (daytime, evenings, summer), adult/continuing education programs, and internships. The most frequently chosen baccalaureate fields are business/marketing, education, protective services/public administration.
Student Body Statistics The student body totals 1,192, of whom 1,057 are undergraduates (231 freshmen). 55 percent are women and 45 percent are men. Students come from 2 states and territories and 10 other countries. 75 percent are from Illinois. 1 percent are international students. 18 percent of the 2002 graduating class went on to graduate and professional schools.
Expenses for 2002–03 *Application fee:* $25. *Comprehensive fee:* $21,680 includes full-time tuition ($15,910), mandatory fees ($450), and college room and board ($5320). Room and board charges vary according to board plan and housing facility. *Part-time tuition:* $455 per credit hour.
Financial Aid Forms of aid include need-based and non-need-based scholarships, athletic grants, and part-time jobs. The average aided 2001–02 undergraduate received an aid package worth $14,444. The priority application deadline for financial aid is April 15.
Freshman Admission Quincy University requires a high school transcript, SAT I or ACT scores, and TOEFL scores for international students. A minimum 2.0 high school GPA and an interview are recommended. The application deadline for regular admission is rolling.
Transfer Admission The application deadline for admission is rolling.
Entrance Difficulty Quincy University assesses its entrance difficulty level as moderately difficult. For the fall 2002 freshman class, 97 percent of the applicants were accepted.

For Further Information Contact Mr. Kevin A. Brown, Director of Admissions, Quincy University, 1800 College Avenue, Quincy, IL 62301-2699. *Telephone:* 217-222-8020 Ext. 5215 or 800-688-4295 (toll-free). *Fax:* 217-228-5479. *E-mail:* admissions@quincy.edu. *Web site:* http://www.quincy.edu/.

See page 326 for a narrative description.

ROBERT MORRIS COLLEGE

Chicago, Illinois

RMC is a coed, private, four-year college, founded in 1913, offering degrees at the associate and bachelor's levels.

Academic Information The faculty has 349 members (35% full-time), 26% with terminal degrees. The student-faculty ratio is 15:1. The library holds 101,130 titles, 709 serial subscriptions, and 9,800 audiovisual materials. Special programs include academic remediation, an honors program, cooperative (work-study) education, study abroad, advanced placement credit, accelerated degree programs, distance learning, summer session for credit, part-time degree programs (evenings), adult/continuing education programs, and internships. The most frequently chosen baccalaureate fields are business/marketing, computer/information sciences, visual/performing arts.
Student Body Statistics The student body is made up of 5,231 undergraduates (1,190 freshmen). 68 percent are women and 32 percent are men. Students come from 10 states and territories and 15 other countries. 99 percent are from Illinois. 0.5 percent are international students.
Expenses for 2003–04 *Application fee:* $20. *Tuition:* $13,500 full-time, $1120 per course part-time.
Financial Aid Forms of aid include need-based and non-need-based scholarships, athletic grants, and part-time jobs. The average aided 2002–03 undergraduate received an aid package worth an estimated $10,032. The application deadline for financial aid is continuous.
Freshman Admission RMC requires a high school transcript, a minimum 2.0 high school GPA, an interview, and TOEFL scores for international students. The application deadline for regular admission is rolling.
Transfer Admission The application deadline for admission is rolling.
Entrance Difficulty RMC assesses its entrance difficulty level as minimally difficult. For the fall 2002 freshman class, 76 percent of the applicants were accepted.

For Further Information Contact Candace Goodwin, Senior Vice President for Enrollment, Robert Morris College, 401 South State Street, Chicago, IL 60605. *Telephone:* 312-935-6600 or 800-225-1520 (toll-free). *Fax:* 312-935-6819. *E-mail:* enroll@robertmorris.edu. *Web site:* http://www.robertmorris.edu/.

See page 330 for a narrative description.

ROCKFORD BUSINESS COLLEGE

Rockford, Illinois

RBC is a coed, primarily women's, private, two-year college, founded in 1862, offering degrees at the associate level. It is located in Rockford near Chicago.

Academic Information The faculty has 26 members (31% full-time). The student-faculty ratio is 15:1. The library holds 1,823 titles, 161 serial subscriptions, and 50 audiovisual materials. Special programs include academic remediation, services for learning-disabled students, an honors program, cooperative (work-study) education, advanced placement credit, independent study, summer session for credit, part-time degree programs (daytime, evenings, weekends, summer), adult/continuing education programs, and internships.
Student Body Statistics The student body is made up of 428 undergraduates (90 freshmen). 89 percent are women and 11 percent are men. Students come from 2 states and territories. 99 percent are from Illinois.
Expenses for 2002–03 *Application fee:* $50. *Tuition:* $13,308 full-time.
Financial Aid Forms of aid include need-based scholarships and part-time jobs. The application deadline for financial aid is continuous.
Freshman Admission RBC requires a high school transcript, an interview, and TOEFL scores for international students. An essay is required for some. The application deadline for regular admission is September 4.
Transfer Admission The application deadline for admission is September 4.

Rockford Business College (continued)
Entrance Difficulty RBC has an open admission policy. It assesses its entrance difficulty as noncompetitive for out-of-state applicants; noncompetitive for transfers.

For Further Information Contact Ms. Barbara Holliman, Director of Admissions, Rockford Business College, 730 North Church Street, Rockford, IL 61103. *Telephone:* 815-965-8616 Ext. 16. *Fax:* 815-965-0360. *Web site:* http://www.rbcsuccess.com/.

ROCKFORD COLLEGE

Rockford, Illinois

RC is a coed, private, comprehensive institution, founded in 1847, offering degrees at the bachelor's and master's levels. It has a 130-acre campus in Rockford near Chicago.

Academic Information The faculty has 162 members (46% full-time), 43% with terminal degrees. The undergraduate student-faculty ratio is 10:1. The library holds 140,000 titles, 831 serial subscriptions, and 9,723 audiovisual materials. Special programs include academic remediation, an honors program, study abroad, advanced placement credit, ESL programs, double majors, self-designed majors, summer session for credit, part-time degree programs (daytime, evenings, summer), adult/continuing education programs, internships, and arrangement for off-campus study with American University, Central College (IA), Drew University.
Student Body Statistics The student body totals 1,280, of whom 976 are undergraduates (131 freshmen). 63 percent are women and 38 percent are men. Students come from 8 states and territories and 10 other countries. 96 percent are from Illinois. 2.7 percent are international students. 8 percent of the 2002 graduating class went on to graduate and professional schools.
Expenses for 2003–04 *Application fee:* $35. *Comprehensive fee:* $26,791 includes full-time tuition ($20,210) and college room and board ($6581). *College room only:* $4034. Room and board charges vary according to board plan and housing facility. *Part-time tuition:* $530 per credit hour.
Financial Aid Forms of aid include need-based and non-need-based scholarships and part-time jobs. The priority application deadline for financial aid is April 15.
Freshman Admission RC requires a high school transcript, SAT I or ACT scores, and TOEFL scores for international students. A minimum 2.5 high school GPA, an interview, and campus visit are recommended. An essay, a minimum 2.5 high school GPA, and 2 recommendations are required for some. The application deadline for regular admission is rolling.
Transfer Admission The application deadline for admission is rolling.
Entrance Difficulty RC assesses its entrance difficulty level as moderately difficult. For the fall 2002 freshman class, 59 percent of the applicants were accepted.

For Further Information Contact Mr. William Laffey, Director of Admission, Rockford College, Nelson Hall, Rockford, IL 61108-2393. *Telephone:* 815-226-4050 or 800-892-2984 (toll-free). *Fax:* 815-226-2822. *E-mail:* admission@rockford.edu. *Web site:* http://www.rockford.edu/.

See page 332 for a narrative description.

ROOSEVELT UNIVERSITY

Chicago, Illinois

Roosevelt is a coed, private, comprehensive institution, founded in 1945, offering degrees at the bachelor's, master's, and doctoral levels.

Academic Information The faculty has 662 members (32% full-time). The undergraduate student-faculty ratio is 11:1. The library holds 233,016 titles, 1,195 serial subscriptions, and 9,897 audiovisual materials. Special programs include academic remediation, services for learning-disabled students, an honors program, advanced placement credit, accelerated degree programs, ESL programs, double majors, independent study, distance learning, self-designed majors, summer session for credit, part-time degree programs (daytime, evenings, weekends, summer), external degree programs, adult/continuing education programs, internships, and arrangement for off-campus study with School of the Art Institute of Chicago. The most frequently chosen baccalaureate fields are business/marketing, psychology, social sciences and history.
Student Body Statistics The student body totals 7,321, of whom 4,307 are undergraduates (286 freshmen). 67 percent are women and 33 percent are men. Students come from 24 states and territories and 70 other countries. 96 percent are from Illinois. 3.4 percent are international students.
Expenses for 2002–03 *Application fee:* $25. *Comprehensive fee:* $21,160 includes full-time tuition ($14,460), mandatory fees ($200), and college room and board ($6500). *College room only:* $4740. Full-time tuition and fees vary according to program. *Part-time tuition:* $482 per semester hour. *Part-time mandatory fees:* $100 per term. Part-time tuition and fees vary according to program.
Financial Aid Forms of aid include need-based and non-need-based scholarships and part-time jobs. The average aided 2002–03 undergraduate received an aid package worth an estimated $11,395. The priority application deadline for financial aid is April 1.
Freshman Admission Roosevelt requires an essay, a high school transcript, a minimum 2.0 high school GPA, audition for music and theater programs, SAT I or ACT scores, and TOEFL scores for international students. Recommendations and an interview are required for some. The application deadline for regular admission is September 1.
Transfer Admission The application deadline for admission is September 1.
Entrance Difficulty Roosevelt assesses its entrance difficulty level as moderately difficult. For the fall 2002 freshman class, 67 percent of the applicants were accepted.

For Further Information Contact Mr. Brian Lynch, Director of Admission, Roosevelt University, 430 South Michigan Avenue, Room 576, Chicago, IL 60605-1394. *Telephone:* 847-619-8620 or 877-APPLYRU (toll-free). *Fax:* 312-341-3523. *E-mail:* applyru@roosevelt.edu. *Web site:* http://www.roosevelt.edu/.

RUSH UNIVERSITY

Chicago, Illinois

Rush is a coed, private, upper-level institution, founded in 1969, offering degrees at the bachelor's, master's, doctoral, and first professional levels and post-master's certificates. It has a 35-acre campus in Chicago.

Academic Information The faculty has 796 members (100% full-time). The undergraduate student-faculty ratio is 8:1. The library holds 120,042 titles, 1,100 serial subscriptions, and 4,750 audiovisual materials. Special programs include accelerated degree programs, distance learning, and part-time degree programs (daytime). The most frequently chosen baccalaureate field is biological/life sciences.
Student Body Statistics The student body totals 1,232, of whom 133 are undergraduates. 92 percent are women and 8 percent are men. Students come from 14 states and territories and 4 other countries. 94 percent are from Illinois. 1.5 percent are international students. 12 percent of the 2002 graduating class went on to graduate and professional schools.
Expenses for 2002–03 *Application fee:* $40. *Tuition:* $14,880 full-time, $430 per quarter hour part-time. *College room only:* $7250.
Financial Aid Forms of aid include need-based and non-need-based scholarships and part-time jobs. The application deadline for financial aid is April 1 with a priority deadline of March 1.
Transfer Admission Rush requires a college transcript. A minimum 2.75 college GPA is recommended. Standardized test scores are required for some. The application deadline for admission is rolling.

Entrance Difficulty Rush assesses its entrance difficulty level as moderately difficult. For the fall 2002 entering class, 54 percent of the applicants were accepted.

For Further Information Contact Ms. Hicela Castruita Woods, Director of College Admission Services, Rush University, 600 S. Paulina—Suite 440, College Admissions Services, Chicago, IL 60612-3878. *Telephone:* 312-942-7100. *Fax:* 312-942-2219. *E-mail:* rush_admissions@rush.edu. *Web site:* http://www.rushu.rush.edu/.

SAINT ANTHONY COLLEGE OF NURSING

Rockford, Illinois

SACN is a coed, primarily women's, private, Roman Catholic, upper-level institution, founded in 1915, offering degrees at the bachelor's level in nursing. It has a 17-acre campus in Rockford near Chicago.

Academic Information The faculty has 13 members (77% full-time), 15% with terminal degrees. The student-faculty ratio is 6:1. The library holds 1,394 titles, 3,136 serial subscriptions, and 163 audiovisual materials. Special programs include services for learning-disabled students, advanced placement credit, accelerated degree programs, independent study, summer session for credit, part-time degree programs (daytime, evenings, summer), internships, and arrangement for off-campus study. The most frequently chosen baccalaureate field is health professions and related sciences.
Student Body Statistics The student body is made up of 91 undergraduates. 95 percent are women and 5 percent are men. Students come from 2 states and territories. 95 percent are from Illinois. 5 percent of the 2002 graduating class went on to graduate and professional schools.
Expenses for 2003–04 *Application fee:* $50. *One-time mandatory fee:* $90. *Tuition:* $13,600 full-time, $425 per credit part-time. *Mandatory fees:* $112 full-time, $55.35 per term part-time. Full-time tuition and fees vary according to course load. Part-time tuition and fees vary according to course load.
Financial Aid Forms of aid include need-based scholarships. The average aided 2002–03 undergraduate received an aid package worth an estimated $6800. The priority application deadline for financial aid is May 1.
Transfer Admission SACN requires a college transcript. A minimum 2.5 college GPA is recommended. The application deadline for admission is rolling.
Entrance Difficulty SACN assesses its entrance difficulty level as moderately difficult.

For Further Information Contact Ms. Nancy Sanders, Director of Student Services, Saint Anthony College of Nursing, 5658 East State Street, Rockford, IL 61108-2468. *Telephone:* 815-395-5100. *Fax:* 815-395-2275. *E-mail:* cheryldelgado@sacn.edu. *Web site:* http://www.sacn.edu/.

ST. AUGUSTINE COLLEGE

Chicago, Illinois

St. Augustine College is a coed, private, four-year college, founded in 1980, offering degrees at the associate and bachelor's levels (bilingual Spanish/English degree programs). It has a 4-acre campus in Chicago.

Academic Information The faculty has 164 members (16% full-time), 12% with terminal degrees. The student-faculty ratio is 13:1. The library holds 15,500 titles. Special programs include academic remediation, cooperative (work-study) education, ESL programs, independent study, summer session for credit, part-time degree programs (daytime, evenings, summer), and internships. The most frequently chosen baccalaureate field is social sciences and history.
Student Body Statistics The student body is made up of 1,769 undergraduates (555 freshmen). 78 percent are women and 22 percent are men. Students come from 1 state or territory.
Expenses for 2003–04 *Application fee:* $0. *Tuition:* $7000 full-time, $290 per credit part-time.
Financial Aid Forms of aid include need-based scholarships and part-time jobs. The average aided 2002–03 undergraduate received an aid package worth an estimated $13,490. The application deadline for financial aid is continuous.
Freshman Admission The application deadline for regular admission is rolling.
Transfer Admission The application deadline for admission is rolling.
Entrance Difficulty St. Augustine College has an open admission policy.

For Further Information Contact Ms. Soledad Ruiz, Director of Admissions, St. Augustine College, 1345 West Argyle Street, Chicago, IL 60604-3501. *Telephone:* 773-878-8756 Ext. 243. *E-mail:* info@staugustinecollege.edu. *Web site:* http://www.staugustinecollege.edu/.

SAINT FRANCIS MEDICAL CENTER COLLEGE OF NURSING

Peoria, Illinois

Saint Francis College of Nursing is a coed, primarily women's, private, Roman Catholic, upper-level institution, founded in 1986, offering degrees at the bachelor's and master's levels in nursing.

Academic Information The faculty has 19 members (100% full-time). The undergraduate student-faculty ratio is 8:1. The library holds 6,215 titles and 125 serial subscriptions. Special programs include advanced placement credit, independent study, distance learning, summer session for credit, and part-time degree programs. The most frequently chosen baccalaureate field is health professions and related sciences.
Student Body Statistics The student body totals 181, of whom 154 are undergraduates. 93 percent are women and 7 percent are men. Students come from 1 state or territory.
Expenses for 2003–04 *Application fee:* $25. *Tuition:* $10,088 full-time, $402 per semester hour part-time. *Mandatory fees:* $200 full-time. Full-time tuition and fees vary according to course load. Part-time tuition varies according to course load. *College room only:* $1680.
Financial Aid Forms of aid include need-based and non-need-based scholarships. The average aided 2001–02 undergraduate received an aid package worth $9543. The priority application deadline for financial aid is March 1.
Transfer Admission Saint Francis College of Nursing requires a college transcript and a minimum 2.5 college GPA. The application deadline for admission is rolling.
Entrance Difficulty Saint Francis College of Nursing assesses its entrance difficulty level as moderately difficult. For the fall 2002 entering class, 100 percent of the applicants were accepted.

For Further Information Contact Mrs. Janice Farquharson, Director of Admissions and Registrar, Saint Francis Medical Center College of Nursing, 511 Greenleaf Street, Peoria, IL 61603-3783. *Telephone:* 309-624-8980. *Fax:* 309-624-8973. *E-mail:* janice.farquharson@osfhealthcare.org. *Web site:* http://www.sfmccon.edu/.

ST. JOHN'S COLLEGE

Springfield, Illinois

St. John's College is a coed, primarily women's, private, Roman Catholic, upper-level institution, founded in 1886, offering degrees at the bachelor's level in nursing.

Academic Information The faculty has 15 members (93% full-time), 7% with terminal degrees. The student-faculty ratio is 4:1. The library holds 7,715 titles, 349 serial subscriptions, and 735 audiovisual materials. Special programs include part-time degree programs (daytime). The most frequently chosen baccalaureate field is health professions and related sciences.
Student Body Statistics The student body is made up of 66 undergraduates. 97 percent are women and 3 percent are men. Students come from 2 states and territories and 1 other country. 99 percent are from Illinois. 1.5 percent are international students.

St. John's College (continued)

Expenses for 2002–03 *Application fee:* $25. *Tuition:* $8780 full-time, $254 per credit hour part-time. *Mandatory fees:* $338 full-time, $148 per semester hour part-time. Full-time tuition and fees vary according to course load and student level. Part-time tuition and fees vary according to course load and student level.

Financial Aid Forms of aid include need-based scholarships and part-time jobs. The average aided 2002–03 undergraduate received an aid package worth an estimated $8927. The priority application deadline for financial aid is May 31.

Transfer Admission St. John's College requires a college transcript and a minimum 2.4 college GPA.

Entrance Difficulty St. John's College assesses its entrance difficulty level as moderately difficult. For the fall 2002 entering class, 100 percent of the applicants were accepted.

For Further Information Contact Ms. Beth Beasley, Student Development Officer, St. John's College, 421 North Ninth Street, Springfield, IL 62702-5317. *Telephone:* 217-525-5628 Ext. 45468. *Fax:* 217-757-6870. *E-mail:* college@st-johns.org. *Web site:* http://www.st-johns.org/education/schools/nursing/.

SAINT JOSEPH COLLEGE OF NURSING

See University of St. Francis

SAINT XAVIER UNIVERSITY

Chicago, Illinois

Saint Xavier is a coed, private, Roman Catholic, comprehensive institution, founded in 1847, offering degrees at the bachelor's and master's levels and post-master's and postbachelor's certificates. It has a 55-acre campus in Chicago.

Academic Information The faculty has 352 members (43% full-time), 47% with terminal degrees. The undergraduate student-faculty ratio is 15:1. The library holds 170,753 titles, 717 serial subscriptions, and 3,112 audiovisual materials. Special programs include academic remediation, services for learning-disabled students, an honors program, cooperative (work-study) education, study abroad, advanced placement credit, accelerated degree programs, ESL programs, double majors, independent study, self-designed majors, summer session for credit, part-time degree programs (daytime, evenings, weekends, summer), adult/continuing education programs, and internships. The most frequently chosen baccalaureate fields are business/marketing, education, health professions and related sciences.

Student Body Statistics The student body totals 5,278, of whom 2,958 are undergraduates (380 freshmen). 72 percent are women and 28 percent are men. Students come from 19 states and territories and 5 other countries. 97 percent are from Illinois. 0.4 percent are international students. 18 percent of the 2002 graduating class went on to graduate and professional schools.

Expenses for 2002–03 *Application fee:* $25. *Comprehensive fee:* $22,163 includes full-time tuition ($15,750), mandatory fees ($180), and college room and board ($6233). *College room only:* $3544. Full-time tuition and fees vary according to course load. Room and board charges vary according to board plan. *Part-time tuition:* $525 per credit hour. *Part-time mandatory fees:* $45 per term. Part-time tuition and fees vary according to course load.

Financial Aid Forms of aid include need-based and non-need-based scholarships, athletic grants, and part-time jobs. The average aided 2002–03 undergraduate received an aid package worth an estimated $13,849. The priority application deadline for financial aid is March 1.

Freshman Admission Saint Xavier requires a high school transcript, SAT I or ACT scores, and TOEFL scores for international students. An essay, a minimum 2.5 high school GPA, and an interview are recommended. An interview is required for some. The application deadline for regular admission is rolling.

Transfer Admission The application deadline for admission is rolling.

Entrance Difficulty Saint Xavier assesses its entrance difficulty level as moderately difficult. For the fall 2002 freshman class, 70 percent of the applicants were accepted.

For Further Information Contact Elizabeth A. Gierach, Director of Enrollment Services, Saint Xavier University, 3700 West 103rd Street, Chicago, IL 60655-3105. *Telephone:* 773-298-3121 or 800-462-9288 (toll-free). *Fax:* 773-298-3076. *E-mail:* admissions@sxu.edu. *Web site:* http://www.sxu.edu/.

SCHOOL OF THE ART INSTITUTE OF CHICAGO

Chicago, Illinois

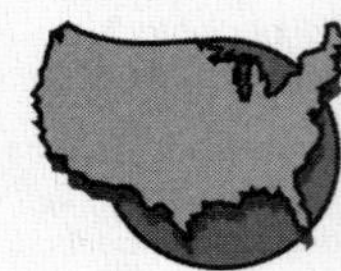

SAIC is a coed, private, comprehensive institution, founded in 1866, offering degrees at the bachelor's and master's levels in art. It has a 1-acre campus in Chicago.

Academic Information The faculty has 491 members (25% full-time). The undergraduate student-faculty ratio is 13:1. The library holds 72,490 titles, 334 serial subscriptions, and 4,067 audiovisual materials. Special programs include academic remediation, services for learning-disabled students, cooperative (work-study) education, study abroad, advanced placement credit, ESL programs, double majors, independent study, self-designed majors, summer session for credit, part-time degree programs (daytime, evenings, weekends, summer), internships, and arrangement for off-campus study with Association of Independent Colleges of Art and Design.

Student Body Statistics The student body totals 2,698, of whom 2,147 are undergraduates (292 freshmen). 67 percent are women and 33 percent are men. Students come from 50 states and territories and 41 other countries. 23 percent are from Illinois. 13.7 percent are international students.

Expenses for 2002–03 *Application fee:* $65. *Tuition:* $22,500 full-time, $750 per credit hour part-time. *College room only:* $6825.

Financial Aid Forms of aid include need-based and non-need-based scholarships and part-time jobs. The priority application deadline for financial aid is March 15.

Freshman Admission SAIC requires an essay, a high school transcript, 1 recommendation, a portfolio, SAT I or ACT scores, and TOEFL scores for international students. An interview is recommended. The application deadline for regular admission is August 15.

Transfer Admission The application deadline for admission is August 15.

Entrance Difficulty SAIC assesses its entrance difficulty level as moderately difficult. For the fall 2002 freshman class, 77 percent of the applicants were accepted.

SPECIAL MESSAGE TO STUDENTS

Social Life Each year, the semester kicks off with an all-school barbecue, featuring free food and a band. Other school-sponsored events include an 80s prom, Thanksgiving dinner, and a holiday art sale, which is open to the public. Students use Chicago as their campus, taking advantage of free jazz and blues festivals and ethnic neighborhood celebrations. Theaters, museums, and the Chicago Symphony are within walking distance, as are parks, beaches, and the zoo.

Academic Highlights The First Year Program ensures that all freshmen paint, draw, sculpt, photograph, take liberal arts and art history courses, and try their hand at video and performance art. At the same time, one studio day is reserved for students to begin working in their chosen area of interest. Unlike many other schools, students do not have to declare a major. Within a prescribed balance of studio, art history, and liberal arts requirements, students are free to experiment with different media and to design their own interdisciplinary program after the first year. Every year the School offers off-campus study opportunities in Saugatuck, Michigan, and New York City. Numerous other domestic and international exchange opportunities are readily available.

Interviews and Campus Visits The Immediate Decision Option (IDO) offers prospective students the opportunity to visit the School of the Art Institute of Chicago for a full day, tour the School and the museum, meet with currently enrolled students, and participate in financial aid and career workshops. The IDO day also includes an admission interview with a faculty member during which the applicant's portfolio and academic credentials are reviewed. At the end of the IDO day, the applicant receives the admission decision. In addition to painting, printmaking, and sculpture studios, the School houses the Video Data Bank (a video library of more than 1,800 interviews and art tapes by contemporary artists), professional galleries for student shows, the nationally acclaimed Gene Siskel Film Center, and the Poetry Center. Technical facilities include a general-access computing lab for the whole school. Current equipment includes more than forty PowerMacintosh G3 and G4 workstations, flatbed and slide scanners, CD burners, a film recorder, video editing equipment, and black and white color output. Daily and weekly authorizations, demos, and workshops are provided during the 100 to 135 weekly hours the lab offers. In addition, the Media Center provides access to technical production tools for the entire community, ranging from the simplest slide projector to state-of-the-art digital editing. For information about appointments and campus visits, students should call the Office of Admissions at 312-899-5219 or 800-232-7242 (toll-free), Monday through Friday, 8:30 a.m. to 4:30 p.m. CDT. The fax number is 312-899-1840. The office is located at 37 South Wabash, Suite 703, on campus. The nearest commercial airport is O'Hare International/Chicago Midway.

For Further Information Write to the Office of Admissions, School of the Art Institute of Chicago, 37 South Wabash, Suite 703, Chicago, IL 60603. *E-mail:* admiss@artic.edu. *Web site:* http://www.artic.edu/saic.

SHIMER COLLEGE

Waukegan, Illinois

Shimer is a coed, private, four-year college, founded in 1853, offering degrees at the bachelor's level and postbachelor's certificates. It has a 3-acre campus in Waukegan near Chicago and Milwaukee.

Academic Information The faculty has 16 members (81% full-time), 88% with terminal degrees. The student-faculty ratio is 10:1. The library holds 200,000 titles and 200 serial subscriptions. Special programs include cooperative (work-study) education, study abroad, double majors, independent study, distance learning, self-designed majors, summer session for credit, part-time degree programs (daytime, weekends, summer), adult/continuing education programs, internships, and arrangement for off-campus study with Barat College, Northwestern University.
Student Body Statistics The student body totals 136, of whom 115 are undergraduates (23 freshmen). 43 percent are women and 57 percent are men. Students come from 12 states and territories and 3 other countries. 70 percent are from Illinois. 3.5 percent are international students.
Expenses for 2003–04 *Application fee:* $25. *Comprehensive fee:* $19,530 includes full-time tuition ($16,100), mandatory fees ($650), and college room and board ($2780). *Part-time tuition:* $575 per credit hour. *Part-time mandatory fees:* $250 per term.
Financial Aid Forms of aid include need-based and non-need-based scholarships and part-time jobs. The application deadline for financial aid is continuous.
Freshman Admission Shimer requires an essay, a high school transcript, 1 recommendation, an interview, and TOEFL scores for international students. SAT I or ACT scores are recommended. SAT I or ACT scores are required for some. The application deadline for regular admission is August 30.
Transfer Admission The application deadline for admission is August 30.
Entrance Difficulty Shimer has an open admission policy.

For Further Information Contact Mr. Bill Paterson, Associate Director of Admissions, Shimer College, PO Box 500, Waukegan, IL 60079-0500. *Telephone:* 847-249-7173 or 800-215-7173 (toll-free). *Fax:* 847-249-8798. *E-mail:* admissions@shimer.edu. *Web site:* http://www.shimer.edu/.

SOUTHERN ILLINOIS UNIVERSITY CARBONDALE

Carbondale, Illinois

SIUC is a coed, public unit of Southern Illinois University, founded in 1869, offering degrees at the associate, bachelor's, master's, doctoral, and first professional levels and post-master's, first professional, and postbachelor's certificates. It has a 1,128-acre campus in Carbondale.

Academic Information The faculty has 1,112 members (80% full-time), 70% with terminal degrees. The undergraduate student-faculty ratio is 17:1. The library holds 4 million titles, 18,271 serial subscriptions, and 371,180 audiovisual materials. Special programs include academic remediation, services for learning-disabled students, an honors program, cooperative (work-study) education, study abroad, advanced placement credit, accelerated degree programs, ESL programs, double majors, independent study, distance learning, summer session for credit, part-time degree programs, adult/continuing education programs, internships, and arrangement for off-campus study with Southern Illinois University School of Medicine. The most frequently chosen baccalaureate fields are education, business/marketing, engineering/engineering technologies.
Student Body Statistics The student body totals 21,873, of whom 16,863 are undergraduates (2,532 freshmen). 44 percent are women and 56 percent are men. Students come from 52 states and territories and 117 other countries. 85 percent are from Illinois. 3.4 percent are international students.
Expenses for 2003–04 *Application fee:* $30. *State resident tuition:* $4245 full-time, $142 per semester hour part-time. *Nonresident tuition:* $8490 full-time, $283 per semester hour part-time. *Mandatory fees:* $1276 full-time. *College room and board:* $4903. *College room only:* $2492.
Financial Aid Forms of aid include need-based and non-need-based scholarships, athletic grants, and part-time jobs. The average aided 2001–02 undergraduate received an aid package worth $7892. The priority application deadline for financial aid is April 1.
Freshman Admission SIUC requires a high school transcript, SAT I or ACT scores, and TOEFL scores for international students. The application deadline for regular admission is rolling.
Transfer Admission The application deadline for admission is rolling.
Entrance Difficulty SIUC assesses its entrance difficulty level as moderately difficult. For the fall 2002 freshman class, 78 percent of the applicants were accepted.

For Further Information Contact Ms. Anne DeLuca, Assistant Vice Chancellor, Student Affairs and Enrollment Management and Director of Admissions, Southern Illinois University Carbondale, Mail Code 4701, Carbondale, IL 62901-4701. *Telephone:* 618-453-2908. *Fax:* 618-453-3250. *E-mail:* admrec@siu.edu. *Web site:* http://www.siuc.edu/.

See page 338 for a narrative description.

SOUTHERN ILLINOIS UNIVERSITY EDWARDSVILLE

Edwardsville, Illinois

SIUE is a coed, public, comprehensive unit of Southern Illinois University, founded in 1957, offering degrees at the bachelor's, master's, and first professional levels and post-master's, first professional, and postbachelor's certificates. It has a 2,660-acre campus in Edwardsville near St. Louis.

Academic Information The faculty has 742 members (67% full-time). The undergraduate student-faculty ratio is 17:1. The library holds 783,050 titles, 14,807 serial subscriptions, and 29,183 audiovisual materials. Special programs include academic remediation, services for learning-disabled students, an honors program, cooperative (work-study) education, study abroad, advanced placement credit, accelerated degree programs, ESL programs, double majors, independent study, distance learning, self-designed majors, summer session for credit, part-time degree programs (daytime, evenings, weekends, summer), adult/continuing education programs, internships, and arrangement for off-campus study with

Southern Illinois University Edwardsville (continued)
University of Missouri–St. Louis, International Student Exchange Program. The most frequently chosen baccalaureate fields are business/marketing, education, social sciences and history.
Student Body Statistics The student body totals 12,708, of whom 10,014 are undergraduates (1,655 freshmen). 56 percent are women and 44 percent are men. Students come from 47 states and territories and 62 other countries. 90 percent are from Illinois. 1.4 percent are international students. 29 percent of the 2002 graduating class went on to graduate and professional schools.
Expenses for 2003–04 *Application fee:* $30. *State resident tuition:* $3198 full-time, $105 per semester hour part-time. *Nonresident tuition:* $6396 full-time, $210 per semester hour part-time. *Mandatory fees:* $823 full-time, $234.40 per term part-time. Full-time tuition and fees vary according to course load. Part-time tuition and fees vary according to course load. *College room and board:* $5364. *College room only:* $3077. Room and board charges vary according to board plan and housing facility.
Financial Aid Forms of aid include need-based and non-need-based scholarships, athletic grants, and part-time jobs. The average aided 2001–02 undergraduate received an aid package worth $7500. The priority application deadline for financial aid is February 15.
Freshman Admission SIUE requires a high school transcript, SAT I or ACT scores, and TOEFL scores for international students. The application deadline for regular admission is May 31.
Transfer Admission The application deadline for admission is July 31.
Entrance Difficulty SIUE assesses its entrance difficulty level as moderately difficult. For the fall 2002 freshman class, 79 percent of the applicants were accepted.

For Further Information Contact Mr. Boyd Bradshaw, Acting Vice Chancellor for Enrollment Management, Southern Illinois University Edwardsville, Edwardsville, IL 62026-0001. *Telephone:* 618-650-3705 or 800-447-SIUE (toll-free). *Fax:* 618-650-5013. *E-mail:* admis@siue.edu. *Web site:* http://www.siue.edu/.

SPRINGFIELD COLLEGE IN ILLINOIS

Springfield, Illinois

SCI is a coed, private, two-year college, founded in 1929, affiliated with the Roman Catholic Church, offering degrees at the associate level. It has an 8-acre campus in Springfield.

Academic Information The faculty has 38 members (55% full-time). The student-faculty ratio is 10:1. The library holds 19,951 titles, 146 serial subscriptions, and 2,490 audiovisual materials. Special programs include academic remediation, advanced placement credit, self-designed majors, summer session for credit, part-time degree programs (daytime, evenings, weekends, summer), adult/continuing education programs, and arrangement for off-campus study with Illinois College, MacMurray College, Sangamon State University, Lincoln Land Community College.
Student Body Statistics The student body is made up of 400 undergraduates. Students come from 13 states and territories and 8 other countries. 96 percent are from Illinois. 2.6 percent are international students. 86 percent of the 2002 graduating class went on to four-year colleges.
Expenses for 2002–03 *Application fee:* $15. *Comprehensive fee:* $9600 includes full-time tuition ($7272), mandatory fees ($84), and college room and board ($2244). *Part-time tuition:* $303 per credit hour. *Part-time mandatory fees:* $42 per term.
Financial Aid Forms of aid include need-based scholarships and part-time jobs. The priority application deadline for financial aid is March 1.
Freshman Admission SCI requires a high school transcript, ACT scores, and TOEFL scores for international students. A minimum 2.0 high school GPA is recommended. An interview is required for some. The application deadline for regular admission is rolling.
Transfer Admission The application deadline for admission is rolling.
Entrance Difficulty SCI assesses its entrance difficulty level as moderately difficult. For the fall 2002 freshman class, 53 percent of the applicants were accepted.

For Further Information Contact Ms. Kim Fontana, Director of Admissions, Springfield College in Illinois, 1500 North Fifth Street, Springfield, IL 62702-2694. *Telephone:* 217-525-1420 Ext. 241 or 800-635-7289 (toll-free). *Fax:* 217-525-1497. *Web site:* http://www.sci.edu/.

TELSHE YESHIVA–CHICAGO

Chicago, Illinois

For Information Write to Telshe Yeshiva–Chicago, Chicago, IL 60625-5598.

TRINITY CHRISTIAN COLLEGE

Palos Heights, Illinois

Trinity Christian College is a coed, private, interdenominational, four-year college, founded in 1959, offering degrees at the bachelor's level. It has a 53-acre campus in Palos Heights near Chicago.

Academic Information The faculty has 110 members (51% full-time), 38% with terminal degrees. The student-faculty ratio is 13:1. The library holds 77,833 titles, 441 serial subscriptions, and 762 audiovisual materials. Special programs include academic remediation, services for learning-disabled students, an honors program, cooperative (work-study) education, study abroad, advanced placement credit, double majors, independent study, part-time degree programs (evenings), adult/continuing education programs, internships, and arrangement for off-campus study with Saint Xavier College, Moraine Valley Community College. The most frequently chosen baccalaureate fields are business/marketing, education, health professions and related sciences.
Student Body Statistics The student body is made up of 1,135 undergraduates (216 freshmen). 62 percent are women and 38 percent are men. Students come from 36 states and territories and 11 other countries. 58 percent are from Illinois. 1.9 percent are international students. 8 percent of the 2002 graduating class went on to graduate and professional schools.
Expenses for 2002–03 *Application fee:* $20. *Comprehensive fee:* $20,340 includes full-time tuition ($14,640) and college room and board ($5700). *College room only:* $2930. Room and board charges vary according to board plan. *Part-time tuition:* $490 per semester hour. Part-time tuition varies according to course load.
Financial Aid Forms of aid include need-based and non-need-based scholarships, athletic grants, and part-time jobs. The average aided 2001–02 undergraduate received an aid package worth $9875. The application deadline for financial aid is continuous.
Freshman Admission Trinity Christian College requires an essay, a high school transcript, a minimum 2.0 high school GPA, an interview, SAT I or ACT scores, and TOEFL scores for international students. 1 recommendation is required for some. The application deadline for regular admission is rolling.
Transfer Admission The application deadline for admission is rolling.
Entrance Difficulty Trinity Christian College assesses its entrance difficulty level as moderately difficult. For the fall 2002 freshman class, 91 percent of the applicants were accepted.

For Further Information Contact Mr. Pete Hamstra, Dean of Admissions, Trinity Christian College, 6601 West College Drive, Palos Heights, IL 60463. *Telephone:* 708-239-4709 or 800-748-0085 (toll-free). *Fax:* 708-239-4826. *E-mail:* admissions@trnty.edu. *Web site:* http://www.trnty.edu/.

TRINITY COLLEGE OF NURSING AND HEALTH SCIENCES SCHOOLS

Moline, Illinois

Trinity College of Nursing and Health Sciences Schools is a coed, primarily women's, private, four-year college, founded in 1994, offering degrees at the associate and bachelor's levels in nursing (general education requirements are taken off campus, usually at Black Hawk College, Eastern Iowa Community College District and Western Illinois University). It has a 1-acre campus in Moline.

Academic Information The faculty has 14 members (86% full-time). The student-faculty ratio is 10:1. Special programs include academic remediation, services for learning-disabled students, an honors program, independent study, distance learning, summer session for credit, part-time degree programs (daytime, evenings), adult/continuing education programs, and arrangement for off-campus study with Black Hawk College, Western Illinois University. The most frequently chosen baccalaureate field is health professions and related sciences.
Student Body Statistics The student body is made up of 108 undergraduates (5 freshmen). 95 percent are women and 5 percent are men. Students come from 2 states and territories. 72 percent are from Illinois.
Expenses for 2003–04 *Application fee:* $50. *Tuition:* $8780 full-time. *Mandatory fees:* $320 full-time.
Financial Aid Forms of aid include need-based scholarships and part-time jobs. The application deadline for financial aid is continuous.
Freshman Admission Trinity College of Nursing and Health Sciences Schools requires a high school transcript, a minimum 2.5 high school GPA, SAT I or ACT scores, and TOEFL scores for international students. The application deadline for regular admission is June 1.
Transfer Admission The application deadline for admission is June 1.
Entrance Difficulty Trinity College of Nursing and Health Sciences Schools assesses its entrance difficulty level as most difficult. For the fall 2002 freshman class, 50 percent of the applicants were accepted.

For Further Information Contact Ms. Barbara Kimpe, Admissions Representative, Trinity College of Nursing and Health Sciences Schools, 2122 25th Avenue, Rock Island, IL 61201. *Telephone:* 309-779-7812. *Fax:* 309-779-7748. *E-mail:* con@trinityqc.com. *Web site:* http://www.trinitycollegeqc.edu/.

TRINITY INTERNATIONAL UNIVERSITY

Deerfield, Illinois

Trinity is a coed, private university, founded in 1897, affiliated with the Evangelical Free Church of America, offering degrees at the bachelor's, master's, doctoral, and first professional levels. It has a 108-acre campus in Deerfield near Chicago.

Academic Information The faculty has 87 members (46% full-time), 38% with terminal degrees. The undergraduate student-faculty ratio is 16:1. The library holds 155,811 titles, 1,332 serial subscriptions, and 4,332 audiovisual materials. Special programs include academic remediation, an honors program, study abroad, advanced placement credit, double majors, independent study, part-time degree programs (daytime, evenings), adult/continuing education programs, internships, and arrangement for off-campus study with 13 members of the Christian College Consortium. The most frequently chosen baccalaureate fields are education, communications/communication technologies, philosophy, religion, and theology.
Student Body Statistics The student body totals 2,078, of whom 1,162 are undergraduates (257 freshmen). 58 percent are women and 42 percent are men. Students come from 29 states and territories and 6 other countries. 62 percent are from Illinois. 1.2 percent are international students.
Expenses for 2002–03 *Application fee:* $25. *Comprehensive fee:* $21,860 includes full-time tuition ($16,100), mandatory fees ($250), and college room and board ($5510). *College room only:* $2880. *Part-time tuition:* $672 per hour. *Part-time mandatory fees:* $125 per term.
Financial Aid Forms of aid include need-based and non-need-based scholarships and part-time jobs. The average aided 2002–03 undergraduate received an aid package worth an estimated $12,955. The priority application deadline for financial aid is April 1.
Freshman Admission Trinity requires an essay, a high school transcript, a minimum 2.5 high school GPA, 1 recommendation, SAT I or ACT scores, and TOEFL scores for international students. A minimum 3.0 high school GPA is recommended. An interview is required for some. The application deadline for regular admission is rolling.
Transfer Admission The application deadline for admission is rolling.
Entrance Difficulty Trinity assesses its entrance difficulty level as moderately difficult. For the fall 2002 freshman class, 84 percent of the applicants were accepted.

For Further Information Contact Mr. Matt Yoder, Director of Undergraduate Admissions, Trinity International University, 2065 Half Day Road, Peterson Wing, McClennan Building, Deerfield, IL 60015-1284. *Telephone:* 847-317-7000 or 800-822-3225 (toll-free out-of-state). *Fax:* 847-317-8097. *E-mail:* tcdadm@tiu.edu. *Web site:* http://www.tiu.edu/.

UNIVERSITY OF CHICAGO

Chicago, Illinois

Chicago is a coed, private university, founded in 1891, offering degrees at the bachelor's, master's, doctoral, and first professional levels. It has a 203-acre campus in Chicago.

Academic Information The faculty has 1,861 members (86% full-time). The undergraduate student-faculty ratio is 4:1. The library holds 6 million titles and 47,000 serial subscriptions. Special programs include study abroad, advanced placement credit, accelerated degree programs, double majors, independent study, self-designed majors, summer session for credit, adult/continuing education programs, internships, and arrangement for off-campus study with Committee on Institutional Cooperation, Associated Colleges of the Midwest. The most frequently chosen baccalaureate fields are biological/life sciences, English, social sciences and history.
Student Body Statistics The student body totals 12,576, of whom 4,075 are undergraduates (1,081 freshmen). 51 percent are women and 49 percent are men. Students come from 52 states and territories and 49 other countries. 22 percent are from Illinois. 7 percent are international students.
Expenses for 2002–03 *Application fee:* $60. *Comprehensive fee:* $36,553 includes full-time tuition ($27,324), mandatory fees ($501), and college room and board ($8728). *Part-time tuition:* varies with course load.
Financial Aid Forms of aid include need-based and non-need-based scholarships and part-time jobs. The priority application deadline for financial aid is February 1.
Freshman Admission Chicago requires an essay, a high school transcript, 3 recommendations, SAT I or ACT scores, and TOEFL scores for international students. An interview is recommended. The application deadline for regular admission is January 1 and for early action it is November 1.
Transfer Admission The application deadline for admission is April 11.
Entrance Difficulty Chicago assesses its entrance difficulty level as most difficult. For the fall 2002 freshman class, 42 percent of the applicants were accepted.

For Further Information Contact Mr. Theodore O'Neill, Dean of Admissions, University of Chicago, 1116 East 59th Street, Chicago, IL 60637-1513. *Telephone:* 773-702-8650. *Fax:* 773-702-4199. *Web site:* http://www.uchicago.edu/.

UNIVERSITY OF ILLINOIS AT CHICAGO

Chicago, Illinois

UIC is a coed, public unit of University of Illinois System, founded in 1946, offering degrees at the bachelor's, master's, doctoral, and first professional levels and first professional certificates. It has a 216-acre campus in Chicago.

University of Illinois at Chicago (continued)

Academic Information The faculty has 1,508 members (82% full-time), 77% with terminal degrees. The undergraduate student-faculty ratio is 15:1. The library holds 2 million titles, 21,571 serial subscriptions, and 28,436 audiovisual materials. Special programs include academic remediation, services for learning-disabled students, an honors program, cooperative (work-study) education, study abroad, advanced placement credit, accelerated degree programs, ESL programs, double majors, independent study, distance learning, self-designed majors, summer session for credit, part-time degree programs (daytime, summer), internships, and arrangement for off-campus study with University Center of Lake County. The most frequently chosen baccalaureate fields are business/marketing, engineering/engineering technologies, psychology.
Student Body Statistics The student body totals 26,138, of whom 16,543 are undergraduates (3,015 freshmen). 55 percent are women and 45 percent are men. Students come from 52 states and territories and 100 other countries. 97 percent are from Illinois. 1.5 percent are international students.
Expenses for 2002–03 *Application fee:* $40. *State resident tuition:* $4664 full-time. *Nonresident tuition:* $11,992 full-time. *Mandatory fees:* $1778 full-time. Full-time tuition and fees vary according to program. *College room and board:* $6428. *College room only:* $4352. Room and board charges vary according to board plan and housing facility.
Financial Aid Forms of aid include need-based and non-need-based scholarships, athletic grants, and part-time jobs. The average aided 2001–02 undergraduate received an aid package worth $11,900. The priority application deadline for financial aid is March 1.
Freshman Admission UIC requires a high school transcript, SAT I or ACT scores, and TOEFL scores for international students. An essay and an interview are required for some. The application deadline for regular admission is April 1.
Transfer Admission The application deadline for admission is May 1.
Entrance Difficulty UIC assesses its entrance difficulty level as moderately difficult; very difficult for honors program, Guaranteed Professional Program. For the fall 2002 freshman class, 63 percent of the applicants were accepted.

For Further Information Contact Mr. Rob Sheinkopf, Executive Director of Admissions, University of Illinois at Chicago, Box 5220, Chicago, IL 60680-5220. *Telephone:* 312-996-4350. *Fax:* 312-413-7628. *E-mail:* uic.admit@uic.edu. *Web site:* http://www.uic.edu/.

UNIVERSITY OF ILLINOIS AT SPRINGFIELD

Springfield, Illinois

UIS is a coed, public, upper-level unit of University of Illinois, founded in 1969, offering degrees at the bachelor's, master's, and doctoral levels. It has a 746-acre campus in Springfield.

Academic Information The faculty has 258 members (66% full-time). The undergraduate student-faculty ratio is 15:1. The library holds 521,389 titles, 2,014 serial subscriptions, and 40,171 audiovisual materials. Special programs include academic remediation, cooperative (work-study) education, self-designed majors, summer session for credit, part-time degree programs (daytime, evenings, weekends, summer), external degree programs, adult/continuing education programs, internships, and arrangement for off-campus study with Springfield College, Illinois College, MacMurray College, Lincoln Land Community College, Western Illinois University, Southern Illinois University, Illinois State University. The most frequently chosen baccalaureate fields are business/marketing, communications/communication technologies, psychology.
Student Body Statistics The student body totals 4,451, of whom 2,445 are undergraduates (29 in entering class). 62 percent are women and 38 percent are men. Students come from 18 states and territories and 33 other countries. 98 percent are from Illinois. 1.3 percent are international students.
Expenses for 2002–03 *State resident tuition:* $3285 full-time, $109.50 per credit part-time. *Nonresident tuition:* $9855 full-time, $328.50 per credit part-time. *Mandatory fees:* $724 full-time, $211.08. *College room and board:* $6370. *College room only:* $4170. Room and board charges vary according to housing facility.
Financial Aid Forms of aid include need-based and non-need-based scholarships, athletic grants, and part-time jobs. The average aided 2001–02 undergraduate received an aid package worth $7501. The application deadline for financial aid is November 15 with a priority deadline of April 1.
Transfer Admission UIS requires a college transcript and a minimum 2.0 college GPA. Standardized test scores are required for some. The application deadline for admission is rolling.
Entrance Difficulty UIS assesses its entrance difficulty level as minimally difficult. For the fall 2002 entering class, 23 percent of the applicants were accepted.

For Further Information Contact Office of Enrollment Services, University of Illinois at Springfield, Building SAB, 1 University Plaza, Springfield, IL 62703-5404. *Telephone:* 217-206-6626 or 888-977-4847 (toll-free). *Fax:* 217-206-6620. *Web site:* http://www.uis.edu/.

See page 344 for a narrative description.

UNIVERSITY OF ILLINOIS AT URBANA–CHAMPAIGN

Champaign, Illinois

Illinois is a coed, public unit of University of Illinois System, founded in 1867, offering degrees at the bachelor's, master's, doctoral, and first professional levels. It has a 1,470-acre campus in Champaign.

Academic Information The faculty has 2,564 members (86% full-time), 86% with terminal degrees. The undergraduate student-faculty ratio is 13:1. The library holds 10 million titles, 90,707 serial subscriptions, and 1 million audiovisual materials. Special programs include services for learning-disabled students, an honors program, cooperative (work-study) education, study abroad, advanced placement credit, accelerated degree programs, double majors, distance learning, self-designed majors, summer session for credit, internships, and arrangement for off-campus study with members of the Committee on Institutional Cooperation, Midwest Universities Consortium for International Activities. The most frequently chosen baccalaureate fields are business/marketing, engineering/engineering technologies, social sciences and history.
Student Body Statistics The student body totals 39,999, of whom 28,947 are undergraduates (6,366 freshmen). 48 percent are women and 52 percent are men. Students come from 49 states and territories and 69 other countries. 89 percent are from Illinois. 2.6 percent are international students. 56 percent of the 2002 graduating class went on to graduate and professional schools.
Expenses for 2002–03 *Application fee:* $40, $50 for international students. *State resident tuition:* $4302 full-time. *Nonresident tuition:* $14,352 full-time. *Mandatory fees:* $1446 full-time. Full-time tuition and fees vary according to course load and student level. *College room and board:* $6360. Room and board charges vary according to board plan and housing facility.
Financial Aid Forms of aid include need-based scholarships, athletic grants, and part-time jobs. The average aided 2002–03 undergraduate received an aid package worth an estimated $9263. The priority application deadline for financial aid is March 15.
Freshman Admission Illinois requires an essay, a high school transcript, SAT I or ACT scores, and TOEFL scores for international students. Audition, statement of professional interest is required for some. The application deadline for regular admission is January 1.
Transfer Admission The application deadline for admission is March 15.
Entrance Difficulty Illinois assesses its entrance difficulty level as very difficult. For the fall 2002 freshman class, 60 percent of the applicants were accepted.

For Further Information Contact Mr. Abel Montoya, Assistant Director of Admissions, University of Illinois at Urbana–Champaign, 901 West Illinois, Urbana, IL 61801. *Telephone:* 217-333-0302. *Fax:* 217-244-7278. *E-mail:* admissions@oar.uiuc.edu. *Web site:* http://www.uiuc.edu/.

UNIVERSITY OF PHOENIX-CHICAGO CAMPUS

Schaumburg, Illinois

University of Phoenix-Chicago Campus is a coed, proprietary, comprehensive institution, founded in 2002, offering degrees at the associate, bachelor's, master's, and doctoral levels and post-master's and postbachelor's certificates (courses conducted at 121 campuses and learning centers in 25 states).

Academic Information The faculty has 4 members (50% full-time), 25% with terminal degrees. The library holds 27 million titles and 11,648 serial subscriptions. Special programs include advanced placement credit, accelerated degree programs, independent study, distance learning, external degree programs, and adult/continuing education programs.
Student Body Statistics The student body totals 119, of whom 92 are undergraduates (16 freshmen). 45 percent are women and 55 percent are men.
Expenses for 2002–03 *Tuition:* $9540 full-time, $318 per credit part-time.
Financial Aid The application deadline for financial aid is continuous.
Freshman Admission University of Phoenix-Chicago Campus requires 1 recommendation, 2 years of work experience, 23 years of age, and TOEFL scores for international students. A high school transcript is required for some. The application deadline for regular admission is rolling.
Transfer Admission The application deadline for admission is rolling.
Entrance Difficulty University of Phoenix-Chicago Campus has an open admission policy.

For Further Information Contact Ms. Beth Barilla, Director of Admissions, University of Phoenix-Chicago Campus, 4615 East Elwood Street, Mail Stop 10-0030, Phoenix, AZ 85040-1958. *Telephone:* 480-557-1712 or 800-228-7240 (toll-free). *Fax:* 480-594-1758. *Web site:* http://www.phoenix.edu/.

UNIVERSITY OF ST. FRANCIS

Joliet, Illinois

USF is a coed, private, Roman Catholic, comprehensive institution, founded in 1920, offering degrees at the bachelor's and master's levels and postbachelor's certificates. It has a 16-acre campus in Joliet near Chicago.

Academic Information The faculty has 219 members (34% full-time). The undergraduate student-faculty ratio is 10:1. The library holds 105,121 titles, 953 serial subscriptions, and 8,601 audiovisual materials. Special programs include academic remediation, study abroad, advanced placement credit, accelerated degree programs, double majors, independent study, distance learning, self-designed majors, summer session for credit, part-time degree programs (daytime, evenings, weekends, summer), external degree programs, adult/continuing education programs, internships, and arrangement for off-campus study. The most frequently chosen baccalaureate fields are education, communications/communication technologies, health professions and related sciences.
Student Body Statistics The student body totals 2,079, of whom 1,362 are undergraduates (148 freshmen). 68 percent are women and 32 percent are men. Students come from 9 states and territories. 97 percent are from Illinois. 0.3 percent are international students. 15 percent of the 2002 graduating class went on to graduate and professional schools.
Expenses for 2002–03 *Application fee:* $20. *Comprehensive fee:* $21,830 includes full-time tuition ($15,710), mandatory fees ($320), and college room and board ($5800). *College room only:* $2810. *Part-time tuition:* $455 per semester hour. *Part-time mandatory fees:* $15 per term. Part-time tuition and fees vary according to course load.
Financial Aid Forms of aid include need-based and non-need-based scholarships, athletic grants, and part-time jobs. The average aided 2002–03 undergraduate received an aid package worth an estimated $14,279. The priority application deadline for financial aid is May 1.
Freshman Admission USF requires a high school transcript, a minimum 2.5 high school GPA, SAT I or ACT scores, and TOEFL scores for international students. An essay, 2 recommendations, and an interview are required for some. The application deadline for regular admission is September 1.
Transfer Admission The application deadline for admission is rolling.
Entrance Difficulty USF assesses its entrance difficulty level as moderately difficult. For the fall 2002 freshman class, 69 percent of the applicants were accepted.

For Further Information Contact Ms. Michelle Mega, Assistant Director On-Campus Admissions, University of St. Francis, 500 North Wilcox Street, Joliet, IL 60435-6188. *Telephone:* 815-740-3385 or 800-735-3500 (toll-free). *Fax:* 815-740-5032. *E-mail:* admissions@stfrancis.edu. *Web site:* http://www.stfrancis.edu/.

See page 346 for a narrative description.

VANDERCOOK COLLEGE OF MUSIC

Chicago, Illinois

VCM is a coed, private, comprehensive institution, founded in 1909, offering degrees at the bachelor's and master's levels in music education. It has a 1-acre campus in Chicago.

Academic Information The faculty has 28 members (25% full-time), 18% with terminal degrees. The undergraduate student-faculty ratio is 7:1. Special programs include advanced placement credit, independent study, and internships. The most frequently chosen baccalaureate field is education.
Student Body Statistics The student body totals 214, of whom 132 are undergraduates (24 freshmen). 39 percent are women and 61 percent are men. Students come from 9 states and territories and 2 other countries. 71 percent are from Illinois. 2.3 percent are international students.
Expenses for 2003–04 *Application fee:* $35. *Comprehensive fee:* $21,490 includes full-time tuition ($14,690), mandatory fees ($600), and college room and board ($6200). Full-time tuition and fees vary according to degree level. Room and board charges vary according to board plan. *Part-time tuition:* $615 per semester hour. *Part-time mandatory fees:* $300. Part-time tuition and fees vary according to course load and degree level.
Financial Aid Forms of aid include need-based and non-need-based scholarships and part-time jobs. The average aided 2001–02 undergraduate received an aid package worth $7983. The application deadline for financial aid is June 7.
Freshman Admission VCM requires an essay, a high school transcript, 3 recommendations, an interview, audition, SAT I or ACT scores, and TOEFL scores for international students. A minimum 3.0 high school GPA is recommended. A minimum 3.0 high school GPA is required for some. The application deadline for regular admission is May 1.
Transfer Admission The application deadline for admission is May 1.
Entrance Difficulty VCM assesses its entrance difficulty level as moderately difficult. For the fall 2002 freshman class, 81 percent of the applicants were accepted.

For Further Information Contact Mr. James Malley, Director of Undergraduate Admission, VanderCook College of Music, 3140 South Federal Street, Chicago, IL 60616. *Telephone:* 800-448-2655 Ext. 241 or 800-448-2655 Ext. 230 (toll-free). *Fax:* 312-225-5211. *E-mail:* admissions@vandercook.edu. *Web site:* http://www.vandercook.edu/.

See page 348 for a narrative description.

WESTERN ILLINOIS UNIVERSITY

Macomb, Illinois

WIU is a coed, public, comprehensive institution, founded in 1899, offering degrees at the bachelor's and master's levels and postbachelor's certificates. It has a 1,050-acre campus in Macomb.

Academic Information The faculty has 689 members (89% full-time), 62% with terminal degrees. The undergraduate student-faculty ratio is 17:1. The library holds 998,041 titles, 3,200 serial subscriptions, and 3,445 audiovisual materials. Special programs include academic remediation, services for learning-disabled students, an honors program, study abroad,

Western Illinois University (continued)

advanced placement credit, Freshman Honors College, ESL programs, double majors, independent study, distance learning, self-designed majors, summer session for credit, part-time degree programs (daytime, evenings, weekends, summer), external degree programs, adult/continuing education programs, internships, and arrangement for off-campus study with Western Illinois Education Consortium. The most frequently chosen baccalaureate fields are education, liberal arts/general studies, protective services/public administration.
Student Body Statistics The student body totals 13,461, of whom 11,033 are undergraduates (1,939 freshmen). 50 percent are women and 50 percent are men. Students come from 42 states and territories and 54 other countries. 94 percent are from Illinois. 1.6 percent are international students. 25 percent of the 2002 graduating class went on to graduate and professional schools.
Expenses for 2002–03 *Application fee:* $30. *State resident tuition:* $3465 full-time, $115.50 per credit hour part-time. *Nonresident tuition:* $6930 full-time, $231 per credit hour part-time. *Mandatory fees:* $1381 full-time, $34 per credit hour part-time. *College room and board:* $5062. *College room only:* $3032.
Financial Aid Forms of aid include need-based and non-need-based scholarships, athletic grants, and part-time jobs. The average aided 2002–03 undergraduate received an aid package worth an estimated $7220. The priority application deadline for financial aid is February 15.
Freshman Admission WIU requires a high school transcript, SAT I or ACT scores, and TOEFL scores for international students. The application deadline for regular admission is August 1.
Transfer Admission The application deadline for admission is rolling.
Entrance Difficulty WIU assesses its entrance difficulty level as moderately difficult. For the fall 2002 freshman class, 64 percent of the applicants were accepted.

For Further Information Contact Ms. Karen Helmers, Director of Admissions, Western Illinois University, 1 University Circle, 115 Sherman Hall, Macomb, IL 61455-1390. *Telephone:* 309-298-3157 or 877-742-5948 (toll-free). *Fax:* 309-298-3111. *E-mail:* kl-helmers@wiu.edu. *Web site:* http://www.wiu.edu/.

WEST SUBURBAN COLLEGE OF NURSING

Oak Park, Illinois

West Suburban College of Nursing is a coed, primarily women's, private, four-year college, founded in 1982, offering degrees at the bachelor's level in nursing. It has a 10-acre campus in Oak Park near Chicago.

Academic Information The faculty has 14 members (71% full-time). The student-faculty ratio is 14:1. Special programs include advanced placement credit, accelerated degree programs, independent study, summer session for credit, part-time degree programs (daytime, summer), and adult/continuing education programs. The most frequently chosen baccalaureate field is health professions and related sciences.
Student Body Statistics The student body is made up of 105 undergraduates (10 freshmen). 97 percent are women and 3 percent are men. Students come from 8 states and territories. 92 percent are from Illinois.
Expenses for 2003–04 *Application fee:* $0. *Tuition:* $17,745 full-time, $600 per semester hour part-time. *Mandatory fees:* $250 full-time, $125 per term part-time.
Freshman Admission West Suburban College of Nursing requires TOEFL scores for international students. The application deadline for regular admission is rolling.
Transfer Admission The application deadline for admission is rolling.
Entrance Difficulty West Suburban College of Nursing assesses its entrance difficulty level as moderately difficult. For the fall 2002 freshman class, 35 percent of the applicants were accepted.

For Further Information Contact Ms. Cindy Valdez, Director of Admission and Records/Registrar, West Suburban College of Nursing, 3 Erie Court, Oak Park, IL 60302. *Telephone:* 708-763-6530. *Fax:* 708-763-1531. *Web site:* http://www.wscn.edu/.

WESTWOOD COLLEGE OF TECHNOLOGY-CHICAGO DU PAGE

Woodridge, Illinois

Westwood College of Technology-Chicago Du Page is a coed, proprietary, primarily two-year college, offering degrees at the associate and bachelor's levels.

Student Body Statistics The student body is made up of 422 undergraduates.
Financial Aid Forms of aid include need-based scholarships and part-time jobs. The application deadline for financial aid is continuous.

For Further Information Contact Mr. Scott Kawall, Director of Admissions, Westwood College of Technology-Chicago Du Page, 7155 James Avenue, Woodridge, IL 60517-2321. *Telephone:* 630-434-8244 or 888-721-7646 (toll-free in-state). *Fax:* 630-434-8244. *E-mail:* info@westwood.edu. *Web site:* http://www.westwood.edu/.

WESTWOOD COLLEGE OF TECHNOLOGY–CHICAGO RIVER OAKS

Calumet City, Illinois

Westwood College of Technology–Chicago River Oaks is a coed, proprietary, primarily two-year college, offering degrees at the associate and bachelor's levels.

Academic Information The faculty has 77 members.
Student Body Statistics The student body is made up of 763 undergraduates.
Financial Aid Forms of aid include need-based scholarships and part-time jobs. The application deadline for financial aid is continuous.

For Further Information Contact Mr. Barry McDonald, Director of Admissions, Westwood College of Technology–Chicago River Oaks, 80 River Oaks Drive, Suite D-49, Calumet City, IL 60409-5820. *Telephone:* 708-832-1988 or 888-549-6873 (toll-free in-state). *Fax:* 708-832-9617. *E-mail:* info@westwood.edu. *Web site:* http://www.westwood.edu/.

WHEATON COLLEGE

Wheaton, Illinois

Wheaton is a coed, private, nondenominational, comprehensive institution, founded in 1860, offering degrees at the bachelor's, master's, and doctoral levels and postbachelor's certificates. It has an 80-acre campus in Wheaton near Chicago.

Academic Information The faculty has 287 members (64% full-time), 74% with terminal degrees. The undergraduate student-faculty ratio is 11:1. The library holds 429,892 titles, 2,751 serial subscriptions, and 38,591 audiovisual materials. Special programs include services for learning-disabled students, study abroad, advanced placement credit, double majors, independent study, self-designed majors, summer session for credit, internships, and arrangement for off-campus study with members of the Christian College Consortium, Council for Christian Colleges and Universities. The most frequently chosen baccalaureate fields are English, philosophy, religion, and theology, trade and industry.
Student Body Statistics The student body totals 2,872, of whom 2,395 are undergraduates (569 freshmen). 51 percent are women and 49 percent are men. Students come from 51 states and territories and 19 other countries. 23 percent are from Illinois. 1.1 percent are international students. 21 percent of the 2002 graduating class went on to graduate and professional schools.
Expenses for 2003–04 *Application fee:* $40. *Tuition:* $771 per hour part-time.

Financial Aid Forms of aid include need-based and non-need-based scholarships and part-time jobs. The average aided 2002–03 undergraduate received an aid package worth an estimated $14,830. The priority application deadline for financial aid is February 15.
Freshman Admission Wheaton requires an essay, a high school transcript, 2 recommendations, SAT I or ACT scores, and TOEFL scores for international students. An interview, SAT II: Writing Test scores, and SAT II Subject Test in French, German, Latin, Spanish or Hebrew are recommended. The application deadline for regular admission is January 15 and for early action it is November 1.
Transfer Admission The application deadline for admission is March 1.
Entrance Difficulty Wheaton assesses its entrance difficulty level as very difficult. For the fall 2002 freshman class, 54 percent of the applicants were accepted.

For Further Information Contact Ms. Shawn Leftwich, Director of Admissions, Wheaton College, 501 College Avenue, Wheaton, IL 60187-5593. *Telephone:* 630-752-5011 or 800-222-2419 (toll-free out-of-state). *Fax:* 630-752-5285. *E-mail:* admissions@wheaton.edu. *Web site:* http://www.wheaton.edu/.

WORSHAM COLLEGE OF MORTUARY SCIENCE

Wheeling, Illinois

Worsham College of Mortuary Science is a coed, private, two-year college, offering degrees at the associate level.

Academic Information The faculty has 12 members. The student-faculty ratio is 17:1.
Student Body Statistics The student body is made up of 150 undergraduates.
Financial Aid Forms of aid include need-based scholarships. The application deadline for financial aid is continuous.
Entrance Difficulty For the fall 2002 freshman class, 100 percent of the applicants were accepted.

For Further Information Contact Ms. Stephanie Kann, President, Worsham College of Mortuary Science, 495 Northgate Parkway, Wheeling, IL 60090-2646. *Telephone:* 847-808-8444. *Fax:* 847-808-8493. *Web site:* http://www.worshamcollege.com/.

Indiana

ANCILLA COLLEGE

Donaldson, Indiana

Ancilla is a coed, private, Roman Catholic, two-year college, founded in 1937, offering degrees at the associate level. It has a 63-acre campus in Donaldson near Chicago.

Academic Information The faculty has 58 members (28% full-time), 22% with terminal degrees. The student-faculty ratio is 15:1. The library holds 28,199 titles, 179 serial subscriptions, and 1,426 audiovisual materials. Special programs include academic remediation, services for learning-disabled students, cooperative (work-study) education, advanced placement credit, double majors, independent study, summer session for credit, part-time degree programs (daytime, evenings, weekends, summer), and adult/continuing education programs.
Student Body Statistics The student body is made up of 565 undergraduates (181 freshmen). 68 percent are women and 32 percent are men. Students come from 2 states and territories and 4 other countries. 99 percent are from Indiana. 0.8 percent are international students. 59 percent of the 2002 graduating class went on to four-year colleges.
Expenses for 2002–03 *Application fee:* $25. *Tuition:* $6600 full-time, $220 per semester hour part-time. *Mandatory fees:* $220 full-time, $50 per term part-time.
Financial Aid Forms of aid include need-based scholarships and part-time jobs. The application deadline for financial aid is March 1.
Freshman Admission Ancilla requires a high school transcript and TOEFL scores for international students. An interview is recommended. The application deadline for regular admission is rolling.
Transfer Admission The application deadline for admission is rolling.
Entrance Difficulty Ancilla has an open admission policy.

For Further Information Contact Mr. Steve Olson, Executive Director of Enrollment Management, Ancilla College, 9601 Union Road, Donaldson, IN 46513. *Telephone:* 574-936-8898 Ext. 350 or 866-262-4552 Ext. 350 (toll-free in-state). *Fax:* 574-935-1773. *E-mail:* admissions@ancilla.edu. *Web site:* http://www.ancilla.edu/.

ANDERSON UNIVERSITY

Anderson, Indiana

Anderson University is a coed, private, comprehensive institution, founded in 1917, affiliated with the Church of God, offering degrees at the associate, bachelor's, master's, doctoral, and first professional levels. It has a 100-acre campus in Anderson near Indianapolis.

Academic Information The faculty has 233 members (56% full-time), 34% with terminal degrees. The undergraduate student-faculty ratio is 13:1. The library holds 245,019 titles, 937 serial subscriptions, and 372 audiovisual materials. Special programs include academic remediation, services for learning-disabled students, an honors program, study abroad, advanced placement credit, accelerated degree programs, double majors, independent study, self-designed majors, summer session for credit, part-time degree programs, adult/continuing education programs, and internships. The most frequently chosen baccalaureate fields are business/marketing, education, philosophy, religion, and theology.
Student Body Statistics The student body totals 2,506, of whom 2,121 are undergraduates (598 freshmen). 58 percent are women and 42 percent are men. Students come from 46 states and territories and 16 other countries. 65 percent are from Indiana. 1.1 percent are international students. 21 percent of the 2002 graduating class went on to graduate and professional schools.
Expenses for 2002–03 *Application fee:* $20. *Comprehensive fee:* $21,760 includes full-time tuition ($16,140) and college room and board ($5620). *College room only:* $3140. Room and board charges vary according to board plan. *Part-time tuition:* $673 per credit hour. Part-time tuition varies according to course load.
Financial Aid Forms of aid include need-based and non-need-based scholarships and part-time jobs. The average aided 2001–02 undergraduate received an aid package worth $15,736. The priority application deadline for financial aid is March 1.
Freshman Admission Anderson University requires a high school transcript, a minimum 2.0 high school GPA, 2 recommendations, lifestyle statement, and SAT I or ACT scores. An essay and TOEFL scores for international students are recommended. An interview is required for some. The application deadline for regular admission is July 1.
Transfer Admission The application deadline for admission is August 25.
Entrance Difficulty Anderson University assesses its entrance difficulty level as moderately difficult. For the fall 2002 freshman class, 72 percent of the applicants were accepted.

For Further Information Contact Mr. Jim King, Director of Admissions, Anderson University, 1100 East 5th Street, Anderson, IN 46012-3495. *Telephone:* 765-641-4080, 800-421-3014 (toll-free in-state), or 800-428-6414 (toll-free out-of-state). *Fax:* 765-641-3851. *E-mail:* info@anderson.edu. *Web site:* http://www.anderson.edu/.

BALL STATE UNIVERSITY

Muncie, Indiana

Ball State is a coed, public university, founded in 1918, offering degrees at the associate, bachelor's, master's, and doctoral levels and post-master's and postbachelor's certificates. It has a 955-acre campus in Muncie near Indianapolis.

Academic Information The faculty has 1,175 members (76% full-time), 62% with terminal degrees. The undergraduate student-faculty ratio is 16:1. The library holds 1 million titles, 2,937 serial subscriptions, and 506,303 audiovisual materials. Special programs include academic remediation, an honors program, cooperative (work-study) education, study abroad, advanced placement credit, Freshman Honors College, ESL programs, double majors, independent study, distance learning, summer session for credit, part-time degree programs, adult/continuing education programs, and internships. The most frequently chosen baccalaureate fields are business/marketing, education, liberal arts/general studies.

Student Body Statistics The student body totals 20,113, of whom 17,061 are undergraduates (4,032 freshmen). 53 percent are women and 47 percent are men. Students come from 49 states and territories. 92 percent are from Indiana.

Expenses for 2002–03 *Application fee:* $25. *State resident tuition:* $4320 full-time. *Nonresident tuition:* $12,100 full-time. *Mandatory fees:* $380 full-time. *College room and board:* $5546. Room and board charges vary according to board plan and housing facility.

Financial Aid Forms of aid include need-based and non-need-based scholarships, athletic grants, and part-time jobs. The average aided 2002–03 undergraduate received an aid package worth an estimated $6368. The priority application deadline for financial aid is March 1.

Freshman Admission Ball State requires a high school transcript and TOEFL scores for international students. An essay, recommendations, an interview, and SAT I or ACT scores are required for some. The application deadline for regular admission is rolling.

Transfer Admission The application deadline for admission is rolling.

Entrance Difficulty Ball State assesses its entrance difficulty level as moderately difficult; very difficult for architecture program. For the fall 2002 freshman class, 76 percent of the applicants were accepted.

SPECIAL MESSAGE TO STUDENTS

Social Life At Ball State, the life lived outside the classroom is important, too. That is why all first-year students must live in residence halls unless they commute from their parents' primary residences. Ball State's thirty-two residence halls are safe, affordable, and convenient. A full-time residence hall director lives in every hall. The amenities in each hall include large-screen televisions, pianos, pool tables, video games, kitchenettes, and on-site computer labs. Residence halls offer a wide range of visitation policies, and there are wellness halls, which offer tobacco-free living environments, fitness and aerobic areas, and special programs that emphasize positive lifestyle choice. Ball State has everything from lasagna to lattes at its five dining hall locations.

Academic Highlights Ball State is a coed public university that offers degrees at the associate, bachelor's, master's, and doctoral levels. Founded in 1918, the 955-acre campus, located in Muncie, Indiana, includes sixty-three major buildings. The University brings together the powerful resources of a large research university and the personal learning of a small liberal arts college. The University operates twenty-one public computer labs and forty departmental labs, which provide a computer terminal for every 11 students. Ranked as a Doctoral I institution by the Carnegie Foundation, the University has seven academic colleges, an Honors College, University College, and a graduate school that offers 125 undergraduate programs, seventy-six master's programs, and nineteen doctoral programs. Ball State awards approximately 4,000 degrees each year. There are 870 full-time faculty members; 83 percent of the tenure-track faculty members hold doctoral degrees in their disciplines. Bracken Library, one of the largest and most modern libraries in Indiana, houses 14 million items and more than 4,000 current periodical titles.

Interviews and Campus Visits Students can experience Ball State during a Cardinal Preview Day or by scheduling an individual visit. During visits, prospective students may talk with students, faculty and staff members, visit a class, and have lunch in a residence hall. An individual visit provides opportunities for students and their families to tour the campus, attend an admissions information session, and enjoy a meal in a dining hall. With advance notice of a visit, Ball State can make arrangements for students to experience a University core curriculum class and meet with faculty members to discuss academic areas of interest. For more information, students should call 765-285-8300 or 800-482-4BSU (toll-free). To arrange a campus visit, students should call 866-770-3163 (toll-free). The nearest commercial airport is Indianapolis International.

For Further Information Write to Dr. Lawrence Waters, Dean of Admissions and Enrollment Services, Office of Admissions, Ball State University, Muncie, IN 47306-1099 , Fax: 765-285-1632. *E-mail:* askus@wp.bsu.edu. *Web site:* http://www.bsu.edu/admissions.

See page 252 for a narrative description.

BETHEL COLLEGE

Mishawaka, Indiana

Bethel is a coed, private, comprehensive institution, founded in 1947, affiliated with the Missionary Church, offering degrees at the associate, bachelor's, and master's levels. It has a 70-acre campus in Mishawaka.

Academic Information The faculty has 109 members (61% full-time), 49% with terminal degrees. The undergraduate student-faculty ratio is 17:1. The library holds 106,584 titles, 450 serial subscriptions, and 3,926 audiovisual materials. Special programs include academic remediation, an honors program, study abroad, advanced placement credit, accelerated degree programs, double majors, independent study, summer session for credit, part-time degree programs (daytime, evenings, summer), adult/continuing education programs, internships, and arrangement for off-campus study with Northern Indiana Consortium for Education, Coalition for Christian Colleges and Universities. The most frequently chosen baccalaureate fields are business/marketing, education, health professions and related sciences.

Student Body Statistics The student body totals 1,746, of whom 1,634 are undergraduates (427 freshmen). 64 percent are women and 36 percent are men. Students come from 33 states and territories and 11 other countries. 72 percent are from Indiana. 10 percent of the 2002 graduating class went on to graduate and professional schools.

Expenses for 2002–03 *Application fee:* $25. *One-time mandatory fee:* $400. *Comprehensive fee:* $18,500 includes full-time tuition ($13,990), mandatory fees ($130), and college room and board ($4380). *College room only:* $2180. Room and board charges vary according to board plan and housing facility. *Part-time tuition:* $260 per hour. *Part-time mandatory fees:* $40 per year. Part-time tuition and fees vary according to course load.

Financial Aid Forms of aid include need-based and non-need-based scholarships, athletic grants, and part-time jobs. The average aided 2002–03 undergraduate received an aid package worth an estimated $12,041. The priority application deadline for financial aid is March 1.

Freshman Admission Bethel requires an essay, a high school transcript, a minimum 2.0 high school GPA, 1 recommendation, SAT I or ACT scores, and TOEFL scores for international students. A minimum 2.5 high school GPA and an interview are recommended. The application deadline for regular admission is August 1.

Transfer Admission The application deadline for admission is August 1.

Entrance Difficulty Bethel assesses its entrance difficulty level as minimally difficult. For the fall 2002 freshman class, 90 percent of the applicants were accepted.

For Further Information Contact Ms. Andrea M. Helmuth, Director of Admissions, Bethel College, 1001 West McKinley Avenue, Mishawaka, IN 46545-5591. *Telephone:* 574-257-3319 or 800-422-4101 (toll-free). *Fax:* 574-257-3335. *E-mail:* admissions@bethelcollege.edu. *Web site:* http://www.bethelcollege.edu/.

BUTLER UNIVERSITY

Indianapolis, Indiana

Butler is a coed, private, comprehensive institution, founded in 1855, offering degrees at the associate, bachelor's, master's, and first professional levels and postbachelor's certificates. It has a 290-acre campus in Indianapolis.

Academic Information The faculty has 435 members (59% full-time), 60% with terminal degrees. The undergraduate student-faculty ratio is 12:1. The library holds 308,689 titles, 2,000 serial subscriptions, and 13,091 audiovisual materials. Special programs include an honors program, cooperative (work-study) education, study abroad, advanced placement credit, ESL programs, double majors, independent study, self-designed majors, summer session for credit, part-time degree programs (daytime, evenings, summer), adult/continuing education programs, internships, and arrangement for off-campus study with 6 members of the Consortium for Urban Education. The most frequently chosen baccalaureate fields are business/marketing, education, health professions and related sciences.
Student Body Statistics The student body totals 4,326, of whom 3,512 are undergraduates (940 freshmen). 63 percent are women and 37 percent are men. Students come from 42 states and territories and 48 other countries. 60 percent are from Indiana. 1.9 percent are international students. 19 percent of the 2002 graduating class went on to graduate and professional schools.
Expenses for 2002–03 *Application fee:* $25. *Comprehensive fee:* $26,900 includes full-time tuition ($19,990), mandatory fees ($200), and college room and board ($6710). *College room only:* $3090. Full-time tuition and fees vary according to program. Room and board charges vary according to board plan and housing facility. *Part-time tuition:* $840 per credit. Part-time tuition varies according to program.
Financial Aid Forms of aid include need-based and non-need-based scholarships, athletic grants, and part-time jobs. The average aided 2001–02 undergraduate received an aid package worth $14,900. The priority application deadline for financial aid is March 1.
Freshman Admission Butler requires an essay, a high school transcript, SAT I or ACT scores, and TOEFL scores for international students. SAT II: Subject Test scores are recommended. An interview and audition are required for some. The application deadline for regular admission is August 15 and for early action it is December 1.
Transfer Admission The application deadline for admission is August 15.
Entrance Difficulty Butler assesses its entrance difficulty level as moderately difficult. For the fall 2002 freshman class, 80 percent of the applicants were accepted.

For Further Information Contact Mr. William Preble, Dean of Admissions, Butler University, 4600 Sunset Avenue, Indianapolis, IN 46208-3485. *Telephone:* 317-940-8100 Ext. 8124 or 888-940-8100 (toll-free). *Fax:* 317-940-8150. *E-mail:* admission@butler.edu. *Web site:* http://www.butler.edu/.

CALUMET COLLEGE OF SAINT JOSEPH

Whiting, Indiana

Calumet College is a coed, private, Roman Catholic, comprehensive institution, founded in 1951, offering degrees at the associate, bachelor's, and master's levels. It has a 25-acre campus in Whiting near Chicago.

Academic Information The faculty has 106 members (22% full-time). The undergraduate student-faculty ratio is 13:1. The library holds 93,055 titles, 354 serial subscriptions, and 6,412 audiovisual materials. Special programs include academic remediation, cooperative (work-study) education, advanced placement credit, accelerated degree programs, double majors, independent study, self-designed majors, summer session for credit, part-time degree programs (daytime, evenings, weekends), external degree programs, adult/continuing education programs, and internships.
Student Body Statistics The student body totals 1,143, of whom 1,079 are undergraduates (85 freshmen). 59 percent are women and 41 percent are men. Students come from 2 states and territories. 71 percent are from Indiana. 0.1 percent are international students.
Expenses for 2003–04 *Application fee:* $25. *Tuition:* $9000 full-time, $300 per credit hour part-time.
Financial Aid Forms of aid include need-based and non-need-based scholarships and part-time jobs. The priority application deadline for financial aid is March 1.
Freshman Admission Calumet College requires a high school transcript and TOEFL scores for international students. A minimum 2.0 high school GPA, an interview, and SAT I or ACT scores are recommended. An essay and ACT COMPASS are required for some. The application deadline for regular admission is rolling.
Transfer Admission The application deadline for admission is rolling.
Entrance Difficulty Calumet College assesses its entrance difficulty level as minimally difficult. For the fall 2002 freshman class, 55 percent of the applicants were accepted.

For Further Information Contact Mr. Chuck Walz, Director of Admissions, Calumet College of Saint Joseph, 2400 New York Avenue, Whiting, IN 46394. *Telephone:* 219-473-4215 Ext. 379 or 877-700-9100 (toll-free). *Fax:* 219-473-4259. *E-mail:* admissions@ccsj.edu. *Web site:* http://www.ccsj.edu/.

CROSSROADS BIBLE COLLEGE

Indianapolis, Indiana

Crossroads Bible College is a coed, private, Baptist, four-year college, founded in 1980, offering degrees at the associate and bachelor's levels. It has a 6-acre campus in Indianapolis.

Academic Information The faculty has 29 members (17% full-time).
Student Body Statistics The student body is made up of 204 undergraduates (29 freshmen). 38 percent are women and 62 percent are men.
Expenses for 2002–03 *Tuition:* $5100 full-time, $170 per credit hour part-time. *Mandatory fees:* $220 full-time, $110 per term part-time.
Financial Aid Forms of aid include need-based scholarships and part-time jobs. The average aided 2001–02 undergraduate received an aid package worth $1100. The priority application deadline for financial aid is May 31.
Entrance Difficulty Crossroads Bible College assesses its entrance difficulty level as noncompetitive. For the fall 2002 freshman class, 100 percent of the applicants were accepted.

For Further Information Contact Ms. Bethanie Holdcroft, Director of Admissions, Crossroads Bible College, 601 North Shortridge Road, Indianapolis, IN 46219. *Telephone:* 317-352-8736 Ext. 230 or 800-273-2224 (toll-free). *Fax:* 317-352-9145. *Web site:* http://www.crossroads.edu/.

DAVENPORT UNIVERSITY

Granger, Indiana

For Information Write to Davenport University, Granger, IN 46530.

DAVENPORT UNIVERSITY

Hammond, Indiana

For Information Write to Davenport University, Hammond, IN 46320.

DAVENPORT UNIVERSITY

Merrillville, Indiana

For Information Write to Davenport University, Merrillville, IN 46410.

DEPAUW UNIVERSITY

Greencastle, Indiana

DePauw is a coed, private, four-year college, founded in 1837, affiliated with the United Methodist Church, offering degrees at the bachelor's level. It has a 175-acre campus in Greencastle near Indianapolis.

Academic Information The faculty has 238 members (82% full-time), 86% with terminal degrees. The student-faculty ratio is 11:1. The library holds 545,736 titles, 2,134 serial subscriptions, and 12,126 audiovisual materials. Special programs include an honors program, study abroad, advanced placement credit, double majors, independent study, self-designed majors, part-time degree programs (daytime, evenings), internships, and arrangement for off-campus study with Great Lakes Colleges Association. The most frequently chosen baccalaureate fields are communications/communication technologies, computer/information sciences, English.
Student Body Statistics The student body is made up of 2,338 undergraduates (685 freshmen). 56 percent are women and 44 percent are men. Students come from 42 states and territories and 15 other countries. 53 percent are from Indiana. 1.5 percent are international students. 21.3 percent of the 2002 graduating class went on to graduate and professional schools.
Expenses for 2002–03 *Application fee:* $0. *Comprehensive fee:* $29,640 includes full-time tuition ($22,400), mandatory fees ($440), and college room and board ($6800). *College room only:* $3400. *Part-time tuition:* $700 per semester hour.
Financial Aid Forms of aid include need-based and non-need-based scholarships and part-time jobs. The average aided 2002–03 undergraduate received an aid package worth an estimated $20,223. The application deadline for financial aid is February 15.
Freshman Admission DePauw requires an essay, a high school transcript, 1 recommendation, and SAT I or ACT scores. A minimum 3.25 high school GPA, an interview, and TOEFL scores for international students are recommended. The application deadline for regular admission is February 1; for early decision it is November 1; and for early action it is December 1.
Transfer Admission The application deadline for admission is March 1.
Entrance Difficulty DePauw assesses its entrance difficulty level as moderately difficult. For the fall 2002 freshman class, 61 percent of the applicants were accepted.

For Further Information Contact Director of Admission, DePauw University, 101 East Seminary Street, Greencastle, IN 46135-0037. *Telephone:* 765-658-4006 or 800-447-2495 (toll-free). *Fax:* 765-658-4007. *E-mail:* admission@depauw.edu. *Web site:* http://www.depauw.edu/.

See page 274 for a narrative description.

EARLHAM COLLEGE

Richmond, Indiana

Earlham is a coed, private, comprehensive institution, founded in 1847, affiliated with the Society of Friends, offering degrees at the bachelor's, master's, and first professional levels. It has an 800-acre campus in Richmond near Cincinnati, Indianapolis, and Dayton.

Academic Information The faculty has 97 members (95% full-time), 98% with terminal degrees. The undergraduate student-faculty ratio is 11:1. The library holds 392,100 titles, 1,660 serial subscriptions, and 53,000 audiovisual materials. Special programs include services for learning-disabled students, study abroad, advanced placement credit, accelerated degree programs, double majors, independent study, self-designed majors, internships, and arrangement for off-campus study with members of the Great Lakes Colleges Association. The most frequently chosen baccalaureate fields are psychology, biological/life sciences, social sciences and history.
Student Body Statistics The student body totals 1,153, of whom 1,080 are undergraduates (282 freshmen). 56 percent are women and 44 percent are men. Students come from 47 states and territories and 35 other countries. 32 percent are from Indiana. 5.3 percent are international students. 19 percent of the 2002 graduating class went on to graduate and professional schools.
Expenses for 2003–04 *Application fee:* $30. *Comprehensive fee:* $29,976 includes full-time tuition ($23,920), mandatory fees ($640), and college room and board ($5416). *College room only:* $2650. Room and board charges vary according to board plan. *Part-time tuition:* $797 per credit hour.
Financial Aid Forms of aid include need-based and non-need-based scholarships and part-time jobs. The average aided 2002–03 undergraduate received an aid package worth an estimated $20,439. The priority application deadline for financial aid is March 1.
Freshman Admission Earlham requires an essay, a high school transcript, a minimum 3.0 high school GPA, 2 recommendations, SAT I or ACT scores, and TOEFL scores for international students. An interview and SAT I scores are recommended. The application deadline for regular admission is February 15; for early decision it is December 1; and for early action it is January 1.
Transfer Admission The application deadline for admission is April 1.
Entrance Difficulty Earlham assesses its entrance difficulty level as moderately difficult. For the fall 2002 freshman class, 78 percent of the applicants were accepted.

For Further Information Contact Mr. Jeff Rickey, Dean of Admissions and Financial Aid, Earlham College, 801 National Road West, Richmond, IN 47374. *Telephone:* 765-983-1600 or 800-327-5426 (toll-free). *Fax:* 765-983-1560. *E-mail:* admission@earlham.edu. *Web site:* http://www.earlham.edu/.

FRANKLIN COLLEGE

Franklin, Indiana

Franklin is a coed, private, four-year college, founded in 1834, affiliated with the American Baptist Churches in the U.S.A., offering degrees at the bachelor's level. It has a 74-acre campus in Franklin near Indianapolis.

Academic Information The faculty has 99 members (60% full-time), 58% with terminal degrees. The student-faculty ratio is 14:1. The library holds 122,605 titles, 484 serial subscriptions, and 7,388 audiovisual materials. Special programs include academic remediation, services for learning-disabled students, study abroad, advanced placement credit, double majors, independent study, summer session for credit, part-time degree programs (daytime, summer), internships, and arrangement for off-campus study with Marian College, University of Indianapolis, Indiana University-Purdue University at Indianapolis, Butler University, Martin University, Ivy Tech State College. The most frequently chosen baccalaureate fields are education, communications/communication technologies, social sciences and history.
Student Body Statistics The student body is made up of 1,048 undergraduates (293 freshmen). 56 percent are women and 44 percent are men. Students come from 21 states and territories and 5 other countries. 94 percent are from Indiana. 0.6 percent are international students. 17 percent of the 2002 graduating class went on to graduate and professional schools.
Expenses for 2002–03 *Application fee:* $30. *Comprehensive fee:* $20,915 includes full-time tuition ($15,500), mandatory fees ($135), and college room and board ($5280). *College room only:* $2960. Room and board charges vary according to board plan and housing facility. *Part-time tuition:* $480 per credit. *Part-time mandatory fees:* $5 per credit. Part-time tuition and fees vary according to course load.
Financial Aid Forms of aid include need-based and non-need-based scholarships and part-time jobs. The average aided 2001–02 undergraduate received an aid package worth $12,302. The priority application deadline for financial aid is March 1.
Freshman Admission Franklin requires an essay, a high school transcript, 1 recommendation, SAT I or ACT scores, and TOEFL scores for international students. An interview is recommended. The application deadline for regular admission is May 1.

Entrance Difficulty Franklin assesses its entrance difficulty level as moderately difficult. For the fall 2002 freshman class, 85 percent of the applicants were accepted.

For Further Information Contact Mr. Alan Hill, Vice President for Enrollment and Student Affairs, Franklin College, 501 East Monroe Street, Franklin, IN 46131-2598. *Telephone:* 317-738-8062 or 800-852-0232 (toll-free). *Fax:* 317-738-8274. *E-mail:* admissions@franklincollege.edu. *Web site:* http://www.franklincollege.edu/.

GOSHEN COLLEGE

Goshen, Indiana

Goshen is a coed, private, Mennonite, four-year college, founded in 1894, offering degrees at the bachelor's level. It has a 135-acre campus in Goshen.

Academic Information The faculty has 123 members (59% full-time), 49% with terminal degrees. The student-faculty ratio is 9:1. The library holds 127,028 titles, 750 serial subscriptions, and 3,250 audiovisual materials. Special programs include academic remediation, services for learning-disabled students, an honors program, cooperative (work-study) education, study abroad, advanced placement credit, accelerated degree programs, Freshman Honors College, ESL programs, double majors, independent study, distance learning, self-designed majors, summer session for credit, part-time degree programs, adult/continuing education programs, internships, and arrangement for off-campus study with Northern Indiana Consortium for Education. The most frequently chosen baccalaureate fields are business/marketing, education, health professions and related sciences.

Student Body Statistics The student body is made up of 871 undergraduates (136 freshmen). 63 percent are women and 37 percent are men. Students come from 36 states and territories and 27 other countries. 45 percent are from Indiana. 9.5 percent are international students. 40 percent of the 2002 graduating class went on to graduate and professional schools.

Expenses for 2003–04 *Application fee:* $25. *Comprehensive fee:* $22,450 includes full-time tuition ($16,320), mandatory fees ($330), and college room and board ($5800). *College room only:* $3000. Room and board charges vary according to board plan and student level. *Part-time tuition:* $640 per credit hour. Part-time tuition varies according to course load.

Financial Aid Forms of aid include need-based and non-need-based scholarships, athletic grants, and part-time jobs. The average aided 2002–03 undergraduate received an aid package worth an estimated $13,629. The priority application deadline for financial aid is February 15.

Freshman Admission Goshen requires a high school transcript, a minimum 2.0 high school GPA, 2 recommendations, an interview, rank in upper 50% of high school class, minimum SAT score of 920, ACT score of 19, SAT I or ACT scores, and TOEFL scores for international students. An essay is recommended. The application deadline for regular admission is August 15.

Transfer Admission The application deadline for admission is August 15.

Entrance Difficulty Goshen assesses its entrance difficulty level as moderately difficult. For the fall 2002 freshman class, 45 percent of the applicants were accepted.

For Further Information Contact Ms. Karen Lowe Raftus, Director of Admission, Goshen College, 1700 South Main Street, Goshen, IN 46526-4794. *Telephone:* 574-535-7535 or 800-348-7422 (toll-free). *Fax:* 574-535-7609. *E-mail:* admissions@goshen.edu. *Web site:* http://www.goshen.edu/.

GRACE COLLEGE

Winona Lake, Indiana

Grace is a coed, private, comprehensive institution, founded in 1948, affiliated with the Fellowship of Grace Brethren Churches, offering degrees at the associate, bachelor's, and master's levels. It has a 160-acre campus in Winona Lake.

Academic Information The faculty has 82 members (51% full-time), 41% with terminal degrees. The undergraduate student-faculty ratio is 19:1. The library holds 142,865 titles, 12,500 serial subscriptions, and 3,583 audiovisual materials. Special programs include academic remediation, services for learning-disabled students, study abroad, advanced placement credit, accelerated degree programs, double majors, independent study, distance learning, summer session for credit, part-time degree programs, adult/continuing education programs, internships, and arrangement for off-campus study with Coalition for Christian Colleges and Universities. The most frequently chosen baccalaureate fields are business/marketing, education, psychology.

Student Body Statistics The student body totals 1,033, of whom 968 are undergraduates (217 freshmen). 59 percent are women and 41 percent are men. Students come from 35 states and territories and 8 other countries. 52 percent are from Indiana. 14 percent of the 2002 graduating class went on to graduate and professional schools.

Expenses for 2002–03 *Application fee:* $20. *Comprehensive fee:* $17,777 includes full-time tuition ($12,126), mandatory fees ($340), and college room and board ($5311). *College room only:* $2539. Room and board charges vary according to board plan and housing facility. *Part-time tuition:* $225 per credit. *Part-time mandatory fees:* $230 per year. Part-time tuition and fees vary according to course load.

Financial Aid Forms of aid include need-based and non-need-based scholarships, athletic grants, and part-time jobs. The average aided 2002–03 undergraduate received an aid package worth an estimated $11,521. The priority application deadline for financial aid is March 1.

Freshman Admission Grace requires a high school transcript, a minimum 2.3 high school GPA, 2 recommendations, SAT I or ACT scores, and TOEFL scores for international students. An interview is required for some. The application deadline for regular admission is August 1.

Transfer Admission The application deadline for admission is August 1.

Entrance Difficulty Grace assesses its entrance difficulty level as moderately difficult. For the fall 2002 freshman class, 75 percent of the applicants were accepted.

For Further Information Contact Ms. Rebecca E. Gehrke, Admission Coordinator, Grace College, 200 Seminary Drive, Winona Lake, IN 46590-1294. *Telephone:* 574-372-5100 Ext. 6411, 800-54-GRACE (toll-free in-state), or 800-54 GRACE (toll-free out-of-state). *Fax:* 574-372-5139. *E-mail:* enroll@grace.edu. *Web site:* http://www.grace.edu/.

HANOVER COLLEGE

Hanover, Indiana

Hanover is a coed, private, Presbyterian, four-year college, founded in 1827, offering degrees at the bachelor's level. It has a 630-acre campus in Hanover near Louisville.

Academic Information The faculty has 102 members (90% full-time), 89% with terminal degrees. The student-faculty ratio is 11:1. The library holds 224,478 titles, 1,035 serial subscriptions, and 5,080 audiovisual materials. Special programs include study abroad, advanced placement credit, accelerated degree programs, double majors, independent study, internships, and arrangement for off-campus study with 8 members of the Spring Term Consortium. The most frequently chosen baccalaureate fields are business/marketing, education, social sciences and history.

Student Body Statistics The student body is made up of 1,050 undergraduates (280 freshmen). 54 percent are women and 46 percent are men. Students come from 35 states and territories and 18 other countries. 70 percent are from Indiana. 3.6 percent are international students. 31.4 percent of the 2002 graduating class went on to graduate and professional schools.

Expenses for 2002–03 *Application fee:* $30. *Comprehensive fee:* $19,000 includes full-time tuition ($13,100), mandatory fees ($400), and college room and board ($5500). *College room only:* $2600. Room and board charges vary according to housing facility. *Part-time tuition:* varies with course load.

Financial Aid Forms of aid include need-based and non-need-based scholarships. The average aided 2002–03 undergraduate received an aid package worth an estimated $12,050. The priority application deadline for financial aid is March 10.

Hanover College (continued)

Freshman Admission Hanover requires an essay, a high school transcript, 1 recommendation, SAT I or ACT scores, and TOEFL scores for international students. An interview is recommended. The application deadline for regular admission is March 1 and for early action it is December 1.

Transfer Admission The application deadline for admission is rolling.

Entrance Difficulty Hanover assesses its entrance difficulty level as moderately difficult. For the fall 2002 freshman class, 76 percent of the applicants were accepted.

For Further Information Contact Mr. Kenneth Moyer, Dean of Admission, Hanover College, PO Box 108, Hanover, IN 47243-0108. *Telephone:* 812-866-7021 or 800-213-2178 (toll-free). *Fax:* 812-866-7098. *E-mail:* info@hanover.edu. *Web site:* http://www.hanover.edu/.

HOLY CROSS COLLEGE

Notre Dame, Indiana

Holy Cross College is a coed, private, Roman Catholic, two-year college, founded in 1966, offering degrees at the associate level. It has a 150-acre campus in Notre Dame.

Academic Information The faculty has 42 members (60% full-time), 29% with terminal degrees. The student-faculty ratio is 17:1. The library holds 15,000 titles and 160 serial subscriptions. Special programs include academic remediation, advanced placement credit, ESL programs, summer session for credit, part-time degree programs (daytime, summer), and arrangement for off-campus study with members of the Northern Indiana Consortium for Education.

Student Body Statistics The student body is made up of 558 undergraduates (304 freshmen). 39 percent are women and 61 percent are men. Students come from 35 states and territories and 12 other countries. 54 percent are from Indiana. 2.3 percent are international students. 85 percent of the 2002 graduating class went on to four-year colleges.

Expenses for 2002–03 *Application fee:* $50. *Tuition:* $9000 full-time, $315 per semester hour part-time.

Financial Aid Forms of aid include need-based scholarships and part-time jobs. The priority application deadline for financial aid is March 1.

Freshman Admission Holy Cross College requires an essay, a high school transcript, a minimum 2.0 high school GPA, SAT I or ACT scores, and TOEFL scores for international students. An interview is recommended. The application deadline for regular admission is rolling.

Transfer Admission The application deadline for admission is rolling.

Entrance Difficulty Holy Cross College assesses its entrance difficulty level as minimally difficult. For the fall 2002 freshman class, 94 percent of the applicants were accepted.

For Further Information Contact Office of Admissions, Holy Cross College, PO Box 308, Notre Dame, IN 46556. *Telephone:* 574-239-8400 Ext. 407. *Fax:* 574-233-7427. *E-mail:* vduke@hcc-nd.edu. *Web site:* http://www.hcc-nd.edu/.

HUNTINGTON COLLEGE

Huntington, Indiana

Huntington is a coed, private, comprehensive institution, founded in 1897, affiliated with the Church of the United Brethren in Christ, offering degrees at the bachelor's and master's levels and postbachelor's certificates. It has a 200-acre campus in Huntington.

Academic Information The faculty has 95 members (59% full-time), 47% with terminal degrees. The undergraduate student-faculty ratio is 16:1. The library holds 91,709 titles, 553 serial subscriptions, and 4,323 audiovisual materials. Special programs include academic remediation, study abroad, advanced placement credit, accelerated degree programs, ESL programs, double majors, independent study, distance learning, summer session for credit, part-time degree programs, adult/continuing education programs, internships, and arrangement for off-campus study with Saint Francis College (IN). The most frequently chosen baccalaureate fields are business/marketing, education, physical sciences.

Student Body Statistics The student body totals 1,016, of whom 868 are undergraduates (240 freshmen). 58 percent are women and 42 percent are men. Students come from 24 states and territories and 15 other countries. 65 percent are from Indiana. 2.3 percent are international students. 15 percent of the 2002 graduating class went on to graduate and professional schools.

Expenses for 2002–03 *Application fee:* $20. *Comprehensive fee:* $21,600 includes full-time tuition ($15,520), mandatory fees ($400), and college room and board ($5680). Room and board charges vary according to board plan. *Part-time tuition:* $475 per semester hour. *Part-time mandatory fees:* $90. Part-time tuition and fees vary according to course load.

Financial Aid Forms of aid include need-based and non-need-based scholarships, athletic grants, and part-time jobs. The average aided 2002–03 undergraduate received an aid package worth an estimated $11,823. The priority application deadline for financial aid is March 1.

Freshman Admission Huntington requires an essay, a high school transcript, a minimum 2.3 high school GPA, SAT I or ACT scores, and TOEFL scores for international students. An interview is recommended. The application deadline for regular admission is August 1.

Transfer Admission The application deadline for admission is rolling.

Entrance Difficulty Huntington assesses its entrance difficulty level as moderately difficult. For the fall 2002 freshman class, 98 percent of the applicants were accepted.

For Further Information Contact Mr. Jeff Berggren, Dean of Enrollment, Huntington College, 2303 College Avenue, Huntington, IN 46750-1299. *Telephone:* 260-356-6000 Ext. 4016 or 800-642-6493 (toll-free). *Fax:* 260-356-9448. *E-mail:* admissions@huntington.edu. *Web site:* http://www.huntington.edu/.

INDIANA INSTITUTE OF TECHNOLOGY

Fort Wayne, Indiana

Indiana Tech is a coed, private, comprehensive institution, founded in 1930, offering degrees at the associate, bachelor's, and master's levels. It has a 25-acre campus in Fort Wayne.

Academic Information The faculty has 207 members (19% full-time), 12% with terminal degrees. The undergraduate student-faculty ratio is 22:1. The library holds 35,200 titles, 158 serial subscriptions, and 92 audiovisual materials. Special programs include academic remediation, services for learning-disabled students, advanced placement credit, accelerated degree programs, ESL programs, double majors, independent study, distance learning, self-designed majors, summer session for credit, part-time degree programs, external degree programs, adult/continuing education programs, and internships. The most frequently chosen baccalaureate fields are business/marketing, computer/information sciences, engineering/engineering technologies.

Student Body Statistics The student body totals 3,019, of whom 2,680 are undergraduates (741 freshmen). 55 percent are women and 45 percent are men. Students come from 34 states and territories and 6 other countries. 84 percent are from Indiana. 1.2 percent are international students. 11 percent of the 2002 graduating class went on to graduate and professional schools.

Expenses for 2003–04 *Application fee:* $50. *Comprehensive fee:* $21,620 includes full-time tuition ($15,590) and college room and board ($6030). Full-time tuition varies according to class time, course load, and program. Room and board charges vary according to housing facility. *Part-time tuition:* $495 per credit hour. Part-time tuition varies according to class time, course load, and program.

Financial Aid Forms of aid include need-based and non-need-based scholarships and part-time jobs. $9125. The priority application deadline for financial aid is March 1.

Freshman Admission Indiana Tech requires a high school transcript, SAT I or ACT scores, and TOEFL scores for international students. A minimum 3.0 high school GPA, an interview, and 2 references are recommended.

Entrance Difficulty Indiana Tech assesses its entrance difficulty level as moderately difficult. For the fall 2002 freshman class, 49 percent of the applicants were accepted.

For Further Information Contact Ms. Allison Carnahan, Director of Admissions, Indiana Institute of Technology, 1600 East Washington Boulevard, Fort Wayne, IN 46803. *Telephone:* 260-422-5561 Ext. 2251, 800-937-2448 (toll-free in-state), or 888-666-TECH (toll-free out-of-state). *Fax:* 260-422-7696. *E-mail:* admissions@indtech.edu. *Web site:* http://www.indtech.edu/.

INDIANA STATE UNIVERSITY

Terre Haute, Indiana

Indiana State is a coed, public university, founded in 1865, offering degrees at the associate, bachelor's, master's, doctoral, and first professional levels and postbachelor's certificates. It has a 91-acre campus in Terre Haute near Indianapolis.

Academic Information The faculty has 673 members (80% full-time). The undergraduate student-faculty ratio is 18:1. The library holds 2 million titles and 2,827 serial subscriptions. Special programs include academic remediation, services for learning-disabled students, an honors program, cooperative (work-study) education, study abroad, advanced placement credit, accelerated degree programs, ESL programs, double majors, independent study, distance learning, summer session for credit, part-time degree programs (daytime, evenings, summer), adult/continuing education programs, internships, and arrangement for off-campus study with Saint Mary-of-the-Woods College, Rose-Hulman Institute of Technology. The most frequently chosen baccalaureate fields are business/marketing, education, social sciences and history.
Student Body Statistics The student body totals 11,714, of whom 9,997 are undergraduates (2,140 freshmen). 52 percent are women and 48 percent are men. Students come from 46 states and territories and 45 other countries. 92 percent are from Indiana. 1.9 percent are international students.
Expenses for 2002–03 *Application fee:* $25. *State resident tuition:* $4116 full-time, $148 per credit part-time. *Nonresident tuition:* $10,276 full-time, $361 per credit part-time. *Mandatory fees:* $100 full-time, $50 per term part-time. *College room and board:* $4998. *College room only:* $2587. Room and board charges vary according to board plan, housing facility, and student level.
Financial Aid Forms of aid include need-based and non-need-based scholarships, athletic grants, and part-time jobs. The average aided 2002–03 undergraduate received an aid package worth an estimated $6532. The priority application deadline for financial aid is March 1.
Freshman Admission Indiana State requires a high school transcript, a minimum 2.0 high school GPA, SAT I or ACT scores, and TOEFL scores for international students. An essay is recommended. Recommendations and an interview are required for some. The application deadline for regular admission is August 15.
Transfer Admission The application deadline for admission is rolling.
Entrance Difficulty Indiana State assesses its entrance difficulty level as moderately difficult. For the fall 2002 freshman class, 83 percent of the applicants were accepted.

For Further Information Contact Mr. Ronald Brown, Director of Admissions, Indiana State University, Tirey Hall 134, 217 North 7th Street, Terre Haute, IN 47809. *Telephone:* 812-237-2121 or 800-742-0891 (toll-free). *Fax:* 812-237-8023. *E-mail:* admisu@amber.indstate.edu. *Web site:* http://web.indstate.edu/.

INDIANA UNIVERSITY BLOOMINGTON

Bloomington, Indiana

IU is a coed, public unit of Indiana University System, founded in 1820, offering degrees at the associate, bachelor's, master's, doctoral, and first professional levels and postbachelor's certificates. It has a 1,931-acre campus in Bloomington near Indianapolis.

Academic Information The faculty has 1,947 members (87% full-time), 71% with terminal degrees. The undergraduate student-faculty ratio is 20:1. The library holds 7 million titles, 60,019 serial subscriptions, and 252,801 audiovisual materials. Special programs include academic remediation, services for learning-disabled students, an honors program, cooperative (work-study) education, study abroad, advanced placement credit, accelerated degree programs, Freshman Honors College, ESL programs, double majors, independent study, distance learning, self-designed majors, summer session for credit, part-time degree programs (daytime, evenings, summer), external degree programs, adult/continuing education programs, internships, and arrangement for off-campus study. The most frequently chosen baccalaureate fields are business/marketing, education, protective services/public administration.
Student Body Statistics The student body totals 38,903, of whom 30,752 are undergraduates (7,080 freshmen). 53 percent are women and 47 percent are men. Students come from 56 states and territories and 135 other countries. 72 percent are from Indiana. 4.1 percent are international students.
Expenses for 2002–03 *Application fee:* $40. *State resident tuition:* $4573 full-time, $142.75 per credit hour part-time. *Nonresident tuition:* $15,184 full-time, $474.50 per credit hour part-time. *Mandatory fees:* $742 full-time. Part-time tuition varies according to course load. *College room and board:* $5676. *College room only:* $3286. Room and board charges vary according to board plan and housing facility.
Financial Aid Forms of aid include need-based and non-need-based scholarships, athletic grants, and part-time jobs. The average aided 2002–03 undergraduate received an aid package worth an estimated $7080. The priority application deadline for financial aid is March 1.
Freshman Admission IU requires a high school transcript and SAT I or ACT scores. An interview and TOEFL scores for international students are recommended. The application deadline for regular admission is February 1.
Transfer Admission The application deadline for admission is rolling.
Entrance Difficulty IU assesses its entrance difficulty level as moderately difficult. For the fall 2002 freshman class, 81 percent of the applicants were accepted.

For Further Information Contact Mr. Don Hossler, Vice Chancellor for Enrollment Services, Indiana University Bloomington, 300 North Jordan Avenue, Bloomington, IN 47405-1106. *Telephone:* 812-855-0661 or 812-855-0661 (toll-free in-state). *Fax:* 812-855-5102. *E-mail:* iuadmit@indiana.edu. *Web site:* http://www.indiana.edu/.

INDIANA UNIVERSITY EAST

Richmond, Indiana

IU East is a coed, public, four-year college of Indiana University System, founded in 1971, offering degrees at the associate and bachelor's levels and postbachelor's certificates. It has a 194-acre campus in Richmond near Indianapolis.

Academic Information The faculty has 69 members (100% full-time), 51% with terminal degrees. The student-faculty ratio is 14:1. The library holds 67,036 titles, 435 serial subscriptions, and 2,222 audiovisual materials. Special programs include academic remediation, services for learning-disabled students, cooperative (work-study) education, advanced placement credit, double majors, independent study, distance learning, summer session for credit, part-time degree programs, external degree programs, adult/continuing education programs, internships, and arrangement for off-campus study with Earlham College. The most frequently chosen baccalaureate fields are education, health professions and related sciences, liberal arts/general studies.
Student Body Statistics The student body totals 2,481, of whom 2,416 are undergraduates (471 freshmen). 70 percent are women and 30 percent are men. Students come from 7 states and territories. 92 percent are from Indiana. 0.1 percent are international students.
Expenses for 2002–03 *Application fee:* $25. *State resident tuition:* $3479 full-time, $115.95 per credit hour part-time. *Nonresident tuition:* $9201 full-time, $306.70 per credit hour part-time. *Mandatory fees:* $310 full-time. Full-time tuition and fees vary according to course load. Part-time tuition varies according to course load.

Indiana University East (continued)

Financial Aid Forms of aid include need-based and non-need-based scholarships and part-time jobs. The average aided 2002–03 undergraduate received an aid package worth an estimated $4786. The priority application deadline for financial aid is March 1.

Freshman Admission IU East requires a high school transcript. A minimum 2.0 high school GPA and SAT I or ACT scores are recommended. The application deadline for regular admission is rolling.

Transfer Admission The application deadline for admission is rolling.

Entrance Difficulty IU East assesses its entrance difficulty level as moderately difficult. For the fall 2002 freshman class, 89 percent of the applicants were accepted.

For Further Information Contact Ms. Susanna Tanner, Admissions Counselor, Indiana University East, 2325 Chester Boulevard, WZ 116, Richmond, IN 47374-1289. *Telephone:* 765-973-8208 or 800-959-EAST (toll-free). *Fax:* 765-973-8288. *E-mail:* eaadmit@indiana.edu. *Web site:* http://www.indiana.edu/.

INDIANA UNIVERSITY KOKOMO

Kokomo, Indiana

IUK is a coed, public, comprehensive unit of Indiana University System, founded in 1945, offering degrees at the associate, bachelor's, and master's levels and postbachelor's certificates. It has a 51-acre campus in Kokomo near Indianapolis.

Academic Information The faculty has 74 members (100% full-time), 65% with terminal degrees. The undergraduate student-faculty ratio is 15:1. The library holds 132,424 titles, 1,513 serial subscriptions, and 1,466 audiovisual materials. Special programs include academic remediation, services for learning-disabled students, an honors program, study abroad, advanced placement credit, Freshman Honors College, independent study, distance learning, summer session for credit, part-time degree programs, external degree programs, adult/continuing education programs, and internships. The most frequently chosen baccalaureate fields are education, business/marketing, liberal arts/general studies.

Student Body Statistics The student body totals 2,772, of whom 2,557 are undergraduates (476 freshmen). 71 percent are women and 29 percent are men. Students come from 3 states and territories. 99 percent are from Indiana. 0.3 percent are international students.

Expenses for 2002–03 *Application fee:* $30. *State resident tuition:* $3479 full-time, $115.95 per credit hour part-time. *Nonresident tuition:* $9201 full-time, $306.70 per credit hour part-time. *Mandatory fees:* $345 full-time. Full-time tuition and fees vary according to course load. Part-time tuition varies according to course load.

Financial Aid Forms of aid include need-based and non-need-based scholarships and part-time jobs. The average aided 2002–03 undergraduate received an aid package worth an estimated $5128. The priority application deadline for financial aid is March 1.

Freshman Admission IUK requires a high school transcript, SAT I or ACT scores, and TOEFL scores for international students. The application deadline for regular admission is August 3.

Transfer Admission The application deadline for admission is August 3.

Entrance Difficulty IUK assesses its entrance difficulty level as minimally difficult. For the fall 2002 freshman class, 87 percent of the applicants were accepted.

For Further Information Contact Ms. Patty Young, Admissions Director, Indiana University Kokomo, PO Box 9003, Kelley Student Center 230A, Kokomo, IN 46904-9003. *Telephone:* 765-455-9217 or 888-875-4485 (toll-free). *Fax:* 765-455-9537. *E-mail:* iuadmis@iuk.edu. *Web site:* http://www.indiana.edu.

INDIANA UNIVERSITY NORTHWEST

Gary, Indiana

IUN is a coed, public, comprehensive unit of Indiana University System, founded in 1959, offering degrees at the associate, bachelor's, and master's levels and postbachelor's certificates. It has a 38-acre campus in Gary near Chicago.

Academic Information The faculty has 349 members (48% full-time), 26% with terminal degrees. The undergraduate student-faculty ratio is 14:1. The library holds 251,508 titles, 1,541 serial subscriptions, and 331 audiovisual materials. Special programs include academic remediation, services for learning-disabled students, an honors program, cooperative (work-study) education, study abroad, advanced placement credit, accelerated degree programs, double majors, independent study, distance learning, self-designed majors, summer session for credit, part-time degree programs, external degree programs, adult/continuing education programs, internships, and arrangement for off-campus study. The most frequently chosen baccalaureate fields are business/marketing, health professions and related sciences, liberal arts/general studies.

Student Body Statistics The student body totals 4,893, of whom 4,322 are undergraduates (813 freshmen). 70 percent are women and 30 percent are men. Students come from 6 states and territories. 99 percent are from Indiana. 0.1 percent are international students.

Expenses for 2002–03 *Application fee:* $25. *State resident tuition:* $3479 full-time, $115.95 per credit hour part-time. *Nonresident tuition:* $9201 full-time, $306.70 per credit hour part-time. *Mandatory fees:* $416 full-time. Full-time tuition and fees vary according to course level. Part-time tuition varies according to course level.

Financial Aid Forms of aid include need-based and non-need-based scholarships, athletic grants, and part-time jobs. The average aided 2002–03 undergraduate received an aid package worth an estimated $5877. The application deadline for financial aid is continuous.

Freshman Admission IUN requires a high school transcript, a minimum 2.0 high school GPA, and SAT I or ACT scores. TOEFL scores for international students are recommended. The application deadline for regular admission is August 1.

Transfer Admission The application deadline for admission is rolling.

Entrance Difficulty IUN assesses its entrance difficulty level as minimally difficult; moderately difficult for out-of-state applicants. For the fall 2002 freshman class, 72 percent of the applicants were accepted.

For Further Information Contact Dr. Linda B. Templeton, Director of Admissions, Indiana University Northwest, Hawthorne 100, 3400 Broadway, Gary, IN 46408-1197. *Telephone:* 219-980-6767 or 800-968-7486 (toll-free). *Fax:* 219-981-4219. *E-mail:* pkeshei@iun.edu. *Web site:* http://www.indiana.edu/.

INDIANA UNIVERSITY–PURDUE UNIVERSITY FORT WAYNE

Fort Wayne, Indiana

IPFW is a coed, public, comprehensive unit of Indiana University System and Purdue University System, founded in 1917, offering degrees at the associate, bachelor's, and master's levels and postbachelor's certificates. It has a 565-acre campus in Fort Wayne.

Academic Information The faculty has 640 members (51% full-time), 50% with terminal degrees. The undergraduate student-faculty ratio is 19:1. The library holds 479,992 titles, 10,964 serial subscriptions, and 1,000 audiovisual materials. Special programs include academic remediation, services for learning-disabled students, an honors program, cooperative (work-study) education, study abroad, advanced placement credit, accelerated degree programs, ESL programs, double majors, independent study, distance learning, self-designed majors, summer session for credit, part-time degree programs (daytime, evenings, weekends, summer), adult/continuing education programs, internships, and arrangement for off-campus study with National Student Exchange. The most frequently chosen baccalaureate fields are business/marketing, education, liberal arts/general studies.

Student Body Statistics The student body totals 11,757, of whom 10,880 are undergraduates (1,732 freshmen). 58 percent are women and 42 percent are men. Students come from 39 states and territories and 66 other countries. 95 percent are from Indiana. 1.5 percent are international students. 15 percent of the 2002 graduating class went on to graduate and professional schools.
Expenses for 2002–03 *Application fee:* $30. *State resident tuition:* $3508 full-time, $145 per semester hour part-time. *Nonresident tuition:* $8136 full-time, $338 per semester hour part-time. *Mandatory fees:* $384 full-time, $16 per semester hour part-time. Full-time tuition and fees vary according to course load. Part-time tuition and fees vary according to course load.
Financial Aid Forms of aid include need-based and non-need-based scholarships, athletic grants, and part-time jobs. The average aided 2001–02 undergraduate received an aid package worth $4601. The priority application deadline for financial aid is March 10.
Freshman Admission IPFW requires a high school transcript, SAT I or ACT scores, and TOEFL scores for international students. Rank in upper 50% of high school class is recommended. The application deadline for regular admission is August 1.
Transfer Admission The application deadline for admission is August 1.
Entrance Difficulty IPFW assesses its entrance difficulty level as minimally difficult; moderately difficult for out-of-state applicants; noncompetitive for students graduating high school over 2 years ago. For the fall 2002 freshman class, 97 percent of the applicants were accepted.

For Further Information Contact Ms. Carol Isaacs, Director of Admissions, Indiana University–Purdue University Fort Wayne, Admissions Office, 2101 East Coliseum Boulevard, Fort Wayne, IN 46805-1499. *Telephone:* 260-481-6812 or 800-324-4739 (toll-free in-state). *Fax:* 260-481-6880. *E-mail:* ipfwadms@ipfw.edu. *Web site:* http://www.ipfw.edu/.

INDIANA UNIVERSITY–PURDUE UNIVERSITY INDIANAPOLIS

Indianapolis, Indiana

IUPUI is a coed, public unit of Indiana University System, founded in 1969, offering degrees at the associate, bachelor's, master's, doctoral, and first professional levels and postbachelor's certificates. It has a 511-acre campus in Indianapolis.

Academic Information The faculty has 2,732 members (70% full-time), 65% with terminal degrees. The undergraduate student-faculty ratio is 18:1. The library holds 1 million titles, 14,673 serial subscriptions, and 1,663 audiovisual materials. Special programs include academic remediation, services for learning-disabled students, an honors program, cooperative (work-study) education, study abroad, advanced placement credit, ESL programs, double majors, independent study, distance learning, summer session for credit, part-time degree programs, external degree programs, adult/continuing education programs, internships, and arrangement for off-campus study with 5 members of the Consortium for Urban Education. The most frequently chosen baccalaureate fields are biological/life sciences, health professions and related sciences, liberal arts/general studies.
Student Body Statistics The student body totals 29,025, of whom 21,060 are undergraduates (2,787 freshmen). 59 percent are women and 41 percent are men. Students come from 40 states and territories. 98 percent are from Indiana. 1.7 percent are international students.
Expenses for 2002–03 *Application fee:* $35. *State resident tuition:* $4184 full-time, $139.45 per credit hour part-time. *Nonresident tuition:* $13,014 full-time, $433.80 per credit hour part-time. *Mandatory fees:* $531 full-time. Full-time tuition and fees vary according to course load. Part-time tuition varies according to course load. *College room only:* $2080. Room charges vary according to housing facility.
Financial Aid Forms of aid include need-based and non-need-based scholarships, athletic grants, and part-time jobs. The average aided 2002–03 undergraduate received an aid package worth an estimated $6139. The application deadline for financial aid is continuous.
Freshman Admission IUPUI requires a high school transcript, SAT I or ACT scores, and TOEFL scores for international students. Portfolio for art program and SAT I scores are recommended. An interview is required for some. The application deadline for regular admission is rolling.
Transfer Admission The application deadline for admission is rolling.
Entrance Difficulty IUPUI assesses its entrance difficulty level as moderately difficult. For the fall 2002 freshman class, 75 percent of the applicants were accepted.

For Further Information Contact Michael Donahue, Director of Admissions, Indiana University–Purdue University Indianapolis, 425 N. University Boulevard, Cavanaugh Hall Room 129, Indianapolis, IN 46202-5143. *Telephone:* 317-274-4591. *Fax:* 317-278-1862. *E-mail:* apply@iupui.edu. *Web site:* http://www.indiana.edu/.

INDIANA UNIVERSITY SOUTH BEND

South Bend, Indiana

IUSB is a coed, public, comprehensive unit of Indiana University System, founded in 1922, offering degrees at the associate, bachelor's, and master's levels and postbachelor's certificates. It has a 73-acre campus in South Bend near Chicago.

Academic Information The faculty has 498 members (52% full-time), 39% with terminal degrees. The undergraduate student-faculty ratio is 14:1. The library holds 300,202 titles, 1,937 serial subscriptions, and 13,001 audiovisual materials. Special programs include an honors program, study abroad, accelerated degree programs, ESL programs, double majors, distance learning, summer session for credit, part-time degree programs, external degree programs, adult/continuing education programs, internships, and arrangement for off-campus study with Bethel College, Saint Mary's College (IN), Holy Cross College, Goshen College. The most frequently chosen baccalaureate fields are business/marketing, education, liberal arts/general studies.
Student Body Statistics The student body totals 7,457, of whom 6,177 are undergraduates (932 freshmen). 64 percent are women and 36 percent are men. Students come from 13 states and territories. 97 percent are from Indiana. 2.7 percent are international students.
Expenses for 2002–03 *Application fee:* $40. *State resident tuition:* $3540 full-time, $118 per credit hour part-time. *Nonresident tuition:* $9879 full-time, $329.30 per credit hour part-time. *Mandatory fees:* $390 full-time. Full-time tuition and fees vary according to course load. Part-time tuition varies according to course load.
Financial Aid Forms of aid include need-based and non-need-based scholarships, athletic grants, and part-time jobs. The average aided 2002–03 undergraduate received an aid package worth an estimated $4854. The priority application deadline for financial aid is March 1.
Freshman Admission IUSB requires a high school transcript, a minimum 2.0 high school GPA, and SAT I or ACT scores. TOEFL scores for international students are recommended. The application deadline for regular admission is July 1.
Transfer Admission The application deadline for admission is June 1.
Entrance Difficulty IUSB assesses its entrance difficulty level as moderately difficult. For the fall 2002 freshman class, 80 percent of the applicants were accepted.

For Further Information Contact Jeff Johnston, Director of Recruitment/Admissions, Indiana University South Bend, 1700 Mishawaka Avenue, Administration Building, Room 169, PO Box 7111, South Bend, IN 46634-7111. *Telephone:* 219-237-4480 or 877-GO-2-IUSB (toll-free). *Fax:* 219-237-4834. *E-mail:* admissions@iusb.edu. *Web site:* http://www.iusb.edu/.

INDIANA UNIVERSITY SOUTHEAST

New Albany, Indiana

IU Southeast is a coed, public, comprehensive unit of Indiana University System, founded in 1941, offering degrees at the associate, bachelor's, and master's levels and postbachelor's certificates. It has a 177-acre campus in New Albany near Louisville.

Academic Information The faculty has 437 members (42% full-time), 40% with terminal degrees. The undergraduate student-faculty ratio is

Indiana University Southeast (continued)
17:1. The library holds 215,429 titles, 962 serial subscriptions, and 9,360 audiovisual materials. Special programs include academic remediation, services for learning-disabled students, study abroad, advanced placement credit, accelerated degree programs, double majors, independent study, summer session for credit, part-time degree programs, external degree programs, adult/continuing education programs, internships, and arrangement for off-campus study with 7 members of the Kentuckiana Metroversity. The most frequently chosen baccalaureate fields are business/marketing, education, law/legal studies.
Student Body Statistics The student body totals 6,716, of whom 5,860 are undergraduates (903 freshmen). 63 percent are women and 37 percent are men. Students come from 3 states and territories. 83 percent are from Indiana. 0.4 percent are international students.
Expenses for 2002–03 *Application fee:* $30. *State resident tuition:* $3479 full-time, $115.95 per credit hour part-time. *Nonresident tuition:* $9201 full-time, $306.70 per credit hour part-time. *Mandatory fees:* $386 full-time. Full-time tuition and fees vary according to course load. Part-time tuition varies according to course load.
Financial Aid Forms of aid include need-based and non-need-based scholarships, athletic grants, and part-time jobs. The average aided 2002–03 undergraduate received an aid package worth an estimated $5053. The priority application deadline for financial aid is March 1.
Freshman Admission IU Southeast requires a high school transcript, SAT I or ACT scores, and TOEFL scores for international students. An interview is required for some. The application deadline for regular admission is July 15.
Transfer Admission The application deadline for admission is July 1.
Entrance Difficulty IU Southeast assesses its entrance difficulty level as minimally difficult; moderately difficult for out-of-state applicants; moderately difficult for transfers. For the fall 2002 freshman class, 89 percent of the applicants were accepted.

For Further Information Contact Mr. David B. Campbell, Director of Admissions, Indiana University Southeast, University Center Building, Room 100, 4201 Grant Line Road, New Albany, IN 47150. *Telephone:* 812-941-2212 or 800-852-8835 (toll-free in-state). *Fax:* 812-941-2595. *E-mail:* admissions@ius.edu. *Web site:* http://www.indiana.edu/.

INDIANA WESLEYAN UNIVERSITY

Marion, Indiana

IWU is a coed, private, Wesleyan, comprehensive institution, founded in 1920, offering degrees at the associate, bachelor's, and master's levels (also offers adult program with significant enrollment not reflected in profile). It has a 132-acre campus in Marion near Indianapolis.

Academic Information The faculty has 167 members (63% full-time), 40% with terminal degrees. The undergraduate student-faculty ratio is 17:1. The library holds 106,362 titles, 5,343 serial subscriptions, and 8,553 audiovisual materials. Special programs include academic remediation, services for learning-disabled students, an honors program, study abroad, advanced placement credit, accelerated degree programs, Freshman Honors College, double majors, independent study, distance learning, self-designed majors, summer session for credit, part-time degree programs (daytime, evenings, weekends, summer), adult/continuing education programs, internships, and arrangement for off-campus study with Taylor University, Council for Christian Colleges and Universities. The most frequently chosen baccalaureate fields are business/marketing, education, health professions and related sciences.
Student Body Statistics The student body totals 8,765, of whom 6,204 are undergraduates (1,036 freshmen). 63 percent are women and 37 percent are men. Students come from 42 states and territories and 17 other countries. 80 percent are from Indiana. 0.8 percent are international students.
Expenses for 2003–04 *Application fee:* $25. *Comprehensive fee:* $19,900 includes full-time tuition ($14,420) and college room and board ($5480). *College room only:* $2550. Room and board charges vary according to board plan. *Part-time tuition:* $482 per credit hour. Part-time tuition varies according to course load.
Financial Aid Forms of aid include need-based and non-need-based scholarships and part-time jobs. The priority application deadline for financial aid is March 1.
Freshman Admission IWU requires an essay, a high school transcript, a minimum 2.0 high school GPA, 1 recommendation, SAT I or ACT scores, and TOEFL scores for international students. An interview is required for some. The application deadline for regular admission is rolling.
Transfer Admission The application deadline for admission is rolling.
Entrance Difficulty IWU assesses its entrance difficulty level as moderately difficult. For the fall 2002 freshman class, 90 percent of the applicants were accepted.

For Further Information Contact Ms. Gaytha Holloway, Director of Admissions, Indiana Wesleyan University, 4201 South Washington Street, Marion, IN 46953. *Telephone:* 765-677-2138 or 800-332-6901 (toll-free). *Fax:* 765-677-2333. *E-mail:* admissions@indwes.edu. *Web site:* http://www.indwes.edu/.

INTERNATIONAL BUSINESS COLLEGE

Fort Wayne, Indiana

IBC is a coed, primarily women's, proprietary, primarily two-year college of Bradford Schools, Inc, founded in 1889, offering degrees at the associate and bachelor's levels. It has a 2-acre campus in Fort Wayne.

Academic Information The faculty has 48 members (25% full-time). The student-faculty ratio is 24:1. The library holds 2,100 titles and 100 serial subscriptions. Special programs include independent study, part-time degree programs (evenings), adult/continuing education programs, and internships.
Student Body Statistics The student body is made up of 800 undergraduates (358 freshmen). 72 percent are women and 28 percent are men.
Expenses for 2003–04 *Application fee:* $50. *Tuition:* $10,100 full-time. *College room only:* $4600.
Financial Aid Forms of aid include need-based scholarships. The priority application deadline for financial aid is March 1.
Freshman Admission IBC requires a high school transcript. The application deadline for regular admission is September 2.
Entrance Difficulty IBC assesses its entrance difficulty level as minimally difficult; moderately difficult for accounting, paralegal programs. For the fall 2002 freshman class, 97 percent of the applicants were accepted.

For Further Information Contact Mr. Steve Kinzer, School Director, International Business College, 5699 Coventry Lane, Fort Wayne, IN 46804. *Telephone:* 219-459-4513 or 800-589-6363 (toll-free). *Fax:* 219-436-1896. *Web site:* http://www.bradfordschools.com/.

ITT TECHNICAL INSTITUTE

Fort Wayne, Indiana

ITT Tech is a coed, proprietary, primarily two-year college of ITT Educational Services, Inc, founded in 1967, offering degrees at the associate and bachelor's levels.

Student Body Statistics The student body is made up of 469 undergraduates.
Expenses for 2002–03 *Application fee:* $100. *Tuition:* $347 per credit hour part-time.
Financial Aid Forms of aid include need-based scholarships and part-time jobs. The application deadline for financial aid is continuous.
Freshman Admission ITT Tech requires a high school transcript, an interview, TOEFL scores for international students, and Wonderlic aptitude test. Recommendations are recommended. The application deadline for regular admission is rolling.
Transfer Admission The application deadline for admission is rolling.

Entrance Difficulty ITT Tech assesses its entrance difficulty level as minimally difficult.

For Further Information Contact Mr. Michael D. Frantom, ITT Technical Institute, 4919 Coldwater Road, Fort Wayne, IN 46825. *Telephone:* 260-484-4107 Ext. 244 or 800-866-4488 (toll-free). *Fax:* 260-484-0860. *Web site:* http://www.itt-tech.edu/.

ITT TECHNICAL INSTITUTE

Indianapolis, Indiana

ITT Tech is a coed, proprietary, primarily two-year college of ITT Educational Services, Inc, founded in 1966, offering degrees at the associate and bachelor's levels. It has a 10-acre campus in Indianapolis.

Academic Information Special programs include distance learning.
Student Body Statistics The student body is made up of 738 undergraduates.
Expenses for 2002–03 *Application fee:* $100.
Financial Aid Forms of aid include need-based scholarships and part-time jobs. The application deadline for financial aid is continuous.
Freshman Admission ITT Tech requires a high school transcript, an interview, and Wonderlic aptitude test. Recommendations are recommended. The application deadline for regular admission is rolling.
Transfer Admission The application deadline for admission is rolling.
Entrance Difficulty ITT Tech assesses its entrance difficulty level as minimally difficult.

For Further Information Contact Ms. Martha Watson, ITT Technical Institute, 9511 Angola Court, Indianapolis, IN 46268. *Telephone:* 317-875-8640 or 800-937-4488 (toll-free). *Fax:* 317-875-8641. *Web site:* http://www.itt-tech.edu/.

ITT TECHNICAL INSTITUTE

Newburgh, Indiana

ITT Tech is a coed, proprietary, primarily two-year college of ITT Educational Services, Inc, founded in 1966, offering degrees at the associate and bachelor's levels.

Student Body Statistics The student body is made up of 357 undergraduates.
Expenses for 2002–03 *Application fee:* $100. *Tuition:* $347 per credit hour part-time.
Financial Aid Forms of aid include need-based scholarships and part-time jobs. The application deadline for financial aid is continuous.
Freshman Admission ITT Tech requires a high school transcript, an interview, and Wonderlic aptitude test. Recommendations and TOEFL scores for international students are recommended. The application deadline for regular admission is rolling.
Transfer Admission The application deadline for admission is rolling.
Entrance Difficulty ITT Tech assesses its entrance difficulty level as minimally difficult.

For Further Information Contact Mr. Jim Smolinski, Director of Recruitment, ITT Technical Institute, 10999 Stahl Road, Newburgh, IN 47630. *Telephone:* 812-858-1600 or 800-832-4488 (toll-free in-state). *Fax:* 812-858-0646. *Web site:* http://www.itt-tech.edu/.

LUTHERAN COLLEGE OF HEALTH PROFESSIONS

See University of Saint Francis

MANCHESTER COLLEGE

North Manchester, Indiana

MC is a coed, private, comprehensive institution, founded in 1889, affiliated with the Church of the Brethren, offering degrees at the associate, bachelor's, and master's levels. It has a 125-acre campus in North Manchester.

Academic Information The faculty has 93 members (72% full-time), 62% with terminal degrees. The undergraduate student-faculty ratio is 14:1. The library holds 172,822 titles, 733 serial subscriptions, and 5,188 audiovisual materials. Special programs include services for learning-disabled students, an honors program, study abroad, advanced placement credit, double majors, independent study, self-designed majors, summer session for credit, part-time degree programs, adult/continuing education programs, internships, and arrangement for off-campus study. The most frequently chosen baccalaureate fields are business/marketing, communications/communication technologies, education.
Student Body Statistics The student body totals 1,140, of whom 1,127 are undergraduates (309 freshmen). 57 percent are women and 43 percent are men. Students come from 23 states and territories and 29 other countries. 88 percent are from Indiana. 6.5 percent are international students. 24 percent of the 2002 graduating class went on to graduate and professional schools.
Expenses for 2002–03 *Application fee:* $20. *Comprehensive fee:* $22,420 includes full-time tuition ($15,980), mandatory fees ($100), and college room and board ($6340). *College room only:* $3940. Room and board charges vary according to board plan and housing facility. *Part-time tuition:* $560 per credit hour.
Financial Aid Forms of aid include need-based and non-need-based scholarships and part-time jobs. The average aided 2002–03 undergraduate received an aid package worth an estimated $15,435. The application deadline for financial aid is continuous.
Freshman Admission MC requires a high school transcript, 1 recommendation, rank in upper 50% of high school class, SAT I or ACT scores, and TOEFL scores for international students. A minimum 2.3 high school GPA and an interview are recommended. An essay, a minimum 3.0 high school GPA, and an interview are required for some. The application deadline for regular admission is rolling.
Transfer Admission The application deadline for admission is rolling.
Entrance Difficulty MC assesses its entrance difficulty level as moderately difficult. For the fall 2002 freshman class, 83 percent of the applicants were accepted.

For Further Information Contact Ms. Jolane Rohr, Director of Admissions, Manchester College, 604 East College Avenue, North Manchester, IN 46962-1225. *Telephone:* 260-982-5055 or 800-852-3648 (toll-free). *Fax:* 260-982-5239. *E-mail:* admitinfo@manchester.edu. *Web site:* http://www.manchester.edu/.

See page 304 for a narrative description.

MARIAN COLLEGE

Indianapolis, Indiana

Marian is a coed, private, Roman Catholic, comprehensive institution, founded in 1851, offering degrees at the associate, bachelor's, and master's levels. It has a 114-acre campus in Indianapolis.

Academic Information The faculty has 132 members (49% full-time). The undergraduate student-faculty ratio is 12:1. The library holds 132,000 titles, 300 serial subscriptions, and 100 audiovisual materials. Special programs include academic remediation, services for learning-disabled students, an honors program, cooperative (work-study) education, study abroad, advanced placement credit, accelerated degree programs, double majors, independent study, summer session for credit, part-time degree programs (daytime, evenings, weekends, summer), adult/continuing education programs, internships, and arrangement for off-campus study with Franklin College of Indiana, Indiana University–Purdue University at Indianapolis, University of Indianapolis, Christian Theological Seminary, Butler University. The most frequently chosen baccalaureate fields are business/marketing, education, health professions and related sciences.

Marian College (continued)

Student Body Statistics The student body totals 1,431, of whom 1,416 are undergraduates (257 freshmen). 68 percent are women and 32 percent are men. Students come from 22 states and territories and 15 other countries. 93 percent are from Indiana. 2 percent are international students. 12 percent of the 2002 graduating class went on to graduate and professional schools.
Expenses for 2002–03 *Application fee:* $20. *Comprehensive fee:* $22,160 includes full-time tuition ($16,000), mandatory fees ($560), and college room and board ($5600). Room and board charges vary according to board plan and housing facility. *Part-time tuition:* $700 per credit. *Part-time mandatory fees:* $250 per credit. Part-time tuition and fees vary according to class time and course load.
Financial Aid Forms of aid include need-based and non-need-based scholarships, athletic grants, and part-time jobs. The average aided 2002–03 undergraduate received an aid package worth an estimated $14,322. The priority application deadline for financial aid is March 1.
Freshman Admission Marian requires a high school transcript, a minimum 2.00 high school GPA, SAT I or ACT scores, and TOEFL scores for international students. The application deadline for regular admission is August 15.
Transfer Admission The application deadline for admission is August 1.
Entrance Difficulty Marian assesses its entrance difficulty level as moderately difficult. For the fall 2002 freshman class, 76 percent of the applicants were accepted.

For Further Information Contact Ms. Karen Kist, Director of Admission, Marian College, 3200 Cold Spring Road, Indianapolis, IN 46222-1997. *Telephone:* 317-955-6300 or 800-772-7264 (toll-free in-state). *Web site:* http://www.marian.edu/.

MARTIN UNIVERSITY

Indianapolis, Indiana

Martin University is a coed, private, comprehensive institution, founded in 1977, offering degrees at the bachelor's and master's levels. It has a 5-acre campus in Indianapolis.

Academic Information The faculty has 38 members (84% full-time). The undergraduate student-faculty ratio is 20:1. Special programs include academic remediation, an honors program, advanced placement credit, accelerated degree programs, double majors, independent study, self-designed majors, summer session for credit, part-time degree programs (daytime, evenings, weekends, summer), adult/continuing education programs, internships, and arrangement for off-campus study with Consortium for Urban Education (CUE).
Student Body Statistics The student body totals 615, of whom 543 are undergraduates. Students come from 1 state or territory and 6 other countries. 20 percent of the 2002 graduating class went on to graduate and professional schools.
Expenses for 2003–04 *Application fee:* $25. *Tuition:* $9750 full-time, $325 per credit part-time.
Financial Aid Forms of aid include need-based scholarships and part-time jobs. The average aided 2001–02 undergraduate received an aid package worth $12,924. The priority application deadline for financial aid is March 1.
Freshman Admission Martin University requires an essay, a high school transcript, an interview, writing sample, and TOEFL scores for international students. Wonderlic aptitude test, Wide Range Achievement Test is required for some. The application deadline for regular admission is rolling.
Transfer Admission The application deadline for admission is rolling.
Entrance Difficulty Martin University has an open admission policy.

For Further Information Contact Ms. Brenda Shaheed, Director of Enrollment Management, Martin University, PO Box 18567, 2171 Avondale Place, Indianapolis, IN 46218-3867. *Telephone:* 317-543-3237. *Fax:* 317-543-4790. *Web site:* http://www.martin.edu/.

MID-AMERICA COLLEGE OF FUNERAL SERVICE

Jeffersonville, Indiana

Mid-America College of Funeral Service is a coed, primarily men's, private, primarily two-year college, founded in 1905, offering degrees at the associate and bachelor's levels in funeral service. It has a 3-acre campus in Jeffersonville near Louisville.

Academic Information The faculty has 7 members (86% full-time). The student-faculty ratio is 13:1. The library holds 1,500 titles and 20 serial subscriptions. Special programs include academic remediation.
Student Body Statistics The student body is made up of 120 undergraduates. 45 percent are women and 55 percent are men. Students come from 6 states and territories.
Expenses for 2002–03 *Application fee:* $25. *Tuition:* $8000 full-time.
Financial Aid Forms of aid include need-based scholarships. The application deadline for financial aid is continuous.
Freshman Admission Mid-America College of Funeral Service requires a high school transcript. The application deadline for regular admission is rolling.
Entrance Difficulty Mid-America College of Funeral Service has an open admission policy. It assesses its entrance difficulty as noncompetitive for transfers.

For Further Information Contact Mr. Richard Nelson, Dean of Students, Mid-America College of Funeral Service, 3111 Hamburg Pike, Jeffersonville, IN 47130-9630. *Telephone:* 812-288-8878 or 800-221-6158 (toll-free). *E-mail:* macfs@mindspring.com. *Web site:* http://www.midamericacollege.com/.

OAKLAND CITY UNIVERSITY

Oakland City, Indiana

OCU is a coed, private, General Baptist, comprehensive institution, founded in 1885, offering degrees at the associate, bachelor's, master's, doctoral, and first professional levels. It has a 20-acre campus in Oakland City.

Academic Information The faculty has 150 members (24% full-time), 18% with terminal degrees. The undergraduate student-faculty ratio is 15:1. The library holds 75,000 titles and 350 serial subscriptions. Special programs include academic remediation, services for learning-disabled students, advanced placement credit, accelerated degree programs, summer session for credit, part-time degree programs (daytime, evenings, summer), external degree programs, and adult/continuing education programs. The most frequently chosen baccalaureate fields are business/marketing, education, philosophy, religion, and theology.
Student Body Statistics The student body totals 1,897, of whom 1,610 are undergraduates (329 freshmen). 52 percent are women and 48 percent are men. Students come from 5 states and territories. 77 percent are from Indiana.
Expenses for 2003–04 *Application fee:* $35. *Comprehensive fee:* $16,880 includes full-time tuition ($12,000), mandatory fees ($320), and college room and board ($4560). *College room only:* $1470. Full-time tuition and fees vary according to location and program. Room and board charges vary according to housing facility. *Part-time tuition:* $400 per hour. Part-time tuition varies according to location and program.
Financial Aid Forms of aid include need-based and non-need-based scholarships and part-time jobs. The priority application deadline for financial aid is March 10.
Freshman Admission OCU requires an essay, a high school transcript, a minimum 2.0 high school GPA, 1 recommendation, SAT I or ACT scores, and TOEFL scores for international students. An interview is recommended. The application deadline for regular admission is rolling.

Entrance Difficulty OCU assesses its entrance difficulty level as minimally difficult. For the fall 2002 freshman class, 100 percent of the applicants were accepted.

For Further Information Contact Mr. Buddy Harris, Director of Admissions, Oakland City University, 143 North Lucretia Street, Oakland City, IN 47660-1099. *Telephone:* 812-749-1222 or 800-737-5125 (toll-free). *Fax:* 812-749-1233. *Web site:* http://www.oak.edu/.

PROFESSIONAL CAREERS INSTITUTE

Indianapolis, Indiana

Professional Careers Institute is a coed, primarily women's, private, two-year college, offering degrees at the associate level.

Expenses for 2002–03 *Application fee:* $100. *Tuition:* $7350 full-time. *Mandatory fees:* $150 full-time.

For Further Information Contact Ms. Paulette M. Clay, Director of Admissions, Professional Careers Institute, 7302 Woodland Drive, Indianapolis, IN 46217. *Telephone:* 317-299-6001 Ext. 320. *E-mail:* lilgeneral9@hotmail.com. *Web site:* http://www.pcicareers.com/.

PURDUE UNIVERSITY

West Lafayette, Indiana

Purdue is a coed, public unit of Purdue University System, founded in 1869, offering degrees at the associate, bachelor's, master's, doctoral, and first professional levels. It has a 1,579-acre campus in West Lafayette near Indianapolis.

Academic Information The faculty has 1,924 members (97% full-time), 98% with terminal degrees. The undergraduate student-faculty ratio is 16:1. The library holds 1 million titles, 18,374 serial subscriptions, and 12,733 audiovisual materials. Special programs include services for learning-disabled students, an honors program, cooperative (work-study) education, study abroad, advanced placement credit, Freshman Honors College, double majors, independent study, distance learning, summer session for credit, part-time degree programs, adult/continuing education programs, and internships. The most frequently chosen baccalaureate fields are business/marketing, education, engineering/engineering technologies.
Student Body Statistics The student body totals 38,546, of whom 30,908 are undergraduates (6,265 freshmen). 42 percent are women and 58 percent are men. Students come from 52 states and territories and 120 other countries. 76 percent are from Indiana. 6.5 percent are international students.
Expenses for 2002–03 *Application fee:* $30. *State resident tuition:* $5228 full-time, $200 per credit hour part-time. *Nonresident tuition:* $15,908 full-time, $540 per credit hour part-time. *Mandatory fees:* $352 full-time. Full-time tuition and fees vary according to program. *College room and board:* $6340. *College room only:* $2676.
Financial Aid Forms of aid include need-based and non-need-based scholarships, athletic grants, and part-time jobs. The average aided 2002–03 undergraduate received an aid package worth an estimated $7387. The priority application deadline for financial aid is March 1.
Freshman Admission Purdue requires a high school transcript, SAT I or ACT scores, and TOEFL scores for international students. The application deadline for regular admission is rolling.
Transfer Admission The application deadline for admission is rolling.
Entrance Difficulty Purdue assesses its entrance difficulty level as moderately difficult; most difficult for engineering, aviation flight, nursing, veterinary technology, computer related, health related programs. For the fall 2002 freshman class, 76 percent of the applicants were accepted.

For Further Information Contact Director of Admissions, Purdue University, 475 Stadium Mall Drive, Schleman Hall, West Lafayette, IN 47907-2050. *Telephone:* 765-494-1776. *Fax:* 765-494-0544. *E-mail:* admissions@purdue.edu. *Web site:* http://www.purdue.edu/.

PURDUE UNIVERSITY CALUMET

Hammond, Indiana

Purdue Cal is a coed, public, comprehensive unit of Purdue University System, founded in 1951, offering degrees at the associate, bachelor's, and master's levels and postbachelor's certificates. It has a 167-acre campus in Hammond near Chicago.

Academic Information The faculty has 291 members (92% full-time), 97% with terminal degrees. The undergraduate student-faculty ratio is 21:1. The library holds 215,830 titles and 1,736 serial subscriptions. Special programs include academic remediation, services for learning-disabled students, an honors program, cooperative (work-study) education, advanced placement credit, summer session for credit, part-time degree programs (daytime, evenings, weekends, summer), adult/continuing education programs, and internships.
Student Body Statistics The student body totals 8,863, of whom 7,920 are undergraduates (1,579 freshmen). 56 percent are women and 44 percent are men. 0.8 percent are international students.
Expenses for 2003–04 *State resident tuition:* $4099 full-time, $146.40 per credit hour part-time. *Nonresident tuition:* $9570 full-time, $341.80 per credit hour part-time. *Mandatory fees:* $316 full-time, $12.20 per credit hour part-time. Full-time tuition and fees vary according to program. Part-time tuition and fees vary according to course load and program.
Financial Aid Forms of aid include need-based and non-need-based scholarships, athletic grants, and part-time jobs. The average aided 2002–03 undergraduate received an aid package worth an estimated $4638. The priority application deadline for financial aid is March 1.
Freshman Admission Purdue Cal requires a high school transcript. SAT I or ACT scores are required for some. The application deadline for regular admission is rolling.
Transfer Admission The application deadline for admission is rolling.
Entrance Difficulty Purdue Cal has an open admission policy.

For Further Information Contact Mr. Paul McGuinness, Director of Admissions, Purdue University Calumet, 173rd and Woodmar Avenue, Hammond, IN 46323-2094. *Telephone:* 219-989-2213 or 800-447-8738 (toll-free in-state). *Fax:* 219-989-2775. *E-mail:* adms@calumet.purdue.edu. *Web site:* http://www.calumet.purdue.edu/.

PURDUE UNIVERSITY NORTH CENTRAL

Westville, Indiana

Purdue University North Central is a coed, public, comprehensive unit of Purdue University System, founded in 1967, offering degrees at the associate, bachelor's, and master's levels. It has a 264-acre campus in Westville near Chicago.

Academic Information The faculty has 242 members (40% full-time), 30% with terminal degrees. The undergraduate student-faculty ratio is 18:1. The library holds 87,675 titles, 403 serial subscriptions, and 602 audiovisual materials. Special programs include academic remediation, services for learning-disabled students, an honors program, cooperative (work-study) education, study abroad, advanced placement credit, double majors, distance learning, self-designed majors, summer session for credit, part-time degree programs (daytime, evenings, summer), adult/continuing education programs, and internships. The most frequently chosen baccalaureate fields are education, liberal arts/general studies, trade and industry.
Student Body Statistics The student body totals 3,658, of whom 3,636 are undergraduates (692 freshmen). 59 percent are women and 41 percent are men. Students come from 5 states and territories. 99 percent are from Indiana. 0.1 percent are international students.
Expenses for 2002–03 *State resident tuition:* $3310 full-time, $137.90 per credit hour part-time. *Nonresident tuition:* $7735 full-time, $322.30 per credit hour part-time. *Mandatory fees:* $280 full-time, $11.65 per credit hour part-time. Full-time tuition and fees vary according to course load, location, and program. Part-time tuition and fees vary according to course load, location, and program.

Purdue University North Central (continued)

Financial Aid Forms of aid include need-based and non-need-based scholarships and part-time jobs. The average aided 2002–03 undergraduate received an aid package worth an estimated $4893. The priority application deadline for financial aid is March 1.

Freshman Admission Purdue University North Central requires a high school transcript and TOEFL scores for international students. SAT I scores and ACT scores are recommended. An essay, a minimum 2.0 high school GPA, an interview, and SAT I or ACT scores are required for some. The application deadline for regular admission is August 6.

Transfer Admission The application deadline for admission is August 1.

Entrance Difficulty Purdue University North Central assesses its entrance difficulty level as minimally difficult; moderately difficult for engineering, nursing programs. For the fall 2002 freshman class, 91 percent of the applicants were accepted.

For Further Information Contact Ms. Cathy Buckman, Director of Admissions, Purdue University North Central, 1401 South U.S. Highway 421, Westville, IN 46391. *Telephone:* 219-785-5458 or 800-872-1231 (toll-free in-state). *Fax:* 219-785-5538. *E-mail:* cbuckman@purduenc.edu. *Web site:* http://www.purduenc.edu/.

ROSE-HULMAN INSTITUTE OF TECHNOLOGY

Terre Haute, Indiana

Rose-Hulman is a coed, primarily men's, private, comprehensive institution, founded in 1874, offering degrees at the bachelor's and master's levels. It has a 130-acre campus in Terre Haute near Indianapolis.

Academic Information The faculty has 133 members (95% full-time), 98% with terminal degrees. The undergraduate student-faculty ratio is 13:1. The library holds 77,348 titles, 280 serial subscriptions, and 493 audiovisual materials. Special programs include services for learning-disabled students, an honors program, cooperative (work-study) education, study abroad, advanced placement credit, accelerated degree programs, double majors, independent study, summer session for credit, adult/continuing education programs, and arrangement for off-campus study with Indiana State University, St. Mary-of-the-Woods College. The most frequently chosen baccalaureate fields are computer/information sciences, engineering/engineering technologies, physical sciences.

Student Body Statistics The student body totals 1,804, of whom 1,642 are undergraduates (451 freshmen). 18 percent are women and 82 percent are men. Students come from 48 states and territories and 9 other countries. 49 percent are from Indiana. 0.9 percent are international students. 14 percent of the 2002 graduating class went on to graduate and professional schools.

Expenses for 2002–03 *Application fee:* $40. *Comprehensive fee:* $29,773 includes full-time tuition ($22,990), mandatory fees ($435), and college room and board ($6348). *College room only:* $3600. Full-time tuition and fees vary according to course load and student level. Room and board charges vary according to board plan. *Part-time tuition:* $654 per credit. Part-time tuition varies according to course load.

Financial Aid Forms of aid include need-based and non-need-based scholarships and part-time jobs. The average aided 2001–02 undergraduate received an aid package worth $14,471. The priority application deadline for financial aid is March 1.

Freshman Admission Rose-Hulman requires a high school transcript, 1 recommendation, SAT I or ACT scores, and TOEFL scores for international students. An essay and an interview are recommended. The application deadline for regular admission is March 1.

Entrance Difficulty Rose-Hulman assesses its entrance difficulty level as very difficult. For the fall 2002 freshman class, 65 percent of the applicants were accepted.

For Further Information Contact Mr. Charles G. Howard, Dean of Admissions/Vice President, Rose-Hulman Institute of Technology, 5500 Wabash Avenue, Terre Haute, IN 47803-3920. *Telephone:* 812-877-8213, 800-552-0725 (toll-free in-state), or 800-248-7448 (toll-free out-of-state). *Fax:* 812-877-8941. *E-mail:* admis.ofc@rose-hulman.edu. *Web site:* http://www.rose-hulman.edu/.

SAINT FRANCIS COLLEGE

See University of Saint Francis

SAINT JOSEPH'S COLLEGE

Rensselaer, Indiana

Saint Joseph's is a coed, private, Roman Catholic, comprehensive institution, founded in 1889, offering degrees at the associate, bachelor's, and master's levels. It has a 340-acre campus in Rensselaer near Chicago.

Academic Information The faculty has 78 members (69% full-time), 73% with terminal degrees. The undergraduate student-faculty ratio is 15:1. The library holds 157,481 titles, 498 serial subscriptions, and 22,416 audiovisual materials. Special programs include academic remediation, services for learning-disabled students, an honors program, study abroad, advanced placement credit, accelerated degree programs, double majors, independent study, self-designed majors, summer session for credit, part-time degree programs (daytime), and internships. The most frequently chosen baccalaureate fields are business/marketing, education, social sciences and history.

Student Body Statistics The student body totals 974, of whom 972 are undergraduates (247 freshmen). 58 percent are women and 42 percent are men. Students come from 22 states and territories. 72 percent are from Indiana. 0.2 percent are international students.

Expenses for 2003–04 *Application fee:* $25. *Comprehensive fee:* $24,250 includes full-time tuition ($17,900), mandatory fees ($160), and college room and board ($6190). *Part-time tuition:* $600 per credit.

Financial Aid Forms of aid include need-based and non-need-based scholarships, athletic grants, and part-time jobs. The average aided 2001–02 undergraduate received an aid package worth $12,500. The priority application deadline for financial aid is March 1.

Freshman Admission Saint Joseph's requires a high school transcript, a minimum 2.0 high school GPA, SAT I or ACT scores, and TOEFL scores for international students. An essay and recommendations are recommended. An interview is required for some. The application deadline for regular admission is rolling and for early decision it is October 1.

Transfer Admission The application deadline for admission is rolling.

Entrance Difficulty Saint Joseph's assesses its entrance difficulty level as moderately difficult. For the fall 2002 freshman class, 77 percent of the applicants were accepted.

For Further Information Contact Mr. Frank P. Bevec, Director of Admissions, Assistant Vice President for Enrollment Management, Saint Joseph's College, PO Box 815, Rensselaer, IN 47978-0850. *Telephone:* 219-866-6170 or 800-447-8781 (toll-free out-of-state). *Fax:* 219-866-6122. *E-mail:* admissions@saintjoe.edu. *Web site:* http://www.saintjoe.edu/.

SAINT MARY-OF-THE-WOODS COLLEGE

Saint Mary-of-the-Woods, Indiana

The Woods is a women's, private, Roman Catholic, comprehensive institution, founded in 1840, offering degrees at the associate, bachelor's, and master's levels and post-master's certificates (also offers external degree program with significant enrollment reflected in profile). It has a 67-acre campus in Saint Mary-of-the-Woods near Indianapolis.

Academic Information The faculty has 62 members (97% full-time), 69% with terminal degrees. The undergraduate student-faculty ratio is 12:1. The library holds 152,162 titles, 301 serial subscriptions, and 522 audiovisual materials. Special programs include academic remediation, study abroad, advanced placement credit, accelerated degree programs, double majors, independent study, distance learning, self-designed majors, summer session for credit, part-time degree programs (evenings, weekends, summer), external degree programs, adult/continuing education programs, internships, and arrangement for off-campus study with Indiana State University, Rose-Hulman Institute of Technology, DePauw University, Wabash College. The most frequently chosen baccalaureate fields are business/marketing, education, liberal arts/general studies.
Student Body Statistics The student body totals 1,612, of whom 1,495 are undergraduates (185 freshmen). Students come from 24 states and territories. 70 percent are from Indiana. 0.3 percent are international students. 25 percent of the 2002 graduating class went on to graduate and professional schools.
Expenses for 2002–03 *Application fee:* $30. *Comprehensive fee:* $22,379 includes full-time tuition ($15,890), mandatory fees ($480), and college room and board ($6009). *College room only:* $2350. *Part-time tuition:* $307 per hour. *Part-time mandatory fees:* $25 per term. Part-time tuition and fees vary according to course load and program.
Financial Aid Forms of aid include need-based and non-need-based scholarships and part-time jobs. The application deadline for financial aid is continuous.
Freshman Admission The Woods requires a minimum 2.0 high school GPA, 1 recommendation, and TOEFL scores for international students. An essay, a high school transcript, an interview, and SAT I or ACT scores are required for some. The application deadline for regular admission is August 15.
Transfer Admission The application deadline for admission is August 15.
Entrance Difficulty The Woods assesses its entrance difficulty level as moderately difficult. For the fall 2002 freshman class, 79 percent of the applicants were accepted.

For Further Information Contact Ms. Jessica Day, Director, Saint Mary-of-the-Woods College, Guerin Hall, Saint Mary-of-the-Woods, IN 47876. *Telephone:* 812-535-5106 or 800-926-SMWC (toll-free). *Fax:* 812-535-4900. *E-mail:* smwcadms@smwc.edu. *Web site:* http://www.smwc.edu/.

SAINT MARY'S COLLEGE

Notre Dame, Indiana

Saint Mary's is a women's, private, Roman Catholic, four-year college, founded in 1844, offering degrees at the bachelor's level. It has a 275-acre campus in Notre Dame.

Academic Information The faculty has 189 members (60% full-time). The student-faculty ratio is 11:1. The library holds 210,812 titles, 776 serial subscriptions, and 2,471 audiovisual materials. Special programs include academic remediation, services for learning-disabled students, cooperative (work-study) education, study abroad, advanced placement credit, accelerated degree programs, double majors, independent study, self-designed majors, summer session for credit, part-time degree programs (daytime), internships, and arrangement for off-campus study with University of Notre Dame, members of the Northern Indiana Consortium for Education. The most frequently chosen baccalaureate fields are business/marketing, education, social sciences and history.
Student Body Statistics The student body is made up of 1,492 undergraduates (376 freshmen). Students come from 46 states and territories and 8 other countries. 26 percent are from Indiana. 0.8 percent are international students. 18 percent of the 2002 graduating class went on to graduate and professional schools.
Expenses for 2003–04 *Application fee:* $30. *Comprehensive fee:* $29,263 includes full-time tuition ($21,624), mandatory fees ($350), and college room and board ($7289). Full-time tuition and fees vary according to program. Room and board charges vary according to housing facility. *Part-time tuition:* $855 per semester hour.
Financial Aid Forms of aid include need-based and non-need-based scholarships and part-time jobs. The average aided 2002–03 undergraduate received an aid package worth an estimated $16,507. The priority application deadline for financial aid is March 1.
Freshman Admission Saint Mary's requires an essay, a high school transcript, 1 recommendation, SAT I and SAT II or ACT scores, and TOEFL scores for international students. An interview is recommended. The application deadline for regular admission is March 1 and for early decision it is November 15.
Transfer Admission The application deadline for admission is rolling.
Entrance Difficulty Saint Mary's assesses its entrance difficulty level as moderately difficult. For the fall 2002 freshman class, 82 percent of the applicants were accepted.

For Further Information Contact Ms. Mary Pat Nolan, Director of Admission, Saint Mary's College, Notre Dame, IN 46556. *Telephone:* 574-284-4587 or 800-551-7621 (toll-free). *Fax:* 574-284-4713. *E-mail:* admission@saintmarys.edu. *Web site:* http://www.saintmarys.edu/.

See page 334 for a narrative description.

TAYLOR UNIVERSITY

Upland, Indiana

Taylor is a coed, private, interdenominational, comprehensive institution, founded in 1846, offering degrees at the associate and bachelor's levels. It has a 250-acre campus in Upland near Indianapolis.

Academic Information The faculty has 157 members (75% full-time), 64% with terminal degrees. The student-faculty ratio is 15:1. The library holds 193,343 titles, 902 serial subscriptions, and 6,653 audiovisual materials. Special programs include academic remediation, services for learning-disabled students, an honors program, cooperative (work-study) education, study abroad, advanced placement credit, double majors, independent study, distance learning, self-designed majors, summer session for credit, part-time degree programs, internships, and arrangement for off-campus study with members of the Christian College Coalition and the Christian College Consortium, Bowling Green University, Trinity Christian College. The most frequently chosen baccalaureate fields are business/marketing, computer/information sciences, education.
Student Body Statistics The student body is made up of 1,869 undergraduates (457 freshmen). 52 percent are women and 48 percent are men. Students come from 47 states and territories and 25 other countries. 31 percent are from Indiana. 1.7 percent are international students. 13 percent of the 2002 graduating class went on to graduate and professional schools.
Expenses for 2002–03 *Application fee:* $25. *Comprehensive fee:* $22,620 includes full-time tuition ($17,270), mandatory fees ($220), and college room and board ($5130). *College room only:* $2490. Room and board charges vary according to housing facility. *Part-time tuition:* $619 per credit. *Part-time mandatory fees:* $30 per term.
Financial Aid Forms of aid include need-based and non-need-based scholarships, athletic grants, and part-time jobs. The average aided 2002–03 undergraduate received an aid package worth an estimated $12,425. The application deadline for financial aid is March 10.
Freshman Admission Taylor requires an essay, a high school transcript, 2 recommendations, an interview, SAT I or ACT scores, and TOEFL scores for international students. A minimum 2.8 high school GPA is recommended. The application deadline for regular admission is February 15 and for early action it is December 15.
Transfer Admission The application deadline for admission is rolling.

Taylor University (continued)

Entrance Difficulty Taylor assesses its entrance difficulty level as very difficult. For the fall 2002 freshman class, 78 percent of the applicants were accepted.

For Further Information Contact Mr. Stephen R. Mortland, Director of Admissions, Taylor University, 236 West Reade Avenue, Upland, IN 46989-1001. *Telephone:* 765-998-5134 or 800-882-3456 (toll-free). *Fax:* 765-998-4925. *E-mail:* admissions_u@tayloru.edu. *Web site:* http://www.tayloru.edu/.

TAYLOR UNIVERSITY, FORT WAYNE CAMPUS

Fort Wayne, Indiana

Taylor Fort Wayne is a coed, private, interdenominational, comprehensive unit of Taylor University, founded in 1992, offering degrees at the associate, bachelor's, and master's levels. It has a 32-acre campus in Fort Wayne.

Academic Information The faculty has 53 members (57% full-time), 45% with terminal degrees. The undergraduate student-faculty ratio is 14:1. The library holds 78,662 titles, 670 serial subscriptions, and 4,699 audiovisual materials. Special programs include academic remediation, services for learning-disabled students, cooperative (work-study) education, study abroad, advanced placement credit, accelerated degree programs, double majors, independent study, distance learning, self-designed majors, summer session for credit, part-time degree programs (daytime, evenings, weekends, summer), internships, and arrangement for off-campus study with Christian College Coalition, Christian College Consortium, Wesleyan Urban Coalition. The most frequently chosen baccalaureate fields are communications/communication technologies, philosophy, religion, and theology, psychology.
Student Body Statistics The student body is made up of 633 undergraduates (142 freshmen). 63 percent are women and 37 percent are men. Students come from 26 states and territories and 2 other countries. 75 percent are from Indiana. 0.6 percent are international students. 11 percent of the 2002 graduating class went on to graduate and professional schools.
Expenses for 2002–03 *Application fee:* $20. *Comprehensive fee:* $19,610 includes full-time tuition ($14,880), mandatory fees ($110), and college room and board ($4620). *College room only:* $1980. Room and board charges vary according to board plan. *Part-time tuition:* $175 per hour. *Part-time mandatory fees:* $25 per hour. Part-time tuition and fees vary according to course load.
Financial Aid Forms of aid include need-based and non-need-based scholarships, athletic grants, and part-time jobs. The average aided 2001–02 undergraduate received an aid package worth $14,469. The priority application deadline for financial aid is March 10.
Freshman Admission Taylor Fort Wayne requires an essay, a high school transcript, a minimum 2.0 high school GPA, 2 recommendations, SAT I or ACT scores, and TOEFL scores for international students. A minimum 3.0 high school GPA and an interview are recommended. The application deadline for regular admission is rolling.
Transfer Admission The application deadline for admission is rolling.
Entrance Difficulty Taylor Fort Wayne assesses its entrance difficulty level as moderately difficult. For the fall 2002 freshman class, 85 percent of the applicants were accepted.

For Further Information Contact Mr. Leo Gonot, Director of Admissions, Taylor University, Fort Wayne Campus, 1025 West Rudisill Boulevard, Fort Wayne, IN 46807-2197. *Telephone:* 219-744-8689 or 800-233-3922 (toll-free). *Fax:* 219-744-8660. *E-mail:* admissions_f@tayloru.edu. *Web site:* http://www.tayloru.edu/fw/.

TRI-STATE UNIVERSITY

Angola, Indiana

Tri-State is a coed, private, comprehensive institution, founded in 1884, offering degrees at the associate, bachelor's, and master's levels. It has a 400-acre campus in Angola.

Academic Information The faculty has 94 members (68% full-time), 47% with terminal degrees. The undergraduate student-faculty ratio is 15:1. The library holds 82,474 titles, 336 serial subscriptions, and 625 audiovisual materials. Special programs include academic remediation, cooperative (work-study) education, study abroad, advanced placement credit, double majors, distance learning, summer session for credit, part-time degree programs (daytime, evenings, summer), adult/continuing education programs, and internships. The most frequently chosen baccalaureate fields are business/marketing, education, engineering/engineering technologies.
Student Body Statistics The student body is made up of 1,267 undergraduates (286 freshmen). 36 percent are women and 64 percent are men. Students come from 22 states and territories and 20 other countries. 60 percent are from Indiana. 2.8 percent are international students. 5 percent of the 2002 graduating class went on to graduate and professional schools.
Expenses for 2002–03 *Application fee:* $20. *Comprehensive fee:* $22,160 includes full-time tuition ($16,910) and college room and board ($5250). *Part-time tuition:* $528 per semester hour.
Financial Aid Forms of aid include need-based and non-need-based scholarships, athletic grants, and part-time jobs. The average aided 2002–03 undergraduate received an aid package worth an estimated $11,128. The priority application deadline for financial aid is March 1.
Freshman Admission Tri-State requires a high school transcript, a minimum 2.0 high school GPA, and SAT I or ACT scores. Recommendations, an interview, and TOEFL scores for international students are recommended. The application deadline for regular admission is June 1.
Transfer Admission The application deadline for admission is August 1.
Entrance Difficulty Tri-State assesses its entrance difficulty level as moderately difficult. For the fall 2002 freshman class, 74 percent of the applicants were accepted.

For Further Information Contact Ms. Sara Yarian, Admissions Officer, Tri-State University, Angola, IN 46703. *Telephone:* 260-665-4365 or 800-347-4TSU (toll-free). *Fax:* 260-665-4578. *E-mail:* admit@tristate.edu. *Web site:* http://www.tristate.edu/.

UNIVERSITY OF EVANSVILLE

Evansville, Indiana

UE is a coed, private, comprehensive institution, founded in 1854, affiliated with the United Methodist Church, offering degrees at the associate, bachelor's, and master's levels. It has a 75-acre campus in Evansville.

Academic Information The faculty has 168 members (99% full-time). The undergraduate student-faculty ratio is 13:1. The library holds 275,980 titles, 1,320 serial subscriptions, and 10,094 audiovisual materials. Special programs include services for learning-disabled students, an honors program, cooperative (work-study) education, study abroad, advanced placement credit, accelerated degree programs, Freshman Honors College, ESL programs, double majors, independent study, distance learning, self-designed majors, summer session for credit, part-time degree programs (daytime), external degree programs, adult/continuing education programs, and internships. The most frequently chosen baccalaureate fields are business/marketing, education, health professions and related sciences.
Student Body Statistics The student body totals 2,668, of whom 2,600 are undergraduates (603 freshmen). 60 percent are women and 40 percent are men. Students come from 47 states and territories and 44 other countries. 66 percent are from Indiana. 5.5 percent are international students. 16 percent of the 2002 graduating class went on to graduate and professional schools.
Expenses for 2002–03 *Application fee:* $35. *Comprehensive fee:* $23,650 includes full-time tuition ($17,900), mandatory fees ($330), and college

room and board ($5420). *College room only:* $2480. Room and board charges vary according to board plan and housing facility. *Part-time tuition:* $500 per hour. *Part-time mandatory fees:* $30 per term. Part-time tuition and fees vary according to course load.
Financial Aid Forms of aid include need-based and non-need-based scholarships, athletic grants, and part-time jobs. The average aided 2002–03 undergraduate received an aid package worth an estimated $16,197. The priority application deadline for financial aid is March 1.
Freshman Admission UE requires an essay, a high school transcript, a minimum 2.0 high school GPA, 1 recommendation, SAT I or ACT scores, and TOEFL scores for international students. A minimum 3.0 high school GPA and an interview are recommended. An interview is required for some. The application deadline for regular admission is February 15 and for early action it is December 1.
Transfer Admission The application deadline for admission is July 1.
Entrance Difficulty UE assesses its entrance difficulty level as moderately difficult; very difficult for engineering, physical therapy programs. For the fall 2002 freshman class, 85 percent of the applicants were accepted.

For Further Information Contact Dr. Tom Bear, Dean of Admission, University of Evansville, 1800 Lincoln Avenue, Evansville, IN 47722-0002. *Telephone:* 812-479-2683 or 800-423-8633 (toll-free out-of-state). *Fax:* 812-474-4076. *E-mail:* admission@evansville.edu. *Web site:* http://www.evansville.edu/.

UNIVERSITY OF INDIANAPOLIS

Indianapolis, Indiana

U of I is a coed, private, comprehensive institution, founded in 1902, affiliated with the United Methodist Church, offering degrees at the associate, bachelor's, master's, and doctoral levels. It has a 60-acre campus in Indianapolis.

Academic Information The faculty has 358 members (45% full-time), 59% with terminal degrees. The undergraduate student-faculty ratio is 14:1. The library holds 173,363 titles, 1,015 serial subscriptions, and 5,324 audiovisual materials. Special programs include academic remediation, services for learning-disabled students, an honors program, cooperative (work-study) education, study abroad, advanced placement credit, accelerated degree programs, ESL programs, double majors, independent study, distance learning, self-designed majors, summer session for credit, part-time degree programs (evenings), adult/continuing education programs, internships, and arrangement for off-campus study with 7 members of the Consortium for Urban Education, 10 members of the May Term Consortium. The most frequently chosen baccalaureate fields are business/marketing, education, psychology.
Student Body Statistics The student body totals 3,776, of whom 2,868 are undergraduates (600 freshmen). 67 percent are women and 33 percent are men. Students come from 31 states and territories and 55 other countries. 92 percent are from Indiana. 4.6 percent are international students. 25 percent of the 2002 graduating class went on to graduate and professional schools.
Expenses for 2002–03 *Application fee:* $20. *Comprehensive fee:* $21,480 includes full-time tuition ($15,820) and college room and board ($5660). Full-time tuition varies according to program. Room and board charges vary according to board plan and housing facility. *Part-time tuition:* $660 per credit hour. Part-time tuition varies according to class time.
Financial Aid Forms of aid include need-based and non-need-based scholarships, athletic grants, and part-time jobs. The average aided 2001–02 undergraduate received an aid package worth $13,688. The priority application deadline for financial aid is March 1.
Freshman Admission U of I requires a high school transcript, a minimum 2.0 high school GPA, SAT I or ACT scores, and TOEFL scores for international students. An interview is required for some. The application deadline for regular admission is rolling.
Transfer Admission The application deadline for admission is rolling.
Entrance Difficulty U of I assesses its entrance difficulty level as moderately difficult. For the fall 2002 freshman class, 80 percent of the applicants were accepted.

For Further Information Contact Mr. Ronald W. Wilks, Director of Admissions, University of Indianapolis, 1400 East Hanna Avenue, Indianapolis, IN 46227-3697. *Telephone:* 317-788-3216 or 800-232-8634 Ext. 3216 (toll-free). *Fax:* 317-778-3300. *E-mail:* admissions@uindy.edu. *Web site:* http://www.uindy.edu/.

UNIVERSITY OF NOTRE DAME

Notre Dame, Indiana

Notre Dame is a coed, private, Roman Catholic university, founded in 1842, offering degrees at the bachelor's, master's, doctoral, and first professional levels. It has a 1,250-acre campus in Notre Dame.

Academic Information The faculty has 1,171 members (65% full-time), 87% with terminal degrees. The library holds 3 million titles, 19,232 serial subscriptions, and 23,497 audiovisual materials. Special programs include services for learning-disabled students, an honors program, cooperative (work-study) education, study abroad, advanced placement credit, accelerated degree programs, double majors, independent study, distance learning, self-designed majors, summer session for credit, internships, and arrangement for off-campus study with Saint Mary's College (IN), Xavier University of Louisiana, Clark Atlanta University, St. Mary's University of San Antonio. The most frequently chosen baccalaureate fields are business/marketing, health professions and related sciences, social sciences and history.
Student Body Statistics The student body totals 11,311, of whom 8,261 are undergraduates (1,946 freshmen). 47 percent are women and 53 percent are men. Students come from 54 states and territories and 68 other countries. 12 percent are from Indiana. 3.2 percent are international students. 32 percent of the 2002 graduating class went on to graduate and professional schools.
Expenses for 2002–03 *Application fee:* $50. *Comprehensive fee:* $32,362 includes full-time tuition ($25,510), mandatory fees ($342), and college room and board ($6510). Room and board charges vary according to board plan and housing facility. *Part-time tuition:* $1063 per credit.
Financial Aid Forms of aid include need-based and non-need-based scholarships, athletic grants, and part-time jobs. The average aided 2002–03 undergraduate received an aid package worth an estimated $23,432. The application deadline for financial aid is February 15.
Freshman Admission Notre Dame requires an essay, a high school transcript, 1 recommendation, SAT I or ACT scores, and TOEFL scores for international students. The application deadline for regular admission is January 9 and for early action it is November 1.
Transfer Admission The application deadline for admission is April 15.
Entrance Difficulty Notre Dame assesses its entrance difficulty level as most difficult. For the fall 2002 freshman class, 34 percent of the applicants were accepted.

For Further Information Contact Mr. Daniel J. Saracino, Assistant Provost for Enrollment, University of Notre Dame, 220 Main Building, Notre Dame, IN 46556-5612. *Telephone:* 574-631-7505. *Fax:* 574-631-8865. *E-mail:* admissions.admissio.1@nd.edu. *Web site:* http://www.nd.edu/.

UNIVERSITY OF SAINT FRANCIS

Fort Wayne, Indiana

University of Saint Francis is a coed, private, Roman Catholic, comprehensive institution, founded in 1890, offering degrees at the associate, bachelor's, and master's levels and postbachelor's certificates. It has a 73-acre campus in Fort Wayne.

Academic Information The faculty has 193 members (55% full-time), 31% with terminal degrees. The undergraduate student-faculty ratio is 11:1. The library holds 47,877 titles and 449 serial subscriptions. Special programs include academic remediation, services for learning-disabled students, an honors program, cooperative (work-study) education, study

University of Saint Francis (continued)

abroad, advanced placement credit, Freshman Honors College, double majors, independent study, distance learning, summer session for credit, part-time degree programs (daytime, evenings, weekends, summer), adult/continuing education programs, and internships. The most frequently chosen baccalaureate fields are education, business/marketing, health professions and related sciences.

Student Body Statistics The student body totals 1,709, of whom 1,515 are undergraduates (269 freshmen). 68 percent are women and 32 percent are men. Students come from 10 states and territories and 15 other countries. 92 percent are from Indiana. 13 percent of the 2002 graduating class went on to graduate and professional schools.

Expenses for 2002–03 *Application fee:* $20. *Comprehensive fee:* $19,800 includes full-time tuition ($14,000), mandatory fees ($560), and college room and board ($5240). *College room only:* $2090. Full-time tuition and fees vary according to class time. *Part-time tuition:* $440 per semester hour. *Part-time mandatory fees:* $11 per semester hour, $75 per term. Part-time tuition and fees vary according to class time and course load.

Financial Aid Forms of aid include need-based and non-need-based scholarships, athletic grants, and part-time jobs. The average aided 2001–02 undergraduate received an aid package worth $10,901. The priority application deadline for financial aid is March 1.

Freshman Admission University of Saint Francis requires a high school transcript and TOEFL scores for international students. An essay, a minimum 2.0 high school GPA, and SAT I or ACT scores are recommended. Recommendations and an interview are required for some. The application deadline for regular admission is rolling.

Transfer Admission The application deadline for admission is rolling.

Entrance Difficulty University of Saint Francis assesses its entrance difficulty level as moderately difficult. For the fall 2002 freshman class, 75 percent of the applicants were accepted.

For Further Information Contact Mr. Ron Schumacher, Vice President for Enrollment Management, University of Saint Francis, 2701 Spring Street, Fort Wayne, IN 46808. *Telephone:* 260-434-3279 or 800-729-4732 (toll-free). *E-mail:* admiss@sfc.edu. *Web site:* http://www.sf.edu/.

UNIVERSITY OF SOUTHERN INDIANA

Evansville, Indiana

USI is a coed, public, comprehensive unit of Indiana Commission for Higher Education, founded in 1965, offering degrees at the associate, bachelor's, and master's levels and postbachelor's certificates. It has a 300-acre campus in Evansville.

Academic Information The faculty has 559 members (51% full-time), 40% with terminal degrees. The undergraduate student-faculty ratio is 18:1. The library holds 234,406 titles, 3,035 serial subscriptions, and 7,924 audiovisual materials. Special programs include academic remediation, services for learning-disabled students, an honors program, cooperative (work-study) education, study abroad, advanced placement credit, ESL programs, double majors, independent study, distance learning, summer session for credit, part-time degree programs (daytime, evenings, weekends, summer), adult/continuing education programs, and internships. The most frequently chosen baccalaureate fields are business/marketing, education, health professions and related sciences.

Student Body Statistics The student body totals 9,675, of whom 8,998 are undergraduates (2,032 freshmen). 60 percent are women and 40 percent are men. Students come from 32 states and territories and 33 other countries. 90 percent are from Indiana. 0.5 percent are international students.

Expenses for 2002–03 *Application fee:* $25. *State resident tuition:* $3390 full-time, $113 per semester hour part-time. *Nonresident tuition:* $8288 full-time, $276.25 per semester hour part-time. *Mandatory fees:* $135 full-time, $22.75 per term part-time. Full-time tuition and fees vary according to course load and reciprocity agreements. Part-time tuition and fees vary according to course load and reciprocity agreements. *College room and board:* $4940. *College room only:* $2640. Room and board charges vary according to board plan and housing facility.

Financial Aid Forms of aid include need-based and non-need-based scholarships, athletic grants, and part-time jobs. The average aided 2002–03 undergraduate received an aid package worth an estimated $5658. The application deadline for financial aid is March 1.

Freshman Admission USI requires a high school transcript, SAT I or ACT scores, and TOEFL scores for international students. An essay and a minimum 2.0 high school GPA are recommended. An interview is required for some. The application deadline for regular admission is August 15.

Transfer Admission The application deadline for admission is August 15.

Entrance Difficulty USI assesses its entrance difficulty level as noncompetitive; minimally difficult for transfers; moderately difficult for allied health, social work programs. For the fall 2002 freshman class, 94 percent of the applicants were accepted.

For Further Information Contact Mr. Eric Otto, Director of Admission, University of Southern Indiana, 8600 University Boulevard, Evansville, IN 47712-3590. *Telephone:* 812-464-1765 or 800-467-1965 (toll-free). *Fax:* 812-465-7154. *E-mail:* enroll@usi.edu. *Web site:* http://www.usi.edu/.

VALPARAISO UNIVERSITY

Valparaiso, Indiana

Valpo is a coed, private, comprehensive institution, founded in 1859, affiliated with the Lutheran Church, offering degrees at the associate, bachelor's, master's, and first professional levels and post-master's and postbachelor's certificates. It has a 310-acre campus in Valparaiso near Chicago.

Academic Information The faculty has 328 members (69% full-time), 71% with terminal degrees. The undergraduate student-faculty ratio is 13:1. The library holds 521,907 titles, 5,282 serial subscriptions, and 13,413 audiovisual materials. Special programs include an honors program, cooperative (work-study) education, study abroad, advanced placement credit, accelerated degree programs, Freshman Honors College, ESL programs, double majors, independent study, distance learning, self-designed majors, summer session for credit, part-time degree programs (daytime, evenings, summer), adult/continuing education programs, internships, and arrangement for off-campus study with Associated Colleges of the Midwest. The most frequently chosen baccalaureate fields are business/marketing, education, engineering/engineering technologies.

Student Body Statistics The student body totals 3,661, of whom 2,910 are undergraduates (717 freshmen). 53 percent are women and 47 percent are men. Students come from 49 states and territories and 37 other countries. 34 percent are from Indiana. 2.5 percent are international students. 23 percent of the 2002 graduating class went on to graduate and professional schools.

Expenses for 2002–03 *Application fee:* $30. *Comprehensive fee:* $24,762 includes full-time tuition ($19,000), mandatory fees ($632), and college room and board ($5130). *College room only:* $3280. *Part-time tuition:* $810 per credit. *Part-time mandatory fees:* $50 per term. Part-time tuition and fees vary according to course load.

Financial Aid Forms of aid include need-based and non-need-based scholarships, athletic grants, and part-time jobs. The average aided 2002–03 undergraduate received an aid package worth an estimated $16,448. The priority application deadline for financial aid is March 1.

Freshman Admission Valpo requires a high school transcript, SAT I or ACT scores, and TOEFL scores for international students. An essay and 2 recommendations are recommended. An interview is required for some. The application deadline for regular admission is August 15 and for early action it is November 1.

Transfer Admission The application deadline for admission is rolling.

Entrance Difficulty Valpo assesses its entrance difficulty level as moderately difficult. For the fall 2002 freshman class, 91 percent of the applicants were accepted.

For Further Information Contact Ms. Karen Foust, Director of Admissions, Valparaiso University, Kretzmann Hall, 1700 Chapel Drive, Valparaiso, IN 46383-6493. *Telephone:* 219-464-5011 or 888-GO-VALPO (toll-free out-of-state). *Fax:* 219-464-6898. *E-mail:* undergrad.admissions@valpo.edu. *Web site:* http://www.valpo.edu/.

WABASH COLLEGE

Crawfordsville, Indiana

Wabash is a men's, private, four-year college, founded in 1832, offering degrees at the bachelor's level. It has a 50-acre campus in Crawfordsville near Indianapolis.

Academic Information The faculty has 83 members (99% full-time), 100% with terminal degrees. The student-faculty ratio is 11:1. The library holds 420,906 titles, 1,634 serial subscriptions, and 10,557 audiovisual materials. Special programs include services for learning-disabled students, cooperative (work-study) education, study abroad, advanced placement credit, accelerated degree programs, double majors, independent study, internships, and arrangement for off-campus study with members of the Great Lakes Colleges Association. The most frequently chosen baccalaureate fields are English, biological/life sciences, social sciences and history.
Student Body Statistics The student body is made up of 912 undergraduates (270 freshmen). Students come from 36 states and territories and 13 other countries. 74 percent are from Indiana. 3.3 percent are international students. 40 percent of the 2002 graduating class went on to graduate and professional schools.
Expenses for 2002–03 *Application fee:* $30. *Comprehensive fee:* $26,602 includes full-time tuition ($19,837), mandatory fees ($368), and college room and board ($6397). *College room only:* $2367. Room and board charges vary according to board plan and housing facility. *Part-time tuition:* $3306 per course. Part-time tuition varies according to course load.
Financial Aid Forms of aid include need-based and non-need-based scholarships and part-time jobs. The average aided 2001–02 undergraduate received an aid package worth $18,585. The application deadline for financial aid is March 1 with a priority deadline of February 15.
Freshman Admission Wabash requires an essay, a high school transcript, a minimum 2.0 high school GPA, 1 recommendation, SAT I or ACT scores, and TOEFL scores for international students. A minimum 3.0 high school GPA and an interview are recommended. The application deadline for regular admission is March 15; for early decision it is November 15; and for early action it is December 15.
Transfer Admission The application deadline for admission is March 15.
Entrance Difficulty Wabash assesses its entrance difficulty level as moderately difficult. For the fall 2002 freshman class, 50 percent of the applicants were accepted.

For Further Information Contact Mr. Steve Klein, Director of Admissions, Wabash College, PO Box 362, Crawfordsville, IN 47933-0352. *Telephone:* 765-361-6225 or 800-345-5385 (toll-free). *Fax:* 765-361-6437. *E-mail:* admissions@wabash.edu. *Web site:* http://www.wabash.edu/.

Iowa

AIB COLLEGE OF BUSINESS

Des Moines, Iowa

AIB is a coed, private, two-year college, founded in 1921, offering degrees at the associate level. It has a 20-acre campus in Des Moines.

Academic Information The faculty has 64 members (36% full-time). The library holds 5,400 titles and 185 serial subscriptions. Special programs include academic remediation, accelerated degree programs, double majors, summer session for credit, part-time degree programs (daytime, evenings, summer), adult/continuing education programs, and internships.
Student Body Statistics The student body is made up of 892 undergraduates (352 freshmen). 69 percent are women and 31 percent are men. Students come from 5 states and territories. 95 percent are from Iowa.
Expenses for 2003–04 *Application fee:* $25. *Tuition:* $8100 full-time, $225 per credit hour part-time. *Mandatory fees:* $81 full-time, $81 per year part-time. Full-time tuition and fees vary according to class time, course load, and program. Part-time tuition and fees vary according to class time, course load, and program. *College room only:* $2520. Room charges vary according to housing facility.
Financial Aid Forms of aid include need-based scholarships and part-time jobs. The priority application deadline for financial aid is April 1.
Freshman Admission AIB requires a high school transcript and TOEFL scores for international students. An interview and ACT scores are recommended. The application deadline for regular admission is rolling.
Transfer Admission The application deadline for admission is rolling.
Entrance Difficulty AIB assesses its entrance difficulty level as minimally difficult; moderately difficult for Realtime Reporting program. For the fall 2002 freshman class, 99 percent of the applicants were accepted.

For Further Information Contact Ms. Gail Cline, Director of Admissions, AIB College of Business, Keith Fenton Administration Building, 2500 Fleur Drive, Des Moines, IA 50321-1799. *Telephone:* 515-244-4221 Ext. 5634 or 800-444-1921 (toll-free). *Fax:* 515-244-6773. *E-mail:* clineg@aib.edu. *Web site:* http://www.aib.edu/.

ALLEN COLLEGE

Waterloo, Iowa

Allen College is a coed, primarily women's, private, comprehensive institution, founded in 1989, offering degrees at the associate, bachelor's, and master's levels (liberal arts and general education courses are taken at either University of North Iowa or Wartburg College). It has a 20-acre campus in Waterloo.

Academic Information The faculty has 17 members (59% full-time), 18% with terminal degrees. The undergraduate student-faculty ratio is 22:1. The library holds 2,797 titles, 184 serial subscriptions, and 421 audiovisual materials. Special programs include advanced placement credit, independent study, distance learning, part-time degree programs (daytime, evenings), internships, and arrangement for off-campus study. The most frequently chosen baccalaureate field is health professions and related sciences.
Student Body Statistics The student body totals 273, of whom 238 are undergraduates (27 freshmen). 97 percent are women and 3 percent are men. Students come from 2 states and territories. 99 percent are from Iowa. 13.7 percent of the 2002 graduating class went on to graduate and professional schools.
Expenses for 2003–04 *Application fee:* $20. *One-time mandatory fee:* $300. *Comprehensive fee:* $15,468 includes full-time tuition ($9324), mandatory fees ($1214), and college room and board ($4930). *College room only:* $2465. Full-time tuition and fees vary according to course load, location, program, and student level. Room and board charges vary according to board plan and housing facility. *Part-time tuition:* $356 per credit hour. *Part-time mandatory fees:* $25 per credit hour, $185 per term. Part-time tuition and fees vary according to program.
Financial Aid Forms of aid include need-based and non-need-based scholarships and part-time jobs. The average aided 2001–02 undergraduate received an aid package worth $8246. The application deadline for financial aid is continuous.
Freshman Admission Allen College requires an essay, a high school transcript, 1 recommendation, SAT I and SAT II or ACT scores, and TOEFL scores for international students. A minimum 2.3 high school GPA is recommended. An interview is required for some. The application deadline for regular admission is August 1.
Transfer Admission The application deadline for admission is August 1.
Entrance Difficulty Allen College assesses its entrance difficulty level as moderately difficult. For the fall 2002 freshman class, 40 percent of the applicants were accepted.

For Further Information Contact Ms. Lois Hagedorn, Student Services Assistant, Allen College, Barrett Forum, 1825 Logan Avenue, Waterloo, IA 50703. *Telephone:* 319-226-2002. *Fax:* 319-226-2051. *E-mail:* hagedole@ihs.org. *Web site:* http://www.allencollege.edu/.

BRIAR CLIFF UNIVERSITY

Sioux City, Iowa

Briar Cliff is a coed, private, Roman Catholic, comprehensive institution, founded in 1930, offering degrees at the associate, bachelor's, and master's levels. It has a 70-acre campus in Sioux City.

Academic Information The faculty has 88 members (59% full-time), 56% with terminal degrees. The undergraduate student-faculty ratio is 12:1. The library holds 83,737 titles, 6,366 serial subscriptions, and 9,791 audiovisual materials. Special programs include academic remediation, services for learning-disabled students, advanced placement credit, accelerated degree programs, ESL programs, double majors, independent study, distance learning, self-designed majors, summer session for credit, part-time degree programs (daytime, evenings, weekends, summer), adult/continuing education programs, internships, and arrangement for off-campus study with Colleges of Mid-America. The most frequently chosen baccalaureate fields are business/marketing, health professions and related sciences, protective services/public administration.

Student Body Statistics The student body is made up of 973 undergraduates (248 freshmen). 59 percent are women and 41 percent are men. Students come from 27 states and territories and 3 other countries. 70 percent are from Iowa. 0.4 percent are international students.

Expenses for 2002–03 *Application fee:* $20. *Comprehensive fee:* $19,491 includes full-time tuition ($14,220), mandatory fees ($360), and college room and board ($4911). *College room only:* $2433. Room and board charges vary according to board plan and housing facility. *Part-time tuition:* $532 per hour. *Part-time mandatory fees:* $390 per year. Part-time tuition and fees vary according to class time and course load.

Financial Aid Forms of aid include need-based and non-need-based scholarships and part-time jobs. The average aided 2001–02 undergraduate received an aid package worth $15,950. The application deadline for financial aid is March 15.

Freshman Admission Briar Cliff requires a high school transcript, a minimum 2.0 high school GPA, minimum ACT score of 18, and SAT I or ACT scores. An essay and TOEFL scores for international students are recommended. 3 recommendations and an interview are required for some. The application deadline for regular admission is rolling.

Transfer Admission The application deadline for admission is rolling.

Entrance Difficulty Briar Cliff assesses its entrance difficulty level as moderately difficult. For the fall 2002 freshman class, 81 percent of the applicants were accepted.

For Further Information Contact Ms. Tammy Namminga, Applications Specialist, Briar Cliff University, 3303 Rebecca Street, Sioux City, IA 51106. *Telephone:* 712-279-5200 Ext. 1628 or 800-662-3303 Ext. 5200 (toll-free). *Fax:* 712-279-1632. *E-mail:* admissions@briarcliff.edu. *Web site:* http://www.briarcliff.edu/.

BUENA VISTA UNIVERSITY

Storm Lake, Iowa

BVU is a coed, private, comprehensive institution, founded in 1891, affiliated with the Presbyterian Church (U.S.A.), offering degrees at the bachelor's and master's levels. It has a 60-acre campus in Storm Lake.

Academic Information The faculty has 112 members (71% full-time), 56% with terminal degrees. The undergraduate student-faculty ratio is 16:1. The library holds 153,084 titles, 698 serial subscriptions, and 4,158 audiovisual materials. Special programs include academic remediation, services for learning-disabled students, an honors program, study abroad, advanced placement credit, Freshman Honors College, ESL programs, double majors, independent study, distance learning, self-designed majors, summer session for credit, part-time degree programs, adult/continuing education programs, internships, and arrangement for off-campus study with Washington University in St. Louis. The most frequently chosen baccalaureate fields are education, communications/communication technologies, social sciences and history.

Student Body Statistics The student body totals 1,345, of whom 1,267 are undergraduates (358 freshmen). 52 percent are women and 48 percent are men. Students come from 22 states and territories and 4 other countries. 84 percent are from Iowa. 0.8 percent are international students. 15 percent of the 2002 graduating class went on to graduate and professional schools.

Expenses for 2002–03 *Application fee:* $0. *Comprehensive fee:* $23,968 includes full-time tuition ($18,738) and college room and board ($5230). *Part-time tuition:* $630 per semester hour.

Financial Aid Forms of aid include need-based and non-need-based scholarships and part-time jobs. The average aided 2002–03 undergraduate received an aid package worth an estimated $18,074. The priority application deadline for financial aid is June 1.

Freshman Admission BVU requires a high school transcript, recommendations, SAT I or ACT scores, and TOEFL scores for international students. A minimum 3.0 high school GPA is recommended. An essay and an interview are required for some. The application deadline for regular admission is June 1.

Transfer Admission The application deadline for admission is June 1.

Entrance Difficulty BVU assesses its entrance difficulty level as moderately difficult. For the fall 2002 freshman class, 84 percent of the applicants were accepted.

For Further Information Contact Ms. Louise Cummings-Simmons, Director of Admissions, Buena Vista University, 610 West Fourth Street, Storm Lake, IA 50588. *Telephone:* 712-749-2235 or 800-383-9600 (toll-free). *Fax:* 712-749-2037. *E-mail:* admissions@bvu.edu. *Web site:* http://www.bvu.edu/.

CENTRAL COLLEGE

Pella, Iowa

Central is a coed, private, four-year college, founded in 1853, affiliated with the Reformed Church in America, offering degrees at the bachelor's level. It has a 133-acre campus in Pella near Des Moines.

Academic Information The faculty has 143 members (64% full-time), 73% with terminal degrees. The student-faculty ratio is 13:1. The library holds 220,526 titles, 1,161 serial subscriptions, and 13,160 audiovisual materials. Special programs include academic remediation, services for learning-disabled students, an honors program, study abroad, double majors, independent study, self-designed majors, summer session for credit, part-time degree programs (daytime, evenings), internships, and arrangement for off-campus study. The most frequently chosen baccalaureate fields are business/marketing, education, parks and recreation.

Student Body Statistics The student body is made up of 1,659 undergraduates (425 freshmen). 57 percent are women and 43 percent are men. Students come from 36 states and territories and 14 other countries. 83 percent are from Iowa. 1 percent are international students. 18 percent of the 2002 graduating class went on to graduate and professional schools.

Expenses for 2002–03 *Application fee:* $25. *Comprehensive fee:* $22,552 includes full-time tuition ($16,612), mandatory fees ($144), and college room and board ($5796). *College room only:* $2842. Room and board charges vary according to board plan. *Part-time tuition:* $576 per credit hour. *Part-time mandatory fees:* $144 per year. Part-time tuition and fees vary according to course load.

Financial Aid Forms of aid include need-based and non-need-based scholarships and part-time jobs. The average aided 2002–03 undergraduate received an aid package worth an estimated $15,658. The priority application deadline for financial aid is March 1.

Freshman Admission Central requires a high school transcript, SAT I or ACT scores, and TOEFL scores for international students. A minimum 2.0 high school GPA and an interview are recommended. An essay, 3 recommendations, and an interview are required for some. The application deadline for regular admission is rolling.

Transfer Admission The application deadline for admission is rolling.

Entrance Difficulty Central assesses its entrance difficulty level as moderately difficult. For the fall 2002 freshman class, 86 percent of the applicants were accepted.

For Further Information Contact Mr. John Olsen, Vice President for Admission and Student Enrollment Services, Central College, 812 University Street, Pella, IA 50219-1999. *Telephone:* 641-628-7600 or 800-458-5503 (toll-free). *Fax:* 641-628-5316. *E-mail:* admissions@central.edu. *Web site:* http://www.central.edu/.

See page 262 for a narrative description.

CLARKE COLLEGE

Dubuque, Iowa

Clarke is a coed, private, Roman Catholic, comprehensive institution, founded in 1843, offering degrees at the associate, bachelor's, and master's levels. It has a 55-acre campus in Dubuque.

Academic Information The faculty has 89 members (87% full-time), 52% with terminal degrees. The undergraduate student-faculty ratio is 10:1. The library holds 127,089 titles, 897 serial subscriptions, and 1,504 audiovisual materials. Special programs include an honors program, cooperative (work-study) education, study abroad, advanced placement credit, ESL programs, double majors, independent study, distance learning, self-designed majors, summer session for credit, part-time degree programs (evenings), adult/continuing education programs, internships, and arrangement for off-campus study with Tri-College Cooperative Effort. The most frequently chosen baccalaureate fields are business/marketing, computer/information sciences, health professions and related sciences.
Student Body Statistics The student body totals 1,126, of whom 998 are undergraduates (180 freshmen). 69 percent are women and 31 percent are men. Students come from 10 states and territories and 10 other countries. 62 percent are from Iowa. 2.4 percent are international students. 29 percent of the 2002 graduating class went on to graduate and professional schools.
Expenses for 2002–03 *Application fee:* $25. *Comprehensive fee:* $21,955 includes full-time tuition ($15,715), mandatory fees ($475), and college room and board ($5765). *College room only:* $2795. Full-time tuition and fees vary according to class time. Room and board charges vary according to board plan and housing facility. *Part-time tuition:* $400 per credit. Part-time tuition varies according to class time.
Financial Aid Forms of aid include need-based and non-need-based scholarships and part-time jobs. The average aided 2002–03 undergraduate received an aid package worth an estimated $13,913. The priority application deadline for financial aid is April 15.
Freshman Admission Clarke requires a high school transcript, a minimum 2.0 high school GPA, rank in upper 50% of high school class, minimum ACT score of 21 or SAT score of 1000, SAT I or ACT scores, and TOEFL scores for international students. An interview is required for some. The application deadline for regular admission is rolling.
Transfer Admission The application deadline for admission is rolling.
Entrance Difficulty Clarke assesses its entrance difficulty level as moderately difficult; very difficult for physical therapy program. For the fall 2002 freshman class, 66 percent of the applicants were accepted.

For Further Information Contact Mr. Omar G. Correa, Executive Director of Admissions and Financial Aid, Clarke College, 1550 Clarke Drive, Dubuque, IA 52001-3198. *Telephone:* 563-588-6316 or 800-383-2345 (toll-free). *Fax:* 319-588-6789. *E-mail:* admissions@clarke.edu. *Web site:* http://www.clarke.edu/.

COE COLLEGE

Cedar Rapids, Iowa

Coe is a coed, private, comprehensive institution, founded in 1851, affiliated with the Presbyterian Church, offering degrees at the bachelor's and master's levels. It has a 55-acre campus in Cedar Rapids.

Academic Information The faculty has 129 members (57% full-time), 67% with terminal degrees. The undergraduate student-faculty ratio is 12:1. The library holds 213,270 titles, 750 serial subscriptions, and 8,653 audiovisual materials. Special programs include services for learning-disabled students, an honors program, study abroad, advanced placement credit, accelerated degree programs, ESL programs, double majors, independent study, self-designed majors, summer session for credit, part-time degree programs (daytime, evenings, summer), adult/continuing education programs, internships, and arrangement for off-campus study with University of Iowa, Mount Mercy College, Associated Colleges of the Midwest, Washington University in St. Louis. The most frequently chosen baccalaureate fields are business/marketing, psychology, social sciences and history.
Student Body Statistics The student body totals 1,325, of whom 1,300 are undergraduates (302 freshmen). 57 percent are women and 43 percent are men. Students come from 40 states and territories and 15 other countries. 66 percent are from Iowa. 3.3 percent are international students. 24 percent of the 2002 graduating class went on to graduate and professional schools.
Expenses for 2002–03 *Application fee:* $0. *Comprehensive fee:* $26,150 includes full-time tuition ($20,280), mandatory fees ($260), and college room and board ($5610). *College room only:* $2640. Room and board charges vary according to board plan and housing facility. *Part-time tuition:* $980 per course.
Financial Aid Forms of aid include need-based and non-need-based scholarships and part-time jobs. The average aided 2002–03 undergraduate received an aid package worth an estimated $18,365. The application deadline for financial aid is April 30 with a priority deadline of March 1.
Freshman Admission Coe requires an essay, a high school transcript, 1 recommendation, SAT I or ACT scores, and TOEFL scores for international students. A minimum 3.0 high school GPA and an interview are recommended. The application deadline for regular admission is March 1 and for early action it is December 15.
Transfer Admission The application deadline for admission is rolling.
Entrance Difficulty Coe assesses its entrance difficulty level as moderately difficult. For the fall 2002 freshman class, 77 percent of the applicants were accepted.

For Further Information Contact Mr. Dennis Trotter, Vice President of Admission and Financial Aid, Coe College, 1220 1st Avenue, NE, Cedar Rapids, IA 52402-5070. *Telephone:* 319-399-8500 or 877-225-5263 (toll-free). *Fax:* 319-399-8816. *E-mail:* admission@coe.edu. *Web site:* http://www.coe.edu/.

CORNELL COLLEGE

Mount Vernon, Iowa

Cornell is a coed, private, Methodist, four-year college, founded in 1853, offering degrees at the bachelor's level. It has a 129-acre campus in Mount Vernon.

Academic Information The faculty has 108 members (76% full-time), 80% with terminal degrees. The student-faculty ratio is 11:1. The library holds 197,780 titles, 1,236 serial subscriptions, and 4,471 audiovisual materials. Special programs include study abroad, advanced placement credit, ESL programs, double majors, independent study, self-designed majors, adult/continuing education programs, internships, and arrangement for off-campus study with Associated Colleges of the Midwest, Fisk University. The most frequently chosen baccalaureate fields are biological/life sciences, education, social sciences and history.
Student Body Statistics The student body is made up of 1,001 undergraduates (314 freshmen). 60 percent are women and 40 percent are men. Students come from 38 states and territories and 7 other countries. 32 percent are from Iowa. 0.9 percent are international students. 33 percent of the 2002 graduating class went on to graduate and professional schools.
Expenses for 2002–03 *Application fee:* $25. *Comprehensive fee:* $26,755 includes full-time tuition ($20,795), mandatory fees ($160), and college room and board ($5800). *College room only:* $2715. Full-time tuition and fees vary according to reciprocity agreements. Room and board charges vary according to board plan. *Part-time tuition:* $628 per semester hour. Part-time tuition varies according to course load.

Cornell College (continued)

Financial Aid Forms of aid include need-based and non-need-based scholarships and part-time jobs. The average aided 2002–03 undergraduate received an aid package worth an estimated $18,795. The priority application deadline for financial aid is March 1.
Freshman Admission Cornell requires an essay, a high school transcript, 1 recommendation, SAT I or ACT scores, and TOEFL scores for international students. A minimum 2.80 high school GPA and an interview are recommended. The application deadline for regular admission is February 1.
Transfer Admission The application deadline for admission is February 1.
Entrance Difficulty Cornell assesses its entrance difficulty level as moderately difficult. For the fall 2002 freshman class, 62 percent of the applicants were accepted.

For Further Information Contact Mr. Jonathan Stroud, Dean of Admissions and Financial Assistance, Cornell College, 600 First Street West, Mount Vernon, IA 52314-1098. *Telephone:* 319-895-4477 or 800-747-1112 (toll-free). *Fax:* 319-895-4451. *E-mail:* admissions@cornellcollege.edu. *Web site:* http://www.cornellcollege.edu/.

See page 272 for a narrative description.

DIVINE WORD COLLEGE

Epworth, Iowa

For Information Write to Divine Word College, Epworth, IA 52045-0380.

DORDT COLLEGE

Sioux Center, Iowa

Dordt is a coed, private, Christian Reformed, comprehensive institution, founded in 1955, offering degrees at the associate, bachelor's, and master's levels. It has a 65-acre campus in Sioux Center.

Academic Information The faculty has 110 members (73% full-time), 64% with terminal degrees. The undergraduate student-faculty ratio is 15:1. The library holds 160,000 titles, 6,597 serial subscriptions, and 1,989 audiovisual materials. Special programs include academic remediation, services for learning-disabled students, study abroad, advanced placement credit, ESL programs, double majors, independent study, distance learning, self-designed majors, part-time degree programs, internships, and arrangement for off-campus study with Christian College Coalition, Chicago Metro Program, American Studies Program, Los Angeles Film Studies Program. The most frequently chosen baccalaureate fields are business/marketing, education, engineering/engineering technologies.
Student Body Statistics The student body totals 1,404, of whom 1,347 are undergraduates (278 freshmen). 55 percent are women and 45 percent are men. Students come from 36 states and territories and 12 other countries. 42 percent are from Iowa. 12 percent are international students. 10 percent of the 2002 graduating class went on to graduate and professional schools.
Expenses for 2002–03 *Application fee:* $25. *Comprehensive fee:* $19,040 includes full-time tuition ($14,700), mandatory fees ($180), and college room and board ($4160). *College room only:* $2180. Room and board charges vary according to board plan and housing facility. *Part-time tuition:* $615 per credit hour. *Part-time mandatory fees:* $75 per term.
Financial Aid Forms of aid include need-based and non-need-based scholarships, athletic grants, and part-time jobs. The average aided 2002–03 undergraduate received an aid package worth an estimated $13,323. The priority application deadline for financial aid is April 1.
Freshman Admission Dordt requires a high school transcript, a minimum 2.25 high school GPA, minimum ACT composite score of 19 or combined SAT I score of 920, SAT I or ACT scores, and TOEFL scores for international students. An essay and an interview are required for some. The application deadline for regular admission is August 1.
Transfer Admission The application deadline for admission is August 1.
Entrance Difficulty Dordt assesses its entrance difficulty level as moderately difficult. For the fall 2002 freshman class, 93 percent of the applicants were accepted.

For Further Information Contact Mr. Quentin Van Essen, Executive Director of Admissions, Dordt College, 498 4th Avenue, NE, Sioux Center, IA 51250-1697. *Telephone:* 712-722-6080 or 800-343-6738 (toll-free). *Fax:* 712-722-1967. *E-mail:* admissions@dordt.edu. *Web site:* http://www.dordt.edu/.

DRAKE UNIVERSITY

Des Moines, Iowa

Drake is a coed, private university, founded in 1881, offering degrees at the bachelor's, master's, doctoral, and first professional levels. It has a 120-acre campus in Des Moines.

Academic Information The faculty has 369 members (66% full-time). The undergraduate student-faculty ratio is 13:1. The library holds 472,110 titles, 2,000 serial subscriptions, and 858 audiovisual materials. Special programs include services for learning-disabled students, an honors program, cooperative (work-study) education, study abroad, advanced placement credit, accelerated degree programs, ESL programs, double majors, independent study, distance learning, self-designed majors, summer session for credit, part-time degree programs (daytime, evenings, weekends, summer), internships, and arrangement for off-campus study with 2 members of the Des Moines Consortium. The most frequently chosen baccalaureate fields are business/marketing, communications/communication technologies, education.
Student Body Statistics The student body totals 5,092, of whom 3,603 are undergraduates (776 freshmen). 60 percent are women and 40 percent are men. Students come from 43 states and territories and 47 other countries. 39 percent are from Iowa. 6.1 percent are international students. 17.2 percent of the 2002 graduating class went on to graduate and professional schools.
Expenses for 2002–03 *Application fee:* $25. *Comprehensive fee:* $24,000 includes full-time tuition ($18,190), mandatory fees ($320), and college room and board ($5490). *College room only:* $2840. Full-time tuition and fees vary according to student level. Room and board charges vary according to board plan. *Part-time tuition:* $370 per hour. *Part-time mandatory fees:* $7 per hour. Part-time tuition and fees vary according to class time.
Financial Aid Forms of aid include need-based and non-need-based scholarships, athletic grants, and part-time jobs. The average aided 2002–03 undergraduate received an aid package worth an estimated $15,701. The priority application deadline for financial aid is March 1.
Freshman Admission Drake requires a high school transcript, SAT I or ACT scores, and TOEFL scores for international students. An essay and an interview are recommended. PCAT for pharmacy transfers is required for some. The application deadline for regular admission is rolling.
Transfer Admission The application deadline for admission is rolling.
Entrance Difficulty Drake assesses its entrance difficulty level as moderately difficult; most difficult for transfer students to the College of Pharmacy. For the fall 2002 freshman class, 86 percent of the applicants were accepted.

For Further Information Contact Mr. Thomas F. Willoughby, Dean of Admission and Financial Aid, Drake University, 2507 University Avenue, Des Moines, IA 50311. *Telephone:* 515-271-3181 or 800-44DRAKE Ext. 3181 (toll-free). *Fax:* 515-271-2831. *E-mail:* admission@drake.edu. *Web site:* http://www.drake.edu/.

EMMAUS BIBLE COLLEGE

Dubuque, Iowa

Emmaus is a coed, private, nondenominational, four-year college, founded in 1941, offering degrees at the associate and bachelor's levels. It has a 22-acre campus in Dubuque.

Academic Information The faculty has 27 members (52% full-time), 30% with terminal degrees. The student-faculty ratio is 12:1. The library

holds 86,000 titles and 330 serial subscriptions. Special programs include advanced placement credit, double majors, independent study, part-time degree programs (daytime, evenings), internships, and arrangement for off-campus study. The most frequently chosen baccalaureate fields are education, philosophy, religion, and theology.
Student Body Statistics The student body is made up of 294 undergraduates (57 freshmen). 56 percent are women and 44 percent are men. Students come from 42 states and territories and 7 other countries. 28 percent are from Iowa. 5.9 percent are international students.
Expenses for 2002–03 *Application fee:* $25. *Comprehensive fee:* $9806 includes full-time tuition ($6116), mandatory fees ($210), and college room and board ($3480). Full-time tuition and fees vary according to program. *Part-time tuition:* $185 per credit hour. *Part-time mandatory fees:* $9 per credit hour. Part-time tuition and fees vary according to course load.
Financial Aid Forms of aid include need-based and non-need-based scholarships. The average aided 2001–02 undergraduate received an aid package worth $4200. The application deadline for financial aid is June 10.
Freshman Admission Emmaus requires an essay, a high school transcript, 3 recommendations, SAT I or ACT scores, and TOEFL scores for international students. The application deadline for regular admission is August 1.
Transfer Admission The application deadline for admission is August 1.
Entrance Difficulty Emmaus has an open admission policy.

For Further Information Contact Mr. Steve Schimpf, Enrollment Services Manager, Emmaus Bible College, 2570 Asbury Road, Dubuque, IA 52001. *Telephone:* 563-588-8000 Ext. 1310 or 800-397-2425 (toll-free). *Fax:* 563-557-0573. *E-mail:* admissions@emmaus.edu. *Web site:* http://www.emmaus.edu/.

FAITH BAPTIST BIBLE COLLEGE AND THEOLOGICAL SEMINARY

Ankeny, Iowa

FBBC&TS is a coed, private, comprehensive institution, founded in 1921, affiliated with the General Association of Regular Baptist Churches, offering degrees at the associate, bachelor's, master's, and first professional levels. It has a 52-acre campus in Ankeny.

Academic Information The faculty has 34 members (59% full-time), 53% with terminal degrees. The undergraduate student-faculty ratio is 18:1. The library holds 63,123 titles, 492 serial subscriptions, and 6,629 audiovisual materials. Special programs include academic remediation, advanced placement credit, double majors, independent study, summer session for credit, part-time degree programs (daytime, summer), adult/continuing education programs, and internships. The most frequently chosen baccalaureate fields are education, philosophy, religion, and theology, visual/performing arts.
Student Body Statistics The student body totals 505, of whom 403 are undergraduates (120 freshmen). 54 percent are women and 46 percent are men. Students come from 27 states and territories. 47 percent are from Iowa. 0.5 percent are international students. 13 percent of the 2002 graduating class went on to graduate and professional schools.
Expenses for 2002–03 *Application fee:* $25. *Comprehensive fee:* $13,418 includes full-time tuition ($9342), mandatory fees ($350), and college room and board ($3726). *College room only:* $1736. Full-time tuition and fees vary according to course load. *Part-time tuition:* $340 per semester hour. *Part-time mandatory fees:* $80 per term.
Financial Aid Forms of aid include need-based and non-need-based scholarships. The average aided 2002–03 undergraduate received an aid package worth an estimated $7450. The priority application deadline for financial aid is March 1.
Freshman Admission FBBC&TS requires an essay, a high school transcript, 2 recommendations, SAT I or ACT scores, and TOEFL scores for international students. An interview is required for some. The application deadline for regular admission is August 1.
Transfer Admission The application deadline for admission is August 1.
Entrance Difficulty FBBC&TS assesses its entrance difficulty level as minimally difficult. For the fall 2002 freshman class, 77 percent of the applicants were accepted.

For Further Information Contact Mrs. Sherie Bartlett, Admissions Office Secretary, Faith Baptist Bible College and Theological Seminary, 1900 NW 4th Street, Ankeny, IA 50021. *Telephone:* 515-964-0601 Ext. 238 or 888-FAITH 4U (toll-free). *Fax:* 515-964-1638. *E-mail:* admissions@faith.edu. *Web site:* http://www.faith.edu/.

THE FRANCISCAN UNIVERSITY

Clinton, Iowa

The Franciscan University is a coed, private, Roman Catholic, four-year college, founded in 1918, offering degrees at the associate and bachelor's levels (offers some graduate classes). It has a 24-acre campus in Clinton near Chicago.

Academic Information The faculty has 52 members (52% full-time), 33% with terminal degrees. The student-faculty ratio is 12:1. The library holds 80,759 titles, 1,442 serial subscriptions, and 363 audiovisual materials. Special programs include academic remediation, an honors program, study abroad, advanced placement credit, Freshman Honors College, ESL programs, double majors, independent study, distance learning, self-designed majors, summer session for credit, part-time degree programs (daytime, evenings, summer), external degree programs, and internships. The most frequently chosen baccalaureate fields are business/marketing, education, liberal arts/general studies.
Student Body Statistics The student body totals 492, of whom 458 are undergraduates (48 freshmen). 57 percent are women and 43 percent are men. Students come from 11 states and territories and 10 other countries. 60 percent are from Iowa. 3.5 percent are international students. 28 percent of the 2002 graduating class went on to graduate and professional schools.
Expenses for 2002–03 *Application fee:* $20. *Comprehensive fee:* $19,060 includes full-time tuition ($13,800), mandatory fees ($260), and college room and board ($5000). *College room only:* $2500. Room and board charges vary according to board plan and housing facility. *Part-time tuition:* $407 per credit hour. *Part-time mandatory fees:* $6 per credit hour.
Financial Aid Forms of aid include need-based and non-need-based scholarships, athletic grants, and part-time jobs. The average aided 2002–03 undergraduate received an aid package worth an estimated $10,654. The application deadline for financial aid is August 1 with a priority deadline of March 1.
Freshman Admission The Franciscan University requires a high school transcript, SAT I or ACT scores, and TOEFL scores for international students. A minimum 2.0 high school GPA and an interview are recommended. Recommendations and an interview are required for some. The application deadline for regular admission is August 15.
Transfer Admission The application deadline for admission is rolling.
Entrance Difficulty The Franciscan University assesses its entrance difficulty level as minimally difficult; moderately difficult for transfers. For the fall 2002 freshman class, 76 percent of the applicants were accepted.

For Further Information Contact Ms. Waunita M. Sullivan, Director of Enrollment, The Franciscan University, 400 North Bluff Boulevard, PO Box 2967, Clinton, IA 52733-2967. *Telephone:* 563-242-4023 Ext. 3401 or 800-242-4153 (toll-free). *Fax:* 563-243-6102. *E-mail:* admissns@clare.edu. *Web site:* http://www.clare.edu/.

GRACELAND UNIVERSITY

Lamoni, Iowa

Graceland is a coed, private, Community of Christ, comprehensive institution, founded in 1895, offering degrees at the bachelor's and master's levels and post-master's certificates. It has a 169-acre campus in Lamoni.

Academic Information The faculty has 106 members (85% full-time), 51% with terminal degrees. The undergraduate student-faculty ratio is 16:1. The library holds 143,523 titles, 5,545 serial subscriptions, and 3,500

Graceland University (continued)
audiovisual materials. Special programs include academic remediation, services for learning-disabled students, an honors program, cooperative (work-study) education, study abroad, advanced placement credit, accelerated degree programs, ESL programs, double majors, independent study, distance learning, self-designed majors, summer session for credit, part-time degree programs (daytime), external degree programs, adult/continuing education programs, internships, and arrangement for off-campus study with American Institute of Business, Indian Hills Community College, North Central Missouri College. The most frequently chosen baccalaureate fields are business/marketing, education, health professions and related sciences.
Student Body Statistics The student body totals 2,297, of whom 2,066 are undergraduates (272 freshmen). 68 percent are women and 32 percent are men. Students come from 49 states and territories and 26 other countries. 32 percent are from Iowa. 5 percent are international students. 17 percent of the 2002 graduating class went on to graduate and professional schools.
Expenses for 2002–03 *Application fee:* $50. *Comprehensive fee:* $18,430 includes full-time tuition ($13,750), mandatory fees ($150), and college room and board ($4530). *College room only:* $1690. Full-time tuition and fees vary according to course load. Room and board charges vary according to board plan, housing facility, and location. *Part-time tuition:* $430 per semester hour. *Part-time mandatory fees:* $60 per term. Part-time tuition and fees vary according to location.
Financial Aid Forms of aid include need-based and non-need-based scholarships, athletic grants, and part-time jobs. The average aided 2002–03 undergraduate received an aid package worth an estimated $13,203. The application deadline for financial aid is continuous.
Freshman Admission Graceland requires a high school transcript, a minimum 2.0 high school GPA, SAT I or ACT scores, and TOEFL scores for international students. Minimum SAT score of 960 or ACT score of 21 is recommended. An essay, 2 recommendations, and an interview are required for some. The application deadline for regular admission is rolling.
Transfer Admission The application deadline for admission is rolling.
Entrance Difficulty Graceland assesses its entrance difficulty level as moderately difficult. For the fall 2002 freshman class, 57 percent of the applicants were accepted.

For Further Information Contact Mr. Brian Shantz, Dean of Admissions, Graceland University, 1 University Place. *Telephone:* 641-784-5118 or 866-GRACELAND (toll-free). *Fax:* 641-784-5480. *E-mail:* admissions@graceland.edu. *Web site:* http://www.graceland.edu/.

See page 280 for a narrative description.

GRAND VIEW COLLEGE

Des Moines, Iowa

Grand View is a coed, private, four-year college, founded in 1896, affiliated with the Evangelical Lutheran Church in America, offering degrees at the associate and bachelor's levels and postbachelor's certificates. It has a 25-acre campus in Des Moines.

Academic Information The faculty has 139 members (55% full-time), 47% with terminal degrees. The student-faculty ratio is 15:1. The library holds 103,468 titles, 3,412 serial subscriptions, and 6,360 audiovisual materials. Special programs include academic remediation, services for learning-disabled students, an honors program, cooperative (work-study) education, study abroad, advanced placement credit, accelerated degree programs, Freshman Honors College, double majors, independent study, distance learning, self-designed majors, summer session for credit, part-time degree programs (daytime, evenings, weekends, summer), adult/continuing education programs, internships, and arrangement for off-campus study with Drake University, Des Moines Area Community College. The most frequently chosen baccalaureate fields are business/marketing, education, health professions and related sciences.
Student Body Statistics The student body is made up of 1,546 undergraduates (198 freshmen). 68 percent are women and 32 percent are men. Students come from 22 states and territories and 19 other countries. 95 percent are from Iowa. 1.6 percent are international students.
Expenses for 2002–03 *Application fee:* $0. *Comprehensive fee:* $18,992 includes full-time tuition ($13,914), mandatory fees ($280), and college room and board ($4798). Room and board charges vary according to board plan and housing facility. *Part-time tuition:* $395 per credit hour. Part-time tuition varies according to class time.
Financial Aid Forms of aid include need-based and non-need-based scholarships, athletic grants, and part-time jobs. The average aided 2002–03 undergraduate received an aid package worth an estimated $12,192. The priority application deadline for financial aid is March 1.
Freshman Admission Grand View requires a high school transcript, SAT I or ACT scores, and TOEFL scores for international students. A minimum 2.0 high school GPA is recommended. The application deadline for regular admission is August 15.
Transfer Admission The application deadline for admission is August 15.
Entrance Difficulty Grand View assesses its entrance difficulty level as minimally difficult; very difficult for honors program. For the fall 2002 freshman class, 94 percent of the applicants were accepted.

For Further Information Contact Ms. Diane Johnson Schaefer, Director of Admissions, Grand View College, 1200 Grandview Avenue, Des Moines, IA 50316-1599. *Telephone:* 515-263-2810 or 800-444-6083 (toll-free). *Fax:* 515-263-2974. *E-mail:* admiss@gvc.edu. *Web site:* http://www.gvc.edu/.

GRINNELL COLLEGE

Grinnell, Iowa

Grinnell College is a coed, private, four-year college, founded in 1846, offering degrees at the bachelor's level. It has a 95-acre campus in Grinnell.

Academic Information The faculty has 141 members (97% full-time), 95% with terminal degrees. The student-faculty ratio is 10:1. The library holds 1 million titles, 3,470 serial subscriptions, and 28,368 audiovisual materials. Special programs include services for learning-disabled students, study abroad, advanced placement credit, accelerated degree programs, double majors, independent study, self-designed majors, internships, and arrangement for off-campus study. The most frequently chosen baccalaureate fields are biological/life sciences, English, social sciences and history.
Student Body Statistics The student body is made up of 1,485 undergraduates (368 freshmen). 55 percent are women and 45 percent are men. Students come from 52 states and territories and 52 other countries. 15 percent are from Iowa. 10.5 percent are international students. 33 percent of the 2002 graduating class went on to graduate and professional schools.
Expenses for 2002–03 *Application fee:* $30. *Comprehensive fee:* $29,860 includes full-time tuition ($22,960), mandatory fees ($570), and college room and board ($6330). *College room only:* $2940. Room and board charges vary according to board plan and housing facility. *Part-time tuition:* $717 per credit hour.
Financial Aid Forms of aid include need-based and non-need-based scholarships and part-time jobs. The average aided 2002–03 undergraduate received an aid package worth an estimated $19,611. The application deadline for financial aid is February 1.
Freshman Admission Grinnell College requires an essay, a high school transcript, 3 recommendations, SAT I or ACT scores, and TOEFL scores for international students. An interview is recommended. The application deadline for regular admission is January 20 and for early decision it is November 20.
Transfer Admission The application deadline for admission is May 1.
Entrance Difficulty Grinnell College assesses its entrance difficulty level as very difficult. For the fall 2002 freshman class, 65 percent of the applicants were accepted.

For Further Information Contact Mr. James Sumner, Dean for Admission and Financial Aid, Grinnell College, Grinnell, IA 50112. *Telephone:* 641-269-3600 or 800-247-0113 (toll-free). *Fax:* 641-269-4800. *E-mail:* askgrin@grinnell.edu. *Web site:* http://www.grinnell.edu/.

HAMILTON COLLEGE

Cedar Rapids, Iowa

Hamilton College is a coed, proprietary, primarily two-year college, founded in 1900, offering degrees at the associate and bachelor's levels (branch locations in Des Moines, Mason City, and Cedar Falls with significant enrollment reflected in profile). It has a 4-acre campus in Cedar Rapids.

Academic Information The faculty has 40 members (18% full-time), 2% with terminal degrees. The student-faculty ratio is 25:1. The library holds 5,500 titles and 40 serial subscriptions. Special programs include academic remediation, cooperative (work-study) education, distance learning, part-time degree programs (daytime, evenings, summer), adult/continuing education programs, and internships.
Student Body Statistics The student body is made up of 511 undergraduates (278 freshmen). 60 percent are women and 40 percent are men. Students come from 1 state or territory.
Expenses for 2003–04 *Application fee:* $25. *Tuition:* $14,160 full-time.
Financial Aid Forms of aid include need-based scholarships and part-time jobs. The application deadline for financial aid is continuous.
Freshman Admission Hamilton College requires a high school transcript, a minimum 2.0 high school GPA, an interview, TOEFL scores for international students, and CPAt. The application deadline for regular admission is rolling.
Entrance Difficulty Hamilton College assesses its entrance difficulty level as moderately difficult.

For Further Information Contact Mr. Brad Knudson, Director of Admissions, Hamilton College, 1924 D Street SW, Cedar Rapids, IA 52404. *Telephone:* 319-363-0481 or 800-728-0481 (toll-free out-of-state). *Fax:* 319-363-3812. *Web site:* http://www.hamiltonia.edu/.

HAMILTON TECHNICAL COLLEGE

Davenport, Iowa

Hamilton Technical College is a coed, proprietary, four-year college, founded in 1969, offering degrees at the associate and bachelor's levels.

Academic Information The faculty has 18 members. The student-faculty ratio is 20:1. The library holds 4,500 titles and 30 serial subscriptions. Special programs include accelerated degree programs.
Student Body Statistics The student body is made up of 420 undergraduates.
Expenses for 2002–03 *Application fee:* $25. *Tuition:* $6300 full-time.
Financial Aid Forms of aid include need-based scholarships. The priority application deadline for financial aid is June 30.
Freshman Admission Hamilton Technical College requires a high school transcript and an interview. The application deadline for regular admission is rolling.
Transfer Admission The application deadline for admission is rolling.
Entrance Difficulty Hamilton Technical College has an open admission policy.

For Further Information Contact Mr. Chad Nelson, Admissions, Hamilton Technical College, 1011 East 53rd Street, Davenport, IA 52807. *Telephone:* 563-386-3570. *Fax:* 319-386-6756. *Web site:* http://www.hamiltontechcollege.com/.

IOWA STATE UNIVERSITY OF SCIENCE AND TECHNOLOGY

Ames, Iowa

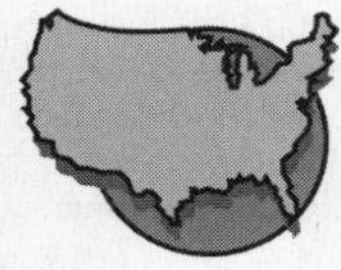

Iowa State is a coed, public university, founded in 1858, offering degrees at the bachelor's, master's, doctoral, and first professional levels and post-master's certificates. It has a 1,788-acre campus in Ames.

Academic Information The faculty has 1,625 members (86% full-time), 88% with terminal degrees. The undergraduate student-faculty ratio is 16:1. The library holds 2 million titles, 29,681 serial subscriptions, and 58,055 audiovisual materials. Special programs include academic remediation, services for learning-disabled students, an honors program, cooperative (work-study) education, study abroad, advanced placement credit, accelerated degree programs, Freshman Honors College, ESL programs, double majors, independent study, distance learning, self-designed majors, summer session for credit, part-time degree programs, external degree programs, adult/continuing education programs, internships, and arrangement for off-campus study with Iowa Regents' Universities Student Exchange, National Student Exchange. The most frequently chosen baccalaureate fields are business/marketing, agriculture, engineering/engineering technologies.
Student Body Statistics The student body totals 27,898, of whom 22,999 are undergraduates (4,219 freshmen). 44 percent are women and 56 percent are men. Students come from 54 states and territories and 113 other countries. 81 percent are from Iowa. 4.6 percent are international students. 16.4 percent of the 2002 graduating class went on to graduate and professional schools.
Expenses for 2002–03 *Application fee:* $30. *State resident tuition:* $3692 full-time, $154 per semester hour part-time. *Nonresident tuition:* $12,384 full-time, $516 per semester hour part-time. *Mandatory fees:* $418 full-time, $85 per semester hour part-time, $170 per term part-time. Full-time tuition and fees vary according to class time, degree level, and program. Part-time tuition and fees vary according to class time, course load, degree level, and program. *College room and board:* $5020. *College room only:* $2822. Room and board charges vary according to board plan and housing facility.
Financial Aid Forms of aid include need-based and non-need-based scholarships, athletic grants, and part-time jobs. The average aided 2001–02 undergraduate received an aid package worth $6772. The priority application deadline for financial aid is March 1.
Freshman Admission Iowa State requires a high school transcript, rank in upper 50% of high school class, SAT I or ACT scores, and TOEFL scores for international students. The application deadline for regular admission is August 1.
Transfer Admission The application deadline for admission is August 1.
Entrance Difficulty Iowa State assesses its entrance difficulty level as moderately difficult. For the fall 2002 freshman class, 89 percent of the applicants were accepted.

SPECIAL MESSAGE TO STUDENTS

Social Life Campus life is energized by a diverse community of 27,823 students living in a variety of housing arrangements, including nineteen residence halls (7,500 students), twelve apartment-style buildings, and thirty-nine fraternities and nineteen sororities (3,000 students). The *Daily* student newspaper and the Web are great resources to access information about Iowa State's more than 500 clubs and organizations, fifty intramural sports, forty sports clubs, four indoor recreation facilities, and Big 12 competition in twenty Division I men's and women's sports. Students catch all the top acts at the Iowa State Center, an on-campus arts and entertainment complex that houses the 2,700-seat Stephens Auditorium, the 452-seat Fisher Theater, and the 15,000-seat Hilton Coliseum. Ames offers arts groups, recreational facilities, biking and hiking trails, more than eighty restaurants, a great downtown, shopping, and a variety of movie theaters. Des Moines, Iowa's capitol, is a 40-minute drive from campus.

Academic Highlights Iowa State, with more than 100 undergraduate degree programs, ranks nineteenth in the nation among all colleges and universities in the enrollment of National Achievement and Merit Scholars; second among universities in the nation for the number of top technologies honored by *R&D Magazine;* and among the 20 Most Wired Universities by *Yahoo! Internet Life* magazine. Academic options include Soar in Four (a four-year graduation guarantee program), the University Honors Program, international exchange programs (more than 100 institutions in forty countries), and the National Student Exchange program (148 reciprocating universities around the country). Computing resources include thousands of workstations, 24-hour availability, and mainframe/Internet access from residence hall rooms.

Interviews and Campus Visits Visitors are always welcome. Visit options include student-guided walking tours, residence hall tours, college advising

Iowa State University of Science and Technology (continued)

appointments, and facility tours. Students and parents can participate in a group visit program called "Experience Iowa State." For more information or to receive a Campus Visit Planner and plan a customized schedule, students should call the Office of Admissions at 800-262-3810 (toll-free), Monday through Friday, 8 a.m. to 5 p.m., and most Saturdays from 9 a.m. to noon. The office is located in Alumni Hall, on campus. The nearest commercial airport is Des Moines International.

For Further Information Write to the Office of Admissions, Alumni Hall, Iowa State University, Ames, IA 50011-2010. *E-mail:* admissions@iastate.edu. *Web site:* http://www.iastate.edu/~admis_info/.

See page 292 for a narrative description.

IOWA WESLEYAN COLLEGE

Mount Pleasant, Iowa

Iowa Wesleyan is a coed, private, United Methodist, four-year college, founded in 1842, offering degrees at the bachelor's level. It has a 60-acre campus in Mount Pleasant.

Academic Information The faculty has 65 members (68% full-time), 37% with terminal degrees. The student-faculty ratio is 14:1. The library holds 107,227 titles, 431 serial subscriptions, and 6,553 audiovisual materials. Special programs include academic remediation, services for learning-disabled students, study abroad, advanced placement credit, ESL programs, double majors, independent study, distance learning, self-designed majors, summer session for credit, part-time degree programs (daytime, evenings, summer), adult/continuing education programs, internships, and arrangement for off-campus study with Southeastern Community College, Muscatine Community College.
Student Body Statistics The student body is made up of 721 undergraduates (106 freshmen). 60 percent are women and 40 percent are men. Students come from 22 states and territories and 7 other countries. 83 percent are from Iowa. 2.6 percent are international students. 2 percent of the 2002 graduating class went on to graduate and professional schools.
Expenses for 2002–03 *One-time mandatory fee:* $100. *Comprehensive fee:* $18,740 includes full-time tuition ($14,280) and college room and board ($4460). *College room only:* $1860. Room and board charges vary according to board plan and housing facility. *Part-time tuition:* $345 per credit hour. Part-time tuition varies according to class time.
Financial Aid Forms of aid include need-based and non-need-based scholarships, athletic grants, and part-time jobs. The average aided 2002–03 undergraduate received an aid package worth an estimated $10,775. The priority application deadline for financial aid is April 1.
Freshman Admission Iowa Wesleyan requires a high school transcript, a minimum 2.0 high school GPA, SAT I or ACT scores, and TOEFL scores for international students. An interview is recommended. An essay and recommendations are required for some. The application deadline for regular admission is August 15.
Transfer Admission The application deadline for admission is August 15.
Entrance Difficulty Iowa Wesleyan assesses its entrance difficulty level as moderately difficult. For the fall 2002 freshman class, 53 percent of the applicants were accepted.

For Further Information Contact Mr. Cary A. Owens, Dean of Enrollment Management, Iowa Wesleyan College, 601 North Main Street, Mount Pleasant, IA 52641-1398. *Telephone:* 319-385-6230 or 800-582-2383 (toll-free). *Fax:* 319-385-6296. *E-mail:* admitrwl@iwc.edu. *Web site:* http://www.iwc.edu/.

KAPLAN COLLEGE

Davenport, Iowa

Kaplan College is a coed, proprietary, primarily two-year college of Quest Education Corporation, founded in 1937, offering degrees at the associate and bachelor's levels.

Academic Information The faculty has 44 members (36% full-time), 11% with terminal degrees. The student-faculty ratio is 11:1. The library holds 7,000 titles, 120 serial subscriptions, and 504 audiovisual materials. Special programs include academic remediation, cooperative (work-study) education, double majors, independent study, distance learning, summer session for credit, part-time degree programs (daytime, evenings), adult/continuing education programs, and internships.
Student Body Statistics The student body is made up of 505 undergraduates (112 freshmen). 66 percent are women and 34 percent are men. Students come from 2 states and territories. 71 percent are from Iowa.
Expenses for 2003–04 *Application fee:* $25. *Tuition:* $10,620 full-time, $236 per credit part-time.
Financial Aid Forms of aid include need-based scholarships and part-time jobs. The application deadline for financial aid is continuous.
Freshman Admission Kaplan College requires a high school transcript, an interview, TOEFL scores for international students, and CPAt. An essay is required for some. The application deadline for regular admission is rolling.
Transfer Admission The application deadline for admission is rolling.
Entrance Difficulty Kaplan College assesses its entrance difficulty level as minimally difficult. For the fall 2002 freshman class, 71 percent of the applicants were accepted.

For Further Information Contact Mr. Robert Hoffmann, Director of Admissions, Kaplan College, 1801 East Kimberly Road, Suite 1, Davenport, IA 52807. *Telephone:* 563-441-2496 or 800-747-1035 (toll-free in-state). *Fax:* 563-355-1320. *E-mail:* infoke@kaplancollege.edu. *Web site:* http://www.kaplancollegeia.com/.

LORAS COLLEGE

Dubuque, Iowa

Loras is a coed, private, Roman Catholic, comprehensive institution, founded in 1839, offering degrees at the associate, bachelor's, and master's levels. It has a 60-acre campus in Dubuque.

Academic Information The faculty has 173 members (68% full-time), 64% with terminal degrees. The undergraduate student-faculty ratio is 12:1. The library holds 290,517 titles, 912 serial subscriptions, and 1,676 audiovisual materials. Special programs include academic remediation, services for learning-disabled students, an honors program, cooperative (work-study) education, study abroad, advanced placement credit, ESL programs, double majors, independent study, self-designed majors, summer session for credit, part-time degree programs (daytime, evenings, summer), adult/continuing education programs, internships, and arrangement for off-campus study. The most frequently chosen baccalaureate fields are business/marketing, communications/communication technologies, education.
Student Body Statistics The student body totals 1,736, of whom 1,614 are undergraduates (373 freshmen). 51 percent are women and 49 percent are men. Students come from 28 states and territories and 7 other countries. 56 percent are from Iowa. 1.5 percent are international students. 11.4 percent of the 2002 graduating class went on to graduate and professional schools.
Expenses for 2002–03 *Application fee:* $25. *Comprehensive fee:* $23,844 includes full-time tuition ($16,860), mandatory fees ($1089), and college room and board ($5895). *College room only:* $2900. Full-time tuition and fees vary according to course load and degree level. *Part-time tuition:* $350 per credit.
Financial Aid Forms of aid include need-based and non-need-based scholarships and part-time jobs. The average aided 2002–03 undergraduate received an aid package worth an estimated $16,812. The priority application deadline for financial aid is April 15.
Freshman Admission Loras requires a high school transcript, a minimum 2.5 high school GPA, SAT I or ACT scores, and TOEFL scores for international students. An essay and 1 recommendation are recommended. An interview is required for some. The application deadline for regular admission is rolling.
Transfer Admission The application deadline for admission is rolling.

Entrance Difficulty Loras assesses its entrance difficulty level as moderately difficult. For the fall 2002 freshman class, 80 percent of the applicants were accepted.

SPECIAL MESSAGE TO STUDENTS

Social Life Loras College students develop a sense of belonging and involvement by choosing from twenty-one men's and women's varsity athletics and more than fifty-five clubs and organizations. In addition, more than 80 percent of students participate in excess of 100 intramural sports. World-renowned speakers and performers punctuate the Loras calendar. Scenic Dubuque boasts two skiing and snowboarding areas, extensive bike trails, and an abundance of restaurants while also offering a vibrant arts community with a beautiful art museum, a symphony, and theater groups.

Academic Highlights Loras students connect with the campus and the world through its technology-enriched environment, integrated into the academic experience. All full-time students receive multimedia laptop computers with wireless network connections, freeing them from traditional computer labs. Loras students are well connected to faculty members and other students and enjoy the close-knit environment of a 12:1 student-faculty ratio and an average class size of 17. Loras offers a choice of more than forty majors and fifteen preprofessional majors, ranging from biochemistry to English writing. The College's 1,736 students hail from twenty-seven states and thirteen countries. Loras's Center for Experiential Learning offers memorable learning opportunities with its study-abroad and internship programs.

Interviews and Campus Visits To make the right college choice, students are encouraged to visit the campus. A campus visit takes the student beyond course listings and faculty members' credentials to get the feel of the College. By arranging an individual campus visit or attending an official campus visit day, students can choose from two different methods to experience the College firsthand. Visit days offer an overview of the college as well as campus tours, which introduce students to a wide array of academic departments, student services, and campus life. Individual appointments allow students to tailor their visit to suit their interests and needs, including a personal tour of the Loras campus, hosted by a current student. Every visit offers the opportunity to meet with an admissions counselor and to tour the campus. Like a Loras education, faculty and staff members make the visit an individual experience. To arrange an appointment, students should call the Admissions Office, Monday through Friday, 9 a.m. to 3 p.m. at 563-588-7236 or 800-245-6727 (toll-free). Dubuque Regional Airport is just 10 minutes from campus.

For Further Information Write to Mr. Tim Hauber, Director of Admissions, Loras College, 1450 Alta Vista, Dubuque, IA 52004-0178. *E-mail:* thauber@loras.edu. *Web site:* http://www.loras.edu.

LUTHER COLLEGE

Decorah, Iowa

Luther is a coed, private, four-year college, founded in 1861, affiliated with the Evangelical Lutheran Church in America, offering degrees at the bachelor's level. It has an 800-acre campus in Decorah.

Academic Information The faculty has 234 members (75% full-time), 64% with terminal degrees. The student-faculty ratio is 13:1. The library holds 336,605 titles, 1,600 serial subscriptions, and 7,000 audiovisual materials. Special programs include academic remediation, an honors program, study abroad, advanced placement credit, double majors, independent study, self-designed majors, summer session for credit, part-time degree programs, internships, and arrangement for off-campus study. The most frequently chosen baccalaureate fields are biological/life sciences, business/marketing, education.

Student Body Statistics The student body is made up of 2,572 undergraduates (609 freshmen). 60 percent are women and 40 percent are men. Students come from 37 states and territories and 41 other countries. 36 percent are from Iowa. 5.8 percent are international students. 22 percent of the 2002 graduating class went on to graduate and professional schools.

Expenses for 2002–03 *Application fee:* $25. *Comprehensive fee:* $24,350 includes full-time tuition ($20,310) and college room and board ($4040). *College room only:* $2070. Full-time tuition varies according to course load. Room and board charges vary according to housing facility. *Part-time tuition:* $726 per semester hour. Part-time tuition varies according to course load.

Financial Aid Forms of aid include need-based and non-need-based scholarships and part-time jobs. The average aided 2001–02 undergraduate received an aid package worth $16,554. The priority application deadline for financial aid is February 15.

Freshman Admission Luther requires an essay, a high school transcript, 1 recommendation, SAT I or ACT scores, and TOEFL scores for international students. An interview is recommended.

Entrance Difficulty Luther assesses its entrance difficulty level as moderately difficult. For the fall 2002 freshman class, 78 percent of the applicants were accepted.

For Further Information Contact Mr. Jon Lund, Vice President for Enrollment and Marketing, Luther College, 700 College Drive, Decorah, IA 52101. *Telephone:* 563-387-1287 or 800-458-8437 (toll-free). *Fax:* 563-387-2159. *E-mail:* admissions@luther.edu. *Web site:* http://www.luther.edu/.

MAHARISHI UNIVERSITY OF MANAGEMENT

Fairfield, Iowa

M.U.M. is a coed, private university, founded in 1971, offering degrees at the associate, bachelor's, master's, and doctoral levels. It has a 262-acre campus in Fairfield.

Academic Information The faculty has 66 members (76% full-time), 68% with terminal degrees. The undergraduate student-faculty ratio is 11:1. The library holds 113,580 titles, 868 serial subscriptions, and 21,850 audiovisual materials. Special programs include academic remediation, services for learning-disabled students, an honors program, cooperative (work-study) education, study abroad, advanced placement credit, ESL programs, double majors, independent study, distance learning, self-designed majors, adult/continuing education programs, and internships. The most frequently chosen baccalaureate fields are business/marketing, biological/life sciences, visual/performing arts.

Student Body Statistics The student body totals 756, of whom 186 are undergraduates (37 freshmen). 51 percent are women and 49 percent are men. Students come from 26 states and territories and 20 other countries. 52 percent are from Iowa. 23.1 percent are international students.

Expenses for 2002–03 *Application fee:* $25. *Comprehensive fee:* $29,250 includes full-time tuition ($23,600), mandatory fees ($450), and college room and board ($5200). *College room only:* $2720. Full-time tuition and fees vary according to program. Room and board charges vary according to housing facility. *Part-time tuition:* $330 per credit. Part-time tuition varies according to program.

Financial Aid Forms of aid include need-based and non-need-based scholarships and part-time jobs. The average aided 2002–03 undergraduate received an aid package worth an estimated $29,462. The priority application deadline for financial aid is April 15.

Freshman Admission M.U.M. requires an essay, a high school transcript, a minimum 2.5 high school GPA, 2 recommendations, minimum SAT score of 950 or ACT score of 19, SAT I or ACT scores, and TOEFL scores for international students. An interview is recommended. The application deadline for regular admission is August 1.

Transfer Admission The application deadline for admission is August 1.

Entrance Difficulty M.U.M. assesses its entrance difficulty level as moderately difficult. For the fall 2002 freshman class, 68 percent of the applicants were accepted.

For Further Information Contact Mr. Brad Mylett, Director of Admissions, Maharishi University of Management, 1000 North 4th Street, Fairfield, IA 52557. *Telephone:* 641-472-1110 or 800-369-6480 (toll-free). *Fax:* 641-472-1179. *E-mail:* admissions@mum.edu. *Web site:* http://www.mum.edu/.

See page 302 for a narrative description.

MERCY COLLEGE OF HEALTH SCIENCES

Des Moines, Iowa

Mercy College of Health Sciences is a coed, primarily women's, private, four-year college, founded in 1995, affiliated with the Roman Catholic Church, offering degrees at the associate and bachelor's levels. It has a 4-acre campus in Des Moines.

Expenses for 2002–03 *Application fee:* $10. *Tuition:* $9700 full-time.
For Further Information Contact Ms. Sandi Nagel, Admissions Representative, Mercy College of Health Sciences, IA. *Telephone:* 515-643-6605 or 800-637-2994 (toll-free). *Fax:* 515-643-6698. *Web site:* http://www.mchs.edu/.

MORNINGSIDE COLLEGE

Sioux City, Iowa

Morningside is a coed, private, United Methodist, comprehensive institution, founded in 1894, offering degrees at the bachelor's and master's levels. It has a 41-acre campus in Sioux City.

Academic Information The faculty has 109 members (61% full-time), 50% with terminal degrees. The undergraduate student-faculty ratio is 10:1. The library holds 114,250 titles, 571 serial subscriptions, and 5,372 audiovisual materials. Special programs include academic remediation, services for learning-disabled students, an honors program, study abroad, advanced placement credit, ESL programs, double majors, independent study, self-designed majors, summer session for credit, part-time degree programs (daytime, evenings, summer), adult/continuing education programs, internships, and arrangement for off-campus study with American University, Drew University. The most frequently chosen baccalaureate fields are business/marketing, education, health professions and related sciences.
Student Body Statistics The student body totals 1,040, of whom 915 are undergraduates (247 freshmen). 57 percent are women and 43 percent are men. Students come from 23 states and territories and 3 other countries. 69 percent are from Iowa. 2.2 percent are international students. 13.4 percent of the 2002 graduating class went on to graduate and professional schools.
Expenses for 2002–03 *Application fee:* $25. *Comprehensive fee:* $20,580 includes full-time tuition ($14,570), mandatory fees ($890), and college room and board ($5120). *College room only:* $2680. Room and board charges vary according to board plan. *Part-time tuition:* $480 per semester hour.
Financial Aid Forms of aid include need-based and non-need-based scholarships, athletic grants, and part-time jobs. The average aided 2002–03 undergraduate received an aid package worth an estimated $15,516. The priority application deadline for financial aid is March 1.
Freshman Admission Morningside requires a high school transcript, minimum SAT score of 930 or ACT score of 20 and rank in top 50% of high school class or achieved GPA of 2.5 or better, SAT I or ACT scores, and TOEFL scores for international students. An interview is recommended. 2 recommendations are required for some. The application deadline for regular admission is rolling.
Transfer Admission The application deadline for admission is rolling.
Entrance Difficulty Morningside assesses its entrance difficulty level as moderately difficult. For the fall 2002 freshman class, 73 percent of the applicants were accepted.

For Further Information Contact Mr. Joel Weyand, Director of Admissions, Morningside College, 1501 Morningside Avenue, Sioux City, IA 51106. *Telephone:* 712-274-5111 or 800-831-0806 Ext. 5111 (toll-free). *Fax:* 712-274-5101. *E-mail:* mscadm@morningside.edu. *Web site:* http://www.morningside.edu/.

See page 312 for a narrative description.

MOUNT MERCY COLLEGE

Cedar Rapids, Iowa

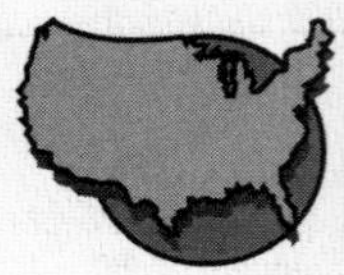

Mount Mercy is a coed, private, Roman Catholic, four-year college, founded in 1928, offering degrees at the bachelor's level. It has a 36-acre campus in Cedar Rapids.

Academic Information The faculty has 119 members (57% full-time), 55% with terminal degrees. The student-faculty ratio is 14:1. The library holds 118,000 titles, 1,000 serial subscriptions, and 5,000 audiovisual materials. Special programs include academic remediation, services for learning-disabled students, an honors program, advanced placement credit, accelerated degree programs, Freshman Honors College, double majors, independent study, self-designed majors, summer session for credit, part-time degree programs (daytime, evenings, weekends, summer), adult/continuing education programs, internships, and arrangement for off-campus study with Coe College. The most frequently chosen baccalaureate fields are education, health professions and related sciences, protective services/public administration.
Student Body Statistics The student body is made up of 1,434 undergraduates (163 freshmen). 68 percent are women and 32 percent are men. Students come from 23 states and territories. 78 percent are from Iowa. 0.1 percent are international students. 11 percent of the 2002 graduating class went on to graduate and professional schools.
Expenses for 2002–03 *Application fee:* $20. *Comprehensive fee:* $20,374 includes full-time tuition ($15,300) and college room and board ($5074). *College room only:* $2060. Full-time tuition varies according to course load. Room and board charges vary according to board plan. *Part-time tuition:* $425 per credit hour. Part-time tuition varies according to course load.
Financial Aid Forms of aid include need-based and non-need-based scholarships and part-time jobs. The average aided 2002–03 undergraduate received an aid package worth an estimated $12,943. The priority application deadline for financial aid is March 1.
Freshman Admission Mount Mercy requires a high school transcript, a minimum 2.5 high school GPA, 1 recommendation, SAT I or ACT scores, and TOEFL scores for international students. An essay and a minimum 3.0 high school GPA are recommended. An interview is required for some. The application deadline for regular admission is August 30.
Transfer Admission The application deadline for admission is August 30.
Entrance Difficulty Mount Mercy assesses its entrance difficulty level as moderately difficult. For the fall 2002 freshman class, 84 percent of the applicants were accepted.

SPECIAL MESSAGE TO STUDENTS

Social Life Shows on campus by musicians and comedians on weekend nights, regular "Club Friday" at Lundy Commons, and the activities of more than thirty clubs and organizations, plus an active student government and newspaper, spark the social life on the Mount Mercy campus. When students are in the mood to expand their entertainment horizons, they are also in the right place, just 2 miles in either direction from downtown or a major mall. With city bus stops at the edge of campus, students have easy access to everything the thriving Midwestern city of Cedar Rapids has to offer—a noted symphony, Theater Cedar Rapids, the Paramount Theater, the Cedar Rapids Museum of Art, minor league baseball and hockey, a downtown arena that hosts popular concerts and shows, and the Science Station with an IMAX theater.

Academic Highlights Known for its high academic quality, moderate cost, and generous scholarships, Mount Mercy College offers outstanding educational value. At Mount Mercy, students achieve more than just a credential; they are molded with the intellectual tools to succeed. Mount Mercy students are prepared to be well-rounded critical thinkers and effective communicators. The Freshman Partnership program helps first-time freshmen make a smooth transition to college life; the Honors Program offers accomplished students unique classes that encourage exploration beyond traditional academic boundaries; and the Academic Achievement Center provides academic counseling and assistance to all students. Classes are small and the faculty members are focused on teaching. At Mount Mercy College, an active learning environment helps students gain confidence in discussing their views and opinions—an environment that well prepares students for a job or graduate school.

Interviews and Campus Visits The best way to learn about the College is to visit, sit in on a class, meet with students and faculty members, and learn about scholarships and other forms of financial assistance. Mount Mercy welcomes students on special visit days throughout the year, and the staff members are happy to arrange individual weekday or weekend appointments. For more information about interviews and campus visits, students should call the Mount Mercy College Office of Admission, Monday through Friday, 8 a.m. to 5 p.m. (CST), at 319-368-6460 or 800-248-4504 (toll-free).

For Further Information Write to the Dean of Admission, Mount Mercy College, 1330 Elmhurst Drive, NE, Cedar Rapids, IA 52402. *E-mail:* admission@mtmercy.edu. *Web site:* http://www.mtmercy.edu.

See page 314 for a narrative description.

MOUNT ST. CLARE COLLEGE

See The Franciscan University

NORTHWESTERN COLLEGE

Orange City, Iowa

Northwestern is a coed, private, four-year college, founded in 1882, affiliated with the Reformed Church in America, offering degrees at the associate and bachelor's levels. It has a 45-acre campus in Orange City.

Academic Information The faculty has 118 members (62% full-time), 53% with terminal degrees. The student-faculty ratio is 16:1. The library holds 125,000 titles, 615 serial subscriptions, and 5,000 audiovisual materials. Special programs include academic remediation, an honors program, cooperative (work-study) education, study abroad, advanced placement credit, accelerated degree programs, Freshman Honors College, ESL programs, double majors, independent study, self-designed majors, summer session for credit, part-time degree programs, internships, and arrangement for off-campus study with 5 members of the Mid-America States Universities Association, Council for Christian Colleges and Universities. The most frequently chosen baccalaureate fields are business/marketing, biological/life sciences, education.
Student Body Statistics The student body is made up of 1,313 undergraduates (347 freshmen). 61 percent are women and 39 percent are men. Students come from 30 states and territories and 12 other countries. 57 percent are from Iowa. 2.4 percent are international students. 9 percent of the 2002 graduating class went on to graduate and professional schools.
Expenses for 2002–03 *Application fee:* $25. *Comprehensive fee:* $18,420 includes full-time tuition ($14,290) and college room and board ($4130). *College room only:* $1714. *Part-time tuition:* $285 per credit. Part-time tuition varies according to course load.
Financial Aid Forms of aid include need-based and non-need-based scholarships, athletic grants, and part-time jobs. The average aided 2002–03 undergraduate received an aid package worth an estimated $11,634. The priority application deadline for financial aid is April 1.
Freshman Admission Northwestern requires an essay, a high school transcript, a minimum 2.0 high school GPA, 1 recommendation, SAT I or ACT scores, and TOEFL scores for international students. A minimum 2.5 high school GPA and an interview are recommended. The application deadline for regular admission is rolling.
Transfer Admission The application deadline for admission is rolling.
Entrance Difficulty Northwestern assesses its entrance difficulty level as moderately difficult. For the fall 2002 freshman class, 83 percent of the applicants were accepted.

For Further Information Contact Mr. Ronald K. DeJong, Director of Admissions, Northwestern College, 101 College Lane, Orange City, IA 51041-1996. *Telephone:* 712-737-7130 or 800-747-4757 (toll-free). *Fax:* 712-707-7164. *E-mail:* markb@nwciowa.edu. *Web site:* http://www.nwciowa.edu/.

PALMER COLLEGE OF CHIROPRACTIC

Davenport, Iowa

PCC is a coed, private, comprehensive unit of Palmer Chiropractic University System, founded in 1897, offering degrees at the associate, incidental bachelor's, master's, and first professional levels in chiropractic. It has a 3-acre campus in Davenport.

Academic Information The faculty has 87 members (100% full-time). The undergraduate student-faculty ratio is 20:1. The library holds 51,445 titles, 894 serial subscriptions, and 22,869 audiovisual materials. Special programs include academic remediation, services for learning-disabled students, summer session for credit, and internships. The most frequently chosen baccalaureate field is health professions and related sciences.
Student Body Statistics The student body totals 1,798, of whom 41 are undergraduates. 76 percent are women and 24 percent are men. Students come from 19 states and territories and 3 other countries. 61 percent are from Iowa. 9.8 percent are international students.
Expenses for 2002–03 *Application fee:* $50. *Tuition:* $18,840 full-time, $245 per term part-time. *Mandatory fees:* $105 full-time, $20 per term part-time.
Financial Aid Forms of aid include need-based and non-need-based scholarships and part-time jobs. The application deadline for financial aid is continuous.
Freshman Admission PCC requires a high school transcript, a minimum 2.0 high school GPA, minimum 2.0 in math, sciences, and English courses, and TOEFL scores for international students. An essay and an interview are required for some. The application deadline for regular admission is rolling.
Entrance Difficulty PCC assesses its entrance difficulty level as moderately difficult. For the fall 2002 freshman class, 90 percent of the applicants were accepted.

For Further Information Contact Dr. David Anderson, Director of Admissions, Palmer College of Chiropractic, 1000 Brady Street, Davenport, IA 52803-5287. *Telephone:* 563-884-5656 or 800-722-3648 (toll-free). *Fax:* 563-884-5414. *E-mail:* pcadmit@palmer.edu. *Web site:* http://www.palmer.edu/.

QUEST COLLEGE

See Kaplan College

ST. AMBROSE UNIVERSITY

Davenport, Iowa

St. Ambrose is a coed, private, Roman Catholic, comprehensive institution, founded in 1882, offering degrees at the bachelor's, master's, and doctoral levels and post-master's and postbachelor's certificates. It has an 11-acre campus in Davenport.

Academic Information The faculty has 269 members (55% full-time), 44% with terminal degrees. The undergraduate student-faculty ratio is 17:1. The library holds 135,920 titles, 735 serial subscriptions, and 2,930 audiovisual materials. Special programs include academic remediation, services for learning-disabled students, cooperative (work-study) education, study abroad, advanced placement credit, accelerated degree programs, double majors, independent study, distance learning, self-designed majors, summer session for credit, part-time degree programs (daytime, evenings, weekends, summer), external degree programs, adult/continuing education programs, internships, and arrangement for off-campus study with Black Hawk College, Eastern Iowa Community Colleges. The most frequently chosen baccalaureate fields are business/marketing, education, psychology.
Student Body Statistics The student body totals 3,500, of whom 2,454 are undergraduates (393 freshmen). 59 percent are women and 41 percent are men. Students come from 23 states and territories and 15 other countries. 63 percent are from Iowa. 0.7 percent are international students. 20 percent of the 2002 graduating class went on to graduate and professional schools.
Expenses for 2003–04 *Application fee:* $25. *One-time mandatory fee:* $100. *Comprehensive fee:* $22,800 includes full-time tuition ($16,650) and college

St. Ambrose University (continued)
room and board ($6150). *College room only:* $2710. Full-time tuition varies according to course load and location. Room and board charges vary according to board plan and housing facility. *Part-time tuition:* $518 per credit. Part-time tuition varies according to course load and location.
Financial Aid Forms of aid include need-based and non-need-based scholarships, athletic grants, and part-time jobs. The average aided 2002–03 undergraduate received an aid package worth an estimated $12,696. The priority application deadline for financial aid is March 15.
Freshman Admission St. Ambrose requires a high school transcript, a minimum 2.5 high school GPA, minimum ACT score of 20 or rank in top 50% of high school class, SAT I or ACT scores, and TOEFL scores for international students. An interview and ACT scores are recommended. Recommendations and an interview are required for some. The application deadline for regular admission is rolling.
Transfer Admission The application deadline for admission is rolling.
Entrance Difficulty St. Ambrose assesses its entrance difficulty level as moderately difficult. For the fall 2002 freshman class, 85 percent of the applicants were accepted.

For Further Information Contact Ms. Meg Higgins, Director of Admissions, St. Ambrose University, 518 West Locust Street, Davenport, IA 52803-2898. *Telephone:* 563-333-6300 Ext. 6311 or 800-383-2627 (toll-free). *Fax:* 563-333-6297. *E-mail:* higginsmegf@sau.edu. *Web site:* http://www.sau.edu/.

ST. LUKE'S COLLEGE OF NURSING AND HEALTH SCIENCES

Sioux City, Iowa

St. Luke's College of Nursing and Health Sciences is a coed, primarily women's, private, two-year college of St., Luke's Regional Medical Center, offering degrees at the associate level.

Academic Information The faculty has 20 members (50% full-time), 25% with terminal degrees. The student-faculty ratio is 7:1. The library holds 115 serial subscriptions and 1,800 audiovisual materials. Special programs include cooperative (work-study) education, advanced placement credit, summer session for credit, and part-time degree programs (daytime, evenings, summer).
Student Body Statistics The student body is made up of 122 undergraduates (10 freshmen). 91 percent are women and 9 percent are men. Students come from 8 states and territories and 1 other country. 75 percent are from Iowa. 0.8 percent are international students.
Expenses for 2003–04 *Application fee:* $25. *One-time mandatory fee:* $75. *Comprehensive fee:* $13,772 includes full-time tuition ($10,080), mandatory fees ($570), and college room and board ($3122). *College room only:* $2622. Full-time tuition and fees vary according to course load and program. Room and board charges vary according to board plan. *Part-time tuition:* $280 per credit hour. Part-time tuition varies according to course load and program.
Financial Aid Forms of aid include need-based scholarships and part-time jobs. The priority application deadline for financial aid is March 1.
Freshman Admission St. Luke's College of Nursing and Health Sciences requires an essay, a high school transcript, a minimum 2.50 high school GPA, and ACT scores. The application deadline for regular admission is August 1.
Entrance Difficulty St. Luke's College of Nursing and Health Sciences assesses its entrance difficulty level as minimally difficult. For the fall 2002 freshman class, 1150 percent of the applicants were accepted.

For Further Information Contact Ms. Sherry McCarthy, Admissions Coordinator, St. Luke's College of Nursing and Health Sciences, 2720 Stone Park Boulevard, 27th and Douglas, Sioux City, IA 51104. *Telephone:* 712-279-3149 or 800-352-4660 Ext. 3149 (toll-free). *Fax:* 712-279-3155. *E-mail:* mccartsj@stlukes.org. *Web site:* http://www.stlukes.org/college/sn_college.htm.

SIMPSON COLLEGE

Indianola, Iowa

Simpson is a coed, private, United Methodist, four-year college, founded in 1860, offering degrees at the bachelor's level and postbachelor's certificates. It has a 68-acre campus in Indianola.

Academic Information The faculty has 142 members (59% full-time), 51% with terminal degrees. The student-faculty ratio is 14:1. The library holds 151,359 titles, 599 serial subscriptions, and 5,357 audiovisual materials. Special programs include academic remediation, services for learning-disabled students, an honors program, cooperative (work-study) education, study abroad, advanced placement credit, accelerated degree programs, Freshman Honors College, double majors, independent study, self-designed majors, summer session for credit, part-time degree programs (daytime, evenings, weekends, summer), adult/continuing education programs, internships, and arrangement for off-campus study with Drew University, American University, Washington Center Internships and Symposia. The most frequently chosen baccalaureate fields are business/marketing, communications/communication technologies, education.
Student Body Statistics The student body is made up of 1,845 undergraduates (381 freshmen). 59 percent are women and 41 percent are men. Students come from 26 states and territories and 13 other countries. 90 percent are from Iowa. 1.7 percent are international students. 11 percent of the 2002 graduating class went on to graduate and professional schools.
Expenses for 2002–03 *Application fee:* $0. *Comprehensive fee:* $22,210 includes full-time tuition ($16,475), mandatory fees ($174), and college room and board ($5561). *College room only:* $2669. Room and board charges vary according to board plan and housing facility. *Part-time tuition:* $215 per credit. Part-time tuition varies according to class time and course load.
Financial Aid Forms of aid include need-based and non-need-based scholarships and part-time jobs. The average aided 2002–03 undergraduate received an aid package worth an estimated $17,200. The application deadline for financial aid is continuous.
Freshman Admission Simpson requires a high school transcript, 1 recommendation, SAT I or ACT scores, and TOEFL scores for international students. An interview and rank in upper 50% of high school class are recommended. The application deadline for regular admission is August 15.
Transfer Admission The application deadline for admission is August 15.
Entrance Difficulty Simpson assesses its entrance difficulty level as moderately difficult. For the fall 2002 freshman class, 85 percent of the applicants were accepted.

SPECIAL MESSAGE TO STUDENTS

Social Life One of the characteristics of Simpson is the number of opportunities available on campus. Activities include vocal and instrumental music groups, Theatre Simpson, honor and professional societies, and religious life council. Simpson competes in Division III of the NCAA and offers eighteen intercollegiate teams for men and women. Students annually elect a president and vice president of the Student Government. Each housing unit elects representatives to Student Senate, and the senate appoints student members to appropriate College committees. Simpson is a residential campus with four traditional residence halls, seven apartment-style residences, ten theme houses, three national fraternities, one local fraternity, and four national sororities. Approximately 35 percent of the students participate in the Greek system.

Academic Highlights Simpson's academic program is based on the best traditions of the liberal arts, enhanced by a genuine respect for the career requirements of today. Simpson's professors are dedicated to teaching. With a student-faculty ratio of 14:1, professors get to know students personally. More than forty different majors and career programs are available. Simpson is on a 4-4-1 calendar, with two 4-month semesters and one 3-week term of concentrated study in May. The May-Term course offerings provide an in-depth exploration of a subject and include internships, study abroad, and career observations. Simpson has exchange programs with international and domestic universities and offers study-abroad programs on a regular basis.

Interviews and Campus Visits Simpson College strongly encourages all prospective students to visit the campus. An interview is not required but is considered an excellent opportunity for prospective students and their parents to discuss academic programs, financial assistance, and scholarship opportunities. During the visit, prospective students tour the campus with a Student Ambassador, perhaps meet with a professor or attend a class, and interview with an admissions counselor. Students can take advantage of music or theater productions, athletic events, or other activities during their visit. Simpson blends tradition with practicality, and this is reflected in the architecture on campus. Buildings of interest include the historic College Hall, built in 1869; Carver Science Center, named after George Washington Carver, who attended Simpson College; McNeill Hall for Business, housing a seminar room, conference center, computer labs, and classrooms; Dunn Library; the Amy Robertson Music Center, housing a 250-seat recital hall, studios, and practice rooms; and Cowles Athletic Center, in which a 25-meter swimming pool, physical education facilities, weight rooms, racquetball courts, and a field house are located. For information about appointments and campus visits, students should call the Office of Admissions at 515-961-1624 or 800-362-2454 (toll-free), Monday through Friday, 8 a.m. to 4:30 p.m., or most Saturdays, 9 a.m. to noon. The fax number is 515-961-1870. The office is located in College Hall, first floor, on campus. The nearest commercial airport is Des Moines International.

For Further Information Write to the Office of Admissions, Simpson College, 701 North C Street, Indianola, IA 50125. *E-mail:* admiss@simpson.edu. *Web site:* http://www.simpson.edu.

See page 336 for a narrative description.

UNIVERSITY OF DUBUQUE

Dubuque, Iowa

UD is a coed, private, Presbyterian, comprehensive institution, founded in 1852, offering degrees at the bachelor's, master's, and first professional levels. It has a 56-acre campus in Dubuque.

Academic Information The faculty has 97 members (46% full-time), 47% with terminal degrees. The undergraduate student-faculty ratio is 14:1. The library holds 166,331 titles, 565 serial subscriptions, and 525 audiovisual materials. Special programs include academic remediation, services for learning-disabled students, study abroad, advanced placement credit, accelerated degree programs, ESL programs, double majors, independent study, distance learning, self-designed majors, summer session for credit, part-time degree programs (daytime, evenings, weekends, summer), adult/continuing education programs, internships, and arrangement for off-campus study with Loras College, Clarke College (IA). The most frequently chosen baccalaureate fields are business/marketing, computer/information sciences, education.

Student Body Statistics The student body totals 1,120, of whom 843 are undergraduates (277 freshmen). 35 percent are women and 65 percent are men. Students come from 30 states and territories. 52 percent are from Iowa. 0.6 percent are international students.

Expenses for 2003–04 *Application fee:* $25. *Comprehensive fee:* $21,575 includes full-time tuition ($16,000), mandatory fees ($155), and college room and board ($5420). *College room only:* $2610. Room and board charges vary according to board plan and housing facility. *Part-time tuition:* $360 per credit.

Financial Aid Forms of aid include need-based and non-need-based scholarships and part-time jobs. The average aided 2002–03 undergraduate received an aid package worth an estimated $15,355. The application deadline for financial aid is continuous.

Freshman Admission UD requires an essay, a high school transcript, a minimum 2.0 high school GPA, 2 recommendations, SAT I or ACT scores, and TOEFL scores for international students. An interview is recommended. The application deadline for regular admission is rolling.

Transfer Admission The application deadline for admission is rolling.

Entrance Difficulty UD assesses its entrance difficulty level as moderately difficult. For the fall 2002 freshman class, 78 percent of the applicants were accepted.

For Further Information Contact Mr. Jesse James, Director of Admissions and Records, University of Dubuque, 2000 University Avenue, Dubuque, IA 52001-5099. *Telephone:* 563-589-3214 or 800-722-5583 (toll-free in-state). *Fax:* 563-589-3690. *E-mail:* admssns@dbq.edu. *Web site:* http://www.dbq.edu/.

THE UNIVERSITY OF IOWA

Iowa City, Iowa

Iowa is a coed, public university, founded in 1847, offering degrees at the bachelor's, master's, doctoral, and first professional levels. It has a 1,900-acre campus in Iowa City.

Academic Information The faculty has 1,679 members (95% full-time), 96% with terminal degrees. The undergraduate student-faculty ratio is 15:1. The library holds 4 million titles, 44,644 serial subscriptions, and 267,192 audiovisual materials. Special programs include academic remediation, services for learning-disabled students, an honors program, cooperative (work-study) education, study abroad, advanced placement credit, accelerated degree programs, ESL programs, double majors, independent study, distance learning, self-designed majors, summer session for credit, part-time degree programs (daytime, evenings, weekends, summer), external degree programs, adult/continuing education programs, internships, and arrangement for off-campus study with Iowa State University of Science and Technology, University of Northern Iowa, Committee on Institutional Cooperation. The most frequently chosen baccalaureate fields are business/marketing, communications/communication technologies, social sciences and history.

Student Body Statistics The student body totals 29,697, of whom 20,487 are undergraduates (4,184 freshmen). 55 percent are women and 45 percent are men. Students come from 52 states and territories and 72 other countries. 67 percent are from Iowa. 1.2 percent are international students.

Expenses for 2003–04 *Application fee:* $30. *State resident tuition:* $4342 full-time, $181 per semester hour part-time. *Nonresident tuition:* $14,634 full-time, $610 per semester hour part-time. *Mandatory fees:* $651 full-time, $326 per term part-time. Full-time tuition and fees vary according to course load. Part-time tuition and fees vary according to course load. *College room and board:* $5930. Room and board charges vary according to board plan and housing facility.

Financial Aid Forms of aid include need-based and non-need-based scholarships, athletic grants, and part-time jobs. The average aided 2001–02 undergraduate received an aid package worth $6806. The application deadline for financial aid is continuous.

Freshman Admission Iowa requires a high school transcript, rank in top 50% for residents, rank in top 30% for nonresidents, SAT I or ACT scores, and TOEFL scores for international students. The application deadline for regular admission is April 1.

Transfer Admission The application deadline for admission is April 1.

Entrance Difficulty Iowa assesses its entrance difficulty level as moderately difficult; very difficult for engineering programs. For the fall 2002 freshman class, 84 percent of the applicants were accepted.

For Further Information Contact Mr. Michael Barron, Director of Admissions, The University of Iowa, 107 Calvin Hall, Iowa City, IA 52242. *Telephone:* 319-335-3847 or 800-553-4692 (toll-free). *Fax:* 319-335-1535. *E-mail:* admissions@uiowa.edu. *Web site:* http://www.uiowa.edu/.

UNIVERSITY OF NORTHERN IOWA

Cedar Falls, Iowa

UNI is a coed, public, comprehensive unit of Board of Regents, State of Iowa, founded in 1876, offering degrees at the bachelor's, master's, and doctoral levels. It has a 940-acre campus in Cedar Falls.

Academic Information The faculty has 842 members (81% full-time), 69% with terminal degrees. The undergraduate student-faculty ratio is

University of Northern Iowa (continued)

16:1. The library holds 760,595 titles, 7,226 serial subscriptions, and 22,883 audiovisual materials. Special programs include academic remediation, services for learning-disabled students, an honors program, cooperative (work-study) education, study abroad, advanced placement credit, accelerated degree programs, ESL programs, double majors, independent study, distance learning, self-designed majors, summer session for credit, part-time degree programs (daytime, evenings, summer), adult/continuing education programs, internships, and arrangement for off-campus study with Iowa Regents' Universities Student Exchange, National Student Exchange. The most frequently chosen baccalaureate fields are business/marketing, education, social sciences and history.

Student Body Statistics The student body totals 14,167, of whom 12,397 are undergraduates (1,858 freshmen). 58 percent are women and 42 percent are men. Students come from 42 states and territories and 72 other countries. 95 percent are from Iowa. 1.7 percent are international students. 13 percent of the 2002 graduating class went on to graduate and professional schools.

Expenses for 2002–03 *Application fee:* $30. *State resident tuition:* $3692 full-time, $154 per hour part-time. *Nonresident tuition:* $10,000 full-time, $417 per hour part-time. *Mandatory fees:* $425 full-time, $35 per term part-time. Full-time tuition and fees vary according to course load. Part-time tuition and fees vary according to course load. *College room and board:* $4640. *College room only:* $2132. Room and board charges vary according to board plan and housing facility.

Financial Aid Forms of aid include need-based and non-need-based scholarships, athletic grants, and part-time jobs. The average aided 2002–03 undergraduate received an aid package worth an estimated $6222. The application deadline for financial aid is continuous.

Freshman Admission UNI requires a high school transcript, SAT I or ACT scores, and TOEFL scores for international students. An interview is required for some. The application deadline for regular admission is August 15.

Transfer Admission The application deadline for admission is August 15.

Entrance Difficulty UNI assesses its entrance difficulty level as moderately difficult. For the fall 2002 freshman class, 80 percent of the applicants were accepted.

For Further Information Contact Mr. Clark Elmer, Director of Enrollment Management and Admissions, University of Northern Iowa, 120 Gilchrist Hall, Cedar Falls, IA 50614-0018. *Telephone:* 319-273-2281 or 800-772-2037 (toll-free). *Fax:* 319-273-2885. *E-mail:* admissions@uni.edu. *Web site:* http://www.uni.edu/.

UPPER IOWA UNIVERSITY

Fayette, Iowa

Upper Iowa is a coed, private, comprehensive institution, founded in 1857, offering degrees at the associate, bachelor's, and master's levels (also offers continuing education program with significant enrollment not reflected in profile). It has an 80-acre campus in Fayette.

Academic Information The faculty has 65 members (88% full-time), 62% with terminal degrees. The undergraduate student-faculty ratio is 14:1. The library holds 64,043 titles, 3,241 serial subscriptions, and 4,031 audiovisual materials. Special programs include academic remediation, study abroad, advanced placement credit, accelerated degree programs, double majors, independent study, distance learning, self-designed majors, summer session for credit, part-time degree programs (daytime, evenings, summer), external degree programs, adult/continuing education programs, and internships.

Student Body Statistics The student body totals 870, of whom 630 are undergraduates (106 freshmen). 36 percent are women and 64 percent are men. Students come from 25 states and territories and 7 other countries. 58 percent are from Iowa. 6.8 percent are international students.

Expenses for 2002–03 *Application fee:* $15. *Comprehensive fee:* $18,838 includes full-time tuition ($14,056) and college room and board ($4782). Full-time tuition varies according to course load. Room and board charges vary according to board plan and housing facility. *Part-time tuition:* $660 per course.

Financial Aid Forms of aid include need-based and non-need-based scholarships and part-time jobs. $6000. The priority application deadline for financial aid is June 1.

Freshman Admission Upper Iowa requires a high school transcript, a minimum 2.0 high school GPA, SAT I or ACT scores, and TOEFL scores for international students. An essay, recommendations, and an interview are required for some. The application deadline for regular admission is rolling.

Transfer Admission The application deadline for admission is rolling.

Entrance Difficulty Upper Iowa assesses its entrance difficulty level as moderately difficult. For the fall 2002 freshman class, 68 percent of the applicants were accepted.

For Further Information Contact Ms. Linda Hoopes, Director of Admissions, Upper Iowa University, Box 1859, 605 Washington Street, Fayette, IA 52142-1857. *Telephone:* 563-425-5281 Ext. 5279 or 800-553-4150 Ext. 2 (toll-free). *Fax:* 563-425-5277. *E-mail:* admission@uiu.edu. *Web site:* http://www.uiu.edu/.

VENNARD COLLEGE

University Park, Iowa

Vennard is a coed, private, interdenominational, four-year college, founded in 1996, offering degrees at the associate and bachelor's levels.

Academic Information The faculty has 13 members (46% full-time), 23% with terminal degrees. The student-faculty ratio is 11:1. The library holds 17,950 titles and 538,323 serial subscriptions. Special programs include academic remediation, services for learning-disabled students, cooperative (work-study) education, advanced placement credit, double majors, independent study, distance learning, self-designed majors, summer session for credit, part-time degree programs (daytime, evenings), external degree programs, internships, and arrangement for off-campus study with William Penn University.

Student Body Statistics The student body is made up of 114 undergraduates. Students come from 19 states and territories and 2 other countries. 45 percent are from Iowa. 1.8 percent are international students.

Expenses for 2003–04 *Application fee:* $20.

Financial Aid The average aided 2002–03 undergraduate received an aid package worth an estimated $7000. The priority application deadline for financial aid is April 1.

Freshman Admission Vennard requires an essay, a high school transcript, a minimum 2.5 high school GPA, and 3 recommendations. SAT I or ACT scores are recommended. SAT I and SAT II or ACT scores are required for some.

Entrance Difficulty For the fall 2002 freshman class, 47 percent of the applicants were accepted.

For Further Information Contact Randy Ozan, Director of Admissions, Vennard College, PO Box 29, University Park, IA 52595. *Telephone:* 641-673-8391 Ext. 218 or 800-686-8391 (toll-free). *Fax:* 641-673-8365. *Web site:* http://www.vennard.edu/.

WALDORF COLLEGE

Forest City, Iowa

Waldorf is a coed, private, Lutheran, four-year college, founded in 1903, offering degrees at the associate and bachelor's levels. It has a 29-acre campus in Forest City.

Academic Information The faculty has 53 members (68% full-time), 30% with terminal degrees. The student-faculty ratio is 13:1. The library holds 33,422 titles, 55,989 serial subscriptions, and 274 audiovisual materials. Special programs include academic remediation, services for learning-disabled students, an honors program, cooperative (work-study) education, study abroad, advanced placement credit, accelerated degree programs, Freshman Honors College, ESL programs, double majors, summer session for credit, part-time degree programs, adult/continuing education programs, and internships.

Student Body Statistics The student body is made up of 547 undergraduates. 46 percent are women and 54 percent are men. 67 percent are from Iowa. 6.2 percent are international students. 2 percent of the 2002 graduating class went on to graduate and professional schools.
Expenses for 2002–03 *Application fee:* $20. *Comprehensive fee:* $18,861 includes full-time tuition ($13,999), mandatory fees ($662), and college room and board ($4200). Room and board charges vary according to board plan and housing facility. *Part-time tuition:* $150 per credit.
Financial Aid Forms of aid include need-based and non-need-based scholarships, athletic grants, and part-time jobs. The average aided 2002–03 undergraduate received an aid package worth an estimated $15,565. The priority application deadline for financial aid is March 1.
Freshman Admission Waldorf requires a high school transcript, 1 recommendation, SAT I or ACT scores, and TOEFL scores for international students. A minimum 2.0 high school GPA is recommended. An interview is required for some. The application deadline for regular admission is rolling.
Transfer Admission The application deadline for admission is rolling.
Entrance Difficulty Waldorf assesses its entrance difficulty level as moderately difficult. For the fall 2002 freshman class, 69 percent of the applicants were accepted.

For Further Information Contact Mr. Steve Hall, Assistant Dean of Admission, Waldorf College, 106 South 6th Street, Forest City, IA 50436. *Telephone:* 641-585-8112 or 800-292-1903 (toll-free). *Fax:* 641-585-8125. *E-mail:* admissions@waldorf.edu. *Web site:* http://www.waldorf.edu/.

WARTBURG COLLEGE

Waverly, Iowa

Wartburg is a coed, private, Lutheran, four-year college, founded in 1852, offering degrees at the bachelor's level. It has a 118-acre campus in Waverly.

Academic Information The faculty has 167 members (60% full-time), 60% with terminal degrees. The student-faculty ratio is 14:1. The library holds 171,852 titles, 826 serial subscriptions, and 3,754 audiovisual materials. Special programs include academic remediation, study abroad, advanced placement credit, accelerated degree programs, double majors, independent study, self-designed majors, summer session for credit, part-time degree programs, internships, and arrangement for off-campus study with members of the May Term Consortium. The most frequently chosen baccalaureate fields are business/marketing, biological/life sciences, education.
Student Body Statistics The student body is made up of 1,695 undergraduates (513 freshmen). 56 percent are women and 44 percent are men. Students come from 29 states and territories and 32 other countries. 80 percent are from Iowa. 3.7 percent are international students.
Expenses for 2003–04 *Application fee:* $20. *Comprehensive fee:* $23,730 includes full-time tuition ($18,150), mandatory fees ($400), and college room and board ($5180). *College room only:* $2530. *Part-time tuition:* $670 per credit. *Part-time mandatory fees:* $15 per term.
Financial Aid Forms of aid include need-based and non-need-based scholarships and part-time jobs. The average aided 2002–03 undergraduate received an aid package worth an estimated $16,135. The priority application deadline for financial aid is March 1.
Freshman Admission Wartburg requires a high school transcript, a minimum 2.0 high school GPA, SAT I or ACT scores, and TOEFL scores for international students. Recommendations and secondary school report are recommended. An interview is required for some.
Entrance Difficulty Wartburg assesses its entrance difficulty level as moderately difficult. For the fall 2002 freshman class, 84 percent of the applicants were accepted.

For Further Information Contact Doug Bowman, Dean of Admissions/Financial Aid, Wartburg College, 100 Wartburg Boulevard, PO Box 1003, Waverly, IA 50677-0903. *Telephone:* 319-352-8264 or 800-772-2085 (toll-free). *Fax:* 319-352-8579. *E-mail:* admissions@wartburg.edu. *Web site:* http://www.wartburg.edu/.

See page 350 for a narrative description.

WILLIAM PENN UNIVERSITY

Oskaloosa, Iowa

William Penn is a coed, private, four-year college, founded in 1873, affiliated with the Society of Friends, offering degrees at the associate and bachelor's levels. It has a 40-acre campus in Oskaloosa near Des Moines.

Academic Information The faculty has 52 members (67% full-time), 37% with terminal degrees. The student-faculty ratio is 14:1. The library holds 72,907 titles, 354 serial subscriptions, and 738 audiovisual materials. Special programs include academic remediation, services for learning-disabled students, cooperative (work-study) education, study abroad, advanced placement credit, ESL programs, double majors, independent study, self-designed majors, summer session for credit, part-time degree programs (daytime, evenings, summer), adult/continuing education programs, and internships. The most frequently chosen baccalaureate fields are business/marketing, education, psychology.
Student Body Statistics The student body is made up of 1,499 undergraduates (230 freshmen). 48 percent are women and 52 percent are men. Students come from 41 states and territories and 10 other countries. 72 percent are from Iowa. 1.1 percent are international students. 15 percent of the 2002 graduating class went on to graduate and professional schools.
Expenses for 2002–03 *Application fee:* $20. *Comprehensive fee:* $18,084 includes full-time tuition ($13,284), mandatory fees ($370), and college room and board ($4430). Room and board charges vary according to board plan and housing facility. *Part-time tuition:* $215 per credit hour. Part-time tuition varies according to course load.
Financial Aid Forms of aid include need-based and non-need-based scholarships, athletic grants, and part-time jobs. The priority application deadline for financial aid is April 15.
Freshman Admission William Penn requires a high school transcript, a minimum 2.0 high school GPA, SAT I or ACT scores, and TOEFL scores for international students. An essay, recommendations, and an interview are required for some.
Entrance Difficulty William Penn assesses its entrance difficulty level as moderately difficult. For the fall 2002 freshman class, 62 percent of the applicants were accepted.

For Further Information Contact Mrs. Mary Boyd, Director of Admissions, William Penn University, 201 Trueblood Avenue, Oskaloosa, IA 52577-1799. *Telephone:* 641-673-1012 or 800-779-7366 (toll-free). *Fax:* 641-673-2113. *E-mail:* admissions@wmpenn.edu. *Web site:* http://www.wmpenn.edu/.

See page 356 for a narrative description.

Kansas

BAKER UNIVERSITY

Baldwin City, Kansas

Baker is a coed, private, United Methodist, comprehensive institution, founded in 1858, offering degrees at the bachelor's level. It has a 26-acre campus in Baldwin City near Kansas City.

Academic Information The faculty has 100 members (69% full-time), 56% with terminal degrees. The student-faculty ratio is 12:1. The library holds 84,114 titles, 507 serial subscriptions, and 1,139 audiovisual materials. Special programs include services for learning-disabled students, an honors program, study abroad, advanced placement credit, double majors, independent study, self-designed majors, summer session for credit, and internships. The most frequently chosen baccalaureate fields are business/marketing, education, health professions and related sciences.
Student Body Statistics The student body is made up of 988 undergraduates (231 freshmen). 60 percent are women and 40 percent are men. Students come from 18 states and territories and 4 other countries.

Baker University (continued)
75 percent are from Kansas. 0.8 percent are international students. 16 percent of the 2002 graduating class went on to graduate and professional schools.
Expenses for 2003–04 *Application fee:* $20. *One-time mandatory fee:* $80. *Comprehensive fee:* $19,860 includes full-time tuition ($14,210), mandatory fees ($350), and college room and board ($5300). Full-time tuition and fees vary according to location and program. Room and board charges vary according to board plan and housing facility. *Part-time tuition:* varies with course load.
Financial Aid Forms of aid include need-based and non-need-based scholarships, athletic grants, and part-time jobs. The average aided 2002–03 undergraduate received an aid package worth an estimated $10,900. The priority application deadline for financial aid is March 1.
Freshman Admission Baker requires a high school transcript, a minimum 3.0 high school GPA, 1 recommendation, SAT I or ACT scores, and TOEFL scores for international students. An essay and an interview are required for some. The application deadline for regular admission is rolling.
Transfer Admission The application deadline for admission is rolling.
Entrance Difficulty Baker assesses its entrance difficulty level as moderately difficult. For the fall 2002 freshman class, 95 percent of the applicants were accepted.

For Further Information Contact Director of Admission, Baker University, PO Box 65, Baldwin City, KS 66006-0065. *Telephone:* 785-594-6451 Ext. 458 or 800-873-4282 (toll-free). *Fax:* 785-594-8372. *E-mail:* admission@bakeru.edu. *Web site:* http://www.bakeru.edu/.

BARCLAY COLLEGE

Haviland, Kansas

Barclay is a coed, private, four-year college, founded in 1917, affiliated with the Society of Friends, offering degrees at the associate and bachelor's levels. It has a 13-acre campus in Haviland.

Academic Information The faculty has 38 members (21% full-time), 8% with terminal degrees. The student-faculty ratio is 7:1. The library holds 60,397 titles, 6,959 serial subscriptions, and 2,291 audiovisual materials. Special programs include academic remediation, advanced placement credit, accelerated degree programs, double majors, independent study, distance learning, self-designed majors, part-time degree programs (daytime, evenings), external degree programs, adult/continuing education programs, and internships. The most frequently chosen baccalaureate fields are business/marketing, philosophy, religion, and theology, psychology.
Student Body Statistics The student body is made up of 194 undergraduates (20 freshmen). 55 percent are women and 45 percent are men. Students come from 18 states and territories and 1 other country. 59 percent are from Kansas. 1.5 percent are international students. 10 percent of the 2002 graduating class went on to graduate and professional schools.
Expenses for 2003–04 *Application fee:* $15. *Comprehensive fee:* $12,450 includes full-time tuition ($8250) and college room and board ($4200). *College room only:* $1650. *Part-time tuition:* $350 per credit hour. *Part-time mandatory fees:* $42 per credit hour.
Financial Aid Forms of aid include need-based and non-need-based scholarships and part-time jobs. The average aided 2002–03 undergraduate received an aid package worth an estimated $6700. The priority application deadline for financial aid is March 15.
Freshman Admission Barclay requires an essay, a high school transcript, a minimum 2.3 high school GPA, 2 recommendations, SAT I or ACT scores, and TOEFL scores for international students. The application deadline for regular admission is September 1.
Transfer Admission The application deadline for admission is September 1.
Entrance Difficulty Barclay assesses its entrance difficulty level as minimally difficult. For the fall 2002 freshman class, 100 percent of the applicants were accepted.

For Further Information Contact Ryan Haase, Director of Admissions, Barclay College, 607 North Kingman, Haviland, KS 67059. *Telephone:* 620-862-5252 Ext. 41 or 800-862-0226 (toll-free). *Fax:* 620-862-5242. *E-mail:* admissions@barclaycollege.edu. *Web site:* http://www.barclaycollege.edu/.

BENEDICTINE COLLEGE

Atchison, Kansas

Benedictine College is a coed, private, Roman Catholic, comprehensive institution, founded in 1859, offering degrees at the associate, bachelor's, and master's levels. It has a 225-acre campus in Atchison near Kansas City.

Academic Information The faculty has 64 members (88% full-time), 69% with terminal degrees. The undergraduate student-faculty ratio is 15:1. The library holds 366,212 titles, 501 serial subscriptions, and 831 audiovisual materials. Special programs include academic remediation, cooperative (work-study) education, study abroad, advanced placement credit, ESL programs, independent study, self-designed majors, summer session for credit, part-time degree programs (daytime, evenings, summer), internships, and arrangement for off-campus study with 16 members of the Kansas City Regional Council for Higher Education, Kansas State University. The most frequently chosen baccalaureate fields are business/marketing, education, social sciences and history.
Student Body Statistics The student body totals 1,375, of whom 1,296 are undergraduates (300 freshmen). 52 percent are women and 48 percent are men. Students come from 34 states and territories and 14 other countries. 47 percent are from Kansas. 2.7 percent are international students.
Expenses for 2002–03 *Application fee:* $25. *Comprehensive fee:* $19,830 includes full-time tuition ($13,400), mandatory fees ($800), and college room and board ($5630). *College room only:* $2430. Full-time tuition and fees vary according to course load and degree level. Room and board charges vary according to board plan and housing facility. *Part-time tuition:* $385 per credit hour. *Part-time mandatory fees:* $400 per year. Part-time tuition and fees vary according to course load and degree level.
Financial Aid Forms of aid include need-based and non-need-based scholarships, athletic grants, and part-time jobs. The average aided 2001–02 undergraduate received an aid package worth $13,523. The application deadline for financial aid is continuous.
Freshman Admission Benedictine College requires a high school transcript, a minimum 2.0 high school GPA, SAT I or ACT scores, and TOEFL scores for international students. An interview is required for some.
Entrance Difficulty Benedictine College assesses its entrance difficulty level as moderately difficult. For the fall 2002 freshman class, 89 percent of the applicants were accepted.

For Further Information Contact Ms. Kelly Vowels, Dean of Enrollment Management, Benedictine College, 1020 North 2nd Street, Atchison, KS 66002. *Telephone:* 913-367-5340 Ext. 2476 or 800-467-5340 (toll-free). *Fax:* 913-367-5462. *E-mail:* bcadmiss@benedictine.edu. *Web site:* http://www.benedictine.edu/.

BETHANY COLLEGE

Lindsborg, Kansas

Bethany is a coed, private, Lutheran, four-year college, founded in 1881, offering degrees at the bachelor's level. It has an 80-acre campus in Lindsborg.

Academic Information The faculty has 73 members (60% full-time), 51% with terminal degrees. The student-faculty ratio is 10:1. The library holds 609 serial subscriptions and 3,518 audiovisual materials. Special programs include services for learning-disabled students, advanced placement credit, accelerated degree programs, double majors, independent

study, self-designed majors, summer session for credit, internships, and arrangement for off-campus study with 6 members of the Associated Colleges of Central Kansas. The most frequently chosen baccalaureate fields are business/marketing, education, social sciences and history.
Student Body Statistics The student body is made up of 623 undergraduates (142 freshmen). 49 percent are women and 51 percent are men. Students come from 28 states and territories. 61 percent are from Kansas. 0.3 percent are international students. 22 percent of the 2002 graduating class went on to graduate and professional schools.
Expenses for 2003–04 *Application fee:* $20. *Comprehensive fee:* $18,710 includes full-time tuition ($14,140) and college room and board ($4570). *College room only:* $2100. Full-time tuition varies according to location. Room and board charges vary according to board plan and housing facility. *Part-time tuition:* $230 per credit hour. Part-time tuition varies according to course load.
Financial Aid Forms of aid include need-based and non-need-based scholarships, athletic grants, and part-time jobs. The average aided 2002–03 undergraduate received an aid package worth an estimated $14,465. The application deadline for financial aid is continuous.
Freshman Admission Bethany requires a high school transcript, a minimum 2.5 high school GPA, SAT I or ACT scores, and TOEFL scores for international students. An essay, recommendations, and an interview are required for some. The application deadline for regular admission is July 1.
Transfer Admission The application deadline for admission is rolling.
Entrance Difficulty Bethany assesses its entrance difficulty level as moderately difficult. For the fall 2002 freshman class, 69 percent of the applicants were accepted.

For Further Information Contact Ms. Brenda Meagher, Interim Dean of Admissions and Financial Aid, Bethany College, 421 North First Street, Lindsborg, KS 67456. *Telephone:* 785-227-3311 Ext. 3248 or 800-826-2281 (toll-free). *Fax:* 785-227-2004. *E-mail:* admissions@bethanylb.edu. *Web site:* http://www.bethanylb.edu/.

BETHEL COLLEGE

North Newton, Kansas

Bethel is a coed, private, four-year college, founded in 1887, affiliated with the General Conference Mennonite Church, offering degrees at the bachelor's level. It has a 60-acre campus in North Newton near Wichita.

Academic Information The faculty has 61 members (72% full-time), 48% with terminal degrees. The student-faculty ratio is 9:1. The library holds 99,287 titles, 560 serial subscriptions, and 161,396 audiovisual materials. Special programs include academic remediation, services for learning-disabled students, cooperative (work-study) education, study abroad, advanced placement credit, double majors, independent study, summer session for credit, part-time degree programs (daytime, evenings, summer), internships, and arrangement for off-campus study with 6 members of the Associated Colleges of Central Kansas, Hesston College. The most frequently chosen baccalaureate fields are education, business/marketing, health professions and related sciences.
Student Body Statistics The student body is made up of 471 undergraduates (99 freshmen). 48 percent are women and 52 percent are men. Students come from 27 states and territories and 12 other countries. 62 percent are from Kansas. 3.2 percent are international students. 11 percent of the 2002 graduating class went on to graduate and professional schools.
Expenses for 2003–04 *Application fee:* $20. *Comprehensive fee:* $19,800 includes full-time tuition ($13,900) and college room and board ($5900). Full-time tuition varies according to course load. Room and board charges vary according to board plan and housing facility. *Part-time tuition:* $495 per credit hour. Part-time tuition varies according to course load.
Financial Aid Forms of aid include need-based and non-need-based scholarships, athletic grants, and part-time jobs. The average aided 2001–02 undergraduate received an aid package worth $13,599. The priority application deadline for financial aid is March 15.
Freshman Admission Bethel requires a high school transcript, a minimum 2.5 high school GPA, SAT I or ACT scores, and TOEFL scores for international students. An interview is recommended. An essay and 2 recommendations are required for some. The application deadline for regular admission is August 1.
Transfer Admission The application deadline for admission is August 1.
Entrance Difficulty Bethel assesses its entrance difficulty level as moderately difficult. For the fall 2002 freshman class, 68 percent of the applicants were accepted.

For Further Information Contact Ms. Pauline Buller, Associate Director of Admissions, Bethel College, 300 East 27th Street, North Newton, KS 67117-0531. *Telephone:* 316-284-5230 or 800-522-1887 Ext. 230 (toll-free). *Fax:* 316-284-5870. *E-mail:* admissions@bethelks.edu. *Web site:* http://www.bethelks.edu/.

See page 256 for a narrative description.

CENTRAL CHRISTIAN COLLEGE OF KANSAS

McPherson, Kansas

Central is a coed, private, Free Methodist, four-year college, founded in 1884, offering degrees at the associate and bachelor's levels. It has a 16-acre campus in McPherson.

Academic Information The faculty has 35 members (51% full-time), 17% with terminal degrees. The student-faculty ratio is 14:1. The library holds 26,700 titles, 95 serial subscriptions, and 988 audiovisual materials. Special programs include academic remediation, services for learning-disabled students, cooperative (work-study) education, study abroad, advanced placement credit, double majors, independent study, self-designed majors, part-time degree programs (daytime, evenings), adult/continuing education programs, internships, and arrangement for off-campus study with McPherson College, Christian Center for Urban Studies. The most frequently chosen baccalaureate fields are liberal arts/general studies, business/marketing, philosophy, religion, and theology.
Student Body Statistics The student body is made up of 337 undergraduates. 54 percent are women and 46 percent are men. Students come from 30 states and territories and 2 other countries. 49 percent are from Kansas. 2.4 percent are international students. 7 percent of the 2002 graduating class went on to graduate and professional schools.
Expenses for 2003–04 *Application fee:* $20. *Comprehensive fee:* $16,600 includes full-time tuition ($12,000), mandatory fees ($500), and college room and board ($4100). *College room only:* $1900. Full-time tuition and fees vary according to course load. Room and board charges vary according to board plan and gender. *Part-time tuition:* $350 per credit hour. Part-time tuition varies according to course load.
Financial Aid Forms of aid include need-based and non-need-based scholarships, athletic grants, and part-time jobs. The average aided 2002–03 undergraduate received an aid package worth an estimated $10,414. The priority application deadline for financial aid is March 1.
Freshman Admission Central requires a high school transcript, a minimum 2.5 high school GPA, 2 recommendations, SAT I or ACT scores, and TOEFL scores for international students. An essay and an interview are recommended. The application deadline for regular admission is rolling.
Transfer Admission The application deadline for admission is rolling.
Entrance Difficulty Central assesses its entrance difficulty level as moderately difficult. For the fall 2002 freshman class, 99 percent of the applicants were accepted.

For Further Information Contact Dr. David Ferrell, Dean of Admissions, Central Christian College of Kansas, PO Box 1403, McPherson, KS 67460. *Telephone:* 620-241-0723 Ext. 380 or 800-835-0078 (toll-free). *Fax:* 620-241-6032. *E-mail:* admissions@centralchristian.edu. *Web site:* http://www.centralchristian.edu/.

DONNELLY COLLEGE

Kansas City, Kansas

Donnelly College is a coed, private, Roman Catholic, two-year college, founded in 1949, offering degrees at the associate level. It has a 4-acre campus in Kansas City.

Academic Information The faculty has 46 members (28% full-time), 15% with terminal degrees. The student-faculty ratio is 10:1. The library holds 33,752 titles, 114 serial subscriptions, and 1,020 audiovisual materials. Special programs include academic remediation, services for learning-disabled students, advanced placement credit, ESL programs, double majors, independent study, summer session for credit, part-time degree programs (daytime, evenings, weekends, summer), external degree programs, and internships.
Student Body Statistics The student body is made up of 697 undergraduates. Students come from 15 states and territories and 39 other countries. 88 percent are from Kansas. 90 percent of the 2002 graduating class went on to four-year colleges.
Expenses for 2003–04 *Application fee:* $0. *Tuition:* $3780 full-time, $145 per credit part-time. *Mandatory fees:* $40 full-time. Full-time tuition and fees vary according to course load. Part-time tuition varies according to course load.
Financial Aid Forms of aid include need-based scholarships and part-time jobs. The priority application deadline for financial aid is April 1.
Freshman Admission Donnelly College requires TOEFL scores for international students. A high school transcript is recommended. The application deadline for regular admission is rolling.
Transfer Admission The application deadline for admission is rolling.
Entrance Difficulty Donnelly College has an open admission policy.

For Further Information Contact Sr. Mary Agnes Patterson, Vice President, Donnelly College, 608 North 18th Street, Kansas City, KS 66102. *Telephone:* 913-621-8724. *Fax:* 913-621-0354. *E-mail:* bernetta@donnelly.edu. *Web site:* http://www.donnelly.edu/.

EMPORIA STATE UNIVERSITY

Emporia, Kansas

ESU is a coed, public, comprehensive unit of Kansas Board of Regents, founded in 1863, offering degrees at the bachelor's, master's, and doctoral levels and post-master's certificates. It has a 207-acre campus in Emporia near Wichita.

Academic Information The faculty has 266 members (92% full-time), 79% with terminal degrees. The undergraduate student-faculty ratio is 19:1. The library holds 558,565 titles, 1,416 serial subscriptions, and 7,649 audiovisual materials. Special programs include academic remediation, services for learning-disabled students, an honors program, study abroad, advanced placement credit, accelerated degree programs, ESL programs, double majors, independent study, distance learning, summer session for credit, part-time degree programs (daytime, evenings, weekends, summer), adult/continuing education programs, internships, and arrangement for off-campus study. The most frequently chosen baccalaureate fields are business/marketing, education, social sciences and history.
Student Body Statistics The student body totals 6,005, of whom 4,393 are undergraduates (803 freshmen). 61 percent are women and 39 percent are men. Students come from 41 states and territories and 55 other countries. 93 percent are from Kansas. 2.6 percent are international students. 18 percent of the 2002 graduating class went on to graduate and professional schools.
Expenses for 2002–03 *Application fee:* $25. *State resident tuition:* $1896 full-time, $63 per credit hour part-time. *Nonresident tuition:* $7188 full-time, $240 per credit hour part-time. *Mandatory fees:* $558 full-time, $34 per credit hour part-time. *College room and board:* $4046. *College room only:* $1968. Room and board charges vary according to board plan and housing facility.
Financial Aid Forms of aid include need-based and non-need-based scholarships, athletic grants, and part-time jobs. The average aided 2001–02 undergraduate received an aid package worth $5139. The priority application deadline for financial aid is March 15.
Freshman Admission ESU requires a high school transcript, SAT I or ACT scores, and TOEFL scores for international students. A minimum 2.0 high school GPA is recommended. The application deadline for regular admission is rolling.
Transfer Admission The application deadline for admission is rolling.
Entrance Difficulty ESU assesses its entrance difficulty level as noncompetitive; minimally difficult for transfers. For the fall 2002 freshman class, 71 percent of the applicants were accepted.

For Further Information Contact Ms. Susan Brinkman, Director of Admissions, Emporia State University, 1200 Commercial Street, Emporia, KS 66801-5087. *Telephone:* 620-341-5465, 877-GOTOESU (toll-free in-state), or 877-468-6378 (toll-free out-of-state). *Fax:* 620-341-5599. *E-mail:* go2esu@emporia.edu. *Web site:* http://www.emporia.edu/.

FORT HAYS STATE UNIVERSITY

Hays, Kansas

FHSU is a coed, public, comprehensive unit of Kansas Board of Regents, founded in 1902, offering degrees at the associate, bachelor's, and master's levels. It has a 200-acre campus in Hays.

Academic Information The faculty has 300 members (85% full-time), 70% with terminal degrees. The undergraduate student-faculty ratio is 17:1. The library holds 624,637 titles and 1,689 serial subscriptions. Special programs include academic remediation, services for learning-disabled students, study abroad, advanced placement credit, ESL programs, double majors, distance learning, self-designed majors, summer session for credit, part-time degree programs (daytime, evenings, weekends, summer), external degree programs, adult/continuing education programs, internships, and arrangement for off-campus study with members of the National Student Exchange. The most frequently chosen baccalaureate fields are business/marketing, education, health professions and related sciences.
Student Body Statistics The student body totals 6,392, of whom 5,570 are undergraduates (850 freshmen). 55 percent are women and 45 percent are men. Students come from 48 states and territories and 15 other countries. 91 percent are from Kansas. 9.9 percent are international students. 19 percent of the 2002 graduating class went on to graduate and professional schools.
Expenses for 2002–03 *Application fee:* $25. *State resident tuition:* $1851 full-time, $61.70 per credit hour part-time. *Nonresident tuition:* $7011 full-time, $233.70 per credit hour part-time. *Mandatory fees:* $477 full-time, $15.90 per credit hour part-time. Full-time tuition and fees vary according to course load, location, and reciprocity agreements. Part-time tuition and fees vary according to course load and location. *College room and board:* $4843. *College room only:* $2461. Room and board charges vary according to board plan, housing facility, and student level.
Financial Aid Forms of aid include need-based and non-need-based scholarships, athletic grants, and part-time jobs. The average aided 2001–02 undergraduate received an aid package worth $5085. The priority application deadline for financial aid is March 15.
Freshman Admission FHSU requires a high school transcript, SAT I or ACT scores, and TOEFL scores for international students. The application deadline for regular admission is rolling.
Transfer Admission The application deadline for admission is rolling.
Entrance Difficulty FHSU assesses its entrance difficulty level as noncompetitive; minimally difficult for out-of-state applicants; minimally difficult for transfers; moderately difficult for radiological technology program, School of Nursing. For the fall 2002 freshman class, 93 percent of the applicants were accepted.

For Further Information Contact Ms. Christy Befort, Senior Administrative Assistant, Office of Admissions, Fort Hays State University, 600 Park Street, Hays, KS 67601-4099. *Telephone:* 785-628-5666 or 800-628-FHSU (toll-free). *Fax:* 785-628-4187. *E-mail:* tigers@fhsu.edu. *Web site:* http://www.fhsu.edu/.

FRIENDS UNIVERSITY

Wichita, Kansas

Friends University is a coed, private, comprehensive institution, founded in 1898, offering degrees at the associate, bachelor's, and master's levels. It has a 45-acre campus in Wichita.

Expenses for 2002–03 *Application fee:* $15. *Comprehensive fee:* $16,855 includes full-time tuition ($12,845), mandatory fees ($120), and college room and board ($3890). *College room only:* $1710. Full-time tuition and fees vary according to course load. Room and board charges vary according to student level. *Part-time tuition:* varies with course load.

For Further Information Contact Mr. Tony Myers, Director of Admissions, Friends University, 2100 West University Street, Wichita, KS 67213. *Telephone:* 316-295-5100 or 800-577-2233 (toll-free). *Fax:* 316-262-5027. *E-mail:* tmyers@friends.edu. *Web site:* http://www.friends.edu/.

HASKELL INDIAN NATIONS UNIVERSITY

Lawrence, Kansas

Haskell is a coed, public, four-year college, founded in 1884, offering degrees at the associate and bachelor's levels. It has a 320-acre campus in Lawrence.

Academic Information The faculty has 48 members (100% full-time). The student-faculty ratio is 15:1. The library holds 50,000 titles and 400 serial subscriptions. Special programs include academic remediation, services for learning-disabled students, advanced placement credit, independent study, distance learning, self-designed majors, summer session for credit, part-time degree programs (daytime, summer), internships, and arrangement for off-campus study with members of the American Indian Higher Education Consortium, Kansas City Regional Council for Higher Education, University of Kansas.

Student Body Statistics The student body is made up of 1,028 undergraduates (350 freshmen). 47 percent are women and 53 percent are men. Students come from 37 states and territories.

Expenses for 2002–03 *Application fee:* $10. *One-time mandatory fee:* $10. *State resident tuition:* $0 full-time. *Nonresident tuition:* $0 full-time. *Mandatory fees:* $210 full-time, $70 per term part-time. *College room and board:* $70.

Financial Aid Forms of aid include need-based scholarships and part-time jobs. The application deadline for financial aid is continuous.

Freshman Admission Haskell requires a high school transcript, a minimum 2.0 high school GPA, ACT scores, and SAT I or ACT scores. 2 recommendations are required for some. The application deadline for regular admission is July 30.

Transfer Admission The application deadline for admission is July 30.

Entrance Difficulty Haskell assesses its entrance difficulty level as minimally difficult.

For Further Information Contact Ms. Patty Grant, Recruitment Officer, Haskell Indian Nations University, 155 Indian Avenue, #5031, Lawrence, KS 66046. *Telephone:* 785-749-8454 Ext. 456. *Fax:* 785-749-8429. *Web site:* http://www.haskell.edu/.

HESSTON COLLEGE

Hesston, Kansas

Hesston College is a coed, private, Mennonite, two-year college, founded in 1909, offering degrees at the associate level. It has a 50-acre campus in Hesston near Wichita.

Academic Information The faculty has 43 members (65% full-time), 23% with terminal degrees. The student-faculty ratio is 12:1. The library holds 35,000 titles, 234 serial subscriptions, and 2,409 audiovisual materials. Special programs include academic remediation, services for learning-disabled students, cooperative (work-study) education, advanced placement credit, ESL programs, double majors, independent study, summer session for credit, part-time degree programs (daytime, evenings), and internships.

Student Body Statistics The student body is made up of 440 undergraduates (177 freshmen). 53 percent are women and 47 percent are men. Students come from 30 states and territories and 12 other countries. 43 percent are from Kansas. 10.5 percent are international students.

Expenses for 2003–04 *Application fee:* $15. *Comprehensive fee:* $18,998 includes full-time tuition ($13,578), mandatory fees ($220), and college room and board ($5200). *Part-time tuition:* $568 per hour. *Part-time mandatory fees:* $55 per term. Part-time tuition and fees vary according to course load.

Financial Aid Forms of aid include need-based scholarships and part-time jobs. The priority application deadline for financial aid is May 1.

Freshman Admission Hesston College requires a high school transcript, recommendations, and TOEFL scores for international students. SAT I or ACT scores are recommended. An interview is required for some. The application deadline for regular admission is rolling.

Transfer Admission The application deadline for admission is rolling.

Entrance Difficulty Hesston College has an open admission policy except for nursing and pastoral ministries programs. It assesses its entrance difficulty as moderately difficult for nursing program.

For Further Information Contact Mr. Clark Roth, Vice President for Admissions, Hesston College, Box 3000, Hesston, KS 67062. *Telephone:* 620-327-8222 or 800-995-2757 (toll-free). *Fax:* 620-327-8300. *E-mail:* admissions@hesston.edu. *Web site:* http://www.hesston.edu/.

KANSAS NEWMAN COLLEGE

See Newman University

KANSAS STATE UNIVERSITY

Manhattan, Kansas

K-State is a coed, public university, founded in 1863, offering degrees at the associate, bachelor's, master's, doctoral, and first professional levels. It has a 668-acre campus in Manhattan near Kansas City.

Academic Information The faculty has 913 members (97% full-time), 85% with terminal degrees. The undergraduate student-faculty ratio is 20:1. The library holds 2 million titles, 1,365 serial subscriptions, and 5,056 audiovisual materials. Special programs include academic remediation, services for learning-disabled students, an honors program, cooperative (work-study) education, study abroad, advanced placement credit, accelerated degree programs, Freshman Honors College, ESL programs, double majors, independent study, distance learning, summer session for credit, part-time degree programs (daytime, evenings, summer), adult/continuing education programs, internships, and arrangement for off-campus study with Manhattan Christian College, University of Missouri-Kansas City, 19 Kansas community colleges. The most frequently chosen baccalaureate fields are agriculture, business/marketing, engineering/engineering technologies.

Student Body Statistics The student body totals 22,732, of whom 19,048 are undergraduates (3,537 freshmen). 48 percent are women and 52 percent are men. Students come from 50 states and territories and 98 other countries. 90 percent are from Kansas. 1.1 percent are international students.

Expenses for 2002–03 *Application fee:* $25. *State resident tuition:* $2918 full-time, $97.25 per semester hour part-time. *Nonresident tuition:* $10,178 full-time, $339.25 per semester hour part-time. *Mandatory fees:* $526 full-time, $18 per semester hour part-time, $65 per term part-time. *College room and board:* $4500. Room and board charges vary according to board plan.

Financial Aid Forms of aid include need-based and non-need-based scholarships, athletic grants, and part-time jobs. The average aided 2001–02 undergraduate received an aid package worth $4882. The priority application deadline for financial aid is March 1.

Kansas State University (continued)

Freshman Admission K-State requires a high school transcript, a minimum 2.0 high school GPA, SAT I or ACT scores, and TOEFL scores for international students. ACT scores are recommended. The application deadline for regular admission is rolling.
Transfer Admission The application deadline for admission is rolling.
Entrance Difficulty K-State assesses its entrance difficulty level as noncompetitive; moderately difficult for out-of-state applicants; moderately difficult for transfers; very difficult for architecture and design program. For the fall 2002 freshman class, 58 percent of the applicants were accepted.

For Further Information Contact Mr. Larry Moeder, Interim Director of Admissions, Kansas State University, 119 Anderson Hall, Manhattan, KS 66506. *Telephone:* 785-532-6250 or 800-432-8270 (toll-free in-state). *Fax:* 785-532-6393. *E-mail:* kstate@ksu.edu. *Web site:* http://www.ksu.edu/.

KANSAS WESLEYAN UNIVERSITY

Salina, Kansas

Kansas Wesleyan is a coed, private, United Methodist, comprehensive institution, founded in 1886, offering degrees at the associate, bachelor's, and master's levels. It has a 28-acre campus in Salina.

Expenses for 2002–03 *Application fee:* $20. *Comprehensive fee:* $18,000 includes full-time tuition ($13,400) and college room and board ($4600). *College room only:* $2200. *Part-time tuition:* varies with course load.

For Further Information Contact Dr. Philip P. Kerstetter, Director of Admissions, Kansas Wesleyan University, 100 East Claflin Avenue, Salina, KS 67401-6196. *Telephone:* 785-829-5541 Ext. 1283 or 800-874-1154 Ext. 1285 (toll-free). *Fax:* 785-827-0927. *E-mail:* admissions@diamond.kwu.edu. *Web site:* http://www.kwu.edu/.

MANHATTAN CHRISTIAN COLLEGE

Manhattan, Kansas

MCC is a coed, private, four-year college, founded in 1927, affiliated with the Christian Churches and Churches of Christ, offering degrees at the associate and bachelor's levels. It has a 10-acre campus in Manhattan.

Academic Information The faculty has 30 members (27% full-time), 20% with terminal degrees. The student-faculty ratio is 17:1. The library holds 2,500 titles and 45 serial subscriptions. Special programs include academic remediation, advanced placement credit, double majors, independent study, distance learning, summer session for credit, adult/continuing education programs, internships, and arrangement for off-campus study with Kansas State University. The most frequently chosen baccalaureate fields are business/marketing, philosophy, religion, and theology.
Student Body Statistics The student body is made up of 362 undergraduates (70 freshmen). 52 percent are women and 48 percent are men. Students come from 17 states and territories. 76 percent are from Kansas. 0.3 percent are international students. 1 percent of the 2002 graduating class went on to graduate and professional schools.
Expenses for 2002–03 *Application fee:* $25. *Comprehensive fee:* $11,920 includes full-time tuition ($7936), mandatory fees ($30), and college room and board ($3954). Room and board charges vary according to board plan. *Part-time tuition:* $331 per hour. Part-time tuition varies according to course load.
Financial Aid Forms of aid include need-based and non-need-based scholarships and part-time jobs. The priority application deadline for financial aid is March 15.
Freshman Admission MCC requires an essay, a high school transcript, a minimum 2.0 high school GPA, 3 recommendations, SAT I or ACT scores, and TOEFL scores for international students. An interview is required for some. The application deadline for regular admission is August 1.
Transfer Admission The application deadline for admission is August 1.
Entrance Difficulty MCC assesses its entrance difficulty level as minimally difficult. For the fall 2002 freshman class, 71 percent of the applicants were accepted.

For Further Information Contact Mr. Scott Jenkins, Director of Admissions, Manhattan Christian College, 1415 Anderson, Manhattan, KS 66502-4081. *Telephone:* 785-539-3571 or 877-246-4622 (toll-free). *Fax:* 785-776-9251. *E-mail:* admit@mccks.edu. *Web site:* http://www.mccks.edu/.

MCPHERSON COLLEGE

McPherson, Kansas

McPherson College is a coed, private, four-year college, founded in 1887, affiliated with the Church of the Brethren, offering degrees at the associate and bachelor's levels. It has a 26-acre campus in McPherson.

Academic Information The faculty has 49 members (73% full-time), 57% with terminal degrees. The student-faculty ratio is 10:1. The library holds 89,946 titles, 345 serial subscriptions, and 4,465 audiovisual materials. Special programs include academic remediation, services for learning-disabled students, study abroad, advanced placement credit, double majors, independent study, self-designed majors, summer session for credit, part-time degree programs (daytime, evenings, summer), adult/continuing education programs, internships, and arrangement for off-campus study with 6 members of the Associated Colleges of Central Kansas. The most frequently chosen baccalaureate fields are business/marketing, education, social sciences and history.
Student Body Statistics The student body is made up of 379 undergraduates (77 freshmen). 44 percent are women and 56 percent are men. Students come from 30 states and territories. 52 percent are from Kansas. 0.6 percent are international students.
Expenses for 2003–04 *Application fee:* $25. *Comprehensive fee:* $19,540 includes full-time tuition ($13,830), mandatory fees ($260), and college room and board ($5450). *College room only:* $2300. Room and board charges vary according to board plan. *Part-time tuition:* $450 per credit hour. *Part-time mandatory fees:* $30 per term. Part-time tuition and fees vary according to course load.
Financial Aid Forms of aid include need-based and non-need-based scholarships, athletic grants, and part-time jobs. The average aided 2002–03 undergraduate received an aid package worth an estimated $14,357. The application deadline for financial aid is continuous.
Freshman Admission McPherson College requires a high school transcript, a minimum 2.0 high school GPA, SAT I or ACT scores, and TOEFL scores for international students. ACT scores are recommended. The application deadline for regular admission is rolling.
Transfer Admission The application deadline for admission is rolling.
Entrance Difficulty McPherson College assesses its entrance difficulty level as moderately difficult. For the fall 2002 freshman class, 68 percent of the applicants were accepted.

For Further Information Contact Mr. Fred Schmidt, Dean of Enrollment, McPherson College, 1600 East Euclid, PO Box 1402, McPherson, KS 67460-1402. *Telephone:* 620-241-0731 Ext. 1270 or 800-365-7402 (toll-free). *Fax:* 620-241-8443. *E-mail:* admiss@mcpherson.edu. *Web site:* http://www.mcpherson.edu/.

MIDAMERICA NAZARENE UNIVERSITY

Olathe, Kansas

MNU is a coed, private, comprehensive institution, founded in 1966, affiliated with the Church of the Nazarene, offering degrees at the associate, bachelor's, and master's levels. It has a 112-acre campus in Olathe near Kansas City.

Academic Information The faculty has 151 members (48% full-time), 26% with terminal degrees. The undergraduate student-faculty ratio is 18:1. The library holds 428,450 titles, 1,225 serial subscriptions, and 7,391 audiovisual materials. Special programs include academic remediation, services for learning-disabled students, study abroad, advanced placement

credit, accelerated degree programs, double majors, independent study, summer session for credit, part-time degree programs (daytime, summer), adult/continuing education programs, internships, and arrangement for off-campus study with Coalition for Christian Colleges and Universities. The most frequently chosen baccalaureate fields are business/marketing, education, health professions and related sciences.
Student Body Statistics The student body totals 1,825, of whom 1,372 are undergraduates (291 freshmen). 52 percent are women and 48 percent are men. Students come from 38 states and territories and 5 other countries. 61 percent are from Kansas.
Expenses for 2003–04 *Application fee:* $15. *Comprehensive fee:* $18,738 includes full-time tuition ($11,910), mandatory fees ($1000), and college room and board ($5828). Full-time tuition and fees vary according to course load. Room and board charges vary according to board plan and housing facility. *Part-time tuition:* $397 per semester hour. *Part-time mandatory fees:* $500 per term. Part-time tuition and fees vary according to course load.
Financial Aid Forms of aid include need-based and non-need-based scholarships, athletic grants, and part-time jobs. The average aided 2002–03 undergraduate received an aid package worth an estimated $10,180. The priority application deadline for financial aid is March 1.
Freshman Admission MNU requires a high school transcript, a minimum 2.0 high school GPA, 1 recommendation, SAT I or ACT scores, and TOEFL scores for international students. The application deadline for regular admission is August 1.
Transfer Admission The application deadline for admission is August 1.
Entrance Difficulty MNU assesses its entrance difficulty level as minimally difficult. For the fall 2002 freshman class, 46 percent of the applicants were accepted.

For Further Information Contact Mr. Mike Redwine, Vice President for Enrollment Development, MidAmerica Nazarene University, 2030 East College Way, Olathe, KS 66062-1899. *Telephone:* 913-791-3380 Ext. 481 or 800-800-8887 (toll-free). *Fax:* 913-791-3481. *E-mail:* admissions@mnu.edu. *Web site:* http://www.mnu.edu/.

NEWMAN UNIVERSITY

Wichita, Kansas

Newman is a coed, private, Roman Catholic, comprehensive institution, founded in 1933, offering degrees at the associate, bachelor's, and master's levels. It has a 53-acre campus in Wichita.

Academic Information The faculty has 198 members (34% full-time), 19% with terminal degrees. The undergraduate student-faculty ratio is 14:1. The library holds 107,911 titles, 478 serial subscriptions, and 2,042 audiovisual materials. Special programs include academic remediation, services for learning-disabled students, cooperative (work-study) education, study abroad, advanced placement credit, accelerated degree programs, double majors, independent study, distance learning, summer session for credit, part-time degree programs (daytime, evenings, weekends, summer), external degree programs, adult/continuing education programs, internships, and arrangement for off-campus study with Friends University. The most frequently chosen baccalaureate field is philosophy, religion, and theology.
Student Body Statistics The student body totals 1,929, of whom 1,678 are undergraduates (133 freshmen). 65 percent are women and 35 percent are men. Students come from 30 states and territories and 33 other countries. 87 percent are from Kansas. 4.3 percent are international students.
Expenses for 2002–03 *Application fee:* $20. *Comprehensive fee:* $16,630 includes full-time tuition ($11,890), mandatory fees ($150), and college room and board ($4590). Full-time tuition and fees vary according to location. Room and board charges vary according to housing facility. *Part-time tuition:* $396 per credit hour. *Part-time mandatory fees:* $5 per credit hour. Part-time tuition and fees vary according to location.
Financial Aid Forms of aid include need-based and non-need-based scholarships, athletic grants, and part-time jobs. The average aided 2001–02 undergraduate received an aid package worth $8364. The priority application deadline for financial aid is March 1.
Freshman Admission Newman requires a high school transcript, a minimum 2.0 high school GPA, SAT I or ACT scores, and TOEFL scores for international students. An interview is recommended. The application deadline for regular admission is rolling.
Transfer Admission The application deadline for admission is rolling.
Entrance Difficulty Newman assesses its entrance difficulty level as minimally difficult; moderately difficult for nursing, occupational therapy programs. For the fall 2002 freshman class, 100 percent of the applicants were accepted.

For Further Information Contact Mrs. Marla Sexson, Dean of Admissions, Newman University, 3100 McCormick Avenue, Wichita, KS 67213. *Telephone:* 316-942-4291 Ext. 144 or 877-NEWMANU Ext. 144 (toll-free). *Fax:* 316-942-4483. *E-mail:* admissions@newmanu.edu. *Web site:* http://www.newmanu.edu/.

OTTAWA UNIVERSITY

Ottawa, Kansas

OU is a coed, private, American Baptist Churches in the USA, comprehensive institution, founded in 1865, offering degrees at the bachelor's level (also offers adult, international and on-line education programs with significant enrollment not reflected in profile). It has a 60-acre campus in Ottawa near Kansas City.

Academic Information The faculty has 43 members (37% full-time), 26% with terminal degrees. The student-faculty ratio is 14:1. The library holds 80,500 titles and 310 serial subscriptions. Special programs include advanced placement credit, ESL programs, double majors, independent study, self-designed majors, summer session for credit, part-time degree programs (daytime), and internships.
Student Body Statistics The student body is made up of 511 undergraduates (144 freshmen). 44 percent are women and 56 percent are men. Students come from 25 states and territories and 4 other countries. 67 percent are from Kansas. 4.1 percent are international students. 20 percent of the 2002 graduating class went on to graduate and professional schools.
Expenses for 2002–03 *Application fee:* $15. *Comprehensive fee:* $17,750 includes full-time tuition ($12,200), mandatory fees ($250), and college room and board ($5300). *College room only:* $2400. Full-time tuition and fees vary according to course load. Room and board charges vary according to board plan and housing facility. *Part-time tuition:* $407 per credit hour. *Part-time mandatory fees:* $65 per term. Part-time tuition and fees vary according to course load.
Financial Aid Forms of aid include need-based and non-need-based scholarships and part-time jobs. The priority application deadline for financial aid is March 15.
Freshman Admission OU requires a high school transcript, a minimum 2.5 high school GPA, SAT I or ACT scores, and TOEFL scores for international students. 2 recommendations and an interview are recommended. An essay is required for some. The application deadline for regular admission is rolling.
Transfer Admission The application deadline for admission is rolling.
Entrance Difficulty OU assesses its entrance difficulty level as moderately difficult. For the fall 2002 freshman class, 94 percent of the applicants were accepted.

For Further Information Contact Mr. Ryan Ficken, Director of Admissions, Ottawa University, 1001 South Cedar #17, Ottawa, KS 66067-3399. *Telephone:* 785-242-5200 Ext. 1051 or 800-755-5200 (toll-free). *Fax:* 785-242-7429. *E-mail:* admiss@ottawa.edu. *Web site:* http://www.ottawa.edu/.

See page 322 for a narrative description.

PITTSBURG STATE UNIVERSITY

Pittsburg, Kansas

Pitt State is a coed, public, comprehensive unit of Kansas Board of Regents, founded in 1903, offering degrees at the associate, bachelor's, and master's levels. It has a 233-acre campus in Pittsburg.

Pittsburg State University (continued)

Academic Information The faculty has 269 members. The undergraduate student-faculty ratio is 23:1. The library holds 290,798 titles and 1,368 serial subscriptions. Special programs include academic remediation, services for learning-disabled students, an honors program, cooperative (work-study) education, study abroad, advanced placement credit, Freshman Honors College, ESL programs, double majors, independent study, self-designed majors, summer session for credit, part-time degree programs (daytime, evenings, summer), external degree programs, adult/continuing education programs, internships, and arrangement for off-campus study with Southside Education Center, Wichita, KS, Kansas City Metro Center, Lenexa, KS.

Student Body Statistics The student body totals 6,751, of whom 5,483 are undergraduates. 49 percent are women and 51 percent are men. Students come from 50 states and territories and 46 other countries. 79 percent are from Kansas. 3.6 percent are international students.

Expenses for 2002–03 *Application fee:* $25. *State resident tuition:* $2534 full-time, $92 per credit hour part-time. *Nonresident tuition:* $7946 full-time, $272 per credit hour part-time. *College room and board:* $2003. Room and board charges vary according to board plan.

Financial Aid Forms of aid include need-based and non-need-based scholarships, athletic grants, and part-time jobs. The average aided 2002–03 undergraduate received an aid package worth an estimated $6439. The priority application deadline for financial aid is March 1.

Freshman Admission Pitt State requires a high school transcript, ACT scores, and TOEFL scores for international students. A minimum 2.0 high school GPA is required for some. The application deadline for regular admission is rolling.

Transfer Admission The application deadline for admission is rolling.

Entrance Difficulty Pitt State has an open admission policy for state residents. It assesses its entrance difficulty as moderately difficult for out-of-state applicants; moderately difficult for transfers; very difficult for international students.

For Further Information Contact Ms. Ange Peterson, Director of Admission and Retention, Pittsburg State University, Pittsburg, KS 66762. *Telephone:* 620-235-4251 or 800-854-7488 Ext. 1 (toll-free). *Fax:* 316-235-6003. *E-mail:* psuadmit@pittstate.edu. *Web site:* http://www.pittstate.edu/.

SAINT MARY UNIVERSITY

Leavenworth, Kansas

Saint Mary is a coed, private, Roman Catholic, comprehensive institution, founded in 1923, offering degrees at the associate, bachelor's, and master's levels. It has a 240-acre campus in Leavenworth near Kansas City.

Academic Information The faculty has 85 members (42% full-time), 36% with terminal degrees. The undergraduate student-faculty ratio is 12:1. The library holds 117,070 titles, 223 serial subscriptions, and 1,907 audiovisual materials. Special programs include an honors program, cooperative (work-study) education, study abroad, advanced placement credit, double majors, independent study, distance learning, self-designed majors, summer session for credit, part-time degree programs (daytime, evenings, summer), adult/continuing education programs, internships, and arrangement for off-campus study with University of Kansas, members of the Council of Independent Colleges. The most frequently chosen baccalaureate fields are communications/communication technologies, engineering/engineering technologies, psychology.

Student Body Statistics The student body totals 891, of whom 543 are undergraduates (71 freshmen). 59 percent are women and 41 percent are men. Students come from 20 states and territories and 3 other countries. 74 percent are from Kansas. 0.9 percent are international students.

Expenses for 2002–03 *Application fee:* $25. *Comprehensive fee:* $18,250 includes full-time tuition ($12,928), mandatory fees ($200), and college room and board ($5122). *Part-time tuition:* $242 per credit hour. *Part-time mandatory fees:* $55 per term. Part-time tuition and fees vary according to course load.

Financial Aid Forms of aid include need-based and non-need-based scholarships and part-time jobs. The application deadline for financial aid is continuous.

Freshman Admission Saint Mary requires a high school transcript, a minimum 2.5 high school GPA, 1 recommendation, SAT I or ACT scores, and TOEFL scores for international students. An interview is recommended. The application deadline for regular admission is rolling.

Transfer Admission The application deadline for admission is rolling.

Entrance Difficulty Saint Mary assesses its entrance difficulty level as moderately difficult. For the fall 2002 freshman class, 57 percent of the applicants were accepted.

For Further Information Contact Ms. Judy Wiedower, Director of Admissions and Financial Aid, Saint Mary University, 4100 South Fourth Street, Leavenworth, KS 66048. *Telephone:* 913-682-5151 Ext. 6118 or 800-752-7043 (toll-free out-of-state). *Fax:* 913-758-6140. *E-mail:* admiss@hub.smcks.edu. *Web site:* http://www.smcks.edu/.

SOUTHWESTERN COLLEGE

Winfield, Kansas

Southwestern is a coed, private, United Methodist, comprehensive institution, founded in 1885, offering degrees at the bachelor's and master's levels. It has a 70-acre campus in Winfield near Wichita.

Academic Information The faculty has 115 members (47% full-time), 26% with terminal degrees. The undergraduate student-faculty ratio is 13:1. The library holds 77,000 titles, 320 serial subscriptions, and 320 audiovisual materials. Special programs include academic remediation, an honors program, study abroad, advanced placement credit, double majors, independent study, self-designed majors, summer session for credit, part-time degree programs (daytime, evenings, weekends, summer), external degree programs, adult/continuing education programs, internships, and arrangement for off-campus study with Urban Life Center, Chicago. The most frequently chosen baccalaureate fields are business/marketing, computer/information sciences, health professions and related sciences.

Student Body Statistics The student body totals 1,298, of whom 1,137 are undergraduates (106 freshmen). 49 percent are women and 51 percent are men. Students come from 22 states and territories and 9 other countries. 85 percent are from Kansas. 2.8 percent are international students.

Expenses for 2002–03 *Application fee:* $20. *Comprehensive fee:* $18,658 includes full-time tuition ($13,922) and college room and board ($4736). *College room only:* $2100. Full-time tuition varies according to degree level and location. Room and board charges vary according to board plan, housing facility, and location. *Part-time tuition:* $580 per semester hour. Part-time tuition varies according to degree level and location.

Financial Aid Forms of aid include need-based and non-need-based scholarships, athletic grants, and part-time jobs. The average aided 2001–02 undergraduate received an aid package worth $12,576. The application deadline for financial aid is August 1 with a priority deadline of July 1.

Freshman Admission Southwestern requires an essay, a high school transcript, a minimum 2.25 high school GPA, SAT I or ACT scores, and TOEFL scores for international students. An interview is required for some. The application deadline for regular admission is August 15.

Transfer Admission The application deadline for admission is August 15.

Entrance Difficulty Southwestern assesses its entrance difficulty level as moderately difficult. For the fall 2002 freshman class, 75 percent of the applicants were accepted.

For Further Information Contact Mr. Todd Moore, Director of Admission, Southwestern College, 100 College Street, Winfield, KS 67156. *Telephone:* 620-229-6236 or 800-846-1543 (toll-free). *Fax:* 620-229-6344. *E-mail:* scadmit@sckans.edu. *Web site:* http://www.sckans.edu/.

STERLING COLLEGE

Sterling, Kansas

Sterling College is a coed, private, Presbyterian, four-year college, founded in 1887, offering degrees at the bachelor's level. It has a 46-acre campus in Sterling.

Academic Information The faculty has 52 members (63% full-time), 46% with terminal degrees. The student-faculty ratio is 11:1. The library holds 76,637 titles, 350 serial subscriptions, and 2,159 audiovisual materials. Special programs include services for learning-disabled students, an honors program, study abroad, advanced placement credit, double majors, independent study, self-designed majors, internships, and arrangement for off-campus study with 6 members of the Associated Colleges of Central Kansas. The most frequently chosen baccalaureate fields are business/marketing, biological/life sciences, education.
Student Body Statistics The student body is made up of 461 undergraduates (106 freshmen). 52 percent are women and 48 percent are men. Students come from 28 states and territories and 14 other countries. 64 percent are from Kansas. 2 percent are international students.
Expenses for 2002–03 *Application fee:* $25. *Comprehensive fee:* $18,360 includes full-time tuition ($12,750), mandatory fees ($370), and college room and board ($5240). Room and board charges vary according to board plan and housing facility. *Part-time tuition:* $275 per credit. Part-time tuition varies according to course load.
Financial Aid Forms of aid include need-based and non-need-based scholarships, athletic grants, and part-time jobs. The average aided 2002–03 undergraduate received an aid package worth an estimated $12,143. The priority application deadline for financial aid is March 15.
Freshman Admission Sterling College requires a high school transcript, a minimum 2.2 high school GPA, SAT I or ACT scores, and TOEFL scores for international students. An essay is recommended. 2 recommendations are required for some. The application deadline for regular admission is rolling and for early action it is November 15.
Transfer Admission The application deadline for admission is rolling.
Entrance Difficulty Sterling College assesses its entrance difficulty level as moderately difficult. For the fall 2002 freshman class, 57 percent of the applicants were accepted.

For Further Information Contact Mr. Chris Burlew, Vice President for Enrollment Services, Sterling College, PO Box 98, Administration Building, 125 West Cooper, Sterling, KS 67579-0098. *Telephone:* 620-278-4364 Ext. 364 or 800-346-1017 (toll-free). *Fax:* 620-278-4416. *E-mail:* admissions@sterling.edu. *Web site:* http://www.sterling.edu/.

TABOR COLLEGE

Hillsboro, Kansas

Tabor is a coed, private, Mennonite Brethren, comprehensive institution, founded in 1908, offering degrees at the associate, bachelor's, and master's levels. It has a 26-acre campus in Hillsboro near Wichita.

Academic Information The faculty has 51 members (57% full-time), 41% with terminal degrees. The undergraduate student-faculty ratio is 12:1. The library holds 80,754 titles, 265 serial subscriptions, and 945 audiovisual materials. Special programs include academic remediation, services for learning-disabled students, an honors program, cooperative (work-study) education, study abroad, advanced placement credit, accelerated degree programs, double majors, independent study, distance learning, self-designed majors, summer session for credit, part-time degree programs (evenings, weekends, summer), adult/continuing education programs, internships, and arrangement for off-campus study with Associated Colleges of Central Kansas. The most frequently chosen baccalaureate fields are business/marketing, education, philosophy, religion, and theology.
Student Body Statistics The student body totals 575, of whom 557 are undergraduates (108 freshmen). 52 percent are women and 48 percent are men. Students come from 27 states and territories and 4 other countries. 70 percent are from Kansas. 1.1 percent are international students.
Expenses for 2002–03 *Application fee:* $20. *Comprehensive fee:* $18,534 includes full-time tuition ($13,314), mandatory fees ($320), and college room and board ($4900). *College room only:* $1900. Full-time tuition and fees vary according to course load. Room and board charges vary according to board plan, housing facility, and location. *Part-time tuition:* $555 per credit hour. *Part-time mandatory fees:* $5 per credit hour. Part-time tuition and fees vary according to course load.
Financial Aid Forms of aid include need-based and non-need-based scholarships, athletic grants, and part-time jobs. The average aided 2002–03 undergraduate received an aid package worth an estimated $13,955. The application deadline for financial aid is August 15 with a priority deadline of March 1.
Freshman Admission Tabor requires an essay, a high school transcript, a minimum 2.0 high school GPA, 2 recommendations, ACT-18, SAT I or ACT scores, and TOEFL scores for international students. A minimum 3.0 high school GPA and an interview are recommended. The application deadline for regular admission is August 1.
Transfer Admission The application deadline for admission is August 1.
Entrance Difficulty Tabor assesses its entrance difficulty level as moderately difficult. For the fall 2002 freshman class, 59 percent of the applicants were accepted.

For Further Information Contact Ms. Cara Marrs, Director of Admissions, Tabor College, 400 South Jefferson, Hillsboro, KS 67063. *Telephone:* 620-947-3121 Ext. 1727 or 800-822-6799 (toll-free). *Fax:* 620-947-2607. *E-mail:* admissions@tabor.edu. *Web site:* http://www.tabor.edu/.

UNIVERSITY OF KANSAS

Lawrence, Kansas

KU is a coed, public university, founded in 1866, offering degrees at the bachelor's, master's, doctoral, and first professional levels and post-master's and first professional certificates (University of Kansas is a single institution with academic programs and facilities at two primary locations: Lawrence and Kansas City. Undergraduate, graduate, and professional education are the principal missions of the Lawrence campus, with medicine and related professional education the focus of the Kansas City campus). It has a 1,000-acre campus in Lawrence near Kansas City.

Academic Information The faculty has 1,332 members (90% full-time), 86% with terminal degrees. The undergraduate student-faculty ratio is 19:1. The library holds 5 million titles, 33,874 serial subscriptions, and 51,153 audiovisual materials. Special programs include academic remediation, services for learning-disabled students, an honors program, cooperative (work-study) education, study abroad, advanced placement credit, accelerated degree programs, ESL programs, double majors, independent study, distance learning, summer session for credit, part-time degree programs (daytime, summer), adult/continuing education programs, and internships. The most frequently chosen baccalaureate fields are business/marketing, English, social sciences and history.
Student Body Statistics The student body totals 28,196, of whom 20,605 are undergraduates (4,074 freshmen). 52 percent are women and 48 percent are men. Students come from 53 states and territories and 118 other countries. 76 percent are from Kansas. 3.3 percent are international students. 23 percent of the 2002 graduating class went on to graduate and professional schools.
Expenses for 2002–03 *Application fee:* $25. *State resident tuition:* $2921 full-time, $97.35 per credit hour part-time. *Nonresident tuition:* $10,124 full-time, $337.45 per credit hour part-time. *Mandatory fees:* $563 full-time, $47 per credit hour part-time. Full-time tuition and fees vary according to program. Part-time tuition and fees vary according to program. *College room and board:* $4642. Room and board charges vary according to board plan and housing facility.
Financial Aid Forms of aid include need-based and non-need-based scholarships, athletic grants, and part-time jobs. The average aided 2001–02 undergraduate received an aid package worth $6173. The priority application deadline for financial aid is March 1.
Freshman Admission KU requires a high school transcript, a minimum 2.0 high school GPA, Kansas Board of Regents admissions criteria with GPA of 2.0/2.5; top third of high school class; minimum ACT score of 24 or minimum SAT score of 1090, and SAT I or ACT scores. TOEFL

University of Kansas (continued)
scores for international students are recommended. A minimum 2.5 high school GPA is required for some. The application deadline for regular admission is April 1.
Transfer Admission The application deadline for admission is rolling.
Entrance Difficulty KU assesses its entrance difficulty level as moderately difficult; very difficult for architecture, architectural engineering programs. For the fall 2002 freshman class, 67 percent of the applicants were accepted.

For Further Information Contact Ms. Lisa Pinamonti, Interim Director of Admissions and Scholarships, University of Kansas, KU Visitor Center, 1502 Iowa Street, Lawrence, KS 66045-7576. *Telephone:* 785-864-3911 or 888-686-7323 (toll-free in-state). *Fax:* 785-864-5006. *E-mail:* adm@ku.edu. *Web site:* http://www.ku.edu/.

WASHBURN UNIVERSITY

Topeka, Kansas

Washburn is a coed, public, comprehensive institution, founded in 1865, offering degrees at the associate, bachelor's, master's, and first professional levels. It has a 160-acre campus in Topeka near Kansas City.

Expenses for 2002–03 *Application fee:* $20. *State resident tuition:* $3600 full-time. *Nonresident tuition:* $8130 full-time. *Mandatory fees:* $56 full-time. *College room and board:* $4786. Room and board charges vary according to housing facility.

For Further Information Contact Kirk R. Haskins, Director of Admission, Washburn University, 1700 SW College Avenue, Topeka, KS 66621. *Telephone:* 785-231-1010 Ext. 1812 or 800-332-0291 (toll-free in-state). *Fax:* 785-231-1089. *E-mail:* zzhansen@acc.washburn.edu. *Web site:* http://www.washburn.edu/.

WICHITA STATE UNIVERSITY

Wichita, Kansas

WSU is a coed, public unit of Kansas Board of Regents, founded in 1895, offering degrees at the associate, bachelor's, master's, and doctoral levels and post-master's and postbachelor's certificates. It has a 335-acre campus in Wichita.

Academic Information The faculty has 530 members (91% full-time), 69% with terminal degrees. The undergraduate student-faculty ratio is 17:1. The library holds 2 million titles, 15,169 serial subscriptions, and 47,558 audiovisual materials. Special programs include academic remediation, services for learning-disabled students, an honors program, cooperative (work-study) education, study abroad, advanced placement credit, accelerated degree programs, Freshman Honors College, ESL programs, double majors, independent study, distance learning, self-designed majors, summer session for credit, part-time degree programs (daytime, evenings, weekends, summer), internships, and arrangement for off-campus study with National Student Exchange, Midwest Student Exchange. The most frequently chosen baccalaureate fields are business/marketing, education, health professions and related sciences.
Student Body Statistics The student body totals 15,534, of whom 11,940 are undergraduates (1,303 freshmen). 57 percent are women and 43 percent are men. Students come from 49 states and territories and 82 other countries. 97 percent are from Kansas. 5.7 percent are international students.
Expenses for 2002–03 *Application fee:* $25. *State resident tuition:* $2412 full-time, $100.70 per credit hour part-time. *Nonresident tuition:* $9189 full-time, $326.60 per credit hour part-time. *Mandatory fees:* $643 full-time, $20.30 per credit hour part-time, $17 per term part-time. Full-time tuition and fees vary according to course load. *College room and board:* $4420. Room and board charges vary according to board plan and housing facility.
Financial Aid Forms of aid include need-based and non-need-based scholarships, athletic grants, and part-time jobs. The average aided 2001–02 undergraduate received an aid package worth $5516. The priority application deadline for financial aid is March 15.
Freshman Admission WSU requires a high school transcript and TOEFL scores for international students. A minimum 2.0 high school GPA and ACT scores are required for some.
Transfer Admission The application deadline for admission is rolling.
Entrance Difficulty WSU has an open admission policy for state residents who graduated from a Kansas high school before May 2001. It assesses its entrance difficulty as moderately difficult for out-of-state applicants; moderately difficult for transfers; very difficult for physical therapy, dental hygiene, nursing, physician assistant programs.

For Further Information Contact Ms. Christine Schneikart-Luebbe, Director of Admissions, Wichita State University, 1845 North Fairmount, Wichita, KS 67260. *Telephone:* 316-978-3085 or 800-362-2594 (toll-free). *Fax:* 316-978-3174. *E-mail:* admissions@wichita.edu. *Web site:* http://www.wichita.edu/.

Michigan

ADRIAN COLLEGE

Adrian, Michigan

Adrian is a coed, private, four-year college, founded in 1859, affiliated with the United Methodist Church, offering degrees at the associate and bachelor's levels. It has a 100-acre campus in Adrian near Detroit and Toledo.

Academic Information The faculty has 102 members (65% full-time), 73% with terminal degrees. The student-faculty ratio is 13:1. The library holds 143,484 titles, 610 serial subscriptions, and 1,178 audiovisual materials. Special programs include academic remediation, services for learning-disabled students, an honors program, cooperative (work-study) education, study abroad, ESL programs, double majors, independent study, self-designed majors, summer session for credit, part-time degree programs (daytime), adult/continuing education programs, internships, and arrangement for off-campus study with Urban Life Center (Chicago), The Washington Center. The most frequently chosen baccalaureate fields are business/marketing, English, social sciences and history.
Student Body Statistics The student body is made up of 1,021 undergraduates (299 freshmen). 58 percent are women and 42 percent are men. Students come from 18 states and territories and 8 other countries. 79 percent are from Michigan. 1.6 percent are international students.
Expenses for 2002–03 *Application fee:* $20. *Comprehensive fee:* $21,100 includes full-time tuition ($15,560), mandatory fees ($100), and college room and board ($5440). *College room only:* $2320. Room and board charges vary according to board plan. *Part-time tuition:* $485 per semester hour.
Financial Aid Forms of aid include need-based and non-need-based scholarships and part-time jobs. The average aided 2002–03 undergraduate received an aid package worth an estimated $14,697. The priority application deadline for financial aid is March 1.
Freshman Admission Adrian requires a high school transcript, SAT I or ACT scores, and TOEFL scores for international students. An interview and ACT scores are recommended. An essay is required for some. The application deadline for regular admission is August 1.
Transfer Admission The application deadline for admission is August 1.
Entrance Difficulty Adrian assesses its entrance difficulty level as moderately difficult. For the fall 2002 freshman class, 88 percent of the applicants were accepted.

For Further Information Contact Ms. Janel Sutkus, Director of Admissions, Adrian College, 110 South Madison Street, Adrian, MI 49221. *Telephone:* 517-265-5161 Ext. 4326 or 800-877-2246 (toll-free). *Fax:* 517-264-3331. *E-mail:* admissions@adrian.edu. *Web site:* http://www.adrian.edu/.

ALBION COLLEGE

Albion, Michigan

Albion is a coed, private, Methodist, four-year college, founded in 1835, offering degrees at the bachelor's level. It has a 225-acre campus in Albion near Detroit.

Academic Information The faculty has 130 members (91% full-time), 91% with terminal degrees. The student-faculty ratio is 12:1. The library holds 363,000 titles, 2,016 serial subscriptions, and 6,540 audiovisual materials. Special programs include services for learning-disabled students, an honors program, study abroad, advanced placement credit, double majors, independent study, self-designed majors, summer session for credit, part-time degree programs (daytime, evenings, summer), internships, and arrangement for off-campus study with Great Lakes Colleges Association. The most frequently chosen baccalaureate fields are business/marketing, biological/life sciences, social sciences and history.

Student Body Statistics The student body is made up of 1,658 undergraduates (526 freshmen). 57 percent are women and 43 percent are men. Students come from 27 states and territories and 14 other countries. 92 percent are from Michigan. 1.1 percent are international students. 40 percent of the 2002 graduating class went on to graduate and professional schools.

Expenses for 2002–03 *Application fee:* $20. *Comprehensive fee:* $26,612 includes full-time tuition ($20,458), mandatory fees ($242), and college room and board ($5912). *College room only:* $2892. Room and board charges vary according to housing facility. *Part-time tuition:* $870 per credit.

Financial Aid Forms of aid include need-based and non-need-based scholarships and part-time jobs. The average aided 2002–03 undergraduate received an aid package worth an estimated $17,700. The priority application deadline for financial aid is February 15.

Freshman Admission Albion requires an essay, a high school transcript, 1 recommendation, SAT I or ACT scores, and TOEFL scores for international students. A minimum 3.0 high school GPA, SAT II: Subject Test scores, and SAT II: Writing Test scores are recommended. An interview is required for some. The application deadline for regular admission is May 1; for early decision it is November 15; and for early action it is December 15.

Transfer Admission The application deadline for admission is rolling.

Entrance Difficulty Albion assesses its entrance difficulty level as moderately difficult. For the fall 2002 freshman class, 85 percent of the applicants were accepted.

For Further Information Contact Mr. Doug Kellar, Associate Vice President for Enrollment, Albion College, 611 East Porter Street, Albion, MI 49224. *Telephone:* 517-629-0600 or 800-858-6770 (toll-free). *Fax:* 517-629-0569. *E-mail:* admissions@albion.edu. *Web site:* http://www.albion.edu/.

See page 248 for a narrative description.

ALMA COLLEGE

Alma, Michigan

Alma is a coed, private, Presbyterian, four-year college, founded in 1886, offering degrees at the bachelor's level. It has a 100-acre campus in Alma.

Academic Information The faculty has 133 members (69% full-time), 60% with terminal degrees. The student-faculty ratio is 12:1. The library holds 246,649 titles, 1,157 serial subscriptions, and 7,962 audiovisual materials. Special programs include academic remediation, services for learning-disabled students, study abroad, advanced placement credit, double majors, independent study, self-designed majors, summer session for credit, internships, and arrangement for off-campus study. The most frequently chosen baccalaureate fields are business/marketing, education, social sciences and history.

Student Body Statistics The student body is made up of 1,317 undergraduates (333 freshmen). 57 percent are women and 43 percent are men. Students come from 22 states and territories. 96 percent are from Michigan. 0.9 percent are international students. 40 percent of the 2002 graduating class went on to graduate and professional schools.

Expenses for 2002–03 *Application fee:* $25. *Comprehensive fee:* $23,918 includes full-time tuition ($17,412), mandatory fees ($170), and college room and board ($6336). *College room only:* $3138. Room and board charges vary according to board plan and housing facility. *Part-time tuition:* $668 per credit. Part-time tuition varies according to course load.

Financial Aid Forms of aid include need-based and non-need-based scholarships and part-time jobs. The average aided 2002–03 undergraduate received an aid package worth an estimated $15,914. The priority application deadline for financial aid is February 21.

Freshman Admission Alma requires a high school transcript, a minimum 3.0 high school GPA, minimum SAT score of 1030 or ACT score of 22, SAT I or ACT scores, and TOEFL scores for international students. An essay and an interview are recommended. The application deadline for regular admission is rolling and for early action it is November 1.

Transfer Admission The application deadline for admission is rolling.

Entrance Difficulty Alma assesses its entrance difficulty level as moderately difficult. For the fall 2002 freshman class, 79 percent of the applicants were accepted.

For Further Information Contact Mr. Paul Pollatz, Director of Admissions, Alma College, Admissions Office, Alma, MI 48801-1599. *Telephone:* 989-463-7139 or 800-321-ALMA (toll-free). *Fax:* 989-463-7057. *E-mail:* admissions@alma.edu. *Web site:* http://www.alma.edu/.

ANDREWS UNIVERSITY

Berrien Springs, Michigan

Andrews is a coed, private, Seventh-day Adventist university, founded in 1874, offering degrees at the associate, bachelor's, master's, doctoral, and first professional levels. It has a 1,650-acre campus in Berrien Springs.

Academic Information The faculty has 247 members (92% full-time), 65% with terminal degrees. The undergraduate student-faculty ratio is 12:1. The library holds 512,100 titles, 3,032 serial subscriptions, and 41,503 audiovisual materials. Special programs include academic remediation, an honors program, cooperative (work-study) education, study abroad, advanced placement credit, accelerated degree programs, Freshman Honors College, ESL programs, double majors, distance learning, self-designed majors, summer session for credit, part-time degree programs (daytime, evenings), external degree programs, adult/continuing education programs, internships, and arrangement for off-campus study. The most frequently chosen baccalaureate fields are biological/life sciences, business/marketing, health professions and related sciences.

Student Body Statistics The student body totals 2,779, of whom 1,657 are undergraduates (319 freshmen). 54 percent are women and 46 percent are men. Students come from 46 states and territories and 50 other countries. 48 percent are from Michigan. 13.7 percent are international students.

Expenses for 2003–04 *Application fee:* $30. *Comprehensive fee:* $19,550 includes full-time tuition ($14,200), mandatory fees ($370), and college room and board ($4980). *College room only:* $2590. Full-time tuition and fees vary according to course load. Room and board charges vary according to board plan. *Part-time tuition:* $595 per credit hour. Part-time tuition varies according to course load.

Financial Aid Forms of aid include need-based and non-need-based scholarships and part-time jobs. The average aided 2001–02 undergraduate received an aid package worth $16,236. The application deadline for financial aid is continuous.

Freshman Admission Andrews requires an essay, a high school transcript, a minimum 2.25 high school GPA, 2 recommendations, and SAT I or ACT scores. ACT scores are recommended. The application deadline for regular admission is rolling.

Transfer Admission The application deadline for admission is rolling.

Andrews University (continued)

Entrance Difficulty Andrews assesses its entrance difficulty level as moderately difficult. For the fall 2002 freshman class, 56 percent of the applicants were accepted.

For Further Information Contact Ms. Charlotte Coy, Admissions Supervisor, Andrews University, Berrien Springs, MI 49104. *Telephone:* 269-471-7771 or 800-253-2874 (toll-free). *Fax:* 616-471-3228. *E-mail:* enroll@andrews.edu. *Web site:* http://www.andrews.edu/.

AQUINAS COLLEGE

Grand Rapids, Michigan

Aquinas College is a coed, private, Roman Catholic, comprehensive institution, founded in 1886, offering degrees at the associate, bachelor's, and master's levels. It has a 107-acre campus in Grand Rapids near Detroit.

Academic Information The faculty has 206 members (48% full-time), 42% with terminal degrees. The undergraduate student-faculty ratio is 16:1. The library holds 112,458 titles, 14,725 serial subscriptions, and 4,907 audiovisual materials. Special programs include academic remediation, services for learning-disabled students, an honors program, cooperative (work-study) education, study abroad, advanced placement credit, accelerated degree programs, double majors, independent study, distance learning, self-designed majors, summer session for credit, part-time degree programs, adult/continuing education programs, internships, and arrangement for off-campus study with members of the Dominican College Interchange. The most frequently chosen baccalaureate fields are business/marketing, education, psychology.

Student Body Statistics The student body totals 2,579, of whom 1,991 are undergraduates (346 freshmen). 66 percent are women and 34 percent are men. Students come from 20 states and territories and 11 other countries. 94 percent are from Michigan. 0.7 percent are international students. 4 percent of the 2002 graduating class went on to graduate and professional schools.

Expenses for 2003–04 *Application fee:* $25. *Comprehensive fee:* $21,894 includes full-time tuition ($16,400) and college room and board ($5494). *College room only:* $2510. Full-time tuition varies according to course load. Room and board charges vary according to board plan and housing facility. *Part-time tuition:* $330 per credit. Part-time tuition varies according to course load.

Financial Aid Forms of aid include need-based and non-need-based scholarships, athletic grants, and part-time jobs. The average aided 2002–03 undergraduate received an aid package worth an estimated $14,634. The priority application deadline for financial aid is February 15.

Freshman Admission Aquinas College requires a high school transcript, a minimum 2.5 high school GPA, ACT scores, and TOEFL scores for international students. An essay and an interview are required for some. The application deadline for regular admission is rolling.

Transfer Admission The application deadline for admission is rolling.

Entrance Difficulty Aquinas College assesses its entrance difficulty level as moderately difficult. For the fall 2002 freshman class, 79 percent of the applicants were accepted.

SPECIAL MESSAGE TO STUDENTS

Social Life Aquinas College, located in Grand Rapids, Michigan, has the advantages of a city that is the cultural, medical, business, and commercial center of western Michigan. Students involve themselves in the Community Senate, intramural and intercollegiate athletics, music performance groups, volunteer and service groups, and campus ministry. Some campus sponsored events include white-water rafting, Spring Fling, Homecoming, dinner nightclubs, a Jazz Festival, a cultural series, Welcome Week, movie nights, Winterfest, a film series, dances, and lectures. Off-campus events include theater, concerts and musical performances by nationally known performers, and a local IHL hockey team as well as minor league baseball.

Academic Highlights Aquinas offers more than forty different majors. The College has three schools within this structure: the School of Education, the School of Liberal Arts and Sciences, and the School of Management. The study program in Ireland provides a semester abroad for 30 students during the second semester of each academic year. The curriculum centers on Irish studies and culture and provides independent travel opportunities to the British Isles and the Continent. Other cultural immersion programs include Costa Rica, France, Germany, Japan, and Spain. A revised general education plan ensures that the student is equipped with the skills necessary for both life and a career. Aquinas also offers a semester of field experience in career-related employment through which the student earns college credit and a salary. The location of the College in Grand Rapids provides myriad experiences for students in medical, business, and commercial fields. More than 200 internships with leading firms and organizations are available.

Interviews and Campus Visits While the admission interview is not a requirement, campus visits are highly recommended. Aquinas provides three Campus Days throughout the year. This program gives the student the opportunity to tour the campus, meet with faculty members, participate in financial aid workshops, and enjoy a complimentary lunch. Parents are also welcome. Individual appointments with the Admissions Office are available. Students are encouraged to see the Holmdene Mansion, part of the original estate on which Aquinas is built, and the Art and Music Center, which houses recital halls, an art gallery, a sculpture studio, a photography lab, and a darkroom. The Albertus Magnus Hall of Science houses laboratories, a greenhouse, and an observatory. For information about appointments and campus visits, students should call the Admissions Office at 616-732-4460 or 800-678-9593 (toll-free), Monday through Friday, 8:30 a.m. to 5 p.m., and Saturdays, 9 a.m. to 1 p.m. The office is located in Hruby Hall, 1760 Fulton Street, on campus.

For Further Information Write to Paula Meehan, Dean of Admissions, Aquinas College, 1607 Robinson Road, SE, Grand Rapids, MI 49506-1799. *E-mail:* admissions@aquinas.edu. *Web site:* http://www.aquinas.edu.

AVE MARIA COLLEGE

Ypsilanti, Michigan

Ave Maria College is a coed, private, Roman Catholic, four-year college, founded in 1998, offering degrees at the bachelor's level.

Academic Information The faculty has 28 members (61% full-time). The student-faculty ratio is 13:1. Special programs include study abroad.

Student Body Statistics The student body is made up of 234 undergraduates. Students come from 34 states and territories and 13 other countries. 38 percent are from Michigan. 21 percent are international students.

Expenses for 2003–04 *Application fee:* $25. *Comprehensive fee:* $14,920 includes full-time tuition ($9650), mandatory fees ($270), and college room and board ($5000).

Financial Aid Forms of aid include need-based and non-need-based scholarships. The average aided 2002–03 undergraduate received an aid package worth an estimated $6992. The priority application deadline for financial aid is April 15.

Freshman Admission Ave Maria College requires an essay, a high school transcript, a minimum 2.4 high school GPA, 2 recommendations, SAT I or ACT scores, and TOEFL scores for international students. An interview is recommended.

Entrance Difficulty Ave Maria College assesses its entrance difficulty level as very difficult. For the fall 2002 freshman class, 83 percent of the applicants were accepted.

For Further Information Contact Admissions Office Manager, Ave Maria College, 300 West Forest Avenue, Ypsilanti, MI 48197. *Telephone:* 734-337-4545 or 866-866-3030 (toll-free). *Fax:* 734-337-4140. *E-mail:* admissions@avemaria.edu. *Web site:* http://www.avemaria.edu/.

BAKER COLLEGE OF AUBURN HILLS

Auburn Hills, Michigan

Baker is a coed, private, four-year college of Baker College System, founded in 1911, offering degrees at the associate and bachelor's levels and postbachelor's certificates. It has a 7-acre campus in Auburn Hills near Detroit.

Academic Information The faculty has 115 members (8% full-time), 10% with terminal degrees. The student-faculty ratio is 22:1. The library holds 5,400 titles and 95 serial subscriptions. Special programs include academic remediation, services for learning-disabled students, cooperative (work-study) education, advanced placement credit, accelerated degree programs, double majors, independent study, distance learning, summer session for credit, part-time degree programs (daytime, evenings, summer), external degree programs, and internships.
Student Body Statistics The student body is made up of 2,596 undergraduates. 68 percent are women and 32 percent are men. Students come from 1 state or territory.
Expenses for 2002–03 *Application fee:* $20. *Tuition:* $5760 full-time, $160 per quarter hour part-time.
Freshman Admission Baker requires a high school transcript and TOEFL scores for international students. SAT I or ACT scores are recommended. The application deadline for regular admission is rolling.
Transfer Admission The application deadline for admission is rolling.
Entrance Difficulty Baker has an open admission policy.

For Further Information Contact Ms. Jan Bohlen, Vice President for Admissions, Baker College of Auburn Hills, 1500 University Drive, Auburn Hills, MI 48326-1586. *Telephone:* 248-340-0600 or 888-429-0410 (toll-free in-state). *Fax:* 248-340-0608. *E-mail:* bohlen_j@auburnhills.baker.edu. *Web site:* http://www.baker.edu/.

BAKER COLLEGE OF CADILLAC

Cadillac, Michigan

Baker is a coed, private, four-year college of Baker College System, founded in 1986, offering degrees at the associate and bachelor's levels. It has a 40-acre campus in Cadillac.

Academic Information The faculty has 73 members (5% full-time). The student-faculty ratio is 16:1. The library holds 4,000 titles and 78 serial subscriptions. Special programs include academic remediation, services for learning-disabled students, cooperative (work-study) education, advanced placement credit, double majors, independent study, distance learning, summer session for credit, part-time degree programs (daytime, evenings, weekends, summer), external degree programs, and internships.
Student Body Statistics The student body is made up of 1,174 undergraduates. 73 percent are women and 27 percent are men. Students come from 4 states and territories.
Expenses for 2002–03 *Application fee:* $20. *Tuition:* $5760 full-time, $160 per quarter hour part-time.
Freshman Admission Baker requires a high school transcript and TOEFL scores for international students. An interview and SAT I or ACT scores are recommended. The application deadline for regular admission is rolling.
Transfer Admission The application deadline for admission is rolling.
Entrance Difficulty Baker has an open admission policy.

For Further Information Contact Mr. Mike Tisdale, Director of Admissions, Baker College of Cadillac, 9600 East 13th Street, Cadillac, MI 49601. *Telephone:* 616-775-8458, 888-313-3463 (toll-free in-state), or 231-876-3100 (toll-free out-of-state). *Fax:* 231-775-8505. *E-mail:* runstr_e@cadillac.baker.edu. *Web site:* http://www.baker.edu/.

BAKER COLLEGE OF CLINTON TOWNSHIP

Clinton Township, Michigan

Baker is a coed, private, four-year college of Baker College System, founded in 1990, offering degrees at the associate and bachelor's levels. It has a 22-acre campus in Clinton Township near Detroit.

Academic Information The faculty has 133 members (6% full-time). The student-faculty ratio is 19:1. The library holds 8,000 titles and 97 serial subscriptions. Special programs include academic remediation, services for learning-disabled students, cooperative (work-study) education, advanced placement credit, summer session for credit, part-time degree programs (daytime, evenings, weekends, summer), external degree programs, and internships.
Student Body Statistics The student body is made up of 3,929 undergraduates. 77 percent are women and 23 percent are men.
Expenses for 2002–03 *Application fee:* $20. *Tuition:* $5760 full-time, $160 per quarter hour part-time.
Freshman Admission Baker requires a high school transcript and TOEFL scores for international students. SAT I or ACT scores are recommended. The application deadline for regular admission is rolling.
Transfer Admission The application deadline for admission is rolling.
Entrance Difficulty Baker has an open admission policy.

For Further Information Contact Ms. Annette M. Looser, Vice President for Admissions, Baker College of Clinton Township, 34950 Little Mack Avenue, Clinton Township, MI 48035. *Telephone:* 810-791-6610 or 888-272-2842 (toll-free). *Fax:* 810-791-6611. *E-mail:* looser_a@mtclemens.baker.edu. *Web site:* http://www.baker.edu/.

BAKER COLLEGE OF FLINT

Flint, Michigan

Baker is a coed, private, four-year college of Baker College System, founded in 1911, offering degrees at the associate and bachelor's levels. It has a 30-acre campus in Flint near Detroit.

Academic Information The faculty has 173 members (15% full-time), 10% with terminal degrees. The student-faculty ratio is 37:1. The library holds 168,700 titles. Special programs include academic remediation, services for learning-disabled students, cooperative (work-study) education, advanced placement credit, accelerated degree programs, double majors, independent study, distance learning, summer session for credit, part-time degree programs, external degree programs, and internships.
Student Body Statistics The student body is made up of 5,291 undergraduates. 69 percent are women and 31 percent are men. Students come from 5 states and territories. 99 percent are from Michigan.
Expenses for 2002–03 *Application fee:* $20. *Tuition:* $5760 full-time, $160 per quarter hour part-time. *College room only:* $2175.
Freshman Admission Baker requires a high school transcript and TOEFL scores for international students. SAT I or ACT scores are recommended. The application deadline for regular admission is September 20.
Transfer Admission The application deadline for admission is September 20.
Entrance Difficulty Baker has an open admission policy.

For Further Information Contact Mr. Troy Crowe, Vice President for Admissions, Baker College of Flint, 1050 West Bristol Road, Flint, MI 48507-5508. *Telephone:* 810-766-4015 or 800-964-4299 (toll-free). *Fax:* 810-766-4049. *E-mail:* heaton_m@fafl.baker.edu. *Web site:* http://www.baker.edu/.

BAKER COLLEGE OF JACKSON

Jackson, Michigan

Baker is a coed, private, four-year college of Baker College System, founded in 1994, offering degrees at the associate and bachelor's levels. It has a 42-acre campus in Jackson near Lansing.

Academic Information The faculty has 90 members (10% full-time), 10% with terminal degrees. The student-faculty ratio is 13:1. The library holds 7,000 titles and 150 serial subscriptions. Special programs include academic remediation, services for learning-disabled students, cooperative (work-study) education, advanced placement credit, accelerated degree programs, double majors, independent study, distance learning, summer session for credit, part-time degree programs (daytime, evenings, weekends, summer), external degree programs, and internships.

Baker College of Jackson (continued)

Student Body Statistics The student body is made up of 1,392 undergraduates. 75 percent are women and 25 percent are men. Students come from 2 states and territories. 99 percent are from Michigan.
Expenses for 2002–03 *Application fee:* $20. *Tuition:* $5760 full-time, $160 per quarter hour part-time.
Freshman Admission Baker requires a high school transcript. SAT I or ACT scores are recommended. The application deadline for regular admission is September 19.
Transfer Admission The application deadline for admission is rolling.
Entrance Difficulty Baker has an open admission policy.

For Further Information Contact Ms. Kelli Stepka, Director of Admissions, Baker College of Jackson, 2800 Springport Road, Jackson, MI 49202. *Telephone:* 517-788-7800 or 888-343-3683 (toll-free). *Fax:* 517-789-7331. *E-mail:* hoban_k@jackson.baker.edu. *Web site:* http://www.baker.edu/.

BAKER COLLEGE OF MUSKEGON

Muskegon, Michigan

Baker is a coed, private, four-year college of Baker College System, founded in 1888, offering degrees at the associate and bachelor's levels. It has a 40-acre campus in Muskegon near Grand Rapids.

Academic Information The faculty has 145 members (10% full-time), 6% with terminal degrees. The student-faculty ratio is 30:1. The library holds 32,000 titles and 140 serial subscriptions. Special programs include academic remediation, services for learning-disabled students, cooperative (work-study) education, advanced placement credit, accelerated degree programs, double majors, independent study, distance learning, summer session for credit, part-time degree programs (daytime, evenings, weekends), external degree programs, adult/continuing education programs, and internships.
Student Body Statistics The student body is made up of 3,422 undergraduates. 69 percent are women and 31 percent are men. Students come from 13 states and territories. 99 percent are from Michigan. 1 percent of the 2002 graduating class went on to graduate and professional schools.
Expenses for 2002–03 *Application fee:* $20. *Tuition:* $5760 full-time, $160 per quarter hour part-time. *College room only:* $2100.
Freshman Admission Baker requires a high school transcript and TOEFL scores for international students. SAT I or ACT scores are recommended. The application deadline for regular admission is September 24.
Transfer Admission The application deadline for admission is rolling.
Entrance Difficulty Baker has an open admission policy.

For Further Information Contact Ms. Kathy Jacobson, Vice President of Admissions, Baker College of Muskegon, 1903 Marquette Avenue, Muskegon, MI 49442-3497. *Telephone:* 231-777-5207 or 800-937-0337 (toll-free in-state). *Fax:* 231-777-5201. *E-mail:* jacobs_k@muskegon.baker.edu. *Web site:* http://www.baker.edu/.

BAKER COLLEGE OF OWOSSO

Owosso, Michigan

Baker is a coed, private, four-year college of Baker College System, founded in 1984, offering degrees at the associate and bachelor's levels. It has a 32-acre campus in Owosso.

Academic Information The faculty has 103 members (5% full-time), 11% with terminal degrees. The student-faculty ratio is 38:1. The library holds 35,424 titles, 215 serial subscriptions, and 344 audiovisual materials. Special programs include academic remediation, services for learning-disabled students, cooperative (work-study) education, advanced placement credit, accelerated degree programs, summer session for credit, part-time degree programs, external degree programs, adult/continuing education programs, and internships.
Student Body Statistics The student body is made up of 2,361 undergraduates. 69 percent are women and 31 percent are men. Students come from 4 states and territories. 100 percent are from Michigan.
Expenses for 2002–03 *Application fee:* $20. *Tuition:* $5760 full-time, $160 per quarter hour part-time. *College room only:* $2100.
Freshman Admission Baker requires a high school transcript and TOEFL scores for international students. SAT I or ACT scores are recommended. The application deadline for regular admission is rolling.
Transfer Admission The application deadline for admission is rolling.
Entrance Difficulty Baker has an open admission policy.

For Further Information Contact Mr. Michael Konopacke, Vice President for Admissions, Baker College of Owosso, 1020 South Washington Street, Owosso, MI 48867-4400. *Telephone:* 517-729-3353 or 800-879-3797 (toll-free). *Fax:* 517-729-3359. *E-mail:* konopa-_m@owosso.baker.edu. *Web site:* http://www.baker.edu/.

BAKER COLLEGE OF PORT HURON

Port Huron, Michigan

Baker is a coed, private, four-year college of Baker College System, founded in 1990, offering degrees at the associate and bachelor's levels. It has a 10-acre campus in Port Huron near Detroit.

Academic Information The faculty has 95 members (11% full-time), 9% with terminal degrees. The student-faculty ratio is 13:1. The library holds 16,823 titles, 181 serial subscriptions, and 135 audiovisual materials. Special programs include academic remediation, services for learning-disabled students, cooperative (work-study) education, advanced placement credit, accelerated degree programs, double majors, independent study, distance learning, summer session for credit, part-time degree programs (daytime, evenings, weekends, summer), external degree programs, and internships.
Student Body Statistics The student body is made up of 1,363 undergraduates. 76 percent are women and 24 percent are men. 90 percent are from Michigan.
Expenses for 2002–03 *Application fee:* $20. *Tuition:* $5760 full-time, $160 per quarter hour part-time. Full-time tuition varies according to program.
Freshman Admission Baker requires a high school transcript, an interview, and TOEFL scores for international students. The application deadline for regular admission is September 24.
Transfer Admission The application deadline for admission is rolling.
Entrance Difficulty Baker has an open admission policy.

For Further Information Contact Mr. Daniel Kenny, Director of Admissions, Baker College of Port Huron, 3403 Lapeer Road, Port Huron, MI 48060-2597. *Telephone:* 810-985-7000 or 888-262-2442 (toll-free). *Fax:* 810-985-7066. *E-mail:* kenny_d@porthuron.baker.edu. *Web site:* http://www.baker.edu/.

CALVIN COLLEGE

Grand Rapids, Michigan

Calvin is a coed, private, comprehensive institution, founded in 1876, affiliated with the Christian Reformed Church, offering degrees at the bachelor's and master's levels and postbachelor's certificates. It has a 370-acre campus in Grand Rapids.

Academic Information The faculty has 374 members (78% full-time), 68% with terminal degrees. The undergraduate student-faculty ratio is 15:1. The library holds 801,802 titles, 2,658 serial subscriptions, and 22,394 audiovisual materials. Special programs include academic remediation, services for learning-disabled students, an honors program, study abroad, advanced placement credit, accelerated degree programs, double majors, independent study, self-designed majors, summer session for credit, part-time degree programs (daytime, evenings, summer), adult/continuing education programs, internships, and arrangement for off-campus study with Council for Christian Colleges and Universities,

Central College, Trinity Christian College, Au Sable Institute. The most frequently chosen baccalaureate fields are business/marketing, education, social sciences and history.
Student Body Statistics The student body totals 4,324, of whom 4,286 are undergraduates (1,049 freshmen). 56 percent are women and 44 percent are men. Students come from 48 states and territories and 38 other countries. 61 percent are from Michigan. 7.7 percent are international students. 20 percent of the 2002 graduating class went on to graduate and professional schools.
Expenses for 2003–04 *Application fee:* $50. *Comprehensive fee:* $22,615 includes full-time tuition ($16,775) and college room and board ($5840). *College room only:* $3180. Room and board charges vary according to board plan. *Part-time tuition:* $410 per credit hour. Part-time tuition varies according to course load.
Financial Aid Forms of aid include need-based and non-need-based scholarships and part-time jobs. The average aided 2002–03 undergraduate received an aid package worth an estimated $12,252. The priority application deadline for financial aid is February 15.
Freshman Admission Calvin requires an essay, a high school transcript, a minimum 2.5 high school GPA, 1 recommendation, SAT I or ACT scores, and TOEFL scores for international students. An interview is recommended. The application deadline for regular admission is August 15.
Transfer Admission The application deadline for admission is rolling.
Entrance Difficulty Calvin assesses its entrance difficulty level as moderately difficult. For the fall 2002 freshman class, 98 percent of the applicants were accepted.

For Further Information Contact Mr. Dale D. Kuiper, Director of Admissions, Calvin College, 3201 Burton Street, SE, Grand Rapids, MI 49546-4388. *Telephone:* 616-957-6106 or 800-688-0122 (toll-free). *Fax:* 616-957-8513. *E-mail:* admissions@calvin.edu. *Web site:* http://www.calvin.edu/.

CENTER FOR CREATIVE STUDIES-COLLEGE OF ART AND DESIGN

See College for Creative Studies

CENTRAL MICHIGAN UNIVERSITY

Mount Pleasant, Michigan

Central Michigan is a coed, public university, founded in 1892, offering degrees at the bachelor's, master's, and doctoral levels and post-master's and postbachelor's certificates. It has an 854-acre campus in Mount Pleasant.

Academic Information The faculty has 1,045 members (69% full-time), 63% with terminal degrees. The undergraduate student-faculty ratio is 22:1. The library holds 998,460 titles, 4,634 serial subscriptions, and 24,630 audiovisual materials. Special programs include academic remediation, an honors program, study abroad, advanced placement credit, accelerated degree programs, Freshman Honors College, ESL programs, double majors, distance learning, self-designed majors, summer session for credit, part-time degree programs, external degree programs, adult/continuing education programs, and internships. The most frequently chosen baccalaureate fields are business/marketing, education, social sciences and history.
Student Body Statistics The student body totals 28,159, of whom 19,696 are undergraduates (3,626 freshmen). 59 percent are women and 41 percent are men. Students come from 45 states and territories and 51 other countries. 98 percent are from Michigan. 1 percent are international students. 9 percent of the 2002 graduating class went on to graduate and professional schools.
Expenses for 2002–03 *Application fee:* $25. *State resident tuition:* $3992 full-time, $133.05 per credit part-time. *Nonresident tuition:* $10,364 full-time, $345.45 per credit part-time. *Mandatory fees:* $755 full-time, $207.50 per term part-time. *College room and board:* $5524. Room and board charges vary according to board plan and housing facility.
Financial Aid Forms of aid include need-based and non-need-based scholarships, athletic grants, and part-time jobs. The average aided 2002–03 undergraduate received an aid package worth an estimated $8495. The priority application deadline for financial aid is February 21.
Freshman Admission Central Michigan requires a high school transcript, ACT scores, and TOEFL scores for international students. A minimum 3.0 high school GPA is recommended. An essay, recommendations, and an interview are required for some. The application deadline for regular admission is rolling.
Transfer Admission The application deadline for admission is rolling.
Entrance Difficulty Central Michigan assesses its entrance difficulty level as moderately difficult. For the fall 2002 freshman class, 71 percent of the applicants were accepted.

For Further Information Contact Mrs. Betty J. Wagner, Director of Admissions, Central Michigan University, Office of Admissions, 105 Warriner Hall, Mt. Pleasant, MI 48859. *Telephone:* 989-774-3076. *Fax:* 989-774-7267. *E-mail:* cmuadmit@cmich.edu. *Web site:* http://www.cmich.edu/.

CLEARY UNIVERSITY

Ann Arbor, Michigan

Cleary is a coed, private, comprehensive institution, founded in 1883, offering degrees at the associate, bachelor's, and master's levels in business. It has a 27-acre campus in Ann Arbor near Detroit and Lansing.

Academic Information The faculty has 112 members (10% full-time), 18% with terminal degrees. The undergraduate student-faculty ratio is 10:1. The library holds 4,500 titles, 22 serial subscriptions, and 100 audiovisual materials. Special programs include cooperative (work-study) education, advanced placement credit, accelerated degree programs, independent study, distance learning, summer session for credit, adult/continuing education programs, and internships.
Student Body Statistics The student body totals 626, of whom 594 are undergraduates. Students come from 2 states and territories. 99 percent are from Michigan. 35 percent of the 2002 graduating class went on to graduate and professional schools.
Expenses for 2003–04 *Application fee:* $25. *Tuition:* $11,040 full-time, $230 per quarter hour part-time. Full-time tuition varies according to degree level.
Financial Aid Forms of aid include need-based and non-need-based scholarships and part-time jobs. The average aided 2001–02 undergraduate received an aid package worth $4598. The priority application deadline for financial aid is March 15.
Freshman Admission Cleary requires a high school transcript, a minimum 2.5 high school GPA, complete the Technology Skills Inventory (TSI), and SAT I or ACT scores. An interview is recommended. An essay and 2 recommendations are required for some. The application deadline for regular admission is August 5.
Transfer Admission The application deadline for admission is August 5.
Entrance Difficulty Cleary assesses its entrance difficulty level as moderately difficult.

For Further Information Contact Ms. Colleen Murphy, Admissions Representative, Cleary University, 3750 Cleary Drive, Howell, MI 48843. *Telephone:* 517-548-3670 Ext. 2213, 888-5-CLEARY (toll-free in-state), or 888-5-CLEARY Ext. 2249 (toll-free out-of-state). *Fax:* 517-552-7805. *E-mail:* admissions@cleary.edu. *Web site:* http://www.cleary.edu/.

COLLEGE FOR CREATIVE STUDIES

Detroit, Michigan

CCS is a coed, private, four-year college, founded in 1926, offering degrees at the bachelor's level in art. It has an 11-acre campus in Detroit.

Academic Information The faculty has 226 members (19% full-time). The student-faculty ratio is 10:1. The library holds 24,000 titles and 75

College for Creative Studies (continued)

serial subscriptions. Special programs include academic remediation, services for learning-disabled students, cooperative (work-study) education, advanced placement credit, ESL programs, double majors, independent study, summer session for credit, part-time degree programs (daytime, evenings, weekends, summer), internships, and arrangement for off-campus study with Association of Independent Colleges of Art and Design. The most frequently chosen baccalaureate field is visual/performing arts.
Student Body Statistics The student body is made up of 1,204 undergraduates (194 freshmen). 41 percent are women and 59 percent are men. Students come from 31 states and territories and 15 other countries. 83 percent are from Michigan. 5.5 percent are international students.
Expenses for 2003–04 *Application fee:* $35. *Comprehensive fee:* $23,098 includes full-time tuition ($18,720), mandatory fees ($1078), and college room and board ($3300). Room and board charges vary according to housing facility. *Part-time tuition:* $624 per credit hour. *Part-time mandatory fees:* $424 per term. Part-time tuition and fees vary according to course load.
Financial Aid Forms of aid include need-based and non-need-based scholarships and part-time jobs. The priority application deadline for financial aid is February 21.
Freshman Admission CCS requires an essay, a high school transcript, a portfolio, SAT I or ACT scores, and TOEFL scores for international students. A minimum 2.5 high school GPA is recommended. Recommendations and an interview are required for some. The application deadline for regular admission is rolling.
Transfer Admission The application deadline for admission is rolling.
Entrance Difficulty CCS assesses its entrance difficulty level as moderately difficult. For the fall 2002 freshman class, 78 percent of the applicants were accepted.

For Further Information Contact Office of Admissions, College for Creative Studies, 201 East Kirby, Detroit, MI 48202-4034. *Telephone:* 313-664-7425 or 800-952-ARTS (toll-free). *Fax:* 313-872-2739. *E-mail:* admissions@ccscad.edu. *Web site:* http://www.ccscad.edu/.

CONCORDIA UNIVERSITY

Ann Arbor, Michigan

Concordia is a coed, private, comprehensive unit of Concordia University System, founded in 1963, affiliated with the Lutheran Church–Missouri Synod, offering degrees at the associate, bachelor's, and master's levels. It has a 234-acre campus in Ann Arbor near Detroit.

Academic Information The faculty has 91 members (44% full-time). The undergraduate student-faculty ratio is 10:1. The library holds 120,000 titles, 3,950 serial subscriptions, and 10,500 audiovisual materials. Special programs include academic remediation, services for learning-disabled students, study abroad, advanced placement credit, accelerated degree programs, double majors, independent study, distance learning, self-designed majors, summer session for credit, part-time degree programs (daytime, evenings, weekends, summer), adult/continuing education programs, internships, and arrangement for off-campus study with Concordia University System. The most frequently chosen baccalaureate fields are business/marketing, education, health professions and related sciences.
Student Body Statistics The student body totals 552, of whom 516 are undergraduates (97 freshmen). 54 percent are women and 46 percent are men. Students come from 22 states and territories and 3 other countries. 76 percent are from Michigan. 0.8 percent are international students.
Expenses for 2002–03 *Application fee:* $25. *Comprehensive fee:* $23,250 includes full-time tuition ($16,200), mandatory fees ($450), and college room and board ($6600). *Part-time tuition:* $540 per semester hour.
Financial Aid Forms of aid include need-based and non-need-based scholarships, athletic grants, and part-time jobs. The average aided 2002–03 undergraduate received an aid package worth an estimated $13,648. The priority application deadline for financial aid is May 1.
Freshman Admission Concordia requires a high school transcript, a minimum 2.5 high school GPA, and SAT I or ACT scores. 1 recommendation and ACT scores are recommended. An essay and an interview are required for some. The application deadline for regular admission is rolling.
Transfer Admission The application deadline for admission is rolling.
Entrance Difficulty Concordia assesses its entrance difficulty level as moderately difficult. For the fall 2002 freshman class, 87 percent of the applicants were accepted.

For Further Information Contact Ms. Sydney Wolf, Director of Admissions, Concordia University, 4090 Geddes Road, Ann Arbor, MI 48105. *Telephone:* 734-995-7322 Ext. 7311 or 800-253-0680 (toll-free). *Fax:* 734-995-7455. *E-mail:* admissions@cuaa.edu. *Web site:* http://www.cuaa.edu/.

CORNERSTONE UNIVERSITY

Grand Rapids, Michigan

Cornerstone University is a coed, private, nondenominational, comprehensive institution, founded in 1941, offering degrees at the associate, bachelor's, master's, and first professional levels. It has a 132-acre campus in Grand Rapids.

Academic Information The faculty has 133 members (55% full-time), 38% with terminal degrees. The undergraduate student-faculty ratio is 16:1. The library holds 109,376 titles, 1,073 serial subscriptions, and 19,702 audiovisual materials. Special programs include academic remediation, advanced placement credit, accelerated degree programs, double majors, independent study, summer session for credit, part-time degree programs, adult/continuing education programs, internships, and arrangement for off-campus study with Calvin College, Reformed Bible College, Grace Bible College. The most frequently chosen baccalaureate fields are business/marketing, education, English.
Student Body Statistics The student body totals 2,450, of whom 2,110 are undergraduates (349 freshmen). 61 percent are women and 39 percent are men. Students come from 31 states and territories and 1 other country. 80 percent are from Michigan. 0.9 percent are international students. 14 percent of the 2002 graduating class went on to graduate and professional schools.
Expenses for 2002–03 *Application fee:* $25. *Comprehensive fee:* $18,988 includes full-time tuition ($13,770) and college room and board ($5218). *College room only:* $2380. *Part-time tuition:* $530 per credit. Part-time tuition varies according to course load.
Financial Aid Forms of aid include need-based and non-need-based scholarships, athletic grants, and part-time jobs. The average aided 2002–03 undergraduate received an aid package worth an estimated $11,570. The application deadline for financial aid is February 3.
Freshman Admission Cornerstone University requires an essay, a high school transcript, a minimum 2.25 high school GPA, 1 recommendation, SAT I or ACT scores, and TOEFL scores for international students. An interview is recommended. The application deadline for regular admission is rolling.
Transfer Admission The application deadline for admission is rolling.
Entrance Difficulty Cornerstone University assesses its entrance difficulty level as moderately difficult. For the fall 2002 freshman class, 79 percent of the applicants were accepted.

For Further Information Contact Mr. Brent Rudin, Director of Admissions, Cornerstone University, 1001 East Beltline Avenue, NE, Grand Rapids, MI 49525. *Telephone:* 616-222-1426 or 800-787-9778 (toll-free). *Fax:* 616-222-1400. *E-mail:* admissions@cornerstone.edu. *Web site:* http://www.cornerstone.edu/.

DAVENPORT UNIVERSITY

Alma, Michigan

For Information Write to Davenport University, Alma, MI 48801.

DAVENPORT UNIVERSITY

Bad Axe, Michigan

For Information Write to Davenport University, Bad Axe, MI 48413.

DAVENPORT UNIVERSITY

Bay City, Michigan

For Information Write to Davenport University, Bay City, MI 48706.

DAVENPORT UNIVERSITY

Caro, Michigan

For Information Write to Davenport University, Caro, MI 48723.

DAVENPORT UNIVERSITY

Dearborn, Michigan

Davenport University is a coed, private, comprehensive institution, founded in 1985, offering degrees at the associate, bachelor's, and master's levels. It has a 17-acre campus in Dearborn near Detroit.

Expenses for 2002–03 *Application fee:* $20. *Tuition:* $7776 full-time. *Mandatory fees:* $110 full-time. Full-time tuition and fees vary according to course load and location. *Part-time tuition:* varies with course load, location.

For Further Information Contact Ms. Jennifer Salloum, Director of Admissions, Davenport University, 4801 Oakman Boulevard, Dearborn, MI 48126-3799. *Telephone:* 313-581-4400 or 800-585-1479 (toll-free). *Fax:* 313-581-1985. *E-mail:* jennifer.salloum@davenport.edu. *Web site:* http://www.davenport.edu/.

DAVENPORT UNIVERSITY

Flint, Michigan

For Information Write to Davenport University, Flint, MI 48504-1700.

DAVENPORT UNIVERSITY

Gaylord, Michigan

For Information Write to Davenport University, Gaylord, MI 49735.

DAVENPORT UNIVERSITY

Grand Rapids, Michigan

Davenport is a coed, private, comprehensive unit of Davenport University, founded in 1866, offering degrees at the associate, bachelor's, and master's levels. It has a 5-acre campus in Grand Rapids.

Academic Information The faculty has 111 members (21% full-time), 18% with terminal degrees. The undergraduate student-faculty ratio is 20:1. The library holds 40,810 titles and 1,500 serial subscriptions. Special programs include academic remediation, cooperative (work-study) education, study abroad, advanced placement credit, accelerated degree programs, ESL programs, independent study, distance learning, summer session for credit, part-time degree programs (daytime, evenings, weekends, summer), external degree programs, adult/continuing education programs, and internships. The most frequently chosen baccalaureate field is law/legal studies.

Student Body Statistics The student body totals 2,216, of whom 2,077 are undergraduates (262 freshmen). 64 percent are women and 36 percent are men. Students come from 4 states and territories and 27 other countries. 1.5 percent are international students. 1.7 percent of the 2002 graduating class went on to graduate and professional schools.

Expenses for 2002–03 *Application fee:* $25. *Comprehensive fee:* $16,425 includes full-time tuition ($8910), mandatory fees ($105), and college room and board ($7410). *College room only:* $4050. *Part-time tuition:* $220 per credit hour. *Part-time mandatory fees:* $35 per term.

Financial Aid Forms of aid include need-based and non-need-based scholarships and part-time jobs. The priority application deadline for financial aid is March 15.

Freshman Admission Davenport requires a high school transcript. An essay, an interview, ACT scores, and TOEFL scores for international students are recommended. The application deadline for regular admission is rolling and for nonresidents it is September 15.

Transfer Admission The application deadline for admission is rolling.

Entrance Difficulty Davenport has an open admission policy.

For Further Information Contact Lynnae Selberg, Executive Director of Enrollment, Davenport University, 415 East Fulton Street, Grand Rapids, MI 49503. *Telephone:* 616-451-3511 Ext. 1213 or 800-632-9569 (toll-free). *Fax:* 616-732-1142. *Web site:* http://www.davenport.edu/.

DAVENPORT UNIVERSITY

Holland, Michigan

For Information Write to Davenport University, Holland, MI 49423.

DAVENPORT UNIVERSITY

Kalamazoo, Michigan

Davenport University is a coed, private, four-year college of Davenport Educational System, founded in 1977, offering degrees at the associate and bachelor's levels and postbachelor's certificates. It has a 5-acre campus in Kalamazoo.

Academic Information The faculty has 110 members (22% full-time), 13% with terminal degrees. The student-faculty ratio is 13:1. The library holds 10,257 titles and 949 audiovisual materials. Special programs include academic remediation, cooperative (work-study) education, study abroad, ESL programs, independent study, distance learning, summer session for credit, part-time degree programs (daytime, evenings, weekends, summer), adult/continuing education programs, internships, and arrangement for off-campus study with Kalamazoo Consortium. The most frequently chosen baccalaureate field is law/legal studies.

Student Body Statistics The student body is made up of 1,063 undergraduates (161 freshmen). 75 percent are women and 25 percent are men. Students come from 2 states and territories and 6 other countries. 99 percent are from Michigan. 0.2 percent are international students.

Expenses for 2002–03 *Application fee:* $25. *One-time mandatory fee:* $50. *Tuition:* $10,042 full-time, $220 per credit hour part-time. *Mandatory fees:* $105 full-time, $35 per term part-time. Full-time tuition and fees vary according to location. Part-time tuition and fees vary according to location and program.

Financial Aid Forms of aid include need-based scholarships and part-time jobs. The priority application deadline for financial aid is February 21.

Freshman Admission Davenport University requires an essay and a high school transcript. TOEFL scores for international students are recommended. The application deadline for regular admission is rolling.

Transfer Admission The application deadline for admission is rolling.

Entrance Difficulty Davenport University has an open admission policy.

For Further Information Contact Ms. Gloria Stender, Admissions Director, Davenport University, 4123 West Main Street, Kalamazoo, MI 49006-2791. *Telephone:* 616-382-2835 Ext. 3309 or 800-632-8928 (toll-free). *Fax:* 616-382-2661. *Web site:* http://www.davenport.edu/.

DAVENPORT UNIVERSITY

Lansing, Michigan

Davenport University is a coed, private, four-year college of Davenport Educational System, founded in 1977, offering degrees at the associate and bachelor's levels. It has a 2-acre campus in Lansing near Detroit.

Academic Information The faculty has 79 members (14% full-time). The student-faculty ratio is 15:1. The library holds 10,680 titles and 850 serial subscriptions. Special programs include academic remediation, services for learning-disabled students, cooperative (work-study) education, advanced placement credit, accelerated degree programs, independent study, distance learning, self-designed majors, summer session for credit, part-time degree programs, external degree programs, adult/continuing education programs, and internships.
Student Body Statistics The student body is made up of 1,209 undergraduates (270 freshmen). 72 percent are women and 28 percent are men. Students come from 1 state or territory. 0.2 percent are international students. 3 percent of the 2002 graduating class went on to graduate and professional schools.
Expenses for 2002–03 *Application fee:* $25. *Tuition:* $8586 full-time, $212 per credit hour part-time. *Mandatory fees:* $70 full-time, $35 per term part-time.
Financial Aid Forms of aid include need-based and non-need-based scholarships and part-time jobs. The priority application deadline for financial aid is March 15.
Freshman Admission Davenport University requires a high school transcript. An interview is recommended. ACT scores are required for some. The application deadline for regular admission is September 15.
Transfer Admission The application deadline for admission is September 15.
Entrance Difficulty Davenport University has an open admission policy.

For Further Information Contact Mr. Tom Woods, Associate Dean of Enrollment, Davenport University, 220 East Kalamazoo, Lansing, MI 48933-2197. *Telephone:* 517-484-2600 Ext. 288 or 800-686-1600 (toll-free). *Fax:* 517-484-9719. *E-mail:* laadmissions@davenport.edu. *Web site:* http://www.davenport.edu/.

DAVENPORT UNIVERSITY

Lapeer, Michigan

For Information Write to Davenport University, Lapeer, MI 48446.

DAVENPORT UNIVERSITY

Midland, Michigan

For Information Write to Davenport University, Midland, MI 48642.

DAVENPORT UNIVERSITY

Romeo, Michigan

For Information Write to Davenport University, Romeo, MI 48065.

DAVENPORT UNIVERSITY

Saginaw, Michigan

For Information Write to Davenport University, Saginaw, MI 48604.

DAVENPORT UNIVERSITY

Traverse City, Michigan

For Information Write to Davenport University, Traverse City, MI 49684.

DAVENPORT UNIVERSITY

Warren, Michigan

Davenport University is a coed, private, comprehensive institution, founded in 1985, offering degrees at the associate, bachelor's, and master's levels. It has a 9-acre campus in Warren near Detroit.

Expenses for 2002–03 *Application fee:* $20. *Tuition:* $7776 full-time. *Mandatory fees:* $110 full-time. Full-time tuition and fees vary according to course load. *Part-time tuition:* varies with course load.

For Further Information Contact Ms. Gerri Pavone, Director of Admissions, Davenport University, 27650 Dequindre Road, Warren, MI 48092-5209. *Telephone:* 586-558-8700 or 800-724-7708 (toll-free). *Fax:* 810-558-7868. *E-mail:* gerripavone@davenport.edu. *Web site:* http://www.davenport.edu/.

EASTERN MICHIGAN UNIVERSITY

Ypsilanti, Michigan

EMU is a coed, public, comprehensive institution, founded in 1849, offering degrees at the bachelor's, master's, and doctoral levels and post-master's certificates. It has a 460-acre campus in Ypsilanti near Detroit.

Academic Information The faculty has 1,224 members (62% full-time). The undergraduate student-faculty ratio is 19:1. The library holds 658,648 titles, 4,457 serial subscriptions, and 11,524 audiovisual materials. Special programs include academic remediation, services for learning-disabled students, an honors program, cooperative (work-study) education, study abroad, advanced placement credit, accelerated degree programs, ESL programs, double majors, independent study, distance learning, self-designed majors, summer session for credit, part-time degree programs (daytime, evenings, weekends, summer), adult/continuing education programs, and internships. The most frequently chosen baccalaureate fields are business/marketing, education, social sciences and history.
Student Body Statistics The student body totals 24,195, of whom 18,757 are undergraduates (2,760 freshmen). 61 percent are women and 39 percent are men. Students come from 44 states and territories and 74 other countries. 93 percent are from Michigan. 1.9 percent are international students. 20 percent of the 2002 graduating class went on to graduate and professional schools.
Expenses for 2002–03 *Application fee:* $25. *State resident tuition:* $4047 full-time, $134.90 per credit hour part-time. *Nonresident tuition:* $12,780 full-time, $426 per credit hour part-time. *Mandatory fees:* $980 full-time, $30 per credit hour part-time, $40 per term part-time. Full-time tuition and fees vary according to reciprocity agreements. Part-time tuition and fees vary according to reciprocity agreements. *College room and board:* $5597. *College room only:* $2630. Room and board charges vary according to housing facility and location.
Financial Aid Forms of aid include need-based and non-need-based scholarships, athletic grants, and part-time jobs. The average aided 2001–02 undergraduate received an aid package worth $10,495. The priority application deadline for financial aid is March 15.
Freshman Admission EMU requires a high school transcript, a minimum 2.0 high school GPA, SAT I or ACT scores, and TOEFL scores for international students. ACT scores are recommended. 1 recommendation and an interview are required for some. The application deadline for regular admission is June 30.
Transfer Admission The application deadline for admission is rolling.

Entrance Difficulty EMU assesses its entrance difficulty level as moderately difficult. For the fall 2002 freshman class, 75 percent of the applicants were accepted.

For Further Information Contact Ms. Judy Benfield-Tatum, Director of Admissions, Eastern Michigan University, 400 Pierce Hall. *Telephone:* 734-487-3060 or 800-GO TO EMU (toll-free). *Fax:* 734-487-6559. *E-mail:* admissions@emich.edu. *Web site:* http://www.emich.edu/.

FERRIS STATE UNIVERSITY

Big Rapids, Michigan

Ferris is a coed, public, comprehensive institution, founded in 1884, offering degrees at the associate, bachelor's, master's, and first professional levels. It has a 600-acre campus in Big Rapids near Grand Rapids.

Academic Information The faculty has 630 members (78% full-time). The undergraduate student-faculty ratio is 16:1. The library holds 340,048 titles, 9,809 serial subscriptions, and 10,199 audiovisual materials. Special programs include academic remediation, an honors program, cooperative (work-study) education, study abroad, advanced placement credit, accelerated degree programs, Freshman Honors College, ESL programs, double majors, distance learning, summer session for credit, part-time degree programs (daytime, evenings, weekends, summer), external degree programs, adult/continuing education programs, internships, and arrangement for off-campus study. The most frequently chosen baccalaureate fields are business/marketing, engineering/engineering technologies, health professions and related sciences.
Student Body Statistics The student body totals 11,074, of whom 10,176 are undergraduates (2,067 freshmen). 46 percent are women and 54 percent are men. Students come from 42 states and territories and 54 other countries. 95 percent are from Michigan. 1.8 percent are international students.
Expenses for 2002–03 *Application fee:* $30. *State resident tuition:* $5734 full-time, $229 per credit hour part-time. *Nonresident tuition:* $11,385 full-time, $466 per credit hour part-time. *Mandatory fees:* $118 full-time, $59 per term part-time. Full-time tuition and fees vary according to program and reciprocity agreements. Part-time tuition and fees vary according to course load. *College room and board:* $5968. *College room only:* $1468. Room and board charges vary according to board plan and housing facility.
Financial Aid Forms of aid include need-based and non-need-based scholarships, athletic grants, and part-time jobs. The average aided 2001–02 undergraduate received an aid package worth $7800. The priority application deadline for financial aid is March 15.
Freshman Admission Ferris requires a high school transcript, a minimum 2.25 high school GPA, SAT I or ACT scores, and TOEFL scores for international students. An interview is recommended. An interview is required for some. The application deadline for regular admission is August 4.
Transfer Admission The application deadline for admission is August 4.
Entrance Difficulty Ferris assesses its entrance difficulty level as minimally difficult; moderately difficult for transfers; very difficult for pharmacy, dental hygiene, nursing, optometry programs. For the fall 2002 freshman class, 74 percent of the applicants were accepted.

For Further Information Contact Dr. Craig Westmann, Director Admissions Records/Associate Dean of Enrollment Services, Ferris State University, CSS201, Big Rapids, MI 49307-2742. *Telephone:* 231-591-2100 or 800-433-7747 (toll-free). *Fax:* 616-592-2978. *E-mail:* admissions@ferris.edu. *Web site:* http://www.ferris.edu/.

FINLANDIA UNIVERSITY

Hancock, Michigan

Finlandia University is a coed, private, four-year college, founded in 1896, affiliated with the Evangelical Lutheran Church in America, offering degrees at the associate and bachelor's levels. It has a 25-acre campus in Hancock.

Academic Information The faculty has 62 members (52% full-time). The student-faculty ratio is 11:1. The library holds 61,631 titles, 313 serial subscriptions, and 15,694 audiovisual materials. Special programs include academic remediation, services for learning-disabled students, study abroad, advanced placement credit, accelerated degree programs, ESL programs, independent study, distance learning, summer session for credit, part-time degree programs (daytime, evenings, summer), adult/continuing education programs, and internships. The most frequently chosen baccalaureate fields are business/marketing, liberal arts/general studies, protective services/public administration.
Student Body Statistics The student body is made up of 503 undergraduates (126 freshmen). 67 percent are women and 33 percent are men. Students come from 8 states and territories. 95 percent are from Michigan.
Expenses for 2003–04 *Application fee:* $30. *One-time mandatory fee:* $75. *Comprehensive fee:* $18,620 includes full-time tuition ($13,750) and college room and board ($4870). Full-time tuition varies according to degree level. Room and board charges vary according to housing facility. *Part-time tuition:* $460 per credit. Part-time tuition varies according to course load and reciprocity agreements.
Financial Aid Forms of aid include need-based and non-need-based scholarships and part-time jobs. The average aided 2002–03 undergraduate received an aid package worth an estimated $10,700. The priority application deadline for financial aid is February 15.
Freshman Admission Finlandia University requires a high school transcript, a minimum 2.5 high school GPA, and TOEFL scores for international students. SAT I or ACT scores are recommended. An essay, recommendations, and an interview are required for some. The application deadline for regular admission is August 15.
Transfer Admission The application deadline for admission is August 15.
Entrance Difficulty Finlandia University assesses its entrance difficulty level as minimally difficult. For the fall 2002 freshman class, 57 percent of the applicants were accepted.

For Further Information Contact Mr. Ben Larson, Executive Director of Admissions, Finlandia University, 601 Quincy Street, Hancock, MI 49930. *Telephone:* 906-487-7324 or 877-202-5491 (toll-free). *Fax:* 906-487-7383. *E-mail:* admissions@finlandia.edu. *Web site:* http://www.finlandia.edu/.

GMI ENGINEERING & MANAGEMENT INSTITUTE

See Kettering University

GRACE BIBLE COLLEGE

Grand Rapids, Michigan

Grace is a coed, private, four-year college, founded in 1945, affiliated with the Grace Gospel Fellowship, offering degrees at the associate and bachelor's levels. It has a 16-acre campus in Grand Rapids.

Academic Information The faculty has 29 members (31% full-time), 21% with terminal degrees. The student-faculty ratio is 11:1. The library holds 32,291 titles, 192 serial subscriptions, and 2,121 audiovisual materials. Special programs include academic remediation, advanced placement credit, ESL programs, independent study, internships, and arrangement for off-campus study with Grand Rapids Community College, Davenport University, Cornerstone University. The most frequently chosen baccalaureate fields are education, philosophy, religion, and theology, visual/performing arts.

Grace Bible College (continued)

Student Body Statistics The student body is made up of 145 undergraduates (31 freshmen). 44 percent are women and 56 percent are men. Students come from 16 states and territories and 2 other countries. 74 percent are from Michigan. 1.4 percent are international students.

Expenses for 2002–03 *Application fee:* $0. *Comprehensive fee:* $13,740 includes full-time tuition ($8300), mandatory fees ($390), and college room and board ($5050). Room and board charges vary according to housing facility. *Part-time tuition:* $345 per semester hour. Part-time tuition varies according to course load.

Financial Aid Forms of aid include need-based and non-need-based scholarships and part-time jobs. The average aided 2001–02 undergraduate received an aid package worth $6873. The priority application deadline for financial aid is February 15.

Freshman Admission Grace requires a high school transcript, 2 recommendations, ACT scores, and TOEFL scores for international students. A minimum 2.5 high school GPA is recommended. An interview is required for some. The application deadline for regular admission is July 15.

Entrance Difficulty Grace assesses its entrance difficulty level as minimally difficult. For the fall 2002 freshman class, 30 percent of the applicants were accepted.

For Further Information Contact Mr. Kevin Gilliam, Director of Enrollment, Grace Bible College, 1101 Aldon Street, SW, PO Box 910, Grand Rapids, MI 49509. *Telephone:* 616-538-2330 or 800-968-1887 (toll-free). *Fax:* 616-538-0599. *E-mail:* gbc@gbcol.edu. *Web site:* http://www.gbcol.edu/.

GRAND VALLEY STATE UNIVERSITY

Allendale, Michigan

GVSU is a coed, public, comprehensive institution, founded in 1960, offering degrees at the bachelor's and master's levels and post-master's and postbachelor's certificates. It has a 900-acre campus in Allendale near Grand Rapids.

Academic Information The faculty has 1,257 members (61% full-time), 43% with terminal degrees. The undergraduate student-faculty ratio is 22:1. The library holds 620,000 titles and 3,207 serial subscriptions. Special programs include academic remediation, services for learning-disabled students, an honors program, cooperative (work-study) education, study abroad, advanced placement credit, accelerated degree programs, Freshman Honors College, ESL programs, double majors, independent study, distance learning, summer session for credit, part-time degree programs (daytime, evenings, weekends, summer), adult/continuing education programs, and internships. The most frequently chosen baccalaureate fields are business/marketing, health professions and related sciences, psychology.

Student Body Statistics The student body totals 20,407, of whom 16,875 are undergraduates (2,894 freshmen). 60 percent are women and 40 percent are men. Students come from 43 states and territories and 39 other countries. 96 percent are from Michigan. 0.6 percent are international students.

Expenses for 2002–03 *Application fee:* $20. *State resident tuition:* $5056 full-time, $221 per semester hour part-time. *Nonresident tuition:* $10,936 full-time, $466 per semester hour part-time. Full-time tuition varies according to student level. Part-time tuition varies according to course load. *College room and board:* $5656. Room and board charges vary according to board plan, housing facility, and location.

Financial Aid Forms of aid include need-based and non-need-based scholarships, athletic grants, and part-time jobs. The average aided 2002–03 undergraduate received an aid package worth an estimated $6428. The priority application deadline for financial aid is February 15.

Freshman Admission GVSU requires a high school transcript, SAT I or ACT scores, and TOEFL scores for international students. An essay and an interview are required for some. The application deadline for regular admission is July 25.

Transfer Admission The application deadline for admission is July 25.

Entrance Difficulty GVSU assesses its entrance difficulty level as moderately difficult. For the fall 2002 freshman class, 71 percent of the applicants were accepted.

For Further Information Contact Ms. Jodi Chycinski, Director of Admissions, Grand Valley State University, 1 Campus Drive, Allendale, MI 49401. *Telephone:* 616-331-2025 or 800-748-0246 (toll-free). *Fax:* 616-331-2000. *E-mail:* go2gvsu@gvsu.edu. *Web site:* http://www.gvsu.edu/.

GREAT LAKES CHRISTIAN COLLEGE

Lansing, Michigan

GLCC is a coed, private, four-year college, founded in 1949, affiliated with the Christian Churches and Churches of Christ, offering degrees at the associate and bachelor's levels. It has a 50-acre campus in Lansing.

Academic Information The faculty has 20 members (50% full-time). The student-faculty ratio is 14:1. The library holds 34,000 titles and 213 serial subscriptions. Special programs include advanced placement credit, double majors, independent study, part-time degree programs (daytime, evenings), external degree programs, adult/continuing education programs, internships, and arrangement for off-campus study with Cornerstone College, Davenport College of Business. The most frequently chosen baccalaureate fields are education, philosophy, religion, and theology, psychology.

Student Body Statistics The student body is made up of 207 undergraduates. Students come from 8 states and territories and 3 other countries. 2.4 percent are international students.

Expenses for 2003–04 *Application fee:* $30. *Comprehensive fee:* $14,080 includes full-time tuition ($7680), mandatory fees ($1600), and college room and board ($4800). *Part-time tuition:* $240 per hour.

Financial Aid Forms of aid include non-need-based scholarships and part-time jobs.

Freshman Admission GLCC requires an essay, a high school transcript, a minimum 2.25 high school GPA, 3 recommendations, SAT I and SAT II or ACT scores, and TOEFL scores for international students. The application deadline for regular admission is August 1.

Transfer Admission The application deadline for admission is August 1.

Entrance Difficulty GLCC assesses its entrance difficulty level as moderately difficult.

For Further Information Contact Mr. Mike Klauka, Dean of Student Affairs, Great Lakes Christian College, 6211 West Willow Highway, Lansing, MI 48917-1299. *Telephone:* 517-321-0242 Ext. 221 or 800-YES-GLCC (toll-free). *Fax:* 517-321-5902. *Web site:* http://www.glcc.edu/.

HILLSDALE COLLEGE

Hillsdale, Michigan

Hillsdale is a coed, private, four-year college, founded in 1844, offering degrees at the bachelor's level. It has a 200-acre campus in Hillsdale.

Academic Information The faculty has 127 members (70% full-time), 81% with terminal degrees. The student-faculty ratio is 11:1. The library holds 205,000 titles, 1,625 serial subscriptions, and 7,950 audiovisual materials. Special programs include an honors program, study abroad, advanced placement credit, accelerated degree programs, double majors, independent study, summer session for credit, part-time degree programs (daytime, summer), and internships. The most frequently chosen baccalaureate fields are business/marketing, education, social sciences and history.

Student Body Statistics The student body is made up of 1,220 undergraduates (422 freshmen). 54 percent are women and 46 percent are men. Students come from 46 states and territories and 11 other countries. 48 percent are from Michigan.

Expenses for 2002–03 *Application fee:* $15. *Comprehensive fee:* $21,386 includes full-time tuition ($15,000), mandatory fees ($300), and college

room and board ($6086). *College room only:* $2900. Room and board charges vary according to board plan. *Part-time tuition:* $590 per semester hour.
Financial Aid Forms of aid include need-based and non-need-based scholarships, athletic grants, and part-time jobs. The average aided 2001–02 undergraduate received an aid package worth $14,000. The priority application deadline for financial aid is March 15.
Freshman Admission Hillsdale requires an essay, a high school transcript, a minimum 3.15 high school GPA, 1 recommendation, SAT I or ACT scores, and TOEFL scores for international students. 2 recommendations, an interview, SAT II: Subject Test scores, and SAT II: Writing Test scores are recommended. An interview is required for some. The application deadline for regular admission is rolling.
Transfer Admission The application deadline for admission is rolling.
Entrance Difficulty Hillsdale assesses its entrance difficulty level as very difficult. For the fall 2002 freshman class, 82 percent of the applicants were accepted.

For Further Information Contact Mr. Jeffrey S. Lantis, Director of Admissions, Hillsdale College, 33 East College Street, Hillsdale, MI 49242-1298. *Telephone:* 517-607-2327 Ext. 2327. *Fax:* 517-607-2223. *E-mail:* admissions@hillsdale.edu. *Web site:* http://www.hillsdale.edu/.

HOPE COLLEGE

Holland, Michigan

Hope is a coed, private, four-year college, founded in 1866, affiliated with the Reformed Church in America, offering degrees at the bachelor's level. It has a 45-acre campus in Holland near Grand Rapids.

Academic Information The faculty has 282 members (71% full-time), 70% with terminal degrees. The student-faculty ratio is 13:1. The library holds 343,865 titles, 2,250 serial subscriptions, and 11,970 audiovisual materials. Special programs include services for learning-disabled students, study abroad, advanced placement credit, ESL programs, double majors, independent study, self-designed majors, summer session for credit, part-time degree programs (daytime), internships, and arrangement for off-campus study with members of the Great Lakes Colleges Association, Associated Colleges of the Midwest, Institute of European Studies, Council for International Educational Exchange. The most frequently chosen baccalaureate fields are business/marketing, English, social sciences and history.
Student Body Statistics The student body is made up of 3,035 undergraduates (725 freshmen). 61 percent are women and 39 percent are men. Students come from 38 states and territories and 40 other countries. 77 percent are from Michigan. 1.5 percent are international students. 27 percent of the 2002 graduating class went on to graduate and professional schools.
Expenses for 2002–03 *Application fee:* $25. *Comprehensive fee:* $23,956 includes full-time tuition ($18,158), mandatory fees ($110), and college room and board ($5688). *College room only:* $2594. Full-time tuition and fees vary according to course load. Room and board charges vary according to board plan. *Part-time tuition:* $640 per credit.
Financial Aid Forms of aid include need-based and non-need-based scholarships and part-time jobs. The average aided 2002–03 undergraduate received an aid package worth an estimated $15,673. The priority application deadline for financial aid is February 15.
Freshman Admission Hope requires an essay, a high school transcript, SAT I or ACT scores, and TOEFL scores for international students. An interview is recommended. 1 recommendation is required for some. The application deadline for regular admission is rolling.
Transfer Admission The application deadline for admission is rolling.
Entrance Difficulty Hope assesses its entrance difficulty level as moderately difficult. For the fall 2002 freshman class, 90 percent of the applicants were accepted.

For Further Information Contact Dr. James R. Bekkering, Vice President for Admissions, Hope College, 69 East 10th Street, PO Box 9000, Holland, MI 49422-9000. *Telephone:* 616-395-7955 or 800-968-7850 (toll-free). *Fax:* 616-395-7130. *E-mail:* admissions@hope.edu. *Web site:* http://www.hope.edu/.

KALAMAZOO COLLEGE

Kalamazoo, Michigan

K-College is a coed, private, four-year college, founded in 1833, affiliated with the American Baptist Churches in the U.S.A., offering degrees at the bachelor's level. It has a 60-acre campus in Kalamazoo.

Academic Information The faculty has 121 members (85% full-time), 82% with terminal degrees. The student-faculty ratio is 12:1. The library holds 342,939 titles, 1,495 serial subscriptions, and 6,967 audiovisual materials. Special programs include services for learning-disabled students, cooperative (work-study) education, study abroad, advanced placement credit, ESL programs, double majors, independent study, internships, and arrangement for off-campus study with Western Michigan University. The most frequently chosen baccalaureate fields are English, biological/life sciences, social sciences and history.
Student Body Statistics The student body is made up of 1,265 undergraduates (337 freshmen). 55 percent are women and 45 percent are men. Students come from 36 states and territories and 14 other countries. 79 percent are from Michigan. 1.7 percent are international students. 35 percent of the 2002 graduating class went on to graduate and professional schools.
Expenses for 2002–03 *Application fee:* $45. *Comprehensive fee:* $27,957 includes full-time tuition ($21,603) and college room and board ($6354). *College room only:* $3147.
Financial Aid Forms of aid include need-based and non-need-based scholarships and part-time jobs. The average aided 2002–03 undergraduate received an aid package worth an estimated $19,000. The priority application deadline for financial aid is February 15.
Freshman Admission K-College requires an essay, a high school transcript, 2 recommendations, SAT I or ACT scores, and TOEFL scores for international students. A minimum 3.0 high school GPA and an interview are recommended. The application deadline for regular admission is February 15; for early decision it is November 15; and for early action it is December 1.
Transfer Admission The application deadline for admission is May 1.
Entrance Difficulty K-College assesses its entrance difficulty level as very difficult. For the fall 2002 freshman class, 73 percent of the applicants were accepted.

For Further Information Contact Mrs. Linda Wirgau, Records Manager, Kalamazoo College, Mandelle Hall, 1200 Academy Street, Kalamazoo, MI 49006-3295. *Telephone:* 616-337-7166 or 800-253-3602 (toll-free). *Fax:* 269-337-7251. *E-mail:* admission@kzoo.edu. *Web site:* http://www.kzoo.edu/.

KENDALL COLLEGE OF ART AND DESIGN OF FERRIS STATE UNIVERSITY

Grand Rapids, Michigan

Kendall is a coed, private, comprehensive institution, founded in 1928, offering degrees at the bachelor's and master's levels in art.

Academic Information The faculty has 105 members (39% full-time). The undergraduate student-faculty ratio is 13:1. The library holds 21,324 titles, 111 serial subscriptions, and 311 audiovisual materials. Special programs include services for learning-disabled students, study abroad, advanced placement credit, independent study, summer session for credit, part-time degree programs, adult/continuing education programs, internships, and arrangement for off-campus study with Art College Exchange, New York Studio Program. The most frequently chosen baccalaureate fields are trade and industry, visual/performing arts.
Student Body Statistics The student body totals 855, of whom 844 are undergraduates. 59 percent are women and 41 percent are men. Students come from 17 states and territories and 5 other countries. 94 percent are from Michigan. 1.4 percent are international students.
Expenses for 2002–03 *Application fee:* $35. *State resident tuition:* $206 per credit hour part-time. *Nonresident tuition:* $446 per credit hour part-time. Part-time tuition varies according to course load and program.

Kendall College of Art and Design of Ferris State University (continued)

Financial Aid Forms of aid include need-based and non-need-based scholarships and part-time jobs. $10,526. The priority application deadline for financial aid is February 15.

Freshman Admission Kendall requires an essay, a high school transcript, a minimum 2.5 high school GPA, a portfolio, ACT scores, and TOEFL scores for international students. An interview is recommended. The application deadline for regular admission is rolling.

Transfer Admission The application deadline for admission is rolling.

Entrance Difficulty Kendall assesses its entrance difficulty level as minimally difficult.

For Further Information Contact Ms. Sandra Britton, Director of Enrollment Management, Kendall College of Art and Design of Ferris State University, 17 Fountain Street, NW, Grand Rapids, MI 49503-3002. *Telephone:* 616-451-2787 Ext. 113 or 800-676-2787 (toll-free). *Fax:* 616-831-9689. *Web site:* http://www.kcad.edu/.

KETTERING UNIVERSITY

Flint, Michigan

Kettering/GMI is a coed, private, comprehensive institution, founded in 1919, offering degrees at the bachelor's and master's levels. It has a 45-acre campus in Flint near Detroit.

Academic Information The faculty has 153 members (92% full-time), 87% with terminal degrees. The undergraduate student-faculty ratio is 9:1. The library holds 115,000 titles, 1,200 serial subscriptions, and 778 audiovisual materials. Special programs include services for learning-disabled students, cooperative (work-study) education, study abroad, advanced placement credit, accelerated degree programs, double majors, independent study, distance learning, and internships. The most frequently chosen baccalaureate fields are business/marketing, computer/information sciences, engineering/engineering technologies.

Student Body Statistics The student body totals 3,166, of whom 2,487 are undergraduates (435 freshmen). 17 percent are women and 83 percent are men. Students come from 48 states and territories and 15 other countries. 63 percent are from Michigan. 2.2 percent are international students. 33 percent of the 2002 graduating class went on to graduate and professional schools.

Expenses for 2002–03 *Application fee:* $35. *Comprehensive fee:* $25,085 includes full-time tuition ($20,170), mandatory fees ($163), and college room and board ($4752). *College room only:* $3052. Full-time tuition and fees vary according to student level. Room and board charges vary according to student level. *Part-time tuition:* $631 per credit.

Financial Aid Forms of aid include need-based and non-need-based scholarships and part-time jobs. The average aided 2001–02 undergraduate received an aid package worth $13,078. The priority application deadline for financial aid is February 14.

Freshman Admission Kettering/GMI requires a high school transcript, SAT I or ACT scores, and TOEFL scores for international students. A minimum 3.0 high school GPA, an interview, and SAT II: Subject Test scores are recommended. An essay is required for some. The application deadline for regular admission is rolling.

Transfer Admission The application deadline for admission is rolling.

Entrance Difficulty Kettering/GMI assesses its entrance difficulty level as very difficult. For the fall 2002 freshman class, 56 percent of the applicants were accepted.

For Further Information Contact Ms. Barbara Sosin, Interim Director of Admissions, Kettering University, 1700 West Third Avenue, Flint, MI 48504-4898. *Telephone:* 810-762-7865, 800-955-4464 Ext. 7865 (toll-free in-state), or 800-955-4464 (toll-free out-of-state). *Fax:* 810-762-9837. *E-mail:* admissions@kettering.edu. *Web site:* http://www.kettering.edu/.

See page 296 for a narrative description.

LAKE SUPERIOR STATE UNIVERSITY

Sault Sainte Marie, Michigan

LSSU is a coed, public, four-year college, founded in 1946, offering degrees at the associate and bachelor's levels. It has a 121-acre campus in Sault Sainte Marie.

Expenses for 2002–03 *Application fee:* $20. *State resident tuition:* $4548 full-time. *Nonresident tuition:* $8904 full-time. *Mandatory fees:* $210 full-time. Full-time tuition and fees vary according to reciprocity agreements. *College room and board:* $5548. *College room only:* $4848. Room and board charges vary according to board plan.

For Further Information Contact Mr. Kevin Pollock, Director of Admissions, Lake Superior State University, 650 West Easterday Avenue, Sault Saint Marie, MI 49783-1699. *Telephone:* 906-635-2670 or 888-800-LSSU Ext. 2231 (toll-free). *Fax:* 906-635-6669. *E-mail:* admissions@gw.lssu.edu. *Web site:* http://www.lssu.edu/.

LAWRENCE TECHNOLOGICAL UNIVERSITY

Southfield, Michigan

Lawrence Tech is a coed, private, comprehensive institution, founded in 1932, offering degrees at the associate, bachelor's, and master's levels. It has a 110-acre campus in Southfield near Detroit.

Academic Information The faculty has 353 members (29% full-time), 54% with terminal degrees. The undergraduate student-faculty ratio is 13:1. The library holds 110,250 titles, 700 serial subscriptions, and 420 audiovisual materials. Special programs include academic remediation, services for learning-disabled students, cooperative (work-study) education, study abroad, advanced placement credit, ESL programs, double majors, independent study, distance learning, summer session for credit, part-time degree programs (daytime, evenings, weekends, summer), adult/continuing education programs, internships, and arrangement for off-campus study with Macomb University Center, Oakland Technical Center.

Student Body Statistics The student body totals 4,054, of whom 2,806 are undergraduates (422 freshmen). 26 percent are women and 74 percent are men. Students come from 11 states and territories. 99 percent are from Michigan. 1.3 percent are international students. 15 percent of the 2002 graduating class went on to graduate and professional schools.

Expenses for 2002–03 *Application fee:* $30. *Comprehensive fee:* $18,130 includes full-time tuition ($13,050), mandatory fees ($240), and college room and board ($4840). *College room only:* $3684. Full-time tuition and fees vary according to course level, course load, degree level, program, and student level. Room and board charges vary according to board plan and housing facility. *Part-time tuition:* $450 per hour. *Part-time mandatory fees:* $220 per term. Part-time tuition and fees vary according to course level, course load, degree level, program, and student level.

Financial Aid Forms of aid include need-based and non-need-based scholarships and part-time jobs. The average aided 2002–03 undergraduate received an aid package worth an estimated $9149. The priority application deadline for financial aid is May 1.

Freshman Admission Lawrence Tech requires a high school transcript, a minimum 2.5 high school GPA, and SAT I or ACT scores. An essay and TOEFL scores for international students are recommended. An essay, recommendations, and an interview are required for some. The application deadline for regular admission is August 15.

Transfer Admission The application deadline for admission is August 15.

Entrance Difficulty Lawrence Tech assesses its entrance difficulty level as moderately difficult. For the fall 2002 freshman class, 84 percent of the applicants were accepted.

For Further Information Contact Ms. Jane Rohrback, Director of Admissions, Lawrence Technological University, 21000 West Ten Mile Road, Southfield, MI 48075. *Telephone:* 248-204-3180 or 800-225-5588 (toll-free). *Fax:* 248-204-3188. *E-mail:* admissions@ltu.edu. *Web site:* http://www.ltu.edu/.

LEWIS COLLEGE OF BUSINESS

Detroit, Michigan

Lewis College is a coed, private, two-year college, founded in 1929, offering degrees at the associate level. It has an 11-acre campus in Detroit.

Academic Information The faculty has 36 members (25% full-time). The student-faculty ratio is 15:1. The library holds 3,355 titles and 90 serial subscriptions. Special programs include academic remediation, cooperative (work-study) education, summer session for credit, and part-time degree programs (daytime, evenings).
Student Body Statistics The student body is made up of 324 undergraduates.
Expenses for 2002–03 *Application fee:* $15. *Tuition:* $8835 full-time, $280 per credit part-time. *Mandatory fees:* $165 full-time, $165 per year part-time.
Financial Aid Forms of aid include need-based scholarships and part-time jobs. The priority application deadline for financial aid is February 1.
Freshman Admission Lewis College requires a high school transcript. The application deadline for regular admission is rolling.
Transfer Admission The application deadline for admission is August 1.
Entrance Difficulty Lewis College has an open admission policy.

For Further Information Contact Ms. Frances Ambrose, Admissions Secretary, Lewis College of Business, 17370 Meyers Road, Detroit, MI 48235-1423. *Telephone:* 313-862-6300 Ext. 230. *Fax:* 313-862-1027. *Web site:* http://www.lewiscollege.edu/.

MADONNA UNIVERSITY

Livonia, Michigan

Madonna University is a coed, private, Roman Catholic, comprehensive institution, founded in 1947, offering degrees at the associate, bachelor's, and master's levels. It has a 49-acre campus in Livonia near Detroit.

Academic Information The faculty has 292 members (34% full-time), 39% with terminal degrees. The undergraduate student-faculty ratio is 17:1. The library holds 199,144 titles and 1,679 serial subscriptions. Special programs include academic remediation, services for learning-disabled students, cooperative (work-study) education, study abroad, advanced placement credit, accelerated degree programs, ESL programs, double majors, independent study, distance learning, summer session for credit, part-time degree programs (daytime, evenings, weekends, summer), adult/continuing education programs, internships, and arrangement for off-campus study with 5 members of the Detroit Area Consortium of Catholic Colleges. The most frequently chosen baccalaureate fields are health professions and related sciences, business/marketing, protective services/public administration.
Student Body Statistics The student body totals 3,808, of whom 2,963 are undergraduates (199 freshmen). 77 percent are women and 23 percent are men. Students come from 9 states and territories and 28 other countries. 99 percent are from Michigan. 2.5 percent are international students. 40 percent of the 2002 graduating class went on to graduate and professional schools.
Expenses for 2003–04 *Application fee:* $0. *Comprehensive fee:* $14,544 includes full-time tuition ($9000), mandatory fees ($100), and college room and board ($5444). *College room only:* $2500. Room and board charges vary according to board plan. *Part-time tuition:* $300 per credit hour.
Financial Aid Forms of aid include need-based and non-need-based scholarships, athletic grants, and part-time jobs. The average aided 2001–02 undergraduate received an aid package worth $1800. The priority application deadline for financial aid is February 21.
Freshman Admission Madonna University requires a high school transcript, a minimum 2.75 high school GPA, ACT scores, and TOEFL scores for international students. 2 recommendations are required for some. The application deadline for regular admission is rolling.
Transfer Admission The application deadline for admission is rolling.
Entrance Difficulty Madonna University assesses its entrance difficulty level as moderately difficult. For the fall 2002 freshman class, 94 percent of the applicants were accepted.

For Further Information Contact Mr. Frank J. Hribar, Director of Enrollment Management, Madonna University, 36600 Schoolcraft Road, Livonia, MI 48150-1173. *Telephone:* 734-432-5317 or 800-852-4951 (toll-free). *Fax:* 734-432-5393. *E-mail:* muinfo@smtp.munet.edu. *Web site:* http://www.madonna.edu/.

MARYGROVE COLLEGE

Detroit, Michigan

Marygrove is a coed, primarily women's, private, Roman Catholic, comprehensive institution, founded in 1905, offering degrees at the associate, bachelor's, and master's levels and postbachelor's certificates. It has a 50-acre campus in Detroit.

Academic Information The faculty has 77 members (92% full-time), 66% with terminal degrees. The undergraduate student-faculty ratio is 15:1. The library holds 98,817 titles, 500 serial subscriptions, and 1,559 audiovisual materials. Special programs include academic remediation, cooperative (work-study) education, advanced placement credit, double majors, distance learning, self-designed majors, summer session for credit, part-time degree programs (daytime, evenings, weekends, summer), internships, and arrangement for off-campus study with Detroit Area Consortium of Catholic Colleges. The most frequently chosen baccalaureate fields are business/marketing, education, social sciences and history.
Student Body Statistics The student body totals 6,465, of whom 866 are undergraduates (40 freshmen). 82 percent are women and 18 percent are men. Students come from 2 states and territories and 3 other countries. 99 percent are from Michigan. 0.9 percent are international students. 35 percent of the 2002 graduating class went on to graduate and professional schools.
Expenses for 2003–04 *Application fee:* $25. *Comprehensive fee:* $17,550 includes full-time tuition ($11,500), mandatory fees ($250), and college room and board ($5800). *Part-time tuition:* $418 per credit. *Part-time mandatory fees:* $10 per credit.
Financial Aid Forms of aid include non-need-based scholarships and part-time jobs.
Freshman Admission Marygrove requires a high school transcript, a minimum 2.7 high school GPA, ACT scores, and TOEFL scores for international students. Recommendations and an interview are required for some. The application deadline for regular admission is August 15.
Transfer Admission The application deadline for admission is August 15.
Entrance Difficulty Marygrove assesses its entrance difficulty level as moderately difficult. For the fall 2002 freshman class, 25 percent of the applicants were accepted.

For Further Information Contact Mr. Fred A. Schebor, Dean of Admissions, Marygrove College, Office of Admissions, Detroit, MI 48221-2599. *Telephone:* 313-927-1570 or 866-313-1297 (toll-free). *Fax:* 313-927-1345. *E-mail:* info@marygrove.edu. *Web site:* http://www.marygrove.edu/.

MICHIGAN CHRISTIAN COLLEGE

See Rochester College

MICHIGAN JEWISH INSTITUTE

Oak Park, Michigan

For Information Write to Michigan Jewish Institute, Oak Park, MI 48237-1304.

MICHIGAN STATE UNIVERSITY

East Lansing, Michigan

Michigan State is a coed, public university, founded in 1855, offering degrees at the bachelor's, master's, doctoral, and first professional levels. It has a 5-acre campus in East Lansing near Detroit.

Academic Information The faculty has 2,647 members (89% full-time), 90% with terminal degrees. The undergraduate student-faculty ratio is 18:1. The library holds 4 million titles, 29,470 serial subscriptions, and 290,206 audiovisual materials. Special programs include academic remediation, services for learning-disabled students, an honors program, cooperative (work-study) education, study abroad, advanced placement credit, accelerated degree programs, Freshman Honors College, ESL programs, double majors, independent study, distance learning, self-designed majors, summer session for credit, part-time degree programs, adult/continuing education programs, internships, and arrangement for off-campus study with Committee on Institutional Cooperation. The most frequently chosen baccalaureate fields are business/marketing, communications/communication technologies, social sciences and history.
Student Body Statistics The student body totals 44,937, of whom 35,197 are undergraduates (7,000 freshmen). 53 percent are women and 47 percent are men. Students come from 54 states and territories and 100 other countries. 94 percent are from Michigan. 2.4 percent are international students.
Expenses for 2002–03 *Application fee:* $35. *State resident tuition:* $5,392 full-time, $179.75 per semester hour part-time. *Nonresident tuition:* $15,884 full-time, $482 per semester hour part-time. *Mandatory fees:* $708 full-time, $708 per year part-time. Full-time tuition and fees vary according to course load, degree level, program, and student level. Part-time tuition and fees vary according to course load, degree level, program, and student level. *College room and board:* $4932. *College room only:* $2280. Room and board charges vary according to housing facility.
Financial Aid Forms of aid include need-based and non-need-based scholarships, athletic grants, and part-time jobs. The average aided 2002–03 undergraduate received an aid package worth an estimated $9355. The application deadline for financial aid is June 30 with a priority deadline of February 21.
Freshman Admission Michigan State requires a high school transcript, SAT I or ACT scores, and TOEFL scores for international students. The application deadline for for early action it is October 1.
Entrance Difficulty Michigan State assesses its entrance difficulty level as moderately difficult. For the fall 2002 freshman class, 67 percent of the applicants were accepted.

For Further Information Contact Ms. Pamela Horne, Assistant to the Provost for Enrollment and Director of Admissions, Michigan State University, 250 Administration Building, East Lansing, MI 48824. *Telephone:* 517-355-8332. *Fax:* 517-353-1647. *E-mail:* admis@msu.edu. *Web site:* http://www.msu.edu/.

MICHIGAN TECHNOLOGICAL UNIVERSITY

Houghton, Michigan

Michigan Tech is a coed, public university, founded in 1885, offering degrees at the associate, bachelor's, master's, and doctoral levels. It has a 240-acre campus in Houghton.

Academic Information The faculty has 407 members (93% full-time), 84% with terminal degrees. The undergraduate student-faculty ratio is 11:1. The library holds 820,414 titles, 10,369 serial subscriptions, and 4,529 audiovisual materials. Special programs include services for learning-disabled students, cooperative (work-study) education, study abroad, advanced placement credit, ESL programs, double majors, distance learning, self-designed majors, summer session for credit, part-time degree programs, internships, and arrangement for off-campus study with National Student Exchange.
Student Body Statistics The student body totals 6,625, of whom 5,915 are undergraduates (1,190 freshmen). 24 percent are women and 76 percent are men. Students come from 41 states and territories and 80 other countries. 81 percent are from Michigan. 5.7 percent are international students. 20 percent of the 2002 graduating class went on to graduate and professional schools.
Expenses for 2002–03 *Application fee:* $30. *State resident tuition:* $5782 full-time, $241 per credit hour part-time. *Nonresident tuition:* $14,152 full-time, $590 per credit hour part-time. *Mandatory fees:* $673 full-time, $336.50 per term part-time. Full-time tuition and fees vary according to course load and student level. Part-time tuition and fees vary according to course load and student level. *College room and board:* $5465. *College room only:* $2561. Room and board charges vary according to board plan and housing facility.
Financial Aid Forms of aid include need-based and non-need-based scholarships, athletic grants, and part-time jobs. The average aided 2002–03 undergraduate received an aid package worth an estimated $7855. The priority application deadline for financial aid is February 21.
Freshman Admission Michigan Tech requires a high school transcript, SAT I or ACT scores, and TOEFL scores for international students. An interview is recommended. The application deadline for regular admission is rolling.
Transfer Admission The application deadline for admission is rolling.
Entrance Difficulty Michigan Tech assesses its entrance difficulty level as moderately difficult; noncompetitive for transfers. For the fall 2002 freshman class, 92 percent of the applicants were accepted.

For Further Information Contact Ms. Nancy Rehling, Director of Undergraduate Admissions, Michigan Technological University, 1400 Townsend Drive, Houghton, MI 49931-1295. *Telephone:* 906-487-2335 or 888-MTU-1885 (toll-free). *Fax:* 906-487-2125. *E-mail:* mtu4u@mtu.edu. *Web site:* http://www.mtu.edu/.

NORTHERN MICHIGAN UNIVERSITY

Marquette, Michigan

NMU is a coed, public, comprehensive unit of Autonomous, founded in 1899, offering degrees at the associate, bachelor's, and master's levels and post-master's and postbachelor's certificates. It has a 300-acre campus in Marquette.

Academic Information The faculty has 428 members (73% full-time), 64% with terminal degrees. The undergraduate student-faculty ratio is 21:1. The library holds 1 million titles, 1,711 serial subscriptions, and 19,167 audiovisual materials. Special programs include academic remediation, services for learning-disabled students, an honors program, study abroad, advanced placement credit, accelerated degree programs, double majors, independent study, distance learning, self-designed majors, summer session for credit, part-time degree programs (daytime, evenings, weekends, summer), adult/continuing education programs, internships, and arrangement for off-campus study with other public institutions in Michigan. The most frequently chosen baccalaureate fields are business/marketing, education, health professions and related sciences.
Student Body Statistics The student body totals 9,016, of whom 8,113 are undergraduates (1,706 freshmen). 52 percent are women and 48 percent are men. 82 percent are from Michigan. 1.4 percent are international students.
Expenses for 2002–03 *Application fee:* $25. *State resident tuition:* $4128 full-time, $198 per credit hour part-time. *Nonresident tuition:* $7080 full-time, $310 per credit hour part-time. *College room and board:* $5630. Room and board charges vary according to board plan and housing facility.
Financial Aid Forms of aid include need-based and non-need-based scholarships, athletic grants, and part-time jobs. The average aided 2002–03 undergraduate received an aid package worth an estimated $7054. The priority application deadline for financial aid is February 20.
Freshman Admission NMU requires a high school transcript, SAT I or ACT scores, and TOEFL scores for international students. A minimum 2.25 high school GPA is required for some. The application deadline for regular admission is rolling.
Transfer Admission The application deadline for admission is rolling.

Entrance Difficulty NMU assesses its entrance difficulty level as minimally difficult. For the fall 2002 freshman class, 86 percent of the applicants were accepted.

For Further Information Contact Ms. Gerri Daniels, Director of Admissions, Northern Michigan University, 1401 Presque Isle Avenue, Marquette, MI 49855. *Telephone:* 906-227-2650, 800-682-9797 Ext. 1 (toll-free in-state), or 800-682-9797 (toll-free out-of-state). *Fax:* 906-227-1747. *E-mail:* admiss@nmu.edu. *Web site:* http://www.nmu.edu/.

NORTHWOOD UNIVERSITY

Midland, Michigan

Northwood is a coed, private, comprehensive institution, founded in 1959, offering degrees at the associate, bachelor's, and master's levels. It has a 434-acre campus in Midland.

Academic Information The faculty has 66 members (65% full-time), 15% with terminal degrees. The undergraduate student-faculty ratio is 34:1. The library holds 40,140 titles and 402 serial subscriptions. Special programs include academic remediation, an honors program, cooperative (work-study) education, study abroad, advanced placement credit, accelerated degree programs, ESL programs, double majors, independent study, distance learning, summer session for credit, part-time degree programs (daytime, evenings, weekends, summer), external degree programs, adult/continuing education programs, internships, and arrangement for off-campus study with Lansing Community College, Delta College. The most frequently chosen baccalaureate fields are business/marketing, computer/information sciences.

Student Body Statistics The student body totals 3,627, of whom 3,361 are undergraduates (489 freshmen). 47 percent are women and 53 percent are men. Students come from 33 states and territories and 23 other countries. 87 percent are from Michigan. 11 percent are international students. 4 percent of the 2002 graduating class went on to graduate and professional schools.

Expenses for 2003–04 *Application fee:* $25. *Comprehensive fee:* $20,265 includes full-time tuition ($13,485), mandatory fees ($510), and college room and board ($6270). *Part-time tuition:* $281 per credit.

Financial Aid Forms of aid include need-based and non-need-based scholarships, athletic grants, and part-time jobs. The average aided 2002–03 undergraduate received an aid package worth an estimated $10,556. The application deadline for financial aid is continuous.

Freshman Admission Northwood requires a high school transcript, SAT I or ACT scores, and TOEFL scores for international students. An essay, a minimum 2.0 high school GPA, 1 recommendation, and an interview are recommended. The application deadline for regular admission is rolling.

Transfer Admission The application deadline for admission is rolling.

Entrance Difficulty Northwood assesses its entrance difficulty level as moderately difficult. For the fall 2002 freshman class, 86 percent of the applicants were accepted.

For Further Information Contact Mr. Daniel F. Toland, Director of Admission, Northwood University, 4000 Whiting Drive, Midland, MI 48640. *Telephone:* 989-837-4367 or 800-457-7878 (toll-free). *Fax:* 989-837-4490. *E-mail:* admissions@northwood.edu. *Web site:* http://www.northwood.edu/.

OAKLAND UNIVERSITY

Rochester, Michigan

Oakland is a coed, public university, founded in 1957, offering degrees at the bachelor's, master's, and doctoral levels and post-master's and postbachelor's certificates. It has a 1,444-acre campus in Rochester near Detroit.

Academic Information The faculty has 806 members (56% full-time). The undergraduate student-faculty ratio is 21:1. The library holds 738,420 titles, 1,660 serial subscriptions, and 5,340 audiovisual materials. Special programs include academic remediation, services for learning-disabled students, an honors program, cooperative (work-study) education, study abroad, advanced placement credit, accelerated degree programs, ESL programs, double majors, independent study, distance learning, self-designed majors, summer session for credit, part-time degree programs (daytime, evenings, weekends, summer), internships, and arrangement for off-campus study with Macomb Community College, Beaumont Hospital-Troy. The most frequently chosen baccalaureate fields are business/marketing, education, health professions and related sciences.

Student Body Statistics The student body totals 16,059, of whom 12,634 are undergraduates (1,868 freshmen). 63 percent are women and 37 percent are men. Students come from 40 states and territories and 49 other countries. 99 percent are from Michigan. 0.8 percent are international students. 16 percent of the 2002 graduating class went on to graduate and professional schools.

Expenses for 2002–03 *Application fee:* $25. *State resident tuition:* $4545 full-time, $144.25 per credit hour part-time. *Nonresident tuition:* $11,340 full-time, $364 per credit hour part-time. *Mandatory fees:* $486 full-time, $243 per term part-time. Full-time tuition and fees vary according to program and student level. Part-time tuition and fees vary according to program and student level. *College room and board:* $5252. Room and board charges vary according to housing facility.

Financial Aid Forms of aid include need-based and non-need-based scholarships, athletic grants, and part-time jobs. The average aided 2001–02 undergraduate received an aid package worth $5866. The application deadline for financial aid is continuous.

Freshman Admission Oakland requires a high school transcript, a minimum 2.5 high school GPA, ACT scores, and TOEFL scores for international students. A minimum 3.0 high school GPA, recommendations, an interview, and audition are required for some. The application deadline for regular admission is rolling.

Transfer Admission The application deadline for admission is rolling.

Entrance Difficulty Oakland assesses its entrance difficulty level as moderately difficult. For the fall 2002 freshman class, 78 percent of the applicants were accepted.

For Further Information Contact Mr. Robert E. Johnson, Vice Provost for Enrollment Management, Oakland University, 101 North Foundation Hall, Rochester, MI 48309-4401. *Telephone:* 248-370-3360 or 800-OAK-UNIV (toll-free). *Fax:* 248-370-4462. *E-mail:* ouinfo@oakland.edu. *Web site:* http://www.oakland.edu/.

OLIVET COLLEGE

Olivet, Michigan

Olivet is a coed, private, comprehensive institution, founded in 1844, affiliated with the Congregational Christian Church, offering degrees at the bachelor's and master's levels. It has a 92-acre campus in Olivet.

Academic Information The faculty has 80 members (58% full-time). The undergraduate student-faculty ratio is 15:1. The library holds 90,000 titles and 415 serial subscriptions. Special programs include services for learning-disabled students, an honors program, cooperative (work-study) education, study abroad, advanced placement credit, accelerated degree programs, double majors, independent study, self-designed majors, summer session for credit, part-time degree programs (daytime, evenings, summer), and internships. The most frequently chosen baccalaureate fields are biological/life sciences, business/marketing, education.

Student Body Statistics The student body totals 941, of whom 912 are undergraduates (309 freshmen). 46 percent are women and 54 percent are men. Students come from 19 states and territories. 78 percent are from Michigan. 5 percent are international students.

Expenses for 2003–04 *Application fee:* $25. *Comprehensive fee:* $19,984 includes full-time tuition ($14,762), mandatory fees ($420), and college room and board ($4802). *College room only:* $2614. Room and board charges vary according to board plan and housing facility. *Part-time tuition:* $480 per credit. Part-time tuition varies according to course load.

Financial Aid Forms of aid include need-based and non-need-based scholarships and part-time jobs. The average aided 2001–02 undergraduate received an aid package worth $12,560. The application deadline for financial aid is continuous.

Freshman Admission Olivet requires a high school transcript and TOEFL scores for international students. A minimum 2.6 high school

Olivet College (continued)
GPA is recommended. An essay, recommendations, an interview, and SAT I or ACT scores are required for some. The application deadline for regular admission is rolling.
Transfer Admission The application deadline for admission is rolling.
Entrance Difficulty Olivet assesses its entrance difficulty level as minimally difficult. For the fall 2002 freshman class, 65 percent of the applicants were accepted.

For Further Information Contact Mr. Kevin Leonard, Director of Admissions, Olivet College, 320 South Main Street, Olivet, MI 49076. *Telephone:* 800-456-7189 Ext. 7161 or 800-456-7189 (toll-free). *Fax:* 269-749-6617. *E-mail:* bmcconnell@olivetcollege.edu. *Web site:* http://www.olivetcollege.edu/.

REFORMED BIBLE COLLEGE

Grand Rapids, Michigan

RBC is a coed, private, four-year college, founded in 1939, offering degrees at the associate and bachelor's levels and postbachelor's certificates in Christian ministries. It has a 27-acre campus in Grand Rapids.

Academic Information The faculty has 36 members (39% full-time), 28% with terminal degrees. The student-faculty ratio is 16:1. The library holds 55,760 titles, 234 serial subscriptions, and 3,855 audiovisual materials. Special programs include academic remediation, services for learning-disabled students, cooperative (work-study) education, study abroad, advanced placement credit, ESL programs, double majors, independent study, summer session for credit, part-time degree programs (daytime, evenings), adult/continuing education programs, internships, and arrangement for off-campus study with Grand Rapids Community College, Cornerstone University. The most frequently chosen baccalaureate field is philosophy, religion, and theology.
Student Body Statistics The student body is made up of 278 undergraduates (61 freshmen). 53 percent are women and 47 percent are men. Students come from 16 states and territories and 12 other countries. 92 percent are from Michigan. 9.3 percent are international students.
Expenses for 2002–03 *Application fee:* $25. *Comprehensive fee:* $14,436 includes full-time tuition ($9070), mandatory fees ($466), and college room and board ($4900). Room and board charges vary according to board plan, housing facility, and student level. *Part-time tuition:* $380 per credit hour. *Part-time mandatory fees:* $90 per term. Part-time tuition and fees vary according to course load.
Financial Aid Forms of aid include need-based and non-need-based scholarships and part-time jobs. The average aided 2002–03 undergraduate received an aid package worth an estimated $8519. The priority application deadline for financial aid is February 15.
Freshman Admission RBC requires an essay, a high school transcript, a minimum 2.5 high school GPA, 2 recommendations, an interview, SAT I or ACT scores, and TOEFL scores for international students. The application deadline for regular admission is rolling.
Transfer Admission The application deadline for admission is rolling.
Entrance Difficulty RBC assesses its entrance difficulty level as moderately difficult. For the fall 2002 freshman class, 70 percent of the applicants were accepted.

For Further Information Contact Ms. Jeanine Kopaska Broek, Assistant Director of Admissions, Reformed Bible College, 3333 East Beltline North East, Grand Rapids, MI 49525. *Telephone:* 616-222-3000 Ext. 634 or 800-511-3749 (toll-free). *Fax:* 616-222-3045. *E-mail:* admissions@reformed.edu. *Web site:* http://www.reformed.edu/.

ROCHESTER COLLEGE

Rochester Hills, Michigan

Rochester College is a coed, private, four-year college, founded in 1959, affiliated with the Church of Christ, offering degrees at the associate and bachelor's levels. It has an 83-acre campus in Rochester Hills near Detroit.

Academic Information The faculty has 104 members (36% full-time), 34% with terminal degrees. The student-faculty ratio is 13:1. The library holds 45,000 titles, 325 serial subscriptions, and 1,000 audiovisual materials. Special programs include academic remediation, study abroad, advanced placement credit, accelerated degree programs, double majors, independent study, distance learning, summer session for credit, part-time degree programs (daytime, evenings, weekends, summer), external degree programs, adult/continuing education programs, internships, and arrangement for off-campus study with Madonna University, Macomb Community College, Oakland Community College, Mott Community College. The most frequently chosen baccalaureate fields are business/marketing, education, psychology.
Student Body Statistics The student body is made up of 932 undergraduates (119 freshmen). 61 percent are women and 39 percent are men. Students come from 18 states and territories and 15 other countries. 87 percent are from Michigan. 3 percent are international students. 12 percent of the 2002 graduating class went on to graduate and professional schools.
Expenses for 2002–03 *Application fee:* $25. *Comprehensive fee:* $16,659 includes full-time tuition ($10,272), mandatory fees ($763), and college room and board ($5624). *Part-time tuition:* $321 per credit hour. *Part-time mandatory fees:* $142 per term. Part-time tuition and fees vary according to course load.
Financial Aid Forms of aid include need-based and non-need-based scholarships, athletic grants, and part-time jobs. The average aided 2002–03 undergraduate received an aid package worth an estimated $9838. The priority application deadline for financial aid is April 1.
Freshman Admission Rochester College requires a high school transcript, SAT I or ACT scores, and TOEFL scores for international students. An essay, a minimum 2.25 high school GPA, and 1 recommendation are recommended. An interview is required for some. The application deadline for regular admission is rolling.
Transfer Admission The application deadline for admission is rolling.
Entrance Difficulty Rochester College assesses its entrance difficulty level as minimally difficult; moderately difficult for early admission applicants. For the fall 2002 freshman class, 42 percent of the applicants were accepted.

For Further Information Contact Mr. Larry Norman, Vice President for Enrollment Management, Rochester College, 800 West Avon Road, Rochester Hills, MI 48307-2764. *Telephone:* 248-218-2032 or 800-521-6010 (toll-free). *Fax:* 248-218-2005. *E-mail:* admissions@rc.edu. *Web site:* http://www.rc.edu/.

SACRED HEART MAJOR SEMINARY

Detroit, Michigan

Sacred Heart Major Seminary is a coed, private, Roman Catholic, comprehensive institution, founded in 1919, offering degrees at the associate, bachelor's, master's, and first professional levels in philosophy. It has a 24-acre campus in Detroit.

Academic Information The faculty has 31 members (45% full-time), 77% with terminal degrees. The undergraduate student-faculty ratio is 9:1. The library holds 160,000 titles and 510 serial subscriptions. Special programs include academic remediation, services for learning-disabled students, advanced placement credit, independent study, part-time degree programs (daytime, evenings), and arrangement for off-campus study with Detroit Area Catholic Higher Education Consortium. The most frequently chosen baccalaureate fields are liberal arts/general studies, philosophy, religion, and theology.
Student Body Statistics The student body totals 387, of whom 260 are undergraduates. Students come from 5 states and territories. 72 percent are from Michigan. 2.4 percent are international students. 90 percent of the 2002 graduating class went on to graduate and professional schools.
Expenses for 2002–03 *Application fee:* $30. *One-time mandatory fee:* $100. *Comprehensive fee:* $12,343 includes full-time tuition ($7369), mandatory fees ($60), and college room and board ($4914). Full-time tuition and fees vary according to course load. *Part-time tuition:* $213 per credit hour. Part-time tuition varies according to course load.

Financial Aid Forms of aid include need-based and non-need-based scholarships and part-time jobs. The average aided 2002–03 undergraduate received an aid package worth an estimated $3000. The application deadline for financial aid is continuous.
Freshman Admission Sacred Heart Major Seminary requires an essay, a high school transcript, a minimum 2.0 high school GPA, 1 recommendation, an interview, and SAT I or ACT scores. The application deadline for regular admission is July 31.
Transfer Admission The application deadline for admission is July 31.
Entrance Difficulty Sacred Heart Major Seminary assesses its entrance difficulty level as moderately difficult. For the fall 2002 freshman class, 100 percent of the applicants were accepted.

For Further Information Contact Fr. Patrick Halfpenny, Vice Rector, Sacred Heart Major Seminary, 2701 Chicago Boulevard, Detroit, MI 48206. *Telephone:* 313-883-8552.

SAGINAW CHIPPEWA TRIBAL COLLEGE

Mount Pleasant, Michigan

For Information Write to Saginaw Chippewa Tribal College, Mount Pleasant, MI 48858.

SAGINAW VALLEY STATE UNIVERSITY

University Center, Michigan

SVSU is a coed, public, comprehensive institution, founded in 1963, offering degrees at the bachelor's and master's levels and post-master's certificates. It has a 782-acre campus in University Center.

Academic Information The faculty has 240 members (97% full-time), 78% with terminal degrees. The undergraduate student-faculty ratio is 29:1. The library holds 631,455 titles, 1,113 serial subscriptions, and 22,713 audiovisual materials. Special programs include academic remediation, services for learning-disabled students, an honors program, cooperative (work-study) education, study abroad, advanced placement credit, accelerated degree programs, ESL programs, double majors, independent study, distance learning, self-designed majors, summer session for credit, part-time degree programs (daytime, evenings, summer), adult/continuing education programs, and internships. The most frequently chosen baccalaureate fields are education, business/marketing, protective services/public administration.
Student Body Statistics The student body totals 9,189, of whom 7,506 are undergraduates (1,162 freshmen). 60 percent are women and 40 percent are men. Students come from 15 states and territories and 50 other countries. 38 percent are from Michigan. 3.3 percent are international students.
Expenses for 2002–03 *Application fee:* $25. *State resident tuition:* $4,382 full-time, $127.45 per credit hour part-time. *Nonresident tuition:* $9288 full-time, $213.40 per credit hour part-time. *Mandatory fees:* $558 full-time, $18.60 per credit hour part-time. Full-time tuition and fees vary according to course load, location, and program. Part-time tuition and fees vary according to course load, location, and program. *College room and board:* $5485. *College room only:* $1970. Room and board charges vary according to board plan and housing facility.
Financial Aid Forms of aid include need-based and non-need-based scholarships, athletic grants, and part-time jobs. The average aided 2002–03 undergraduate received an aid package worth an estimated $5382. The priority application deadline for financial aid is February 14.
Freshman Admission SVSU requires a high school transcript, SAT I or ACT scores, and TOEFL scores for international students. A minimum 2.5 high school GPA is recommended. The application deadline for regular admission is rolling.
Transfer Admission The application deadline for admission is rolling.
Entrance Difficulty SVSU assesses its entrance difficulty level as moderately difficult. For the fall 2002 freshman class, 88 percent of the applicants were accepted.

For Further Information Contact Mr. James P. Dwyer, Director of Admissions, Saginaw Valley State University, 7400 Bay Road, University Center, MI 48710-0001. *Telephone:* 989-964-4200 or 800-968-9500 (toll-free). *Fax:* 517-790-0180. *E-mail:* admissions@svsu.edu. *Web site:* http://www.svsu.edu/.

SAINT MARY'S COLLEGE OF MADONNA UNIVERSITY

Orchard Lake, Michigan

Saint Mary's is a coed, private, Roman Catholic, four-year college, founded in 1885, offering degrees at the bachelor's level. It has a 120-acre campus in Orchard Lake near Detroit.

Academic Information The faculty has 60 members (42% full-time), 50% with terminal degrees. The student-faculty ratio is 12:1. The library holds 79,103 titles, 335 serial subscriptions, and 1,400 audiovisual materials. Special programs include academic remediation, cooperative (work-study) education, study abroad, advanced placement credit, accelerated degree programs, ESL programs, double majors, independent study, part-time degree programs (daytime, evenings, weekends), internships, and arrangement for off-campus study with members of the Detroit Area Consortium of Catholic Colleges. The most frequently chosen baccalaureate fields are biological/life sciences, business/marketing, communications/communication technologies.
Student Body Statistics The student body totals 628, of whom 459 are undergraduates (40 freshmen). 44 percent are women and 56 percent are men. Students come from 9 states and territories and 12 other countries. 98 percent are from Michigan. 31 percent are international students.
Expenses for 2002–03 *Application fee:* $25. *Comprehensive fee:* $13,728 includes full-time tuition ($7800), mandatory fees ($288), and college room and board ($5640). Full-time tuition and fees vary according to course load. Room and board charges vary according to board plan and housing facility. *Part-time tuition:* $325 per credit hour. Part-time tuition varies according to course load.
Financial Aid Forms of aid include need-based and non-need-based scholarships and part-time jobs. The average aided 2002–03 undergraduate received an aid package worth an estimated $6770. The application deadline for financial aid is April 30 with a priority deadline of February 21.
Freshman Admission Saint Mary's requires an essay, a high school transcript, a minimum 2.5 high school GPA, minimum ACT score of 19 or SAT I score of 900, SAT I or ACT scores, and TOEFL scores for international students. 2 recommendations are recommended. An interview is required for some. The application deadline for regular admission is rolling.
Transfer Admission The application deadline for admission is rolling.
Entrance Difficulty Saint Mary's assesses its entrance difficulty level as moderately difficult. For the fall 2002 freshman class, 74 percent of the applicants were accepted.

For Further Information Contact Mr. Jim Bass, Director of Enrollment, Saint Mary's College of Madonna University, 3535 Indian Trail, Orchard Lake, MI 48324-1623. *Telephone:* 248-683-0523 or 877-252-3131 (toll-free in-state). *Fax:* 248-683-1756. *E-mail:* admissions@stmarys.avemaria.edu. *Web site:* http://www.stmarys.avemaria.edu/.

SIENA HEIGHTS UNIVERSITY

Adrian, Michigan

Siena is a coed, private, Roman Catholic, comprehensive institution, founded in 1919, offering degrees at the associate, bachelor's, and master's levels. It has a 140-acre campus in Adrian near Detroit.

Academic Information The faculty has 65 full-time members. The undergraduate student-faculty ratio is 14:1. The library holds 120,407 titles

Siena Heights University (continued)
and 451 serial subscriptions. Special programs include academic remediation, services for learning-disabled students, cooperative (work-study) education, study abroad, advanced placement credit, accelerated degree programs, double majors, independent study, self-designed majors, summer session for credit, part-time degree programs, external degree programs, adult/continuing education programs, internships, and arrangement for off-campus study with Adrian College. The most frequently chosen baccalaureate field is philosophy, religion, and theology.
Student Body Statistics The student body totals 2,024, of whom 1,810 are undergraduates. Students come from 8 states and territories. 9 percent of the 2002 graduating class went on to graduate and professional schools.
Expenses for 2002–03 *Application fee:* $25. *Comprehensive fee:* $18,760 includes full-time tuition ($13,330), mandatory fees ($300), and college room and board ($5130). Room and board charges vary according to board plan and housing facility. *Part-time tuition:* $350 per credit. *Part-time mandatory fees:* $50 per term. Part-time tuition and fees vary according to course load.
Financial Aid Forms of aid include need-based and non-need-based scholarships and part-time jobs. The average aided 2002–03 undergraduate received an aid package worth an estimated $12,200. The priority application deadline for financial aid is March 15.
Freshman Admission Siena requires a high school transcript, SAT I or ACT scores, and TOEFL scores for international students. A minimum 2.3 high school GPA and an interview are recommended. An essay, recommendations, and an interview are required for some. The application deadline for regular admission is rolling.
Transfer Admission The application deadline for admission is rolling.
Entrance Difficulty Siena assesses its entrance difficulty level as moderately difficult. For the fall 2002 freshman class, 72 percent of the applicants were accepted.

For Further Information Contact Mr. Kevin Kucera, Dean of Admissions and Enrollment Services, Siena Heights University, 1247 East Siena Heights Drive, Adrian, MI 49221-1796. *Telephone:* 517-264-7180 or 800-521-0009 (toll-free). *Fax:* 517-264-7745. *E-mail:* admissions@sienahts.edu. *Web site:* http://www.sienahts.edu/.

SPRING ARBOR UNIVERSITY

Spring Arbor, Michigan

Spring Arbor is a coed, private, Free Methodist, comprehensive institution, founded in 1873, offering degrees at the associate, bachelor's, and master's levels. It has a 70-acre campus in Spring Arbor.

Academic Information The faculty has 91 members (75% full-time), 52% with terminal degrees. The undergraduate student-faculty ratio is 16:1. The library holds 90,042 titles, 667 serial subscriptions, and 2,025 audiovisual materials. Special programs include academic remediation, services for learning-disabled students, an honors program, advanced placement credit, accelerated degree programs, ESL programs, double majors, independent study, self-designed majors, summer session for credit, part-time degree programs (daytime, evenings, weekends, summer), external degree programs, adult/continuing education programs, internships, and arrangement for off-campus study with Christian College Consortium. The most frequently chosen baccalaureate fields are business/marketing, health professions and related sciences, home economics/vocational home economics.
Student Body Statistics The student body totals 3,124, of whom 2,441 are undergraduates (304 freshmen). 70 percent are women and 30 percent are men. 87 percent are from Michigan. 1.2 percent are international students.
Expenses for 2002–03 *Application fee:* $30. *Comprehensive fee:* $19,096 includes full-time tuition ($13,800), mandatory fees ($216), and college room and board ($5080). *College room only:* $2310. Room and board charges vary according to board plan, housing facility, and location. *Part-time tuition:* $280 per credit. Part-time tuition varies according to course load.
Financial Aid Forms of aid include need-based and non-need-based scholarships and part-time jobs. The average aided 2002–03 undergraduate received an aid package worth an estimated $11,293. The priority application deadline for financial aid is February 15.
Freshman Admission Spring Arbor requires a high school transcript, SAT I or ACT scores, and TOEFL scores for international students. An essay, an interview, and guidance counselor's evaluation form are recommended. Recommendations are required for some. The application deadline for regular admission is rolling.
Transfer Admission The application deadline for admission is rolling.
Entrance Difficulty Spring Arbor assesses its entrance difficulty level as moderately difficult. For the fall 2002 freshman class, 87 percent of the applicants were accepted.

For Further Information Contact Mr. Jim Weidman, Director of Admissions, Spring Arbor University, 106 East Main Street, Spring Arbor, MI 49283-9799. *Telephone:* 517-750-1200 Ext. 1475 or 800-968-0011 (toll-free). *Fax:* 517-750-6620. *E-mail:* shellya@admin.arbor.edu. *Web site:* http://www.arbor.edu/.

UNIVERSITY OF DETROIT MERCY

Detroit, Michigan

For Information Write to University of Detroit Mercy, Detroit, MI 48219-0900.

UNIVERSITY OF MICHIGAN

Ann Arbor, Michigan

Michigan is a coed, public university, founded in 1817, offering degrees at the bachelor's, master's, doctoral, and first professional levels and post-master's certificates. It has a 2,861-acre campus in Ann Arbor near Detroit.

Academic Information The faculty has 2,799 members (78% full-time), 88% with terminal degrees. The undergraduate student-faculty ratio is 15:1. The library holds 7 million titles, 69,849 serial subscriptions, and 73,568 audiovisual materials. Special programs include services for learning-disabled students, an honors program, cooperative (work-study) education, study abroad, advanced placement credit, accelerated degree programs, ESL programs, double majors, independent study, distance learning, self-designed majors, summer session for credit, part-time degree programs, adult/continuing education programs, internships, and arrangement for off-campus study with Committee on Institutional Cooperation. The most frequently chosen baccalaureate fields are engineering/engineering technologies, psychology, social sciences and history.
Student Body Statistics The student body totals 38,972, of whom 24,472 are undergraduates (5,187 freshmen). 51 percent are women and 49 percent are men. Students come from 54 states and territories and 87 other countries. 69 percent are from Michigan. 4.4 percent are international students. 34 percent of the 2002 graduating class went on to graduate and professional schools.
Expenses for 2002–03 *Application fee:* $40. *State resident tuition:* $7090 full-time, $279 per credit part-time. *Nonresident tuition:* $23,314 full-time, $940 per credit part-time. *Mandatory fees:* $187 full-time. Full-time tuition and fees vary according to program and student level. Part-time tuition varies according to course load, program, and student level. *College room and board:* $6366. Room and board charges vary according to board plan and housing facility.
Financial Aid Forms of aid include need-based and non-need-based scholarships, athletic grants, and part-time jobs. The average aided 2001–02 undergraduate received an aid package worth $10,022. The priority application deadline for financial aid is February 15.
Freshman Admission Michigan requires an essay, a high school transcript, SAT I or ACT scores, and TOEFL scores for international students. Recommendations, an interview, SAT II: Subject Test scores, and SAT II: Writing Test scores are required for some. The application deadline for regular admission is February 1.

Transfer Admission The application deadline for admission is February 1.
Entrance Difficulty Michigan assesses its entrance difficulty level as very difficult. For the fall 2002 freshman class, 49 percent of the applicants were accepted.

For Further Information Contact Mr. Ted Spencer, Director of Undergraduate Admissions, University of Michigan, 1220 Student Activities Building, 515 East Jefferson, Ann Arbor, MI 48109-1316. *Telephone:* 734-764-7433. *Fax:* 734-936-0740. *E-mail:* ugadmiss@umich.edu. *Web site:* http://www.umich.edu/.

UNIVERSITY OF MICHIGAN–DEARBORN

Dearborn, Michigan

UM-D is a coed, public, comprehensive unit of University of Michigan System, founded in 1959, offering degrees at the bachelor's and master's levels and postbachelor's certificates. It has a 210-acre campus in Dearborn near Detroit.

Academic Information The faculty has 503 members (52% full-time), 64% with terminal degrees. The undergraduate student-faculty ratio is 17:1. The library holds 340,897 titles, 1,099 serial subscriptions, and 4,734 audiovisual materials. Special programs include academic remediation, services for learning-disabled students, an honors program, cooperative (work-study) education, study abroad, accelerated degree programs, double majors, independent study, self-designed majors, summer session for credit, part-time degree programs (daytime, evenings, weekends, summer), adult/continuing education programs, internships, and arrangement for off-campus study with University of Michigan. The most frequently chosen baccalaureate fields are business/marketing, education, engineering/engineering technologies.
Student Body Statistics The student body totals 8,725, of whom 6,556 are undergraduates (815 freshmen). 54 percent are women and 46 percent are men. Students come from 25 states and territories and 22 other countries. 97 percent are from Michigan. 2 percent are international students. 22.8 percent of the 2002 graduating class went on to graduate and professional schools.
Expenses for 2002–03 *Application fee:* $30. *State resident tuition:* $5136 full-time, $203.25 per credit hour part-time. *Nonresident tuition:* $12,697 full-time, $505.30 per credit hour part-time. *Mandatory fees:* $196 full-time, $97.80 per term part-time. Full-time tuition and fees vary according to course level, course load, program, and student level. Part-time tuition and fees vary according to course level, course load, program, and student level.
Financial Aid Forms of aid include need-based and non-need-based scholarships, athletic grants, and part-time jobs. The average aided 2001–02 undergraduate received an aid package worth $7252. The application deadline for financial aid is continuous.
Freshman Admission UM-D requires a high school transcript, a minimum 3.0 high school GPA, SAT I or ACT scores, and TOEFL scores for international students. ACT scores are recommended. An interview is required for some. The application deadline for regular admission is rolling.
Transfer Admission The application deadline for admission is rolling.
Entrance Difficulty UM-D assesses its entrance difficulty level as moderately difficult. For the fall 2002 freshman class, 67 percent of the applicants were accepted.

For Further Information Contact Mr. David Placey, Director of Admissions, University of Michigan–Dearborn, 4901 Evergreen Road, Dearborn, MI 48128-1491. *Telephone:* 313-593-5100. *Fax:* 313-436-9167. *E-mail:* admissions@umd.umich.edu. *Web site:* http://www.umd.umich.edu/.

UNIVERSITY OF MICHIGAN–FLINT

Flint, Michigan

UM-Flint is a coed, public, comprehensive unit of University of Michigan System, founded in 1956, offering degrees at the bachelor's, master's, and first professional levels and postbachelor's certificates. It has a 72-acre campus in Flint near Detroit.

Academic Information The faculty has 400 members (52% full-time), 47% with terminal degrees. The undergraduate student-faculty ratio is 16:1. The library holds 267,062 titles, 1,111 serial subscriptions, and 18,063 audiovisual materials. Special programs include academic remediation, services for learning-disabled students, an honors program, cooperative (work-study) education, study abroad, advanced placement credit, double majors, independent study, distance learning, self-designed majors, summer session for credit, part-time degree programs (daytime, evenings, weekends, summer), and internships. The most frequently chosen baccalaureate fields are business/marketing, education, health professions and related sciences.
Student Body Statistics The student body totals 6,434, of whom 5,877 are undergraduates (527 freshmen). 64 percent are women and 36 percent are men. Students come from 21 states and territories and 3 other countries. 99 percent are from Michigan. 0.4 percent are international students. 20 percent of the 2002 graduating class went on to graduate and professional schools.
Expenses for 2002–03 *Application fee:* $30. *State resident tuition:* $4494 full-time, $187.25 per credit part-time. *Nonresident tuition:* $8988 full-time, $374.50 per credit part-time. *Mandatory fees:* $258 full-time, $129 per term part-time. Full-time tuition and fees vary according to program and student level. Part-time tuition and fees vary according to program and student level.
Financial Aid Forms of aid include need-based and non-need-based scholarships and part-time jobs. The average aided 2002–03 undergraduate received an aid package worth an estimated $6562. The priority application deadline for financial aid is February 21.
Freshman Admission UM-Flint requires a high school transcript and TOEFL scores for international students. An essay and SAT I or ACT scores are recommended. The application deadline for regular admission is September 2.
Transfer Admission The application deadline for admission is August 19.
Entrance Difficulty UM-Flint assesses its entrance difficulty level as moderately difficult. For the fall 2002 freshman class, 79 percent of the applicants were accepted.

For Further Information Contact Dr. Virginia R. Allen, Vice Chancellor for Student Services and Enrollment, University of Michigan–Flint, 303 East Kearsley Street, Flint, MI 48502-1950. *Telephone:* 810-762-3434 or 800-742-5363 (toll-free in-state). *Fax:* 810-762-3272. *E-mail:* admissions@list.flint.umich.edu. *Web site:* http://www.flint.umich.edu/.

UNIVERSITY OF PHOENIX–METRO DETROIT CAMPUS

Troy, Michigan

University of Phoenix–Metro Detroit Campus is a coed, proprietary, comprehensive institution, offering degrees at the associate, bachelor's, master's, and doctoral levels and post-master's and postbachelor's certificates (courses conducted at 121 campuses and learning centers in 25 states).

Academic Information The faculty has 388 members (2% full-time), 20% with terminal degrees. The undergraduate student-faculty ratio is 11:1. The library holds 27 million titles and 11,648 serial subscriptions. Special programs include advanced placement credit, accelerated degree programs, independent study, distance learning, and external degree programs. The most frequently chosen baccalaureate fields are business/marketing, computer/information sciences, health professions and related sciences.

University of Phoenix–Metro Detroit Campus (continued)
Student Body Statistics The student body totals 3,318, of whom 2,511 are undergraduates (1 freshman). 66 percent are women and 34 percent are men. 2.2 percent are international students.
Expenses for 2002–03 *Application fee:* $85. *Tuition:* $9540 full-time, $318 per credit part-time.
Financial Aid The application deadline for financial aid is continuous.
Freshman Admission University of Phoenix–Metro Detroit Campus requires 1 recommendation, 2 years of work experience, 23 years of age, and TOEFL scores for international students. A high school transcript is required for some. The application deadline for regular admission is rolling.
Transfer Admission The application deadline for admission is rolling.
Entrance Difficulty University of Phoenix–Metro Detroit Campus has an open admission policy.

For Further Information Contact Ms. Beth Barilla, Director of Admissions, University of Phoenix–Metro Detroit Campus, 4615 East Elwood Street, Mail Stop 10-0030, Phoenix, AZ 85040-1958. *Telephone:* 480-557-1712 or 800-834-2438 (toll-free). *Fax:* 480-594-1758. *E-mail:* beth.barilla@apollogrp.edu. *Web site:* http://www.phoenix.edu/.

UNIVERSITY OF PHOENIX–WEST MICHIGAN CAMPUS

Grand Rapids, Michigan

University of Phoenix–West Michigan Campus is a coed, proprietary, comprehensive institution, founded in 2000, offering degrees at the associate, bachelor's, master's, and doctoral levels and post-master's and postbachelor's certificates (courses conducted at 121 campuses and learning centers in 25 states).

Academic Information The faculty has 98 members (5% full-time), 11% with terminal degrees. The undergraduate student-faculty ratio is 11:1. The library holds 27 million titles and 11,648 serial subscriptions. Special programs include advanced placement credit, accelerated degree programs, independent study, distance learning, external degree programs, and adult/continuing education programs. The most frequently chosen baccalaureate field is business/marketing.
Student Body Statistics The student body totals 786, of whom 572 are undergraduates (1 freshman). 51 percent are women and 49 percent are men. 0.5 percent are international students.
Expenses for 2002–03 *Application fee:* $85. *Tuition:* $9210 full-time, $307 per credit part-time.
Financial Aid The application deadline for financial aid is continuous.
Freshman Admission University of Phoenix–West Michigan Campus requires 1 recommendation, 2 years of work experience, 23 years of age, and TOEFL scores for international students. A high school transcript is required for some. The application deadline for regular admission is rolling.
Transfer Admission The application deadline for admission is rolling.
Entrance Difficulty University of Phoenix–West Michigan Campus has an open admission policy.

For Further Information Contact Ms. Beth Barilla, Director of Admissions, University of Phoenix–West Michigan Campus, 4615 East Elwood Street, Mail Stop 10-0030, Phoenix, AZ 85040-1958. *Telephone:* 480-557-1712 or 800-228-7240 (toll-free). *E-mail:* beth.barilla@apollogrp.edu. *Web site:* http://www.phoenix.edu/.

WALSH COLLEGE OF ACCOUNTANCY AND BUSINESS ADMINISTRATION

Troy, Michigan

Walsh College is a coed, private, upper-level institution, founded in 1922, offering degrees at the bachelor's and master's levels. It has a 29-acre campus in Troy near Detroit.

Academic Information The faculty has 130 members (12% full-time), 28% with terminal degrees. The undergraduate student-faculty ratio is 20:1. The library holds 26,180 titles, 437 serial subscriptions, and 121 audiovisual materials. Special programs include services for learning-disabled students, advanced placement credit, double majors, independent study, distance learning, summer session for credit, part-time degree programs, adult/continuing education programs, internships, and arrangement for off-campus study. The most frequently chosen baccalaureate field is business/marketing.
Student Body Statistics The student body totals 3,216, of whom 1,098 are undergraduates. 61 percent are women and 39 percent are men. Students come from 1 state or territory. 1.5 percent are international students.
Expenses for 2002–03 *Application fee:* $25. *Tuition:* $6870 full-time, $229 per credit part-time. *Mandatory fees:* $230 full-time, $110 per term part-time.
Financial Aid Forms of aid include need-based and non-need-based scholarships and part-time jobs. The average aided 2002–03 undergraduate received an aid package worth an estimated $10,937. The application deadline for financial aid is continuous.
Transfer Admission Walsh College requires a college transcript and a minimum 2.0 college GPA. Standardized test scores are required for some. The application deadline for admission is rolling.
Entrance Difficulty Walsh College has an open admission policy.

For Further Information Contact Ms. Karen Mahaffy, Director of Admissions, Walsh College of Accountancy and Business Administration, 3838 Livernois Road, PO Box 7006, Troy, MI 48007-7006. *Telephone:* 248-823-1610 or 800-925-7401 (toll-free in-state). *Fax:* 248-524-2520. *E-mail:* admissions@walshcollege.edu. *Web site:* http://www.walshcollege.edu/.

WAYNE STATE UNIVERSITY

Detroit, Michigan

Wayne State is a coed, public university, founded in 1868, offering degrees at the bachelor's, master's, doctoral, and first professional levels and post-master's and postbachelor's certificates. It has a 203-acre campus in Detroit.

Academic Information The faculty has 1,735 members (52% full-time). The undergraduate student-faculty ratio is 11:1. The library holds 2 million titles, 18,645 serial subscriptions, and 70,131 audiovisual materials. Special programs include academic remediation, services for learning-disabled students, an honors program, cooperative (work-study) education, study abroad, advanced placement credit, accelerated degree programs, ESL programs, double majors, independent study, distance learning, self-designed majors, summer session for credit, part-time degree programs (daytime, evenings, weekends, summer), adult/continuing education programs, internships, and arrangement for off-campus study with University of Michigan, University of Windsor. The most frequently chosen baccalaureate fields are business/marketing, education, health professions and related sciences.
Student Body Statistics The student body totals 31,167, of whom 18,408 are undergraduates. 60 percent are women and 40 percent are men. Students come from 39 states and territories and 100 other countries. 99 percent are from Michigan. 7.1 percent are international students.
Expenses for 2002–03 *Application fee:* $20. *State resident tuition:* $4242 full-time, $141 per semester hour part-time. *Nonresident tuition:* $9720 full-time, $324 per semester hour part-time. *Mandatory fees:* $481 full-time, $12.75 per semester hour part-time, $87.50 per term part-time. Full-time tuition and fees vary according to course level and student level. Part-time tuition and fees vary according to course level and student level. *College room and board:* $6100. Room and board charges vary according to housing facility.
Financial Aid Forms of aid include need-based and non-need-based scholarships, athletic grants, and part-time jobs. The average aided 2001–02 undergraduate received an aid package worth $6488. The priority application deadline for financial aid is March 1.
Freshman Admission Wayne State requires a high school transcript, a minimum 2.0 high school GPA, SAT I or ACT scores, and TOEFL scores

for international students. Recommendations, an interview, and a portfolio are required for some. The application deadline for regular admission is August 1.
Transfer Admission The application deadline for admission is August 1.
Entrance Difficulty Wayne State assesses its entrance difficulty level as moderately difficult. For the fall 2002 freshman class, 69 percent of the applicants were accepted.

For Further Information Contact Ms. Susan Swieg, Director of University Admissions, Wayne State University, 3E HNJ, Detroit, MI 48202. *Telephone:* 313-577-3581. *Fax:* 313-577-7536. *E-mail:* admissions@wayne.edu. *Web site:* http://www.wayne.edu/.

WESTERN MICHIGAN UNIVERSITY

Kalamazoo, Michigan

WMU is a coed, public university, founded in 1903, offering degrees at the bachelor's, master's, and doctoral levels and post-master's certificates. It has a 504-acre campus in Kalamazoo.

Academic Information The faculty has 1,189 members (83% full-time). The undergraduate student-faculty ratio is 16:1. The library holds 4 million titles, 6,707 serial subscriptions, and 32,535 audiovisual materials. Special programs include academic remediation, services for learning-disabled students, an honors program, cooperative (work-study) education, study abroad, advanced placement credit, accelerated degree programs, Freshman Honors College, ESL programs, double majors, independent study, distance learning, self-designed majors, summer session for credit, part-time degree programs (daytime, evenings, weekends, summer), adult/continuing education programs, internships, and arrangement for off-campus study with Kalamazoo College, Kalamazoo Valley Community College, Davenport College of Business. The most frequently chosen baccalaureate fields are business/marketing, education, engineering/engineering technologies.
Student Body Statistics The student body totals 29,732, of whom 23,643 are undergraduates (4,474 freshmen). 51 percent are women and 49 percent are men. Students come from 52 states and territories and 102 other countries. 93 percent are from Michigan. 3.8 percent are international students.
Expenses for 2002–03 *Application fee:* $25. *State resident tuition:* $4322 full-time, $144.08 per credit hour part-time. *Nonresident tuition:* $11,007 full-time, $366.90 per credit hour part-time. *Mandatory fees:* $602 full-time, $132 per term part-time. Full-time tuition and fees vary according to course load and student level. Part-time tuition and fees vary according to course load and student level. *College room and board:* $6128. Room and board charges vary according to board plan.
Financial Aid Forms of aid include need-based and non-need-based scholarships, athletic grants, and part-time jobs. The average aided 2002–03 undergraduate received an aid package worth an estimated $7006. The application deadline for financial aid is continuous.
Freshman Admission WMU requires a high school transcript, SAT I or ACT scores, and TOEFL scores for international students. An interview is required for some. The application deadline for regular admission is rolling.
Transfer Admission The application deadline for admission is August 1.
Entrance Difficulty WMU assesses its entrance difficulty level as moderately difficult. For the fall 2002 freshman class, 80 percent of the applicants were accepted.

For Further Information Contact Mr. John Fraire, Dean, Office of Admissions and Orientation, Western Michigan University, 1903 West Michigan Avenue, Kalamazoo, MI 49008. *Telephone:* 269-387-2000 or 800-400-4968 (toll-free in-state). *Fax:* 269-387-2096. *E-mail:* ask-wmu@wmich.edu. *Web site:* http://www.wmich.edu/.

See page 352 for a narrative description.

WILLIAM TYNDALE COLLEGE

Farmington Hills, Michigan

Tyndale is a coed, private, four-year college, founded in 1945, offering degrees at the associate and bachelor's levels. It has a 28-acre campus in Farmington Hills near Detroit.

Expenses for 2002–03 *Application fee:* $50. *Comprehensive fee:* $12,050 includes full-time tuition ($8550) and college room and board ($3500). Room and board charges vary according to housing facility.

For Further Information Contact Ms. Ann Corwell, Acting Director of Admissions, William Tyndale College, 37500 West Twelve Mile Road, Farmington Hills, MI 48331. *Telephone:* 248-553-7200 Ext. 204 or 800-483-0707 (toll-free). *Fax:* 248-553-5963. *E-mail:* admissions@williamtyndale.edu. *Web site:* http://www.williamtyndale.edu.

YESHIVA GEDDOLAH OF GREATER DETROIT RABBINICAL COLLEGE

Oak Park, Michigan

For Information Write to Yeshiva Geddolah of Greater Detroit Rabbinical College, Oak Park, MI 48237-1544.

Minnesota

ACADEMY COLLEGE

Minneapolis, Minnesota

Academy College is a coed, proprietary, primarily two-year college, offering degrees at the associate and bachelor's levels.

Academic Information The faculty has 34 members (12% full-time). Special programs include academic remediation, services for learning-disabled students, an honors program, cooperative (work-study) education, accelerated degree programs, ESL programs, double majors, summer session for credit, part-time degree programs (daytime, evenings, weekends, summer), adult/continuing education programs, and internships.
Student Body Statistics The student body is made up of 400 undergraduates.
Expenses for 2002–03 *Tuition:* $13,618 full-time. *Mandatory fees:* $200 full-time. Full-time tuition and fees vary according to program. *Part-time tuition:* varies with program.
Financial Aid Forms of aid include need-based scholarships and part-time jobs. The application deadline for financial aid is continuous.
Freshman Admission Academy College requires a high school transcript and an interview.
Entrance Difficulty Academy College has an open admission policy.

For Further Information Contact Mr. Dave Quade, Director of Education, Academy College, 3050 Metro Drive, Minneapolis, MN 55425. *Telephone:* 952-851-0066 or 800-292-9149 (toll-free). *Fax:* 952-851-0094. *E-mail:* info@academycollege.edu. *Web site:* http://www.academycollege.edu/.

ARGOSY UNIVERSITY-TWIN CITIES

Eagan, Minnesota

For Information Write to Argosy University-Twin Cities, Eagan, MN 55121.

THE ART INSTITUTES INTERNATIONAL MINNESOTA

Minneapolis, Minnesota

The Art Institutes International Minnesota is a coed, proprietary, primarily two-year college of The Art Institute, founded in 1964, offering degrees at the associate and bachelor's levels.

Academic Information The faculty has 57 members (44% full-time). The student-faculty ratio is 20:1. The library holds 1,450 titles and 25 serial subscriptions. Special programs include academic remediation, services for learning-disabled students, cooperative (work-study) education, advanced placement credit, summer session for credit, part-time degree programs (daytime, evenings), and internships. The most frequently chosen baccalaureate field is visual/performing arts.
Student Body Statistics The student body is made up of 989 undergraduates. Students come from 27 states and territories. 0.3 percent are international students. 2.8 percent of the 2002 graduating class went on to four-year colleges.
Expenses for 2003–04 *Application fee:* $50. *Tuition:* $17,658 full-time, $327 per credit part-time. Full-time tuition varies according to course load, degree level, and program. Part-time tuition varies according to course load, degree level, and program. *College room only:* $4995.
Financial Aid Forms of aid include need-based scholarships and part-time jobs. The application deadline for financial aid is continuous.
Freshman Admission The Art Institutes International Minnesota requires an essay, a high school transcript, an interview, TOEFL scores for international students, and Thurston Mental Alertness Test. ACT scores are recommended. The application deadline for regular admission is rolling.
Transfer Admission The application deadline for admission is rolling.
Entrance Difficulty The Art Institutes International Minnesota assesses its entrance difficulty level as minimally difficult. For the fall 2002 freshman class, 53 percent of the applicants were accepted.

For Further Information Contact Mr. Russ Gill, Director of Admissions, The Art Institutes International Minnesota, 15 South 9th Street, Minneapolis, MN 55402. *Telephone:* 612-332-3361 Ext. 120 or 800-777-3643 (toll-free). *Fax:* 612-332-3934. *E-mail:* kozela@aii.edu. *Web site:* http://www.aim.artinstitutes.edu/.

AUGSBURG COLLEGE

Minneapolis, Minnesota

Augsburg is a coed, private, Lutheran, comprehensive institution, founded in 1869, offering degrees at the bachelor's and master's levels and postbachelor's certificates. It has a 23-acre campus in Minneapolis.

Academic Information The faculty has 294 members (50% full-time), 64% with terminal degrees. The undergraduate student-faculty ratio is 14:1. The library holds 146,166 titles, 754 serial subscriptions, and 2,908 audiovisual materials. Special programs include academic remediation, services for learning-disabled students, an honors program, cooperative (work-study) education, study abroad, advanced placement credit, Freshman Honors College, ESL programs, double majors, independent study, self-designed majors, summer session for credit, part-time degree programs (daytime, weekends, summer), adult/continuing education programs, internships, and arrangement for off-campus study with Associated Colleges of the Twin Cities. The most frequently chosen baccalaureate fields are business/marketing, education, social sciences and history.
Student Body Statistics The student body totals 2,994, of whom 2,763 are undergraduates (352 freshmen). 58 percent are women and 42 percent are men. Students come from 42 states and territories and 35 other countries. 90 percent are from Minnesota. 1.5 percent are international students. 15 percent of the 2002 graduating class went on to graduate and professional schools.
Expenses for 2002–03 *Application fee:* $25. *Comprehensive fee:* $23,883 includes full-time tuition ($17,825), mandatory fees ($368), and college room and board ($5690). *College room only:* $2900. Room and board charges vary according to board plan and housing facility. *Part-time tuition:* $2100 per course. *Part-time mandatory fees:* $66.25 per course. Part-time tuition and fees vary according to course load.
Financial Aid Forms of aid include need-based and non-need-based scholarships and part-time jobs. The average aided 2001–02 undergraduate received an aid package worth $12,808. The application deadline for financial aid is April 15.
Freshman Admission Augsburg requires an essay, a high school transcript, a minimum 2.5 high school GPA, an interview, SAT I or ACT scores, and TOEFL scores for international students. 2 recommendations are required for some. The application deadline for regular admission is August 15.
Transfer Admission The application deadline for admission is August 10.
Entrance Difficulty Augsburg assesses its entrance difficulty level as moderately difficult. For the fall 2002 freshman class, 80 percent of the applicants were accepted.

For Further Information Contact Ms. Sally Daniels, Director of Undergraduate Day Admissions, Augsburg College, 2211 Riverside Avenue, Minneapolis, MN 55454-1351. *Telephone:* 612-330-1001 or 800-788-5678 (toll-free). *Fax:* 612-330-1590. *E-mail:* admissions@augsburg.edu. *Web site:* http://www.augsburg.edu/.

BEMIDJI STATE UNIVERSITY

Bemidji, Minnesota

Bemidji State University is a coed, public, comprehensive unit of Minnesota State Colleges and Universities System, founded in 1919, offering degrees at the associate, bachelor's, and master's levels. It has an 89-acre campus in Bemidji.

Academic Information The faculty has 328 members (65% full-time), 54% with terminal degrees. The undergraduate student-faculty ratio is 19:1. The library holds 554,087 titles, 991 serial subscriptions, and 5,521 audiovisual materials. Special programs include academic remediation, services for learning-disabled students, an honors program, cooperative (work-study) education, study abroad, advanced placement credit, ESL programs, double majors, independent study, distance learning, summer session for credit, part-time degree programs (daytime, evenings, summer), external degree programs, adult/continuing education programs, internships, and arrangement for off-campus study with other colleges in the Minnesota State College and University System. The most frequently chosen baccalaureate fields are business/marketing, education, protective services/public administration.
Student Body Statistics The student body totals 4,941, of whom 4,614 are undergraduates (603 freshmen). 54 percent are women and 46 percent are men. Students come from 28 states and territories and 47 other countries. 95 percent are from Minnesota. 5.8 percent are international students.
Expenses for 2002–03 *Application fee:* $20. *State resident tuition:* $3782 full-time, $138 per credit part-time. *Nonresident tuition:* $8022 full-time, $268 per credit part-time. *Mandatory fees:* $693 full-time, $74.83 per credit part-time. Full-time tuition and fees vary according to reciprocity agreements. Part-time tuition and fees vary according to course load and reciprocity agreements. *College room and board:* $4597. *College room only:* $2448. Room and board charges vary according to board plan and housing facility.
Financial Aid Forms of aid include need-based and non-need-based scholarships, athletic grants, and part-time jobs. The average aided 2002–03 undergraduate received an aid package worth an estimated $7189. The priority application deadline for financial aid is May 15.
Freshman Admission Bemidji State University requires a high school transcript, ACT scores, and TOEFL scores for international students. An essay, recommendations, and an interview are required for some. The application deadline for regular admission is rolling.
Transfer Admission The application deadline for admission is rolling.

Entrance Difficulty Bemidji State University assesses its entrance difficulty level as moderately difficult. For the fall 2002 freshman class, 70 percent of the applicants were accepted.

For Further Information Contact Mr. Kevin Drexel, Director of Admissions, Bemidji State University, Deputy-102, Bemidji, MN 56601. *Telephone:* 218-755-2040, 800-475-2001 (toll-free in-state), or 800-652-9747 (toll-free out-of-state). *Fax:* 218-755-2074. *E-mail:* admissions@bemidjistate.edu. *Web site:* http://www.bemidjistate.edu/.

BETHANY LUTHERAN COLLEGE

Mankato, Minnesota

Bethany is a coed, private, Lutheran, four-year college, founded in 1927, offering degrees at the associate and bachelor's levels. It has a 50-acre campus in Mankato near Minneapolis–St. Paul.

Academic Information The faculty has 64 members (52% full-time), 22% with terminal degrees. The student-faculty ratio is 8:1. The library holds 63,436 titles, 237 serial subscriptions, and 4,002 audiovisual materials. Special programs include academic remediation, services for learning-disabled students, an honors program, advanced placement credit, and ESL programs. The most frequently chosen baccalaureate fields are communications/communication technologies, liberal arts/general studies.
Student Body Statistics The student body is made up of 470 undergraduates (218 freshmen). 57 percent are women and 43 percent are men. Students come from 20 states and territories and 13 other countries. 70 percent are from Minnesota. 4.3 percent are international students. 2 percent of the 2002 graduating class went on to graduate and professional schools.
Expenses for 2003–04 *Application fee:* $20. *Comprehensive fee:* $18,708 includes full-time tuition ($13,760), mandatory fees ($260), and college room and board ($4688). *College room only:* $1718. Room and board charges vary according to board plan. *Part-time tuition:* $540 per credit. *Part-time mandatory fees:* $130 per term.
Financial Aid Forms of aid include need-based scholarships and part-time jobs. The application deadline for financial aid is July 15 with a priority deadline of May 1.
Freshman Admission Bethany requires an essay, a high school transcript, a minimum 2.4 high school GPA, SAT I or ACT scores, and TOEFL scores for international students. A minimum 3.2 high school GPA and an interview are recommended. An interview is required for some. The application deadline for regular admission is July 15.
Transfer Admission The application deadline for admission is rolling.
Entrance Difficulty Bethany assesses its entrance difficulty level as moderately difficult; minimally difficult for transfers. For the fall 2002 freshman class, 90 percent of the applicants were accepted.

For Further Information Contact Mr. Donald Westphal, Dean of Admissions, Bethany Lutheran College, 700 Luther Drive, Mankato, MN 56001. *Telephone:* 507-344-7320 or 800-944-3066 (toll-free). *Fax:* 507-344-7376. *E-mail:* admiss@blc.edu. *Web site:* http://www.blc.edu/.

BETHEL COLLEGE

St. Paul, Minnesota

Bethel is a coed, private, comprehensive institution, founded in 1871, affiliated with the Baptist General Conference, offering degrees at the associate, bachelor's, and master's levels. It has a 231-acre campus in St. Paul.

Academic Information The faculty has 303 members (51% full-time), 48% with terminal degrees. The undergraduate student-faculty ratio is 9:1. The library holds 173,000 titles, 14,678 serial subscriptions, and 12,204 audiovisual materials. Special programs include services for learning-disabled students, an honors program, study abroad, advanced placement credit, accelerated degree programs, Freshman Honors College, ESL programs, double majors, independent study, self-designed majors, summer session for credit, part-time degree programs (daytime, evenings, summer), external degree programs, adult/continuing education programs, internships, and arrangement for off-campus study with members of the Christian College Consortium, Au Sable Institute, Coalition for Christian Colleges and Universities. The most frequently chosen baccalaureate fields are business/marketing, education, health professions and related sciences.
Student Body Statistics The student body totals 3,091, of whom 2,772 are undergraduates (579 freshmen). 61 percent are women and 39 percent are men. Students come from 41 states and territories. 74 percent are from Minnesota. 0.1 percent are international students.
Expenses for 2003–04 *Application fee:* $25. *Comprehensive fee:* $25,180 includes full-time tuition ($18,700), mandatory fees ($100), and college room and board ($6380). *College room only:* $3790. Room and board charges vary according to board plan. *Part-time tuition:* $710 per credit. Part-time tuition varies according to course load.
Financial Aid Forms of aid include need-based and non-need-based scholarships and part-time jobs. The average aided 2002–03 undergraduate received an aid package worth an estimated $14,097. The priority application deadline for financial aid is April 15.
Freshman Admission Bethel requires an essay, a high school transcript, 2 recommendations, TOEFL scores for international students, and SAT I, ACT, or PSAT. An interview is recommended. An interview is required for some. The application deadline for regular admission is March 1 and for early action it is December 1.
Transfer Admission The application deadline for admission is December 1.
Entrance Difficulty Bethel assesses its entrance difficulty level as moderately difficult. For the fall 2002 freshman class, 89 percent of the applicants were accepted.

SPECIAL MESSAGE TO STUDENTS

Social Life The social atmosphere at Bethel is exciting, with many student-run campus activities. Bethel has excellent music performance groups, varsity and intramural sports, student government, theater productions, and a wide variety of student clubs and spiritual growth groups. Spiritual life is a priority at Bethel. Community chapel services, residence hall Bible studies, and discipleship programs offer opportunities for Christian growth. There are also many opportunities for students to get involved in ministry through campus outreach events, Habitat for Humanity, community service programs, inner-city projects, and missions trips.

Academic Highlights With sixty-four majors within seventy-six areas of study, Bethel ranks in the top Midwestern Universities category of the *U.S. News & World Report* "America's Best Colleges." Bethel's general education curriculum has become a model for many other liberal arts colleges nationwide. General education courses give students a broad view of the world and their role as Christians in it. The courses are grouped around the following themes: Bible and theology, Western culture, world citizenship, self-understanding, math, science, technology, health and wholeness, and final integration. Bethel strongly encourages and provides students with the opportunity to participate in a number of off-campus study programs, such as the Latin American Studies Program in Costa Rica, the Los Angeles Film Studies Program, American Studies Program in Washington, D.C., AuSable Institute for Environmental Studies in Michigan, England Term, Jerusalem University College, Australia Term, and Daystar University in Kenya.

Interviews and Campus Visits On-campus interviews are strongly encouraged but not required. An interview gives the prospective student the opportunity to learn more about the college, ask questions, and better determine if the college is a good fit. A campus visit at Bethel gives students opportunities to stay in a residence hall, attend classes and chapel, meet with professors and coaches, enjoy free meals with Bethel students, and attend on-campus events. Bethel's beautiful wooded campus is located on the shores of Lake Valentine in Arden Hills, Minnesota—just 15 minutes from downtown St. Paul and Minneapolis. The Bethel campus offers modern academic, housing, and recreation facilities. The Community Life Center houses the 1,700-seat Benson Great Hall, hailed as one of the best music performance halls in the upper Midwest. For more information about Bethel College or to arrange a campus visit, students can call the Office of Admissions at 651-638-6242 or 800-255-8706 (toll-free), Monday through Friday, 8:30 a.m. to 4:30 p.m. The

Bethel College (continued)

fax number is 651-635-1490. The Office of Admissions is located on campus in RC 341, Robertson Center building. The nearest commercial airport is Minneapolis-St. Paul International.

For Further Information Write to Office of Admissions, Bethel College, 3900 Bethel Drive, St. Paul, MN 55112. *E-mail:* bcoll-admit@bethel.edu. *Web site:* http://www.bethel.edu. *Fax:* 651–635–1490.

BROWN COLLEGE

Mendota Heights, Minnesota

Brown College is a coed, proprietary, primarily two-year college of Career Education Corporation, founded in 1946, offering degrees at the associate and bachelor's levels. It has a 20-acre campus in Mendota Heights near Minneapolis–St. Paul.

Academic Information The faculty has 200 members (38% full-time). The student-faculty ratio is 24:1. The library holds 768 titles and 33 serial subscriptions. Special programs include academic remediation, summer session for credit, part-time degree programs (daytime, evenings), and internships.
Student Body Statistics The student body is made up of 2,250 undergraduates. Students come from 15 states and territories.
Expenses for 2002–03 *Application fee:* $50. *Tuition:* $16,800 full-time. *Mandatory fees:* $50 full-time.
Financial Aid Forms of aid include need-based scholarships and part-time jobs. The application deadline for financial aid is continuous.
Freshman Admission Brown College requires a high school transcript, an interview, TOEFL scores for international students, and CPAt, SAT I, or ACT. Recommendations are recommended. A minimum 2.0 high school GPA is required for some. The application deadline for regular admission is rolling.
Transfer Admission The application deadline for admission is rolling.
Entrance Difficulty Brown College assesses its entrance difficulty level as moderately difficult.

For Further Information Contact Mr. Mike Price, Director of Admissions, Brown College, 1440 Northland Drive, Mendota Heights, MN 55120. *Telephone:* 651-905-3400 or 800-6BROWN6 (toll-free). *Fax:* 651-905-3510. *Web site:* http://www.browncollege.edu/.

CAPELLA UNIVERSITY

Minneapolis, Minnesota

Capella University is a coed, proprietary, upper-level institution, founded in 1993, offering degrees at the bachelor's, master's, doctoral, and first professional levels and first professional certificates (offers only distance learning degree programs).

Academic Information The faculty has 350 members (13% full-time), 89% with terminal degrees. The undergraduate student-faculty ratio is 12:1. Special programs include services for learning-disabled students, double majors, independent study, distance learning, self-designed majors, summer session for credit, part-time degree programs, external degree programs, adult/continuing education programs, internships, and arrangement for off-campus study. The most frequently chosen baccalaureate field is computer/information sciences.
Student Body Statistics The student body totals 6,500, of whom 600 are undergraduates. 15 percent are from Minnesota.
Expenses for 2002–03 *One-time mandatory fee:* $250. *Tuition:* $14,250 full-time, $1425 per course part-time. Full-time tuition varies according to degree level and program. Part-time tuition varies according to degree level and program.
Financial Aid Forms of aid include need-based scholarships. The average aided 2002–03 undergraduate received an aid package worth an estimated $10,500. The application deadline for financial aid is continuous.
Transfer Admission Capella University requires a college transcript and a minimum 2.0 college GPA. The application deadline for admission is rolling.
Entrance Difficulty Capella University assesses its entrance difficulty level as moderately difficult.

For Further Information Contact Ms. Liz Hinz, Associate Director, Enrollment Services, Capella University, 222 South 9th Street, 20th Floor, Minneapolis, MN 55402. *Telephone:* 612-659-5871 or 888-CAPELLA (toll-free). *Fax:* 612-339-8022. *E-mail:* info@capella.edu. *Web site:* http://www.capellauniversity.edu/.

CARLETON COLLEGE

Northfield, Minnesota

Carleton is a coed, private, four-year college, founded in 1866, offering degrees at the bachelor's level. It has a 955-acre campus in Northfield near Minneapolis–St. Paul.

Academic Information The faculty has 231 members (84% full-time), 89% with terminal degrees. The student-faculty ratio is 9:1. The library holds 662,871 titles, 10,964 serial subscriptions, and 778 audiovisual materials. Special programs include services for learning-disabled students, study abroad, advanced placement credit, accelerated degree programs, double majors, independent study, self-designed majors, internships, and arrangement for off-campus study with St. Olaf College, Associated Colleges of the Midwest, Higher Education Consortium for Urban Affairs. The most frequently chosen baccalaureate fields are physical sciences, biological/life sciences, social sciences and history.
Student Body Statistics The student body is made up of 1,932 undergraduates (502 freshmen). 52 percent are women and 48 percent are men. Students come from 50 states and territories and 37 other countries. 23 percent are from Minnesota. 3.4 percent are international students. 16 percent of the 2002 graduating class went on to graduate and professional schools.
Expenses for 2002–03 *Application fee:* $30. *Comprehensive fee:* $32,445 includes full-time tuition ($26,745), mandatory fees ($165), and college room and board ($5535).
Financial Aid Forms of aid include need-based and non-need-based scholarships and part-time jobs. The average aided 2001–02 undergraduate received an aid package worth $18,832. The priority application deadline for financial aid is February 15.
Freshman Admission Carleton requires an essay, a high school transcript, 2 recommendations, SAT I or ACT scores, and TOEFL scores for international students. An interview, SAT II: Subject Test scores, and SAT II: Writing Test scores are recommended. The application deadline for regular admission is January 15; for early decision plan 1 it is November 15; and for early decision plan 2 it is January 15.
Transfer Admission The application deadline for admission is March 31.
Entrance Difficulty Carleton assesses its entrance difficulty level as very difficult; most difficult for transfers. For the fall 2002 freshman class, 35 percent of the applicants were accepted.

For Further Information Contact Mr. Paul Thiboutot, Dean of Admissions, Carleton College, 100 South College Street, Northfield, MN 55057. *Telephone:* 507-646-4190 or 800-995-2275 (toll-free). *Fax:* 507-646-4526. *E-mail:* admissions@acs.carleton.edu.

COLLEGE OF SAINT BENEDICT

Saint Joseph, Minnesota

St. Ben's is a coed, primarily women's, private, Roman Catholic, four-year college, founded in 1887, coordinate with Saint John's University (MN), offering degrees at the bachelor's level (coordinate with Saint John's University for men). It has a 315-acre campus in Saint Joseph near Minneapolis–St. Paul.

Academic Information The faculty has 159 members (87% full-time), 77% with terminal degrees. The student-faculty ratio is 13:1. The library holds 805,376 titles, 5,735 serial subscriptions, and 22,452 audiovisual materials. Special programs include services for learning-disabled students, an honors program, study abroad, advanced placement credit, accelerated degree programs, ESL programs, double majors, independent study,

self-designed majors, internships, and arrangement for off-campus study with Tri-College Exchange Program (MN), Saint John's University (MN). The most frequently chosen baccalaureate fields are business/marketing, English, health professions and related sciences.
Student Body Statistics The student body is made up of 2,072 undergraduates (516 freshmen). 100 percent are women and 100 percent are men. Students come from 31 states and territories and 20 other countries. 86 percent are from Minnesota. 3.6 percent are international students. 11 percent of the 2002 graduating class went on to graduate and professional schools.
Expenses for 2002–03 *Application fee:* $30. *Comprehensive fee:* $25,015 includes full-time tuition ($18,916), mandatory fees ($310), and college room and board ($5789). *College room only:* $3053. Room and board charges vary according to board plan and housing facility. *Part-time tuition:* $788 per credit. *Part-time mandatory fees:* $155 per term.
Financial Aid Forms of aid include need-based and non-need-based scholarships and part-time jobs. The average aided 2002–03 undergraduate received an aid package worth an estimated $16,190. The priority application deadline for financial aid is March 15.
Freshman Admission St. Ben's requires an essay, a high school transcript, 1 recommendation, SAT I or ACT scores, and TOEFL scores for international students. A minimum 3.0 high school GPA and an interview are recommended. The application deadline for regular admission is rolling and for early action it is December 1.
Transfer Admission The application deadline for admission is rolling.
Entrance Difficulty St. Ben's assesses its entrance difficulty level as moderately difficult. For the fall 2002 freshman class, 85 percent of the applicants were accepted.

For Further Information Contact Karen Backes, Associate Dean of Admissions, College of Saint Benedict, 37 South College Avenue, St. Joseph, MN 56374. *Telephone:* 320-363-5308 or 800-544-1489 (toll-free). *Fax:* 320-363-5010. *E-mail:* admissions@csbsju.edu. *Web site:* http://www.csbsju.edu/.

COLLEGE OF ST. CATHERINE

St. Paul, Minnesota

CSC is a women's, private, Roman Catholic, comprehensive institution, founded in 1905, offering degrees at the associate, bachelor's, master's, and doctoral levels and postbachelor's certificates. It has a 110-acre campus in St. Paul near Minneapolis.

Academic Information The faculty has 367 members (46% full-time), 54% with terminal degrees. The undergraduate student-faculty ratio is 12:1. The library holds 263,495 titles, 1,141 serial subscriptions, and 13,627 audiovisual materials. Special programs include academic remediation, services for learning-disabled students, an honors program, study abroad, advanced placement credit, ESL programs, double majors, independent study, distance learning, self-designed majors, summer session for credit, part-time degree programs (daytime, weekends, summer), external degree programs, adult/continuing education programs, internships, and arrangement for off-campus study with Associated Colleges of the Twin Cities, Sisters of St. Joseph College Consortium, Higher Education Consortium for Urban Affairs. The most frequently chosen baccalaureate fields are education, business/marketing, health professions and related sciences.
Student Body Statistics The student body totals 4,704, of whom 3,569 are undergraduates (405 freshmen). Students come from 31 states and territories and 30 other countries. 90 percent are from Minnesota. 2 percent are international students. 19 percent of the 2002 graduating class went on to graduate and professional schools.
Expenses for 2002–03 *Application fee:* $20. *Comprehensive fee:* $23,532 includes full-time tuition ($18,240), mandatory fees ($122), and college room and board ($5170). *College room only:* $2920. Full-time tuition and fees vary according to class time and degree level. Room and board charges vary according to board plan and housing facility. *Part-time tuition:* $570 per credit. *Part-time mandatory fees:* $61 per term. Part-time tuition and fees vary according to class time and degree level.
Financial Aid Forms of aid include need-based and non-need-based scholarships and part-time jobs. The average aided 2002–03 undergraduate received an aid package worth an estimated $18,319. The priority application deadline for financial aid is April 1.
Freshman Admission CSC requires a high school transcript, 1 recommendation, SAT I or ACT scores, and TOEFL scores for international students. An interview is recommended. An essay and an interview are required for some. The application deadline for regular admission is August 15.
Transfer Admission The application deadline for admission is rolling.
Entrance Difficulty CSC assesses its entrance difficulty level as moderately difficult. For the fall 2002 freshman class, 78 percent of the applicants were accepted.

For Further Information Contact Ms. Cory Piper-Hauswirth, Associate Director of Admission and Financial Aid, College of St. Catherine, 2004 Randolph Avenue, St. Paul, MN 55105-1789. *Telephone:* 651-690-6505 or 800-945-4599 (toll-free in-state). *Fax:* 651-690-8824. *E-mail:* admissions@stkate.edu. *Web site:* http://www.stkate.edu/.

COLLEGE OF ST. CATHERINE–MINNEAPOLIS

Minneapolis, Minnesota

College of St. Catherine–Minneapolis is a coed, primarily women's, private, Roman Catholic, two-year college, founded in 1964, offering degrees at the associate level. It has a 1-acre campus in Minneapolis.

Academic Information The faculty has 525 members (38% full-time), 50% with terminal degrees. The student-faculty ratio is 9:1. The library holds 267,558 titles, 1,141 serial subscriptions, and 13,627 audiovisual materials. Special programs include academic remediation, services for learning-disabled students, ESL programs, independent study, summer session for credit, part-time degree programs (daytime, evenings, weekends, summer), adult/continuing education programs, and internships. The most frequently chosen baccalaureate fields are education, business/marketing, health professions and related sciences.
Student Body Statistics The student body is made up of 3,569 undergraduates (405 freshmen). 98 percent are women and 2 percent are men. Students come from 18 states and territories. 96 percent are from Minnesota.
Expenses for 2003–04 *Application fee:* $20. *Comprehensive fee:* $19,090 includes full-time tuition ($13,600), mandatory fees ($30), and college room and board ($5460). *College room only:* $3060. Room and board charges vary according to board plan and housing facility. *Part-time tuition:* $425 per credit. *Part-time mandatory fees:* $15 per term.
Financial Aid Forms of aid include need-based scholarships and part-time jobs. The priority application deadline for financial aid is June 1.
Freshman Admission College of St. Catherine–Minneapolis requires an essay, a high school transcript, and 2 recommendations. A minimum 2.0 high school GPA, an interview, and ACT scores are recommended. A minimum 3.0 high school GPA is required for some. The application deadline for regular admission is rolling.
Transfer Admission The application deadline for admission is rolling.
Entrance Difficulty College of St. Catherine–Minneapolis assesses its entrance difficulty level as minimally difficult; moderately difficult for transfers. For the fall 2002 freshman class, 67 percent of the applicants were accepted.

For Further Information Contact Mr. Cal Mosley, Assistant to the President for Admission, College of St. Catherine–Minneapolis, 601 25th Avenue South, Minneapolis, MN 55454-1494. *Telephone:* 651-690-8600 or 800-945-4599 Ext. 7800 (toll-free). *Fax:* 651-690-8119. *E-mail:* career-info@stkate.edu. *Web site:* http://www.stkate.edu/.

THE COLLEGE OF ST. SCHOLASTICA

Duluth, Minnesota

St. Scholastica is a coed, private, comprehensive institution, founded in 1912, affiliated with the Roman Catholic Church, offering degrees at

The College of St. Scholastica (continued)
the bachelor's and master's levels and post-master's and postbachelor's certificates. It has a 160-acre campus in Duluth.

Academic Information The faculty has 194 members (60% full-time), 64% with terminal degrees. The undergraduate student-faculty ratio is 13:1. The library holds 125,091 titles, 1,135 serial subscriptions, and 15,262 audiovisual materials. Special programs include academic remediation, services for learning-disabled students, an honors program, study abroad, advanced placement credit, accelerated degree programs, double majors, independent study, distance learning, self-designed majors, summer session for credit, part-time degree programs (evenings), external degree programs, adult/continuing education programs, internships, and arrangement for off-campus study with University of Wisconsin-Superior, University of Minnesota, Duluth. The most frequently chosen baccalaureate fields are business/marketing, biological/life sciences, health professions and related sciences.
Student Body Statistics The student body totals 2,512, of whom 1,981 are undergraduates (402 freshmen). 70 percent are women and 30 percent are men. Students come from 23 states and territories and 11 other countries. 89 percent are from Minnesota. 1.1 percent are international students. 31 percent of the 2002 graduating class went on to graduate and professional schools.
Expenses for 2002–03 *Application fee:* $25. *Comprehensive fee:* $23,622 includes full-time tuition ($18,106), mandatory fees ($110), and college room and board ($5406). Full-time tuition and fees vary according to class time. Room and board charges vary according to board plan. *Part-time tuition:* $567 per credit. *Part-time mandatory fees:* $55 per term. Part-time tuition and fees vary according to class time and course load.
Financial Aid Forms of aid include need-based and non-need-based scholarships and part-time jobs. The average aided 2002–03 undergraduate received an aid package worth an estimated $15,908. The priority application deadline for financial aid is March 15.
Freshman Admission St. Scholastica requires a high school transcript, SAT I or ACT scores, and TOEFL scores for international students. An essay, recommendations, an interview, and PSAT are recommended. A minimum 2.0 high school GPA and an interview are required for some. The application deadline for regular admission is rolling.
Transfer Admission The application deadline for admission is rolling.
Entrance Difficulty St. Scholastica assesses its entrance difficulty level as moderately difficult. For the fall 2002 freshman class, 88 percent of the applicants were accepted.

For Further Information Contact Mr. Brian Dalton, Vice President for Enrollment Management, The College of St. Scholastica, 1200 Kenwood Avenue, Duluth, MN 55811-4199. *Telephone:* 218-723-6053 or 800-249-6412 (toll-free). *Fax:* 218-723-5991. *E-mail:* admissions@css.edu. *Web site:* http://www.css.edu/.

COLLEGE OF VISUAL ARTS

St. Paul, Minnesota

CVA is a coed, private, four-year college, founded in 1924, offering degrees at the bachelor's level in art and design. It has a 2-acre campus in St. Paul near Minneapolis.

Academic Information The faculty has 59 members (17% full-time), 92% with terminal degrees. The student-faculty ratio is 8:1. The library holds 7,100 titles, 55 serial subscriptions, and 30,370 audiovisual materials. Special programs include academic remediation, an honors program, study abroad, advanced placement credit, double majors, independent study, summer session for credit, part-time degree programs (daytime, evenings, summer), and internships. The most frequently chosen baccalaureate field is visual/performing arts.
Student Body Statistics The student body is made up of 228 undergraduates (27 freshmen). 53 percent are women and 47 percent are men. Students come from 13 states and territories. 90 percent are from Minnesota. 0.4 percent are international students.
Expenses for 2002–03 *Application fee:* $40. *One-time mandatory fee:* $50. *Tuition:* $13,908 full-time, $696 per credit part-time. *Mandatory fees:* $510 full-time, $17 per credit part-time. Full-time tuition and fees vary according to course load. Part-time tuition and fees vary according to course load.
Financial Aid Forms of aid include need-based and non-need-based scholarships and part-time jobs. The average aided 2001–02 undergraduate received an aid package worth $8625. The application deadline for financial aid is continuous.
Freshman Admission CVA requires an essay, a high school transcript, a minimum 2.7 high school GPA, an interview, a portfolio, SAT I or ACT scores, and TOEFL scores for international students. A minimum 3.0 high school GPA and recommendations are recommended. The application deadline for regular admission is rolling.
Transfer Admission The application deadline for admission is rolling.
Entrance Difficulty CVA assesses its entrance difficulty level as moderately difficult. For the fall 2002 freshman class, 44 percent of the applicants were accepted.

For Further Information Contact Ms. Elizabeth Catron, Associate Director of Admissions, College of Visual Arts, 344 Summit Avenue, St. Paul, MN 55102-2124. *Telephone:* 651-224-3416 or 800-224-1536 (toll-free). *Fax:* 651-224-8854. *E-mail:* info@cva.edu. *Web site:* http://www.cva.edu/.

CONCORDIA COLLEGE

Moorhead, Minnesota

Concordia is a coed, private, four-year college, founded in 1891, affiliated with the Evangelical Lutheran Church in America, offering degrees at the bachelor's level. It has a 120-acre campus in Moorhead.

Academic Information The faculty has 254 members (78% full-time). The student-faculty ratio is 15:1. The library holds 299,808 titles, 1,433 serial subscriptions, and 20,778 audiovisual materials. Special programs include services for learning-disabled students, an honors program, cooperative (work-study) education, study abroad, advanced placement credit, ESL programs, double majors, independent study, summer session for credit, part-time degree programs (daytime, summer), adult/continuing education programs, internships, and arrangement for off-campus study with Tri-College University. The most frequently chosen baccalaureate fields are business/marketing, education, foreign language/literature.
Student Body Statistics The student body is made up of 2,775 undergraduates (748 freshmen). 63 percent are women and 37 percent are men. Students come from 37 states and territories and 41 other countries. 66 percent are from Minnesota. 6.1 percent are international students. 23 percent of the 2002 graduating class went on to graduate and professional schools.
Expenses for 2003–04 *Application fee:* $20. *Comprehensive fee:* $20,077 includes full-time tuition ($15,635), mandatory fees ($132), and college room and board ($4310). *College room only:* $1960. Room and board charges vary according to board plan and housing facility. *Part-time tuition:* $2435 per course. Part-time tuition varies according to course load.
Financial Aid Forms of aid include need-based and non-need-based scholarships and part-time jobs. The average aided 2001–02 undergraduate received an aid package worth $12,375. The application deadline for financial aid is continuous.
Freshman Admission Concordia requires a high school transcript, 2 recommendations, SAT I or ACT scores, and TOEFL scores for international students. ACT scores are recommended. The application deadline for regular admission is rolling.
Transfer Admission The application deadline for admission is rolling.
Entrance Difficulty Concordia assesses its entrance difficulty level as moderately difficult. For the fall 2002 freshman class, 87 percent of the applicants were accepted.

For Further Information Contact Mr. Scott E. Ellingson, Director of Admissions, Concordia College, 901 8th Street South, Moorhead, MN 56562. *Telephone:* 218-299-3004 or 800-699-9897 (toll-free). *Fax:* 218-299-3947. *E-mail:* admissions@cord.edu. *Web site:* http://www.concordiacollege.edu/.

CONCORDIA UNIVERSITY

St. Paul, Minnesota

Concordia-St. Paul is a coed, private, comprehensive unit of Concordia University System, founded in 1893, affiliated with the Lutheran Church–Missouri Synod, offering degrees at the associate, bachelor's, and master's levels. It has a 37-acre campus in St. Paul.

Academic Information The faculty has 391 members (20% full-time). The undergraduate student-faculty ratio is 10:1. The library holds 131,242 titles, 1,400 serial subscriptions, and 6,843 audiovisual materials. Special programs include academic remediation, services for learning-disabled students, cooperative (work-study) education, study abroad, advanced placement credit, accelerated degree programs, ESL programs, double majors, independent study, distance learning, self-designed majors, summer session for credit, part-time degree programs (daytime, evenings, summer), external degree programs, adult/continuing education programs, internships, and arrangement for off-campus study with University of Minnesota–Twin Cities Campus. The most frequently chosen baccalaureate fields are business/marketing, education, philosophy, religion, and theology.
Student Body Statistics The student body totals 1,921, of whom 1,677 are undergraduates (175 freshmen). 61 percent are women and 39 percent are men. Students come from 40 states and territories and 4 other countries. 75 percent are from Minnesota. 0.4 percent are international students.
Expenses for 2002–03 *Application fee:* $30. *Comprehensive fee:* $22,856 includes full-time tuition ($17,326) and college room and board ($5530). Full-time tuition varies according to program. *Part-time tuition:* $362 per credit. Part-time tuition varies according to course load.
Financial Aid Forms of aid include need-based and non-need-based scholarships, athletic grants, and part-time jobs. The average aided 2002–03 undergraduate received an aid package worth an estimated $11,051. The application deadline for financial aid is continuous.
Freshman Admission Concordia-St. Paul requires a high school transcript, 2 recommendations, and ACT scores. A minimum 2.0 high school GPA and an interview are recommended. An essay is required for some. The application deadline for regular admission is August 15.
Transfer Admission The application deadline for admission is August 15.
Entrance Difficulty Concordia-St. Paul assesses its entrance difficulty level as minimally difficult. For the fall 2002 freshman class, 53 percent of the applicants were accepted.

For Further Information Contact Ms. Rhonda Behm-Severeid, Director of Undergraduate Admissions, Concordia University, 275 Syndicate North, St. Paul, MN 55104-5494. *Telephone:* 651-641-8230 or 800-333-4705 (toll-free). *Fax:* 651-659-0207. *E-mail:* admiss@csp.edu. *Web site:* http://www.csp.edu/.

CROSSROADS COLLEGE

Rochester, Minnesota

Crossroads College is a coed, private, four-year college, founded in 1913, affiliated with the Christian Churches and Churches of Christ, offering degrees at the associate and bachelor's levels. It has a 40-acre campus in Rochester near Minneapolis–St. Paul.

Academic Information The faculty has 20 members (40% full-time), 30% with terminal degrees. The student-faculty ratio is 10:1. The library holds 31,059 titles, 300 serial subscriptions, and 1,532 audiovisual materials. Special programs include academic remediation, advanced placement credit, double majors, independent study, self-designed majors, and internships. The most frequently chosen baccalaureate fields are liberal arts/general studies, philosophy, religion, and theology.
Student Body Statistics The student body is made up of 110 undergraduates (27 freshmen). 48 percent are women and 52 percent are men. Students come from 6 states and territories and 4 other countries. 72 percent are from Minnesota. 6.2 percent are international students. 8 percent of the 2002 graduating class went on to graduate and professional schools.
Expenses for 2002–03 *Application fee:* $30. *Tuition:* $6900 full-time, $230 per semester hour part-time. *Mandatory fees:* $110 full-time. Full-time tuition and fees vary according to course load. Part-time tuition varies according to course load. *College room only:* $1750. Room charges vary according to housing facility.
Financial Aid Forms of aid include need-based and non-need-based scholarships and part-time jobs. The average aided 2001–02 undergraduate received an aid package worth $7326. The priority application deadline for financial aid is April 1.
Freshman Admission Crossroads College requires an essay, a high school transcript, 3 recommendations, SAT I or ACT scores, and TOEFL scores for international students. An interview is required for some. The application deadline for regular admission is August 15.
Transfer Admission The application deadline for admission is August 15.
Entrance Difficulty Crossroads College assesses its entrance difficulty level as noncompetitive. For the fall 2002 freshman class, 100 percent of the applicants were accepted.

For Further Information Contact Mr. Michael Golembiesky, Director of Admissions, Crossroads College, 920 Mayowood Road, SW, Rochester, MN 55902-2382. *Telephone:* 507-288-4563 Ext. 313 or 800-456-7651 (toll-free). *Fax:* 507-288-9046. *E-mail:* admissions@crossroadscollege.edu. *Web site:* http://www.crossroadscollege.edu/.

CROWN COLLEGE

St. Bonifacius, Minnesota

Crown College is a coed, private, comprehensive institution, founded in 1916, affiliated with The Christian and Missionary Alliance, offering degrees at the associate, bachelor's, and master's levels. It has a 193-acre campus in St. Bonifacius near Minneapolis–St. Paul.

Academic Information The faculty has 53 members (62% full-time), 42% with terminal degrees. The undergraduate student-faculty ratio is 14:1. The library holds 78,000 titles, 1,780 serial subscriptions, and 2,400 audiovisual materials. Special programs include academic remediation, services for learning-disabled students, an honors program, study abroad, advanced placement credit, ESL programs, double majors, independent study, distance learning, summer session for credit, part-time degree programs (daytime, evenings, weekends, summer), adult/continuing education programs, and internships. The most frequently chosen baccalaureate fields are education, business/marketing, philosophy, religion, and theology.
Student Body Statistics The student body totals 912, of whom 898 are undergraduates (137 freshmen). 57 percent are women and 43 percent are men. Students come from 33 states and territories. 64 percent are from Minnesota. 11 percent of the 2002 graduating class went on to graduate and professional schools.
Expenses for 2002–03 *Application fee:* $35. *Comprehensive fee:* $16,962 includes full-time tuition ($11,236), mandatory fees ($746), and college room and board ($4980). *College room only:* $2324. Room and board charges vary according to board plan. *Part-time tuition:* $469 per credit. *Part-time mandatory fees:* $28 per credit hour. Part-time tuition and fees vary according to course load.
Financial Aid Forms of aid include need-based and non-need-based scholarships and part-time jobs. The average aided 2002–03 undergraduate received an aid package worth an estimated $10,286. The priority application deadline for financial aid is April 1.
Freshman Admission Crown College requires an essay, a high school transcript, a minimum 2.0 high school GPA, 2 recommendations, SAT I or ACT scores, and TOEFL scores for international students. An interview is required for some. The application deadline for regular admission is rolling.
Transfer Admission The application deadline for admission is rolling.
Entrance Difficulty Crown College assesses its entrance difficulty level as minimally difficult. For the fall 2002 freshman class, 75 percent of the applicants were accepted.

For Further Information Contact Ms. Kimberely LaQuay, Application Coordinator/Office Systems Manager, Crown College, 6425 County Road 30, St. Bonifacius, MN 55375-9001. *Telephone:* 952-446-4144 or 800-68-CROWN (toll-free). *Fax:* 952-446-4149. *E-mail:* info@crown.edu. *Web site:* http://www.crown.edu/.

DUNWOODY COLLEGE OF TECHNOLOGY

Minneapolis, Minnesota

Dunwoody is a coed, primarily men's, private, two-year college, founded in 1914, offering degrees at the associate level. It has a 12-acre campus in Minneapolis.

For Further Information Contact Ms. Yun-bok Christenson, Records Coordinator, Dunwoody College of Technology, 818 Dunwoody Boulevard, Minneapolis, MN 55403. *Telephone:* 612-374-5800 Ext. 2014 or 800-292-4625 (toll-free). *Fax:* 612-374-4128. *E-mail:* aylreb@dunwoody.tec.mn.us. *Web site:* http://www.dunwoody.edu/.

GLOBE COLLEGE

Oakdale, Minnesota

Globe College is a private, primarily two-year college, founded in 1885, offering degrees at the associate and bachelor's levels.

Academic Information The faculty has 49 members (51% full-time), 16% with terminal degrees. The student-faculty ratio is 15:1. The library holds 1,700 titles, 85 serial subscriptions, and 100 audiovisual materials. Special programs include academic remediation, advanced placement credit, independent study, distance learning, part-time degree programs (daytime, evenings, weekends, summer), external degree programs, adult/continuing education programs, and internships.
Student Body Statistics The student body is made up of 879 undergraduates (323 freshmen). 92 percent are from Minnesota. 0.1 percent are international students.
Expenses for 2003–04 *Tuition:* $13,050 full-time, $290 per credit part-time. *Mandatory fees:* $150 full-time, $10 per credit part-time. Full-time tuition and fees vary according to course load. Part-time tuition and fees vary according to course load.
Financial Aid Forms of aid include need-based scholarships. The application deadline for financial aid is continuous.
Freshman Admission Globe College requires an interview. SAT I or ACT scores are recommended.
Entrance Difficulty Globe College has an open admission policy.

For Further Information Contact Mr. Nathan Herrmann, Director of Admissions, Globe College, 7166 10th Street North, Oakdale, MN 55128. *Telephone:* 651-730-5100 Ext. 315. *Fax:* 651-730-5151. *E-mail:* admissions@globecollege.edu. *Web site:* http://www.globecollege.com/.

GUSTAVUS ADOLPHUS COLLEGE

St. Peter, Minnesota

Gustavus is a coed, private, four-year college, founded in 1862, affiliated with the Evangelical Lutheran Church in America, offering degrees at the bachelor's level. It has a 330-acre campus in St. Peter near Minneapolis–St. Paul.

Academic Information The faculty has 238 members (75% full-time), 69% with terminal degrees. The student-faculty ratio is 13:1. The library holds 287,761 titles, 1,001 serial subscriptions, and 16,063 audiovisual materials. Special programs include services for learning-disabled students, an honors program, cooperative (work-study) education, study abroad, advanced placement credit, accelerated degree programs, double majors, independent study, self-designed majors, summer session for credit, internships, and arrangement for off-campus study with Minnesota State University, Mankato. The most frequently chosen baccalaureate fields are business/marketing, biological/life sciences, social sciences and history.
Student Body Statistics The student body is made up of 2,536 undergraduates (662 freshmen). 58 percent are women and 42 percent are men. Students come from 42 states and territories and 17 other countries. 78 percent are from Minnesota. 1.4 percent are international students. 36 percent of the 2002 graduating class went on to graduate and professional schools.
Expenses for 2002–03 *Application fee:* $25. *Comprehensive fee:* $25,620 includes full-time tuition ($19,945), mandatory fees ($505), and college room and board ($5170). *College room only:* $2770. Full-time tuition and fees vary according to student level. Room and board charges vary according to board plan, housing facility, and student level. *Part-time tuition:* $2160 per course. *Part-time mandatory fees:* $100.
Financial Aid Forms of aid include need-based and non-need-based scholarships and part-time jobs. The average aided 2001–02 undergraduate received an aid package worth $14,501. The priority application deadline for financial aid is February 15.
Freshman Admission Gustavus requires an essay, a high school transcript, 2 recommendations, SAT I or ACT scores, and TOEFL scores for international students. An interview is recommended. The application deadline for regular admission is April 1; for early decision it is November 15; and for early action it is December 31.
Transfer Admission The application deadline for admission is April 1.
Entrance Difficulty Gustavus assesses its entrance difficulty level as very difficult. For the fall 2002 freshman class, 77 percent of the applicants were accepted.

For Further Information Contact Mr. Mark H. Anderson, Dean of Admission, Gustavus Adolphus College, 800 West College Avenue, St. Peter, MN 56082-1498. *Telephone:* 507-933-7676 or 800-GUSTAVU(S) (toll-free). *Fax:* 507-933-7474. *E-mail:* admission@gac.edu. *Web site:* http://www.gustavus.edu/.

HAMLINE UNIVERSITY

St. Paul, Minnesota

Hamline is a coed, private, comprehensive institution, founded in 1854, affiliated with the United Methodist Church, offering degrees at the bachelor's, master's, doctoral, and first professional levels and post-master's, first professional, and postbachelor's certificates. It has a 50-acre campus in St. Paul.

Academic Information The faculty has 341 members (51% full-time), 75% with terminal degrees. The undergraduate student-faculty ratio is 13:1. The library holds 556,450 titles, 3,858 serial subscriptions, and 2,642 audiovisual materials. Special programs include academic remediation, services for learning-disabled students, an honors program, cooperative (work-study) education, study abroad, advanced placement credit, ESL programs, double majors, independent study, self-designed majors, summer session for credit, part-time degree programs, adult/continuing education programs, internships, and arrangement for off-campus study with members of the Associated Colleges of the Twin Cities, American University, Southern College Student Exchange Program, Higher Education Consortium for Urban Affairs, Drew University. The most frequently chosen baccalaureate fields are psychology, business/marketing, social sciences and history.
Student Body Statistics The student body totals 4,479, of whom 1,918 are undergraduates (417 freshmen). 64 percent are women and 36 percent are men. Students come from 35 states and territories and 32 other countries. 3.4 percent are international students. 21 percent of the 2002 graduating class went on to graduate and professional schools.
Expenses for 2002–03 *One-time mandatory fee:* $150. *Comprehensive fee:* $25,184 includes full-time tuition ($18,970), mandatory fees ($243), and college room and board ($5971). *College room only:* $3075. Full-time tuition and fees vary according to student level. Room and board charges vary according to board plan and housing facility. *Part-time tuition:* $593 per credit. *Part-time mandatory fees:* $175 per term. Part-time tuition and fees vary according to course load and student level.
Financial Aid Forms of aid include need-based and non-need-based scholarships and part-time jobs. The average aided 2002–03 undergraduate received an aid package worth an estimated $16,865. The priority application deadline for financial aid is May 1.
Freshman Admission Hamline requires an essay, a high school transcript, 2 recommendations, SAT I or ACT scores, and TOEFL scores for international students. An interview is recommended. The application deadline for regular admission is rolling and for early action it is December 1.
Transfer Admission The application deadline for admission is rolling.

Entrance Difficulty Hamline assesses its entrance difficulty level as moderately difficult. For the fall 2002 freshman class, 79 percent of the applicants were accepted.

For Further Information Contact Mr. Steven Bjork, Director of Undergraduate Admission, Hamline University, 1536 Hewitt Avenue C1930, St. Paul, MN 55104-1284. *Telephone:* 651-523-2207 or 800-753-9753 (toll-free). *Fax:* 651-523-2458. *E-mail:* cla-admis@gw.hamline.edu. *Web site:* http://www.hamline.edu/.

HERZING COLLEGE, MINNEAPOLIS DRAFTING SCHOOL CAMPUS

Minneapolis, Minnesota

Herzing College, Minneapolis Drafting School Campus is a coed, proprietary, primarily two-year college of Herzing College, offering degrees at the associate and bachelor's levels.

Academic Information The faculty has 34 members (53% full-time), 15% with terminal degrees. The student-faculty ratio is 11:1. Special programs include part-time degree programs (daytime, evenings) and adult/continuing education programs.

Student Body Statistics The student body is made up of 332 undergraduates (87 freshmen). 72 percent are women and 28 percent are men. Students come from 5 states and territories. 99 percent are from Minnesota.

Expenses for 2003–04 *Application fee:* $0. *Tuition:* $8560 full-time, $287 per credit part-time. *Mandatory fees:* $25 full-time. Full-time tuition and fees vary according to course load. Part-time tuition varies according to course load.

Freshman Admission Herzing College, Minneapolis Drafting School Campus requires a high school transcript, an interview, and Wonderlic aptitude test.

Entrance Difficulty Herzing College, Minneapolis Drafting School Campus has an open admission policy.

For Further Information Contact Mr. James Decker, Director of Admissions, Herzing College, Minneapolis Drafting School Campus, 5700 West Broadway, Minneapolis, MN 55428. *Telephone:* 763-231-3152 or 800-878-DRAW (toll-free). *Fax:* 763-535-9205. *E-mail:* info@mpls.herzing.edu. *Web site:* http://www.herzing.edu.

LEECH LAKE TRIBAL COLLEGE

Cass Lake, Minnesota

For Information Write to Leech Lake Tribal College, Cass Lake, MN 56633-0180.

LOWTHIAN COLLEGE

See The Art Institutes International Minnesota

MACALESTER COLLEGE

St. Paul, Minnesota

Mac is a coed, private, Presbyterian, four-year college, founded in 1874, offering degrees at the bachelor's level. It has a 53-acre campus in St. Paul.

Academic Information The faculty has 221 members (68% full-time), 83% with terminal degrees. The student-faculty ratio is 10:1. The library holds 407,321 titles, 2,119 serial subscriptions, and 9,288 audiovisual materials. Special programs include an honors program, study abroad, double majors, independent study, self-designed majors, part-time degree programs, internships, and arrangement for off-campus study with College of St. Catherine, University of St. Thomas, Augsburg College, Hamline University, Minneapolis College of Art and Design. The most frequently chosen baccalaureate fields are biological/life sciences, psychology, social sciences and history.

Student Body Statistics The student body is made up of 1,840 undergraduates (441 freshmen). 58 percent are women and 42 percent are men. Students come from 50 states and territories and 88 other countries. 27 percent are from Minnesota. 14.7 percent are international students.

Expenses for 2002–03 *Application fee:* $40. *Comprehensive fee:* $30,288 includes full-time tuition ($23,604), mandatory fees ($168), and college room and board ($6516). *College room only:* $3383. *Part-time tuition:* $740 per semester hour. *Part-time mandatory fees:* $84 per term.

Financial Aid Forms of aid include need-based and non-need-based scholarships and part-time jobs. The average aided 2002–03 undergraduate received an aid package worth an estimated $20,539. The priority application deadline for financial aid is February 7.

Freshman Admission Mac requires an essay, a high school transcript, 3 recommendations, SAT I or ACT scores, and TOEFL scores for international students. An interview is recommended. The application deadline for regular admission is January 15; for early decision plan 1 it is November 15; and for early decision plan 2 it is January 15.

Transfer Admission The application deadline for admission is April 1.

Entrance Difficulty Mac assesses its entrance difficulty level as very difficult. For the fall 2002 freshman class, 44 percent of the applicants were accepted.

For Further Information Contact Mr. Lorne T. Robinson, Dean of Admissions and Financial Aid, Macalester College, 1600 Grand Avenue, St. Paul, MN 55105-1899. *Telephone:* 651-696-6357 or 800-231-7974 (toll-free). *Fax:* 651-696-6724. *E-mail:* admissions@macalester.edu. *Web site:* http://www.macalester.edu/.

MANKATO STATE UNIVERSITY

See Minnesota State University, Mankato

MARTIN LUTHER COLLEGE

New Ulm, Minnesota

MLC is a coed, private, four-year college, founded in 1995, affiliated with the Wisconsin Evangelical Lutheran Synod, offering degrees at the bachelor's level. It has a 50-acre campus in New Ulm.

Academic Information The faculty has 97 members (88% full-time), 40% with terminal degrees. The student-faculty ratio is 13:1. The library holds 115,309 titles, 519 serial subscriptions, and 5,786 audiovisual materials. Special programs include academic remediation, advanced placement credit, ESL programs, double majors, independent study, summer session for credit, and internships. The most frequently chosen baccalaureate fields are education, philosophy, religion, and theology.

Student Body Statistics The student body is made up of 1,063 undergraduates (242 freshmen). 50 percent are women and 50 percent are men. Students come from 35 states and territories and 9 other countries. 27 percent are from Minnesota. 1.3 percent are international students.

Expenses for 2002–03 *Application fee:* $25. *Comprehensive fee:* $13,560 includes full-time tuition ($11,080), mandatory fees ($630), and college room and board ($1850). *College room only:* $680. *Part-time tuition:* $150 per credit hour.

Financial Aid Forms of aid include need-based and non-need-based scholarships and part-time jobs. The average aided 2001–02 undergraduate received an aid package worth $6131. The application deadline for financial aid is April 15.

Freshman Admission MLC requires a high school transcript, a minimum 2.0 high school GPA, recommendations, ACT scores, and TOEFL scores for international students. The application deadline for regular admission is April 15.

Transfer Admission The application deadline for admission is April 15.

Martin Luther College (continued)

Entrance Difficulty MLC assesses its entrance difficulty level as moderately difficult. For the fall 2002 freshman class, 93 percent of the applicants were accepted.

For Further Information Contact Prof. Ronald B. Brutlag, Associate Director of Admissions, Martin Luther College, 1995 Luther Court, New Ulm, MN 56073. *Telephone:* 507-354-8221 Ext. 211. *Fax:* 507-354-8225. *E-mail:* mlcadmit@mlc-wels.edu. *Web site:* http://www.mlc-wels.edu/.

MAYO SCHOOL OF HEALTH SCIENCES

Rochester, Minnesota

Mayo School of Health Sciences is a coed, private, upper-level institution, founded in 1973, offering degrees at the associate, bachelor's, and master's levels and postbachelor's certificates.

Academic Information The library holds 341,170 titles, 6,466 serial subscriptions, and 17,497 audiovisual materials. Special programs include cooperative (work-study) education, independent study, internships, and arrangement for off-campus study.
Student Body Statistics The student body totals 1,354, of whom 281 are undergraduates. 83 percent are women and 17 percent are men.
Financial Aid Forms of aid include need-based and non-need-based scholarships. The average aided 2002–03 undergraduate received an aid package worth an estimated $7868. The application deadline for financial aid is continuous.
Transfer Admission Mayo School of Health Sciences requires standardized test scores and a college transcript.
Entrance Difficulty Mayo School of Health Sciences assesses its entrance difficulty level as moderately difficult.

For Further Information Contact Ms. Kate Ray, Enrollment and Student Services, Mayo School of Health Sciences, 200 First Street, SW, Siebens Building, Room 1138, Rochester, MN 55901. *Telephone:* 507-266-4077 or 800-626-9041 (toll-free). *Fax:* 507-284-0656. *E-mail:* kray@mayo.edu. *Web site:* http://www.mayo.edu/mshs/.

METROPOLITAN STATE UNIVERSITY

St. Paul, Minnesota

Metro State is a coed, public, comprehensive unit of Minnesota State Colleges and Universities System, founded in 1971, offering degrees at the bachelor's and master's levels (offers primarily part-time evening degree programs).

Academic Information The faculty has 619 members (19% full-time), 35% with terminal degrees. The undergraduate student-faculty ratio is 12:1. The library holds 9,856 titles, 235 serial subscriptions, and 507 audiovisual materials. Special programs include ESL programs, double majors, independent study, self-designed majors, summer session for credit, part-time degree programs (daytime, evenings, weekends, summer), external degree programs, adult/continuing education programs, internships, and arrangement for off-campus study with other colleges in the Minnesota State College and University System. The most frequently chosen baccalaureate fields are business/marketing, interdisciplinary studies, protective services/public administration.
Student Body Statistics The student body totals 6,419, of whom 5,990 are undergraduates (113 freshmen). 60 percent are women and 40 percent are men. Students come from 16 states and territories and 53 other countries. 98 percent are from Minnesota. 2.2 percent are international students. 23 percent of the 2002 graduating class went on to graduate and professional schools.
Expenses for 2002–03 *Application fee:* $20. *State resident tuition:* $3136 full-time, $105 per credit part-time. *Nonresident tuition:* $6930 full-time, $231 per credit part-time. *Mandatory fees:* $222 full-time, $7.39 per credit part-time. Full-time tuition and fees vary according to reciprocity agreements. Part-time tuition and fees vary according to course load and reciprocity agreements.
Financial Aid Forms of aid include need-based and non-need-based scholarships and part-time jobs. The average aided 2002–03 undergraduate received an aid package worth an estimated $7500. The priority application deadline for financial aid is June 1.
Freshman Admission Metro State requires a high school transcript, a minimum 2.0 high school GPA, and TOEFL scores for international students. SAT I or ACT scores are required for some. The application deadline for regular admission is rolling.
Transfer Admission The application deadline for admission is rolling.
Entrance Difficulty Metro State assesses its entrance difficulty level as minimally difficult.

For Further Information Contact Dr. Janice Harring Hendon, Director, Metropolitan State University, 700 East 7th Street, St. Paul, MN 55106-5000. *Telephone:* 651-793-1303. *Fax:* 651-793-1310. *E-mail:* admissionsmetro@metrostate.edu. *Web site:* http://www.metrostate.edu/.

MINNEAPOLIS COLLEGE OF ART AND DESIGN

Minneapolis, Minnesota

MCAD is a coed, private, comprehensive institution, founded in 1886, offering degrees at the bachelor's and master's levels and postbachelor's certificates in art. It has a 7-acre campus in Minneapolis.

Academic Information The faculty has 106 members (34% full-time), 25% with terminal degrees. The undergraduate student-faculty ratio is 15:1. The library holds 47,166 titles, 196 serial subscriptions, and 139,245 audiovisual materials. Special programs include services for learning-disabled students, cooperative (work-study) education, study abroad, advanced placement credit, independent study, distance learning, summer session for credit, part-time degree programs, adult/continuing education programs, internships, and arrangement for off-campus study with members of the Association of Independent Colleges of Art and Design, Macalester College. The most frequently chosen baccalaureate field is visual/performing arts.
Student Body Statistics The student body totals 659, of whom 606 are undergraduates (123 freshmen). 43 percent are women and 57 percent are men. Students come from 30 states and territories. 61 percent are from Minnesota. 10 percent of the 2002 graduating class went on to graduate and professional schools.
Expenses for 2003–04 *Application fee:* $35. *Comprehensive fee:* $27,840 includes full-time tuition ($22,400), mandatory fees ($140), and college room and board ($5300). *College room only:* $2042. *Part-time tuition:* $747 per credit.
Financial Aid Forms of aid include need-based and non-need-based scholarships and part-time jobs. The average aided 2002–03 undergraduate received an aid package worth an estimated $12,761. The priority application deadline for financial aid is March 15.
Freshman Admission MCAD requires an essay, a high school transcript, 1 recommendation, an interview, SAT I or ACT scores, and TOEFL scores for international students. A portfolio is required for some. The application deadline for regular admission is rolling.
Transfer Admission The application deadline for admission is rolling.
Entrance Difficulty MCAD assesses its entrance difficulty level as moderately difficult. For the fall 2002 freshman class, 73 percent of the applicants were accepted.

For Further Information Contact Mr. William Mullen, Director of Admissions, Minneapolis College of Art and Design, 2501 Stevens Avenue South, Minneapolis, MN 55404-4347. *Telephone:* 612-874-3762 or 800-874-6223 (toll-free). *Fax:* 612-874-3704. *E-mail:* admissions@mn.mcad.edu. *Web site:* http://www.mcad.edu/.

MINNESOTA BIBLE COLLEGE

See Crossroads College

MINNESOTA SCHOOL OF BUSINESS-RICHFIELD

Richfield, Minnesota

MSB is a coed, proprietary, primarily two-year college, founded in 1877, offering degrees at the associate and bachelor's levels. It has a 3-acre campus in Richfield near Minneapolis–St. Paul.

Academic Information The student-faculty ratio is 12:1. The library holds 3,000 titles and 5 serial subscriptions. Special programs include academic remediation, cooperative (work-study) education, accelerated degree programs, distance learning, adult/continuing education programs, and internships.
Student Body Statistics The student body is made up of 2,600 undergraduates. Students come from 5 states and territories.
Expenses for 2003–04 *Application fee:* $50. *Tuition:* $290 per credit part-time.
Financial Aid Forms of aid include need-based scholarships. The application deadline for financial aid is continuous.
Freshman Admission MSB requires a high school transcript, an interview, and CPAt. An essay is required for some. The application deadline for regular admission is rolling.
Entrance Difficulty MSB has an open admission policy.

For Further Information Contact Ms. Patricia Murray, Director of Marketing, Minnesota School of Business-Richfield, 1401 West 76th Street, Richfield, MN 55430. *Telephone:* 612-861-2000 Ext. 712 or 800-752-4223 (toll-free in-state). *Fax:* 612-861-5548. *E-mail:* rkuhl@msbcollege.com. *Web site:* http://www.msbcollege.edu/.

MINNESOTA STATE UNIVERSITY, MANKATO

Mankato, Minnesota

Mankato State is a coed, public, comprehensive unit of Minnesota State Colleges and Universities System, founded in 1868, offering degrees at the associate, bachelor's, and master's levels and post-master's certificates. It has a 303-acre campus in Mankato near Minneapolis–St. Paul.

Academic Information The faculty has 630 members (72% full-time), 59% with terminal degrees. The undergraduate student-faculty ratio is 24:1. The library holds 468,567 titles, 3,275 serial subscriptions, and 31,078 audiovisual materials. Special programs include academic remediation, services for learning-disabled students, an honors program, study abroad, advanced placement credit, ESL programs, double majors, independent study, distance learning, self-designed majors, summer session for credit, part-time degree programs (daytime, evenings, weekends, summer), adult/continuing education programs, internships, and arrangement for off-campus study with other colleges in the Minnesota State College and University System. The most frequently chosen baccalaureate fields are business/marketing, education, protective services/public administration.
Student Body Statistics The student body totals 13,795, of whom 12,087 are undergraduates (2,083 freshmen). 52 percent are women and 48 percent are men. Students come from 40 states and territories and 71 other countries. 88 percent are from Minnesota. 4.2 percent are international students.
Expenses for 2002–03 *Application fee:* $20. *State resident tuition:* $3310 full-time, $132 per credit part-time. *Nonresident tuition:* $7020 full-time, $280 per credit part-time. *Mandatory fees:* $671 full-time, $27.90 per credit part-time. Full-time tuition and fees vary according to course load and reciprocity agreements. Part-time tuition and fees vary according to course load and reciprocity agreements. *College room and board:* $4018. Room and board charges vary according to board plan.
Financial Aid Forms of aid include need-based and non-need-based scholarships and part-time jobs. The average aided 2002–03 undergraduate received an aid package worth an estimated $5992. The priority application deadline for financial aid is March 15.
Freshman Admission Mankato State requires a high school transcript, ACT scores, and TOEFL scores for international students. An essay and 3 recommendations are required for some. The application deadline for regular admission is rolling.
Transfer Admission The application deadline for admission is rolling.
Entrance Difficulty Mankato State assesses its entrance difficulty level as moderately difficult. For the fall 2002 freshman class, 89 percent of the applicants were accepted.

For Further Information Contact Mr. Walt Wolff, Director of Admissions, Minnesota State University, Mankato, 122 Taylor Center, Mankato, MN 56001. *Telephone:* 507-389-6670 or 800-722-0544 (toll-free). *Fax:* 507-389-1511. *E-mail:* admissions@mnsu.edu. *Web site:* http://www.mnsu.edu/.

MINNESOTA STATE UNIVERSITY, MOORHEAD

Moorhead, Minnesota

Minnesota State University, Moorhead is a coed, public, comprehensive unit of Minnesota State Colleges and Universities System, founded in 1885, offering degrees at the associate, bachelor's, and master's levels and post-master's certificates. It has a 118-acre campus in Moorhead.

Academic Information The faculty has 334 members (90% full-time). The undergraduate student-faculty ratio is 18:1. The library holds 367,334 titles and 1,539 serial subscriptions. Special programs include academic remediation, services for learning-disabled students, an honors program, study abroad, advanced placement credit, Freshman Honors College, double majors, independent study, distance learning, self-designed majors, summer session for credit, part-time degree programs (daytime, evenings, weekends, summer), external degree programs, adult/continuing education programs, internships, and arrangement for off-campus study with North Dakota State University, Concordia College (Moorhead, MN), other colleges of the Minnesota State Colleges and Universities System. The most frequently chosen baccalaureate fields are law/legal studies, philosophy, religion, and theology.
Student Body Statistics The student body totals 7,431, of whom 7,048 are undergraduates. 62 percent are women and 38 percent are men. Students come from 34 states and territories and 32 other countries. 62 percent are from Minnesota. 1.9 percent are international students. 6.9 percent of the 2002 graduating class went on to graduate and professional schools.
Expenses for 2002–03 *Application fee:* $20. *State resident tuition:* $3388 full-time, $105.15 per credit hour part-time. *Nonresident tuition:* $6958 full-time, $105.15 per credit hour part-time. Part-time tuition varies according to reciprocity agreements. *College room and board:* $3706. *College room only:* $2016. Room and board charges vary according to board plan.
Financial Aid Forms of aid include need-based and non-need-based scholarships, athletic grants, and part-time jobs. The average aided 2002–03 undergraduate received an aid package worth an estimated $4094. The priority application deadline for financial aid is March 1.
Freshman Admission Minnesota State University, Moorhead requires a high school transcript, SAT I or ACT scores, TOEFL scores for international students, and PSAT. The application deadline for regular admission is August 7.
Transfer Admission The application deadline for admission is August 7.
Entrance Difficulty Minnesota State University, Moorhead assesses its entrance difficulty level as moderately difficult.

For Further Information Contact Ms. Gina Monson, Director of Admissions, Minnesota State University, Moorhead, Owens Hall, Moorhead, MN 56563-0002. *Telephone:* 218-236-2161 or 800-593-7246 (toll-free). *Fax:* 218-236-2168. *Web site:* http://www.mnstate.edu/.

NATIONAL AMERICAN UNIVERSITY–ST. PAUL CAMPUS

St. Paul, Minnesota

National is a coed, proprietary, four-year college of National American University, founded in 1974, offering degrees at the associate and bachelor's levels. It has a 1-acre campus in St. Paul.

Expenses for 2002–03 *Application fee:* $25. *Tuition:* $259 per credit hour part-time.

For Further Information Contact Mr. Steve Grunlan, Director of Admissions, National American University–St. Paul Campus, 1500 West Highway 36, Roseville, MN. *Telephone:* 651-644-1265. *Fax:* 651-644-0690. *Web site:* http://www.nationalcollege.edu/.

NORTH CENTRAL UNIVERSITY

Minneapolis, Minnesota

For Information Write to North Central University, Minneapolis, MN 55404-1322.

NORTHWESTERN COLLEGE

St. Paul, Minnesota

Northwestern is a coed, private, nondenominational, four-year college, founded in 1902, offering degrees at the associate and bachelor's levels. It has a 100-acre campus in St. Paul.

Academic Information The faculty has 177 members (44% full-time), 42% with terminal degrees. The student-faculty ratio is 15:1. The library holds 75,082 titles, 560 serial subscriptions, and 3,716 audiovisual materials. Special programs include academic remediation, an honors program, study abroad, advanced placement credit, ESL programs, double majors, independent study, distance learning, summer session for credit, part-time degree programs (evenings, weekends), adult/continuing education programs, internships, and arrangement for off-campus study with Coalition for Christian Colleges and Universities, Focus on the Family Institute, William Mitchell College of Law. The most frequently chosen baccalaureate fields are education, business/marketing, philosophy, religion, and theology.

Student Body Statistics The student body is made up of 2,448 undergraduates (470 freshmen). 62 percent are women and 38 percent are men. Students come from 34 states and territories. 61 percent are from Minnesota. 0.3 percent are international students. 4 percent of the 2002 graduating class went on to graduate and professional schools.

Expenses for 2003–04 *Application fee:* $25. *Comprehensive fee:* $23,020 includes full-time tuition ($17,400) and college room and board ($5620). *College room only:* $3000. Room and board charges vary according to board plan. *Part-time tuition:* $735 per credit.

Financial Aid Forms of aid include need-based and non-need-based scholarships and part-time jobs. The average aided 2001–02 undergraduate received an aid package worth $13,183. The application deadline for financial aid is July 1 with a priority deadline of March 1.

Freshman Admission Northwestern requires an essay, a high school transcript, a minimum 2.0 high school GPA, 2 recommendations, lifestyle agreement, statement of Christian faith, SAT I or ACT scores, and TOEFL scores for international students. A minimum 3.0 high school GPA and an interview are recommended. An interview is required for some. The application deadline for regular admission is August 1.

Transfer Admission The application deadline for admission is August 1.

Entrance Difficulty Northwestern assesses its entrance difficulty level as moderately difficult. For the fall 2002 freshman class, 91 percent of the applicants were accepted.

For Further Information Contact Mr. Kenneth K. Faffler, Director of Recruitment, Northwestern College, 3003 Snelling Avenue North, Nazareth Hall, Room 229, St. Paul, MN 55113-1598. *Telephone:* 651-631-5111 or 800-827-6827 (toll-free). *Fax:* 651-631-5680. *E-mail:* admissions@nwc.edu. *Web site:* http://www.nwc.edu/.

OAK HILLS CHRISTIAN COLLEGE

Bemidji, Minnesota

Oak Hills is a coed, private, interdenominational, four-year college, founded in 1946, offering degrees at the associate and bachelor's levels. It has a 180-acre campus in Bemidji.

Academic Information The faculty has 23 members (35% full-time), 35% with terminal degrees. The student-faculty ratio is 13:1. The library holds 25,079 titles, 99 serial subscriptions, and 1,338 audiovisual materials. Special programs include academic remediation, services for learning-disabled students, an honors program, advanced placement credit, double majors, independent study, part-time degree programs (daytime, evenings), internships, and arrangement for off-campus study with Bemidji State University, Crown College. The most frequently chosen baccalaureate field is philosophy, religion, and theology.

Student Body Statistics The student body is made up of 147 undergraduates. Students come from 15 states and territories. 75 percent are from Minnesota.

Expenses for 2003–04 *Application fee:* $20. *Comprehensive fee:* $13,990 includes full-time tuition ($10,180) and college room and board ($3810). *College room only:* $1830. Full-time tuition varies according to course load. Room and board charges vary according to board plan and housing facility. *Part-time tuition:* $125 per semester hour. Part-time tuition varies according to course load.

Financial Aid Forms of aid include need-based and non-need-based scholarships and part-time jobs. The average aided 2001–02 undergraduate received an aid package worth $8481. The application deadline for financial aid is continuous.

Freshman Admission Oak Hills requires an essay, a high school transcript, 2 recommendations, and ACT scores. A minimum 2.0 high school GPA is required for some. The application deadline for regular admission is rolling.

Transfer Admission The application deadline for admission is rolling.

Entrance Difficulty Oak Hills assesses its entrance difficulty level as minimally difficult. For the fall 2002 freshman class, 80 percent of the applicants were accepted.

For Further Information Contact Mr. Dan Hovestol, Admissions Director, Oak Hills Christian College, Bemidji, MN 56601. *Telephone:* 218-751-8670 Ext. 220 or 888-751-8670 Ext. 285 (toll-free). *Fax:* 218-751-8825. *E-mail:* admissions@oakhills.edu. *Web site:* http://www.oakhills.edu/.

PILLSBURY BAPTIST BIBLE COLLEGE

Owatonna, Minnesota

Pillsbury is a coed, private, Baptist, four-year college, founded in 1957, offering degrees at the associate and bachelor's levels. It has a 14-acre campus in Owatonna near Minneapolis–St. Paul.

Academic Information The faculty has 31 members (48% full-time), 6% with terminal degrees. The student-faculty ratio is 10:1. The library holds 52,340 titles, 245 serial subscriptions, and 817 audiovisual materials. Special programs include academic remediation, services for learning-disabled students, advanced placement credit, accelerated degree programs, double majors, independent study, summer session for credit, part-time degree programs (daytime, evenings, summer), and internships. The most frequently chosen baccalaureate fields are business/marketing, education, philosophy, religion, and theology.

Student Body Statistics The student body is made up of 206 undergraduates (49 freshmen). 53 percent are women and 47 percent are men. Students come from 28 states and territories and 2 other countries. 46 percent are from Minnesota. 1.5 percent are international students.
Expenses for 2003–04 *Application fee:* $25. *Comprehensive fee:* $11,720 includes full-time tuition ($6560), mandatory fees ($1560), and college room and board ($3600). *Part-time tuition:* $205 per credit hour. *Part-time mandatory fees:* $896 per year. Part-time tuition and fees vary according to course load.
Financial Aid Forms of aid include need-based and non-need-based scholarships. The application deadline for financial aid is continuous.
Freshman Admission Pillsbury requires an essay, a high school transcript, 2 recommendations, 2 photographs, and TOEFL scores for international students. An interview is recommended. The application deadline for regular admission is August 20.
Transfer Admission The application deadline for admission is August 20.
Entrance Difficulty Pillsbury has an open admission policy.

For Further Information Contact Mr. Gene Young, Director of Admissions, Pillsbury Baptist Bible College, 315 South Grove Avenue, Owatonna, MN 55060-3097. *Telephone:* 507-451-2710 Ext. 279 or 800-747-4557 (toll-free). *Fax:* 507-451-6459. *E-mail:* ppbc@pillsbury.edu. *Web site:* http://www.pillsbury.edu/.

ROCHESTER COMMUNITY AND TECHNICAL COLLEGE

Rochester, Minnesota

RCTC is a coed, public, primarily two-year college of Minnesota State Colleges and Universities System, founded in 1915, offering degrees at the associate and bachelor's levels (also offers 13 programs that lead to a bachelor's degree with Winona State University or University of Minnesota). It has a 160-acre campus in Rochester.

Academic Information The faculty has 225 members (41% full-time). The library holds 62,000 titles and 600 serial subscriptions. Special programs include academic remediation, services for learning-disabled students, an honors program, advanced placement credit, ESL programs, independent study, distance learning, summer session for credit, part-time degree programs (daytime, evenings, weekends, summer), internships, and arrangement for off-campus study with other colleges in the Minnesota State Colleges and Universities System, Winona State University–Rochester Center.
Student Body Statistics The student body is made up of 5,411 undergraduates. Students come from 39 states and territories and 36 other countries. 90 percent are from Minnesota.
Expenses for 2002–03 *Application fee:* $20. *State resident tuition:* $2492 full-time, $103.85 per credit part-time. *Nonresident tuition:* $4608 full-time, $192 per credit part-time.
Financial Aid Forms of aid include need-based scholarships and part-time jobs. The application deadline for financial aid is continuous.
Freshman Admission RCTC requires a high school transcript and TOEFL scores for international students. The application deadline for regular admission is August 24.
Transfer Admission The application deadline for admission is August 24.
Entrance Difficulty RCTC has an open admission policy except for allied health, technology programs. It assesses its entrance difficulty as moderately difficult for allied health programs.

For Further Information Contact Mr. Troy Tynsky, Director of Admissions, Rochester Community and Technical College, 851 30th Avenue, SE, Rochester, MN 55904-4999. *Telephone:* 507-280-3509. *Fax:* 507-285-7496. *Web site:* http://www.roch.edu/.

ST. CLOUD STATE UNIVERSITY

St. Cloud, Minnesota

SCSU is a coed, public, comprehensive unit of Minnesota State Colleges and Universities System, founded in 1869, offering degrees at the associate, bachelor's, and master's levels and first professional and postbachelor's certificates. It has a 108-acre campus in St. Cloud near Minneapolis–St. Paul.

Academic Information The faculty has 809 members (81% full-time). The undergraduate student-faculty ratio is 19:1. The library holds 560,251 titles, 1,487 serial subscriptions, and 33,900 audiovisual materials. Special programs include academic remediation, services for learning-disabled students, an honors program, study abroad, advanced placement credit, accelerated degree programs, ESL programs, double majors, independent study, distance learning, self-designed majors, summer session for credit, part-time degree programs (daytime, evenings, weekends, summer), adult/continuing education programs, internships, and arrangement for off-campus study with members of the Tri-College Exchange Program, other colleges in the Minnesota State Colleges and University System. The most frequently chosen baccalaureate fields are business/marketing, communications/communication technologies, social sciences and history.
Student Body Statistics The student body totals 15,719, of whom 14,513 are undergraduates (2,449 freshmen). 54 percent are women and 46 percent are men. Students come from 50 states and territories and 84 other countries. 86 percent are from Minnesota. 5.1 percent are international students. 10 percent of the 2002 graduating class went on to graduate and professional schools.
Expenses for 2002–03 *Application fee:* $20. *State resident tuition:* $3461 full-time, $115.35 per credit part-time. *Nonresident tuition:* $7512 full-time, $250.40 per credit part-time. *Mandatory fees:* $537 full-time, $21.28 per credit part-time. Full-time tuition and fees vary according to course load and reciprocity agreements. Part-time tuition and fees vary according to course load and reciprocity agreements. *College room and board:* $3788. *College room only:* $2450. Room and board charges vary according to board plan and housing facility.
Financial Aid Forms of aid include need-based and non-need-based scholarships, athletic grants, and part-time jobs. The average aided 2002–03 undergraduate received an aid package worth an estimated $5911. The priority application deadline for financial aid is May 1.
Freshman Admission SCSU requires a high school transcript, ACT scores, and TOEFL scores for international students. Recommendations are required for some.
Entrance Difficulty SCSU assesses its entrance difficulty level as moderately difficult; most difficult for honors program. For the fall 2002 freshman class, 76 percent of the applicants were accepted.

For Further Information Contact Ms. Debbie Tamte-Horan, Director of Admissions, St. Cloud State University, 115 AS Building, 720 4th Avenue South, St. Cloud, MN 56301-4498. *Telephone:* 320-255-2286 or 877-654-7278 (toll-free). *Fax:* 320-255-2243. *E-mail:* scsu4u@stcloudstate.edu. *Web site:* http://www.stcloudstate.edu/.

SAINT JOHN'S UNIVERSITY

Collegeville, Minnesota

St. John's is a coed, primarily men's, private, Roman Catholic, comprehensive institution, founded in 1857, coordinate with College of Saint Benedict, offering degrees at the bachelor's, master's, and first professional levels (coordinate with College of Saint Benedict for women). It has a 2,400-acre campus in Collegeville near Minneapolis–St. Paul.

Academic Information The faculty has 178 members (83% full-time), 93% with terminal degrees. The undergraduate student-faculty ratio is 13:1. The library holds 805,376 titles, 5,735 serial subscriptions, and 22,452 audiovisual materials. Special programs include services for learning-disabled students, an honors program, study abroad, advanced placement credit, accelerated degree programs, ESL programs, double majors, independent study, self-designed majors, internships, and arrangement for off-campus study with College of Saint Benedict,

Saint John's University (continued)

Tri-College Exchange Program. The most frequently chosen baccalaureate fields are business/marketing, English, social sciences and history.
Student Body Statistics The student body totals 2,046, of whom 1,897 are undergraduates (468 freshmen). 100 percent are men. Students come from 30 states and territories and 27 other countries. 86 percent are from Minnesota. 3 percent are international students. 22 percent of the 2002 graduating class went on to graduate and professional schools.
Expenses for 2002–03 *Application fee:* $30. *Comprehensive fee:* $24,780 includes full-time tuition ($18,916), mandatory fees ($310), and college room and board ($5554). *College room only:* $2737. Room and board charges vary according to board plan and housing facility. *Part-time tuition:* $788 per credit. *Part-time mandatory fees:* $155 per term.
Financial Aid Forms of aid include need-based and non-need-based scholarships and part-time jobs. The average aided 2002–03 undergraduate received an aid package worth an estimated $16,895. The priority application deadline for financial aid is March 15.
Freshman Admission St. John's requires an essay, a high school transcript, 1 recommendation, SAT I or ACT scores, and TOEFL scores for international students. A minimum 3.0 high school GPA and an interview are recommended. The application deadline for regular admission is rolling and for early action it is December 1.
Transfer Admission The application deadline for admission is rolling.
Entrance Difficulty St. John's assesses its entrance difficulty level as moderately difficult. For the fall 2002 freshman class, 87 percent of the applicants were accepted.

For Further Information Contact Ms. Renee Miller, Director of Admission, Saint John's University, PO Box 7155, Collegeville, MN 56321-7155. *Telephone:* 320-363-2196 or 800-24JOHNS (toll-free). *Fax:* 320-363-3206. *E-mail:* admissions@csbsju.edu. *Web site:* http://www.csbsju.edu/.

SAINT MARY'S UNIVERSITY OF MINNESOTA

Winona, Minnesota

Saint Mary's is a coed, private, Roman Catholic, comprehensive institution, founded in 1912, offering degrees at the bachelor's, master's, and doctoral levels and post-master's and postbachelor's certificates. It has a 350-acre campus in Winona.

Academic Information The faculty has 513 members (21% full-time), 40% with terminal degrees. The undergraduate student-faculty ratio is 12:1. The library holds 130,944 titles, 708 serial subscriptions, and 8,281 audiovisual materials. Special programs include academic remediation, services for learning-disabled students, an honors program, study abroad, advanced placement credit, accelerated degree programs, ESL programs, double majors, independent study, self-designed majors, summer session for credit, part-time degree programs (daytime, evenings, summer), adult/continuing education programs, internships, and arrangement for off-campus study with Winona State University. The most frequently chosen baccalaureate fields are business/marketing, communications/ communication technologies, social sciences and history.
Student Body Statistics The student body totals 5,065, of whom 1,654 are undergraduates (396 freshmen). 53 percent are women and 47 percent are men. Students come from 25 states and territories and 21 other countries. 69 percent are from Minnesota. 2.4 percent are international students. 23 percent of the 2002 graduating class went on to graduate and professional schools.
Expenses for 2002–03 *Application fee:* $25. *Comprehensive fee:* $20,615 includes full-time tuition ($15,280), mandatory fees ($415), and college room and board ($4920). *College room only:* $2750. Full-time tuition and fees vary according to course load, location, and program. Room and board charges vary according to housing facility. *Part-time tuition:* $510 per credit. Part-time tuition varies according to location and program.
Financial Aid Forms of aid include need-based and non-need-based scholarships and part-time jobs. The priority application deadline for financial aid is March 15.
Freshman Admission Saint Mary's requires an essay, a high school transcript, a minimum 2.5 high school GPA, SAT I or ACT scores, and TOEFL scores for international students. 2 recommendations are recommended. An interview is required for some. The application deadline for regular admission is May 1.
Transfer Admission The application deadline for admission is rolling.
Entrance Difficulty Saint Mary's assesses its entrance difficulty level as moderately difficult. For the fall 2002 freshman class, 79 percent of the applicants were accepted.

For Further Information Contact Mr. Anthony M. Piscitiello, Vice President for Admission, Saint Mary's University of Minnesota, Winona, MN 55987-1399. *Telephone:* 507-457-1700 or 800-635-5987 (toll-free). *Fax:* 507-457-1722. *E-mail:* admissions@smumn.edu. *Web site:* http://www.smumn.edu/.

ST. OLAF COLLEGE

Northfield, Minnesota

St. Olaf is a coed, private, Lutheran, four-year college, founded in 1874, offering degrees at the bachelor's level. It has a 350-acre campus in Northfield near Minneapolis–St. Paul.

Academic Information The faculty has 322 members (60% full-time), 75% with terminal degrees. The student-faculty ratio is 13:1. The library holds 654,950 titles, 1,616 serial subscriptions, and 16,194 audiovisual materials. Special programs include services for learning-disabled students, study abroad, advanced placement credit, double majors, independent study, self-designed majors, summer session for credit, part-time degree programs (daytime), internships, and arrangement for off-campus study with Carleton College, Augsburg College, Minnesota Intercollegiate Nursing Consortium, Washington University. The most frequently chosen baccalaureate fields are biological/life sciences, social sciences and history, visual/performing arts.
Student Body Statistics The student body is made up of 3,041 undergraduates (779 freshmen). 59 percent are women and 41 percent are men. Students come from 49 states and territories and 27 other countries. 53 percent are from Minnesota. 1.3 percent are international students. 25.1 percent of the 2002 graduating class went on to graduate and professional schools.
Expenses for 2003–04 *Application fee:* $35. *Comprehensive fee:* $28,500 includes full-time tuition ($23,650) and college room and board ($4850). *College room only:* $2250. Room and board charges vary according to board plan. *Part-time tuition:* $740 per credit hour.
Financial Aid Forms of aid include need-based and non-need-based scholarships and part-time jobs. The average aided 2002–03 undergraduate received an aid package worth an estimated $16,873. The priority application deadline for financial aid is February 15.
Freshman Admission St. Olaf requires an essay, a high school transcript, 2 recommendations, SAT I or ACT scores, and TOEFL scores for international students. An interview is recommended. The application deadline for regular admission is rolling; for early decision it is November 15; and for early action it is December 15.
Transfer Admission The application deadline for admission is June 1.
Entrance Difficulty St. Olaf assesses its entrance difficulty level as very difficult. For the fall 2002 freshman class, 73 percent of the applicants were accepted.

For Further Information Contact Jeff McLaughlin, Director of Admissions, St. Olaf College, 1520 St. Olaf Avenue, Northfield, MN 55057. *Telephone:* 507-646-3025 or 800-800-3025 (toll-free). *Fax:* 507-646-3832. *E-mail:* admiss@stolaf.edu. *Web site:* http://www.stolaf.edu/.

SOUTHWEST MINNESOTA STATE UNIVERSITY

Marshall, Minnesota

SSU is a coed, public, comprehensive unit of Minnesota State Colleges and Universities System, founded in 1963, offering degrees at the associate, bachelor's, and master's levels. It has a 216-acre campus in Marshall.

Academic Information The faculty has 159 members (77% full-time), 58% with terminal degrees. The undergraduate student-faculty ratio is 18:1. The library holds 167,888 titles, 695 serial subscriptions, and 4,324 audiovisual materials. Special programs include academic remediation, services for learning-disabled students, an honors program, study abroad, advanced placement credit, accelerated degree programs, Freshman Honors College, double majors, independent study, distance learning, self-designed majors, summer session for credit, part-time degree programs (daytime, evenings, weekends, summer), external degree programs, adult/continuing education programs, internships, and arrangement for off-campus study with other colleges in the Minnesota State College and University System.
Student Body Statistics The student body totals 5,636, of whom 5,167 are undergraduates (1,232 freshmen). 60 percent are women and 40 percent are men. Students come from 27 states and territories and 29 other countries. 88 percent are from Minnesota. 2.5 percent are international students. 4 percent of the 2002 graduating class went on to graduate and professional schools.
Expenses for 2002–03 *Application fee:* $20. *State resident tuition:* $3435 full-time, $114.50 per credit part-time. *Nonresident tuition:* $3435 full-time, $114.50 per credit part-time. *Mandatory fees:* $656 full-time, $26.19 per credit part-time. Full-time tuition and fees vary according to course load, location, and reciprocity agreements. Part-time tuition and fees vary according to course load, location, and reciprocity agreements. *College room and board:* $4248. *College room only:* $3160. Room and board charges vary according to board plan and housing facility.
Financial Aid Forms of aid include need-based and non-need-based scholarships, athletic grants, and part-time jobs. The average aided 2002–03 undergraduate received an aid package worth an estimated $5810. The priority application deadline for financial aid is April 1.
Freshman Admission SSU requires an essay, a high school transcript, an interview, SAT I or ACT scores, and TOEFL scores for international students. SAT I and SAT II or ACT scores are recommended. The application deadline for regular admission is rolling.
Transfer Admission The application deadline for admission is rolling.
Entrance Difficulty SSU assesses its entrance difficulty level as minimally difficult.

For Further Information Contact Richard Shearer, Director of Enrollment Services, Southwest Minnesota State University, 1501 State Street, Marshall, MN 56258-1598. *Telephone:* 507-537-6286 or 800-642-0684 (toll-free). *Fax:* 507-537-7154. *E-mail:* shearerr@southwest.msus.edu. *Web site:* http://www.southwest.msus.edu/.

UNIVERSITY OF MINNESOTA, CROOKSTON

Crookston, Minnesota

UMC is a coed, public, four-year college of University of Minnesota System, founded in 1966, offering degrees at the associate and bachelor's levels. It has a 95-acre campus in Crookston.

Academic Information The faculty has 103 members (53% full-time), 40% with terminal degrees. The student-faculty ratio is 15:1. The library holds 30,000 titles and 700 serial subscriptions. Special programs include academic remediation, services for learning-disabled students, study abroad, advanced placement credit, double majors, independent study, distance learning, summer session for credit, part-time degree programs, adult/continuing education programs, and internships. The most frequently chosen baccalaureate fields are agriculture, business/marketing, computer/information sciences.
Student Body Statistics The student body is made up of 2,387 undergraduates (276 freshmen). 55 percent are women and 45 percent are men. Students come from 21 states and territories and 18 other countries. 72 percent are from Minnesota. 2.8 percent are international students.
Expenses for 2002–03 *Application fee:* $25. *State resident tuition:* $5116 full-time, $160.52 per credit part-time. *Nonresident tuition:* $5116 full-time, $160.52 per credit part-time. *Mandatory fees:* $1306 full-time. Full-time tuition and fees vary according to reciprocity agreements. Part-time tuition varies according to course load. *College room and board:* $4464. Room and board charges vary according to board plan and housing facility.
Financial Aid Forms of aid include need-based and non-need-based scholarships, athletic grants, and part-time jobs. The average aided 2001–02 undergraduate received an aid package worth $8069. The priority application deadline for financial aid is March 31.
Freshman Admission UMC requires a high school transcript, ACT scores, and TOEFL scores for international students. The application deadline for regular admission is July 15.
Transfer Admission The application deadline for admission is July 15.
Entrance Difficulty UMC assesses its entrance difficulty level as moderately difficult. For the fall 2002 freshman class, 81 percent of the applicants were accepted.

For Further Information Contact Mr. Russell L. Kreager, Director of Admissions, University of Minnesota, Crookston, 2900 University Avenue, 170 Owen Hall, Crookston, MN 56716-5001. *Telephone:* 218-281-8569 or 800-862-6466 (toll-free). *Fax:* 218-281-8575. *E-mail:* info@mail.crk.umn.edu. *Web site:* http://www.crk.umn.edu/.

UNIVERSITY OF MINNESOTA, DULUTH

Duluth, Minnesota

UMD is a coed, public, comprehensive unit of University of Minnesota System, founded in 1947, offering degrees at the bachelor's, master's, and first professional levels. It has a 250-acre campus in Duluth.

Academic Information The faculty has 466 members (78% full-time), 68% with terminal degrees. The undergraduate student-faculty ratio is 20:1. The library holds 709,145 titles, 4,500 serial subscriptions, and 15,245 audiovisual materials. Special programs include academic remediation, services for learning-disabled students, an honors program, study abroad, advanced placement credit, ESL programs, double majors, independent study, distance learning, self-designed majors, summer session for credit, part-time degree programs (daytime, evenings, summer), adult/continuing education programs, internships, and arrangement for off-campus study with University of Wisconsin-Superior, College of St. Scholastica. The most frequently chosen baccalaureate fields are business/marketing, education, social sciences and history.
Student Body Statistics The student body totals 9,815, of whom 9,144 are undergraduates (2,051 freshmen). 51 percent are women and 49 percent are men. Students come from 36 states and territories and 32 other countries. 88 percent are from Minnesota. 2.3 percent are international students. 23 percent of the 2002 graduating class went on to graduate and professional schools.
Expenses for 2002–03 *Application fee:* $35. *One-time mandatory fee:* $300. *State resident tuition:* $5580 full-time, $186 per credit part-time. *Nonresident tuition:* $15,840 full-time, $528 per credit part-time. *Mandatory fees:* $887 full-time, $444 per term part-time. Full-time tuition and fees vary according to course load, degree level, program, and reciprocity agreements. Part-time tuition and fees vary according to course load, degree level, program, and reciprocity agreements. *College room and board:* $4960.
Financial Aid Forms of aid include need-based and non-need-based scholarships, athletic grants, and part-time jobs. The average aided 2002–03 undergraduate received an aid package worth an estimated $7371. The priority application deadline for financial aid is March 1.
Freshman Admission UMD requires a high school transcript, SAT I or ACT scores, and TOEFL scores for international students. The application deadline for regular admission is February 1.
Transfer Admission The application deadline for admission is August 1.
Entrance Difficulty UMD assesses its entrance difficulty level as moderately difficult. For the fall 2002 freshman class, 77 percent of the applicants were accepted.

For Further Information Contact Ms. Beth Esselstrom, Director of Admissions, University of Minnesota, Duluth, 23 Solon Campus Center, 1117 University Drive, Duluth, MN 55812-3000. *Telephone:* 218-726-7171 or 800-232-1339 (toll-free). *Fax:* 218-726-7040. *E-mail:* umdadmis@d.umn.edu. *Web site:* http://www.d.umn.edu/.

UNIVERSITY OF MINNESOTA, MORRIS

Morris, Minnesota

UMM is a coed, public, four-year college of University of Minnesota System, founded in 1959, offering degrees at the bachelor's level. It has a 130-acre campus in Morris.

Academic Information The faculty has 120 full-time members. The student-faculty ratio is 14:1. The library holds 191,469 titles, 9,042 serial subscriptions, and 2,140 audiovisual materials. Special programs include services for learning-disabled students, an honors program, study abroad, advanced placement credit, accelerated degree programs, Freshman Honors College, ESL programs, double majors, distance learning, self-designed majors, summer session for credit, part-time degree programs (daytime, summer), external degree programs, adult/continuing education programs, internships, and arrangement for off-campus study with other units of the University of Minnesota System. The most frequently chosen baccalaureate fields are English, biological/life sciences, social sciences and history.
Student Body Statistics The student body is made up of 1,910 undergraduates (477 freshmen). 60 percent are women and 40 percent are men. Students come from 31 states and territories and 13 other countries. 85 percent are from Minnesota. 1.1 percent are international students. 30 percent of the 2002 graduating class went on to graduate and professional schools.
Expenses for 2002–03 *Application fee:* $35. *State resident tuition:* $6381 full-time, $212.70 per credit part-time. *Nonresident tuition:* $212.70 per credit part-time. *Mandatory fees:* $878 full-time, $439 per term part-time. Part-time tuition and fees vary according to course load. *College room and board:* $4680. *College room only:* $2200. Room and board charges vary according to board plan and housing facility.
Financial Aid Forms of aid include need-based and non-need-based scholarships, athletic grants, and part-time jobs. The average aided 2002–03 undergraduate received an aid package worth an estimated $9754. The priority application deadline for financial aid is March 1.
Freshman Admission UMM requires an essay, a high school transcript, SAT I or ACT scores, and TOEFL scores for international students. A minimum 3.0 high school GPA is recommended. An interview is required for some. The application deadline for regular admission is March 15.
Transfer Admission The application deadline for admission is May 1.
Entrance Difficulty UMM assesses its entrance difficulty level as moderately difficult. For the fall 2002 freshman class, 82 percent of the applicants were accepted.

For Further Information Contact Mr. Scott K. Hagg, Director of Admissions, University of Minnesota, Morris, 600 East 4th Street, Morris, MN 56267-2199. *Telephone:* 320-539-6035 or 800-992-8863 (toll-free). *Fax:* 320-589-1673. *E-mail:* admissions@mrs.umn.edu. *Web site:* http://www.mrs.umn.edu/.

UNIVERSITY OF MINNESOTA, TWIN CITIES CAMPUS

Minneapolis, Minnesota

U of M-Twin Cities Campus is a coed, public unit of University of Minnesota System, founded in 1851, offering degrees at the bachelor's, master's, doctoral, and first professional levels and post-master's and postbachelor's certificates. It has a 2,000-acre campus in Minneapolis.

Academic Information The faculty has 3,079 members (88% full-time), 95% with terminal degrees. The undergraduate student-faculty ratio is 15:1. The library holds 6 million titles, 45,000 serial subscriptions, and 1 million audiovisual materials. Special programs include academic remediation, services for learning-disabled students, an honors program, cooperative (work-study) education, study abroad, advanced placement credit, accelerated degree programs, Freshman Honors College, ESL programs, double majors, independent study, distance learning, self-designed majors, summer session for credit, part-time degree programs, external degree programs, adult/continuing education programs, internships, and arrangement for off-campus study with National Student Exchange, Minnesota Community College System. The most frequently chosen baccalaureate fields are engineering/engineering technologies, business/marketing, social sciences and history.
Student Body Statistics The student body totals 48,677, of whom 32,457 are undergraduates (5,188 freshmen). 53 percent are women and 47 percent are men. Students come from 55 states and territories and 85 other countries. 74 percent are from Minnesota. 2.1 percent are international students.
Expenses for 2002–03 *Application fee:* $35. *State resident tuition:* $5420 full-time, $208.45 per credit part-time. *Nonresident tuition:* $15,994 full-time, $615.12 per credit part-time. *Mandatory fees:* $860 full-time. Full-time tuition and fees vary according to program. Part-time tuition varies according to course load and program. *College room and board:* $5696. Room and board charges vary according to board plan, housing facility, and location.
Financial Aid Forms of aid include need-based and non-need-based scholarships, athletic grants, and part-time jobs. The average aided 2002–03 undergraduate received an aid package worth an estimated $8496. The priority application deadline for financial aid is January 15.
Freshman Admission U of M-Twin Cities Campus requires a high school transcript, SAT I or ACT scores, and TOEFL scores for international students. A minimum 2.0 high school GPA is recommended. The application deadline for regular admission is rolling.
Transfer Admission The application deadline for admission is March 1.
Entrance Difficulty U of M-Twin Cities Campus assesses its entrance difficulty level as moderately difficult; very difficult for Institute of Technology, management, biological science programs. For the fall 2002 freshman class, 74 percent of the applicants were accepted.

For Further Information Contact Ms. Patricia Jones Whyte, Associate Director of Admissions, University of Minnesota, Twin Cities Campus, 240 Williamson Hall, Minneapolis, MN 55455-0115. *Telephone:* 612-625-2008 or 800-752-1000 (toll-free). *Fax:* 612-626-1693. *E-mail:* admissions@tc.umn.edu. *Web site:* http://www.umn.edu/tc/.

UNIVERSITY OF ST. THOMAS

St. Paul, Minnesota

St. Thomas is a coed, private, Roman Catholic university, founded in 1885, offering degrees at the bachelor's, master's, doctoral, and first professional levels and post-master's and postbachelor's certificates. It has a 78-acre campus in St. Paul near Minneapolis.

Academic Information The faculty has 800 members (50% full-time), 60% with terminal degrees. The undergraduate student-faculty ratio is 14:1. The library holds 440,023 titles, 4,168 serial subscriptions, and 3,516 audiovisual materials. Special programs include services for learning-disabled students, an honors program, study abroad, advanced placement credit, ESL programs, double majors, independent study, self-designed majors, summer session for credit, part-time degree programs (daytime, evenings, weekends, summer), adult/continuing education programs, internships, and arrangement for off-campus study with 5 members of the Associated Colleges of the Twin Cities. The most frequently chosen baccalaureate fields are business/marketing, communications/communication technologies, social sciences and history.
Student Body Statistics The student body totals 11,321, of whom 5,429 are undergraduates (1,104 freshmen). 52 percent are women and 48 percent are men. 83 percent are from Minnesota. 0.9 percent are international students. 15 percent of the 2002 graduating class went on to graduate and professional schools.
Expenses for 2002–03 *Application fee:* $30. *Comprehensive fee:* $25,597 includes full-time tuition ($19,120), mandatory fees ($348), and college room and board ($6129). *College room only:* $3499. Full-time tuition and fees vary according to course load. Room and board charges vary according to board plan and housing facility. *Part-time tuition:* $597.50 per credit. *Part-time mandatory fees:* $82 per term. Part-time tuition and fees vary according to course load.
Financial Aid Forms of aid include need-based and non-need-based scholarships and part-time jobs. The average aided 2002–03 undergraduate received an aid package worth an estimated $15,313. The priority application deadline for financial aid is April 1.

Freshman Admission St. Thomas requires an essay, a high school transcript, SAT I or ACT scores, and TOEFL scores for international students. Recommendations, an interview, and ACT scores are recommended. The application deadline for regular admission is rolling.
Transfer Admission The application deadline for admission is August 1.
Entrance Difficulty St. Thomas assesses its entrance difficulty level as moderately difficult. For the fall 2002 freshman class, 87 percent of the applicants were accepted.

For Further Information Contact Ms. Marla Friederichs, Associate Vice President of Enrollment Management, University of St. Thomas, Mail #32F-1, 2115 Summit Avenue, St. Paul, MN 55105-1096. *Telephone:* 651-962-6150 or 800-328-6819 Ext. 26150 (toll-free). *Fax:* 651-962-6160. *E-mail:* admissions@stthomas.edu. *Web site:* http://www.stthomas.edu/.

WINONA STATE UNIVERSITY

Winona, Minnesota

Winona State is a coed, public, comprehensive unit of Minnesota State Colleges and Universities System, founded in 1858, offering degrees at the associate, bachelor's, and master's levels and post-master's certificates. It has a 40-acre campus in Winona.

Academic Information The faculty has 357 members (88% full-time), 62% with terminal degrees. The undergraduate student-faculty ratio is 19:1. The library holds 243,500 titles and 1,950 serial subscriptions. Special programs include academic remediation, services for learning-disabled students, an honors program, study abroad, advanced placement credit, accelerated degree programs, ESL programs, double majors, independent study, distance learning, self-designed majors, summer session for credit, part-time degree programs (daytime, evenings, weekends, summer), external degree programs, adult/continuing education programs, internships, and arrangement for off-campus study with Saint Mary's University of Minnesota, other colleges in the Minnesota State Colleges and Universities System. The most frequently chosen baccalaureate field is law/legal studies.
Student Body Statistics The student body totals 7,760, of whom 7,130 are undergraduates. 64 percent are women and 36 percent are men. Students come from 39 states and territories and 55 other countries. 60 percent are from Minnesota. 4.1 percent are international students. 25 percent of the 2002 graduating class went on to graduate and professional schools.
Expenses for 2002–03 *Application fee:* $20. *State resident tuition:* $3490 full-time. *Nonresident tuition:* $7370 full-time. *Mandatory fees:* $675 full-time. *College room and board:* $4140. Room and board charges vary according to board plan and housing facility.
Financial Aid Forms of aid include need-based and non-need-based scholarships, athletic grants, and part-time jobs. The average aided 2001–02 undergraduate received an aid package worth $5406. The application deadline for financial aid is continuous.
Freshman Admission Winona State requires a high school transcript, class rank, SAT I or ACT scores, and TOEFL scores for international students. An essay, recommendations, and an interview are required for some. The application deadline for regular admission is rolling.
Transfer Admission The application deadline for admission is August 1.
Entrance Difficulty Winona State assesses its entrance difficulty level as moderately difficult; minimally difficult for adult students. For the fall 2002 freshman class, 82 percent of the applicants were accepted.

For Further Information Contact Mr. Douglas Schacke, Director of Admissions, Winona State University, PO Box 5838, Winona, MN 55987. *Telephone:* 507-457-5100 or 800-DIAL WSU (toll-free). *Fax:* 507-457-5620. *E-mail:* admissions@winona.edu. *Web site:* http://www.winona.edu/.

Missouri

AVILA UNIVERSITY

Kansas City, Missouri

Avila is a coed, private, Roman Catholic, comprehensive institution, founded in 1916, offering degrees at the bachelor's and master's levels. It has a 50-acre campus in Kansas City.

Academic Information The faculty has 190 members (33% full-time), 38% with terminal degrees. The undergraduate student-faculty ratio is 13:1. The library holds 80,865 titles, 7,179 serial subscriptions, and 3,265 audiovisual materials. Special programs include academic remediation, services for learning-disabled students, cooperative (work-study) education, study abroad, advanced placement credit, accelerated degree programs, ESL programs, double majors, independent study, distance learning, summer session for credit, part-time degree programs (daytime, evenings, weekends, summer), adult/continuing education programs, internships, and arrangement for off-campus study with Sisters of St. Joseph Consortium, Council of Independent Colleges Exchange Program. The most frequently chosen baccalaureate fields are business/marketing, education, health professions and related sciences.
Student Body Statistics The student body totals 1,746, of whom 1,236 are undergraduates (131 freshmen). 65 percent are women and 35 percent are men. Students come from 17 states and territories and 24 other countries. 77 percent are from Missouri. 2.7 percent are international students. 14 percent of the 2002 graduating class went on to graduate and professional schools.
Expenses for 2002–03 *Application fee:* $0. *Comprehensive fee:* $19,460 includes full-time tuition ($13,900), mandatory fees ($260), and college room and board ($5300). Full-time tuition and fees vary according to course load. Room and board charges vary according to board plan and housing facility. *Part-time tuition:* $316 per credit hour. *Part-time mandatory fees:* $8 per credit hour. Part-time tuition and fees vary according to course load.
Financial Aid Forms of aid include need-based and non-need-based scholarships and part-time jobs. The application deadline for financial aid is continuous.
Freshman Admission Avila requires a high school transcript, a minimum 2.5 high school GPA, SAT I or ACT scores, and TOEFL scores for international students. An interview is recommended. An essay and recommendations are required for some. The application deadline for regular admission is rolling.
Transfer Admission The application deadline for admission is rolling.
Entrance Difficulty Avila assesses its entrance difficulty level as minimally difficult. For the fall 2002 freshman class, 48 percent of the applicants were accepted.

For Further Information Contact Ms. Paige Illum, Director of Admissions, Avila University, 11901 Wornall Rd, Kansas City, MO 64145. *Telephone:* 816-501-3773 or 800-GO-AVILA (toll-free). *Fax:* 816-501-2453. *E-mail:* admissions@mail.avila.edu. *Web site:* http://www.avila.edu/.

BAPTIST BIBLE COLLEGE

Springfield, Missouri

Baptist Bible College is a coed, private, Baptist, comprehensive institution, founded in 1950, offering degrees at the associate, bachelor's, and master's levels. It has a 38-acre campus in Springfield.

Academic Information The faculty has 42 members (76% full-time). The library holds 36,844 titles and 226 serial subscriptions. Special programs include academic remediation, summer session for credit, part-time degree programs (daytime, summer), and internships.
Student Body Statistics The student body is made up of 653 undergraduates. Students come from 46 states and territories and 5 other countries. 20 percent are from Missouri.

Baptist Bible College (continued)

Expenses for 2002–03 *Application fee:* $40. *Comprehensive fee:* $8350 includes full-time tuition ($3238), mandatory fees ($522), and college room and board ($4590). Full-time tuition and fees vary according to program.
Financial Aid Forms of aid include need-based scholarships. The application deadline for financial aid is continuous.
Freshman Admission Baptist Bible College requires a high school transcript, 1 recommendation, and ACT scores. The application deadline for regular admission is rolling.
Transfer Admission The application deadline for admission is rolling.
Entrance Difficulty Baptist Bible College has an open admission policy.

For Further Information Contact Dr. Joseph Gleason, Director of Admissions, Baptist Bible College, 628 East Kearney, Springfield, MO 65803-3498. *Telephone:* 417-268-6000 Ext. 6013. *Fax:* 417-268-6694. *Web site:* http://www.bbcnet.edu/bbgst.html.

CALVARY BIBLE COLLEGE AND THEOLOGICAL SEMINARY

Kansas City, Missouri

Calvary is a coed, private, interdenominational, comprehensive institution, founded in 1932, offering degrees at the associate, bachelor's, master's, and first professional levels. It has a 55-acre campus in Kansas City.

Expenses for 2002–03 *Application fee:* $25. *Comprehensive fee:* $9730 includes full-time tuition ($5720), mandatory fees ($410), and college room and board ($3600).

For Further Information Contact Mr. Timothy Smith, Director of Admissions, Calvary Bible College and Theological Seminary, 15800 Calvary Road, Kansas City, MO 64147-1341. *Telephone:* 816-322-0110 Ext. 1326 or 800-326-3960 (toll-free). *Fax:* 816-331-4474. *E-mail:* admissions@calvary.edu. *Web site:* http://www.calvary.edu/.

CENTRAL BIBLE COLLEGE

Springfield, Missouri

CBC is a coed, private, Assemblies of God, four-year college, founded in 1922, offering degrees at the associate and bachelor's levels in religious studies. It has a 108-acre campus in Springfield.

Academic Information The faculty has 66 members (61% full-time), 17% with terminal degrees. The student-faculty ratio is 18:1. The library holds 107,023 titles, 1,074 serial subscriptions, and 6,894 audiovisual materials. Special programs include academic remediation, services for learning-disabled students, advanced placement credit, double majors, independent study, distance learning, summer session for credit, part-time degree programs (daytime, evenings, summer), and internships. The most frequently chosen baccalaureate field is philosophy, religion, and theology.
Student Body Statistics The student body is made up of 817 undergraduates (189 freshmen). 40 percent are women and 60 percent are men. Students come from 48 states and territories. 26 percent are from Missouri. 0.9 percent are international students.
Expenses for 2002–03 *Application fee:* $25. *Comprehensive fee:* $10,693 includes full-time tuition ($6476), mandatory fees ($540), and college room and board ($3677). Full-time tuition and fees vary according to course load. *Part-time tuition:* $245 per credit. *Part-time mandatory fees:* $90 per term. Part-time tuition and fees vary according to course load.
Financial Aid Forms of aid include need-based and non-need-based scholarships and part-time jobs. The average aided 2002–03 undergraduate received an aid package worth an estimated $6469. The priority application deadline for financial aid is April 1.
Freshman Admission CBC requires an essay, a high school transcript, 3 recommendations, SAT I or ACT scores, and TOEFL scores for international students. A minimum 2.0 high school GPA is recommended. An interview is required for some. The application deadline for regular admission is rolling.
Transfer Admission The application deadline for admission is rolling.
Entrance Difficulty CBC assesses its entrance difficulty level as moderately difficult; noncompetitive for out-of-state applicants. For the fall 2002 freshman class, 71 percent of the applicants were accepted.

For Further Information Contact Mrs. Eunice A. Bruegman, Director of Admissions and Records, Central Bible College, 3000 North Grant Avenue, Springfield, MO 65803-1096. *Telephone:* 417-833-2551 Ext. 1184 or 800-831-4222 Ext. 1184 (toll-free). *Fax:* 417-833-5141. *E-mail:* info@cbcag.edu. *Web site:* http://www.cbcag.edu/.

CENTRAL CHRISTIAN COLLEGE OF THE BIBLE

Moberly, Missouri

Central Christian College is a coed, private, four-year college, founded in 1957, affiliated with the Christian Churches and Churches of Christ, offering degrees at the associate and bachelor's levels. It has a 40-acre campus in Moberly.

Expenses for 2002–03 *Application fee:* $25. *Comprehensive fee:* $8260 includes full-time tuition ($4200), mandatory fees ($550), and college room and board ($3510). Room and board charges vary according to board plan. *Part-time tuition:* varies with course load.

For Further Information Contact Ms. Misty Rodda, Director of Admissions, Central Christian College of the Bible, 911 Urbandale Drive East, Moberly, MO 65270-1997. *Telephone:* 660-263-3900 or 888-263-3900 (toll-free in-state). *Fax:* 660-263-3936. *E-mail:* iwant2be@cccb.edu. *Web site:* http://www.cccb.edu/.

CENTRAL METHODIST COLLEGE

Fayette, Missouri

CMC is a coed, private, Methodist, comprehensive institution, founded in 1854, offering degrees at the associate, bachelor's, and master's levels. It has a 52-acre campus in Fayette.

Academic Information The faculty has 112 members (46% full-time), 31% with terminal degrees. The undergraduate student-faculty ratio is 14:1. The library holds 97,793 titles, 316 serial subscriptions, and 379 audiovisual materials. Special programs include academic remediation, services for learning-disabled students, an honors program, study abroad, advanced placement credit, accelerated degree programs, double majors, independent study, distance learning, self-designed majors, summer session for credit, part-time degree programs (daytime, evenings, summer), internships, and arrangement for off-campus study with Mineral Area College, East Central College. The most frequently chosen baccalaureate fields are business/marketing, education, health professions and related sciences.
Student Body Statistics The student body totals 1,361, of whom 1,288 are undergraduates (236 freshmen). 58 percent are women and 42 percent are men. Students come from 20 states and territories. 97 percent are from Missouri. 0.9 percent are international students.
Expenses for 2003–04 *Application fee:* $0. *Comprehensive fee:* $18,680 includes full-time tuition ($13,160), mandatory fees ($600), and college room and board ($4920). *College room only:* $2420. *Part-time tuition:* $140 per credit hour. *Part-time mandatory fees:* $26 per credit hour. Part-time tuition and fees vary according to course load.
Financial Aid Forms of aid include need-based and non-need-based scholarships, athletic grants, and part-time jobs. The average aided 2001–02 undergraduate received an aid package worth $9801. The priority application deadline for financial aid is March 15.
Freshman Admission CMC requires a high school transcript, a minimum 2.0 high school GPA, SAT I or ACT scores, and TOEFL scores for international students. ACT scores are recommended. 2 recommendations are required for some. The application deadline for regular admission is August 1.
Transfer Admission The application deadline for admission is August 15.

Entrance Difficulty CMC assesses its entrance difficulty level as moderately difficult. For the fall 2002 freshman class, 76 percent of the applicants were accepted.

For Further Information Contact Mr. Don Hapward, Dean of Admissions and Financial Assistance, Central Methodist College, 411 Central Methodist Square, Fayette, MO 65248-1198. *Telephone:* 660-248-6247 or 888-CMC-1854 (toll-free in-state). *Fax:* 660-248-1872. *E-mail:* admissions@cmc.edu. *Web site:* http://www.cmc.edu/.

CENTRAL MISSOURI STATE UNIVERSITY

Warrensburg, Missouri

Central is a coed, public, comprehensive institution, founded in 1871, offering degrees at the associate, bachelor's, and master's levels and post-master's and postbachelor's certificates. It has a 1,240-acre campus in Warrensburg near Kansas City.

Academic Information The faculty has 592 members (72% full-time), 57% with terminal degrees. The undergraduate student-faculty ratio is 17:1. The library holds 567,934 titles, 3,582 serial subscriptions, and 23,690 audiovisual materials. Special programs include academic remediation, services for learning-disabled students, an honors program, cooperative (work-study) education, study abroad, advanced placement credit, ESL programs, double majors, distance learning, self-designed majors, summer session for credit, part-time degree programs (daytime, evenings, weekends, summer), adult/continuing education programs, internships, and arrangement for off-campus study. The most frequently chosen baccalaureate fields are business/marketing, education, protective services/public administration.

Student Body Statistics The student body totals 10,313, of whom 8,732 are undergraduates (1,327 freshmen). 54 percent are women and 46 percent are men. Students come from 43 states and territories and 65 other countries. 94 percent are from Missouri. 3.9 percent are international students. 11 percent of the 2002 graduating class went on to graduate and professional schools.

Expenses for 2003–04 *Application fee:* $25. *State resident tuition:* $4350 full-time, $145 per credit part-time. *Nonresident tuition:* $8700 full-time, $290 per credit part-time. *Mandatory fees:* $60 full-time. *College room and board:* $4630. *College room only:* $2900.

Financial Aid Forms of aid include need-based and non-need-based scholarships, athletic grants, and part-time jobs. The average aided 2001–02 undergraduate received an aid package worth $5929. The application deadline for financial aid is continuous.

Freshman Admission Central requires a high school transcript, rank in upper two-thirds of high school class, minimum ACT score of 20, ACT scores, and TOEFL scores for international students. Recommendations are required for some. The application deadline for regular admission is rolling.

Transfer Admission The application deadline for admission is rolling.

Entrance Difficulty Central assesses its entrance difficulty level as moderately difficult; very difficult for business, teacher education, nursing programs. For the fall 2002 freshman class, 79 percent of the applicants were accepted.

For Further Information Contact Mr. Matt Melvin, Director of Admissions, Central Missouri State University, 1401 Ward Edwards, Warrensburg, MO 64093. *Telephone:* 660-543-4290 or 800-729-2678 (toll-free in-state). *Fax:* 660-543-8517. *E-mail:* admit@cmsuvmb.cmsu.edu. *Web site:* http://www.cmsu.edu/.

CLEVELAND CHIROPRACTIC COLLEGE-KANSAS CITY CAMPUS

Kansas City, Missouri

Cleveland Chiropractic College-Kansas City Campus is a coed, private, upper-level institution, founded in 1922, offering degrees at the bachelor's and first professional levels.

Academic Information The faculty has 45 full-time members. The undergraduate student-faculty ratio is 15:1. The library holds 14,000 titles, 268 serial subscriptions, and 12,320 audiovisual materials. Special programs include academic remediation, services for learning-disabled students, cooperative (work-study) education, accelerated degree programs, summer session for credit, and internships.

Student Body Statistics The student body totals 467, of whom 61 are undergraduates. 39 percent are women and 61 percent are men. Students come from 18 states and territories. 20 percent are from Missouri. 41 percent are international students.

Expenses for 2003–04 *Application fee:* $35. *Tuition:* $3670 full-time. *Mandatory fees:* $150 full-time.

Transfer Admission Cleveland Chiropractic College-Kansas City Campus requires a college transcript and a minimum 2.5 college GPA.

Entrance Difficulty Cleveland Chiropractic College-Kansas City Campus has an open admission policy except cumulative college GPA of 2.0 or 2.0 high school GPA required to enter BS degree program.

For Further Information Contact Ms. Melissa Denton, Director of Admissions, Cleveland Chiropractic College-Kansas City Campus, 6401 Rockhill Road, Kansas City, MO 64131. *Telephone:* 816-501-0100 or 800-467-2252 (toll-free). *Fax:* 816-501-0205. *E-mail:* kc.admissions@cleveland.edu. *Web site:* http://www.cleveland.edu/.

COLLEGE OF THE OZARKS

Point Lookout, Missouri

C of O is a coed, private, Presbyterian, four-year college, founded in 1906, offering degrees at the bachelor's level. It has a 1,000-acre campus in Point Lookout.

Academic Information The faculty has 110 members (66% full-time), 48% with terminal degrees. The student-faculty ratio is 14:1. The library holds 118,235 titles, 503 serial subscriptions, and 5,193 audiovisual materials. Special programs include academic remediation, an honors program, cooperative (work-study) education, study abroad, advanced placement credit, accelerated degree programs, self-designed majors, summer session for credit, part-time degree programs, and internships. The most frequently chosen baccalaureate fields are business/marketing, education, protective services/public administration.

Student Body Statistics The student body is made up of 1,348 undergraduates (269 freshmen). 57 percent are women and 43 percent are men. Students come from 26 states and territories and 22 other countries. 67 percent are from Missouri. 1.6 percent are international students. 8 percent of the 2002 graduating class went on to graduate and professional schools.

Expenses for 2003–04 *Application fee:* $0. *Comprehensive fee:* $3040 includes full-time tuition ($0), mandatory fees ($200), and college room and board ($2840). *Part-time tuition:* $250 per credit. *Part-time mandatory fees:* $125 per term.

Financial Aid Forms of aid include need-based and non-need-based scholarships, athletic grants, and part-time jobs. The average aided 2001–02 undergraduate received an aid package worth $12,484. The priority application deadline for financial aid is March 15.

Freshman Admission C of O requires a high school transcript, 2 recommendations, an interview, medical history, financial statement, SAT I or ACT scores, and TOEFL scores for international students. An essay and a minimum 2.0 high school GPA are recommended. The application deadline for regular admission is February 15.

Transfer Admission The application deadline for admission is February 1.

Entrance Difficulty C of O assesses its entrance difficulty level as moderately difficult. For the fall 2002 freshman class, 12 percent of the applicants were accepted.

For Further Information Contact Mrs. Gayle Groves, Admissions Secretary, College of the Ozarks, PO Box 17, Point Lookout, MO 65726. *Telephone:* 417-334-6411 Ext. 4218 or 800-222-0525 (toll-free). *Fax:* 417-335-2618. *E-mail:* admiss4@cofo.edu. *Web site:* http://www.cofo.edu/.

COLUMBIA COLLEGE

Columbia, Missouri

Columbia College is a coed, private, comprehensive institution, founded in 1851, affiliated with the Christian Church (Disciples of Christ), offering degrees at the associate, bachelor's, and master's levels (offers continuing education program with significant enrollment not reflected in profile). It has a 29-acre campus in Columbia.

Academic Information The faculty has 85 members (60% full-time), 51% with terminal degrees. The undergraduate student-faculty ratio is 12:1. The library holds 62,265 titles, 382 serial subscriptions, and 3,613 audiovisual materials. Special programs include academic remediation, an honors program, cooperative (work-study) education, study abroad, advanced placement credit, accelerated degree programs, ESL programs, double majors, independent study, distance learning, self-designed majors, summer session for credit, part-time degree programs (daytime, evenings, summer), adult/continuing education programs, internships, and arrangement for off-campus study with 6 members of the Mid-Missouri Associated Colleges and Universities. The most frequently chosen baccalaureate fields are business/marketing, education, liberal arts/general studies.

Student Body Statistics The student body totals 1,038, of whom 886 are undergraduates (160 freshmen). 57 percent are women and 43 percent are men. Students come from 19 states and territories and 32 other countries. 94 percent are from Missouri. 6.6 percent are international students.

Expenses for 2002–03 *Application fee:* $25. *Comprehensive fee:* $15,592 includes full-time tuition ($10,926) and college room and board ($4666). *College room only:* $2936. Full-time tuition varies according to class time and course load. Room and board charges vary according to board plan. *Part-time tuition:* $234 per credit hour. Part-time tuition varies according to class time, course load, and location.

Financial Aid Forms of aid include need-based and non-need-based scholarships, athletic grants, and part-time jobs. The average aided 2002–03 undergraduate received an aid package worth an estimated $12,167. The priority application deadline for financial aid is March 1.

Freshman Admission Columbia College requires a high school transcript, a minimum 2.0 high school GPA, ACT scores, and TOEFL scores for international students. Rank in upper 50% of high school class and SAT I scores are recommended. An essay, recommendations, and an interview are required for some. The application deadline for regular admission is rolling.

Transfer Admission The application deadline for admission is rolling.

Entrance Difficulty Columbia College assesses its entrance difficulty level as minimally difficult. For the fall 2002 freshman class, 63 percent of the applicants were accepted.

SPECIAL MESSAGE TO STUDENTS

Social Life A strong Student Government Association plans and organizes social activities. There are more than thirty clubs and organizations, ranging from academic associations to special interest groups, providing myriad choices for students to get involved and experience leadership opportunities. Strong athletics are a tradition at Columbia College with a history of nationally ranked NAIA Division I teams. One of three institutions of higher education in town, Columbia College provides a vibrant small campus environment within a larger college community.

Academic Highlights Columbia College is known for its excellence in teaching and learning. Among the nearly thirty programs offered, those in criminal justice, art, education, and business are quite distinctive. The Writing and Math Centers build upon quality teaching in the classroom to provide opportunities for students to enhance their learning experience. INCC 111, Introduction to Columbia College, is a popular freshman orientation course team-taught by a full-time professor and an upperclass student. Study-abroad opportunities are available, and internships can be obtained for a more hands-on experience in any field.

Interviews and Campus Visits Located in a small city consistently recognized by national magazines as an exceptional place to live, Columbia College welcomes visitors to its beautiful historic campus. The campus dates from 1851 and has several distinct architectural features in its older buildings. Williams Hall is the oldest building west of the Mississippi still in continuous use for education purposes. Visitors have the opportunity to sit in on a class and meet faculty members and students as well as financial aid officials. Campus visits may be arranged weekdays from 8 a.m. to 5 p.m. by calling the Admissions Office at 573-875-7352 or 800-231-2391 Ext. 7352 (toll-free).

For Further Information Write to Ms. Regina M. Morin, Director of Admissions, Columbia College, 1001 Rogers Street, Columbia, MO 65216. *E-mail:* admissions@ccis.edu. *Web site:* http://www.ccis.edu.

See page 268 for a narrative description.

CONCEPTION SEMINARY COLLEGE

Conception, Missouri

Conception Seminary College is a men's, private, Roman Catholic, four-year college, founded in 1886, offering degrees at the bachelor's level. It has a 30-acre campus in Conception.

Academic Information The faculty has 21 members (95% full-time), 81% with terminal degrees. The student-faculty ratio is 4:1. The library holds 115,000 titles, 300 serial subscriptions, and 5,000 audiovisual materials. Special programs include academic remediation, advanced placement credit, ESL programs, double majors, independent study, and arrangement for off-campus study with Northwest Missouri State University. The most frequently chosen baccalaureate fields are liberal arts/general studies, philosophy, religion, and theology.

Student Body Statistics The student body is made up of 100 undergraduates (17 freshmen). Students come from 18 states and territories and 5 other countries. 33 percent are from Missouri.

Expenses for 2003–04 *Application fee:* $0. *Comprehensive fee:* $17,044 includes full-time tuition ($10,584), mandatory fees ($170), and college room and board ($6290). *College room only:* $2660. Room and board charges vary according to board plan. *Part-time tuition:* $100 per credit.

Financial Aid Forms of aid include need-based and non-need-based scholarships and part-time jobs. The average aided 2002–03 undergraduate received an aid package worth an estimated $8864. The application deadline for financial aid is continuous.

Freshman Admission Conception Seminary College requires an essay, a high school transcript, a minimum 2.0 high school GPA, 2 recommendations, church certificate, medical history, and ACT scores. The application deadline for regular admission is July 31.

Transfer Admission The application deadline for admission is July 31.

Entrance Difficulty Conception Seminary College assesses its entrance difficulty level as noncompetitive. For the fall 2002 freshman class, 100 percent of the applicants were accepted.

For Further Information Contact Mr. Keith Jiron, Director of Recruitment and Admissions, Conception Seminary College, PO Box 502, Highway 136 & VV, 37174 State Highway VV, Conception, MO 64433. *Telephone:* 660-944-2886. *Fax:* 660-944-2829. *E-mail:* vocations@conception.edu. *Web site:* http://www.conceptionabbey.org/.

COTTEY COLLEGE

Nevada, Missouri

Cottey is a women's, private, two-year college, founded in 1884, offering degrees at the associate level. It has a 51-acre campus in Nevada.

Academic Information The faculty has 37 members (95% full-time). The student-faculty ratio is 10:1. The library holds 54,200 titles and 246 serial subscriptions. Special programs include advanced placement credit and part-time degree programs (daytime).

Student Body Statistics The student body is made up of 350 undergraduates. Students come from 42 states and territories and 15 other countries. 22 percent are from Missouri. 13.5 percent are international students. 100 percent of the 2002 graduating class went on to four-year colleges.

Expenses for 2003–04 *Application fee:* $20. *Comprehensive fee:* $15,330 includes full-time tuition ($10,000), mandatory fees ($530), and college room and board ($4800).

Financial Aid Forms of aid include need-based scholarships and part-time jobs. The priority application deadline for financial aid is April 1.

Freshman Admission Cottey requires an essay, a high school transcript, 1 recommendation, SAT I or ACT scores, and TOEFL scores for international students. A minimum 2.6 high school GPA and an interview are recommended. The application deadline for regular admission is rolling.

Transfer Admission The application deadline for admission is rolling.

Entrance Difficulty Cottey assesses its entrance difficulty level as moderately difficult. For the fall 2002 freshman class, 58 percent of the applicants were accepted.

For Further Information Contact Ms. Marjorie J. Cooke, Dean of Enrollment Management, Cottey College, 1000 West Austin, Nevada, MO 64772. *Telephone:* 417-667-8181 or 888-526-8839 (toll-free). *Fax:* 417-667-8103. *E-mail:* enrollmgt@cottey.edu. *Web site:* http://www.cottey.edu/.

CULVER-STOCKTON COLLEGE

Canton, Missouri

Culver-Stockton is a coed, private, four-year college, founded in 1853, affiliated with the Christian Church (Disciples of Christ), offering degrees at the bachelor's level. It has a 143-acre campus in Canton.

Academic Information The faculty has 73 members (79% full-time), 66% with terminal degrees. The student-faculty ratio is 12:1. The library holds 155,487 titles, 777 serial subscriptions, and 4,327 audiovisual materials. Special programs include an honors program, study abroad, advanced placement credit, double majors, independent study, self-designed majors, summer session for credit, part-time degree programs, internships, and arrangement for off-campus study with Central College. The most frequently chosen baccalaureate fields are business/marketing, education, health professions and related sciences.

Student Body Statistics The student body is made up of 828 undergraduates (224 freshmen). 57 percent are women and 43 percent are men. Students come from 28 states and territories and 8 other countries. 56 percent are from Missouri. 1.3 percent are international students. 10 percent of the 2002 graduating class went on to graduate and professional schools.

Expenses for 2002–03 *Application fee:* $25. *Comprehensive fee:* $17,000 includes full-time tuition ($11,800) and college room and board ($5200). *College room only:* $2400. Room and board charges vary according to board plan. *Part-time tuition:* $325 per credit hour.

Financial Aid Forms of aid include need-based and non-need-based scholarships, athletic grants, and part-time jobs. The average aided 2002–03 undergraduate received an aid package worth an estimated $11,614. The application deadline for financial aid is June 15.

Freshman Admission Culver-Stockton requires a high school transcript, a minimum 2.0 high school GPA, SAT I or ACT scores, and TOEFL scores for international students. An essay, recommendations, and an interview are recommended. An interview is required for some.

Transfer Admission The application deadline for admission is rolling.

Entrance Difficulty Culver-Stockton assesses its entrance difficulty level as moderately difficult. For the fall 2002 freshman class, 77 percent of the applicants were accepted.

For Further Information Contact Mr. Ron Cronacher, Director of Enrollment Services, Culver-Stockton College, One College Hill, Canton, MO 63435-1299. *Telephone:* 800-537-1883 or 800-537-1883 (toll-free out-of-state). *Fax:* 217-231-6618. *E-mail:* enrollment@culver.edu. *Web site:* http://www.culver.edu/.

DEACONESS COLLEGE OF NURSING

St. Louis, Missouri

Deaconess is a coed, primarily women's, proprietary, four-year college, founded in 1889, offering degrees at the associate and bachelor's levels in nursing. It has a 15-acre campus in St. Louis.

Academic Information The faculty has 14 members (79% full-time), 79% with terminal degrees. The student-faculty ratio is 12:1. The library holds 8,700 titles and 233 serial subscriptions. Special programs include academic remediation, advanced placement credit, ESL programs, summer session for credit, part-time degree programs, and arrangement for off-campus study with Fontbonne College. The most frequently chosen baccalaureate field is health professions and related sciences.

Student Body Statistics The student body is made up of 324 undergraduates (160 freshmen). 98 percent are women and 2 percent are men. Students come from 15 states and territories.

Expenses for 2002–03 *Application fee:* $30. *Comprehensive fee:* $15,136 includes full-time tuition ($9800), mandatory fees ($136), and college room and board ($5200). Room and board charges vary according to housing facility.

Financial Aid Forms of aid include need-based and non-need-based scholarships and part-time jobs. The average aided 2002–03 undergraduate received an aid package worth an estimated $7081. The priority application deadline for financial aid is April 1.

Freshman Admission Deaconess requires an essay, a high school transcript, ACT scores, and TOEFL scores for international students. A minimum 2.5 high school GPA is recommended. Recommendations and an interview are required for some. The application deadline for regular admission is rolling.

Transfer Admission The application deadline for admission is rolling.

Entrance Difficulty Deaconess assesses its entrance difficulty level as moderately difficult.

For Further Information Contact Ms. Lisa Mancini, Dean of Enrollment and Student Services, Deaconess College of Nursing, 6150 Oakland Avenue, St. Louis, MO 63139-3215. *Telephone:* 314-768-3179 or 800-942-4310 (toll-free). *Fax:* 314-768-5673. *Web site:* http://www.deaconess.edu/.

DEVRY UNIVERSITY

Kansas City, Missouri

DeVry is a coed, proprietary, four-year college of DeVry University, founded in 1931, offering degrees at the associate and bachelor's levels and postbachelor's certificates. It has a 12-acre campus in Kansas City.

Academic Information The faculty has 133 members (52% full-time). The student-faculty ratio is 18:1. The library holds 15,000 titles, 68 serial subscriptions, and 457 audiovisual materials. Special programs include academic remediation, services for learning-disabled students, cooperative (work-study) education, advanced placement credit, accelerated degree programs, distance learning, summer session for credit, part-time degree programs (daytime, evenings, weekends, summer), and adult/continuing education programs. The most frequently chosen baccalaureate fields are business/marketing, computer/information sciences, engineering/engineering technologies.

Student Body Statistics The student body totals 2,590, of whom 2,374 are undergraduates (395 freshmen). 24 percent are women and 76 percent are men. Students come from 28 states and territories and 8 other countries. 58 percent are from Missouri. 0.8 percent are international students.

Expenses for 2003–04 *Application fee:* $50. *Tuition:* $9990 full-time, $355 per credit hour part-time. *Mandatory fees:* $165 full-time. Full-time tuition and fees vary according to course load. Part-time tuition varies according to course load.

Financial Aid Forms of aid include need-based and non-need-based scholarships and part-time jobs. The average aided 2001–02 undergraduate received an aid package worth $7095. The application deadline for financial aid is continuous.

DeVry University (continued)

Freshman Admission DeVry requires a high school transcript, an interview, CPT, TOEFL scores for international students, and CPT. SAT I or ACT scores are recommended. The application deadline for regular admission is rolling.
Transfer Admission The application deadline for admission is rolling.
Entrance Difficulty DeVry assesses its entrance difficulty level as minimally difficult; moderately difficult for electronics engineering technology program. For the fall 2002 freshman class, 71 percent of the applicants were accepted.

For Further Information Contact Ms. Anna Diamond, New Student Coordinator, DeVry University, 11224 Holmes Street, Kansas City, MO 64131. *Telephone:* 816-941-2810 or 800-821-3766 (toll-free out-of-state). *Fax:* 816-941-0896. *Web site:* http://www.kc.devry.edu/.

DRURY UNIVERSITY

Springfield, Missouri

Drury is a coed, private, comprehensive institution, founded in 1873, offering degrees at the bachelor's and master's levels (also offers evening program with significant enrollment not reflected in profile). It has a 60-acre campus in Springfield.

Academic Information The faculty has 154 members (75% full-time), 77% with terminal degrees. The undergraduate student-faculty ratio is 11:1. The library holds 177,794 titles, 868 serial subscriptions, and 60,098 audiovisual materials. Special programs include services for learning-disabled students, an honors program, cooperative (work-study) education, study abroad, advanced placement credit, accelerated degree programs, ESL programs, double majors, independent study, distance learning, self-designed majors, summer session for credit, part-time degree programs (daytime, evenings, summer), adult/continuing education programs, internships, and arrangement for off-campus study. The most frequently chosen baccalaureate fields are biological/life sciences, business/marketing, communications/communication technologies.
Student Body Statistics The student body totals 1,805, of whom 1,494 are undergraduates (381 freshmen). 56 percent are women and 44 percent are men. Students come from 35 states and territories and 50 other countries. 80 percent are from Missouri. 5.8 percent are international students. 26 percent of the 2002 graduating class went on to graduate and professional schools.
Expenses for 2003–04 *Application fee:* $25. *Comprehensive fee:* $18,099 includes full-time tuition ($12,995), mandatory fees ($219), and college room and board ($4885). Room and board charges vary according to board plan and housing facility. *Part-time tuition:* $428 per semester hour.
Financial Aid Forms of aid include need-based and non-need-based scholarships, athletic grants, and part-time jobs. The average aided 2002–03 undergraduate received an aid package worth an estimated $7985. The priority application deadline for financial aid is March 15.
Freshman Admission Drury requires an essay, a high school transcript, a minimum 2.7 high school GPA, 1 recommendation, minimum ACT score of 21, SAT I or ACT scores, and TOEFL scores for international students. An interview is recommended. The application deadline for regular admission is March 15.
Transfer Admission The application deadline for admission is rolling.
Entrance Difficulty Drury assesses its entrance difficulty level as moderately difficult. For the fall 2002 freshman class, 83 percent of the applicants were accepted.

For Further Information Contact Mr. Chip Parker, Director of Admission, Drury University, 900 North Benton, Bay Hall, Springfield, MO 65802. *Telephone:* 417-873-7205 or 800-922-2274 (toll-free). *Fax:* 417-866-3873. *E-mail:* druryad@drury.edu. *Web site:* http://www.drury.edu/.

EVANGEL UNIVERSITY

Springfield, Missouri

Evangel University is a coed, private, Assemblies of God, comprehensive institution, founded in 1955, affiliated with the Assemblies of God, offering degrees at the associate, bachelor's, and master's levels. It has an 80-acre campus in Springfield.

Academic Information The faculty has 144 members (67% full-time), 41% with terminal degrees. The undergraduate student-faculty ratio is 18:1. The library holds 100,691 titles, 1,060 serial subscriptions, and 6,962 audiovisual materials. Special programs include academic remediation, services for learning-disabled students, advanced placement credit, accelerated degree programs, double majors, summer session for credit, part-time degree programs (daytime, summer), adult/continuing education programs, and internships. The most frequently chosen baccalaureate fields are business/marketing, education, psychology.
Student Body Statistics The student body totals 1,666, of whom 1,597 are undergraduates (442 freshmen). 60 percent are women and 40 percent are men. Students come from 51 states and territories. 49 percent are from Missouri. 0.4 percent are international students.
Expenses for 2003–04 *Application fee:* $25. *Comprehensive fee:* $15,435 includes full-time tuition ($10,610), mandatory fees ($695), and college room and board ($4130). *College room only:* $1960. Full-time tuition and fees vary according to course load. Room and board charges vary according to board plan. *Part-time tuition:* $414 per credit hour. *Part-time mandatory fees:* $235 per term.
Financial Aid Forms of aid include need-based and non-need-based scholarships, athletic grants, and part-time jobs. The average aided 2001–02 undergraduate received an aid package worth $7795. The priority application deadline for financial aid is March 1.
Freshman Admission Evangel University requires a high school transcript, SAT I or ACT scores, and TOEFL scores for international students. A minimum 2.0 high school GPA is recommended. The application deadline for regular admission is August 1.
Transfer Admission The application deadline for admission is August 1.
Entrance Difficulty Evangel University assesses its entrance difficulty level as moderately difficult. For the fall 2002 freshman class, 89 percent of the applicants were accepted.

For Further Information Contact Ms. Charity Waltner, Director of Admissions, Evangel University, 1111 North Glenstone, Springfield, MO 65802. *Telephone:* 417-865-2811 Ext. 7262 or 800-382-6435 (toll-free in-state). *Fax:* 417-865-9599. *E-mail:* admissions@evangel.edu. *Web site:* http://www.evangel.edu/.

FONTBONNE UNIVERSITY

St. Louis, Missouri

Fontbonne University is a coed, private, Roman Catholic, comprehensive institution, founded in 1917, offering degrees at the bachelor's and master's levels and postbachelor's certificates. It has a 13-acre campus in St. Louis.

Academic Information The faculty has 194 members (28% full-time), 48% with terminal degrees. The undergraduate student-faculty ratio is 12:1. The library holds 102,552 titles, 333 serial subscriptions, and 14,983 audiovisual materials. Special programs include academic remediation, services for learning-disabled students, an honors program, cooperative (work-study) education, advanced placement credit, accelerated degree programs, ESL programs, double majors, independent study, distance learning, self-designed majors, summer session for credit, adult/continuing education programs, internships, and arrangement for off-campus study with Webster University, Maryville College, Lindenwood College, Missouri Baptist College. The most frequently chosen baccalaureate fields are business/marketing, education, visual/performing arts.
Student Body Statistics The student body totals 2,344, of whom 1,611 are undergraduates (190 freshmen). 76 percent are women and 24 percent are men. Students come from 21 states and territories and 1 other country. 86 percent are from Missouri. 0.5 percent are international students. 25 percent of the 2002 graduating class went on to graduate and professional schools.
Expenses for 2002–03 *Application fee:* $25. *Comprehensive fee:* $20,249 includes full-time tuition ($13,414), mandatory fees ($300), and college room and board ($6535). Full-time tuition and fees vary according to class time, program, and reciprocity agreements. Room and board charges vary according to board plan and housing facility. *Part-time tuition:* $380 per

credit hour. *Part-time mandatory fees:* $15 per hour. Part-time tuition and fees vary according to class time, course load, program, and reciprocity agreements.
Financial Aid Forms of aid include need-based and non-need-based scholarships and part-time jobs. The average aided 2002–03 undergraduate received an aid package worth an estimated $15,600. The priority application deadline for financial aid is April 30.
Freshman Admission Fontbonne University requires an essay, a high school transcript, a minimum 2.5 high school GPA, SAT I or ACT scores, and TOEFL scores for international students. 2 recommendations and an interview are recommended. The application deadline for regular admission is August 1.
Transfer Admission The application deadline for admission is rolling.
Entrance Difficulty Fontbonne University assesses its entrance difficulty level as moderately difficult. For the fall 2002 freshman class, 81 percent of the applicants were accepted.

For Further Information Contact Ms. Peggy Musen, Associate Dean for Enrollment Management, Fontbonne University, 6800 Wydown Boulevard, St. Louis, MO 63105-3098. *Telephone:* 314-889-1400. *Fax:* 314-719-8021. *E-mail:* pmusen@fontbonne.edu. *Web site:* http://www.fontbonne.edu/.

GLOBAL UNIVERSITY OF THE ASSEMBLIES OF GOD

Springfield, Missouri

Global University of the Assemblies of God is a coed, private, comprehensive institution, founded in 1948, affiliated with the Assemblies of God, offering degrees at the associate, bachelor's, and master's levels in biblical studies (offers only external degree programs).

Academic Information The faculty has 480 members (11% full-time), 31% with terminal degrees. The library holds 180 serial subscriptions. Special programs include academic remediation, an honors program, cooperative (work-study) education, advanced placement credit, accelerated degree programs, independent study, distance learning, part-time degree programs, external degree programs, adult/continuing education programs, and internships. The most frequently chosen baccalaureate field is philosophy, religion, and theology.
Student Body Statistics The student body totals 6,547, of whom 6,252 are undergraduates. 35 percent are women and 65 percent are men. Students come from 50 states and territories and 123 other countries. 3 percent are from Missouri.
Expenses for 2002–03 *Application fee:* $35. *Tuition:* $2040 full-time, $85 per credit hour part-time. Full-time tuition varies according to location and reciprocity agreements. Part-time tuition varies according to course load, location, and reciprocity agreements.
Freshman Admission Global University of the Assemblies of God requires a high school transcript. An essay is recommended. 1 recommendation is required for some. The application deadline for regular admission is rolling.
Transfer Admission The application deadline for admission is rolling.
Entrance Difficulty Global University of the Assemblies of God has an open admission policy.

For Further Information Contact Ms. Jessica Dorn, Director of US Enrollments, Global University of the Assemblies of God, 1211 South Glenstone Avenue, Springfield, MO 65804. *Telephone:* 800-443-1083 or 800-443-1083 (toll-free). *Fax:* 417-862-5318. *Web site:* http://www.globaluniversity.edu/.

HANNIBAL-LAGRANGE COLLEGE

Hannibal, Missouri

HLG is a coed, private, Southern Baptist, four-year college, founded in 1858, offering degrees at the associate and bachelor's levels. It has a 110-acre campus in Hannibal.

Academic Information The faculty has 87 members (59% full-time), 30% with terminal degrees. The student-faculty ratio is 13:1. The library holds 71,680 titles, 516 serial subscriptions, and 6,605 audiovisual materials. Special programs include academic remediation, services for learning-disabled students, an honors program, cooperative (work-study) education, study abroad, advanced placement credit, accelerated degree programs, Freshman Honors College, double majors, independent study, self-designed majors, summer session for credit, part-time degree programs, adult/continuing education programs, and internships. The most frequently chosen baccalaureate fields are business/marketing, education, protective services/public administration.
Student Body Statistics The student body is made up of 1,117 undergraduates. Students come from 24 states and territories and 8 other countries. 76 percent are from Missouri. 1.6 percent are international students. 3 percent of the 2002 graduating class went on to graduate and professional schools.
Expenses for 2003–04 *Application fee:* $25. *Comprehensive fee:* $13,670 includes full-time tuition ($9660), mandatory fees ($300), and college room and board ($3710). Full-time tuition and fees vary according to course load and program. Room and board charges vary according to board plan and housing facility. *Part-time tuition:* $322 per credit hour. *Part-time mandatory fees:* $70 per term. Part-time tuition and fees vary according to course load and program.
Financial Aid Forms of aid include need-based and non-need-based scholarships and part-time jobs. The average aided 2001–02 undergraduate received an aid package worth $5310. The application deadline for financial aid is continuous.
Freshman Admission HLG requires a high school transcript, 2 recommendations, SAT I or ACT scores, and TOEFL scores for international students. The application deadline for regular admission is August 26.
Transfer Admission The application deadline for admission is rolling.
Entrance Difficulty HLG assesses its entrance difficulty level as moderately difficult. For the fall 2002 freshman class, 97 percent of the applicants were accepted.

For Further Information Contact Mr. Raymond Carty, Dean of Enrollment Management, Hannibal-LaGrange College, 2800 Palmyra Road, Hannibal, MO 63401-1999. *Telephone:* 573-221-3113 or 800-HLG-1119 (toll-free). *Fax:* 573-221-6594. *E-mail:* admissio@hlg.edu. *Web site:* http://www.hlg.edu/.

HARRIS-STOWE STATE COLLEGE

St. Louis, Missouri

Harris-Stowe State College is a coed, public, four-year college of Missouri Coordinating Board for Higher Education, founded in 1857, offering degrees at the bachelor's level. It has a 22-acre campus in St. Louis.

Academic Information The faculty has 68 members (76% full-time), 66% with terminal degrees. The student-faculty ratio is 18:1. The library holds 60,000 titles, 340 serial subscriptions, and 15 audiovisual materials. Special programs include academic remediation, services for learning-disabled students, cooperative (work-study) education, advanced placement credit, self-designed majors, summer session for credit, part-time degree programs (daytime, evenings, weekends, summer), internships, and arrangement for off-campus study with Saint Louis University, University of Missouri–St. Louis. The most frequently chosen baccalaureate fields are business/marketing, education, protective services/public administration.
Student Body Statistics The student body is made up of 1,968 undergraduates (1,322 freshmen). 66 percent are women and 34 percent are men. Students come from 5 states and territories and 21 other countries. 91 percent are from Missouri. 1.9 percent are international students.
Expenses for 2002–03 *Application fee:* $15. *State resident tuition:* $2880 full-time, $120 per credit hour part-time. *Nonresident tuition:* $5674 full-time, $236.40 per credit hour part-time. *Mandatory fees:* $160 full-time, $80 per term part-time. Full-time tuition and fees vary according to program. Part-time tuition and fees vary according to program.

Harris-Stowe State College (continued)

Financial Aid Forms of aid include need-based and non-need-based scholarships, athletic grants, and part-time jobs. The priority application deadline for financial aid is April 1.
Freshman Admission Harris-Stowe State College requires a high school transcript, a minimum 2.0 high school GPA, SAT I or ACT scores, and TOEFL scores for international students. The application deadline for regular admission is rolling.
Transfer Admission The application deadline for admission is rolling.
Entrance Difficulty Harris-Stowe State College assesses its entrance difficulty level as moderately difficult.

For Further Information Contact Ms. LaShanda Boone, Interim Director of Admissions, Harris-Stowe State College, 3026 Laclede Avenue, St. Louis, MO 63103. *Telephone:* 314-340-3301. *Fax:* 314-340-3555. *E-mail:* admissions@hssc.edu. *Web site:* http://www.hssc.edu/.

IHM HEALTH STUDIES CENTER

St. Louis, Missouri

For Information Write to IHM Health Studies Center, St. Louis, MO 63143-2636.

ITT TECHNICAL INSTITUTE

Arnold, Missouri

ITT Technical Institute is a coed, proprietary, primarily two-year college of ITT Educational Services, Inc, offering degrees at the associate and bachelor's levels.

Student Body Statistics The student body is made up of 460 undergraduates.
Expenses for 2003–04 *Application fee:* $100.
Financial Aid Forms of aid include need-based scholarships and part-time jobs. The application deadline for financial aid is continuous.
Freshman Admission ITT Technical Institute requires a high school transcript, an interview, and Wonderlic aptitude test. Recommendations are recommended. The application deadline for regular admission is rolling.
Transfer Admission The application deadline for admission is rolling.
Entrance Difficulty ITT Technical Institute assesses its entrance difficulty level as minimally difficult.

For Further Information Contact Mr. James R. Rowe, Director of Recruitment, ITT Technical Institute, 1930 Meyer Drury Drive, Arnold, MO 63010. *Telephone:* 636-464-6600 or 888-488-1082 (toll-free). *Fax:* 636-464-6611. *Web site:* http://www.itt-tech.edu/.

ITT TECHNICAL INSTITUTE

Earth City, Missouri

ITT Tech is a coed, proprietary, primarily two-year college of ITT Educational Services, Inc, founded in 1936, offering degrees at the associate and bachelor's levels. It has a 2-acre campus in Earth City near St. Louis.

Student Body Statistics The student body is made up of 607 undergraduates.
Expenses for 2002–03 *Application fee:* $100. *Tuition:* $347 per credit hour part-time.
Financial Aid Forms of aid include need-based scholarships and part-time jobs. The application deadline for financial aid is continuous.
Freshman Admission ITT Tech requires a high school transcript, an interview, TOEFL scores for international students, and Wonderlic aptitude test. Recommendations are recommended. The application deadline for regular admission is rolling.
Transfer Admission The application deadline for admission is rolling.
Entrance Difficulty ITT Tech assesses its entrance difficulty level as minimally difficult.

For Further Information Contact Mr. Randal Hayes, ITT Technical Institute, 13505 Lakefront Drive, Earth City, MO 63045. *Telephone:* 314-298-7800 or 800-235-5488 (toll-free). *Fax:* 314-298-0559. *Web site:* http://www.itt-tech.edu/.

JEWISH HOSPITAL COLLEGE OF NURSING AND ALLIED HEALTH

St. Louis, Missouri

Jewish Hospital College is a coed, primarily women's, private, comprehensive institution, founded in 1902, offering degrees at the associate, bachelor's, and master's levels and post-master's and postbachelor's certificates.

Academic Information The faculty has 43 members (77% full-time), 40% with terminal degrees. The undergraduate student-faculty ratio is 10:1. The library holds 3,765 titles, 232 serial subscriptions, and 400 audiovisual materials. Special programs include services for learning-disabled students, advanced placement credit, double majors, independent study, summer session for credit, part-time degree programs (daytime, evenings, weekends, summer), and arrangement for off-campus study with Washington University in St. Louis. The most frequently chosen baccalaureate field is health professions and related sciences.
Student Body Statistics The student body totals 640, of whom 563 are undergraduates (48 freshmen). 88 percent are women and 12 percent are men. Students come from 7 states and territories. 60 percent are from Missouri. 10 percent of the 2002 graduating class went on to graduate and professional schools.
Expenses for 2002–03 *Application fee:* $25. *Tuition:* $11,319 full-time, $343 per term part-time. *Mandatory fees:* $200 full-time, $35 per term part-time. Full-time tuition and fees vary according to course load. Part-time tuition and fees vary according to course load. *College room only:* $2385.
Financial Aid Forms of aid include need-based and non-need-based scholarships and part-time jobs. The average aided 2002–03 undergraduate received an aid package worth an estimated $12,000. The priority application deadline for financial aid is April 1.
Freshman Admission Jewish Hospital College requires a high school transcript, a minimum 2.5 high school GPA, 2 recommendations, and SAT I or ACT scores. An interview and SCAT are required for some. The application deadline for regular admission is rolling.
Transfer Admission The application deadline for admission is rolling.
Entrance Difficulty Jewish Hospital College assesses its entrance difficulty level as moderately difficult. For the fall 2002 freshman class, 100 percent of the applicants were accepted.

For Further Information Contact Ms. Christie Schneider, Chief Admissions Officer, Jewish Hospital College of Nursing and Allied Health, 306 S. Kingshighway Boulevard, St. Louis, MO 63110. *Telephone:* 314-454-7538 or 800-832-9009 (toll-free in-state). *Fax:* 314-454-5239. *E-mail:* jhcollegeinguiry@bjc.org. *Web site:* http://jhconah.edu.

KANSAS CITY ART INSTITUTE

Kansas City, Missouri

KCAI is a coed, private, four-year college, founded in 1885, offering degrees at the bachelor's level in art. It has a 12-acre campus in Kansas City.

Academic Information The faculty has 86 members (51% full-time), 73% with terminal degrees. The student-faculty ratio is 9:1. The library holds 30,000 titles and 125 serial subscriptions. Special programs include academic remediation, services for learning-disabled students, cooperative (work-study) education, study abroad, advanced placement credit, ESL programs, double majors, independent study, summer session for credit, adult/continuing education programs, internships, and arrangement for off-campus study with New York Studio Program, AICAD School Exchange. The most frequently chosen baccalaureate field is visual/performing arts.

Student Body Statistics The student body is made up of 548 undergraduates (113 freshmen). 54 percent are women and 46 percent are men. Students come from 33 states and territories and 9 other countries. 39 percent are from Missouri. 2.2 percent are international students. 35 percent of the 2002 graduating class went on to graduate and professional schools.

Expenses for 2002–03 *Application fee:* $25. *Comprehensive fee:* $26,850 includes full-time tuition ($19,274), mandatory fees ($1036), and college room and board ($6540). *College room only:* $3900. Room and board charges vary according to board plan and housing facility. *Part-time tuition:* $800 per credit hour.

Financial Aid Forms of aid include need-based and non-need-based scholarships and part-time jobs. The average aided 2002–03 undergraduate received an aid package worth an estimated $15,661. The priority application deadline for financial aid is March 1.

Freshman Admission KCAI requires an essay, a high school transcript, a minimum 2.5 high school GPA, 2 recommendations, portfolio, statement of purpose, SAT I or ACT scores, and TOEFL scores for international students. An interview is recommended. The application deadline for regular admission is rolling.

Transfer Admission The application deadline for admission is rolling.

Entrance Difficulty KCAI assesses its entrance difficulty level as moderately difficult. For the fall 2002 freshman class, 83 percent of the applicants were accepted.

For Further Information Contact Mr. Gerald Valet, Director of Admission Technology, Kansas City Art Institute, 4415 Warwick Boulevard, Kansas City, MO 64111-1874. *Telephone:* 816-474-5224 or 800-522-5224 (toll-free). *Fax:* 816-802-3309. *E-mail:* admiss@kcai.edu. *Web site:* http://www.kcai.edu/.

KANSAS CITY COLLEGE OF LEGAL STUDIES

Kansas City, Missouri

Kansas City College of Legal Studies is a coed, proprietary, four-year college, offering degrees at the associate and bachelor's levels.

For Further Information Contact Mrs. Rosemary Velez, Admissions Director, Kansas City College of Legal Studies, 402 East Bannister Road, Suite A, Kansas City, MO 64131. *Telephone:* 816-444-2232, 816-444-2232 (toll-free in-state), or 877-582-3963 (toll-free out-of-state). *Fax:* 816-444-3142. *Web site:* http://www.metropolitancollege.edu/.

LESTER L. COX COLLEGE OF NURSING AND HEALTH SCIENCES

Springfield, Missouri

Lester L. Cox College of Nursing and Health Sciences is a coed, primarily women's, private, four-year college, founded in 1994, offering degrees at the associate and bachelor's levels.

Academic Information The faculty has 22 members (73% full-time), 5% with terminal degrees. The student-faculty ratio is 15:1. Special programs include academic remediation, accelerated degree programs, summer session for credit, and part-time degree programs (daytime, evenings). The most frequently chosen baccalaureate field is health professions and related sciences.

Student Body Statistics The student body is made up of 445 undergraduates (58 freshmen). 92 percent are women and 8 percent are men. Students come from 4 states and territories. 99 percent are from Missouri.

Expenses for 2003–04 *Application fee:* $30. *One-time mandatory fee:* $40. *Tuition:* $6600 full-time, $284 per credit hour part-time. *Mandatory fees:* $330 full-time, $165 per term part-time. Full-time tuition and fees vary according to course load and program. Part-time tuition and fees vary according to course load and program. *College room only:* $2000.

Financial Aid The average aided 2002–03 undergraduate received an aid package worth an estimated $8500. The priority application deadline for financial aid is April 1.

Freshman Admission Lester L. Cox College of Nursing and Health Sciences requires a high school transcript, a minimum 2.5 high school GPA, and ACT scores. The application deadline for regular admission is February 1 and for early decision it is November 1.

Entrance Difficulty For the fall 2002 freshman class, 51 percent of the applicants were accepted.

For Further Information Contact Ms. Jennifer Plimmer, Admission Coordinator, Lester L. Cox College of Nursing and Health Sciences, 1423 North Jefferson, Springfield, MO 65802. *Telephone:* 417-269-3069 or 866-898-5355 (toll-free in-state). *Fax:* 417-269-3581. *E-mail:* jplimme@coxcollege.edu. *Web site:* http://www.coxcollege.edu.

LINCOLN UNIVERSITY

Jefferson City, Missouri

LU is a coed, public, comprehensive unit of Missouri Coordinating Board for Higher Education, founded in 1866, offering degrees at the associate, bachelor's, and master's levels. It has a 152-acre campus in Jefferson City.

For Further Information Contact Executive Director of Enrollment Management, Lincoln University, 820 Chestnut, Jefferson City, MO 65102. *Telephone:* 573-681-5599 or 800-521-5052 (toll-free). *Fax:* 573-681-6074. *Web site:* http://www.lincolnu.edu/.

LINDENWOOD UNIVERSITY

St. Charles, Missouri

Lindenwood is a coed, private, Presbyterian, comprehensive institution, founded in 1827, offering degrees at the bachelor's and master's levels and post-master's certificates. It has a 358-acre campus in St. Charles near St. Louis.

Academic Information The faculty has 330 members (47% full-time). The undergraduate student-faculty ratio is 17:1. The library holds 130,412 titles, 3,789 serial subscriptions, and 2,748 audiovisual materials. Special programs include academic remediation, services for learning-disabled students, an honors program, cooperative (work-study) education, study abroad, advanced placement credit, accelerated degree programs, Freshman Honors College, double majors, independent study, self-designed majors, summer session for credit, part-time degree programs (daytime, evenings, weekends, summer), external degree programs, adult/continuing education programs, internships, and arrangement for off-campus study with St. Louis Private College Consortium, Washington University in St. Louis, University of Missouri–Columbia. The most frequently chosen baccalaureate fields are business/marketing, communications/communication technologies, education.

Student Body Statistics The student body totals 6,937, of whom 4,446 are undergraduates (674 freshmen). 54 percent are women and 46 percent are men. Students come from 47 states and territories and 63 other countries. 89 percent are from Missouri. 8.4 percent are international students.

Expenses for 2002–03 *Application fee:* $25. *One-time mandatory fee:* $200. *Comprehensive fee:* $17,250 includes full-time tuition ($11,200), mandatory fees ($450), and college room and board ($5600). *College room only:* $2800. *Part-time tuition:* $300 per credit hour. Part-time tuition varies according to course load.

Financial Aid Forms of aid include need-based and non-need-based scholarships and part-time jobs. The priority application deadline for financial aid is March 15.

Freshman Admission Lindenwood requires a high school transcript, a minimum 2.0 high school GPA, minimum ACT score of 20 or minimum SAT score of 900, SAT I or ACT scores, and TOEFL scores for

Lindenwood University (continued)
international students. An essay, recommendations, and an interview are required for some. The application deadline for regular admission is rolling.
Transfer Admission The application deadline for admission is rolling.
Entrance Difficulty Lindenwood assesses its entrance difficulty level as moderately difficult. For the fall 2002 freshman class, 47 percent of the applicants were accepted.

For Further Information Contact Mr. John Guffey, Dean of Admissions, Lindenwood University, 209 South Kingshighway, St. Charles, MO 63301-1695. *Telephone:* 636-949-4933. *Fax:* 636-949-4989. *Web site:* http://www.lindenwood.edu/.

LOGAN UNIVERSITY-COLLEGE OF CHIROPRACTIC

Chesterfield, Missouri

Logan is a coed, private, upper-level institution, founded in 1935, offering degrees at the incidental bachelor's and first professional levels in health sciences. It has a 100-acre campus in Chesterfield near St. Louis.

Academic Information The faculty has 90 members (54% full-time), 97% with terminal degrees. The undergraduate student-faculty ratio is 12:1. The library holds 12,838 titles, 225 serial subscriptions, and 2,078 audiovisual materials. Special programs include services for learning-disabled students, advanced placement credit, independent study, distance learning, adult/continuing education programs, and internships. The most frequently chosen baccalaureate field is biological/life sciences.
Student Body Statistics The student body totals 874, of whom 92 are undergraduates. 33 percent are women and 67 percent are men. Students come from 24 states and territories and 4 other countries. 30 percent are from Missouri. 2.2 percent are international students.
Expenses for 2003–04 *Application fee:* $50. *Tuition:* $3000 full-time, $1500 per semester hour part-time. *Mandatory fees:* $220 full-time, $110.
Financial Aid Forms of aid include need-based and non-need-based scholarships and part-time jobs. The priority application deadline for financial aid is April 30.
Transfer Admission Logan requires a minimum 2.0 college GPA and a college transcript. Standardized test scores are required for some. The application deadline for admission is rolling.
Entrance Difficulty Logan assesses its entrance difficulty level as moderately difficult.

For Further Information Contact Dr. Patrick Browne, Vice President of Enrollment, Logan University-College of Chiropractic, 1851 Schoettler Road, Chesterfield, MO 63006-1065. *Telephone:* 636-227-2100 Ext. 149 or 800-533-9210 (toll-free). *Fax:* 636-227-9338. *E-mail:* loganadm@logan.edu. *Web site:* http://www.logan.edu/.

MARYVILLE UNIVERSITY OF SAINT LOUIS

St. Louis, Missouri

Maryville is a coed, private, comprehensive institution, founded in 1872, offering degrees at the bachelor's and master's levels. It has a 130-acre campus in St. Louis.

Academic Information The faculty has 313 members (28% full-time). The undergraduate student-faculty ratio is 13:1. The library holds 205,512 titles, 9,004 serial subscriptions, and 10,933 audiovisual materials. Special programs include services for learning-disabled students, an honors program, cooperative (work-study) education, study abroad, advanced placement credit, accelerated degree programs, Freshman Honors College, ESL programs, double majors, independent study, distance learning, self-designed majors, summer session for credit, part-time degree programs (daytime, evenings, weekends, summer), adult/continuing education programs, internships, and arrangement for off-campus study with Fontbonne University, Lindenwood University, Webster University, Missouri Baptist University. The most frequently chosen baccalaureate fields are law/legal studies, philosophy, religion, and theology.
Student Body Statistics The student body totals 3,265, of whom 2,710 are undergraduates (303 freshmen). 74 percent are women and 26 percent are men. Students come from 15 states and territories and 34 other countries. 92 percent are from Missouri. 3.4 percent are international students.
Expenses for 2002–03 *Application fee:* $25. *Comprehensive fee:* $20,860 includes full-time tuition ($14,400), mandatory fees ($160), and college room and board ($6300). Room and board charges vary according to housing facility. *Part-time tuition:* $410 per credit hour. *Part-time mandatory fees:* $40 per term. Part-time tuition and fees vary according to class time.
Financial Aid Forms of aid include need-based and non-need-based scholarships and part-time jobs. The average aided 2002–03 undergraduate received an aid package worth an estimated $8110. The priority application deadline for financial aid is April 1.
Freshman Admission Maryville requires a high school transcript, a minimum 2.5 high school GPA, SAT I or ACT scores, and TOEFL scores for international students. An essay, recommendations, an interview, and audition, portfolio are required for some. The application deadline for regular admission is August 15.
Transfer Admission The application deadline for admission is rolling.
Entrance Difficulty Maryville assesses its entrance difficulty level as moderately difficult; very difficult for physical therapy, occupational therapy, education, actuarial science programs. For the fall 2002 freshman class, 76 percent of the applicants were accepted.

For Further Information Contact Ms. Lynn Jackson, Admissions Director, Maryville University of Saint Louis, 13550 Conway Road, St. Louis, MO 63141-7299. *Telephone:* 314-529-9350 or 800-627-9855 (toll-free). *Fax:* 314-529-9927. *E-mail:* admissions@maryville.edu. *Web site:* http://www.maryville.edu/.

MESSENGER COLLEGE

Joplin, Missouri

Messenger College is a coed, private, Pentecostal, four-year college, founded in 1987, offering degrees at the associate and bachelor's levels. It has a 16-acre campus in Joplin near Springfield.

Academic Information The faculty has 14 members (29% full-time), 29% with terminal degrees. The library holds 28,874 titles, 114 serial subscriptions, and 326 audiovisual materials. Special programs include academic remediation, an honors program, cooperative (work-study) education, double majors, independent study, distance learning, part-time degree programs (daytime, evenings), external degree programs, and internships. The most frequently chosen baccalaureate fields are philosophy, religion, and theology, visual/performing arts.
Student Body Statistics The student body is made up of 100 undergraduates (23 freshmen). 41 percent are women and 59 percent are men. Students come from 18 states and territories. 48 percent are from Missouri.
Expenses for 2002–03 *Application fee:* $10. *Comprehensive fee:* $7970 includes full-time tuition ($4500), mandatory fees ($370), and college room and board ($3100). *Part-time tuition:* $150 per credit hour.
Financial Aid Forms of aid include need-based and non-need-based scholarships and part-time jobs. The average aided 2001–02 undergraduate received an aid package worth $4175. The application deadline for financial aid is continuous.
Freshman Admission Messenger College requires an essay, a high school transcript, a minimum 2.0 high school GPA, 2 recommendations, SAT I or ACT scores, and TOEFL scores for international students. An interview is required for some. The application deadline for regular admission is September 1.
Transfer Admission The application deadline for admission is September 1.

Entrance Difficulty Messenger College assesses its entrance difficulty level as moderately difficult. For the fall 2002 freshman class, 98 percent of the applicants were accepted.

For Further Information Contact Ms. Gwen Minor, Vice President of Academic Affairs, Messenger College, 300 East 50th, PO Box 4050, Joplin, MO 64803. *Telephone:* 417-624-7070 Ext. 102 or 800-385-8940 (toll-free in-state). *Fax:* 417-624-5070. *E-mail:* mc@pcg.org.

METRO BUSINESS COLLEGE

Cape Girardeau, Missouri

Metro Business College is a coed, proprietary, primarily two-year college, offering degrees at the associate and bachelor's levels.

Academic Information The faculty has 11 members (82% full-time).
Student Body Statistics The student body is made up of 118 undergraduates. 89 percent are women and 11 percent are men.
Financial Aid Forms of aid include need-based scholarships. The application deadline for financial aid is continuous.
Entrance Difficulty Metro Business College assesses its entrance difficulty level as minimally difficult.

For Further Information Contact Ms. Kyla Evans, Admissions Director, Metro Business College, 1732 North Kings Highway, Cape Girardeau, MO 63701. *Telephone:* 573-334-9181. *Fax:* 573-334-0617. *Web site:* http://www.metrobusinesscollege.edu/.

MISSOURI BAPTIST UNIVERSITY

St. Louis, Missouri

Missouri Baptist University is a coed, private, Southern Baptist, comprehensive institution, founded in 1964, offering degrees at the associate, bachelor's, and master's levels and postbachelor's certificates (also offers some graduate courses). It has a 65-acre campus in St. Louis.

Expenses for 2002–03 *Application fee:* $25. *Comprehensive fee:* $16,790 includes full-time tuition ($11,100), mandatory fees ($210), and college room and board ($5480). Full-time tuition and fees vary according to course load and location. Room and board charges vary according to housing facility. *Part-time tuition:* varies with course load, location.

For Further Information Contact Mr. Robert Cornwell, Associate Director of Admissions, Missouri Baptist University, One College Park Drive, St. Louis, MO 63141-8660. *Telephone:* 314-392-2291 or 877-434-1115 Ext. 2290 (toll-free). *Fax:* 314-434-7596. *E-mail:* admissions@mobap.edu. *Web site:* http://www.mobap.edu/.

MISSOURI SOUTHERN STATE COLLEGE

Joplin, Missouri

Missouri Southern State is a coed, public, four-year college, founded in 1937, offering degrees at the associate and bachelor's levels. It has a 350-acre campus in Joplin.

Academic Information The faculty has 297 members (68% full-time), 48% with terminal degrees. The student-faculty ratio is 18:1. The library holds 157,362 titles, 1,574 serial subscriptions, and 10,417 audiovisual materials. Special programs include academic remediation, services for learning-disabled students, an honors program, cooperative (work-study) education, study abroad, advanced placement credit, accelerated degree programs, ESL programs, double majors, independent study, distance learning, summer session for credit, part-time degree programs (daytime, evenings, weekends, summer), external degree programs, adult/continuing education programs, internships, and arrangement for off-campus study with Crowder College and Nevada Telecenter. The most frequently chosen baccalaureate fields are business/marketing, education, protective services/public administration.
Student Body Statistics The student body is made up of 5,782 undergraduates (725 freshmen). 59 percent are women and 41 percent are men. Students come from 31 states and territories and 32 other countries. 87 percent are from Missouri. 2 percent are international students. 10 percent of the 2002 graduating class went on to graduate and professional schools.
Expenses for 2002–03 *Application fee:* $15. *State resident tuition:* $3720 full-time, $124 per credit part-time. *Nonresident tuition:* $7440 full-time, $248 per credit part-time. *Mandatory fees:* $166 full-time, $53 per term part-time. Full-time tuition and fees vary according to course load. *College room and board:* $4000. Room and board charges vary according to housing facility.
Financial Aid Forms of aid include need-based and non-need-based scholarships, athletic grants, and part-time jobs. The average aided 2002–03 undergraduate received an aid package worth an estimated $4682. The priority application deadline for financial aid is February 15.
Freshman Admission Missouri Southern State requires a high school transcript, SAT I or ACT scores, and TOEFL scores for international students. ACT scores and Michigan Test of English Language Proficiency are required for some. The application deadline for regular admission is August 3.
Transfer Admission The application deadline for admission is August 3.
Entrance Difficulty Missouri Southern State assesses its entrance difficulty level as moderately difficult; noncompetitive for transfers. For the fall 2002 freshman class, 74 percent of the applicants were accepted.

For Further Information Contact Mr. Derek Skaggs, Director of Enrollment Services, Missouri Southern State College, 3950 East Newman Road, Joplin, MO 64801-1595. *Telephone:* 417-625-9537 or 800-606-MSSC (toll-free). *Fax:* 417-659-4429. *E-mail:* admissions@mail.mssc.edu. *Web site:* http://www.mssc.edu/.

MISSOURI TECH

St. Louis, Missouri

Missouri Tech is a coed, primarily men's, proprietary, four-year college, founded in 1932, offering degrees at the associate and bachelor's levels in electronics engineering technology.

Academic Information The faculty has 13 members (54% full-time), 15% with terminal degrees. The student-faculty ratio is 10:1. Special programs include advanced placement credit, accelerated degree programs, summer session for credit, part-time degree programs (daytime, evenings), adult/continuing education programs, and internships. The most frequently chosen baccalaureate field is engineering/engineering technologies.
Student Body Statistics The student body is made up of 193 undergraduates (13 freshmen). 11 percent are women and 89 percent are men. Students come from 4 states and territories and 8 other countries. 10 percent of the 2002 graduating class went on to graduate and professional schools.
Expenses for 2003–04 *Tuition:* $11,387 full-time, $345 per semester hour part-time. *Mandatory fees:* $380 full-time. *College room only:* $3224.
Financial Aid Forms of aid include need-based and non-need-based scholarships. The application deadline for financial aid is continuous.
Freshman Admission Missouri Tech requires a high school transcript and TOEFL scores for international students. ACT scores are recommended. An interview and minimum ACT score of 20 are required for some. The application deadline for regular admission is rolling.
Entrance Difficulty Missouri Tech assesses its entrance difficulty level as moderately difficult. For the fall 2002 freshman class, 65 percent of the applicants were accepted.

For Further Information Contact Mr. Bob Honaker, Director of Admissions, Missouri Tech, 1167 Corporate Lake Drive, St. Louis, MO 63132. *Telephone:* 314-569-3600 Ext. 363 or 800-960-8324 (toll-free out-of-state). *Fax:* 314-569-1167. *Web site:* http://www.motech.edu/.

MISSOURI VALLEY COLLEGE

Marshall, Missouri

Missouri Valley is a coed, private, four-year college, founded in 1889, affiliated with the Presbyterian Church, offering degrees at the associate and bachelor's levels. It has a 140-acre campus in Marshall near Kansas City.

Academic Information The faculty has 103 members (66% full-time), 30% with terminal degrees. The student-faculty ratio is 17:1. The library holds 61,907 titles, 391 serial subscriptions, and 1,399 audiovisual materials. Special programs include services for learning-disabled students, cooperative (work-study) education, advanced placement credit, ESL programs, double majors, independent study, summer session for credit, part-time degree programs (daytime, evenings), adult/continuing education programs, and internships. The most frequently chosen baccalaureate fields are business/marketing, education, protective services/public administration.

Student Body Statistics The student body is made up of 1,600 undergraduates (430 freshmen). 44 percent are women and 56 percent are men. Students come from 40 states and territories and 29 other countries. 66 percent are from Missouri. 5.8 percent are international students.

Expenses for 2003–04 *Application fee:* $15. *Comprehensive fee:* $18,300 includes full-time tuition ($12,600), mandatory fees ($500), and college room and board ($5200). *Part-time tuition:* $350 per credit hour.

Financial Aid Forms of aid include need-based and non-need-based scholarships and part-time jobs. The average aided 2002–03 undergraduate received an aid package worth an estimated $12,141. The application deadline for financial aid is September 15 with a priority deadline of March 20.

Freshman Admission Missouri Valley requires a high school transcript, SAT I or ACT scores, and TOEFL scores for international students. A minimum 2.0 high school GPA, an interview, and SAT II: Writing Test scores are recommended. An essay, 3 recommendations, and an interview are required for some. The application deadline for regular admission is rolling.

Transfer Admission The application deadline for admission is rolling.

Entrance Difficulty Missouri Valley assesses its entrance difficulty level as minimally difficult. For the fall 2002 freshman class, 85 percent of the applicants were accepted.

For Further Information Contact Ms. Debbie Bultman, Admissions, Missouri Valley College, 500 East College, Marshall, MO 65340-3197. *Telephone:* 660-831-4157. *Fax:* 660-831-4039. *E-mail:* admissions@moval.edu. *Web site:* http://www.moval.edu/.

See page 310 for a narrative description.

MISSOURI WESTERN STATE COLLEGE

St. Joseph, Missouri

MWSC is a coed, public, four-year college, founded in 1915, offering degrees at the associate and bachelor's levels. It has a 744-acre campus in St. Joseph near Kansas City.

Academic Information The faculty has 330 members (56% full-time), 48% with terminal degrees. The student-faculty ratio is 19:1. The library holds 147,509 titles, 1,068 serial subscriptions, and 13,705 audiovisual materials. Special programs include academic remediation, an honors program, advanced placement credit, accelerated degree programs, Freshman Honors College, double majors, distance learning, summer session for credit, part-time degree programs (daytime, evenings, weekends, summer), and internships. The most frequently chosen baccalaureate fields are business/marketing, education, protective services/public administration.

Student Body Statistics The student body is made up of 5,197 undergraduates (1,234 freshmen). 61 percent are women and 39 percent are men. Students come from 33 states and territories and 7 other countries. 94 percent are from Missouri. 0.2 percent are international students. 22 percent of the 2002 graduating class went on to graduate and professional schools.

Expenses for 2002–03 *Application fee:* $15. *State resident tuition:* $3768 full-time, $135 per credit part-time. *Nonresident tuition:* $7074 full-time, $247 per credit part-time. *Mandatory fees:* $296 full-time, $11 per credit part-time, $10 per term part-time. *College room and board:* $3804. Room and board charges vary according to board plan and housing facility.

Financial Aid Forms of aid include need-based and non-need-based scholarships, athletic grants, and part-time jobs. The average aided 2001–02 undergraduate received an aid package worth $6677. The priority application deadline for financial aid is April 1.

Freshman Admission MWSC requires a high school transcript, ACT scores, and TOEFL scores for international students. The application deadline for regular admission is July 30.

Transfer Admission The application deadline for admission is July 30.

Entrance Difficulty MWSC has an open admission policy. It assesses its entrance difficulty as moderately difficult for nursing, computer science, education, criminal justice, leisure management, math, history, political science, social work programs.

For Further Information Contact Mr. Howard McCauley, Director of Admissions, Missouri Western State College, 4525 Downs Drive, St. Joseph, MO 64507-2294. *Telephone:* 816-271-4267 or 800-662-7041 Ext. 60 (toll-free). *Fax:* 816-271-5833. *E-mail:* admissn@mwsc.edu. *Web site:* http://www.mwsc.edu/.

NATIONAL AMERICAN UNIVERSITY

Kansas City, Missouri

For Information Write to National American University, Kansas City, MO 64133-1612.

NORTHWEST MISSOURI STATE UNIVERSITY

Maryville, Missouri

Northwest is a coed, public, comprehensive unit of Missouri Coordinating Board for Higher Education, founded in 1905, offering degrees at the bachelor's and master's levels. It has a 240-acre campus in Maryville near Kansas City.

Academic Information The faculty has 247 members (98% full-time), 69% with terminal degrees. The undergraduate student-faculty ratio is 24:1. The library holds 358,274 titles, 5,381 serial subscriptions, and 4,691 audiovisual materials. Special programs include academic remediation, services for learning-disabled students, study abroad, advanced placement credit, accelerated degree programs, ESL programs, double majors, independent study, distance learning, summer session for credit, part-time degree programs (daytime, evenings, summer), internships, and arrangement for off-campus study with Missouri Western State College, Truman State University, North Central Missouri College. The most frequently chosen baccalaureate fields are business/marketing, computer/information sciences, education.

Student Body Statistics The student body totals 6,514, of whom 5,601 are undergraduates (1,198 freshmen). 57 percent are women and 43 percent are men. Students come from 30 states and territories and 11 other countries. 64 percent are from Missouri. 2.8 percent are international students.

Expenses for 2002–03 *Application fee:* $15. *State resident tuition:* $3930 full-time, $137 per credit hour part-time. *Nonresident tuition:* $6832 full-time, $233 per credit hour part-time. *Mandatory fees:* $180 full-time, $10 per credit hour part-time. Full-time tuition and fees vary according to course load. Part-time tuition and fees vary according to course load. *College room and board:* $4556. Room and board charges vary according to board plan.

Financial Aid Forms of aid include need-based and non-need-based scholarships, athletic grants, and part-time jobs. The average aided 2001–02 undergraduate received an aid package worth $6047. The priority application deadline for financial aid is March 1.

Freshman Admission Northwest requires a high school transcript, a minimum 2.0 high school GPA, SAT I or ACT scores, and TOEFL scores for international students. An interview is required for some. The application deadline for regular admission is rolling.

Transfer Admission The application deadline for admission is rolling.
Entrance Difficulty Northwest assesses its entrance difficulty level as moderately difficult; minimally difficult for transfers. For the fall 2002 freshman class, 87 percent of the applicants were accepted.

For Further Information Contact Ms. Deb Powers, Associate Director of Admission, Northwest Missouri State University, Office of Admissions, 800 University Drive, Maryville, MO 64468. *Telephone:* 660-562-1587 or 800-633-1175 (toll-free). *Fax:* 660-562-1121. *E-mail:* admissions@acad.nwmissouri.edu. *Web site:* http://www.nwmissouri.edu/.

OZARK CHRISTIAN COLLEGE

Joplin, Missouri

OCC is a coed, private, Christian, four-year college, founded in 1942, offering degrees at the associate and bachelor's levels. It has a 110-acre campus in Joplin.

Academic Information The faculty has 60 members (50% full-time), 17% with terminal degrees. The student-faculty ratio is 19:1. The library holds 59,808 titles, 362 serial subscriptions, and 21,289 audiovisual materials. Special programs include academic remediation, services for learning-disabled students, ESL programs, double majors, summer session for credit, part-time degree programs (daytime, evenings, summer), adult/continuing education programs, and internships. The most frequently chosen baccalaureate field is philosophy, religion, and theology.
Student Body Statistics The student body is made up of 799 undergraduates. 48 percent are women and 52 percent are men. Students come from 33 states and territories and 13 other countries. 43 percent are from Missouri. 1.6 percent are international students.
Expenses for 2002–03 *Application fee:* $30. *Comprehensive fee:* $9625 includes full-time tuition ($5280), mandatory fees ($515), and college room and board ($3830). *College room only:* $1880. Room and board charges vary according to board plan. *Part-time tuition:* $165 per credit.
Financial Aid Forms of aid include need-based and non-need-based scholarships and part-time jobs. The application deadline for financial aid is April 1.
Freshman Admission OCC requires an essay, a high school transcript, 4 recommendations, SAT I or ACT scores, and TOEFL scores for international students. An interview is required for some. The application deadline for regular admission is March 5.
Transfer Admission The application deadline for admission is rolling.
Entrance Difficulty OCC has an open admission policy.

For Further Information Contact Mr. Troy B. Nelson, Executive Director of Admissions, Ozark Christian College, 1111 North Main Street, Joplin, MO 64801-4804. *Telephone:* 417-624-2518 Ext. 2006 or 800-299-4622 (toll-free). *Fax:* 417-624-0090. *E-mail:* occadmin@occ.edu. *Web site:* http://www.occ.edu/.

PARK UNIVERSITY

Parkville, Missouri

Park is a coed, private, comprehensive institution, founded in 1875, offering degrees at the associate, bachelor's, and master's levels. It has an 800-acre campus in Parkville near Kansas City.

Academic Information The faculty has 765 members (7% full-time). The undergraduate student-faculty ratio is 14:1. The library holds 144,870 titles, 775 serial subscriptions, and 850 audiovisual materials. Special programs include academic remediation, services for learning-disabled students, an honors program, advanced placement credit, ESL programs, double majors, independent study, distance learning, self-designed majors, summer session for credit, part-time degree programs, external degree programs, adult/continuing education programs, internships, and arrangement for off-campus study with members of the Kansas City Professional Development Council. The most frequently chosen baccalaureate fields are business/marketing, protective services/public administration, psychology.
Student Body Statistics The student body totals 10,123, of whom 9,870 are undergraduates (159 freshmen). 50 percent are women and 50 percent are men. Students come from 47 states and territories and 90 other countries. 23 percent are from Missouri. 2.1 percent are international students. 7 percent of the 2002 graduating class went on to graduate and professional schools.
Expenses for 2002–03 *Application fee:* $25. *Comprehensive fee:* $10,332 includes full-time tuition ($5152) and college room and board ($5180). Room and board charges vary according to board plan and housing facility. *Part-time tuition:* $184 per credit hour.
Financial Aid Forms of aid include need-based and non-need-based scholarships, athletic grants, and part-time jobs. The average aided 2002–03 undergraduate received an aid package worth an estimated $4753. The priority application deadline for financial aid is April 1.
Freshman Admission Park requires a high school transcript, a minimum 2.0 high school GPA, SAT I or ACT scores, and TOEFL scores for international students. An essay is recommended. 2 recommendations and an interview are required for some. The application deadline for regular admission is August 1.
Transfer Admission The application deadline for admission is August 1.
Entrance Difficulty Park assesses its entrance difficulty level as moderately difficult. For the fall 2002 freshman class, 72 percent of the applicants were accepted.

For Further Information Contact Office of Admissions, Park University, 8700 NW River Park Drive, Campus Box 1, Parkville, MO 64152. *Telephone:* 816-584-6215 or 800-745-7275 (toll-free). *Fax:* 816-741-4462. *E-mail:* admissions@mail.park.edu. *Web site:* http://www.park.edu/.

RANKEN TECHNICAL COLLEGE

St. Louis, Missouri

Ranken is a coed, primarily men's, private, primarily two-year college, founded in 1907, offering degrees at the associate and bachelor's levels. It has a 10-acre campus in St. Louis.

Academic Information The faculty has 67 members (88% full-time). The student-faculty ratio is 15:1. The library holds 11,000 titles and 182 serial subscriptions. Special programs include academic remediation, services for learning-disabled students, cooperative (work-study) education, advanced placement credit, independent study, distance learning, summer session for credit, part-time degree programs (daytime, evenings, weekends, summer), adult/continuing education programs, and internships.
Student Body Statistics The student body is made up of 1,423 undergraduates (321 freshmen). 4 percent are women and 96 percent are men. Students come from 3 states and territories. 60 percent are from Missouri. 5 percent of the 2002 graduating class went on to four-year colleges.
Expenses for 2002–03 *Application fee:* $95. *Tuition:* $9000 full-time.
Financial Aid Forms of aid include need-based scholarships and part-time jobs. The application deadline for financial aid is continuous.
Freshman Admission Ranken requires an essay, a high school transcript, and an interview. TOEFL scores for international students are recommended. The application deadline for regular admission is rolling.
Entrance Difficulty Ranken assesses its entrance difficulty level as moderately difficult. For the fall 2002 freshman class, 92 percent of the applicants were accepted.

For Further Information Contact Ms. Elizabeth Darr, Director of Admissions, Ranken Technical College, 4431 Finney Avenue, St. Louis, MO 63113. *Telephone:* 314-371-0233 Ext. 4811 or 866-4RANKEN (toll-free out-of-state). *Fax:* 314-371-0241. *E-mail:* admissions@ranken.edu. *Web site:* http://www.ranken.edu/.

RESEARCH COLLEGE OF NURSING

Kansas City, Missouri

Research College of Nursing is a coed, primarily women's, private, comprehensive unit of Rockhurst University, founded in 1980, offering

Research College of Nursing (continued)
degrees at the bachelor's and master's levels in nursing (bachelor's degree offered jointly with Rockhurst College). It has a 66-acre campus in Kansas City.

Academic Information The faculty has 35 members (71% full-time). The undergraduate student-faculty ratio is 7:1. The library holds 150,000 titles and 675 serial subscriptions. Special programs include services for learning-disabled students, an honors program, study abroad, advanced placement credit, accelerated degree programs, double majors, independent study, and summer session for credit. The most frequently chosen baccalaureate field is health professions and related sciences.
Student Body Statistics The student body totals 203, of whom 176 are undergraduates (20 freshmen). 92 percent are women and 8 percent are men. Students come from 7 states and territories.
Expenses for 2003–04 *Application fee:* $25. *Comprehensive fee:* $22,850 includes full-time tuition ($16,950), mandatory fees ($450), and college room and board ($5450). *Part-time tuition:* $495 per credit hour. *Part-time mandatory fees:* $15 per term.
Financial Aid Forms of aid include need-based and non-need-based scholarships. The average aided 2001–02 undergraduate received an aid package worth $10,300. The priority application deadline for financial aid is March 15.
Freshman Admission Research College of Nursing requires a high school transcript, 1 recommendation, SAT I or ACT scores, and TOEFL scores for international students. A minimum 2.8 high school GPA, an interview, and minimum ACT score of 20 are recommended. The application deadline for regular admission is June 30.
Transfer Admission The application deadline for admission is January 31.
Entrance Difficulty Research College of Nursing assesses its entrance difficulty level as moderately difficult. For the fall 2002 freshman class, 74 percent of the applicants were accepted.

For Further Information Contact Ms. Marisa Ferrara, Rockhurst College Admission Office, Research College of Nursing, 1100 Rockhurst Road, Kansas City, MO 64110. *Telephone:* 816-276-4733 or 800-842-6776 (toll-free). *Fax:* 816-501-4588. *E-mail:* mendenhall@vax2.rockhurst.edu. *Web site:* http://www.researchcollege.edu/.

ROCKHURST UNIVERSITY

Kansas City, Missouri

Rockhurst is a coed, private, Roman Catholic (Jesuit), comprehensive institution, founded in 1910, offering degrees at the bachelor's and master's levels and postbachelor's certificates. It has a 35-acre campus in Kansas City.

Academic Information The faculty has 226 members (58% full-time), 62% with terminal degrees. The undergraduate student-faculty ratio is 10:1. The library holds 597,800 titles, 750 serial subscriptions, and 3,339 audiovisual materials. Special programs include academic remediation, services for learning-disabled students, an honors program, cooperative (work-study) education, study abroad, advanced placement credit, accelerated degree programs, Freshman Honors College, double majors, independent study, distance learning, summer session for credit, part-time degree programs (daytime, evenings, weekends, summer), adult/continuing education programs, internships, and arrangement for off-campus study with Kansas City Area Student Exchange. The most frequently chosen baccalaureate fields are business/marketing, health professions and related sciences, psychology.
Student Body Statistics The student body totals 2,870, of whom 2,020 are undergraduates (214 freshmen). 56 percent are women and 44 percent are men. Students come from 26 states and territories and 13 other countries. 72 percent are from Missouri. 2.5 percent are international students. 26 percent of the 2002 graduating class went on to graduate and professional schools.
Expenses for 2002–03 *Application fee:* $25. *Comprehensive fee:* $21,580 includes full-time tuition ($15,980), mandatory fees ($400), and college room and board ($5200). Full-time tuition and fees vary according to course load. Room and board charges vary according to housing facility. *Part-time tuition:* $540 per semester hour. *Part-time mandatory fees:* $15 per term. Part-time tuition and fees vary according to class time, course load, and program.
Financial Aid Forms of aid include need-based and non-need-based scholarships, athletic grants, and part-time jobs. The average aided 2002–03 undergraduate received an aid package worth an estimated $14,306. The priority application deadline for financial aid is March 1.
Freshman Admission Rockhurst requires a high school transcript, a minimum 2.0 high school GPA, 1 recommendation, SAT I or ACT scores, and TOEFL scores for international students. An essay and an interview are required for some. The application deadline for regular admission is June 30 and for early action it is July 1.
Transfer Admission The application deadline for admission is rolling.
Entrance Difficulty Rockhurst assesses its entrance difficulty level as moderately difficult. For the fall 2002 freshman class, 83 percent of the applicants were accepted.

For Further Information Contact Mr. Lane Ramey, Director of Freshman Admissions, Rockhurst University, 1100 Rockhurst Road, Kansas City, MO 64110-2561. *Telephone:* 816-501-4100 or 800-842-6776 (toll-free). *Fax:* 816-501-4142. *E-mail:* admission@rockhurst.edu. *Web site:* http://www.rockhurst.edu/.

ST. LOUIS CHRISTIAN COLLEGE

Florissant, Missouri

SLCC is a coed, private, Christian, four-year college, founded in 1956, offering degrees at the associate and bachelor's levels. It has a 20-acre campus in Florissant near St. Louis.

Academic Information The faculty has 35 members (31% full-time), 26% with terminal degrees. The student-faculty ratio is 12:1. The library holds 39,728 titles and 144 serial subscriptions. Special programs include academic remediation, services for learning-disabled students, advanced placement credit, accelerated degree programs, part-time degree programs (daytime), adult/continuing education programs, and internships. The most frequently chosen baccalaureate field is philosophy, religion, and theology.
Student Body Statistics The student body is made up of 232 undergraduates (29 freshmen). 42 percent are women and 58 percent are men. Students come from 11 states and territories and 3 other countries. 63 percent are from Missouri. 3 percent are international students. 21 percent of the 2002 graduating class went on to graduate and professional schools.
Expenses for 2003–04 *Application fee:* $0. *Comprehensive fee:* $11,724 includes full-time tuition ($6944) and college room and board ($4780). Room and board charges vary according to housing facility. *Part-time tuition:* $217 per hour.
Financial Aid Forms of aid include need-based and non-need-based scholarships and part-time jobs. The average aided 2002–03 undergraduate received an aid package worth an estimated $6332. The priority application deadline for financial aid is May 1.
Freshman Admission SLCC requires an essay, a high school transcript, 2 recommendations, ACT scores, and TOEFL scores for international students. A minimum 2.0 high school GPA is recommended. An interview is required for some. The application deadline for regular admission is August 15.
Transfer Admission The application deadline for admission is August 15.
Entrance Difficulty SLCC assesses its entrance difficulty level as minimally difficult. For the fall 2002 freshman class, 76 percent of the applicants were accepted.

For Further Information Contact Mr. Richard Fordyce, Registrar, St. Louis Christian College, 1360 Grandview Drive, Florissant, MO 63033-6499. *Telephone:* 314-837-6777 Ext. 1500 or 800-887-SLCC (toll-free). *Fax:* 314-837-8291. *E-mail:* questions@slcc4ministry.edu. *Web site:* http://www.slcc4ministry.edu/.

ST. LOUIS COLLEGE OF PHARMACY

St. Louis, Missouri

St. Louis College of Pharmacy is a coed, private, comprehensive institution, founded in 1864, offering degrees at the bachelor's, master's, and first professional levels (bachelor of science degree program in pharmaceutical studies cannot be applied to directly; students have the option to transfer in after their second year in the PharmD program. Bachelor's degree candidates are not eligible to take the pharmacist's licensing examination). It has a 5-acre campus in St. Louis.

Academic Information The faculty has 100 members (64% full-time). The undergraduate student-faculty ratio is 12:1. The library holds 59,012 titles, 234 serial subscriptions, and 802 audiovisual materials. Special programs include advanced placement credit, summer session for credit, adult/continuing education programs, and internships. The most frequently chosen baccalaureate field is health professions and related sciences.
Student Body Statistics The student body totals 900, of whom 825 are undergraduates (203 freshmen). 64 percent are women and 36 percent are men. Students come from 24 states and territories and 3 other countries. 50 percent are from Missouri. 0.4 percent are international students. 6 percent of the 2002 graduating class went on to graduate and professional schools.
Expenses for 2003–04 *Application fee:* $35. *Comprehensive fee:* $23,280 includes full-time tuition ($16,030), mandatory fees ($250), and college room and board ($7000). Full-time tuition and fees vary according to student level. Room and board charges vary according to housing facility. *Part-time tuition:* $690 per credit.
Financial Aid Forms of aid include need-based and non-need-based scholarships and part-time jobs. $11,324. The application deadline for financial aid is November 15 with a priority deadline of April 1.
Freshman Admission St. Louis College of Pharmacy requires an essay, a high school transcript, a minimum 3.0 high school GPA, recommendations, SAT I or ACT scores, and TOEFL scores for international students. An interview is required for some. The application deadline for regular admission is rolling.
Transfer Admission The application deadline for admission is March 1.
Entrance Difficulty St. Louis College of Pharmacy assesses its entrance difficulty level as moderately difficult; most difficult for transfers. For the fall 2002 freshman class, 65 percent of the applicants were accepted.

For Further Information Contact Ms. Patty Kulage, Admissions and Financial Aid Coordinator, St. Louis College of Pharmacy, 4588 Parkview Place, St. Louis, MO 63110-1088. *Telephone:* 314-367-8700 Ext. 1067 or 800-278-5267 (toll-free in-state). *Fax:* 314-367-2784. *E-mail:* pkulage@stlcop.edu. *Web site:* http://www.stlcop.edu/.

SAINT LOUIS UNIVERSITY

St. Louis, Missouri

SLU is a coed, private, Roman Catholic (Jesuit) university, founded in 1818, offering degrees at the associate, bachelor's, master's, doctoral, and first professional levels and post-master's and postbachelor's certificates. It has a 279-acre campus in St. Louis.

Academic Information The faculty has 930 members (64% full-time). The undergraduate student-faculty ratio is 12:1. The library holds 1 million titles, 12,881 serial subscriptions, and 195,651 audiovisual materials. Special programs include academic remediation, services for learning-disabled students, an honors program, cooperative (work-study) education, study abroad, advanced placement credit, accelerated degree programs, ESL programs, double majors, independent study, distance learning, self-designed majors, summer session for credit, part-time degree programs (daytime, evenings, weekends, summer), adult/continuing education programs, internships, and arrangement for off-campus study with Washington University in St. Louis. The most frequently chosen baccalaureate fields are business/marketing, communications/communication technologies, health professions and related sciences.
Student Body Statistics The student body totals 11,272, of whom 7,178 are undergraduates (1,539 freshmen). 54 percent are women and 46 percent are men. Students come from 52 states and territories and 73 other countries. 53 percent are from Missouri. 2.7 percent are international students. 21 percent of the 2002 graduating class went on to graduate and professional schools.
Expenses for 2002–03 *Application fee:* $25. *Comprehensive fee:* $28,318 includes full-time tuition ($20,840), mandatory fees ($168), and college room and board ($7310). *College room only:* $3940. Room and board charges vary according to board plan and housing facility. *Part-time tuition:* $730 per credit hour. *Part-time mandatory fees:* $55 per term. Part-time tuition and fees vary according to class time and program.
Financial Aid Forms of aid include need-based and non-need-based scholarships, athletic grants, and part-time jobs. The average aided 2002–03 undergraduate received an aid package worth an estimated $20,707. The priority application deadline for financial aid is March 1.
Freshman Admission SLU requires an essay, a high school transcript, secondary school report form, and SAT I or ACT scores. A minimum 2.5 high school GPA, 2 recommendations, an interview, and TOEFL scores for international students are recommended. The application deadline for regular admission is August 1.
Transfer Admission The application deadline for admission is August 1.
Entrance Difficulty SLU assesses its entrance difficulty level as moderately difficult. For the fall 2002 freshman class, 72 percent of the applicants were accepted.

For Further Information Contact Ms. Shani Lenore, Director, Saint Louis University, 221 North Grand Boulevard, St. Louis, MO 63103-2097. *Telephone:* 314-977-3415 or 800-758-3678 (toll-free out-of-state). *Fax:* 314-977-7136. *E-mail:* admitme@slu.edu. *Web site:* http://www.slu.edu/.

SAINT LUKE'S COLLEGE

Kansas City, Missouri

Saint Luke's College is a coed, primarily women's, private, Episcopal, upper-level institution, founded in 1903, offering degrees at the bachelor's level in nursing. It has a 3-acre campus in Kansas City.

Academic Information The faculty has 19 members (89% full-time), 5% with terminal degrees. The student-faculty ratio is 7:1. Special programs include cooperative (work-study) education and summer session for credit. The most frequently chosen baccalaureate field is health professions and related sciences.
Student Body Statistics The student body is made up of 129 undergraduates. 95 percent are women and 5 percent are men.
Expenses for 2002–03 *Application fee:* $20. *Tuition:* $9000 full-time. *Mandatory fees:* $510 full-time.
Financial Aid Forms of aid include need-based and non-need-based scholarships and part-time jobs. The average aided 2002–03 undergraduate received an aid package worth an estimated $6500. The application deadline for financial aid is continuous.
Transfer Admission Saint Luke's College requires a college transcript and a minimum 2.5 college GPA. Standardized test scores are required for some. The application deadline for admission is December 31.
Entrance Difficulty Saint Luke's College assesses its entrance difficulty level as very difficult.

For Further Information Contact Ms. Marsha Thomas, Director of Admissions, Saint Luke's College, 4426 Wornall Road, Kansas City, MO 64111. *Telephone:* 816-932-2073. *E-mail:* slc-admissions@saint-lukes.org. *Web site:* http://www.saint-lukes.org/.

SANFORD-BROWN COLLEGE

Fenton, Missouri

Sanford-Brown is a coed, proprietary, primarily two-year college, founded in 1868, offering degrees at the associate and bachelor's levels. It has a 6-acre campus in Fenton near St. Louis.

Sanford-Brown College (continued)
Academic Information The faculty has 28 members (46% full-time). The student-faculty ratio is 9:1. Special programs include services for learning-disabled students, independent study, adult/continuing education programs, and internships.
Student Body Statistics The student body is made up of 440 undergraduates (79 freshmen). 65 percent are women and 35 percent are men. Students come from 2 states and territories. 92 percent are from Missouri.
Expenses for 2002–03 *Application fee:* $25.
Financial Aid Forms of aid include need-based scholarships and part-time jobs. The application deadline for financial aid is continuous.
Freshman Admission Sanford-Brown requires a high school transcript, an interview, and CPAt.
Entrance Difficulty Sanford-Brown has an open admission policy.

For Further Information Contact Ms. Judy Wilga, Director of Admissions, Sanford-Brown College, 1203 Smizer Mill Road, Fenton, MO 63026. *Telephone:* 636-349-4900 Ext. 102 or 800-456-7222 (toll-free). *Fax:* 636-349-9170. *Web site:* http://www.sanford-brown.edu/.

SOUTHEAST MISSOURI HOSPITAL COLLEGE OF NURSING AND HEALTH SCIENCES

Cape Girardeau, Missouri

For Information Write to Southeast Missouri Hospital College of Nursing and Health Sciences, Cape Girardeau, MO 63701.

SOUTHEAST MISSOURI STATE UNIVERSITY

Cape Girardeau, Missouri

Southeast is a coed, public, comprehensive unit of Missouri Coordinating Board for Higher Education, founded in 1873, offering degrees at the associate, bachelor's, and master's levels. It has a 693-acre campus in Cape Girardeau near St. Louis.

Academic Information The faculty has 517 members (75% full-time), 67% with terminal degrees. The undergraduate student-faculty ratio is 18:1. The library holds 411,992 titles, 2,781 serial subscriptions, and 9,400 audiovisual materials. Special programs include academic remediation, services for learning-disabled students, an honors program, cooperative (work-study) education, study abroad, advanced placement credit, ESL programs, double majors, independent study, distance learning, self-designed majors, summer session for credit, part-time degree programs, adult/continuing education programs, and internships. The most frequently chosen baccalaureate fields are business/marketing, education, protective services/public administration.
Student Body Statistics The student body totals 9,534, of whom 8,351 are undergraduates (1,566 freshmen). 59 percent are women and 41 percent are men. Students come from 37 states and territories and 35 other countries. 87 percent are from Missouri. 2.2 percent are international students.
Expenses for 2002–03 *Application fee:* $20. *State resident tuition:* $3744 full-time, $124.80 per credit part-time. *Nonresident tuition:* $6819 full-time, $227.30 per credit part-time. *Mandatory fees:* $291 full-time, $9.70 per credit part-time. Full-time tuition and fees vary according to degree level. Part-time tuition and fees vary according to degree level. *College room and board:* $4938. *College room only:* $3052. Room and board charges vary according to board plan and housing facility.
Financial Aid Forms of aid include need-based and non-need-based scholarships, athletic grants, and part-time jobs. The average aided 2001–02 undergraduate received an aid package worth $5506. The application deadline for financial aid is continuous.
Freshman Admission Southeast requires a high school transcript, a minimum 2.0 high school GPA, SAT I or ACT scores, and TOEFL scores for international students. The application deadline for regular admission is August 1.
Entrance Difficulty Southeast assesses its entrance difficulty level as moderately difficult; minimally difficult for transfers. For the fall 2002 freshman class, 53 percent of the applicants were accepted.

For Further Information Contact Ms. Deborah Below, Director of Admissions, Southeast Missouri State University, MS 3550, Cape Girardeau, MO 63701. *Telephone:* 573-651-2590. *Fax:* 573-651-5936. *E-mail:* admissions@semo.edu. *Web site:* http://www.semo.edu/.

SOUTHWEST BAPTIST UNIVERSITY

Bolivar, Missouri

SBU is a coed, private, Southern Baptist, comprehensive institution, founded in 1878, offering degrees at the associate, bachelor's, and master's levels. It has a 152-acre campus in Bolivar.

Academic Information The faculty has 295 members (35% full-time), 41% with terminal degrees. The undergraduate student-faculty ratio is 21:1. The library holds 108,128 titles, 2,518 serial subscriptions, and 9,370 audiovisual materials. Special programs include academic remediation, an honors program, cooperative (work-study) education, study abroad, advanced placement credit, accelerated degree programs, ESL programs, double majors, independent study, summer session for credit, part-time degree programs (daytime, evenings, summer), and internships. The most frequently chosen baccalaureate fields are education, health professions and related sciences, psychology.
Student Body Statistics The student body totals 3,534, of whom 2,663 are undergraduates (463 freshmen). 67 percent are women and 33 percent are men. Students come from 40 states and territories and 11 other countries. 49 percent are from Missouri. 0.7 percent are international students.
Expenses for 2003–04 *Application fee:* $25. *Comprehensive fee:* $15,309 includes full-time tuition ($11,200), mandatory fees ($409), and college room and board ($3700). *College room only:* $2100. Room and board charges vary according to board plan and housing facility. *Part-time tuition:* $475 per credit hour. *Part-time mandatory fees:* $5 per credit hour, $66 per term. Part-time tuition and fees vary according to course load.
Financial Aid Forms of aid include need-based and non-need-based scholarships, athletic grants, and part-time jobs. The average aided 2002–03 undergraduate received an aid package worth an estimated $9613. The priority application deadline for financial aid is March 15.
Freshman Admission SBU requires a high school transcript, SAT I or ACT scores, and TOEFL scores for international students. An interview is recommended. The application deadline for regular admission is rolling and for early action it is December 31.
Transfer Admission The application deadline for admission is rolling.
Entrance Difficulty SBU assesses its entrance difficulty level as moderately difficult. For the fall 2002 freshman class, 89 percent of the applicants were accepted.

For Further Information Contact Mr. Rob Harris, Director of Admissions, Southwest Baptist University, 1600 University Avenue, Bolivar, MO 65613-2597. *Telephone:* 417-328-1809 or 800-526-5859 (toll-free). *Fax:* 417-328-1514. *E-mail:* rharris@sbuniv.edu. *Web site:* http://www.sbuniv.edu/.

SOUTHWEST MISSOURI STATE UNIVERSITY

Springfield, Missouri

SMSU is a coed, public, comprehensive institution, founded in 1905, offering degrees at the bachelor's and master's levels and postbachelor's certificates. It has a 225-acre campus in Springfield.

Academic Information The faculty has 1,000 members (73% full-time), 64% with terminal degrees. The undergraduate student-faculty ratio is

18:1. The library holds 2 million titles, 4,238 serial subscriptions, and 33,547 audiovisual materials. Special programs include services for learning-disabled students, an honors program, cooperative (work-study) education, study abroad, advanced placement credit, accelerated degree programs, Freshman Honors College, ESL programs, double majors, independent study, distance learning, self-designed majors, summer session for credit, part-time degree programs, adult/continuing education programs, internships, and arrangement for off-campus study with National Student Exchange. The most frequently chosen baccalaureate fields are business/marketing, communications/communication technologies, education.
Student Body Statistics The student body totals 18,718, of whom 15,448 are undergraduates (2,761 freshmen). 55 percent are women and 45 percent are men. Students come from 49 states and territories and 91 other countries. 92 percent are from Missouri. 2.2 percent are international students. 20 percent of the 2002 graduating class went on to graduate and professional schools.
Expenses for 2002–03 *Application fee:* $25. *State resident tuition:* $4274 full-time, $128 per credit hour part-time. *Nonresident tuition:* $8114 full-time, $256 per credit hour part-time. *Mandatory fees:* $434 full-time. *College room and board:* $4850. *College room only:* $2898. Room and board charges vary according to board plan and housing facility.
Financial Aid Forms of aid include need-based and non-need-based scholarships, athletic grants, and part-time jobs. The average aided 2001–02 undergraduate received an aid package worth $7253. The priority application deadline for financial aid is March 30.
Freshman Admission SMSU requires a high school transcript, SAT I or ACT scores, and TOEFL scores for international students. ACT scores are recommended. An essay and an interview are required for some. The application deadline for regular admission is August 2.
Transfer Admission The application deadline for admission is August 2.
Entrance Difficulty SMSU assesses its entrance difficulty level as moderately difficult. For the fall 2002 freshman class, 80 percent of the applicants were accepted.

For Further Information Contact Ms. Jill Duncan, Associate Director of Admissions, Southwest Missouri State University, 901 South National, Springfield, MO 65804-0094. *Telephone:* 417-836-5521 or 800-492-7900 (toll-free). *Fax:* 417-836-6334. *E-mail:* smsuinfo@smsu.edu. *Web site:* http://www.smsu.edu/.

STEPHENS COLLEGE

Columbia, Missouri

Stephens is a women's, private, comprehensive institution, founded in 1833, offering degrees at the associate, bachelor's, and master's levels. It has a 202-acre campus in Columbia.

Academic Information The faculty has 74 members (69% full-time), 61% with terminal degrees. The undergraduate student-faculty ratio is 10:1. The library holds 121,084 titles, 534 serial subscriptions, and 4,764 audiovisual materials. Special programs include academic remediation, services for learning-disabled students, an honors program, cooperative (work-study) education, study abroad, advanced placement credit, accelerated degree programs, Freshman Honors College, ESL programs, double majors, independent study, distance learning, self-designed majors, part-time degree programs (daytime, weekends), external degree programs, adult/continuing education programs, internships, and arrangement for off-campus study with University of Missouri, Columbia College (MO). The most frequently chosen baccalaureate fields are business/marketing, education, visual/performing arts.
Student Body Statistics The student body totals 669, of whom 618 are undergraduates (128 freshmen). Students come from 41 states and territories and 3 other countries. 48 percent are from Missouri. 3 percent are international students.
Expenses for 2003–04 *Application fee:* $25. *Comprehensive fee:* $24,260 includes full-time tuition ($17,360) and college room and board ($6900). Room and board charges vary according to board plan.
Financial Aid Forms of aid include need-based and non-need-based scholarships and part-time jobs. The average aided 2002–03 undergraduate received an aid package worth an estimated $17,694. The priority application deadline for financial aid is March 15.
Freshman Admission Stephens requires an essay, a high school transcript, a minimum 2.5 high school GPA, 1 recommendation, SAT I or ACT scores, and TOEFL scores for international students. An interview is recommended. The application deadline for regular admission is July 31 and for early decision it is December 15.
Transfer Admission The application deadline for admission is July 31.
Entrance Difficulty Stephens assesses its entrance difficulty level as moderately difficult. For the fall 2002 freshman class, 85 percent of the applicants were accepted.

For Further Information Contact Ms. Amy Shaver, Director of Admissions, Stephens College, Box 2121, Columbia, MO 65215-0002. *Telephone:* 573-876-7207 or 800-876-7207 (toll-free). *Fax:* 573-876-7237. *E-mail:* apply@stephens.edu. *Web site:* http://www.stephens.edu/.

TRUMAN STATE UNIVERSITY

Kirksville, Missouri

Truman is a coed, public, comprehensive institution, founded in 1867, offering degrees at the bachelor's and master's levels. It has a 140-acre campus in Kirksville.

Academic Information The faculty has 399 members (92% full-time), 80% with terminal degrees. The undergraduate student-faculty ratio is 15:1. The library holds 481,424 titles, 3,197 serial subscriptions, and 36,724 audiovisual materials. Special programs include services for learning-disabled students, an honors program, study abroad, advanced placement credit, accelerated degree programs, ESL programs, double majors, summer session for credit, part-time degree programs (daytime, summer), internships, and arrangement for off-campus study with Gulf Coast Research Laboratory, Reis Biological Station, Kirksville College of Osteopathic Medicine. The most frequently chosen baccalaureate fields are biological/life sciences, business/marketing, English.
Student Body Statistics The student body totals 5,867, of whom 5,636 are undergraduates (1,448 freshmen). 59 percent are women and 41 percent are men. Students come from 38 states and territories and 49 other countries. 76 percent are from Missouri. 4.1 percent are international students. 35.4 percent of the 2002 graduating class went on to graduate and professional schools.
Expenses for 2002–03 *Application fee:* $0. *State resident tuition:* $4144 full-time, $172 per credit hour part-time. *Nonresident tuition:* $7544 full-time, $314 per credit hour part-time. *Mandatory fees:* $56 full-time. Part-time tuition varies according to course load. *College room and board:* $4928. Room and board charges vary according to board plan and housing facility.
Financial Aid Forms of aid include need-based and non-need-based scholarships, athletic grants, and part-time jobs. The average aided 2001–02 undergraduate received an aid package worth $5263. The priority application deadline for financial aid is April 1.
Freshman Admission Truman requires an essay, a high school transcript, SAT I or ACT scores, and TOEFL scores for international students. A minimum 3.0 high school GPA, an interview, and ACT scores are recommended. The application deadline for regular admission is March 1 and for early action it is November 15.
Transfer Admission The application deadline for admission is May 1.
Entrance Difficulty Truman assesses its entrance difficulty level as moderately difficult. For the fall 2002 freshman class, 79 percent of the applicants were accepted.

For Further Information Contact Mr. Brad Chambers, Co-Director of Admissions, Truman State University, 205 McClain Hall, Kirksville, MO 63501-4221. *Telephone:* 660-785-4114 or 800-892-7792 (toll-free in-state). *Fax:* 660-785-7456. *E-mail:* admissions@truman.edu. *Web site:* http://www.truman.edu/.

See page 340 for a narrative description.

UNIVERSITY OF MISSOURI–COLUMBIA

Columbia, Missouri

MU is a coed, public unit of University of Missouri System, founded in 1839, offering degrees at the bachelor's, master's, doctoral, and first professional levels and post-master's certificates. It has a 1,348-acre campus in Columbia.

Academic Information The faculty has 1,748 members (96% full-time), 86% with terminal degrees. The undergraduate student-faculty ratio is 18:1. The library holds 3 million titles, 16,073 serial subscriptions, and 19,383 audiovisual materials. Special programs include academic remediation, services for learning-disabled students, an honors program, cooperative (work-study) education, study abroad, advanced placement credit, accelerated degree programs, Freshman Honors College, ESL programs, double majors, independent study, distance learning, self-designed majors, summer session for credit, part-time degree programs (daytime, evenings), external degree programs, adult/continuing education programs, internships, and arrangement for off-campus study with Mid-Missouri Associated Colleges and Universities, National Student Exchange. The most frequently chosen baccalaureate fields are business/marketing, communications/communication technologies, engineering/engineering technologies.

Student Body Statistics The student body totals 26,124, of whom 19,698 are undergraduates (4,439 freshmen). 52 percent are women and 48 percent are men. Students come from 51 states and territories and 88 other countries. 88 percent are from Missouri. 1.3 percent are international students.

Expenses for 2002–03 *Application fee:* $35. *State resident tuition:* $4872 full-time, $162.40 per credit hour part-time. *Nonresident tuition:* $14,025 full-time, $467.50 per credit hour part-time. *Mandatory fees:* $680 full-time, $20.25 per credit hour part-time. *College room and board:* $5374. Room and board charges vary according to board plan and housing facility.

Financial Aid Forms of aid include need-based and non-need-based scholarships, athletic grants, and part-time jobs. The average aided 2002–03 undergraduate received an aid package worth an estimated $7544. The priority application deadline for financial aid is March 1.

Freshman Admission MU requires a high school transcript, specific high school curriculum, ACT scores, and TOEFL scores for international students. The application deadline for regular admission is rolling.

Transfer Admission The application deadline for admission is rolling.

Entrance Difficulty MU assesses its entrance difficulty level as moderately difficult. For the fall 2002 freshman class, 88 percent of the applicants were accepted.

For Further Information Contact Ms. Georgeanne Porter, Director of Admissions, University of Missouri–Columbia, 230 Jesse Hall, Columbia, MO 65211. *Telephone:* 573-882-7786 or 800-225-6075 (toll-free in-state). *Fax:* 573-882-7887. *E-mail:* mu4u@missouri.edu. *Web site:* http://www.missouri.edu.

UNIVERSITY OF MISSOURI–KANSAS CITY

Kansas City, Missouri

UMKC is a coed, public unit of University of Missouri System, founded in 1929, offering degrees at the bachelor's, master's, doctoral, and first professional levels and first professional certificates. It has a 191-acre campus in Kansas City.

Academic Information The faculty has 910 members (58% full-time), 65% with terminal degrees. The undergraduate student-faculty ratio is 9:1. The library holds 1 million titles, 6,951 serial subscriptions, and 449,074 audiovisual materials. Special programs include services for learning-disabled students, an honors program, cooperative (work-study) education, study abroad, advanced placement credit, accelerated degree programs, ESL programs, self-designed majors, summer session for credit, part-time degree programs (daytime, evenings, weekends, summer), adult/continuing education programs, internships, and arrangement for off-campus study with other campuses of the University of Missouri System. The most frequently chosen baccalaureate fields are business/marketing, education, liberal arts/general studies.

Student Body Statistics The student body totals 13,881, of whom 8,870 are undergraduates (763 freshmen). 60 percent are women and 40 percent are men. Students come from 45 states and territories and 105 other countries. 81 percent are from Missouri. 4.5 percent are international students.

Expenses for 2002–03 *Application fee:* $25. *State resident tuition:* $4872 full-time. *Nonresident tuition:* $14,023 full-time. *Mandatory fees:* $60 full-time. Full-time tuition and fees vary according to course load, program, and student level. *College room and board:* $5235. *College room only:* $3070. Room and board charges vary according to board plan and housing facility.

Financial Aid Forms of aid include need-based and non-need-based scholarships, athletic grants, and part-time jobs. The average aided 2002–03 undergraduate received an aid package worth an estimated $10,778. The priority application deadline for financial aid is March 1.

Freshman Admission UMKC requires a high school transcript, ACT scores, and TOEFL scores for international students. The application deadline for regular admission is rolling.

Transfer Admission The application deadline for admission is rolling.

Entrance Difficulty UMKC assesses its entrance difficulty level as moderately difficult; most difficult for medicine programs. For the fall 2002 freshman class, 78 percent of the applicants were accepted.

For Further Information Contact Ms. Jennifer DeHaemers, Director of Admissions, University of Missouri–Kansas City, Office of Admissions, 5100 Rockhill Road, Kansas City, MO 64110-2499. *Telephone:* 816-235-1111 or 800-775-8652 (toll-free out-of-state). *Fax:* 816-235-5544. *E-mail:* admit@umkc.edu. *Web site:* http://www.umkc.edu/.

UNIVERSITY OF MISSOURI–ROLLA

Rolla, Missouri

UMR is a coed, public unit of University of Missouri System, founded in 1870, offering degrees at the bachelor's, master's, and doctoral levels. It has a 284-acre campus in Rolla.

Academic Information The faculty has 354 members (88% full-time), 85% with terminal degrees. The undergraduate student-faculty ratio is 14:1. The library holds 255,768 titles, 1,495 serial subscriptions, and 6,353 audiovisual materials. Special programs include academic remediation, services for learning-disabled students, an honors program, cooperative (work-study) education, study abroad, advanced placement credit, accelerated degree programs, Freshman Honors College, ESL programs, double majors, independent study, distance learning, summer session for credit, part-time degree programs, adult/continuing education programs, internships, and arrangement for off-campus study with University of Missouri–Columbia. The most frequently chosen baccalaureate fields are computer/information sciences, engineering/engineering technologies, physical sciences.

Student Body Statistics The student body totals 5,240, of whom 3,849 are undergraduates (795 freshmen). 23 percent are women and 77 percent are men. Students come from 47 states and territories and 38 other countries. 78 percent are from Missouri. 3.2 percent are international students. 17 percent of the 2002 graduating class went on to graduate and professional schools.

Expenses for 2002–03 *Application fee:* $25. *State resident tuition:* $4872 full-time, $162.40 per credit hour part-time. *Nonresident tuition:* $13,917 full-time, $467.50 per credit hour part-time. *Mandatory fees:* $778 full-time, $26.44 per credit hour part-time. *College room and board:* $5230. *College room only:* $3170.

Financial Aid Forms of aid include need-based and non-need-based scholarships, athletic grants, and part-time jobs. The average aided 2001–02 undergraduate received an aid package worth $8203. The priority application deadline for financial aid is March 1.

Freshman Admission UMR requires a high school transcript and SAT I or ACT scores. TOEFL scores for international students are recommended. The application deadline for regular admission is July 1.

Transfer Admission The application deadline for admission is July 1.

Entrance Difficulty UMR assesses its entrance difficulty level as very difficult; moderately difficult for transfers. For the fall 2002 freshman class, 92 percent of the applicants were accepted.

For Further Information Contact Ms. Lynn Stichnote, Director of Admissions, University of Missouri–Rolla, 106 Parker Hall, Rolla, MO 65409. *Telephone:* 573-341-4164 or 800-522-0938 (toll-free). *Fax:* 573-341-4082. *E-mail:* umrolla@umr.edu. *Web site:* http://www.umr.edu/.

UNIVERSITY OF MISSOURI–ST. LOUIS

St. Louis, Missouri

UM-St. Louis is a coed, public unit of University of Missouri System, founded in 1963, offering degrees at the bachelor's, master's, doctoral, and first professional levels and postbachelor's certificates. It has a 250-acre campus in St. Louis.

Academic Information The faculty has 661 members (45% full-time), 59% with terminal degrees. The undergraduate student-faculty ratio is 19:1. The library holds 782,431 titles, 3,570 serial subscriptions, and 3,878 audiovisual materials. Special programs include services for learning-disabled students, an honors program, cooperative (work-study) education, study abroad, advanced placement credit, accelerated degree programs, Freshman Honors College, ESL programs, double majors, independent study, distance learning, self-designed majors, summer session for credit, part-time degree programs (daytime, evenings, weekends, summer), adult/continuing education programs, internships, and arrangement for off-campus study with Southern Illinois University, Saint Louis University, Washington University in St. Louis, St. Charles Community College, Mineral Area Community College, East Central Community College, Jefferson Community College. The most frequently chosen baccalaureate fields are business/marketing, education, social sciences and history.
Student Body Statistics The student body totals 15,658, of whom 12,715 are undergraduates (519 freshmen). 60 percent are women and 40 percent are men. Students come from 38 states and territories and 61 other countries. 96 percent are from Missouri. 2.6 percent are international students.
Expenses for 2002–03 *Application fee:* $25. *State resident tuition:* $3682 full-time, $153.40 per credit hour part-time. *Nonresident tuition:* $11,004 full-time, $458.40 per credit hour part-time. *Mandatory fees:* $884 full-time, $36.82 per credit hour part-time. Full-time tuition and fees vary according to reciprocity agreements. Part-time tuition and fees vary according to course load. *College room and board:* $5400. *College room only:* $4100. Room and board charges vary according to board plan and housing facility.
Financial Aid Forms of aid include need-based and non-need-based scholarships, athletic grants, and part-time jobs. The average aided 2002–03 undergraduate received an aid package worth an estimated $6680. The priority application deadline for financial aid is April 1.
Freshman Admission UM-St. Louis requires a high school transcript, SAT I or ACT scores, and TOEFL scores for international students. The application deadline for regular admission is rolling.
Transfer Admission The application deadline for admission is rolling.
Entrance Difficulty UM-St. Louis assesses its entrance difficulty level as moderately difficult. For the fall 2002 freshman class, 45 percent of the applicants were accepted.

For Further Information Contact Ms. Melissa Hattman, Director of Admissions, University of Missouri–St. Louis, 351 Millennuim Student Center, 8001 National Bridge Road, St. Louis, MO 63121-4499. *Telephone:* 314-516-5460 or 888-GO2-UMSL (toll-free in-state). *Fax:* 314-516-5310. *E-mail:* mhattman@umsl.edu. *Web site:* http://www.umsl.edu/.

UNIVERSITY OF PHOENIX-KANSAS CITY CAMPUS

Kansas City, Missouri

University of Phoenix-Kansas City Campus is a coed, proprietary, comprehensive institution, founded in 2002, offering degrees at the associate, bachelor's, master's, and doctoral levels and post-master's and postbachelor's certificates (courses conducted at 121 campuses and learning centers in 25 states).

Academic Information The faculty has 65 members (5% full-time). The library holds 27 million titles and 11,648 serial subscriptions. Special programs include advanced placement credit, accelerated degree programs, independent study, distance learning, external degree programs, and adult/continuing education programs.
Student Body Statistics The student body totals 260, of whom 178 are undergraduates (20 freshmen). 55 percent are women and 45 percent are men.
Expenses for 2002–03 *Tuition:* $9600 full-time, $320 per credit part-time.
Financial Aid The application deadline for financial aid is continuous.
Freshman Admission University of Phoenix-Kansas City Campus requires 1 recommendation, 2 years of work experience, 23 years of age, and TOEFL scores for international students. A high school transcript is required for some. The application deadline for regular admission is rolling.
Transfer Admission The application deadline for admission is rolling.
Entrance Difficulty University of Phoenix-Kansas City Campus has an open admission policy.

For Further Information Contact Ms. Beth Barilla, Director of Admissions, University of Phoenix-Kansas City Campus, 4615 East Elwood Street, Mail Stop 10-0030, Phoenix, AZ 85040-1958. *Telephone:* 480-557-1712 or 800-228-7240 (toll-free). *Fax:* 480-594-1758. *E-mail:* beth.barilla@apollogrp.edu. *Web site:* http://www.phoenix.edu/.

UNIVERSITY OF PHOENIX–ST. LOUIS CAMPUS

St. Louis, Missouri

University of Phoenix–St. Louis Campus is a coed, proprietary, comprehensive institution, founded in 2000, offering degrees at the associate, bachelor's, master's, and doctoral levels and post-master's and postbachelor's certificates (courses conducted at 121 campuses and learning centers in 25 states).

Academic Information The faculty has 62 members (3% full-time), 18% with terminal degrees. The undergraduate student-faculty ratio is 10:1. The library holds 27 million titles and 11,648 serial subscriptions. Special programs include advanced placement credit, accelerated degree programs, independent study, distance learning, external degree programs, and adult/continuing education programs.
Student Body Statistics The student body totals 447, of whom 328 are undergraduates. 59 percent are women and 41 percent are men. 0.6 percent are international students.
Expenses for 2002–03 *Application fee:* $85. *Tuition:* $10,080 full-time, $336 per credit part-time.
Financial Aid The application deadline for financial aid is continuous.
Freshman Admission University of Phoenix–St. Louis Campus requires 1 recommendation, 2 years of work experience, 23 years of age, and TOEFL scores for international students. A high school transcript is required for some. The application deadline for regular admission is rolling.
Transfer Admission The application deadline for admission is rolling.
Entrance Difficulty University of Phoenix–St. Louis Campus has an open admission policy.

For Further Information Contact Ms. Beth Barilla, Director of Admissions, University of Phoenix–St. Louis Campus, 4615 East Elwood Street, Mail Stop 10-0030, Phoenix, AZ 85040-1958. *Telephone:* 480-557-1712, 888-326-7737 (toll-free in-state), or 800-228-7240 (toll-free out-of-state). *Fax:* 480-594-1758. *E-mail:* beth.barilla@apollogrp.edu. *Web site:* http://www.phoenix.edu/.

VATTEROTT COLLEGE

St. Ann, Missouri

Vatterott College is a coed, proprietary, primarily two-year college, founded in 1969, offering degrees at the associate and bachelor's levels. It is located in St. Ann near St. Louis.

Student Body Statistics The student body is made up of 600 undergraduates.

Financial Aid Forms of aid include need-based scholarships. The application deadline for financial aid is continuous.

For Further Information Contact Ms. Michelle Tinsley, Co-Director of Admissions, Vatterott College, 3925 Industrial Drive, St. Ann, MO 63074-1807. *Telephone:* 314-843-4200 or 800-345-6018 (toll-free). *Fax:* 314-428-5956. *Web site:* http://www.vatterott-college.edu/.

VATTEROTT COLLEGE

Sunset Hills, Missouri

Vatterott College is a coed, proprietary, primarily two-year college, offering degrees at the associate and bachelor's levels.

Student Body Statistics The student body is made up of 600 undergraduates.

For Further Information Contact Ms. Michelle Tinsley, Director of Admission, Vatterott College, 12970 Maurer Industrial Drive, St. Louis, MO 63127. *Telephone:* 314-843-4200. *Fax:* 314-843-1709. *E-mail:* sunsethills@vatterott-college.edu. *Web site:* http://www.vatterott-college.edu/.

WASHINGTON UNIVERSITY IN ST. LOUIS

St. Louis, Missouri

Washington is a coed, private university, founded in 1853, offering degrees at the bachelor's, master's, doctoral, and first professional levels and postbachelor's certificates. It has a 169-acre campus in St. Louis.

Academic Information The faculty has 1,062 members (76% full-time), 75% with terminal degrees. The undergraduate student-faculty ratio is 7:1. The library holds 2 million titles, 18,316 serial subscriptions, and 69,422 audiovisual materials. Special programs include services for learning-disabled students, cooperative (work-study) education, study abroad, advanced placement credit, accelerated degree programs, ESL programs, double majors, independent study, self-designed majors, summer session for credit, part-time degree programs, adult/continuing education programs, internships, and arrangement for off-campus study with Consortium on Financing Higher Education. The most frequently chosen baccalaureate fields are business/marketing, engineering/engineering technologies, social sciences and history.

Student Body Statistics The student body totals 12,767, of whom 7,219 are undergraduates (1,342 freshmen). 53 percent are women and 47 percent are men. Students come from 52 states and territories and 104 other countries. 11 percent are from Missouri. 4.6 percent are international students. 33 percent of the 2002 graduating class went on to graduate and professional schools.

Expenses for 2003–04 *Application fee:* $55. *Comprehensive fee:* $38,293 includes full-time tuition ($28,300), mandatory fees ($753), and college room and board ($9240). *College room only:* $5424. Room and board charges vary according to board plan and housing facility. *Part-time tuition:* varies with class time.

Financial Aid Forms of aid include need-based and non-need-based scholarships and part-time jobs. The average aided 2002–03 undergraduate received an aid package worth an estimated $22,979. The application deadline for financial aid is February 15.

Freshman Admission Washington requires an essay, a high school transcript, 2 recommendations, SAT I or ACT scores, and TOEFL scores for international students. A minimum 3.0 high school GPA and portfolio for art and architecture programs are recommended. The application deadline for regular admission is January 15; for early decision plan 1 it is November 15; and for early decision plan 2 it is January 1.

Transfer Admission The application deadline for admission is April 15.

Entrance Difficulty Washington assesses its entrance difficulty level as most difficult. For the fall 2002 freshman class, 24 percent of the applicants were accepted.

For Further Information Contact Ms. Nanette Tarbouni, Director of Admissions, Washington University in St. Louis, Campus Box 1089, One Brookings Drive, St. Louis, MO 63130-4899. *Telephone:* 314-935-6000 or 800-638-0700 (toll-free). *Fax:* 314-935-4290. *E-mail:* admissions@wustl.edu. *Web site:* http://www.wustl.edu/.

WEBSTER UNIVERSITY

St. Louis, Missouri

Webster is a coed, private, comprehensive institution, founded in 1915, offering degrees at the bachelor's, master's, and doctoral levels. It has a 47-acre campus in St. Louis.

Academic Information The faculty has 1,947 members (7% full-time), 38% with terminal degrees. The undergraduate student-faculty ratio is 13:1. The library holds 268,000 titles, 1,480 serial subscriptions, and 14,800 audiovisual materials. Special programs include academic remediation, services for learning-disabled students, cooperative (work-study) education, study abroad, advanced placement credit, accelerated degree programs, ESL programs, double majors, independent study, distance learning, self-designed majors, summer session for credit, part-time degree programs (daytime, evenings, summer), adult/continuing education programs, internships, and arrangement for off-campus study with Fontbonne College, Lindenwood College, Maryville University of Saint Louis, Eden Theological Seminary, Missouri Baptist College. The most frequently chosen baccalaureate fields are business/marketing, communications/communication technologies, computer/information sciences.

Student Body Statistics The student body totals 6,890, of whom 3,458 are undergraduates (393 freshmen). 62 percent are women and 38 percent are men. Students come from 48 states and territories and 104 other countries. 72 percent are from Missouri. 3.7 percent are international students.

Expenses for 2002–03 *Application fee:* $25. *Comprehensive fee:* $20,720 includes full-time tuition ($14,600) and college room and board ($6120). *College room only:* $3018. Full-time tuition varies according to program. Room and board charges vary according to board plan and housing facility. *Part-time tuition:* $410 per credit hour. Part-time tuition varies according to location.

Financial Aid Forms of aid include need-based and non-need-based scholarships and part-time jobs. The average aided 2002–03 undergraduate received an aid package worth an estimated $15,236. The priority application deadline for financial aid is April 1.

Freshman Admission Webster requires a high school transcript, a minimum 2.5 high school GPA, 1 recommendation, SAT I or ACT scores, and TOEFL scores for international students. An essay, a minimum 3.0 high school GPA, and an interview are recommended. Audition is required for some. The application deadline for regular admission is July 1.

Transfer Admission The application deadline for admission is August 1.

Entrance Difficulty Webster assesses its entrance difficulty level as moderately difficult. For the fall 2002 freshman class, 58 percent of the applicants were accepted.

For Further Information Contact Mr. Andrew Laue, Associate Director of Undergraduate Admission, Webster University, 470 East Lockwood Avenue, St. Louis, MO 63119-3194. *Telephone:* 314-968-6991 or 800-75-ENROL (toll-free). *Fax:* 314-968-7115. *E-mail:* admit@webster.edu. *Web site:* http://www.webster.edu/.

WENTWORTH MILITARY ACADEMY AND JUNIOR COLLEGE

Lexington, Missouri

WMA is a coed, private, two-year college, founded in 1880, offering degrees at the associate level. It has a 130-acre campus in Lexington near Kansas City.

Academic Information The faculty has 32 members (22% full-time). The student-faculty ratio is 9:1. The library holds 18,890 titles, 49 serial subscriptions, and 919 audiovisual materials. Special programs include academic remediation, advanced placement credit, ESL programs, self-designed majors, summer session for credit, part-time degree programs (daytime, evenings, summer), and adult/continuing education programs.
Student Body Statistics The student body is made up of 290 undergraduates. Students come from 22 states and territories and 4 other countries. 82 percent are from Missouri. 0.6 percent are international students. 76 percent of the 2002 graduating class went on to four-year colleges.
Expenses for 2002–03 *Application fee:* $100. *Comprehensive fee:* $17,035 includes full-time tuition ($10,390), mandatory fees ($2065), and college room and board ($4580). *College room only:* $2060. *Part-time tuition:* $125 per credit.
Financial Aid Forms of aid include need-based scholarships and part-time jobs. The application deadline for financial aid is continuous.
Freshman Admission WMA requires a high school transcript and TOEFL scores for international students. SAT I or ACT scores are recommended. The application deadline for regular admission is rolling.
Transfer Admission The application deadline for admission is rolling.
Entrance Difficulty WMA assesses its entrance difficulty level as moderately difficult. For the fall 2002 freshman class, 95 percent of the applicants were accepted.

For Further Information Contact Maj. Todd Kitchen, Dean of Admissions, Wentworth Military Academy and Junior College, 1880 Washington Avenue, Lexington, MO 64067. *Telephone:* 660-259-2221. *Fax:* 660-259-2677. *E-mail:* admissions@wma1880.org. *Web site:* http://www.wma1880.org/.

WESTMINSTER COLLEGE

Fulton, Missouri

Westminster is a coed, private, four-year college, founded in 1851, affiliated with the Presbyterian Church, offering degrees at the bachelor's level. It has a 65-acre campus in Fulton.

Academic Information The faculty has 79 members (71% full-time), 72% with terminal degrees. The student-faculty ratio is 12:1. The library holds 111,922 titles, 3,081 serial subscriptions, and 9,082 audiovisual materials. Special programs include academic remediation, services for learning-disabled students, an honors program, cooperative (work-study) education, study abroad, advanced placement credit, double majors, independent study, self-designed majors, summer session for credit, part-time degree programs (daytime), internships, and arrangement for off-campus study with Chicago Urban Studies Semester, American University, Beaver College. The most frequently chosen baccalaureate fields are education, psychology, social sciences and history.
Student Body Statistics The student body is made up of 789 undergraduates (208 freshmen). 45 percent are women and 55 percent are men. Students come from 28 states and territories and 15 other countries. 73 percent are from Missouri. 5.3 percent are international students.
Expenses for 2003–04 *Application fee:* $25. *Comprehensive fee:* $17,970 includes full-time tuition ($12,300), mandatory fees ($240), and college room and board ($5430). *College room only:* $2740. Room and board charges vary according to board plan and housing facility. *Part-time tuition:* $513 per credit hour. *Part-time mandatory fees:* $120 per term.
Financial Aid Forms of aid include need-based and non-need-based scholarships and part-time jobs. The average aided 2002–03 undergraduate received an aid package worth an estimated $14,906. The priority application deadline for financial aid is February 28.
Freshman Admission Westminster requires a high school transcript, 1 recommendation, and SAT I or ACT scores. An essay is recommended. An interview is required for some. The application deadline for regular admission is rolling.
Transfer Admission The application deadline for admission is rolling.
Entrance Difficulty Westminster assesses its entrance difficulty level as moderately difficult. For the fall 2002 freshman class, 66 percent of the applicants were accepted.

For Further Information Contact Dr. Patrick Kirby, Dean of Enrollment Services, Westminster College, 501 Westminster Avenue, Fulton, MO 65251-1299. *Telephone:* 573-592-5251 or 800-475-3361 (toll-free). *Fax:* 573-592-5255. *E-mail:* admissions@jaynet.wcmo.edu. *Web site:* http://www.westminster-mo.edu/.

WILLIAM JEWELL COLLEGE

Liberty, Missouri

William Jewell is a coed, private, Baptist, four-year college, founded in 1849, offering degrees at the bachelor's level (also offers evening program with significant enrollment not reflected in profile). It has a 149-acre campus in Liberty near Kansas City.

Academic Information The faculty has 128 members (59% full-time), 55% with terminal degrees. The student-faculty ratio is 12:1. The library holds 260,119 titles, 868 serial subscriptions, and 27,617 audiovisual materials. Special programs include academic remediation, an honors program, cooperative (work-study) education, study abroad, advanced placement credit, double majors, independent study, self-designed majors, summer session for credit, part-time degree programs (daytime, evenings, weekends, summer), adult/continuing education programs, and internships. The most frequently chosen baccalaureate fields are business/marketing, education, psychology.
Student Body Statistics The student body is made up of 1,168 undergraduates (345 freshmen). 58 percent are women and 42 percent are men. Students come from 32 states and territories and 12 other countries. 97 percent are from Missouri. 1.8 percent are international students. 19 percent of the 2002 graduating class went on to graduate and professional schools.
Expenses for 2002–03 *Application fee:* $25. *Comprehensive fee:* $19,950 includes full-time tuition ($15,400) and college room and board ($4550). *College room only:* $1920. Full-time tuition varies according to class time and course load. Room and board charges vary according to board plan and housing facility. *Part-time tuition:* $600 per semester hour. Part-time tuition varies according to class time.
Financial Aid Forms of aid include need-based and non-need-based scholarships, athletic grants, and part-time jobs. The average aided 2002–03 undergraduate received an aid package worth an estimated $11,899. The priority application deadline for financial aid is March 1.
Freshman Admission William Jewell requires a high school transcript, a minimum 2.0 high school GPA, SAT I or ACT scores, and TOEFL scores for international students. An essay, a minimum 2.5 high school GPA, 2 recommendations, and an interview are recommended. The application deadline for regular admission is rolling and for early action it is November 15.
Transfer Admission The application deadline for admission is rolling.
Entrance Difficulty William Jewell assesses its entrance difficulty level as moderately difficult. For the fall 2002 freshman class, 96 percent of the applicants were accepted.

For Further Information Contact Mr. Chad Jolly, Dean of Enrollment Development, William Jewell College, 500 College Hill, Liberty, MO 64068. *Telephone:* 816-781-7700 or 800-753-7009 (toll-free). *Fax:* 816-415-5027. *E-mail:* admission@william.jewell.edu. *Web site:* http://www.jewell.edu/.

WILLIAM WOODS UNIVERSITY

Fulton, Missouri

William Woods is a coed, private, comprehensive institution, founded in 1870, affiliated with the Christian Church (Disciples of Christ), offering degrees at the associate, bachelor's, and master's levels. It has a 170-acre campus in Fulton near St. Louis.

Academic Information The faculty has 58 members (74% full-time), 59% with terminal degrees. The undergraduate student-faculty ratio is 13:1. The library holds 93,917 titles and 26,773 audiovisual materials. Special programs include academic remediation, an honors program, study abroad, advanced placement credit, accelerated degree programs, double majors, independent study, self-designed majors, summer session for credit, part-time degree programs (evenings, weekends), adult/continuing education programs, internships, and arrangement for off-campus study with University of Missouri–Columbia, Westminster College (MO), Stephens College, Lincoln University (MO). The most frequently chosen baccalaureate fields are business/marketing, computer/information sciences, visual/performing arts.

Student Body Statistics The student body totals 1,813, of whom 912 are undergraduates (247 freshmen). 73 percent are women and 27 percent are men. Students come from 38 states and territories and 11 other countries. 78 percent are from Missouri. 4.2 percent are international students.

Expenses for 2003–04 *Application fee:* $25. *Comprehensive fee:* $20,120 includes full-time tuition ($14,000), mandatory fees ($420), and college room and board ($5700). Full-time tuition and fees vary according to program. Room and board charges vary according to board plan. *Part-time tuition:* $467 per credit hour. *Part-time mandatory fees:* $15 per term.

Financial Aid Forms of aid include need-based and non-need-based scholarships, athletic grants, and part-time jobs. The average aided 2002–03 undergraduate received an aid package worth an estimated $14,162. The priority application deadline for financial aid is March 1.

Freshman Admission William Woods requires a high school transcript, SAT I or ACT scores, and TOEFL scores for international students. An interview is recommended. An essay and 2 recommendations are required for some. The application deadline for regular admission is rolling.

Transfer Admission The application deadline for admission is rolling.

Entrance Difficulty William Woods assesses its entrance difficulty level as moderately difficult. For the fall 2002 freshman class, 94 percent of the applicants were accepted.

For Further Information Contact Ms. Laura Archuleta, Executive Director of Enrollment Services, William Woods University, One University Avenue, Fulton, MO 65251. *Telephone:* 573-592-4221 or 800-995-3159 Ext. 4221 (toll-free). *Fax:* 573-592-1146. *E-mail:* admissions@williamwoods.edu. *Web site:* http://www.williamwoods.edu/.

Nebraska

BELLEVUE UNIVERSITY

Bellevue, Nebraska

Bellevue University is a coed, private, comprehensive institution, founded in 1965, offering degrees at the bachelor's and master's levels. It has a 19-acre campus in Bellevue near Omaha.

Academic Information The faculty has 152 members (41% full-time), 29% with terminal degrees. The undergraduate student-faculty ratio is 17:1. The library holds 87,000 titles, 7,564 serial subscriptions, and 3,955 audiovisual materials. Special programs include academic remediation, cooperative (work-study) education, advanced placement credit, accelerated degree programs, ESL programs, double majors, independent study, distance learning, summer session for credit, part-time degree programs, external degree programs, adult/continuing education programs, and internships.

Student Body Statistics The student body totals 4,057, of whom 3,321 are undergraduates (226 freshmen). 51 percent are women and 49 percent are men. Students come from 40 states and territories and 67 other countries. 80 percent are from Nebraska. 9.5 percent are international students. 15 percent of the 2002 graduating class went on to graduate and professional schools.

Expenses for 2002–03 *Application fee:* $25. *Tuition:* $4200 full-time, $140 per credit hour part-time. *Mandatory fees:* $70 full-time, $45 per term part-time. Full-time tuition and fees vary according to program. Part-time tuition and fees vary according to program.

Financial Aid Forms of aid include need-based and non-need-based scholarships, athletic grants, and part-time jobs. The application deadline for financial aid is continuous.

Freshman Admission Bellevue University requires a high school transcript, an interview, and TOEFL scores for international students. 3 recommendations and SAT I or ACT scores are required for some. The application deadline for regular admission is rolling.

Transfer Admission The application deadline for admission is rolling.

Entrance Difficulty Bellevue University has an open admission policy.

For Further Information Contact Ms. Kelley Dengel, Information Center Manager, Bellevue University, 1000 Galvin Road South, Bellevue, NE 68005-3098. *Telephone:* 402-293-3769 or 800-756-7920 (toll-free). *Fax:* 402-293-2020. *E-mail:* set@scholars.bellevue.edu. *Web site:* http://www.bellevue.edu/.

CHADRON STATE COLLEGE

Chadron, Nebraska

Chadron State is a coed, public, comprehensive unit of Nebraska State College System, founded in 1911, offering degrees at the bachelor's and master's levels and post-master's certificates. It has a 281-acre campus in Chadron.

Academic Information The faculty has 121 members (82% full-time), 58% with terminal degrees. The undergraduate student-faculty ratio is 22:1. The library holds 213,231 titles, 720 serial subscriptions, and 5,596 audiovisual materials. Special programs include services for learning-disabled students, an honors program, cooperative (work-study) education, study abroad, advanced placement credit, Freshman Honors College, double majors, independent study, distance learning, self-designed majors, summer session for credit, part-time degree programs (daytime, evenings, summer), adult/continuing education programs, and internships. The most frequently chosen baccalaureate fields are business/marketing, education, protective services/public administration.

Student Body Statistics The student body totals 2,712, of whom 2,392 are undergraduates (417 freshmen). 58 percent are women and 42 percent are men. Students come from 31 states and territories and 10 other countries. 74 percent are from Nebraska. 1 percent are international students.

Expenses for 2002–03 *Application fee:* $15. *State resident tuition:* $2640 full-time, $76 per credit hour part-time. *Nonresident tuition:* $5280 full-time, $153 per credit hour part-time. *Mandatory fees:* $650 full-time, $17.75 per credit hour part-time, $15 per term part-time. *College room and board:* $3655. *College room only:* $1778.

Financial Aid Forms of aid include need-based scholarships and part-time jobs. The average aided 2001–02 undergraduate received an aid package worth $2375. The priority application deadline for financial aid is June 1.

Freshman Admission Chadron State requires a high school transcript, health forms, and TOEFL scores for international students. SAT I or ACT scores are recommended. The application deadline for regular admission is rolling.

Transfer Admission The application deadline for admission is rolling.

Entrance Difficulty Chadron State has an open admission policy. It assesses its entrance difficulty as minimally difficult for transfers.

For Further Information Contact Ms. Tena Cook Gould, Director of Admissions, Chadron State College, 1000 Main Street, Chadron, NE 69337-2690. *Telephone:* 308-432-6263 or 800-242-3766 (toll-free in-state). *Fax:* 308-432-6229. *E-mail:* inquire@csc1.csc.edu. *Web site:* http://www.csc.edu/.

CLARKSON COLLEGE

Omaha, Nebraska

Clarkson is a coed, primarily women's, private, comprehensive unit of Nebraska Health System, founded in 1888, offering degrees at the associate, bachelor's, and master's levels. It has a 3-acre campus in Omaha.

Academic Information The faculty has 64 members (97% full-time), 11% with terminal degrees. The undergraduate student-faculty ratio is 12:1. The library holds 8,807 titles, 262 serial subscriptions, and 530 audiovisual materials. Special programs include cooperative (work-study) education, study abroad, advanced placement credit, accelerated degree programs, double majors, independent study, distance learning, summer session for credit, part-time degree programs (daytime, evenings, summer), external degree programs, adult/continuing education programs, and internships. The most frequently chosen baccalaureate fields are business/marketing, health professions and related sciences.
Student Body Statistics The student body totals 507, of whom 421 are undergraduates (142 freshmen). 91 percent are women and 9 percent are men. Students come from 35 states and territories. 67 percent are from Nebraska. 10 percent of the 2002 graduating class went on to graduate and professional schools.
Expenses for 2003–04 *Application fee:* $15. *Comprehensive fee:* $12,662 includes full-time tuition ($9300), mandatory fees ($462), and college room and board ($2900). Room and board charges vary according to housing facility and location. *Part-time tuition:* $310 per credit hour. *Part-time mandatory fees:* $18 per credit hour, $15 per term.
Financial Aid Forms of aid include need-based and non-need-based scholarships and part-time jobs. The average aided 2001–02 undergraduate received an aid package worth $8291. The priority application deadline for financial aid is April 1.
Freshman Admission Clarkson requires an essay, a high school transcript, and a minimum 2.5 high school GPA. A minimum 3.0 high school GPA is recommended. 2 recommendations and SAT I or ACT scores are required for some. The application deadline for regular admission is rolling.
Transfer Admission The application deadline for admission is rolling.
Entrance Difficulty Clarkson assesses its entrance difficulty level as moderately difficult.

For Further Information Contact Ms. Nicole Wegenast, Dean of Enrollment Services, Clarkson College, 101 South 42nd Street, Omaha, NE 68131-2739. *Telephone:* 402-552-3100 or 800-647-5500 (toll-free). *Fax:* 402-552-6057. *E-mail:* admiss@clarksoncollege.edu. *Web site:* http://www.clarksoncollege.edu/.

COLLEGE OF SAINT MARY

Omaha, Nebraska

CSM is a women's, private, Roman Catholic, four-year college, founded in 1923, offering degrees at the associate and bachelor's levels. It has a 25-acre campus in Omaha.

Academic Information The faculty has 53 members (79% full-time), 34% with terminal degrees. The student-faculty ratio is 10:1. The library holds 70,514 titles, 12,675 serial subscriptions, and 1,300 audiovisual materials. Special programs include academic remediation, services for learning-disabled students, study abroad, advanced placement credit, accelerated degree programs, double majors, independent study, summer session for credit, part-time degree programs, adult/continuing education programs, and internships. The most frequently chosen baccalaureate fields are business/marketing, education, health professions and related sciences.
Student Body Statistics The student body is made up of 852 undergraduates (97 freshmen). Students come from 18 states and territories and 6 other countries. 88 percent are from Nebraska. 0.8 percent are international students. 10 percent of the 2002 graduating class went on to graduate and professional schools.
Expenses for 2002–03 *Application fee:* $25. *Comprehensive fee:* $20,140 includes full-time tuition ($14,940) and college room and board ($5200). Room and board charges vary according to housing facility. *Part-time tuition:* $415 per credit hour. Part-time tuition varies according to class time.
Financial Aid Forms of aid include need-based and non-need-based scholarships and part-time jobs. The average aided 2002–03 undergraduate received an aid package worth an estimated $10,109. The priority application deadline for financial aid is April 1.
Freshman Admission CSM requires a high school transcript, a minimum 2.0 high school GPA, SAT I or ACT scores, and TOEFL scores for international students. An essay is recommended. A minimum 3.0 high school GPA, 2 recommendations, and an interview are required for some. The application deadline for regular admission is rolling.
Transfer Admission The application deadline for admission is rolling.
Entrance Difficulty CSM assesses its entrance difficulty level as minimally difficult. For the fall 2002 freshman class, 66 percent of the applicants were accepted.

For Further Information Contact Ms. Natalie Vrbka, Senior Admissions Counselor, College of Saint Mary, 1901 South 72nd Street, Omaha, NE 68124-2377. *Telephone:* 402-399-2407 or 800-926-5534 (toll-free). *Fax:* 402-399-2412. *E-mail:* enroll@csm.edu. *Web site:* http://www.csm.edu/.

CONCORDIA UNIVERSITY

Seward, Nebraska

Concordia University is a coed, private, comprehensive unit of Concordia University System, founded in 1894, affiliated with the Lutheran Church–Missouri Synod, offering degrees at the bachelor's and master's levels. It has a 120-acre campus in Seward near Omaha.

Academic Information The faculty has 123 members (54% full-time), 50% with terminal degrees. The undergraduate student-faculty ratio is 14:1. The library holds 171,688 titles, 575 serial subscriptions, and 12,068 audiovisual materials. Special programs include academic remediation, services for learning-disabled students, an honors program, cooperative (work-study) education, study abroad, advanced placement credit, accelerated degree programs, ESL programs, double majors, independent study, distance learning, summer session for credit, part-time degree programs (daytime, evenings, summer), adult/continuing education programs, internships, and arrangement for off-campus study with University of Nebraska–Lincoln.
Student Body Statistics The student body totals 1,425, of whom 1,320 are undergraduates (318 freshmen). 56 percent are women and 44 percent are men. Students come from 37 states and territories. 42 percent are from Nebraska.
Expenses for 2002–03 *Application fee:* $15. *Comprehensive fee:* $18,934 includes full-time tuition ($14,546) and college room and board ($4388). Room and board charges vary according to board plan. *Part-time tuition:* $409 per credit. Part-time tuition varies according to course load.
Financial Aid Forms of aid include need-based and non-need-based scholarships, athletic grants, and part-time jobs. The average aided 2002–03 undergraduate received an aid package worth an estimated $13,280. The application deadline for financial aid is May 31 with a priority deadline of March 1.
Freshman Admission Concordia University requires a high school transcript, SAT I or ACT scores, and TOEFL scores for international students. A minimum 2.0 high school GPA and an interview are recommended. Recommendations are required for some. The application deadline for regular admission is August 1.
Transfer Admission The application deadline for admission is August 1.
Entrance Difficulty Concordia University assesses its entrance difficulty level as moderately difficult. For the fall 2002 freshman class, 93 percent of the applicants were accepted.

For Further Information Contact Mr. Pete Kenow, Director of Admissions, Concordia University, 800 North Columbia Avenue, Seward, NE 68434-1599. *Telephone:* 402-643-7233 or 800-535-5494 (toll-free). *Fax:* 402-643-4073. *E-mail:* admiss@seward.ccsn.edu. *Web site:* http://www.cune.edu/.

CREIGHTON UNIVERSITY

Omaha, Nebraska

Creighton is a coed, private, Roman Catholic (Jesuit) university, founded in 1878, offering degrees at the associate, bachelor's, master's, doctoral, and first professional levels. It has a 90-acre campus in Omaha.

Academic Information The faculty has 860 members (72% full-time), 92% with terminal degrees. The undergraduate student-faculty ratio is 14:1. The library holds 481,848 titles, 1,666 serial subscriptions, and 2,500 audiovisual materials. Special programs include academic remediation, services for learning-disabled students, an honors program, study abroad, advanced placement credit, accelerated degree programs, ESL programs, double majors, independent study, summer session for credit, part-time degree programs (daytime, evenings, weekends, summer), adult/continuing education programs, internships, and arrangement for off-campus study with Creighton University; West Omaha Campus. The most frequently chosen baccalaureate fields are business/marketing, biological/life sciences, health professions and related sciences.

Student Body Statistics The student body totals 6,327, of whom 3,607 are undergraduates (802 freshmen). 60 percent are women and 40 percent are men. Students come from 41 states and territories and 64 other countries. 50 percent are from Nebraska. 1.9 percent are international students.

Expenses for 2002–03 *Application fee:* $40. *Comprehensive fee:* $25,320 includes full-time tuition ($18,200), mandatory fees ($682), and college room and board ($6438). *College room only:* $3650. Room and board charges vary according to board plan and housing facility. *Part-time tuition:* $569 per credit. *Part-time mandatory fees:* $57 per term.

Financial Aid Forms of aid include need-based and non-need-based scholarships, athletic grants, and part-time jobs. The average aided 2002–03 undergraduate received an aid package worth an estimated $17,552. The priority application deadline for financial aid is May 15.

Freshman Admission Creighton requires a high school transcript, a minimum 2.75 high school GPA, 1 recommendation, SAT I or ACT scores, and TOEFL scores for international students. An essay is recommended. The application deadline for regular admission is August 1.

Transfer Admission The application deadline for admission is rolling.

Entrance Difficulty Creighton assesses its entrance difficulty level as moderately difficult. For the fall 2002 freshman class, 90 percent of the applicants were accepted.

For Further Information Contact Mr. Don Bishop, Associate Vice President of Enrollment Management, Creighton University, 2500 California Plaza, Omaha, NE 68178-0001. *Telephone:* 402-280-2703 Ext. 2162 or 800-282-5835 (toll-free). *Fax:* 402-280-2685. *E-mail:* admissions@creighton.edu. *Web site:* http://www.creighton.edu/.

DANA COLLEGE

Blair, Nebraska

Dana is a coed, private, four-year college, founded in 1884, affiliated with the Evangelical Lutheran Church in America, offering degrees at the bachelor's level. It has a 150-acre campus in Blair near Omaha.

Academic Information The faculty has 72 members (56% full-time), 35% with terminal degrees. The student-faculty ratio is 12:1. The library holds 157,860 titles, 27,150 serial subscriptions, and 4,092 audiovisual materials. Special programs include services for learning-disabled students, an honors program, study abroad, advanced placement credit, accelerated degree programs, ESL programs, double majors, independent study, self-designed majors, summer session for credit, part-time degree programs (daytime), adult/continuing education programs, internships, and arrangement for off-campus study with Consortium of Eastern Nebraska Colleges. The most frequently chosen baccalaureate fields are business/marketing, education, protective services/public administration.

Student Body Statistics The student body is made up of 580 undergraduates (140 freshmen). 45 percent are women and 55 percent are men. Students come from 34 states and territories and 6 other countries. 58 percent are from Nebraska. 1 percent are international students.

Expenses for 2003–04 *Application fee:* $0. *Comprehensive fee:* $20,630 includes full-time tuition ($15,200), mandatory fees ($550), and college room and board ($4880). *College room only:* $1900. Full-time tuition and fees vary according to course load. Room and board charges vary according to board plan. *Part-time tuition:* $465 per semester hour. *Part-time mandatory fees:* $30 per term. Part-time tuition and fees vary according to course load.

Financial Aid Forms of aid include need-based and non-need-based scholarships, athletic grants, and part-time jobs. The average aided 2002–03 undergraduate received an aid package worth an estimated $13,864. The priority application deadline for financial aid is March 15.

Freshman Admission Dana requires a high school transcript, a minimum 2.0 high school GPA, SAT I or ACT scores, and TOEFL scores for international students. ACT scores are recommended. An essay, 1 recommendation, and an interview are required for some. The application deadline for regular admission is rolling.

Entrance Difficulty Dana assesses its entrance difficulty level as moderately difficult. For the fall 2002 freshman class, 95 percent of the applicants were accepted.

For Further Information Contact Ms. Judy Mathiesen, Office Manager, Dana College, 2848 College Drive, Blair, NE 68008-1099. *Telephone:* 402-426-7220 or 800-444-3262 (toll-free). *Fax:* 402-426-7386. *E-mail:* admissions@acad2.dana.edu. *Web site:* http://www.dana.edu/.

DOANE COLLEGE

Crete, Nebraska

Doane is a coed, private, comprehensive institution, founded in 1872, affiliated with the United Church of Christ, offering degrees at the bachelor's and master's levels (nontraditional undergraduate programs and graduate programs offered at Lincoln campus). It has a 300-acre campus in Crete near Omaha.

Academic Information The faculty has 127 members (57% full-time), 39% with terminal degrees. The undergraduate student-faculty ratio is 12:1. The library holds 257,560 titles, 3,500 serial subscriptions, and 1,313 audiovisual materials. Special programs include academic remediation, an honors program, cooperative (work-study) education, study abroad, advanced placement credit, accelerated degree programs, ESL programs, double majors, independent study, self-designed majors, summer session for credit, part-time degree programs (daytime, evenings), adult/continuing education programs, internships, and arrangement for off-campus study with Association of Nebraska Interterm Colleges. The most frequently chosen baccalaureate fields are business/marketing, education, social sciences and history.

Student Body Statistics The student body is made up of 1,015 undergraduates (275 freshmen). 51 percent are women and 49 percent are men. Students come from 23 states and territories and 7 other countries. 83 percent are from Nebraska. 0.9 percent are international students.

Expenses for 2002–03 *Application fee:* $15. *Comprehensive fee:* $18,580 includes full-time tuition ($13,960), mandatory fees ($320), and college room and board ($4300). *College room only:* $1650. Full-time tuition and fees vary according to location. Room and board charges vary according to board plan, housing facility, and location. *Part-time tuition:* $465 per credit hour. *Part-time mandatory fees:* $128 per credit hour. Part-time tuition and fees vary according to course load and location.

Financial Aid Forms of aid include need-based and non-need-based scholarships, athletic grants, and part-time jobs. The average aided 2002–03 undergraduate received an aid package worth an estimated $12,570. The priority application deadline for financial aid is March 1.

Freshman Admission Doane requires a high school transcript, 2 recommendations, SAT I or ACT scores, and TOEFL scores for international students. A minimum 2.0 high school GPA is recommended. An interview is required for some. The application deadline for regular admission is rolling.

Transfer Admission The application deadline for admission is rolling.

Entrance Difficulty Doane assesses its entrance difficulty level as moderately difficult. For the fall 2002 freshman class, 86 percent of the applicants were accepted.

For Further Information Contact Mr. Dan Kunzman, Dean of Admissions, Doane College, Crete, NE 68333. *Telephone:* 402-826-8222 or 800-333-6263 (toll-free). *Fax:* 402-826-8600. *E-mail:* admissions@doane.edu. *Web site:* http://www.doane.edu/.

GRACE UNIVERSITY

Omaha, Nebraska

Grace is a coed, private, interdenominational, comprehensive institution, founded in 1943, offering degrees at the associate, bachelor's, and master's levels. It has a 15-acre campus in Omaha.

Academic Information The faculty has 56 members (34% full-time), 27% with terminal degrees. The undergraduate student-faculty ratio is 18:1. The library holds 46,736 titles, 3,721 serial subscriptions, and 3,882 audiovisual materials. Special programs include services for learning-disabled students, cooperative (work-study) education, study abroad, advanced placement credit, accelerated degree programs, double majors, independent study, distance learning, self-designed majors, summer session for credit, part-time degree programs, external degree programs, adult/continuing education programs, internships, and arrangement for off-campus study with Iowa Western Community College, Metropolitan Community College (NE), University of Nebraska at Omaha, Bellevue University, Clarkson College. The most frequently chosen baccalaureate fields are business/marketing, philosophy, religion, and theology, social sciences and history.

Student Body Statistics The student body totals 507, of whom 431 are undergraduates (94 freshmen). 53 percent are women and 47 percent are men. Students come from 29 states and territories. 77 percent are from Nebraska. 0.7 percent are international students.

Expenses for 2002–03 *Application fee:* $35. *Comprehensive fee:* $13,665 includes full-time tuition ($8850), mandatory fees ($625), and college room and board ($4190). Room and board charges vary according to board plan and housing facility. *Part-time tuition:* $295 per credit hour. Part-time tuition varies according to course load.

Financial Aid Forms of aid include need-based and non-need-based scholarships and part-time jobs. The average aided 2001–02 undergraduate received an aid package worth $6160. The priority application deadline for financial aid is February 1.

Freshman Admission Grace requires an essay, a high school transcript, a minimum 2.0 high school GPA, 3 recommendations, SAT I or ACT scores, and TOEFL scores for international students. ACT scores are recommended. An interview is required for some. The application deadline for regular admission is rolling.

Transfer Admission The application deadline for admission is rolling.

Entrance Difficulty Grace assesses its entrance difficulty level as moderately difficult. For the fall 2002 freshman class, 45 percent of the applicants were accepted.

For Further Information Contact Mrs. Terri L. Dingfield, Director of Admissions, Grace University, 1311 South Ninth Street, Omaha, NE 68108. *Telephone:* 402-449-2831 or 800-383-1422 (toll-free). *Fax:* 402-341-9587. *E-mail:* admissions@graceuniversity.com. *Web site:* http://www.graceuniversity.edu/.

HASTINGS COLLEGE

Hastings, Nebraska

Hastings is a coed, private, Presbyterian, comprehensive institution, founded in 1882, offering degrees at the bachelor's and master's levels. It has an 88-acre campus in Hastings.

Academic Information The faculty has 108 members (69% full-time), 59% with terminal degrees. The undergraduate student-faculty ratio is 13:1. The library holds 101,000 titles, 607 serial subscriptions, and 714 audiovisual materials. Special programs include services for learning-disabled students, study abroad, advanced placement credit, double majors, independent study, self-designed majors, summer session for credit, part-time degree programs (daytime, summer), adult/continuing education programs, internships, and arrangement for off-campus study. The most frequently chosen baccalaureate fields are business/marketing, communications/communication technologies, education.

Student Body Statistics The student body totals 1,078, of whom 1,033 are undergraduates (276 freshmen). 52 percent are women and 48 percent are men. Students come from 25 states and territories and 5 other countries. 76 percent are from Nebraska. 1 percent are international students. 19 percent of the 2002 graduating class went on to graduate and professional schools.

Expenses for 2002–03 *Application fee:* $20. *Comprehensive fee:* $18,952 includes full-time tuition ($13,972), mandatory fees ($582), and college room and board ($4398). *College room only:* $1854. Full-time tuition and fees vary according to degree level and program. Room and board charges vary according to board plan. *Part-time tuition:* $578 per semester hour. *Part-time mandatory fees:* $153 per term. Part-time tuition and fees vary according to course load, degree level, and program.

Financial Aid Forms of aid include need-based and non-need-based scholarships, athletic grants, and part-time jobs. The average aided 2002–03 undergraduate received an aid package worth an estimated $11,407. The application deadline for financial aid is September 1 with a priority deadline of May 1.

Freshman Admission Hastings requires a high school transcript, a minimum 2.0 high school GPA, counselor's recommendation, SAT I or ACT scores, and TOEFL scores for international students. An essay, 2 recommendations, and an interview are required for some. The application deadline for regular admission is August 1.

Transfer Admission The application deadline for admission is rolling.

Entrance Difficulty Hastings assesses its entrance difficulty level as moderately difficult. For the fall 2002 freshman class, 85 percent of the applicants were accepted.

For Further Information Contact Ms. Mary Molliconi, Director of Admissions, Hastings College, 800 Turner Avenue, Hastings, NE 68901-7696. *Telephone:* 402-461-7320 or 800-532-7642 (toll-free). *Fax:* 402-461-7490. *E-mail:* admissions@hastings.edu. *Web site:* http://www.hastings.edu/.

LITTLE PRIEST TRIBAL COLLEGE

Winnebago, Nebraska

Little Priest Tribal College is a private, two-year college, offering degrees at the associate level.

Academic Information The faculty has 20 members (25% full-time).

Student Body Statistics The student body is made up of 146 undergraduates.

Expenses for 2002–03 *Tuition:* $2020 full-time, $4 per credit hour part-time. *Mandatory fees:* $635 full-time, $18.50 per credit hour part-time.

Financial Aid Forms of aid include need-based scholarships and part-time jobs. The application deadline for financial aid is continuous.

Freshman Admission Little Priest Tribal College requires TOEFL scores for international students.

Entrance Difficulty For the fall 2002 freshman class, 100 percent of the applicants were accepted.

For Further Information Contact Ms. Karen Kemling, Dean of Admissions and Records, Little Priest Tribal College, PO Box 270, Winnebago, NE 68071. *Telephone:* 402-878-2380. *Fax:* 402-878-2355. *Web site:* http://www.lptc.bia.edu/.

MIDLAND LUTHERAN COLLEGE

Fremont, Nebraska

Midland is a coed, private, Lutheran, four-year college, founded in 1883, offering degrees at the associate and bachelor's levels. It has a 27-acre campus in Fremont near Omaha.

Academic Information The faculty has 82 members (70% full-time), 59% with terminal degrees. The student-faculty ratio is 15:1. The library

Midland Lutheran College (continued)

holds 110,000 titles and 900 serial subscriptions. Special programs include academic remediation, services for learning-disabled students, an honors program, cooperative (work-study) education, study abroad, advanced placement credit, accelerated degree programs, ESL programs, double majors, independent study, self-designed majors, summer session for credit, part-time degree programs (daytime), internships, and arrangement for off-campus study with Concordia University, Doane College, Dana College, Hastings College, Central College. The most frequently chosen baccalaureate fields are business/marketing, education, social sciences and history.

Student Body Statistics The student body is made up of 946 undergraduates (261 freshmen). 58 percent are women and 42 percent are men. Students come from 24 states and territories. 77 percent are from Nebraska. 0.4 percent are international students. 12 percent of the 2002 graduating class went on to graduate and professional schools.

Expenses for 2002–03 *Application fee:* $30. *Comprehensive fee:* $19,710 includes full-time tuition ($15,400) and college room and board ($4310). Full-time tuition varies according to course load. Room and board charges vary according to board plan. *Part-time tuition:* $625 per credit hour. Part-time tuition varies according to course load.

Financial Aid Forms of aid include need-based and non-need-based scholarships, athletic grants, and part-time jobs. The average aided 2002–03 undergraduate received an aid package worth an estimated $13,600. The application deadline for financial aid is continuous.

Freshman Admission Midland requires a high school transcript, SAT I or ACT scores, and TOEFL scores for international students. An essay, a minimum 3.0 high school GPA, and recommendations are recommended. An interview is required for some. The application deadline for regular admission is rolling.

Transfer Admission The application deadline for admission is rolling.

Entrance Difficulty Midland assesses its entrance difficulty level as moderately difficult. For the fall 2002 freshman class, 86 percent of the applicants were accepted.

For Further Information Contact Ms. Stacy Poggendorf, Assistant Vice President for Admissions, Midland Lutheran College, Admissions Office, Fremont, NE 68025-4200. *Telephone:* 402-941-6508 or 800-642-8382 Ext. 6501 (toll-free). *Fax:* 402-941-6513. *E-mail:* admissions@admin.mlc.edu. *Web site:* http://www.mlc.edu/.

NEBRASKA CHRISTIAN COLLEGE

Norfolk, Nebraska

Nebraska Christian College is a coed, private, four-year college, founded in 1944, affiliated with the Christian Churches and Churches of Christ, offering degrees at the associate and bachelor's levels. It has an 85-acre campus in Norfolk.

Academic Information The faculty has 16 members, 19% with terminal degrees. The student-faculty ratio is 17:1. The library holds 250,000 titles and 149 serial subscriptions. Special programs include part-time degree programs, internships, and arrangement for off-campus study with Northeast Community College, Wayne State College, York College (NE), Fort Hays State University. The most frequently chosen baccalaureate field is philosophy, religion, and theology.

Student Body Statistics The student body is made up of 167 undergraduates (60 freshmen). 49 percent are women and 51 percent are men. Students come from 15 states and territories and 3 other countries. 51 percent are from Nebraska. 1.8 percent are international students. 8 percent of the 2002 graduating class went on to graduate and professional schools.

Expenses for 2002–03 *Application fee:* $25. *Comprehensive fee:* $9700 includes full-time tuition ($4950), mandatory fees ($490), and college room and board ($4260). *Part-time tuition:* $175 per credit. Part-time tuition varies according to course load.

Financial Aid Forms of aid include need-based and non-need-based scholarships and part-time jobs. The priority application deadline for financial aid is June 1.

Freshman Admission Nebraska Christian College requires a high school transcript, 2 recommendations, ACT scores, and TOEFL scores for international students. An interview is required for some. The application deadline for regular admission is rolling.

Transfer Admission The application deadline for admission is rolling.

Entrance Difficulty Nebraska Christian College assesses its entrance difficulty level as minimally difficult. For the fall 2002 freshman class, 45 percent of the applicants were accepted.

For Further Information Contact Mr. Jason Epperson, Associate Director of Admissions, Nebraska Christian College, 1800 Syracuse Avenue, Norfolk, NE 68701. *Telephone:* 402-379-5000 Ext. 411. *Fax:* 402-379-5100. *E-mail:* admissions@nechristian.edu. *Web site:* http://www.nechristian.edu/.

NEBRASKA INDIAN COMMUNITY COLLEGE

Macy, Nebraska

NICC is a coed, private, two-year college, founded in 1979, offering degrees at the associate level. It has a 2-acre campus in Macy.

Academic Information The faculty has 30 members (20% full-time). Special programs include academic remediation, double majors, summer session for credit, part-time degree programs (daytime, evenings, summer), and adult/continuing education programs.

Student Body Statistics The student body is made up of 118 undergraduates (25 freshmen). 69 percent are women and 31 percent are men. Students come from 3 states and territories and 19 other countries.

Expenses for 2002–03 *Application fee:* $10. *Tuition:* $2160 full-time, $60 per credit hour part-time. *Mandatory fees:* $580 full-time. Full-time tuition and fees vary according to course load. Part-time tuition varies according to course load.

Financial Aid Forms of aid include need-based scholarships and part-time jobs. The application deadline for financial aid is continuous.

Freshman Admission NICC requires a high school transcript and certificate of tribal enrollment. The application deadline for regular admission is rolling.

Transfer Admission The application deadline for admission is rolling.

Entrance Difficulty NICC has an open admission policy.

For Further Information Contact Mr. Ed Stevens, Admission Counselor, Nebraska Indian Community College, 2451 Saint Mary's Avenue, Omaha, NE 68105. *Telephone:* 402-344-8428. *Fax:* 402-344-8358. *Web site:* http://www.thenicc.edu/.

NEBRASKA METHODIST COLLEGE

Omaha, Nebraska

Nebraska Methodist College is a coed, private, comprehensive institution, founded in 1891, affiliated with the United Methodist Church, offering degrees at the associate, bachelor's, and master's levels and post-master's certificates. It has a 5-acre campus in Omaha.

Academic Information The faculty has 55 members (56% full-time), 24% with terminal degrees. The undergraduate student-faculty ratio is 10:1. The library holds 8,656 titles, 475 serial subscriptions, and 985 audiovisual materials. Special programs include academic remediation, services for learning-disabled students, advanced placement credit, accelerated degree programs, independent study, distance learning, summer session for credit, and internships. The most frequently chosen baccalaureate field is health professions and related sciences.

Student Body Statistics The student body totals 343, of whom 304 are undergraduates (32 freshmen). 91 percent are women and 9 percent are men. Students come from 6 states and territories and 1 other country. 80 percent are from Nebraska. 0.3 percent are international students. 3 percent of the 2002 graduating class went on to graduate and professional schools.

Expenses for 2002–03 *Application fee:* $25. *Tuition:* $9300 full-time, $310 per credit hour part-time. *Mandatory fees:* $600 full-time, $35 per credit hour part-time. *College room only:* $1600. Room charges vary according to housing facility and location.
Financial Aid Forms of aid include need-based and non-need-based scholarships and part-time jobs. The average aided 2001–02 undergraduate received an aid package worth $6021. The priority application deadline for financial aid is May 1.
Freshman Admission Nebraska Methodist College requires an essay, a high school transcript, a minimum 2.0 high school GPA, 3 recommendations, an interview, SAT I or ACT scores, and TOEFL scores for international students. The application deadline for regular admission is April 1.
Transfer Admission The application deadline for admission is April 1.
Entrance Difficulty Nebraska Methodist College assesses its entrance difficulty level as moderately difficult. For the fall 2002 freshman class, 83 percent of the applicants were accepted.

For Further Information Contact Ms. Deann Sterner, Director of Admissions, Nebraska Methodist College, Omaha, NE 68114. *Telephone:* 402-354-4922 or 800-335-5510 (toll-free). *Fax:* 402-354-8875. *E-mail:* dsterne@methodistcollege.edu. *Web site:* http://www.methodistcollege.edu/.

NEBRASKA WESLEYAN UNIVERSITY

Lincoln, Nebraska

NWU is a coed, private, United Methodist, comprehensive institution, founded in 1887, offering degrees at the bachelor's and master's levels. It has a 50-acre campus in Lincoln near Omaha.

Academic Information The faculty has 142 members (67% full-time), 69% with terminal degrees. The undergraduate student-faculty ratio is 14:1. The library holds 178,531 titles, 743 serial subscriptions, and 7,951 audiovisual materials. Special programs include services for learning-disabled students, study abroad, advanced placement credit, double majors, independent study, summer session for credit, part-time degree programs (evenings, summer), adult/continuing education programs, internships, and arrangement for off-campus study with Chicago Urban Life Center. The most frequently chosen baccalaureate fields are business/marketing, parks and recreation, psychology.
Student Body Statistics The student body totals 1,684, of whom 1,559 are undergraduates (336 freshmen). 55 percent are women and 45 percent are men. Students come from 25 states and territories and 9 other countries. 94 percent are from Nebraska. 0.5 percent are international students.
Expenses for 2003–04 *Application fee:* $20. *Comprehensive fee:* $20,954 includes full-time tuition ($16,140), mandatory fees ($284), and college room and board ($4530). Room and board charges vary according to board plan and housing facility. *Part-time tuition:* $609 per hour. Part-time tuition varies according to class time and course load.
Financial Aid Forms of aid include need-based and non-need-based scholarships and part-time jobs. The average aided 2002–03 undergraduate received an aid package worth an estimated $11,866. The application deadline for financial aid is continuous.
Freshman Admission NWU requires a high school transcript, a minimum 2.0 high school GPA, SAT I or ACT scores, and TOEFL scores for international students. An interview is recommended. An essay and resume of activities are required for some. The application deadline for regular admission is May 1 and for early decision it is November 15.
Transfer Admission The application deadline for admission is rolling.
Entrance Difficulty NWU assesses its entrance difficulty level as moderately difficult. For the fall 2002 freshman class, 93 percent of the applicants were accepted.

For Further Information Contact Mr. Kendal E. Sieg, Assistant Vice President for Admissions, Nebraska Wesleyan University, 5000 Saint Paul Avenue, Lincoln, NE 68504. *Telephone:* 402-465-2218 or 800-541-3818 (toll-free). *Fax:* 402-465-2179. *E-mail:* admissions@nebrwesleyan.edu. *Web site:* http://www.nebrwesleyan.edu/.

PERU STATE COLLEGE

Peru, Nebraska

PSC is a coed, public, comprehensive unit of Nebraska State College System, founded in 1867, offering degrees at the bachelor's and master's levels. It has a 103-acre campus in Peru.

Academic Information The faculty has 87 members (47% full-time). The undergraduate student-faculty ratio is 16:1. The library holds 177,373 titles and 232 serial subscriptions. Special programs include academic remediation, services for learning-disabled students, an honors program, cooperative (work-study) education, advanced placement credit, Freshman Honors College, summer session for credit, part-time degree programs (daytime, evenings, summer), external degree programs, adult/continuing education programs, internships, and arrangement for off-campus study with Southeast Community College, Beatrice Campus; Metropolitan Community College.
Student Body Statistics The student body totals 1,687, of whom 1,482 are undergraduates (178 freshmen). 58 percent are women and 42 percent are men. Students come from 27 states and territories and 3 other countries. 90 percent are from Nebraska. 0.7 percent are international students. 13 percent of the 2002 graduating class went on to graduate and professional schools.
Expenses for 2002–03 *Application fee:* $10. *State resident tuition:* $2288 full-time, $76.25 per semester hour part-time. *Nonresident tuition:* $4575 full-time, $152.50 per semester hour part-time. *Mandatory fees:* $614 full-time. Full-time tuition and fees vary according to course load, location, and reciprocity agreements. Part-time tuition varies according to course load, location, and reciprocity agreements. *College room and board:* $4010. *College room only:* $1966. Room and board charges vary according to board plan and housing facility.
Financial Aid Forms of aid include need-based and non-need-based scholarships and part-time jobs. The priority application deadline for financial aid is March 1.
Freshman Admission PSC requires a high school transcript and TOEFL scores for international students. A minimum 2.0 high school GPA, recommendations, and SAT I or ACT scores are required for some. The application deadline for regular admission is rolling.
Transfer Admission The application deadline for admission is rolling.
Entrance Difficulty PSC has an open admission policy. It assesses its entrance difficulty as minimally difficult for out-of-state applicants.

For Further Information Contact Ms. Janelle Moran, Director of Recruitment and Admissions, Peru State College, PO Box 10, Peru, NE 68421. *Telephone:* 402-872-2221 or 800-742-4412 (toll-free in-state). *Fax:* 402-872-2296. *E-mail:* jmoran@oakmail.peru.edu. *Web site:* http://www.peru.edu/.

UNION COLLEGE

Lincoln, Nebraska

Union is a coed, private, Seventh-day Adventist, four-year college, founded in 1891, offering degrees at the associate and bachelor's levels. It has a 26-acre campus in Lincoln near Omaha.

Academic Information The faculty has 95 members (52% full-time). The student-faculty ratio is 14:1. The library holds 147,813 titles, 1,357 serial subscriptions, and 3,278 audiovisual materials. Special programs include services for learning-disabled students, an honors program, cooperative (work-study) education, study abroad, advanced placement credit, accelerated degree programs, ESL programs, double majors, independent study, self-designed majors, summer session for credit, part-time degree programs (daytime, summer), adult/continuing education programs, internships, and arrangement for off-campus study with University of Nebraska, Southeast Community College. The most frequently chosen baccalaureate fields are education, business/marketing, health professions and related sciences.
Student Body Statistics The student body is made up of 951 undergraduates (184 freshmen). 57 percent are women and 43 percent are men. Students come from 41 states and territories and 34 other countries. 23 percent are from Nebraska. 13.5 percent are international students.

Union College (continued)

Expenses for 2002–03 *Application fee:* $0. *Comprehensive fee:* $15,764 includes full-time tuition ($12,158), mandatory fees ($122), and college room and board ($3484). *College room only:* $2394. *Part-time tuition:* $507 per semester hour.
Financial Aid Forms of aid include need-based and non-need-based scholarships and part-time jobs. The average aided 2002–03 undergraduate received an aid package worth an estimated $8376. The priority application deadline for financial aid is May 1.
Freshman Admission Union requires a high school transcript, a minimum 2.5 high school GPA, 3 recommendations, and ACT scores. An essay is recommended. An interview is required for some. The application deadline for regular admission is rolling.
Transfer Admission The application deadline for admission is rolling.
Entrance Difficulty Union has an open admission policy except for nursing, elementary education, physician assistant programs.

For Further Information Contact Huda McClelland, Director of Admissions, Union College, 3800 South 48th Street, Lincoln, NE 68506-4300. *Telephone:* 402-486-2504 or 800-228-4600 (toll-free out-of-state). *Fax:* 402-486-2895. *E-mail:* ucenrol@ucollege.edu. *Web site:* http://www.ucollege.edu/.

UNIVERSITY OF NEBRASKA AT KEARNEY

Kearney, Nebraska

UNK is a coed, public, comprehensive unit of University of Nebraska System, founded in 1903, offering degrees at the bachelor's and master's levels. It has a 235-acre campus in Kearney.

Academic Information The faculty has 374 members (82% full-time). The undergraduate student-faculty ratio is 16:1. The library holds 320,915 titles, 1,657 serial subscriptions, and 75,881 audiovisual materials. Special programs include academic remediation, services for learning-disabled students, an honors program, cooperative (work-study) education, study abroad, advanced placement credit, ESL programs, double majors, independent study, distance learning, summer session for credit, part-time degree programs (daytime, evenings, weekends, summer), internships, and arrangement for off-campus study with National Student Exchange. The most frequently chosen baccalaureate fields are business/marketing, education, protective services/public administration.
Student Body Statistics The student body totals 6,395, of whom 5,366 are undergraduates (1,138 freshmen). 55 percent are women and 45 percent are men. Students come from 38 states and territories and 46 other countries. 94 percent are from Nebraska. 5.4 percent are international students.
Expenses for 2002–03 *Application fee:* $25. *State resident tuition:* $2715 full-time. *Nonresident tuition:* $5550 full-time. *Mandatory fees:* $668 full-time. Full-time tuition and fees vary according to course load, reciprocity agreements, and student level. *College room and board:* $4156. Room and board charges vary according to board plan and housing facility.
Financial Aid Forms of aid include need-based and non-need-based scholarships and part-time jobs. The average aided 2001–02 undergraduate received an aid package worth $5417. The priority application deadline for financial aid is March 1.
Freshman Admission UNK requires a high school transcript, SAT I or ACT scores, and TOEFL scores for international students. ACT scores are recommended. 3 recommendations are required for some. The application deadline for regular admission is August 1.
Transfer Admission The application deadline for admission is August 1.
Entrance Difficulty UNK assesses its entrance difficulty level as moderately difficult. For the fall 2002 freshman class, 88 percent of the applicants were accepted.

For Further Information Contact Mr. John Kundel, Director of Admissions, University of Nebraska at Kearney, 905 West 25th Street, Kearney, NE 68849-0001. *Telephone:* 308-865-8702 or 800-532-7639 (toll-free). *Fax:* 308-865-8987. *E-mail:* admissionsug@unk.edu. *Web site:* http://www.unk.edu/.

UNIVERSITY OF NEBRASKA AT OMAHA

Omaha, Nebraska

UNO is a coed, public unit of University of Nebraska System, founded in 1908, offering degrees at the bachelor's, master's, and doctoral levels and post-master's and postbachelor's certificates. It has an 88-acre campus in Omaha.

Academic Information The faculty has 849 members (54% full-time), 55% with terminal degrees. The undergraduate student-faculty ratio is 18:1. The library holds 750,000 titles, 3,000 serial subscriptions, and 7,000 audiovisual materials. Special programs include services for learning-disabled students, an honors program, cooperative (work-study) education, study abroad, advanced placement credit, ESL programs, double majors, distance learning, self-designed majors, summer session for credit, part-time degree programs (daytime, evenings, summer), adult/continuing education programs, internships, and arrangement for off-campus study with other units of the University of Nebraska System. The most frequently chosen baccalaureate fields are business/marketing, education, protective services/public administration.
Student Body Statistics The student body totals 14,451, of whom 11,333 are undergraduates (1,723 freshmen). 53 percent are women and 47 percent are men. Students come from 48 states and territories and 83 other countries. 92 percent are from Nebraska. 2.8 percent are international students.
Expenses for 2002–03 *Application fee:* $40. *State resident tuition:* $3060 full-time, $102 per semester hour part-time. *Nonresident tuition:* $9008 full-time, $300 per semester hour part-time. *Mandatory fees:* $492 full-time, $12.50 per semester hour part-time, $56 per term part-time. Full-time tuition and fees vary according to course load and student level. Part-time tuition and fees vary according to course load and student level. *College room and board:* $4517. *College room only:* $2727.
Financial Aid Forms of aid include need-based and non-need-based scholarships, athletic grants, and part-time jobs. The priority application deadline for financial aid is March 1.
Freshman Admission UNO requires a high school transcript, minimum ACT score of 20 or rank in upper 50% of high school class, SAT I or ACT scores, and TOEFL scores for international students. The application deadline for regular admission is August 1.
Transfer Admission The application deadline for admission is August 1.
Entrance Difficulty UNO assesses its entrance difficulty level as minimally difficult; moderately difficult for engineering program; noncompetitive for nontraditional, adult applicants. For the fall 2002 freshman class, 86 percent of the applicants were accepted.

For Further Information Contact Ms. Jolene Adams, Associate Director of Admissions, University of Nebraska at Omaha, 6001 Dodge Street, Omaha, NE 68182. *Telephone:* 402-554-2416 or 800-858-8648 (toll-free in-state). *Fax:* 402-554-3472. *Web site:* http://www.unomaha.edu/.

UNIVERSITY OF NEBRASKA–LINCOLN

Lincoln, Nebraska

UNL is a coed, public unit of University of Nebraska System, founded in 1869, offering degrees at the associate, bachelor's, master's, doctoral, and first professional levels and post-master's certificates. It has a 623-acre campus in Lincoln near Omaha.

Academic Information The faculty has 1,071 members (99% full-time), 93% with terminal degrees. The undergraduate student-faculty ratio is 19:1. The library holds 1 million titles, 21,309 serial subscriptions, and 73,405 audiovisual materials. Special programs include services for learning-disabled students, an honors program, cooperative (work-study) education, study abroad, advanced placement credit, accelerated degree programs, ESL programs, double majors, independent study, distance learning, self-designed majors, summer session for credit, part-time degree programs (daytime, evenings, summer), adult/continuing education programs, internships, and arrangement for off-campus study with University of Missouri, Kansas State University, University of South

Dakota. The most frequently chosen baccalaureate fields are business/marketing, communications/communication technologies, engineering/engineering technologies.

Student Body Statistics The student body totals 22,988, of whom 18,118 are undergraduates (3,653 freshmen). 48 percent are women and 52 percent are men. Students come from 52 states and territories and 101 other countries. 86 percent are from Nebraska. 3.1 percent are international students.

Expenses for 2002–03 *Application fee:* $25. *State resident tuition:* $3345 full-time, $111.50 per credit hour part-time. *Nonresident tuition:* $9,938 full-time, $331.25 per credit hour part-time. *Mandatory fees:* $780 full-time, $5 per credit hour part-time, $153.65 per term part-time. Full-time tuition and fees vary according to course load. Part-time tuition and fees vary according to course load. *College room and board:* $4875. *College room only:* $2255. Room and board charges vary according to board plan and housing facility.

Financial Aid Forms of aid include need-based and non-need-based scholarships, athletic grants, and part-time jobs. The average aided 2002–03 undergraduate received an aid package worth an estimated $6334. The application deadline for financial aid is continuous.

Freshman Admission UNL requires a high school transcript, SAT I or ACT scores, and TOEFL scores for international students. Rank in upper 50% of high school class is required for some. The application deadline for regular admission is June 30.

Transfer Admission The application deadline for admission is June 30.

Entrance Difficulty UNL assesses its entrance difficulty level as moderately difficult; very difficult for architecture, engineering programs. For the fall 2002 freshman class, 90 percent of the applicants were accepted.

For Further Information Contact Mr. Alan Cerveny, Dean of Admissions, University of Nebraska–Lincoln, 1410 Q Street, Lincoln, NE 68588-0417. *Telephone:* 402-472-2030 or 800-742-8800 (toll-free). *Fax:* 402-472-0670. *E-mail:* nuhusker@unl.edu. *Web site:* http://www.unl.edu/.

UNIVERSITY OF NEBRASKA MEDICAL CENTER

Omaha, Nebraska

UNMC is a coed, public, upper-level unit of University of Nebraska System, founded in 1869, offering degrees at the bachelor's, master's, doctoral, and first professional levels and post-master's, first professional, and postbachelor's certificates. It has a 51-acre campus in Omaha.

Academic Information The faculty has 831 members (81% full-time). The library holds 247,434 titles, 1,741 serial subscriptions, and 849 audiovisual materials. Special programs include services for learning-disabled students, an honors program, distance learning, summer session for credit, part-time degree programs (daytime, summer), internships, and arrangement for off-campus study with University of Nebraska–Lincoln, University of Nebraska at Omaha, University of Nebraska at Kearney. The most frequently chosen baccalaureate field is health professions and related sciences.

Student Body Statistics The student body totals 2,724, of whom 663 are undergraduates. 92 percent are women and 8 percent are men. Students come from 12 states and territories. 91 percent are from Nebraska. 0.2 percent are international students.

Expenses for 2002–03 *Application fee:* $25. *State resident tuition:* $4237 full-time, $141.25 per semester hour part-time. *Nonresident tuition:* $12,420 full-time, $414 per semester hour part-time. *Mandatory fees:* $260 full-time. Full-time tuition and fees vary according to program. Part-time tuition varies according to program.

Financial Aid Forms of aid include need-based and non-need-based scholarships and part-time jobs. The priority application deadline for financial aid is February 1.

Transfer Admission UNMC requires a college transcript and a minimum 2.0 college GPA. Standardized test scores and a minimum 3.0 college GPA are required for some. The application deadline for admission is rolling.

Entrance Difficulty UNMC assesses its entrance difficulty level as moderately difficult. For the fall 2002 entering class, 33 percent of the applicants were accepted.

For Further Information Contact Crystal Oldham, Administrative Technician, University of Nebraska Medical Center, 984230 Nebraska Medical Center, Omaha, NE 68198-4230. *Telephone:* 402-559-7262 or 800-626-8431 Ext. 6468 (toll-free). *Fax:* 402-559-6796. *E-mail:* thorton@unmc.edu. *Web site:* http://www.unmc.edu/.

WAYNE STATE COLLEGE

Wayne, Nebraska

WSC is a coed, public, comprehensive unit of Nebraska State College System, founded in 1910, offering degrees at the bachelor's and master's levels and post-master's certificates. It has a 128-acre campus in Wayne.

Academic Information The faculty has 215 members (59% full-time), 51% with terminal degrees. The undergraduate student-faculty ratio is 18:1. The library holds 147,205 titles, 656 serial subscriptions, and 5,300 audiovisual materials. Special programs include services for learning-disabled students, an honors program, cooperative (work-study) education, double majors, independent study, distance learning, self-designed majors, summer session for credit, part-time degree programs (daytime, evenings, weekends, summer), adult/continuing education programs, internships, and arrangement for off-campus study with Northeast Community College, Central Community College. The most frequently chosen baccalaureate fields are business/marketing, education, psychology.

Student Body Statistics The student body totals 3,220, of whom 2,743 are undergraduates (607 freshmen). 58 percent are women and 42 percent are men. Students come from 25 states and territories and 22 other countries. 85 percent are from Nebraska. 1 percent are international students.

Expenses for 2002–03 *Application fee:* $20. *State resident tuition:* $2288 full-time, $76.25 per credit hour part-time. *Nonresident tuition:* $4575 full-time, $152.50 per credit hour part-time. *Mandatory fees:* $726 full-time, $26 per credit hour part-time. *College room and board:* $3760. *College room only:* $1770. Room and board charges vary according to board plan and housing facility.

Financial Aid Forms of aid include need-based and non-need-based scholarships, athletic grants, and part-time jobs. The average aided 2002–03 undergraduate received an aid package worth an estimated $2996. The priority application deadline for financial aid is June 1.

Freshman Admission WSC requires a high school transcript and TOEFL scores for international students. SAT I or ACT scores are recommended. The application deadline for regular admission is rolling.

Transfer Admission The application deadline for admission is rolling.

Entrance Difficulty WSC has an open admission policy for state residents. It assesses its entrance difficulty as minimally difficult for transfers.

For Further Information Contact R. Lincoln Morris, Director of Admissions, Wayne State College, 1111 Main Street, Wayne, NE 68787. *Telephone:* 402-375-7234 or 800-228-9972 (toll-free in-state). *Fax:* 402-375-7204. *E-mail:* admit1@wsc.edu. *Web site:* http://www.wsc.edu/.

YORK COLLEGE

York, Nebraska

York is a coed, private, four-year college, founded in 1890, affiliated with the Church of Christ, offering degrees at the associate and bachelor's levels. It has a 44-acre campus in York.

Academic Information The faculty has 56 members (43% full-time), 29% with terminal degrees. The student-faculty ratio is 12:1. The library holds 49,891 titles, 339 serial subscriptions, and 5,867 audiovisual materials. Special programs include academic remediation, services for learning-disabled students, an honors program, cooperative (work-study) education, study abroad, advanced placement credit, double majors,

York College (continued)

independent study, summer session for credit, part-time degree programs, external degree programs, adult/continuing education programs, and internships. The most frequently chosen baccalaureate fields are business/marketing, education, psychology.

Student Body Statistics The student body is made up of 462 undergraduates (123 freshmen). 53 percent are women and 47 percent are men. Students come from 32 states and territories. 28 percent are from Nebraska. 0.6 percent are international students. 5 percent of the 2002 graduating class went on to graduate and professional schools.

Expenses for 2002–03 *Application fee:* $20. *Comprehensive fee:* $14,500 includes full-time tuition ($10,300), mandatory fees ($800), and college room and board ($3400). *College room only:* $1200. Full-time tuition and fees vary according to course load. Room and board charges vary according to board plan and housing facility. *Part-time tuition:* $325 per credit hour. *Part-time mandatory fees:* $50 per hour. Part-time tuition and fees vary according to course load.

Financial Aid Forms of aid include need-based and non-need-based scholarships and part-time jobs. The priority application deadline for financial aid is April 30.

Freshman Admission York requires a high school transcript, 2 recommendations, SAT I or ACT scores, and TOEFL scores for international students. A minimum 2.0 high school GPA is recommended. A minimum 2.0 high school GPA is required for some. The application deadline for regular admission is rolling.

Transfer Admission The application deadline for admission is rolling.

Entrance Difficulty York assesses its entrance difficulty level as moderately difficult. For the fall 2002 freshman class, 68 percent of the applicants were accepted.

For Further Information Contact Ms. Kristin Mathews, Associate Director of Admissions, York College, 1125 East 8th Street, York, NE 68467-2699. *Telephone:* 402-363-5608 or 800-950-9675 (toll-free). *Fax:* 402-363-5623. *E-mail:* enroll@york.edu. *Web site:* http://www.york.edu/.

North Dakota

DICKINSON STATE UNIVERSITY

Dickinson, North Dakota

Dickinson State University is a coed, public, four-year college of North Dakota University System, founded in 1918, offering degrees at the associate and bachelor's levels. It has a 100-acre campus in Dickinson.

Academic Information The faculty has 140 members (52% full-time), 35% with terminal degrees. The student-faculty ratio is 19:1. The library holds 87,324 titles, 5,450 serial subscriptions, and 4,668 audiovisual materials. Special programs include academic remediation, services for learning-disabled students, an honors program, cooperative (work-study) education, study abroad, advanced placement credit, accelerated degree programs, double majors, independent study, distance learning, self-designed majors, summer session for credit, part-time degree programs (daytime, evenings, weekends, summer), external degree programs, adult/continuing education programs, internships, and arrangement for off-campus study. The most frequently chosen baccalaureate fields are business/marketing, education, health professions and related sciences.

Student Body Statistics The student body is made up of 2,326 undergraduates (433 freshmen). 56 percent are women and 44 percent are men. Students come from 26 states and territories and 26 other countries. 72 percent are from North Dakota. 3.7 percent are international students. 10 percent of the 2002 graduating class went on to graduate and professional schools.

Expenses for 2002–03 *Application fee:* $35. *State resident tuition:* $2202 full-time, $91.75 per semester hour part-time. *Nonresident tuition:* $5879 full-time, $245 per semester hour part-time. *Mandatory fees:* $596 full-time, $24.83 per semester hour part-time. Full-time tuition and fees vary according to location, program, and reciprocity agreements. Part-time tuition and fees vary according to course load, location, program, and reciprocity agreements. *College room and board:* $2050. Room and board charges vary according to board plan.

Financial Aid Forms of aid include need-based and non-need-based scholarships, athletic grants, and part-time jobs. The priority application deadline for financial aid is April 15.

Freshman Admission Dickinson State University requires a high school transcript, medical history, proof of measles-rubella shot, SAT I or ACT scores, and TOEFL scores for international students. The application deadline for regular admission is rolling.

Transfer Admission The application deadline for admission is rolling.

Entrance Difficulty Dickinson State University has an open admission policy for all United States students. It assesses its entrance difficulty as minimally difficult for out-of-state applicants; minimally difficult for transfers; moderately difficult for nursing program.

For Further Information Contact Ms. Deb Dazell, Director of Student Recruitment, Dickinson State University, Campus Box 169, Dickinson, ND 58601. *Telephone:* 701-483-2331 or 800-279-4295 (toll-free). *Fax:* 701-483-2409. *E-mail:* dsu.hawks@dsu.nodak.edu. *Web site:* http://www.dsu.nodak.edu/.

See page 276 for a narrative description.

FORT BERTHOLD COMMUNITY COLLEGE

New Town, North Dakota

FBCC is a coed, private, two-year college, founded in 1973, offering degrees at the associate level.

For Further Information Contact Mr. Russell Mason Jr., Registrar and Admissions Director, Fort Berthold Community College, PO Box 490, New Town, ND 58763-0490. *Telephone:* 701-627-3665. *Fax:* 701-627-3629. *E-mail:* rmason@nt1.fort.berthold.cc.nd.us. *Web site:* http://www.fort-berthold.cc.nd.us/.

JAMESTOWN COLLEGE

Jamestown, North Dakota

Jamestown College is a coed, private, Presbyterian, four-year college, founded in 1883, offering degrees at the bachelor's level. It has a 107-acre campus in Jamestown.

Academic Information The faculty has 65 members (86% full-time), 49% with terminal degrees. The student-faculty ratio is 17:1. The library holds 128,915 titles, 675 serial subscriptions, and 5,219 audiovisual materials. Special programs include services for learning-disabled students, an honors program, cooperative (work-study) education, study abroad, advanced placement credit, double majors, independent study, self-designed majors, summer session for credit, part-time degree programs (daytime, evenings), internships, and arrangement for off-campus study. The most frequently chosen baccalaureate fields are business/marketing, education, health professions and related sciences.

Student Body Statistics The student body is made up of 1,185 undergraduates (353 freshmen). 56 percent are women and 44 percent are men. Students come from 34 states and territories and 12 other countries. 62 percent are from North Dakota. 3.1 percent are international students. 5 percent of the 2002 graduating class went on to graduate and professional schools.

Expenses for 2003–04 *Application fee:* $20. *Comprehensive fee:* $12,600 includes full-time tuition ($8750) and college room and board ($3850). *College room only:* $1650. Room and board charges vary according to board plan. *Part-time tuition:* $260 per credit hour. Part-time tuition varies according to course load.

Financial Aid Forms of aid include need-based and non-need-based scholarships, athletic grants, and part-time jobs. The average aided 2002–03 undergraduate received an aid package worth an estimated $7828. The application deadline for financial aid is continuous.

Freshman Admission Jamestown College requires a high school transcript and TOEFL scores for international students. A minimum 2.5

high school GPA, minimum ACT score of 18 or minimum SAT score of 860, and SAT I or ACT scores are recommended. Recommendations, minimum ACT score of 18 or minimum SAT score of 860, and SAT I or ACT scores are required for some. The application deadline for regular admission is rolling.
Transfer Admission The application deadline for admission is rolling.
Entrance Difficulty Jamestown College assesses its entrance difficulty level as minimally difficult. For the fall 2002 freshman class, 99 percent of the applicants were accepted.

For Further Information Contact Ms. Judy Erickson, Director of Admissions, Jamestown College, 6081 College Lane, Jamestown, ND 58405. *Telephone:* 701-252-3467 Ext. 2548 or 800-336-2554 (toll-free). *Fax:* 701-253-4318. *E-mail:* admissions@jc.edu. *Web site:* http://www.jc.edu/.

MAYVILLE STATE UNIVERSITY

Mayville, North Dakota

Mayville State University is a coed, public, four-year college of North Dakota University System, founded in 1889, offering degrees at the associate and bachelor's levels. It has a 60-acre campus in Mayville.

Academic Information The faculty has 68 members (53% full-time), 31% with terminal degrees. The student-faculty ratio is 14:1. The library holds 71,595 titles, 599 serial subscriptions, and 20,679 audiovisual materials. Special programs include academic remediation, services for learning-disabled students, cooperative (work-study) education, advanced placement credit, accelerated degree programs, double majors, distance learning, self-designed majors, summer session for credit, part-time degree programs (daytime, evenings, summer), adult/continuing education programs, and internships. The most frequently chosen baccalaureate fields are business/marketing, computer/information sciences, education.
Student Body Statistics The student body is made up of 746 undergraduates (175 freshmen). 56 percent are women and 44 percent are men. Students come from 17 states and territories and 4 other countries. 77 percent are from North Dakota. 3.1 percent are international students. 4 percent of the 2002 graduating class went on to graduate and professional schools.
Expenses for 2002–03 *Application fee:* $35. *State resident tuition:* $2202 full-time, $92 per credit hour part-time. *Nonresident tuition:* $5879 full-time, $245 per credit hour part-time. *Mandatory fees:* $1331 full-time. Full-time tuition and fees vary according to reciprocity agreements. Part-time tuition varies according to reciprocity agreements. *College room and board:* $3138. *College room only:* $1356. Room and board charges vary according to board plan and housing facility.
Financial Aid Forms of aid include need-based and non-need-based scholarships, athletic grants, and part-time jobs. The average aided 2001–02 undergraduate received an aid package worth $6008. The priority application deadline for financial aid is March 15.
Freshman Admission Mayville State University requires a high school transcript, SAT I or ACT scores, and TOEFL scores for international students. An interview is recommended. The application deadline for regular admission is rolling.
Transfer Admission The application deadline for admission is rolling.
Entrance Difficulty Mayville State University has an open admission policy. It assesses its entrance difficulty as minimally difficult for transfers.

For Further Information Contact Mr. Brian Larson, Director of Enrollment Services, Mayville State University, 330 3rd Street, NE, Mayville, ND 58257-1299. *Telephone:* 701-788-4773 Ext. 34773 or 800-437-4104 (toll-free). *Fax:* 701-788-4748. *E-mail:* admit@mail.masu.nodak.edu. *Web site:* http://www.mayvillestate.edu/.

MEDCENTER ONE COLLEGE OF NURSING

Bismarck, North Dakota

Medcenter One College of Nursing is a coed, primarily women's, private, upper-level institution, founded in 1988, offering degrees at the bachelor's level in nursing. It has a 15-acre campus in Bismarck.

Academic Information The faculty has 12 members (83% full-time). The student-faculty ratio is 9:1. The library holds 28,470 titles, 331 serial subscriptions, and 1,467 audiovisual materials. Special programs include an honors program, independent study, and internships. The most frequently chosen baccalaureate field is health professions and related sciences.
Student Body Statistics The student body is made up of 99 undergraduates. 94 percent are women and 6 percent are men. Students come from 5 states and territories. 92 percent are from North Dakota.
Expenses for 2003–04 *Application fee:* $40. *Tuition:* $8000 full-time, $334 per credit part-time. *Mandatory fees:* $500 full-time, $5 per credit part-time, $190 per term part-time. *College room only:* $900.
Financial Aid Forms of aid include need-based and non-need-based scholarships and part-time jobs. The average aided 2002–03 undergraduate received an aid package worth an estimated $6532. The priority application deadline for financial aid is May 1.
Transfer Admission Medcenter One College of Nursing requires a college transcript and a minimum 2.5 college GPA. The application deadline for admission is November 7.
Entrance Difficulty Medcenter One College of Nursing assesses its entrance difficulty level as moderately difficult. For the fall 2002 entering class, 75 percent of the applicants were accepted.

For Further Information Contact Ms. Mary Smith, Director of Student Services, Medcenter One College of Nursing, 512 North 7th Street, Bismarck, ND 58501-4494. *Telephone:* 701-323-6271. *Fax:* 701-323-6967. *Web site:* http://www.medcenterone.com/nursing/nursing.htm.

MINOT STATE UNIVERSITY

Minot, North Dakota

Minot State is a coed, public, comprehensive unit of North Dakota University System, founded in 1913, offering degrees at the bachelor's and master's levels and post-master's certificates. It has a 103-acre campus in Minot.

Academic Information The faculty has 225 members (73% full-time), 40% with terminal degrees. The undergraduate student-faculty ratio is 16:1. The library holds 240,395 titles, 805 serial subscriptions, and 11,073 audiovisual materials. Special programs include academic remediation, services for learning-disabled students, an honors program, cooperative (work-study) education, study abroad, advanced placement credit, accelerated degree programs, double majors, independent study, distance learning, self-designed majors, summer session for credit, part-time degree programs (daytime, evenings, summer), adult/continuing education programs, and internships. The most frequently chosen baccalaureate fields are business/marketing, education, protective services/public administration.
Student Body Statistics The student body totals 3,625, of whom 3,425 are undergraduates (567 freshmen). 63 percent are women and 37 percent are men. Students come from 40 states and territories and 18 other countries. 89 percent are from North Dakota. 5.1 percent are international students. 9 percent of the 2002 graduating class went on to graduate and professional schools.
Expenses for 2002–03 *Application fee:* $35. *State resident tuition:* $2344 full-time, $98 per semester hour part-time. *Nonresident tuition:* $6258 full-time, $277 per semester hour part-time. *Mandatory fees:* $462 full-time, $16 per semester hour part-time. Full-time tuition and fees vary according to course load, location, and reciprocity agreements. Part-time tuition and fees vary according to location and reciprocity agreements. *College room and board:* $3162. *College room only:* $1432. Room and board charges vary according to housing facility.
Financial Aid Forms of aid include need-based and non-need-based scholarships, athletic grants, and part-time jobs. The average aided 2002–03 undergraduate received an aid package worth an estimated $5217. The priority application deadline for financial aid is April 15.
Freshman Admission Minot State requires a high school transcript, SAT I or ACT scores, and TOEFL scores for international students. A minimum 2.75 high school GPA is required for some. The application deadline for regular admission is rolling.
Transfer Admission The application deadline for admission is rolling.

Minot State University (continued)

Entrance Difficulty Minot State assesses its entrance difficulty level as minimally difficult. For the fall 2002 freshman class, 86 percent of the applicants were accepted.

For Further Information Contact Ms. Lauralee Moseanko, Admissions Specialist, Minot State University, 500 University Avenue West, Minot, ND 58707-0002. *Telephone:* 701-858-3350 or 800-777-0750 Ext. 3350 (toll-free). *Fax:* 701-839-6933. *E-mail:* askmsu@misu.nodak.edu. *Web site:* http://www.minotstateu.edu/.

NORTH DAKOTA STATE UNIVERSITY

Fargo, North Dakota

NDSU is a coed, public unit of North Dakota University System, founded in 1890, offering degrees at the bachelor's, master's, doctoral, and first professional levels. It has a 2,100-acre campus in Fargo.

Academic Information The faculty has 593 members (83% full-time), 74% with terminal degrees. The undergraduate student-faculty ratio is 18:1. The library holds 303,274 titles, 4,497 serial subscriptions, and 2,757 audiovisual materials. Special programs include academic remediation, services for learning-disabled students, an honors program, cooperative (work-study) education, study abroad, advanced placement credit, ESL programs, double majors, independent study, distance learning, self-designed majors, summer session for credit, part-time degree programs (daytime, evenings, summer), internships, and arrangement for off-campus study with members of the Tri-College University-Concordia College, Moorhead, MN, Minnesota State University Moorhead. The most frequently chosen baccalaureate fields are business/marketing, engineering/engineering technologies, health professions and related sciences.
Student Body Statistics The student body totals 11,146, of whom 9,874 are undergraduates (1,856 freshmen). 43 percent are women and 57 percent are men. Students come from 44 states and territories and 54 other countries. 60 percent are from North Dakota. 1.1 percent are international students. 17.7 percent of the 2002 graduating class went on to graduate and professional schools.
Expenses for 2002–03 *Application fee:* $35. *One-time mandatory fee:* $45. *State resident tuition:* $2904 full-time, $121 per credit part-time. *Nonresident tuition:* $3396 full-time, $323.08 per credit part-time. *Mandatory fees:* $602 full-time, $25.08 per credit part-time. Full-time tuition and fees vary according to reciprocity agreements. Part-time tuition and fees vary according to course load and reciprocity agreements. *College room and board:* $4175. *College room only:* $1555. Room and board charges vary according to board plan and housing facility.
Financial Aid Forms of aid include need-based and non-need-based scholarships, athletic grants, and part-time jobs. The average aided 2001–02 undergraduate received an aid package worth $5210. The priority application deadline for financial aid is April 15.
Freshman Admission NDSU requires a high school transcript, a minimum 2.5 high school GPA, SAT I or ACT scores, and TOEFL scores for international students. The application deadline for regular admission is August 15.
Transfer Admission The application deadline for admission is August 15.
Entrance Difficulty NDSU assesses its entrance difficulty level as moderately difficult. For the fall 2002 freshman class, 60 percent of the applicants were accepted.

For Further Information Contact Dr. Kate Haugen, Director of Admission, North Dakota State University, PO Box 5454, Fargo, ND 58105-5454. *Telephone:* 701-231-8643 or 800-488-NDSU (toll-free). *Fax:* 701-231-8802. *E-mail:* ndsu.admission@ndsu.nodak.edu. *Web site:* http://www.ndsu.edu/.

SITTING BULL COLLEGE

Fort Yates, North Dakota

Sitting Bull College is a coed, private, two-year college, founded in 1973, offering degrees at the associate level.

Academic Information The faculty has 32 members (50% full-time), 9% with terminal degrees. The student-faculty ratio is 6:1. The library holds 10,000 titles and 130 serial subscriptions. Special programs include academic remediation, part-time degree programs (daytime, evenings, weekends, summer), adult/continuing education programs, and arrangement for off-campus study with members of the American Indian Higher Education Consortium.
Student Body Statistics The student body is made up of 214 undergraduates. Students come from 2 states and territories.
Expenses for 2002–03 *Tuition:* $2400 full-time, $80 per credit part-time. Full-time tuition varies according to program. Part-time tuition varies according to program.
Financial Aid Forms of aid include need-based scholarships and part-time jobs. The priority application deadline for financial aid is May 15.
Freshman Admission Sitting Bull College requires a high school transcript, medical questionnaire, and TABE. The application deadline for regular admission is September 6.
Transfer Admission The application deadline for admission is September 6.
Entrance Difficulty Sitting Bull College has an open admission policy.

For Further Information Contact Ms. Melody Silk, Director of Registration and Admissions, Sitting Bull College, 1341 92nd Street, Fort Yates, ND 58538-9701. *Telephone:* 701-854-3864. *Fax:* 701-854-3403. *Web site:* http://www.sittingbull.edu/.

TRINITY BIBLE COLLEGE

Ellendale, North Dakota

TBC is a coed, private, Assemblies of God, four-year college, founded in 1948, offering degrees at the associate and bachelor's levels. It has a 28-acre campus in Ellendale.

Academic Information The student-faculty ratio is 11:1. The library holds 67,868 titles, 227 serial subscriptions, and 2,258 audiovisual materials. Special programs include academic remediation, advanced placement credit, accelerated degree programs, double majors, distance learning, summer session for credit, part-time degree programs (evenings), and internships. The most frequently chosen baccalaureate fields are education, philosophy, religion, and theology.
Student Body Statistics The student body is made up of 287 undergraduates (59 freshmen). 53 percent are women and 47 percent are men. Students come from 30 states and territories. 34 percent are from North Dakota. 5 percent of the 2002 graduating class went on to graduate and professional schools.
Expenses for 2003–04 *Application fee:* $25. *Comprehensive fee:* $14,686 includes full-time tuition ($8080), mandatory fees ($2296), and college room and board ($4310). Full-time tuition and fees vary according to course load. Room and board charges vary according to gender and housing facility. *Part-time tuition:* varies with course load.
Financial Aid Forms of aid include need-based and non-need-based scholarships and part-time jobs. The application deadline for financial aid is September 1 with a priority deadline of March 1.
Freshman Admission TBC requires an essay, a high school transcript, a minimum 2.0 high school GPA, 2 recommendations, health form, evidence of Christian conversion, and ACT scores. TOEFL scores for international students are recommended. An interview and SAT I scores are required for some. The application deadline for regular admission is rolling.
Transfer Admission The application deadline for admission is rolling.
Entrance Difficulty TBC assesses its entrance difficulty level as noncompetitive. For the fall 2002 freshman class, 51 percent of the applicants were accepted.

For Further Information Contact Rev. Steve Tvedt, Vice President of College Relations, Trinity Bible College, 50 South Sixth Avenue, Ellendale, ND 58436. *Telephone:* 701-349-3621 Ext. 2045 or 888-TBC-2DAY (toll-free). *Fax:* 701-349-5443. *E-mail:* admissions@trinitybiblecollege.edu. *Web site:* http://www.trinitybiblecollege.edu/.

TURTLE MOUNTAIN COMMUNITY COLLEGE

Belcourt, North Dakota

For Information Write to Turtle Mountain Community College, Belcourt, ND 58316-0340.

UNIVERSITY OF MARY

Bismarck, North Dakota

Mary is a coed, private, Roman Catholic, comprehensive institution, founded in 1959, offering degrees at the associate, bachelor's, and master's levels. It has a 107-acre campus in Bismarck.

Academic Information The faculty has 184 members (48% full-time), 29% with terminal degrees. The undergraduate student-faculty ratio is 16:1. The library holds 74,205 titles, 597 serial subscriptions, and 5,382 audiovisual materials. Special programs include academic remediation, services for learning-disabled students, cooperative (work-study) education, study abroad, advanced placement credit, accelerated degree programs, double majors, independent study, distance learning, summer session for credit, part-time degree programs (daytime, evenings, weekends, summer), external degree programs, adult/continuing education programs, internships, and arrangement for off-campus study. The most frequently chosen baccalaureate fields are business/marketing, education, health professions and related sciences.
Student Body Statistics The student body totals 2,546, of whom 2,100 are undergraduates (402 freshmen). 60 percent are women and 40 percent are men. Students come from 25 states and territories and 15 other countries. 72 percent are from North Dakota. 1.6 percent are international students. 13 percent of the 2002 graduating class went on to graduate and professional schools.
Expenses for 2002–03 *Application fee:* $15. *Comprehensive fee:* $13,135 includes full-time tuition ($9200), mandatory fees ($200), and college room and board ($3735). *College room only:* $1735. Full-time tuition and fees vary according to course load and program. Room and board charges vary according to board plan, housing facility, and location. *Part-time tuition:* $290 per credit hour. *Part-time mandatory fees:* $5 per credit hour. Part-time tuition and fees vary according to degree level.
Financial Aid Forms of aid include need-based and non-need-based scholarships and part-time jobs. The priority application deadline for financial aid is May 1.
Freshman Admission Mary requires a high school transcript, 1 recommendation, ACT scores, SAT I and SAT II or ACT scores, and TOEFL scores for international students. 2.5 GPA is recommended. An essay and an interview are required for some. The application deadline for regular admission is rolling.
Transfer Admission The application deadline for admission is rolling.
Entrance Difficulty Mary assesses its entrance difficulty level as moderately difficult. For the fall 2002 freshman class, 94 percent of the applicants were accepted.

For Further Information Contact Dr. Dave Hebinger, Vice President for Enrollment Services, University of Mary, 7500 University Drive, Bismarck, ND 58504-9652. *Telephone:* 701-255-7500 Ext. 8190 or 800-288-6279 (toll-free). *Fax:* 701-255-7687. *E-mail:* marauder@umary.edu. *Web site:* http://www.umary.edu/.

UNIVERSITY OF NORTH DAKOTA

Grand Forks, North Dakota

UND is a coed, public unit of North Dakota University System, founded in 1883, offering degrees at the bachelor's, master's, doctoral, and first professional levels and post-master's certificates. It has a 570-acre campus in Grand Forks.

Academic Information The faculty has 593 members (79% full-time). The undergraduate student-faculty ratio is 18:1. The library holds 658,957 titles, 10,438 serial subscriptions, and 14,306 audiovisual materials. Special programs include services for learning-disabled students, an honors program, cooperative (work-study) education, study abroad, advanced placement credit, accelerated degree programs, double majors, independent study, distance learning, self-designed majors, summer session for credit, part-time degree programs, adult/continuing education programs, internships, and arrangement for off-campus study. The most frequently chosen baccalaureate fields are business/marketing, health professions and related sciences, trade and industry.
Student Body Statistics The student body totals 12,423, of whom 10,277 are undergraduates (2,020 freshmen). 47 percent are women and 53 percent are men. Students come from 54 states and territories and 45 other countries. 58 percent are from North Dakota. 2.4 percent are international students. 12 percent of the 2002 graduating class went on to graduate and professional schools.
Expenses for 2002–03 *Application fee:* $35. *State resident tuition:* $3662 full-time, $173.41 per credit hour part-time. *Nonresident tuition:* $8594 full-time, $378.96 per credit hour part-time. *Mandatory fees:* $708 full-time, $50.33 per credit hour part-time, $328.63 per term part-time. Full-time tuition and fees vary according to degree level, program, and reciprocity agreements. Part-time tuition and fees vary according to course load, degree level, program, and reciprocity agreements. *College room and board:* $3987. *College room only:* $1579. Room and board charges vary according to board plan and housing facility.
Financial Aid Forms of aid include need-based and non-need-based scholarships, athletic grants, and part-time jobs. The average aided 2002–03 undergraduate received an aid package worth an estimated $9107. The priority application deadline for financial aid is April 15.
Freshman Admission UND requires a high school transcript, SAT I or ACT scores, and TOEFL scores for international students. A minimum 2.25 high school GPA and ACT scores are recommended. The application deadline for regular admission is July 1.
Transfer Admission The application deadline for admission is rolling.
Entrance Difficulty UND assesses its entrance difficulty level as minimally difficult; moderately difficult for transfers. For the fall 2002 freshman class, 72 percent of the applicants were accepted.

For Further Information Contact Ms. Heidi Kippenhan, Director of Admissions, University of North Dakota, Box 8382, Grand Forks, ND 58202. *Telephone:* 701-777-4463 or 800-CALL UND (toll-free). *Fax:* 701-777-2696. *E-mail:* enrolser@sage.und.nodak.edu. *Web site:* http://www.und.edu/.

VALLEY CITY STATE UNIVERSITY

Valley City, North Dakota

VCSU is a coed, public, four-year college of North Dakota University System, founded in 1890, offering degrees at the bachelor's level. It has a 55-acre campus in Valley City.

Academic Information The faculty has 85 members (72% full-time), 29% with terminal degrees. The student-faculty ratio is 12:1. The library holds 94,236 titles, 392 serial subscriptions, and 15,305 audiovisual materials. Special programs include academic remediation, services for learning-disabled students, cooperative (work-study) education, double majors, distance learning, self-designed majors, summer session for credit, part-time degree programs (daytime, evenings, summer), internships, and arrangement for off-campus study with North Dakota State University, Mayville State University. The most frequently chosen baccalaureate fields are business/marketing, education, liberal arts/general studies.
Student Body Statistics The student body is made up of 1,022 undergraduates (162 freshmen). 55 percent are women and 45 percent are men. Students come from 27 states and territories and 8 other countries. 75 percent are from North Dakota. 4.6 percent are international students.
Expenses for 2002–03 *Application fee:* $35. *State resident tuition:* $2202 full-time, $92 per semester hour part-time. *Nonresident tuition:* $5879 full-time, $245 per semester hour part-time. *Mandatory fees:* $54 per semester hour part-time. *College room and board:* $3130. *College room only:* $1165. Room and board charges vary according to board plan.
Financial Aid Forms of aid include need-based and non-need-based scholarships, athletic grants, and part-time jobs. The average aided 2001–02 undergraduate received an aid package worth $6043. The priority application deadline for financial aid is March 15.

Valley City State University (continued)

Freshman Admission VCSU requires a high school transcript, SAT I or ACT scores, and TOEFL scores for international students. The application deadline for regular admission is rolling.
Transfer Admission The application deadline for admission is rolling.
Entrance Difficulty VCSU has an open admission policy.

For Further Information Contact Mr. Monte Johnson, Director of Admissions, Valley City State University, 101 College Street Southwest, Valley City, ND 58072. *Telephone:* 701-845-7101 Ext. 37297 or 800-532-8641 Ext. 37101 (toll-free). *Fax:* 701-845-7299. *E-mail:* enrollment_services@mail.vcsu.nodak.edu. *Web site:* http://www.vcsu.edu/.

Ohio

ALLEGHENY WESLEYAN COLLEGE

Salem, Ohio

Allegheny Wesleyan College is a coed, private, four-year college, offering degrees at the bachelor's level.

Student Body Statistics The student body is made up of 70 undergraduates.
Expenses for 2002–03 *Tuition:* $6050 full-time, $125 per hour part-time.

For Further Information Contact Admissions Office, Allegheny Wesleyan College, 2161 Woodsdale Road, Salem, OH 44460. *Telephone:* 330-337-6403 or 800-292-3153 (toll-free). *Fax:* 330-337-6255. *Web site:* http://www.awc.edu/.

ANTIOCH COLLEGE

Yellow Springs, Ohio

Antioch is a coed, private, four-year college of Antioch University, founded in 1852, offering degrees at the bachelor's level. It has a 100-acre campus in Yellow Springs near Dayton.

Academic Information The faculty has 60 members (95% full-time), 100% with terminal degrees. The student-faculty ratio is 10:1. The library holds 300,000 titles, 10,504 serial subscriptions, and 6,259 audiovisual materials. Special programs include academic remediation, services for learning-disabled students, cooperative (work-study) education, study abroad, advanced placement credit, double majors, independent study, self-designed majors, summer session for credit, internships, and arrangement for off-campus study with members of the Great Lakes Colleges Association, Southwestern Ohio Council for Higher Education.
Student Body Statistics The student body totals 597, of whom 581 are undergraduates (155 freshmen). 61 percent are women and 39 percent are men. Students come from 42 states and territories and 2 other countries. 24 percent are from Ohio. 0.3 percent are international students.
Expenses for 2002–03 *Application fee:* $35. *Comprehensive fee:* $27,705 includes full-time tuition ($21,190), mandatory fees ($913), and college room and board ($5602). *College room only:* $2740.
Financial Aid Forms of aid include need-based and non-need-based scholarships and part-time jobs. The average aided 2001–02 undergraduate received an aid package worth $16,692. The priority application deadline for financial aid is March 1.
Freshman Admission Antioch requires an essay, a high school transcript, a minimum 2.5 high school GPA, and 2 recommendations. An interview is recommended. The application deadline for regular admission is February 1 and for early action it is November 15.
Transfer Admission The application deadline for admission is rolling.
Entrance Difficulty Antioch assesses its entrance difficulty level as moderately difficult. For the fall 2002 freshman class, 75 percent of the applicants were accepted.

For Further Information Contact Ms. Cathy Paige, Information Manager, Antioch College, 795 Livermore Street, Yellow Springs, OH 45387-1697. *Telephone:* 937-769-1100 Ext. 1107 or 800-543-9436 (toll-free). *Fax:* 937-769-1111. *E-mail:* admissions@antioch-college.edu. *Web site:* http://www.antioch-college.edu/.

ANTIOCH UNIVERSITY MCGREGOR

Yellow Springs, Ohio

Antioch University McGregor is a coed, private, upper-level unit of Antioch University, founded in 1988, offering degrees at the bachelor's and master's levels. It has a 100-acre campus in Yellow Springs near Dayton.

Academic Information The faculty has 107 members (19% full-time), 61% with terminal degrees. The undergraduate student-faculty ratio is 7:1. The library holds 285,000 titles and 1,000 serial subscriptions. Special programs include cooperative (work-study) education, advanced placement credit, accelerated degree programs, double majors, independent study, distance learning, summer session for credit, part-time degree programs (evenings, weekends, summer), adult/continuing education programs, and internships. The most frequently chosen baccalaureate fields are business/marketing, liberal arts/general studies, psychology.
Student Body Statistics The student body totals 703, of whom 163 are undergraduates. 77 percent are women and 23 percent are men. Students come from 1 state or territory.
Expenses for 2003–04 *Application fee:* $45. *Tuition:* $10,755 full-time. *Mandatory fees:* $225 full-time.
Financial Aid Forms of aid include need-based scholarships and part-time jobs. The average aided 2001–02 undergraduate received an aid package worth $10,500. The application deadline for financial aid is continuous.
Transfer Admission Antioch University McGregor requires a college transcript and a minimum 2.0 college GPA. The application deadline for admission is rolling.
Entrance Difficulty Antioch University McGregor assesses its entrance difficulty level as noncompetitive.

For Further Information Contact Mr. Oscar Robinson, Enrollment Services Manager, Antioch University McGregor, Student and Alumni Services Division, Enrollment Services, 800 Livermore Street, Yellow Springs, OH 45387. *Telephone:* 937-769-1823 or 937-769-1818 (toll-free). *Fax:* 937-769-1805. *E-mail:* sas@mcgregor.edu. *Web site:* http://www.mcgregor.edu/.

ART ACADEMY OF CINCINNATI

Cincinnati, Ohio

Art Academy of Cincinnati is a coed, private, comprehensive institution, founded in 1887, offering degrees at the associate, bachelor's, and master's levels in art. It has a 184-acre campus in Cincinnati.

Academic Information The faculty has 51 members (33% full-time), 84% with terminal degrees. The undergraduate student-faculty ratio is 12:1. The library holds 66,404 titles, 150 serial subscriptions, and 588 audiovisual materials. Special programs include services for learning-disabled students, study abroad, advanced placement credit, double majors, independent study, self-designed majors, summer session for credit, part-time degree programs (daytime, evenings, summer), adult/continuing education programs, internships, and arrangement for off-campus study with members of the Greater Cincinnati Consortium of Colleges and Universities, Association of Independent Colleges of Art and Design. The most frequently chosen baccalaureate field is visual/performing arts.
Student Body Statistics The student body totals 207, of whom 188 are undergraduates (38 freshmen). 49 percent are women and 51 percent are men. Students come from 14 states and territories and 3 other countries.

79 percent are from Ohio. 1.6 percent are international students. 5 percent of the 2002 graduating class went on to graduate and professional schools.
Expenses for 2003–04 *Application fee:* $25. *Tuition:* $17,000 full-time, $700 per credit hour part-time. *Mandatory fees:* $300 full-time, $150 per term part-time. Part-time tuition and fees vary according to course load.
Financial Aid Forms of aid include need-based and non-need-based scholarships and part-time jobs. The average aided 2002–03 undergraduate received an aid package worth an estimated $10,735. The priority application deadline for financial aid is March 1.
Freshman Admission Art Academy of Cincinnati requires an essay, a high school transcript, a minimum 2.5 high school GPA, 1 recommendation, an interview, a portfolio, SAT I or ACT scores, and TOEFL scores for international students. The application deadline for regular admission is June 30.
Transfer Admission The application deadline for admission is June 30.
Entrance Difficulty Art Academy of Cincinnati assesses its entrance difficulty level as moderately difficult. For the fall 2002 freshman class, 73 percent of the applicants were accepted.

For Further Information Contact Ms. Mary Jane Zumwalde, Director of Admissions, Art Academy of Cincinnati, 1125 Saint Gregory Street, Cincinnati, OH 45202. *Telephone:* 513-562-8744 or 800-323-5692 (toll-free in-state). *Fax:* 513-562-8778. *E-mail:* admissions@artacademy.edu. *Web site:* http://www.artacademy.edu/.

ASHLAND UNIVERSITY

Ashland, Ohio

AU is a coed, private, comprehensive institution, founded in 1878, affiliated with the Brethren Church, offering degrees at the associate, bachelor's, master's, doctoral, and first professional levels. It has a 98-acre campus in Ashland near Cleveland.

Academic Information The faculty has 502 members (42% full-time), 43% with terminal degrees. The undergraduate student-faculty ratio is 16:1. The library holds 205,200 titles, 1,625 serial subscriptions, and 3,550 audiovisual materials. Special programs include academic remediation, services for learning-disabled students, an honors program, study abroad, advanced placement credit, ESL programs, double majors, independent study, self-designed majors, summer session for credit, part-time degree programs (daytime, evenings, weekends, summer), adult/continuing education programs, internships, and arrangement for off-campus study with Case Western Reserve University, Art Institute of Pittsburgh, Purdue University, Drew University, American University, Merrill-Palmer Institute, Hunter College of the City University of New York. The most frequently chosen baccalaureate fields are business/marketing, communications/communication technologies, education.
Student Body Statistics The student body totals 6,430, of whom 2,748 are undergraduates (560 freshmen). 58 percent are women and 42 percent are men. Students come from 27 states and territories and 14 other countries. 95 percent are from Ohio. 1.5 percent are international students.
Expenses for 2002–03 *Application fee:* $25. *Comprehensive fee:* $23,482 includes full-time tuition ($16,764), mandatory fees ($506), and college room and board ($6212). *College room only:* $3274. Full-time tuition and fees vary according to location and reciprocity agreements. Room and board charges vary according to board plan and housing facility. *Part-time tuition:* $515 per credit hour. *Part-time mandatory fees:* $13 per credit hour. Part-time tuition and fees vary according to location and program.
Financial Aid Forms of aid include need-based and non-need-based scholarships, athletic grants, and part-time jobs. The average aided 2002–03 undergraduate received an aid package worth an estimated $15,818. The application deadline for financial aid is March 15.
Freshman Admission AU requires an essay, a high school transcript, a minimum 2.5 high school GPA, SAT I or ACT scores, and TOEFL scores for international students. An interview is recommended. Recommendations and an interview are required for some. The application deadline for regular admission is rolling.
Transfer Admission The application deadline for admission is rolling.
Entrance Difficulty AU assesses its entrance difficulty level as moderately difficult. For the fall 2002 freshman class, 88 percent of the applicants were accepted.

For Further Information Contact Mr. Thomas Mansperger, Director of Admission, Ashland University, 401 College Avenue, Ashland, OH 44805. *Telephone:* 419-289-5052 or 800-882-1548 (toll-free). *Fax:* 419-289-5999. *E-mail:* auadmsn@ashland.edu. *Web site:* http://www.ashland.edu/.

BALDWIN-WALLACE COLLEGE

Berea, Ohio

B-W is a coed, private, Methodist, comprehensive institution, founded in 1845, offering degrees at the bachelor's and master's levels. It has a 92-acre campus in Berea near Cleveland.

Academic Information The faculty has 396 members (41% full-time), 42% with terminal degrees. The undergraduate student-faculty ratio is 15:1. The library holds 200,000 titles and 883 serial subscriptions. Special programs include academic remediation, services for learning-disabled students, an honors program, study abroad, advanced placement credit, accelerated degree programs, ESL programs, double majors, independent study, distance learning, self-designed majors, summer session for credit, part-time degree programs (daytime, evenings, weekends, summer), adult/continuing education programs, internships, and arrangement for off-campus study with Drew University, American University. The most frequently chosen baccalaureate fields are business/marketing, education, social sciences and history.
Student Body Statistics The student body totals 4,719, of whom 3,910 are undergraduates (735 freshmen). 62 percent are women and 38 percent are men. Students come from 31 states and territories and 29 other countries. 91 percent are from Ohio. 0.9 percent are international students. 24 percent of the 2002 graduating class went on to graduate and professional schools.
Expenses for 2002–03 *Application fee:* $15. *Comprehensive fee:* $23,454 includes full-time tuition ($17,432) and college room and board ($6022). *College room only:* $3042. *Part-time tuition:* $555 per hour. Part-time tuition varies according to class time.
Financial Aid Forms of aid include need-based and non-need-based scholarships and part-time jobs. The average aided 2002–03 undergraduate received an aid package worth an estimated $14,893. The application deadline for financial aid is September 1 with a priority deadline of May 1.
Freshman Admission B-W requires an essay, a high school transcript, a minimum 2.6 high school GPA, 1 recommendation, SAT I or ACT scores, and TOEFL scores for international students. A minimum 3.2 high school GPA and an interview are recommended. The application deadline for regular admission is rolling.
Transfer Admission The application deadline for admission is rolling.
Entrance Difficulty B-W assesses its entrance difficulty level as moderately difficult. For the fall 2002 freshman class, 84 percent of the applicants were accepted.

For Further Information Contact Ms. Grace B. Chalker, Interim Associate Director of Admissions, Baldwin-Wallace College, 275 Eastland Road, Berea, OH 44017-2088. *Telephone:* 440-826-2222 or 877-BWAPPLY (toll-free in-state). *Fax:* 440-826-3830. *E-mail:* admit@bw.edu. *Web site:* http://www.bw.edu/.

BLUFFTON COLLEGE

Bluffton, Ohio

Bluffton College is a coed, private, Mennonite, comprehensive institution, founded in 1899, offering degrees at the bachelor's and master's levels. It has a 65-acre campus in Bluffton near Toledo.

Academic Information The faculty has 106 members (70% full-time), 52% with terminal degrees. The undergraduate student-faculty ratio is 14:1. The library holds 163,448 titles, 385 serial subscriptions, and 1,259 audiovisual materials. Special programs include academic remediation, an honors program, study abroad, advanced placement credit, independent

Bluffton College (continued)
study, self-designed majors, summer session for credit, part-time degree programs, adult/continuing education programs, internships, and arrangement for off-campus study with Christian College Coalition, Council of Independent Colleges. The most frequently chosen baccalaureate fields are business/marketing, education, protective services/ public administration.
Student Body Statistics The student body totals 1,110, of whom 1,053 are undergraduates (263 freshmen). 59 percent are women and 41 percent are men. Students come from 14 states and territories and 11 other countries. 89 percent are from Ohio. 2 percent are international students.
Expenses for 2002–03 *Application fee:* $20. *Comprehensive fee:* $22,066 includes full-time tuition ($16,130), mandatory fees ($300), and college room and board ($5636). *Part-time tuition:* varies with course load.
Financial Aid Forms of aid include need-based and non-need-based scholarships and part-time jobs. The average aided 2002–03 undergraduate received an aid package worth an estimated $15,795. The application deadline for financial aid is October 1 with a priority deadline of May 1.
Freshman Admission Bluffton College requires a high school transcript, 2 recommendations, rank in upper 50% of high school class or 2.3 high school GPA, SAT I or ACT scores, and TOEFL scores for international students. An interview is recommended. An essay is required for some. The application deadline for regular admission is May 31.
Transfer Admission The application deadline for admission is rolling.
Entrance Difficulty Bluffton College assesses its entrance difficulty level as moderately difficult. For the fall 2002 freshman class, 78 percent of the applicants were accepted.

For Further Information Contact Mr. Eric Fulcomer, Director of Admissions, Associate Dean for Enrollment Management, Bluffton College, 280 West College Avenue, Bluffton, OH 45817. *Telephone:* 419-358-3254 or 800-488-3257 (toll-free). *Fax:* 419-358-3232. *E-mail:* admissions@bluffton.edu. *Web site:* http://www.bluffton.edu/.

See page 258 for a narrative description.

BOHECKER'S BUSINESS COLLEGE
Ravenna, Ohio

For Information Write to Bohecker's Business College, Ravenna, OH 44266.

BOWLING GREEN STATE UNIVERSITY
Bowling Green, Ohio

BGSU is a coed, public university, founded in 1910, offering degrees at the bachelor's, master's, and doctoral levels and post-master's certificates. It has a 1,230-acre campus in Bowling Green near Toledo.

Academic Information The faculty has 1,045 members (77% full-time). The undergraduate student-faculty ratio is 19:1. The library holds 2 million titles, 4,833 serial subscriptions, and 718,734 audiovisual materials. Special programs include academic remediation, services for learning-disabled students, an honors program, cooperative (work-study) education, study abroad, advanced placement credit, accelerated degree programs, ESL programs, double majors, independent study, distance learning, self-designed majors, summer session for credit, part-time degree programs (daytime, evenings, summer), adult/continuing education programs, internships, and arrangement for off-campus study with University of Toledo, Medical College of Ohio. The most frequently chosen baccalaureate fields are business/marketing, education, English.
Student Body Statistics The student body totals 18,773, of whom 15,703 are undergraduates (3,605 freshmen). 56 percent are women and 44 percent are men. Students come from 52 states and territories and 86 other countries. 94 percent are from Ohio. 0.7 percent are international students.
Expenses for 2002–03 *Application fee:* $35. *State resident tuition:* $5358 full-time, $263 per credit hour part-time. *Nonresident tuition:* $11,986 full-time, $579 per credit hour part-time. *Mandatory fees:* $1144 full-time, $57 per credit hour part-time. Part-time tuition and fees vary according to course load. *College room and board:* $6490. *College room only:* $3760. Room and board charges vary according to board plan and housing facility.
Financial Aid Forms of aid include need-based and non-need-based scholarships, athletic grants, and part-time jobs. The average aided 2001–02 undergraduate received an aid package worth $6122. The application deadline for financial aid is continuous.
Freshman Admission BGSU requires a high school transcript, a minimum 2.5 high school GPA, SAT I or ACT scores, and TOEFL scores for international students. An interview is recommended. The application deadline for regular admission is July 15.
Transfer Admission The application deadline for admission is July 15.
Entrance Difficulty BGSU assesses its entrance difficulty level as moderately difficult. For the fall 2002 freshman class, 91 percent of the applicants were accepted.

For Further Information Contact Mr. Gary Swegan, Director of Admissions, Bowling Green State University, 110 McFall, Bowling Green, OH 43403. *Telephone:* 419-372-2086. *Fax:* 419-372-6955. *E-mail:* admissions@bgnet.bgsu.edu. *Web site:* http://www.bgsu.edu/.

BRYANT AND STRATTON COLLEGE
Cleveland, Ohio

Bryant and Stratton is a coed, proprietary, four-year college of Bryant and Stratton Business Institute, Inc, founded in 1929, offering degrees at the associate and bachelor's levels.

Academic Information The faculty has 20 members (25% full-time). The student-faculty ratio is 10:1. The library holds 4,466 titles, 80 serial subscriptions, and 159 audiovisual materials. Special programs include academic remediation, services for learning-disabled students, cooperative (work-study) education, double majors, independent study, distance learning, summer session for credit, part-time degree programs (evenings, weekends, summer), adult/continuing education programs, and internships. The most frequently chosen baccalaureate field is engineering/engineering technologies.
Student Body Statistics The student body is made up of 203 undergraduates. Students come from 2 states and territories.
Expenses for 2002–03 *Application fee:* $25. *Tuition:* $9900 full-time. *Mandatory fees:* $200 full-time. *College room only:* $3200.
Financial Aid Forms of aid include need-based and non-need-based scholarships and part-time jobs. The average aided 2001–02 undergraduate received an aid package worth $6200. The application deadline for financial aid is continuous.
Freshman Admission Bryant and Stratton requires an essay, a high school transcript, an interview, TOEFL scores for international students, and TABE. SAT I or ACT scores are recommended. The application deadline for regular admission is rolling.
Transfer Admission The application deadline for admission is rolling.
Entrance Difficulty Bryant and Stratton assesses its entrance difficulty level as minimally difficult. For the fall 2002 freshman class, 93 percent of the applicants were accepted.

For Further Information Contact Ms. Marilyn Scheaffer, Director of Admissions, Bryant and Stratton College, 1700 East 13th Street, Cleveland, OH 44114-3203. *Telephone:* 216-771-1700. *Fax:* 216-771-7787. *Web site:* http://www.bryantstratton.edu/.

CAPITAL UNIVERSITY
Columbus, Ohio

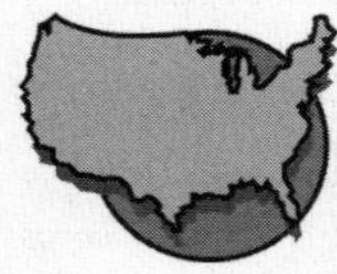

Capital is a coed, private, comprehensive institution, founded in 1830, affiliated with the Evangelical Lutheran Church in America, offering degrees at the bachelor's, master's, and first professional levels. It has a 48-acre campus in Columbus.

Academic Information The faculty has 444 members (41% full-time), 58% with terminal degrees. The undergraduate student-faculty ratio is 11:1. The library holds 187,281 titles, 3,741 serial subscriptions, and 6,048 audiovisual materials. Special programs include services for learning-disabled students, study abroad, advanced placement credit, Freshman Honors College, ESL programs, double majors, independent study, self-designed majors, summer session for credit, part-time degree programs (evenings, weekends, summer), adult/continuing education programs, internships, and arrangement for off-campus study with members of the Higher Education Council of Columbus. The most frequently chosen baccalaureate fields are business/marketing, interdisciplinary studies, social sciences and history.

Student Body Statistics The student body totals 3,947, of whom 2,785 are undergraduates. 64 percent are women and 36 percent are men. Students come from 24 states and territories and 14 other countries. 92 percent are from Ohio. 0.7 percent are international students. 21 percent of the 2002 graduating class went on to graduate and professional schools.

Expenses for 2003–04 *Application fee:* $25. *One-time mandatory fee:* $200. *Comprehensive fee:* $26,550 includes full-time tuition ($20,500) and college room and board ($6050). Room and board charges vary according to board plan and housing facility.

Financial Aid Forms of aid include need-based and non-need-based scholarships and part-time jobs. The average aided 2001–02 undergraduate received an aid package worth $14,904. The priority application deadline for financial aid is February 28.

Freshman Admission Capital requires a high school transcript, a minimum 2.6 high school GPA, SAT I or ACT scores, and TOEFL scores for international students. An interview is recommended. An essay, 1 recommendation, and audition are required for some. The application deadline for regular admission is April 15.

Transfer Admission The application deadline for admission is rolling.

Entrance Difficulty Capital assesses its entrance difficulty level as moderately difficult. For the fall 2002 freshman class, 83 percent of the applicants were accepted.

SPECIAL MESSAGE TO STUDENTS

Social Life A Lutheran university, Capital has varied programs that attract students from all backgrounds and religions. Capital offers more than seventy athletic and extracurricular activities that support student involvement and leadership. The sororities and fraternities on campus attract about 20 percent of the students. Approximately 65 percent of the traditional undergraduates live on campus. Students organize and enjoy numerous campus events, including live music performances, movies, all-campus parties, spring-break trips, Homecoming, and speakers.

Academic Highlights Capital's many features include small class sizes; a location within a major metropolitan area that offers unlimited educational, cultural, recreational, and social activities; internships and cooperative education opportunities with national companies and organizations; an innovative General Education curriculum that brings together the University's academic, scientific, religious, and artistic disciplines; study-abroad programs; and special University resources, including a television studio, computer labs, an art gallery, and CAPNet, a campuswide voice, data, and video network that connects every residence room, classroom, and office to the Internet and the World Wide Web.

Interviews and Campus Visits A student should visit the campus to see if Capital is the right choice. The Admission Office can arrange a campus tour and interview and provide an opportunity to talk with professors and students and sample the food in the main dining room. Capital's compact campus makes it easy for visitors to experience its many features, including The Capital Center (athletic and recreation facility), The Schumacher Gallery, the Campus Center (which includes the snack bar, dining hall, bookstore, and student government and organization offices), Kerns Religious Life Center, Ruff Learning Center, Mees Auditorium, and the library and residence halls. For information about appointments and campus visits, students should call the Admission Office at 614-236-6101 or 800-289-6289 (toll-free), Monday through Friday, 9 a.m. to 4 p.m. The office is located in Yochum Hall on campus. The nearest commercial airport is Port Columbus International.

For Further Information Write to Ms. Kimberly V. Ebbrecht, Director of Admission, Capital University, Columbus, OH 43209-2394. *E-mail:* admissions@capital.edu. *Web site:* http://www.capital.edu.

CASE WESTERN RESERVE UNIVERSITY

Cleveland, Ohio

CWRU is a coed, private university, founded in 1826, offering degrees at the bachelor's, master's, doctoral, and first professional levels and postbachelor's certificates. It has a 128-acre campus in Cleveland.

Academic Information The faculty has 594 members (100% full-time), 95% with terminal degrees. The undergraduate student-faculty ratio is 8:1. The library holds 2 million titles, 17,506 serial subscriptions, and 49,889 audiovisual materials. Special programs include services for learning-disabled students, an honors program, cooperative (work-study) education, study abroad, advanced placement credit, accelerated degree programs, ESL programs, double majors, independent study, self-designed majors, summer session for credit, part-time degree programs (daytime, evenings), adult/continuing education programs, internships, and arrangement for off-campus study with Cleveland Institute of Art, Cleveland Institute of Music, 11 other Cleveland area institutions. The most frequently chosen baccalaureate fields are biological/life sciences, business/marketing, engineering/engineering technologies.

Student Body Statistics The student body totals 9,097, of whom 3,457 are undergraduates (836 freshmen). 39 percent are women and 61 percent are men. Students come from 50 states and territories and 26 other countries. 60 percent are from Ohio. 3.7 percent are international students. 39 percent of the 2002 graduating class went on to graduate and professional schools.

Expenses for 2002–03 *Application fee:* $35. *Comprehensive fee:* $29,880 includes full-time tuition ($22,500), mandatory fees ($230), and college room and board ($7150). *College room only:* $4450. Room and board charges vary according to board plan and housing facility. *Part-time tuition:* $938 per credit. Part-time tuition varies according to course load.

Financial Aid Forms of aid include need-based and non-need-based scholarships and part-time jobs. The average aided 2002–03 undergraduate received an aid package worth an estimated $21,815. The priority application deadline for financial aid is February 1.

Freshman Admission CWRU requires an essay, a high school transcript, 1 recommendation, SAT I or ACT scores, and TOEFL scores for international students. An interview and SAT II: Subject Test scores are recommended. The application deadline for regular admission is February 1 and for early decision it is January 1.

Transfer Admission The application deadline for admission is June 30.

Entrance Difficulty CWRU assesses its entrance difficulty level as very difficult. For the fall 2002 freshman class, 78 percent of the applicants were accepted.

For Further Information Contact Ms. Elizabeth H. Woyczynski, Acting Dean of Undergraduate Admission, Case Western Reserve University, 10900 Euclid Avenue, Cleveland, OH 44106. *Telephone:* 216-368-4450. *Fax:* 216-368-5111. *E-mail:* admission@po.cwru.edu. *Web site:* http://www.cwru.edu/.

See page 260 for a narrative description.

CEDARVILLE UNIVERSITY

Cedarville, Ohio

Cedarville is a coed, private, Baptist, comprehensive institution, founded in 1887, offering degrees at the associate, bachelor's, and master's levels. It has a 300-acre campus in Cedarville near Columbus and Dayton.

Academic Information The faculty has 247 members (79% full-time), 45% with terminal degrees. The undergraduate student-faculty ratio is 16:1. The library holds 149,164 titles, 4,932 serial subscriptions, and 15,452 audiovisual materials. Special programs include academic remediation, services for learning-disabled students, an honors program, study abroad, advanced placement credit, accelerated degree programs, double majors, independent study, distance learning, summer session for credit, part-time degree programs (daytime), internships, and arrangement for off-campus study with Au Sable Institute. The most frequently chosen baccalaureate fields are education, business/marketing, philosophy, religion, and theology.

Cedarville University (continued)

Student Body Statistics The student body totals 3,005, of whom 2,986 are undergraduates (774 freshmen). 54 percent are women and 46 percent are men. Students come from 49 states and territories. 33 percent are from Ohio. 0.5 percent are international students.

Expenses for 2002–03 *Application fee:* $30. *Comprehensive fee:* $18,706 includes full-time tuition ($13,696) and college room and board ($5010). *College room only:* $2684. Room and board charges vary according to board plan. *Part-time tuition:* $428 per credit hour. Part-time tuition varies according to course load.

Financial Aid Forms of aid include need-based and non-need-based scholarships, athletic grants, and part-time jobs. The average aided 2001–02 undergraduate received an aid package worth $10,749. The priority application deadline for financial aid is March 1.

Freshman Admission Cedarville requires an essay, a high school transcript, a minimum 3.0 high school GPA, 2 recommendations, SAT I or ACT scores, and TOEFL scores for international students. An interview is required for some. The application deadline for regular admission is rolling.

Transfer Admission The application deadline for admission is rolling.

Entrance Difficulty Cedarville assesses its entrance difficulty level as moderately difficult. For the fall 2002 freshman class, 82 percent of the applicants were accepted.

For Further Information Contact Mr. Roscoe Smith, Director of Admissions, Cedarville University, 251 North Main Street, Cedarville, OH 45314-0601. *Telephone:* 937-766-7700 or 800-CEDARVILLE (toll-free). *Fax:* 937-766-7575. *E-mail:* admiss@cedarville.edu. *Web site:* http://www.cedarville.edu/.

CENTRAL STATE UNIVERSITY

Wilberforce, Ohio

Central is a coed, public, comprehensive unit of Ohio Board of Regents, founded in 1887, offering degrees at the bachelor's and master's levels and postbachelor's certificates. It has a 60-acre campus in Wilberforce near Dayton.

For Further Information Contact Mr. Thandabantu Maceo, Director, Admissions, Central State University, PO Box 1004, 1400 Blush Row Road, Wilberforce, OH 45384. *Telephone:* 937-376-6348 or 800-388-CSU1 (toll-free in-state). *Fax:* 937-376-6648. *E-mail:* admissions@csu.ces.edu. *Web site:* http://www.centralstate.edu/.

CHATFIELD COLLEGE

St. Martin, Ohio

Chatfield is a coed, primarily women's, private, two-year college, founded in 1970, affiliated with the Roman Catholic Church, offering degrees at the associate level. It has a 200-acre campus in St. Martin near Cincinnati and Dayton.

Academic Information The faculty has 42 members (7% full-time), 7% with terminal degrees. The student-faculty ratio is 12:1. The library holds 15,000 titles and 30 serial subscriptions. Special programs include academic remediation, advanced placement credit, summer session for credit, part-time degree programs (daytime, evenings, summer), adult/continuing education programs, internships, and arrangement for off-campus study with 14 members of the Greater Cincinnati Consortium of Colleges and Universities.

Student Body Statistics The student body is made up of 282 undergraduates. 88 percent are women and 12 percent are men. Students come from 1 state or territory. 39 percent of the 2002 graduating class went on to four-year colleges.

Expenses for 2003–04 *Application fee:* $10. *Tuition:* $7050 full-time, $235 per credit hour part-time. *Mandatory fees:* $90 full-time, $50 per term part-time.

Financial Aid Forms of aid include need-based scholarships and part-time jobs. The application deadline for financial aid is August 1 with a priority deadline of April 26.

Freshman Admission Chatfield requires a high school transcript. TOEFL scores for international students are recommended. The application deadline for regular admission is rolling.

Transfer Admission The application deadline for admission is rolling.

Entrance Difficulty Chatfield has an open admission policy.

For Further Information Contact Ms. Julie Burdick, Director of Admissions, Chatfield College, St. Martin, OH 45118. *Telephone:* 513-875-3344. *Fax:* 513-875-3912. *Web site:* http://www.chatfield.edu/.

CINCINNATI BIBLE COLLEGE AND SEMINARY

Cincinnati, Ohio

Cincinnati Bible College is a coed, private, comprehensive institution, founded in 1924, affiliated with the Church of Christ, offering degrees at the associate, bachelor's, master's, and first professional levels. It has a 40-acre campus in Cincinnati.

Academic Information The faculty has 63 members (48% full-time). The undergraduate student-faculty ratio is 16:1. The library holds 93,000 titles and 656 serial subscriptions. Special programs include academic remediation, advanced placement credit, double majors, independent study, summer session for credit, part-time degree programs (daytime, evenings, summer), adult/continuing education programs, internships, and arrangement for off-campus study with College of Mount St. Joseph, Greater Cincinnati Consortium of Colleges and Universities.

Student Body Statistics The student body totals 922, of whom 626 are undergraduates (135 freshmen). 44 percent are women and 56 percent are men. Students come from 33 states and territories and 6 other countries. 67 percent are from Ohio. 12 percent of the 2002 graduating class went on to graduate and professional schools.

Expenses for 2002–03 *Application fee:* $35. *Comprehensive fee:* $13,730 includes full-time tuition ($8320), mandatory fees ($570), and college room and board ($4840). *College room only:* $2450. Room and board charges vary according to board plan. *Part-time tuition:* $260 per credit hour. *Part-time mandatory fees:* $10 per credit hour.

Financial Aid Forms of aid include need-based and non-need-based scholarships and part-time jobs. The average aided 2001–02 undergraduate received an aid package worth $6714. The priority application deadline for financial aid is March 15.

Freshman Admission Cincinnati Bible College requires an essay, a high school transcript, 3 recommendations, SAT I or ACT scores, and TOEFL scores for international students. A minimum 2.0 high school GPA and an interview are recommended. The application deadline for regular admission is August 10.

Transfer Admission The application deadline for admission is August 10.

Entrance Difficulty Cincinnati Bible College assesses its entrance difficulty level as minimally difficult. For the fall 2002 freshman class, 99 percent of the applicants were accepted.

For Further Information Contact Mr. Alex Eady, Director of Undergraduate Admissions, Cincinnati Bible College and Seminary, 2700 Glenway Avenue, Cincinnati, OH 45204-1799. *Telephone:* 800-949-4222 Ext. 8610 or 800-949-4CBC (toll-free). *Fax:* 513-244-8140. *E-mail:* admissions@cincybible.edu. *Web site:* http://www.cincybible.edu/.

CINCINNATI COLLEGE OF MORTUARY SCIENCE

Cincinnati, Ohio

Cincinnati Mortuary College is a coed, private, primarily two-year college, founded in 1882, offering degrees at the associate and bachelor's levels in funeral service. It has a 10-acre campus in Cincinnati.

Academic Information The faculty has 12 members (58% full-time). The student-faculty ratio is 5:1. The library holds 5,000 titles and 30 serial subscriptions. Special programs include academic remediation, advanced placement credit, summer session for credit, and adult/continuing education programs.
Student Body Statistics The student body is made up of 111 undergraduates (10 freshmen). 45 percent are women and 55 percent are men. Students come from 17 states and territories.
Expenses for 2002–03 *Application fee:* $25. *Tuition:* $11,845 full-time, $155 per credit part-time.
Financial Aid Forms of aid include need-based scholarships. The application deadline for financial aid is continuous.
Freshman Admission Cincinnati Mortuary College requires a high school transcript. Recommendations and TOEFL scores for international students are recommended. The application deadline for regular admission is rolling.
Transfer Admission The application deadline for admission is rolling.
Entrance Difficulty Cincinnati Mortuary College assesses its entrance difficulty level as minimally difficult.

For Further Information Contact Ms. Pat Leon, Director of Financial Aid, Cincinnati College of Mortuary Science, 645 West North Bend Road, Cincinnati, OH 45224-1462. *Telephone:* 513-761-2020. *Fax:* 513-761-3333. *Web site:* http://www.ccms.edu/.

CIRCLEVILLE BIBLE COLLEGE

Circleville, Ohio

CBC is a coed, private, four-year college, founded in 1948, affiliated with the Churches of Christ in Christian Union, offering degrees at the associate and bachelor's levels. It has a 40-acre campus in Circleville near Columbus.

Academic Information The faculty has 38 members (26% full-time). The student-faculty ratio is 13:1. The library holds 37,521 titles, 111 serial subscriptions, and 1,995 audiovisual materials. Special programs include academic remediation, services for learning-disabled students, an honors program, advanced placement credit, double majors, independent study, self-designed majors, summer session for credit, part-time degree programs (daytime, evenings), adult/continuing education programs, internships, and arrangement for off-campus study with Columbus State Community College. The most frequently chosen baccalaureate field is philosophy, religion, and theology.
Student Body Statistics The student body is made up of 317 undergraduates (45 freshmen). 47 percent are women and 53 percent are men. Students come from 11 states and territories. 74 percent are from Ohio.
Expenses for 2003–04 *Application fee:* $25. *Comprehensive fee:* $14,394 includes full-time tuition ($8460), mandatory fees ($844), and college room and board ($5090). Full-time tuition and fees vary according to course load, location, and reciprocity agreements. Room and board charges vary according to board plan. *Part-time tuition:* varies with course load, location, reciprocity agreements.
Financial Aid Forms of aid include need-based and non-need-based scholarships and part-time jobs. The average aided 2002–03 undergraduate received an aid package worth an estimated $10,000. The priority application deadline for financial aid is April 1.
Freshman Admission CBC requires an essay, a high school transcript, 4 recommendations, medical form, and TOEFL scores for international students. SAT I scores are recommended. An interview and ACT scores are required for some. The application deadline for regular admission is rolling.
Transfer Admission The application deadline for admission is rolling.
Entrance Difficulty CBC assesses its entrance difficulty level as minimally difficult; noncompetitive for transfers. For the fall 2002 freshman class, 61 percent of the applicants were accepted.

For Further Information Contact Rev. James Schroeder, Acting Director of Enrollment, Circleville Bible College, PO Box 458, Circleville, OH 43113-9487. *Telephone:* 740-477-7741 or 800-701-0222 (toll-free). *Fax:* 740-477-7755. *E-mail:* enroll@biblecollege.edu. *Web site:* http://www.biblecollege.edu/.

CLEVELAND COLLEGE OF JEWISH STUDIES

See Laura and Alvin Siegal College of Judaic Studies

THE CLEVELAND INSTITUTE OF ART

Cleveland, Ohio

CIA is a coed, private, comprehensive institution, founded in 1882, offering degrees at the bachelor's and master's levels in art. It has a 488-acre campus in Cleveland.

Academic Information The faculty has 85 members (51% full-time), 56% with terminal degrees. The undergraduate student-faculty ratio is 10:1. The library holds 42,000 titles, 250 serial subscriptions, and 95,000 audiovisual materials. Special programs include academic remediation, services for learning-disabled students, an honors program, study abroad, advanced placement credit, independent study, part-time degree programs (daytime), internships, and arrangement for off-campus study with Case Western Reserve University, Northeast Ohio Commission on Higher Education, Association of Independent Colleges of Art and Design. The most frequently chosen baccalaureate field is visual/performing arts.
Student Body Statistics The student body totals 641, of whom 636 are undergraduates (107 freshmen). 53 percent are women and 47 percent are men. Students come from 28 states and territories and 10 other countries. 68 percent are from Ohio. 3.3 percent are international students. 17 percent of the 2002 graduating class went on to graduate and professional schools.
Expenses for 2002–03 *Application fee:* $30. *Comprehensive fee:* $27,450 includes full-time tuition ($19,744), mandatory fees ($1280), and college room and board ($6426). Room and board charges vary according to board plan and housing facility. *Part-time tuition:* $825 per credit. *Part-time mandatory fees:* $65 per credit.
Financial Aid Forms of aid include need-based and non-need-based scholarships and part-time jobs. The average aided 2002–03 undergraduate received an aid package worth an estimated $13,424. The priority application deadline for financial aid is March 15.
Freshman Admission CIA requires an essay, a high school transcript, a minimum 2.0 high school GPA, 2 recommendations, a portfolio, SAT I or ACT scores, and TOEFL scores for international students. An interview is recommended. The application deadline for regular admission is rolling.
Transfer Admission The application deadline for admission is rolling.
Entrance Difficulty CIA assesses its entrance difficulty level as moderately difficult. For the fall 2002 freshman class, 65 percent of the applicants were accepted.

For Further Information Contact Office of Admissions, The Cleveland Institute of Art, 11141 East Boulevard, Cleveland, OH 44106. *Telephone:* 216-421-7418 or 800-223-4700 (toll-free). *Fax:* 216-754-3634. *E-mail:* admiss@gate.cia.edu. *Web site:* http://www.cia.edu/.

CLEVELAND INSTITUTE OF MUSIC

Cleveland, Ohio

Cleveland Institute of Music is a coed, private, comprehensive institution, founded in 1920, offering degrees at the bachelor's, master's, and doctoral levels. It has a 488-acre campus in Cleveland.

Academic Information The faculty has 96 members (33% full-time), 4% with terminal degrees. The undergraduate student-faculty ratio is 7:1. The library holds 48,128 titles, 115 serial subscriptions, and 19,633 audiovisual materials. Special programs include academic remediation, advanced placement credit, accelerated degree programs, ESL programs, summer session for credit, internships, and arrangement for off-campus study with Case Western Reserve University.
Student Body Statistics The student body totals 387, of whom 226 are undergraduates (63 freshmen). 55 percent are women and 45 percent are men. Students come from 38 states and territories and 11 other countries.

Cleveland Institute of Music (continued)
11 percent are from Ohio. 10.6 percent are international students. 90 percent of the 2002 graduating class went on to graduate and professional schools.
Expenses for 2002–03 *Application fee:* $70. *Comprehensive fee:* $28,180 includes full-time tuition ($20,625), mandatory fees ($880), and college room and board ($6675). *College room only:* $3975. *Part-time tuition:* $937.50 per credit hour. *Part-time mandatory fees:* $440 per term.
Financial Aid Forms of aid include need-based and non-need-based scholarships and part-time jobs. The average aided 2001–02 undergraduate received an aid package worth $13,980. The application deadline for financial aid is February 15.
Freshman Admission Cleveland Institute of Music requires an essay, a high school transcript, 2 recommendations, audition, SAT I or ACT scores, and TOEFL scores for international students. An interview is recommended. The application deadline for regular admission is December 1.
Transfer Admission The application deadline for admission is December 1.
Entrance Difficulty Cleveland Institute of Music assesses its entrance difficulty level as very difficult. For the fall 2002 freshman class, 39 percent of the applicants were accepted.

For Further Information Contact Mr. William Fay, Director of Admission, Cleveland Institute of Music, 11021 East Boulevard, Cleveland, OH 44106-1776. *Telephone:* 216-795-3107. *Fax:* 216-791-1530. *E-mail:* cimadmission@po.cwru.edu. *Web site:* http://www.cim.edu/.

CLEVELAND STATE UNIVERSITY

Cleveland, Ohio

Cleveland State is a coed, public university, founded in 1964, offering degrees at the bachelor's, master's, doctoral, and first professional levels and post-master's, first professional, and postbachelor's certificates. It has a 70-acre campus in Cleveland.

Academic Information The faculty has 905 members (54% full-time), 60% with terminal degrees. The undergraduate student-faculty ratio is 17:1. The library holds 484,914 titles, 6,186 serial subscriptions, and 101,376 audiovisual materials. Special programs include academic remediation, an honors program, cooperative (work-study) education, study abroad, advanced placement credit, accelerated degree programs, Freshman Honors College, ESL programs, independent study, self-designed majors, summer session for credit, part-time degree programs, adult/continuing education programs, internships, and arrangement for off-campus study with 7 members of the Cleveland Commission on Higher Education, University of Akron, Baldwin-Wallace College, University of Toledo. The most frequently chosen baccalaureate fields are business/marketing, education, social sciences and history.
Student Body Statistics The student body totals 15,974, of whom 10,356 are undergraduates (1,011 freshmen). 55 percent are women and 45 percent are men. Students come from 38 states and territories and 22 other countries. 98 percent are from Ohio. 2.4 percent are international students.
Expenses for 2002–03 *Application fee:* $30. *State resident tuition:* $5184 full-time, $216 per semester hour part-time. *Nonresident tuition:* $10,219 full-time, $426 per semester hour part-time. Full-time tuition varies according to program. Part-time tuition varies according to program. *College room and board:* $5880. *College room only:* $3336. Room and board charges vary according to board plan and housing facility.
Financial Aid Forms of aid include need-based and non-need-based scholarships, athletic grants, and part-time jobs. The average aided 2002–03 undergraduate received an aid package worth an estimated $6557. The priority application deadline for financial aid is February 15.
Freshman Admission Cleveland State requires a high school transcript, SAT I or ACT scores, and TOEFL scores for international students. The application deadline for regular admission is rolling.
Transfer Admission The application deadline for admission is July 15.
Entrance Difficulty Cleveland State has an open admission policy for state residents. It assesses its entrance difficulty as moderately difficult for out-of-state applicants; moderately difficult for transfers; moderately difficult for engineering, education, health science programs.

For Further Information Contact Mr. Tom Steffen, Office of Admissions, Cleveland State University, 2121 Euclid Avenue, Box A, Cleveland, OH 44115. *Telephone:* 216-523-7244 or 888-CSU-OHIO (toll-free). *Fax:* 216-687-9210. *E-mail:* registrar@csuohio.edu. *Web site:* http://www.csuohio.edu/.

COLLEGE OF MOUNT ST. JOSEPH

Cincinnati, Ohio

The Mount is a coed, private, Roman Catholic, comprehensive institution, founded in 1920, offering degrees at the associate, bachelor's, and master's levels and postbachelor's certificates. It has a 75-acre campus in Cincinnati.

Academic Information The faculty has 211 members (56% full-time), 44% with terminal degrees. The undergraduate student-faculty ratio is 14:1. The library holds 98,849 titles, 429 serial subscriptions, and 3,109 audiovisual materials. Special programs include academic remediation, services for learning-disabled students, an honors program, cooperative (work-study) education, study abroad, advanced placement credit, accelerated degree programs, Freshman Honors College, ESL programs, double majors, independent study, distance learning, summer session for credit, part-time degree programs (daytime, evenings, weekends, summer), external degree programs, adult/continuing education programs, internships, and arrangement for off-campus study with Greater Cincinnati Consortium of Colleges and Universities. The most frequently chosen baccalaureate fields are business/marketing, education, health professions and related sciences.
Student Body Statistics The student body totals 2,067, of whom 1,842 are undergraduates (348 freshmen). 69 percent are women and 31 percent are men. Students come from 16 states and territories and 13 other countries. 88 percent are from Ohio. 1.5 percent are international students. 15 percent of the 2002 graduating class went on to graduate and professional schools.
Expenses for 2002–03 *Application fee:* $25. *Comprehensive fee:* $21,860 includes full-time tuition ($14,950), mandatory fees ($890), and college room and board ($6020). Full-time tuition and fees vary according to course load, program, and reciprocity agreements. Room and board charges vary according to board plan and housing facility. *Part-time tuition:* $382 per semester hour. *Part-time mandatory fees:* $15 per term. Part-time tuition and fees vary according to course load, location, and reciprocity agreements.
Financial Aid Forms of aid include need-based and non-need-based scholarships and part-time jobs. The average aided 2002–03 undergraduate received an aid package worth an estimated $11,400. The priority application deadline for financial aid is March 1.
Freshman Admission The Mount requires a high school transcript, a minimum 2.25 high school GPA, minimum SAT score of 960 or ACT score of 19, SAT I or ACT scores, and TOEFL scores for international students. A minimum 3.0 high school GPA is recommended. An essay, 1 recommendation, and an interview are required for some. The application deadline for regular admission is August 15.
Transfer Admission The application deadline for admission is August 15.
Entrance Difficulty The Mount assesses its entrance difficulty level as moderately difficult; minimally difficult for transfers; very difficult for physical therapy. For the fall 2002 freshman class, 75 percent of the applicants were accepted.

For Further Information Contact Ms. Peggy Minnich, Director of Admission, College of Mount St. Joseph, 5701 Delhi Road, Cincinnati, OH 45233-1672. *Telephone:* 513-244-4814 or 800-654-9314 (toll-free). *Fax:* 513-244-4629. *E-mail:* peggy_minnich@mail.msj.edu. *Web site:* http://www.msj.edu/.

See page 264 for a narrative description.

THE COLLEGE OF WOOSTER

Wooster, Ohio

Wooster is a coed, private, four-year college, founded in 1866, affiliated with the Presbyterian Church (U.S.A.), offering degrees at the bachelor's level. It has a 320-acre campus in Wooster near Cleveland.

Academic Information The faculty has 168 members (79% full-time), 92% with terminal degrees. The student-faculty ratio is 13:1. The library holds 581,518 titles and 12,416 audiovisual materials. Special programs include services for learning-disabled students, study abroad, advanced placement credit, double majors, independent study, self-designed majors, summer session for credit, internships, and arrangement for off-campus study. The most frequently chosen baccalaureate fields are English, biological/life sciences, social sciences and history.
Student Body Statistics The student body is made up of 1,856 undergraduates (512 freshmen). 53 percent are women and 47 percent are men. Students come from 39 states and territories and 21 other countries. 56 percent are from Ohio. 7.3 percent are international students.
Expenses for 2003–04 *Application fee:* $40. *Comprehensive fee:* $31,300 includes full-time tuition ($25,040) and college room and board ($6260). *College room only:* $2850.
Financial Aid Forms of aid include need-based and non-need-based scholarships and part-time jobs. The average aided 2002–03 undergraduate received an aid package worth an estimated $20,629. The priority application deadline for financial aid is February 15.
Freshman Admission Wooster requires an essay, a high school transcript, 2 recommendations, SAT I or ACT scores, and TOEFL scores for international students. An interview is recommended. The application deadline for regular admission is February 15; for early decision plan 1 it is December 1; and for early decision plan 2 it is January 15.
Transfer Admission The application deadline for admission is June 1.
Entrance Difficulty Wooster assesses its entrance difficulty level as moderately difficult. For the fall 2002 freshman class, 72 percent of the applicants were accepted.

For Further Information Contact Ms. Ruth Vedvik, Director of Admissions, The College of Wooster, 1189 Beall Avenue, Wooster, OH 44691. *Telephone:* 330-263-2270 Ext. 2118 or 800-877-9905 (toll-free). *Fax:* 330-263-2621. *E-mail:* admissions@wooster.edu. *Web site:* http://www.wooster.edu/.

See page 266 for a narrative description.

COLUMBUS COLLEGE OF ART AND DESIGN

Columbus, Ohio

CCAD is a coed, private, four-year college, founded in 1879, offering degrees at the bachelor's level in art. It has a 7-acre campus in Columbus.

Academic Information The faculty has 193 members (41% full-time), 40% with terminal degrees. The student-faculty ratio is 11:1. The library holds 45,257 titles, 275 serial subscriptions, and 126,726 audiovisual materials. Special programs include academic remediation, services for learning-disabled students, advanced placement credit, ESL programs, double majors, independent study, summer session for credit, part-time degree programs (daytime, evenings, summer), internships, and arrangement for off-campus study with members of the Higher Education Council of Columbus.
Student Body Statistics The student body is made up of 1,681 undergraduates (188 freshmen). 52 percent are women and 48 percent are men. Students come from 30 states and territories and 11 other countries. 76 percent are from Ohio. 4.6 percent are international students. 10 percent of the 2002 graduating class went on to graduate and professional schools.
Expenses for 2002–03 *Application fee:* $25. *Comprehensive fee:* $23,960 includes full-time tuition ($17,160), mandatory fees ($500), and college room and board ($6300). *Part-time tuition:* $715 per credit. *Part-time mandatory fees:* $100 per term.
Financial Aid Forms of aid include need-based and non-need-based scholarships and part-time jobs. The average aided 2001–02 undergraduate received an aid package worth $11,226. The priority application deadline for financial aid is March 3.
Freshman Admission CCAD requires an essay, a high school transcript, a minimum 2.0 high school GPA, a portfolio, SAT I or ACT scores, and TOEFL scores for international students. An interview is recommended. Recommendations are required for some. The application deadline for regular admission is rolling.
Transfer Admission The application deadline for admission is rolling.
Entrance Difficulty CCAD assesses its entrance difficulty level as moderately difficult. For the fall 2002 freshman class, 71 percent of the applicants were accepted.

For Further Information Contact Mr. Thomas E. Green, Director of Admissions, Columbus College of Art and Design, 107 North Ninth Street, Columbus, OH 43215-1758. *Telephone:* 614-224-9101. *Fax:* 614-232-8344. *E-mail:* brooke@ccad.edu. *Web site:* http://www.ccad.edu/.

DAVID N. MYERS UNIVERSITY

Cleveland, Ohio

Myers University is a coed, private, comprehensive institution, founded in 1848, offering degrees at the associate, bachelor's, and master's levels. It has a 1-acre campus in Cleveland.

Expenses for 2002–03 *Application fee:* $25. *Tuition:* $16,608 full-time.

For Further Information Contact Ms. Tiffiney Payton, Interim Director of Admissions, David N. Myers University, 112 Prospect Avenue, Cleveland, OH 44115. *Telephone:* 216-523-3806 Ext. 805 or 800-424-3953 (toll-free). *Fax:* 216-696-6430. *E-mail:* tpayton@dnmyers.edu. *Web site:* http://www.dnmyers.edu/.

DEFIANCE COLLEGE

Defiance, Ohio

Defiance College is a coed, private, comprehensive institution, founded in 1850, affiliated with the United Church of Christ, offering degrees at the associate, bachelor's, and master's levels. It has a 150-acre campus in Defiance near Toledo.

Academic Information The faculty has 75 members (55% full-time), 33% with terminal degrees. The undergraduate student-faculty ratio is 14:1. The library holds 88,000 titles, 424 serial subscriptions, and 25,000 audiovisual materials. Special programs include academic remediation, an honors program, cooperative (work-study) education, study abroad, advanced placement credit, double majors, independent study, distance learning, self-designed majors, summer session for credit, part-time degree programs (daytime, evenings, weekends, summer), external degree programs, adult/continuing education programs, internships, and arrangement for off-campus study with Bowling Green State University. The most frequently chosen baccalaureate fields are business/marketing, education, law/legal studies.
Student Body Statistics The student body totals 998, of whom 894 are undergraduates (178 freshmen). 56 percent are women and 44 percent are men. Students come from 12 states and territories and 3 other countries. 0.6 percent are international students.
Expenses for 2002–03 *Application fee:* $25. *Comprehensive fee:* $21,805 includes full-time tuition ($16,360), mandatory fees ($375), and college room and board ($5070). *College room only:* $2550. Room and board charges vary according to board plan and housing facility. *Part-time tuition:* $290 per credit hour. *Part-time mandatory fees:* $25 per term.
Financial Aid Forms of aid include need-based and non-need-based scholarships and part-time jobs. The average aided 2001–02 undergraduate received an aid package worth $15,477. The priority application deadline for financial aid is March 1.
Freshman Admission Defiance College requires a high school transcript, a minimum 2.25 high school GPA, SAT I or ACT scores, and TOEFL scores for international students. Recommendations and an

Defiance College (continued)
interview are recommended. An essay and an interview are required for some. The application deadline for regular admission is August 15.
Transfer Admission The application deadline for admission is August 15.
Entrance Difficulty Defiance College assesses its entrance difficulty level as moderately difficult. For the fall 2002 freshman class, 78 percent of the applicants were accepted.

For Further Information Contact Mr. Brad M. Harsha, Acting Director of Admissions, Defiance College, 701 North Clinton Street, Defiance, OH 43512-1610. *Telephone:* 419-783-2365 or 800-520-4632 Ext. 2359 (toll-free). *Fax:* 419-783-2468. *E-mail:* admissions@defiance.edu. *Web site:* http://www.defiance.edu/.

DENISON UNIVERSITY

Granville, Ohio

Denison is a coed, private, four-year college, founded in 1831, offering degrees at the bachelor's level. It has a 1,200-acre campus in Granville near Columbus.

Academic Information The faculty has 190 members (96% full-time), 95% with terminal degrees. The student-faculty ratio is 11:1. The library holds 728,949 titles, 4,445 serial subscriptions, and 25,452 audiovisual materials. Special programs include services for learning-disabled students, an honors program, cooperative (work-study) education, study abroad, advanced placement credit, double majors, independent study, self-designed majors, part-time degree programs (daytime), internships, and arrangement for off-campus study with American University, Great Lakes Colleges Association, Marine Science Consortium. The most frequently chosen baccalaureate fields are communications/communication technologies, biological/life sciences, social sciences and history.
Student Body Statistics The student body is made up of 2,096 undergraduates (633 freshmen). 56 percent are women and 44 percent are men. Students come from 48 states and territories and 29 other countries. 45 percent are from Ohio. 5.1 percent are international students. 22 percent of the 2002 graduating class went on to graduate and professional schools.
Expenses for 2002–03 *Application fee:* $40. *Comprehensive fee:* $31,120 includes full-time tuition ($23,680), mandatory fees ($560), and college room and board ($6880). *College room only:* $3760. Room and board charges vary according to housing facility. *Part-time tuition:* $740 per credit hour. Part-time tuition varies according to course load.
Financial Aid Forms of aid include need-based and non-need-based scholarships and part-time jobs. The average aided 2002–03 undergraduate received an aid package worth an estimated $21,560. The priority application deadline for financial aid is February 15.
Freshman Admission Denison requires an essay, a high school transcript, 2 recommendations, and SAT I or ACT scores. An interview, SAT II: Subject Test scores, and TOEFL scores for international students are recommended. The application deadline for regular admission is February 1; for early decision plan 1 it is November 15; and for early decision plan 2 it is January 15.
Transfer Admission The application deadline for admission is May 1.
Entrance Difficulty Denison assesses its entrance difficulty level as moderately difficult. For the fall 2002 freshman class, 61 percent of the applicants were accepted.

For Further Information Contact Mr. Perry Robinson, Director of Admissions, Denison University, Box H, Granville, OH 43023. *Telephone:* 740-587-6276 or 800-DENISON (toll-free). *Fax:* 740-587-6306. *E-mail:* admissions@denison.edu. *Web site:* http://www.denison.edu/.

DEVRY UNIVERSITY

Columbus, Ohio

DeVry is a coed, proprietary, four-year college of DeVry University, founded in 1952, offering degrees at the associate and bachelor's levels and postbachelor's certificates. It has a 21-acre campus in Columbus.

Academic Information The faculty has 157 members (53% full-time). The student-faculty ratio is 22:1. The library holds 30,000 titles, 5,892 serial subscriptions, and 1,050 audiovisual materials. Special programs include academic remediation, services for learning-disabled students, cooperative (work-study) education, advanced placement credit, accelerated degree programs, distance learning, summer session for credit, part-time degree programs (daytime, evenings, weekends, summer), and adult/continuing education programs. The most frequently chosen baccalaureate fields are business/marketing, computer/information sciences, engineering/engineering technologies.
Student Body Statistics The student body totals 3,632, of whom 3,493 are undergraduates (942 freshmen). 24 percent are women and 76 percent are men. Students come from 32 states and territories and 3 other countries. 88 percent are from Ohio. 0.9 percent are international students.
Expenses for 2003–04 *Application fee:* $50. *Tuition:* $9990 full-time, $355 per credit hour part-time. *Mandatory fees:* $165 full-time. Full-time tuition and fees vary according to course load. Part-time tuition varies according to course load.
Financial Aid Forms of aid include need-based and non-need-based scholarships and part-time jobs. The average aided 2001–02 undergraduate received an aid package worth $7409. The application deadline for financial aid is continuous.
Freshman Admission DeVry requires a high school transcript, an interview, CPT, TOEFL scores for international students, and CPT. SAT I or ACT scores are recommended. The application deadline for regular admission is rolling.
Transfer Admission The application deadline for admission is rolling.
Entrance Difficulty DeVry assesses its entrance difficulty level as minimally difficult; moderately difficult for electronics engineering technology program.

For Further Information Contact Ms. Shelia Brown, New Student Coordinator, DeVry University, 1350 Alum Creek Drive, Columbus, OH 43209-2705. *Telephone:* 614-253-7291 Ext. 700, 800-426-3916 (toll-free in-state), or 800-426-3090 (toll-free out-of-state). *E-mail:* admissions@devrycol5.edu. *Web site:* http://www.devrycols.edu/.

FRANCISCAN UNIVERSITY OF STEUBENVILLE

Steubenville, Ohio

Franciscan University of Steubenville is a coed, private, Roman Catholic, comprehensive institution, founded in 1946, offering degrees at the associate, bachelor's, and master's levels. It has a 116-acre campus in Steubenville near Pittsburgh.

Academic Information The faculty has 189 members (54% full-time), 42% with terminal degrees. The undergraduate student-faculty ratio is 14:1. The library holds 231,176 titles, 578 serial subscriptions, and 1,260 audiovisual materials. Special programs include services for learning-disabled students, an honors program, study abroad, advanced placement credit, accelerated degree programs, double majors, independent study, distance learning, summer session for credit, part-time degree programs (daytime, evenings, summer), adult/continuing education programs, and internships. The most frequently chosen baccalaureate fields are business/marketing, education, philosophy, religion, and theology.
Student Body Statistics The student body totals 2,253, of whom 1,799 are undergraduates (359 freshmen). 60 percent are women and 40 percent are men. Students come from 52 states and territories and 24 other countries. 21 percent are from Ohio. 2.5 percent are international students. 17 percent of the 2002 graduating class went on to graduate and professional schools.

Expenses for 2002–03 *Application fee:* $20. *Comprehensive fee:* $19,600 includes full-time tuition ($14,020), mandatory fees ($380), and college room and board ($5200). Room and board charges vary according to board plan. *Part-time tuition:* $465 per credit. *Part-time mandatory fees:* $10 per credit. Part-time tuition and fees vary according to class time.
Financial Aid Forms of aid include need-based and non-need-based scholarships and part-time jobs. The average aided 2002–03 undergraduate received an aid package worth an estimated $8570. The priority application deadline for financial aid is April 15.
Freshman Admission Franciscan University of Steubenville requires an essay, a high school transcript, a minimum 2.4 high school GPA, recommendations, SAT I or ACT scores, and TOEFL scores for international students. An interview is recommended. The application deadline for regular admission is May 1.
Transfer Admission The application deadline for admission is May 1.
Entrance Difficulty Franciscan University of Steubenville assesses its entrance difficulty level as moderately difficult. For the fall 2002 freshman class, 89 percent of the applicants were accepted.

For Further Information Contact Mrs. Margaret Weber, Director of Admissions, Franciscan University of Steubenville, 1235 University Boulevard, Steubenville, OH 43952-1763. *Telephone:* 740-283-6226 or 800-783-6220 (toll-free). *Fax:* 740-284-5456. *E-mail:* admissions@franciscan.edu. *Web site:* http://www.franciscan.edu/.

FRANKLIN UNIVERSITY

Columbus, Ohio

Franklin University is a coed, private, comprehensive institution, founded in 1902, offering degrees at the associate, bachelor's, and master's levels. It has a 14-acre campus in Columbus.

Academic Information The faculty has 425 members (8% full-time), 20% with terminal degrees. The undergraduate student-faculty ratio is 17:1. The library holds 73,702 titles, 432 serial subscriptions, and 220 audiovisual materials. Special programs include academic remediation, services for learning-disabled students, cooperative (work-study) education, study abroad, advanced placement credit, accelerated degree programs, ESL programs, independent study, distance learning, self-designed majors, summer session for credit, part-time degree programs (daytime, evenings, weekends, summer), adult/continuing education programs, internships, and arrangement for off-campus study with members of the Higher Education Council of Columbus. The most frequently chosen baccalaureate fields are business/marketing, computer/information sciences, health professions and related sciences.
Student Body Statistics The student body totals 5,808, of whom 4,863 are undergraduates (71 freshmen). 54 percent are women and 46 percent are men. Students come from 40 states and territories and 69 other countries. 84 percent are from Ohio. 8.7 percent are international students.
Expenses for 2002–03 *Application fee:* $0. *Tuition:* $7704 full-time, $214 per credit hour part-time. Full-time tuition varies according to program. Part-time tuition varies according to program.
Financial Aid Forms of aid include need-based and non-need-based scholarships and part-time jobs. The priority application deadline for financial aid is June 15.
Freshman Admission Franklin University requires TOEFL scores for international students. A high school transcript is required for some. The application deadline for regular admission is rolling.
Transfer Admission The application deadline for admission is rolling.
Entrance Difficulty Franklin University has an open admission policy except for international students. It assesses its entrance difficulty as moderately difficult for international students.

For Further Information Contact Mr. Wayne Miller, Assistant Vice President for Students, Franklin University, 201 South Grant Avenue, Columbus, OH 43215. *Telephone:* 614-797-4700 Ext. 7500 or 877-341-6300 (toll-free). *Fax:* 614-224-8027. *E-mail:* info@franklin.edu. *Web site:* http://www.franklin.edu/.

GALLIPOLIS CAREER COLLEGE

Gallipolis, Ohio

Gallipolis Career College is a coed, primarily women's, private, two-year college, founded in 1962, offering degrees at the associate level.

Academic Information The faculty has 20 members. The student-faculty ratio is 8:1. The library holds 94 audiovisual materials. Special programs include academic remediation, double majors, independent study, summer session for credit, part-time degree programs (daytime, evenings, summer), adult/continuing education programs, and internships.
Student Body Statistics The student body is made up of 160 undergraduates. Students come from 2 states and territories.
Expenses for 2002–03 *Application fee:* $50. *Tuition:* $5760 full-time, $160 per credit hour part-time. *Mandatory fees:* $50 full-time.
Freshman Admission Gallipolis Career College requires a high school transcript, an interview, and Wonderlic aptitude test. The application deadline for regular admission is rolling.
Transfer Admission The application deadline for admission is rolling.
Entrance Difficulty Gallipolis Career College assesses its entrance difficulty level as minimally difficult.

For Further Information Contact Mr. Jack Henson, Director of Admissions, Gallipolis Career College, 1176 Jackson Pike, Suite 312, Gallipolis, OH 45631. *Telephone:* 740-446-4367 Ext. 12 or 800-214-0452 (toll-free). *Fax:* 740-446-4124. *E-mail:* admissions@gallipoliscareercollege.com. *Web site:* http://www.gallipoliscareercollege.com/.

GOD'S BIBLE SCHOOL AND COLLEGE

Cincinnati, Ohio

God's Bible College is a coed, private, interdenominational, four-year college, founded in 1900, offering degrees at the associate and bachelor's levels. It has a 14-acre campus in Cincinnati.

Academic Information The student-faculty ratio is 15:1. The library holds 28,452 titles and 240 serial subscriptions. Special programs include academic remediation, advanced placement credit, independent study, summer session for credit, part-time degree programs (daytime), and internships.
Student Body Statistics The student body is made up of 247 undergraduates. Students come from 24 states and territories and 12 other countries. 18 percent of the 2002 graduating class went on to graduate and professional schools.
Expenses for 2002–03 *Application fee:* $50. *Comprehensive fee:* $7280 includes full-time tuition ($3900), mandatory fees ($480), and college room and board ($2900). *College room only:* $1150. *Part-time tuition:* $150 per credit hour.
Financial Aid Forms of aid include need-based and non-need-based scholarships. The application deadline for financial aid is continuous.
Freshman Admission God's Bible College requires a high school transcript, 3 recommendations, an interview, SAT I or ACT scores, and TOEFL scores for international students. The application deadline for regular admission is rolling.
Transfer Admission The application deadline for admission is rolling.
Entrance Difficulty God's Bible College assesses its entrance difficulty level as minimally difficult. For the fall 2002 freshman class, 74 percent of the applicants were accepted.

For Further Information Contact Ms. Laura Ellison, Director of Admissions, God's Bible School and College, 1810 Young Street, Cincinnati, OH 45210-1599. *Telephone:* 513-721-7944 Ext. 204 or 800-486-4637 (toll-free). *Fax:* 513-721-3971. *E-mail:* admissions@gbs.edu.

HEIDELBERG COLLEGE

Tiffin, Ohio

Heidelberg is a coed, private, comprehensive institution, founded in 1850, affiliated with the United Church of Christ, offering degrees at the bachelor's and master's levels. It has a 110-acre campus in Tiffin near Toledo.

Academic Information The faculty has 122 members (61% full-time), 54% with terminal degrees. The undergraduate student-faculty ratio is 13:1. The library holds 260,055 titles and 829 serial subscriptions. Special programs include academic remediation, services for learning-disabled students, an honors program, study abroad, advanced placement credit, accelerated degree programs, ESL programs, double majors, summer session for credit, part-time degree programs (daytime, evenings, weekends, summer), adult/continuing education programs, internships, and arrangement for off-campus study with members of the East Central College Consortium. The most frequently chosen baccalaureate fields are business/marketing, education, parks and recreation.
Student Body Statistics The student body totals 1,468, of whom 1,264 are undergraduates (280 freshmen). 55 percent are women and 45 percent are men. Students come from 25 states and territories and 7 other countries. 87 percent are from Ohio. 1.8 percent are international students. 20 percent of the 2002 graduating class went on to graduate and professional schools.
Expenses for 2003–04 *Application fee:* $25. *Comprehensive fee:* $19,948 includes full-time tuition ($13,364), mandatory fees ($308), and college room and board ($6276). *College room only:* $2852. Room and board charges vary according to housing facility. *Part-time tuition:* $430 per semester hour. *Part-time mandatory fees:* $50 per term. Part-time tuition and fees vary according to location.
Financial Aid Forms of aid include need-based and non-need-based scholarships and part-time jobs. The average aided 2002–03 undergraduate received an aid package worth an estimated $15,414. The priority application deadline for financial aid is March 1.
Freshman Admission Heidelberg requires a high school transcript, a minimum 2.4 high school GPA, and SAT I or ACT scores. 1 recommendation, an interview, and TOEFL scores for international students are recommended. The application deadline for regular admission is August 1.
Transfer Admission The application deadline for admission is August 1.
Entrance Difficulty Heidelberg assesses its entrance difficulty level as moderately difficult. For the fall 2002 freshman class, 82 percent of the applicants were accepted.

For Further Information Contact Director of Admission, Heidelberg College, 310 East Market Street, Tiffin, OH 44883. *Telephone:* 419-448-2330 or 800-434-3352 (toll-free). *Fax:* 419-448-2334. *E-mail:* admininfo@heidelberg.edu. *Web site:* http://www.heidelberg.edu/.

See page 284 for a narrative description.

HIRAM COLLEGE

Hiram, Ohio

Hiram is a coed, private, four-year college, founded in 1850, affiliated with the Christian Church (Disciples of Christ), offering degrees at the bachelor's level. It has a 110-acre campus in Hiram near Cleveland.

Academic Information The faculty has 137 members (53% full-time), 51% with terminal degrees. The student-faculty ratio is 11:1. The library holds 187,451 titles, 3,993 serial subscriptions, and 10,351 audiovisual materials. Special programs include services for learning-disabled students, study abroad, advanced placement credit, accelerated degree programs, ESL programs, double majors, independent study, self-designed majors, summer session for credit, part-time degree programs (weekends), adult/continuing education programs, internships, and arrangement for off-campus study. The most frequently chosen baccalaureate fields are biological/life sciences, business/marketing, social sciences and history.
Student Body Statistics The student body is made up of 1,134 undergraduates (241 freshmen). 59 percent are women and 41 percent are men. Students come from 31 states and territories and 20 other countries. 76 percent are from Ohio. 3.3 percent are international students.
Expenses for 2002–03 *Application fee:* $35. *Comprehensive fee:* $27,132 includes full-time tuition ($19,650), mandatory fees ($662), and college room and board ($6820). *College room only:* $3040. Room and board charges vary according to board plan and housing facility. *Part-time tuition:* varies with class time.
Financial Aid Forms of aid include need-based and non-need-based scholarships and part-time jobs. The average aided 2002–03 undergraduate received an aid package worth an estimated $20,675. The priority application deadline for financial aid is February 15.
Freshman Admission Hiram requires an essay, a high school transcript, 2 recommendations, SAT I or ACT scores, and TOEFL scores for international students. 3 recommendations and an interview are recommended. An interview is required for some. The application deadline for regular admission is February 1 and for early decision it is December 1.
Transfer Admission The application deadline for admission is July 15.
Entrance Difficulty Hiram assesses its entrance difficulty level as very difficult. For the fall 2002 freshman class, 69 percent of the applicants were accepted.

For Further Information Contact Ms. Brenda Swihart Meyer, Director of Admission, Hiram College, Box 96, Hiram, OH 44234-0067. *Telephone:* 330-569-5169 or 800-362-5280 (toll-free). *Fax:* 330-569-5944. *E-mail:* admission@hiram.edu. *Web site:* http://www.hiram.edu/.

See page 286 for a narrative description.

JOHN CARROLL UNIVERSITY

University Heights, Ohio

John Carroll is a coed, private, Roman Catholic (Jesuit), comprehensive institution, founded in 1886, offering degrees at the bachelor's and master's levels. It has a 60-acre campus in University Heights near Cleveland.

Academic Information The faculty has 397 members (63% full-time). The undergraduate student-faculty ratio is 14:1. The library holds 620,000 titles, 2,198 serial subscriptions, and 5,820 audiovisual materials. Special programs include an honors program, cooperative (work-study) education, study abroad, advanced placement credit, accelerated degree programs, double majors, independent study, self-designed majors, summer session for credit, part-time degree programs, adult/continuing education programs, internships, and arrangement for off-campus study with Northeast Ohio Commission on Higher Education. The most frequently chosen baccalaureate fields are business/marketing, communications/communication technologies, social sciences and history.
Student Body Statistics The student body totals 4,294, of whom 3,281 are undergraduates. Students come from 35 states and territories. 73 percent are from Ohio. 22 percent of the 2002 graduating class went on to graduate and professional schools.
Expenses for 2002–03 *Application fee:* $25. *Comprehensive fee:* $25,746 includes full-time tuition ($18,832), mandatory fees ($350), and college room and board ($6564). Room and board charges vary according to board plan. *Part-time tuition:* $544 per credit hour. *Part-time mandatory fees:* $10 per credit hour. Part-time tuition and fees vary according to course load.
Financial Aid Forms of aid include need-based and non-need-based scholarships and part-time jobs. $14,104. The priority application deadline for financial aid is March 1.
Freshman Admission John Carroll requires a high school transcript, 1 recommendation, SAT I or ACT scores, and TOEFL scores for international students. An essay and an interview are recommended. An interview is required for some. The application deadline for regular admission is February 1.
Transfer Admission The application deadline for admission is rolling.
Entrance Difficulty John Carroll assesses its entrance difficulty level as moderately difficult. For the fall 2002 freshman class, 86 percent of the applicants were accepted.

For Further Information Contact Mr. Thomas P. Fanning, Director of Admission, John Carroll University, 20700 North Park Boulevard, University Heights, OH 44118. *Telephone:* 216-397-4294. *Fax:* 216-397-4981. *E-mail:* admission@jcu.edu. *Web site:* http://www.jcu.edu/.

KENT STATE UNIVERSITY

Kent, Ohio

Kent is a coed, public unit of Kent State University System, founded in 1910, offering degrees at the associate, bachelor's, master's, and doctoral levels. It has a 1,200-acre campus in Kent near Cleveland.

Academic Information The faculty has 1,300 members (62% full-time). The undergraduate student-faculty ratio is 20:1. The library holds 1 million titles, 8,771 serial subscriptions, and 27,447 audiovisual materials. Special programs include academic remediation, services for learning-disabled students, an honors program, cooperative (work-study) education, study abroad, advanced placement credit, accelerated degree programs, Freshman Honors College, ESL programs, double majors, independent study, distance learning, self-designed majors, summer session for credit, part-time degree programs (daytime, evenings, weekends, summer), adult/continuing education programs, internships, and arrangement for off-campus study with Cuyahoga Community College, Lorain County Community College, Lakeland Community College. The most frequently chosen baccalaureate fields are business/marketing, education, health professions and related sciences.

Student Body Statistics The student body totals 23,504, of whom 18,813 are undergraduates (3,729 freshmen). 59 percent are women and 41 percent are men. Students come from 46 states and territories and 24 other countries. 93 percent are from Ohio. 1 percent are international students. 20 percent of the 2002 graduating class went on to graduate and professional schools.

Expenses for 2002–03 *Application fee:* $30. *State resident tuition:* $6374 full-time, $290 per semester hour part-time. *Nonresident tuition:* $12,330 full-time, $561 per semester hour part-time. Full-time tuition varies according to course level, course load, degree level, location, reciprocity agreements, and student level. Part-time tuition varies according to course level, course load, degree level, location, program, reciprocity agreements, and student level. *College room and board:* $5570. *College room only:* $3330. Room and board charges vary according to board plan.

Financial Aid Forms of aid include need-based and non-need-based scholarships, athletic grants, and part-time jobs. The average aided 2002–03 undergraduate received an aid package worth an estimated $6368. The priority application deadline for financial aid is March 1.

Freshman Admission Kent requires a high school transcript, a minimum 2.5 high school GPA, and TOEFL scores for international students. SAT I or ACT scores are recommended. SAT I or ACT scores are required for some. The application deadline for regular admission is May 1.

Entrance Difficulty Kent assesses its entrance difficulty level as moderately difficult; minimally difficult for transfers; very difficult for architecture, 6-year medical programs. For the fall 2002 freshman class, 90 percent of the applicants were accepted.

For Further Information Contact Mr. Christopher Buttenschon, Assistant Director of Admissions, Kent State University, 161 Michael Schwartz Center, Kent, OH 44242-0001. *Telephone:* 330-672-2444 or 800-988-KENT (toll-free). *Fax:* 330-672-2499. *E-mail:* kentadm@admissions.kent.edu. *Web site:* http://www.kent.edu/.

KENT STATE UNIVERSITY, ASHTABULA CAMPUS

Ashtabula, Ohio

Kent Ashtabula is a coed, public, primarily two-year college of Kent State University System, founded in 1958, offering degrees at the associate and bachelor's levels (also offers some upper-level and graduate courses). It has a 120-acre campus in Ashtabula near Cleveland.

Academic Information The faculty has 80 members (45% full-time). The library holds 51,884 titles and 225 serial subscriptions. Special programs include academic remediation, an honors program, advanced placement credit, Freshman Honors College, self-designed majors, summer session for credit, part-time degree programs (daytime, evenings, summer), and internships.

Student Body Statistics The student body is made up of 1,396 undergraduates. 0.4 percent are international students.

Expenses for 2002–03 *State resident tuition:* $1837 full-time, $167 per credit hour part-time. *Nonresident tuition:* $4815 full-time, $438 per credit hour part-time.

Financial Aid Forms of aid include need-based scholarships and part-time jobs. The priority application deadline for financial aid is March 1.

Freshman Admission Kent Ashtabula requires TOEFL scores for international students. SAT I or ACT scores are recommended. The application deadline for regular admission is August 1 and for nonresidents it is July 15.

Transfer Admission The application deadline for admission is July 15.

Entrance Difficulty Kent Ashtabula has an open admission policy except for nursing program. It assesses its entrance difficulty as moderately difficult for nursing program.

For Further Information Contact Ms. Kelly Sanford, Director, Enrollment Management and Student Services, Kent State University, Ashtabula Campus, 3325 West 13th Street, Ashtabula, OH 44004-2299. *Telephone:* 440-964-4217. *Fax:* 440-964-4269. *E-mail:* robinson@ashtabula.kent.edu. *Web site:* http://www.ashtabula.kent.edu/.

KENT STATE UNIVERSITY, GEAUGA CAMPUS

Burton, Ohio

Kent State Geauga is a coed, public, primarily two-year college of Kent State University System, founded in 1964, offering degrees at the associate, bachelor's, and master's levels. It has an 87-acre campus in Burton near Cleveland.

Academic Information The faculty has 64 members (17% full-time), 8% with terminal degrees. The undergraduate student-faculty ratio is 14:1. The library holds 8,300 titles and 6,600 serial subscriptions. Special programs include academic remediation, services for learning-disabled students, advanced placement credit, double majors, distance learning, self-designed majors, summer session for credit, part-time degree programs (daytime, evenings, weekends, summer), adult/continuing education programs, and internships.

Student Body Statistics The student body totals 806, of whom 785 are undergraduates (103 freshmen). 59 percent are women and 41 percent are men. Students come from 6 states and territories and 2 other countries. 99 percent are from Ohio. 1 percent are international students.

Expenses for 2002–03 *Application fee:* $30. *State resident tuition:* $1837 full-time, $167 per credit hour part-time. *Nonresident tuition:* $4815 full-time, $438 per credit hour part-time.

Financial Aid Forms of aid include need-based scholarships and part-time jobs. The priority application deadline for financial aid is March 1.

Freshman Admission Kent State Geauga requires a high school transcript, an interview, and TOEFL scores for international students. A minimum 2.0 high school GPA and ACT scores are recommended. The application deadline for regular admission is rolling.

Transfer Admission The application deadline for admission is rolling.

Entrance Difficulty Kent State Geauga has an open admission policy.

For Further Information Contact Ms. Betty Landrus, Admissions and Records Secretary, Kent State University, Geauga Campus, 14111 Claridon-Troy Road, Burton, OH 44021. *Telephone:* 440-834-4187. *Fax:* 440-834-8846. *E-mail:* cbaker@geauga.kent.edu. *Web site:* http://www.geauga.kent.edu/.

KENT STATE UNIVERSITY, SALEM CAMPUS

Salem, Ohio

Kent Salem is a coed, public, primarily two-year college of Kent State University System, founded in 1966, offering degrees at the associate and bachelor's levels (also offers some upper-level and graduate courses). It has a 98-acre campus in Salem.

Academic Information The faculty has 93 members (40% full-time). The student-faculty ratio is 13:1. The library holds 19,000 titles, 163 serial subscriptions, and 158 audiovisual materials. Special programs include academic remediation, services for learning-disabled students, an honors program, advanced placement credit, Freshman Honors College, distance learning, summer session for credit, part-time degree programs (daytime, evenings, weekends), adult/continuing education programs, and internships.
Student Body Statistics The student body totals 1,220, of whom 1,203 are undergraduates. Students come from 2 states and territories.
Expenses for 2002–03 *Application fee:* $30. *State resident tuition:* $3674 full-time, $167 per credit part-time. *Nonresident tuition:* $9630 full-time, $438 per credit part-time. Full-time tuition varies according to course level. Part-time tuition varies according to course level.
Financial Aid Forms of aid include need-based scholarships and part-time jobs. The priority application deadline for financial aid is March 1.
Freshman Admission Kent Salem requires a high school transcript and TOEFL scores for international students. SAT I or ACT scores are recommended. An essay, a minimum X high school GPA, recommendations, ACT scores, and SAT I or ACT scores are required for some. The application deadline for regular admission is rolling.
Transfer Admission The application deadline for admission is rolling.
Entrance Difficulty Kent Salem has an open admission policy except for radiological technology, human services programs, and honors program. It assesses its entrance difficulty as very difficult for radiological technology, human services programs.

For Further Information Contact Ms. Malinda Shean, Admissions Secretary, Kent State University, Salem Campus, 2491 State Route 45 South, Salem, OH 44460-9412. *Telephone:* 330-332-0361. *Fax:* 330-332-9256. *Web site:* http://www.salem.kent.edu/.

KENT STATE UNIVERSITY, STARK CAMPUS

Canton, Ohio

Kent Stark is a coed, public, primarily two-year college of Kent State University System, founded in 1967, offering degrees at the associate and bachelor's levels (also offers some graduate courses). It has a 200-acre campus in Canton near Cleveland.

Academic Information The student-faculty ratio is 19:1. The library holds 72,807 titles and 313 serial subscriptions. Special programs include academic remediation, services for learning-disabled students, an honors program, study abroad, advanced placement credit, Freshman Honors College, ESL programs, independent study, self-designed majors, summer session for credit, part-time degree programs (daytime, evenings, weekends, summer), adult/continuing education programs, internships, and arrangement for off-campus study with Stark State College of Technology.
Student Body Statistics The student body is made up of 3,736 undergraduates. Students come from 2 states and territories.
Expenses for 2002–03 *Application fee:* $30. *State resident tuition:* $3674 full-time, $167 per credit part-time. *Nonresident tuition:* $9630 full-time, $438 per credit part-time.
Financial Aid Forms of aid include need-based scholarships and part-time jobs. The priority application deadline for financial aid is March 1.
Freshman Admission Kent Stark requires a high school transcript and TOEFL scores for international students. An interview and SAT I or ACT scores are required for some. The application deadline for regular admission is rolling.
Transfer Admission The application deadline for admission is rolling.
Entrance Difficulty Kent Stark has an open admission policy.

For Further Information Contact Mrs. Deborah Ann Speck, Director of Admissions, Kent State University, Stark Campus, 6000 Frank Avenue NW, Canton, OH 44720-7599. *Telephone:* 330-499-9600. *Fax:* 330-499-0301. *E-mail:* aspeck@stark.kent.edu. *Web site:* http://www.stark.kent.edu/.

KENT STATE UNIVERSITY, TUSCARAWAS CAMPUS

New Philadelphia, Ohio

Kent Tuscarawas is a coed, public, primarily two-year college of Kent State University System, founded in 1962, offering degrees at the associate and bachelor's levels (also offers some upper-level and graduate courses). It has a 172-acre campus in New Philadelphia near Cleveland.

Academic Information The faculty has 154 members (31% full-time), 38% with terminal degrees. The student-faculty ratio is 16:1. The library holds 58,946 titles, 400 serial subscriptions, and 520 audiovisual materials. Special programs include academic remediation, services for learning-disabled students, an honors program, advanced placement credit, accelerated degree programs, Freshman Honors College, double majors, distance learning, self-designed majors, summer session for credit, part-time degree programs (daytime, evenings, weekends, summer), adult/continuing education programs, and internships. The most frequently chosen baccalaureate fields are business/marketing, engineering/engineering technologies, protective services/public administration.
Student Body Statistics The student body totals 1,853, of whom 1,841 are undergraduates. 0.2 percent are international students.
Expenses for 2002–03 *Application fee:* $30. *State resident tuition:* $3674 full-time, $167 per credit hour part-time. *Nonresident tuition:* $8832 full-time, $438 per credit hour part-time. Full-time tuition varies according to course level, course load, and program. Part-time tuition varies according to course level, course load, and program.
Financial Aid Forms of aid include need-based scholarships and part-time jobs. The priority application deadline for financial aid is February 1.
Freshman Admission Kent Tuscarawas requires a high school transcript and TOEFL scores for international students. SAT I or ACT scores are required for some. The application deadline for regular admission is September 1.
Transfer Admission The application deadline for admission is September 1.
Entrance Difficulty Kent Tuscarawas has an open admission policy except for business administration, education, nursing, fine and performing arts programs. It assesses its entrance difficulty as moderately difficult for nursing, education, business administration, fine and performing arts programs.

For Further Information Contact Ms. Denise L. Testa, Director of Admissions, Kent State University, Tuscarawas Campus, 330 University Drive NE, New Philadelphia, OH 44663-9403. *Telephone:* 330-339-3391 Ext. 47425. *Fax:* 330-339-3321. *Web site:* http://www.tusc.kent.edu/.

KENYON COLLEGE

Gambier, Ohio

Kenyon is a coed, private, four-year college, founded in 1824, offering degrees at the bachelor's level. It has an 800-acre campus in Gambier near Columbus.

Academic Information The faculty has 168 members (86% full-time), 90% with terminal degrees. The student-faculty ratio is 9:1. The library holds 858,000 titles, 5,300 serial subscriptions, and 171,230 audiovisual materials. Special programs include services for learning-disabled students, an honors program, study abroad, advanced placement credit, accelerated degree programs, double majors, independent study, self-designed majors, internships, and arrangement for off-campus study. The most frequently chosen baccalaureate fields are English, social sciences and history, visual/performing arts.

Student Body Statistics The student body is made up of 1,576 undergraduates (440 freshmen). 54 percent are women and 46 percent are men. 2.6 percent are international students. 26.5 percent of the 2002 graduating class went on to graduate and professional schools.

Expenses for 2002–03 *Application fee:* $45. *Comprehensive fee:* $33,400 includes full-time tuition ($27,900), mandatory fees ($810), and college room and board ($4690). *College room only:* $2090. Room and board charges vary according to housing facility. *Part-time tuition:* $3490 per course.

Financial Aid Forms of aid include need-based and non-need-based scholarships and part-time jobs. The average aided 2002–03 undergraduate received an aid package worth an estimated $21,499. The priority application deadline for financial aid is February 15.

Freshman Admission Kenyon requires an essay, a high school transcript, a minimum 2.0 high school GPA, 1 recommendation, SAT I or ACT scores, and TOEFL scores for international students. A minimum 3.0 high school GPA, 2 recommendations, and an interview are recommended. The application deadline for regular admission is February 1; for early decision plan 1 it is December 1; and for early decision plan 2 it is January 15.

Transfer Admission The application deadline for admission is April 1.

Entrance Difficulty Kenyon assesses its entrance difficulty level as very difficult. For the fall 2002 freshman class, 52 percent of the applicants were accepted.

For Further Information Contact Ms. M. Beverly Morse, Acting Dean of Admissions, Kenyon College, Gambier, OH 43022-9623. *Telephone:* 740-427-5776 or 800-848-2468 (toll-free). *Fax:* 740-427-5770. *E-mail:* admissions@kenyon.edu. *Web site:* http://www.kenyon.edu/.

KETTERING COLLEGE OF MEDICAL ARTS

Kettering, Ohio

KCMA is a coed, private, Seventh-day Adventist, primarily two-year college, founded in 1967, offering degrees at the associate and bachelor's levels. It has a 35-acre campus in Kettering.

Academic Information The faculty has 44 members (52% full-time). The library holds 29,390 titles and 266 serial subscriptions. Special programs include advanced placement credit, summer session for credit, part-time degree programs (daytime, evenings), internships, and arrangement for off-campus study with members of the Southwestern Ohio Council for Higher Education.

Student Body Statistics The student body is made up of 599 undergraduates. 79 percent are women and 21 percent are men. Students come from 29 states and territories and 3 other countries.

Expenses for 2002–03 *Application fee:* $25. *Tuition:* $12,200 full-time. *College room only:* $2425.

Financial Aid Forms of aid include need-based scholarships and part-time jobs. The priority application deadline for financial aid is March 31.

Freshman Admission KCMA requires a high school transcript, a minimum 2.0 high school GPA, 3 recommendations, ACT scores, and TOEFL scores for international students. A minimum 3.0 high school GPA, an interview, and SAT I scores are recommended. The application deadline for regular admission is rolling.

Transfer Admission The application deadline for admission is rolling.

Entrance Difficulty KCMA assesses its entrance difficulty level as moderately difficult; most difficult for physician's assistant program.

For Further Information Contact Mr. David Lofthouse, Director of Enrollment Services, Kettering College of Medical Arts, 3737 Southern Boulevard, Kettering, OH 45429-1299. *Telephone:* 937-296-7228 or 800-433-5262 (toll-free). *Fax:* 937-296-4238. *Web site:* http://www.kcma.edu/.

LAKE ERIE COLLEGE

Painesville, Ohio

Lake Erie is a coed, private, comprehensive institution, founded in 1856, offering degrees at the bachelor's and master's levels. It has a 57-acre campus in Painesville near Cleveland.

Academic Information The faculty has 88 members (41% full-time), 47% with terminal degrees. The undergraduate student-faculty ratio is 13:1. The library holds 86,600 titles, 6,020 serial subscriptions, and 1,093 audiovisual materials. Special programs include academic remediation, services for learning-disabled students, cooperative (work-study) education, study abroad, advanced placement credit, accelerated degree programs, double majors, independent study, self-designed majors, summer session for credit, part-time degree programs (daytime, evenings, weekends, summer), external degree programs, adult/continuing education programs, internships, and arrangement for off-campus study with Northeast Ohio Commission on Higher Education. The most frequently chosen baccalaureate fields are business/marketing, agriculture, computer/information sciences.

Student Body Statistics The student body totals 977, of whom 690 are undergraduates (135 freshmen). 76 percent are women and 24 percent are men. Students come from 19 states and territories and 8 other countries. 85 percent are from Ohio. 2.5 percent are international students.

Expenses for 2002–03 *Application fee:* $25. *Comprehensive fee:* $22,910 includes full-time tuition ($16,370), mandatory fees ($840), and college room and board ($5700). *College room only:* $3010. Full-time tuition and fees vary according to course load and program. Room and board charges vary according to board plan. *Part-time tuition:* $445 per credit hour. *Part-time mandatory fees:* $25 per credit hour.

Financial Aid Forms of aid include need-based and non-need-based scholarships and part-time jobs. The application deadline for financial aid is continuous.

Freshman Admission Lake Erie requires a high school transcript, a minimum 2.0 high school GPA, SAT I or ACT scores, and TOEFL scores for international students. An interview is recommended.

Entrance Difficulty Lake Erie assesses its entrance difficulty level as minimally difficult. For the fall 2002 freshman class, 84 percent of the applicants were accepted.

For Further Information Contact Ms. Alison Dewey, Director of Admissions, Lake Erie College, 391 West Washington Street, Painesville, OH 44077-3389. *Telephone:* 440-639-7885 or 800-916-0904 (toll-free). *Fax:* 440-352-3533. *E-mail:* lecadmit@lec.edu. *Web site:* http://www.lec.edu/.

LAURA AND ALVIN SIEGAL COLLEGE OF JUDAIC STUDIES

Beachwood, Ohio

Siegal College is a coed, private, comprehensive institution, founded in 1963, offering degrees at the bachelor's and master's levels. It has a 2-acre campus in Beachwood near Cleveland.

Academic Information The faculty has 34 members (35% full-time), 62% with terminal degrees. The undergraduate student-faculty ratio is 8:1. The library holds 28,000 titles and 100 serial subscriptions. Special programs include cooperative (work-study) education, double majors, independent study, distance learning, summer session for credit, part-time degree programs, external degree programs, adult/continuing education programs, internships, and arrangement for off-campus study with John Carroll University, Ursuline College, Case Western Reserve University. The most frequently chosen baccalaureate field is philosophy, religion, and theology.

Student Body Statistics The student body totals 129, of whom 17 are undergraduates (2 freshmen). 94 percent are women and 6 percent are men. Students come from 1 state or territory and 1 other country. 17.6 percent are international students.

Laura and Alvin Siegal College of Judaic Studies (continued)

Expenses for 2003–04 *Application fee:* $50. *Tuition:* $9750 full-time, $325 per credit part-time. *Mandatory fees:* $25 full-time, $25 per year part-time. Full-time tuition and fees vary according to course load. Part-time tuition and fees vary according to course load.
Financial Aid Forms of aid include need-based and non-need-based scholarships. The average aided 2002–03 undergraduate received an aid package worth an estimated $200. The application deadline for financial aid is continuous.
Freshman Admission Siegal College requires an essay, a high school transcript, 2 recommendations, and an interview. The application deadline for regular admission is rolling.
Transfer Admission The application deadline for admission is rolling.
Entrance Difficulty Siegal College has an open admission policy.

For Further Information Contact Ms. Linda L. Rosen, Director of Student Services, Laura and Alvin Siegal College of Judaic Studies, 26500 Shaker Boulevard, Beachwood, OH 44122-7116. *Telephone:* 216-464-4050 Ext. 101 or 888-336-2257 (toll-free). *Fax:* 216-464-5827. *E-mail:* admissions@siegalcollege.edu. *Web site:* http://www.siegalcollege.edu/.

LOURDES COLLEGE

Sylvania, Ohio

Lourdes is a coed, private, Roman Catholic, four-year college, founded in 1958, offering degrees at the associate and bachelor's levels. It has a 90-acre campus in Sylvania near Toledo.

Academic Information The faculty has 123 members (50% full-time), 22% with terminal degrees. The student-faculty ratio is 14:1. The library holds 57,730 titles, 448 serial subscriptions, and 1,571 audiovisual materials. Special programs include academic remediation, services for learning-disabled students, cooperative (work-study) education, study abroad, advanced placement credit, accelerated degree programs, double majors, independent study, self-designed majors, summer session for credit, part-time degree programs (daytime, evenings, weekends, summer), adult/continuing education programs, and internships. The most frequently chosen baccalaureate fields are business/marketing, health professions and related sciences, protective services/public administration.
Student Body Statistics The student body totals 1,300, of whom 1,272 are undergraduates (73 freshmen). 81 percent are women and 19 percent are men. Students come from 2 states and territories and 1 other country. 93 percent are from Ohio. 0.1 percent are international students. 24 percent of the 2002 graduating class went on to graduate and professional schools.
Expenses for 2002–03 *Application fee:* $25. *Tuition:* $13,700 full-time, $315 per credit hour part-time. *Mandatory fees:* $900 full-time, $40 per credit hour part-time. Full-time tuition and fees vary according to course load and program. Part-time tuition and fees vary according to course load and program.
Financial Aid Forms of aid include need-based and non-need-based scholarships and part-time jobs. The average aided 2002–03 undergraduate received an aid package worth an estimated $12,527. The application deadline for financial aid is continuous.
Freshman Admission Lourdes requires a high school transcript, SAT I or ACT scores, and TOEFL scores for international students. An interview is required for some. The application deadline for regular admission is rolling.
Transfer Admission The application deadline for admission is rolling.
Entrance Difficulty Lourdes assesses its entrance difficulty level as moderately difficult; minimally difficult for transfers. For the fall 2002 freshman class, 27 percent of the applicants were accepted.

For Further Information Contact Office of Admissions, Lourdes College, 6832 Convent Boulevard, Sylvania, OH 43560. *Telephone:* 419-885-5291 or 800-878-3210 Ext. 1299 (toll-free). *Fax:* 419-882-3987. *E-mail:* lcadmits@lourdes.edu. *Web site:* http://www.lourdes.edu/.

MALONE COLLEGE

Canton, Ohio

Malone is a coed, private, comprehensive institution, founded in 1892, affiliated with the Evangelical Friends Church–Eastern Region, offering degrees at the bachelor's and master's levels. It has a 78-acre campus in Canton near Cleveland.

Academic Information The faculty has 189 members (53% full-time), 41% with terminal degrees. The undergraduate student-faculty ratio is 14:1. The library holds 158,974 titles, 1,517 serial subscriptions, and 9,693 audiovisual materials. Special programs include academic remediation, services for learning-disabled students, an honors program, cooperative (work-study) education, study abroad, advanced placement credit, accelerated degree programs, double majors, independent study, distance learning, self-designed majors, summer session for credit, part-time degree programs (daytime, evenings, summer), adult/continuing education programs, internships, and arrangement for off-campus study with members of the Christian College Consortium, Council for Christian Colleges and Universities. The most frequently chosen baccalaureate fields are business/marketing, education, health professions and related sciences.
Student Body Statistics The student body totals 2,137, of whom 1,878 are undergraduates (355 freshmen). 60 percent are women and 40 percent are men. Students come from 27 states and territories and 9 other countries. 90 percent are from Ohio. 0.7 percent are international students. 30 percent of the 2002 graduating class went on to graduate and professional schools.
Expenses for 2002–03 *Application fee:* $20. *Comprehensive fee:* $19,980 includes full-time tuition ($13,910), mandatory fees ($240), and college room and board ($5830). *College room only:* $3150. Room and board charges vary according to board plan. *Part-time tuition:* $315 per semester hour. *Part-time mandatory fees:* $60 per term. Part-time tuition and fees vary according to course load.
Financial Aid Forms of aid include need-based and non-need-based scholarships, athletic grants, and part-time jobs. The average aided 2002–03 undergraduate received an aid package worth an estimated $11,397. The application deadline for financial aid is July 31 with a priority deadline of March 1.
Freshman Admission Malone requires an essay, a high school transcript, a minimum 2.5 high school GPA, SAT I or ACT scores, and TOEFL scores for international students. An interview is required for some. The application deadline for regular admission is July 1.
Transfer Admission The application deadline for admission is July 1.
Entrance Difficulty Malone assesses its entrance difficulty level as moderately difficult. For the fall 2002 freshman class, 91 percent of the applicants were accepted.

For Further Information Contact Mr. John Chopka, Vice President of Enrollment Management, Malone College, 515 25th Street, NW, Canton, OH 44709-3897. *Telephone:* 330-471-8145 or 800-521-1146 (toll-free). *Fax:* 330-471-8149. *E-mail:* admissions@malone.edu. *Web site:* http://www.malone.edu/.

MARIETTA COLLEGE

Marietta, Ohio

Marietta is a coed, private, comprehensive institution, founded in 1835, offering degrees at the associate, bachelor's, and master's levels. It has a 120-acre campus in Marietta.

Academic Information The faculty has 116 members (67% full-time), 66% with terminal degrees. The undergraduate student-faculty ratio is 12:1. The library holds 250,000 titles, 7,100 serial subscriptions, and 5,800 audiovisual materials. Special programs include academic remediation, services for learning-disabled students, an honors program, study abroad, advanced placement credit, accelerated degree programs, ESL programs, double majors, independent study, self-designed majors, summer session for credit, part-time degree programs (daytime, evenings, summer), adult/continuing education programs, internships, and arrangement for off-campus study with American University, Stillman College, Central

College, Institute of European Studies, Institute of Asian Studies. The most frequently chosen baccalaureate fields are business/marketing, education, parks and recreation.
Student Body Statistics The student body totals 1,208, of whom 1,112 are undergraduates (268 freshmen). 50 percent are women and 50 percent are men. Students come from 37 states and territories and 11 other countries. 64 percent are from Ohio. 5.2 percent are international students. 22 percent of the 2002 graduating class went on to graduate and professional schools.
Expenses for 2002–03 *Application fee:* $25. *Comprehensive fee:* $25,886 includes full-time tuition ($19,762), mandatory fees ($350), and college room and board ($5774). *Part-time tuition:* $565 per credit. Part-time tuition varies according to class time.
Financial Aid Forms of aid include need-based and non-need-based scholarships and part-time jobs. The average aided 2001–02 undergraduate received an aid package worth $17,455. The priority application deadline for financial aid is March 1.
Freshman Admission Marietta requires an essay, a high school transcript, a minimum 2.0 high school GPA, 2 recommendations, SAT I or ACT scores, and TOEFL scores for international students. A minimum 3.0 high school GPA, an interview, and SAT II: Subject Test scores are recommended. The application deadline for regular admission is April 15.
Transfer Admission The application deadline for admission is rolling.
Entrance Difficulty Marietta assesses its entrance difficulty level as moderately difficult. For the fall 2002 freshman class, 94 percent of the applicants were accepted.

For Further Information Contact Ms. Marke Vickers, Director of Admission, Marietta College, 215 Fifth Street, Marietta, OH 45750-4000. *Telephone:* 740-376-4600 or 800-331-7896 (toll-free). *Fax:* 740-376-8888. *E-mail:* admit@marietta.edu. *Web site:* http://www.marietta.edu/.

See page 306 for a narrative description.

THE MCGREGOR SCHOOL OF ANTIOCH UNIVERSITY

See Antioch University McGregor

MEDCENTRAL COLLEGE OF NURSING

Mansfield, Ohio

For Information Write to MedCentral College of Nursing, Mansfield, OH 44903.

MERCY COLLEGE OF NORTHWEST OHIO

Toledo, Ohio

Mercy College of Northwest Ohio is a coed, primarily women's, private, primarily two-year college, founded in 1993, affiliated with the Roman Catholic Church, offering degrees at the associate and bachelor's levels. It is located in Toledo near Detroit.

Academic Information The faculty has 36 members (97% full-time), 42% with terminal degrees. The student-faculty ratio is 10:1. The library holds 5,900 titles, 171 serial subscriptions, and 331 audiovisual materials. Special programs include academic remediation, services for learning-disabled students, advanced placement credit, independent study, summer session for credit, part-time degree programs (daytime, evenings, summer), and internships.
Student Body Statistics The student body is made up of 406 undergraduates (101 freshmen). 92 percent are women and 8 percent are men. Students come from 3 states and territories. 90 percent are from Ohio.
Expenses for 2002–03 *Application fee:* $25. *Tuition:* $6234 full-time, $228 per semester hour part-time. *Mandatory fees:* $160 full-time, $50 per term part-time. Full-time tuition and fees vary according to course load and program. Part-time tuition and fees vary according to course load and program. *College room only:* $2000. Room charges vary according to housing facility.
Financial Aid Forms of aid include need-based scholarships and part-time jobs. The application deadline for financial aid is continuous.
Freshman Admission Mercy College of Northwest Ohio requires a high school transcript. SAT I or ACT scores are recommended. A minimum 2.3 high school GPA and SAT I or ACT scores are required for some. The application deadline for regular admission is rolling.
Transfer Admission The application deadline for admission is rolling.
Entrance Difficulty Mercy College of Northwest Ohio assesses its entrance difficulty level as moderately difficult.

For Further Information Contact Ms. Janice Bernard, Secretary, Mercy College of Northwest Ohio, 2221 Madison Avenue, Toledo, OH 43624-1197. *Telephone:* 419-251-1313 Ext. 11203 or 888-80-Mercy (toll-free). *Fax:* 419-251-1462. *E-mail:* admissions@mercycollege.edu. *Web site:* http://www.mercycollege.edu/.

MIAMI UNIVERSITY

Oxford, Ohio

Miami University is a coed, public unit of Miami University System, founded in 1809, offering degrees at the associate, bachelor's, master's, and doctoral levels and post-master's certificates. It has a 2,000-acre campus in Oxford near Cincinnati.

Academic Information The faculty has 1,033 members (78% full-time), 76% with terminal degrees. The undergraduate student-faculty ratio is 17:1. The library holds 3 million titles, 14,089 serial subscriptions, and 143,868 audiovisual materials. Special programs include services for learning-disabled students, an honors program, cooperative (work-study) education, study abroad, advanced placement credit, double majors, independent study, self-designed majors, summer session for credit, adult/continuing education programs, internships, and arrangement for off-campus study with Greater Cincinnati Consortium of Colleges and Universities. The most frequently chosen baccalaureate fields are business/marketing, education, social sciences and history.
Student Body Statistics The student body totals 16,730, of whom 15,384 are undergraduates (3,549 freshmen). 54 percent are women and 46 percent are men. Students come from 49 states and territories and 70 other countries. 73 percent are from Ohio. 0.7 percent are international students.
Expenses for 2002–03 *Application fee:* $45. *State resident tuition:* $6386 full-time, $317 per credit hour part-time. *Nonresident tuition:* $15,110 full-time, $680 per credit hour part-time. *Mandatory fees:* $1214 full-time, $51 per credit hour part-time, $18 per term part-time. *College room and board:* $6240. *College room only:* $3060.
Financial Aid Forms of aid include need-based and non-need-based scholarships, athletic grants, and part-time jobs. The average aided 2002–03 undergraduate received an aid package worth an estimated $6997. The priority application deadline for financial aid is February 15.
Freshman Admission Miami University requires a high school transcript, SAT I or ACT scores, and TOEFL scores for international students. An essay and 1 recommendation are recommended. The application deadline for regular admission is January 31 and for early decision it is November 1.
Transfer Admission The application deadline for admission is May 1.
Entrance Difficulty Miami University assesses its entrance difficulty level as moderately difficult; noncompetitive for district residents. For the fall 2002 freshman class, 77 percent of the applicants were accepted.

For Further Information Contact Mr. Michael E. Mills, Director of Undergraduate Admissions, Miami University, 301 South Campus Avenue, Oxford, OH 45056. *Telephone:* 513-529-5040. *Fax:* 513-529-1550. *E-mail:* admission@muohio.edu. *Web site:* http://www.muohio.edu/.

MIAMI UNIVERSITY–HAMILTON CAMPUS

Hamilton, Ohio

Miami University Hamilton is a coed, public, primarily two-year college of Miami University System, founded in 1968, offering degrees at the associate, bachelor's, and master's levels (degrees awarded by Miami University main campus). It has a 78-acre campus in Hamilton near Cincinnati.

Academic Information The faculty has 207 members (40% full-time). The undergraduate student-faculty ratio is 16:1. The library holds 68,000 titles and 400 serial subscriptions. Special programs include academic remediation, services for learning-disabled students, an honors program, cooperative (work-study) education, study abroad, advanced placement credit, ESL programs, double majors, self-designed majors, summer session for credit, part-time degree programs (daytime, evenings, weekends, summer), adult/continuing education programs, and internships.
Student Body Statistics The student body totals 3,317, of whom 3,261 are undergraduates (645 freshmen). 55 percent are women and 45 percent are men.
Expenses for 2002–03 *Application fee:* $25. *State resident tuition:* $2988 full-time, $124 per credit part-time. *Nonresident tuition:* $11,712 full-time, $488 per credit part-time. *Mandatory fees:* $344 full-time, $13 per credit part-time, $16 per term part-time.
Financial Aid Forms of aid include need-based scholarships and part-time jobs. The application deadline for financial aid is continuous.
Freshman Admission Miami University Hamilton requires a high school transcript and TOEFL scores for international students. SAT I or ACT scores are required for some. The application deadline for regular admission is rolling.
Transfer Admission The application deadline for admission is rolling.
Entrance Difficulty Miami University Hamilton has an open admission policy except for nursing program, transfer students. It assesses its entrance difficulty as minimally difficult for transfers; moderately difficult for nursing program.

For Further Information Contact Ms. Triana Adlon, Director of Admission and Financial Aid, Miami University–Hamilton Campus, 1601 Peck Boulevard, Hamilton, OH 45011-3399. *Telephone:* 513-785-3111. *Fax:* 513-785-3148. *E-mail:* adlontm@muohio.edu. *Web site:* http://www.ham.muohio.edu/.

MIAMI UNIVERSITY–MIDDLETOWN CAMPUS

Middletown, Ohio

Miami University–Middletown Campus is a coed, public, primarily two-year college of Miami University System, founded in 1966, offering degrees at the associate and bachelor's levels (also offers up to 2 years of most bachelor's degree programs offered at Miami University main campus). It has a 141-acre campus in Middletown near Cincinnati and Dayton.

Academic Information The faculty has 209 members (38% full-time). The student-faculty ratio is 13:1. The library holds 540 serial subscriptions and 4,857 audiovisual materials. Special programs include academic remediation, services for learning-disabled students, cooperative (work-study) education, study abroad, advanced placement credit, double majors, independent study, distance learning, self-designed majors, summer session for credit, part-time degree programs, adult/continuing education programs, internships, and arrangement for off-campus study with members of the Greater Cincinnati Consortium of Colleges and Universities.
Student Body Statistics The student body is made up of 2,660 undergraduates. 99 percent are from Ohio.
Expenses for 2003–04 *Application fee:* $25. *State resident tuition:* $3498 full-time, $145.75 per credit hour part-time. *Nonresident tuition:* $13,248 full-time, $552 per credit hour part-time. *Mandatory fees:* $201 full-time. Full-time tuition and fees vary according to student level. Part-time tuition varies according to student level.
Financial Aid Forms of aid include need-based scholarships and part-time jobs. The priority application deadline for financial aid is February 15.
Freshman Admission Miami University–Middletown Campus requires a high school transcript and TOEFL scores for international students. SAT I or ACT scores are recommended. The application deadline for regular admission is rolling.
Transfer Admission The application deadline for admission is rolling.
Entrance Difficulty Miami University–Middletown Campus has an open admission policy except for nursing program. It assesses its entrance difficulty as moderately difficult for nursing program.

For Further Information Contact Mrs. Mary Lou Flynn, Director of Enrollment Services, Miami University–Middletown Campus, 4200 East University Boulevard, Middletown, OH 45042. *Telephone:* 513-727-3346 or 800-622-2262 (toll-free in-state). *Fax:* 513-727-3223. *E-mail:* flynnml@muohio.edu. *Web site:* http://www.mid.muohio.edu/.

MOUNT CARMEL COLLEGE OF NURSING

Columbus, Ohio

Mount Carmel College of Nursing is a coed, primarily women's, private, comprehensive institution, offering degrees at the bachelor's level.

Academic Information The faculty has 31 members (74% full-time). The student-faculty ratio is 11:1. The most frequently chosen baccalaureate field is health professions and related sciences.
Student Body Statistics The student body is made up of 424 undergraduates (42 freshmen). 91 percent are women and 9 percent are men.
Expenses for 2002–03 *Comprehensive fee:* $15,807 includes full-time tuition ($11,215), mandatory fees ($292), and college room and board ($4300). *College room only:* $1870. Full-time tuition and fees vary according to student level. *Part-time tuition:* varies with student level.
Financial Aid Forms of aid include need-based and non-need-based scholarships and part-time jobs. The average aided 2002–03 undergraduate received an aid package worth an estimated $9000. The application deadline for financial aid is continuous.
Entrance Difficulty For the fall 2002 freshman class, 71 percent of the applicants were accepted.

For Further Information Contact Ms. Merschel Menefield, Director of Admissions, Mount Carmel College of Nursing, 127 South Davis Avenue, Columbus, OH 43222. *Telephone:* 614-234-5800. *Web site:* http://www.mccn.edu/.

MOUNT UNION COLLEGE

Alliance, Ohio

Mount Union is a coed, private, United Methodist, four-year college, founded in 1846, offering degrees at the bachelor's level. It has a 105-acre campus in Alliance near Cleveland.

Academic Information The faculty has 216 members (58% full-time), 51% with terminal degrees. The student-faculty ratio is 14:1. The library holds 228,850 titles, 972 serial subscriptions, and 500 audiovisual materials. Special programs include services for learning-disabled students, an honors program, cooperative (work-study) education, study abroad, advanced placement credit, accelerated degree programs, ESL programs, double majors, independent study, self-designed majors, summer session for credit, part-time degree programs (daytime, evenings, summer), external degree programs, adult/continuing education programs, internships, and arrangement for off-campus study with 6 members of the East Central College Consortium. The most frequently chosen baccalaureate fields are business/marketing, education, parks and recreation.
Student Body Statistics The student body is made up of 2,372 undergraduates (586 freshmen). 57 percent are women and 43 percent are men. Students come from 23 states and territories and 14 other countries. 91 percent are from Ohio. 1.4 percent are international students. 16 percent of the 2002 graduating class went on to graduate and professional schools.

Expenses for 2002–03 *Application fee:* $1.50. *Comprehensive fee:* $22,220 includes full-time tuition ($16,240), mandatory fees ($910), and college room and board ($5070). *College room only:* $2060. Room and board charges vary according to housing facility. *Part-time tuition:* $685 per semester hour.
Financial Aid Forms of aid include need-based and non-need-based scholarships and part-time jobs. The average aided 2002–03 undergraduate received an aid package worth an estimated $14,667. The application deadline for financial aid is continuous.
Freshman Admission Mount Union requires an essay, a high school transcript, a minimum 2.0 high school GPA, 1 recommendation, SAT I or ACT scores, and TOEFL scores for international students. An interview is recommended. The application deadline for regular admission is rolling.
Transfer Admission The application deadline for admission is rolling.
Entrance Difficulty Mount Union assesses its entrance difficulty level as moderately difficult. For the fall 2002 freshman class, 78 percent of the applicants were accepted.

For Further Information Contact Mr. Vince Heslop, Director of Admissions, Mount Union College, 1972 Clark Avenue, Alliance, OH 44601. *Telephone:* 330-823-2590, 800-334-6682 (toll-free in-state), or 800-992-6682 (toll-free out-of-state). *Fax:* 330-823-3487. *E-mail:* admissn@muc.edu. *Web site:* http://www.muc.edu/.

MOUNT VERNON NAZARENE UNIVERSITY

Mount Vernon, Ohio

MVNU is a coed, private, Nazarene, comprehensive institution, founded in 1964, offering degrees at the associate, bachelor's, and master's levels. It has a 210-acre campus in Mount Vernon near Columbus.

Academic Information The faculty has 197 members (37% full-time), 37% with terminal degrees. The undergraduate student-faculty ratio is 18:1. The library holds 92,169 titles, 586 serial subscriptions, and 4,744 audiovisual materials. Special programs include academic remediation, services for learning-disabled students, an honors program, study abroad, advanced placement credit, Freshman Honors College, double majors, independent study, summer session for credit, part-time degree programs (evenings), adult/continuing education programs, internships, and arrangement for off-campus study with Kenyon College, Capital University, Coalition for Christian Colleges and Universities. The most frequently chosen baccalaureate fields are business/marketing, education, social sciences and history.
Student Body Statistics The student body totals 2,337, of whom 2,235 are undergraduates (352 freshmen). 57 percent are women and 43 percent are men. Students come from 29 states and territories. 90 percent are from Ohio. 0.4 percent are international students.
Expenses for 2002–03 *Application fee:* $25. *One-time mandatory fee:* $146. *Comprehensive fee:* $17,815 includes full-time tuition ($12,810), mandatory fees ($478), and college room and board ($4527). *College room only:* $2511. Full-time tuition and fees vary according to course load, program, and reciprocity agreements. Room and board charges vary according to board plan and housing facility. *Part-time tuition:* $458 per credit hour. *Part-time mandatory fees:* $17 per credit hour. Part-time tuition and fees vary according to course load, program, and reciprocity agreements.
Financial Aid Forms of aid include need-based and non-need-based scholarships, athletic grants, and part-time jobs. The average aided 2001–02 undergraduate received an aid package worth $8025. The priority application deadline for financial aid is March 15.
Freshman Admission MVNU requires an essay, a high school transcript, a minimum 2.5 high school GPA, 2 recommendations, SAT I or ACT scores, and TOEFL scores for international students. An interview is recommended. The application deadline for regular admission is May 31.
Transfer Admission The application deadline for admission is May 31.
Entrance Difficulty MVNU assesses its entrance difficulty level as moderately difficult. For the fall 2002 freshman class, 77 percent of the applicants were accepted.

For Further Information Contact Dr. Jeff Williamson, Interim Director of Admissions and Student Recruitment, Mount Vernon Nazarene University, 800 Martinsburg Road, Mount Vernon, OH 43050. *Telephone:* 740-392-6868 Ext. 4510 or 866-462-6868 (toll-free). *Fax:* 740-393-0511. *E-mail:* admissions@mvnu.edu. *Web site:* http://www.mvnu.edu/.

MUSKINGUM COLLEGE

New Concord, Ohio

Muskingum is a coed, private, comprehensive institution, founded in 1837, affiliated with the Presbyterian Church (U.S.A.), offering degrees at the bachelor's and master's levels. It has a 215-acre campus in New Concord near Columbus.

Academic Information The faculty has 152 members (61% full-time), 67% with terminal degrees. The undergraduate student-faculty ratio is 16:1. The library holds 233,000 titles, 900 serial subscriptions, and 6,000 audiovisual materials. Special programs include services for learning-disabled students, study abroad, advanced placement credit, accelerated degree programs, ESL programs, double majors, independent study, self-designed majors, summer session for credit, part-time degree programs (daytime, evenings, summer), external degree programs, internships, and arrangement for off-campus study with Case Western Reserve University.
Student Body Statistics The student body totals 2,049, of whom 1,686 are undergraduates (450 freshmen). 50 percent are women and 50 percent are men. Students come from 26 states and territories and 19 other countries. 88 percent are from Ohio. 2.1 percent are international students.
Expenses for 2003–04 *Application fee:* $0. *Comprehensive fee:* $20,680 includes full-time tuition ($14,200), mandatory fees ($600), and college room and board ($5880). *College room only:* $2940. Room and board charges vary according to board plan and housing facility. *Part-time tuition:* $240 per credit hour. Part-time tuition varies according to course load.
Financial Aid Forms of aid include need-based and non-need-based scholarships and part-time jobs. The average aided 2002–03 undergraduate received an aid package worth an estimated $12,693. The priority application deadline for financial aid is March 15.
Freshman Admission Muskingum requires a high school transcript, a minimum 2.0 high school GPA, 1 recommendation, SAT I or ACT scores, and TOEFL scores for international students. An essay, a minimum 3.0 high school GPA, and an interview are recommended. The application deadline for regular admission is June 1.
Transfer Admission The application deadline for admission is August 1.
Entrance Difficulty Muskingum assesses its entrance difficulty level as moderately difficult. For the fall 2002 freshman class, 79 percent of the applicants were accepted.

For Further Information Contact Mrs. Beth DaLonzo, Director of Admission, Muskingum College, 163 Stormont Street, New Concord, OH 43762. *Telephone:* 740-826-8137 or 800-752-6082 (toll-free). *Fax:* 740-826-8100. *E-mail:* adminfo@muskingum.edu. *Web site:* http://www.muskingum.edu/.

NORTHWESTERN COLLEGE

See University of Northwestern Ohio

NOTRE DAME COLLEGE

South Euclid, Ohio

Notre Dame College is a coed, private, Roman Catholic, comprehensive institution, founded in 1922, offering degrees at the associate, bachelor's, and master's levels. It has a 53-acre campus in South Euclid near Cleveland.

Notre Dame College (continued)

Academic Information The faculty has 84 members (31% full-time). The undergraduate student-faculty ratio is 12:1. The library holds 9,983 audiovisual materials. Special programs include academic remediation, cooperative (work-study) education, study abroad, advanced placement credit, accelerated degree programs, double majors, independent study, self-designed majors, summer session for credit, part-time degree programs (daytime, evenings, weekends, summer), adult/continuing education programs, internships, and arrangement for off-campus study with members of the Northeast Ohio Commission on Higher Education. The most frequently chosen baccalaureate fields are business/marketing, computer/information sciences, education.

Student Body Statistics The student body totals 925, of whom 767 are undergraduates. Students come from 8 states and territories and 15 other countries. 90 percent are from Ohio. 0.9 percent are international students. 7 percent of the 2002 graduating class went on to graduate and professional schools.

Expenses for 2003–04 *Application fee:* $30. *Comprehensive fee:* $23,740 includes full-time tuition ($16,990), mandatory fees ($550), and college room and board ($6200). *College room only:* $3114. Full-time tuition and fees vary according to class time. Room and board charges vary according to board plan. *Part-time tuition:* $405 per credit. Part-time tuition varies according to class time.

Financial Aid Forms of aid include need-based and non-need-based scholarships, athletic grants, and part-time jobs. The average aided 2001–02 undergraduate received an aid package worth $15,336. The application deadline for financial aid is continuous.

Freshman Admission Notre Dame College requires an essay, a high school transcript, a minimum 2.0 high school GPA, an interview, SAT I or ACT scores, and TOEFL scores for international students. A minimum 2.5 high school GPA and an interview are recommended. The application deadline for regular admission is rolling.

Transfer Admission The application deadline for admission is rolling.

Entrance Difficulty Notre Dame College assesses its entrance difficulty level as moderately difficult. For the fall 2002 freshman class, 78 percent of the applicants were accepted.

For Further Information Contact Karen Poelkiz, Vice President for Recruitment, Notre Dame College, South Euclid, OH 44121-4293. *Telephone:* 216-381-1680 Ext. 5239 or 800-NDC-1680 (toll-free). *Fax:* 216-381-3802. *E-mail:* admissions@ndc.edu. *Web site:* http://www.ndc.edu/.

OBERLIN COLLEGE

Oberlin, Ohio

Oberlin is a coed, private, comprehensive institution, founded in 1833, offering degrees at the bachelor's and master's levels and postbachelor's certificates. It has a 440-acre campus in Oberlin near Cleveland.

Academic Information The faculty has 292 members (93% full-time). The undergraduate student-faculty ratio is 10:1. The library holds 2 million titles, 4,560 serial subscriptions, and 59,186 audiovisual materials. Special programs include services for learning-disabled students, an honors program, study abroad, advanced placement credit, ESL programs, double majors, independent study, self-designed majors, part-time degree programs (daytime), internships, and arrangement for off-campus study with Great Lakes Colleges Association. The most frequently chosen baccalaureate fields are social sciences and history, biological/life sciences, visual/performing arts.

Student Body Statistics The student body totals 2,861, of whom 2,848 are undergraduates (746 freshmen). 55 percent are women and 45 percent are men. Students come from 54 states and territories and 28 other countries. 11 percent are from Ohio. 6.2 percent are international students. 30 percent of the 2002 graduating class went on to graduate and professional schools.

Expenses for 2002–03 *Application fee:* $35. *Comprehensive fee:* $35,880 includes full-time tuition ($27,880), mandatory fees ($170), and college room and board ($7830). *College room only:* $3260. Room and board charges vary according to housing facility. *Part-time tuition:* $1160 per credit. Part-time tuition varies according to course load.

Financial Aid Forms of aid include need-based and non-need-based scholarships and part-time jobs. The average aided 2002–03 undergraduate received an aid package worth an estimated $23,099. The priority application deadline for financial aid is February 15.

Freshman Admission Oberlin requires an essay, a high school transcript, 2 recommendations, SAT I or ACT scores, and TOEFL scores for international students. SAT II: Subject Test scores are recommended. An interview is required for some. The application deadline for regular admission is January 15; for early decision plan 1 it is November 15; and for early decision plan 2 it is January 2.

Transfer Admission The application deadline for admission is May 1.

Entrance Difficulty Oberlin assesses its entrance difficulty level as very difficult. For the fall 2002 freshman class, 33 percent of the applicants were accepted.

For Further Information Contact Ms. Debra Chermonte, Dean of Admissions and Financial Aid, Oberlin College, Admissions Office, Carnegie Building, Oberlin, OH 44074-1090. *Telephone:* 440-775-8411 or 800-622-OBIE (toll-free). *Fax:* 440-775-6905. *E-mail:* college.admissions@oberlin.edu. *Web site:* http://www.oberlin.edu/.

OHIO DOMINICAN UNIVERSITY

Columbus, Ohio

ODU is a coed, private, Roman Catholic, comprehensive institution, founded in 1911, offering degrees at the associate, bachelor's, and master's levels. It has a 62-acre campus in Columbus.

Academic Information The faculty has 163 members (38% full-time), 55% with terminal degrees. The undergraduate student-faculty ratio is 15:1. The library holds 110,953 titles, 553 serial subscriptions, and 4,302 audiovisual materials. Special programs include academic remediation, an honors program, study abroad, advanced placement credit, ESL programs, independent study, self-designed majors, summer session for credit, part-time degree programs (daytime, evenings, weekends, summer), adult/continuing education programs, internships, and arrangement for off-campus study with members of the Higher Education Council of Columbus. The most frequently chosen baccalaureate fields are business/marketing, education, social sciences and history.

Student Body Statistics The student body totals 2,317, of whom 2,250 are undergraduates (265 freshmen). 71 percent are women and 29 percent are men. Students come from 18 states and territories and 13 other countries. 99 percent are from Ohio. 1.4 percent are international students.

Expenses for 2003–04 *Comprehensive fee:* $22,700 includes full-time tuition ($17,200) and college room and board ($5500). Room and board charges vary according to housing facility. *Part-time tuition:* $360 per credit hour. *Part-time mandatory fees:* $100 per term.

Financial Aid Forms of aid include need-based and non-need-based scholarships, athletic grants, and part-time jobs. The average aided 2002–03 undergraduate received an aid package worth an estimated $12,467. The priority application deadline for financial aid is April 1.

Freshman Admission ODU requires an essay, a high school transcript, a minimum 2.0 high school GPA, and an interview. TOEFL scores for international students are recommended. Recommendations and SAT I and SAT II or ACT scores are required for some. The application deadline for regular admission is rolling.

Transfer Admission The application deadline for admission is rolling.

Entrance Difficulty ODU assesses its entrance difficulty level as moderately difficult. For the fall 2002 freshman class, 64 percent of the applicants were accepted.

For Further Information Contact Ms. Vicki Thompson-Campbell, Director of Admissions, Ohio Dominican University, 1216 Sunbury Road, Columbus, OH 43219-2099. *Telephone:* 614-251-4588 or 800-854-2670 (toll-free). *Fax:* 614-251-0156. *E-mail:* admissions@ohiodominican.edu. *Web site:* http://www.ohiodominican.edu/.

OHIO NORTHERN UNIVERSITY

Ada, Ohio

Ohio Northern is a coed, private, United Methodist, comprehensive institution, founded in 1871, offering degrees at the bachelor's and first professional levels. It has a 260-acre campus in Ada.

Academic Information The faculty has 291 members (68% full-time), 67% with terminal degrees. The undergraduate student-faculty ratio is 13:1. The library holds 250,231 titles, 9,220 serial subscriptions, and 9,776 audiovisual materials. Special programs include academic remediation, services for learning-disabled students, an honors program, cooperative (work-study) education, study abroad, advanced placement credit, double majors, independent study, distance learning, summer session for credit, part-time degree programs (daytime, evenings), internships, and arrangement for off-campus study. The most frequently chosen baccalaureate fields are business/marketing, engineering/engineering technologies, health professions and related sciences.

Student Body Statistics The student body totals 3,430, of whom 2,281 are undergraduates (533 freshmen). 47 percent are women and 53 percent are men. Students come from 42 states and territories. 87 percent are from Ohio. 0.6 percent are international students. 16 percent of the 2002 graduating class went on to graduate and professional schools.

Expenses for 2002–03 *Application fee:* $30. *Comprehensive fee:* $29,115 includes full-time tuition ($23,310) and college room and board ($5805). *College room only:* $2835. Full-time tuition varies according to program. Room and board charges vary according to board plan and housing facility. *Part-time tuition:* $648 per quarter hour. Part-time tuition varies according to course load and program.

Financial Aid Forms of aid include need-based and non-need-based scholarships and part-time jobs. The average aided 2002–03 undergraduate received an aid package worth an estimated $19,711. The application deadline for financial aid is June 1 with a priority deadline of April 15.

Freshman Admission Ohio Northern requires a high school transcript, SAT I or ACT scores, and TOEFL scores for international students. An essay, a minimum 2.5 high school GPA, and an interview are recommended. 2 recommendations are required for some. The application deadline for regular admission is August 15.

Transfer Admission The application deadline for admission is August 15.

Entrance Difficulty Ohio Northern assesses its entrance difficulty level as moderately difficult. For the fall 2002 freshman class, 89 percent of the applicants were accepted.

SPECIAL MESSAGE TO STUDENTS

Social Life More than 150 campus organizations make life outside the classroom a rewarding, learning experience. Weekend activities are geared for students on a residential campus and include sporting events, concerts, plays, and a variety of entertainment. Ohio Northern University (ONU) students also become active in Greek life and religious groups. A strong student government is in place.

Academic Highlights Internships, externships, and cooperative education programs are available in each of the four undergraduate colleges. These real-life work experiences provide an invaluable asset to those entering the professional workplace after graduation. Ohio Northern's academic programs begin with a liberal arts philosophy and are strengthened by professional training in the Colleges of Business Administration, Engineering, and Pharmacy. The math and science departments are exceptionally strong to provide academic support for these programs. The physical plant at Northern is extensive and impressive. The 280-acre campus includes the Freed Center for the Performing Arts, home to a beautiful theater/concert hall, classrooms for the Communication Arts Department, and the 3,000-watt FM radio station, WONB.

Interviews and Campus Visits While interviews are not required for admission to Ohio Northern, they are encouraged. Depending upon a student's preference, there are opportunities to attend class, tour campus, speak to a professor about a specific area of interest, meet an athletic coach, and meet with an admissions or financial aid representative. Among the many modern facilities at Ohio Northern, the ONU Sports Center, home to varsity athletics, is both impressive and functional. It has been the site of three NCAA Division III Indoor Track and Field Championships and two NCAA Division III Wrestling Championships and again served as the proud host for the 2003 Wrestling Championships. Students have recreational use of three gymnasiums, a wrestling room, a six-lane swimming pool, three racquetball courts, and gymnastics rooms. The center also includes a 200-meter indoor running track, two weight-training rooms, and modern athletic training and fitness areas. For information about appointments and campus visits, students should call the Office of Admissions at 888-408-4ONU (4668) (toll-free), Monday through Friday, 8 a.m. to 4:30 p.m., or Saturday, 8 a.m. to noon. The fax number is 419-772-2313. The nearest commercial airport is Port Columbus International.

For Further Information Write to Ms. Karen P. Condeni, Vice President and Dean of Admissions and Financial Aid, Admissions Office, Ohio Northern University, Ada, OH 45810. *E-mail:* admissions-ug@onu.edu. *Web site:* http://www.onu.edu.

THE OHIO STATE UNIVERSITY

Columbus, Ohio

Ohio State is a coed, public university, founded in 1870, offering degrees at the bachelor's, master's, doctoral, and first professional levels and post-master's certificates.

Academic Information The faculty has 3,542 members (77% full-time). The undergraduate student-faculty ratio is 14:1. The library holds 6 million titles, 43,086 serial subscriptions, and 46,705 audiovisual materials. Special programs include academic remediation, services for learning-disabled students, an honors program, cooperative (work-study) education, study abroad, advanced placement credit, accelerated degree programs, Freshman Honors College, ESL programs, double majors, independent study, distance learning, self-designed majors, summer session for credit, part-time degree programs (daytime, evenings, weekends, summer), adult/continuing education programs, internships, and arrangement for off-campus study with Higher Education Council of Columbus. The most frequently chosen baccalaureate fields are business/marketing, home economics/vocational home economics, social sciences and history.

Student Body Statistics The student body totals 49,676, of whom 36,855 are undergraduates (5,982 freshmen). 48 percent are women and 52 percent are men. Students come from 53 states and territories and 89 other countries. 89 percent are from Ohio. 4.2 percent are international students. 10 percent of the 2002 graduating class went on to graduate and professional schools.

Expenses for 2002–03 *Application fee:* $30. *State resident tuition:* $5664 full-time. *Nonresident tuition:* $15,087 full-time. Full-time tuition varies according to course load, location, program, and reciprocity agreements. *College room and board:* $6291. Room and board charges vary according to board plan and housing facility.

Financial Aid Forms of aid include need-based and non-need-based scholarships, athletic grants, and part-time jobs. The average aided 2002–03 undergraduate received an aid package worth an estimated $8211. The priority application deadline for financial aid is February 15.

Freshman Admission Ohio State requires a high school transcript, SAT I or ACT scores, and TOEFL scores for international students. The application deadline for regular admission is February 15.

Transfer Admission The application deadline for admission is June 25.

Entrance Difficulty Ohio State assesses its entrance difficulty level as moderately difficult. For the fall 2002 freshman class, 74 percent of the applicants were accepted.

For Further Information Contact Dr. Mabel G. Freeman, Director of Undergraduate Admissions and Vice President for First-Year Experience, The Ohio State University, 3rd Floor, Lincoln Tower, 1800 Cannon Drive, Columbus, OH 43210. *Telephone:* 614-292-3974. *Fax:* 614-292-4818. *E-mail:* askabuckeye@osu.edu. *Web site:* http://www.osu.edu/.

THE OHIO STATE UNIVERSITY AT LIMA

Lima, Ohio

OSU-Lima is a coed, public, four-year college of Ohio State University, founded in 1960, offering degrees at the associate and bachelor's levels (also offers some graduate courses). It has a 565-acre campus in Lima.

Academic Information The faculty has 91 members (62% full-time). The student-faculty ratio is 13:1. The library holds 74,619 titles and 592 serial subscriptions. Special programs include academic remediation, services for learning-disabled students, an honors program, advanced placement credit, accelerated degree programs, ESL programs, summer session for credit, part-time degree programs, and adult/continuing education programs.

Student Body Statistics The student body totals 1,412, of whom 1,293 are undergraduates (389 freshmen). 57 percent are women and 43 percent are men. Students come from 1 state or territory and 1 other country.

Expenses for 2002–03 *Application fee:* $30. *State resident tuition:* $3927 full-time. *Nonresident tuition:* $13,350 full-time.

Freshman Admission OSU-Lima requires a high school transcript and ACT scores. The application deadline for regular admission is July 1.

Transfer Admission The application deadline for admission is July 1.

Entrance Difficulty OSU-Lima has an open admission policy for state residents. It assesses its entrance difficulty as moderately difficult for out-of-state applicants; moderately difficult for transfers.

For Further Information Contact Ms. Marissa Christoff Snyder, Admissions Counselor, The Ohio State University at Lima, 4240 Campus Drive, Lima, OH 45804. *Telephone:* 419-995-8220. *E-mail:* admissions@lima.ohio-state.edu. *Web site:* http://www.ohio-state.edu/.

THE OHIO STATE UNIVERSITY AT MARION

Marion, Ohio

OSU-Marion is a coed, public, four-year college of Ohio State University, founded in 1958, offering degrees at the associate and bachelor's levels (also offers some graduate courses). It has a 180-acre campus in Marion near Columbus.

Expenses for 2002–03 *Application fee:* $30. *State resident tuition:* $3927 full-time. *Nonresident tuition:* $13,350 full-time.

For Further Information Contact Mr. Mathrey Moreau, Admissions Coordinator, The Ohio State University at Marion, 1465 Mount Vernon Avenue, Marion, OH 43302-5695. *Telephone:* 740-389-6786 Ext. 6337. *Web site:* http://www.ohio-state.edu/.

THE OHIO STATE UNIVERSITY–MANSFIELD CAMPUS

Mansfield, Ohio

OSU-Mansfield is a coed, public, four-year college of Ohio State University, founded in 1958, offering degrees at the associate and bachelor's levels (also offers some graduate courses). It has a 593-acre campus in Mansfield near Columbus and Cleveland.

Expenses for 2002–03 *Application fee:* $30. *State resident tuition:* $3927 full-time. *Nonresident tuition:* $13,350 full-time.

For Further Information Contact Mr. Henry D. Thomas, Coordinator of Admissions and Financial Aid, The Ohio State University–Mansfield Campus, 1680 University Drive, Mansfield, OH 44906-1599. *Telephone:* 419-755-4226. *Web site:* http://www.ohio-state.edu/.

THE OHIO STATE UNIVERSITY–NEWARK CAMPUS

Newark, Ohio

OSU-Newark is a coed, public, four-year college of Ohio State University, founded in 1957, offering degrees at the associate and bachelor's levels (also offers some graduate courses). It has a 101-acre campus in Newark near Columbus.

Expenses for 2002–03 *Application fee:* $30. *State resident tuition:* $3927 full-time. *Nonresident tuition:* $13,350 full-time.

For Further Information Contact Ms. Ann Donahue, Director of Enrollment, The Ohio State University–Newark Campus, 1179 University Drive, Newark, OH 43055-1797. *Telephone:* 614-366-9333. *Web site:* http://www.ohio-state.edu/.

OHIO UNIVERSITY

Athens, Ohio

Ohio is a coed, public unit of Ohio Board of Regents, founded in 1804, offering degrees at the associate, bachelor's, master's, doctoral, and first professional levels. It has a 1,700-acre campus in Athens.

Academic Information The faculty has 1,158 members (73% full-time), 82% with terminal degrees. The undergraduate student-faculty ratio is 20:1. The library holds 2 million titles, 15,906 serial subscriptions, and 111,579 audiovisual materials. Special programs include academic remediation, services for learning-disabled students, an honors program, cooperative (work-study) education, study abroad, advanced placement credit, accelerated degree programs, ESL programs, double majors, independent study, distance learning, self-designed majors, summer session for credit, part-time degree programs, external degree programs, adult/continuing education programs, internships, and arrangement for off-campus study. The most frequently chosen baccalaureate fields are business/marketing, communications/communication technologies, education.

Student Body Statistics The student body totals 20,528, of whom 17,343 are undergraduates (3,700 freshmen). 55 percent are women and 45 percent are men. Students come from 52 states and territories and 52 other countries. 91 percent are from Ohio. 2.2 percent are international students. 25 percent of the 2002 graduating class went on to graduate and professional schools.

Expenses for 2002–03 *Application fee:* $40. *State resident tuition:* $6336 full-time, $193 per quarter hour part-time. *Nonresident tuition:* $13,818 full-time, $413 per quarter hour part-time. *College room and board:* $6777. *College room only:* $3333. Room and board charges vary according to board plan.

Financial Aid Forms of aid include need-based and non-need-based scholarships, athletic grants, and part-time jobs. The average aided 2002–03 undergraduate received an aid package worth an estimated $6581. The priority application deadline for financial aid is March 15.

Freshman Admission Ohio requires a high school transcript and SAT I or ACT scores. 2 recommendations are recommended. An essay and an interview are required for some. The application deadline for regular admission is February 1.

Transfer Admission The application deadline for admission is May 15.

Entrance Difficulty Ohio assesses its entrance difficulty level as moderately difficult; very difficult for transfers; very difficult for business, engineering, journalism, radio-television programs, Honors Tutorial College. For the fall 2002 freshman class, 75 percent of the applicants were accepted.

For Further Information Contact Mr. N. Kip Howard Jr., Director of Admissions, Ohio University, Athens, OH 45701-2979. *Telephone:* 740-593-4100. *Fax:* 740-593-4229. *E-mail:* admissions.freshmen@ohiou.edu. *Web site:* http://www.ohio.edu/.

OHIO UNIVERSITY–CHILLICOTHE

Chillicothe, Ohio

Ohio University–Chillicothe is a coed, public, four-year college of Ohio Board of Regents, founded in 1946, offering degrees at the associate, bachelor's, and master's levels (offers first 2 years of most bachelor's degree programs available at the main campus in Athens; also offers several bachelor's degree programs that can be completed at this campus and several programs exclusive to this campus; also offers some graduate programs). It has a 124-acre campus in Chillicothe near Columbus.

Academic Information The faculty has 106 members (39% full-time). The library holds 47,900 titles and 418 serial subscriptions. Special programs include academic remediation, services for learning-disabled students, advanced placement credit, accelerated degree programs, double majors, independent study, distance learning, self-designed majors, summer session for credit, part-time degree programs (daytime, evenings, summer), adult/continuing education programs, and internships.
Student Body Statistics The student body totals 1,999, of whom 1,816 are undergraduates. Students come from 2 states and territories. 10 percent of the 2002 graduating class went on to graduate and professional schools.
Expenses for 2002–03 *Application fee:* $20. *State resident tuition:* $3564 full-time, $108 per quarter hour part-time. *Nonresident tuition:* $9150 full-time, $293 per quarter hour part-time.
Financial Aid Forms of aid include need-based and non-need-based scholarships and part-time jobs. The average aided 2002–03 undergraduate received an aid package worth an estimated $6435. The priority application deadline for financial aid is March 15.
Freshman Admission Ohio University–Chillicothe requires a high school transcript and SAT I or ACT scores. The application deadline for regular admission is September 1.
Transfer Admission The application deadline for admission is September 1.
Entrance Difficulty Ohio University–Chillicothe has an open admission policy for state residents. It assesses its entrance difficulty as minimally difficult for transfers.

For Further Information Contact Mr. Richard R. Whitney, Director of Student Services, Ohio University–Chillicothe, 571 West Fifth Street, Chillicothe, OH 45601. *Telephone:* 740-774-7200 Ext. 242 or 877-462-6824 (toll-free in-state). *Fax:* 740-774-7295. *Web site:* http://www.ohio.edu/chillicothe/.

OHIO UNIVERSITY–EASTERN

St. Clairsville, Ohio

For Information Write to Ohio University–Eastern, St. Clairsville, OH 43950-9724.

OHIO UNIVERSITY–LANCASTER

Lancaster, Ohio

Ohio University–Lancaster is a coed, public, comprehensive unit of Ohio Board of Regents, founded in 1968, offering degrees at the associate, bachelor's, and master's levels. It has a 360-acre campus in Lancaster near Columbus.

Academic Information The faculty has 104 members (30% full-time), 66% with terminal degrees. The undergraduate student-faculty ratio is 30:1. The library holds 94,688 titles, 399 serial subscriptions, and 2,759 audiovisual materials. Special programs include academic remediation, advanced placement credit, accelerated degree programs, double majors, independent study, distance learning, self-designed majors, summer session for credit, part-time degree programs (daytime, evenings, weekends, summer), external degree programs, adult/continuing education programs, and internships. The most frequently chosen baccalaureate fields are communications/communication technologies, business/marketing, education.
Student Body Statistics The student body totals 1,744, of whom 1,617 are undergraduates (308 freshmen). 67 percent are women and 33 percent are men. Students come from 12 states and territories and 1 other country. 0.2 percent are international students.
Expenses for 2002–03 *Application fee:* $20. *State resident tuition:* $4095 full-time, $117 per credit hour part-time. *Nonresident tuition:* $9150 full-time, $302 per credit hour part-time. Full-time tuition varies according to course level, course load, location, and student level. Part-time tuition varies according to course level, course load, location, and student level.
Financial Aid Forms of aid include need-based and non-need-based scholarships and part-time jobs. The average aided 2002–03 undergraduate received an aid package worth an estimated $6073. The priority application deadline for financial aid is March 15.
Freshman Admission Ohio University–Lancaster requires a high school transcript and SAT I or ACT scores. An interview is recommended. The application deadline for regular admission is rolling.
Transfer Admission The application deadline for admission is rolling.
Entrance Difficulty Ohio University–Lancaster has an open admission policy.

For Further Information Contact Mr. Nathan Thomas, Admissions Officer, Ohio University–Lancaster, 1570 Granville Pike, Lancaster, OH 43130-1097. *Telephone:* 740-654-6711 Ext. 215 or 888-446-4468 Ext. 215 (toll-free). *Fax:* 740-687-9497. *E-mail:* fox@ohio.edu. *Web site:* http://www.ohiou.edu/lancaster/.

OHIO UNIVERSITY–SOUTHERN CAMPUS

Ironton, Ohio

Ohio University–Southern Campus is a coed, public, comprehensive unit of Ohio Board of Regents, founded in 1956, offering degrees at the associate, bachelor's, and master's levels. It has a 9-acre campus in Ironton.

Academic Information The faculty has 155 members (6% full-time). The library holds 26,000 titles, 275 serial subscriptions, and 524 audiovisual materials. Special programs include academic remediation, self-designed majors, summer session for credit, part-time degree programs (daytime, evenings, weekends, summer), and adult/continuing education programs.
Student Body Statistics The student body totals 1,746, of whom 1,630 are undergraduates (348 freshmen). 63 percent are women and 37 percent are men. Students come from 4 states and territories. 86 percent are from Ohio. 0.1 percent are international students.
Expenses for 2002–03 *Application fee:* $20. *State resident tuition:* $3282 full-time, $100 per hour part-time. *Nonresident tuition:* $4272 full-time, $130 per hour part-time. Full-time tuition varies according to student level. Part-time tuition varies according to student level.
Financial Aid Forms of aid include need-based and non-need-based scholarships and part-time jobs. The average aided 2002–03 undergraduate received an aid package worth an estimated $6718. The priority application deadline for financial aid is April 1.
Freshman Admission SAT I or ACT scores are recommended. A high school transcript is required for some. The application deadline for regular admission is rolling.
Transfer Admission The application deadline for admission is rolling.
Entrance Difficulty Ohio University–Southern Campus has an open admission policy.

For Further Information Contact Dr. Kim K. Lawson, Coordinator of Admissions, Ohio University–Southern Campus, 1804 Liberty Avenue, Ironton, OH 45638. *Telephone:* 740-533-4612 or 800-626-0513 (toll-free). *Fax:* 740-593-0560. *Web site:* http://www.ohiou.edu/.

OHIO UNIVERSITY–ZANESVILLE

Zanesville, Ohio

OUZ is a coed, public, comprehensive unit of Ohio Board of Regents, founded in 1946, offering degrees at the associate, bachelor's, and master's levels (offers first 2 years of most bachelor's degree

Ohio University–Zanesville (continued)

programs available at the main campus in Athens; also offers several bachelor's degree programs that can be completed at this campus; also offers some graduate courses). It has a 179-acre campus in Zanesville near Columbus.

Academic Information The faculty has 109 members (26% full-time), 24% with terminal degrees. The undergraduate student-faculty ratio is 23:1. The library holds 64,227 titles and 489 serial subscriptions. Special programs include academic remediation, services for learning-disabled students, advanced placement credit, self-designed majors, summer session for credit, part-time degree programs, external degree programs, adult/continuing education programs, and arrangement for off-campus study with Muskingum Area Technical College.

Student Body Statistics The student body totals 1,635, of whom 1,506 are undergraduates (348 freshmen). 72 percent are women and 28 percent are men. Students come from 4 states and territories. 99 percent are from Ohio.

Expenses for 2002–03 *Application fee:* $20. *State resident tuition:* $3564 full-time, $108 per credit hour part-time. *Nonresident tuition:* $9150 full-time, $293 per credit hour part-time. Full-time tuition varies according to course level. Part-time tuition varies according to course level.

Financial Aid Forms of aid include need-based and non-need-based scholarships and part-time jobs. The average aided 2002–03 undergraduate received an aid package worth an estimated $6145. The priority application deadline for financial aid is April 1.

Freshman Admission OUZ requires a high school transcript. SAT I or ACT scores and nursing examination are required for some. The application deadline for regular admission is rolling.

Transfer Admission The application deadline for admission is rolling.

Entrance Difficulty OUZ has an open admission policy except for nursing, engineering, business, communications programs. It assesses its entrance difficulty as moderately difficult for nursing, business, engineering, communications programs.

For Further Information Contact Mrs. Karen Ragsdale, Student Services Secretary, Ohio University–Zanesville, 1425 Newark Road, Zanesville, OH 43701-2695. *Telephone:* 740-588-1439 Ext. 1446. *Fax:* 740-453-6161. *Web site:* http://www.zanesville.ohiou.edu/.

OHIO WESLEYAN UNIVERSITY

Delaware, Ohio

Ohio Wesleyan is a coed, private, United Methodist, four-year college, founded in 1842, offering degrees at the bachelor's level. It has a 200-acre campus in Delaware near Columbus.

Academic Information The faculty has 183 members (71% full-time), 80% with terminal degrees. The student-faculty ratio is 13:1. The library holds 420,936 titles, 1,084 serial subscriptions, and 2,980 audiovisual materials. Special programs include services for learning-disabled students, an honors program, study abroad, advanced placement credit, Freshman Honors College, double majors, independent study, self-designed majors, summer session for credit, part-time degree programs (daytime, summer), internships, and arrangement for off-campus study with Great Lakes Colleges Association, New York City Arts Program. The most frequently chosen baccalaureate fields are business/marketing, biological/life sciences, social sciences and history.

Student Body Statistics The student body is made up of 1,935 undergraduates (546 freshmen). 54 percent are women and 46 percent are men. Students come from 44 states and territories and 47 other countries. 60 percent are from Ohio. 11.1 percent are international students. 34 percent of the 2002 graduating class went on to graduate and professional schools.

Expenses for 2002–03 *Application fee:* $35. *Comprehensive fee:* $31,210 includes full-time tuition ($24,000), mandatory fees ($200), and college room and board ($7010). *College room only:* $3530. Room and board charges vary according to board plan. *Part-time tuition:* $2610 per course.

Financial Aid Forms of aid include need-based and non-need-based scholarships and part-time jobs. The average aided 2002–03 undergraduate received an aid package worth an estimated $20,866. The priority application deadline for financial aid is March 15.

Freshman Admission Ohio Wesleyan requires an essay, a high school transcript, 1 recommendation, SAT I or ACT scores, and TOEFL scores for international students. A minimum 2.5 high school GPA, 2 recommendations, an interview, and SAT II: Subject Test scores are recommended. The application deadline for regular admission is March 15; for early decision it is December 1; and for early action it is December 15.

Transfer Admission The application deadline for admission is May 15.

Entrance Difficulty Ohio Wesleyan assesses its entrance difficulty level as very difficult; most difficult for honors program. For the fall 2002 freshman class, 80 percent of the applicants were accepted.

For Further Information Contact Ms. Carol Wheatley, Director of Admission, Ohio Wesleyan University, 61 South Sandusky Street, Delaware, OH 43015. *Telephone:* 740-368-3020 or 800-922-8953 (toll-free). *Fax:* 740-368-3314. *E-mail:* owuadmit@owu.edu. *Web site:* http://web.owu.edu/.

See page 318 for a narrative description.

OTTERBEIN COLLEGE

Westerville, Ohio

Otterbein is a coed, private, United Methodist, comprehensive institution, founded in 1847, offering degrees at the bachelor's and master's levels. It has a 140-acre campus in Westerville near Columbus.

Academic Information The faculty has 249 members (58% full-time). The undergraduate student-faculty ratio is 13:1. The library holds 182,629 titles, 1,012 serial subscriptions, and 8,971 audiovisual materials. Special programs include academic remediation, services for learning-disabled students, an honors program, study abroad, advanced placement credit, double majors, self-designed majors, summer session for credit, part-time degree programs (daytime, evenings, weekends, summer), adult/continuing education programs, internships, and arrangement for off-campus study with American University, University of Pittsburgh (Semester at Sea), members of the Higher Education Council of Columbus. The most frequently chosen baccalaureate fields are business/marketing, education, health professions and related sciences.

Student Body Statistics The student body totals 3,064, of whom 2,622 are undergraduates (550 freshmen). 64 percent are women and 36 percent are men. Students come from 34 states and territories. 92 percent are from Ohio. 13 percent of the 2002 graduating class went on to graduate and professional schools.

Expenses for 2003–04 *Application fee:* $25. *Comprehensive fee:* $26,085 includes full-time tuition ($20,133) and college room and board ($5952). *College room only:* $2712. Full-time tuition varies according to course load and program. Room and board charges vary according to housing facility. *Part-time tuition:* $242 per credit hour. Part-time tuition varies according to course load and program.

Financial Aid Forms of aid include need-based and non-need-based scholarships and part-time jobs. The priority application deadline for financial aid is April 1.

Freshman Admission Otterbein requires a high school transcript, SAT I or ACT scores, and TOEFL scores for international students. A minimum 2.5 high school GPA and an interview are recommended. The application deadline for regular admission is March 1.

Transfer Admission The application deadline for admission is rolling.

Entrance Difficulty Otterbein assesses its entrance difficulty level as moderately difficult. For the fall 2002 freshman class, 81 percent of the applicants were accepted.

SPECIAL MESSAGE TO STUDENTS

Social Life Students participate in more than ninety campus organizations, from music performance groups such as the marching band, concert choir, and orchestra to student government to student-run radio and television studios to intramural sports. Thirty-five percent join one of the six fraternities and six sororities. Many students are involved in campus service organizations, such as Habitat for Humanity. Religious activities are also available for students in most denominations. Cultural activities on campus include a professional Artist Series, the Otterbein College Theatre, and musical performances. Off-campus activities in nearby Columbus include many social and cultural offerings.

Academic Highlights The curriculum revolves around Otterbein's nationally recognized liberal arts curriculum, Integrative Studies, combined with professional and career preparation. Otterbein offers forty-nine majors and seven baccalaureate and four graduate degrees. Internships are encouraged in order to give students hands-on work experience to complement their course work. Programs in theater and equine science have each achieved national recognition.

Interviews and Campus Visits Individual interviews are not required of all applicants, but campus visits are strongly recommended for all accepted students. The visit is structured so that students can gain a thorough understanding of the campus from a variety of perspectives. Faculty conferences, student-conducted tours, admission and financial aid conferences, and classroom observation are part of each campus visit. Roush Hall, the multipurpose, state-of-the-art classroom building; Battelle Fine Arts Center; the Rike Physical Education Building; the Science Hall–Observatory; the campus center; residence halls; Towers Hall; the computer center; Courtright Memorial Library; and the new Clements Recreation Center should not be missed. For information about appointments and campus visits, students should call the Office of Admission at 614-823-1500 (collect) or 800-488-8144 (toll-free), Monday through Friday, 8:30 a.m. to 5 p.m., or Saturday, 9:30 a.m. to 1 p.m. The office is located in the Clippinger Administration Building on campus.

For Further Information Write to Dr. Cass Johnson, Director of Admission, Otterbein College, Westerville, OH 43081.

See page 324 for a narrative description.

PONTIFICAL COLLEGE JOSEPHINUM

Columbus, Ohio

Josephinum is a coed, primarily men's, private, Roman Catholic, comprehensive institution, founded in 1888, offering degrees at the bachelor's, master's, and first professional levels. It has a 100-acre campus in Columbus.

Academic Information The faculty has 19 members (53% full-time). The undergraduate student-faculty ratio is 4:1. The library holds 124,742 titles and 520 serial subscriptions. Special programs include academic remediation, services for learning-disabled students, an honors program, advanced placement credit, ESL programs, double majors, internships, and arrangement for off-campus study with 2 members of the Theological Cluster. The most frequently chosen baccalaureate fields are area/ethnic studies, philosophy, religion, and theology.
Student Body Statistics The student body totals 130, of whom 69 are undergraduates (9 freshmen). 100 percent are men. Students come from 16 states and territories. 60 percent are from Ohio. 2.9 percent are international students. 85 percent of the 2002 graduating class went on to graduate and professional schools.
Expenses for 2002–03 *Application fee:* $25. *Comprehensive fee:* $15,400 includes full-time tuition ($9640), mandatory fees ($100), and college room and board ($5660). *College room only:* $2830. *Part-time tuition:* $325 per credit.
Financial Aid Forms of aid include need-based and non-need-based scholarships and part-time jobs. The average aided 2002–03 undergraduate received an aid package worth an estimated $13,560. The priority application deadline for financial aid is September 2.
Freshman Admission Josephinum requires an essay, a high school transcript, 3 recommendations, and TOEFL scores for international students. An interview and SAT I and SAT II or ACT scores are recommended. The application deadline for regular admission is rolling.
Transfer Admission The application deadline for admission is rolling.
Entrance Difficulty Josephinum assesses its entrance difficulty level as minimally difficult. For the fall 2002 freshman class, 64 percent of the applicants were accepted.

For Further Information Contact Arminda Crawford, Secretary for Admissions, Pontifical College Josephinum, Columbus, OH 43235. *Telephone:* 614-985-2241 or 888-252-5812 (toll-free). *Fax:* 614-885-2307. *E-mail:* acrawford@pcj.edu. *Web site:* http://www.pcj.edu/.

ROSEDALE BIBLE COLLEGE

Irwin, Ohio

For Information Write to Rosedale Bible College, Irwin, OH 43029-9501.

SHAWNEE STATE UNIVERSITY

Portsmouth, Ohio

Shawnee State is a coed, public, four-year college of Ohio Board of Regents, founded in 1986, offering degrees at the associate and bachelor's levels. It has a 52-acre campus in Portsmouth.

Academic Information The faculty has 263 members (46% full-time). The student-faculty ratio is 18:1. The library holds 152,961 titles, 6,909 serial subscriptions, and 19,316 audiovisual materials. Special programs include academic remediation, services for learning-disabled students, an honors program, study abroad, advanced placement credit, double majors, independent study, distance learning, summer session for credit, part-time degree programs, adult/continuing education programs, internships, and arrangement for off-campus study. The most frequently chosen baccalaureate fields are business/marketing, liberal arts/general studies, social sciences and history.
Student Body Statistics The student body is made up of 3,606 undergraduates (730 freshmen). 62 percent are women and 38 percent are men. Students come from 10 states and territories and 9 other countries. 91 percent are from Ohio. 0.4 percent are international students.
Expenses for 2002–03 *Application fee:* $0. *State resident tuition:* $4347 full-time, $98 per credit hour part-time. *Nonresident tuition:* $7443 full-time, $184 per credit hour part-time. *Mandatory fees:* $522 full-time, $14.50 per credit hour part-time. *College room and board:* $5421. *College room only:* $3342.
Financial Aid Forms of aid include need-based and non-need-based scholarships, athletic grants, and part-time jobs. $3972. The priority application deadline for financial aid is April 1.
Freshman Admission Shawnee State requires a high school transcript and TOEFL scores for international students. ACT scores are recommended. Recommendations and an interview are required for some. The application deadline for regular admission is rolling.
Transfer Admission The application deadline for admission is rolling.
Entrance Difficulty Shawnee State has an open admission policy except for allied health programs, nonresident aliens. It assesses its entrance difficulty as moderately difficult for allied health programs.

For Further Information Contact Mr. Bob Trusz, Director of Admission, Shawnee State University, 940 Second Street, Commons Building, Portsmouth, OH 45662. *Telephone:* 740-351-3610 Ext. 610 or 800-959-2SSU (toll-free). *Fax:* 740-351-3111. *E-mail:* to_ssu@shawnee.edu. *Web site:* http://www.shawnee.edu/.

SOUTHEASTERN BUSINESS COLLEGE

See Gallipolis Career College

TIFFIN UNIVERSITY

Tiffin, Ohio

Tiffin is a coed, private, comprehensive institution, founded in 1888, offering degrees at the associate, bachelor's, and master's levels. It has a 108-acre campus in Tiffin near Toledo.

Academic Information The faculty has 232 members (18% full-time), 30% with terminal degrees. The undergraduate student-faculty ratio is 10:1. The library holds 29,779 titles, 250 serial subscriptions, and 544 audiovisual materials. Special programs include study abroad, advanced placement credit, accelerated degree programs, double majors, independent study, distance learning, summer session for credit, adult/continuing education programs, and internships. The most frequently chosen baccalaureate fields are business/marketing, liberal arts/general studies, protective services/public administration.
Student Body Statistics The student body totals 1,533, of whom 1,204 are undergraduates (265 freshmen). 56 percent are women and 44 percent are men. Students come from 22 states and territories and 19 other countries. 91 percent are from Ohio. 2.4 percent are international students. 18 percent of the 2002 graduating class went on to graduate and professional schools.
Expenses for 2003–04 *Application fee:* $20. *Comprehensive fee:* $19,490 includes full-time tuition ($13,590) and college room and board ($5900). *College room only:* $3100. Room and board charges vary according to board plan and housing facility. *Part-time tuition:* $453 per credit hour.
Financial Aid Forms of aid include need-based and non-need-based scholarships, athletic grants, and part-time jobs. The average aided 2002–03 undergraduate received an aid package worth an estimated $9770. The priority application deadline for financial aid is March 31.
Freshman Admission Tiffin requires an essay, a high school transcript, SAT I or ACT scores, and TOEFL scores for international students. A minimum 2.50 high school GPA and an interview are recommended. Recommendations and an interview are required for some. The application deadline for regular admission is rolling.
Transfer Admission The application deadline for admission is rolling.
Entrance Difficulty Tiffin assesses its entrance difficulty level as minimally difficult. For the fall 2002 freshman class, 73 percent of the applicants were accepted.

SPECIAL MESSAGE TO STUDENTS

Social Life Tiffin University's (TU) student government is one of the most active organizations on campus. It is responsible for planning, organizing, and implementing social, cultural, and educational programs and activities. Students' activities also revolve around sixteen varsity sports, intramural sports, four Greek organizations, two honor societies, and a variety of academic clubs. Approximately 50 percent of students live on or near campus.

Academic Highlights The programs of emphasis at Tiffin University are accounting, criminal justice, hospitality management, and liberal studies. The Sworn Internship Program for law enforcement majors is unequaled in Ohio. After two years, a student can be hired by a police department as a reserve officer, complete the police academy training, and participate in two internships in his or her senior year as a sworn police officer. In addition to excellent internship possibilities, hospitality management majors receive hands-on experience at a chosen workplace.

Interviews and Campus Visits The best way to learn about TU is to visit the campus. As part of the visitation program, students may attend at least one course in their area of interest, meet with representatives of various campus activities and functions, and sample the dining hall's cuisine. TU's dining facilities and staff were rated number one in overall services and performance among all mid-Atlantic colleges within its membership services. Most students who come to Tiffin discover the best about themselves. It is the people who make Tiffin University special, and students are encouraged to take advantage of the opportunities to grow with and learn from the University community. For information about appointments and campus visits, students should call the Office of Undergraduate Admission at 419-447-6443 (collect) or 800-968-6446 (toll-free), Monday through Friday, 9 a.m. to 4 p.m., or Saturday, 9 a.m. to 1 p.m. The office is located in Seitz Hall, 155 Miami Street, on campus.

For Further Information Write to Mr. Darby M. Roggow, Director of Admissions, Tiffin University, 155 Miami Street, Tiffin, OH 44883. *E-mail:* droggow@tiffin.edu.

TRI-STATE BIBLE COLLEGE

South Point, Ohio

For Information Write to Tri-State Bible College, South Point, OH 45680-8402.

UNION INSTITUTE & UNIVERSITY

Cincinnati, Ohio

Union is a coed, private university, founded in 1969, offering degrees at the bachelor's, master's, and doctoral levels and post-master's certificates. It has a 5-acre campus in Cincinnati.

Academic Information The faculty has 286 members (38% full-time), 65% with terminal degrees. The undergraduate student-faculty ratio is 16:1. The library holds 50,000 titles and 300 audiovisual materials. Special programs include services for learning-disabled students, advanced placement credit, accelerated degree programs, double majors, independent study, distance learning, self-designed majors, summer session for credit, part-time degree programs (daytime, evenings, weekends, summer), external degree programs, and adult/continuing education programs. The most frequently chosen baccalaureate fields are education, business/marketing, protective services/public administration.
Student Body Statistics The student body totals 2,801, of whom 1,153 are undergraduates. 69 percent are women and 31 percent are men. Students come from 42 states and territories and 8 other countries. 76 percent are from Ohio. 1.1 percent are international students. 39 percent of the 2002 graduating class went on to graduate and professional schools.
Expenses for 2002–03 *Application fee:* $50. *Tuition:* $7224 full-time, $301 per semester hour part-time. *Mandatory fees:* $67 full-time. Full-time tuition and fees vary according to course load and program.
Financial Aid Forms of aid include need-based and non-need-based scholarships and part-time jobs. $8000. The priority application deadline for financial aid is April 15.
Freshman Admission Union requires an essay, a high school transcript, 2 recommendations, and an interview. The application deadline for regular admission is October 1.
Transfer Admission The application deadline for admission is October 1.
Entrance Difficulty Union assesses its entrance difficulty level as moderately difficult.

For Further Information Contact Ms. Lisa Schrenger, Director, Admissions, Union Institute & University, 36 College Street, Montpelier, VT 05602. *Telephone:* 800-486-3116 or 800-486-3116 (toll-free). *Fax:* 513-861-0779. *E-mail:* admissions@tui.edu. *Web site:* http://www.tui.edu/.

THE UNIVERSITY OF AKRON

Akron, Ohio

Akron is a coed, public university, founded in 1870, offering degrees at the associate, bachelor's, master's, doctoral, and first professional levels. It has a 170-acre campus in Akron near Cleveland.

Academic Information The faculty has 1,647 members (47% full-time), 59% with terminal degrees. The undergraduate student-faculty ratio is 17:1. The library holds 1 million titles, 12,849 serial subscriptions, and 43,448 audiovisual materials. Special programs include academic remediation, services for learning-disabled students, an honors program, cooperative (work-study) education, study abroad, advanced placement credit, accelerated degree programs, ESL programs, double majors,

independent study, distance learning, self-designed majors, summer session for credit, part-time degree programs (daytime, evenings, weekends, summer), adult/continuing education programs, and internships. The most frequently chosen baccalaureate fields are business/marketing, education, protective services/public administration.
Student Body Statistics The student body totals 24,348, of whom 20,182 are undergraduates (3,668 freshmen). 55 percent are women and 45 percent are men. Students come from 32 states and territories and 70 other countries. 98 percent are from Ohio. 0.8 percent are international students.
Expenses for 2002–03 *Application fee:* $35. *One-time mandatory fee:* $300. *State resident tuition:* $5020 full-time, $209 per credit part-time. *Nonresident tuition:* $11,834 full-time, $436 per credit part-time. *Mandatory fees:* $778 full-time, $22 per credit part-time. Full-time tuition and fees vary according to course load, location, and student level. Part-time tuition and fees vary according to course load, location, and student level. *College room and board:* $5959. *College room only:* $3765. Room and board charges vary according to board plan and housing facility.
Financial Aid Forms of aid include need-based and non-need-based scholarships, athletic grants, and part-time jobs. The average aided 2002–03 undergraduate received an aid package worth an estimated $5969. The priority application deadline for financial aid is March 1.
Freshman Admission Akron requires a high school transcript, SAT I or ACT scores, and TOEFL scores for international students. An essay, 3 recommendations, and an interview are required for some. The application deadline for regular admission is August 15 and for early action it is February 1.
Transfer Admission The application deadline for admission is August 15.
Entrance Difficulty Akron assesses its entrance difficulty level as minimally difficult; moderately difficult for transfers; noncompetitive for Community and Technical College. For the fall 2002 freshman class, 85 percent of the applicants were accepted.

For Further Information Contact Ms. Diane Raybuck, Director of Admissions, The University of Akron, 381 Buchtel Common, Akron, OH 44325-2001. *Telephone:* 330-972-6425 or 800-655-4884 (toll-free). *Fax:* 330-972-7676. *E-mail:* admissions@uakron.edu. *Web site:* http://www.uakron.edu/.

UNIVERSITY OF CINCINNATI

Cincinnati, Ohio

UC is a coed, public unit of University of Cincinnati System, founded in 1819, offering degrees at the associate, bachelor's, master's, doctoral, and first professional levels and postbachelor's certificates. It has a 137-acre campus in Cincinnati.

Academic Information The faculty has 1,333 members (100% full-time), 58% with terminal degrees. The undergraduate student-faculty ratio is 18:1. The library holds 16,560 serial subscriptions and 51,224 audiovisual materials. Special programs include academic remediation, services for learning-disabled students, an honors program, cooperative (work-study) education, study abroad, advanced placement credit, accelerated degree programs, ESL programs, double majors, independent study, distance learning, summer session for credit, part-time degree programs, adult/continuing education programs, internships, and arrangement for off-campus study with Greater Cincinnati Consortium of Colleges and Universities. The most frequently chosen baccalaureate fields are business/marketing, engineering/engineering technologies, social sciences and history.
Student Body Statistics The student body totals 26,552, of whom 19,204 are undergraduates (3,943 freshmen). 49 percent are women and 51 percent are men. Students come from 46 states and territories and 50 other countries. 93 percent are from Ohio. 1 percent are international students. 36 percent of the 2002 graduating class went on to graduate and professional schools.
Expenses for 2002–03 *Application fee:* $35. *State resident tuition:* $5715 full-time, $193 per credit hour part-time. *Nonresident tuition:* $16,089 full-time, $480 per credit hour part-time. *Mandatory fees:* $1221 full-time. Full-time tuition and fees vary according to location. Part-time tuition varies according to location. *College room and board:* $6774. Room and board charges vary according to board plan and housing facility.
Financial Aid Forms of aid include need-based and non-need-based scholarships, athletic grants, and part-time jobs. The average aided 2002–03 undergraduate received an aid package worth an estimated $7125. The application deadline for financial aid is continuous.
Freshman Admission UC requires a high school transcript, SAT I or ACT scores, and TOEFL scores for international students. An interview and ACT scores are recommended. 2 recommendations and audition are required for some. The application deadline for regular admission is rolling.
Transfer Admission The application deadline for admission is rolling.
Entrance Difficulty UC assesses its entrance difficulty level as moderately difficult; most difficult for engineering, architecture programs. For the fall 2002 freshman class, 88 percent of the applicants were accepted.

For Further Information Contact Terry Davis, Director of Admissions, University of Cincinnati, Cincinnati, OH 45221-0091. *Telephone:* 513-556-6999. *Fax:* 513-556-1105. *E-mail:* admissions@uc.edu. *Web site:* http://www.uc.edu/.

UNIVERSITY OF DAYTON

Dayton, Ohio

UD is a coed, private, Roman Catholic university, founded in 1850, offering degrees at the bachelor's, master's, doctoral, and first professional levels. It has a 110-acre campus in Dayton near Cincinnati.

Academic Information The faculty has 801 members (51% full-time). The undergraduate student-faculty ratio is 15:1. The library holds 849,244 titles, 7,318 serial subscriptions, and 1,763 audiovisual materials. Special programs include academic remediation, services for learning-disabled students, an honors program, cooperative (work-study) education, study abroad, advanced placement credit, accelerated degree programs, ESL programs, double majors, independent study, summer session for credit, part-time degree programs (daytime, evenings, summer), adult/continuing education programs, internships, and arrangement for off-campus study with Southwestern Ohio Council for Higher Education, Chaminade University of Honolulu, St. Mary's University. The most frequently chosen baccalaureate fields are business/marketing, education, engineering/engineering technologies.
Student Body Statistics The student body totals 10,126, of whom 7,085 are undergraduates (1,666 freshmen). 50 percent are women and 50 percent are men. Students come from 48 states and territories and 29 other countries. 67 percent are from Ohio. 0.7 percent are international students.
Expenses for 2002–03 *Application fee:* $0. *One-time mandatory fee:* $90. *Comprehensive fee:* $23,600 includes full-time tuition ($17,450), mandatory fees ($550), and college room and board ($5600). *College room only:* $3100. Full-time tuition and fees vary according to program. Room and board charges vary according to board plan, housing facility, and student level. *Part-time tuition:* $582 per credit hour. *Part-time mandatory fees:* $25 per term. Part-time tuition and fees vary according to course load and program.
Financial Aid Forms of aid include need-based and non-need-based scholarships, athletic grants, and part-time jobs. The average aided 2001–02 undergraduate received an aid package worth $9410. The priority application deadline for financial aid is March 31.
Freshman Admission UD requires a high school transcript, 1 recommendation, SAT I or ACT scores, and TOEFL scores for international students. An essay and an interview are recommended. Audition required for music, music therapy, music education programs is required for some.
Transfer Admission The application deadline for admission is June 15.
Entrance Difficulty UD assesses its entrance difficulty level as moderately difficult. For the fall 2002 freshman class, 84 percent of the applicants were accepted.

University of Dayton (continued)

SPECIAL MESSAGE TO STUDENTS

Social Life The residential character of the University of Dayton (UD) campus supports a stimulating academic and extracurricular life for approximately 6,500 full-time undergraduate students, of whom more than 95 percent choose to live on campus. Participation in clubs and organizations—whether service, performance, professional, religious, social, or athletic—is a distinguishing characteristic of the active UD student body. More than 200 clubs and organizations are active on campus. One of the most notable interests of students, however, is service to others. Virtually every organization offers some type of service.

Academic Highlights The University of Dayton is a place where students are encouraged and challenged to reach their full potential in and out of the classroom. Students are the most important part of UD, and teaching and advising are the University's highest priorities. The University of Dayton provides cooperative education, internships, study abroad, the University Honors and John W. Berry, Sr. Scholars programs, and opportunities in undergraduate research to supplement academic course work. UD's campus is completely wired, providing 24-hour access to the library, the Internet, and class registration. In fact, all University-owned housing is fully wired for the Internet, and a wireless network covers several academic buildings, the library, and the student union and expands each year to include more areas.

Interviews and Campus Visits The campus interview is not required for admission but is recommended as a means of sharing information. Campus visits may include interviews with admissions and financial aid counselors, meetings with faculty members, campus and residence hall tours, attending class, and accompanying a UD student through his or her day. The University of Dayton urges visitors to see the Jesse Philips Center for the Humanities, a $163-million facility for use by all undergraduates; the Ryan C. Harris Learning Teaching Center; Virginia Kettering Residence Hall for sophomores; the Center for Portfolio Management and Security Analysis; Roesch Library, which holds more than 1.2 million volumes; the Physical Activity Center (PAC) recreational facility; and the newly renovated University of Dayton Arena, which has a seating capacity of approximately 13,500. More information about appointments and campus visits can be found online at http://admission.udayton.edu/visitud/ or by calling the Office of Admission at 937-229-4411 or 800-837-7433 (toll-free), Monday through Friday, 8:30 a.m. to 4:30 p.m. Open-house programs are available in the fall, and individual appointments may be scheduled on Saturday mornings, January through May. The nearest commercial airport is Dayton International.

For Further Information Write to Mr. Robert Durkle, Director of Admission, University of Dayton, 300 College Park, Dayton, OH 45469-1300. *E-mail:* admission@udayton.edu. *Web site:* http://admission.udayton.edu.

THE UNIVERSITY OF FINDLAY

Findlay, Ohio

Findlay is a coed, private, comprehensive institution, founded in 1882, affiliated with the Church of God, offering degrees at the associate, bachelor's, and master's levels. It has a 160-acre campus in Findlay near Toledo.

Academic Information The faculty has 340 members (47% full-time). The undergraduate student-faculty ratio is 19:1. The library holds 135,000 titles, 1,050 serial subscriptions, and 2,000 audiovisual materials. Special programs include academic remediation, services for learning-disabled students, an honors program, cooperative (work-study) education, study abroad, advanced placement credit, accelerated degree programs, ESL programs, double majors, independent study, distance learning, self-designed majors, summer session for credit, part-time degree programs (daytime, evenings, weekends, summer), adult/continuing education programs, internships, and arrangement for off-campus study. The most frequently chosen baccalaureate fields are business/marketing, education, health professions and related sciences.
Student Body Statistics The student body totals 4,591, of whom 3,384 are undergraduates (910 freshmen). 56 percent are women and 44 percent are men. Students come from 45 states and territories and 34 other countries. 87 percent are from Ohio. 2 percent are international students. 15.7 percent of the 2002 graduating class went on to graduate and professional schools.
Expenses for 2002–03 *Application fee:* $0. *Comprehensive fee:* $25,516 includes full-time tuition ($18,114), mandatory fees ($610), and college room and board ($6792). *College room only:* $3356. Full-time tuition and fees vary according to location and program. Room and board charges vary according to housing facility. *Part-time tuition:* $399 per semester hour. *Part-time mandatory fees:* $65 per term. Part-time tuition and fees vary according to location and program.
Financial Aid Forms of aid include need-based and non-need-based scholarships, athletic grants, and part-time jobs. The average aided 2002–03 undergraduate received an aid package worth an estimated $13,850. The application deadline for financial aid is continuous.
Freshman Admission Findlay requires a high school transcript, a minimum 2.3 high school GPA, and SAT I or ACT scores. TOEFL scores for international students are recommended. An essay, recommendations, and an interview are required for some. The application deadline for regular admission is June 1.
Transfer Admission The application deadline for admission is August 1.
Entrance Difficulty Findlay assesses its entrance difficulty level as moderately difficult. For the fall 2002 freshman class, 71 percent of the applicants were accepted.

For Further Information Contact Mr. Michael Momany, Executive Director of Enrollment Services, The University of Findlay, 1000 North Main Street, Findlay, OH 45840-3653. *Telephone:* 419-434-4732 or 800-548-0932 (toll-free). *Fax:* 419-434-4898. *E-mail:* admissions@findlay.edu. *Web site:* http://www.findlay.edu/.

See page 342 for a narrative description.

UNIVERSITY OF NORTHWESTERN OHIO

Lima, Ohio

University of Northwestern Ohio is a coed, private, primarily two-year college, founded in 1920, offering degrees at the associate and bachelor's levels. It has a 35-acre campus in Lima near Dayton and Toledo.

Academic Information The faculty has 95 members (72% full-time), 9% with terminal degrees. The student-faculty ratio is 24:1. The library holds 8,857 titles, 117 serial subscriptions, and 10 audiovisual materials. Special programs include academic remediation, cooperative (work-study) education, advanced placement credit, accelerated degree programs, double majors, distance learning, summer session for credit, part-time degree programs, and adult/continuing education programs. The most frequently chosen baccalaureate field is health professions and related sciences.
Student Body Statistics The student body is made up of 2,205 undergraduates (1,557 freshmen). 27 percent are women and 73 percent are men. Students come from 37 states and territories. 85 percent are from Ohio. 40 percent of the 2002 graduating class went on to four-year colleges.
Expenses for 2002–03 *Application fee:* $50. *Tuition:* $9612 full-time, $195 per credit part-time. *College room only:* $2400.
Financial Aid Forms of aid include need-based scholarships and part-time jobs. The priority application deadline for financial aid is April 1.
Freshman Admission University of Northwestern Ohio requires a high school transcript and TOEFL scores for international students. The application deadline for regular admission is rolling.
Transfer Admission The application deadline for admission is rolling.
Entrance Difficulty University of Northwestern Ohio has an open admission policy.

For Further Information Contact Mr. Dan Klopp, Vice President for Enrollment Management, University of Northwestern Ohio, 1441 North Cable Road, Lima, OH 45805-1498. *Telephone:* 419-227-3141. *Fax:* 419-229-6926. *E-mail:* info@nc.edu. *Web site:* http://www.unoh.edu/.

UNIVERSITY OF PHOENIX–OHIO CAMPUS

Independence, Ohio

University of Phoenix–Ohio Campus is a coed, proprietary, comprehensive institution, founded in 2000, offering degrees at the associate, bachelor's, master's, and doctoral levels and post-master's and postbachelor's certificates (courses conducted at 121 campuses and learning centers in 25 states).

Academic Information The faculty has 107 members (2% full-time), 21% with terminal degrees. The undergraduate student-faculty ratio is 13:1. The library holds 27 million titles and 11,648 serial subscriptions. Special programs include advanced placement credit, accelerated degree programs, independent study, distance learning, external degree programs, and adult/continuing education programs.
Student Body Statistics The student body totals 740, of whom 480 are undergraduates. 57 percent are women and 43 percent are men. 0.8 percent are international students.
Expenses for 2002–03 *Application fee:* $85. *Tuition:* $11,250 full-time, $375 per credit part-time.
Financial Aid The application deadline for financial aid is continuous.
Freshman Admission University of Phoenix–Ohio Campus requires 1 recommendation, 2 years of work experience, 23 years of age, and TOEFL scores for international students. A high school transcript is required for some. The application deadline for regular admission is rolling.
Transfer Admission The application deadline for admission is rolling.
Entrance Difficulty University of Phoenix–Ohio Campus has an open admission policy.

For Further Information Contact Ms. Beth Barilla, Director of Admissions, University of Phoenix–Ohio Campus, 4615 East Elwood Street, Mail Stop 10-0030, Phoenix, AZ 85040-1958. *Telephone:* 480-557-1712. *Fax:* 480-594-1758. *E-mail:* beth.barilla@apollogrp.edu. *Web site:* http://www.phoenix.edu/.

UNIVERSITY OF RIO GRANDE

Rio Grande, Ohio

Rio Grande is a coed, private, comprehensive institution, founded in 1876, offering degrees at the associate, bachelor's, and master's levels. It has a 170-acre campus in Rio Grande.

Academic Information The faculty has 146 members (58% full-time). The undergraduate student-faculty ratio is 18:1. The library holds 96,731 titles and 850 serial subscriptions. Special programs include academic remediation, services for learning-disabled students, an honors program, cooperative (work-study) education, advanced placement credit, accelerated degree programs, Freshman Honors College, ESL programs, independent study, self-designed majors, summer session for credit, part-time degree programs (daytime, evenings), adult/continuing education programs, and internships. The most frequently chosen baccalaureate fields are business/marketing, communications/communication technologies, education.
Student Body Statistics The student body totals 2,076, of whom 1,932 are undergraduates (343 freshmen). 59 percent are women and 41 percent are men. Students come from 11 states and territories and 15 other countries. 95 percent are from Ohio.
Expenses for 2002–03 *Application fee:* $15. *Area resident tuition:* $8976 full-time. *State resident tuition:* $9168 full-time. *Nonresident tuition:* $9936 full-time. *Mandatory fees:* $510 full-time. *College room and board:* $5442.
Financial Aid Forms of aid include need-based and non-need-based scholarships, athletic grants, and part-time jobs. The average aided 2001–02 undergraduate received an aid package worth $7406. The application deadline for financial aid is continuous.
Freshman Admission Rio Grande requires a high school transcript, medical history, ACT scores, and TOEFL scores for international students. The application deadline for regular admission is rolling.
Transfer Admission The application deadline for admission is rolling.
Entrance Difficulty Rio Grande has an open admission policy.
For Further Information Contact Mr. Mark F. Abell, Executive Director of Admissions, University of Rio Grande, PO Box 500, Rio Grande, OH 45674. *Telephone:* 740-245-5353 Ext. 7206, 800-288-2746 (toll-free in-state), or 800-282-7204 (toll-free out-of-state). *Fax:* 740-245-7260. *E-mail:* mabell@urgrgcc.edu. *Web site:* http://www.rio.edu/.

UNIVERSITY OF TOLEDO

Toledo, Ohio

UT is a coed, public university, founded in 1872, offering degrees at the associate, bachelor's, master's, doctoral, and first professional levels and post-master's and postbachelor's certificates. It has a 407-acre campus in Toledo near Detroit.

Academic Information The faculty has 1,180 members (58% full-time), 57% with terminal degrees. The undergraduate student-faculty ratio is 18:1. The library holds 1 million titles, 4,754 serial subscriptions, and 4,695 audiovisual materials. Special programs include academic remediation, services for learning-disabled students, an honors program, cooperative (work-study) education, study abroad, advanced placement credit, double majors, independent study, distance learning, self-designed majors, summer session for credit, part-time degree programs (daytime, evenings, weekends, summer), adult/continuing education programs, internships, and arrangement for off-campus study with Bowling Green State University, Medical College of Ohio, Consortium for Health Education, The Central States Universities, Inc. The most frequently chosen baccalaureate fields are business/marketing, education, engineering/engineering technologies.
Student Body Statistics The student body totals 20,889, of whom 17,563 are undergraduates (3,895 freshmen). 51 percent are women and 49 percent are men. Students come from 42 states and territories and 82 other countries. 91 percent are from Ohio. 2.3 percent are international students.
Expenses for 2002–03 *Application fee:* $40. *State resident tuition:* $4805 full-time, $250 per semester hour part-time. *Nonresident tuition:* $13,258 full-time, $602 per semester hour part-time. *Mandatory fees:* $1044 full-time. *College room and board:* $6511. Room and board charges vary according to board plan, housing facility, and location.
Financial Aid Forms of aid include need-based and non-need-based scholarships, athletic grants, and part-time jobs. The average aided 2002–03 undergraduate received an aid package worth an estimated $5539. The priority application deadline for financial aid is March 15.
Freshman Admission UT requires a high school transcript. TOEFL scores for international students are recommended. A minimum 2.0 high school GPA and SAT I or ACT scores are required for some. The application deadline for regular admission is rolling.
Transfer Admission The application deadline for admission is rolling.
Entrance Difficulty UT has an open admission policy for state residents. It assesses its entrance difficulty as moderately difficult for out-of-state applicants; moderately difficult for transfers; very difficult for physical therapy, engineering, pharmacy, legal assisting technology, pre-medicine, pre-dentistry programs.

For Further Information Contact Ms. Nancy Hintz, Assistant Director, University of Toledo, 2801 West Bancroft, Toledo, OH 43606-3398. *Telephone:* 419-530-5737 or 800-5TOLEDO (toll-free in-state). *Fax:* 419-530-5872. *E-mail:* enroll@utnet.utoledo.edu. *Web site:* http://www.utoledo.edu/.

URBANA UNIVERSITY

Urbana, Ohio

Urbana is a coed, private, comprehensive institution, founded in 1850, affiliated with the Church of the New Jerusalem, offering degrees at the associate, bachelor's, and master's levels. It has a 128-acre campus in Urbana near Columbus and Dayton.

Academic Information The faculty has 115 members (43% full-time), 39% with terminal degrees. The undergraduate student-faculty ratio is 16:1. The library holds 61,600 titles, 800 serial subscriptions, and 22,036

Urbana University (continued)

audiovisual materials. Special programs include academic remediation, services for learning-disabled students, an honors program, cooperative (work-study) education, advanced placement credit, accelerated degree programs, double majors, independent study, self-designed majors, summer session for credit, part-time degree programs (daytime, evenings, summer), adult/continuing education programs, internships, and arrangement for off-campus study with members of the Southwestern Ohio Council for Higher Education. The most frequently chosen baccalaureate fields are business/marketing, communications/communication technologies, education.
Student Body Statistics The student body totals 1,411, of whom 1,338 are undergraduates (159 freshmen). 56 percent are women and 44 percent are men. Students come from 11 states and territories and 2 other countries. 99 percent are from Ohio. 0.3 percent are international students. 11 percent of the 2002 graduating class went on to graduate and professional schools.
Expenses for 2003–04 *Application fee:* $25. *Comprehensive fee:* $18,950 includes full-time tuition ($13,540) and college room and board ($5410). Room and board charges vary according to board plan. *Part-time tuition:* $280 per semester hour. *Part-time mandatory fees:* $80 per year.
Financial Aid Forms of aid include need-based and non-need-based scholarships and part-time jobs. The average aided 2002–03 undergraduate received an aid package worth an estimated $11,636. The priority application deadline for financial aid is April 1.
Freshman Admission Urbana requires an essay, a high school transcript, a minimum 2.0 high school GPA, SAT I or ACT scores, and TOEFL scores for international students. An interview is recommended. 2 recommendations and an interview are required for some. The application deadline for regular admission is rolling.
Transfer Admission The application deadline for admission is rolling.
Entrance Difficulty Urbana assesses its entrance difficulty level as moderately difficult. For the fall 2002 freshman class, 57 percent of the applicants were accepted.

For Further Information Contact Ms. Melissa Tolle, Associate Director of Admissions, Urbana University, 579 College Way, Urbana, OH 93078. *Telephone:* 937-484-1356 or 800-7-URBANA (toll-free). *Fax:* 937-484-1389. *E-mail:* admiss@urbana.edu. *Web site:* http://www.urbana.edu/.

URSULINE COLLEGE

Pepper Pike, Ohio

Ursuline is a women's, private, Roman Catholic, comprehensive institution, founded in 1871, offering degrees at the bachelor's and master's levels (applications from men are also accepted). It has a 112-acre campus in Pepper Pike near Cleveland.

Academic Information The faculty has 186 members (33% full-time), 39% with terminal degrees. The undergraduate student-faculty ratio is 9:1. The library holds 126,491 titles, 332 serial subscriptions, and 6,926 audiovisual materials. Special programs include academic remediation, services for learning-disabled students, cooperative (work-study) education, advanced placement credit, accelerated degree programs, double majors, independent study, distance learning, summer session for credit, part-time degree programs (daytime, evenings, weekends, summer), adult/continuing education programs, internships, and arrangement for off-campus study with Baldwin-Wallace College, Case Western Reserve University, Cleveland State University, Cuyahoga Community College, David N. Myers College, Notre Dame College of Ohio, John Carroll University. The most frequently chosen baccalaureate fields are business/marketing, health professions and related sciences, psychology.
Student Body Statistics The student body totals 1,319, of whom 1,008 are undergraduates (97 freshmen). Students come from 8 states and territories and 7 other countries. 98 percent are from Ohio. 0.9 percent are international students.
Expenses for 2002–03 *Application fee:* $25. *Comprehensive fee:* $20,930 includes full-time tuition ($15,750), mandatory fees ($150), and college room and board ($5030). Room and board charges vary according to board plan. *Part-time tuition:* $525 per credit hour. *Part-time mandatory fees:* $40 per term.
Financial Aid Forms of aid include need-based and non-need-based scholarships, athletic grants, and part-time jobs. The average aided 2002–03 undergraduate received an aid package worth an estimated $13,976. The priority application deadline for financial aid is March 15.
Freshman Admission Ursuline requires a high school transcript, SAT I or ACT scores, and TOEFL scores for international students. An essay, a minimum 2.0 high school GPA, recommendations, and an interview are recommended. The application deadline for regular admission is rolling and for early action it is November 15.
Transfer Admission The application deadline for admission is rolling.
Entrance Difficulty Ursuline assesses its entrance difficulty level as minimally difficult. For the fall 2002 freshman class, 65 percent of the applicants were accepted.

For Further Information Contact Ms. Sarah Carr, Director of Admissions, Ursuline College, 2550 Lander Road, Pepper Pike, OH 44124. *Telephone:* 440-449-4203 or 888-URSULINE (toll-free). *Fax:* 440-684-6138. *E-mail:* admission@ursuline.edu. *Web site:* http://www.ursuline.edu/.

WALSH UNIVERSITY

North Canton, Ohio

Walsh is a coed, private, Roman Catholic, comprehensive institution, founded in 1958, offering degrees at the associate, bachelor's, and master's levels. It has a 100-acre campus in North Canton near Cleveland.

Academic Information The faculty has 177 members (38% full-time), 43% with terminal degrees. The undergraduate student-faculty ratio is 15:1. The library holds 132,957 titles, 663 serial subscriptions, and 1,434 audiovisual materials. Special programs include academic remediation, services for learning-disabled students, an honors program, advanced placement credit, accelerated degree programs, Freshman Honors College, ESL programs, double majors, self-designed majors, summer session for credit, part-time degree programs (daytime, evenings, weekends, summer), adult/continuing education programs, internships, and arrangement for off-campus study with University of Michigan, Case Western Reserve University, Stark State College of Technology. The most frequently chosen baccalaureate fields are business/marketing, education, health professions and related sciences.
Student Body Statistics The student body totals 1,648, of whom 1,480 are undergraduates (302 freshmen). 58 percent are women and 42 percent are men. Students come from 14 states and territories and 12 other countries. 98 percent are from Ohio. 1.2 percent are international students.
Expenses for 2003–04 *Application fee:* $25. *Comprehensive fee:* $23,450 includes full-time tuition ($14,250), mandatory fees ($450), and college room and board ($8750). *College room only:* $5650. Full-time tuition and fees vary according to course load. Room and board charges vary according to housing facility. *Part-time tuition:* $475 per credit. *Part-time mandatory fees:* $15 per credit.
Financial Aid Forms of aid include need-based and non-need-based scholarships, athletic grants, and part-time jobs. The average aided 2002–03 undergraduate received an aid package worth an estimated $9778. The application deadline for financial aid is continuous.
Freshman Admission Walsh requires a high school transcript, a minimum 2.1 high school GPA, SAT I or ACT scores, and TOEFL scores for international students. An interview is recommended. An essay, a minimum 3.0 high school GPA, and 2 recommendations are required for some. The application deadline for regular admission is rolling.
Transfer Admission The application deadline for admission is rolling.
Entrance Difficulty Walsh assesses its entrance difficulty level as moderately difficult. For the fall 2002 freshman class, 79 percent of the applicants were accepted.

For Further Information Contact Mr. Brett Freshour, Dean of Enrollment Management, Walsh University, 2020 Easton Street, NW, North Canton, OH 44720-3396. *Telephone:* 330-490-7171, 800-362-9846 (toll-free in-state), or 800-362-8846 (toll-free out-of-state). *Fax:* 330-490-7165. *E-mail:* admissions@walsh.edu. *Web site:* http://www.walsh.edu/.

WILBERFORCE UNIVERSITY

Wilberforce, Ohio

Wilberforce University is a coed, private, four-year college, founded in 1856, affiliated with the African Methodist Episcopal Church, offering degrees at the bachelor's level. It has a 125-acre campus in Wilberforce near Dayton.

Academic Information The faculty has 70 members (74% full-time). The student-faculty ratio is 14:1. The library holds 63,000 titles, 650 serial subscriptions, and 500 audiovisual materials. Special programs include academic remediation, an honors program, cooperative (work-study) education, study abroad, advanced placement credit, Freshman Honors College, external degree programs, and arrangement for off-campus study with 18 members of the Southwestern Ohio Council for Higher Education.
Student Body Statistics The student body is made up of 1,190 undergraduates (212 freshmen). 60 percent are women and 40 percent are men. Students come from 34 states and territories and 8 other countries. 46 percent are from Ohio. 1.4 percent are international students.
Expenses for 2002–03 *Application fee:* $20. *Comprehensive fee:* $16,100 includes full-time tuition ($9720), mandatory fees ($1060), and college room and board ($5320). *College room only:* $2820. *Part-time tuition:* $376 per credit hour.
Financial Aid Forms of aid include need-based and non-need-based scholarships and part-time jobs. The application deadline for financial aid is June 1 with a priority deadline of April 30.
Freshman Admission Wilberforce University requires an essay, a high school transcript, a minimum 2.0 high school GPA, 2 recommendations, SAT I or ACT scores, and TOEFL scores for international students. An interview is recommended. The application deadline for regular admission is July 1.
Transfer Admission The application deadline for admission is July 1.
Entrance Difficulty Wilberforce University assesses its entrance difficulty level as minimally difficult. For the fall 2002 freshman class, 28 percent of the applicants were accepted.

For Further Information Contact Mr. Kenneth C. Christmon, Director of Admissions, Wilberforce University, PO Box 1001, Wilberforce, OH 45384-1001. *Telephone:* 937-708-5789 or 800-367-8568 (toll-free). *Fax:* 937-376-4751. *E-mail:* kchristm@wilberforce.edu. *Web site:* http://www.wilberforce.edu/.

See page 354 for a narrative description.

WILMINGTON COLLEGE

Wilmington, Ohio

Wilmington College is a coed, private, Friends, comprehensive institution, founded in 1870, offering degrees at the bachelor's and master's levels. It has a 1,465-acre campus in Wilmington near Cincinnati and Columbus.

Academic Information The faculty has 131 members (50% full-time), 41% with terminal degrees. The undergraduate student-faculty ratio is 16:1. The library holds 103,706 titles, 408 serial subscriptions, and 1,280 audiovisual materials. Special programs include academic remediation, services for learning-disabled students, an honors program, study abroad, advanced placement credit, double majors, independent study, self-designed majors, summer session for credit, part-time degree programs (daytime, evenings, summer), adult/continuing education programs, internships, and arrangement for off-campus study with members of the Southwestern Ohio Council for Higher Education, Greater Cincinnati Consortium of Colleges and Universities. The most frequently chosen baccalaureate fields are business/marketing, agriculture, education.
Student Body Statistics The student body totals 1,262, of whom 1,231 are undergraduates (339 freshmen). 56 percent are women and 44 percent are men. Students come from 15 states and territories and 6 other countries. 95 percent are from Ohio. 0.6 percent are international students.
Expenses for 2003–04 *Application fee:* $25. *Comprehensive fee:* $24,172 includes full-time tuition ($17,256), mandatory fees ($426), and college room and board ($6490). *College room only:* $3080. Room and board charges vary according to board plan and housing facility. *Part-time tuition:* varies with course load.
Financial Aid Forms of aid include need-based and non-need-based scholarships and part-time jobs. The average aided 2001–02 undergraduate received an aid package worth $15,091. The application deadline for financial aid is June 1 with a priority deadline of March 1.
Freshman Admission Wilmington College requires a high school transcript, SAT I or ACT scores, and TOEFL scores for international students. A minimum 2.5 high school GPA, 1 recommendation, and an interview are recommended. The application deadline for regular admission is rolling.
Transfer Admission The application deadline for admission is rolling.
Entrance Difficulty Wilmington College assesses its entrance difficulty level as moderately difficult. For the fall 2002 freshman class, 83 percent of the applicants were accepted.

For Further Information Contact Ms. Tina Garland, Interim Director of Admission and Financial Aid, Wilmington College, Pyle Center Box 1325, 251 Ludovic Street, Wilmington, OH 45177. *Telephone:* 937-382-6661 Ext. 260 or 800-341-9318 Ext. 260 (toll-free). *Fax:* 937-382-7077. *E-mail:* admission@wilmington.edu. *Web site:* http://www.wilmington.edu/.

WITTENBERG UNIVERSITY

Springfield, Ohio

Wittenberg University is a coed, private, comprehensive institution, founded in 1845, affiliated with the Evangelical Lutheran Church, offering degrees at the bachelor's and master's levels. It has a 71-acre campus in Springfield near Columbus and Dayton.

Academic Information The faculty has 204 members (68% full-time), 70% with terminal degrees. The undergraduate student-faculty ratio is 14:1. The library holds 350,000 titles and 1,300 serial subscriptions. Special programs include academic remediation, an honors program, cooperative (work-study) education, study abroad, advanced placement credit, accelerated degree programs, Freshman Honors College, ESL programs, double majors, independent study, self-designed majors, summer session for credit, part-time degree programs (daytime, evenings, summer), external degree programs, adult/continuing education programs, internships, and arrangement for off-campus study with 21 members of the Southwestern Ohio Council for Higher Education.
Student Body Statistics The student body totals 2,346, of whom 2,320 are undergraduates (652 freshmen). 57 percent are women and 43 percent are men. Students come from 46 states and territories and 32 other countries. 57 percent are from Ohio. 2.5 percent are international students. 24 percent of the 2002 graduating class went on to graduate and professional schools.
Expenses for 2002–03 *Application fee:* $40. *One-time mandatory fee:* $150. *Comprehensive fee:* $29,826 includes full-time tuition ($23,610), mandatory fees ($150), and college room and board ($6066). *College room only:* $3134. Full-time tuition and fees vary according to course load. Room and board charges vary according to board plan. *Part-time tuition:* $787 per credit hour. *Part-time mandatory fees:* $150 per credit hour. Part-time tuition and fees vary according to course load.
Financial Aid Forms of aid include need-based and non-need-based scholarships and part-time jobs. The average aided 2002–03 undergraduate received an aid package worth an estimated $21,286. The application deadline for financial aid is March 15 with a priority deadline of February 15.
Freshman Admission Wittenberg University requires an essay, a high school transcript, 1 recommendation, SAT I or ACT scores, and TOEFL scores for international students. An interview and SAT II: Subject Test scores are recommended. An interview is required for some. The application deadline for regular admission is March 15; for early decision it is November 15; and for early action it is December 1.
Transfer Admission The application deadline for admission is rolling.
Entrance Difficulty Wittenberg University assesses its entrance difficulty level as moderately difficult; very difficult for International United Nations

Wittenberg University (continued)

Scholars Program, Institute of International Education Program. For the fall 2002 freshman class, 85 percent of the applicants were accepted.

For Further Information Contact Mr. Kenneth G. Benne, Dean of Admissions and Financial Aid, Wittenberg University, PO Box 720, Springfield, OH 45501-0720. *Telephone:* 937-327-6314 Ext. 6366 or 800-677-7558 Ext. 6314 (toll-free). *Fax:* 937-327-6379. *E-mail:* admission@wittenberg.edu. *Web site:* http://www.wittenberg.edu/.

WRIGHT STATE UNIVERSITY

Dayton, Ohio

Wright State is a coed, public university, founded in 1964, offering degrees at the associate, bachelor's, master's, doctoral, and first professional levels and postbachelor's certificates. It has a 557-acre campus in Dayton near Cincinnati and Columbus.

Academic Information The faculty has 850 members (60% full-time). The undergraduate student-faculty ratio is 20:1. The library holds 695,805 titles and 5,312 serial subscriptions. Special programs include academic remediation, services for learning-disabled students, an honors program, cooperative (work-study) education, study abroad, advanced placement credit, ESL programs, self-designed majors, summer session for credit, part-time degree programs, adult/continuing education programs, internships, and arrangement for off-campus study with members of the Southwestern Ohio Council for Higher Education. The most frequently chosen baccalaureate fields are business/marketing, communications/communication technologies, education.
Student Body Statistics The student body totals 16,517, of whom 12,531 are undergraduates (2,356 freshmen). 57 percent are women and 43 percent are men. Students come from 49 states and territories and 69 other countries. 97 percent are from Ohio. 1.1 percent are international students.
Expenses for 2002–03 *Application fee:* $30. *State resident tuition:* $5361 full-time, $166 per hour part-time. *Nonresident tuition:* $10,524 full-time, $326 per hour part-time. *College room and board:* $5772. Room and board charges vary according to board plan and housing facility.
Financial Aid Forms of aid include need-based and non-need-based scholarships and part-time jobs. The average aided 2002–03 undergraduate received an aid package worth an estimated $7857. The priority application deadline for financial aid is February 15.
Freshman Admission Wright State requires a high school transcript, SAT I or ACT scores, and TOEFL scores for international students. A minimum 2.0 high school GPA is recommended. The application deadline for regular admission is rolling.
Transfer Admission The application deadline for admission is rolling.
Entrance Difficulty Wright State assesses its entrance difficulty level as minimally difficult; moderately difficult for out-of-state applicants. For the fall 2002 freshman class, 92 percent of the applicants were accepted.

For Further Information Contact Ms. Cathy Davis, Director of Undergraduate Admissions, Wright State University, 3640 Colonel Glenn Highway, Dayton, OH 45435. *Telephone:* 937-775-5700 or 800-247-1770 (toll-free). *Fax:* 937-775-5795. *E-mail:* admissions@wright.edu. *Web site:* http://www.wright.edu/.

XAVIER UNIVERSITY

Cincinnati, Ohio

Xavier is a coed, private, Roman Catholic, comprehensive institution, founded in 1831, offering degrees at the associate, bachelor's, master's, and doctoral levels and post-master's and postbachelor's certificates. It has a 100-acre campus in Cincinnati.

Academic Information The faculty has 577 members (46% full-time), 47% with terminal degrees. The undergraduate student-faculty ratio is 13:1. The library holds 191,923 titles, 1,633 serial subscriptions, and 8,371 audiovisual materials. Special programs include academic remediation, services for learning-disabled students, an honors program, cooperative (work-study) education, study abroad, advanced placement credit, ESL programs, double majors, independent study, summer session for credit, part-time degree programs (daytime, evenings, weekends, summer), adult/continuing education programs, internships, and arrangement for off-campus study with 13 members of the Greater Cincinnati Consortium of Colleges and Universities. The most frequently chosen baccalaureate fields are business/marketing, communications/communication technologies, liberal arts/general studies.
Student Body Statistics The student body totals 6,573, of whom 3,942 are undergraduates (757 freshmen). 58 percent are women and 42 percent are men. Students come from 46 states and territories and 51 other countries. 66 percent are from Ohio. 2.6 percent are international students. 19.8 percent of the 2002 graduating class went on to graduate and professional schools.
Expenses for 2002–03 *Application fee:* $30. *Comprehensive fee:* $25,620 includes full-time tuition ($17,780), mandatory fees ($240), and college room and board ($7600). *College room only:* $4190. Full-time tuition and fees vary according to program. Room and board charges vary according to board plan and housing facility. *Part-time tuition:* $385 per credit hour. Part-time tuition varies according to course load.
Financial Aid Forms of aid include need-based and non-need-based scholarships, athletic grants, and part-time jobs. The average aided 2002–03 undergraduate received an aid package worth an estimated $12,947. The priority application deadline for financial aid is February 15.
Freshman Admission Xavier requires an essay, a high school transcript, 1 recommendation, SAT I or ACT scores, and TOEFL scores for international students. An interview is recommended. The application deadline for regular admission is February 1.
Transfer Admission The application deadline for admission is rolling.
Entrance Difficulty Xavier assesses its entrance difficulty level as moderately difficult; very difficult for occupational therapy program; dual enrollment medical program with University of Cincinnati. For the fall 2002 freshman class, 83 percent of the applicants were accepted.

For Further Information Contact Mr. Marc Camille, Dean of Admission, Xavier University, 3800 Victory Parkway, Cincinnati, OH 45207-5311. *Telephone:* 513-745-3301 or 800-344-4698 (toll-free). *Fax:* 513-745-4319. *E-mail:* xuadmit@xu.edu. *Web site:* http://www.xu.edu/.

YOUNGSTOWN STATE UNIVERSITY

Youngstown, Ohio

YSU is a coed, public, comprehensive institution, founded in 1908, offering degrees at the associate, bachelor's, master's, and doctoral levels and postbachelor's certificates. It has a 150-acre campus in Youngstown near Cleveland and Pittsburgh.

Academic Information The faculty has 894 members (45% full-time), 50% with terminal degrees. The undergraduate student-faculty ratio is 18:1. The library holds 991,501 titles, 2,908 serial subscriptions, and 16,976 audiovisual materials. Special programs include academic remediation, services for learning-disabled students, an honors program, cooperative (work-study) education, study abroad, advanced placement credit, accelerated degree programs, ESL programs, double majors, distance learning, self-designed majors, summer session for credit, part-time degree programs (daytime, evenings, weekends, summer), adult/continuing education programs, internships, and arrangement for off-campus study with Lorain County Community College. The most frequently chosen baccalaureate fields are business/marketing, education, protective services/public administration.
Student Body Statistics The student body totals 12,698, of whom 11,375 are undergraduates (2,172 freshmen). 54 percent are women and 46 percent are men. Students come from 37 states and territories and 51 other countries. 91 percent are from Ohio. 0.8 percent are international students.
Expenses for 2003–04 *Application fee:* $30. *State resident tuition:* $4344 full-time, $181 per credit part-time. *Nonresident tuition:* $9524 full-time, $412 per credit part-time. *Mandatory fees:* $1128 full-time, $42 per credit part-time. Full-time tuition and fees vary according to course load. Part-time tuition and fees vary according to course load. *College room and board:* $5700. Room and board charges vary according to board plan and housing facility.
Financial Aid Forms of aid include need-based and non-need-based scholarships, athletic grants, and part-time jobs. The priority application deadline for financial aid is February 15.

Freshman Admission YSU requires a high school transcript, SAT I or ACT scores, and TOEFL scores for international students. An interview is required for some. The application deadline for regular admission is August 15 and for early action it is February 15.
Transfer Admission The application deadline for admission is August 15.
Entrance Difficulty YSU has an open admission policy for state residents, students from Mercer and Lawrence Counties in Pennsylvania. It assesses its entrance difficulty as minimally difficult for out-of-state applicants; minimally difficult for transfers; moderately difficult for nursing, engineering, engineering technology, health occupations programs.

For Further Information Contact Ms. Sue Davis, Director of Undergraduate Admissions, Youngstown State University, One University Plaza, Youngstown, OH 44555-0001. *Telephone:* 330-941-2000, 877-468-6978 (toll-free in-state), or 877-466-6978 (toll-free out-of-state). *Fax:* 330-941-3674. *E-mail:* enroll@ysu.edu. *Web site:* http://www.ysu.edu/.

See page 358 for a narrative description.

Oklahoma

AMERICAN CHRISTIAN COLLEGE AND SEMINARY

Oklahoma City, Oklahoma

American Christian College and Seminary is a coed, private, interdenominational, comprehensive institution, founded in 1976, offering degrees at the associate, bachelor's, master's, doctoral, and first professional levels. It has a 1-acre campus in Oklahoma City near Oklahoma City.

Academic Information The faculty has 36 members (47% full-time), 75% with terminal degrees. The undergraduate student-faculty ratio is 8:1. The library holds 14,652 titles, 47 serial subscriptions, and 554 audiovisual materials. Special programs include cooperative (work-study) education, advanced placement credit, independent study, distance learning, summer session for credit, part-time degree programs (daytime, evenings, weekends, summer), external degree programs, adult/continuing education programs, and internships. The most frequently chosen baccalaureate field is philosophy, religion, and theology.
Student Body Statistics The student body totals 484, of whom 292 are undergraduates. 45 percent are women and 55 percent are men.
Expenses for 2002–03 *Application fee:* $50. *Tuition:* $3420 full-time, $420 per course part-time. *Mandatory fees:* $156 full-time, $80 per year part-time.
Financial Aid Forms of aid include need-based scholarships and part-time jobs. The priority application deadline for financial aid is July 15.
Freshman Admission American Christian College and Seminary requires a high school transcript. The application deadline for regular admission is September 9.
Transfer Admission The application deadline for admission is September 9.
Entrance Difficulty American Christian College and Seminary has an open admission policy.

For Further Information Contact Dr. Mitchel Beville, Vice President of Business Affairs/Admissions, American Christian College and Seminary, 4300 Highline Boulevard #202, Oklahoma City, OK 73108. *Telephone:* 405-945-0100 Ext. 120 or 800-488-2528 (toll-free). *Fax:* 405-945-0311. *E-mail:* info@accs.edu. *Web site:* http://www.accs.edu/.

BACONE COLLEGE

Muskogee, Oklahoma

Bacone is a coed, private, primarily two-year college, founded in 1880, affiliated with the American Baptist Churches in the U.S.A., offering degrees at the associate and bachelor's levels. It has a 187-acre campus in Muskogee near Tulsa.

Academic Information The faculty has 34 members, 29% with terminal degrees. The student-faculty ratio is 15:1. The library holds 34,564 titles, 121 serial subscriptions, and 185 audiovisual materials. Special programs include academic remediation, services for learning-disabled students, cooperative (work-study) education, advanced placement credit, accelerated degree programs, self-designed majors, summer session for credit, part-time degree programs (daytime, evenings, weekends, summer), adult/continuing education programs, and internships.
Student Body Statistics Students come from 29 states and territories and 16 other countries. 95 percent are from Oklahoma. 3.4 percent are international students. 80 percent of the 2002 graduating class went on to four-year colleges.
Expenses for 2003–04 *Application fee:* $25.
Financial Aid Forms of aid include need-based scholarships and part-time jobs. The priority application deadline for financial aid is March 31.
Freshman Admission Bacone requires a high school transcript, a minimum 2.0 high school GPA, minimum ACT score of 14, SAT I or ACT scores, and TOEFL scores for international students. The application deadline for regular admission is rolling.
Transfer Admission The application deadline for admission is rolling.
Entrance Difficulty Bacone assesses its entrance difficulty level as minimally difficult; moderately difficult for nursing, radiological technology programs.

For Further Information Contact Ms. Jean Kay, Administrative Assistant, Bacone College, 2299 Old Bacone Road, Muskogee, OK 74403. *Telephone:* 918-781-7349 or 888-682-5514 Ext. 7340 (toll-free). *Fax:* 918-682-5514. *E-mail:* admissions@bacone.edu. *Web site:* http://www.bacone.edu/.

BARTLESVILLE WESLEYAN COLLEGE

See Oklahoma Wesleyan University

CAMERON UNIVERSITY

Lawton, Oklahoma

Cameron is a coed, public, comprehensive unit of Oklahoma State Regents for Higher Education, founded in 1908, offering degrees at the associate, bachelor's, and master's levels. It has a 160-acre campus in Lawton.

Academic Information The faculty has 458 members (41% full-time), 24% with terminal degrees. The undergraduate student-faculty ratio is 19:1. The library holds 258,000 titles, 3,840 serial subscriptions, and 7,053 audiovisual materials. Special programs include academic remediation, services for learning-disabled students, an honors program, advanced placement credit, accelerated degree programs, double majors, independent study, distance learning, summer session for credit, part-time degree programs (daytime, evenings, weekends, summer), adult/continuing education programs, and arrangement for off-campus study with University of Oklahoma, East Central University, Oklahoma State University. The most frequently chosen baccalaureate fields are business/marketing, protective services/public administration, social sciences and history.
Student Body Statistics The student body totals 5,298, of whom 4,811 are undergraduates (899 freshmen). 58 percent are women and 42 percent are men. Students come from 22 states and territories and 21 other countries. 98 percent are from Oklahoma. 2.4 percent are international students.
Expenses for 2002–03 *Application fee:* $15. *State resident tuition:* $2370 full-time, $78.65 per hour part-time. *Nonresident tuition:* $5700 full-time, $189.10 per hour part-time. *Mandatory fees:* $150 full-time, $80 per term part-time. Full-time tuition and fees vary according to course level, course

Cameron University (continued)
load, degree level, and student level. Part-time tuition and fees vary according to course level, course load, degree level, and student level. *College room and board:* $2830. Room and board charges vary according to board plan.
Financial Aid Forms of aid include need-based and non-need-based scholarships, athletic grants, and part-time jobs. The average aided 2002–03 undergraduate received an aid package worth an estimated $3825. The application deadline for financial aid is continuous.
Freshman Admission Cameron requires a high school transcript, SAT I or ACT scores, and TOEFL scores for international students. The application deadline for regular admission is rolling.
Transfer Admission The application deadline for admission is rolling.
Entrance Difficulty Cameron assesses its entrance difficulty level as minimally difficult. For the fall 2002 freshman class, 95 percent of the applicants were accepted.

For Further Information Contact Ms. Brenda Dally, Coordinator of Student Recruitment, Cameron University, Cameron University, Attention: Admissions, 2800 West Gore Boulevard, Lawton, OK 73505. *Telephone:* 580-581-2288 or 888-454-7600 (toll-free). *Fax:* 580-581-5514. *E-mail:* admiss@cua.cameron.edu. *Web site:* http://www.cameron.edu/.

EAST CENTRAL UNIVERSITY

Ada, Oklahoma

East Central is a coed, public, comprehensive unit of Oklahoma State Regents for Higher Education, founded in 1909, offering degrees at the bachelor's and master's levels. It has a 140-acre campus in Ada near Oklahoma City.

Academic Information The undergraduate student-faculty ratio is 19:1. The library holds 213,000 titles and 800 serial subscriptions. Special programs include academic remediation, services for learning-disabled students, an honors program, advanced placement credit, accelerated degree programs, double majors, distance learning, summer session for credit, part-time degree programs, adult/continuing education programs, internships, and arrangement for off-campus study with Ardmore Higher Education Center. The most frequently chosen baccalaureate field is law/legal studies.
Student Body Statistics The student body totals 4,195, of whom 3,423 are undergraduates (1,197 freshmen). 59 percent are women and 41 percent are men. Students come from 20 states and territories and 25 other countries. 97 percent are from Oklahoma. 2.6 percent are international students.
Expenses for 2002–03 *State resident tuition:* $1718 full-time. *Nonresident tuition:* $3314 full-time. *Mandatory fees:* $653 full-time. Full-time tuition and fees vary according to course level, course load, and student level. *College room and board:* $2646. *College room only:* $910. Room and board charges vary according to board plan and housing facility.
Financial Aid Forms of aid include need-based and non-need-based scholarships, athletic grants, and part-time jobs. The average aided 2002–03 undergraduate received an aid package worth an estimated $7105. The priority application deadline for financial aid is March 1.
Freshman Admission East Central requires a high school transcript, SAT I or ACT scores, and TOEFL scores for international students. ACT scores are recommended. A minimum 2.7 high school GPA and rank in upper 50% of high school class are required for some. The application deadline for regular admission is September 1.
Transfer Admission The application deadline for admission is September 1.
Entrance Difficulty East Central assesses its entrance difficulty level as moderately difficult; minimally difficult for transfers.

For Further Information Contact Ms. Pamela Armstrong, Registrar, East Central University, PMBJ8, 1100 East 14th Street, Ada, OK 74820-6999. *Telephone:* 580-332-8000 Ext. 239. *Fax:* 580-310-5432. *E-mail:* parmstro@mailclerk.ecok.edu. *Web site:* http://www.ecok.edu/.

HILLSDALE FREE WILL BAPTIST COLLEGE

Moore, Oklahoma

Hillsdale is a coed, private, Free Will Baptist, comprehensive institution, founded in 1959, offering degrees at the associate, bachelor's, and master's levels. It has a 40-acre campus in Moore near Oklahoma City.

Academic Information The faculty has 51 members (49% full-time), 22% with terminal degrees. The undergraduate student-faculty ratio is 14:1. The library holds 20,102 titles, 363 serial subscriptions, and 1,800 audiovisual materials. Special programs include academic remediation, advanced placement credit, accelerated degree programs, ESL programs, double majors, independent study, summer session for credit, part-time degree programs (daytime, evenings, summer), adult/continuing education programs, and internships. The most frequently chosen baccalaureate fields are business/marketing, interdisciplinary studies, philosophy, religion, and theology.
Student Body Statistics The student body totals 290, of whom 282 are undergraduates (74 freshmen). 41 percent are women and 59 percent are men. Students come from 15 states and territories and 13 other countries. 81 percent are from Oklahoma. 7.6 percent are international students. 17 percent of the 2002 graduating class went on to graduate and professional schools.
Expenses for 2003–04 *Application fee:* $20. *Comprehensive fee:* $10,890 includes full-time tuition ($5900), mandatory fees ($890), and college room and board ($4100). *College room only:* $1900. Full-time tuition and fees vary according to course load. Room and board charges vary according to board plan and housing facility. *Part-time tuition:* $215 per credit hour. *Part-time mandatory fees:* $10 per credit hour, $145 per term. Part-time tuition and fees vary according to course load.
Financial Aid Forms of aid include need-based and non-need-based scholarships and part-time jobs. The application deadline for financial aid is continuous.
Freshman Admission Hillsdale requires an essay, a high school transcript, 1 recommendation, Biblical foundation statement, student conduct pledge; medical form required for some, SAT I or ACT scores, and TOEFL scores for international students. A minimum 2.0 high school GPA and 2 recommendations are recommended. 1 recommendation and an interview are required for some. The application deadline for regular admission is rolling.
Transfer Admission The application deadline for admission is rolling.
Entrance Difficulty Hillsdale assesses its entrance difficulty level as noncompetitive. For the fall 2002 freshman class, 98 percent of the applicants were accepted.

For Further Information Contact Ms. Sue Chaffin, Registrar/Assistant Director of Admissions, Hillsdale Free Will Baptist College, PO Box 7208, Moore, OK 73153-1208. *Telephone:* 405-912-9006. *Fax:* 405-912-9050. *E-mail:* hillsdale@hc.edu. *Web site:* http://www.hc.edu/.

LANGSTON UNIVERSITY

Langston, Oklahoma

Langston University is a coed, public, comprehensive unit of Oklahoma State Regents for Higher Education, founded in 1897, offering degrees at the associate, bachelor's, and master's levels. It has a 40-acre campus in Langston near Oklahoma City.

Academic Information The undergraduate student-faculty ratio is 30:1. The library holds 97,565 titles, 1,235 serial subscriptions, and 4,974 audiovisual materials. Special programs include academic remediation, services for learning-disabled students, an honors program, cooperative (work-study) education, advanced placement credit, accelerated degree programs, summer session for credit, part-time degree programs (daytime, evenings, weekends, summer), adult/continuing education programs, and internships. The most frequently chosen baccalaureate fields are education, health professions and related sciences, psychology.
Student Body Statistics The student body totals 3,008, of whom 2,898 are undergraduates (481 freshmen). 57 percent are women and 43 percent are men. Students come from 37 states and territories and 8 other countries. 0.5 percent are international students.

Expenses for 2002–03 *Area resident tuition:* $54.50 per credit hour part-time. *State resident tuition:* $1635 full-time. *Nonresident tuition:* $4547 full-time, $155.55 per credit hour part-time. *Mandatory fees:* $922 full-time, $19.70 per credit hour part-time, $122.50 per term part-time. Full-time tuition and fees vary according to course level. *College room and board:* $1680.
Financial Aid Forms of aid include need-based and non-need-based scholarships, athletic grants, and part-time jobs. The average aided 2002–03 undergraduate received an aid package worth an estimated $6391. The priority application deadline for financial aid is March 15.
Freshman Admission Langston University requires a high school transcript, a minimum 2.70 high school GPA, SAT I or ACT scores, and TOEFL scores for international students. Recommendations are required for some. The application deadline for regular admission is rolling.
Transfer Admission The application deadline for admission is rolling.
Entrance Difficulty Langston University has an open admission policy. It assesses its entrance difficulty as moderately difficult for out-of-state applicants; moderately difficult for transfers.

For Further Information Contact Brent Russell, Assistant Director of Admission, Langston University, Langston University, PO Box 728, Langston, OK 73120. *Telephone:* 405-466-2980 or 405-466-3428 (toll-free). *Fax:* 405-466-3391. *Web site:* http://www.lunet.edu/.

METROPOLITAN COLLEGE
Oklahoma City, Oklahoma

Metropolitan College is a coed, primarily women's, proprietary, four-year college of Wyandotte Collegiate Systems, offering degrees at the associate and bachelor's levels.

Academic Information The faculty has 18 members (17% full-time), 61% with terminal degrees.
Student Body Statistics The student body is made up of 140 undergraduates. 94 percent are women and 6 percent are men. 0.7 percent are international students.
Expenses for 2002–03 *Application fee:* $50. *Tuition:* $6718 full-time, $4357 per year part-time.
Financial Aid The application deadline for financial aid is continuous.
Freshman Admission Metropolitan College requires a high school transcript, an interview, and Wonderlic aptitude test.
Entrance Difficulty Metropolitan College has an open admission policy.

For Further Information Contact Ms. Pamela Picken, Admissions Director, Metropolitan College, 1900 NW Expressway R-302, Oklahoma City, OK 73118. *Telephone:* 405-843-1000. *Fax:* 405-528-0320. *Web site:* http://www.metropolitancollege.edu/.

METROPOLITAN COLLEGE
Tulsa, Oklahoma

Metropolitan College is a coed, primarily women's, proprietary, four-year college, offering degrees at the associate and bachelor's levels.

Academic Information The faculty has 16 members (25% full-time), 50% with terminal degrees. The student-faculty ratio is 15:1. Special programs include academic remediation, accelerated degree programs, part-time degree programs (daytime, evenings), adult/continuing education programs, and internships.
Student Body Statistics The student body is made up of 149 undergraduates (30 freshmen). 94 percent are women and 6 percent are men. Students come from 3 states and territories. 99 percent are from Oklahoma.
Expenses for 2002–03 *Application fee:* $50. *Tuition:* $6535 full-time, $200 per credit hour part-time. Full-time tuition varies according to course load and program.
Financial Aid The application deadline for financial aid is continuous.
Freshman Admission Metropolitan College requires a high school transcript, an interview, and Wonderlic aptitude test.
Entrance Difficulty Metropolitan College has an open admission policy.

For Further Information Contact Ms. Toby Quoss, Admissions Director, Metropolitan College, 4528 South Sheridan Road, Suite 105, Tulsa, OK 74145-1011. *Telephone:* 918-627-9300. *Fax:* 918-627-2122. *Web site:* http://www.metropolitancollege.edu/.

MID-AMERICA CHRISTIAN UNIVERSITY
Oklahoma City, Oklahoma

For Information Write to Mid-America Christian University, Oklahoma City, OK 73170-4504.

NORTHEASTERN STATE UNIVERSITY
Tahlequah, Oklahoma

NSU is a coed, public, comprehensive unit of Oklahoma State Regents for Higher Education, founded in 1846, offering degrees at the bachelor's, master's, and first professional levels. It has a 160-acre campus in Tahlequah near Tulsa.

Academic Information The faculty has 446 members. The undergraduate student-faculty ratio is 24:1. The library holds 424,818 titles, 3,983 serial subscriptions, and 6,804 audiovisual materials. Special programs include academic remediation, services for learning-disabled students, an honors program, advanced placement credit, ESL programs, double majors, distance learning, summer session for credit, part-time degree programs, adult/continuing education programs, and internships. The most frequently chosen baccalaureate fields are business/marketing, education, protective services/public administration.
Student Body Statistics The student body totals 8,985, of whom 7,777 are undergraduates (1,231 freshmen). 59 percent are women and 41 percent are men. Students come from 31 states and territories and 40 other countries. 100 percent are from Oklahoma. 1.3 percent are international students.
Expenses for 2003–04 *Application fee:* $0. *State resident tuition:* $2275 full-time, $75.85 per credit hour part-time. *Nonresident tuition:* $5268 full-time, $175.60 per credit hour part-time. *Mandatory fees:* $150 full-time. Full-time tuition and fees vary according to course level and student level. Part-time tuition varies according to course level and student level. *College room and board:* $2960. Room and board charges vary according to board plan and housing facility.
Financial Aid Forms of aid include need-based and non-need-based scholarships, athletic grants, and part-time jobs. The average aided 2001–02 undergraduate received an aid package worth $7200. The priority application deadline for financial aid is April 1.
Freshman Admission NSU requires a high school transcript, ACT scores, and TOEFL scores for international students. Recommendations and an interview are required for some. The application deadline for regular admission is August 5.
Transfer Admission The application deadline for admission is August 5.
Entrance Difficulty NSU assesses its entrance difficulty level as moderately difficult; minimally difficult for transfers. For the fall 2002 freshman class, 87 percent of the applicants were accepted.

For Further Information Contact Mr. Todd Essary, Director of High School and College Relations, Northeastern State University, 601 North Grand, Tahlequah, OK 74464. *Telephone:* 918-456-5511 Ext. 2200 or 800-722-9614 (toll-free in-state). *Fax:* 918-458-2342. *E-mail:* nsuadmis@nsuok.edu. *Web site:* http://www.nsuok.edu/.

NORTHWESTERN OKLAHOMA STATE UNIVERSITY
Alva, Oklahoma

NWOSU is a coed, public, comprehensive unit of Oklahoma State Regents for Higher Education, founded in 1897, offering degrees at

Northwestern Oklahoma State University (continued)
the bachelor's and master's levels and post-master's and postbachelor's certificates. It has a 70-acre campus in Alva.

Academic Information The faculty has 131 members (56% full-time), 39% with terminal degrees. The undergraduate student-faculty ratio is 16:1. The library holds 299,974 titles, 1,411 serial subscriptions, and 3,466 audiovisual materials. Special programs include academic remediation, services for learning-disabled students, study abroad, advanced placement credit, double majors, independent study, distance learning, summer session for credit, part-time degree programs (daytime, evenings, weekends, summer), adult/continuing education programs, internships, and arrangement for off-campus study with Northern Oklahoma College, Southwestern Oklahoma State University. The most frequently chosen baccalaureate fields are business/marketing, education, protective services/ public administration.
Student Body Statistics The student body totals 2,013, of whom 1,776 are undergraduates (302 freshmen). 57 percent are women and 43 percent are men. Students come from 28 states and territories and 25 other countries. 84 percent are from Oklahoma. 1.7 percent are international students.
Expenses for 2002–03 *Application fee:* $15. *State resident tuition:* $2237 full-time, $73.95 per credit hour part-time. *Nonresident tuition:* $5390 full-time, $173.70 per credit hour part-time. *Mandatory fees:* $86 full-time, $16 per term part-time. Full-time tuition and fees vary according to course load, location, and student level. Part-time tuition and fees vary according to course load, location, and student level. *College room and board:* $2600. *College room only:* $860. Room and board charges vary according to board plan.
Financial Aid Forms of aid include need-based and non-need-based scholarships, athletic grants, and part-time jobs. The average aided 2001–02 undergraduate received an aid package worth $3780. The priority application deadline for financial aid is March 1.
Freshman Admission NWOSU requires a high school transcript, SAT I or ACT scores, and TOEFL scores for international students. An essay, a minimum 2.0 high school GPA, and 3 recommendations are required for some. The application deadline for regular admission is rolling.
Transfer Admission The application deadline for admission is rolling.
Entrance Difficulty NWOSU assesses its entrance difficulty level as moderately difficult. For the fall 2002 freshman class, 96 percent of the applicants were accepted.

For Further Information Contact Mrs. Shirley Murrow, Registrar, Northwestern Oklahoma State University, 709 Oklahoma Boulevard, Alva, OK 73717-2799. *Telephone:* 580-327-8550. *Fax:* 580-327-8699. *E-mail:* smmurrow@nwosu.edu. *Web site:* http://www.nwosu.edu/.

OKLAHOMA BAPTIST UNIVERSITY

Shawnee, Oklahoma

OBU is a coed, private, Southern Baptist, comprehensive institution, founded in 1910, offering degrees at the bachelor's and master's levels. It has a 125-acre campus in Shawnee near Oklahoma City.

Academic Information The faculty has 119 members. The undergraduate student-faculty ratio is 15:1. The library holds 230,000 titles, 1,800 serial subscriptions, and 1,600 audiovisual materials. Special programs include academic remediation, services for learning-disabled students, an honors program, cooperative (work-study) education, study abroad, advanced placement credit, double majors, independent study, self-designed majors, summer session for credit, part-time degree programs (daytime, summer), internships, and arrangement for off-campus study with St. Gregory's University. The most frequently chosen baccalaureate fields are education, business/marketing, health professions and related sciences.
Student Body Statistics The student body totals 1,933, of whom 1,911 are undergraduates (435 freshmen). 56 percent are women and 44 percent are men. Students come from 42 states and territories and 19 other countries. 61 percent are from Oklahoma.
Expenses for 2002–03 *Application fee:* $25. *Comprehensive fee:* $14,790 includes full-time tuition ($10,300), mandatory fees ($740), and college room and board ($3750). *College room only:* $1650. Full-time tuition and fees vary according to course load. Room and board charges vary according to board plan and housing facility. *Part-time tuition:* $325 per credit hour. Part-time tuition varies according to course load.
Financial Aid Forms of aid include need-based and non-need-based scholarships, athletic grants, and part-time jobs. The average aided 2002–03 undergraduate received an aid package worth an estimated $11,142. The priority application deadline for financial aid is March 1.
Freshman Admission OBU requires a high school transcript, a minimum 2.5 high school GPA, SAT I or ACT scores, and TOEFL scores for international students. An essay, recommendations, and an interview are required for some. The application deadline for regular admission is August 1.
Transfer Admission The application deadline for admission is August 1.
Entrance Difficulty OBU assesses its entrance difficulty level as moderately difficult. For the fall 2002 freshman class, 86 percent of the applicants were accepted.

For Further Information Contact Mr. Michael Cappo, Dean of Admissions, Oklahoma Baptist University, Box 61174, Shawnee, OK 74804. *Telephone:* 405-878-2033 or 800-654-3285 (toll-free). *Fax:* 405-878-2046. *E-mail:* admissions@mail.okbu.edu. *Web site:* http://www.okbu.edu/.

OKLAHOMA CHRISTIAN UNIVERSITY

Oklahoma City, Oklahoma

Oklahoma Christian is a coed, private, comprehensive institution, founded in 1950, affiliated with the Church of Christ, offering degrees at the bachelor's and master's levels. It has a 200-acre campus in Oklahoma City.

Academic Information The faculty has 204 members (53% full-time), 52% with terminal degrees. The undergraduate student-faculty ratio is 13:1. The library holds 99,916 titles, 990 serial subscriptions, and 10,232 audiovisual materials. Special programs include academic remediation, services for learning-disabled students, an honors program, study abroad, advanced placement credit, accelerated degree programs, ESL programs, double majors, distance learning, summer session for credit, adult/ continuing education programs, internships, and arrangement for off-campus study with University of Central Oklahoma. The most frequently chosen baccalaureate fields are business/marketing, biological/ life sciences, education.
Student Body Statistics The student body totals 1,718, of whom 1,599 are undergraduates (426 freshmen). 53 percent are women and 47 percent are men. 45 percent are from Oklahoma.
Expenses for 2002–03 *Application fee:* $25. *One-time mandatory fee:* $45. *Comprehensive fee:* $17,200 includes full-time tuition ($11,100), mandatory fees ($1600), and college room and board ($4500). Full-time tuition and fees vary according to course load. Room and board charges vary according to housing facility. *Part-time tuition:* $465 per credit hour. *Part-time mandatory fees:* $767 per term. Part-time tuition and fees vary according to course load.
Financial Aid Forms of aid include need-based and non-need-based scholarships, athletic grants, and part-time jobs. The average aided 2002–03 undergraduate received an aid package worth an estimated $11,048. The application deadline for financial aid is August 31 with a priority deadline of March 15.
Freshman Admission Oklahoma Christian requires a high school transcript, SAT I or ACT scores, and TOEFL scores for international students. The application deadline for regular admission is rolling.
Transfer Admission The application deadline for admission is rolling.
Entrance Difficulty Oklahoma Christian has an open admission policy.

For Further Information Contact Ms. Rita Forrester, Director of Admissions, Oklahoma Christian University, Box 11000, Oklahoma City, OK 73136-1100. *Telephone:* 405-425-5050 or 800-877-5010 (toll-free in-state). *Fax:* 405-425-5208. *E-mail:* info@oc.edu. *Web site:* http://www.oc.edu/.

OKLAHOMA CITY UNIVERSITY

Oklahoma City, Oklahoma

OCU is a coed, private, United Methodist, comprehensive institution, founded in 1904, offering degrees at the bachelor's, master's, and first professional levels. It has a 68-acre campus in Oklahoma City.

Academic Information The faculty has 304 members (57% full-time), 56% with terminal degrees. The undergraduate student-faculty ratio is 14:1. The library holds 321,093 titles, 5,498 serial subscriptions, and 10,132 audiovisual materials. Special programs include academic remediation, services for learning-disabled students, an honors program, cooperative (work-study) education, study abroad, advanced placement credit, accelerated degree programs, ESL programs, double majors, independent study, self-designed majors, summer session for credit, part-time degree programs (daytime, evenings, summer), external degree programs, adult/continuing education programs, internships, and arrangement for off-campus study with American University. The most frequently chosen baccalaureate fields are liberal arts/general studies, business/marketing, visual/performing arts.

Student Body Statistics The student body totals 3,529, of whom 1,710 are undergraduates (258 freshmen). 60 percent are women and 40 percent are men. Students come from 49 states and territories and 75 other countries. 32 percent are from Oklahoma. 22 percent are international students.

Expenses for 2002–03 *Application fee:* $30. *Comprehensive fee:* $17,200 includes full-time tuition ($11,600), mandatory fees ($400), and college room and board ($5200). Full-time tuition and fees vary according to program. Room and board charges vary according to board plan and housing facility. *Part-time tuition:* $395 per semester hour. *Part-time mandatory fees:* $100 per term. Part-time tuition and fees vary according to program.

Financial Aid Forms of aid include need-based and non-need-based scholarships, athletic grants, and part-time jobs. The average aided 2001–02 undergraduate received an aid package worth $8796. The priority application deadline for financial aid is March 1.

Freshman Admission OCU requires a high school transcript, a minimum 2.5 high school GPA, SAT I or ACT scores, and TOEFL scores for international students. An interview and audition for music and dance programs are required for some. The application deadline for regular admission is August 22.

Transfer Admission The application deadline for admission is rolling.

Entrance Difficulty OCU assesses its entrance difficulty level as moderately difficult. For the fall 2002 freshman class, 67 percent of the applicants were accepted.

For Further Information Contact Ms. Shery Boyles, Director of Admissions, Oklahoma City University, 2501 North Blackwelder, Oklahoma City, OK 73106. *Telephone:* 405-521-5050 or 800-633-7242 (toll-free). *Fax:* 405-521-5916. *E-mail:* uadmissions@okcu.edu. *Web site:* http://www.okcu.edu/.

OKLAHOMA PANHANDLE STATE UNIVERSITY

Goodwell, Oklahoma

OPSU is a coed, public, four-year college of Oklahoma State Regents for Higher Education, founded in 1909, offering degrees at the associate and bachelor's levels. It has a 40-acre campus in Goodwell.

Academic Information The faculty has 65 members (82% full-time), 31% with terminal degrees. The student-faculty ratio is 22:1. The library holds 106,000 titles, 308 serial subscriptions, and 2,079 audiovisual materials. Special programs include academic remediation, cooperative (work-study) education, advanced placement credit, accelerated degree programs, ESL programs, double majors, distance learning, summer session for credit, part-time degree programs (daytime, evenings, summer), adult/continuing education programs, and internships. The most frequently chosen baccalaureate fields are agriculture, business/marketing, education.

Student Body Statistics The student body is made up of 1,226 undergraduates (222 freshmen). 53 percent are women and 47 percent are men. Students come from 36 states and territories and 26 other countries. 48 percent are from Oklahoma. 5 percent are international students.

Expenses for 2002–03 *Application fee:* $0. *State resident tuition:* $1718 full-time, $56.05 per credit hour part-time. *Nonresident tuition:* $3134 full-time, $99.75 per credit hour part-time. *Mandatory fees:* $454 full-time, $12.40 per credit hour part-time, $41 per term part-time. Full-time tuition and fees vary according to course level. Part-time tuition and fees vary according to course level. *College room and board:* $2810. *College room only:* $930. Room and board charges vary according to board plan, housing facility, and student level.

Financial Aid Forms of aid include need-based and non-need-based scholarships and part-time jobs. The average aided 2002–03 undergraduate received an aid package worth an estimated $9200. The priority application deadline for financial aid is January 1.

Freshman Admission OPSU requires a high school transcript, SAT I or ACT scores, and TOEFL scores for international students. The application deadline for regular admission is rolling.

Transfer Admission The application deadline for admission is rolling.

Entrance Difficulty OPSU has an open admission policy.

For Further Information Contact Mr. Vic Shrock, Registrar and Director of Admissions, Oklahoma Panhandle State University, PO Box 430, 323 Eagle Boulevard, Goodwell, OK 73939-0430. *Telephone:* 580-349-1376 or 800-664-6778 (toll-free). *Fax:* 580-349-2302. *E-mail:* opsu@opsu.edu. *Web site:* http://www.opsu.edu/.

OKLAHOMA STATE UNIVERSITY

Stillwater, Oklahoma

OSU is a coed, public unit of Oklahoma State University, founded in 1890, offering degrees at the bachelor's, master's, doctoral, and first professional levels. It has an 840-acre campus in Stillwater near Oklahoma City and Tulsa.

Academic Information The faculty has 1,122 members (86% full-time), 83% with terminal degrees. The undergraduate student-faculty ratio is 19:1. The library holds 2 million titles, 24,806 serial subscriptions, and 510,548 audiovisual materials. Special programs include academic remediation, services for learning-disabled students, an honors program, cooperative (work-study) education, study abroad, advanced placement credit, accelerated degree programs, Freshman Honors College, ESL programs, double majors, independent study, distance learning, self-designed majors, summer session for credit, part-time degree programs (daytime, evenings, weekends, summer), adult/continuing education programs, internships, and arrangement for off-campus study with National Student Exchange. The most frequently chosen baccalaureate fields are business/marketing, agriculture, engineering/engineering technologies.

Student Body Statistics The student body totals 22,992, of whom 18,043 are undergraduates (3,265 freshmen). 49 percent are women and 51 percent are men. Students come from 50 states and territories and 122 other countries. 88 percent are from Oklahoma. 4.6 percent are international students.

Expenses for 2002–03 *Application fee:* $25. *State resident tuition:* $2163 full-time, $69.80 per credit hour part-time. *Nonresident tuition:* $7217 full-time, $228.35 per credit hour part-time. *Mandatory fees:* $862 full-time, $22.73 per credit part-time, $90 per term part-time. Full-time tuition and fees vary according to course level. Part-time tuition and fees vary according to course level. *College room and board:* $5150. *College room only:* $2374. Room and board charges vary according to board plan, housing facility, and location.

Financial Aid Forms of aid include need-based and non-need-based scholarships, athletic grants, and part-time jobs. The average aided 2001–02 undergraduate received an aid package worth $7550. The application deadline for financial aid is continuous.

Freshman Admission OSU requires a high school transcript, a minimum 3.0 high school GPA, class rank, SAT I or ACT scores, and TOEFL scores for international students. ACT scores are recommended. An interview is required for some. The application deadline for regular admission is rolling.

Transfer Admission The application deadline for admission is rolling.

Oklahoma State University (continued)

Entrance Difficulty OSU assesses its entrance difficulty level as moderately difficult. For the fall 2002 freshman class, 92 percent of the applicants were accepted.

For Further Information Contact Ms. Paulette Cundiff, Coordinator of Admissions Processing, Oklahoma State University, 324 Student Union, Stillwater, OK 74078. *Telephone:* 405-744-7275, 800-233-5019 (toll-free in-state), or 800-852-1255 (toll-free out-of-state). *Fax:* 405-744-5285. *E-mail:* admit@okstate.edu. *Web site:* http://www.okstate.edu/.

OKLAHOMA WESLEYAN UNIVERSITY

Bartlesville, Oklahoma

Oklahoma Wesleyan University is a coed, private, comprehensive institution, founded in 1909, affiliated with the Wesleyan Church, offering degrees at the associate, bachelor's, and master's levels. It has a 127-acre campus in Bartlesville near Tulsa.

Academic Information The faculty has 37 members. The undergraduate student-faculty ratio is 14:1. The library holds 124,722 titles and 300 serial subscriptions. Special programs include academic remediation, cooperative (work-study) education, advanced placement credit, ESL programs, independent study, distance learning, self-designed majors, summer session for credit, part-time degree programs, adult/continuing education programs, internships, and arrangement for off-campus study with Tri-County Technical College, Coalition for Christian Colleges and Universities.
Student Body Statistics The student body is made up of 675 undergraduates. Students come from 26 states and territories and 8 other countries. 54 percent are from Oklahoma. 10 percent of the 2002 graduating class went on to graduate and professional schools.
Expenses for 2002–03 *Application fee:* $25. *Comprehensive fee:* $14,500 includes full-time tuition ($9800), mandatory fees ($600), and college room and board ($4100). *College room only:* $2000. Room and board charges vary according to board plan and housing facility. *Part-time tuition:* $360 per semester hour. *Part-time mandatory fees:* $40 per semester hour.
Financial Aid Forms of aid include need-based and non-need-based scholarships, athletic grants, and part-time jobs. The average aided 2001–02 undergraduate received an aid package worth $6466. The priority application deadline for financial aid is March 31.
Freshman Admission Oklahoma Wesleyan University requires a high school transcript, recommendations, minimum ACT of 18 or SAT 860, and SAT I or ACT scores. A minimum 2.0 high school GPA and TOEFL scores for international students are recommended. The application deadline for regular admission is rolling.
Transfer Admission The application deadline for admission is rolling.
Entrance Difficulty Oklahoma Wesleyan University assesses its entrance difficulty level as minimally difficult. For the fall 2002 freshman class, 60 percent of the applicants were accepted.

For Further Information Contact Mr. Jim Weidman, Director of Enrollment Services, Oklahoma Wesleyan University, 2201 Silver Lake Road, Bartlesville, OK 74006-6299. *Telephone:* 800-468-6292 or 800-468-6292 (toll-free in-state). *Fax:* 918-335-6229. *E-mail:* admissions@okwu.edu. *Web site:* http://www.okwu.edu/.

ORAL ROBERTS UNIVERSITY

Tulsa, Oklahoma

ORU is a coed, private, interdenominational, comprehensive institution, founded in 1963, offering degrees at the bachelor's, master's, doctoral, and first professional levels. It has a 263-acre campus in Tulsa.

Academic Information The faculty has 289 members (72% full-time), 47% with terminal degrees. The undergraduate student-faculty ratio is 16:1. The library holds 216,691 titles, 600 serial subscriptions, and 25,445 audiovisual materials. Special programs include academic remediation, services for learning-disabled students, an honors program, study abroad, advanced placement credit, Freshman Honors College, ESL programs, double majors, independent study, distance learning, self-designed majors, summer session for credit, part-time degree programs, external degree programs, adult/continuing education programs, internships, and arrangement for off-campus study with Christian College Coalition. The most frequently chosen baccalaureate fields are business/marketing, communications/communication technologies, philosophy, religion, and theology.
Student Body Statistics The student body totals 3,542, of whom 3,041 are undergraduates (582 freshmen). 59 percent are women and 41 percent are men. 36 percent are from Oklahoma. 3.3 percent are international students.
Expenses for 2002–03 *Application fee:* $35. *Comprehensive fee:* $18,550 includes full-time tuition ($12,600), mandatory fees ($380), and college room and board ($5570). *College room only:* $2720. Room and board charges vary according to board plan. *Part-time tuition:* $525 per credit hour. *Part-time mandatory fees:* $90 per term.
Financial Aid Forms of aid include need-based and non-need-based scholarships, athletic grants, and part-time jobs. The average aided 2001–02 undergraduate received an aid package worth $12,448. The priority application deadline for financial aid is March 15.
Freshman Admission ORU requires an essay, a high school transcript, a minimum 2.0 high school GPA, 1 recommendation, proof of immunization, SAT I or ACT scores, and TOEFL scores for international students. An interview is required for some. The application deadline for regular admission is rolling and for early action it is September 1.
Transfer Admission The application deadline for admission is rolling.
Entrance Difficulty ORU assesses its entrance difficulty level as moderately difficult; noncompetitive for transfers. For the fall 2002 freshman class, 72 percent of the applicants were accepted.

For Further Information Contact Chris Miller, Director of Undergraduate Admissions, Oral Roberts University, Tulsa, OK 74171. *Telephone:* 918-495-6518 or 800-678-8876 (toll-free). *Fax:* 918-495-6222. *E-mail:* admissions@oru.edu. *Web site:* http://www.oru.edu/.

ROGERS STATE UNIVERSITY

Claremore, Oklahoma

Rogers State University is a coed, public, four-year college of Oklahoma State Regents for Higher Education, founded in 1909, offering degrees at the associate and bachelor's levels. It has a 40-acre campus in Claremore near Tulsa.

Academic Information The faculty has 151 members (58% full-time), 38% with terminal degrees. The student-faculty ratio is 19:1. The library holds 57,283 titles, 524 serial subscriptions, and 4,844 audiovisual materials. Special programs include academic remediation, services for learning-disabled students, cooperative (work-study) education, advanced placement credit, double majors, independent study, distance learning, summer session for credit, part-time degree programs (daytime, evenings, weekends, summer), external degree programs, adult/continuing education programs, internships, and arrangement for off-campus study with Northeast Technology Centers, Claremore and Pryor, OK; Tri-County Technology Center, Bartlesville, OK; University Learning Center of Northern Oklahoma; Central Technology Center, Drumright, OK.
Student Body Statistics The student body is made up of 3,300 undergraduates (763 freshmen). 63 percent are women and 37 percent are men. 97 percent are from Oklahoma.
Expenses for 2002–03 *Application fee:* $0. *State resident tuition:* $1345 full-time, $56 per credit part-time. *Nonresident tuition:* $3739 full-time, $156 per credit part-time. *Mandatory fees:* $494 full-time, $20 per credit part-time, $15 per term part-time. Full-time tuition and fees vary according to course level and course load. Part-time tuition and fees vary according to course level and course load. *College room only:* $3321.
Financial Aid Forms of aid include need-based scholarships and part-time jobs. The application deadline for financial aid is continuous.
Freshman Admission Rogers State University requires a high school transcript and TOEFL scores for international students. A minimum 2.7 high school GPA, ACT scores, and ACT COMPASS (for students over 21) are required for some. The application deadline for regular admission is rolling.
Transfer Admission The application deadline for admission is rolling.

Entrance Difficulty Rogers State University has an open admission policy for applicants to the Associate's degree program or the Certificate program.

For Further Information Contact Ms. Becky Noah, Director of Enrollment Management, Rogers State University, Roger's State University, Office of Admissions, 1701 West Will Rogers Boulevard, Claremore, OK 74017. *Telephone:* 918-343-7545 or 800-256-7511 (toll-free). *Fax:* 918-343-7595. *E-mail:* shunter@rsu.edu. *Web site:* http://www.rsu.edu/.

ST. GREGORY'S UNIVERSITY

Shawnee, Oklahoma

St. Gregory's University is a coed, private, Roman Catholic, four-year college, founded in 1875, offering degrees at the associate and bachelor's levels. It has a 640-acre campus in Shawnee near Oklahoma City.

Academic Information The faculty has 87 members (40% full-time), 26% with terminal degrees. The student-faculty ratio is 17:1. The library holds 55,500 titles and 284 serial subscriptions. Special programs include academic remediation, services for learning-disabled students, an honors program, study abroad, advanced placement credit, ESL programs, double majors, independent study, self-designed majors, summer session for credit, part-time degree programs (daytime, evenings, summer), external degree programs, adult/continuing education programs, internships, and arrangement for off-campus study with Oklahoma Baptist University; Edge Hill College, England. The most frequently chosen baccalaureate fields are business/marketing, health professions and related sciences, social sciences and history.
Student Body Statistics The student body is made up of 793 undergraduates (162 freshmen). 51 percent are women and 49 percent are men. Students come from 20 states and territories and 17 other countries. 91 percent are from Oklahoma. 10.2 percent are international students. 20 percent of the 2002 graduating class went on to graduate and professional schools.
Expenses for 2003–04 *Application fee:* $25. *Comprehensive fee:* $15,254 includes full-time tuition ($9680), mandatory fees ($770), and college room and board ($4804). Room and board charges vary according to board plan and housing facility. *Part-time tuition:* $322 per hour. Part-time tuition varies according to course load and reciprocity agreements.
Financial Aid Forms of aid include need-based and non-need-based scholarships, athletic grants, and part-time jobs. The average aided 2001–02 undergraduate received an aid package worth $8037. The application deadline for financial aid is continuous.
Freshman Admission St. Gregory's University requires a high school transcript, a minimum 2.0 high school GPA, SAT I or ACT scores, and TOEFL scores for international students. An essay, recommendations, and an interview are required for some. The application deadline for regular admission is rolling.
Transfer Admission The application deadline for admission is rolling.
Entrance Difficulty St. Gregory's University assesses its entrance difficulty level as minimally difficult. For the fall 2002 freshman class, 86 percent of the applicants were accepted.

For Further Information Contact Mr. Dan Rutledge, Director of Admissions, St. Gregory's University, 1900 West MacArthur Drive, Shawnee, OK 74804. *Telephone:* 405-878-5447 or 888-STGREGS (toll-free). *Fax:* 405-878-5198. *E-mail:* admissions@sgc.edu. *Web site:* http://www.sgc.edu/.

SOUTHEASTERN OKLAHOMA STATE UNIVERSITY

Durant, Oklahoma

SOSU is a coed, public, comprehensive unit of Oklahoma State Regents for Higher Education, founded in 1909, offering degrees at the bachelor's and master's levels and post-master's certificates. It has a 176-acre campus in Durant.

Academic Information The faculty has 226 members (69% full-time), 53% with terminal degrees. The undergraduate student-faculty ratio is 19:1. The library holds 187,971 titles, 671 serial subscriptions, and 5,291 audiovisual materials. Special programs include academic remediation, services for learning-disabled students, an honors program, advanced placement credit, accelerated degree programs, double majors, independent study, distance learning, summer session for credit, part-time degree programs (daytime, evenings), adult/continuing education programs, internships, and arrangement for off-campus study with Ardmore Higher Education Center, E.T. Dunlap Higher Education Center. The most frequently chosen baccalaureate fields are business/marketing, education, engineering/engineering technologies.
Student Body Statistics The student body totals 4,033, of whom 3,637 are undergraduates (593 freshmen). 53 percent are women and 47 percent are men. Students come from 34 states and territories and 25 other countries. 78 percent are from Oklahoma. 1.8 percent are international students.
Expenses for 2003–04 *Application fee:* $20. *State resident tuition:* $1,682 full-time, $56.05 per credit hour part-time. *Nonresident tuition:* $4674 full-time, $155.80 per credit hour part-time. *Mandatory fees:* $722 full-time, $20.70 per semester hour part-time, $50.50 per term part-time. Full-time tuition and fees vary according to course level. Part-time tuition and fees vary according to course level and course load. *College room and board:* $2670. *College room only:* $1000. Room and board charges vary according to board plan and housing facility.
Financial Aid Forms of aid include need-based and non-need-based scholarships, athletic grants, and part-time jobs. The average aided 2001–02 undergraduate received an aid package worth $3111. The priority application deadline for financial aid is March 1.
Freshman Admission SOSU requires a high school transcript and TOEFL scores for international students. An interview, ACT scores, and SAT II: Subject Test scores are required for some. The application deadline for regular admission is rolling.
Transfer Admission The application deadline for admission is rolling.
Entrance Difficulty SOSU has an open admission policy for adults over 21. It assesses its entrance difficulty as minimally difficult for transfers; very difficult for honors program.

For Further Information Contact Mr. Kyle Stafford, Director of Admissions and Enrollment Services, Southeastern Oklahoma State University, 1405 North 4th Avenue PMB 4225, Durant, OK 74701-0609. *Telephone:* 580-745-2060 or 800-435-1327 Ext. 2060 (toll-free). *Fax:* 580-745-7502. *E-mail:* admissions@sosu.edu. *Web site:* http://www.sosu.edu/.

SOUTHERN NAZARENE UNIVERSITY

Bethany, Oklahoma

SNU is a coed, private, Nazarene, comprehensive institution, founded in 1899, offering degrees at the associate, bachelor's, and master's levels. It has a 40-acre campus in Bethany near Oklahoma City.

Academic Information The faculty has 203 members (36% full-time). The undergraduate student-faculty ratio is 21:1. The library holds 115,564 titles and 2,748 audiovisual materials. Special programs include academic remediation, services for learning-disabled students, an honors program, study abroad, advanced placement credit, accelerated degree programs, double majors, self-designed majors, summer session for credit, part-time degree programs (daytime, evenings, summer), external degree programs, adult/continuing education programs, internships, and arrangement for off-campus study with Christian College Coalition Council for Christian Colleges and Universities. The most frequently chosen baccalaureate fields are business/marketing, health professions and related sciences, social sciences and history.
Student Body Statistics The student body totals 2,120, of whom 1,780 are undergraduates (310 freshmen). 54 percent are women and 46 percent are men. Students come from 32 states and territories and 17 other countries. 53 percent are from Oklahoma. 1.1 percent are international students. 22 percent of the 2002 graduating class went on to graduate and professional schools.

Southern Nazarene University (continued)

Expenses for 2003–04 *Application fee:* $25. *Comprehensive fee:* $16,948 includes full-time tuition ($11,310), mandatory fees ($680), and college room and board ($4958). *College room only:* $2362. Room and board charges vary according to board plan.
Financial Aid Forms of aid include need-based and non-need-based scholarships and part-time jobs. The priority application deadline for financial aid is March 1.
Freshman Admission SNU requires a high school transcript, SAT I or ACT scores, and TOEFL scores for international students. An interview is recommended. The application deadline for regular admission is August 15.
Transfer Admission The application deadline for admission is August 15.
Entrance Difficulty SNU has an open admission policy.

For Further Information Contact Mr. Larry Hess, Director of Admissions, Southern Nazarene University, 6729 Northwest 39th Expressway, Bethany, OK 73008. *Telephone:* 405-491-6324 or 800-648-9899 (toll-free). *Fax:* 405-491-6320. *E-mail:* admiss@snu.edu.

SOUTHWESTERN CHRISTIAN UNIVERSITY

Bethany, Oklahoma

For Information Write to Southwestern Christian University, Bethany, OK 73008-0340.

SOUTHWESTERN OKLAHOMA STATE UNIVERSITY

Weatherford, Oklahoma

Southwestern is a coed, public, comprehensive unit of Southwestern Oklahoma State University, founded in 1901, offering degrees at the bachelor's, master's, and first professional levels. It has a 73-acre campus in Weatherford near Oklahoma City.

Academic Information The faculty has 228 members (86% full-time), 57% with terminal degrees. The undergraduate student-faculty ratio is 20:1. The library holds 217,051 titles, 1,230 serial subscriptions, and 6,718 audiovisual materials. Special programs include academic remediation, services for learning-disabled students, cooperative (work-study) education, advanced placement credit, accelerated degree programs, double majors, independent study, distance learning, self-designed majors, summer session for credit, part-time degree programs (daytime, evenings, summer), adult/continuing education programs, internships, and arrangement for off-campus study with Academic Common Market. The most frequently chosen baccalaureate fields are business/marketing, education, health professions and related sciences.
Student Body Statistics The student body totals 4,652, of whom 4,015 are undergraduates (912 freshmen). 56 percent are women and 44 percent are men. Students come from 32 states and territories and 32 other countries. 90 percent are from Oklahoma. 2.6 percent are international students.
Expenses for 2002–03 *Application fee:* $15. *State resident tuition:* $1700 full-time, $56 per hour part-time. *Nonresident tuition:* $4853 full-time, $156 per hour part-time. *Mandatory fees:* $748 full-time, $23.05 per hour part-time, $57 per term part-time. *College room and board:* $2680. *College room only:* $1050. Room and board charges vary according to board plan.
Financial Aid Forms of aid include need-based and non-need-based scholarships, athletic grants, and part-time jobs. The average aided 2002–03 undergraduate received an aid package worth an estimated $3377. The application deadline for financial aid is March 1.
Freshman Admission Southwestern requires a high school transcript, a minimum 2.0 high school GPA, ACT scores, and TOEFL scores for international students.
Entrance Difficulty Southwestern assesses its entrance difficulty level as moderately difficult. For the fall 2002 freshman class, 94 percent of the applicants were accepted.

For Further Information Contact Ms. Connie Phillips, Admission Counselor, Southwestern Oklahoma State University, 100 Campus Drive, Weatherford, OK 73096. *Telephone:* 580-774-3777. *Fax:* 580-774-3795. *E-mail:* phillic@swosu.edu. *Web site:* http://www.swosu.edu/.

SPARTAN SCHOOL OF AERONAUTICS

Tulsa, Oklahoma

Spartan School of Aeronautics is a coed, primarily men's, proprietary, primarily two-year college of National Education Centers, Inc, founded in 1928, offering degrees at the associate and bachelor's levels. It has a 26-acre campus in Tulsa.

Academic Information The faculty has 150 members (80% full-time). The library holds 18,000 titles and 160 serial subscriptions. Special programs include academic remediation, advanced placement credit, and ESL programs.
Student Body Statistics The student body is made up of 1,625 undergraduates. 4 percent are women and 96 percent are men. Students come from 52 states and territories and 40 other countries. 85 percent are from Oklahoma. 11.7 percent are international students. 2 percent of the 2002 graduating class went on to four-year colleges.
Financial Aid Forms of aid include need-based scholarships and part-time jobs. The application deadline for financial aid is continuous.
Freshman Admission Spartan School of Aeronautics requires a high school transcript, TOEFL scores for international students, and ACT ASSET. An interview is recommended. The application deadline for regular admission is rolling.
Transfer Admission The application deadline for admission is rolling.
Entrance Difficulty Spartan School of Aeronautics has an open admission policy.

For Further Information Contact Mr. John Buck, Vice President of Marketing, Spartan School of Aeronautics, 8820 East Pine Street, PO Box 582833, Tulsa, OK 74158-2833. *Telephone:* 918-836-6886 Ext. 231. *Web site:* http://www.spartan.edu/.

UNIVERSITY OF BIBLICAL STUDIES AND SEMINARY

See American Christian College and Seminary

UNIVERSITY OF CENTRAL OKLAHOMA

Edmond, Oklahoma

UCO is a coed, public, comprehensive unit of Oklahoma State Regents for Higher Education, founded in 1890, offering degrees at the bachelor's and master's levels. It has a 200-acre campus in Edmond near Oklahoma City.

Academic Information The faculty has 713 members (53% full-time), 52% with terminal degrees. The undergraduate student-faculty ratio is 20:1. The library holds 254,478 titles, 3,707 serial subscriptions, and 37,484 audiovisual materials. Special programs include services for learning-disabled students, an honors program, advanced placement credit, accelerated degree programs, ESL programs, double majors, independent study, distance learning, summer session for credit, part-time degree programs (daytime, evenings, weekends, summer), adult/continuing education programs, and internships. The most frequently chosen baccalaureate fields are business/marketing, education, law/legal studies.
Student Body Statistics The student body totals 14,099, of whom 11,790 are undergraduates (2,045 freshmen). 57 percent are women and 43

percent are men. Students come from 38 states and territories and 108 other countries. 98 percent are from Oklahoma. 10 percent are international students.
Expenses for 2002–03 *Application fee:* $15. *State resident tuition:* $1681 full-time, $56.05 per semester hour part-time. *Nonresident tuition:* $4674 full-time, $155.80 per semester hour part-time. *Mandatory fees:* $529 full-time, $17.65 per semester hour part-time. Full-time tuition and fees vary according to course level, course load, program, and student level. Part-time tuition and fees vary according to course level, course load, program, and student level. *College room and board:* $3600. Room and board charges vary according to board plan and housing facility.
Financial Aid Forms of aid include need-based and non-need-based scholarships, athletic grants, and part-time jobs. The average aided 2001–02 undergraduate received an aid package worth $5000. The application deadline for financial aid is continuous.
Freshman Admission UCO requires a high school transcript, a minimum 2.7 high school GPA, rank in upper 50% of high school class, SAT I or ACT scores, and TOEFL scores for international students. The application deadline for regular admission is rolling.
Transfer Admission The application deadline for admission is rolling.
Entrance Difficulty UCO assesses its entrance difficulty level as minimally difficult. For the fall 2002 freshman class, 96 percent of the applicants were accepted.

For Further Information Contact Ms. Linda Lofton, Director, Admissions and Records Processing, University of Central Oklahoma, Office of Enrollment Services, 100 North University Drive, Box 151, Edmond, OK 73034. *Telephone:* 405-974-2338 Ext. 2338 or 800-254-4215 (toll-free in-state). *Fax:* 405-341-4964. *E-mail:* admituco@ucok.edu. *Web site:* http://www.ucok.edu/.

UNIVERSITY OF OKLAHOMA

Norman, Oklahoma

OU is a coed, public university, founded in 1890, offering degrees at the bachelor's, master's, doctoral, and first professional levels and post-master's certificates. It has a 3,500-acre campus in Norman near Oklahoma City.

Academic Information The faculty has 1,177 members (82% full-time), 80% with terminal degrees. The undergraduate student-faculty ratio is 21:1. The library holds 4 million titles, 26,696 serial subscriptions, and 7,647 audiovisual materials. Special programs include academic remediation, services for learning-disabled students, an honors program, cooperative (work-study) education, study abroad, advanced placement credit, accelerated degree programs, Freshman Honors College, ESL programs, double majors, independent study, distance learning, self-designed majors, summer session for credit, part-time degree programs (daytime, evenings, weekends, summer), external degree programs, adult/continuing education programs, internships, and arrangement for off-campus study with Oklahoma State University, Langston University, Northeastern State University, Rose State College, Oklahoma City Community College, Rogers University, Cameron University. The most frequently chosen baccalaureate fields are business/marketing, engineering/engineering technologies, social sciences and history.
Student Body Statistics The student body totals 23,799, of whom 19,570 are undergraduates (3,833 freshmen). 49 percent are women and 51 percent are men. Students come from 50 states and territories and 79 other countries. 81 percent are from Oklahoma. 2.8 percent are international students.
Expenses for 2002–03 *Application fee:* $25. *State resident tuition:* $2163 full-time, $72 per credit hour part-time. *Nonresident tuition:* $7311 full-time, $244 per credit hour part-time. *Mandatory fees:* $766 full-time, $20.62 per credit part-time, $74 per term part-time. Full-time tuition and fees vary according to course level, course load, location, program, and reciprocity agreements. Part-time tuition and fees vary according to course level, course load, location, program, and reciprocity agreements. *College room and board:* $5030. *College room only:* $2564. Room and board charges vary according to board plan and housing facility.
Financial Aid Forms of aid include need-based and non-need-based scholarships, athletic grants, and part-time jobs. The average aided 2001–02 undergraduate received an aid package worth $7635. The application deadline for financial aid is continuous.
Freshman Admission OU requires a high school transcript, a minimum 3.0 high school GPA, SAT I or ACT scores, and TOEFL scores for international students. An essay is required for some. The application deadline for regular admission is June 1.
Transfer Admission The application deadline for admission is rolling.
Entrance Difficulty OU assesses its entrance difficulty level as moderately difficult; most difficult for honors college program. For the fall 2002 freshman class, 89 percent of the applicants were accepted.

For Further Information Contact Karen Renfroe, Executive Director of Recruitment Services, University of Oklahoma, 1000 Asp Avenue, Norman, OK 73019. *Telephone:* 405-325-4521 or 800-234-6868 (toll-free). *Fax:* 405-325-7124. *E-mail:* admrec@ou.edu. *Web site:* http://www.ou.edu/.

UNIVERSITY OF OKLAHOMA HEALTH SCIENCES CENTER

Oklahoma City, Oklahoma

OU Health Sciences Center is a coed, public, upper-level unit of University of Oklahoma, founded in 1890, offering degrees at the bachelor's, master's, doctoral, and first professional levels and post-master's, first professional, and postbachelor's certificates. It has a 200-acre campus in Oklahoma City.

Academic Information The faculty has 347 members (65% full-time), 95% with terminal degrees. The library holds 234,000 titles and 2,658 serial subscriptions. Special programs include an honors program, advanced placement credit, distance learning, summer session for credit, part-time degree programs (daytime, evenings, summer), and internships. The most frequently chosen baccalaureate field is health professions and related sciences.
Student Body Statistics The student body totals 2,935, of whom 621 are undergraduates. 90 percent are women and 10 percent are men. Students come from 18 states and territories and 4 other countries. 91 percent are from Oklahoma. 1.6 percent are international students.
Expenses for 2002–03 *Application fee:* $25. *State resident tuition:* $1,786 full-time, $74.40 per credit part-time. *Nonresident tuition:* $6,148 full-time, $256.15 per credit part-time. *Mandatory fees:* $544 full-time, $10.50 per credit hour part-time, $61 per term part-time.
Financial Aid Forms of aid include non-need-based scholarships.
Transfer Admission OU Health Sciences Center requires a college transcript and a minimum 2.0 college GPA. Standardized test scores are required for some. The application deadline for admission is October 1.
Entrance Difficulty OU Health Sciences Center assesses its entrance difficulty level as moderately difficult. For the fall 2002 entering class, 52 percent of the applicants were accepted.

For Further Information Contact Ms. Leslie Wilbourn, Director of Admissions and Records, University of Oklahoma Health Sciences Center, BSE-200, PO Box 26901, 941 S. L. Young Boulevard, Oklahoma City, OK 73190. *Telephone:* 405-271-2359 Ext. 48902. *Fax:* 405-271-2480. *E-mail:* admissions@ouhsc.edu. *Web site:* http://www.ouhsc.edu/.

UNIVERSITY OF PHOENIX–OKLAHOMA CITY CAMPUS

Oklahoma City, Oklahoma

University of Phoenix–Oklahoma City Campus is a coed, proprietary, comprehensive institution, founded in 1976, offering degrees at the associate, bachelor's, master's, and doctoral levels and post-master's and postbachelor's certificates (courses conducted at 121 campuses and learning centers in 25 states).

University of Phoenix–Oklahoma City Campus (continued)

Academic Information The faculty has 85 members (4% full-time), 25% with terminal degrees. The undergraduate student-faculty ratio is 14:1. The library holds 27 million titles and 11,648 serial subscriptions. Special programs include advanced placement credit, accelerated degree programs, independent study, distance learning, external degree programs, and adult/continuing education programs. The most frequently chosen baccalaureate field is business/marketing.
Student Body Statistics The student body totals 874, of whom 683 are undergraduates. 48 percent are women and 52 percent are men. 1 percent are international students.
Expenses for 2002–03 *Application fee:* $85. *Tuition:* $8250 full-time, $275 per credit part-time.
Financial Aid The application deadline for financial aid is continuous.
Freshman Admission University of Phoenix–Oklahoma City Campus requires 1 recommendation, 2 years of work experience, 23 years of age, and TOEFL scores for international students. A high school transcript is required for some. The application deadline for regular admission is rolling.
Transfer Admission The application deadline for admission is rolling.
Entrance Difficulty University of Phoenix–Oklahoma City Campus has an open admission policy.

For Further Information Contact Ms. Beth Barilla, Director of Admissions, University of Phoenix–Oklahoma City Campus, 4615 East Elwood Street, Mail Stop 10-0030, Phoenix, AZ 85040-1958. *Telephone:* 480-557-1712 or 800-228-7240 (toll-free). *Fax:* 480-594-1758. *E-mail:* beth.barilla@apollogrp.edu. *Web site:* http://www.phoenix.edu/.

UNIVERSITY OF PHOENIX–TULSA CAMPUS

Tulsa, Oklahoma

University of Phoenix–Tulsa Campus is a coed, proprietary, comprehensive institution, founded in 1998, offering degrees at the associate, bachelor's, master's, and doctoral levels and post-master's and postbachelor's certificates (courses conducted at 121 campuses and learning centers in 25 states).

Academic Information The faculty has 102 members (3% full-time), 20% with terminal degrees. The undergraduate student-faculty ratio is 14:1. The library holds 27 million titles and 11,648 serial subscriptions. Special programs include advanced placement credit, accelerated degree programs, independent study, distance learning, external degree programs, and adult/continuing education programs. The most frequently chosen baccalaureate field is business/marketing.
Student Body Statistics The student body totals 912, of whom 705 are undergraduates (3 freshmen). 51 percent are women and 49 percent are men. 21.7 percent are international students.
Expenses for 2002–03 *Application fee:* $85. *Tuition:* $8250 full-time, $275 per credit part-time.
Financial Aid The application deadline for financial aid is continuous.
Freshman Admission University of Phoenix–Tulsa Campus requires 1 recommendation, 2 years of work experience, 23 years of age, and TOEFL scores for international students. A high school transcript is required for some. The application deadline for regular admission is rolling.
Transfer Admission The application deadline for admission is rolling.
Entrance Difficulty University of Phoenix–Tulsa Campus has an open admission policy.

For Further Information Contact Ms. Beth Barilla, Director of Admissions, University of Phoenix–Tulsa Campus, 4615 East Elwood Street, Mail Stop 10-0030, Phoenix, AZ 85040-1958. *Telephone:* 480-557-1712 or 800-228-7240 (toll-free). *Fax:* 480-594-1758. *E-mail:* beth.barilla@apollogrp.edu. *Web site:* http://www.phoenix.edu/.

UNIVERSITY OF SCIENCE AND ARTS OF OKLAHOMA

Chickasha, Oklahoma

USAO is a coed, public, four-year college of Oklahoma State Regents for Higher Education, founded in 1908, offering degrees at the bachelor's level. It has a 75-acre campus in Chickasha near Oklahoma City.

Academic Information The faculty has 88 members (60% full-time), 65% with terminal degrees. The student-faculty ratio is 19:1. The library holds 72,395 titles, 137 serial subscriptions, and 4,187 audiovisual materials. Special programs include academic remediation, services for learning-disabled students, advanced placement credit, accelerated degree programs, double majors, independent study, distance learning, self-designed majors, summer session for credit, part-time degree programs (daytime, evenings, summer), adult/continuing education programs, internships, and arrangement for off-campus study. The most frequently chosen baccalaureate fields are business/marketing, education, social sciences and history.
Student Body Statistics The student body is made up of 1,490 undergraduates (289 freshmen). 64 percent are women and 36 percent are men. 96 percent are from Oklahoma. 2.2 percent are international students. 25 percent of the 2002 graduating class went on to graduate and professional schools.
Expenses for 2002–03 *Application fee:* $15. *State resident tuition:* $1698 full-time, $56.65 per hour part-time. *Nonresident tuition:* $4794 full-time, $159.80 per hour part-time. *Mandatory fees:* $610 full-time, $20.35 per hour part-time. Full-time tuition and fees vary according to course load. Part-time tuition and fees vary according to course load. *College room and board:* $2790. *College room only:* $1250. Room and board charges vary according to board plan and housing facility.
Financial Aid Forms of aid include need-based and non-need-based scholarships, athletic grants, and part-time jobs. The average aided 2002–03 undergraduate received an aid package worth an estimated $6231. The priority application deadline for financial aid is March 15.
Freshman Admission USAO requires a high school transcript, SAT I or ACT scores, and TOEFL scores for international students. A minimum 2.7 high school GPA is recommended. The application deadline for regular admission is September 3.
Transfer Admission The application deadline for admission is rolling.
Entrance Difficulty USAO assesses its entrance difficulty level as moderately difficult. For the fall 2002 freshman class, 82 percent of the applicants were accepted.

For Further Information Contact Mr. Joseph Evans, Registrar and Director of Admissions and Records, University of Science and Arts of Oklahoma, 1727 West Alabama, Chickasha, OK 73018-5322. *Telephone:* 405-574-1204 or 800-933-8726 Ext. 1204 (toll-free). *Fax:* 405-574-1220. *E-mail:* jwevans@usao.edu. *Web site:* http://www.usao.edu/.

UNIVERSITY OF TULSA

Tulsa, Oklahoma

TU is a coed, private university, founded in 1894, affiliated with the Presbyterian Church, offering degrees at the bachelor's, master's, doctoral, and first professional levels and first professional certificates. It has a 160-acre campus in Tulsa.

Academic Information The faculty has 398 members (75% full-time), 96% with terminal degrees. The undergraduate student-faculty ratio is 11:1. The library holds 940,105 titles, 6,317 serial subscriptions, and 13,320 audiovisual materials. Special programs include services for learning-disabled students, an honors program, study abroad, advanced placement credit, accelerated degree programs, ESL programs, double majors, independent study, self-designed majors, summer session for credit, part-time degree programs (daytime, evenings, summer), adult/continuing education programs, and internships. The most frequently chosen baccalaureate fields are business/marketing, engineering/engineering technologies, visual/performing arts.

Student Body Statistics The student body totals 4,049, of whom 2,691 are undergraduates (552 freshmen). 52 percent are women and 48 percent are men. Students come from 38 states and territories and 56 other countries. 76 percent are from Oklahoma. 10.8 percent are international students. 29 percent of the 2002 graduating class went on to graduate and professional schools.
Expenses for 2002–03 *Application fee:* $35. *Comprehensive fee:* $20,078 includes full-time tuition ($14,910), mandatory fees ($80), and college room and board ($5088). *College room only:* $2688. Room and board charges vary according to board plan and housing facility. *Part-time tuition:* $535 per credit hour. *Part-time mandatory fees:* $3 per credit hour.
Financial Aid Forms of aid include need-based and non-need-based scholarships, athletic grants, and part-time jobs. The average aided 2002–03 undergraduate received an aid package worth an estimated $13,737. The priority application deadline for financial aid is April 1.
Freshman Admission TU requires a high school transcript, 1 recommendation, SAT I or ACT scores, and TOEFL scores for international students. An essay, a minimum 3.0 high school GPA, and an interview are recommended.
Transfer Admission The application deadline for admission is rolling.
Entrance Difficulty TU assesses its entrance difficulty level as very difficult; moderately difficult for transfers. For the fall 2002 freshman class, 73 percent of the applicants were accepted.

For Further Information Contact Mr. John C. Corso, Associate Vice President for Administration/Dean of Admission, University of Tulsa, 600 South College Avenue, Tulsa, OK 74104. *Telephone:* 918-631-2307 or 800-331-3050 (toll-free). *Fax:* 918-631-5003. *E-mail:* admission@utulsa.edu. *Web site:* http://www.utulsa.edu/.

South Dakota

AUGUSTANA COLLEGE

Sioux Falls, South Dakota

Augustana is a coed, private, comprehensive institution, founded in 1860, affiliated with the Evangelical Lutheran Church in America, offering degrees at the bachelor's and master's levels. It has a 100-acre campus in Sioux Falls.

Academic Information The faculty has 161 members (67% full-time), 66% with terminal degrees. The undergraduate student-faculty ratio is 12:1. The library holds 268,645 titles, 1,418 serial subscriptions, and 7,280 audiovisual materials. Special programs include academic remediation, services for learning-disabled students, an honors program, cooperative (work-study) education, study abroad, advanced placement credit, accelerated degree programs, double majors, independent study, self-designed majors, summer session for credit, part-time degree programs (daytime, evenings, summer), adult/continuing education programs, internships, and arrangement for off-campus study with 10 other colleges in the upper Midwest. The most frequently chosen baccalaureate fields are business/marketing, education, health professions and related sciences.
Student Body Statistics The student body totals 1,834, of whom 1,804 are undergraduates (455 freshmen). 64 percent are women and 36 percent are men. Students come from 30 states and territories. 50 percent are from South Dakota. 1.8 percent are international students. 21 percent of the 2002 graduating class went on to graduate and professional schools.
Expenses for 2002–03 *Application fee:* $25. *Comprehensive fee:* $20,756 includes full-time tuition ($15,892), mandatory fees ($196), and college room and board ($4668). Room and board charges vary according to board plan and housing facility. *Part-time tuition:* $235 per credit. Part-time tuition varies according to course load.
Financial Aid Forms of aid include need-based and non-need-based scholarships, athletic grants, and part-time jobs. The average aided 2002–03 undergraduate received an aid package worth an estimated $13,811. The priority application deadline for financial aid is March 1.
Freshman Admission Augustana requires a high school transcript, a minimum 2.5 high school GPA, 1 recommendation, minimum ACT score of 20, SAT I or ACT scores, and TOEFL scores for international students. An interview is recommended. An essay is required for some. The application deadline for regular admission is August 1.
Transfer Admission The application deadline for admission is rolling.
Entrance Difficulty Augustana assesses its entrance difficulty level as moderately difficult; minimally difficult for transfers. For the fall 2002 freshman class, 79 percent of the applicants were accepted.

For Further Information Contact Mr. Robert Preloger, Vice President for Enrollment, Augustana College, 2001 South Summit Avenue, Sioux Falls, SD 57197. *Telephone:* 605-274-5516 Ext. 5504, 800-727-2844 Ext. 5516 (toll-free in-state), or 800-727-2844 (toll-free out-of-state). *Fax:* 605-274-5518. *E-mail:* info@augie.edu. *Web site:* http://www.augie.edu/.

BLACK HILLS STATE UNIVERSITY

Spearfish, South Dakota

Black Hills State University is a coed, public, comprehensive unit of South Dakota University System, founded in 1883, offering degrees at the associate, bachelor's, and master's levels and post-master's and postbachelor's certificates. It has a 123-acre campus in Spearfish.

Academic Information The faculty has 192 members (56% full-time). The undergraduate student-faculty ratio is 24:1. The library holds 209,738 titles, 4,481 serial subscriptions, and 23,901 audiovisual materials. Special programs include academic remediation, services for learning-disabled students, cooperative (work-study) education, advanced placement credit, accelerated degree programs, double majors, independent study, distance learning, summer session for credit, part-time degree programs (daytime, evenings, summer), internships, and arrangement for off-campus study with South Dakota State University. The most frequently chosen baccalaureate fields are business/marketing, education, psychology.
Student Body Statistics The student body totals 3,747, of whom 3,542 are undergraduates (592 freshmen). 63 percent are women and 37 percent are men. Students come from 36 states and territories and 6 other countries. 80 percent are from South Dakota. 0.2 percent are international students.
Expenses for 2002–03 *Application fee:* $15. *One-time mandatory fee:* $20. *State resident tuition:* $2080 full-time, $65 per credit part-time. *Nonresident tuition:* $6613 full-time, $206.65 per credit part-time. *Mandatory fees:* $2113 full-time, $66.03 per credit part-time. Full-time tuition and fees vary according to course load and reciprocity agreements. Part-time tuition and fees vary according to course load and reciprocity agreements. *College room and board:* $3127. Room and board charges vary according to board plan and housing facility.
Financial Aid Forms of aid include need-based and non-need-based scholarships, athletic grants, and part-time jobs. The average aided 2001–02 undergraduate received an aid package worth $5463. The priority application deadline for financial aid is March 1.
Freshman Admission Black Hills State University requires a high school transcript, minimum 2.0 high school GPA in core curriculum, SAT I or ACT scores, and TOEFL scores for international students. The application deadline for regular admission is rolling.
Transfer Admission The application deadline for admission is rolling.
Entrance Difficulty Black Hills State University assesses its entrance difficulty level as minimally difficult. For the fall 2002 freshman class, 94 percent of the applicants were accepted.

For Further Information Contact Mr. Steve Ochsner, Dean of Admissions, Black Hills State University, University Street Box 9502, Spearfish, SD 57799-9502. *Telephone:* 605-642-6343 or 800-255-2478 (toll-free). *E-mail:* admissions@bhsu.edu. *Web site:* http://www.bhsu.edu/.

COLORADO TECHNICAL UNIVERSITY SIOUX FALLS CAMPUS

Sioux Falls, South Dakota

Colorado Technical University Sioux Falls Campus is a coed, proprietary, comprehensive unit of Colorado Technical University—Main Campus Colorado Springs, CO, founded in 1965, offering degrees at the associate, bachelor's, and master's levels. It has a 3-acre campus in Sioux Falls.

Academic Information The faculty has 61 members (15% full-time), 13% with terminal degrees. The undergraduate student-faculty ratio is 18:1. The library holds 5,787 titles, 25 serial subscriptions, and 280 audiovisual materials. Special programs include cooperative (work-study) education, accelerated degree programs, double majors, distance learning, summer session for credit, part-time degree programs (daytime, evenings, weekends, summer), adult/continuing education programs, and internships. The most frequently chosen baccalaureate fields are business/marketing, computer/information sciences, protective services/public administration.
Student Body Statistics The student body totals 923, of whom 837 are undergraduates (133 freshmen). 56 percent are women and 44 percent are men. Students come from 3 states and territories. 95 percent are from South Dakota.
Expenses for 2003–04 *Application fee:* $25. *Tuition:* $8775 full-time, $195 per credit hour part-time. *Mandatory fees:* $513 full-time, $50 per term part-time. Full-time tuition and fees vary according to course load. Part-time tuition and fees vary according to course load.
Financial Aid Forms of aid include need-based scholarships and part-time jobs. $3500. The application deadline for financial aid is continuous.
Freshman Admission Colorado Technical University Sioux Falls Campus requires a high school transcript, an interview, and TOEFL scores for international students. ACT scores are recommended. The application deadline for regular admission is rolling.
Transfer Admission The application deadline for admission is rolling.
Entrance Difficulty Colorado Technical University Sioux Falls Campus has an open admission policy. It assesses its entrance difficulty as noncompetitive for transfers.

For Further Information Contact Ms. Angela Haley, Admissions Advisor/Mentor, Colorado Technical University Sioux Falls Campus, 3901 West 59th Street, Sioux Falls, SD 57108. *Telephone:* 605-361-0200 Ext. 103. *Fax:* 605-361-5954. *E-mail:* callen@sf.coloradotech.edu. *Web site:* http://www.colotechu.edu/.

DAKOTA STATE UNIVERSITY

Madison, South Dakota

Dakota State is a coed, public, comprehensive institution, founded in 1881, offering degrees at the associate, bachelor's, and master's levels. It has a 40-acre campus in Madison near Sioux Falls.

Academic Information The faculty has 94 members (82% full-time), 54% with terminal degrees. The undergraduate student-faculty ratio is 23:1. The library holds 98,156 titles, 350 serial subscriptions, and 2,435 audiovisual materials. Special programs include academic remediation, services for learning-disabled students, an honors program, cooperative (work-study) education, study abroad, advanced placement credit, ESL programs, double majors, independent study, distance learning, summer session for credit, part-time degree programs (daytime, evenings, summer), external degree programs, adult/continuing education programs, internships, and arrangement for off-campus study with South Dakota State University, University of Sioux Falls, University of South Dakota. The most frequently chosen baccalaureate fields are computer/information sciences, business/marketing, engineering/engineering technologies.
Student Body Statistics The student body totals 2,188, of whom 1,965 are undergraduates (294 freshmen). 51 percent are women and 49 percent are men. Students come from 12 states and territories and 6 other countries. 84 percent are from South Dakota. 0.9 percent are international students. 2 percent of the 2002 graduating class went on to graduate and professional schools.
Expenses for 2002–03 *Application fee:* $20. *State resident tuition:* $3774 full-time, $126 per credit hour part-time. *Nonresident tuition:* $7857 full-time, $262 per credit hour part-time. *College room and board:* $3130.
Financial Aid Forms of aid include need-based and non-need-based scholarships, athletic grants, and part-time jobs. The average aided 2001–02 undergraduate received an aid package worth $5297. The priority application deadline for financial aid is March 1.
Freshman Admission Dakota State requires a high school transcript, rank in upper two-thirds of high school class, and ACT scores. TOEFL scores for international students are recommended. The application deadline for regular admission is rolling.
Transfer Admission The application deadline for admission is rolling.
Entrance Difficulty Dakota State assesses its entrance difficulty level as minimally difficult; moderately difficult for out-of-state applicants; moderately difficult for transfers. For the fall 2002 freshman class, 86 percent of the applicants were accepted.

For Further Information Contact Ms. Katy O'Hara, Admissions Secretary, Dakota State University, 820 North Washington, Madison, SD 57042-1799. *Telephone:* 605-256-5696 or 888-DSU-9988 (toll-free). *Fax:* 605-256-5316. *E-mail:* yourfuture@dsu.edu. *Web site:* http://www.dsu.edu/.

DAKOTA WESLEYAN UNIVERSITY

Mitchell, South Dakota

DWU is a coed, private, United Methodist, four-year college, founded in 1885, offering degrees at the associate and bachelor's levels. It has a 40-acre campus in Mitchell.

Academic Information The faculty has 64 members (66% full-time), 41% with terminal degrees. The student-faculty ratio is 14:1. The library holds 61,000 titles, 404 serial subscriptions, and 7,600 audiovisual materials. Special programs include academic remediation, services for learning-disabled students, an honors program, study abroad, advanced placement credit, ESL programs, double majors, independent study, distance learning, self-designed majors, summer session for credit, part-time degree programs (daytime, evenings, summer), adult/continuing education programs, and internships. The most frequently chosen baccalaureate fields are business/marketing, education, protective services/public administration.
Student Body Statistics The student body is made up of 717 undergraduates (148 freshmen). 59 percent are women and 41 percent are men. Students come from 30 states and territories. 73 percent are from South Dakota. 0.4 percent are international students. 8 percent of the 2002 graduating class went on to graduate and professional schools.
Expenses for 2003–04 *Application fee:* $25. *Comprehensive fee:* $17,814 includes full-time tuition ($12,998), mandatory fees ($400), and college room and board ($4416). *College room only:* $1910. Full-time tuition and fees vary according to program. Room and board charges vary according to board plan and student level. *Part-time tuition:* $266 per credit. *Part-time mandatory fees:* $15 per credit. Part-time tuition and fees vary according to course load and program.
Financial Aid Forms of aid include need-based and non-need-based scholarships, athletic grants, and part-time jobs. The average aided 2002–03 undergraduate received an aid package worth an estimated $11,061. The priority application deadline for financial aid is April 1.
Freshman Admission DWU requires a high school transcript, SAT I or ACT scores, and TOEFL scores for international students. A minimum 2.0 high school GPA is recommended. The application deadline for regular admission is August 25.
Transfer Admission The application deadline for admission is August 25.
Entrance Difficulty DWU assesses its entrance difficulty level as moderately difficult. For the fall 2002 freshman class, 84 percent of the applicants were accepted.

For Further Information Contact Ms. Laura Miller, Director of Admissions Operations and Outreach Programming, Dakota Wesleyan University, 1200 West University Avenue, Mitchell, SD 57301-4398. *Telephone:* 605-995-2650 or 800-333-8506 (toll-free). *Fax:* 605-995-2699. *E-mail:* admissions@dwu.edu. *Web site:* http://www.dwu.edu/.

HURON UNIVERSITY

See Si Tanka Huron University

KILIAN COMMUNITY COLLEGE

Sioux Falls, South Dakota

Kilian is a coed, private, two-year college, founded in 1977, offering degrees at the associate level. It has a 1-acre campus in Sioux Falls.

Expenses for 2003–04 *Application fee:* $25. *Tuition:* $3408 full-time, $178 per credit part-time.

For Further Information Contact Ms. Christiana Hasenmueller, Director of Admissions, Kilian Community College, 224 North Phillips Avenue, Sioux Falls, SD 57104-6014. *Telephone:* 605-336-1711 or 800-888-1147 (toll-free). *Fax:* 605-336-2606. *E-mail:* info@kcc.cc.sd.us. *Web site:* http://www.kilian.edu/.

MOUNT MARTY COLLEGE

Yankton, South Dakota

Mount Marty is a coed, private, Roman Catholic, comprehensive institution, founded in 1936, offering degrees at the associate, bachelor's, and master's levels. It has an 80-acre campus in Yankton.

Academic Information The faculty has 102 members (41% full-time), 22% with terminal degrees. The undergraduate student-faculty ratio is 13:1. The library holds 79,167 titles, 439 serial subscriptions, and 8,537 audiovisual materials. Special programs include academic remediation, services for learning-disabled students, an honors program, cooperative (work-study) education, advanced placement credit, accelerated degree programs, double majors, independent study, self-designed majors, summer session for credit, part-time degree programs (daytime, evenings), adult/continuing education programs, internships, and arrangement for off-campus study with members of the Colleges of Mid-America. The most frequently chosen baccalaureate fields are business/marketing, education, health professions and related sciences.
Student Body Statistics The student body totals 1,123, of whom 1,030 are undergraduates (167 freshmen). 68 percent are women and 32 percent are men. Students come from 29 states and territories and 2 other countries. 78 percent are from South Dakota. 0.6 percent are international students.
Expenses for 2002–03 *Application fee:* $35. *Comprehensive fee:* $17,260 includes full-time tuition ($11,580), mandatory fees ($1080), and college room and board ($4600). *Part-time tuition:* $196 per credit.
Financial Aid Forms of aid include need-based and non-need-based scholarships, athletic grants, and part-time jobs. The average aided 2002–03 undergraduate received an aid package worth an estimated $12,118. The priority application deadline for financial aid is March 1.
Freshman Admission Mount Marty requires a high school transcript, a minimum 2.0 high school GPA, ACT scores, and TOEFL scores for international students. An interview is recommended. Recommendations are required for some. The application deadline for regular admission is rolling.
Transfer Admission The application deadline for admission is rolling.
Entrance Difficulty Mount Marty assesses its entrance difficulty level as moderately difficult. For the fall 2002 freshman class, 90 percent of the applicants were accepted.

For Further Information Contact Ms. Brandi Tschumper, Director of Enrollment, Mount Marty College, 1105 West 8th Street, Yankton, SD 57078. *Telephone:* 605-668-1545 or 800-658-4552 (toll-free). *Fax:* 605-668-1607. *E-mail:* mmcadmit@mtmc.edu. *Web site:* http://www.mtmc.edu/.

NATIONAL AMERICAN UNIVERSITY

Rapid City, South Dakota

National American University is a coed, proprietary, comprehensive unit of National College, founded in 1941, offering degrees at the associate, bachelor's, and master's levels. It has an 8-acre campus in Rapid City.

Academic Information The library holds 31,018 titles and 268 serial subscriptions. Special programs include academic remediation, services for learning-disabled students, cooperative (work-study) education, advanced placement credit, accelerated degree programs, ESL programs, independent study, distance learning, summer session for credit, part-time degree programs (daytime, evenings, summer), external degree programs, adult/continuing education programs, and internships.
Student Body Statistics The student body totals 749, of whom 714 are undergraduates (166 freshmen). 48 percent are women and 52 percent are men. Students come from 25 states and territories. 79 percent are from South Dakota. 0.7 percent are international students.
Expenses for 2002–03 *Application fee:* $25. *One-time mandatory fee:* $50. *Comprehensive fee:* $13,740 includes full-time tuition ($9840), mandatory fees ($315), and college room and board ($3585). *College room only:* $1605. Room and board charges vary according to board plan. *Part-time tuition:* $205 per credit. *Part-time mandatory fees:* $75 per term.
Financial Aid Forms of aid include need-based and non-need-based scholarships and part-time jobs. The application deadline for financial aid is continuous.
Freshman Admission National American University requires a high school transcript and TOEFL scores for international students. An interview and ACT scores are recommended. The application deadline for regular admission is rolling.
Transfer Admission The application deadline for admission is rolling.
Entrance Difficulty National American University has an open admission policy.

For Further Information Contact Mr. Tom Shea, Vice President of Enrollment Management, National American University, 321 Kansas City Street, Rapid City, SD 57701. *Telephone:* 605-394-4902 or 800-843-8892 (toll-free). *Fax:* 605-394-4871. *E-mail:* apply@server1.natcol-rcy.edu. *Web site:* http://www.national.edu/.

NATIONAL AMERICAN UNIVERSITY–SIOUX FALLS BRANCH

Sioux Falls, South Dakota

National American University–Sioux Falls Branch is a coed, primarily women's, proprietary, four-year college of National College, founded in 1941, offering degrees at the associate and bachelor's levels.

Academic Information The faculty has 35 members. The library holds 1,580 titles and 57 serial subscriptions. Special programs include academic remediation, cooperative (work-study) education, advanced placement credit, accelerated degree programs, ESL programs, double majors, distance learning, summer session for credit, part-time degree programs (daytime, evenings, summer), adult/continuing education programs, and internships. The most frequently chosen baccalaureate fields are business/marketing, computer/information sciences, law/legal studies.
Student Body Statistics The student body is made up of 350 undergraduates. Students come from 5 states and territories. 10 percent of the 2002 graduating class went on to graduate and professional schools.
Expenses for 2003–04 *Application fee:* $25. *Tuition:* $7560 full-time, $200 per credit part-time. *Mandatory fees:* $315 full-time.
Financial Aid Forms of aid include need-based and non-need-based scholarships and part-time jobs. The application deadline for financial aid is continuous.
Freshman Admission National American University–Sioux Falls Branch requires a high school transcript, an interview, and TOEFL scores for international students. The application deadline for regular admission is rolling.
Transfer Admission The application deadline for admission is rolling.

National American University–Sioux Falls Branch (continued)
Entrance Difficulty National American University–Sioux Falls Branch has an open admission policy.

For Further Information Contact Ms. Lisa Houtsma, Director of Admissions, National American University–Sioux Falls Branch, 2801 South Kiwanis Avenue, Suite 100, Sioux Falls, SD 57105. *Telephone:* 605-334-5430. *E-mail:* lhautsma@national.edu.

NORTHERN STATE UNIVERSITY

Aberdeen, South Dakota

NSU is a coed, public, comprehensive unit of South Dakota Board of Regents, founded in 1901, offering degrees at the associate, bachelor's, and master's levels and postbachelor's certificates. It has a 52-acre campus in Aberdeen.

Academic Information The faculty has 110 members (100% full-time), 77% with terminal degrees. The undergraduate student-faculty ratio is 20:1. The library holds 187,961 titles and 880 serial subscriptions. Special programs include academic remediation, services for learning-disabled students, an honors program, cooperative (work-study) education, study abroad, advanced placement credit, accelerated degree programs, ESL programs, distance learning, self-designed majors, summer session for credit, part-time degree programs, adult/continuing education programs, internships, and arrangement for off-campus study with National Student Exchange. The most frequently chosen baccalaureate fields are business/marketing, education, social sciences and history.
Student Body Statistics The student body totals 3,020, of whom 2,740 are undergraduates (411 freshmen). 59 percent are women and 41 percent are men. Students come from 31 states and territories and 10 other countries. 85 percent are from South Dakota.
Expenses for 2002–03 *Application fee:* $15. *State resident tuition:* $1950 full-time, $65 per credit hour part-time. *Nonresident tuition:* $6199 full-time, $206.65 per credit hour part-time. *Mandatory fees:* $1924 full-time, $64.15 per credit hour part-time. Full-time tuition and fees vary according to course level, course load, and reciprocity agreements. Part-time tuition and fees vary according to course level, course load, and reciprocity agreements. *College room and board:* $3234. *College room only:* $1446. Room and board charges vary according to board plan.
Financial Aid Forms of aid include need-based and non-need-based scholarships, athletic grants, and part-time jobs. The average aided 2001–02 undergraduate received an aid package worth $4988. The priority application deadline for financial aid is March 1.
Freshman Admission NSU requires a high school transcript, a minimum X high school GPA, SAT I or ACT scores, and TOEFL scores for international students. Recommendations are required for some. The application deadline for regular admission is September 1.
Transfer Admission The application deadline for admission is September 1.
Entrance Difficulty NSU assesses its entrance difficulty level as minimally difficult; moderately difficult for transfers. For the fall 2002 freshman class, 92 percent of the applicants were accepted.

For Further Information Contact Ms. Sara Hanson, Interim Director of Admissions-Campus, Northern State University, 1200 South Jay Street, Aberdeen, SD 57401. *Telephone:* 605-626-2544 or 800-678-5330 (toll-free). *Fax:* 605-626-2587. *E-mail:* admissions1@northern.edu. *Web site:* http://www.northern.edu/.

OGLALA LAKOTA COLLEGE

Kyle, South Dakota

For Information Write to Oglala Lakota College, Kyle, SD 57752-0490.

PRESENTATION COLLEGE

Aberdeen, South Dakota

Presentation College is a coed, private, Roman Catholic, four-year college, founded in 1951, offering degrees at the associate and bachelor's levels. It has a 100-acre campus in Aberdeen.

Academic Information The faculty has 68 members (38% full-time), 13% with terminal degrees. The student-faculty ratio is 12:1. The library holds 40,000 titles, 430 serial subscriptions, and 2,900 audiovisual materials. Special programs include academic remediation, cooperative (work-study) education, advanced placement credit, accelerated degree programs, double majors, distance learning, summer session for credit, part-time degree programs (daytime, evenings, summer), external degree programs, adult/continuing education programs, and internships. The most frequently chosen baccalaureate fields are business/marketing, health professions and related sciences, protective services/public administration.
Student Body Statistics The student body is made up of 594 undergraduates. 87 percent are women and 13 percent are men. Students come from 1 state or territory. 73 percent are from South Dakota. 0.2 percent are international students.
Expenses for 2002–03 *Application fee:* $20. *Comprehensive fee:* $13,175 includes full-time tuition ($8850), mandatory fees ($175), and college room and board ($4150). *College room only:* $3400. Full-time tuition and fees vary according to course load, location, and program. Room and board charges vary according to board plan, housing facility, and student level. *Part-time tuition:* $350 per credit hour. Part-time tuition varies according to course load, location, and program.
Financial Aid Forms of aid include need-based and non-need-based scholarships and part-time jobs. The average aided 2001–02 undergraduate received an aid package worth $8574. The application deadline for financial aid is April 1.
Freshman Admission Presentation College requires a high school transcript, TOEFL scores for international students, and ACT ASSET. ACT scores are recommended. A minimum 2.0 high school GPA and ACT scores are required for some. The application deadline for regular admission is rolling.
Transfer Admission The application deadline for admission is rolling.
Entrance Difficulty Presentation College has an open admission policy except for allied health programs, nursing. It assesses its entrance difficulty as minimally difficult for allied health programs.

For Further Information Contact Mr. Joddy Meidinger, Director of Admissions, Presentation College, 1500 North Main Street, Aberdeen, SD 57401. *Telephone:* 605-229-8493 Ext. 492 or 800-437-6060 (toll-free). *Fax:* 605-229-8518. *E-mail:* admit@presentation.edu. *Web site:* http://www.presentation.edu/.

SINTE GLESKA UNIVERSITY

Rosebud, South Dakota

Sinte Gleska is a coed, private, comprehensive institution, founded in 1970, offering degrees at the associate, bachelor's, and master's levels. It has a 52-acre campus in Rosebud.

Expenses for 2002–03 *Application fee:* $0. *Tuition:* $75 per credit hour part-time. *Mandatory fees:* $3 per credit hour part-time, $65 per term part-time.

For Further Information Contact Mr. Jack Herman, Registrar and Director of Admissions, Sinte Gleska University, PO Box 490, Rosebud, SD 57570-0490. *Telephone:* 605-747-2263 Ext. 224. *Fax:* 605-747-2098. *Web site:* http://www.sinte.edu/.

SI TANKA HURON UNIVERSITY

Huron, South Dakota

Si Tanka Huron University is a coed, proprietary, four-year college, founded in 1883, offering degrees at the associate and bachelor's levels. It has a 15-acre campus in Huron.

Academic Information The faculty has 61 members (30% full-time). The student-faculty ratio is 12:1. The library holds 50,000 titles and 1,300 audiovisual materials. Special programs include an honors program, cooperative (work-study) education, advanced placement credit, accelerated degree programs, Freshman Honors College, double majors, independent study, summer session for credit, part-time degree programs (daytime, evenings, summer), and adult/continuing education programs. The most frequently chosen baccalaureate field is law/legal studies.
Student Body Statistics The student body is made up of 528 undergraduates (175 freshmen). 45 percent are women and 55 percent are men. Students come from 27 states and territories. 62 percent are from South Dakota.
Expenses for 2002–03 *Application fee:* $35. *Comprehensive fee:* $11,650 includes full-time tuition ($8400), mandatory fees ($300), and college room and board ($2950). *Part-time tuition:* $300 per credit.
Financial Aid Forms of aid include need-based and non-need-based scholarships and part-time jobs. The average aided 2001–02 undergraduate received an aid package worth $5250. The application deadline for financial aid is continuous.
Freshman Admission Si Tanka Huron University requires a high school transcript, a minimum 2.0 high school GPA, applicants for athletic scholarship programs must meet approved ACT requirement, and TOEFL scores for international students. An interview and SAT I or ACT scores are recommended. The application deadline for regular admission is rolling.
Transfer Admission The application deadline for admission is rolling.
Entrance Difficulty Si Tanka Huron University assesses its entrance difficulty level as minimally difficult; moderately difficult for nursing program. For the fall 2002 freshman class, 39 percent of the applicants were accepted.

For Further Information Contact Mr. Tyler Fisher, Director of Admissions, Si Tanka Huron University, 333 9th Street Southwest, Huron, SD 57350. *Telephone:* 605-352-8721 Ext. 41 or 800-710-7159 (toll-free). *Fax:* 605-352-7421. *E-mail:* admissions@huron.edu. *Web site:* http://www.huron.edu/.

SOUTH DAKOTA SCHOOL OF MINES AND TECHNOLOGY

Rapid City, South Dakota

SDSM&T is a coed, public unit of South Dakota State University System, founded in 1885, offering degrees at the associate, bachelor's, master's, and doctoral levels. It has a 120-acre campus in Rapid City.

Academic Information The faculty has 125 members (81% full-time), 74% with terminal degrees. The undergraduate student-faculty ratio is 16:1. The library holds 219,961 titles, 496 serial subscriptions, and 1,610 audiovisual materials. Special programs include academic remediation, services for learning-disabled students, cooperative (work-study) education, study abroad, advanced placement credit, ESL programs, double majors, independent study, distance learning, summer session for credit, part-time degree programs (daytime, evenings), adult/continuing education programs, and internships.
Student Body Statistics The student body totals 2,447, of whom 2,094 are undergraduates (446 freshmen). 32 percent are women and 68 percent are men. Students come from 34 states and territories and 8 other countries. 74 percent are from South Dakota. 1.3 percent are international students. 18 percent of the 2002 graduating class went on to graduate and professional schools.
Expenses for 2002–03 *Application fee:* $20. *State resident tuition:* $1950 full-time, $65 per credit hour part-time. *Nonresident tuition:* $6200 full-time, $206.65 per credit hour part-time. *Mandatory fees:* $2142 full-time, $66.95 per credit hour part-time. Full-time tuition and fees vary according to course load, program, and reciprocity agreements. Part-time tuition and fees vary according to course load, program, and reciprocity agreements. *College room and board:* $3484. *College room only:* $1590. Room and board charges vary according to board plan and housing facility.
Financial Aid Forms of aid include need-based and non-need-based scholarships, athletic grants, and part-time jobs. The average aided 2001–02 undergraduate received an aid package worth $6067. The priority application deadline for financial aid is March 15.
Freshman Admission SDSM&T requires a high school transcript, SAT I or ACT scores, and TOEFL scores for international students. A minimum 2.6 high school GPA is recommended. ACT scores and are required for some. The application deadline for regular admission is rolling.
Transfer Admission The application deadline for admission is rolling.
Entrance Difficulty SDSM&T assesses its entrance difficulty level as moderately difficult. For the fall 2002 freshman class, 98 percent of the applicants were accepted.

For Further Information Contact Mr. Joseph Mueller, Director of Admissions, South Dakota School of Mines and Technology, 501 East Saint Joseph, Rapid City, SD 57701-3995. *Telephone:* 605-394-2414 Ext. 1266 or 800-544-8162 Ext. 2414 (toll-free). *Fax:* 605-394-1268. *E-mail:* admissions@sdsmt.edu. *Web site:* http://www.sdsmt.edu/.

SOUTH DAKOTA STATE UNIVERSITY

Brookings, South Dakota

SDSU is a coed, public university, founded in 1881, offering degrees at the associate, bachelor's, master's, doctoral, and first professional levels. It has a 260-acre campus in Brookings.

Academic Information The faculty has 508 members (96% full-time), 73% with terminal degrees. The undergraduate student-faculty ratio is 18:1. The library holds 555,523 titles, 6,023 serial subscriptions, and 2,504 audiovisual materials. Special programs include academic remediation, services for learning-disabled students, an honors program, cooperative (work-study) education, study abroad, advanced placement credit, accelerated degree programs, Freshman Honors College, ESL programs, double majors, independent study, distance learning, summer session for credit, part-time degree programs (daytime, evenings, summer), adult/continuing education programs, internships, and arrangement for off-campus study with National Student Exchange. The most frequently chosen baccalaureate fields are agriculture, engineering/engineering technologies, health professions and related sciences.
Student Body Statistics The student body totals 9,952, of whom 8,445 are undergraduates. Students come from 39 states and territories and 19 other countries. 74 percent are from South Dakota. 5 percent of the 2002 graduating class went on to graduate and professional schools.
Expenses for 2003–04 *Application fee:* $20. *State resident tuition:* $2308 full-time, $72.10 per credit part-time. *Nonresident tuition:* $7332 full-time, $229.15 per credit part-time. *Mandatory fees:* $2228 full-time, $69.70 per credit part-time. *College room and board:* $3586. *College room only:* $1862.
Financial Aid Forms of aid include need-based and non-need-based scholarships, athletic grants, and part-time jobs. The average aided 2002–03 undergraduate received an aid package worth an estimated $6912. The priority application deadline for financial aid is March 7.
Freshman Admission SDSU requires a high school transcript, a minimum 2.6 high school GPA, minimum ACT score of 18, ACT scores, and TOEFL scores for international students. The application deadline for regular admission is rolling.
Transfer Admission The application deadline for admission is rolling.
Entrance Difficulty SDSU assesses its entrance difficulty level as moderately difficult. For the fall 2002 freshman class, 94 percent of the applicants were accepted.

For Further Information Contact Ms. Michelle Kuebler, Assistant Director of Admissions, South Dakota State University, PO Box 2201, Brookings, SD 57007. *Telephone:* 605-688-4121 or 800-952-3541 (toll-free). *Fax:* 605-688-6891. *E-mail:* sdsu_admissions@sdstate.edu. *Web site:* http://www.sdstate.edu/.

UNIVERSITY OF SIOUX FALLS

Sioux Falls, South Dakota

USF is a coed, private, American Baptist Churches in the USA, comprehensive institution, founded in 1883, offering degrees at the associate, bachelor's, master's, and doctoral levels. It has a 22-acre campus in Sioux Falls.

Academic Information The faculty has 97 members (48% full-time), 35% with terminal degrees. The undergraduate student-faculty ratio is 17:1. The library holds 57,750 titles, 382 serial subscriptions, and 4,480 audiovisual materials. Special programs include academic remediation, services for learning-disabled students, an honors program, cooperative (work-study) education, study abroad, advanced placement credit, accelerated degree programs, double majors, independent study, distance learning, self-designed majors, summer session for credit, part-time degree programs (daytime, evenings, weekends, summer), external degree programs, adult/continuing education programs, internships, and arrangement for off-campus study with Colleges of Mid-America, Augustana College (SD), North American Baptist Seminary, Christian College Coalition. The most frequently chosen baccalaureate fields are business/marketing, education, psychology.
Student Body Statistics The student body totals 1,405, of whom 1,186 are undergraduates (209 freshmen). 56 percent are women and 44 percent are men. Students come from 22 states and territories and 6 other countries. 67 percent are from South Dakota. 0.8 percent are international students. 17 percent of the 2002 graduating class went on to graduate and professional schools.
Expenses for 2003–04 *Application fee:* $25. *Comprehensive fee:* $18,000 includes full-time tuition ($13,900) and college room and board ($4100). *College room only:* $1790. Room and board charges vary according to board plan and housing facility. *Part-time tuition:* $215 per semester hour.
Financial Aid Forms of aid include need-based and non-need-based scholarships and part-time jobs. The priority application deadline for financial aid is March 1.
Freshman Admission USF requires a high school transcript, SAT I and SAT II or ACT scores, and TOEFL scores for international students. An essay and a minimum 2.0 high school GPA are recommended. 2 recommendations and an interview are required for some. The application deadline for regular admission is rolling.
Transfer Admission The application deadline for admission is rolling.
Entrance Difficulty USF assesses its entrance difficulty level as moderately difficult. For the fall 2002 freshman class, 94 percent of the applicants were accepted.

For Further Information Contact Ms. Laura A. Olson, Assistant Director of Admissions, University of Sioux Falls, 1101 West 22nd Street, Sioux Falls, SD 57105. *Telephone:* 605-331-6600 or 800-888-1047 (toll-free). *Fax:* 605-331-6615. *E-mail:* admissions@usiouxfalls.edu. *Web site:* http://www.usiouxfalls.edu/.

THE UNIVERSITY OF SOUTH DAKOTA

Vermillion, South Dakota

USD is a coed, public university, founded in 1862, offering degrees at the associate, bachelor's, master's, doctoral, and first professional levels and post-master's and postbachelor's certificates. It has a 216-acre campus in Vermillion.

Academic Information The faculty has 295 members (96% full-time), 78% with terminal degrees. The undergraduate student-faculty ratio is 14:1. The library holds 335,757 titles, 2,852 serial subscriptions, and 30,885 audiovisual materials. Special programs include services for learning-disabled students, an honors program, study abroad, advanced placement credit, ESL programs, double majors, independent study, distance learning, summer session for credit, part-time degree programs, internships, and arrangement for off-campus study with National Student Exchange. The most frequently chosen baccalaureate fields are business/marketing, education, health professions and related sciences.
Student Body Statistics The student body totals 8,873, of whom 5,769 are undergraduates (1,109 freshmen). 61 percent are women and 39 percent are men. Students come from 40 states and territories and 57 other countries. 77 percent are from South Dakota. 1.3 percent are international students.
Expenses for 2002–03 *Application fee:* $20. *State resident tuition:* $1950 full-time, $65 per credit hour part-time. *Nonresident tuition:* $6200 full-time, $206.65 per credit hour part-time. *Mandatory fees:* $1922 full-time, $64.08 per credit hour part-time. Full-time tuition and fees vary according to course load. Part-time tuition and fees vary according to course load. *College room and board:* $3278. *College room only:* $1631. Room and board charges vary according to board plan and housing facility.
Financial Aid Forms of aid include need-based and non-need-based scholarships, athletic grants, and part-time jobs. The average aided 2001–02 undergraduate received an aid package worth $6565. The priority application deadline for financial aid is March 15.
Freshman Admission USD requires a high school transcript, SAT I or ACT scores, and TOEFL scores for international students. A minimum 2.6 high school GPA is recommended. Recommendations are required for some. The application deadline for regular admission is rolling.
Transfer Admission The application deadline for admission is rolling.
Entrance Difficulty USD assesses its entrance difficulty level as moderately difficult. For the fall 2002 freshman class, 86 percent of the applicants were accepted.

For Further Information Contact Ms. Paula Tacke, Director of Admissions, The University of South Dakota, 414 East Clark Street, Vermillion, SD 57069. *Telephone:* 605-677-5434 or 877-269-6837 (toll-free). *Fax:* 605-677-6753. *E-mail:* admiss@usd.edu. *Web site:* http://www.usd.edu/.

Wisconsin

ALVERNO COLLEGE

Milwaukee, Wisconsin

Alverno is a women's, private, Roman Catholic, comprehensive institution, founded in 1887, offering degrees at the associate, bachelor's, and master's levels (also offers weekend program with significant enrollment not reflected in profile). It has a 46-acre campus in Milwaukee.

Academic Information The faculty has 199 members (50% full-time), 74% with terminal degrees. The undergraduate student-faculty ratio is 14:1. The library holds 92,076 titles, 1,001 serial subscriptions, and 34,795 audiovisual materials. Special programs include academic remediation, services for learning-disabled students, study abroad, advanced placement credit, double majors, summer session for credit, part-time degree programs (daytime, evenings, weekends, summer), adult/continuing education programs, and internships. The most frequently chosen baccalaureate fields are business/marketing, communications/communication technologies, health professions and related sciences.
Student Body Statistics The student body totals 1,999, of whom 1,800 are undergraduates (196 freshmen). Students come from 13 states and territories. 98 percent are from Wisconsin. 0.6 percent are international students. 13 percent of the 2002 graduating class went on to graduate and professional schools.
Expenses for 2002–03 *Application fee:* $20. *Comprehensive fee:* $17,710 includes full-time tuition ($12,600), mandatory fees ($150), and college room and board ($4960). *College room only:* $1870. Full-time tuition and fees vary according to class time and program. Room and board charges vary according to board plan. *Part-time tuition:* $525 per credit hour. *Part-time mandatory fees:* $75 per term. Part-time tuition and fees vary according to class time and program.
Financial Aid Forms of aid include need-based and non-need-based scholarships and part-time jobs. The priority application deadline for financial aid is April 1.
Freshman Admission Alverno requires an essay, a high school transcript, and TOEFL scores for international students. An interview and

ACT scores are recommended. Recommendations are required for some. The application deadline for regular admission is rolling.
Transfer Admission The application deadline for admission is rolling.
Entrance Difficulty Alverno assesses its entrance difficulty level as moderately difficult. For the fall 2002 freshman class, 82 percent of the applicants were accepted.

For Further Information Contact Ms. Mary Kay Farrell, Director of Admissions, Alverno College, 3400 South 43 Street, PO Box 343922, Milwaukee, WI 53234-3922. *Telephone:* 414-382-6113 or 800-933-3401 (toll-free). *Fax:* 414-382-6354. *E-mail:* admissions@alverno.edu. *Web site:* http://www.alverno.edu/.

BELLIN COLLEGE OF NURSING

Green Bay, Wisconsin

Bellin College is a coed, primarily women's, private, four-year college, founded in 1909, offering degrees at the bachelor's level in nursing.

Academic Information The faculty has 17 members (88% full-time), 12% with terminal degrees. The student-faculty ratio is 10:1. The library holds 7,000 titles, 225 serial subscriptions, and 600 audiovisual materials. Special programs include advanced placement credit, accelerated degree programs, independent study, summer session for credit, and arrangement for off-campus study with University of Wisconsin-Green Bay. The most frequently chosen baccalaureate field is health professions and related sciences.
Student Body Statistics The student body is made up of 176 undergraduates (30 freshmen). 94 percent are women and 6 percent are men. Students come from 3 states and territories and 1 other country. 97 percent are from Wisconsin. 0.6 percent are international students. 2 percent of the 2002 graduating class went on to graduate and professional schools.
Expenses for 2002–03 *Application fee:* $20. *Tuition:* $11,264 full-time, $547 per credit part-time. *Mandatory fees:* $279 full-time.
Financial Aid Forms of aid include need-based and non-need-based scholarships and part-time jobs. The average aided 2002–03 undergraduate received an aid package worth an estimated $12,091. The priority application deadline for financial aid is March 1.
Freshman Admission Bellin College requires a high school transcript, 3 recommendations, an interview, and ACT scores. A minimum 3.0 high school GPA is recommended. The application deadline for regular admission is rolling.
Transfer Admission The application deadline for admission is rolling.
Entrance Difficulty Bellin College assesses its entrance difficulty level as moderately difficult.

For Further Information Contact Dr. Penny Croghan, Admissions Director, Bellin College of Nursing, 725 South Webster Avenue, Green Bay, WI 54301. *Telephone:* 920-433-5803 or 800-236-8707 (toll-free in-state). *Fax:* 920-433-7416. *E-mail:* admissio@bcon.edu. *Web site:* http://www.bcon.edu.

BELOIT COLLEGE

Beloit, Wisconsin

Beloit is a coed, private, four-year college, founded in 1846, offering degrees at the bachelor's level. It has a 65-acre campus in Beloit near Chicago and Milwaukee.

Academic Information The faculty has 126 members (79% full-time), 98% with terminal degrees. The student-faculty ratio is 11:1. The library holds 183,736 titles, 946 serial subscriptions, and 7,285 audiovisual materials. Special programs include services for learning-disabled students, study abroad, advanced placement credit, ESL programs, double majors, independent study, self-designed majors, summer session for credit, adult/continuing education programs, internships, and arrangement for off-campus study with University of Wisconsin-Madison, University of Chicago, Spelman College, Morehouse College, Associated Colleges of the Midwest. The most frequently chosen baccalaureate fields are social sciences and history, biological/life sciences, visual/performing arts.
Student Body Statistics The student body is made up of 1,281 undergraduates (304 freshmen). 62 percent are women and 38 percent are men. Students come from 49 states and territories and 59 other countries. 20 percent are from Wisconsin. 7.6 percent are international students. 31 percent of the 2002 graduating class went on to graduate and professional schools.
Expenses for 2002–03 *Application fee:* $30. *Comprehensive fee:* $28,504 includes full-time tuition ($23,016), mandatory fees ($220), and college room and board ($5268). *College room only:* $2570. Room and board charges vary according to board plan.
Financial Aid Forms of aid include need-based and non-need-based scholarships and part-time jobs. The average aided 2001–02 undergraduate received an aid package worth $17,839. The priority application deadline for financial aid is March 1.
Freshman Admission Beloit requires an essay, a high school transcript, 1 recommendation, SAT I or ACT scores, and TOEFL scores for international students. An interview is recommended. An interview is required for some. The application deadline for regular admission is February 1 and for early action it is December 15.
Transfer Admission The application deadline for admission is rolling.
Entrance Difficulty Beloit assesses its entrance difficulty level as very difficult. For the fall 2002 freshman class, 70 percent of the applicants were accepted.

For Further Information Contact Mr. James S. Zielinski, Director of Admissions, Beloit College, 700 College Street, Beloit, WI 53511-5596. *Telephone:* 608-363-2380 or 800-356-0751 (toll-free). *Fax:* 608-363-2075. *E-mail:* admiss@beloit.edu. *Web site:* http://www.beloit.edu/.

BRYANT AND STRATTON COLLEGE

Milwaukee, Wisconsin

Bryant & Stratton is a coed, proprietary, primarily two-year college of Bryant and Stratton Business Institute, Inc, founded in 1863, offering degrees at the associate and bachelor's levels. It has a 2-acre campus in Milwaukee.

Academic Information The faculty has 37 members (16% full-time). The student-faculty ratio is 14:1. The library holds 120 serial subscriptions and 100 audiovisual materials. Special programs include academic remediation, cooperative (work-study) education, advanced placement credit, double majors, independent study, distance learning, summer session for credit, part-time degree programs (daytime, evenings), adult/continuing education programs, and internships.
Student Body Statistics The student body is made up of 487 undergraduates. 80 percent are women and 20 percent are men. Students come from 1 state or territory. 9 percent of the 2002 graduating class went on to four-year colleges.
Expenses for 2003–04 *Application fee:* $25. *One-time mandatory fee:* $25. *Tuition:* $10,200 full-time, $340 per credit hour part-time. *Mandatory fees:* $200 full-time, $100 per term part-time. Full-time tuition and fees vary according to class time and course load. Part-time tuition and fees vary according to class time and course load.
Financial Aid Forms of aid include need-based scholarships and part-time jobs. The application deadline for financial aid is continuous.
Freshman Admission Bryant & Stratton requires a high school transcript, TOEFL scores for international students, and TABE. A minimum 2.0 high school GPA and SAT I or ACT scores are recommended. Recommendations and an interview are required for some. The application deadline for regular admission is rolling.
Transfer Admission The application deadline for admission is rolling.
Entrance Difficulty Bryant & Stratton assesses its entrance difficulty level as minimally difficult. For the fall 2002 freshman class, 69 percent of the applicants were accepted.

For Further Information Contact Ms. Kathryn Cotey, Director of Admissions, Bryant and Stratton College, 310 West Wisconsin Avenue, Milwaukee, WI 53203-2214. *Telephone:* 414-276-5200.

CARDINAL STRITCH UNIVERSITY

Milwaukee, Wisconsin

Stritch is a coed, private, Roman Catholic, comprehensive institution, founded in 1937, offering degrees at the associate, bachelor's, master's, and doctoral levels and postbachelor's certificates. It has a 40-acre campus in Milwaukee.

Academic Information The undergraduate student-faculty ratio is 18:1. The library holds 124,897 titles, 667 serial subscriptions, and 6,250 audiovisual materials. Special programs include academic remediation, services for learning-disabled students, an honors program, cooperative (work-study) education, advanced placement credit, accelerated degree programs, ESL programs, double majors, independent study, distance learning, self-designed majors, summer session for credit, part-time degree programs (daytime, evenings, weekends, summer), external degree programs, adult/continuing education programs, internships, and arrangement for off-campus study with Concordia University Wisconsin, Saint Francis Seminary, Sacred Heart School of Theology. The most frequently chosen baccalaureate fields are business/marketing, education, health professions and related sciences.
Student Body Statistics The student body totals 6,854, of whom 3,146 are undergraduates (262 freshmen). 69 percent are women and 31 percent are men. Students come from 16 states and territories and 27 other countries. 1.9 percent are international students.
Expenses for 2002–03 *Application fee:* $25. *Comprehensive fee:* $18,570 includes full-time tuition ($13,280), mandatory fees ($300), and college room and board ($4990). Full-time tuition and fees vary according to program. Room and board charges vary according to board plan. *Part-time tuition:* $415 per credit. *Part-time mandatory fees:* $100 per term. Part-time tuition and fees vary according to course load and program.
Financial Aid Forms of aid include need-based and non-need-based scholarships and part-time jobs. $7115. The application deadline for financial aid is continuous.
Freshman Admission Stritch requires an essay, a high school transcript, a minimum 2.0 high school GPA, SAT I or ACT scores, and TOEFL scores for international students. An interview and ACT scores are recommended. Recommendations are required for some. The application deadline for regular admission is rolling.
Transfer Admission The application deadline for admission is rolling.
Entrance Difficulty Stritch assesses its entrance difficulty level as moderately difficult.

For Further Information Contact Mr. David Wegener, Director of Admissions, Cardinal Stritch University, 6801 North Yates Road, Milwaukee, WI 53217-3985. *Telephone:* 414-410-4040 or 800-347-8822 Ext. 4040 (toll-free). *Fax:* 414-410-4058. *E-mail:* admityou@stritch.edu. *Web site:* http://www.stritch.edu/.

CARROLL COLLEGE

Waukesha, Wisconsin

Carroll is a coed, private, Presbyterian, comprehensive institution, founded in 1846, offering degrees at the bachelor's and master's levels (master's degrees in education and physical therapy). It has a 52-acre campus in Waukesha near Milwaukee.

Academic Information The faculty has 221 members (45% full-time), 48% with terminal degrees. The undergraduate student-faculty ratio is 16:1. The library holds 200,000 titles, 520 serial subscriptions, and 362 audiovisual materials. Special programs include academic remediation, services for learning-disabled students, an honors program, study abroad, advanced placement credit, double majors, independent study, distance learning, self-designed majors, summer session for credit, part-time degree programs (daytime, evenings, weekends, summer), adult/continuing education programs, and internships. The most frequently chosen baccalaureate fields are business/marketing, education, health professions and related sciences.
Student Body Statistics The student body totals 2,968, of whom 2,705 are undergraduates (538 freshmen). 66 percent are women and 34 percent are men. Students come from 29 states and territories and 24 other countries. 78 percent are from Wisconsin. 2.2 percent are international students. 11 percent of the 2002 graduating class went on to graduate and professional schools.
Expenses for 2003–04 *Application fee:* $0. *Comprehensive fee:* $22,740 includes full-time tuition ($17,020), mandatory fees ($360), and college room and board ($5360). *College room only:* $2900. Full-time tuition and fees vary according to program. Room and board charges vary according to board plan and housing facility. *Part-time tuition:* $210 per credit. Part-time tuition varies according to course load and program.
Financial Aid Forms of aid include need-based and non-need-based scholarships and part-time jobs. The average aided 2001–02 undergraduate received an aid package worth $12,532. The application deadline for financial aid is continuous.
Freshman Admission Carroll requires a high school transcript, a minimum 2.0 high school GPA, 1 recommendation, SAT I and SAT II or ACT scores, and TOEFL scores for international students. An interview is recommended. An essay is required for some. The application deadline for regular admission is rolling.
Transfer Admission The application deadline for admission is rolling.
Entrance Difficulty Carroll assesses its entrance difficulty level as moderately difficult. For the fall 2002 freshman class, 84 percent of the applicants were accepted.

For Further Information Contact Mr. James V. Wiseman III, Vice President of Enrollment, Carroll College, 100 North East Avenue, Waukesha, WI 53186-5593. *Telephone:* 262-524-7221 or 800-CARROLL (toll-free). *Fax:* 262-524-7139. *E-mail:* cc.info@ccadmin.cc.edu. *Web site:* http://www.cc.edu/.

CARTHAGE COLLEGE

Kenosha, Wisconsin

Carthage is a coed, private, comprehensive institution, founded in 1847, affiliated with the Evangelical Lutheran Church in America, offering degrees at the bachelor's and master's levels. It has a 72-acre campus in Kenosha near Chicago and Milwaukee.

Academic Information The faculty has 161 members (70% full-time), 58% with terminal degrees. The undergraduate student-faculty ratio is 16:1. The library holds 128,551 titles, 425 serial subscriptions, and 4,361 audiovisual materials. Special programs include services for learning-disabled students, an honors program, cooperative (work-study) education, study abroad, advanced placement credit, accelerated degree programs, double majors, independent study, self-designed majors, summer session for credit, part-time degree programs, adult/continuing education programs, internships, and arrangement for off-campus study with University of Wisconsin-Parkside, Marquette University. The most frequently chosen baccalaureate fields are business/marketing, education, social sciences and history.
Student Body Statistics The student body totals 2,520, of whom 2,388 are undergraduates (615 freshmen). 59 percent are women and 41 percent are men. Students come from 27 states and territories and 12 other countries. 49 percent are from Wisconsin. 0.8 percent are international students. 14 percent of the 2002 graduating class went on to graduate and professional schools.
Expenses for 2003–04 *Application fee:* $25. *Comprehensive fee:* $26,220 includes full-time tuition ($20,150) and college room and board ($6070). Full-time tuition varies according to reciprocity agreements. Room and board charges vary according to board plan. *Part-time tuition:* $300 per credit hour. Part-time tuition varies according to class time and course load.
Financial Aid Forms of aid include need-based and non-need-based scholarships and part-time jobs. The average aided 2002–03 undergraduate received an aid package worth an estimated $16,277. The priority application deadline for financial aid is February 15.
Freshman Admission Carthage requires a high school transcript, a minimum 2.0 high school GPA, SAT I or ACT scores, and TOEFL scores for international students. An essay, a minimum 3.0 high school GPA, and an interview are recommended. An essay and 2 recommendations are required for some. The application deadline for regular admission is rolling and for early action it is July 1.
Transfer Admission The application deadline for admission is rolling.

Entrance Difficulty Carthage assesses its entrance difficulty level as moderately difficult. For the fall 2002 freshman class, 83 percent of the applicants were accepted.

For Further Information Contact Mr. Tom Augustine, Director of Admission, Carthage College, 2001 Alford Park Drive, Kenosha, WI 53140-1994. *Telephone:* 262-551-5850 or 800-351-4058 (toll-free). *Fax:* 262-551-5762. *E-mail:* admissions@carthage.edu. *Web site:* http://www.carthage.edu/.

COLLEGE OF MENOMINEE NATION

Keshena, Wisconsin

College of Menominee Nation is a coed, private, two-year college, offering degrees at the associate level.

Academic Information The faculty has 14 full-time members.
Student Body Statistics The student body is made up of 530 undergraduates.
Expenses for 2002–03 *Application fee:* $10. *State resident tuition:* $3240 full-time, $135 per credit part-time. *Mandatory fees:* $15 full-time.
Financial Aid Forms of aid include need-based scholarships and part-time jobs. The application deadline for financial aid is continuous.
Freshman Admission College of Menominee Nation requires TABE. The application deadline for regular admission is August 14.
Entrance Difficulty College of Menominee Nation has an open admission policy.

For Further Information Contact Ms. Cynthia Norton, Dean, College of Menominee Nation, PO Box 1179, Keshena, WI 54135. *Telephone:* 715-799-5600. *Fax:* 715-799-1326. *Web site:* http://www.menominee.com/.

COLUMBIA COLLEGE OF NURSING

Milwaukee, Wisconsin

Columbia College of Nursing is a coed, primarily women's, private, four-year college, founded in 1901, offering degrees at the bachelor's level in nursing.

Academic Information The faculty has 13 members (77% full-time), 38% with terminal degrees. The student-faculty ratio is 18:1. The library holds 9,060 titles, 253 serial subscriptions, and 508 audiovisual materials. Special programs include an honors program, advanced placement credit, double majors, independent study, summer session for credit, part-time degree programs (daytime, evenings, summer), and arrangement for off-campus study with Carroll College. The most frequently chosen baccalaureate field is health professions and related sciences.
Student Body Statistics The student body is made up of 175 undergraduates. 87 percent are from Wisconsin. 18 percent of the 2002 graduating class went on to graduate and professional schools.
Expenses for 2002–03 *Application fee:* $0. *Comprehensive fee:* $18,365 includes full-time tuition ($13,995), mandatory fees ($620), and college room and board ($3750). *College room only:* $2750. Room and board charges vary according to board plan, housing facility, location, and student level. *Part-time tuition:* $420 per credit hour. *Part-time mandatory fees:* $500 per term. Part-time tuition and fees vary according to program.
Financial Aid Forms of aid include need-based and non-need-based scholarships and part-time jobs. $13,219. The application deadline for financial aid is continuous.
Freshman Admission Columbia College of Nursing requires a high school transcript, SAT I or ACT scores, and TOEFL scores for international students. An essay, 1 recommendation, and an interview are recommended. An essay is required for some. The application deadline for regular admission is rolling.
Transfer Admission The application deadline for admission is rolling.
Entrance Difficulty Columbia College of Nursing assesses its entrance difficulty level as moderately difficult.

For Further Information Contact Ms. Amy Dobson, Dean of Admissions, Columbia College of Nursing, Carroll College, 100 North East Avenue, Milwaukee, WI 53186. *Telephone:* 414-256-1219. *Fax:* 262-524-7646. *E-mail:* jwiseman@ccadmin.cc.edu. *Web site:* http://www.ccon.edu/.

CONCORDIA UNIVERSITY WISCONSIN

Mequon, Wisconsin

CUW is a coed, private, comprehensive institution, founded in 1881, affiliated with the Lutheran Church–Missouri Synod, offering degrees at the bachelor's and master's levels. It has a 155-acre campus in Mequon near Milwaukee.

Academic Information The faculty has 167 members (56% full-time), 43% with terminal degrees. The undergraduate student-faculty ratio is 11:1. The library holds 110,929 titles, 1,411 serial subscriptions, and 4,645 audiovisual materials. Special programs include academic remediation, services for learning-disabled students, an honors program, study abroad, advanced placement credit, accelerated degree programs, ESL programs, double majors, independent study, distance learning, self-designed majors, summer session for credit, part-time degree programs, adult/continuing education programs, internships, and arrangement for off-campus study with Milwaukee Area Technical College, Milwaukee Institute of Art and Design, Cardinal Stritch University, Mount Mary College. The most frequently chosen baccalaureate fields are business/marketing, health professions and related sciences, interdisciplinary studies.
Student Body Statistics The student body totals 4,904, of whom 3,975 are undergraduates (294 freshmen). 65 percent are women and 35 percent are men. Students come from 41 states and territories and 21 other countries. 65 percent are from Wisconsin. 0.8 percent are international students.
Expenses for 2003–04 *Application fee:* $35. *Comprehensive fee:* $21,365 includes full-time tuition ($15,515), mandatory fees ($60), and college room and board ($5790). *Part-time tuition:* $645 per credit hour. Part-time tuition varies according to class time and program.
Financial Aid Forms of aid include need-based and non-need-based scholarships and part-time jobs. The average aided 2001–02 undergraduate received an aid package worth $11,938. The priority application deadline for financial aid is May 1.
Freshman Admission CUW requires a high school transcript, a minimum 2.0 high school GPA, SAT I or ACT scores, and TOEFL scores for international students. An interview is recommended. An essay, a minimum 3.0 high school GPA, and 3 recommendations are required for some. The application deadline for regular admission is August 15.
Transfer Admission The application deadline for admission is August 15.
Entrance Difficulty CUW assesses its entrance difficulty level as moderately difficult; minimally difficult for transfers. For the fall 2002 freshman class, 79 percent of the applicants were accepted.

For Further Information Contact Mr. Ken Gaschk, Director of Admissions, Concordia University Wisconsin, 12800 North Lake Shore Drive, Mequon, WI 53097. *Telephone:* 262-243-4305 Ext. 4305 or 888-628-9472 (toll-free). *Fax:* 262-243-4351. *E-mail:* admissions@cuw.edu. *Web site:* http://www.cuw.edu/.

EDGEWOOD COLLEGE

Madison, Wisconsin

Edgewood is a coed, private, Roman Catholic, comprehensive institution, founded in 1927, offering degrees at the associate, bachelor's, and master's levels. It has a 55-acre campus in Madison.

Academic Information The faculty has 221 members (39% full-time), 52% with terminal degrees. The undergraduate student-faculty ratio is 12:1. The library holds 90,253 titles, 447 serial subscriptions, and 4,359 audiovisual materials. Special programs include academic remediation,

Edgewood College (continued)

services for learning-disabled students, advanced placement credit, independent study, summer session for credit, part-time degree programs (daytime, evenings, weekends, summer), adult/continuing education programs, and arrangement for off-campus study with University of Wisconsin-Madison. The most frequently chosen baccalaureate field is philosophy, religion, and theology.

Student Body Statistics The student body totals 2,264, of whom 1,731 are undergraduates (271 freshmen). 73 percent are women and 27 percent are men. Students come from 16 states and territories and 22 other countries. 92 percent are from Wisconsin. 2.8 percent are international students. 8 percent of the 2002 graduating class went on to graduate and professional schools.

Expenses for 2003–04 *Application fee:* $25. *Comprehensive fee:* $20,450 includes full-time tuition ($15,100) and college room and board ($5350). *College room only:* $2708. Room and board charges vary according to housing facility and location. *Part-time tuition:* $457 per credit.

Financial Aid Forms of aid include need-based and non-need-based scholarships and part-time jobs. The average aided 2002–03 undergraduate received an aid package worth an estimated $11,172. The priority application deadline for financial aid is March 15.

Freshman Admission Edgewood requires a high school transcript, a minimum 2.5 high school GPA, SAT I or ACT scores, and TOEFL scores for international students. An essay, 2 recommendations, and an interview are required for some. The application deadline for regular admission is rolling.

Transfer Admission The application deadline for admission is rolling.

Entrance Difficulty Edgewood assesses its entrance difficulty level as moderately difficult. For the fall 2002 freshman class, 79 percent of the applicants were accepted.

For Further Information Contact Mr. Jim Krystofiak, Associate Director of Admissions, Edgewood College, 1000 Edgewood College Drive, Madison, WI 53711-1997. *Telephone:* 608-663-2254 or 800-444-4861 (toll-free). *Fax:* 608-663-3291. *E-mail:* admissions@edgewood.edu. *Web site:* http://www.edgewood.edu/.

HERZING COLLEGE

Madison, Wisconsin

Herzing College is a coed, primarily men's, proprietary, primarily two-year college of Herzing Institutes, Inc, founded in 1948, offering degrees at the associate and bachelor's levels. It is located in Madison near Milwaukee.

Academic Information The faculty has 46 members (33% full-time), 15% with terminal degrees. The student-faculty ratio is 13:1. The library holds 1,500 titles and 15 serial subscriptions. Special programs include academic remediation, advanced placement credit, accelerated degree programs, double majors, independent study, distance learning, part-time degree programs (evenings), and adult/continuing education programs.

Student Body Statistics The student body is made up of 650 undergraduates. Students come from 5 states and territories and 2 other countries. 67 percent are from Wisconsin. 20 percent of the 2002 graduating class went on to four-year colleges.

Expenses for 2002–03 *Application fee:* $0. *Tuition:* $8500 full-time, $260 per credit part-time. *Mandatory fees:* $100 full-time. Full-time tuition and fees vary according to course level and program. Part-time tuition varies according to course level and program.

Financial Aid Forms of aid include need-based scholarships and part-time jobs. The application deadline for financial aid is June 30.

Freshman Admission Herzing College requires a high school transcript, an interview, and TOEFL scores for international students. The application deadline for regular admission is October 10.

Transfer Admission The application deadline for admission is October 10.

Entrance Difficulty Herzing College assesses its entrance difficulty level as moderately difficult.

For Further Information Contact Ms. Renee Herzing, Admissions Director, Herzing College, 5218 E. Terrace Drive, Madison, WI 53718. *Telephone:* 608-249-6611 or 800-582-1227 (toll-free). *Fax:* 608-249-8593. *E-mail:* mailbag@msn.herzing.edu. *Web site:* http://www.herzing.edu/.

ITT TECHNICAL INSTITUTE

Green Bay, Wisconsin

ITT Tech is a coed, proprietary, primarily two-year college of ITT Educational Services, Inc., founded in 2000, offering degrees at the associate and bachelor's levels.

Student Body Statistics The student body is made up of 254 undergraduates.

Expenses for 2003–04 *Application fee:* $100.

Financial Aid Forms of aid include need-based scholarships and part-time jobs. The application deadline for financial aid is continuous.

Freshman Admission ITT Tech requires a high school transcript, an interview, Recommendations are recommended. The application deadline for regular admission is rolling.

Transfer Admission The application deadline for admission is rolling.

Entrance Difficulty ITT Tech assesses its entrance difficulty level as minimally difficult.

For Further Information Contact Mr. Raymond Sweetman, ITT Technical Institute, 470 Security Boulevard, Green Bay, WI 54313. *Telephone:* 920-662-9000. *Fax:* 920-662-9384. *Web site:* http://www.itt-tech.edu/.

ITT TECHNICAL INSTITUTE

Greenfield, Wisconsin

ITT Tech is a coed, proprietary, primarily two-year college of ITT Educational Services, Inc, founded in 1968, offering degrees at the associate and bachelor's levels. It is located in Greenfield near Milwaukee.

Student Body Statistics The student body is made up of 530 undergraduates.

Expenses for 2002–03 *Application fee:* $100. *Tuition:* $347 per credit hour part-time.

Financial Aid Forms of aid include need-based scholarships and part-time jobs. The application deadline for financial aid is continuous.

Freshman Admission ITT Tech requires a high school transcript, an interview, and Wonderlic aptitude test. Recommendations are recommended. The application deadline for regular admission is rolling.

Transfer Admission The application deadline for admission is rolling.

Entrance Difficulty ITT Tech assesses its entrance difficulty level as minimally difficult.

For Further Information Contact Mr. Al Hedin, Director of Recruitment, ITT Technical Institute, 6300 West Layton Avenue, Greenfield, WI 53220. *Telephone:* 414-282-9494. *Fax:* 414-282-9698. *Web site:* http://www.itt-tech.edu/.

LAKELAND COLLEGE

Sheboygan, Wisconsin

Lakeland is a coed, private, comprehensive institution, founded in 1862, affiliated with the United Church of Christ, offering degrees at the bachelor's and master's levels. It has a 240-acre campus in Sheboygan near Milwaukee.

Academic Information The faculty has 52 members (92% full-time), 65% with terminal degrees. The undergraduate student-faculty ratio is 19:1. The library holds 64,970 titles, 317 serial subscriptions, and 647

audiovisual materials. Special programs include academic remediation, services for learning-disabled students, an honors program, study abroad, advanced placement credit, ESL programs, independent study, distance learning, summer session for credit, part-time degree programs (evenings, summer), adult/continuing education programs, internships, and arrangement for off-campus study. The most frequently chosen baccalaureate fields are business/marketing, computer/information sciences, education.
Student Body Statistics The student body totals 3,586, of whom 3,254 are undergraduates (160 freshmen). 60 percent are women and 40 percent are men. Students come from 41 states and territories and 37 other countries. 85 percent are from Wisconsin. 4.6 percent are international students. 10 percent of the 2002 graduating class went on to graduate and professional schools.
Expenses for 2003–04 *Application fee:* $20. *Comprehensive fee:* $19,766 includes full-time tuition ($13,715), mandatory fees ($610), and college room and board ($5441). *College room only:* $2551. Full-time tuition and fees vary according to location. Room and board charges vary according to board plan and housing facility. *Part-time tuition:* $1523 per course. Part-time tuition varies according to class time and location.
Financial Aid Forms of aid include need-based and non-need-based scholarships and part-time jobs. The average aided 2002–03 undergraduate received an aid package worth an estimated $9976. The application deadline for financial aid is July 1 with a priority deadline of May 1.
Freshman Admission Lakeland requires an essay, a high school transcript, a minimum 2.0 high school GPA, SAT I or ACT scores, and TOEFL scores for international students. Recommendations are recommended. An interview is required for some. The application deadline for regular admission is July 15.
Transfer Admission The application deadline for admission is July 15.
Entrance Difficulty Lakeland assesses its entrance difficulty level as minimally difficult. For the fall 2002 freshman class, 77 percent of the applicants were accepted.

For Further Information Contact Mr. Leo Gavrilos, Director of Admissions, Lakeland College, PO Box 359, Nash Visitors Center, Sheboygan, WI 53082-0359. *Telephone:* 920-565-1217 or 800-242-3347 (toll-free in-state). *Fax:* 920-565-1206. *E-mail:* admissions@lakeland.edu. *Web site:* http://www.lakeland.edu/.

LAWRENCE UNIVERSITY

Appleton, Wisconsin

Lawrence is a coed, private, four-year college, founded in 1847, offering degrees at the bachelor's level. It has an 84-acre campus in Appleton.

Academic Information The faculty has 170 members (81% full-time), 81% with terminal degrees. The student-faculty ratio is 11:1. The library holds 376,814 titles, 1,586 serial subscriptions, and 21,086 audiovisual materials. Special programs include services for learning-disabled students, study abroad, advanced placement credit, double majors, independent study, self-designed majors, internships, and arrangement for off-campus study with Associated Colleges of the Midwest, Great Lakes Colleges Association. The most frequently chosen baccalaureate fields are social sciences and history, biological/life sciences, visual/performing arts.
Student Body Statistics The student body is made up of 1,389 undergraduates (352 freshmen). 52 percent are women and 48 percent are men. Students come from 49 states and territories and 45 other countries. 41 percent are from Wisconsin. 10.4 percent are international students. 30 percent of the 2002 graduating class went on to graduate and professional schools.
Expenses for 2002–03 *Application fee:* $30. *Comprehensive fee:* $29,124 includes full-time tuition ($23,487), mandatory fees ($180), and college room and board ($5457). *College room only:* $2346. Room and board charges vary according to board plan.
Financial Aid Forms of aid include need-based and non-need-based scholarships and part-time jobs. The average aided 2002–03 undergraduate received an aid package worth an estimated $20,275. The priority application deadline for financial aid is March 15.
Freshman Admission Lawrence requires an essay, a high school transcript, 2 recommendations, audition for music program, and SAT I or ACT scores. A minimum 3.0 high school GPA, an interview, and TOEFL scores for international students are recommended. The application deadline for regular admission is January 15; for early decision it is November 15; and for early action it is December 1.
Transfer Admission The application deadline for admission is rolling.
Entrance Difficulty Lawrence assesses its entrance difficulty level as very difficult. For the fall 2002 freshman class, 68 percent of the applicants were accepted.

For Further Information Contact Mr. Michael Thorp, Director of Admissions, Lawrence University, PO Box 599, Appleton, WI 54912-0599. *Telephone:* 920-832-6500 or 800-227-0982 (toll-free). *Fax:* 920-832-6782. *E-mail:* excel@lawrence.edu. *Web site:* http://www.lawrence.edu.

MARANATHA BAPTIST BIBLE COLLEGE

Watertown, Wisconsin

Maranatha is a coed, private, Baptist, comprehensive institution, founded in 1968, offering degrees at the associate, bachelor's, and master's levels. It has a 60-acre campus in Watertown near Milwaukee.

Academic Information The faculty has 67 full-time members. The undergraduate student-faculty ratio is 16:1. The library holds 99,390 titles, 515 serial subscriptions, and 3,441 audiovisual materials. Special programs include academic remediation, accelerated degree programs, double majors, independent study, distance learning, summer session for credit, part-time degree programs (daytime, evenings, summer), internships, and arrangement for off-campus study with Madison Area Technical College.
Student Body Statistics The student body totals 803, of whom 776 are undergraduates (186 freshmen). 53 percent are women and 47 percent are men. Students come from 29 states and territories and 5 other countries. 34 percent are from Wisconsin. 1.2 percent are international students. 28 percent of the 2002 graduating class went on to graduate and professional schools.
Expenses for 2002–03 *Application fee:* $40. *Comprehensive fee:* $10,920 includes full-time tuition ($6720) and college room and board ($4200). *Part-time tuition:* $210 per semester hour.
Financial Aid Forms of aid include need-based and non-need-based scholarships and part-time jobs. The average aided 2002–03 undergraduate received an aid package worth an estimated $2597. The priority application deadline for financial aid is March 1.
Freshman Admission Maranatha requires an essay, a high school transcript, 3 recommendations, and TOEFL scores for international students. ACT scores are recommended. The application deadline for regular admission is rolling.
Transfer Admission The application deadline for admission is rolling.
Entrance Difficulty Maranatha has an open admission policy.

For Further Information Contact Mr. James H. Harrison, Director of Admissions, Maranatha Baptist Bible College, 745 West Main Street, Watertown, WI 53094. *Telephone:* 920-206-2327 or 800-622-2947 (toll-free). *Fax:* 920-261-9109. *E-mail:* admissions@mbbc.edu. *Web site:* http://www.mbbc.edu/.

MARIAN COLLEGE OF FOND DU LAC

Fond du Lac, Wisconsin

Marian College is a coed, private, Roman Catholic, comprehensive institution, founded in 1936, offering degrees at the bachelor's and master's levels. It has a 77-acre campus in Fond du Lac near Milwaukee.

Academic Information The faculty has 141 members (52% full-time), 42% with terminal degrees. The undergraduate student-faculty ratio is 14:1. The library holds 91,708 titles, 698 serial subscriptions, and 397 audiovisual materials. Special programs include academic remediation, services for learning-disabled students, an honors program, cooperative (work-study) education, study abroad, advanced placement credit, accelerated degree programs, double majors, independent study, distance

Marian College of Fond du Lac (continued)

learning, self-designed majors, summer session for credit, part-time degree programs (daytime, evenings, weekends, summer), external degree programs, adult/continuing education programs, and internships. The most frequently chosen baccalaureate fields are business/marketing, education, health professions and related sciences.
Student Body Statistics The student body totals 2,672, of whom 1,745 are undergraduates (246 freshmen). 71 percent are women and 29 percent are men. Students come from 25 states and territories and 11 other countries. 94 percent are from Wisconsin. 1.7 percent are international students.
Expenses for 2002–03 *Application fee:* $20. *Comprehensive fee:* $18,995 includes full-time tuition ($13,880), mandatory fees ($315), and college room and board ($4800). *College room only:* $2500. Room and board charges vary according to board plan, housing facility, and location. *Part-time tuition:* $270 per credit. Part-time tuition varies according to class time, course load, and program.
Financial Aid Forms of aid include need-based and non-need-based scholarships and part-time jobs. The average aided 2002–03 undergraduate received an aid package worth an estimated $15,490. The priority application deadline for financial aid is March 1.
Freshman Admission Marian College requires a high school transcript, SAT I or ACT scores, and TOEFL scores for international students. A minimum 2.0 high school GPA and recommendations are recommended. An interview is required for some. The application deadline for regular admission is rolling.
Transfer Admission The application deadline for admission is rolling.
Entrance Difficulty Marian College assesses its entrance difficulty level as moderately difficult. For the fall 2002 freshman class, 83 percent of the applicants were accepted.

For Further Information Contact Stacey L. Akey, Dean of Admissions, Marian College of Fond du Lac, 45 South National Avenue, Fond du Lac, WI 54935. *Telephone:* 920-923-7652 or 800-2-MARIAN Ext. 7652 (toll-free in-state). *Fax:* 920-923-8755. *E-mail:* admit@mariancollege.edu. *Web site:* http://www.mariancollege.edu/.

MARQUETTE UNIVERSITY

Milwaukee, Wisconsin

Marquette is a coed, private, Roman Catholic (Jesuit) university, founded in 1881, offering degrees at the associate, bachelor's, master's, doctoral, and first professional levels and post-master's and postbachelor's certificates. It has an 80-acre campus in Milwaukee.

Academic Information The faculty has 1,002 members (62% full-time). The undergraduate student-faculty ratio is 15:1. The library holds 1 million titles, 5,894 serial subscriptions, and 9,332 audiovisual materials. Special programs include services for learning-disabled students, an honors program, cooperative (work-study) education, study abroad, advanced placement credit, ESL programs, double majors, summer session for credit, part-time degree programs (daytime, evenings, weekends, summer), adult/continuing education programs, internships, and arrangement for off-campus study with Milwaukee Institute of Art and Design, Les Aspin Center for Government, Washington, DC. The most frequently chosen baccalaureate fields are business/marketing, communications/communication technologies, engineering/engineering technologies.
Student Body Statistics The student body totals 11,042, of whom 7,644 are undergraduates (1,856 freshmen). 56 percent are women and 44 percent are men. Students come from 54 states and territories and 80 other countries. 47 percent are from Wisconsin. 2 percent are international students. 28 percent of the 2002 graduating class went on to graduate and professional schools.
Expenses for 2002–03 *Application fee:* $30. *Comprehensive fee:* $26,056 includes full-time tuition ($19,400), mandatory fees ($306), and college room and board ($6350). *College room only:* $3810. Full-time tuition and fees vary according to course load, program, and reciprocity agreements. Room and board charges vary according to board plan, housing facility, and location. *Part-time tuition:* $570 per credit. Part-time tuition varies according to program.
Financial Aid Forms of aid include need-based and non-need-based scholarships, athletic grants, and part-time jobs. The average aided 2002–03 undergraduate received an aid package worth an estimated $16,400. The application deadline for financial aid is continuous.
Freshman Admission Marquette requires an essay, a high school transcript, a minimum 2.5 high school GPA, SAT I or ACT scores, and TOEFL scores for international students. A minimum 3.4 high school GPA, 1 recommendation, an interview, and SAT I scores are recommended. SAT I and SAT II or ACT scores, SAT II: Subject Test scores, SAT II: Writing Test scores, are required for some. The application deadline for regular admission is rolling.
Transfer Admission The application deadline for admission is rolling.
Entrance Difficulty Marquette assesses its entrance difficulty level as moderately difficult; very difficult for physical therapy and athletic training. For the fall 2002 freshman class, 82 percent of the applicants were accepted.

For Further Information Contact Mr. Robert Blust, Dean of Undergraduate Admissions, Marquette University, PO Box 1881, Milwaukee, WI 53201-1881. *Telephone:* 414-288-7004 or 800-222-6544 (toll-free). *Fax:* 414-288-3764. *E-mail:* admissions@marquette.edu. *Web site:* http://www.marquette.edu/.

MILWAUKEE INSTITUTE OF ART AND DESIGN

Milwaukee, Wisconsin

MIAD is a coed, private, four-year college, founded in 1974, offering degrees at the bachelor's level in art and design.

Academic Information The faculty has 100 members (36% full-time), 69% with terminal degrees. The student-faculty ratio is 16:1. The library holds 23,000 titles, 84 serial subscriptions, and 360 audiovisual materials. Special programs include academic remediation, services for learning-disabled students, cooperative (work-study) education, study abroad, advanced placement credit, double majors, independent study, summer session for credit, adult/continuing education programs, internships, and arrangement for off-campus study with Marquette University, Association of Independent Colleges of Art and Design. The most frequently chosen baccalaureate field is visual/performing arts.
Student Body Statistics The student body is made up of 632 undergraduates (141 freshmen). 51 percent are women and 49 percent are men. Students come from 16 states and territories and 5 other countries. 72 percent are from Wisconsin. 2.4 percent are international students. 1 percent of the 2002 graduating class went on to graduate and professional schools.
Expenses for 2002–03 *Application fee:* $25. *Comprehensive fee:* $26,568 includes full-time tuition ($19,900), mandatory fees ($130), and college room and board ($6538). Room and board charges vary according to board plan. *Part-time tuition:* $665 per credit. *Part-time mandatory fees:* $65 per term. Part-time tuition and fees vary according to course load.
Financial Aid Forms of aid include need-based and non-need-based scholarships and part-time jobs. The average aided 2001–02 undergraduate received an aid package worth $14,115. The application deadline for financial aid is March 1.
Freshman Admission MIAD requires an essay, a high school transcript, an interview, a portfolio, and TOEFL scores for international students. A minimum 2.0 high school GPA and SAT I or ACT scores are recommended. Recommendations are required for some. The application deadline for regular admission is rolling.
Transfer Admission The application deadline for admission is rolling.
Entrance Difficulty MIAD assesses its entrance difficulty level as moderately difficult. For the fall 2002 freshman class, 84 percent of the applicants were accepted.

For Further Information Contact Mr. Mark Fetherston, Director of Admissions, Milwaukee Institute of Art and Design, 273 East Erie Street, Milwaukee, WI 53202. *Telephone:* 414-847-3259 or 888-749-MIAD (toll-free). *Fax:* 414-291-8077. *E-mail:* admissions@miad.edu. *Web site:* http://www.miad.edu/.

MILWAUKEE SCHOOL OF ENGINEERING

Milwaukee, Wisconsin

MSOE is a coed, primarily men's, private, comprehensive institution, founded in 1903, offering degrees at the bachelor's and master's levels. It has a 12-acre campus in Milwaukee.

Academic Information The faculty has 271 members (44% full-time), 37% with terminal degrees. The undergraduate student-faculty ratio is 11:1. The library holds 56,044 titles, 416 serial subscriptions, and 852 audiovisual materials. Special programs include academic remediation, services for learning-disabled students, study abroad, advanced placement credit, accelerated degree programs, double majors, independent study, distance learning, summer session for credit, part-time degree programs (daytime, evenings, weekends, summer), adult/continuing education programs, and internships. The most frequently chosen baccalaureate fields are business/marketing, communications/communication technologies, engineering/engineering technologies.
Student Body Statistics The student body totals 2,586, of whom 2,272 are undergraduates (508 freshmen). 16 percent are women and 84 percent are men. Students come from 31 states and territories and 19 other countries. 79 percent are from Wisconsin. 3.1 percent are international students. 6 percent of the 2002 graduating class went on to graduate and professional schools.
Expenses for 2003–04 *Application fee:* $25. *Comprehensive fee:* $28,479 includes full-time tuition ($23,034) and college room and board ($5445). *College room only:* $3500. Full-time tuition varies according to student level. Room and board charges vary according to board plan and housing facility. *Part-time tuition:* $402 per quarter hour. Part-time tuition varies according to course load.
Financial Aid Forms of aid include need-based and non-need-based scholarships and part-time jobs. The average aided 2001–02 undergraduate received an aid package worth $15,348. The application deadline for financial aid is continuous.
Freshman Admission MSOE requires a high school transcript, a minimum 2.5 high school GPA, SAT I or ACT scores, and TOEFL scores for international students. An essay and an interview are required for some. The application deadline for regular admission is rolling.
Transfer Admission The application deadline for admission is rolling.
Entrance Difficulty MSOE assesses its entrance difficulty level as moderately difficult. For the fall 2002 freshman class, 72 percent of the applicants were accepted.

For Further Information Contact Mr. Tim A. Valley, Dean of Enrollment Management, Milwaukee School of Engineering, 1025 North Broadway, Milwaukee, WI 53202-3109. *Telephone:* 414-277-6763 or 800-332-6763 (toll-free). *Fax:* 414-277-7475. *E-mail:* explore@msoe.edu. *Web site:* http://www.msoe.edu/.

See page 308 for a narrative description.

MOUNT MARY COLLEGE

Milwaukee, Wisconsin

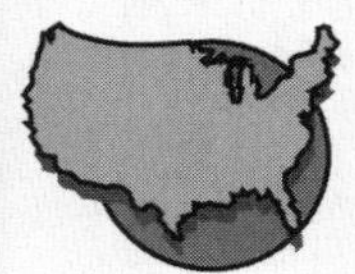

MMC is a women's, private, Roman Catholic, comprehensive institution, founded in 1913, offering degrees at the bachelor's and master's levels. It has an 80-acre campus in Milwaukee.

Academic Information The faculty has 163 members (42% full-time), 42% with terminal degrees. The undergraduate student-faculty ratio is 9:1. The library holds 113,006 titles, 500 serial subscriptions, and 9,832 audiovisual materials. Special programs include academic remediation, services for learning-disabled students, an honors program, study abroad, advanced placement credit, accelerated degree programs, double majors, independent study, self-designed majors, summer session for credit, part-time degree programs (daytime, evenings, weekends, summer), adult/continuing education programs, and internships. The most frequently chosen baccalaureate fields are health professions and related sciences, business/marketing, visual/performing arts.
Student Body Statistics The student body totals 1,401, of whom 1,223 are undergraduates (121 freshmen). Students come from 8 states and territories and 6 other countries. 97 percent are from Wisconsin. 0.7 percent are international students. 6.3 percent of the 2002 graduating class went on to graduate and professional schools.
Expenses for 2002–03 *Application fee:* $25. *Comprehensive fee:* $19,060 includes full-time tuition ($13,995), mandatory fees ($170), and college room and board ($4895). *College room only:* $2180. Room and board charges vary according to board plan. *Part-time tuition:* $420 per credit. *Part-time mandatory fees:* $42.50 per term. Part-time tuition and fees vary according to course load.
Financial Aid Forms of aid include need-based and non-need-based scholarships and part-time jobs. The average aided 2002–03 undergraduate received an aid package worth an estimated $11,037. The priority application deadline for financial aid is March 1.
Freshman Admission MMC requires a high school transcript, a minimum 2.5 high school GPA, SAT I or ACT scores, and TOEFL scores for international students. An interview is recommended. An essay and 2 recommendations are required for some. The application deadline for regular admission is rolling.
Transfer Admission The application deadline for admission is rolling.
Entrance Difficulty MMC assesses its entrance difficulty level as moderately difficult. For the fall 2002 freshman class, 71 percent of the applicants were accepted.

SPECIAL MESSAGE TO STUDENTS

Social Life Students attending Mount Mary College venture from eight countries, thirteen states, and many diverse backgrounds. Mount Mary's enrollment is approximately 1,400 students, producing an inclusive, family atmosphere. Mount Mary's park-like campus features stately stone buildings, gorgeous green lawns, and a beautiful wooded area only 15 minutes from downtown Milwaukee. The campus and the surrounding major metropolitan area features entertainment, including more than twenty campus organizations, concerts, plays, and dances. Students are encouraged to organize activities with other Milwaukee colleges and universities. Mount Mary also offers intercollegiate varsity sports and much more.

Academic Highlights Mount Mary, as a Catholic college sponsored by the School Sisters of Notre Dame, provides the highest quality of values-based education, integrating a strong liberal arts foundation with more than thirty professional majors. Due to its smaller class size, Mount Mary's students are able to participate more and are encouraged to succeed. Mount Mary is not a college where students get lost in the crowd. Learning is involved and interactive. Students express their opinions in a friendly environment, discovering their potential with the close attention of their fellow students and faculty members. Outside the classroom, students participate in club activities, internships, community service, and campus ministry programs.

Interviews and Campus Visits Students can visit campus throughout the year, and the Enrollment Office is open year-round. Students may take a tour, meet with admissions counselors, financial aid officers, faculty members, and current students. To schedule a visit or for more information, students should call the Enrollment Office at 414-256-1219 or 800-321-6265 (toll-free), Monday through Friday, 8:00 a.m. to 5:00 p.m.

For Further Information Write to Enrollment Office, Mount Mary College, 2900 North Menomonee River Parkway, Milwaukee, WI 53222-4597. *E-mail:* admiss@mtmary.edu. *Web site:* http://www.mtmary.edu.

NORTHLAND COLLEGE

Ashland, Wisconsin

Northland is a coed, private, four-year college, founded in 1892, affiliated with the United Church of Christ, offering degrees at the bachelor's level. It has a 130-acre campus in Ashland.

Academic Information The faculty has 88 members (55% full-time), 55% with terminal degrees. The student-faculty ratio is 14:1. The library holds 75,000 titles and 260 serial subscriptions. Special programs include services for learning-disabled students, an honors program, cooperative (work-study) education, study abroad, advanced placement credit, accelerated degree programs, double majors, independent study, distance learning, self-designed majors, summer session for credit, part-time degree

Northland College (continued)
programs (daytime, evenings, summer), adult/continuing education programs, internships, and arrangement for off-campus study with members of the May Term Consortium, Allegheny College, Beloit College. The most frequently chosen baccalaureate fields are education, biological/life sciences, natural resources/environmental science.
Student Body Statistics The student body is made up of 752 undergraduates (186 freshmen). 55 percent are women and 45 percent are men. Students come from 46 states and territories and 13 other countries. 33 percent are from Wisconsin. 3.2 percent are international students. 26 percent of the 2002 graduating class went on to graduate and professional schools.
Expenses for 2003–04 *Application fee:* $0. *Comprehensive fee:* $22,750 includes full-time tuition ($17,070), mandatory fees ($580), and college room and board ($5100). *College room only:* $2080. Room and board charges vary according to board plan and housing facility. *Part-time tuition:* $350 per credit.
Financial Aid Forms of aid include need-based and non-need-based scholarships and part-time jobs. The average aided 2002–03 undergraduate received an aid package worth an estimated $15,203. The priority application deadline for financial aid is April 15.
Freshman Admission Northland requires an essay, a high school transcript, 1 recommendation, SAT I or ACT scores, and TOEFL scores for international students. A minimum 2.0 high school GPA and an interview are recommended. The application deadline for regular admission is August 1.
Transfer Admission The application deadline for admission is August 1.
Entrance Difficulty Northland assesses its entrance difficulty level as moderately difficult. For the fall 2002 freshman class, 94 percent of the applicants were accepted.

For Further Information Contact Mr. Eric Peterson, Director of Admission, Northland College, 1411 Ellis Avenue, Ashland, WI 54806. *Telephone:* 715-682-1224, 800-753-1840 (toll-free in-state), or 800-753-1040 (toll-free out-of-state). *Fax:* 715-682-1258. *E-mail:* admit@northland.edu. *Web site:* http://www.northland.edu/.

RIPON COLLEGE

Ripon, Wisconsin

Ripon is a coed, private, four-year college, founded in 1851, offering degrees at the bachelor's level. It has a 250-acre campus in Ripon near Milwaukee.

Academic Information The faculty has 74 members (64% full-time), 80% with terminal degrees. The student-faculty ratio is 15:1. The library holds 169,523 titles, 985 serial subscriptions, and 662 audiovisual materials. Special programs include services for learning-disabled students, study abroad, advanced placement credit, accelerated degree programs, double majors, self-designed majors, part-time degree programs (daytime), internships, and arrangement for off-campus study with American University, Newberry Library, Oak Ridge National Laboratory, University of Chicago, Associated Colleges of the Midwest Wilderness Field Station. The most frequently chosen baccalaureate fields are English, education, trade and industry.
Student Body Statistics The student body is made up of 987 undergraduates (250 freshmen). 53 percent are women and 47 percent are men. Students come from 36 states and territories and 14 other countries. 68 percent are from Wisconsin. 1.9 percent are international students. 30 percent of the 2002 graduating class went on to graduate and professional schools.
Expenses for 2002–03 *Application fee:* $30. *Comprehensive fee:* $24,320 includes full-time tuition ($19,260), mandatory fees ($240), and college room and board ($4820). *College room only:* $2195. *Part-time tuition:* $825 per credit.
Financial Aid Forms of aid include need-based and non-need-based scholarships and part-time jobs. The average aided 2002–03 undergraduate received an aid package worth an estimated $18,573. The priority application deadline for financial aid is March 1.
Freshman Admission Ripon requires a high school transcript, a minimum 2.0 high school GPA, 1 recommendation, SAT I or ACT scores, and TOEFL scores for international students. An essay and an interview are recommended. The application deadline for regular admission is rolling.
Transfer Admission The application deadline for admission is rolling.
Entrance Difficulty Ripon assesses its entrance difficulty level as moderately difficult. For the fall 2002 freshman class, 84 percent of the applicants were accepted.

For Further Information Contact Mr. Scott J. Goplin, Vice President and Dean of Admission and Financial Aid, Ripon College, 300 Seward Street, PO Box 248, Ripon, WI 54971. *Telephone:* 920-748-8185 or 800-947-4766 (toll-free). *Fax:* 920-748-8335. *E-mail:* adminfo@ripon.edu. *Web site:* http://www.ripon.edu/.

See page 328 for a narrative description.

ST. NORBERT COLLEGE

De Pere, Wisconsin

St. Norbert is a coed, private, Roman Catholic, comprehensive institution, founded in 1898, offering degrees at the bachelor's and master's levels. It has an 84-acre campus in De Pere.

Academic Information The faculty has 181 members (67% full-time), 66% with terminal degrees. The library holds 115,553 titles, 690 serial subscriptions, and 7,625 audiovisual materials. Special programs include academic remediation, services for learning-disabled students, an honors program, cooperative (work-study) education, study abroad, advanced placement credit, ESL programs, double majors, independent study, distance learning, self-designed majors, summer session for credit, part-time degree programs (daytime, summer), internships, and arrangement for off-campus study with Higher Education Consortium for Urban Affairs, American University. The most frequently chosen baccalaureate fields are business/marketing, communications/communication technologies, social sciences and history.
Student Body Statistics The student body totals 2,133, of whom 2,072 are undergraduates (499 freshmen). 57 percent are women and 43 percent are men. Students come from 26 states and territories and 27 other countries. 71 percent are from Wisconsin. 2.2 percent are international students.
Expenses for 2002–03 *Application fee:* $25. *Comprehensive fee:* $24,524 includes full-time tuition ($18,834), mandatory fees ($250), and college room and board ($5440). *College room only:* $2900. Full-time tuition and fees vary according to course load. Room and board charges vary according to board plan, housing facility, and student level. *Part-time tuition:* $2354 per course. *Part-time mandatory fees:* $12.50 per course, $50 per term. Part-time tuition and fees vary according to course load.
Financial Aid Forms of aid include need-based and non-need-based scholarships and part-time jobs. The average aided 2002–03 undergraduate received an aid package worth an estimated $14,718. The priority application deadline for financial aid is March 1.
Freshman Admission St. Norbert requires an essay, a high school transcript, 1 recommendation, SAT I or ACT scores, and TOEFL scores for international students. An interview is recommended. The application deadline for regular admission is rolling and for early decision it is December 1.
Transfer Admission The application deadline for admission is rolling.
Entrance Difficulty St. Norbert assesses its entrance difficulty level as moderately difficult. For the fall 2002 freshman class, 83 percent of the applicants were accepted.

For Further Information Contact Mr. Daniel L. Meyer, Dean of Admission and Enrollment Management, St. Norbert College, 100 Grant Street, De Pere, WI 54115-2099. *Telephone:* 920-403-3005 or 800-236-4878 (toll-free). *Fax:* 920-403-4072. *E-mail:* admit@snc.edu. *Web site:* http://www.snc.edu/.

SILVER LAKE COLLEGE

Manitowoc, Wisconsin

SLC is a coed, private, Roman Catholic, comprehensive institution, founded in 1869, offering degrees at the associate, bachelor's, and master's levels and postbachelor's certificates. It has a 30-acre campus in Manitowoc near Milwaukee.

Academic Information The faculty has 128 members (34% full-time), 34% with terminal degrees. The undergraduate student-faculty ratio is 8:1. The library holds 60,466 titles, 296 serial subscriptions, and 11,458 audiovisual materials. Special programs include academic remediation, cooperative (work-study) education, advanced placement credit, accelerated degree programs, ESL programs, double majors, independent study, distance learning, self-designed majors, summer session for credit, part-time degree programs (daytime, evenings, weekends, summer), adult/continuing education programs, and internships. The most frequently chosen baccalaureate fields are business/marketing, education, engineering/engineering technologies.
Student Body Statistics The student body totals 1,146, of whom 733 are undergraduates (35 freshmen). 69 percent are women and 31 percent are men. Students come from 3 states and territories and 1 other country. 98 percent are from Wisconsin. 0.2 percent are international students. 10 percent of the 2002 graduating class went on to graduate and professional schools.
Expenses for 2003–04 *Application fee:* $35. *Tuition:* $14,350 full-time, $360 per credit part-time. Full-time tuition varies according to location and program. Part-time tuition varies according to course load, location, and program. *College room only:* $4100.
Financial Aid Forms of aid include need-based and non-need-based scholarships, athletic grants, and part-time jobs. The average aided 2001–02 undergraduate received an aid package worth $6443. The application deadline for financial aid is June 1 with a priority deadline of April 15.
Freshman Admission SLC requires a high school transcript, a minimum 2.0 high school GPA, SAT I or ACT scores, and TOEFL scores for international students. An interview and audition are required for some. The application deadline for regular admission is August 31.
Transfer Admission The application deadline for admission is August 31.
Entrance Difficulty SLC assesses its entrance difficulty level as minimally difficult. For the fall 2002 freshman class, 47 percent of the applicants were accepted.

For Further Information Contact Ms. Janis Algozine, Vice President, Dean of Students, Silver Lake College, 2406 South Alverno Road, Manitowoc, WI. *Telephone:* 920-684-5955 Ext. 175 or 800-236-4752 Ext. 175 (toll-free in-state). *Fax:* 920-684-7082. *E-mail:* admslc@silver.sl.edu. *Web site:* http://www.sl.edu/.

STRATTON COLLEGE

See Bryant and Stratton College

UNIVERSITY OF PHOENIX-WISCONSIN CAMPUS

Brookfield, Wisconsin

University of Phoenix-Wisconsin Campus is a coed, proprietary, comprehensive institution, founded in 2001, offering degrees at the associate, bachelor's, master's, and doctoral levels and post-master's and postbachelor's certificates (courses conducted at 121 campuses and learning centers in 25 states).

Academic Information The faculty has 50 members, 18% with terminal degrees. The undergraduate student-faculty ratio is 13:1. The library holds 27 million titles and 11,648 serial subscriptions. Special programs include advanced placement credit, accelerated degree programs, independent study, distance learning, external degree programs, and adult/continuing education programs.
Student Body Statistics The student body totals 533, of whom 376 are undergraduates (1 freshman). 51 percent are women and 49 percent are men. 4.8 percent are international students.
Expenses for 2002–03 *Tuition:* $9210 full-time, $307 per credit part-time.
Financial Aid The application deadline for financial aid is continuous.
Freshman Admission University of Phoenix-Wisconsin Campus requires 1 recommendation, 2 years of work experience, 23 years of age, and TOEFL scores for international students. A high school transcript is required for some. The application deadline for regular admission is rolling.
Transfer Admission The application deadline for admission is rolling.
Entrance Difficulty University of Phoenix-Wisconsin Campus has an open admission policy.

For Further Information Contact Ms. Beth Barilla, Director of Admissions, University of Phoenix-Wisconsin Campus, 4615 East Elwood Street, Mail Stop 10-0030, Phoenix, AZ 85040-1958. *Telephone:* 480-557-1712 or 800-228-7240 (toll-free). *Fax:* 262-785-0608. *E-mail:* beth.barilla@apollogrp.edu. *Web site:* http://www.phoenix.edu/.

UNIVERSITY OF WISCONSIN–EAU CLAIRE

Eau Claire, Wisconsin

UWEC is a coed, public, comprehensive unit of University of Wisconsin System, founded in 1916, offering degrees at the associate, bachelor's, and master's levels and post-master's, first professional, and postbachelor's certificates. It has a 333-acre campus in Eau Claire.

Academic Information The faculty has 484 members (86% full-time), 78% with terminal degrees. The undergraduate student-faculty ratio is 21:1. The library holds 605,639 titles, 2,570 serial subscriptions, and 14,545 audiovisual materials. Special programs include academic remediation, services for learning-disabled students, an honors program, cooperative (work-study) education, study abroad, advanced placement credit, ESL programs, double majors, independent study, distance learning, summer session for credit, part-time degree programs (daytime, evenings, summer), adult/continuing education programs, internships, and arrangement for off-campus study with National Student Exchange. The most frequently chosen baccalaureate fields are business/marketing, education, health professions and related sciences.
Student Body Statistics The student body totals 10,861, of whom 10,364 are undergraduates (2,053 freshmen). 60 percent are women and 40 percent are men. Students come from 22 states and territories and 47 other countries. 78 percent are from Wisconsin. 1.1 percent are international students. 9 percent of the 2002 graduating class went on to graduate and professional schools.
Expenses for 2002–03 *Application fee:* $35. *State resident tuition:* $3722 full-time, $155.04 per credit part-time. *Nonresident tuition:* $13,768 full-time, $573.59 per credit part-time. Full-time tuition varies according to reciprocity agreements. Part-time tuition varies according to reciprocity agreements. *College room and board:* $3910. *College room only:* $2270. Room and board charges vary according to board plan.
Financial Aid Forms of aid include need-based and non-need-based scholarships and part-time jobs. The average aided 2001–02 undergraduate received an aid package worth $5830. The priority application deadline for financial aid is April 15.
Freshman Admission UWEC requires a high school transcript, rank in upper 50% of high school class, SAT I or ACT scores, and TOEFL scores for international students. The application deadline for regular admission is rolling.
Transfer Admission The application deadline for admission is July 1.
Entrance Difficulty UWEC assesses its entrance difficulty level as moderately difficult. For the fall 2002 freshman class, 68 percent of the applicants were accepted.

For Further Information Contact Mr. Robert Lopez, Executive Director of Enrollment Management and Director of Admissions, University of Wisconsin–Eau Claire, PO Box 4004, Eau Claire, WI 54702-4004. *Telephone:* 715-836-5415. *Fax:* 715-836-2409. *E-mail:* admissions@uwec.edu. *Web site:* http://www.uwec.edu/.

UNIVERSITY OF WISCONSIN–GREEN BAY

Green Bay, Wisconsin

UW-Green Bay is a coed, public, comprehensive unit of University of Wisconsin System, founded in 1968, offering degrees at the associate, bachelor's, and master's levels and postbachelor's certificates. It has a 700-acre campus in Green Bay.

Academic Information The faculty has 259 members (67% full-time), 64% with terminal degrees. The undergraduate student-faculty ratio is 23:1. The library holds 333,482 titles, 5,512 serial subscriptions, and 45,396 audiovisual materials. Special programs include academic remediation, services for learning-disabled students, cooperative (work-study) education, study abroad, advanced placement credit, accelerated degree programs, ESL programs, double majors, independent study, distance learning, self-designed majors, summer session for credit, part-time degree programs (daytime, evenings, weekends, summer), external degree programs, adult/continuing education programs, internships, and arrangement for off-campus study with National Student Exchange. The most frequently chosen baccalaureate fields are business/marketing, biological/life sciences, interdisciplinary studies.
Student Body Statistics The student body totals 5,255, of whom 5,101 are undergraduates (901 freshmen). 66 percent are women and 34 percent are men. Students come from 25 states and territories and 31 other countries. 96 percent are from Wisconsin. 1.1 percent are international students. 10 percent of the 2002 graduating class went on to graduate and professional schools.
Expenses for 2002–03 *Application fee:* $35. *State resident tuition:* $3000 full-time, $125 per credit part-time. *Nonresident tuition:* $13,046 full-time, $544 per credit part-time. *Mandatory fees:* $1023 full-time, $34 per credit part-time. Full-time tuition and fees vary according to reciprocity agreements. Part-time tuition and fees vary according to reciprocity agreements. *College room and board:* $3700. *College room only:* $2201. Room and board charges vary according to board plan and housing facility.
Financial Aid Forms of aid include need-based and non-need-based scholarships, athletic grants, and part-time jobs. The average aided 2002–03 undergraduate received an aid package worth an estimated $6666. The priority application deadline for financial aid is April 15.
Freshman Admission UW-Green Bay requires an essay, a high school transcript, rank in upper 45% of high school class, minimum ACT score of 17, SAT I or ACT scores, and TOEFL scores for international students. A minimum 2.25 high school GPA is recommended. Recommendations and an interview are required for some. The application deadline for regular admission is February 1.
Transfer Admission The application deadline for admission is February 1.
Entrance Difficulty UW-Green Bay assesses its entrance difficulty level as moderately difficult. For the fall 2002 freshman class, 76 percent of the applicants were accepted.

For Further Information Contact Ms. Pam Harvey-Jacobs, Interim Director of Admissions, University of Wisconsin–Green Bay, 2420 Nicolet Drive, Green Bay, WI 54311-7001. *Telephone:* 920-465-2111 or 888-367-8942 (toll-free out-of-state). *Fax:* 920-465-5754. *E-mail:* admissions@uwgb.edu. *Web site:* http://www.uwgb.edu/.

UNIVERSITY OF WISCONSIN–LA CROSSE

La Crosse, Wisconsin

UW-La Crosse is a coed, public, comprehensive unit of University of Wisconsin System, founded in 1909, offering degrees at the associate, bachelor's, and master's levels. It has a 121-acre campus in La Crosse.

Academic Information The faculty has 410 members (91% full-time), 74% with terminal degrees. The undergraduate student-faculty ratio is 21:1. The library holds 660,159 titles, 1,603 serial subscriptions, and 1,648 audiovisual materials. Special programs include academic remediation, services for learning-disabled students, an honors program, study abroad, advanced placement credit, Freshman Honors College, ESL programs, double majors, distance learning, summer session for credit, part-time degree programs, adult/continuing education programs, internships, and arrangement for off-campus study with Viterbo College. The most frequently chosen baccalaureate fields are business/marketing, parks and recreation, social sciences and history.
Student Body Statistics The student body totals 8,770, of whom 8,158 are undergraduates (1,562 freshmen). 59 percent are women and 41 percent are men. Students come from 33 states and territories and 43 other countries. 83 percent are from Wisconsin. 0.5 percent are international students. 21 percent of the 2002 graduating class went on to graduate and professional schools.
Expenses for 2002–03 *Application fee:* $35. *State resident tuition:* $3804 full-time, $169 per credit part-time. *Nonresident tuition:* $13,850 full-time, $588 per credit part-time. *Mandatory fees:* $36 per credit hour part-time. Full-time tuition varies according to program and reciprocity agreements. Part-time tuition and fees vary according to course load, program, and reciprocity agreements. *College room and board:* $3800. *College room only:* $2100.
Financial Aid Forms of aid include need-based and non-need-based scholarships and part-time jobs. The average aided 2001–02 undergraduate received an aid package worth $5658. The priority application deadline for financial aid is March 15.
Freshman Admission UW-La Crosse requires a high school transcript and SAT I or ACT scores. An essay and TOEFL scores for international students are recommended. An interview is required for some. The application deadline for regular admission is rolling.
Transfer Admission The application deadline for admission is rolling.
Entrance Difficulty UW-La Crosse assesses its entrance difficulty level as moderately difficult. For the fall 2002 freshman class, 65 percent of the applicants were accepted.

For Further Information Contact Mr. Tim Lewis, Director of Admissions, University of Wisconsin–La Crosse, 1725 State Street, LaCrosse, WI 54601. *Telephone:* 608-785-8939. *Fax:* 608-785-8940. *E-mail:* admissions@uwlax.edu. *Web site:* http://www.uwlax.edu/.

UNIVERSITY OF WISCONSIN–MADISON

Madison, Wisconsin

Wisconsin is a coed, public unit of University of Wisconsin System, founded in 1848, offering degrees at the bachelor's, master's, doctoral, and first professional levels and post-master's and postbachelor's certificates. It has a 1,050-acre campus in Madison.

Academic Information The faculty has 2,219 full-time members. The undergraduate student-faculty ratio is 14:1. The library holds 6 million titles and 66,000 serial subscriptions. Special programs include services for learning-disabled students, an honors program, cooperative (work-study) education, study abroad, advanced placement credit, Freshman Honors College, ESL programs, double majors, independent study, distance learning, self-designed majors, summer session for credit, part-time degree programs (daytime), adult/continuing education programs, and internships.
Student Body Statistics The student body totals 41,515, of whom 29,708 are undergraduates (5,514 freshmen). 54 percent are women and 46 percent are men. Students come from 52 states and territories and 116 other countries. 61 percent are from Wisconsin. 3.2 percent are international students. 69 percent of the 2002 graduating class went on to graduate and professional schools.
Expenses for 2002–03 *Application fee:* $35. *State resident tuition:* $4470 full-time. *Nonresident tuition:* $18,390 full-time. *College room and board:* $5940.
Financial Aid Forms of aid include need-based and non-need-based scholarships, athletic grants, and part-time jobs. The average aided 2001–02 undergraduate received an aid package worth $8722. The application deadline for financial aid is continuous.
Freshman Admission Wisconsin requires an essay, a high school transcript, SAT I or ACT scores, and TOEFL scores for international students. SAT II: Subject Test scores are recommended. SAT II: Subject Test scores are required for some. The application deadline for regular admission is February 1.
Transfer Admission The application deadline for admission is February 1.

Entrance Difficulty Wisconsin assesses its entrance difficulty level as very difficult. For the fall 2002 freshman class, 71 percent of the applicants were accepted.

For Further Information Contact Mr. Keith White, Associate Director of Admission, University of Wisconsin–Madison, 716 Langdon Street, Madison, WI 53706-1481. *Telephone:* 608-262-3961. *Fax:* 608-262-7706. *E-mail:* on.wisconsin@mail.admin.wisc.edu. *Web site:* http://www.wisc.edu/.

UNIVERSITY OF WISCONSIN–MILWAUKEE

Milwaukee, Wisconsin

UWM is a coed, public unit of University of Wisconsin System, founded in 1956, offering degrees at the bachelor's, master's, and doctoral levels and post-master's certificates. It has a 90-acre campus in Milwaukee.

Academic Information The library holds 1 million titles, 8,240 serial subscriptions, and 37,376 audiovisual materials. Special programs include academic remediation, services for learning-disabled students, an honors program, cooperative (work-study) education, study abroad, advanced placement credit, accelerated degree programs, ESL programs, double majors, independent study, distance learning, self-designed majors, summer session for credit, part-time degree programs, adult/continuing education programs, internships, and arrangement for off-campus study with University of Wisconsin-Parkside. The most frequently chosen baccalaureate fields are business/marketing, education, health professions and related sciences.

Student Body Statistics The student body totals 24,587, of whom 20,259 are undergraduates (3,277 freshmen). 55 percent are women and 45 percent are men. Students come from 53 states and territories. 98 percent are from Wisconsin. 0.9 percent are international students.

Expenses for 2002–03 *Application fee:* $35. *State resident tuition:* $3738 full-time, $155.75 per credit part-time. *Nonresident tuition:* $16,490 full-time, $687.10 per credit part-time. *Mandatory fees:* $618 full-time. Full-time tuition and fees vary according to location, program, and reciprocity agreements. Part-time tuition varies according to course load, location, program, and reciprocity agreements. *College room and board:* $4400. *College room only:* $2700. Room and board charges vary according to board plan.

Financial Aid Forms of aid include need-based and non-need-based scholarships, athletic grants, and part-time jobs. $6669. The priority application deadline for financial aid is March 1.

Freshman Admission UWM requires a high school transcript, SAT I or ACT scores, TOEFL scores for international students, and ACT for state residents. ACT scores are recommended. The application deadline for regular admission is August 1.

Transfer Admission The application deadline for admission is rolling.

Entrance Difficulty UWM assesses its entrance difficulty level as moderately difficult. For the fall 2002 freshman class, 78 percent of the applicants were accepted.

For Further Information Contact Ms. Jan Ford, Director, Recruitment and Outreach, University of Wisconsin–Milwaukee, PO Box 749, Milwaukee, WI 53201. *Telephone:* 414-229-3800. *Fax:* 414-229-6940. *E-mail:* uwmlook@des.uwm.edu. *Web site:* http://www.uwm.edu/.

UNIVERSITY OF WISCONSIN–OSHKOSH

Oshkosh, Wisconsin

UW Oshkosh is a coed, public, comprehensive unit of University of Wisconsin System, founded in 1871, offering degrees at the associate, bachelor's, and master's levels. It has a 192-acre campus in Oshkosh near Milwaukee.

Academic Information The faculty has 575 members (73% full-time), 99% with terminal degrees. The undergraduate student-faculty ratio is 20:1. The library holds 446,774 titles, 5,219 serial subscriptions, and 9,102 audiovisual materials. Special programs include academic remediation, services for learning-disabled students, an honors program, cooperative (work-study) education, study abroad, advanced placement credit, accelerated degree programs, ESL programs, double majors, independent study, distance learning, self-designed majors, summer session for credit, part-time degree programs (daytime, evenings, weekends, summer), adult/continuing education programs, and internships. The most frequently chosen baccalaureate fields are business/marketing, education, protective services/public administration.

Student Body Statistics The student body totals 11,211, of whom 9,749 are undergraduates (1,805 freshmen). 59 percent are women and 41 percent are men. Students come from 30 states and territories and 32 other countries. 98 percent are from Wisconsin. 0.8 percent are international students.

Expenses for 2003–04 *Application fee:* $35. *State resident tuition:* $3670 full-time, $145 per credit part-time. *Nonresident tuition:* $14,320 full-time, $564 per credit part-time. Full-time tuition varies according to reciprocity agreements. Part-time tuition varies according to reciprocity agreements. *College room and board:* $3970. *College room only:* $2148. Room and board charges vary according to board plan and housing facility.

Financial Aid Forms of aid include need-based and non-need-based scholarships and part-time jobs. The average aided 2002–03 undergraduate received an aid package worth an estimated $5000. The priority application deadline for financial aid is March 15.

Freshman Admission UW Oshkosh requires a high school transcript, rank in upper 50% of high school class or ACT composite score of 23 or above, TOEFL scores for international students, and SAT I or ACT for nonresidents, ACT for state residents. An essay is recommended. The application deadline for regular admission is August 1.

Transfer Admission The application deadline for admission is August 1.

Entrance Difficulty UW Oshkosh assesses its entrance difficulty level as moderately difficult. For the fall 2002 freshman class, 57 percent of the applicants were accepted.

For Further Information Contact Mr. Richard Hillman, Associate Director of Admissions, University of Wisconsin–Oshkosh, Oshkosh, WI 54901-8602. *Telephone:* 920-424-0202. *Fax:* 920-424-1098. *E-mail:* oshadmuw@uwosh.edu. *Web site:* http://www.uwosh.edu/.

UNIVERSITY OF WISCONSIN–PARKSIDE

Kenosha, Wisconsin

University of Wisconsin–Parkside is a coed, public, comprehensive unit of University of Wisconsin System, founded in 1968, offering degrees at the bachelor's and master's levels. It has a 700-acre campus in Kenosha near Chicago and Milwaukee.

Academic Information The faculty has 186 members (99% full-time), 77% with terminal degrees. The undergraduate student-faculty ratio is 21:1. The library holds 400,000 titles, 1,590 serial subscriptions, and 21,220 audiovisual materials. Special programs include academic remediation, services for learning-disabled students, advanced placement credit, accelerated degree programs, ESL programs, double majors, independent study, distance learning, summer session for credit, part-time degree programs, external degree programs, internships, and arrangement for off-campus study with Carthage College. The most frequently chosen baccalaureate fields are business/marketing, communications/communication technologies, social sciences and history.

Student Body Statistics The student body totals 4,972, of whom 4,815 are undergraduates (831 freshmen). 58 percent are women and 42 percent are men. Students come from 21 states and territories and 21 other countries. 91 percent are from Wisconsin. 1.5 percent are international students. 15 percent of the 2002 graduating class went on to graduate and professional schools.

Expenses for 2002–03 *Application fee:* $35. *State resident tuition:* $3532 full-time, $171 per credit part-time. *Nonresident tuition:* $13,578 full-time, $590 per credit part-time. Full-time tuition varies according to course load and reciprocity agreements. Part-time tuition varies according to course load. *College room and board:* $5056. *College room only:* $3156. Room and board charges vary according to board plan and housing facility.

Financial Aid Forms of aid include need-based and non-need-based scholarships, athletic grants, and part-time jobs. The average aided 2002–03 undergraduate received an aid package worth an estimated $5953. The priority application deadline for financial aid is April 1.

University of Wisconsin–Parkside (continued)

Freshman Admission University of Wisconsin–Parkside requires a high school transcript, minimum of 17 high school units distributed as specified in the UW-Parkside catalog, and TOEFL scores for international students. SAT I or ACT scores are required for some. The application deadline for regular admission is August 1.

Transfer Admission The application deadline for admission is August 1.

Entrance Difficulty University of Wisconsin–Parkside assesses its entrance difficulty level as moderately difficult; very difficult for international students. For the fall 2002 freshman class, 91 percent of the applicants were accepted.

For Further Information Contact Mr. Matthew Jensen, Director of Admissions, University of Wisconsin–Parkside, PO Box 2000, 900 Wood Road, Kenosha, WI 53141-2000. *Telephone:* 262-595-2757 or 877-633-3897 (toll-free in-state). *Fax:* 262-595-2008. *E-mail:* matthew.jensen@uwp.edu. *Web site:* http://www.uwp.edu/.

UNIVERSITY OF WISCONSIN–PLATTEVILLE

Platteville, Wisconsin

UW Platteville is a coed, public, comprehensive unit of University of Wisconsin System, founded in 1866, offering degrees at the associate, bachelor's, and master's levels. It has a 380-acre campus in Platteville.

Academic Information The faculty has 289 members (84% full-time), 64% with terminal degrees. The undergraduate student-faculty ratio is 22:1. The library holds 321,456 titles, 1,280 serial subscriptions, and 13,879 audiovisual materials. Special programs include academic remediation, services for learning-disabled students, an honors program, cooperative (work-study) education, study abroad, advanced placement credit, double majors, independent study, distance learning, self-designed majors, summer session for credit, part-time degree programs (daytime, evenings), external degree programs, adult/continuing education programs, internships, and arrangement for off-campus study with Westfield State College. The most frequently chosen baccalaureate fields are business/marketing, agriculture, engineering/engineering technologies.

Student Body Statistics The student body totals 6,017, of whom 5,506 are undergraduates (1,119 freshmen). 39 percent are women and 61 percent are men. Students come from 34 states and territories and 47 other countries. 89 percent are from Wisconsin. 0.7 percent are international students.

Expenses for 2002–03 *Application fee:* $35. *Area resident tuition:* $125 per credit part-time. *State resident tuition:* $3000 full-time, $151.19 per credit part-time. *Nonresident tuition:* $13,046 full-time, $543 per credit part-time. *Mandatory fees:* $723 full-time. *College room and board:* $3978. *College room only:* $2000.

Financial Aid Forms of aid include need-based and non-need-based scholarships and part-time jobs. The average aided 2001–02 undergraduate received an aid package worth $4836. The priority application deadline for financial aid is March 15.

Freshman Admission UW Platteville requires a high school transcript, SAT I or ACT scores, and TOEFL scores for international students. ACT scores are recommended. Recommendations are required for some. The application deadline for regular admission is rolling.

Transfer Admission The application deadline for admission is rolling.

Entrance Difficulty UW Platteville assesses its entrance difficulty level as moderately difficult. For the fall 2002 freshman class, 87 percent of the applicants were accepted.

For Further Information Contact Dr. Richard Schumacher, Dean of Admissions and Enrollment Management, University of Wisconsin–Platteville, 1 University Plaza, Platteville, WI 53818-3099. *Telephone:* 608-342-1125 or 800-362-5515 (toll-free in-state). *Fax:* 608-342-1122. *E-mail:* admit@uwplatt.edu. *Web site:* http://www.uwplatt.edu/.

UNIVERSITY OF WISCONSIN–RIVER FALLS

River Falls, Wisconsin

UW River Falls is a coed, public, comprehensive unit of University of Wisconsin System, founded in 1874, offering degrees at the bachelor's and master's levels. It has a 225-acre campus in River Falls near Minneapolis–St. Paul.

Academic Information The faculty has 302 members (71% full-time). The undergraduate student-faculty ratio is 19:1. The library holds 448,088 titles, 1,660 serial subscriptions, and 7,500 audiovisual materials. Special programs include academic remediation, services for learning-disabled students, an honors program, cooperative (work-study) education, study abroad, advanced placement credit, accelerated degree programs, double majors, independent study, distance learning, self-designed majors, summer session for credit, part-time degree programs (daytime, summer), external degree programs, adult/continuing education programs, internships, and arrangement for off-campus study with National Student Exchange.

Student Body Statistics The student body totals 5,670, of whom 5,285 are undergraduates (1,052 freshmen). 61 percent are women and 39 percent are men. Students come from 26 states and territories and 12 other countries. 52 percent are from Wisconsin. 1 percent are international students. 22 percent of the 2002 graduating class went on to graduate and professional schools.

Expenses for 2002–03 *Application fee:* $35. *State resident tuition:* $3876 full-time. *Nonresident tuition:* $13,922 full-time. Full-time tuition varies according to course load and reciprocity agreements. *College room and board:* $3806. *College room only:* $2148. Room and board charges vary according to board plan.

Financial Aid Forms of aid include need-based and non-need-based scholarships and part-time jobs. $4429. The priority application deadline for financial aid is March 15.

Freshman Admission UW River Falls requires a high school transcript, ACT scores, and TOEFL scores for international students. Rank in upper 40% of high school class is recommended. The application deadline for regular admission is rolling.

Transfer Admission The application deadline for admission is rolling.

Entrance Difficulty UW River Falls assesses its entrance difficulty level as moderately difficult; very difficult for elementary education majors. For the fall 2002 freshman class, 76 percent of the applicants were accepted.

For Further Information Contact Mr. Alan Tuchtenhagen, Director of Admissions, University of Wisconsin–River Falls, 410 South Third Street, 112 South Hall, River Falls, WI 54022-5001. *Telephone:* 715-425-3500. *Fax:* 715-425-0676. *E-mail:* admit@uwrf.edu. *Web site:* http://www.uwrf.edu/.

UNIVERSITY OF WISCONSIN–STEVENS POINT

Stevens Point, Wisconsin

UWSP is a coed, public, comprehensive unit of University of Wisconsin System, founded in 1894, offering degrees at the associate, bachelor's, and master's levels. It has a 335-acre campus in Stevens Point.

Academic Information The faculty has 440 members (83% full-time), 75% with terminal degrees. The undergraduate student-faculty ratio is 20:1. The library holds 978,112 titles, 8,470 serial subscriptions, and 32,916 audiovisual materials. Special programs include academic remediation, services for learning-disabled students, cooperative (work-study) education, study abroad, advanced placement credit, accelerated degree programs, ESL programs, double majors, independent study, distance learning, self-designed majors, summer session for credit, part-time degree programs (daytime, evenings, summer), adult/continuing education programs, internships, and arrangement for off-campus study with University of Wisconsin-Oshkosh, University of Wisconsin-Eau Claire. The most frequently chosen baccalaureate fields are business/marketing, biological/life sciences, natural resources/environmental science.

Student Body Statistics The student body totals 8,954, of whom 8,466 are undergraduates (1,457 freshmen). 56 percent are women and 44 percent are men. Students come from 28 states and territories and 26 other countries. 94 percent are from Wisconsin. 1.9 percent are international students. 16 percent of the 2002 graduating class went on to graduate and professional schools.
Expenses for 2002–03 *Application fee:* $35. *State resident tuition:* $3000 full-time, $125 per credit part-time. *Nonresident tuition:* $13,046 full-time, $544 per credit part-time. *Mandatory fees:* $631 full-time, $57 per credit part-time. Full-time tuition and fees vary according to reciprocity agreements. Part-time tuition and fees vary according to course load and reciprocity agreements. *College room and board:* $3816. *College room only:* $2232.
Financial Aid Forms of aid include need-based and non-need-based scholarships and part-time jobs. The average aided 2001–02 undergraduate received an aid package worth $5817. The priority application deadline for financial aid is June 15.
Freshman Admission UWSP requires a high school transcript, SAT I or ACT scores, and TOEFL scores for international students. Campus visit is recommended. The application deadline for regular admission is rolling.
Transfer Admission The application deadline for admission is rolling.
Entrance Difficulty UWSP assesses its entrance difficulty level as moderately difficult. For the fall 2002 freshman class, 72 percent of the applicants were accepted.

For Further Information Contact Ms. Catherine Glennon, Director of Admissions, University of Wisconsin–Stevens Point, 2100 Main Street, Stevens Point, WI 54481. *Telephone:* 715-346-2441. *Fax:* 715-346-3296. *E-mail:* admiss@uwsp.edu. *Web site:* http://www.uwsp.edu/.

UNIVERSITY OF WISCONSIN–STOUT

Menomonie, Wisconsin

UW Stout is a coed, public, comprehensive unit of University of Wisconsin System, founded in 1891, offering degrees at the bachelor's and master's levels and post-master's certificates. It has a 120-acre campus in Menomonie near Minneapolis–St. Paul.

Academic Information The faculty has 392 members (75% full-time), 62% with terminal degrees. The undergraduate student-faculty ratio is 19:1. The library holds 229,986 titles, 1,784 serial subscriptions, and 16,142 audiovisual materials. Special programs include academic remediation, services for learning-disabled students, an honors program, cooperative (work-study) education, study abroad, advanced placement credit, accelerated degree programs, double majors, independent study, distance learning, summer session for credit, part-time degree programs, external degree programs, adult/continuing education programs, internships, and arrangement for off-campus study with Fashion Institute of Technology, University of Wisconsin–Eau Claire. The most frequently chosen baccalaureate fields are business/marketing, education, engineering/engineering technologies.
Student Body Statistics The student body totals 7,902, of whom 7,316 are undergraduates (1,308 freshmen). 48 percent are women and 52 percent are men. Students come from 30 states and territories and 30 other countries. 71 percent are from Wisconsin. 0.4 percent are international students. 6 percent of the 2002 graduating class went on to graduate and professional schools.
Expenses for 2002–03 *Application fee:* $35. *State resident tuition:* $3150 full-time, $131 per credit part-time. *Nonresident tuition:* $13,196 full-time, $550 per credit part-time. *Mandatory fees:* $607 full-time. Full-time tuition and fees vary according to reciprocity agreements. Part-time tuition varies according to reciprocity agreements. *College room and board:* $3830. *College room only:* $2144. Room and board charges vary according to board plan.
Financial Aid Forms of aid include need-based and non-need-based scholarships and part-time jobs. The average aided 2002–03 undergraduate received an aid package worth an estimated $6197. The priority application deadline for financial aid is April 1.
Freshman Admission UW Stout requires a high school transcript, SAT I or ACT scores, and TOEFL scores for international students. A minimum 2.75 high school GPA is required for some. The application deadline for regular admission is rolling.
Transfer Admission The application deadline for admission is rolling.
Entrance Difficulty UW Stout assesses its entrance difficulty level as moderately difficult. For the fall 2002 freshman class, 70 percent of the applicants were accepted.

For Further Information Contact Ms. Cynthia Jenkins, Director of Admissions, University of Wisconsin–Stout, Menomonie, WI 54751. *Telephone:* 715-232-2639 or 800-HI-STOUT (toll-free in-state). *Fax:* 715-232-1667. *E-mail:* admissions@uwstout.edu. *Web site:* http://www.uwstout.edu/.

UNIVERSITY OF WISCONSIN–SUPERIOR

Superior, Wisconsin

UW-Superior is a coed, public, comprehensive unit of University of Wisconsin System, founded in 1893, offering degrees at the associate, bachelor's, master's, and first professional levels and postbachelor's certificates. It has a 230-acre campus in Superior.

Academic Information The faculty has 103 members (98% full-time), 83% with terminal degrees. The undergraduate student-faculty ratio is 17:1. The library holds 467,700 titles, 753 serial subscriptions, and 5,467 audiovisual materials. Special programs include academic remediation, services for learning-disabled students, an honors program, cooperative (work-study) education, study abroad, advanced placement credit, Freshman Honors College, ESL programs, double majors, independent study, distance learning, self-designed majors, summer session for credit, part-time degree programs (daytime, evenings, weekends, summer), external degree programs, adult/continuing education programs, internships, and arrangement for off-campus study with College of St. Scholastica, Northland College, University of Minnesota, Duluth. The most frequently chosen baccalaureate fields are business/marketing, education, social sciences and history.
Student Body Statistics The student body totals 2,887, of whom 2,513 are undergraduates (313 freshmen). 59 percent are women and 41 percent are men. Students come from 17 states and territories and 32 other countries. 55 percent are from Wisconsin. 5.7 percent are international students. 18 percent of the 2002 graduating class went on to graduate and professional schools.
Expenses for 2002–03 *Application fee:* $35. *State resident tuition:* $3464 full-time, $163.29 per credit part-time. *Nonresident tuition:* $13,510 full-time, $450.29 per credit part-time. *Mandatory fees:* $464 full-time, $7 per credit part-time, $71 per term part-time. Full-time tuition and fees vary according to course load and reciprocity agreements. Part-time tuition and fees vary according to course load and reciprocity agreements. *College room and board:* $3962. *College room only:* $2208. Room and board charges vary according to housing facility and location. Minnesota full-time tuition $8,844.
Financial Aid Forms of aid include need-based and non-need-based scholarships and part-time jobs. The average aided 2002–03 undergraduate received an aid package worth an estimated $8020. The application deadline for financial aid is May 15 with a priority deadline of April 15.
Freshman Admission UW-Superior requires a high school transcript, SAT I or ACT scores, and TOEFL scores for international students. An interview and ACT scores are recommended. A minimum 2.6 high school GPA and recommendations are required for some. The application deadline for regular admission is April 1.
Transfer Admission The application deadline for admission is rolling.
Entrance Difficulty UW-Superior assesses its entrance difficulty level as moderately difficult. For the fall 2002 freshman class, 76 percent of the applicants were accepted.

For Further Information Contact Ms. Lorraine Washa, Student Application Contact, University of Wisconsin–Superior, Belknap and Catlin, PO Box 2000, Superior, WI 54880-4500. *Telephone:* 715-394-8298 or 715-394-8230 (toll-free in-state). *Fax:* 715-394-8407. *E-mail:* admissions@uwsuper.edu. *Web site:* http://www.uwsuper.edu/.

UNIVERSITY OF WISCONSIN–WHITEWATER

Whitewater, Wisconsin

UW-Whitewater is a coed, public, comprehensive unit of University of Wisconsin System, founded in 1868, offering degrees at the associate, bachelor's, and master's levels. It has a 385-acre campus in Whitewater near Milwaukee.

Academic Information The faculty has 511 members (77% full-time), 64% with terminal degrees. The undergraduate student-faculty ratio is 20:1. The library holds 647,029 titles, 3,358 serial subscriptions, and 15,974 audiovisual materials. Special programs include academic remediation, services for learning-disabled students, an honors program, cooperative (work-study) education, study abroad, advanced placement credit, accelerated degree programs, double majors, independent study, distance learning, self-designed majors, summer session for credit, part-time degree programs, external degree programs, adult/continuing education programs, and internships. The most frequently chosen baccalaureate fields are business/marketing, communications/communication technologies, education.
Student Body Statistics The student body totals 10,796, of whom 9,513 are undergraduates (2,035 freshmen). 54 percent are women and 46 percent are men. Students come from 29 states and territories and 37 other countries. 93 percent are from Wisconsin. 0.6 percent are international students. 10 percent of the 2002 graduating class went on to graduate and professional schools.
Expenses for 2002–03 *Application fee:* $35. *State resident tuition:* $3375 full-time, $155.70 per credit part-time. *Nonresident tuition:* $13,783 full-time, $574.30 per credit part-time. *Mandatory fees:* $631 full-time. *College room and board:* $3570. *College room only:* $2150.
Financial Aid Forms of aid include need-based and non-need-based scholarships and part-time jobs. The average aided 2002–03 undergraduate received an aid package worth an estimated $6411. The priority application deadline for financial aid is March 15.
Freshman Admission UW-Whitewater requires a high school transcript and TOEFL scores for international students. SAT I or ACT scores are recommended. Recommendations and SAT I or ACT scores are required for some. The application deadline for regular admission is rolling.
Transfer Admission The application deadline for admission is rolling.
Entrance Difficulty UW-Whitewater assesses its entrance difficulty level as moderately difficult. For the fall 2002 freshman class, 74 percent of the applicants were accepted.

For Further Information Contact Dr. Tori A. McGuire, Executive Director of Admissions, University of Wisconsin–Whitewater, 800 West Main Street, Whitewater, WI 53190-1790. *Telephone:* 262-472-1440 Ext. 1512. *Fax:* 262-472-1515. *E-mail:* uwwadmit@mail.uww.edu. *Web site:* http://www.uww.edu/.

VITERBO UNIVERSITY

La Crosse, Wisconsin

Viterbo is a coed, private, Roman Catholic, comprehensive institution, founded in 1890, offering degrees at the bachelor's and master's levels. It has a 5-acre campus in La Crosse.

Academic Information The faculty has 183 members (59% full-time), 45% with terminal degrees. The undergraduate student-faculty ratio is 12:1. The library holds 1 million titles, 3,541 serial subscriptions, and 6,181 audiovisual materials. Special programs include academic remediation, cooperative (work-study) education, study abroad, advanced placement credit, accelerated degree programs, double majors, independent study, distance learning, self-designed majors, summer session for credit, part-time degree programs (evenings, weekends, summer), adult/continuing education programs, internships, and arrangement for off-campus study with University of Wisconsin-La Crosse, Western Wisconsin Technical College. The most frequently chosen baccalaureate fields are business/marketing, education, health professions and related sciences.
Student Body Statistics The student body totals 2,331, of whom 1,778 are undergraduates (325 freshmen). 75 percent are women and 25 percent are men. Students come from 21 states and territories and 11 other countries. 78 percent are from Wisconsin. 1 percent are international students. 9 percent of the 2002 graduating class went on to graduate and professional schools.
Expenses for 2003–04 *Application fee:* $25. *Comprehensive fee:* $20,430 includes full-time tuition ($14,900), mandatory fees ($420), and college room and board ($5110). *College room only:* $2250. Room and board charges vary according to board plan and housing facility. *Part-time tuition:* $435 per credit. *Part-time mandatory fees:* $25 per credit. Part-time tuition and fees vary according to course load.
Financial Aid Forms of aid include need-based and non-need-based scholarships, athletic grants, and part-time jobs. The average aided 2001–02 undergraduate received an aid package worth $11,826. The priority application deadline for financial aid is March 15.
Freshman Admission Viterbo requires a high school transcript, a minimum 2.0 high school GPA, audition for theater and music; portfolio for art, ACT scores, and TOEFL scores for international students. An essay, 1 recommendation, and an interview are required for some. The application deadline for regular admission is rolling.
Transfer Admission The application deadline for admission is rolling.
Entrance Difficulty Viterbo assesses its entrance difficulty level as moderately difficult. For the fall 2002 freshman class, 80 percent of the applicants were accepted.

For Further Information Contact Admission Counselor, Viterbo University, 815 South 9th Street, LaCrosse, WI 54601. *Telephone:* 608-796-3010 Ext. 3010 or 800-VIT-ERBO Ext. 3010 (toll-free). *Fax:* 608-796-3020. *E-mail:* admission@viterbo.edu. *Web site:* http://www.viterbo.edu/.

WISCONSIN LUTHERAN COLLEGE

Milwaukee, Wisconsin

Wisconsin Lutheran is a coed, private, four-year college, founded in 1973, affiliated with the Wisconsin Evangelical Lutheran Synod, offering degrees at the bachelor's level. It has a 16-acre campus in Milwaukee.

Academic Information The faculty has 78 members (62% full-time), 46% with terminal degrees. The student-faculty ratio is 11:1. The library holds 71,731 titles, 614 serial subscriptions, and 4,409 audiovisual materials. Special programs include services for learning-disabled students, study abroad, advanced placement credit, double majors, independent study, self-designed majors, summer session for credit, part-time degree programs (daytime, evenings), and internships. The most frequently chosen baccalaureate fields are communications/communication technologies, education, visual/performing arts.
Student Body Statistics The student body is made up of 669 undergraduates (160 freshmen). 61 percent are women and 39 percent are men. Students come from 27 states and territories and 4 other countries. 81 percent are from Wisconsin. 0.9 percent are international students.
Expenses for 2003–04 *Application fee:* $20. *Comprehensive fee:* $21,171 includes full-time tuition ($15,720), mandatory fees ($126), and college room and board ($5325). *College room only:* $2775. *Part-time tuition:* $480 per credit. *Part-time mandatory fees:* $50 per year.
Financial Aid Forms of aid include need-based and non-need-based scholarships and part-time jobs. The average aided 2002–03 undergraduate received an aid package worth an estimated $13,268. The application deadline for financial aid is continuous.
Freshman Admission Wisconsin Lutheran requires a high school transcript, a minimum 2.70 high school GPA, 1 recommendation, minimum ACT score of 21, SAT I or ACT scores, and TOEFL scores for international students. An interview is required for some.
Entrance Difficulty Wisconsin Lutheran assesses its entrance difficulty level as moderately difficult. For the fall 2002 freshman class, 79 percent of the applicants were accepted.

For Further Information Contact Mr. Craig Swiontek, Director of Admissions, Wisconsin Lutheran College, 8800 West Bluemound Road, Milwaukee, WI 53226-9942. *Telephone:* 414-443-8713 or 888-WIS LUTH (toll-free). *Fax:* 414-443-8514. *E-mail:* admissions@wlc.edu. *Web site:* http://www.wlc.edu/.

In-Depth Descriptions of Colleges in the Midwest

The descriptions presented in this section provide a wealth of statistics that are crucial components in the college decision-making equation—components such as tuition, financial aid, and major fields of study. This section shifts the focus to a variety of other factors, some of them intangible, that should also be considered. The following two-page descriptions are offered to provide a greater overview of some of the colleges and universities profiled in this book. Prepared exclusively by college officials, they are designed to help give students a better sense of the individuality of each institution, in terms that include campus environment, student activities, and lifestyle. Such quality-of-life intangibles can be the deciding factors in the college selection process. The absence from this section of any college or university does not constitute an editorial decision on the part of Peterson's. In essence, this section is an open forum for colleges and universities, on a voluntary basis, to communicate their particular messages to prospective college students. The colleges included have paid a fee to Peterson's to provide this information to you. The descriptions are arranged alphabetically by the official name of the institution.

ALBION COLLEGE

ALBION, MICHIGAN

The College

"The Liberal Arts At Work" is the theme adopted by Albion College to demonstrate the relationship between a liberal arts education in college and success in the professions after graduation. At Albion, the liberal arts will work for students who aspire to successful careers in medicine, law, teaching, business, the arts, and many other areas. Six academic institutes are available: the Gerald R. Ford Institute for Public Service, the Carl A. Gerstacker Liberal Arts Program in Professional Management, the Pre-Med/Allied Health Institute, the Honors Institute, the Fritz Shurmur Education Institute, and the Institute for the Study of the Environment.

Albion ranks fourth in the nation for the percentage of undergraduate students involved in summer research, seventh in Yahoo!/Internet Life's Most Wired Colleges in the U.S.A., and first among colleges and universities in Michigan. In addition, 46 percent of Albion's alumni regularly support the college, the highest percentage among schools in Michigan and among the top forty in the nation. Albion is among the top eighty-five private, liberal arts colleges for the number of alumni who are corporate executives, including top executives and CEOs of *Newsweek*, the Lahey Clinic (MA), PricewaterhouseCoopers, Dow Corning, the NCAA, NYNEX, and the Federal Accounting Standards Board (FASB). Albion's graduate school placement reflects 98 percent for law, 96 percent for dental, and 89 percent for medical schools, including Harvard, Michigan, Columbia, Northwestern, Notre Dame, Vanderbilt, and Wisconsin.

Albion's 2003 fall enrollment is 1,658 students (763 men and 895 women). Approximately 87 percent of Albion's students are from Michigan; the rest come from twenty-eight states and nineteen countries. Albion is a residential college and campus life is important for every student. A student-run Union Board selects first-run movies, concerts, and other entertainment, and nationally known speakers and entertainers are sponsored by the Albion Performing Arts and Lecture Series. The Kellogg Center, completed in 1996, provides space for concerts and dances, meeting rooms and offices for student organizations, the college bookstore, and a snack bar. More than 100 student organizations include clubs in academic departments, student publications, a campus radio station, religious fellowship groups, the Black Student Alliance, intercollegiate and intramural athletics, and national fraternities and sororities.

Ninety-six percent of students live on campus. Residence halls, located within walking distance of other campus buildings, are coed, with separate sections for men and women. A comprehensive student services program includes a career development office that assists students in exploring career options and arranges on-campus interviews with employers and graduate schools. More than 40 percent of Albion graduates go directly to graduate or professional school each year; virtually everyone seeking immediate employment has found a position six months after graduation. Within five years of graduation, more than 75 percent of Albion alumni have enrolled for graduate work.

Location

A 1½-hour drive west of Detroit and a 3-hour drive east of Chicago, the College is located on I-94 in the small city of Albion (population 10,000). Eight other colleges and universities, including Michigan State and the University of Michigan, are located within an hour's drive. The 225-acre main campus is a few blocks from the downtown business section. Students and faculty members are very involved in community activities such as volunteer efforts and internships. The College's Student Volunteer Bureau organizes involvement with programs serving children and adults. Albion faculty members founded the all-volunteer Albion Area Ambulance Service.

Majors and Degrees

Albion College awards the Bachelor of Arts and Bachelor of Fine Arts degrees. Majors include American studies, anthropology and sociology, art, art history, biology, chemistry, computer science, economics and management, English, French, geological sciences, German, history, international studies, mathematics, music, philosophy, physical education, physics, political science, psychology, public policy, religious studies, Spanish, and speech communication and theater. Individually designed majors, created with faculty approval, are also offered.

Students may be certified in secondary education and for grades K–12 in art, music, and physical education. Elementary certification is offered through a four-year, on-campus program leading to a bachelor's degree and through a five-year B.A./M.S. program with Bank Street College of Education in New York City.

Preprofessional programs include business management, dentistry, law, medicine, and the ministry. Combined three-year preprofessional programs, involving three years of study at Albion and additional work at other institutions, are available in engineering, health services and nursing, natural resources management, and public policy. Students in these programs are awarded the bachelor's degree from Albion after completing one additional year of study at the participating institutions.

Academic Program

Albion expects its students to gain a broad knowledge in the arts and sciences while also developing an area of specialization. To graduate with the Bachelor of Arts degree, students must complete 31 units (124 semester hours); to earn the Bachelor of Fine Arts degree, art majors must complete 34 units (136 semester hours). All students must pass a writing examination.

To introduce students to important areas of knowledge, Albion has a core curriculum requirement for study in the natural sciences and mathematics, the social sciences, the humanities, interdisciplinary studies, and the fine arts, together with additional studies in gender and ethnicity studies. The core curriculum and the requirements for a major total about one half to two thirds of a student's program at Albion. The remainder can be used for electives, to complete a second major, or for a six- to eight-course sequence in business management, computer science, human services, mass communication, public service, or women's studies. Independent study and on-the-job internships for academic credit are also available. College credit can be obtained through Advanced Placement examinations, College-Level Examination Program (CLEP) tests, or Albion departmental examinations.

Off-Campus Arrangements

Albion College, together with the Great Lakes Colleges Association, offers off-campus study in Australia, Costa Rica, the Dominican Republic, France, Germany, Great Britain, India, Israel, Japan, Mexico, Russia, Spain, and several African countries. Semester-long programs are available in the United States through the Washington (D.C.) Center for Learning Alternatives, the New York City Arts Program, the Philadelphia Center, the Chicago Urban Life Center, the Newberry Library Program in the Humanities (Chicago), and the Oak Ridge National Laboratory (Tennessee). All arrangements are supervised by the director of off-campus programs.

Academic Facilities

Olin Hall, the $4.5-million home of the biology and psychology departments, features excellent laboratory equipment, including scanning and transmission electron microscopes. In the Stockwell/Mudd Libraries, researchers are helped by a computerized catalog of the College's book and periodical collections and by access to national databases in many different academic areas.

Other prominent campus facilities include the Herrick Center for Speech and Theatre and the 144-acre Whitehouse Nature Center, a preserve used for both science instruction and recreation. The Dow Recreation and Wellness Center offers a 1/9-mile indoor track, multipurpose court space, a swimming pool, weight-training facilities for physical education courses, intramural sports, individual conditioning, and wellness programs.

Albion students also have access to Digital Equipment Corporation VAX 4000-200 computers and to the Internet through PCs located throughout the campus and in individual rooms. More than 500 microcomputers are available for various research activities.

Costs

Costs for the 2002–03 academic year were $20,458 for tuition and $5912 for room and board; there was a $242 student activity fee. Laboratory fees and music lessons are additional, as are personal expenses and travel. Costs are the same for both in-state and out-of-state students.

Financial Aid

Every student admitted to Albion College will receive financial assistance if need is determined from the Free Application for Federal Student Aid (FAFSA). Families should file the FAFSA as soon as possible after January 1 so that the College receives the analysis from the federal government by February 15. For each student, Albion will build a financial aid package using federal grants and loans and College aid funds. Many Michigan residents are eligible for state scholarships and grants of more than $2000 that are reserved for people attending private colleges and universities in the state. More than 50 percent of Albion students also have jobs on campus. Students must apply for admission and be accepted before a financial aid package is prepared. Students with strong academic records are also eligible for academic scholarships. These range from a few thousand dollars to full tuition. The scholarship application deadline is February 1. Students with special talent in art, music, and theater may qualify for scholarships in these areas of up to $3000.

Faculty

Ninety-two percent of Albion's faculty members hold the doctorate or terminal degree in their field. There are 121 full-time faculty members. Courses and laboratories are taught by regular faculty members and not by graduate teaching assistants. The average class size is 19. First- and second-year courses have average enrollments of 24 students, with the exception of special First Year Experience courses, which limit enrollment to 16 students. Upper-level courses average 15 students.

Albion's faculty members are dedicated to teaching at a liberal arts college. Faculty members know their students personally and are available outside class hours for discussion and counseling. They are also active scholars and researchers, as shown by the grants that they receive from the National Science Foundation, the National Endowment for the Humanities, and many other sources.

Student Government

An elected Student Senate oversees the operation of campus organizations and disburses student activity fee funds to these groups. The Board of Trustees invites Student Senate members to sit on its committees for academic and student affairs, institutional advancement, and buildings and grounds. Student representatives also sit on the faculty's Educational Policies Committee, which reviews the College curriculum.

Admission Requirements

Albion is a selective national liberal arts college, and admission is mainly based on the applicant's academic record in high school with special attention to the college-preparatory courses completed. Standard test scores from either the ACT or SAT are also an important factor, as are personal qualifications and accomplishments outside the classroom. The College seeks a diverse enrollment without regard to race, religion, or national origin. In 2002, entering freshmen had an average GPA of 3.6, and 63 percent ranked in the top 25 percent of their high school class. The middle 50 percent of enrolled freshmen had ACT scores between 23 and 28. Prospective freshmen can take either the SAT I or ACT. These exams are not required of transfer students who have earned at least a semester of college credit. Candidates for admission are expected to be graduates of an accredited high school or preparatory school and have at least 15 acceptable credit units. Applicants should have a strong background in English, mathematics, and the laboratory and social sciences. Home-schooled applicants are reviewed on an individual basis and need to complete either the SAT I or ACT. International applicants are welcome and must have a minimum TOEFL score of 550 and submit a Declaration of Finances form to show adequate financial resources. An interview may be required. Arrangements for a personal campus visit should be made in advance in writing, by phone, or by e-mail.

Application and Information

Applications for admission are accepted at any time, but most students apply after September 1 of their senior year in high school. Before a decision is made, applicants must submit an application form and $20 application fee (there is no fee for Web applications), high school transcripts, test score results, and recommendations. Students should submit all materials by April 1. Albion is also a member of the Common Application and will accept applications completed on its Web site. Students who have decided that Albion College is their first choice can apply by November 15 under the Early Decision Program and will receive an admissions decision by December 15. Applications received before December 1 that are not for the Early Decision Program are considered under the Early Action Program and are reviewed before January 1. Albion has a Regular Decision Program for applications received after December 1; notification begins no later than February 1. Financial aid applicants will also receive a preliminary financial aid award. For further information, students should contact:

Albion College
611 East Porter Street
Albion, Michigan 49224
Telephone: 800-858-6770 (toll-free)
Fax: 517-629-0569
E-mail: admissions@albion.edu
World Wide Web: http://www.albion.edu

Robinson Hall.

AURORA UNIVERSITY

AURORA, ILLINOIS

The University

Aurora University was founded in 1893. The school has grown substantially over the years and has taken on many new challenges. In 1938, it was one of the first small colleges to achieve regional accreditation. In 1947, the college's evening program was instituted—one of the nation's first adult education programs at a liberal arts college. In 1985, Aurora College was reorganized as Aurora University, reflecting both the increased size of the institution and the needs associated with its many new programs. In addition to the College of Arts, Science, and Business, the University comprises the College of Education and George Williams College (social work, nursing, and human services). Today, the University enrolls 4,000 students in more than forty undergraduate programs and four graduate programs in business, recreation administration, social work, and education. An Ed.D. is offered in educational leadership. Courses are offered at other sites in Illinois, Iowa, and Wisconsin, in addition to the Aurora campus.

The University's student body includes 550 on-campus, traditional-age students; 1,000 undergraduate commuters; 1,200 graduate students; and more than 1,600 students at off-campus sites. The majority of Aurora's students come from the upper-Midwest region, but twenty states and five countries are also represented.

Social life is based on campus, and most activities are campuswide. Aurora has more than forty musical, literary, religious, social, and service clubs and organizations. There are also nine fraternities and sororities for students interested in Greek life. Aurora University has a long history of excellence in both intercollegiate and intramural athletics. A member of the NCAA Division III, Aurora fields intercollegiate teams in baseball, basketball, football, golf, soccer, softball, tennis, and volleyball, often with championship results.

Aurora University is accredited at the bachelor's, master's, and doctoral degree levels by the Commission on Institutions of Higher Education of the North Central Association of Colleges and Schools, and its programs are accredited by the Commission on Collegiate Nursing Education, National League for Nursing Accrediting Commission, Illinois Department of Professional Regulation, Council on Social Work Education, National Recreation and Park Association/American Association of Leisure and Recreation, and Association of Collegiate Business Schools and Programs.

Location

Aurora University is located in an attractive residential neighborhood on the southwest side of Aurora, Illinois, which has a population of more than 144,000 and is the state's third-largest city. The 27-acre main campus is located only minutes from the Illinois Research and Development Corridor, the site of dozens of nationally and internationally based businesses and industries. Located within an hour's drive or train ride is Chicago, one of the most vibrant cities in the world.

Majors and Degrees

The Bachelor of Arts degree is awarded in accounting, biology, business administration, communication (corporate and professional, interdisciplinary, and mass communication/TV production), computer science, computer science/business information systems, computer science/electronics, criminal justice, elementary education, English, finance, history, management, marketing, mathematics, physical education (athletic training, fitness leadership, and K–12 teacher certification), political science, psychology, and sociology. The Bachelor of Science degree is awarded in accounting, biology, biology–environmental science, business administration, computer science, finance, health science (predentistry, premedicine, pre–physical therapy, and pre–veterinary studies), management, marketing, physical education (athletic training and fitness leadership), and recreation administration (commercial recreation management, outdoor leadership, program management, and therapeutic recreation). The Bachelor of Science in human services is awarded in youth development, programming, and management. The Bachelor of Science in Nursing and the Bachelor of Science in Social Work are also offered. The University offers supplemental majors in prelaw and secondary education as well as the YMCA Senior Director Certificate Program.

Academic Program

Aurora University offers academic programs combining a liberal arts foundation with majors emphasizing career preparation and selected concentrations. Graduates are educated to be purposeful, ethical, and proficient—equipped for worthwhile careers and productive lives and for venturing out into a changing world.

To earn a bachelor's degree, students are required to fulfill the general degree requirements of the University and the major requirements for an approved major; complete at least 120 semester hours with a GPA of at least 2.0 on a 4.0 scale, including at least 52 semester hours at a senior college; and complete at least 30 semester hours, including the last 24 for the degree and at least 18 semester hours in the major, at Aurora University.

Aurora University accepts credits earned through the CLEP, DANTES, ACT-PREP, and NLN Mobility testing programs. In addition, credit based on portfolio assessment is available to students who have significant prior learning from career experience or individual study.

The University observes a trimester calendar year (one 11-week term and two 10-week terms), with classes beginning in early September and concluding in late May.

Off-Campus Arrangements

There is a three-week travel-study program in the American West as well as travel-study programs to Mexico and England. The University also has off-campus classes in Chicago (nursing and group work programs) and at the University's Lake Geneva campus in Williams Bay, Wisconsin.

Academic Facilities

The major buildings at Aurora are marked by the distinctive, red-tiled roofs specified by Charles Eckhart in his donation for the original campus. Dunham Hall houses state-of-the-art computer facilities as well as the Schingoethe Center for Native American Cultures. A television studio with professional-grade equipment, serving both the University's communication program and the local cable system, is located in Stephens Hall; other facilities include the fully equipped Perry Theatre, science labs, flora-fauna complex, and the College Commons. Music practice rooms, piano labs, and a spacious art studio are also available. Charles B. Phillips Library has more than 112,000 volumes, 190,000 microform units, and approximately 700 current periodical subscriptions. In addition, the library provides access to approximately 3,700 journals in electronic full-text.

Costs

Tuition for the 2002–03 school year is $13,767 for full-time students (24 to 33 semester hours per year), while yearly room and board costs are $5328.

Financial Aid

Aurora University's financial aid program has been designed to make it possible for any academically qualified student to afford the benefits of a private education. The University works with students to determine the amount of their costs and to identify all available resources so that students can meet these expenses. Financial aid is awarded based on financial need as reported on the FAFSA. In addition to need-based financial aid, Aurora University offers academic scholarships, including the Board of Trustees Scholarship, Crimi Scholarship, Deans' Scholarship, Solon B. Cousins Scholarship, Aurora University Opportunity Grant, and transfer scholarships.

Faculty

The favorable student-faculty ratio of 15:1 ensures that students receive plenty of individual attention in class. Instructors also make time for students outside of class, acting as mentors, advisers, and friends who are eager to answer questions and to join students in sports and social activities.

Student Government

The student body is represented by the AUSA (Aurora University Student Association), which provides funding for various student groups on campus. Students are also active members of committees ranging from faculty searches to academic standards and are provided with certain voting privileges.

Admission Requirements

The Aurora University Committee on Admissions considers the complete record of a candidate for admission. The University seeks qualified students from varied geographical, cultural, economic, racial, and religious backgrounds. No single, inflexible set of admission standards is applied. Two general qualities are considered in each candidate: academic ability, enabling the student to benefit from a high-quality academic program, and a diversity of talents and interests that can contribute to making the campus community a better and more interesting place for learning. An application for admission to Aurora University is considered on the basis of the academic ability, achievements, activities, and motivation of the student. Transfer students with fewer than 30 semester hours of credit should apply in the same manner as freshman applicants. Transfer students with more than 15 semester hours may be admitted to Aurora University if they have a transferable overall GPA of 2.0 or higher. Aurora accepts a maximum of 90 semester hours of transfer credits from a combination of two- and four-year schools. A maximum of 68 semester hours may be transferred from two-year schools. For further information, students should contact a transfer counselor in the Office of Admission and Financial Aid.

Application and Information

To apply for admission to Aurora University, the following items should be sent to the Office of Admission and Financial Aid: a completed application form, an official transcript from the guidance counselor, and official ACT or SAT I scores. Transfer students should submit official transcripts from each college or university attended, along with the completed application.

Applications and further information may be obtained by contacting:

Office of Admission and Financial Aid
Aurora University
347 South Gladstone Avenue
Aurora, Illinois 60506
Telephone: 630-844-5533
800-742-5281 (toll-free)
E-mail: admissions@aurora.edu
World Wide Web: http://www.aurora.edu

An aerial view of Aurora University in Aurora, Illinois.

BALL STATE UNIVERSITY

MUNCIE, INDIANA

The University

Ball State University was founded as a state institution in 1918, but its antecedents date from the late nineteenth century when the Ball family, prominent industrialists, purchased and donated to the state of Indiana the campus and buildings of the Muncie Normal Institute. In 1922 the Board of Trustees gave the school the name of Ball Teachers College, and in 1929 the school became Ball State Teachers College. In 1965 the Indiana General Assembly renamed the institution Ball State University in recognition of its phenomenal growth in enrollment, in physical facilities, and in the variety and quality of its educational programs and services. The fifty-eight buildings on the 955-acre campus reflect the changing architectural styles of the twentieth century.

The total University enrollment stands at 17,662. In fall 2001, undergraduate enrollment was 7,814 men and 9,848 women. The majority of entering freshmen were 18 to 19 years old and single; they had come from families with 2 or more children and from cities of moderate to large size; 7 percent belonged to a minority group. About 10 percent of Ball State freshmen came from outside the state of Indiana. There were 384 students from eighty-six countries other than the United States.

There are more than 300 student organizations that provide extracurricular activities. These include leadership programs, departmental organizations, honorary societies, music groups, religious organizations, fraternities, sororities, governing groups, special interest organizations, and service groups. The University Health Service staff members offer health education, provide care in cases of acute illness and injury while a student is in attendance, and serve as medical advisers for the University.

Location

The Ball State campus is in a pleasant, residential area of Muncie, an industrial city of 78,000 people in east-central Indiana, 56 miles northeast of Indianapolis. The city's cultural features include the Muncie Symphony Orchestra, the Civic Theater, and the Artists Series and Concert Series presented in the John R. Emens University-Community Auditorium located on the Ball State campus.

Majors and Degrees

Ball State's academic programs are offered through the University's seven colleges, which are the College of Applied Sciences and Technology; College of Architecture and Planning; College of Business; College of Communication, Information, and Media; College of Fine Arts; College of Sciences and Humanities; and Teachers College. The degrees awarded are associate degrees in arts and science, bachelor's degrees in arts, fine arts, music, and science, and bachelor's degrees in architecture (five-year program), landscape architecture (five-year program), and urban planning and development (five-year program). The fields of study include accounting, actuarial science, administrative information technology (two years), advertising, anthropology, apparel design, architecture (five years), art, athletic training, biochemistry, biology, business administration (two or four years), business education and office administration, chemical technology (two years), chemistry, classical culture, classical languages (Latin and Greek), communication studies, computer science, criminal justice and criminology (two or four years), dance, dietetics, dietetic technology (two years), early childhood education, economics, elementary education, English, exercise science and wellness, family and consumer sciences (general), family and consumer sciences (vocational education), fashion merchandising, finance, food management (two years), French, general studies (two or four years), geography, geology, German, graphic arts management, graphic design, health and safety education, health science, hearing impairments, history (American and world), industrial supervision (two years), industrial technology, interior design/housing, Japanese, journalism (two or four years), journalism education, junior high/middle school education, kindergarten/primary education, landscape architecture (five years), Latin American studies, legal assistance (two or four years), management, manufacturing engineering technology, manufacturing technology (two years), marketing, marketing education, mathematical economics, mathematics, mechanical engineering technology (two years), medical technology, merchandising, modern languages (French, German, Japanese, and Spanish), music (composition, guitar, music education, music engineering technology, organ, piano, symphonic instruments, and voice), natural resources and environmental management, nuclear medicine technology (two years), nursing, philosophy, physical education, physics, political science, printing technology (two years), psychology, public relations, public service (two years), radiation therapy (two years), radiography (two years), religious studies, residential property management, school media services, science teaching, secondary education, social studies teaching, social work, sociology, Spanish, special education (mentally and physically handicapped and hearing impairments), speech communication and theater, speech pathology and audiology, sport administration, technology education, telecommunications, theater, urban planning (five years), visual arts education, and vocational trade. Preprofessional programs are offered in audiology, dental hygiene, dentistry, engineering (chemical, general, and metallurgical), law, medicine, optometry, pharmacy, and veterinary medicine.

Academic Program

Undergraduate programs combine general studies with majors and minors. Most degrees require 126 semester hours, at least a 2.0 grade point average, and the last year in residence. The academic calendar consists of fall and spring semesters and two summer terms.

The Honors College, a four-year University-wide program featuring special course offerings, colloquia, seminars, and independent study, is especially designed to challenge the talented student. University College is organized to provide support services to students undecided about their majors. The Learning Center is structured to meet the needs of certain recent Indiana high school graduates, GED awardees, veterans, and students whose past academic records indicate underpreparedness in basic skills.

The University, recognizing that there are other ways to obtain an education than through regular enrollment in a class, grants a maximum of 63 credit hours through any combination of credit for successful scores on Advanced Placement tests or College-Level Examination Program tests, credit for military service, credit by departmental examination, and credit by departmental authorization.

Off-Campus Arrangements

Numerous opportunities for study abroad are available to students who have completed at least one semester of their studies. The London Centre offers students a living and learning experience in Regent's Park of central London. The Honors College offers study at Westminster College in Oxford, England. Departments offering University-sponsored programs in Great Britain and optional continental tours are elementary education at Middlesex Polytechnic, architecture in London, and nursing in London. Anthropology students have the opportunity to study in Jamaica. Foreign language students are encouraged to polish their skills through summer programs in Canada, Latin America, and Europe.

Academic Facilities

The library collections total 1.1 million volumes, 343,104 microforms, 551,770 units of audiovisual materials, and 3,568 current periodicals. Professional collections are housed in the Architecture Library and the Science–Health Science Library. A K–12 school library is maintained at the Burris Laboratory School. Separate materials in the main library are the music collection, special collections, archives, government publications, maps, and educational resources.

Facilities on campus also include an art gallery, an observatory and planetarium, outdoor laboratories, a solar-energy research center, fully equipped science laboratories, a human-performance laboratory, state-of-the-art teaching classrooms, and music laboratories. University Computing Services provides a full range of computing and systems services for students, faculty members, and the administration.

Costs

Expenses for 2001–02 were $3924 for general fees for Indiana residents or $10,800 for general fees for nonresident (out-of-state) students, $5200 for room and board, and $800 (average) for books and supplies. Between $1800 and $2100 is considered reasonable for personal expenses and transportation.

Financial Aid

Through a program of scholarships, grants, loans, and employment, Ball State's Office of Scholarships and Financial Aid provides aid for deserving students. The Free Application for Federal Student Aid, obtainable from a high school guidance counselor, should be filed no later than March 1.

Faculty

Ball State's instructional programs are carried out by 893 full-time faculty members, approximately 67 percent of whom hold earned doctoral degrees. Faculty members serve on the University Senate and on numerous senate and campus committees. Full-time academic advisers work with freshmen. Six advising centers around campus work with departments and their faculty advisers.

Student Government

The all-campus student governing group is the Ball State University Student Association, composed of executive, legislative, and judicial branches. All students are encouraged to participate in such activities as proposing changes in University policy, working for expanded and improved educational programs at Ball State, and lobbying at the city and state levels. One student is appointed to serve on the University's Board of Trustees. In addition, representatives from the Student Association are appointed to serve on numerous boards, committees, and councils on campus, including the University Senate and its committees.

Admission Requirements

Undergraduate applicants are considered for admission to Ball State University after the Office of Admissions has received the application for admission, the $25 nonrefundable application fee, the secondary school record (official transcript) or GED high school equivalency scores and certificate, and scores on either the SAT I or ACT.

Transfer students must, in addition, submit a transcript from each vocational or advanced educational institution attended beyond high school. The transcripts must be forwarded to Ball State directly from the institutions attended.

It is suggested that prospective applicants visit the campus and talk with a member of the admission staff.

Application and Information

High school students should complete an application in the fall of their senior year. Application materials must be submitted by March 1 for priority consideration for the autumn semester and by December 1 for the spring semester. Requests for appointments and information should be addressed to:

Dean of Admissions and Enrollment Services
Ball State University
Muncie, Indiana 47306

Telephone: 765-285-8300
800-482-4BSU (toll-free)
765-285-2205 (TDD users only)
E-mail: askus@bsu.edu
visitus@bsu.edu
World Wide Web: http://www.bsu.edu

BENEDICTINE UNIVERSITY

LISLE, ILLINOIS

The University

Benedictine University was founded in 1887 as St. Procopius College. One hundred fifteen years later, the University remains committed to providing a high-quality, Catholic, liberal education for men and women. The undergraduate enrollment is nearly 2,000 students. The student body comprises students of diverse ages, religions, races, and national origins. Twenty-eight percent of the full-time students reside on campus.

Benedictine University is situated on a rolling, tree-covered 108-acre campus of ten major buildings with air-conditioned classrooms and modern, well-equipped laboratories. A student athletic center features three full-size basketball courts, a competition-size swimming pool, three tennis courts, and training facilities. All of the residence halls are comfortable and spacious and have access to the Internet. On-campus apartments recently opened, offering one-, two-, and four-bedroom residences. Other features include a scenic campus pond, spacious and well-kept athletic fields, a student center with dining halls, a game room, lounges, a chapel, a bookstore, and meeting rooms.

At Benedictine University, the environment is strengthened by success, not size. Renowned faculty members know students by name and care as much about each student's progress as they do about their own research. Those personal relationships have produced superb results. Benedictine graduates are accepted into some of the most prestigious graduate programs in the country. Approximately two thirds of Benedictine graduates who apply to medical school are accepted, as well as similar numbers for other health-related professional schools (optometry, pharmacy, physical therapy, and podiatry). The liberal arts curriculum has helped place the University among some of the finest small private schools in the nation.

U.S. News & World Report's 2003 rankings listed Benedictine University as one of the top schools and a best value in the Midwest. The magazine also ranked the school sixth in the region for campus diversity.

Benedictine University is highly competitive in varsity sports. Men's varsity sports are baseball, basketball, cross-country, football, golf, soccer, swimming, and track. Women's varsity sports are basketball, cross-country, golf, soccer, softball, swimming, tennis, track, and volleyball. Aside from varsity and intramural athletic programs, a variety of organizations exist, including student government, a student newspaper, an orchestra, jazz groups, an African-American Student Union, an Indian Student Union, the Coalition of Latin American Students, campus ministry, a drama club, and various other extracurricular and academic organizations.

The graduate division offers the following graduate degrees in the business, education, and health-care areas: the Doctor of Philosophy (Ph.D.) degree in organization development; the Master of Business Administration (M.B.A.); the Master of Arts in Education (M.A.Ed.); the Master of Education (M.Ed.); the Master of Science (M.S.) in clinical psychology, exercise physiology, fitness management, management and organizational behavior, and management information systems; and the Master of Public Health (M.P.H.).

Adult undergraduate accelerated programs, taught by distinguished faculty members, are available in the following areas: accounting (B.B.A.), business and economics (B.A.), computer science (B.S.), health administration (B.B.A.), information systems (B.S.), management and organizational behavior (B.B.A.), nursing and health (degree completion for B.S.N.), organizational leadership (B.A.), and psychology (B.A.). The University also offers an Associate of Arts degree in business administration in an accelerated format.

Location

Benedictine University is 25 miles west of Chicago, in suburban Lisle near Naperville, and is easily accessible from the city and suburbs via the interstate highway system. The Burlington Northern train stops in Lisle, and O'Hare International Airport is only a 30-minute drive away. In addition to the many social and cultural offerings of the Chicago metropolitan area, the University enjoys the proximity and use of Argonne National Laboratory, Fermi National Accelerator Laboratory, the Morton Arboretum, a ski hill, a riding stable, and several golf courses. The University's location in the high-tech East-West Tollway corridor gives students opportunities for internships and employment.

Majors and Degrees

Benedictine University offers programs leading to the Bachelor of Arts, Bachelor of Business Administration, and Bachelor of Science degrees. Programs are offered in accounting, arts administration, biochemistry, biology, business and economics, chemistry (concentrations in chemical business and marketing and forensic chemistry), clinical laboratory science, communication arts (concentrations in advertising and public relations, broadcasting and cable, journalism, and mass media), computer science, economics, elementary education, engineering science, English language and literature, environmental science, finance, health administration, health science, history, information systems, international business and economics, international studies, management and organizational behavior, marketing, mathematics (concentration in actuarial science), molecular biology, music (concentrations in instrumental and vocal), nuclear medicine technology, nursing (completion), nutrition (concentrations in dietetics and management), organizational leadership, philosophy, physics (concentrations in engineering physics and physics), political science (concentration in prelaw), prenursing, psychology (concentrations in pre–occupational therapy and pre–physical therapy), social science, sociology (concentrations in criminal justice and social work), Spanish, special education (concentrations in learning disabilities and social-emotional disorders), studio art, and writing and publishing.

In education, the University partners with the Golden Apple Foundation. Students selected as a Golden Apple Scholar of Illinois have the opportunity to study elementary, secondary, or special education at Benedictine while receiving the $5000 scholarship through the foundation.

In many areas of study, students may opt for a double major. Preprofessional programs include dentistry, engineering, law, medicine, occupational therapy, optometry, pharmacy, physical therapy, podiatry, and veterinary medicine. Combined professional programs are available with cooperating institutions in clinical laboratory science, nuclear medicine technology, and engineering. A joint engineering program is offered with the Illinois Institute of Technology. A nursing program is offered in cooperation with Rush University in Chicago; a registered nurse may earn a Bachelor of Science degree in nursing. Secondary education certification is available in the following majors: biology, business and economics, chemistry, English, mathematics, music education, physics, and social science.

Academic Program

For graduation, a student must earn at least 120 semester hours, at least 55 of which must be completed at a four-year regionally accredited college. At least the final 45 semester hours must be completed at Benedictine University. The University makes selective exceptions to the normal academic residency requirement of 45 semester hours for adults who are eligible for the Degree Completion Program. Eligibility is limited to those who have nearly completed their undergraduate studies but who, for reasons of employment, career change, or family situation, found it necessary to interrupt their studies.

The Second Major Program is designed for people who already have a degree in one area and would like to gain expertise in another. This program allows the student to concentrate on courses that fulfill the requirements of a second major. The student receives a certificate upon completion.

Each year, a select number of talented and motivated prospective students are invited to participate in the Scholars Program. The program is designed to enhance the college experience by developing students' international awareness and strengthening their leadership ability.

Off-Campus Arrangements

Benedictine University is a member of a three-school consortium in the west suburban Chicago area through which students are able to take classes at the other member colleges. Study abroad and internships abroad are encouraged to complement a liberal education.

Academic Facilities

New buildings that opened in fall 2001, the Kindlon Hall of Learning and the Birck Hall of Science, bring science and technology to new levels. The Birck Hall of Science houses state-of-the art computer labs, specialized science labs, a research center, and the Jurica Nature Museum.

The Kindlon Hall of Learning houses computer labs, classrooms, multimedia labs, offices, and student lounges. It is also home to the Benedictine Library which houses more than 160,000 volumes and can be found in the buildings impressive four-story tower. The library is also equipped with eleven group study rooms, a computer lab, and an instruction room.

Benedictine University has distance education classrooms that provide students with the capability to interact globally with other colleges and universities in a classroom setting.

Costs

The cost of tuition for the 2002–03 academic year was $16,150. The average cost of room and board was $5900. Mandatory fees totaled $510 and included health, technology, and student activity fees.

Financial Aid

In 2001–02, Benedictine University freshmen received assistance totaling $2.9 million from sources that included loans, scholarships and grants, tuition remission, and employment opportunities. Nearly 80 percent of the freshman class participated, receiving an average package of $11,905. Benedictine University has dedicated more than $5 million of the annual budget to providing grants and scholarships to students and separate scholarship programs designed to attract and serve members of minority groups. Students who wish to apply for aid must complete the Free Application for Federal Student Aid (FAFSA), the Benedictine University application for financial aid, and the Benedictine University application for admission.

Faculty

The 13:1 student-faculty ratio allows for close interaction between students and faculty members. Of the 84 full-time faculty members, 86 percent hold a Ph.D. or the terminal professional degree in their respective fields. All students are assigned a faculty member as an adviser to help plan programs of study.

Student Government

All full-time enrolled students are automatically members of the student government. The Student Government Association (SGA) is a representative body elected annually by the students to represent their interests. The SGA is responsible for the annual allocation of the student activity fee.

Admission Requirements

The Benedictine University admission philosophy is to select students who will perform successfully in the University's academic programs and become active members of the University community. Typically, Benedictine University's freshman students are in the top third of their high school graduating class, with about 50 percent in the top quarter, and report better-than-average ACT or SAT I scores. A minimum of 16 units in academic subjects is required, including 4 units of English, 1 unit of algebra, 1 unit of geometry, 1 unit of history, 1 unit of laboratory science, and 2 units of foreign language. Benedictine University does admit some students who fall below these standards. These applicants receive individual consideration by the Committee on Admission. When appropriate, the committee will place conditions and/or restrictions upon students to help them reach their academic potential.

Students interested in transferring to Benedictine University must have a minimum cumulative average of C (2.0 on a 4.0 scale) or better from all colleges previously attended. Official transcripts from high school and all colleges attended must be submitted directly to the Office of Admissions for evaluation. If fewer than 20 semester hours of transfer credit are submitted, SAT I or ACT scores are required, and the general admission requirements previously described for incoming freshmen with regard to high school curriculum must also be satisfied. High school information is not required with A.A. or A.S. degrees. Credits transferred from other institutions are evaluated on the basis of their equivalent at Benedictine University. Grades of D are accepted as transfer credit but do not satisfy Benedictine University requirements, which demand a minimum grade of C.

Requests for admission are considered without regard to the applicant's race, religion, gender, age, or disability.

Application and Information

Applications are reviewed on a rolling basis. Students are encouraged to apply for admission at any time after completing their junior year of high school. Transfer students may apply for admission during their last semester or quarter before anticipated transfer to Benedictine University. Earlier applications are encouraged for scholarship and financial aid opportunities.

For further information, students should contact:

Undergraduate Admissions
Benedictine University
5700 College Road
Lisle, Illinois 60532-0900
Telephone: 630-829-6300
888-829-6363 (toll-free oustide Illinois)
Fax: 630-829-6301
E-mail: admissions@ben.edu
World Wide Web: http://www.ben.edu

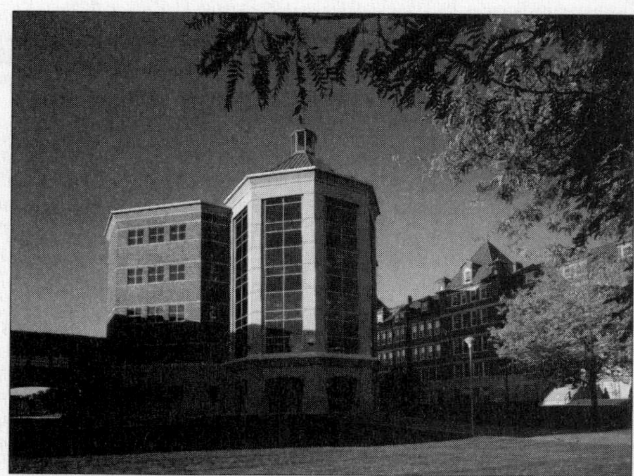

The Kindlon Hall of Learning houses computer labs, classrooms, multimedia labs, offices, and student lounges.

BETHEL COLLEGE

NORTH NEWTON, KANSAS

The College

Founded in 1887, Bethel College is a liberal arts and sciences undergraduate college affiliated with the Mennonite Church USA. Students are encouraged to live and work together and become the kind of leaders who blend faith and learning. To these ends, Bethel maintains a residential environment designed to foster integrative learning experiences, including student organizations, campus worship services, public lectures, symposia, and cultural events. At Bethel, 85 percent of the freshmen and two thirds of the entire student body of more than 500 students live on campus. The sense of community afforded by the residential nature of the campus is invigorating.

Bethel's curriculum is founded on a general education program in the liberal arts and sciences and is geared toward students of moderate to high academic ability who want to be leaders. Distinctive elements include requirements in the study of religion and global issues. The College offers twenty-seven majors and ten specialized programs in traditional liberal arts and selected career areas. Bethel is a diverse community of learners, with students from twenty-three states, seventeen countries, and more than thirty religious denominations.

Bethel's programs are informed by four central values of the mission statement: discipleship, scholarship, service, and integrity. Bethel emphasizes faith, learning, and leadership.

The Bethel campus includes the historic Administration Building, two libraries, a performing arts center, a science center, a student center, two gymnasiums, a natural history museum, an art center, athletic fields, and three residence halls.

The Administration Building is the dominating landmark of the College. Home to the campus Chapel and its Dobson pipe organ, the Administration Building was built in 1888 and is listed in the National Register of Historic Places. Thresher Gymnasium (seating capacity of 2,000) is home to varsity women's volleyball and men's and women's basketball. The Schultz Student Center is a hub of student activity, with a cafeteria, snack bar, game room, bookstore, and meeting rooms. The campus facilities are clustered around an open, grassy area referred to as The Green. The Green, with its benches and fountain, is a gathering place for students.

More than two thirds of Bethel students live on campus in one of three residence halls: Voth Hall, Haury Hall, and Warkentin Court. Each residence hall is supervised by an on-site staff and offers recreational and lounge areas and laundry and vending facilities.

Location

The 90-acre, tree-lined Bethel College campus is in North Newton, which is adjacent to the city of Newton (population 20,000). Located in the rich agricultural and industrial region of south-central Kansas, Bethel borders Interstate 135 and Kansas Highway 15. Wichita, the largest city in Kansas, lies 30 minutes to the south, and Hutchinson is 30 minutes west of the campus. Between Newton, Wichita, and Hutchinson, a wide variety of services and attractions are available to students. These include the Kansas Cosmosphere and Space Center, a world-renowned space museum; several art museums; music theater; opera; symphonies; professional baseball, hockey, and soccer; an ice sports center; and multiple malls and shopping centers. Wichita is served by eleven major airlines, and Amtrak train service is available in Newton.

Majors and Degrees

Bethel College grants Bachelor of Arts and Bachelor of Science degrees. Majors include art, athletic training, Bible and religion, biology, business administration, chemistry, communication arts, computer science, computer system administration, elementary education, English, fine arts, German, global peace and justice, health management, history, history and social sciences, management information systems, mathematical sciences, music, natural science, nursing, physics, psychology, restorative community justice, social work, and Spanish. Within these majors, students may concentrate in the following specialized areas: accounting, economics, environmental studies, finance, general management, marketing, mass media, software development, speech, and theater arts. Preprofessional programs are offered in engineering, law, medicine, and ministry.

Academic Program

Bethel operates on a 4-1-4 academic calendar. Four-month semesters in the spring and fall are supported by the one-month Interterm in January. Interterm allows for a time of focused study in one selected class, either on campus or through several off-campus options. Interterm study-travel options have included English literature in London, biology in the jungle of Belize, theater in New York, history in Russia, religion in Jerusalem, and art in a snowbound cabin in the Colorado Rockies. Through this multifaceted learning environment, Bethel is committed to the diverse educational goals of its students. Courses facilitate intellectual, cultural, and spiritual learning in the Bethel community. The general education requirement of 55 credit hours ensures development of academic skills and disciplines and of integrative learning. Graduation from Bethel requires at least 124 credit hours with a minimum grade point average of 2.0.

Off-Campus Arrangements

Bethel offers a wide variety of formal study-abroad programs. Students enrolled in these programs are considered to be enrolled as full-time Bethel students living off campus. Academic progress and financial aid are generally the same as for on-campus programs. Bethel students may participate in study-abroad programs at sixteen colleges and universities in thirteen countries.

Academic Facilities

The Mantz Library has a collection of 130,000 volumes and more than 500 periodical subscriptions. The library also houses the Career Development Office and the Center for Academic Development, which provides academic support in the form of tutoring and supplemental instruction. Additional support is available for postbaccalaureate placement exams, including the GRE, MCAT, and LSAT. Adjacent to the Mantz Library is the Mennonite Library and Archives, which houses more than 45,000 volumes of Mennonite historical and genealogical information.

The Fine Arts Center includes Krehbiel Auditorium, which is used for theater, concerts, and lectures. The Fine Arts Center also houses an art gallery; music rehearsal areas; a computerized music composition lab; studios of KBCU, the campus radio station; and offices of the *Collegian,* the student newspaper.

Krehbiel Science Center, opened in 2002, provides classrooms and laboratories for biology, chemistry, physics, and psychology. Two networked computer laboratories are available in the Academic Center.

Memorial Hall houses the nursing department (classrooms, labs, and research computers), the Wellness Center (exercise and weight rooms), the Academic Health Center (student clinic), Harms Sports Medicine Center (athletic training), and an auditorium and intramural gymnasium (seating capacity of 2,000).

The Franz Art Center has multiple art studios for painting, drawing, ceramics, and photography.

Costs

Tuition and fees for a full-time student for the 2003–04 academic year are $13,900; room and board costs total $5900. Interterm is included in these costs if a student is enrolled full-time for either the spring or fall term.

Financial Aid

Bethel College administers a broad spectrum of financial aid intended to make the educational experience affordable for qualified students. Through merit-based financial aid (academic and performance), students may receive assistance ranging from $2500 to $7400 per year. For qualified students, need-based aid is available in the form of Bethel, state, and federal grant and loan programs. More than 94 percent of Bethel students receive some form of financial assistance.

Faculty

Bethel has 44 full-time and 9 part-time faculty members. Of the full-time faculty members, 85 percent have terminal degrees. Faculty members of all ranks teach first-year students in addition to upperclassmen. Bethel faculty members are active in scholarly research and regularly enlist students as collaborators in their research. No classes at Bethel are taught by teaching assistants or graduate assistants. The student-faculty ratio is 11:1. As is consistent with the emphasis Bethel places on global awareness and service, more than half of Bethel faculty members have been engaged in overseas service and travel.

Student Government

Student government at Bethel is based on the federal model and consists of twenty-seven elected offices and several appointed positions. The executive branch comprises the Student Body President and Vice-President. The Senate has 5 senators from each class, 3 commuter senators, one senator from the International Club, and one from the multicultural organization. Bethel's active student government provides an opportunity for student advocacy and leadership development.

Admission Requirements

Bethel seeks to enroll a broad range of students with a demonstrated desire and ability to learn. Admission is competitive, and applicants must provide school transcripts and standardized test scores. Freshman applicants should present a minimum GPA of 2.5 and a minimum ACT score of 19 or SAT I score of 890. Transfer applicants should present a minimum college GPA of 2.0 on 24 hours or more of credit accepted in transfer. International applicants are required to present a minimum TOEFL score of 540 on the paper-based version or 207 on the computer-based version. All prospective students are encouraged to visit campus, either during a group-visit event or an individual campus visit. The College admits students without regard to race, color, sex, disability, or national or ethnic origin.

Application and Information

Interested students are invited to request an application for admission from the Admissions Office or to complete the application online at http://www.bethelks.edu/admissions/application.html. Although admission is granted on a rolling basis through the beginning of each semester, early application is encouraged for priority consideration for financial aid, class selection, and housing.

For more information, students should contact:

Office of Admissions
Bethel College
300 East 27th Street
North Newton, Kansas 67117
Telephone: 316-283-2500
800-522-1887 (toll-free)
Fax: 316-284-5870
E-mail: admissions@bethelks.edu
World Wide Web: http://www.bethelks.edu

Bethel College students in front of Memorial Hall.

BLUFFTON COLLEGE

BLUFFTON, OHIO

The College

Bluffton College is a fully accredited, four-year Christian liberal arts college in northwestern Ohio. Founded in 1899 by regional leaders of the General Conference Mennonite Church, it is today affiliated with the Mennonite Church USA. Shaped by this historic peace church tradition and coupled with its desire for excellence in all programs, Bluffton College seeks to prepare students of all backgrounds for life as well as vocation, for responsible citizenship, for service to all peoples, and ultimately for the purposes of God's universal kingdom.

More than 1,100 students from twenty states and eighteen countries study at Bluffton College, which is accredited by the North Central Association of Colleges and Schools (30 North LaSalle Street, Suite 2400, Chicago, Illinois 60602; 800-621-7440, toll-free). The College continues to receive national recognition in *Barron's Best Buys in College Education* for providing outstanding quality at a reasonable price. Bluffton is one of only a handful of Ohio colleges to be included in the prestigious *John Templeton Foundation Honor Roll of Character-Building Colleges.*

The student life program is rich with opportunities for personal and spiritual growth. Weekly chapel services and biweekly Sunday morning worship services provide a community context for joint worship. Examples of the many groups in which students participate include BASIC (Brothers And Sisters In Christ), Diakonia (Christian service/outreach groups), Habitat for Humanity, and PALS Drug Awareness programs. The Honor System, practiced in all classes and throughout campus life, promotes honest, open communication between all members of the campus community.

Students participate in many organizations and activities, including vocal and instrumental music, departmental and preprofessional clubs, student newspaper, student government, and many others. As a member of the NCAA Division III and the Heartland Collegiate Athletic Conference, Bluffton fields varsity athletic teams for both men and women. Men's sports include baseball, basketball, cross-country, football, golf, soccer, tennis, and track. Varsity teams for women include basketball, cross-country, golf, soccer, softball, tennis, track, and volleyball. Bluffton is the first NCAA Division III college in Ohio and the nation to be selected for the NCAA Life Skills program, which helps prepare student athletes for life after college.

Residence life is integral to the campus community. All students are required to live in campus housing unless they are married or commuting from home. No self-selective fraternities or sororities are permitted, and students are expected to adhere to campus standards of conduct, which prohibit the use of tobacco, alcohol, and drugs. A satisfaction guarantee is offered to new residential students.

In addition to its undergraduate degrees, Bluffton offers a Master of Arts in Education and a Master of Organizational Management.

Location

Bluffton College is located just off Interstate 75, midway between Lima and Findlay, Ohio, in the Allen County village of Bluffton (population 3,400). Several restaurants and a movie theater are within walking distance of campus, and easy access to I-75 provides many additional opportunities in Findlay, Lima, Toledo, Dayton, and Columbus.

The campus is situated on 60 beautifully wooded acres and is adjacent to the 130-acre Bluffton College Nature Preserve.

Majors and Degrees

Bluffton College offers Bachelor of Arts degrees. Bachelor's degrees are available in accounting; adolescent/young adult, multiage, and vocational education; apparel/textiles merchandising and design; art; biology; business administration; chemistry; child development; communication; computer science; criminal justice; dietetics; early childhood education; economics; English; family and consumer sciences; food and nutrition–dietetics; food and nutrition–wellness, health, physical education, and recreation (HPER); history; information systems; intervention specialist studies (special education); mathematics; middle childhood education; music; music education; physics; premedicine; psychology; recreation management; religion; social studies; social work; sociology; Spanish; Spanish/economics; sport management; writing; and youth ministries and recreation. In addition, a number of minors, preprofessional programs, and special programs are available, including graphic design, prelaw, peace and conflict studies, TESOL studies, women's studies, and self-designed majors.

Academic Program

The Bluffton College curriculum is centered on a liberal arts and sciences general education program. The strength of this program lies in the many integrated courses in social science, humanities, fine arts, and natural sciences that build upon one another as students advance toward earning their degree. Courses in Bible and theology, an integrated cross-cultural course, and a capstone course titled Christian Values in a Global Community complete the general education program. Key components of the general education curriculum include the First Year Seminar for new students and the cross-cultural requirement. Students seeking a bachelor's degree must complete a minimum of 122 semester hours of academic work and maintain a minimum overall grade point average of 2.0.

Off-Campus Arrangements

Bluffton College offers several semester-long international and cross-cultural opportunities. Current programs include study in Central America, Mexico, Northern Ireland, and Vietnam. Bluffton is also a member of the Council of Christian Colleges and Universities, which offers study programs at various U.S. locations, including Washington, D.C., as well as international programs in the Middle East, Russia, and Central America. Many Bluffton students participate in short-term off-campus projects with organizations such as Habitat for Humanity, Witness for Peace, and the Urban Life Center in Chicago. In addition, Bluffton students may complete up to four supervised independent study courses, which may be used for off-campus study.

Academic Facilities

The Musselman Library, a 1930 building of Georgian colonial architecture, was the gift of Mr. and Mrs. C. H. Musselman. It holds approximately 150,000 volumes, 116,000 microfilm units, approximately 4,000 current periodicals, and more than 350 CD-ROMs. The library has about 4,500 maps and receives many important U.S. government publications as a selective depository library. The library is a member of both the OPAL (Ohio Private Academic Libraries) and the OhioLINK consortia. Through OhioLINK, Bluffton College students and faculty and staff members have access to more than 24 million library items held at more than seventy college and university libraries throughout the state, to more than 60 separate databases, and to hundreds of full-text periodicals.

The newest facility on campus is the Centennial Hall academic center. The academic center is a multilevel building at the center of the campus and contains state-of-the-art computer facilities, a new media center, technology-enhanced classrooms, and faculty offices.

Completed in 1991, the Sauder Visual Arts Center contains an art gallery and classroom and offers studio facilities for printing, painting, drawing, sculpture, ceramics, woodworking, welding, and photography. Shoker Science Center is a unique underground science facility that houses integrated laboratories for all the sciences, a science library, and instructional computers. College Hall serves as the main administrative building and includes the Education Department, several classrooms, and the Educational Media Center.

Founders Hall is a complete physical education facility, containing a main gymnasium, a newly renovated auxiliary gymnasium, and a weight room. Other recent additions to campus include the Salzman Stadium and Ramseyer Hall, a new residence hall for 111 students.

The Al and Marie Yoder Recital Hall provides a state-of-the-art performance facility for student recitals and guest artists. Weekly forums and chapel services are also held in Yoder Hall.

Primary student computer access is provided through the microcomputer center located in Centennial Hall. All students may have e-mail addresses, and Internet access is provided in the lab. In addition, computers are located in residence halls, academic departments, and other locations on campus. All residence halls are equipped for students who wish to bring their own computer.

Costs

Tuition for the 2003–04 school year (based on 24 to 34 semester hours per year) is $17,260. Board is $3272 and room is $2758, for a total of $23,290. There is also a $400 technology fee. Books and personal expenses are additional.

Financial Aid

Nearly 100 percent of Bluffton College students receive some form of financial aid. Some awards are based solely on financial need, such as the Bluffton College Grant, while others are tied to academic achievement or demonstrated leadership and service to others. Scholarships and grants unique to Bluffton include the Presidential Scholarship Competition; the Academic Honors Scholarship; the Academic Merit Scholarship; the Tuition Equalization Scholarship Program, for students scoring at least 23 on the ACT or 1050 on the SAT I and ranking in the top 25 percent of their class or achieving at least a 3.0 grade point average; the Bluffton College Incentive Scholarship, for students with at least a 2.8 grade point average and 21 on the ACT or 970 on the SAT I; Leadership/Service Grants, which are available to students who demonstrate significant contributions outside the classroom in school, church, and community activities; and Church Matching Scholarships to students whose church has awarded them a scholarship to attend Bluffton. Additional College awards include scholarships for music and art and need-based grants to dependents of ministers and those serving in foreign missions. The Learn and Earn program provides an opportunity for many students to work on campus to help with expenses and gain valuable work experience.

Faculty

A high-quality program depends on a superior faculty. Students at Bluffton are taught by 64 full-time faculty members and 37 part-time faculty members. More than 70 percent of the full-time faculty members have earned the doctorate or appropriate terminal degree, and all faculty members teach on a regular basis. Many faculty members continue to research and write yet remain committed to teaching. The faculty members are very approachable and work together with students to create a unique learning environment based on mutual trust and respect.

Student Government

A democratic atmosphere prevails in the Bluffton College campus community. The Student Senate is a very important part of the campus community and actively represents the interests of the student body to the administration. Composed of students elected from each of the four classes, the Senate has primary responsibility in the areas of cocurricular activities. Hall associations are organized for the purpose of self-government and social activities.

Admission Requirements

Requirements for admission to the first-year class include graduation from a secondary school or a GED certificate; satisfactory secondary school work, with preference given to students ranking in the top half of their class and who have taken the recommended secondary preparation of 4 units of English, 3 units of mathematics, and 3 units each of social sciences, science, and a foreign language; and satisfactory performance on either the ACT or SAT I. Also considered are participation in cocurricular activities, moral character, purpose for college study, and recommendations.

Application and Information

Application for admission should be made at the end of the junior year or early in the senior year of high school. The deadline for submitting the application for the fall term is May 31. For all other terms the deadline is fifteen days prior to the intended date of enrollment.

Applicants must complete and return the application with a $20 fee along with recommendations from the school guidance counselor and a teacher, a high school transcript, and scores from either the ACT or the SAT I. A personal campus visit and interview are strongly encouraged.

The Office of Admissions operates on a rolling basis and makes its decision and notifies the applicant soon after receiving the required items. Students wishing to receive additional information may contact:

Office of Admissions
Bluffton College
280 West College Avenue
Bluffton, Ohio 45817-1196
Telephone: 419-358-3257
800-488-3257 (toll-free)
Fax: 419-358-3232
E-mail: admissions@bluffton.edu
World Wide Web: http://www.bluffton.edu

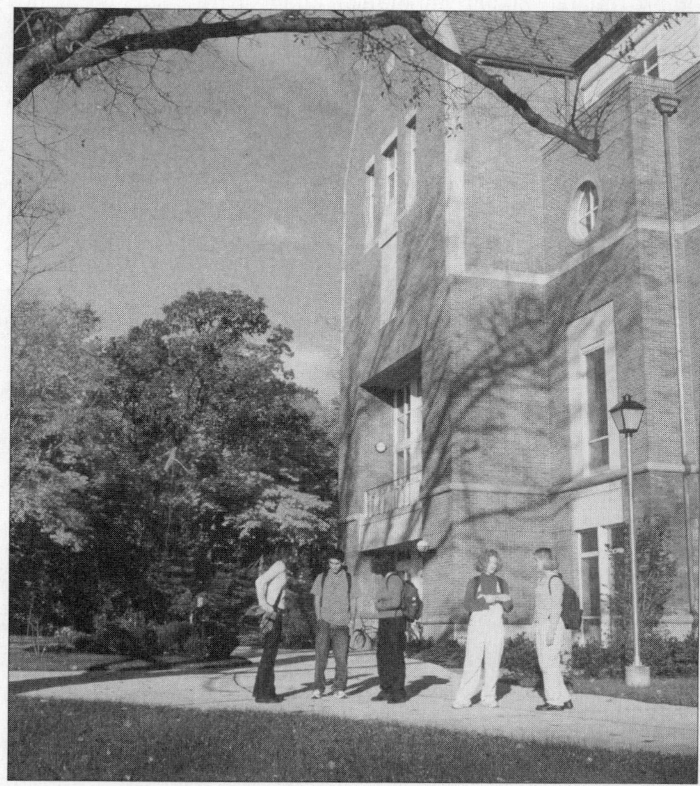

Students enjoy Bluffton College's wooded campus.

CASE WESTERN RESERVE UNIVERSITY

CLEVELAND, OHIO

The University

Formed in 1967 by the federation of Case Institute of Technology and Western Reserve University, Case Western Reserve University is today one of the nation's major independent universities. Currently, 3,457 undergraduates (2,094 men, 1,363 women) are enrolled in programs in engineering, science, management, nursing, the arts, humanities, and the social and behavioral sciences. Students have access to the facilities of a comprehensive university, including graduate and professional schools in applied social sciences, dentistry, graduate studies (humanities, the social and natural sciences, and engineering), nursing, medicine, law, and management. Several undergraduate programs and majors combine the resources of the undergraduate colleges and the graduate and professional schools. Examples include biochemistry and biomedical engineering (CWRU School of Medicine) and accounting and management (Weatherhead School of Management). In addition, collaborative arrangements with neighboring cultural and health-care institutions enable the University to provide special opportunities in other fields.

There are numerous college activities, including those of dozens of professional, religious, political, social, and academic organizations. Nearly every type of interest group, from political organizations to a film society, is represented on campus, and sports are offered at both the varsity and intramural levels. There are eighteen national fraternities and five sororities; approximately 30 percent of the students participate. Residence halls are coeducational, with the exception of one hall for women. Seventy-five percent of the students reside on campus. Automobiles and motorcycles are permitted.

Students at Case Western Reserve enjoy an especially close interaction with the faculty.

Location

The University is located in University Circle, a cultural extension of the campus, which comprises 500 acres of parks, gardens, museums, schools, hospitals, churches, and human service institutions. The Cleveland Museum of Art, the Cleveland Museum of Natural History, and Severance Hall, home of the Cleveland Orchestra, are within walking distance; downtown Cleveland is 10 minutes away by RTA rapid transit. Cooperation in education and research among University Circle institutions enables students to make full use of resources beyond those of the University itself.

Majors and Degrees

Programs of study leading to the Bachelor of Arts degree comprise the following: American studies, anthropology, art history (joint program with the Cleveland Museum of Art), Asian studies, astronomy, biochemistry, biology, chemistry, classics (Greek and Latin), communication sciences (collaborative program with Cleveland Hearing and Speech Center), comparative literature, computer science, economics, English, environmental geology, environmental studies, evolutionary biology, French, French studies, geological sciences, German, German studies, gerontological studies, history, history and philosophy of science, international studies, Japanese studies, mathematics, music (joint program with the Cleveland Institute of Music), natural sciences, nutrition, nutritional biochemistry and metabolism, philosophy, physics, political science, prearchitecture, psychology, religion, sociology, Spanish, statistics, theater arts, and women's studies. Minor areas of concentration within the B.A. curriculum include artificial intelligence, art studio, childhood studies, Chinese, electronics, entrepreneurial studies, history of science and technology, human development, Italian, Japanese, management information and decision systems, public policy, Russian, and sports medicine.

Bachelor of Science degrees are offered in the following fields: accounting, aerospace engineering, applied mathematics, art education (joint program with the Cleveland Institute of Art), astronomy, biochemistry, biology, biomedical engineering, chemical engineering, chemistry, civil engineering, computer engineering, computer science, electrical engineering, engineering physics, fluid and thermal engineering sciences, geological sciences, management (business), materials science and engineering, mathematics, mathematics and physics (combined major), mechanical engineering, music education, nursing, nutrition, nutritional biochemistry and metabolism, physics, polymer science, statistics, systems and control engineering, and an undesignated engineering major. Course sequences emphasizing architecture, energy, environmental/water resources studies, and power are offered in conjunction with some engineering and science fields.

Exceptionally well qualified high school seniors in some fields are eligible for the Pre-Professional Scholars Program offered in association with the Schools of Dentistry, Law, and Medicine. In addition to being accepted as an undergraduate, each student selected is also awarded a conditional acceptance for admission to the appropriate professional school upon completion of the entrance requirements set by each school. A six-year dental program leading to the D.D.S. degree is also available.

Students may work toward a combined B.A./B.S. degree or integrate undergraduate and graduate studies to complete both the bachelor's and master's degrees in five years or less. Combined B.A./B.S. (3-2) programs in astronomy, biochemistry, and engineering are offered in conjunction with a number of four-year liberal arts colleges.

Academic Program

Through a combination of core curricula, major requirements, and minors or approved course sequences, all undergraduates receive a broad educational base as well as specialized knowledge in their chosen fields.

The University offers students opportunities for independent research and internships or professional practicums in business, health-care, government, arts, or service fields. A five-year co-op option providing two 7-month work periods in industry or government is available for majors in engineering, science, management, accounting, and computer science.

The Undergraduate Scholars Program allows a small number of highly motivated and responsible students to pursue individually tailored baccalaureate programs without the normal credit-hour and course requirements. The program, administered by a faculty committee, must be one that cannot be accomplished within the regular curricula.

Candidates for the B.A. who have been accepted at a school of medicine or dentistry other than one of those at CWRU may exercise the Senior Year In Absentia Privilege, which permits them to substitute the first year of professional studies at an approved school for the final year at Case Western Reserve. The Senior Year in Professional Studies option allows B.A. candidates who are admitted during their junior year to CWRU's school of dentistry, management, medicine, nursing, or social work to substitute the first year of professional school for the final undergraduate year.

The Minority Engineers Industrial Opportunity Program offers a special orientation and support to minority students in secondary schools and academic and financial support to minority undergraduates in engineering.

The University has two 4-month semesters and one 8-week summer program.

Off-Campus Arrangements

Selected students may enroll as juniors and seniors in the Washington Semester, which is conducted each spring at the American University. Students with a B average or higher may participate in the Junior Year Abroad program. Up to 36 hours of credit may be granted for study at a foreign university. Students may also cross-register at other Cleveland-area colleges and universities for one course per semester.

Academic Facilities

The $30-million Kelvin Smith Library opened in 1997. Through reciprocal borrowing arrangements, CWRU students have access to the holdings of the Cleveland Public Library, as well as the libraries of five University Circle institutions; the members of OhioLINK, a network that includes state colleges and universities; the State Library of Ohio; and several private institutions. In addition to more traditional departmental research facilities, the University operates two astronomical observatories, a biological field station, and nearly 100 designated research centers and laboratories, many of them interdisciplinary. CWRUnet, the University's high-speed fiber-optic communications network, links every residence hall room with computing centers, libraries, and databases on and off campus. Other computer facilities on campus offer various models of microcomputers and a wide variety of software programs.

Costs

For 2003–04, tuition and compulsory health and laboratory fees total $24,100. The student activity fee is $242. Room and board cost an average of $7660. Books and supplies come to about $800, and incidental expenses are estimated at $1178. The approximate total cost for the year is $33,980.

Financial Aid

Financial aid consisting of grants, loans, and work assistance is awarded on the basis of a student's need. Last year, all students demonstrating need received financial aid. Applicants must file the Free Application for Federal Student Aid (FAFSA) and the Financial Aid PROFILE of the College Scholarship Service by February 1. A signed copy of the most recent federal tax return (Form 1040) is also required. The University also awards merit-based scholarships ranging from $500 to full tuition. These awards are based solely on the student's academic, creative, or leadership ability.

Faculty

The full-time instructional staff of 2,223, of whom 95 percent hold the Ph.D. or equivalent, is shared by all University students: graduate, undergraduate, and professional. The undergraduate student-faculty ratio is 8:1. Each college provides counselors who are always available for both academic and personal advice. Once a major has been chosen, a member of the department in which the student is majoring acts as his or her academic adviser.

Student Government

The Undergraduate Student Government of Case Western Reserve University represents all undergraduate students. The assembly acts as a liaison between undergraduate students and the faculty, administration, and other groups; grants recognition to undergraduate organizations; and has the responsibility and authority to allocate funds from student activity fees to student organizations.

Admission Requirements

The University requires at least 16 units of full-credit high school work in solid academic subjects, including 4 years of English or its equivalent. All applicants are expected to have completed 3 years of high school mathematics, and students interested in mathematics, science, or engineering majors should have 4. At least 2 years of laboratory science are required of all applicants, and prospective mathematics and science majors must present 3 years. For all engineering candidates, physics and chemistry are required. Two years of foreign language study are recommended for students considering majors in the humanities, arts, and social and behavioral sciences. An interview is not a required part of the admission process, but it is strongly recommended as the best way to learn about the University. Applicants should take the ACT or the SAT I not later than January of their senior year in secondary school. For candidates submitting the SAT I, three SAT II Subject Tests are strongly recommended, including the Writing Test for all students, the Level I or II mathematics test and physics or chemistry for engineering candidates, and two tests of their choice for others.

Application and Information

Freshmen matriculate in August. Students for whom Case Western Reserve University is a definite first choice must apply for early decision by January 1. They are notified within two weeks of receipt of a completed application. The final application deadline is February 1 for April 1 notification. Application deadlines for transfer students are June 30 for fall admission and November 15 for spring admission. The application deadline for the Pre-Professional Scholars Program (medicine, dentistry, or law) is December 15. In addition to its own application form, Case Western Reserve University accepts the Common Application and offers online application options.

To obtain an application form and financial aid information, students should contact:

Office of Undergraduate Admission
Case Western Reserve University
10900 Euclid Avenue
Cleveland, Ohio 44106-7055
Telephone: 216-368-4450
E-mail: admission@po.cwru.edu
World Wide Web: http://www.cwru.edu

Students at Case Western Reserve University in Cleveland, Ohio.

CENTRAL COLLEGE

PELLA, IOWA

The College

At Central College in Pella, Iowa, students are not just getting an education, they are taking off on one of life's greatest journeys. Students learn to be critical thinkers, to communicate effectively, and to see the interconnected nature of knowledge, wisdom, and experience. Central College offers opportunities for students to realize their potential and discover who they were always meant to be.

Established in 1853, Central enrolls 1,623 students. More than 75 percent of these students are from Iowa, but the opportunities at Central often take them far from the campus. Students can study in Paris at the Sorbonne, have a semester's internship in Britain's Parliament, and gain professional experience working with children at an orphanage in the Yucatan. Nearly half of Central's graduates have studied in one of its international programs in Austria, China, England, France, Kenya, Mexico, the Netherlands, Spain, and Wales. Central also offers metropolitan study programs in Chicago and Washington, D.C.

Participation in the arts is open to all students and includes symphonic ensembles; jazz, classical, and pop music; painting classes; the only glass-blowing program of its kind in the Midwest; and the light, sound, costume, and set design of the theater.

Central's men and women have achieved great athletic success. The Central Dutch teams have won ten NCAA Division III national championships, placed in the top ten in the nation sixty-one times, and earned 131 Iowa Conference championships. The Dutch field teams in baseball, basketball, cross-country, football, golf, soccer, softball, tennis, track and field, volleyball, and wrestling.

Location

Central's home in Pella, Iowa, is a community with a legacy from Europe, founded by Dutch immigrants in 1847. Many of Pella's 10,000 residents are of Dutch ancestry, and the downtown square is surrounded by shops fashioned after the architecture of Holland. Red-brick shops line a Dutch-style canal, and in the spring, the city's three-day celebration of its heritage attracts more than 100,000 visitors. Pella is home to several international companies, including Pella Corporation and Vermeer Manufacturing. The 13,000-acre Lake Red Rock and Bos Landen Golf Resort are both just 5 minutes from the campus. Des Moines, the state capital, is only 40 minutes away.

Majors and Degrees

Central awards the Bachelor of Arts degree, and students can work directly with their adviser to create their own major. Majors are available in accounting, art, biology, business management, chemistry, communication studies, computer science, cultural anthropology, economics, elementary education, English, environmental studies, exercise science, French, general studies, German, history, individualized interdisciplinary studies, information systems, international management, international studies, linguistics, mathematics, mathematics/computer science, music, music education, natural science, philosophy, physics, political science, psychology, religion, social science, sociology, Spanish, and theater.

Central offers a 3-4 cooperative program in architecture with Washington University in St. Louis, Missouri, and a 3-2 cooperative program in engineering with Iowa State University, the University of Iowa, and Washington University.

Academic Program

The academic program at Central College is designed to help students launch careers, develop their identities, define their values, and discover their special talents. Central is dedicated to the liberal arts tradition and engages students in the broad spectrum of areas that they will encounter in today's world. At the heart of Central's liberal arts philosophy is the conviction that the fully educated person must be able to read and listen critically, write clearly, and speak in an articulate manner. Communication is essential in today's job market, and Central students acquire strong communication skills. Central offers honors courses to its top students, beginning in the freshman year.

Off-Campus Arrangements

Central students can travel the world, see the sights, learn another culture, and understand what it means to have a global perspective. The international campuses in Mexico and Europe offer opportunities to study another culture; not all programs require foreign language proficiency. English-language programs are offered in Hangzhou, China; London and Colchester, England; Eldoret, Kenya; Leiden, the Netherlands; Carmarthen, Wales; and Mérida, Mexico. Students of Spanish, German, and French can perfect their language skills through programs in Granada, Spain; Vienna, Austria; and Paris, France.

The Chicago Metropolitan Center and the Washington Center provide students with another experience away from the Pella campus. The course work emphasizes the urban experience, and a wide range of internships is available. Central's off-campus programs offer full college credit.

Academic Facilities

New construction and significant renovations are changing Central's campus. Students benefit from state-of-the-art classrooms and athletic facilities. Each campus building is connected by high-speed fiber-optic cable. The College's distinctive library is spacious enough to seat nearly one third of the student body at the same time, and it has won numerous architectural awards for innovative use of space and materials. It is a popular study haven, with more than 210,000 volumes, computer stations, a multimedia collection, and an extensive online computerized catalog.

The Vermeer Science Center is designed so that students from across scientific disciplines can share knowledge and collaborate—an example of Central's approach to community learning. The science center underwent a $20-million renovation that was completed in 2003.

The Carlson-Kuyper Field Station is Central College's 62-acre nature preserve and outdoor laboratory. Located about 12 miles from the campus, it is adjacent to extensive wildlife areas managed by the Corps of Engineers around Lake Red Rock, Iowa's largest lake.

The Kruidenier Center for Communication and Theatre, home of two theaters, a scene shop, a costume shop, a makeup room, a seminar room, a classroom, and offices, hosts at least three major theater productions each year, as well as numerous smaller shows.

The Cox-Snow Music Center houses the newly renovated recital hall, rehearsal spaces, classrooms, and keyboard and computer labs. In the Lubbers Center for the Visual Arts, the Mills Gallery provides excellent exhibition space for student, faculty, and visiting art shows adjacent to studio space for ceramics, glass blowing, painting, and graphic arts.

Completed in 1999, the Weller Center for Business and International Studies is filled with the latest in technology, including multimedia classrooms, a large classroom equipped with a computer at each student's desk, seminar rooms, and a 24-hour computer lab.

Other classroom buildings include Jordan Hall and Central Hall. There are also classrooms in the P. H. Kuyper Gymnasium, the H. S. Kuyper Fieldhouse, the Media Center, and the Maytag Student Center.

The campuswide computer network connects all classrooms, labs, offices, and student residence hall rooms to shared file servers and the Internet. Many students bring their own computers to the campus, but there are also twenty-two computer labs distributed around the campus where students can use standard applications or special discipline-specific software. Both PCs and Macs are available. Each student is provided with an e-mail account and a personal home folder on a network file server and Web server. The Computer Help Center provides technical support to students and faculty and staff members. The same fiber-optic backbone that services the computer network also provides cable TV service to each residence hall room and many other locations around the campus.

Costs

For 2002–03, costs were $17,609 for tuition, $3013 for room, $3132 for board (twenty-meal plan), and $144 for activity fees, for a total of $23,898.

Financial Aid

Types of financial assistance include scholarships, grants, loans, and campus employment. More than 98 percent of the student body receive financial assistance, totaling more than $27 million in 2001–02. The average freshman financial aid package in 2002–03 was $15,275. To apply for assistance, students must first apply for admission and complete the financial aid section of the application form. In addition, students are strongly encouraged to file the Free Application for Federal Student Aid (FAFSA) after January 1. (Iowa residents must file before June 1.) Students must name Central (code 001850) in order for the College to receive the needs analysis report. To receive the results more quickly, students should file electronically through Central College or on FAFSA's Web site at http://www.fafsa.ed.gov.

Students who apply for aid after March 1 are funded on a funds-available basis.

Each year, Central reserves a significant number of Presidential Scholar Awards, worth up to full tuition, for the most promising freshmen. Eligible students must have a 3.75 cumulative GPA or higher (on a 4.0 scale) and an ACT composite score of at least 28, or ranked first in their graduating class.

Faculty

More than 81 percent of the faculty members hold doctorates or terminal degrees in their fields. There are 93 full-time and 49 part-time faculty members, and the student-faculty ratio is 14:1. The average class size is 20. Faculty members serve as academic advisers and make time to take a personal interest in their students.

Student Government

The Student Senate works with a budget of more than $145,000, and assigned senators have voting membership on nearly all College committees. Students also have nonvoting representation on the Board of Trustees. The Campus Activities Board is made up of students who plan and implement social events throughout the year.

Admission Requirements

The admission committee reviews all applications for admission and seeks students who demonstrate the desired skills and potential to compete successfully at the college level. A student should graduate from an accredited high school or the equivalent, rank in the upper half of the high school graduating class, have at least a 2.5 cumulative grade point average, and achieve test scores on either the ACT or SAT I that are high enough to predict probable success at Central. While specific courses are not required for admission, Central recommends 4 years of English, including literature; 2 or more years of mathematics, including algebra and geometry; 2 or more years of social studies, including American and European history; 2 or more years of lab science; and 2 or more years of foreign languages.

Application and Information

Offers of admission begin on October 1. Applications completed after October 1 are reviewed on a rolling basis. To apply, students submit a completed application with a nonrefundable $25 application fee and have an official transcript of all high school and college credits and a report of ACT or SAT I scores sent to the Office of Admission. The application fee is waived for students who apply before January 20, for those who apply after a personal campus visit, for those who are children of an alumnus, or for those who apply online.

Application forms may be obtained by contacting the Office of Admission or applying online at:

Office of Admission
Central College
812 University
Pella, Iowa 50219
Telephone: 641-628-5285
877-462-3687 (toll-free)
E-mail: admission@central.edu
World Wide Web: http://www.central.edu

The pond is a favorite gathering place for students.

THE COLLEGE OF MOUNT ST. JOSEPH

CINCINNATI, OHIO

The College

As a private liberal arts college founded in 1920, the College of Mount St. Joseph has a rich history of preparing students for the future. Today, the Mount is a coeducational college with more than 2,000 students, offering an outstanding liberal arts curriculum that emphasizes values, integrity, and social responsibility, as well as practical career preparation. Required courses in humanities, science, and the arts are complemented by opportunities for cooperative work experience, a universal computing requirement, specialized and professionally oriented courses, and extracurricular opportunities, which give students the broad-based background that is in high demand among employers.

Catholic in tradition, the Mount emphasizes a value-centered education and supports the personal growth of each student. A warm, close-knit campus community encourages students to exercise their talents to their fullest potential in academic, athletic, and leadership activities. Mount students come primarily from the Midwest, but many other regions of the United States and nearly fifteen countries are also represented. Spacious rooms are available in Seton Center Residence Hall. Resident students may keep cars on campus.

The College is accredited by the North Central Association of Colleges and Schools.

Campus organizations include the student government, student newspaper, academic honor societies, international club, departmental clubs, marching and concert band, chamber singers, and intramural athletics. The Mount offers a full intercollegiate athletics program in the NCAA Division III for men and women and is a member of the Heartland Collegiate Athletic Conference (HCAC). Women's programs include basketball, cross-country, golf, soccer, softball, tennis, and volleyball. For men, there are baseball, basketball, cross-country, football, golf, tennis, and wrestling.

Location

Located just 10 minutes from downtown Cincinnati, the College sits on a beautiful, 75-acre suburban campus overlooking the Ohio River. The campus is easily accessible from the airport, bus terminal, railway station, and interstate. Well known for its scenic and rolling hills, greater Cincinnati offers numerous parks, cultural and arts events, professional athletics, shopping areas, and a wide assortment of fine restaurants. In addition to their own on-campus activities, Mount students frequently participate in social and service activities with students from other area colleges.

Majors and Degrees

The College of Mount St. Joseph awards bachelor's degrees in the following areas: accounting, art, art education, athletic training, biological chemistry, biology, business administration, chemistry, chemistry/mathematics, communication arts, computer information systems, computer science with minor in math, education (early childhood, middle childhood, physical education, and special education), English, fine arts, gerontological studies, graphic design, history, humanities, interior design, liberal arts and sciences, liberal studies, mathematics, mathematics/chemistry, medical technology, music, natural history, natural science with biology or chemistry concentration, nursing, paralegal studies, paralegal studies for nurses, psychology, recreational therapy, rehabilitation science, religious education, religious pastoral ministry, religious studies, social work, and sociology.

Associate degrees are offered in accounting, art, business administration, communication arts, computer information systems, gerontological studies, graphic design, interior design, and paralegal studies.

Certificate programs are offered in gerontological studies, graphic design, interior design, paralegal studies, paralegal studies for nurses, and parish nurse/health ministries.

For state of Ohio licensure in education, the Mount offers programs in inclusive early childhood, middle childhood, adolescent and young adults, multiage, and intervention specialist/special education. Licensure programs in other states are also available.

Preprofessional programs are available in allied medical professions, law, and medicine.

Academic Program

All majors are backed by a strong liberal arts curriculum that encourages students to develop skills in analytical thinking, problem solving, decision making, and communication. Students must earn 128 credit hours for a bachelor's degree, with 52 of those credits from the liberal arts and science core. For an associate degree, students must earn 64 credit hours, with 27–28 of those credits from the liberal arts and science core.

The academic year consists of fall and spring semesters and three summer terms, with classes offered in day, evening, or weekend time frames.

The Mount offers a highly respected Cooperative Education program, making available to students the benefits of hands-on work experience within their field of study as early as the second semester of their sophomore year. In addition to the financial advantage of being able to work through college, a student can also make the personal contacts that are so important in professional experiences. Students can also gain practical experience and career development before graduation through participation in programs such as the Kaleidoscope of Careers, Career Advising, e-recruiting, and on-campus recruiting.

Project EXCEL is a special program that offers tutorial services, audiotapes of textbooks, and self-instructional materials for students with learning disabilities. Students learn skills that facilitate success in the college environment. Project EXCEL carries an additional fee for testing and for services while in the program. Interested students must apply for admission through Project EXCEL.

The Mount's Academic Performance Center is a centralized system of support for the enhancement of students' academic skills. It encompasses a Math Center, Peer Tutoring Program, COMPASS testing, makeup testing, Skills and Reading Center, Listening Lab, instructional software, courses in basic academic skills, and academic support for students with disabilities.

Off-Campus Arrangements

Opportunities are available to study abroad in Heidelberg, Germany, through the Congress/Bundestag program; in London, England, at Thames Valley College and through the

Mount's affiliation with Huron University; and in Seville, Spain, through the Spanish American Institute.

Academic Facilities

The Mount's campus features modern buildings with state-of-the-art learning facilities. The Computer Learning Center offers all students access to IBM and Macintosh systems, supporting more than 500 different software packages. Students in the nursing department have access to on-campus laboratories and benefit from the department's relationship with nearby hospitals of outstanding quality and reputation.

The Harrington Center offers space for clubs and organizations and is home to the campus bookstore, food court, and entertainment center. Other recreation facilities include a running track, racquetball courts, a fitness center, a 2,000-seat gymnasium, and an athletic training center. A beautiful College theater seats more than 1,000 people.

Costs

For the 2002–03 academic year, tuition was $14,950 and room and board were $5920 (based on a semiprivate room and the fifteen-meals-per-week plan, with $150 flex dollars to use at the food court). The College offers private and semiprivate housing accommodations and a variety of meal plans. There are a $45 activities fee per semester and a technology fee of $400 per semester, which provides students with a wireless laptop/learning environment to use during their years at the Mount. The cost of books varies depending on course load and major.

Financial Aid

The College of Mount St. Joseph assists as many students as possible who require financial aid. About 94 percent of full-time undergraduate students receive some form of assistance, usually as federal, state, or College grants; work-study awards; and loans. In addition, part-time employment may be available in the metropolitan area for those students with transportation. The Mount offers academic scholarship programs in the areas of scholastic achievement and leadership based on merit or on a combination of merit and need.

Students who wish to apply for financial aid must complete, by April 15, the Free Application for Federal Student Aid (FAFSA). Most scholarships are awarded on a rolling basis. Interested students should inquire as early in their senior year as possible.

Faculty

Because the Mount is a small liberal arts college, the faculty's focus is on teaching. Many faculty members have been recognized regionally and nationally for their research and expertise outside the classroom as well as for their contributions as teachers, particularly in the fields of art, science, math, sociology, and education. The student-faculty ratio of 15:1 encourages personal interaction between students and professors.

Student Government

All matriculated students at the College of Mount St. Joseph are members of the Student Government Association (SGA). The SGA represents and serves as the voice of the entire student body. It strives to help students understand their rights, privileges, and responsibilities and to maintain effective communication among the students, faculty and staff members, and administration.

One of the functions of the SGA is that of appointing students to serve on various College committees to represent the common values of the Mount students and to participate in College government. The SGA works toward avoiding conflict by assisting with developing campus policies that directly affect student life.

The SGA supports and monitors all student club activities and functions through the Fiscal Committee. There are many opportunities for interested students to participate in SGA-sponsored programs and activities, including Campus Fair, movies, dances, fund-raising events, and community service activities.

A Student Affairs staff member serves as the adviser to the SGA.

Admission Requirements

Admission decisions are based on high school course selection, ACT or SAT scores, class rank, and grade point average. The College requires 4 units of English, 2 of math (algebra and geometry), 2 of social studies, 2 of science, 2 of foreign language, and 1 of fine arts. Two electives from the areas listed above may be substituted for foreign language. Students are encouraged to submit recommendation letters and personal essays.

Application and Information

Decisions on offers of admission are generally made within two weeks of the date the file is complete. The application fee is $25; the Project EXCEL fee is $60. The physical therapy fee is $50, with an application deadline of January 15. Application fees are nonrefundable and do not apply toward tuition. Students who want to know more about the Mount may arrange a visit by contacting the Office of Admission. In addition to scheduling individual appointments, the College holds Get Acquainted Days throughout the year, giving students the opportunity to visit the campus, explore academic programs, and take a tour.

Office of Admission
College of Mount St. Joseph
5701 Delhi Road
Cincinnati, Ohio 45233-1672
Telephone: 513-244-4531
800-654-9314 (toll-free)
World Wide Web: http://www.msj.edu

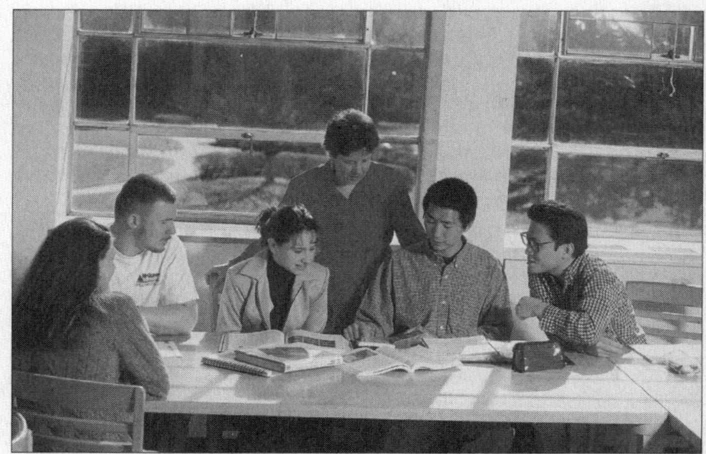

The College of Mount St. Joseph provides a liberal arts and professional education that integrates life and learning while embracing excellence, respect, diversity, and service.

THE COLLEGE OF WOOSTER

WOOSTER, OHIO

The College

One of the first coeducational colleges in the country, the College of Wooster was founded in 1866 by Presbyterians who wanted to do "their proper part in the great work of educating those who are to mold society and give shape to all its institutions." Today it is a fully independent, privately endowed liberal arts college with a rich tradition of academic excellence. That tradition defines student life at Wooster, beginning with the First-Year Seminar in Critical Inquiry and culminating in the Independent Study program.

The current enrollment is about 1,800 men and women. Almost all students live on campus, selecting from a variety of housing options. These include Babcock International House for students interested in international studies, Andrews Hall for students with an interest in the humanities and sciences, and Kenarden Lodge, a modern facility arranged in living suites. There are also thirty-three houses on the edge of campus, many of which serve as living-learning centers for those in community service and volunteer programs.

Wooster's 240-acre campus has thirty-nine major buildings. With its distinctive arch, Kauke Hall is instantly recognizable as an icon for Wooster. Kauke is home to many academic departments, classrooms, and faculty offices. Wooster has excellent facilities for physical education, including a fully equipped fitness center, a nine-hole golf course, an all-weather track, and eight hard-surfaced tennis courts. Three new buildings opened in 2002, beginning in March with the $2-million, 10,000-square-foot Longbrake Student Wellness Center. The Student Wellness Center is a state-of-the-art student facility that includes six treatment rooms, eight in-patient beds, and a pharmacy. The Gault Center for Admissions opened in June 2002, and the $8-million, 44,000-square-foot Burton D. Morgan Hall opened in fall 2002. Morgan Hall houses the Departments of Economics (including Business Economics), Psychology, and Education, and is the future home of the College's Information Technology Center. Severance Chemistry Building reopened in 1999 after a multimillion dollar renovation that made it one of the top chemistry facilities among small liberal arts colleges. Severance Chemistry features spaces for both student and faculty member research, as well as classrooms, offices, computer rooms, and laboratories for several fields of chemistry. Other facilities include Scheide Music Center; the Flo K. Gault Library for Independent Study, which adjoins the Andrews Library; the Ebert Art Center, which contains an art gallery and substantial facilities for studio art and art history; and the Timken Science Library, which opened in fall 1998.

Most of the social life at Wooster originates from Lowry Center, the student union. The Student Activities Board organizes dances, concerts, films, off-campus outings, and many other activities. The music and theater departments and local social clubs also contribute to the activities on campus. The student entertainment center (The Underground) hosts live bands, comedians, dance parties, and folksingers, and sometimes serves as a dinner theater.

Location

The College is located in Wooster, Ohio, a city of approximately 26,000. Wooster is 55 miles south of Cleveland and 30 miles west of Akron. An unusually close relationship exists between the College and the community. College-community activities include the Wooster Symphony, a college-community theatrical production, and a variety of volunteer and internship experiences. The community and the College also sponsor an annual performance by the Cleveland Orchestra on campus.

Majors and Degrees

The College of Wooster offers the degrees of Bachelor of Arts, Bachelor of Music, and Bachelor of Music Education. A student may choose from thirty-seven possible majors, including seven interdepartmental majors: anthropology, archaeology, art history, art/studio, biochemistry and molecular biology, biology, black studies, business economics, chemical physics, chemistry, classical studies, communication sciences and disorders, communication studies, comparative literature, computer science, cultural area studies, economics, English, French, geology, German, history, international relations, mathematics, music, philosophy, physics, political science, psychology, religious studies, Russian studies, sociology, Spanish, theater, theater/dance, urban studies, and women's studies. In addition, minors are available in many of the areas above as well as physical education. Students also have the option of designing their own major, contingent upon the approval of the Upperclass Programs Committee. The Department of Education offers all courses necessary for either elementary or secondary teaching licensure.

Wooster offers combined-degree opportunities in cooperation with other institutions; such programs lead to either two bachelor's degrees (one from each institution) or a bachelor's from Wooster and a master's from the cooperating institution. Specific programs are in operation with Columbia University (law), Dartmouth College (business administration), the University of Michigan (economics, engineering, mathematics, and physics), Duke University (forestry and environmental management), Washington University (engineering), and Case Western Reserve University (dentistry, engineering, nursing, and social work).

Academic Program

Wooster's academic program is designed to provide a liberal education that prepares undergraduates for a lifetime of inquiry, discovery, and responsible citizenship. In fall 2001, Wooster instituted a new curriculum, which focuses directly on these curricular goals. To be eligible for a Bachelor of Arts degree, a student must successfully complete thirty-two courses, including a First-Year Seminar in Critical Inquiry and three courses of Independent Study (IS). IS, as it is universally known on campus, gives each Wooster senior the opportunity to create an original research project, written scholarly work, exhibit of artwork or performance in a yearlong project, supported one-on-one by a faculty mentor. An overall grade point average of at least 2.0 (on a 4.0 scale) is required for graduation. Students may receive credit for work done at other colleges and for scores of 4 or better on the Advanced Placement tests offered by the College Board. Courses are graded A–D or No Credit unless the student exercises an option to take certain courses on a Satisfactory/No Credit basis.

Off-Campus Arrangements

Students who wish to enrich their undergraduate experience by overseas study may choose from a variety of fully accredited programs. Wooster sponsors a number of off-campus programs in the United States and abroad, and, as a member of the Great Lakes Colleges Association, offers off-campus study opportunities in thirteen countries on four continents. There are also programs available through the Institute of European Studies in seven university centers throughout Europe.

A variety of off-campus opportunities within the United States provide both academic and internship experiences. The Washington Semester and the Semester at the United Nations offer extensive possibilities in national and international government. Urban studies centers in Birmingham, Philadelphia, Portland, St. Louis, and San Diego provide many different experiential options. There is also a fine-arts semester in New York City. Other internship possibilities exist in business, the humanities, the natural sciences, and psychology.

Academic Facilities

The College libraries consist of the Andrews Library, the adjacent Flo K. Gault Library for Independent Study, and the nearby Timken Science Library in Frick Hall. Together, the libraries contain more than 1 million books, periodicals, microforms, electronic journals, videotapes, and audio recordings. As a member of CONSORT and OhioLINK, the libraries can provide almost any book from Ohio's academic libraries within two to three days. The libraries subscribe to a wide variety of electronic databases and to some 5,000 periodicals in electronic form, all available campuswide via the computing network. The libraries house more than 300 study carrels, each of which is equipped with electrical and data connections.

Computing is an important part of Wooster's academic environment. All academic buildings and every residence hall room are connected in an interactive computing network. Every residence hall has 24-hour access to a computer room with two to four computers and a laser printer, and the Taylor Hall computer center houses sixty-four terminals for student use. Computer seminar rooms have recently been built for foreign language and English classes.

The College's science facilities contain the most up-to-date laboratory equipment, libraries, computer terminals, and instrumentation, including ultraviolet, visible, fluorescence, and infrared spectrometers; a scanning electron microscope; an atomic force microscope; a nuclear magnetic resonance spectrometer; a mass spectrometer; an X-ray diffractometer; and various chromatographs.

Wooster's Learning Center provides academic support for students, and priority is given to students with identified learning disabilities. Adult tutors work with individual students on time management, organization skills, and effective study strategies. Wooster's Writing Center provides writing assistance through one-to-one tutorial sessions and group workshops covering all aspects of the writing process.

The Freedlander Theatre complex contains excellent technical equipment and a separate theater for students' experimental productions. The speech facility itself houses a radio station, TV studios, and a speech and hearing clinic that also serves the community.

The Scheide Music Center, a 35,000-square-foot complex, contains five classrooms, eleven teaching studios, twenty-three soundproof practice rooms, a music library, and a listening lab. The Timken Rehearsal Hall and the acoustically balanced Gault Recital Hall are "tunable" so that the halls can be rendered "live" to greater or lesser degrees.

The Ebert Art Center, which opened in the fall of 1997, has expansive space for studio art and art history. The building includes classrooms, individual studios for senior studio art majors, and the Sussel Art Gallery.

Costs

The comprehensive fee (room, board, tuition, and fees) for 2002–03 was $29,800.

Financial Aid

Almost all financial assistance is awarded on the basis of need, as determined by the Free Application for Federal Student Aid (FAFSA). Aid is allocated when students are admitted to the College. Financial assistance information and forms should be requested at the time of application. Applications for aid should be submitted by February 15.

Merit aid is available on a competitive basis. The College Scholar program offers ten awards of $18,000 each per year, based on an essay competition. Additional awards of $14,000 per year are available. Selected entering students receive academic and achievement awards independent of the College Scholar program. Synod of the Covenant Scholarships for Presbyterian communicants are available, as are Scottish Arts awards (which require an audition).

The Clarence B. Allen Scholarship program awards up to ten scholarships of $18,000 a year to entering African-American students with a demonstrated record of academic achievement and promise of continued success in college. Multicultural scholarships, ranging from $9000 to $13,000 a year, honor students of color with a demonstrated record of academic achievement, intellectual promise, and community involvement. Students named National Merit Finalists by the National Merit Scholarship Corporation, and who list Wooster as their first college choice, are eligible for awards of $750 to $2000.

The Arthur Holly Compton Scholarships of $9000 to $16,000 a year are awarded annually to students who demonstrate unusual aptitude for Wooster's program of Independent Study. Music and theater scholarships are awarded to entering first-year students based on an audition. Science and mathematics scholarships, ranging from $9000 to $13,000 a year, reward sustained achievement and interest in the natural, physical, or computer sciences. Byron E. Morris Scholarships of up to $6000 are awarded to students who have a demonstrated record of achievement in their school or community in the areas of volunteer/community service or leadership.

Faculty

The faculty members and administration, 95 percent of whom (excluding those in performance areas) hold a doctoral degree, are dedicated to meeting the educational needs of individual students; they strive to help them realize their inherent potential. The student-faculty ratio is less than 12:1.

Student Government

The Campus Council, which consists of representatives from the student body, faculty, and administration, is the main legislative body in the areas of student life and cocurricular affairs. The Student Government Association, the Black Students Association, and the International Student Association also contribute to policymaking at Wooster. Students may attend open meetings of the faculty and are represented on virtually all faculty committees; they may also send representatives to observe meetings of the Board of Trustees.

Admission Requirements

A candidate for admission to the College should have earned a minimum of 16 academic units in high school, with emphases in English, foreign language, mathematics, natural science, and social studies. The student must present satisfactory scores on either the SAT I or the ACT. No College Board Subject Test scores are required.

The deadline for regular admission is February 15. Students are notified of the decision by April 1 and must reply by May 1. Early Decision I applicants must apply by December 1 and are notified on December 15. Early Decision II candidates must apply by January 15 and are notified by February 1. Deferred admission is available, as is admission at the end of the junior year of high school. Students are encouraged to visit the campus and have a personal interview.

The College of Wooster does not discriminate on the basis of age, sex, race, creed, national origin, handicap, sexual orientation, or political affiliation in the admission of students or in their participation in College educational programs, activities, financial aid, or employment.

Application and Information

Director of Admissions
The College of Wooster
Wooster, Ohio 44691

Telephone: 330-263-2000 Ext. 2270 or 2322
800-877-9905 (toll-free)
Fax: 330-263-2621
E-mail: admissions@wooster.edu
World Wide Web: http://www.wooster.edu

COLUMBIA COLLEGE

COLUMBIA, MISSOURI

The College

Columbia College is a four-year, private, coeducational college offering master's, bachelor's, and associate degrees. It was founded in 1851 as Christian College and is affiliated with the Disciples of Christ. The institution is accredited by the North Central Association of Colleges and Schools. Today, 890 students representing fifteen states and twenty-five other countries attend the College.

The College's 29-acre campus, located four blocks from the downtown area of Columbia, Missouri, has twenty buildings, ranging from Williams Hall, constructed in 1851, through administration and classroom buildings erected in the early 1900s, to more modern residence halls and classroom facilities completed in the 1960s and 1970s. A gymnasium was erected in 1988, the Stafford Library was erected in 1989, and the Cultural Arts Center was remodeled in 1992. Brown Hall, the arts and humanities building, became operational in 1995. Three spacious residence halls provide housing for students who live on campus. Miller Hall and Banks Hall offer coeducational housing. Banks Hall features a popular Wellness Floor. Every residence hall provides a computer lab and cooking and laundry facilities. Student academic programmers enhance the academic environment within the residence hall system through specialized programming, peer academic counseling, and research and referral information sharing. Every student is entitled to have an automobile, motorcycle, or bicycle on campus. Student service facilities include a Student Center, a central dining facility, a health center, a counseling center, and a career planning and placement center.

Recreational and athletic opportunities are furnished through the College's remodeled fitness center, gymnasium, softball field, soccer field, tennis courts, and a large back-campus area for intramural sports programs, which are quite popular. The College is a member of the NAIA Division I and the American Midwest Conference, and its teams compete in men's basketball and soccer and women's basketball, softball, and volleyball.

Graduate degrees are available in business, criminal justice, and teaching.

Location

Columbia, Missouri (population 75,000 plus 25,000 college students), is situated halfway between St. Louis and Kansas City. Five hospitals, a major mental health center, social service agencies of all kinds, a large network of parks, and a well-educated populace accustomed to a rich cultural life make Columbia a pleasant place to live, work, and study. *Money* magazine has often ranked it as one of the top twenty cities in the nation.

Majors and Degrees

Columbia College awards the Bachelor of Arts and Bachelor of Science degrees with majors in accounting, art, biology, business administration, chemistry, computer information systems, computer science, criminal justice administration, English, financial services, forensic science, general studies, history, interdisciplinary studies, international business, management, marketing, mathematics, natural sciences, political science, psychology, social work, and sociology. Preprofessional programs in dentistry, law, medicine, and veterinary science are available. The BEACON and DAYSTAR are new, innovative programs in teacher education. The College also confers the Bachelor of Fine Arts and Bachelor of Social Work degrees. Students can choose minors in art history, ethics/philosophy/religion, music, geology, physics, Spanish, and studio art. Columbia College also awards the associate degree with majors in business administration, computer information systems, and criminal justice administration.

Academic Program

The academic curriculum supports the mission of the College to provide career degree programs based on a solid background in the liberal arts and sciences. Each of the degree programs can include an internship, enabling students to obtain practical experience in addition to the more theoretical classroom instruction.

The College follows a two-semester plan with an eight-week summer session. Each degree program sets its own sequence of requirements. To be eligible for graduation, students pursuing an associate degree must complete 60 semester hours with a cumulative grade point average of 2.0 (C) or better. Each associate degree program has a general education component. To receive a bachelor's degree, students must complete 120 semester hours of credit with a cumulative grade point average of 2.0 (C) or better. Students pursuing a baccalaureate degree must complete a series of general education courses, including 6 semester hours of English composition, and earn at least 39 semester hours of credit in junior- or senior-level courses.

Off-Campus Arrangements

Full-time Columbia College students may enroll, at no extra cost, in courses at two neighboring institutions through a cooperative arrangement. ROTC programs (all branches) are available through this arrangement as well. Study-abroad opportunities are also offered.

Academic Facilities

Stafford Library is fully automated and contains more than 70,000 volumes, 500 periodicals, and 6,000 audiovisual materials. Students also have access to materials through the College's interlibrary loan and exchange program with neighboring institutions and the statewide electronic MOBIUS system.

An art and humanities facility, completed in 1995, provides resources for the art degree programs and a public gallery for promoting cultural growth. The College has a large computer and Internet laboratory; science and psychology lab facilities; an educational curriculum/materials library; the Writing Center and Math Center, which have a variety of individual assistance and tutorial programs; and major classroom buildings for traditional instruction.

Costs

For 2002–03, student fees included $10,926 for tuition and $4666 for room and board. Students should plan to spend about $400 per semester for books, supplies, and incidentals. *The Student Guide to America's Best College Scholarships* has rated Columbia College as one of the top colleges with the lowest costs.

Financial Aid

Most Columbia College students receive some type of financial assistance. The College awards to students more than $4 million annually in federal, state, and institutional funds. Financial aid packages may include need-based and merit-based scholarships, grants, loans, and work-study opportunities in a variety of combinations. The most prestigious awards are the Columbia College Scholarship (full tuition, room, and board) and the Presidential Scholarship (full tuition). Five each are awarded annually. Many other competitive scholarships are available. Some awards and scholarships are automatic if certain criteria are met. Talent awards in athletics, art, and music are also available. Half-tuition scholarships are awarded automatically to upperclassmen who maintain a 3.4 grade point average with 30 hours earned annually.

To be considered for financial assistance, students must complete the Free Application for Federal Student Aid (FAFSA) and submit the Columbia College financial assistance application.

Faculty

Excellence in teaching has been a common goal throughout the history of the College. Teaching is the faculty's primary responsibility. The faculty-student ratio of 1:14 fosters personal attention and animated discussion in the classroom. Faculty members also serve as advisers to students. The relatively small size of the student body promotes excellent communication and rapport among students and faculty members. Nearly 80 percent of the faculty members have terminal degrees.

Student Government

All students at Columbia College are members of the Student Government Association (SGA). The SGA Cabinet, elected from this body, serves as a formal liaison between students and the administration. One branch of SGA, the Student Activities Commission, plans and organizes social activities on campus, from programs of interest to specialized groups to campuswide recreational activities. Each residence hall has representation to SGA through its Hall Council, which is composed of elected students.

Admission Requirements

Columbia College evaluates each applicant individually on the basis of the total application, including academic records, ACT/SAT scores, activities, references, goals, and recommendations of high school counselors. A high school diploma or equivalent certification is required for admission. English and math tests are given on campus to appropriately place students. Admission requirements at Columbia College are moderately selective.

Transfer students must submit transcripts of all college work attempted and may need to submit high school academic transcripts. There are no restrictions on the number of transfer students accepted each semester.

Application and Information

Descriptive brochures and application forms are available from the Office of Admissions. A campus visit is highly recommended. The completed application should be returned along with a $25 nonrefundable application fee. There is no fee if the application is submitted before January 1 for the fall semester. Notification of the admission decision is made on a rolling basis following the fulfillment of all admission requirements.

For more information and application materials, students should contact:

Director of Admissions
Columbia College
1001 Rogers Street
Columbia, Missouri 65216
Telephone: 573-875-7352
800-231-2391 (toll-free in the U.S. and Canada)
E-mail: admissions@ccis.edu
World Wide Web: http://www.ccis.edu

Rogers Gates at the entrance of the historic Columbia College campus.

COLUMBIA COLLEGE CHICAGO

CHICAGO, ILLINOIS

The College

Columbia College was established during the World's Columbian Exposition of 1893. The College's original emphasis on communication arts has expanded to include media arts, applied and fine arts, theatrical and performing arts, and management and marketing arts. Today, Columbia College Chicago is the nation's premier visual, performing, and media arts college. The foundation of a Columbia education continues to include small class sizes that ensure close interaction with a faculty of working professionals, abundant internship opportunities with major employers in the Chicago marketplace, and outstanding professional facilities that foster learning by doing. All students are encouraged to begin course work in their chosen fields during their freshman year, allowing them four full years in which to master their craft and build professional portfolios, audition tapes, resumes, and clip books. The College provides a strong liberal arts background for the developing artist or communicator and supports student employment goals through a full range of career services.

Columbia's enrollment of more than 9,250 students is drawn from Chicago and its suburbs, the Midwest, across the United States, and more than forty-five other countries. The student body is almost equally divided between men and women. Creative students who enjoy a supportive but challenging environment thrive at Columbia.

The College provides comfortable and affordable apartment-style housing for approximately 450 full-time students in two separate facilities. The apartment-style suites include a full kitchen and are fully furnished. The 731 South Plymouth Court facility is intended to house freshmen and sophomores. The 18 East Congress facility is a smoke-free environment intended to house juniors and seniors. Both buildings are just minutes from the main campus and are close to public transportation. Life in the residence hall extends the supportive philosophy of the College, and student residents have access to computer and study rooms, drawing and painting studio space, and a fitness room as well as recreational and party areas. The Residence Life staff generates a variety of opportunities to support and enhance student endeavors. On-campus housing is limited; costs vary according to accommodations. Many students live off campus; assistance in locating housing is available through the Off-Campus Housing Coordinator.

Outside the classroom, students participate in activities that include the College's award-winning student newspaper, radio station, electronic newsletter, two student magazines, cable television soap opera, three theaters, dance center, photography and art museums, and film and video festival. Many of the fifty student clubs on campus are linked to an academic discipline and offer opportunities to expand social and professional networking experiences. The Hermann D. Conaway Multicultural Center and the Myron Hokin Center provide gallery/café environments in which students can relax or study between classes. These centers feature a variety of activities, including art exhibits, film screenings, lectures, and live performances of music, comedy, readings, or dance. The 11th Street and Glass Curtain Galleries and the Narrative Arts Center provide additional exhibition spaces for students, faculty members, and others.

At the graduate level, Columbia awards the Master of Arts (M.A.) in arts, entertainment, and media management; creative writing and writing instruction; dance/movement therapy; interdisciplinary arts; journalism; photography; photography–museum studies; and writing instruction. The College awards the Master of Fine Arts (M.F.A.) in architectural studies; creative writing; creative writing and writing instruction; film and video; interdisciplinary book and paper arts; interior architecture; and photography. The Master of Arts in Teaching (M.A.T.) is also offered in elementary education (K–9), interdisciplinary arts education (K–12), and urban teaching.

Location

Columbia's campus is set in Chicago's dynamic South Loop neighborhood, across from Grant Park and Lake Michigan. Close to the Art Institute, Navy Pier, the Adler Planetarium, the Field Museum, the Chicago Symphony, and several other colleges and universities, Columbia's faculty members and students utilize the city of Chicago as a social, educational, and professional resource. Convenient public transportation makes all cultural and educational opportunities easily accessible.

Majors and Degrees

Columbia College grants the Bachelor of Arts (B.A.) and the Bachelor of Fine Arts (B.F.A.) degrees and the Bachelor of Music (B.M.) degree in composition. The School of Fine and Performing Arts offers majors in art and design (advertising art direction, fashion design, fine arts, graphic design, illustration, interior architecture, and product design); arts, entertainment, and media management (arts entrepreneurship and small business, fashion/retail, media, music business, performing arts, and visual arts); dance (choreography, musical theater performance, and teaching); fiction writing; music (contemporary music, including composition, instrumental performance, and vocal performance, and jazz studies, including instrumental and vocal); photography; and theater (acting, directing, playwriting, technical theater, and theater design). The School of Media Arts offers majors in academic computing (digital media technology), audio arts and acoustics (recording, sound contracting, sound reinforcement, and sound technology), film and video (alternative forms, audio, cinematography, computer animation, critical studies, directing, documentary, editing, producing, screenwriting, and traditional animation), interactive multimedia (animation, graphic design, photography, programming, project management, sound design, video, and writing), interdisciplinary (self-designed major), journalism (broadcast, magazine program, news reporting and writing, radio broadcast, and reporting on health, science, and the environment), marketing communication (advertising, creative sports marketing, marketing, and public relations), radio (business and talent/production), and television (interactive, postproduction/effects, production/directing, and writing/producing). The School of Liberal Arts and Sciences offers majors in American Sign Language–English interpretation, early childhood education (center director, infant-toddler studies, language and culture, performing arts, and visual arts), English (poetry), and liberal education (cultural studies).

Academic Program

Columbia supports creative and integrated approaches to education and encourages interdisciplinary study. The B.A. degree is awarded to students who successfully complete 120 semester hours, and the B.F.A. degree is awarded to students who successfully complete 128 semester hours of study in designated programs. Of the required hours, 48 are distributed among courses in the humanities and literature, science and mathematics, English composition, oral communications, social sciences, and computer applications.

The College continues to expand its extensive internship program. Columbia's location allows students to intern with major employers in Chicago. Chicago provides professional settings, classrooms, and internship opportunities for Columbia students.

The Career Center for Arts and Media offers a full range of services designed to help students launch their careers. Services include career counseling; seminars on interviewing, resume writing, and job-search strategies; internships; placement assistance; job fairs; and alumni activities and assistance.

Off-Campus Arrangements

Columbia has an affiliation agreement with the American Institute for Foreign Study, which enables students to participate in study-abroad programs in numerous countries. Columbia also sponsors and participates in a variety of its own study-abroad programs. These programs include trips to Moscow and Prague. Summer programs are also offered with Dartington College in Dartington, England; the Santa Reparata International School of Art in Florence, Italy; and the University of Guadalajara in Mexico. Open to all Columbia students, the Semester in Los Angeles program is a five-week immersion program in which the student maintains full-time status while gaining invaluable real-world experience. Located in Bungalow 25 on the CBS Studio Lot in Culver City, Columbia is the only institution of higher learning permanently located on a studio lot. Students are given Lot ID badges and enter the gates of the lot everyday just like working producers, directors, stars, and craft personnel.

Academic Facilities

Columbia College consists of thirteen campus buildings located primarily in the historic South Loop neighborhood of downtown Chicago. Advanced facilities for radio, television, art, computer graphics, photography, interactive multimedia, fashion design, and film are state-of-the-industry and include professionally equipped color and black-and-white darkrooms, digital imaging computer facilities, photography and film stages, film and video editing suites, and studios for painting, drawing, and 3-D design. The campus also includes the Museum of Contemporary Photography, one of only a few such facilities in the United States, and the Audio Technology Center, a recording production and research facility. In addition, Columbia has extensive computer facilities used by basic computer classes as well as dedicated computer facilities utilized by the departments. The centers for dance, music, and theater are separate but conveniently located and are designed for their specific performance needs, including individual and group rehearsal and specialized performance spaces.

The College's 200,000-volume library and instructional service center provides comprehensive information and study facilities. Reading/study rooms and special audiovisual equipment are available for use in individual projects and research. As a member of a statewide online computer catalog and resource-sharing network, Columbia's library provides students with access to the resources of forty-five academic institutions in Illinois, effectively creating an information base of several million volumes. The library also houses special collections, such as the George S. Lurie Memorial collection of books and resource materials on art, photography, and film; the Black Music Resource Center of books and sound recordings; the Screenwriters' Collection of film and television manuscripts; the History of Photography microfilm collection of books and periodicals; and a nonprint collection of 100,000 slides and more than 7,300 videotapes and films. The latest addition to the library is the Albert P. Weisman Center for the Study of Contemporary Issues in Chicago Journalism. The center includes a print and audiovisual collection and a learning center that explores the development of Chicago's political and social history.

Costs

For the 2002–03 academic year, full tuition (12 to 16 credit hours) averaged $6857 per each fifteen-week semester, or $13,714 per year. Part-time tuition (up to 11 credit hours) was $468 per credit hour. Summer school tuition was $371 per credit hour. Some courses require additional service or laboratory fees. Required nonrefundable fees charged each semester include the registration fee, $50; the student activity fee, $50 ($25 for part-time students); the U-Pass, $70 (for unlimited access to the public transportation system); and a health center fee, $25 ($15 for part-time students). There is also a one-time $30 library deposit that is refunded when the student leaves the College.

Financial Aid

Columbia College makes every effort to help students obtain financial assistance, including grants, on-campus work, and loans. The Office of Student Financial Services administers federal and state grant and loan programs. The College also provides information for students seeking part-time employment both on- and off-campus. On-campus jobs are available in technical, clerical, secretarial, and food service areas. Columbia offers institution-based scholarships, such as Presidential Scholarships for freshmen, scholarships for transfer students, academic excellence awards, leadership awards, and housing grants. The Fischetti Scholarships support the efforts of outstanding Columbia journalism students, and the Weisman Scholarships support special communication-related projects. Appropriate scholarship and applications forms for financial aid are available through the Office of Undergraduate Admissions.

Faculty

Many of Columbia's 1,267 full- and part-time faculty members are working professionals (artists, writers, filmmakers, dancers, etc.) with national reputations. The College is constantly seeking individuals who are both gifted teachers and talented professionals. Many faculty members work nearby in the disciplines in which they teach and share practical expertise with students in informal workshop settings and in the classroom. Interaction with faculty members who are practicing professionals provides students with invaluable access to the latest information in their fields. Students also begin developing their own professional network as faculty members share contacts and information on how to break into the market.

Student Government

Through the Student Government Association (SGA) and the Student Organization Council (SOC), students are able to address college-wide and departmental issues and sponsor services and activities. SGA and SOC work closely with the Office of Student Affairs and serve as liaisons to the administration and departments. The fifty campus clubs and organizations reflect the interests and the diversity of Columbia's student body. Film screenings, student-produced television shows, dance recitals, poetry readings, plays, campus radio, music concerts, and a nationally award-winning newspaper are just some of the campus events and activities available to students.

Admissions Requirements

Columbia College invites applications from all students with creative ability in or inclination to the arts, media, and communication disciplines in which the College specializes. To apply for admissions, students must submit high school transcripts, college transcripts (if applicable), a letter of recommendation, a personal essay, and a $25 application fee. ACT Assessment or SAT I scores are not required but are strongly encouraged. Graduation from high school or an earned GED is required prior to enrollment. Freshmen applicants whose application materials suggest they are likely to be underprepared to meet the College's standards are required to successfully complete the Bridge Program to be admitted to the College. Columbia has a liberal transfer policy.

Application and Information

Students are strongly advised to apply early. The priority date is July 15 for the fall semester, December 15 for the spring semester, and May 1 for the summer term. Applicants are notified within two to four weeks after the College receives all the required information and documents. Students who want to live in campus housing are strongly advised to apply early. Housing assignments are offered on a first-come, first-served basis until full occupancy is achieved.

All students are invited to tour the College and meet with an admissions counselor. To arrange for a tour and an appointment with an admissions counselor, students should call the telephone number below.

For more information, students should contact:

Office of Undergraduate Admissions
Columbia College Chicago
600 South Michigan Avenue
Chicago, Illinois 60605

Telephone: 312-344-7130
Fax: 312-344-8024
E-mail admissions@colum.edu
World Wide Web: http://www.colum.edu

CORNELL COLLEGE

MOUNT VERNON, IOWA

The College

Cornell College is unique in U.S. higher education in that it offers the combination of liberal arts study within the One-Course-At-A-Time framework, an active residential community, an emphasis on service and leadership, and an ideal, wooded-hilltop setting that is one of only two campuses listed on the National Register of Historic Places.

Cornell College is a leader in educational innovation. A private, independent college founded in 1853, Cornell employs the One-Course-At-A-Time academic calendar; it is one of only three colleges in the United States to implement this advancement in postsecondary teaching and learning. Cornell is historically a place of "firsts": the first coeducational college west of the Mississippi, the first college in Iowa to grant a baccalaureate degree to a woman, the first college in the United States to confer upon a woman a full professorship with the same salary received by the male professors, and the first college in the nation to have its entire campus listed on the National Register of Historic Places. The College was among the first schools in the nation to offer its students a choice of degree programs, establish a teacher-education program, and introduce sociology into its curriculum. Cornell offers a strong leadership-training program and actively promotes community service opportunities. Nearly 70 percent of the student body take part in volunteer projects.

In 2002–03, 1,050 students from forty states and eleven other countries were enrolled at this residential college, which is situated atop a high hill overlooking the Cedar River valley. Centered on a pedestrian mall, the campus covers 129 acres and has more than forty buildings, including nine residence halls. A student center, the Commons, houses central dining rooms, a bookstore, meeting rooms, and recreation rooms. Cornell's sports and recreation center has facilities for wellness and fitness programs as well as year-round recreation and athletics space for practice and play. Cornell has 25 NCAA Postgraduate Scholars, ranking seventh in the nation among NCAA Division III schools. It competes in the Iowa Intercollegiate Athletic Conference in nineteen sports. Nearly 60 percent of students participate in sixty-six intramural sports. More than 100 clubs and organizations offer a wide range of activities, from participation in the KRNL-FM radio station to Habitat for Humanity to Greek social groups.

Location

Mount Vernon provides the best of both worlds—a classically beautiful campus in a small college town minutes from Cedar Rapids and Iowa City. These two metropolitan areas contain three additional colleges and universities and 350,000 people. Chicago, St. Louis, and Minneapolis can be reached in about 5 hours by automobile or in less than an hour by air from Cedar Rapids. Palisades–Kepler State Park, site of the annual Pal Day picnic, is 5 miles away. Cornell is 15 minutes from Cedar Rapids (airport, movies, malls) and 20 minutes from Iowa City and Hancher Auditorium, a regular concert and theater tour stop.

Majors and Degrees

Cornell College awards the Bachelor of Arts, Bachelor of Music, Bachelor of Philosophy, and Bachelor of Special Studies degrees. Majors are offered in art, biochemistry and molecular biology, biology, chemistry, classical studies, computer science, economics and business, elementary and secondary education, English, environmental studies, French, geology, German, history, international business, international relations, Latin American studies, mathematics, medieval and Renaissance studies, music education (general, instrumental, and vocal), music performance, philosophy, physical education, physics, politics, psychology, religion, Russian, Russian studies, sociology, sociology and anthropology, Spanish, theater, theater and speech, and women's studies. Prelaw and premedicine programs are available, as are programs to prepare for graduate study in social work/human services and theology. Students may design their own interdisciplinary majors.

Combined-degree programs include a 3-2 program in forestry and environmental management offered in cooperation with Duke University, 3-2 programs in engineering and occupational therapy, and a 3-4 program in architecture with Washington University in St. Louis.

The College also offers cooperative professional programs in nursing and allied health sciences with Rush University in Chicago and in medical technology with St. Luke's Hospital in Cedar Rapids. For students interested in dentistry, the University of Iowa College of Dentistry offers early acceptance into its program.

Academic Program

Cornell encourages the creative structuring of students' educational experiences by offering a choice of four degree programs within the framework of a liberal education. Programs range from a traditional curriculum, with course requirements designed to ensure both breadth and depth, to a nontraditional combination of courses, independent studies, and internships that meet specific goals. For the Bachelor of Arts, Bachelor of Music, and Bachelor of Philosophy degree programs, faculty members set the goals. The Bachelor of Special Studies degree program permits students to define their own educational objectives and design a curriculum to meet those objectives.

To increase the quality and intensity of a Cornell education, the College's academic calendar incorporates the One-Course-At-A-Time schedule. Cornell divides the traditional September–May academic year into nine 3½-week terms. During each term, students concentrate on one course chosen from the more than sixty offered and take one final examination. After a four-day break, the next term begins. Students take eight terms per year, which leaves a ninth term free for internships, off-campus programs, international study, travel, independent study, rest and relaxation, or another course.

The College's emphasis on One-Course-At-A-Time enhances the quality of liberal education offered by allowing students increased contact with faculty members, no interference from competing courses, and greater efficiency of study. It also provides rapid feedback to students about their progress. The work assigned on one day is discussed on the following day, when the material is fresh for both students and instructor. In addition, the pressure of having to prepare for several courses and examinations at the same time is eliminated.

Another liberalizing feature of One-Course-At-A-Time is the possibility of having classes meet for periods longer or shorter than the typical 50-minute period. Professors may opt to divide the day into a series of short meetings, with work assignments given and completed from one session to the next. Laboratories are not necessarily limited to one afternoon. Faculty members are also able to take students on daylong field trips or teach their courses off campus, either in the United States or abroad.

Recent Cornell College graduates are studying public health at Harvard, architecture at Washington University (St. Louis), medicine at Iowa, law at Loyola Chicago, and studio art at the Art Institute of Chicago, to name a few. Among the employers of recent graduates are the Peace Corps; Houston Grand Opera; Cheetah Outreach; Visa International; Wells Fargo; AT&T Wireless; U.S. Agency for International Development; New York Life Insurance; RBC Dain Rauscher, Inc.; and the Red Cross.

Off-Campus Arrangements

Student internship experiences can be central to understanding the realities, demands, and rewards of the workplace. Internships arranged within Cornell's One-Course-At-A-Time academic calendar are distinctly different from those arranged within a semester system. Students are able to become immersed in the experience every day for an entire month without the distractions of other course demands. Employers/mentors can count on a full-time commitment. This availability earns the attention of many nearby

Cedar Rapids businesses and corporations that have offered opportunities from engineering to telecommunications, health-related fields, and art history. More distant internships have also been completed. The intensive internship learning experience makes Cornell students very appealing to prospective employers.

Through Cornell courses abroad and College-affiliated off-campus programs, students may work and travel in other countries and become acquainted with other cultures. Recent classes have journeyed to Mexico to observe local potters, to Montreal to study French, to Mexico and Spain to study Hispanic and Spanish social development, to London for courses in English literature and drama, and to Brazil and Guatemala to experience firsthand the politics of revolutionary movements.

Cornell students have done tropical field research in Costa Rica, studied Chinese culture in Hong Kong, worked with Hispanic communities in urban Chicago, and visited Europe's great cultural centers through off-campus programs administered by the Associated Colleges of the Midwest, of which Cornell is a charter member, and the School for International Training.

Academic Facilities

Cornell's entire campus has been designated a National Historic District, and its carefully restored nineteenth-century academic architecture is combined with contemporary facilities on a fully wired campus, with Internet access in every residence hall room. King Chapel is the historic landmark of the campus and has a 130-foot clock tower. Armstrong Hall and McWethy Hall have recently been renovated and expanded for art, music, and theater. Law Hall Technology Center opened in 2000, and Cole Library was renovated recently.

Costs

The cost for 2002–03 was $26,755, including tuition, fees, and room and board. Students generally enroll for eight courses a year, but, at no extra cost, they may accelerate or broaden their studies by taking nine courses.

Financial Aid

Cornell is committed to making higher education available for all students. The majority of Cornell's students receive financial assistance, and the average aid package exceeds $18,000. A competitive scholarship program recognizes students with strong academic records or special talents. Federal aid programs include Federal Pell Grants, Federal Supplemental Educational Opportunity Grants (FSEOG), and student loans. Federal Work-Study Program awards can provide additional income through part-time, on-campus employment. Additional funds are available through the Iowa Tuition Grant Program and State of Iowa Scholarships. Need is determined by the Free Application for Federal Student Aid (FAFSA). An early financial aid evaluation is available from the College upon request. Students applying for Cornell-funded scholarships must complete their scholarship application by March 1.

Faculty

The members of the College's faculty are distinguished by their desire to teach undergraduates in a small, informal environment. Classes are capped at 25 students. Faculty members outside the department of physical education are required to have a Ph.D. or other terminal degree and are appointed, retained, and promoted based on their ability to teach. Many also distinguish themselves through scholarly and creative activities. The faculty-student ratio is 1:11, and only faculty members, not teaching assistants, teach classes.

Student Government

Student life at Cornell complements the academic program and provides a feeling of community at the College. Students participate actively in the governance of the College, serving on faculty-student committees, the Student Senate, the Residence Hall Council, and the Performing Arts and Activities Council.

Admission Requirements

The courses and degree programs offered at Cornell are intended for students who have been well prepared at the secondary school level, have obvious motivation and a desire to learn, and have the ability and potential to complete a carefully planned degree program and graduate from Cornell College. Admission to Cornell is selective. Applicants are judged on their high school records, test scores, interests, and achievements in such cocurricular activities as debate, student government, music, theater, athletics, and school publications as well as through personal recommendations and, in some cases, interviews. These are not exclusive criteria. Motivation, energy, and persistence are basic to Cornell. Students with the desire to succeed at Cornell and the motivation to benefit from a Cornell education may apply with confidence, knowing that these are important factors in the admission decision.

Application and Information

Cornell College follows a program of rolling admissions, and applicants are notified of admission decisions soon after their files are complete. Special consideration is given to students who apply by December 1. After March 1, applications are accepted on a space-available basis.

To apply for admission to Cornell, prospective students should obtain an application form online or from the Office of Admissions, complete and file the application with Cornell with a $25 application fee, have their high school forward an official transcript and a school recommendation, and have their ACT or SAT I scores sent to Cornell. Cornell welcomes transfer students from accredited two- and four-year institutions.

Additional information, catalogs, application forms, and financial aid forms are available from:

Office of Admissions
Cornell College
600 First Street West
Mount Vernon, Iowa 52314-1098
Telephone: 319-895-4477
800-747-1112 (toll-free)
E-mail: admissions@cornellcollege.edu
World Wide Web: http://www.cornellcollege.edu

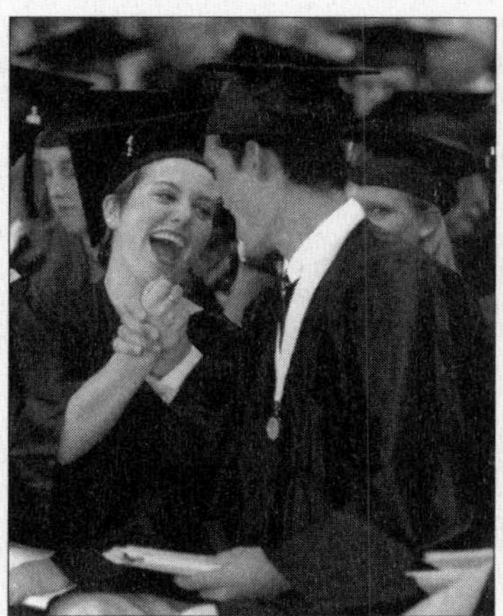

Graduation time at Cornell College.

DEPAUW UNIVERSITY

GREENCASTLE, INDIANA

The University

"DePauw is not a spectator sport" is the way one graduate described the DePauw experience. Indeed, DePauw students expect and seek a challenge. In small classes, students are challenged by professors who are leading scholars with a passion for teaching. There are countless opportunities to excel in more than forty programs of study, five honors programs, numerous leadership positions with student organizations and living units, athletic programs, and more. DePauw students have a tradition of volunteerism, as demonstrated by the fact that three fourths of the student body of 2,300 participate in community service each year. In the first annual *Guide to Campuses Where You Can Make a Difference,* DePauw ranked among the top fifteen colleges where students are truly making a difference in terms of service, both on campus and in the community. In brief, DePauw provides a broad, liberal arts education that is intended to serve as a foundation for the student's lifetime of learning and growth.

At DePauw, the traditional liberal arts curriculum is complemented by perhaps the largest per capita student internship program in the country. Eighty-five percent of DePauw students complete at least one internship during a semester, Winter Term, or summer, and many students complete at least two internships. As a result, DePauw offers a unique opportunity for students to explore various interests and career possibilities, which have a significant impact for students following graduation. More than 96 percent of DePauw graduates are employed or enrolled in graduate/professional school within nine months of graduation. The figure increases to more than 99 percent after one year. Of those students obtaining employment after graduation, approximately 1 out of 4 students accept jobs at companies and organizations where they served a student internship.

Much of DePauw's reputation for excellence can be attributed to the uncommon success of its alumni. DePauw ranked eleventh in the nation in terms of the likelihood that its graduates will become chief executive officers of major American companies, according to *Fortune* magazine in 1990. DePauw ranked eighth in the nation and first in the Midwest as the undergraduate origin of the nation's top executives, according to a 1994 study by Standard & Poor's Corp. DePauw also ranked sixteenth as a baccalaureate source for Ph.D. degree recipients in all fields, according to a 1998 survey by Franklin and Marshall College.

DePauw guarantees graduation in four years for students in forty standard programs, or the University waives tuition and fees for any subsequent course work necessary for graduation.

Location

DePauw is located in a town of 10,000 people set amid the gently rolling hills of west-central Indiana. The campus is exceptionally well maintained, blending new, state-of-the-art facilities with buildings, such as the historic East College, that exemplify the University's heritage. DePauw students are very active in the community, as indicated by the fact that about three fourths of the student body volunteers each year for public service in twenty-five community organizations. Greencastle is 45 miles west of Indianapolis and within a 3-hour drive of Chicago, St. Louis, Louisville, Cincinnati, and Columbus.

Majors and Degrees

DePauw offers the Bachelor of Arts (B.A.), Bachelor of Music (B.Mus.), Bachelor of Musical Arts (B.M.A.), and Bachelor of Music Education (B.M.E.).

DePauw offers majors in more than forty areas, including anthropology, art (history), art (studio), biochemistry, biology, black studies, chemistry, classical civilization, communication, computer science, conflict studies, earth sciences, East Asian studies, economics, elementary education, English (literature), English (writing), environmental geoscience, French, geography, geology, German, Greek, history, interdisciplinary, Latin, mathematics, music, music/business, music performance, music education, philosophy, physical education (sports medicine and sports science), physics, political science, psychology, religious studies, Romance languages, Russian studies, sociology, sociology and anthropology, Spanish, and women's studies. Preprofessional programs are available in dentistry, law, medicine, and secondary education. In addition, DePauw offers a 3-2 program in pre-engineering.

Academic Program

DePauw is committed to providing its students with a traditional, liberal arts education complemented by internship opportunities, and degree requirements reflect this approach. The University follows a 4-1-4 calendar, with four-month fall and spring semesters and a January Winter Term. The normal course load in a semester is four courses, but course loads may vary from three to 4½ courses. During the January Winter Term, first-year students study on campus, and upperclass students participate in research, internships, and travel abroad. DePauw's distinctive honors programs include Honor Scholars, Information Technology Associates Program, Management Fellows, Media Fellows, and Science Research Fellows.

During the 1999–2000 academic year, DePauw began a new first-year experience program, called depauw.year1, that is designed to build a sense of community among first-year students. The program includes special seminars, speakers, programs, and other activities.

Thirty-one courses are required for students earning a Bachelor of Arts, Bachelor of Music, or Bachelor of Musical Arts degree. The Bachelor of Music Education degree requires thirty-two courses. Each student must complete a major, achieve at least a 2.0 GPA (on a 4.0 scale) in that major, and satisfy the senior major requirement. Students must attain a minimum cumulative GPA of 2.0, while students in the B.M.A. and B.M.E. programs need a minimum 2.5 GPA. Fifteen courses leading to a bachelor's degree, including six of the last eight courses, must be completed in residence at DePauw or in a University-approved program. Students in the College of Liberal Arts must achieve certification in writing (W), quantitative reasoning (Q), and oral communication skills (S). Students must complete three Winter Term projects with satisfactory grades, including an on-campus Winter Term for first-year students. A maximum of 3 internship course credits and five internship experiences (including Winter Terms) may be applied toward the bachelor's degree.

Off-Campus Arrangements

DePauw offers extensive off-campus study programs. Domestic programs include the Washington Semester, United Nations Semester, Sea Semester, New York Arts Program, Newberry Library Program, Oak Ridge Science Semester, and Philadelphia Urban Semester. Study abroad is available in Africa, Asia-Pacific, Australia, Austria, Belgium, Canada, the Caribbean, China, the Czech Republic, Denmark, England, France, Germany, Greece, Hungary, India, Indonesia, Ireland, Italy, Japan, Latin America, Mexico, the Middle East, the Netherlands, Poland, Russia, Scotland, Singapore, Spain, Switzerland, Vietnam, and Wales. Many students also participate in off-campus Winter Term projects. More than 40 percent of students study off-campus as part of their DePauw experience. In order to receive course credit, a student must have approval from the International Center; other restrictions may apply.

Academic Facilities

The new blends with the old on DePauw's 175-acre campus, which features thirty-nine major buildings and a nearby 40-acre nature preserve. DePauw's facilities provide an excellent environment for teaching and learning. The physical plant is equal to or superior to that of other liberal arts universities.

The centerpiece of the campus is historic East College, built in 1877 and listed on the Register of Historic Landmarks. New buildings on campus include the Indoor Tennis and Track Center, which opened in 2001 and was recognized by the United States Tennis Association as an outstanding public tennis facility for 2002. The Julian Science and Math Center is currently undergoing a $38 million expansion and renovation project, adding 110,000 square feet of new classroom and laboratory space, including the 361 degrees Technology Center. The new Peeler Art Center gives students a state-of-the-art space optimal to the teaching, creation, and presentation of art. The Center for Contemporary Media has superb facilities and equipment for *The DePauw,* the oldest student newspaper in the state; student-operated WGRE-FM radio; and a television unit in which students produce programs for broadcast statewide and nationwide. The Performing Arts Center is home to the School of Music and features outstanding performance halls.

Costs

Expenses for the 2002–03 academic year included $22,400 for tuition, $6800 for room and board, and $440 in fees for health services and activities. Books and supplies are approximately $600 per year, and personal expenses are approximately $1000 per year.

Financial Aid

Admission to DePauw is need-blind. Ninety-five percent of all DePauw students receive scholarships, grants, loans, or work-study assistance. The average financial aid package covers slightly more than half of total costs. DePauw's financial aid program is designed to recognize achievement and potential and to assist students who otherwise would be unable to attend the University due to financial constraints. DePauw maintains its own scholarship, work, and loan programs and participates in all traditional forms of state and federal financial aid.

February 15 is the priority filing date for applications for fall financial aid. FAFSA and institutional financial aid applications are required. Scholarships/grants available include federal and state scholarships/grants, University scholarships/grants, private scholarships/grants, ROTC scholarships and academic merit scholarships. Approximately 40 percent of students work on campus during the academic year. DePauw participates in the Federal Work-Study Program, and 45 percent of students who receive financial aid participate in work-study.

Faculty

DePauw professors are devoted to teaching students. The University has 223 full-time faculty members, and 92 percent have the terminal degree in their field. The student-faculty ratio is 10:1. All classes at DePauw are taught by professors and not by graduate assistants. Ninety-seven percent of full-time faculty members serve as academic advisers to students.

Student Government

Leadership opportunities in a wide variety of organizations are an integral part of the DePauw experience. Students have numerous opportunities to be involved in student government as well as committees and councils representing student concerns. The president of the student body presides over the many committees of the Student Congress; each committee has several student representatives as members. Sororities, fraternities, and residence halls all have annual elections of officers and representatives to various campus organizations.

Admission Requirements

DePauw does not conduct admission by the numbers. Along with grades and SAT I or ACT scores, the University looks at the required student essays, record of other achievements, and examples of any special talent a student may have. Also considered are the quality of courses selected in the high school; the high school attended; the recommendations of high school counselors, teachers, coaches, and employers; and the personal interview. DePauw examines each individual's application carefully.

To be admitted to the first-year class at DePauw, students must have graduated from an accredited secondary school or offer evidence of equivalent education. Students should have completed the following work in a college-preparatory program: 4 units of English, 4 units of mathematics, 3-4 units of a foreign language, 3-4 units of social science, and 3-4 units of science (2 or more laboratory sciences). In addition, School of Music candidates must audition.

Application and Information

Prospective students can apply online or obtain an application for admission by calling or writing the Office of Admission. DePauw also is a member of the Common Application Group and gives the common application the same consideration as the University's application.

Students interested in early decision must submit applications by November 1, students interested in early notification must submit applications by December 1, and students interested in regular decision must submit applications by February 1. Admission decisions are mailed by mid-December for early decision applicants and by February 1 for early notification applicants. Regular decision applicants are notified by April 1. Early decision applicants who are admitted must respond by February 15; other admitted applicants who decide to enroll must submit an enrollment deposit by May 1. Students should contact:

Madeleine R. Eagon
Vice President for Admission and Financial Aid
DePauw University
P.O. Box 37
Greencastle, Indiana 46135-0037
Telephone: 765-658-4006
800-447-2495 (toll-free)
Fax: 765-658-4007
E-mail: admission@depauw.edu
World Wide Web: http://www.depauw.edu

Historic East College is the centerpiece of DePauw University's campus. The East College bell summons students to class and also signals victories in football.

DICKINSON STATE UNIVERSITY

DICKINSON, NORTH DAKOTA

The University

Student success, both inside and outside the classroom, has been the focus of Dickinson State University since 1918 when the University was established as Dickinson Normal School and Model High. The tradition continues today, allowing easy access and meaningful relationships with qualified professors, supportive and comfortable living arrangements on campus, and with student activities, providing something for everyone.

Dickinson State, with an enrollment of approximately 2,000 students, is the only comprehensive, four-year public university in West River North Dakota. The University is proud of its safe campus. Its location offers students a secure environment in which to pursue their educational and social interests.

The University's mission, as dictated by the North Dakota University System, is to provide high-quality, accessible programs; to promote excellence in teaching and learning; to support scholarly and creative activities; and to provide service relevant to the economy, health, and quality of life of the citizens of North Dakota. With a wide range of academic programs, Dickinson State University prepares students to live, learn, and lead in the twenty-first century.

Dickinson State University is accredited by the North Central Association of Colleges and Schools (NCA), the North Central Association for Teacher Education (NCATE), and the National League for Nursing Accrediting Commission (NLNAC).

At Dickinson State, there are approximately forty-five different organizations to help every student find a niche. Students choose from intramural sports, band, chorus, drama, art, forensics, student government, honorary societies, academic clubs, and cheerleading, to name just a few.

Living in a residence hall at Dickinson State offers many conveniences and countless opportunities to build friendships in an exciting environment close to classes and University activities. Meal plans are available on campus for five or seven days per week. For added ease, students can also opt to purchase meals at the snack bar. Rooms have free access to the campus computer network and cable television. Features in each hall include game room, exercise equipment, computer stations, laundry facilities, and kitchenette. Students can select to live in women's, men's, or coed halls, or student apartments. Family student housing complexes provide apartments at reasonable housing rates to nontraditional students.

Location

Dickinson State is located in Dickinson, North Dakota, near the rugged and beautiful Badlands. With a population of more than 17,000, Dickinson is the hub of West River North Dakota. The community lies only 30 miles from Theodore Roosevelt National Park, and it is just one hour's drive south of Lake Sakakawea. Dickinson is served by both commercial air and bus transportation.

Dickinson's location provides abundant opportunities for people to enjoy outdoor recreational activities year-round. The area's picturesque rivers, lakes, and Badlands are ideal for hiking, fishing, boating, hunting, cross-country skiing, and much more.

As the state's fifth-largest community, Dickinson offers a wide array of restaurants, shopping malls, specialty stores, historic landmarks, museums, movie theaters, and other entertainment outlets. The region offers abundant dinosaur fossils and geological phenomena for explorers of all ages. Many of these treasures are displayed in Dickinson's impressive Dakota Dinosaur Museum.

Health-care services are provided by a 109-bed acute-care hospital, two major clinics, and numerous specialty clinics. The University's Student Health Service provides prompt care on campus for routine health concerns.

Majors and Degrees

Programs offered at Dickinson State University include liberal arts along with specialized programs in education, business, health services, agriculture, and computer science. There are opportunities for preprofessional study and vocational training in selected areas as well.

Dickinson State offers Bachelor of Arts and Bachelor of Science degrees in ten departments, including majors and/or minors (indicated with a *) in accounting, agriculture (with options in natural resource management, integrated ranch management, and business/marketing), art, biology, business administration (with concentrations in accounting, agribusiness, banking and finance, business management, management information systems, manufacturing technology, marketing, office administration, and organizational psychology), business education, chemistry, coaching*, computer science, earth science*, elementary education, English, environmental health, geography*, graphic design*, history, journalism*, mathematics, music, music education, nursing, physical education, political science, psychology, science composite, secondary education, social science composite, social science (elementary education)*, sociology*, social work (linked with University of North Dakota), Spanish, theater and communication, university studies, and writing.

Associate degree and certificate programs include agriculture with specialty areas in agriculture sales and service (with options in agriculture business management and equine management) or farm and ranch management, nursing, office administration (with concentrations in accounting, agribusiness, computer science, legal, management, and medical studies), and university studies.

Preprofessional programs include athletic training, chiropractic, dentistry, dental hygiene, engineering, forestry, law, medicine, medical/lab technology, mortuary science, optometry, physics, seminary, social work, veterinary, and wildlife management.

Academic Program

While many of the majors that Dickinson State University offers have unique academic requirements, the basic baccalaureate degree academic curriculum consists of approximately 39 semester hours of general education courses from the areas of communications, scientific inquiry, expression of human civilization, understanding human civilization, multicultural studies, and physical education; a specific major core curriculum of 32 to 60 or more semester hours; approximately 24 semester hours of credit in a minor field of study (when a minor is required); and professional education course work for those students entering the teaching profession. Students seeking a Bachelor of Arts degree must also complete a minimum of 16 semester hours of a foreign language. A minimum of 128 semester hours is required for graduation in a baccalaureate degree program. Associate degree programs require 64 credit hours for graduation.

Academic Facilities

The commitment to technology at Dickinson State is evident in the number of cutting-edge computers provided for student use. There is an outstanding student-to-personal computer ratio, resulting in easy access to the type of technology students need to excel. Computer labs are located in academic areas, the library, and all residence halls. Students also have free access to e-mail and the Internet, including the World Wide Web.

Stoxen Library is proud of its highly sophisticated automated library. The On-line Dakota Information Network allows students to access resources from across the United States.

Costs

In 2003–04, tuition and fees were $1570 per semester for North Dakota residents; $1774 per semester for Minnesota residents; $1889 per semester for residents of Montana, South Dakota, Manitoba (Canada), and Saskatchewan (Canada); $2208 per semester for residents of Alaska, Arizona, California, Colorado, Hawaii, Idaho, Kansas, Michigan, Missouri, Nebraska, Nevada, New Mexico, Oregon, Utah, Washington, and Wyoming; and for residents of other states, tuition and fees were $3703 per semester. Room and board costs averaged $1675 per semester. Books were approximately $350 per semester. These figures reflect current costs, which are subject to change.

Financial Aid

College is a valuable investment in the future, and Dickinson State realizes financing it can be challenging. One of the best college buys in the region, Dickinson State's tuition and housing rates are among the lowest in the upper Midwest. In addition, attractive tuition rates are offered for students living in states and provinces bordering on North Dakota. Special rates also exist for students who live in those states participating in the Western Undergraduate Exchange (WUE) and the Midwest Student Exchange Program (MSEP). These include Alaska, Arizona, California, Colorado, Hawaii, Idaho, Kansas, Michigan, Missouri, Nebraska, Nevada, New Mexico, Oregon, Utah, Washington, and Wyoming.

The Office of Financial Aid is ready to help ease the cost of a college education through a number of financial aid programs, including scholarships, grants, loans, student employment opportunities, cultural diversity awards, and international awards. More than 85 percent of Dickinson State's students received financial assistance last year.

Faculty

Dickinson State University has 75 full-time and 70 part-time faculty members. Students develop close relationships with their teachers since three fourths of classes have fewer than 30 students.

Student Government

The Student Senate is the governing body and official voice of Dickinson State University students. The Senate is composed of a cross-section of students elected by the campus community. The Campus Activity Board (CAB) offers a broad range of social and recreational activities, including dances, films, comedians, and other special events. The Campus Programming Committee (CPC) provides a variety of educational, instructional, and cultural programs. Residence Hall Councils are made up of elected student residents and deal with matters relating to campus housing. The Student Policies Council is composed of students, faculty, and staff members. The Council recommends policies and programs related to student affairs.

Admission Requirements

Dickinson State's admission policy allows students to enroll if they are high school graduates or have successfully completed the GED examination along with completion of the ACT or SAT. The completion of a high school college-preparatory course core curriculum is also required for admission into a baccalaureate program.

The nursing program has special enrollment and admissions requirements. Students should apply early for this program.

All students under the age of 21 who have not completed 60 credit hours are required to live on campus. Exceptions to this policy include married students; students living locally with parents, grandparents, or a legal guardian; students who live with a brother or sister who is a head of a household; and single parents with one or more dependents.

Application and Information

The admissions staff is anxious to discuss the variety of programs the University has to offer and give a tour of the beautiful campus, its classrooms, facilities, and residence halls. When students are on campus, they should meet with the financial aid staff to discuss concerns about financing an education. Admissions representatives are available Monday through Friday, 8 a.m. to 4 p.m., Mountain Time. Students should contact:

Office of Student Recruitment
Dickinson State University
Dickinson, North Dakota 58601-4896
Telephone: 701-483-2175
800-279-HAWK Ext. 2175 (toll-free)
E-mail: dsu.hawks@dsu.nodak.edu
World Wide Web: http://www.dickinsonstate.com

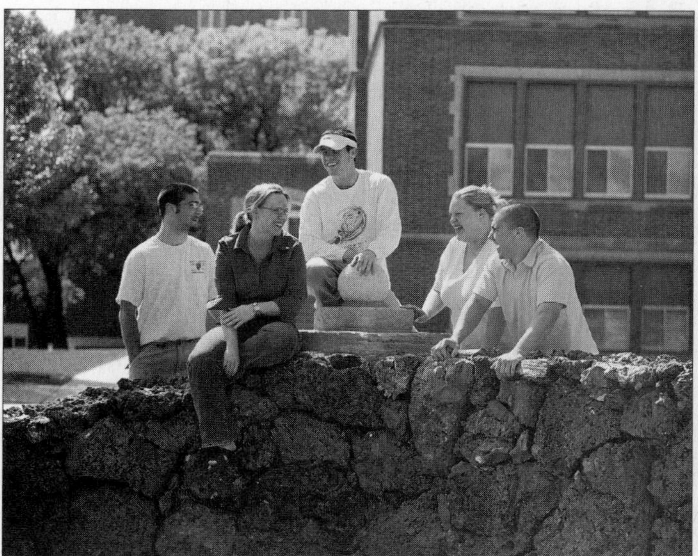

Dickinson State University ensures student success with flexible schedules and by providing numerous group activities for students to live, learn, and lead as they grow together at Dickinson State University.

ELMHURST COLLEGE

ELMHURST, ILLINOIS

The College

Elmhurst College is a private, comprehensive liberal arts college located near the center of metropolitan Chicago. Founded in 1871, the College advances the practical and professional relevance of the liberal arts tradition. The academic programs are characterized by their connections with the professional world and their responsiveness to the intellectual needs of today's diverse student population. In forty-six undergraduate majors and seven graduate programs, Elmhurst students strengthen their skills of critical and creative inquiry and develop their capacity for lives of learning, service, and meaningful work.

The College enrolls 2,600 undergraduate and graduate students. Seventeen percent are students of color. Sixty-five percent are full-time undergraduates; 31 percent are over age 25. Twenty-two states and seventeen countries are represented in the student body. More than one third of Elmhurst's full-time undergraduates live on campus in one of five residence halls.

The Center for Professional Excellence (CPE) is a distinctive component of an Elmhurst education. Established in 1997, the CPE offers internships, mentorships, international study programs, service-learning opportunities, guidance through career launches and transitions, and other student-centered programs. The goal of this innovative center is to enhance the traditional college experience with additional, purposeful challenges, both intellectual and professional, on campus and beyond.

While Elmhurst is small enough to offer students opportunities to make real contributions to campus life, it also is large enough to offer an extensive range of choices among cocurricular and extracurricular activities. Eighty-seven registered clubs, organizations, and athletic teams are active on campus. The jazz band, radio station, and student newspaper, *The Leader,* have a professional edge. The Mill Theatre presents dramas, musicals, and student-directed productions of original scripts. The Elmhurst College Jazz Festival is an annual, nationally recognized celebration of the supremely American artform. Eminent artists and business, political, and religious leaders regularly speak to campus audiences. Examples include Lech Walesa and Elie Wiesel, winners of the Nobel Prize for Peace; the acclaimed poets Maya Angelou and Gwendolyn Brooks; and the explorer Robert Ballard, who discovered the wreckage of the *R.M.S. Titanic.*

The College fields sixteen teams in NCAA Division III and is a charter member of the highly competitive College Conference of Illinois and Wisconsin (CCIW). During the 1990s, the Bluejays won CCIW championships in baseball, softball, and volleyball, and qualified for postseason play in men's basketball and women's volleyball.

Elmhurst is affiliated with the United Church of Christ. Like the church, the College is open, welcoming, and ecumenical. Nearly half of the students are Roman Catholic. Jews, Muslims, Orthodox, and many Protestant denominations are represented on the faculty and in the student body. In short, people of all creeds (and of none) come to the campus to learn and thrive.

Master's degrees are offered in seven disciplines: business administration, computer network systems, early childhood special education, English studies, industrial/organizational psychology, professional accountancy, and supply chain management.

Location

Elmhurst's lush suburban campus, located 16 miles west of Chicago's Loop, is a registered arboretum, with twenty-three red brick buildings and more than 600 varieties of trees and other plants. The students benefit enormously from the College's location near the heart of one of the world's most important and appealing urban regions. The Chicago area offers world-class opportunities for internships and other professional opportunities and for cultural, social, and sporting events. A commuter railroad stops two blocks from the campus, and city and suburban attractions are also accessible via several interstate highways. The city of Elmhurst, a charming suburb with more than 42,000 residents, is located on the eastern edge of DuPage County, which is 6 miles southwest of O'Hare International Airport.

Majors and Degrees

Undergraduates at Elmhurst can choose from among forty-six majors. Through the interdepartmental major, students can develop individualized programs of study with the guidance of a faculty adviser. The College awards the Bachelor of Arts, Bachelor of Liberal Studies, Bachelor of Music, and Bachelor of Science degrees.

Elmhurst offers undergraduate degree programs in accounting; American studies; art; biology; business administration; chemistry; communication studies; computer science; early childhood education; economics; elementary education; English; environmental management; exercise science; finance; French; geography and environmental planning; German; history; information systems; interdepartmental, interdisciplinary communication studies; international business; logistics and transportation management; management; marketing; mathematics; music; music business; music education; musical theater; nursing; philosophy; physical education; physics; political science; professional communication; psychology; secondary education; sociology; Spanish; special education; speech-language pathology; theater; theology; and urban studies.

The College offers preprofessional programs in actuarial science, allied health sciences, dentistry, engineering, law, library science, medicine, seminary, and veterinary medicine.

Academic Program

About one third of Elmhurst students are transfers from other four-year institutions or community colleges. The Office of Admission addresses specific policies regarding transfer credit with students on an individual basis. Elmhurst provides alternatives by which students may obtain credit for areas of study in which they demonstrate prior competence. Such programs include Advanced Placement, departmental examinations, the College-Level Examination Program (CLEP), credit for experiential learning, and credit for noncollegiate instruction.

Academic Facilities

The A. C. Buehler Library, the academic heart of the College, contains more than 225,000 books and subscribes to more than 1,000 periodicals. Through computer-supported consortia, students have access to 20 million books and other resources. The campus has state-of-the-art academic technology. It includes PC and Macintosh laboratories; mainframe, graphics, robotics, and cartography laboratories; an instructional media center; a weather station; a 24-track digital music recording studio; and a

750,000-volt proton accelerator. All students have Internet access. The Deicke Center for Nursing Education occupies its own well-equipped building, Memorial Hall, and uses health-care facilities throughout metropolitan Chicago. One of the nine academic buildings, Old Main, is listed on the National Register of Historic Places.

Costs

Tuition and fees for full-time students totaled $17,500 for 2002–03. Room and board were $5796; books and other expenses averaged $1500. Part-time tuition was $498 per semester hour. Graduate tuition was $555 per semester hour.

Financial Aid

In 2002, Elmhurst awarded approximately $15.6 million in grants and scholarships. About 75 percent of full-time students received some type of aid. The typical package offered to eligible full-time students was about $15,500. Approximately 65 percent of all aid is in the form of grants and scholarships. Roughly 45 percent of all freshmen were awarded scholarships based on prior academic accomplishments. All awards are renewable. To apply for financial aid, students should complete the Elmhurst Application for Financial Aid and the Free Application for Federal Student Aid (FAFSA). New students must be admitted before an aid offer is made.

Faculty

Elmhurst College has 113 full-time faculty members. More than 90 percent hold the highest academic degree in their fields. The College has 226 adjunct faculty members. The academic atmosphere attracts scholars who love to teach on a campus where they can work with students as individuals. The average class has 19 students; the largest class has about 35 students. The student-faculty ratio is 13:1. A faculty member, not a teaching assistant, teaches every class.

Student Government

Elmhurst College believes in shared governance. Students are voting members of such important groups as the College Council. The Student Government Association (SGA) is the primary avenue through which students make recommendations to faculty members and administrators. The SGA consists of an elected student chairperson, 14 student members, 3 faculty members, 4 administrators, and the Dean of Student Affairs.

Admission Requirements

Elmhurst seeks students whose academic profile provides a sound basis for success in the classroom and the larger College community. Typically, successful applicants for freshmen admission rank in the top half of their high school class; present a college-preparatory curriculum, including at least 3 units in English and 2 or more in laboratory science, in math, and in social studies (foreign language is recommended but not required); and score at or above the national average on the ACT or SAT I. The most important single element in admission review is the quality of a student's classroom performance. A faculty committee reviews applicants who fall short of the stated criteria. This committee may issue a positive decision with certain conditions, such as requiring the student to take a lighter full-time course load.

Transfer applicants should present an overall college grade point average of 2.4 or higher on a 4.0 scale and be in good standing at the college they most recently attended. High school records are required. As part of the admission process, the College provides an evaluation of previous credits in relation to both graduation requirements at Elmhurst and major department regulations. Thus, official transcripts from each college attended are required with the application.

Elmhurst College does not discriminate on the basis of race, color, creed, age, gender, disability, marital status, sexual orientation, national origin, or ethnic origin.

Application and Information

Elmhurst College admits freshman and transfer students to both the fall and spring terms. Most new students enroll in the fall. Admission decisions are made on a rolling basis. For fall term, the preferred application deadline is April 15 for freshman admission and July 1 for transfer admission. For the spring term, the preferred application deadline is January 15 for all applicants.

For additional information and admission materials, students are encouraged to contact:

Office of Admission
Elmhurst College
190 Prospect Avenue
Elmhurst, Illinois 60126-3296
Telephone: 630-617-3400
800-697-1871 (toll-free)
Fax: 630-617-5501
E-mail: admit@elmhurst.edu
World Wide Web: http://www.elmhurst.edu

A picturesque, traditional college setting.

GRACELAND UNIVERSITY

LAMONI, IOWA

The University

Graceland University offers a strong academic program firmly rooted in the liberal arts tradition with an emphasis on career preparation. Since its founding in 1895 as a private, coeducational university, Graceland has maintained a tradition of academic excellence based on a commitment to the Christian view of the wholeness, worth, and dignity of every person. The University, sponsored by the Community of Christ, is nonsectarian and offers a varied religious life program for those who wish to participate. Thirty-one percent of Graceland students come from Iowa, and the remaining 69 percent represent forty-nine states and twenty-six nations.

Graceland believes that an important part of a student's learning experience is achieved through association with other students in residence hall living. This belief is supported by an on-campus housing system that provides students with the camaraderie of a fraternity or sorority without the competition. Within the residence halls, there are men's and women's houses. Members of each house elect a house council to plan social, intramural athletic, religious, and academic support activities. Residence halls are equipped with voice mail, e-mail, Internet connections, and cable TV.

The North Central Association of Universities and Schools accredits Graceland as a bachelor's and master's degree–granting institution. Graceland's teacher-education program has been approved by the Iowa Department of Education and is accredited by the National Council for Accreditation of Teacher Education (NCATE). The nursing program is accredited by the National League for Nursing Accrediting Commission and is approved by the Missouri Board of Nursing and the Iowa Board of Nursing.

In addition to its undergraduate programs, Graceland offers a Master of Science in Nursing and an RN to M.S.N. course of study through the Outreach Program. The M.S.N. program has three tracks: family nurse practitioner studies, clinical nurse specialist studies, and health-care administration. Graceland also offers Master of Education, Master of Arts in religion, and Master of Arts in Christian ministries degree programs.

Location

Lamoni, in south-central Iowa, is on Interstate 35 3 miles north of the Missouri border. It is 1 hour from Des Moines, 2 hours from Kansas City, and 3 hours from Omaha. Lamoni is the home of Liberty Hall Historic Center and antique shops. A county lake, Slip Bluff County Park, and Nine Eagles State Park are within 10 miles.

Majors and Degrees

Graceland awards the degrees of Bachelor of Arts, Bachelor of Science, and Bachelor of Science in Nursing. These degrees represent study in liberal arts with a concentration of courses in a major. The majors and concentrations offered in the Bachelor of Arts programs are accounting, art, athletic training, business administration, chemistry, communications, criminal justice, economics, elementary education, English–literature, English–writing, entrepreneurship and free enterprise, finance, German, health, history, human services, information technology, international business, international studies, management, management of information systems, marketing, mathematics, modern foreign language, music, music education, peace studies, philosophy and religion, physical education and health, political science, psychology, publications design, recreation, religion, secondary education, social science, sociology, Spanish, speech communication, theater, visual communications, and wellness program management. Bachelor of Science programs and majors are addiction studies, basic science, biology, chemistry, clinical laboratory science/medical technology, computer science, nursing, pre-engineering, premedicine/predentistry, and pre–veterinary medicine. In addition, a special liberal studies program is offered at Graceland allowing individualized program design by students. Nursing majors complete their last two years at the Graceland Independence Campus in Independence, Missouri.

Graceland offers four undergraduate Outreach Programs: a Bachelor of Science in addiction studies, a Bachelor of Arts in liberal studies (with emphases in health-care administration and health-care psychology), and an RN to B.S.N. program. (Applicants for the B.S.N. must be registered nurses.) These programs allow individuals to complete their degrees through a combination of directed independent study, preceptor-guided practicums, and short residences. For more information, students interested in the addiction studies major should call 800-585-6310 (toll-free); those interested in the nursing and health-care programs should call 877-471-1456 (toll-free).

Academic Program

Graceland is committed to helping develop the lives of its students—intellectually, socially, physically, and ethically—through a curriculum that is strongly rooted in the liberal arts. General education requirements are based on ten core competencies and can be satisfied by course selections, internships, portfolios, proficiency exams, work experience, independent studies, and performance and achievement. Graceland offers majors that foster conceptual thinking, emphasize general principles, develop communication skills, and accommodate growth and enrichment.

Two programs at Graceland give attention to the special needs of students. The honors program is designed for highly motivated students who want to expand their learning beyond the regular academic curriculum. Honors students are required to develop and complete an honors thesis or project. Chance is a program for bright students who have the aptitude for university education but have experienced learning difficulties. The Lindamood and Bell clinical models are used for remediation in reading, spelling, and language comprehension.

The University operates on a 4-1-4 academic calendar. The regular semesters are separated by a one-month winter term in January. Full tuition for either the fall or the spring semester includes the winter term. This program is geared toward innovative and exceptional approaches and action-oriented learning experiences. On-campus programs vary from dance basics to science fiction to philosophy. Off-campus winter term experiences range from scuba diving in Grand Cayman to touring Italy. Winter term is also the ideal time to explore career interests through an internship.

Off-Campus Arrangements

Many students see the world during the winter term by visiting such places as Australia, China, England, France, Grand Cayman Island in the British West Indies, Hungary, Italy, India, Israel, Japan, and Mexico. Students who major in a foreign language may study abroad during their junior or senior year under the auspices of a recognized study program.

Academic Facilities

The Shaw Center for the Performing Arts includes an 800-seat auditorium, a 150-seat studio theater, a 40-foot proscenium stage with orchestra pit, a Casavant pipe organ, a full fly gallery, a spacious scene shop, an art gallery, classrooms, rehearsal rooms, and faculty offices. The Helene Center for the Visual Arts, opening in 2004, includes 29,000 square feet for classrooms, studios, and exhibits. An important feature, the large north-facing windows, will provide optimum light for artists.

Computer facilities include three primary microcomputer laboratories with Macintosh and IBM-compatible computers. Students have access to equipment of commercial quality for desktop publishing and graphics design and to a music laboratory that provides computer-assisted tutoring, synthesis, and composition as well as professional-quality manuscript printing. The centerpiece of this laboratory is the Kurzweil synthesizer. Graceland's Enter.Net.C@fe provides 24-hour Internet access for student research and recreation.

The Frederick Madison Smith Library uses the latest technologies to provide the information services that students need. Ten fully networked computer workstations offer access to the Internet and many research databases, including 2 databases that provide full-text newspaper articles and periodicals for online reading. Access to LIBBIE, the computerized library catalog, is available from residence hall rooms. Articles and books may be ordered from a worldwide network of research libraries. Students log on to the library's home page to ask reference questions. Holdings include 119,615 books and bound journals, 3,383 audiovisual materials, 77,371 government documents, 569 magazine and newspaper subscriptions, and 5,322 items in the Teacher Curriculum Lab. Three microcomputer labs and the Iowa Communications Network (ICN) classroom are located in the library. Students across the state take classes from Graceland via the ICN.

Students have the opportunity to use the ABT 52 scanning electron microscope, nuclear magnetic resonance spectroscope, Fourier transform infrared spectroscope, and a computer lab with PCs that provide access to a multiple-operating system environment.

The Eugene E. Closson Physical Education Center includes an indoor junior Olympic-size pool; an indoor track; a weight room; basketball, tennis, and volleyball courts; and a racquetball court. The Bruce Jenner Sports Complex contains the outdoor track, the football stadium, three soccer fields, five intramural fields, and eight tennis courts. The campus borders on a nine-hole golf course and two small ponds for fishing and canoeing.

Costs

Full-time tuition for 2003–04 is $14,650. All freshmen and sophomores are required to live on campus.

Financial Aid

Graceland's financial aid program is designed to assist qualified students attending the University. Ninety-one percent of Graceland's students receive financial aid such as academic scholarships, performance grants, work-study, federal and state grants, and government loans. Academic scholarships are based on the high school GPA and composite ACT or combined SAT I scores for entering freshmen and on cumulative GPA for transfer and continuing students. Grants are available for achievement in athletics and performing arts and for international students. The University matches a grant up to $1000 annually for a contribution made by a church and designated for a student attending Graceland.

Faculty

The majority of faculty members have earned a doctorate or the highest degree in their field. Faculty members are active in their professional fields, but consider teaching their primary responsibility. The student-faculty ratio is 16:1.

Student Government

Students are actively involved in the decision-making process of the University. Executive members of the Graceland Student Government attend faculty meetings and participate with voice and vote. Each academic department has student representatives who participate in business sessions and serve on faculty search committees. Students provide leadership for the housing system and for the campus social program. There are many avenues through which students can gain practical leadership experience.

Admission Requirements

Admission to Graceland is competitive. To be considered, high school graduates must qualify in two of the following three areas: (1) rank in the upper 50 percent of their class; (2) have a minimum 2.0 GPA, based on a 4.0 system; and (3) have either a minimum composite ACT Assessment score of 21 or a minimum combined SAT I score of 960. No one is denied admission to the University on the basis of race, color, religion, age, sex, national origin, disability, or sexual orientation. Prospective students and their families are encouraged to visit the campus.

Application and Information

Students are encouraged to apply as early as possible. For more information and application materials, students should contact:

Brian Shantz
Dean of Admissions
Graceland University
1 University Place
Lamoni, Iowa 50140

Telephone: 641-784-5196 (local)
866-GRACELAND (toll-free in the United States and Canada)
800-346-9208 (toll-free in Canada only)
Fax: 641-784-5480
E-mail: admissions@graceland.edu
World Wide Web: http://www.graceland.edu

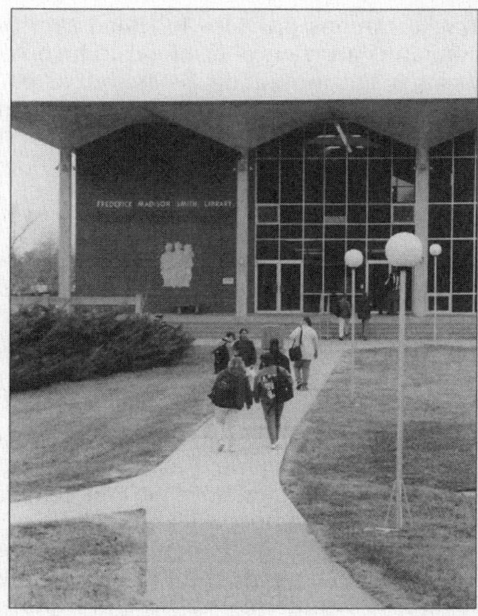

From computer labs with Internet access to thousands of books, journals, and periodicals, the Frederick Madison Smith Library provides students with free access to a world of information.

GREENVILLE COLLEGE

GREENVILLE, ILLINOIS

The College

Since 1892, Greenville College (GC) has provided high-quality Christian higher education. Affiliated with the Free Methodist Church and accredited by the North Central Association, the College welcomes students of any denomination. Its mission is to transform students for lives of character and service through a Christ-centered education in the liberating arts and sciences. Students help with homeless projects in St. Louis, raise funds for missions, work in Big Brother/Big Sister programs, donate blood, sponsor needy children, tutor area youth, and lead discipleship groups.

Greenville's 950 students come from thirty-six states and nine countries. Numbers of men and women are about equal, and most students are 18–22 years old. Nearly half of them graduated in the top quarter of their high school classes. Ten percent of the student body are members of ethnic minority groups.

Greenville College's familylike atmosphere communicates a clear message that faculty members, administration, and students care for each other. The school has adopted Gallup's StrengthsFinder to help faculty and staff members and students identify and develop their individual talents and strengths. New students participate in an introductory program designed to help them develop the foundational skills necessary for success in any discipline. Career services personnel help students with career counseling, resume writing, and job placement.

Unmarried students live in noncoed residence halls (freshman roommates are usually assigned by the College). Students attend chapel—a time of community and worship—three times a week. Students agree to a Christian code of conduct. Covenant groups and opportunities for personal growth abound.

A large dining commons provides full food service, while the Student Union offers a variety of fast foods. The bookstore offers Christian books, magazines, and CDs as well as many varieties of "GC wear," gifts, and vital college gear. The school sponsors movies, concerts, and many other activities, and residence halls often plan activities with the brother or sister floors. Dinners, parties, and ball games appeal to many.

The first weekend in May each year is AGAPE weekend at the local county fairgrounds. Billed as the Midwest's largest Christian music festival, AGAPE provides two days of the biggest names in Christian music. Students organize all details and coordinate the event.

Through competition with the NCAA Division III and the National Christian College Athletic Association (NCCAA), Greenville offers fourteen intercollegiate sports. Men participate in baseball, basketball, cross-country, football, soccer, tennis, and track and field while women take part in basketball, cross-country, soccer, softball, tennis, track and field, and volleyball. Intramural tournaments are common. Two large gymnasiums allow for athletic activities year-round. A fully equipped health club offers exercise, swimming, and weight training.

Location

Greenville is located on I-70, 45 miles east of St. Louis. The historic southern Illinois town (population 7,000) provides a picturesque public square just two blocks from campus. Students can catch a movie at the downtown theater, drive 20 minutes south to the Carlyle water recreation area, or drive 45 minutes west to major shopping malls in the St. Louis metropolitan area.

Majors and Degrees

The College grants Bachelor of Arts and Bachelor of Science degrees. Students major in accounting, adult fitness, art, biology, chemistry, contemporary Christian music, digital media, English, environmental biology, French, history and political science, management, management information systems, marketing, mass communication, mathematics, media promotions, modern languages, music, pastoral ministry, philosophy, physics, predentistry, predietician, prelaw, premedicine, pre–medical research lab studies, pre–medical technology, prenursing, pre–occupational therapy, preoptometry, prepharmacy, pre–physical therapy/occupational therapy, pre–veterinary medicine, psychology, psychology/religion, public relations, recreation leadership, religion, religion/philosophy, secondary education, social work, sociology, Spanish, speech communication, sports management, urban/cross-cultural ministry, or youth ministry.

Greenville offers fully certified teacher training in early childhood through secondary education and special education. It has a 3-2 engineering co-op with the University of Illinois and Washington University in St. Louis and a 2-2 program with the University of Illinois and Washington University in St. Louis and a 2-2 program with St. John's College of Nursing in Springfield, Illinois, and Mennonite College of Nursing at Illinois State University.

Students with varied interests occasionally pursue multiple majors and/or participate in honors programs. In addition, the school offers an individually tailored education plan (ITEP), which allows qualified students to design their own majors.

Academic Program

Along with developing competence in at least one area of study through the completion of an academic major, the College requires each student to complete a curriculum in the liberal arts and sciences. It includes four required "core" classes in addition to general education courses. One hundred twenty-six credits are required for graduation.

Classes meet during two semesters, three summer sessions, and a mini-semester in January called Interterm. Interterm allows students to take nontraditional courses or travel to international locations with Greenville faculty members. Free tutoring for many classes is available. Most departments encourage or require an internship, co-op experience, senior project, or recital.

Greenville graduates do well. Teacher-education graduates are placed at more than twice the national average. The premedicine program places more than 90 percent of its graduates into medical school. Management students often find that summer-long internships lead to jobs after graduation.

Off-Campus Arrangements

Through associations with other Christian colleges and organizations, students may spend a semester, at little or no additional charge, at international locations, including China, Costa Rica, Egypt, England, Israel, Kenya, Mozambique, Russia, and

Zimbabwe. In the United States, students may study government in Washington, D.C., social programs in Chicago, contemporary Christian music at Martha's Vineyard in Massachusetts, film at the Los Angeles Film Center, ecology at the Au Sable Institute in Michigan, or psychology at the Focus on the Family Center in Colorado.

Academic Facilities

Greenville's library houses 130,000 books, 500 periodicals and newspapers, and more than 4,000 audiovisual items in a variety of formats. The library provides online access to many databases including an online catalog and indexes to periodicals, articles, and reference works. The media resource center, educational resource center, and the teacher education project room provide students and faculty members with media equipment and teacher education materials.

The College provides computers with Internet access for student use; computer labs are staffed with tutors, and one is open 24 hours a day. Freshmen composition classes are taught in a fully equipped computer classroom.

Science classes have well-equipped laboratories for physics, chemistry, biology, and the physical sciences. Their equipment includes an ion accelerator, mass spectrometer, and scanning tunneling microscopes. A new observatory, located at the field station a few miles from town, houses several large and small telescopes.

Music facilities offer practice rooms with pianos (both acoustic and electronic) and organs, a piano classroom, and several digital recording studios.

Costs

Greenville's comprehensive fee for 2002–03 was $21,342, including $15,776 for full-time tuition (12–17 credit hours) and $5566 for room and board. Books, supplies, and laboratory fees are extra.

Financial Aid

Students receive financial aid based on merit, need, or a combination of both. Each year, hundreds of highly qualified high school seniors come to campus to compete for four-year honor scholarships of $12,000 to $28,000. Other aid is available for leadership and service in high school.

Many students receive need-based scholarships as well. Students complete the Free Application for Federal Student Aid (FAFSA) in early spring to determine their eligibility for college, state, and federal assistance during the academic year. The Financial Aid Office assists students in getting loans from the College and external sources and in finding campus employment.

Faculty

Greenville's teaching faculty consists of 57 full-time members and 33 adjuncts; the student-faculty ratio is 16:1. All professors teach and advise students. Faculty members regularly publish articles in scholarly journals and author textbooks. Sixty percent have doctoral or terminal degrees.

The Council of Independent Colleges identified Greenville as one of the top ten liberal arts colleges in the nation for excellence in the academic workplace and for an extraordinarily high level of faculty involvement. Faculty members coach sports, advise clubs, and help in all areas of campus life. Recently, the Coalition for Christian Colleges and Universities recognized Greenville College for meeting students' expectations for a caring faculty. Most live less than 1 mile from campus and invite students into their homes regularly.

Student Government

The Senate is the student governing body. Its elected president is an ex-officio member of Faculty Council, the faculty governing body. Students manage the student newspaper, yearbook, radio station, AGAPE music festival, homecoming, concerts, social activities, and all clubs and student organizations.

Admission Requirements

In addition to an application, prospective students submit ACT or SAT I scores, transcripts, and references. The College encourages all prospects to visit the campus prior to making a final enrollment decision. A personal interview and/or testing may be required.

A college-preparatory program is recommended in high school, including four years of English and three years each of science, math, and foreign language. International students receive individual evaluation and may need to provide a TOEFL score.

Application and Information

Students may call, write or visit the Web site for application materials. Greenville encourages students to apply as early as possible during their senior year. Applicants generally receive admission notice within two weeks of the College receiving all necessary materials. For further information, applicants should call or write:

Office of Admissions
Greenville College
315 East College Avenue
Greenville, Illinois 62246
Telephone: 618-664-2800
800-345-4440 (toll-free)
Fax: 618-664-9841
E-mail: admissions@greenville.edu
World Wide Web: http://www.greenville.edu

Students walking on the campus of Greenville College.

HEIDELBERG COLLEGE

TIFFIN, OHIO

The College

Heidelberg College, founded in 1850, is a selective, private coeducational liberal arts college that is affiliated with the United Church of Christ. Believing that a liberal education is the best career preparation a person can have to confront the challenges of the future creatively, Heidelberg College offers students a solid base on which to grow in their professional and personal lives. Heidelberg's dynamic community maintains a touch of its Old World heritage yet continually brings innovative ideas into the classroom.

The current undergraduate enrollment is about 1,200 men and women. Students come to Heidelberg from twenty-two states and nine other countries. This cross-cultural mix helps to keep the campus diverse and to broaden students' knowledge and understanding of ethnic and cultural differences.

Heidelberg has more than sixty campus organizations that offer opportunities for leadership, service, and fellowship. Included in these organizations are thirteen departmental clubs and fifteen departmental honorary societies that sponsor discussions, lectures, and field trips. Other cocurricular activities include a student-edited and student-managed newspaper, a television station that broadcasts daily news, forensic programs, choral and instrumental groups, and intramural sports. The Communication and Theatre Arts Department presents four or more dramatic productions each year.

A member of the Ohio Athletic Conference, NCAA Division III, Heidelberg offers nine varsity men's sports: baseball, basketball, cross-country, football, golf, soccer, tennis, track, and wrestling. The women's varsity sports program, among the first in Ohio to be affiliated with the NCAA Division III, fields eight intercollegiate teams: basketball, cross-country, golf, soccer, softball, tennis, track, and volleyball. Athletic facilities include a weight room, handball/racquetball courts, locker rooms, and an eight-lane, all-weather track, which is considered one of the finest in Ohio.

Heidelberg College also offers Master of Arts degree programs in counseling and education as well as a Master of Business Administration (M.B.A.) degree program.

Location

Heidelberg's 110-acre campus is located in Tiffin, Ohio, a town of 20,000. It is the center of a prosperous agricultural and business area. Downtown Tiffin, within half a mile of campus, is traditional in appearance; its charming brickwork stores and large lampposts trimmed in wrought iron resemble an old German town. Four metropolitan areas are within easy driving distance: Toledo, 50 miles; Columbus, 86 miles; Cleveland, 92 miles; and Detroit, 103 miles.

Majors and Degrees

Heidelberg offers a wide variety of undergraduate majors and several preprofessional programs within nineteen academic departments. It awards the Bachelor of Arts, Bachelor of Science, and Bachelor of Music degrees. Majors are available in accounting, anthropology, athletic training, biology, business administration, chemistry, communication and theater arts (communication/media, theater), computer information systems, computer science, economics, education (early childhood, middle childhood, adolescence to young adult, intervention specialist studies, multiage German, multiage Spanish, multiage health and physical education, multiage music education), English (literature, writing), environmental biology, German, health–physical education and recreation, health services administration, history, international studies (international relations, cross-cultural studies), management science, mathematics, music, music education, music industry, music performance, music performance pedagogy, music theory/composition, philosophy, physics, political science, psychology (child and adolescent, mental health, biopsychology, general), public relations, religion, Spanish, and water resources (biology, chemistry, geology). Preprofessional and cooperative degree programs include dentistry, engineering, environmental management, law, medical technology, medicine, nursing, occupational therapy, optometry, osteopathy, physical therapy, physician assistant studies, podiatry, and veterinary science.

Academic Program

To graduate, a student must complete 120 academic semester hours, comprising 36–45 semester hours of general education, 40 semester hours in a selected major, and 35–44 hours of electives. Two credits in health and physical education and 1 credit for Total Student Development (TSD) are also required.

Off-Campus Arrangements

To supplement their course work, students may choose from a variety of off-campus study programs that provide practical, career-related experience. For example, students interested in studying habitats not found in northwestern Ohio may do on-site field research in Caribbean biogeography in Belize and on-site field research in the Appalachian mountains of West Virginia. Students may also participate in the excavation of an archaeological site.

Opportunities for practical experience in research are also available through Heidelberg's nationally recognized Water Quality Laboratory, which has ongoing research in water-quality studies involving both northern Ohio streams and Lake Erie. Heidelberg's internship program also enables students to participate in on-the-job internships in several area businesses and industries.

Students interested in studying in Washington, D.C., may take part in the Washington Semester at American University; those interested in studying abroad may participate in Heidelberg's own programs in Germany (at Heidelberg University) and Spain or may participate in programs arranged cooperatively with other colleges and universities in such locations as England, Latin America, Africa, and the Far East.

Heidelberg also has cooperative degree programs in engineering with Case Western Reserve University and in forestry with Duke University.

Academic Facilities

Beeghly Library, containing 154,000 volumes, is the intellectual heart of Heidelberg College. The three-story circular library holds a seventy-seat audiovisual room, a seminar and computer room, the Rickard-Mayer Rare Books Room, and the Besse Collection of Letters. Bareis Hall of Science has excellent laboratories and facilities where students may observe demonstrations and experiments. Also located in Bareis Hall are the computer center and the Heidelberg Water Quality Laboratory.

The computer center provides access to Macintosh and PC-compatible computers. All of these systems are connected to a campuswide network providing e-mail, file transfer, World Wide Web, and full access to the Internet. The high number of computers and terminals available for student use in addition to the convenience of the computer center hours are outstanding strengths of the College. Additional computer facilities are located in Brenneman Music Hall, the Pfleiderer Center for Religion and the Humanities, and the Aigler Alumni Building. Founders Hall houses a 250-seat performance theater and a rehearsal theater; an FM radio station, WHEI; television studio WHEI-TV; video taping rooms; costume rooms; a dance studio; and offices and classrooms for the Departments of Communication and Theatre Arts and the Languages.

Costs

For the academic year 2003–04, new student tuition and fees are $13,672; room and board are approximately $6275.

Financial Aid

More than 95 percent of the undergraduate student body at Heidelberg receive financial aid. College and government programs—including scholarships, grants, loans, and jobs—total about $11.3 million annually. Government assistance includes the Federal Pell Grant, direct loan programs, the Federal Supplemental Educational Opportunity Grant, and the Federal Work-Study Program. Heidelberg offers students who meet various academic requirements a number of grants and scholarships that are renewable if eligibility is maintained.

Faculty

Close personal interaction between students and professors is one of Heidelberg's primary strengths. Sixty-two full-time professors serve the student body, and the faculty-student ratio is 1:12. More than 80 percent of the faculty members hold doctoral degrees in their disciplines. Heidelberg's faculty members are readily available to answer questions and meet with students outside of the classroom.

Student Government

Because students are voting members of 90 percent of the faculty committees, their concerns are heard and have an impact on academic standards, athletics, educational policies, and religious life. Heidelberg's Student Senate is made up of 25 students and a Student Affairs adviser.

Admission Requirements

Heidelberg's selective admission policy seeks to admit those students who will benefit from the educational offerings of the College and who will contribute to the shared life of the campus community. The Admission Committee considers each applicant individually to determine if the student will be able to successfully fulfill the academic responsibilities of a Heidelberg student. The applicant's high school achievement record is the single most important factor considered. Other factors considered are ACT or SAT I scores, cocurricular involvement, character, talent, and teacher recommendations.

Application and Information

Although Heidelberg follows a rolling admission policy, applicants are strongly encouraged to complete this process before January 1. Once all admission credentials are received, applicants are notified of the College's admission decision within two weeks.

For additional information, students should contact:

Office of Admission
Heidelberg College
310 East Market Street
Tiffin, Ohio 44883
Telephone: 419-448-2330
800-HEIDELBERG (toll-free)
Fax: 419-448-2334
E-mail: adminfo@heidelberg.edu

Founders Hall (1851), the oldest building on the Heidelberg campus, is one of ten listed on the National Register of Historic Places.

HIRAM COLLEGE

HIRAM, OHIO

The College

Founded in 1850, Hiram College cherishes its heritage as an institution of academic excellence and rare distinction. Hiram's 900 students come from twenty-five states and nineteen countries and represent more than twenty-five different religions. SAT I and ACT scores of Hiram's entering freshmen exceed national norms: in 2002, SAT I medians were 570 (verbal) and 570 (math); the ACT composite median was 24. Between 50 and 60 percent of the College's graduates go on to graduate school or professional school within five years. The College was awarded a Phi Beta Kappa chapter in 1971.

Ninety-five percent of Hiram's students live in the eleven residence halls and eat their meals on campus. Newer College buildings are designed to complement Hiram's old, distinguished Western Reserve architecture. Student services include a health center, a fitness center, a sports medicine clinic, a career placement office, professional counseling on a wide range of personal and academic concerns, optional religious services and activities, and sports for everyone. There are honorary societies, social clubs, music and drama groups, student publications, religious groups, and student government and political and social-action groups. The campus radio station, TV station, and student publications are directed by the students themselves.

Location

Hiram's campus is in the scenic, rural Western Reserve area of northeastern Ohio. Located in Portage County, the campus is about 35 miles southeast of Cleveland. The area is served by excellent state and federal highway systems, which make the College easily accessible. Cleveland Hopkins Airport and the Canton Akron Airport are a 45-minute drive from Hiram, and campus cars can be commissioned on advance request, providing transportation to and from the airport. The campus is a day's drive or less from New England and northern East Coast cities and about a 6-hour drive from Baltimore, Chicago, and Washington, D.C. By air, it is an hour from the East Coast and less than an hour from Chicago and the Middle Atlantic coast.

Majors and Degrees

Hiram College awards the Bachelor of Arts (B.A.). Areas of major concentration are: art, art history, biology, biomedical humanities, chemistry, classical studies, communication, computer science, economics, elementary and secondary education, English, environmental studies, French, German, history, integrated language arts, integrated social studies, management, mathematics, music, philosophy, physics, political science, psychobiology, psychology, religious studies, social science, sociology, Spanish, and theater arts. Minors are available in most areas of study as well as in exercise and sport science, health care humanities, international studies, photography, and writing.

Preprofessional programs offer preparation for study in a wide variety of fields, including dentistry, engineering, law, medicine, physical therapy, and veterinary medicine.

Hiram also offers a cooperative, dual-degree program in engineering with Case Western Reserve University and Washington University, leading to a Bachelor of Arts degree from Hiram in a field of science or mathematics and a Bachelor of Science in engineering from the cooperating engineering school.

Academic Program

Hiram's academic calendar, the Hiram Plan, is unique among colleges and universities. Each fifteen-week semester is divided into a twelve-week and a three-week session. During the three-week session, students take only one intensive course. The plan provides two formats for learning, which increases opportunity for small group study with faculty, study in special topics, hands-on learning through field trips and internships, and study abroad.

Hiram College's commitment to the liberal arts is manifested in a core curriculum required of all students. Required courses include the Freshman Colloquium, a small, seminar course on a special topic taught by a student's adviser; First Year Seminar, emphasizing critical thinking, effective writing, and speaking; and a sequence of interdisciplinary courses.

The course of study in most areas of major concentration is specified by the departments and divisions. Students generally take ten courses from within a department, as well as two or three courses from related or supporting departments. Alternatively, a student, with the assistance of the adviser, may develop an area of concentration that consists of related courses from different academic areas, crossing departmental lines to focus on particular needs or interests. A student may also submit a proposal for an individually designed program to the Area of Concentration Board.

Off-Campus Arrangements

A number of domestic and international off-campus programs and study opportunities are available. Programs in Australia, England, France, Germany, Italy, Mexico, Turkey, and other locations are conducted by the College's own teaching staff. Study-abroad programs are available to students regardless of their major discipline, and more than 50 percent of the College's graduates have participated. Hiram students may also spend a semester at the School of Social Sciences and Public Affairs of the American University in Washington, D.C. Another facet of Hiram's off-campus opportunities is study at John Cabot University, a Hiram affiliate, which is the major American university in Rome. Students may also take advantage of exchange programs with Mithibai College of the University of Bombay, India, and Kansai University of Foreign Studies in Osaka, Japan. Other opportunities are offered through the College's affiliation with the Institute for European Studies and the Institute for Asian Studies.

Internships with corporations and agencies are also available in all academic departments, and arrangements are made for students on an individual basis.

Other opportunities for off-campus study in marine science are described in the section below.

Academic Facilities

The Esther and Carl Gerstacker Science Hall opened in January 2000. This $6.2-million state-of-the-art facility includes modern chemical laboratories specially designed for undergraduate instruction and research, plus a substantial amount of new chemical instrumentation. A $12-million addition to the Student Recreation Center is scheduled to begin in 2004. Plans for this addition include new classrooms, offices, and recreation areas. Hiram opened a $7.2-million library in 1995. This five-level facility contains nearly 180,000 volumes in open stacks and features a reference area that includes recent government documents (the library is one of only 1,400 federal depositories in the U.S.); a media center featuring a listening library, a videotape collection, and a video production room; a computer area equipped with CD-ROM and printers, with access to the Internet and other resources on the information superhighway; and an archival pavilion that houses a number of special collections relating to the history of the Western Reserve, including the papers of notable Hiram alumni James A. Garfield, twentieth president of the United States, and poet Vachel Lindsay.

Other resources include the Stephens Memorial Observatory; the Center for International Studies; the Center for Literature, Medicine, and the Health Care Professions; the Writing Center; InterVIEW™, a PC-based video conferencing and interview system; and SIGI Career Guidance System. The computer facilities at Hiram include an AlphaServer and IBM pSeries UNIX servers for administrative use and workstations and servers for word processing and office automation. These computers are networked, via a fast Ethernet connection, to all campus buildings and offices, including the residence halls. In addition, personal computers are available for student use in several computer labs located in the library, residence halls, and other locations throughout the campus. Hiram is one of only a few undergraduate colleges in Ohio directly connected to the Cray Supercomputer at the Ohio Supercomputer Center in Columbus.

The 260-acre James H. Barrow Field Station encompasses a diversity of habitats that allow for the investigation of both aquatic and terrestrial ecosystems. These include permanent and temporary ponds, a natural and a simulated stream, old fields, and early- and late-successional forests, including a unique beech-maple climax forest. Facilities at the station include the Frohring Laboratory Building, which houses laboratories as well as natural history display areas open to the public; an observation building; a solar-heated, earth-bermed Aquatics Building that houses an experimental stream; and the Ruth E. Kennedy Memorial Nature Trail. The station buildings and the nature trail were built and are maintained by faculty members and students. Recent independent and/or team research projects involving students and faculty members from a variety of disciplines include examinations of the effects of fertilizer enrichment on an old-field ecosystem, the distribution of blood parasites in natural populations of small mammals, and the nesting success of bluebirds.

Northwoods Field Station in upper Michigan, a day's drive from Hiram, offers an additional facility for field trips, summer course work, and research activities.

Students interested in marine science have opportunities for advanced work at Shoals Marine Laboratory off the coast of New Hampshire and at the Gulf Coast Research Laboratory in Mississippi. The College's affiliations with these facilities provide students with field experience in Hiram courses and the opportunity to enroll in any of more than twenty specialized summer courses.

Costs

Costs for 2002–03 were $19,650 for tuition and $6820 for room and board. Fees were $789, including a one-time fee of $225 that was charged to freshmen for the orientation program.

Financial Aid

More than 75 percent of Hiram's students receive financial aid based on need. All financial aid awards are made on a one-year basis, and each year a new Free Application for Federal Student Aid (FAFSA) must be submitted to determine eligibility. Most financial aid at Hiram is a combination of a loan, a job, and a scholarship or grant-in-aid. Scholarships awarded on the basis of merit are also available and range from $3000 to $12,000 per year. Aid includes Federal Pell Grants, Federal Supplemental Educational Opportunity Grants, Federal Perkins Loans, Federal Stafford Student Loans, state grants, Federal Work-Study awards, and veterans' benefits. Campus employment is available regardless of aid eligibility.

Faculty

Hiram has a teaching faculty of 68 full-time members, 95 percent of whom hold earned doctorates or the appropriate terminal degree. The student-faculty ratio is 11:1. The ideal of a "community of scholars" thrives at Hiram, where students engage in research side by side with their professors, enjoy extracurricular activities with their teachers, and reach out with the faculty to serve the community. Faculty concern and guidance begin even before the formal opening of the academic year. One week prior to opening, faculty members work with their advisees, groups of about 15 freshmen, as part of the first-year orientation program. This one-week program, the New Student Institute, is followed by a semester-long seminar in which the freshmen continue to meet as a group. Seminar topics introduce students to scholarship in the liberal arts tradition. Approximately twenty seminars are offered each year.

Student Government

The student governing body, or Student Senate, composed in part of members elected from the academic departments and residence halls, is very active at Hiram. The Senate administers a $150,000 student activities budget and is involved in almost all aspects of college policymaking and governance. It holds seats with faculty, staff, and administrators on most College committees, the College Executive Committee, and the Student Life Subcommittee of Hiram's Board of Trustees. The Kennedy Center Programming Board, an arm of the student government, plans recreational and cultural activities for the campus community.

Admission Requirements

Admission to Hiram College is competitive. The admission process attempts to bring to Hiram students who have the ability and desire to benefit from the College's educational programs. Candidates should have pursued a strong secondary school program of college preparation in the humanities, sciences, and social sciences. All applicants are required to submit SAT I or ACT scores.

Application and Information

Application materials include the completed application form; a secondary school report, which must be completed and returned to Hiram directly by the high school guidance counselor; the results of the SAT I or ACT; and an essay. Teacher recommendations are also required. Hiram employs a rolling admission plan, but for maximum scholarship consideration, applications should be submitted by February 1. An early decision option is also available. Applicants are encouraged to visit the campus. The Office of Admission, located in Teachout-Price Hall, is open year-round for interviews from 9 a.m. to 4 p.m. on weekdays and from 9 a.m. to noon on Saturdays (except during the summer months). Prospective students should address questions to:

Director of Admission
Hiram College
Hiram, Ohio 44234
Telephone: 330-569-5169
800-362-5280 (toll-free)
E-mail: admission@hiram.edu
World Wide Web: http://www.hiram.edu

Esther and Carl Gerstacker Science Hall.

ILLINOIS INSTITUTE OF TECHNOLOGY

CHICAGO, ILLINOIS

The Institute

Illinois Institute of Technology (IIT) is a private, Ph.D.-granting research university with undergraduate programs in architecture, engineering, humanities, psychology, and science. One of the sixteen institutions in the Association of Independent Technological Universities (AITU), IIT offers exceptional preparation for professions that require technological sophistication. Through a committed faculty and close personal attention, IIT provides a challenging academic program focused on the rigor of the real world. The internationally famous main campus is based on a master plan developed by the late Ludwig Mies van der Rohe, one of the most influential architects of the century, who served for twenty years as director of IIT's College of Architecture. An independent university, the Institute includes the College of Architecture, the Armour College of Engineering and Science, the Institute of Psychology, the Stuart School of Business, the Institute of Design, and the Chicago-Kent College of Law.

The more than 6,000 students at IIT (more than 1,800 of whom are undergraduates) are encouraged to participate in the many social, cultural, and athletic opportunities available. Student activities include the campus newspaper, the radio station, special interest clubs, theater and music groups, intramural and varsity athletics, fraternities and sororities, honor societies, professional societies, student government, residence hall organizations, and the student-run Union Board. Campus facilities include the union building, which has its own bowling alley and recreation area; a new campus center; a convenience store and campus book store; a gymnasium; seven residence halls; six new residence halls for fall 2003; one resident sorority house; and seven resident fraternity houses. Counseling, job placement, and student health services are included in the various campus services.

Location

IIT stands in the midst of a developing urban area. It is 1 mile west of Lake Michigan and 1 block from the White Sox ballpark. The campus is located approximately 3 miles south of the Chicago Loop, offering students unlimited opportunities to enjoy art, music, drama, films, museums, and other entertainment. Also convenient to the campus are a number of recreational areas, including McCormick Place exhibition hall, Soldier Field, Grant Park, Lincoln Park Zoo, various bicycle paths, and lakefront beaches. IIT is easily accessible to the rest of Chicago via two major expressways. Bus and elevated railroad lines have stops on campus, and the IIT shuttle bus provides free transportation between the campus and the university's Downtown Campus in Chicago's West Loop area.

Majors and Degrees

The Armour College of Engineering and Science offers the Bachelor of Science in Engineering with specializations in aerospace, architectural, biomedical, chemical, civil, computer, electrical, mechanical, and metallurgical and materials engineering and engineering management, and applied computer science as well as a Bachelor of Science degree in biology, chemistry, computer information systems, humanities, Internet communication, applied mathematics, molecular biochemistry and biophysics, physics, political science, professional and technical communication, and psychology.

The College of Architecture awards the Bachelor of Architecture degree through its five-year professional degree program.

There are various options and minors available within each curriculum, such as artificial intelligence, bioengineering, business, computer-aided drafting, law, management, manufacturing technology, military science, psychology, public administration, and technical communications. Other individualized specializations may be arranged with approval of the dean. Combined undergraduate/graduate degrees include those offered in conjunction with business administration (B.S. and M.B.A.), law (B.S. and J.D.), and public administration (B.S. and M.P.A.).

Along with its traditional premed program, IIT has also established an honors combined program in engineering and medicine (B.S. and M.D.) with the Finch University of Health Sciences/Chicago Medical School and Rush Medical College and an honors research program. IIT also offers an honors combined program in law (B.S. and J.D.) with the Chicago-Kent College of Law. Students interested in an honors program must submit an undergraduate application and a supplemental application for the graduate portion of the program. All application materials are available online.

Academic Program

While requirements vary according to the major, all IIT students complete a general education core, which includes a minimum of 7 semester hours in mathematics and computer science, 11 semester hours in natural science or engineering, 12 semester hours in the humanities, and 12 semester hours in the social sciences. Students pursuing a Bachelor of Science in Engineering or in the physical sciences take, in addition, a program that includes further study in mathematics and computer science, chemistry, and physics.

IIT's mission is to educate students for complex professional roles in a changing world and to advance knowledge through research and scholarship. The Institute is committed to the educational ideal of small undergraduate classes and individual mentoring. IIT's unique Introduction to the Professions program brings students and senior faculty members together each week in small groups, where students interact with their advisers as both teachers and mentors. Throughout the curricula, the IIT interprofessional projects provide a learning environment in which interdisciplinary teams of students apply theoretical knowledge gained in the classroom and laboratory to real-world projects sponsored by industry and government. Many IIT students further enhance their education through a wide variety of research and entrepreneurial projects.

Cooperative education is encouraged. This career development program begins with a freshman year of full-time study and then alternates semesters of study and employment in industry for approximately four additional years. Placement services are provided by the university. Ninety-four percent of recent graduates were placed in jobs in the fields of their majors or went on to graduate or professional schools.

Study abroad is available in several academic disciplines.

Academic Facilities

As the central library, the Paul V. Galvin Library provides a broad range of services, including information on engineering, business, science, mathematics, the humanities, architecture, and design via the Internet; numerous electronic and paper-based databases; a document delivery service; interlibrary loan; and special collections. The main campus operates DEC minicomputers, a Silicon Graphics "Challenge" UNIX multiprocessor, and local UNIX servers. Terminals and microcomputers are located in most academic buildings across the campus, in residence halls, and in Galvin Library. Seminars, tutorials, and computer lab work are conducted in microcomputer classrooms. Among IIT's thirty-two research centers are the Center for Synchrotron Radiation Research, the Fluid Dynamics Research Center, and the Research Laboratory in Human Biomechanics. Most research centers offer undergraduates opportunities to participate on their projects.

Costs

Annual tuition for 2002–03 was $19,200. Other expenses are $5882 for room and board and approximately $1000 for books, $1200 for transportation costs, and $2100 for personal expenses. Additional fees are $100. The estimated annual total for freshmen is $29,482. Annual tuition covers the fall and spring semesters.

Financial Aid

Most full-time undergraduates at IIT receive financial aid from a variety of sources. IIT participates in the Federal Perkins Loan, Federal Work-Study, Federal Pell Grant, Federal Supplemental Educational Opportunity Grant, federally insured student loan, Illinois State Scholarship Commission Monetary Award, Illinois Guaranteed Loan, and Federal PLUS loan programs and similar programs. In addition, IIT provides generous merit-based and need-based scholarships and loans from its own funds and from those supported by a number of companies and other organizations. The NEXT Initiative offers four-year scholarships ranging from $57,600 to $88,500 for the study of any major. A supplemental application is required for NEXT scholarships. All admitted students are automatically reviewed for tuition scholarships. More than 500 are awarded each year. Athletic scholarships are also available for qualified students. Two other programs may be utilized by students working to supplement their financial aid: on-campus employment and the cooperative education program. IIT requires the Free Application for Federal Student Aid (FAFSA). No additional applications or forms are required.

Army, Naval, and Air Force ROTC programs are offered. ROTC scholarship winners receive supplemental scholarships from IIT.

Faculty

There are 317 full-time faculty members and 270 industry professionals as part-time faculty members. The student-faculty ratio is approximately 12:1. All members of the senior teaching faculty instruct in both upper- and lower-division courses. Ninety-eight percent hold doctoral degrees or the highest professional degree in their area.

Student Government

The Student Leadership Committee (SLC) is a vital force in the IIT community. It acts as the students' official voice in communications with faculty and administration, and it plans, develops, and supervises most of the activities pertaining to campus life. In addition to having its own standing committees, SLC is represented on seven of the ten institutional committees pertaining to undergraduates.

Admission Requirements

Admission evaluation is a thorough, personal process. Of paramount consideration is the student's academic performance in high school, specifically in areas that are vital to the student's major at IIT. Minimum high school preparation includes 16 units of credit, including at least 4 units in English, 4 units in mathematics through pre-calculus, and 3 units of science with 2 lab sciences (chemistry and physics required). Calculus is encouraged but not required. Chemistry is strongly recommended.

A completed application, recommendations, test scores—either SAT I or ACT—and an official high school transcript are required for admission. Interviews are not required. Supplemental applications and materials are required for the Honors Program in Engineering and Medicine, the Honors Law Program, and for the NEXT Initiative Scholarship Program. Special deadlines apply to these programs. All materials are available online.

Application and Information

Applications are reviewed on a rolling basis. Students are encouraged to apply as early as possible; an online application is available at http://www.iit.edu/~apply. In general, applicants can expect notification within two weeks after their completed applications are received.

For further information, students should contact:

Office of Admission
Illinois Institute of Technology
10 West 33rd Street
Chicago, Illinois 60616-3793
Telephone: 312-567-3025 (from Chicago)
800-448-2329 (toll-free outside Chicago)
Fax: 312-567-6939
E-mail: admission@iit.edu
World Wide Web: http://www.iit.edu

INTERNATIONAL ACADEMY OF DESIGN & TECHNOLOGY

CHICAGO, ILLINOIS

The Academy

The International Academy of Design & Technology–Chicago is a postsecondary, degree and certification granting institution with career-based curricula and professional staff members who contribute to students' development in their chosen fields. The objectives of the Academy are to provide a high-quality education and prepare students for positions in fields related to their area of study; to provide students with a professional environment that fosters cultural enrichment and personal development; to sustain a diverse faculty and staff of professionals; to maintain high-quality curricula that are sensitive to industry needs as defined by the Academy's advisory board; and to offer career-planning services leading to employment opportunities for graduates that allow them to utilize their knowledge, skills, and talents.

The International Academy of Design & Technology was founded in 1977 by Clem Stein Jr. as a private, coeducational institution. In 1983, the Academy opened a campus in Toronto, Canada. The Tampa, Florida campus was opened in 1984, and in 1987, the fourth campus in Montreal, Canada was opened. In 1997, Career Education Corporation acquired the Academy. Career Education Corporation operates postsecondary institutions throughout the United States and abroad. In 2001, the Academy changed its name from the International Academy of Merchandising & Design to the International Academy of Design & Technology, which better reflects the infusion of technology into all of the program curricula.

The Academy is approved by the Illinois State Board of Education and authorized by the Illinois Board of Higher Education to grant the Bachelor of Arts degree in merchandising management; the Bachelor of Fine Arts degree in advertising and design, fashion design, interior design, and multimedia production and design; and the Associate of Applied Science degree in advertising and design, computer graphics, e-commerce, fashion design, interactive media, merchandising management, and PC/LAN. The Academy also offers PC/LAN certification.

The International Academy of Design & Technology–Chicago is incorporated under the laws of the state of Illinois. The Accrediting Council for Independent Colleges and Schools (ACICS), a nationally recognized accrediting agency, accredits this privately supported educational institution as a senior college. The interior design program is accredited by the Foundation for Interior Design Education Research (FIDER).

The Academy's campus opened in downtown Chicago in 1978, and its enrollment has grown from 160 students in its first class to more than 2,000 students.

In its ongoing commitment to provide innovative, practical education, the Academy depends on the industries it serves for advice and counsel, and each department has an advisory board of leaders in business and education to provide such services.

Location

The Academy's campus is located at historic One North State Street in the center of Chicago's fashion, interior design, and advertising industries. All forms of public transportation easily access the facility. Ample parking is available nearby.

Within walking distance of the campus are the Merchandise Mart and Apparel Center Complex, the retail shops of North Michigan Avenue, Marshall Field's, Carson Pirie Scott, and a multitude of graphic design and interior design firms. Nearby cultural and educational resources include the Art Institute of Chicago, the Harold Washington Library, the Cultural Center of the Chicago Public Library, the Athenaeum Museum of Architecture and Design, the Chicago Architecture Foundation, and the Goodman Theatre, among others. The natural beauty of Grant Park is the ideal complement to the Academy's exciting urban location.

The Academy strives to provide a safe environment for its students and staff. Trespassing and solicitation laws are strictly enforced. The facility is secured each evening, with all offices and records locked.

Majors and Degrees

The International Academy of Design & Technology's Chicago campus awards the Bachelor of Arts degree in merchandising management and the Bachelor of Fine Arts degree in advertising and design, fashion design, interior design, and multimedia production and design.

The Chicago campus also offers two-year programs leading to the Associate of Applied Science degree in advertising and design, computer graphics, e-commerce, fashion design, interactive media, merchandising management, and PC/LAN. The Academy also offers a certificate program in PC/LAN.

Academic Program

The programs of the Academy involve both classroom education and supervised activities off campus that are designed to prepare students for entry-level positions in their chosen field. Students must take a minimum of 180 quarter hours of study to earn the baccalaureate degree. Transfer credits are acceptable in all programs. Students must take a minimum of 90 quarter hours to earn the Associate of Applied Science degree and must complete all prescribed courses satisfactorily with a minimum grade point average of 2.0.

Although working in the field is not mandatory, most Academy students are employed on a part-time basis in a fashion or design-related business or industry. Often, these part-time efforts lead to full-time placement upon graduation. Job-evaluation conferences are held quarterly, and students attend these conferences prior to placement interviews.

The curriculum for each program is reviewed periodically by the faculty members, program directors, and members of the faculty advisory council, who, along with the president and deans, constitute the curriculum advisory committee. Members of the faculty advisory council are experienced professionals in the fields of fashion, interior design, advertising, merchandising, multimedia production and design, computer graphics, interactive media, and PC/LAN who provide the Academy with counsel on a variety of subjects and also participate in seminars. These successful practitioners form an essential link between the academic world and the world that students enter upon graduation.

The Academy's programs are arranged into four quarters of eleven weeks each. A normal full-time load is 15 credit hours per quarter. As a result of the career-oriented emphasis of the Academy, course work is highly specialized and prepares students for entry into a career field. From the point at which they begin their studies at the Academy and continuing through graduation, students are given personal, one-on-one academic guidance. Students are regularly advised by the Academy's faculty members regarding their progress in classes.

Off-Campus Arrangements

The Academy has a tradition of going beyond the classroom for educational opportunities. Students regularly engage in learning activities within the local community. Recent domestic trips have included visits to New York City. The Academy encourages students to study abroad and assists students with finding suitable programs.

Academic Facilities

The Academy's classrooms are designed to facilitate learning and consist of lecture rooms, computer labs, drafting labs, design studios, and sewing and pattern-making rooms. The computer labs are equipped with Macintosh and IBM-compatible personal computers used for instruction and practice in computer-aided design (CAD), graphic design, word processing, database management, and spreadsheet analysis. Each student has his own computer on which to work. Classrooms are available for independent study when they are not occupied by classes.

Costs

Full-time tuition for the 2002–03 academic year at the Chicago campus ranges from $12,300 to $12,900. Books and supplies range from $300 to $2000.

Financial Aid

The Academy helps students find the financial resources they need to achieve their educational goals. The college participates in the Federal Pell Grant, Federal Supplemental Education Opportunity Grant (FSEOG), Federal Work-Study Program, Federal Stafford Student Loans, and the Federal PLUS Programs. In addition to state and federal aid, the Academy has its own scholarship programs. The Career Development Office assists students in finding part-time employment, which provides valuable hands-on experience and helps to meet the cost of their education.

Faculty

The Academy's faculty has more than 100 members who serve on an adjunct and full-time basis. Each faculty member comes directly from industry and professional work, and all have had appropriate education in their teaching field. About one half of the teaching staff has advanced degrees. The ratio of students to faculty members is 15:1. As a result of their close relationships with other professionals, the Academy's faculty and staff members can easily arrange for well-qualified guest speakers and for field trips to normally inaccessible locations.

Student Government

The Academy has a Student Council, and there are a variety of student activities available. The Student Council meets quarterly to discuss issues pertaining to student campus life at the Academy. The Academy's student organizations are geared to the enhancement of career preparation and the development of leadership skills. There are student chapters of the American Society of Interior Designers (ASID), the American Marketing Association (AMA), and Fashion Group International (FGI) on campus. These groups introduce students to the standards set by professional organizations and provide access to professional seminars and workshops.

Admission Requirements

Pursuant to the mission of the institution, the Academy seeks to admit to degree programs students who possess appropriate credentials and have demonstrated capacity or potential for successful completion of the educational programs offered by the institution. To that end, the institution evaluates all students and makes admission decisions on an individual basis. To assist the admissions personnel in making informed decisions, an admissions interview is required.

Transfer students meeting admission requirements are accepted. It is the student's responsibility to have a transcript from the postsecondary institution previously attended forwarded to the Academy. Credit may be given for a course taken at the previous institution if it is comparable in scope and length to an Academy course.

Application and Information

Prospective students should apply for admissions as soon as possible in order to be officially accepted for a specific program and starting date. Applicants and their families are given an opportunity to tour the Academy and to see its equipment and facilities. There is also an opportunity to ask questions relating to the Academy's curricula and career goals.

Once the applicant has submitted a complete application, a $50 application fee, an enrollment agreement, and evidence of graduation from a high school or the equivalent, the Academy reviews the information and informs the applicant of its decision.

For further information, students should contact:

Robyn Palmersheim, Vice President of Admissions
International Academy of Design & Technology
One North State Street, Suite 400
Chicago, Illinois 60602-3300
Telephone: 312-980-9200
877-222-3369 (toll-free)
Fax: 312-541-3929
E-mail: info@iadtchicago.com
World Wide Web: http://www.iadtchicago.com

IOWA STATE UNIVERSITY OF SCIENCE AND TECHNOLOGY

IOWA STATE UNIVERSITY

AMES, IOWA

The University

Iowa State University of Science and Technology (Iowa State), a public, broad-based international university of 27,898 students, was established in 1858 as one of the first U.S. land-grant colleges. It is a member of the prestigious Association of American Universities and is accredited by the North Central Association of Colleges and Schools. All fifty states and 118 countries are represented in the student body, exposing students to ideas from other cultures both in and out of the classroom.

Iowa State has grown in size and reputation to become one of the nation's leading educational institutions and has made significant contributions to the development of the United States and the world. Revolutionary innovations include the world's first electronic digital computer, the digital encoding process that led to the development of facsimile machines, and LoSatSoy, a new cooking oil low in saturated fat. Iowa State's graduates include George Washington Carver, one of the nation's most distinguished educators and plant scientists; Carrie Chapman Catt, a leader in the women's suffrage movement; and John Vincent Atanasoff who, as a faculty member at Iowa State, invented the electronic digital computer.

Nearly 8,000 students live on campus in nineteen residence halls and twelve apartment-style buildings. Each of the nineteen residence halls are divided into houses, which are small-group living arrangements of about 60 residents. Wellness houses, learning communities, honors houses, and alcohol- and smoke-free houses are a few of the options available. The Department of Residence is in the midst of a $105-million renovation and improvement project. In addition, 3,000 undergraduates participate in Iowa State's national award-winning Greek system, which encompasses twenty-eight fraternities, fifteen sororities, and seven National Pan-Hellenic chapters conveniently located near the campus.

More than 500 clubs and organizations provide unlimited leadership, social, and cultural opportunities. Annually, 3,000 teams participate in fifty intramural sports, 2,500 people participate in forty sports clubs, and 20,000 students, staff members, and faculty members participate in outdoor recreation activities. Facilities include the Lied Recreation/Athletic Center, which houses twenty courts for basketball and volleyball, a rock climbing wall, a 300-meter track, an artificial turf area, and a weightlifting and fitness center; Beyer Hall; the Physical Education Building; the State Gym; and many outdoor facilities. The Cyclones have twenty Division I intercollegiate men's and women's sports and belong to the Big 12, one of the premier sports conferences in the country.

Outstanding facilities for the cultural and performing arts include the 2,700-seat Stephens Auditorium, the 452-seat Fisher Theater, and the 15,000-seat Hilton Coliseum. Iowa State attracts the top entertainment acts and world-renowned speakers. Recent performers include Shermie Alexie, Bill Cosby, the Dave Matthews Band, Simon Estes, Mae Jemmison, George Strait, Jars of Clay, Prince, Wynton Marsalis, Nikki Giovanni, The Washington Week in Review, Michael W. Smith, Yanni, Sarah McLachlan, Aerosmith, Dixie Chicks, and Harry Connick Jr.

Personal support services, available to help students become their best, include the following: assertiveness training; career counseling; communication skills workshops; medical, physical, and learning disabled services; and stress management, study skills, and test-taking workshops.

Iowa State University offers 111 master's programs, eighty-two Ph.D. programs, and one professional degree program—the Doctor of Veterinary Medicine.

Location

Iowa State is located in Ames, just 30 minutes north of Iowa's capital, Des Moines. Minneapolis, Chicago, Kansas City, St. Louis, Omaha, and other metropolitan areas are a short drive from Ames or easily accessible by plane and train.

The campus environment rates high with students and faculty and staff members. The book *The Campus as a Work of Art* rated Iowa State among the twenty-five most beautiful campuses in the nation. The American Society of Landscape Architects recently chose Iowa State as a "medallion site," one of the three best central campuses in the nation. Iowa State students spend most of their time on the 24-acre central campus, part of the 1,984 acres.

Ames was recently ranked the second-best "micropolitan" area (population 50,000 or fewer) in the nation. Students take advantage of arts groups, recreational facilities, biking and hiking trails, more than eighty restaurants, a great downtown, many shopping areas, and a variety of movie theaters.

Majors and Degrees

Iowa State University offers 101 bachelor's degree programs. The College of Agriculture includes programs in agricultural biochemistry, agricultural business, agricultural education, agricultural extension education, agricultural studies, agricultural systems technology, agronomy, animal ecology, animal science, dairy science, dietetics, entomology, environmental science, food science, forestry, genetics, horticulture, international agriculture, microbiology, nutritional science, pest management, plant health and protection, professional agriculture, public service and administration in agriculture, seed science, and zoology. The College of Business offers programs in accounting, finance, management, management information systems, marketing, and transportation and logistics. The College of Design offers programs in architecture, art and design, community and regional planning, graphic design, interior design, and landscape architecture. The College of Education offers programs in community health education, early childhood education, elementary education, environmental studies, exercise and sport science, industrial technology, and secondary education. The College of Engineering offers programs in aerospace engineering, agricultural engineering, ceramic engineering, chemical engineering, civil engineering, computer engineering, construction engineering, electrical engineering, engineering applications, engineering operations, engineering science, industrial engineering, mechanical engineering, and metallurgical engineering. The College of Family and Consumer Sciences offers programs in apparel merchandising, design, and production; child and family services; dietetics; early childhood education; family and consumer sciences education; family resource management and consumer sciences; food science; hotel, restaurant, and institution management; housing and the near environment; nutritional science; and studies in family and consumer sciences. The College of Liberal Arts and Sciences is the largest college and offers programs in advertising, African-American studies, American Indian studies, anthropology, astronomy, biochemistry, biology, biology/premedical illustration, biophysics, botany, chemistry, classical studies, computer science, earth science, economics, English, environmental science, environmental studies, French, genetics, geology, German, gerontology, history, interdisciplinary studies, international studies, journalism and mass communication, Latin, liberal studies, linguistics, mathematics, meteorology, music, naval science, performing arts, philosophy, physics, political science, Portuguese, psychology, religious studies, Russian, secondary education, sociology, Spanish, speech communication, statistics, technical communications, technology and social change, women's studies, and zoology.

Academic Program

Each college provides academic support through advising offices. Additional academic services include academic learning labs, learning communities, learning teams, peer education, supplemental instruction, and tutoring services. The University Honors Program provides academically talented students an opportunity to stretch their minds through individualized programs, special courses and seminars, unique off-campus opportunities, and 24-hour access to the Martin C. Jischke Honors Building, home of the Honors Program. The academic year is divided into two semesters of sixteen weeks each, beginning in late August and ending in early May. A program called Soar in Four guarantees graduation in four years in all majors except architecture and landscape architecture.

Off-Campus Arrangements

Students can take advantage of internships, cooperative education programs, and research programs, which provide the opportunity for professional work with national and international companies. International exchange programs are available at more than 100 colleges and universities in forty countries. The National Student Exchange program provides students an opportunity to study at one of 177 reciprocating universities around the country.

Academic Facilities

Iowa State's 173 campus buildings include several recent state-of-the-art additions. Among the newest are the Durham Center for Computation and Communication, the Molecular Biology Building, the Martin C. Jischke Honors Building, the Palmer Educational Building, and Howe Hall, the $61-million engineering facility that is the home of the Engineering Teaching and Research Center (ETRC). Construction is nearly complete on Hoover Hall, a new engineering building, and the Gerdin Building, which will house the College of Business. Technology is utilized to provide students the resources to succeed in a competitive global market. Iowa State is home to C2 and C6, two of the world's most advanced virtual reality rooms. C6 is the only six-sided virtual reality environment in the United States and one of three worldwide. Students are provided free e-mail and Internet access and space to create their own Web page. Students use AccessPlus via the Web or at kiosks for instant access to jobs, grades, schedules, and more. Computing resources include thousands of workstations, 24-hour availability, and mainframe/Internet access from residence hall rooms.

Costs

For the 2003–04 academic year, in-state tuition and fees are $5028 and out-of-state tuition and fees are approximately $14,370 (based upon full-time undergraduate status for two semesters). Room and board are approximately $5740 for two semesters. Books and supplies are estimated at $820 per year.

Financial Aid

Need- and merit-based financial assistance is available to qualified applicants. Approximately 66 percent of students receive some type of financial aid, such as grants, scholarships, loans, and jobs. Students should apply for admission early to receive maximum consideration for merit scholarships. All applicants are encouraged to file the FAFSA by February 14 (for fall semester enrollment). Links to scholarships and financial aid resources may be found at Iowa State's Web site at http://www.iastate.edu/~fin_aid_info/.

Faculty

Iowa State has 1,720 faculty members, 88 percent of whom hold doctorates. The student-faculty ratio is 18:1.

Student Government

The Government of the Student Body (GSB) legislates and administers student policy and provides services to meet the needs of students. The functions of GSB are carried out by executives and senators elected by Iowa State students. GSB's primary function is the allocation of student activity fees, through which a number of diverse services and student organizations are funded.

Admission Requirements

Students seeking admission directly from high school must have a minimum of 4 years of English, 3 years of math (including 1 year each of algebra, geometry, and advanced algebra), 3 years of science (including 1 year each of courses from two of the following fields: biology, chemistry, and physics), and 2 years of social studies. In addition, students applying to the College of Liberal Arts and Sciences must have completed an additional year of social studies, for a total of 3 years, plus 2 years of a single foreign language. Grades, class rank, and quality of course work are the most important criteria in the admissions decision.

Transfer applicants are typically admitted if they have a minimum of 24 transferable credit hours and have earned at least a C (2.0) average in all college-level courses attempted. However, some programs may require a transfer grade point average higher than the 2.0 minimum. Higher academic standards may be required of students who are not residents of Iowa, including international students. Applicants who have not completed 24 transferable semester (or 36 quarter) hours prior to enrolling at Iowa State must submit a high school transcript and an ACT or SAT I score and meet all admission requirements for entering freshmen, as well as earn at least a 2.0 average in all college-level courses attempted.

Applicants must submit an application along with a $30 application fee ($50 for international students) and have their secondary school provide an official transcript of their academic record, including credits and grades, rank in class, and certification of graduation. Applicants must also arrange to have their ACT or SAT I scores reported to Iowa State directly from the testing agency. The Test of English as a Foreign Language (TOEFL) is required of international students whose first language is not English. Applicants may be required to submit additional information or data to support their applications.

Application and Information

Students interested in applying for the fall semester should apply during the preceding fall. Students should submit applications for the other terms six to nine months in advance. Interested students should contact the Office of Admissions for an application or other enrollment information or to arrange a campus visit. Online enrollment and downloadable applications are available at the Web site listed below.

Office of Admissions
Alumni Hall
Iowa State University of Science and Technology
Ames, Iowa 50011-2010

Telephone: 800-262-3810 (toll-free)
515-294-3094 (TTY/TDD)
Fax: 515-294-2592
E-mail: admissions@iastate.edu
World Wide Web: http://www.admissions.iastate.edu

KENDALL COLLEGE

EVANSTON, ILLINOIS

The College

Since 1934, Kendall College has provided its students with a small, personal, and supportive academic environment. At Kendall, the College helps to create an environment where each student, regardless of his or her major, learns basic composition, humanities, and ethics. This foundation prepares students for the real world with the skills and attitudes that are critical for success. Even in today's very competitive marketplace, there are still many attractive opportunities for the well-rounded student who can speak, write, and think intelligently.

Kendall College offers five major degree programs from which the student can choose an area of study. Kendall offers associate and bachelor's degrees in the areas of business, culinary arts, early childhood education, hospitality management, and human services. Each area of study is taught with the individual in mind, in a hands-on context with a low student-faculty ratio. Kendall requires an internship as part of each degree program. As a result, Kendall's students graduate with a solid liberal arts education and hands-on experience in their chosen field. The College uses the rich resources of the Chicago metropolitan environment to relate academic theory to experience.

Outside of class, Kendall is also committed to providing an active social, cultural, and athletic life to its students. In 1997, Kendall College introduced varsity sports. Men's and women's teams are fielded in basketball and volleyball; there is also a men's soccer team. Kendall is committed to building better citizens through a healthy combination of academics and athletics.

Kendall College is accredited by the Higher Learning Commission of the North Central Association of Colleges and Schools The College is also accredited by the University Senate of the United Methodist Church. The School of Culinary Arts is accredited by the American Culinary Federation Accrediting Commission.

Location

Kendall College is located in Evanston, Illinois, a suburb bordering Chicago to the north. Evanston provides an idyllic college setting only two blocks from Lake Michigan, surrounded by tree-lined streets and historic homes. Downtown Evanston is just a short walk down the street, where students can find an abundance of restaurants, shopping, and entertainment.

Evanston is conveniently located about 20 minutes from downtown Chicago. A short ride on the Metra train or on the Chicago Transit Authority's (CTA) "L" takes students into a world of opportunities for finding excellent internships, job opportunities and, of course, world-class art, food, culture, and entertainment. Kendall's proximity to Chicago offers numerous opportunities for internships and job placement after graduation.

Majors and Degrees

Kendall College awards the Bachelor of Arts (B.A.) degree in four of its major programs. The programs include business and technology, early childhood education (leading to Type 04 Illinois state certification), hospitality management, and human services. The College also awards the Associate of Arts (A.A.) degree in business and technology and human services as well as the Associate of Applied Science (A.A.S.) degree in culinary arts.

In addition, Kendall offers concentrations and certificates in each of its major programs. The business and technology program offers concentrations in business administration, marketing, and Web design and certificates in entrepreneurship and marketing. The culinary arts program offers certificates in baking and pastry arts and professional cookery. Early childhood education offers a concentration in special education approval. Hospitality management offers one certificate in bed and breakfast operations and five concentrations: convention and meeting planning, culinary management, food and beverage operations, hotel management, and international hospitality management. Students may also pursue concentrations in human services in crime, justice and rehabilitation, gerontology, psychology, or substance abuse treatment studies.

Academic Program

Kendall College operates on a quarter program. The first quarter term extends from September to early December, the second extends from January to March, and the third extends from April to June. Summer sessions are offered from July to September. A student must fulfill a minimum of 92 quarter hours for an associate degree and a minimum of 184 quarter hours for a bachelor's degree and maintain at least a 2.0 GPA.

Academic Facilities

The campus encompasses one square block in the residential area of Evanston. In the main academic building, Westerberg Hall, the College houses classrooms, seven laboratory kitchens, and a fine-dining restaurant. It is also home to an interactive videoconferencing classroom capable of connecting to other colleges and universities nationally and internationally. The campus has four recently upgraded computer labs, and the two dorms on campus are wired for Internet access.

Kendall's library currently has more than 37,000 books, 250 periodicals, and a growing video collection. It also houses special collections of culinary, business, early childhood, human services, and hospitality materials. The library offers other excellent resources through local consortia and electronic connections.

Native American materials are displayed at the Mitchell Museum of the American Indian. The museum is located near the campus and is an outstanding educational asset to students and the community at large. Adjacent to the Mitchell Museum is the Creative Kids Corner, a classroom environment for young children designed for observation by early childhood education students.

Costs

In 2003–04, full-time tuition and fees for the School of Arts and Sciences were $14,445 for three quarters (12–19 quarter hours), and College room and board were $5853 for three quarters. Part-time tuition for the arts and sciences program was $436 per quarter hour.

Full-time tuition and fees for the School of Culinary Arts were $17,550 for three quarters and include culinary facilities usage. Room and board for the culinary arts program were $3831 for three terms. Part-time culinary arts tuition was $450 per quarter hour.

Financial Aid

The College offers institutional awards. A needs analysis and the determination of eligibility culminate in the financial aid package, which comprises different types of financial aid combined to meet the student's demonstrated need. The financial aid packaging process ensures effective use of available funds and provides fair and equitable treatment of all applicants. It is the goal of Kendall College to seek funding and to package aid to fully meet the needs of all applicants. Awards are made giving priority to applicants who meet the April 1 preferential filing date.

The Kendall College Financial Aid Office believes that self-help (loan and work) should be a part of the Kendall aid package. Students are encouraged to make a commitment of current and future earnings to their education. The College administers aid for undergraduates, including need-based scholarships; athletic, merit-based, and curriculum-specific scholarships; state and federal awards; Federal Supplemental Educational Opportunity Grants; Federal Work-Study Program; and campus employment.

Faculty

The undergraduate academic faculty has 31 full-time and 40 part-time members; 55 percent of the full-time faculty members have doctoral and/or professional degrees. The student-faculty ratio is 17:1. The faculty members at Kendall College believe that students work best when they are actively involved in making choices about their own learning. As Kendall students develop clear ideas of what they wish to study, they are provided with the opportunities to use tutorials to continue their education.

Student Government

Kendall College's Student Government Federation is designed to give students a leadership role and voice in building and improving their campus community. The Student Government Federation is elected annually in the fall term and is composed of a president, vice president, and a group of senators. This group serves in an advisory capacity to the Board of Trustees, the Faculty Senate, and various other faculty committees.

Admission Requirements

Kendall assesses its entrance difficulty level as moderate. Admission to Kendall College is open to men and women of all races and religious affiliations. Each applicant is considered on the basis of probable success at Kendall, as indicated primarily by high school grades, class rank, and ACT or SAT I test scores. A minimum GPA of 2.0 and an 18 on the ACT or an SAT I score of 850 are required for acceptance. If the student falls below either the minimum GPA or the standardized test requirements, the student must complete an entrance examination and submit two letters of recommendation. An essay accompanying the application is required. Qualities of character are also important at Kendall. Therefore, personal interviews and campus visits are encouraged, though not required, to help determine admission.

Application and Information

High school seniors may obtain applications from the Office of Admissions and may submit the admission application at any time. The Office of Admissions must be sent an official transcript of high school records. Some students may be admitted on probation after consultation with the Admissions Committee.

For further information, students should contact:

Office of Admissions
Kendall College
2408 Orrington Avenue
Evanston, Illinois 60201-2899
Telephone: 847-448-2304
877-588-8860 (toll-free)
Fax: 847-448-2120
E-mail: admissions@kendall.edu
World Wide Web: http://www.kendall.edu

Kendall College, located just north of Chicago, has been educating students for more than sixty-five years.

KETTERING UNIVERSITY

FLINT, MICHIGAN

The University

Kettering University (formerly GMI Engineering & Management Institute) offers education for the real world. Nearly 100 percent of Kettering's students receive a job offer or are accepted by graduate schools before receiving their diplomas. Kettering University has a unique partnership that offers students, business, and industry an opportunity found at no other undergraduate college in America. Kettering, a professional cooperative engineering, management, science, and math university, is the only institution that assists incoming freshmen to be selected by companies for cooperative employment, a process initiated for all accepted students. Kettering University successfully integrates the practical aspects of the workplace into the world of higher education through its more than 700 corporate partners, corporations, and agencies located throughout the United States, Canada, and selected countries. Kettering's corporate partners represent most major industrial groups; many are recognized as worldwide leaders in business innovation and manufacturing technology. These corporations share a commitment to "grow their own" engineers and managers by employing exceptionally talented young men and women in one of the nine baccalaureate degree programs. Kettering's corporate partners invest in students' futures by providing a program of progressive work experience that exposes them to processes, products, corporate culture, and the technology necessary to compete in tomorrow's business environment.

Founded in 1919, Kettering University is private and enrolls about 2,400 undergraduate students. The University is accredited by the North Central Association of Colleges and Schools. Its engineering curricula are accredited by the Accreditation Board for Engineering and Technology, Inc. (ABET). The management program is accredited by the Association of Collegiate Business Schools and Programs (ACBSP).

The combination of academics and professional, paid work experience offered through Kettering University is not only highly effective, it is without equal, even among other cooperative education programs. The advantages of a Kettering education have enabled thousands of graduates to rise to key executive leadership positions in the world's finest corporations.

A varied program of sports, fitness, and recreational activities is offered. A 445-student residence hall and a new apartment complex are located on campus. Recreation facilities include athletic fields, tennis courts, and a recreation center with an Olympic-size, six-lane swimming pool, aerobic fitness rooms, a full line of Nautilus equipment, and basketball, tennis, and racquetball courts. A public golf course is adjacent to the campus.

Professional counseling, support services, and health care are available.

Location

Located in east-central Michigan, 60 miles west of Lake Huron and Canada and 60 miles north of Detroit, Flint is a city of 135,000 residents with a metropolitan area population of 450,000. Flint is particularly proud of its distinctive College and Cultural Center Complex, which is about 1½ miles from campus. Built and endowed entirely by the gifts of private citizens, the center includes the Alfred P. Sloan Museum; the Whiting Auditorium, home of the Flint Symphony and host to leading stage shows and entertainers; the Robert T. Longway Planetarium, Michigan's largest and best-equipped sky show facility; the Flint Institute of Arts; the F. A. Bower Theatre; the Dort Institute of Music; the University of Michigan–Flint Campus; the C. S. Mott Community College; and the Flint Public Library. The IMA Sports Arena is home to the Flint Generals professional hockey team, as well as the University hockey club, and is the site of many special events.

Outdoor and indoor recreational opportunities are abundant. Within a few minutes' drive are downhill and cross-country skiing facilities, several fine lakes for the entire range of water sports, a wide selection of good golf courses open to the public, and excellent indoor and outdoor skating rinks.

Majors and Degrees

Kettering University offers a 4½-year, professional cooperative education program with curricula leading to designated Bachelor of Science degrees in Computer Engineering, Electrical Engineering, Industrial Engineering, and Mechanical Engineering degrees; a designated Bachelor of Science in Business Management degree with concentrations in accounting/finance, information systems, manufacturing management, marketing, and materials management; and designated Bachelor of Science degrees in applied mathematics, applied physics, computer science, and environmental chemistry. Minors are available in applied chemistry, applied mathematics, applied optics, computer science, liberal arts, and management.

Academic Program

Although each program at Kettering University has its own sequence requirements, 160 credit hours are generally required, including thesis credit hours. The program involves nine academic terms and nine co-op terms, two of which are focused on the capstone thesis project, which is done on behalf of the student's co-op employer. Students alternate between eleven-week periods of academic study on the campus in Flint and twelve-week periods of related work experience with their corporate employer. The academic year consists of two 3–month academic terms on campus and two 3–month terms of paid work experience. A typical Kettering University cooperative student may earn up to $65,000 in co-op wages through the complete program.

Academic Facilities

A new, $42-million Mechanical Engineering and Chemistry Center opened in spring 2003. This state-of-the-art facility houses a fuel cell lab, an emissions lab, and much more. Kettering University has the traditional laboratory facilities expected of any top engineering school, but also has labs to demonstrate and experiment with a wide range of technologies found in industry—from basic machining to emerging technologies. The instrumentation in some labs is generally found only in graduate school facilities at other colleges. There are manufacturing, laser, radioisotope, heat transfer, electricity and solid-state electronics, metallurgy, computer-aided design (CAD), computer-integrated manufacturing (CIM), acoustics, mechatronics, human factors, digital and analog computer, robotics, holography, and electron microscopy laboratories and the Polymer Optimization Center. The campus is fully networked and allows access to computer resources from dormitory rooms, dedicated labs, and other locations. Course materials are offered online through Blackboard. Each student has unlimited 24-hour access to computer resources and the World Wide Web. The library contains more than 94,000 cataloged volumes and currently subscribes to more than 540 periodicals and various online services. Special facilities include a microfilm area, database search services, record and tape listening and videocassette viewing facilities, and a special collection of SAE, SME, and ASME technical papers.

Costs

Tuition in 2003-04 is $21,184 per year. Room and board are $4900 per year (nineteen meals per week).

Financial Aid

In addition to all traditional sources of aid, all Kettering students benefit from a special resource that is significant and not need based. One of the many advantages of attending Kettering University is the opportunity for students to earn a salary during their co-op work terms. Co-op income is substantial and can help cover part of the cost of a Kettering education by supplementing the family contribution and the standard forms of need-based and merit-based financial aid. Students who live at home during work experience periods are able to contribute a greater proportion of earnings directly to educational expenses. About 70 percent of students are able to live at home during work terms. The typical range of co-op earnings over the five-year program is $40,000 to $65,000.

Kettering University offers all the traditional forms of financial aid, both need- and merit-based. The new Kettering Merit Scholarship program rewards all qualified applicants. Because of their talents, many students win scholarships from agencies and organizations from their local communities. Michigan residents are often recipients of the Michigan Competitive Scholarship/Tuition Grant. Traditionally, more than 92 percent of the entering class receives some form of financial aid, making a private education at Kettering very affordable.

The primary purpose of financial aid at Kettering University is to supplement a student's unmet financial need after cooperative earnings and parents' contributions. Students who wish to apply for financial aid should complete the Free Application for Federal Student Aid (FAFSA) and request that a copy of the analysis be sent to Kettering University. Aid is given as grants, scholarships, loans, and work-study awards.

Faculty

Kettering University's full-time faculty of 144 have teaching as their prime responsibility. Most professors in degree disciplines have industrial experience in addition to academic credentials and maintain contact with industry through consulting, sponsored research, and advising on student thesis projects. More than 80 percent hold the doctorate. Because only half of the students are on campus at any one time, class sizes are small and opportunities for enrichment and extra help are readily available. Kettering faculty members find the challenge of teaching talented students who share their experiences from co-op especially refreshing and rewarding.

Student Government

Kettering University students enjoy an active college life with a wide range of clubs and organizations and an exciting intramural athletic program. Eleven professional societies are active on campus, and there are fourteen national fraternities and six sororities. More than half of all students are active in fraternities and sororities. Kettering students tend to enjoy competition, whether it be in service activities or on the athletic field. The student government represents the interests and needs of the students and contributes to their educational development in the areas of leadership skills, self-confidence, interpersonal relations, and organizational operations.

Admission Requirements

Admission to Kettering University is competitive and based on scholastic achievement and nonscholastic interests, activities, and achievements. Applicants are required to have earned the following credits (a credit represents two semesters or one year of study): algebra, 2 credits; geometry, 1 credit; trigonometry, ½ credit; laboratory science, 2 credits (physics and chemistry are strongly recommended for all students; at least 1 credit of chemistry or physics is required); and English, 3 credits. A minimum of 16 credits is required; however, the University encourages students to complete at least 20 credits. Applicants must submit results of the SAT I or ACT. (Kettering's ACT code number is 1998; the SAT I code number is 1246.) The staff of the Cooperative Education and Career Services Office initiates the process and assists all enrolled students with the process of securing cooperative employment. The process begins upon confirmation of enrollment and continues until each student is employed.

Most Kettering University students achieve at or near the top 10 percent of their graduating class on traditional criteria such as grades, rank, and test scores. Corporate employers are also very interested in activities, career goals, experiences, leadership, and other personal qualities. Kettering University also welcomes students wishing to transfer from other colleges and universities. The transfer alternative is an excellent way to gain admission for students who do not enroll as freshmen.

Application and Information

Prospective freshmen are encouraged to file their application early in their senior year. Admission decisions for transfer applicants are based on college record for those who have completed at least 30 credits. Applications are accepted all year long; however, early application greatly increases visibility for early employment possibilities in the co-op search process. The application fee is $35. Students can also apply online at the Web site listed below.

Admissions Office
Kettering University
1700 West Third Avenue
Flint, Michigan 48504-4898

Telephone: 810-762-7865
800-955-4464 (toll-free in the United States and Canada)
E-mail: admissions@kettering.edu
World Wide Web: http://www.admissions.kettering.edu

Kettering University graduates expect a good job or entrance into a top graduate school.

KNOX COLLEGE

GALESBURG, ILLINOIS

The College

Knox College is a vital community of teachers and students that provides a challenging liberal arts curriculum, a faculty of national distinction, and a campus atmosphere noted for its informality. Knox invites students who seek a strong education and who relish the chance to explore their own ideas within a community of friends and mentors. Founded in 1837, Knox is one of the Midwest's great liberal arts colleges and among the nation's best. Site of the fifth Lincoln-Douglas debate, Knox has enrolled women and African-American students since the 1850s and international students since the 1860s. Knox has been known for its high academic quality since the nineteenth century and has many distinguished alumni in the professions—business, journalism, the natural sciences, and higher education.

Knox is an independent, coeducational four-year college. The student body of 1,120 comes from forty-five states and forty-two countries. Approximately 53 percent of students are women and 47 percent are men; 14 percent of students are students of color (5 percent African American, 5 percent Asian American, 3 percent Latino, and 1 percent Native American), and 8 percent are international students. Knox is very much a residential college, with more than 90 percent of students living on its spacious 82-acre campus. Most student residences are organized in 8- to 15-person suites with double and single rooms; options include coeducational residence halls, former private homes, and apartment-style units. Campus life is characterized by wide participation in more than 100 student organizations and extracurricular activities. The student-run Union Board provides a full entertainment calendar throughout the year. Musical groups run the gamut from rock, folk, and jazz combos to the Chamber Singers and the Knox-Galesburg Symphony. There are frequent theater productions and a modern dance ensemble. Knox has a 1,000-watt FM station, a biweekly student newspaper, and a student literary magazine twice named the nation's best. Student groups provide activities ranging from political activism to community service to religious meditation. There are five fraternities and two sororities. Knox competes at the NCAA Division III level in eleven men's and ten women's sports. Varsity sports are baseball, basketball, cross-country, football, golf, indoor and outdoor track, soccer, swimming, tennis, and wrestling for men and basketball, cross-country, golf, indoor and outdoor track, soccer, softball, swimming, tennis, and volleyball for women.

Location

Galesburg is an historic city of 33,500 located about 180 miles west of Chicago, 200 miles north of St. Louis, and about an hour away from the Mississippi River. It is accessible by transcontinental Amtrak trains, commercial airlines, bus lines, and interstate highways. Community service and internship and employment opportunities are available in local social service agencies, hospitals, financial institutions, and a variety of manufacturing firms. The campus is located three blocks from downtown shops, movie theaters, and restaurants. Notable features are the Orpheum Theater (a restored 1,000-seat concert hall), specialty shops on historic Seminary Street, and Lake Storey on the city's north side.

Majors and Degrees

Knox awards the Bachelor of Arts degree in the following major fields: American Studies, anthropology and sociology, art (history and studio), biochemistry, biology, black studies, chemistry, classics, computer science, economics, education (elementary and secondary), English (creative writing and literature), environmental studies, French, gender and women's studies, German, history, integrated international studies, international relations, mathematics, mathematical finance, modern languages, modern languages and classics, music, philosophy, physics, political science, psychology, Russian, Russian area studies, Spanish, and theater. Students may also design their own interdisciplinary majors and minors. Minors are offered in American politics, anthropology and sociology, applied computer science, art history, behavioral neuroscience, biochemistry, biology, black studies, business, ceramics, comparative politics, computing systems, creative writing, dance, design and technology, directing, dramatic literature and history, English literature, environmental studies, French, gender and women's studies, German, history, international relations, journalism, Latin American studies, mathematics, mathematical finance, painting, performance, philosophy, photography, physics, printmaking, psychology, religious studies, Russian, Russian area studies, sculpture, social services, Spanish, and theory of computing. Course work is also offered in Greek, Japanese, Latin, and sports studies. Preprofessional preparation is provided in architecture, engineering, law, and medicine. In addition, Knox offers teacher certification in elementary and secondary education.

Knox offers special programs in cooperation with several other institutions, including dual-degree programs in the following fields: architecture, engineering, environmental management, forestry, law, nursing/medical technology, and occupational therapy.

The Knox-Rush Early Identification Program identifies selected Knox first-year students for admission to Rush Medical College upon completion of their Knox degree.

Academic Program

The goal of Knox College is to provide students with a strong education in the liberal arts and to prepare them for rewarding professional and personal lives. The curriculum is designed to integrate the skills of critical inquiry and communication with study in breadth and depth. The required First-Year Preceptorial encourages students to engage the fundamental questions and concerns of a liberal education and fosters thoughtful debate, careful reasoning, and clear writing. Other requirements include enhancing specialized knowledge through a major, a second major or a minor, and the study of four broad areas of human inquiry—the arts, humanities, sciences, and social sciences. Students are also required to acquire competencies in writing, oral presentation, quantitative literacy, informed use of technology, foreign language, understanding diversity, and applying classroom learning through hands-on experiences such as internships, study abroad, community service, independent research, and teaching assistantships. The academic calendar is three 10-week terms, with a normal load of three 1-credit courses per term. Thirty-six credits are required for graduation.

The close relationship of faculty and students is key to Knox's program. Students work with faculty advisers to develop their programs of study; the ratio of first-year students to faculty advisers is held to no more than 8:1, while the overall student-faculty ratio is 12:1. Students with declared majors work with an adviser in their major field. Small classes (averaging 17 students) are the rule, and independent study is common in every department. Student research is a distinctive feature at Knox, which regularly sends one of the largest contingents to national conferences on undergraduate research. Promising students are encouraged to apply for one of the several available research opportunities, including the Ford Research Fellows, Richter Fellows, and ACM Minority/McNair Fellows Programs, to pursue an independent project under the supervision of a faculty mentor. Similarly, seniors are encouraged to pursue College Honors. Other special features worthy of note are the nationally recognized Writing Program, the theater department's Repertory Term, and the art department's Open Studio experience.

Off-Campus Arrangements

Knox maintains its own programs abroad in Buenos Aires, Argentina; Besançon, France; and Barcelona, Spain, in cooperation with the universities of those cities. In addition, Knox recognizes and gives credit for twenty-eight programs in twenty countries, as well as eight programs in the United States. Students normally participate in these programs during the junior year.

Academic Facilities

The Knox campus has forty-two academic and residential buildings. Old Main, built in 1857, is the sole intact site of the 1858 Lincoln-Douglas debates and is on the National Register of Historic Buildings. Library holdings include more than 291,000 volumes and 672 periodicals in addition to OCLC interlibrary loan, online databases, and an automated catalog accessible from remote workstations around campus. Seymour Library's Special Collections Center houses manuscripts and rare book collections of national importance, such as the Finley Collection on the Old Northwest and the Hughes Collection on Hemingway and the "Lost Generation." Umbeck Science-Mathematics Center contains spacious teaching and research labs, extensive research equipment including electron microscopes and NMR, and a science library. Computer technology features a campuswide fiber-optic network, Internet access, five student computer labs (including 24-hour access), several specialized departmental labs, and more than 200 Windows and Macintosh workstations for student use. Davis Hall, housing the social sciences and modern languages, includes a data analysis microcomputer lab and a language center equipped with audio, video, and computer equipment. The Fine Arts Center contains two theaters, a recital hall, music rehearsal studios, and art studios for painting, drawing, sculpture, printmaking, and ceramics. In addition, there is a Student Union, an outstanding gymnasium, and a recreational field house.

Costs

The comprehensive fee for 2003–04 is $30,294. This includes $24,105 for tuition, $5925 for room and board, and a $264 student activities fee. Extra expenses for books, travel, supplies, laundry, and incidentals are estimated at $1200.

Financial Aid

Knox is committed to being accessible to all qualified students. Admission decisions are made without regard for ability to pay, and Knox awards need-based financial aid according to each student's eligibility. Financial aid awards may include federal and state grants, student loans, and campus employment. New students must file an official financial aid application by March 1 for priority consideration. Knox offers a number of supplemental loan options as well as a variety of payment plans.

Knox also awards merit-based scholarships not based on financial need to recognize outstanding academic achievement as well as special abilities in art, chemistry, community service, dance, mathematics, music, theater, and writing.

Faculty

Knox has 93 full-time and 21 part-time faculty members, of whom 94 percent hold the Ph.D. or equivalent. Faculty members teach all courses. More than two thirds have published or presented scholarly or creative work in the past five years. National recognition includes major research awards from the National Science Foundation, the National Institutes of Health, and the National Endowment for the Humanities; an ASCAP Award–winning composer; and an NSF Shannon Award–winning geneticist.

Student Government

At Knox, students are treated as full members of the community. Students administer the campuswide honor and judicial systems, regulating academic and social behavior. They are appointed to all faculty committees (except two personnel committees), have formal observer status to the Board of Trustees, and are a majority of the members on the committee regulating student affairs. In addition, there is an elected Student Senate.

Admission Requirements

Applicants to Knox must demonstrate the ability to do successful college-level work and to make a positive contribution to the campus community. The fundamental requirement is successful completion of a challenging college-preparatory program. Of the first-year students in 2002, 32 percent were in the top tenth of their high school class and roughly 65 percent were in the top quarter. The middle 50 percent of students scored between 550 and 660 on the mathematics portion of the SAT I and between 540 and 680 on the verbal; on the ACT composite, the mid-50 percent range was 23 to 29. Applicants must complete the application form, file a nonrefundable $35 fee, and provide Knox with their SAT I or ACT scores, their academic transcripts, and recommendations from a teacher and counselor. Interviews are strongly recommended. Applications from transfer and international students are strongly encouraged.

Application and Information

For more information, students should contact:

Paul Steenis
Director of Admission
Knox College
Galesburg, Illinois 61401
Telephone: 309-341-7100
800-678-KNOX (toll-free)
Fax: 309-341-7070
E-mail: admission@knox.edu
World Wide Web: http://www.knox.edu

Knox College's Old Main, the last remaining site of the Lincoln-Douglas debates of 1858.

LOYOLA UNIVERSITY CHICAGO

CHICAGO, ILLINOIS

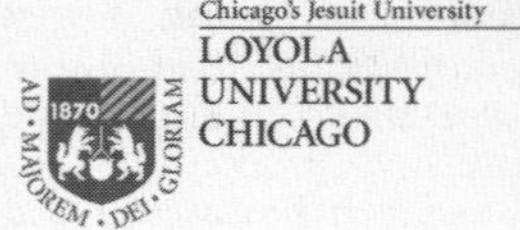

The University

Loyola University Chicago is the most comprehensive Jesuit university in the United States. Founded in 1870 by priests of the Society of Jesus, Loyola continues the Jesuit commitment to education, which is well-grounded in the liberal arts and based on excellence in teaching and research.

Loyola attracts students from all fifty states and seventy-four countries to its nine schools and colleges: the Stritch School of Medicine, the School of Law, the College of Arts and Sciences, the School of Business Administration, the Niehoff School of Nursing, the School of Education, the School of Social Work, the Graduate School, and Mundelein College (for adult and lifelong learning).

Each year, Loyola University Chicago enrolls more than 1,600 freshmen and more than 400 transfer students. These students choose Loyola because of its personal attention, its environment of academic excellence, and its reputation for career preparation. Loyola students take advantage of Chicago as an educational resource, often combining their studies with internships and part-time work experience.

The University seeks to provide an environment that will enhance the academic, social, and spiritual growth of students. More than 130 student organizations, including eleven fraternities and sororities, and extensive recreational sports programs and facilities are provided. NCAA Division I teams include basketball, cross-country, golf, soccer, track, and volleyball for men and basketball, cross-country, golf, soccer, softball, track, and volleyball for women.

The University provides thirteen undergraduate residence halls on the Lake Shore Campus. There are both coed and single-sex halls. Freshmen and sophomores are expected to live on campus. There is also convenient and affordable off-campus housing in the immediate vicinity of campus for upperclass students.

Location

The Lake Shore Campus is located 8 miles north of the city's center and sits on the shore of Lake Michigan in the Rogers Park/Edgewater area, a desirable residential neighborhood where many Loyola faculty and staff members reside. Students at the Lake Shore Campus also can take advantage of the city's vast business and cultural resources, with downtown Chicago being less than 30 minutes away via university-run shuttle bus or via convenient public transportation.

Loyola's Water Tower Campus is located on Chicago's "Magnificent Mile," a fashionable area on the near north side. Close to theaters, museums, major corporate and financial institutions, and some of Chicago's most elegant shops and boutiques, the Water Tower Campus is a vibrant educational center.

Majors and Degrees

Loyola's four undergraduate colleges offer the Bachelor of Arts (B.A.), Bachelor of Science (B.S.), Bachelor of Business Administration (B.B.A.), Bachelor of Science in Education (B.S.Ed.), and the Bachelor of Science in Nursing (B.S.N.) degrees. The College of Arts and Sciences offers majors in anthropology, biology, chemistry (biochemistry), classical civilization, communication (communication and social justice, journalism, and organizational communication/business), computer science, criminal justice, economics, English (creative writing), environmental studies, environmental studies (chemistry), fine arts (art history, studio art, and visual communication), French, German, Greek (ancient), history, international studies, Italian, Latin, mathematics, mathematics and computer science (operations research), music, pharmacy, philosophy, physics, physics and engineering (theoretical physics and applied mathematics), political science, psychology (applied social psychology, human services, natural sciences, and social sciences), social work, sociology, sociology and anthropology, Spanish, statistical science (actuarial science), theology, and women's studies. The School of Business Administration offers majors in accounting, economics, finance, human resource management, information systems management, international business, marketing, and operations management. The School of Education offers a major in elementary education as well as secondary school certification in fourteen majors. The Niehoff School of Nursing offers the Bachelor of Science in Nursing and a baccalaureate completion program for registered nurses, an accelerated B.S.N. program. Five-year dual-degree (bachelor's/master's) programs are available in applied social psychology, biology/M.B.A., business administration/accountancy, business administration/information systems management, computer science, criminal justice, environmental sciences/M.B.A., mathematics, political science, social work, and sociology.

Minors are available in most of the fields listed above as well as in Asian and Asian-American studies, black world studies, Catholic studies, international studies, Latin American studies, medieval studies, neuroscience, peace studies, and psychology of crime and justice.

Preprofessional programs prepare students for future study in bioethics and health policy, cell biology, cell and molecular physiology, divinity, law, medicine, microbiology and immunology, molecular biology, molecular and cellular biochemistry, neurobiology and anatomy, pastoral studies, pharmacology and experimental therapeutics, religious education, and social work. A 3+3 Law Program, in conjunction with the Loyola University School of Law, allows talented undergraduates to enter law school at the conclusion of their junior year of college. An early assurance program to the Loyola Stritch School of Medicine provides students with an articulated admission to medical school.

Academic Program

Jesuit educators believe that a solid foundation in the liberal arts and sciences is essential for students entering all professions. Loyola's Core Curriculum is designed to give students this foundation. The core requirements vary by college but usually include courses in expressive arts, history, literature, mathematical and natural sciences, philosophy, social sciences, and theology. The core allows students who are undecided about their majors to explore all possibilities before deciding upon a field of study.

Most majors require 128 semester hours for graduation. Exceptionally well-qualified students may apply to the Honors Program. Students may receive credit through the Advanced Placement Program (AP Program) tests, the International Baccalaureate (I.B.), and certain College-Level Examination

Program (CLEP) tests are accepted. Loyola students may participate in the Army and Naval ROTC programs through neighboring universities.

Off-Campus Arrangements

Students can choose to attend Loyola's Rome Center of Liberal Arts in Rome, Italy, for a semester or year, or they can choose to enroll in Loyola's study-abroad programs in Chile, China, England, France, Ireland, Japan, and Mexico.

Academic Facilities

The University's library system, including the Cudahy Library at the Lake Shore Campus and the Lewis Library at the Water Tower Campus, contains more than 1.3 million books and 12,000 periodical subscriptions. Other academic facilities include extensive laboratories for the biology, chemistry, and physics departments; a nursing resource center; and computing facilities on all campuses. The School of Business is located in a $38-million building on the Water Tower Campus.

The Martin D'Arcy Gallery of Medieval and Renaissance Art is located on the Lake Shore Campus along with the Fine Art Department's gallery and studios. The theater department's facilities include the Mullady Theatre, where the most sophisticated computerized lighting system in Chicago was recently installed, and the Studio Theatre, an experimental black-box facility. Loyola's FM radio station provides communication majors with on-campus production experience.

The Medical Center Campus in Maywood, a suburb of Chicago, consists of the Foster G. McGaw Hospital and the Stritch School of Medicine as well as the Mulcahy Outpatient Center, the Russo Surgical Pavilion, and the Cardinal Bernardin Cancer Center.

Costs

For the 2003–04 academic year, tuition for full-time undergraduates is $20,544. Based on double occupancy, room and board costs average $7900. Books and fees total about $1715 per year.

Financial Aid

Loyola attempts to meet the financial need of as many students as possible. Ninety-four percent of Loyola freshman receive some form of aid, including University-funded scholarships and grants, federal and state grants, work-study, and loans. Students are encouraged to file the Free Application for Federal Student Aid (FAFSA) by mid-February in order to receive consideration for all types of aid.

Merit scholarships are awarded to entering freshmen who have outstanding academic records. Presidential, Damen, and Loyola Scholarships are awarded to students who rank at the top of their high school graduating class and score well on the ACT or SAT I. Scholarship amounts for these programs are $5000–$12,500 per year. These awards are renewable for up to three years.

Other scholarships available include competitive awards for students admitted to the Honors Program and students from Jesuit/BVM/Sisters of Christian Charity high schools, National Merit/National Achievement finalists, theater scholarships (awarded by audition), and debate, leadership, nursing, and public accounting awards.

Transfer students who have completed 30 hours of college credit with an outstanding record of academic achievement may receive a Transfer Academic Scholarship. These awards are renewable for up to three years.

Faculty

More than 95 percent of the University's full-time faculty members hold the Ph.D. or the highest degree in their field. Faculty members generally teach both graduate and undergraduate students, and senior faculty members often teach Core Curriculum courses. At 13:1 the student-faculty ratio is far below the national average, giving undergraduates ready access to faculty members both as teachers and as advisers.

Student Government

Student government at Loyola provides a liaison between students and administration, emphasizes concerns for student rights, and provides a forum for debate, recommendation, and action on issues that pertain to students. Students also take an active role on University policy and advisory committees and as elected representatives in the residence halls.

Admission Requirements

Students seeking admission to Loyola University Chicago are evaluated on the basis of their overall academic record, including ACT or SAT scores. Most Loyola students rank in the upper quarter of their graduating class, but consideration is given to students in the upper half. Candidates should be graduating from an accredited secondary school with a minimum of 15 units, including courses in English, math, social studies, and science. Study of a foreign language is strongly recommended. Students must submit the application for admission along with high school transcripts, test scores, and a secondary school counselor recommendation. Admission counselors are available to meet and talk with students individually either before or after the application is submitted.

Transfer students with 20 semester hours or more of acceptable credit are evaluated on the basis of their college work only. Minimum acceptable grade point averages are 2.0 (C) for the College of Arts and Sciences and the School of Education and 2.5 (C+) for the Schools of Business Administration and Nursing. Candidates must also have been in good standing at the last college attended.

Application and Information

Applicants are notified of the admission decision three to four weeks after the application, supporting credentials, secondary school counselor recommendation, and $25 application fee are received.

Prospective students are encouraged to visit the campus. The Undergraduate Admission Office encourages students to schedule individual appointments and campus tours or to participate in one of the many campus programs offered throughout the year.

To obtain an application and further information and to arrange a visit, students should contact:

Undergraduate Admission Office
Loyola University Chicago
820 North Michigan Avenue
Chicago, Illinois 60611
Telephone: 312-915-6500
800-262-2373 (toll-free)
E-mail: admission@luc.edu
World Wide Web: http://www.luc.edu/

MAHARISHI UNIVERSITY OF MANAGEMENT

FAIRFIELD, IOWA

The University

Since its founding in 1971 by Maharishi Mahesh Yogi, the goal of Maharishi University of Management (Maharishi International University, 1971–95) has been to make education complete so that every student may enjoy academic excellence, development of consciousness and creativity, and a high quality of life in accord with natural law. One of the greatest strengths of the University is its emphasis on personal development. The practice of the Transcendental Meditation® and TM-Sidhi® programs is incorporated into students' daily schedules. The Consciousness-Based℠ approach provides students with a means to develop their full potential for inner and outer success. A substantial body of more than 600 scientific research studies has validated the effectiveness of this approach. Students make rapid academic progress while studying both traditional and innovative courses and show a marked enhancement in creativity, intelligence, and overall quality of life.

The private accredited University offers bachelor's, master's, and doctoral programs in a broad range of academic disciplines in the sciences, arts, and humanities. Faculty members include internationally recognized scholars and researchers who teach at both the undergraduate and graduate levels. Many faculty members are also involved in research at affiliated institutes such as the University's Center for Natural Medicine and Prevention (CNMP). The CNMP is one of eight institutes funded by the National Institutes of Health focusing on research in natural medicine and the only one specializing in minorities. Its research collaborators include the University of Iowa College of Medicine, Morehouse School of Medicine, Charles R. Drew University of Medicine and Science, and Cedars-Sinai Medical Center. The CNMP and other institutes at the University attract significant funding and peer recognition for their research.

Students study one course at a time through a four-week block system, with five blocks per semester. This allows students to focus in depth on each subject without the conflicting demands of other classes. Students report enthusiastically that with the block system at Maharishi University of Management their academic work is challenging, but at the same time less stressful. The block system affords other opportunities to the students, including the ability to participate in internships and study-abroad programs.

Maharishi University of Management graduates are accepted at leading professional and graduate schools and are successful in careers in business, government, natural health care, the arts, and other fields. Students gain a head start on their careers through business internships or research projects, for example, on-site ecological study in Arizona, Costa Rica, or Ecuador.

Students come to Maharishi University of Management from every state and more than fifty countries. The student body is a world family, excited about knowledge, openhearted and friendly, and dedicated to world peace. Most of the University's undergraduate students live on campus in single rooms. The campus is undergoing an ambitious reconstruction project to incorporate "green" principles such as sustainable energy, organic agriculture, and energy-efficient buildings. The architects utilize the principles of Maharishi Sthapatya Veda® design to promote harmony between individual life and the surrounding environment.

Students enjoy a positive and nourishing atmosphere that is virtually free of crime, drug abuse, and other problems that plague college campuses. Two national surveys of alumni indicate a remarkably high level of satisfaction with the education received at the University, in contrast to the reference group. Responses to the recent National Survey of Student Engagement, the most comprehensive assessment of effective practices in higher education, place Maharishi University of Management among the top in the nation.

There are numerous campus clubs representing the variety of student backgrounds, including international associations, an active student environmental organization, sports teams, and many others. Activities also include a wide variety of recreational events, including movies, dances, visiting speakers, and Student Government–sponsored conferences. Sports include aerobics, basketball, cross-country skiing, fitness training, floor hockey, golf, soccer, and tennis. The three-day breaks given after each monthlong academic block provide opportunities throughout the Midwest to participate in adventure sports such as kayaking, canoeing, mountain biking, and rock climbing.

Location

The University is located on the edge of Fairfield, Iowa (population 10,000), a surprisingly lively city that, through the University, has drawn long-term residents from across America and around the world. Students enjoy a wide variety of shops and restaurants, including a dozen restaurants serving international cuisine. Students take advantage of diverse cultural and recreational activities and a community that is a lively center for the arts. Many students find internships within the dynamic local business community, which has been called "the entrepreneurial capital of Iowa" by a former governor of Iowa. The community also offers opportunities for field trips, projects, consulting, and careers for graduates.

Majors and Degrees

The University offers a comprehensive range of bachelor's, master's, and doctoral programs, including the B.A. in fine arts (or B.F.A.) with emphases, majors, or minors available in digital media, theater arts, and visual arts; the B.A. or B.S. in computer science; the B.S. in biology, which qualifies as premedicine and includes emphasis in environmental studies; the B.S. in mathematics and physics; and the B.A. in education, electronics, literature (emphasis available in writing), Maharishi Vedic Medicine℠, Maharishi Vedic Science℠, management, and Sustainable Living, a holistic program focusing on renewable energy, organic agriculture, and green entrepreneurship. Undergraduate minors are also available in most of these areas.

Academic Program

Students study one subject at a time through a four-week block system in a forty-four week academic year. This allows in-depth focus on each subject and greater retention of knowledge without the conflicting demands of other classes. Faculty members relate each part of the discipline students study to the whole of the discipline, and the whole to the deepest level of the student's own intelligence. This approach makes learning personally relevant—students feel at home with all knowledge. First-year undergraduate students explore up to twenty disciplines in light of the Science of Creative Intelligence® course, the study of consciousness, which connects each branch of knowledge to the whole tree of knowledge. Through these first-year Natural Law Seminars, students thoroughly prepare to choose their major fields of study.

Off-Campus Arrangements

The University's block system easily accommodates overseas study. One-month courses are available at different times throughout the year in some of the world's most beautiful settings, including Australia, Greece, India, Italy, New Zealand, and the Swiss Alps.

Academic Facilities

The University's 262-acre campus includes 1 million square feet of academic, research, residential, administrative, and recreational facilities. Dining halls serve organic foods and a rich and wholesome vegetarian and dairy menu. Facilities also include research and teaching laboratories, a library offering the latest computer technology, a radio station, a student union building, movie and drama theaters, recreational and sports facilities, and an outstanding elementary and secondary school. All buildings on campus are smokefree. The redevelopment of the campus began in 1998 with the construction of the first building designed according to the principles of Maharishi Sthapatya Veda℠ design, ensuring that the campus can be more than environmentally friendly and actually promote clearer thinking, better health, and good fortune.

The library provides excellent resources for study and research, including access to extensive databases, the Internet, and CD-ROM reference sources, and holds tape, record, and CD-ROM collections. The library oversees a campuswide, closed-circuit television network and Internet videoconferencing capabilities. The library's catalog and serials list is accessible online, as are many items in its expanding electronic library.

The University is equipped with a campus computing network using fiber-optic cable to connect academic buildings and provide access to the Internet. Current development of a campus intranet is expected to allow students online access to Registrar's Office information. All student dorms have Ethernet connections. Students are provided with e-mail and voice mail accounts and access to the World Wide Web. There are five computer laboratories available, as well as a bank of library computers and an array of high-speed Internet ports. The University has more than one computer in departmental and public-access labs for every 4 on-campus students. (This compares to an approximate ratio of 1:16 at other universities.) Students also have access to specialized laboratories within their major departments, such as a state-of-the-art digital media laboratory.

Costs

Undergraduate tuition and fees for 2003–04 (for a forty-four-week academic year) total $24,030. Room and board are $5200, with students receiving private rooms.

Faculty

Maharishi University of Management has 67 full-time teaching and research faculty members and more than 18 adjunct and visiting faculty members. Seventy percent of the full-time faculty members have a Ph.D. or the highest degree in their field. The faculty members include internationally recognized scholars and researchers. With the University's 12:1 student-faculty ratio, students are assured maximum access to faculty members. Eighty-five percent of undergraduate courses and all of the first-year Natural Law Seminars are taught by senior faculty members, including the most distinguished professors in each academic department. The University has been awarded grants and contracts in excess of $32 million since 1977 from federal, state, and private sources, including prestigious research grants for which the University has competed successfully with large state universities and major research institutions.

Student Government

The Student Government Executive Committee, together with its sister organizations World Congress and Student Senate, serves as the official voice of the University's students. It provides communication channels between students and members of the faculty, administration; includes various committees to enhance the quality of student life; and sponsors and funds clubs, movies, concerts, dances, speakers, and many other activities. Its 9-member executive committee is elected every spring by the student body.

Admission Requirements

Applicants are considered for admission after a comprehensive evaluation of their completed application. While an applicant's previous academic performance is a primary consideration, commitment to gaining maximum benefit from educational opportunities offered at the University is also an important consideration. For bachelor's programs, a high school diploma, SAT I or ACT test scores (SAT I required for engineering majors), and essays are required. Three high school units each of English, mathematics, science, and social studies are recommended. For admission requirements for nondegree programs, students should contact the Office of Admissions.

Application by April 15 for fall admission and October 15 for spring admission ensures maximum financial assistance and space availability. Applications are accepted after those dates but are then considered on a space-available basis.

Application and Information

Applicants may download and print application forms from the University's Web site and mail them to the address below or submit them online. For more information, students should contact:

Brad Mylett, Director of Admissions
Maharishi University of Management
Fairfield, Iowa 52557

Telephone: 641-472-1110
800-369-6480 (toll-free)
Fax: 641-472-1179
E-mail: admissions@mum.edu
World Wide Web: http://www.mum.edu

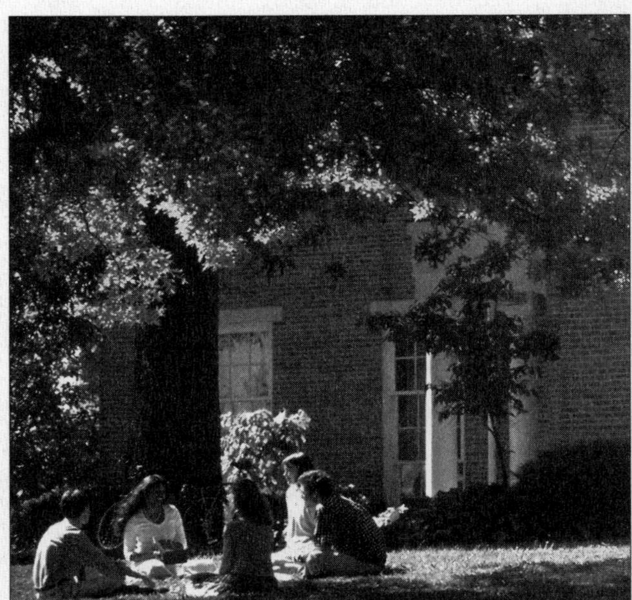

Students on the campus of Maharishi University of Management.

MANCHESTER COLLEGE

NORTH MANCHESTER, INDIANA

The College

Manchester College, founded in 1889, is an independent, coeducational, liberal arts college of the Church of the Brethren. Throughout its history, the College has held that values are central in the study of all majors and that the liberal arts provide a foundation of critical skills and sound scholarship.

An emphasis on service produces exceptional graduates who possess both professional ability and personal convictions, prepared for responsible lives that make a difference in the world.

Located at the edge of North Manchester, Indiana, Manchester College is primarily a residential school; 75 percent of the students live on the beautiful 124-acre campus. The academic buildings are constructed around a tree-lined central mall, and manicured flower gardens dot the campus. In addition, the resource-rich 100-acre Koinonia Environmental Retreat Center is located 12 miles from the academic campus.

The undergraduate enrollment is 1,150. Most students are between the ages of 18 and 22. Approximately 85 percent of the full-time students are from Indiana. Students from twenty-three states and twenty-nine countries were also enrolled during 2002–03. Sixteen percent of the students are members of the Church of the Brethren, but many different religious backgrounds are represented, and all are welcomed.

At Manchester, students get to know the members of the College's well-trained, concerned faculty on both a personal and an academic level. Faculty members take the time to assist students in a caring way, both in the classroom and as advisers.

There are five residence halls on campus that provide a variety of living experiences for students to choose from.

Manchester is a member of the National Collegiate Athletic Association Division III and offers nine men's and eight women's sports. The Physical Education and Recreation Center houses physical education classes, a fitness center, intercollegiate and intramural sports, and recreational activities. The College has a very strong intramural program that involves about 80 percent of its students.

In addition to its undergraduate program, Manchester College offers the Master of Accountancy and Master of Arts in contemporary leadership degrees.

Location

Located in the heart of Indiana's beautiful lake country, North Manchester is a thriving community of 6,000 people. It is within a half hour's drive of the Fort Wayne metropolitan area and is only 3½ hours from Chicago. Wide streets with large shade trees, graceful homes, and a beautiful park combine to provide a setting for classic college living.

Majors and Degrees

Manchester College grants Bachelor of Arts and Bachelor of Science degrees. Areas of study include accounting, adapted physical education, art, athletic training, biology, business administration, chemistry, coaching, communication studies, computer science, corporate finance, criminal justice, early childhood education, economics, elementary education, engineering science, English, environmental studies, exercise science, French, gender studies, German, gerontology, health and fitness instruction, history, journalism, mathematics, media studies, medical technology, music, nonprofit management, peace studies, philosophy, physical education, physics, political science, prelaw, premedicine, prenursing, pre–occupational therapy, pre–physical therapy, psychology, religion, secondary education, small-business administration, social work, sociology, Spanish, and theater arts. Individualized interdisciplinary majors can also be arranged to meet a student's particular goals.

Academic Program

The curriculum reflects a commitment to sound training in a specific area of study, the major, and broad development of skills and understanding through the liberal arts. In addition, students may explore interests different from specific career or professional areas through elective courses. This combination prepares students for careers or graduate school immediately after graduation and equips them for the challenges and changes of the coming century.

Manchester College operates on a 4-1-4 calendar and offers three summer sessions. Qualifying scores on the Advanced Placement Program and College-Level Examination Program tests of the College Board are recognized for college credit or advanced placement.

Off-Campus Arrangements

Manchester College students may study abroad for a semester or year in thirteen countries: at Philipps-Universität Marburg in Marburg/Lahn (Germany), the Institut International d'Études Françaises of the University of Strasbourg (France), the University of Nancy (France), the University of Barcelona (Spain), St. Mary's College in Cheltenham (England), Hokkai Gakuen University in Sapporo (Japan), the Dalian Institute of Foreign Languages in Dalian (People's Republic of China), the University of La Verne Athens Center (Greece), the Catholic University of Ecuador, the Federal University of Ouro Preto (Brazil), Satya Wacana University (Indonesia), Marmara University (Turkey), Cochin (India), and Universidad Veracruzana (Mexico).

During January session, numerous classes are held off campus. In the past several years, professors have taken classes to India, Africa, England, Mexico, Russia, France, Ghana, Vietnam, Nicaragua, Haiti, Germany, Costa Rica, Cuba, and Hawaii as well as destinations in the continental United States.

Field experiences and internships are offered for credit in accounting, broadcasting, business, criminal justice, early childhood education, elementary education, forensic chemistry, gerontology, health sciences practicum, journalism, peace studies, physical education, political science, psychology, secondary education, and social work.

Academic Facilities

Manchester College has a local area network of 165 IBM-compatible workstations, one for every 6 students. In addition, the Clark Computer Center houses file servers, three computer labs, and an AS400 for student use. PC labs tied to the network are located in each residence hall and the library.

Cordier Auditorium, dedicated in 1978, seats 1,300 people and has modern facilities for staging, lighting, and sound.

The Holl-Kintner Hall of Science has extensive laboratory facilities for biology, botany, physics, and geology as well as four separate chemistry laboratories and a number of research laboratories. Students in astronomy use the 10-inch Newtonian reflector telescope in the Charles S. Morris Observatory.

The Funderburg Library is a newly renovated, three-story building that houses more than 170,000 books, 800 periodicals, and 4,500 audio recordings available for student use. Computer connections allow access to major libraries across the country.

Costs

Tuition for 2003–04 is $17,040 for full-time students. Room and board costs for the residence halls (double occupancy) are $6340. The total charges are $23,380 for the academic year.

Financial Aid

Manchester offers extensive scholarship and grant assistance through institutional resources. Academic awards include Honors, Trustee, Presidential, and Dean's Scholarships. Special scholarships based on academic merit and interest are awarded in art, broadcasting, journalism, music, theater, and the video arts. Service scholarships and modern language scholarships are also awarded. International students can receive scholarships based on academic accomplishments and financial need. Manchester awards significant need-based grants. More than $7 million in College funds were awarded in 2002–03.

Approximately 97 percent of Manchester's students have some type of financial assistance, whether it is a scholarship, a grant, a loan, or campus employment. Questions about financial aid should be referred to the Office of Admissions.

Faculty

Manchester's faculty consists of 72 full-time and 19 part-time members. Ninety-three percent of full-time faculty members hold the highest degrees in their fields, and 94 percent of all courses are taught by full-time faculty members. The primary emphasis of the faculty members is teaching, but many are actively engaged in research as well. Faculty members serve as academic advisers, with a specially trained group of faculty members acting as primary advisers for new students. There is a 14:1 student-faculty ratio.

Student Government

Students at Manchester assume responsibility for the governmental and judicial activities of the College. The Community Council provides a forum for discussion and investigation of community concerns and a channel for evaluating and solving community problems.

Each of the residence halls elects a governing body, which is responsible for providing leadership.

The judicial system of the College includes three courts: the Judicial Board, the Community Court, and an administrative hearing panel. The Student Budget Board is charged with responsibility for receiving requests for funds to support the activity program of the College and for making the necessary appropriations.

The Manchester Activities Council organizes programming of student events. Students are offered a wide variety of leadership and participation opportunities as part of the College's student development program.

Admission Requirements

Manchester College seeks to enroll students whose scholastic record, test scores, and personality give promise of success in college. Graduation from an accredited high school or its equivalent is required.

The College recommends that students take 4 years of English, 3 years of laboratory science, 3 years of mathematics, 2 years of foreign language, and 2 years of social studies in high school. Students may take either the ACT or the SAT I, and personal recommendations from a high school principal or guidance counselor are required.

For transfer students, transcripts of all previous college work are required.

Application and Information

Students may apply for admission prior to each term. Applications are accepted on a rolling basis. There is a nonrefundable $20 application fee.

Interested students and their parents are encouraged to visit Manchester College and meet faculty members, coaches, and current students; sit in on classes; and take a campus tour. Arrangements can be made by writing or calling the Office of Admissions.

Application forms and further information may be obtained from:

Office of Admissions
Manchester College
North Manchester, Indiana 46962-0365
Telephone: 800-852-3648 (toll-free)
E-mail: admitinfo@manchester.edu
World Wide Web: http://www.manchester.edu

Students from the First Year Colloquium course Bodies in Motion lead residents of Peabody Retirement Community in Tai Chi.

MARIETTA COLLEGE

MARIETTA, OHIO

The College

Founded in 1835, Marietta College traces its roots to the Muskingum Academy, which was founded in 1797 as the first institution of higher learning in the Northwest Territory. Marietta's chapter of Phi Beta Kappa was the sixteenth in the nation, showing the College's early dedication to scholarship. Women were first admitted in 1897. About half of Marietta's 1,100 students come from a variety of states along the Eastern Seaboard, the South, and the Midwest; the rest come primarily from Ohio, the surrounding states, and nine other countries. More than forty states are represented in the Marietta student body. Situated on 120 acres within a block of downtown Marietta, the College has a number of academic and extracurricular facilities. Highlights of the campus include the McDonough Leadership Center, home to the most comprehensive program in leadership studies in the country; the McKinney Media Center, which houses two radio stations, a cable television station, and an award-winning student newspaper; and a pedestrian mall that enhances the central campus. A new recreation center will open in fall 2002, and it will feature a 200-meter competition track, performances, a gymnasium, indoor rowing tanks, and more. The new Rickey Science Center is scheduled to open in fall 2002, and it will offer state-of-the-art science labs to house biology, chemistry, biochemistry, environmental science, math, computer science, and physics.

Marietta is one of the few colleges in Ohio with intercollegiate crew, a sport in which it has excelled. Marietta's premier men's baseball program has earned twenty-two conference championships, fifteen world series appearances, and three world series titles for NCAA Division III. Students become involved with the campus radio and television stations, the student newspaper, the literary magazine, the yearbook, drama productions, and musical groups, plus service and special interest clubs. National invitational art exhibits are sponsored annually by the College for the educational and cultural enrichment of students.

Location

Historic Marietta, Ohio, was the first permanent settlement in the Northwest Territory, settled by New Englanders in 1787. The city of 17,000 people retains a New England flavor with its wide, tree-lined brick streets, Colonial architecture, and large parks. Marietta is readily accessible by car via Interstate 77 (2 miles from campus) or by air from Wood County/Parkersburg Airport in West Virginia (6 miles from campus). The Ohio and Muskingum Rivers meet in Marietta, contributing to the economic, cultural, and recreational vitality of the area.

Majors and Degrees

Marietta offers all students foundation study in the liberal arts and sciences and the opportunity to gain concentrated study in either the traditional liberal arts disciplines or a number of preprofessional programs. Among the liberal arts are strong programs in biochemistry, biology, chemistry, English, physics, and psychology. Preprofessional programs include accounting, computer science, education, environmental science, graphic design, journalism, musical theater, petroleum engineering, radio/television studies, and a nationally renowned program in sports medicine.

Marietta College grants four baccalaureate degrees: the Bachelor of Arts, the Bachelor of Fine Arts, the Bachelor of Science, and the Bachelor of Science in Petroleum Engineering. Marietta is the only liberal arts college in the nation offering the petroleum engineering degree, which is accredited by the Accreditation Board for Engineering and Technology. Marietta also offers a major in sports medicine, the first such program at a small college to be accredited by the National Athletic Trainers Association. Students have the opportunity to be involved in the Bernard McDonough Leadership Program. The program, known as "the Marietta Model," allows students to study leadership through a multidisciplinary liberal arts perspective. Students involved in the McDonough Leadership Program have the option of completing a minor in leadership or receiving a certificate. Along with the core courses of problem solving, critical thinking, and leadership, the program also requires an internship and community service involvement at one of the many organizations in the Marietta area or throughout the world.

"Binary" programs—cooperative study programs with other institutions—enable qualified Marietta students to earn two degrees in such fields as engineering, forestry, natural resources, and nursing. Preprofessional programs are offered in dentistry, law, medicine, physical therapy, and veterinary medicine.

The College's Education Department is accredited by the State of Ohio Department of Education and offers programs leading to licensure in early childhood, middle childhood, and secondary school education. Ohio has reciprocity with many other states. In addition, the College's programs are accredited by the North Central Association of Colleges and Schools.

Academic Program

Marietta students are known for both their breadth and depth of study. Freshmen take a special first-year program that begins with the College Experience Seminar and includes courses in composition (English 101), oral presentation (Speech 101), and mathematics. Every student also completes a liberal arts core of sequence courses in the humanities, social sciences, science, and the fine arts. There is an honors program for students who are prepared for and desire an extra challenge and who wish to graduate with honors.

Off-Campus Arrangements

Students seeking international study experience may make use of Marietta's association with the Institute for the International Education of Students (IES), the international study program of Central College of Iowa, or the programs of the East Central College Exchange. The programs have centers in Austria, the British Isles, France, Germany, Mexico, and Spain and in Asia. Students may also choose other accredited international-study programs. Finally, the College has numerous exchange programs with the People's Republic of China and annually has both faculty members and students teaching and studying in China.

Students whose interests range from economics to government and politics may take advantage of programs offered through the College's affiliation with two institutions located in the nation's capital. Courses are offered through the Washington Semester program of American University, and internships are available through the Washington Center for Learning Alternatives.

Academic Facilities

Marietta's Dawes Memorial Library will undergo a $1-million renovation next year. The library houses 250,000 volumes, 1,500 periodicals, and an online card catalog. As a member of OhioLINK, the Library provides access to a substantial number of books, materials, and databases. Among the special collections are the Rodney M. Stimson Collection of Americana, a collection of rare fifteenth- through nineteenth-century books, and an extraordinary collection of historic documents pertaining to the Northwest Territory and early Ohio. The card catalog and database are computerized through OCLC (Online Computer Library Center). The Hermann Fine Arts Center includes a laboratory theater, providing study and performance facilities for the College's art, drama, and music departments. Modern computing facilities include 200 personal computers connected by campus network. The campuswide network provides e-mail, Internet, and World Wide Web access. Students can work in computer labs, the library, and the student center, as well as in five academic buildings. The College has well-equipped science labs and its own astronomical observatory and a state-of-the-art computer lab for graphic design students. For instructional and communications purposes, the College operates a media center with a 9,200-watt stereo FM station, a 10-watt FM station, and a television station that reaches more than 12,000 homes via a community cable system. All programs are run by students.

Costs

The total two-semester cost for 2002–03 for a resident student was $25,958. This figure included $3084 for room, $2690 for board, and $350 for fees, but did not include the cost of books (approximately $500 per year) and personal expenses. Tuition was $19,762.

Financial Aid

About 85 percent of current Marietta students receive financial aid based on need. The average award for 2002–03 was $17,200. A number of merit-based scholarships are available in addition to funds allocated through College grants and federal and state sources. Members of the entering freshman class receive academic merit scholarships for three different levels of achievement. Students with a minimum GPA of 3.75, a minimum score of 30 on the ACT, or a minimum score of 1350 on the SAT I receive a Trustees scholarship ranging from $9000 to $13,000. Students with a GPA of 3.5, a score of 27 on the ACT, or a score of 1200 on the SAT I receive a President's scholarship ranging from $6000 to $9000. Finally, those students with a GPA of 3.25, a score of 25 on the ACT, or a score of 1150 on the SAT I receive a Dean's scholarship ranging from $4000 to $6000. Fine Arts Scholarships are awarded annually to winners of an art, music, and drama competition. Numerous work-study jobs are available to students in many campus departments. Grants are available for children and grandchildren of alumni.

Faculty

Close personal contact between students and professors is one of Marietta's primary features. All departmental faculty members, regardless of rank, teach courses. Full professors teach freshman courses. More than 80 percent of the College's full-time faculty members hold doctorates. Professors share their homes, outside interests, and hobbies with students. A 12:1 student-faculty ratio makes this possible.

Student Government

Through the Student Senate and its committee system, students have responsibility for the cocurricular aspects of College life. Students hold memberships on most faculty and trustee committees, as well as on various departmental committees. Housing boards in both men's and women's residence halls provide programming and dormitory governance. In addition, there are more than sixty-five active clubs and organizations on campus.

Admission Requirements

Admission decisions are based upon the high school record, scores on national exams (SAT or ACT), an essay, extracurricular involvement, and recommendations from guidance counselors or teachers. While admission is selective and competitive, individual consideration is given to each application. The admission committee seeks a cross section of students whose ability and past performance indicate that they can compete successfully. Credit is granted for Advanced Placement and International Baccalaureate higher-level 1B exams.

Application and Information

Students should apply early in their senior year of high school to guarantee a place in the fall. Marietta operates on a rolling admission plan, and students are notified of acceptance within one month after all application materials are complete. Students applying for financial aid should apply before March 1 of their senior year to be considered for merit scholarships.

To receive information about Marietta or to apply for admission, students should contact:

Office of Admission
Marietta College
Marietta, Ohio 45750-4005

Telephone: 800-331-7896 (toll-free)
E-mail: admit@marietta.edu
World Wide Web: http://www.marietta.edu

Erwin Hall (1850), the oldest building on the Marietta campus, is listed on the National Register of Historic Places.

MILWAUKEE SCHOOL OF ENGINEERING

MILWAUKEE, WISCONSIN

The School

Advancing beyond acquisition to the highly sophisticated application of knowledge has been the foundation of MSOE's educational philosophy for 100 years. This approach, the university's educational niche, produces graduates who are fully prepared to begin their first jobs and pursue challenging careers. MSOE graduates start their careers as work-ready problem solvers and develop into leaders: creating new products, starting or heading companies, and working to better their communities. MSOE is governed by a Board of Regents of more than 50 members who are elected from leaders in business and industry nationwide who are members of the more than 200-member MSOE Corporation.

The student body of 2,600 men and women comes from throughout the United States and numerous countries. Since its founding, the university has encouraged the enrollment of students of any race, color, creed, or gender. Approximately half of the full-time students live in three modern high-rise residence halls.

Representatives from hundreds of firms from throughout the country, including representatives from Fortune 500 companies, visit MSOE during the academic year to interview graduating students for employment and to discuss career opportunities. The University had a 98 percent placement rate over the past five years.

MSOE's Counseling Services Office provides individual assistance for students with educational, personal, or vocational concerns. Free, on-campus tutoring is provided by the Learning Resource Center and Tau Omega Mu, an honorary fraternity founded in 1953 for the purpose of aiding students who need extra help with their studies.

The Student Life and Campus Center provides on-campus recreational activities. This facility houses student activity rooms, student organization offices, a TV viewing area, a cafeteria, and a game room. Additional recreation areas can be found in the residence halls and the MSOE Sports Center.

There are more than fifty professional societies, fraternities, and other special interest groups on campus. Many students participate in intramural sports programs. MSOE is a member of the National Collegiate Athletic Association (NCAA) Division III Lake Michigan Conference. The Athletic Department sponsors NCAA student teams in men's baseball, basketball, cross-country, golf, ice hockey, soccer, tennis, indoor and outdoor track and field, volleyball, and wrestling and women's basketball, cross-country, golf, softball, tennis, indoor and outdoor track and field, and volleyball that compete with teams from other private colleges and universities in the Midwest.

In addition to the undergraduate degree programs listed below, MSOE offers six Master of Science degree programs: engineering, engineering management, environmental engineering, medical informatics (jointly offered with the Medical College of Wisconsin), perfusion, and structural engineering.

Milwaukee School of Engineering (MSOE) is a member of, and accredited by, the North Central Association of Colleges and Schools. Discipline-specific accrediting agencies are identified in the MSOE academic catalogs.

Location

The MSOE campus is located in the East Town section of downtown Milwaukee. Nearby are the Bradley Center, the Midwest Express Center, the Marcus Center for the Performing Arts, the theater district, churches of most denominations, major hotels and office buildings, restaurants, and department stores. Famous for its friendly atmosphere, Milwaukee offers students many opportunities for educational, cultural, and professional growth. The metropolitan area has more than 15,000 acres of parks and river parkways. A few blocks east of the MSOE campus is Lake Michigan, a place of year-round natural beauty. MSOE also offers classes in Appleton, Wisconsin, for students who wish to pursue select programs in the evening on a part-time basis.

Majors and Degrees

Four-year programs are offered that lead to Bachelor of Science degrees in business, construction management, engineering (architectural, biomedical, computer, electrical, industrial, mechanical, and software), engineering technology—transfer programs only (electrical and mechanical), international business, management, management information systems, and nursing. A Bachelor of Science or Bachelor of Arts degree is offered in technical communication. A two-degree, five-year option is available in a combination of engineering, business, construction management, and technical communication programs. An engineering/environmental engineering degree (B.S./M.S. combination) is also available. An RN to B.S.N. program is available through the MSOE School of Nursing. International study opportunities also exist.

Academic Program

MSOE guarantees graduation in four years for full-time undergraduate students who start on track as freshmen, follow the prescribed curriculum, and meet graduation requirements.

The degree programs at MSOE combine study in degree specialty courses with basic study in sciences, communication, mathematics, and humanities in a high-technology, applications-oriented atmosphere. Students who are admitted with advanced credit to a program leading to a bachelor's degree must complete at least 50 percent of the curriculum in residence at MSOE. MSOE operates on a quarter system. Students average between 16 and 19 credits per quarter, which represent a combination of lecture and laboratory courses. Undergraduate students also average 600 hours of laboratory experience.

MSOE offers students the opportunity to participate in the Air Force Reserve Officer Training Corps (AFROTC) program, the Army ROTC program, or the Navy ROTC program, which are offered in conjunction with Marquette University.

Academic Facilities

The Fred Loock Engineering Center adjoins the Allen-Bradley Hall of Science, forming a prime technical education and applied research complex. The Walter Schroeder Library houses more than 60,000 volumes, with collections that represent the specialized curricula of the university. Electronic technology enables the library to connect with libraries, government agencies, and other sources of information throughout the world. Academic computing facilities are available to all MSOE students and faculty members on an unlimited basis.

Full-time freshmen are required to participate in a Technology Package program that includes a notebook computer and affiliated services. A full range of software is available on these systems and via the local area network linked by a fiber-optic ring around the campus. State-of-the-art electrical, mechanical, industrial, and nursing laboratories complement the respective areas of study. The Rader School of Business has recently moved into a new facility with computer technology integrated throughout. The Applied Technology Center® (ATC) utilizes faculty and student expertise to solve technological problems confronting business and industry. The ATC is heavily involved in the transferring of new technologies into real business practice through the Rapid Prototyping Center (MSOE is the only university in the world to possess the four leading rapid prototyping technologies), Fluid Power Institute™, Photonics and Applied Optics Center, High Impact Materials and Structures Center, Construction Science and Engineering Center, and the Center for BioMolecular Modeling.

There are more than sixty laboratories at MSOE, many with industrial sponsorship from such companies as Johnson Controls, Aeroquip-Vickers, Harley-Davidson, Rockwell Automation/Allen-Bradley, Master Lock, Snap-On Tools, General Electric, and Outboard Marine Corporation. The key to the Rapid Prototyping Center's success is a high level of industrial parts design and fabrication activity using stereolithography, laminated object manufacturing, and fused deposition modeling systems.

Costs

For 2002–03, tuition was $21,855 per year, plus $1140 for the Technology Package (notebook computer, software, insurance, maintenance, Internet access, and user services). The cost of room and board in the residence halls is approximately $5115 per year. Books and supplies average $400 per quarter but may be somewhat higher the first quarter.

Financial Aid

Qualified students are assisted by a comprehensive financial aid program, including MSOE and industry-supported scholarships, student loans, and part-time employment; Federal Perkins Loan, Federal Stafford Student Loan, Federal Work-Study, Federal Pell Grant, and Federal Supplemental Educational Opportunity Grant Programs; and state-supported grant programs. Students can also visit MSOE's Web site (listed at the end of this description) for a financial aid estimate.

Faculty

There are 265 men and women on the MSOE faculty (full-time and part-time). Many are registered professional engineers, architects, and nurses in Wisconsin and other states. They and their colleagues in nontechnical academic areas are active in related professional societies. The student-faculty ratio is 11:1. MSOE does not utilize teaching assistants.

Student Government

The MSOE Student Government Association (SGA) represents clubs and fraternities as well as residence halls and commuting students. SGA appoints representatives to the Campus Security and Disciplinary Hearing committees and the Alumni Association's Board of Directors.

Admission Requirements

Each applicant to MSOE is reviewed individually on the basis of his or her potential for success as determined by academic preparation. Admission may be gained by submitting an application for admission and the appropriate transcripts. High school students are encouraged to complete math through precalculus (including algebra and geometry), chemistry, biology (nursing), physics, and 4 years of English. All entering freshmen are also required to provide results from the ACT or the SAT.

Transfer opportunities exist into the junior year of the Bachelor of Science in electrical engineering technology, management, mechanical engineering technology, and technical communication programs with the appropriate associate degree or equivalent credits.

Application and Information

Classes start in September, November, March, and late May. Freshmen and transfer students may enter at the beginning of any quarter; however, entry in the fall quarter is recommended. An application for admission may be obtained by contacting the address below or by visiting MSOE's Web site listed below. Applicants are encouraged to visit MSOE and have a preadmission counseling interview. Transfer students are required to submit transcripts from all prior institutions attended. An applicant's prior course work is reviewed to determine eligibility for admission. Required course work varies depending on the desired course of study.

Admission Office
Milwaukee School of Engineering
1025 North Broadway
Milwaukee, Wisconsin 53202-3109
Telephone: 414-277-6763
800-332-6763 (toll-free)
E-mail: explore@msoe.edu
World Wide Web: http://www.msoe.edu

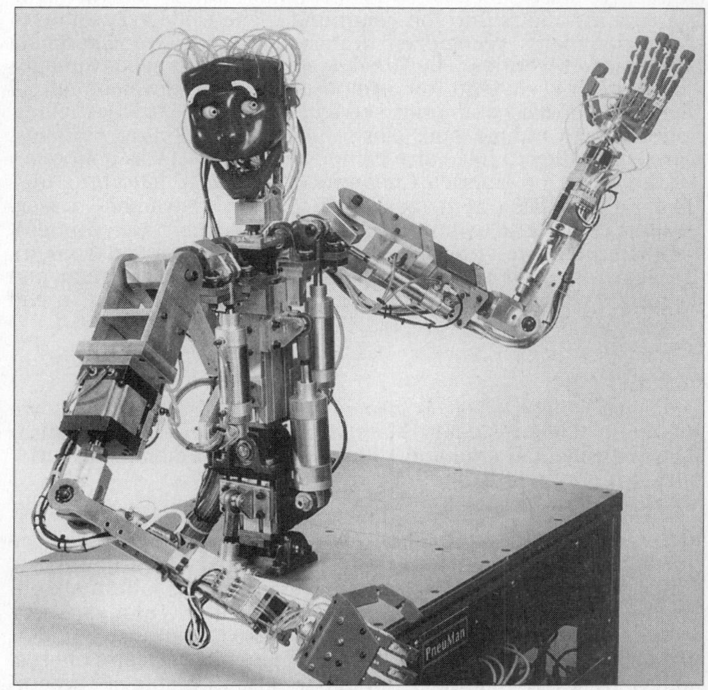

PneuMan, 3 students' senior project and MSOE's spokesman, is just one example of what MSOE students can achieve.

MISSOURI VALLEY COLLEGE

MARSHALL, MISSOURI

The College

Missouri Valley College (MVC) is a private, coeducational liberal arts college related to the Presbyterian Church (U.S.A.). It is committed to preparing young people to become active and contributing members of their communities. MVC is situated on 150 acres; its student body in 2003 is made up of 1,395 students from forty-one states and twenty-nine countries. The College offers a rich tradition of personalized liberal arts education with a focus on career preparation.

Founded in 1889 by a group of Presbyterian and civic leaders in Marshall, Missouri, the College has been accredited by the North Central Association of Colleges and Schools since 1916. Missouri Valley College is approved by the Missouri State Department of Education and the Board of Christian Education of the Presbyterian Church (U.S.A.).

In addition to academic facilities, including the historic Baity Hall, the newly built Technology Center, Ferguson Center, and Collins Science Center, there are four men's dormitories, one women's dormitory, and numerous on-campus houses and apartments available for students. Built in 1991, the Georgia Robertson Burns Multi-purpose Athletic Complex is recognized as one of the premier small-college facilities in the country. The building includes a full recreational area (basketball courts, indoor track, and other facilities) as well as classrooms, locker rooms, a concession area, the Missouri Valley College Athletic Hall of Fame trophy room, and seating to satisfy numerous events.

Missouri Valley College offers many opportunities to be involved on campus and within the community. The College is home to four nationally recognized fraternities and two nationally recognized sororities. The Greek system offers many advantages in improving students on campus, including development of leadership skills, community service, a variety of social activities, career networking, and close bonds with fellow students. Missouri Valley College also competes in the NAIA as a member of the Heart of America Conference. Viking athletic programs include baseball (men), basketball (men and women), cheerleading (men and women), cross-country (men and women), football (men), golf (men and women), rodeo (men and women), soccer (men and women), softball (women), track (men and women), volleyball (men and women), and wrestling (men and women).

Location

Missouri Valley College is located in Marshall, Missouri, a town of about 13,000 residents. Marshall is 1 hour east of the Kansas City metropolitan area and 1 hour west of Columbia, Missouri.

Majors and Degrees

The Arts and Humanities Division of Missouri Valley College offers Bachelor of Arts degrees in the areas of art, English, English education, mass communication, philosophy and religion, speech communication and theater, and speech/communication/theater education. Courses in music, Spanish, French, Latin, and English as a second language are also offered. Dance, English, and music minors are also available at Missouri Valley College.

The College's Business Division offers Bachelor of Arts, Bachelor of Science, and Associate of Arts degrees in the following areas: accounting, actuarial science, agribusiness, business administration (with the following concentrations: finance, management, marketing, and small-business development), and economics. The division also offers a two-year Associate of Arts degree with a major in small-business management. Students are encouraged to seek double majors within the division or in a complementary discipline such as computer information systems. Minors are available in accounting, agribusiness, business administration, and economics.

Offered through the Division of Education and Physical Education, the Missouri Valley College Teacher Education Program is approved by the Missouri State Board of Education and accredited by the North Central Association of Colleges and Schools. MVC offers certification in the following areas: early childhood, elementary grades, middle school, secondary school, and special education cross-categorical. Missouri Valley Teacher Education Program graduates are well represented throughout the nation, with a 95 percent employment rate.

The Human Services Division offers Bachelor of Arts degrees in human services/agency management and recreation administration. Students may apply for the specialized American Humanics Program, qualifying them to become certified American Humanics graduates. Academic courses stress the knowledge students need to become successful nonprofit youth agency administrators. American Humanics was founded at Missouri Valley College in 1948, and Missouri Valley College is the first institution to bring American Humanics into international light.

In the Math and Science Division, Bachelor of Science degrees are obtainable in biology, computer information systems, and mathematics. MVC also offers a Bachelor of Arts degree in biology. Minors are available in biology, chemistry, and mathematics. The division collaborates with the Teacher Education Program to offer certification to teach science and mathematics.

The Social Science Division offers Bachelor of Arts and Bachelor of Science degrees in the following areas: alcohol and drug studies, criminal justice, history, political science/public administration, psychology, and sociology; a Bachelor of Science degree is offered in social studies education. A prelaw curriculum is an option for those interested in law school. Practicum and internship experiences are available, as are service learning and volunteer opportunities.

Academic Program

The academic program of Missouri Valley College has been formulated to promote the development of the student within the mission and goals of the College. Educational policy is intended to ensure the academic growth of the student within a framework of social, physical, and spiritual growth.

The academic year consists of two semesters, with summer courses available. While the number of semester hours required for graduation varies with the program chosen, a minimum of 128 hours is required for a degree. A student must complete the required semester hours in a major as well as the basic requirements of the core curriculum. With an emphasis in liberal arts education, the core curriculum provides general education through approximately 40 hours of core classes.

Academic Facilities

The campus of Missouri Valley College has a changed look that goes well beyond mere appearances. The College has made great strides in enhancing the technology offered to both students and teachers, as evidenced by completion of the Eckilson-Mabee Theatre and the addition of 18,000 square feet of classroom and library space geared toward education students and computer lab space. The new addition onto Mabee includes two presentation rooms on the second floor, one of which is complete with wireless laptop computers, which have Internet access, and an instructor's station, where a professor can access everything from compact discs and DVDs to the Internet for sharing as part of a presentation. There is also a high-technology version of the old overhead projector that digitizes information and can even convert a three-dimensional object into a computer picture for sharing on the large screen at the front of the room, which replaces the traditional chalkboard.

Other major projects within the last year have involved renovations of the old chapel on the upper floor of Baity Hall into a learning center with computers and tutors available to assist fellow students and an extensive remodeling of Murrell Library. The Main Library is located in the Murrell Memorial Library building, and the Library Annex is located in the Tech Center building. This part of the library houses library collections that include art, business and economics, English, humanities, psychology, science and mathematics, and the social sciences.

Costs

Tuition and fees at Missouri Valley College for 2002–03 were $12,300 per year, and room and board averaged $5200. For resident students, a nonrefundable deposit of $500 is required; a $250 deposit is required for commuter students.

Financial Aid

Financial need may be met through a combination of state, federal, and institutional aid, which is available to all qualified students. Institutional awards and grants are offered in many areas.

To be eligible for financial aid, a student must be admitted to the College. All students receiving federal or state-based program aid must file the Free Application for Federal Student Aid. New students need to file the financial aid application by the date of enrollment. International students are required to fill out a standard Affidavit of Support, in addition to their application for admission, to document their ability to pay their education expenses.

The College participates in the following federally sponsored aid programs: the Federal Pell Grant, Federal Supplemental Educational Opportunity Grant, Federal Work-Study Program, and Subsidized and Unsubsidized Federal Stafford Student Loan Program. Missouri Student Grants are available to Missouri students carrying a minimum of 12 hours per semester who can prove financial need. Full-time resident students are able to defray a portion of their College costs by participating in the Missouri Valley College Work & Learn Program on campus. Generally, compensation that would otherwise be provided for this work is credited toward the student's account.

A variety of scholarships are awarded to students who have excelled in fields of study, community activities, or athletic competition, but continuing in the activity is not required to maintain the scholarship. Missouri Valley College's admissions counselors can advise prospective students of the full program of available scholarships.

Faculty

The total number of faculty members the College employs is 103, of whom 67 are full-time. The student-faculty ratio is 17:1, with more than 53 percent of faculty members holding terminal degrees. The College prides itself on the good rapport and excellent personal relationships students and faculty members share.

Student Government

This is the inaugural year for the Student Government Association (SGA) at Missouri Valley College. In October 2002, a group of students started meeting, with the intention of creating a working SGA. In spring 2003, the mission was accomplished. Elections for the 2003–04 academic year are to be held in April 2003. There are numerous ways in which students—including incoming freshmen—can be involved in the SGA. The mission of the SGA is to uphold and enhance all areas of student life on campus.

Admission Requirements

The College desires to select freshmen and transfer students who will benefit from the College's full-service program and who demonstrate the potential for academic success. Each application for admission is reviewed individually.

Students should take the following steps to satisfy admission procedures: complete an application form and submit it in person or by mail to the Office of Admissions, along with a $10 nonrefundable application fee; provide the Office of Admissions an official high school transcript indicating graduation from high school (applicants may provide a copy of the General Educational Development (GED) certificate in lieu of transcripts); and provide a copy of the results of either the ACT or SAT. A student's high school counselor may assist in arranging for the test and obtaining the results. Students who have not taken the SAT or ACT by the time of their arrival on campus are contacted by the Office of Admissions and required to take the ACT during their first semester.

Students who wish to transfer from another institution, including those who have completed junior college work, should submit the following materials to ensure that their applications are processed promptly: the Missouri Valley College application for admission; a high school transcript or the recognized equivalent of a high school diploma; official transcripts of all previous collegiate work, including financial aid transcripts; and the ACT or SAT score (not necessary for students with more than 27 transfer hours). Students should provide a copy of the previous college's catalog to ensure proper credit transfer. If official transcripts are not received within a reasonable time, the student's academic and financial aid status may change.

Application and Information

An application and additional information may be obtained by contacting:

Office of Admissions
Missouri Valley College
500 East College Street
Marshall, Missouri 65340
Telephone: 660-831-4000 or 4114
E-mail: admissions@moval.edu
World Wide Web: http://www.moval.edu

Baity Hall, on the campus of Missouri Valley College.

MORNINGSIDE COLLEGE

SIOUX CITY, IOWA

The College

The Morningside College experience cultivates a passion for lifelong learning and a dedication to ethical leadership and civic responsibility. For more than 100 years, the goal of Morningside College has been to provide students with an education of the highest quality. Morningside is rooted in a strong church-related, liberal arts tradition, and its challenge is to prepare students to be flexible in thought, open in attitude, and confident in themselves.

Founded in 1894, Morningside College is a private, four-year, coeducational, liberal arts institution affiliated with the United Methodist Church. The College seeks both students and faculty members representing diverse social, cultural, ethnic, racial, and national backgrounds.

At the graduate level, Morningside confers a Master of Arts in Teaching, with specialization in elementary education, special education, and technology-based learning.

Morningside College's approximately 1,000 students are encouraged to participate in a wide variety of activities, including departmental, professional, and religious organizations; honor societies; and sororities and fraternities. A newspaper, literary magazine, yearbook, and campus radio station are all under student direction. These activities provide students with many opportunities to develop leadership, interpersonal, and social skills. Since nearly all activities on campus are student initiated and student directed, ample opportunities for leadership development exist. Music recitals and concerts, theater productions, and an academic and cultural arts and lecture series are held each semester. Intercollegiate athletics are available for men in baseball, basketball, cross-country, football, golf, soccer, and track and field and for women in basketball, cross-country, golf, soccer, softball, track, and volleyball. A variety of intramural activities are available.

The Hindman-Hobbs Recreation Center includes a pool, saunas, racquetball courts, a weight room, three basketball courts, and a jogging track.

Location

Morningside College is located on a 41-acre campus in Sioux City, the fourth-largest city in Iowa. The campus is based in a residential section of the community, adjacent to a city park, swimming pool, and tennis courts and within 5 minutes of a major regional shopping mall. The Sioux City metropolitan area offers a blend of urban shopping, commerce, and recreation in a scenic, rural setting. Students find Morningside's Sioux City location to be advantageous in seeking internship opportunities and full- or part-time employment.

Majors and Degrees

The five undergraduate degrees conferred by Morningside College are the Bachelor of Arts, Bachelor of Science, Bachelor of Science in Nursing, Bachelor of Music, and Bachelor of Music Education. Career programs consist of accounting, art, biology, business administration, chemistry, computer science, corporate communications, elementary education, engineering physics, English, graphic arts, history, interdisciplinary studies, mass communications, mathematics, music, nursing, philosophy, photography, political science, psychology, religious studies, Spanish, special education, and theater. Students choosing to teach in secondary school may be certified in most academic majors.

In cooperation with other institutions, Morningside offers preprofessional programs in engineering, law, medical technology, medicine, the ministry, pharmacy, physical therapy, physician assistant studies, and veterinary medicine.

Academic Program

Morningside operates on a two-semester system; sessions are held from late August to December and from January to early May. Evening classes are offered each semester. A 3-week May interim and two 5-week summer sessions are also available.

Morningside College is committed to the liberal arts as a foundation for every field of concentration at the undergraduate level. Requirements in general education consist of a distribution of studies in the humanities, natural sciences, social sciences, and some interdisciplinary courses.

Special opportunities include a voluntary Honors Program, in which students meet weekly to discuss such focus topics as Ancient Rome and the Eighteenth Century. Friday is Writing Day is a weekly discussion format that allows students and faculty members to read aloud and react to one another's writing.

The College's commitment to technology cuts across the academic divisions. In the music and art departments, for example, students produce movies and multimedia productions, arrange music, and create CD-ROMs. Mass communication majors work in state-of-the-art radio and television studio environments. Engineering, physics, and chemistry students learn through computerized labs beginning their first year, and behavioral and health studies majors gain clinical experience in the computerized animal laboratory.

Virtually all Morningside students use computers to complete papers and projects. The College also provides student computer facilities on campus that link students to the world via free e-mail and Internet use.

Off-Campus Arrangements

Morningside students who qualify have the opportunity to take advantage of special programs for off-campus study. Programs are available for a semester or the entire school year. The College has agreements with schools in England, Japan, and Northern Ireland.

Students participate in exchange programs with Kansai Gadai University in Japan, Queen's University, the University of Ulster, and Belfast Institute for Further and Higher Education in Northern Ireland.

In addition, Morningside has opportunities for students to enroll for a semester at American University to study the U.S. government in action. Students can also enroll for a semester at Drew University to study the United Nations. Students who participate in these programs maintain their enrollment at Morningside College.

Academic Facilities

The Hickman-Johnson-Furrow Library has more than 114,000 volumes, more than 5,000 audio recordings and video materials, and more than 500 current print periodical subscriptions. The library also subscribes to a database indexing 1,700 journals, of which 700 are full-text and available online to students in the library. In addition, the library houses a closed-circuit television system, a television studio, a microcomputer lab, and classrooms.

The Eugene C. Eppley Fine Arts Building is one of the finest music and art facilities in the Midwest. The auditorium seats 1,500 people and is noted for its acoustical qualities and the majestic Sanford Memorial Organ. The MacCollin Classroom Building, adjoining the auditorium, houses offices, art studios, practice rooms, and classrooms for music and art students.

The Robert M. Lincoln Center houses the College's division of business administration and economics and contains a library, auditorium, microcomputer lab, conference room, and several classrooms.

Costs

Tuition and fees for 2002–03 were $14,570, and room and board were $5120. These figures do not include books and personal expenses.

Financial Aid

In 2001–02, more than $12 million was awarded in financial aid to Morningside students, with an average financial aid package of $16,010. The financial aid resources of federal, state, and College programs are available to Morningside students through a combination of scholarships, grants, loans, and work-study employment. Morningside values students who achieve both in and out of the classroom—people who are thinkers and doers. Morningside Celebration of Excellence Scholarships recognize academic excellence and outstanding service, and awards of up to $10,000 per year are renewable for four years. Morningside also values its ties with alumni and the United Methodist Church, and those awards are also renewable for four years. Students are encouraged to submit the Free Application for Federal Student Aid (FAFSA) as early as possible. The College's code number is 001879. The annual priority deadline for need-based financial aid is March 1.

Faculty

Eighty-one percent of Morningside College's 67 full-time faculty members have earned the terminal degree in their chosen field. The College also employs 42 part-time instructors and has a 10:1 student-faculty ratio.

Student Government

Student government is directly responsible for regulation, supervision, and coordination of student campus activities. The president of the student body is a voting member of the Board of Directors, allowing for student input in decisions facing the Board.

Admission Requirements

Morningside College selects students for admission whose scholastic achievement and personal abilities provide a foundation for success at the college level. While the College seeks students who rank in the upper half of their graduating class, each application is considered on an individual basis. The student's academic record, class rank, and test scores are considered. Transfer students must have a minimum 2.0 GPA on previous college work to qualify for automatic admission. It is the policy and practice of Morningside College to not discriminate against persons on the basis of age, sex, religion, creed, race, color, national or ethnic origin, sexual orientation, or physical or mental disability.

Application and Information

Rolling admission allows for flexibility; however, prospective students are encouraged to apply as early as possible before the semester in which they wish to enroll. Transfer and international students are welcome. Catalogs, application forms, and financial aid forms are available from the Office of Admissions.

For further information, students should contact:

Office of Admissions
Morningside College
1501 Morningside Avenue
Sioux City, Iowa 51106
Telephone: 712-274-5111
800-831-0806 (toll-free)
E-mail: mscadm@morningside.edu
World Wide Web: http://www.morningside.edu

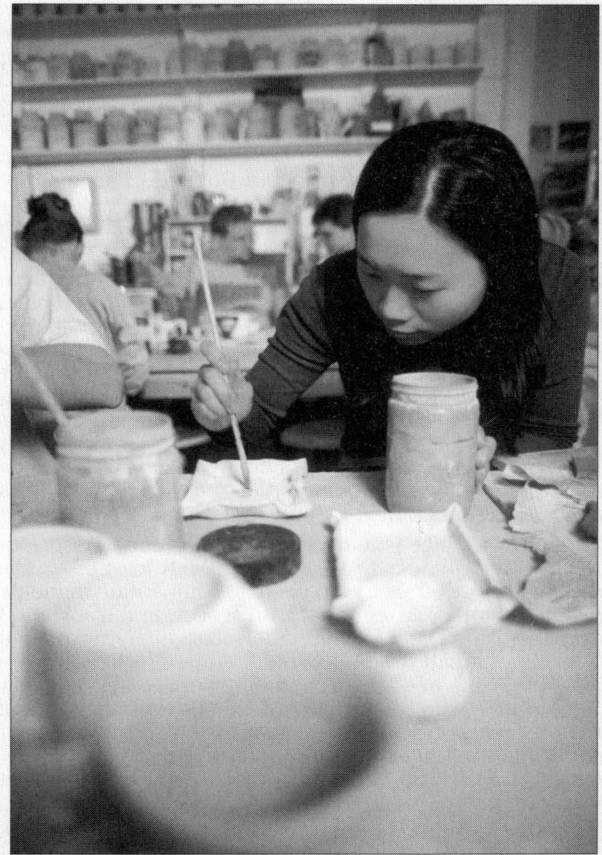

Morningside College provides a welcoming environment for art majors.

MOUNT MERCY COLLEGE

CEDAR RAPIDS, IOWA

The College

Mount Mercy College is distinguished by a unique blend of career preparation and liberal arts, strengthened by a strong emphasis on leadership and service. A Catholic, coeducational four-year college, Mount Mercy is fully accredited by the North Central Association of Colleges and Schools.

Although the College offers a number of professional programs, its career preparation is not limited to those areas. Students majoring in English or history, for example, are just as likely to benefit from internships as students in business or social work. There is a focus on workplace skills such as group process and presentations—competencies that help graduates begin their careers. Mount Mercy believes strongly in a firm liberal arts foundation of analysis, critical thinking, and communication—skills that help graduates adapt to a changing world and find long-term career success.

Through its Emerging Leaders and Campus Ministry programs, the College supports the concept of servant leadership. This tradition of service is a legacy of the Sisters of Mercy, who founded the College in 1928. The College welcomes students of all faiths.

Mount Mercy's high academic quality and its relatively moderate cost make it one of the best values in Midwest higher education. The College offers thirty-six major fields of study, including several interdisciplinary majors. In the College's Partnership program, professors are paired with freshman students to support their transition to college and to enhance the intellectual growth needed to assure academic success.

Student activities include more than thirty clubs and organizations, a student newspaper, a choir and hand-bell ensemble, and a pom squad and cheerleaders, along with such annual events as Hillfest and Spring Fling. Each May, commencement exercises are followed by a celebration for graduates and their families on Mount Mercy's hilltop. During the school year, many student activities—including Club Friday, a Friday afternoon gathering of students, faculty members, and staff members—take place in the Lundy Commons, which houses a game room, TV rooms, convenience store, conference rooms, student organization offices, the *Mount Mercy Times* office, lounge areas, and a bookstore.

Mount Mercy College is a member of the National Association of Intercollegiate Athletics (NAIA) and the Midwest Classic Conference. The College offers intercollegiate competition in men's basketball, baseball, cross-country, golf, soccer, and track and field. In women's sports, the College offers basketball, cross-country, golf, soccer, softball, track and field, and volleyball. These programs have combined for more than twenty conference championship Mount Mercy teams and individuals that regularly qualify for regional and national championship events. In addition, Mount Mercy student-athletes are annually recognized as NAIA academic all-Americans. Intramural activities include basketball, cross-country, flag football, golf, softball, and volleyball.

About 400 of Mount Mercy's 1,432 students live in campus housing. The College offers a variety of living arrangements. Mount Mercy's newest residence, which opened in fall 1999, houses 144 students in eight homelike, four-bedroom suites. A network of tunnels connects campus buildings; many students wear shorts all winter.

Location

Mount Mercy is just minutes from downtown Cedar Rapids' museums, malls, movie theaters, and restaurants. Local businesses offer numerous internships and employment opportunities. The 40-acre, tree-lined campus is tucked into a residential neighborhood of well-kept homes, neat lawns, and good neighbors. Mount Mercy's hilltop, with its sweeping view of the city skyline, is said to be the highest point in Linn County. The city bus stops at the College's "front door," providing convenient in-town transportation. Cedar Rapids is served by six major airlines and is just a 4- or 5-hour drive from Chicago, Minneapolis–St. Paul, Omaha, and St. Louis. Mount Mercy's location in a thriving Midwestern city helps students explore career possibilities and, when they graduate, find promising opportunities. Both economically and culturally, Cedar Rapids offers an outstanding quality of life.

Majors and Degrees

Mount Mercy awards the Bachelor of Arts, Bachelor of Science, Bachelor of Business Administration, Bachelor of Applied Science, Bachelor of Applied Arts, and Bachelor of Science in Nursing degrees.

The Bachelor of Arts degree is awarded to graduates who major in applied philosophy, art, biology, communication, criminal justice, criminal justice/business administration–interdisciplinary, English, English/business administration–interdisciplinary, history, international studies, mathematics, music, music/business administration–interdisciplinary, music education, political science, political science/business administration–interdisciplinary, psychology, psychology/business administration–interdisciplinary, religious studies, secondary education, social work, sociology, sociology/business administration–interdisciplinary, speech/drama, urban and community services, and visual arts/business administration–interdisciplinary.

The Bachelor of Science degree is awarded to graduates who major in biology, business, computer information systems, computer science, elementary education, health services administration, mathematics, medical technology, nursing, and secondary education.

Original endorsements, coupled with the secondary education major, may be completed in art, biology–education, business–marketing/management, English/language arts, history, mathematics–education, music–education, social science American government, social science American history, social science psychology, social science sociology, social science world history, and speech communication theater.

The Bachelor of Business Administration is awarded to graduates who major in accounting, administrative management, marketing, and secondary education. The Bachelor of Science in Nursing is awarded to graduates in nursing.

The Bachelor of Applied Science and Bachelor of Applied Arts degree programs are designed for students with technical training who wish to broaden their specialized background to include a liberal arts education. The Bachelor of Applied Science degree is awarded to graduates who major in accounting, administrative management, biology, business, computer information systems, computer science, health services administration, marketing, and mathematics. The Bachelor of Applied Arts degree is awarded to graduates who major in art, biology, criminal justice, history, mathematics, music, political science, psychology, religious studies, sociology, and speech drama.

Academic Program

Mount Mercy College requires 123 semester hours for graduation, with a cumulative grade point average of at least 2.0 (on a 4.0 scale). General education requirements include two courses in English, two in social sciences, and one each in fine arts, history, mathematics, multicultural studies, natural science, philosophy, religious studies, and speech. Students apply for admission to their major program in the spring of the sophomore year. The College gives credit for related experience based on portfolio presentations and for independent study arranged by the student and the instructor. Graduation requirements may vary according to the major field of study.

Special academic opportunities are offered to outstanding students through special honors sections of general education courses. Students graduating in the honors program receive special recognition at commencement.

Mount Mercy's academic year consists of fall and spring semesters, plus a winter term. This four-week term offers required courses as well as exploratory electives, allowing students to make more rapid progress toward their degrees. In addition, two five-week summer sessions are held.

Off-Campus Arrangements

Mount Mercy College has an exchange program with the University of Palacky in Olomouc, Czech Republic.

Academic Facilities

The Busse Library provides an inviting study and research environment. Internet access opens other major libraries to students as well. The library houses the computer center; a computer classroom used for instruction in writing, accounting, and computer skills; a media center; individual study carrels; group study rooms; and a variety of other comfortable study areas.

Basile Hall is a new business and biology building that opened in summer 2003, providing thirteen technology-ready classrooms and teaching labs, four seminar rooms, and a computer-teaching laboratory.

All on-campus student rooms and faculty/staff offices are connected to a campus network. The College also has an ICN (Iowa Communications Network) fiber-optics classroom, making it possible for students in more than one location to take the same course, interacting with other students and with the instructor.

Costs

Full-time tuition for the 2002–03 academic year was $15,300, about at the midpoint among Iowa private colleges. Major fees are included in this figure. Room costs were $2060 in residence halls and $2640 in apartments. Two meal plans are offered: the nineteen-meal-per-week plan, which cost $3014, and the fifteen-meal plan, $2804. Estimated annual costs for a resident student, including books, supplies, and personal expenses, were $24,695.

Financial Aid

Nearly all Mount Mercy freshmen receive some form of financial aid, including Mount Mercy scholarships or grants, federal or state grants, loans, on-campus employment, or a combination of these sources. The College awarded forty-two Presidential Scholarships of up to $6700 for the 2002–03 school year to high school seniors who had an ACT score of at least 26 and a high school grade point average of at least 3.5. Other awards also are made on the basis of ACT score and GPA. Each year, students who have been admitted to Mount Mercy and identified as Presidential Scholars are invited to campus to compete for the Holland Scholarship, a full-tuition award named for the first president of Mount Mercy. Three Holland Scholarships were awarded for the 2002–03 school year. Students may also apply for the Merit Award, given to entering freshmen and transfer students on the basis of their demonstrated leadership in school and community activities. In addition, scholarships are available to students with records of achievement in art, drama, and music and to those who are planning to major in social work. In 2002–03, the College awarded more than $5 million in institutional scholarships and grants to qualified students.

Students who show financial need may be eligible for the Federal Pell Grant, the Iowa Tuition Grant, Federal Stafford Student Loan, and on-campus employment. Students in work-study positions typically earn from $1000 to $1500 a year.

To apply for Mount Mercy scholarships and grants, students must first be admitted to the College. Early application is advised. The priority deadline for filing the FAFSA (Free Application for Federal Student Aid) is March 1. Students should check other deadlines with their high school counselors or call the Mount Mercy financial aid office.

Faculty

Most of Mount Mercy's 68 full-time and 71 part-time faculty members hold the terminal degree in their fields. Many have been recognized for their achievements: 2 have been Fulbright Fellows, several have received grants from the National Endowment for the Humanities and the National Endowment for the Arts, and many others have been recognized by their professional organizations. With a faculty-student ratio of 14:1, Mount Mercy offers students the opportunity to know their teachers well and to learn from them in an informal, friendly, and supportive environment.

Student Government

The official voice of the student at Mount Mercy is the Student Government Association (SGA). Its officers serve on College committees, and SGA is represented at regular faculty meetings. An SGA petition to the faculty resulted in adding a fall break to the academic calendar. SGA is the body through which all other campus organizations are formed and funded.

Admission Requirements

Mount Mercy admits students whose academic preparation, abilities, interests, and personal qualities give promise of success in college. Applicants are considered on the basis of academic record, class rank, test scores, and recommendations. An Admission Committee reviews the applications of students with minimum qualifications. Students may apply online. To apply, students must submit an application for admission, a transcript of high school credits, scores from ACT or SAT examinations, and a $20 application fee. Transfer students must submit official transcripts from all colleges attended. Mount Mercy College has an agreement with several two-year colleges in Iowa through which degree graduates of these colleges may be admitted to Mount Mercy with junior standing.

Prospective students are encouraged to visit the campus and meet with a faculty member in their area of interest. Special campus visit days are scheduled each year, and individual appointments also may be made. Overnight accommodations in residence halls can be arranged.

Application and Information

Students who wish to be considered for Mount Mercy scholarships and grants should submit their applications for admission as early as possible after their junior year in high school. Admission decisions are made on a rolling basis, and the College notifies students of its decision within ten days of receiving the necessary forms.

Application forms and additional information may be obtained by contacting:

Office of Admission
Mount Mercy College
1330 Elmhurst Drive, NE
Cedar Rapids, Iowa 52402
Telephone: 319-368-6460
319-363-5270
800-248-4504 (toll-free)
E-mail: admission@mtmercy.edu
World Wide Web: http://www.mtmercy.edu

Students talking with a professor on the campus of Mount Mercy.

NORTH CENTRAL COLLEGE

NAPERVILLE, ILLINOIS

The College

Founded in 1861, North Central College has a distinctive heritage as a comprehensive college that educates students in both the liberal arts and sciences and in preprofessional fields.

A private, United Methodist–affiliated institution, the College has long been recognized for academic excellence, with its educational philosophy of incorporating leadership, ethics, and values into academic and cocurricular activities. North Central's 2,600 students include traditional-age undergraduate, part-time, and graduate students. Master's degree programs are offered in business administration, computer science, education, information systems, leadership studies, and liberal studies. New graduate certificates are now available in business foundations, change management, dispute resolution, finance, gender studies, history and nature of science, human resource management, investments and financial planning, leadership studies, management, marketing, and multicultural studies.

Twenty-four states are represented (88 percent of the students are Illinois residents), 17 percent of the members of the 2002 freshman class are members of minority groups, and 80 percent of freshmen live in one of nine residence halls. Twenty-six other countries are represented. Kaufman Dining Hall serves the entire campus.

Cocurricular programs parallel many academic majors and include the nationally acclaimed Students in Free Enterprise, Cardinals in Action (a community service organization), campus radio station WONC, Mock Trial, Model United Nations, and forensics. North Central student athletes compete in nineteen NCAA Division III intercollegiate varsity sports within the College Conference of Illinois and Wisconsin. The varsity sports include baseball, basketball, cross-country, football, golf, soccer, swimming, tennis, track and field, and wrestling for men. Women participate in basketball, cross-country, golf, soccer, softball, swimming, tennis, track and field, and volleyball. Students have many options for social activities: programmed events through the College Union Activities Board, residence life activities, an active intramural program, and travel to both downtown Naperville and Chicago. Student services include centers for academic advising, counseling, writing, foreign language, and career development.

Location

Naperville, a city of 155,000 people and one of the ten fastest-growing communities in the nation, is situated in the center of the Illinois Research and Development Corridor. Chicago, the nation's third-largest metropolitan area, is 29 miles to the east. The cultural, sporting, and social events in that city are easily accessible by commuter trains that stop frequently just two blocks from campus. Students find Naperville safe, friendly, and a great place to relax.

The Illinois Research and Development Corridor, which is bounded on the east by Argonne National Laboratory and on the west by Fermi National Accelerator Laboratory, offers North Central students numerous internships and a wealth of job and research opportunities.

Majors and Degrees

North Central College awards the Bachelor of Arts (B.A.) degree in accounting, actuarial science, applied mathematics, art, art education, arts and letters, athletic training, biochemistry, biology, broadcast communication, chemistry, classical civilization, computer science, East Asian studies, economics, education (elementary and secondary), English, entrepreneurship and small business management, exercise science, finance, French, German, history, humanities, international business, international studies, Japanese, management, management information systems, marketing, mathematics, music, musical theater, music education, organizational communication, philosophy, physical education, physics, political science, print journalism, psychology, religious studies, science, social studies, sociology, sociology and anthropology, Spanish, speech communication, theater, and urban and suburban studies. The Bachelor of Science (B.S.) degree is awarded in biochemistry, biology, chemistry, computer science, mathematics, and psychology and in all economics and business areas.

Preprofessional programs are offered in dentistry, law, medical technology, medicine, physical therapy, and veterinary medicine. A 3-2 engineering program is offered in cooperation with Marquette University, the University of Minnesota, the University of Illinois at Urbana-Champaign, and Washington University in St. Louis. Both 2-2 and 3-2 programs in nursing are available in cooperation with Rush University in Chicago. Students may also design other majors that bridge two or more areas of study.

Academic Program

North Central provides a comprehensive education with the goal of preparing students to live free, ethically responsible, and intellectually rewarding lives. Each student must complete a minimum of 120 credit hours, including all general education requirements and an approved major. CLEP, AP, and IB exams are considered for college credit and/or advanced course placement.

The academic year comprises three 10½-week terms and a monthlong Interim Term between Thanksgiving and the beginning of the new calendar year. Students usually take three courses during each term, while the Interim Term is used for independent study, taking courses, travel, research, work, or simply relaxation. The College actively supports internships as part of career preparation, and the College Scholars Honors Program is open to select students.

Off-Campus Arrangements

The Student-in-Residence-on-Leave (SIROL) program gives North Central students the opportunity to pursue a special program at another accredited college or university while remaining officially enrolled at North Central. An example of a SIROL program is the popular Washington Semester at American University in Washington, D.C. Other off-campus programs include research at the Gulf Coast Research Laboratory in Ocean Springs, Mississippi, and in Roatan, Honduras; study field trips to the deserts of the Southwest; study-abroad programs to Costa Rica and London; and the North Central–sponsored student and faculty exchange programs in France, Japan, Korea, Northern Ireland, and Taiwan.

North Central is also one of only twelve colleges and universities in the nation to offer the distinctive Richter Independent Study Fellowship Program, which provides funds of up to $5000 for a single specialized project. Richter Independent Study projects have included travel and research on every continent.

Academic Facilities

North Central's 56-acre campus, in the heart of the historic district of Naperville, has more than twenty major buildings.

Facilities range from the restored 1906 Carnegie Library building and the 1870 Old Main to the modern Cardinal Stadium. Pfeiffer Hall, with its 1,050-seat auditorium, is the cultural center for both the campus and the community. Oesterle Library provides access to more than 22 million volumes in forty-five college and university libraries in Illinois.

WONC (89.1 FM), the College's 1,500-watt radio station, is one of the most powerful student-staffed stations in the Midwest. With two fully operational state-of-the-art studios, a stereo console, an Associated Press Newsdesk Wireservice, and computerized music programming, the station is one of the most modern educational facilities in the region. WONC has won twenty national Marconi Awards, including Best College Radio Station in America. No other radio station has won more. All students, faculty members, and staff members have access to a voice, video, and data network, with full Internet access from their residence halls, classrooms, computer laboratories, and offices. In the sciences, students can use a scintillation counter; a nuclear magnetic resonance spectrometer; gas and liquid chromatographs; ultraviolet, visible, and infrared spectrophotometers; a pulsed nitrogen laser; and an environmental chamber to pursue laboratory research. Recently, the College raised funds to complete a $2-million challenge to purchase and create an endowment for scientific equipment, supported by a $500,000 commitment from the Kresge Foundation. North Central also has state-of-the-art language and market research laboratories.

Costs

For 2002–03, tuition at North Central College was $17,997. Room and board were $6045. Resident students paid a $225 technology fee. The student activity fee was $180 and estimated additional expenses were $425 for books and supplies. Students should also budget personal expenses and transportation costs.

Financial Aid

The Offices of Admission and Financial Aid believe that no student should be excluded from attending North Central College for financial reasons. Scholarships, loans, grants, and work-study assistance are awarded on the basis of demonstrated financial need and the academic record. Students are required to submit the Free Application for Federal Student Aid (FAFSA). Funds are also available through the Illinois State Monetary Award Program (for Illinois residents only), the Federal Pell Grant Program, Federal Supplemental Educational Opportunity Grant, and the Federal Stafford Student Loan Program. The College awarded more than $11.5 million from institutional sources for 2002–03. A large portion of those funds was allocated through the academic-based Presidential Scholarship Program. Awards range from $4500 to full tuition, renewable annually. Students may also audition for scholarships in theater, forensics, vocal and instrumental music, as well as submit art portfolios.

Faculty

Members of the North Central faculty, 83 percent of whom hold the Ph.D. or another terminal degree, are first—and foremost—teachers. A student-faculty ratio of 14:1 and an average class size of 17 students ensure opportunities for a stimulating exchange of ideas. All faculty members also serve as academic advisers to provide guidance and counseling for students. Students get to know their professors on a personal basis, and the list of independent study projects is extensive. Faculty members teach both undergraduate and graduate courses.

Student Government

All undergraduates are members of the Student Association, which is governed by its elected officers. The Student Association is a vital and influential force in campus activities, and it takes an active role in the development and implementation of policies concerning student life on campus. Representatives of the student body have a voice on faculty, trustee, and administrative committees, while the College Union Activities Board plans social and service events.

Admission Requirements

New students are accepted individually on the basis of their overall academic preparation, character, and potential for success at North Central College. Graduation from an accredited secondary school is a basic requirement for admission. Other criteria used in the selection of prospective students are the high school academic record, personal recommendations of high school counselors, ACT or SAT I scores, and involvement in extracurricular activities. Members of the North Central freshman class of 2001–02 scored an average of 25 on the ACT and ranked in the 75th percentile of their high school graduating class. North Central does not discriminate on the basis of sex, race, ethnic background, age, or physical handicap.

Application and Information

North Central College operates on a rolling admission basis, which allows students to apply at any time during or after their senior year in high school. Applicants receive notification within three weeks after the College receives all documentation. Early application is recommended to ensure availability of campus housing. The application must be accompanied by a $25 fee, an official high school transcript, and official reports of ACT or SAT I scores from the testing agency. For additional information or application forms, students should contact:

Office of Admission
North Central College
30 North Brainard Street
Naperville, Illinois 60540
Telephone: 630-637-5800
800-411-1861 (toll-free)
Fax: 630-637-5819
E-mail: ncadm@noctrl.edu
World Wide Web: http://www.northcentralcollege.edu

Historic Old Main, built in 1870 and renovated in 1998, houses the Offices of Admission, Financial Aid, and the Registrar.

OHIO WESLEYAN UNIVERSITY

DELAWARE, OHIO

The University

An unusual synthesis of liberal arts learning and preprofessional preparation has set Ohio Wesleyan University (OWU) apart. It is one of the country's five independent four-year colleges to rank among the top twenty in both the number of graduates earning Ph.D.'s and the number who are U.S. business leaders. Founded by the United Methodist Church in 1842, the University is strongly committed to developing the service ethic in students, to fusing theory with its practical applications, and to confronting specific issues of long-range public importance.

Undergraduate enrollment is about 1,850 men and women. Students come to Ohio Wesleyan from forty-four states and fifty-two countries, and most reside on the attractive 200-acre campus. OWU ranks fourth in the nation (among schools in its class) in the proportion of students with international origins. Housing options include six large residence halls with special-interest corridors; a number of smaller special-interest units, such as the Tree House and the Peace and Justice House; and eleven fraternity houses. The five sorority houses are nonresidential.

There is a wide range of cocurricular activities. Students initiate discussion groups, service projects, and intramural athletics. Other activities include a fully independent student newspaper, cultural- and ethnic-interest groups such as the Student Union on Black Awareness and the Christian Fellowship, crisis intervention work, the College Republicans and Young Democrats, and prelaw and premed clubs. In the course of a year, students may enjoy more than 100 concerts, plays, dance programs, films, exhibits, and timely speakers. The Theatre and Dance Department stages four major productions and much additional studio work each year, while the Music Department sponsors four large groups and other small ensembles. An impressive $12-million campus center is the hub of cocurricular life on campus.

There are twenty-three varsity athletic teams—eleven for men, eleven for women, and a coed sailing team. Many teams often earn NCAA Division III national ranking; recent rankings have included the men's teams in baseball, golf, lacrosse, soccer, and tennis, and the women's cross-country, field hockey, soccer, swimming, and track teams. In 2001, the OWU women's soccer team was an NCAA Division III national champion. In recent years, individual All-Americans have been named in these sports and in football, men's cross-country, and men's track. Intramural programs are extensive, and all students have access to racquet sports, swimming, and weight-lifting facilities in the Branch Rickey Physical Education Center. Fitness equipment and health services are housed in the new Health and Wellness Center, conveniently located near the residence halls. Off-campus opportunities for backpacking, boating, camping, golf, skiing, and swimming are abundant.

Location

Delaware combines the small-town pace and maple-lined streets of the county seat (population 25,000) with easy access to the state capital, Columbus, the fifteenth-largest city in America. Thirty minutes south of the campus, Columbus provides rich internship opportunities, international research centers, fine dining and shopping, and cultural events that complement campus life. Delaware, founded in 1808, retains a stately, post-Colonial charm in many of its sections. Because the campus is in the town, students find a degree of solitude but not a sense of isolation. About half of the faculty members live a short walk from campus.

Majors and Degrees

Ohio Wesleyan offers the Bachelor of Arts degree in accounting, astronomy, biological sciences (botany, microbiology, and zoology), chemistry, computer science, economics (including accounting, international business, and management), education (elementary and secondary licensing in seventeen areas), English literature and writing, environmental science, fine arts, French, geography, geology, German, history, humanities-classics, journalism, mathematics, music (applied or history/literature), neuroscience, philosophy, physical education, physics, politics and government, psychology, religion, sociology/anthropology, Spanish, and theater and dance. Fifteen interdisciplinary majors include black studies, East Asian studies, environmental studies, international studies, urban studies, and women's studies, as well as prelaw and premedicine. Students may also design majors in topical, period, or regional studies.

Two professional degrees are awarded: the Bachelor of Fine Arts in art history, arts education, and studio art, and the Bachelor of Music in music education and performance. Combined-degree (generally 3-2) programs are offered in engineering, medical technology, optometry, and physical therapy.

Academic Program

Ohio Wesleyan provides opportunities for students to acquire not only depth in a major area but also knowledge about their cultural past through the insight provided by a broad curriculum. At Ohio Wesleyan, education is placed in a context of values, and students are encouraged to develop the intellectual skills of effective communication, independent and logical thought, and creative problem solving. To these ends, students are required to demonstrate competence in English composition and a foreign language (often through placement testing) and to complete distributional study in the natural and social sciences, the humanities, and the arts. With few exceptions, the major requires the completion of eight to fifteen courses; double majors and minors are encouraged. Completion of thirty-four courses is required for graduation.

Advanced placement is available with or without credit. Under the four-year honors program, freshmen may be named Merit Scholars and work individually with faculty mentors on research, directed readings, or original creative work. Upperclass students are also encouraged to participate in independent study. Phi Beta Kappa is one of more than twenty scholastic honorary societies with chapters on campus.

The objectives of an Ohio Wesleyan education are crystallized in the distinctive Sagan National Colloquium, a program focused annually on one issue of compelling public importance, such as "A Wired World: The Internet and Beyond." Through weekly speakers and semester-long seminars, the colloquium stimulates campuswide dialogue and encourages students to integrate knowledge from many different disciplines and apply what is studied to life. Participants should discover not only what they think about the issue but also why they think as they do, as well as how to make important decisions based on their beliefs.

Off-Campus Arrangements

Full-semester internships and apprenticeships, as well as programs of advanced research, are actively developed through most departments. Many are approved by the Great Lakes Colleges Association, Inc. (GLCA), a highly regarded academic consortium of twelve independent institutions. Programs include the Philadelphia Center, the GLCA Arts Program in New York, and the Oak Ridge National Laboratory Science Semester. Other cooperative arrangements include the Newberry Library Program, Wesleyan in Washington, and the Drew University United Nations Semester. Research is done locally at the U.S. Department of Agriculture (USDA) Laboratories in Delaware, the nearby Columbus Zoo, and several other sites.

Ohio Wesleyan has been long committed to education for a global society. Consequently, the curriculum has an international perspective, a significant portion of the student body is drawn from other countries, and a wide variety of opportunities are offered overseas. Individual work may be arranged elsewhere, but formal programs are offered in more than twenty countries. These include Ohio Wesleyan's affiliation with the University of Salamanca in Salamanca, Spain, and its program in Strasbourg, France, as well as programs in Africa, China, Colombia, England, India/Nepal, Japan, Russia, and Scotland.

Academic Facilities

The University has recently completed, and exceeded the goal of, a $100-million campaign. This campaign, which has substantially enhanced the endowment, has also provided funding for extensive building renovations, athletic facility enhancements, and technology improvements. The Beeghly Library houses 503,000 volumes, one of the largest collections in the country for a private university of Ohio Wesleyan's size. The library's federal documents depository is among the nation's oldest and largest, providing an additional 200,000 reference publications. Beeghly also offers the Online Computer Library Center's most advanced cataloging system. The collection is enhanced by OhioLINK and CONSORT membership.

The comprehensive academic computing system is accessible to students 24 hours per day, and all residence hall rooms are wired for network and Internet access. University-wide computing systems at Ohio Wesleyan include IBM xSeries 232 servers for e-mail, general communications, Web hosting, and timesharing; an IBM RS/6000 system for administrative data processing; and a Compaq ProLiant ML350 running Windows 2000. Approximately 200 MS Windows-based microcomputers in twelve public computer laboratories are accessible to the campus community.

Three science buildings house an unusually wide variety of state-of-the-art instrumentation, including a scanning electron microscope in Stewart Hall and scanning and transmission electron microscopes, which are co-owned by the USDA Labs. The Wotemade Center for Economics, Business, and Entrepreneurship; the Economics Department; the Learning Resource Center; and Information Systems are located in the new R. W. Corns Building. The University has a state-of-the-art Geographic Information Systems Computer Laboratory. Perkins Observatory houses a 32-inch reflector telescope and two smaller instruments. Two University wilderness preserves cover a total of 100 acres. Other special facilities are the multistage Chappelear Drama Center; Sanborn Hall, home to the Music Department; and Gray Chapel, which houses one of the three Klais concert organs in the United States.

Costs

The general fee for 2002–03 was $31,010. This amount covered tuition ($24,000), room ($3530), and board ($3480). Books and personal expenses averaged $1100. Nominal fees are charged for some studio art courses, off-campus study, private music lessons for students who are not majoring in music, and student teaching.

Financial Aid

Nearly all freshmen who demonstrate need have been awarded an aid package. Packages include grant, loan, and employment assistance from Ohio Wesleyan and the standard federal and state programs (such as Federal Pell Grant, Federal Stafford Student Loan, Federal Perkins Loan, and Federal Work-Study). More than two thirds of the student body receive some form of need-based aid, and another quarter receive merit- or non-need-based aid. More than 75 percent of all aid is provided by grants and scholarships. On the average, students on financial aid at Ohio Wesleyan receive more scholarship and grant assistance and rely less on loan support than do students at most other institutions.

Several merit scholarship programs worth as much as $24,000 per year, private loan programs, and flexible payment plans are available without regard to financial need. This year, more than 140 enrolling freshmen received merit awards.

Faculty

The full-time faculty numbers 133, providing a student-faculty ratio of approximately 13:1. All of the full-time faculty members hold the highest degree in their fields. Although committed first to teaching and advising, most faculty members maintain active research programs and publish important articles and books. Some members of the faculty are practicing artists whose contributions include the creation and exhibition of original works of art and theater.

Student Government

Students have a significant voice in the government of campus life. The Wesleyan Council on Student Affairs, more than two thirds of whose members are students, formulates basic policy. Students also sit on judicial boards and nine faculty committees and are represented at all meetings of the Board of Trustees.

Admission Requirements

The admission process is competitive. Each application is carefully studied on an individual basis. Although the applicant's academic record is most important, followed closely by teacher and counselor evaluations and SAT I or ACT scores, many other factors are considered, such as evidence of creativity, community service, and leadership. A sixteen-course preparatory program is required. Four units of English and 3 each of mathematics, social studies, science, and foreign language are recommended, but variations of this program are considered. SAT II Subject Tests are not required but may qualify students for advanced placement. Candidates for the B.Mus. degree must audition (tapes are accepted). Early action, early decision, and transfer admission are offered. Campus interviews are strongly recommended but not required. In 2002, approximately 2,250 applications were received; about 1,750 of the applicants gained admission.

Application and Information

Students are urged to complete the application process as early as possible in the senior year of secondary school, especially if they are applying for financial aid. Once complete credentials (application, transcript, recommendations, and SAT I or ACT scores) are received, decisions are made on a rolling basis after January 1. The student's response is required by May 1. The deadline for early action and early decision application is December 1; notification is given within four weeks. After April 1, students are admitted on a space-available, rolling admission basis.

For further information, students should contact:

Office of Admission
Ohio Wesleyan University
Delaware, Ohio 43015
Telephone: 800-922-8953 (toll-free)
Fax: 740-368-3314
E-mail: owuadmit@owu.edu
World Wide Web: http://web.owu.edu

The Hamilton-Williams Campus Center is a magnificent meeting place for the campus community.

OLIVET NAZARENE UNIVERSITY

BOURBONNAIS, ILLINOIS

The University

Olivet Nazarene University (ONU) is a Christian liberal arts university with a strong emphasis on both academic excellence and Christ-centered living. ONU offers one of the finest liberal arts educations in the Midwest, world-class facilities for learning and entertainment, and an atmosphere that promotes fun, relationship building, and spiritual growth.

Olivet's high retention, graduation, and employment/placement rates demonstrate the University's commitment to the students' success. The faculty, staff, and administration members are dedicated to teaching, encouraging, and mentoring each student as a whole person—academically, socially, and spiritually.

With 3,800 total students (2,200 undergraduates), Olivet offers an ideal student population for a private institution, maintaining diversity without sacrificing personalized attention. About half of the student body comes from the Nazarene denomination, while the remainder come from some thirty other denominations. Most U.S. states are represented, as are nearly twenty countries.

The campus offers a championship-caliber athletics department (eighteen intercollegiate men's and women's sports in all) and a large intramural sports program. Music and drama groups involve hundreds of students, and many clubs are organized for a wide variety of interests. Olivet students are also heavily involved in dozens of ministry groups and volunteer efforts, small-group Bible studies, and weekly student-led services.

The University recently completed a $10-million capital campaign, including a completely renovated dining hall, the new Admissions Welcome Center and campus entrance, new furniture in every dorm room, and the new, 56,700-square-foot Weber Center for the Divisions of Education and Social Sciences, which was completed in August 2001. The Larsen Fine Arts Center, housing the Kresge Auditorium and the Brandenberg Gallery, received a complete renovation in 2002.

Location

The University is located just 50 minutes south of Chicago's Loop in the historic village of Bourbonnais. The area includes mall shopping, restaurants, entertainment, and natural recreation centered on the Kankakee River State Park system. Olivet students enjoy many activities nearby and often make the quick trip north to sample the limitless offerings of Chicago and its surroundings.

In addition to recreation, students find numerous opportunities for employment and internships in the area, which is ranked as one of the top locations in the nation for small businesses, and the vast professional resources of Chicago. Students, faculty members, and staff members also find themselves working side by side in local and regional ministry projects. Olivet students are recognized professionally and ministerially as a valuable commodity by area businesses, churches, and parachurch organizations.

Majors and Degrees

Olivet confers Bachelor of Arts (B.A.) and/or Bachelor of Science (B.S.) degrees in the following fields of study (includes all majors, minors, and concentrations): accounting, art, art history, athletic training, biblical literature, biblical studies, biochemistry, biology, broadcasting, business administration, chemistry, Christian education, church music, clinical laboratory science, commercial graphics, computer information systems, computer science, counseling, cross-cultural ministries, dietetics, drawing, early childhood education, earth and space science, economics and finance, elementary education, engineering (electrical), engineering (mechanical), English, environmental science, family and consumer sciences, fashion merchandising, film studies, finance, French, general studies, geochemistry, geoengineering, geology, Greek, history, housing and environmental design, international business, journalism, literature, management, marketing, mathematics, music education, music performance, nursing, nutrition, personnel psychology, philosophy and religion, physical education, physical science, physics, political science, predentistry, prelaw, premedicine, prepharmacy, pre–physical therapy, pre–veterinary medicine, psychology, public policy, religion, religious studies, Romance languages, secondary education, social justice, social science, social work, sociology, Spanish, speech communication, theater, writing, youth ministry, and zoology.

Academic Program

Olivet seeks to offer an "Education with a Christian Purpose." The University believes this commitment to Christ mandates nothing less than the highest-quality academic programs. Olivet's liberal arts curriculum requires that students complete 53 to 61 hours of general education courses. With the addition of major and minor programs of study, students must complete a minimum of 128 credit hours to obtain a bachelor's degree. Credit may be earned through AP and CLEP tests. Students may also participate in ROTC.

Olivet operates on a two-semester schedule, from August to May. Two summer sessions are also available.

Off-Campus Arrangements

Olivet students are encouraged to participate in the various off-campus study programs offered each semester. International locations include Beijing, China; San José, Costa Rica; Cairo, Egypt; Oxford, England, and western Europe; Irian Jaya, Indonesia; Tokyo, Japan; Moscow, Nizhni Novgorod, and St. Petersburg, Russia; and Sighisoara, Transylvania (Romania). Domestic opportunities include the American Studies Program in Washington, D.C.; the Los Angeles Film Studies Program in Burbank, California; Focus on the Family Institute in Colorado Springs, Colorado; and the AuSable Institute (environmental science) in northern Michigan. Costs are usually comparable to a semester at Olivet, and credit is given for these programs. In addition, financial aid is applicable.

In addition, many Olivet students participate in numerous educational and missions-oriented short-term trips, which are available during the Christmas, spring, and summer breaks.

Academic Facilities

Olivet's 200-acre, $150-million campus offers leading-edge academic facilities. These include high-quality performance halls and athletic arenas; excellent natural science, engineering, and nursing laboratories; "smart" classrooms in most departments; and an observatory. It is one of only a handful of small college campuses in the nation to have a planetarium. Each department uses the top software in its field. More than a dozen campus computer labs are available for student use, and two network ports in each dorm room give students access to e-mail, the Internet, and classroom applications 24 hours a day.

Benner Library and Resource Center provides unlimited access to any material a student needs, either on-site from its 160,000 volumes, 1,000 periodicals, government documents, and CD-ROMs or through the interlibrary loan system.

Costs

Tuition, based on 12 to 18 credit hours, was $13,380 in 2002–03. Room and board, based on double occupancy and the twenty-one-meals-per-week plan, were $6080.

Financial Aid

More than 95 percent of Olivet students receive some form of financial aid each year. Merit- and need-based scholarships range from $500 to full tuition. The Olivet Nazarene University Leadership Scholarship for Freshmen provides a significant award for those students who qualify through an application and essay process.

Olivet's cost is below average for private colleges nationwide, and more than 90 percent of ONU students receive financial aid. The University also participates in all federal and state financial aid programs. The priority deadline for filing the Free Application for Federal Student Aid (FAFSA) is March 1. To apply for aid, students must fill out the FAFSA as well as Olivet's application for financial aid. The student must be an accepted applicant before a financial aid package can be created. Olivet offers a monthly installment plan in addition to the traditional three-payment plan. Olivet believes funding a student's education is a partnership between each family, Olivet, and the state and federal governments. The friendly staff is committed to making an Olivet education affordable to every young person.

Faculty

Olivet's more than 100 full-time faculty members are the key to excellence in and out of the classroom. Teaching is a ministry for these dedicated Christian individuals, and Olivet's 18:1 student-faculty ratio gives them an opportunity to teach, mentor, and encourage students on a personal level. To that end, the faculty is heavily involved in campus life, whether sponsoring social organizations or participating in talent shows.

Within the traditional liberal arts curriculum, more than 75 percent of Olivet's faculty members have terminal degrees. Including the more practical programs of study, such as nursing and family and consumer sciences, the total is a strong 68 percent.

Student Government

The Associated Student Council is the student government organization on campus. Its Executive Council consists of a President, Vice President of Finance, Vice President of Spiritual Life, Vice President of Social Affairs, Vice President of Women's Residential Life, Vice President of Men's Residential Life, Vice President of Office Management, the *Glimmerglass* (student newspaper) editor, and the *Aurora* (yearbook) editor. They work alongside the University's administrative team to ensure the health and promotion of campus activities and organizations.

Admission Requirements

Admission to the University is moderately difficult. Students are considered for admission on the basis of their high school GPA, ACT or SAT I scores, and personal recommendations. An ACT score is required for placement in courses. For international students, TOEFL results are an additional factor in the admission decision. Students with low test scores and GPAs may be admitted on a provisional basis. A campus visit and interview are strongly recommended for all prospective students.

Application and Information

Admission is on a rolling basis, although an early decision is required for some scholarships. Students may apply at Olivet's home page on the World Wide Web or in print. The application process includes the written (or electronic) application, high school transcripts, two letters of recommendation, ACT or SAT I scores, and a health form. There is no application fee, but a $30 room deposit places the student on the list for housing.

For more information or to arrange a campus visit, students should contact:

Office of Admissions
Olivet Nazarene University
One University Avenue
Bourbonnais, Illinois 60914
Telephone: 815-939-5203
800-648-1463 (toll-free)
E-mail: admissions@olivet.edu
World Wide Web: http://www.olivet.edu

A view of the campus at Olivet Nazarene University.

OTTAWA UNIVERSITY

OTTAWA, KANSAS

The University

With the college (residential campus); adult centers located in Kansas City, Phoenix, Milwaukee, and Jeffersonville; and the International Program in the Pacific Rim, Ottawa University is a complex institution. The Ottawa Plan of Education, however, is the unique concept of learning that defines the University's progress in all of its various settings. While the following description focuses on the campus program, the fundamental principles noted have characterized the entire University program.

Ottawa University is a church-related college, and believes a university that combines the Christian faith and liberal education, is best able to achieve the full individual development of each student. The University maintains an active relationship with American Baptist Churches, U.S.A. but includes members of many denominations among its students and faculty members.

Ottawa seeks to present the Christian faith in a setting where students are free to accept or reject it but not to ignore it. Confident in the belief that all truth is of God, Ottawa promotes an atmosphere of free and open inquiry into all aspects of knowledge.

Ottawa seeks to help each student develop moral clarity and moral seriousness. The total educational program is designed to assist students in clarifying their beliefs, determining the relationships among them, and learning to act responsibly on the basis of these convictions.

The phrase "Education for Service" is a mandate for Ottawa University. The University seeks to prepare students for lives of service, and the servant ministry of Jesus Christ is upheld as the example most worthy of emulation.

There is diversity among Ottawa University students. Students come to Ottawa from more than twenty-seven different states and fifteen countries. The majority of students come from the Midwest, but the rest of the country is also well represented. Students also come in significant numbers from rural, urban, and suburban areas of major metropolitan centers, small towns, and moderate to large cities. The cosmopolitan nature of the University enriches the total learning experience as students learn from each other.

Location

Ottawa University's 65-acre campus is ideally located within 45 minutes of Kansas City and 30 minutes from Lawrence, Kansas.

Majors and Degrees

Ottawa University offers more than twenty majors that lead to Bachelor of Arts degrees in accounting, art, biology, business administration, communication, education, English, health-care management, history and political science, human service, information technology, mathematics, music, physical education, psychology, religion and philosophy, sociology, and theater. Students can also design an individual major to fit their special interests.

Academic Program

Ottawa University's philosophy of education provides the learning students need to match the changes in the world. The University focuses on expanding career options by helping students learn how to think, write, speak, reason, compute, analyze, and solve problems—the skills necessary for any career, from doctor or lawyer to teacher or business leader.

Ottawa takes a less traditional approach to the liberal arts because it focuses on skills development in addition to well-roundness. Through Ottawa's innovative style of teaching liberal arts, the student's experience starts with a freshman class, Writing, Freedom And Responsibility, and ends with the capstone course, Group Problem Solving.

The University gets results from this approach. More than 50 percent of Ottawa graduates attend graduate school, and the University has a 90 percent acceptance rate into law and medical schools. The career placement rate is more than 95 percent, with 90 percent being within the student's field of study. Ottawa alumni say their education has prepared them for today's changing workplace.

Academic Facilities

As part of its mission to provide the highest-quality education possible for the development of individual students, Ottawa University's academic facilities have undergone many changes.

A capital campaign is underway to improve current academic facilities, including a fully renovated, state-of-the-art library building that is scheduled for completion in 2003.

Computing facilities are provided by the University for the use of students, faculty and staff members, and, in some circumstances, the public. Computers and labs with Internet access are located in various campus buildings. Students can also have access to the Internet in their residence hall rooms.

Costs

Tuition for the 2002–03 academic year was $12,200 per year for all full-time undergraduate students. A typical full-time semester schedule consists of 12 to 16 credit hours. Room and board cost $5300 for 2002–03. Books and supplies range between $200 and $450 per semester.

Financial Aid

Ottawa University is able to help students meet a significant portion of the direct cost of education through a combination of resources.

All full-time students accepted for admission to Ottawa University's residential campus are considered for scholarships and awards. Students are urged to make application early, as some assistance may be limited. Students are strongly encouraged to complete the Free Application for Federal Student Aid (FAFSA) to determine eligibility for additional grants, work-study programs and low-interest loans.

Faculty

With a 15:1 student-faculty ratio, students are encouraged to develop relationships with their professors and even be informal with them. When the professors know the students, they understand their struggles, strengths, and aspirations, and the student's learning experience is greatly enhanced.

The professors pay attention to the student's needs. Each student has a conference with his or her adviser at the beginning of the college career. During this conference, the student and adviser map out the student's class schedule for the next four years, which means students have time to take the classes they want as well as the classes they need.

Student Government

Student Government represents students regarding the issues they face. In essence, Student Government is the student's voice to faculty members and administration.

Student Government is elected by the student body and consists of the student body president, vice-president, and 19 senators. The student body president and vice-president are elected each spring semester to serve the following year. The student body president's main responsibility is serving as a liaison between the faculty members and administration and the students. The student body vice-president primarily serves as the student senate president.

Admission Requirements

Freshman applicants are automatically admitted if two of the following three criteria are met: a score of 18 or above on the ACT (860 SAT), a cumulative GPA of 2.5 or above, or ranking in the top half of their senior class. If the applicant does not meet two of these three criteria, the applicant is taken to the admissions committee.

Application and Information

For more information, students should contact:

Office of Admissions
Ottawa University
1001 S. Cedar #17
Ottawa, Kansas 66067-3399
Telephone: 785-242-5200 Ext. 5421
800-755-5200 (toll-free)
E-mail: admiss@ottawa.edu
World Wide Web: http://www.ottawa.edu

The campus at Ottawa University.

OTTERBEIN COLLEGE

WESTERVILLE, OHIO

The College

Otterbein College, a private, coeducational institution affiliated with the United Methodist Church, blends the traditional and contemporary and continues to pride itself on offering a broad-based liberal arts education. Its 1,969 full-time and 1,095 part-time students come from all over the United States and several countries, but the majority, including 440 graduate students, are from Ohio. Founded in 1847 with only two buildings on 8 acres of land, Otterbein has since grown to twenty-seven buildings on 140 acres in the heart of historic Westerville, Ohio, a suburb of Columbus.

The College offers a wide range of extracurricular activities. They include theater productions, vocal and instrumental ensembles, religious programming activities, the ca weekly student newspaper, the campus radio station (WOBN), the Otterbein-Westerville television station (WOCC), and intramural and intercollegiate athletics. Otterbein men and women compete in the Ohio Athletic Conference, NCAA Division III. There are eight varsity sports for men and eight for women. The Rike Physical Education–Recreation Center is the home for men's and women's athletics and physical education facilities and includes racquetball and tennis courts, an indoor track, a weight room, and seating for 3,000. The $9.5-million Clements Recreation Center opened in fall 2002. Five local fraternities and six local sororities attract approximately 27 percent of Otterbein's students. Roush Hall, a multipurpose, handicapped-accessible building, houses academic departments, multimedia classrooms, contemporary conference rooms, a gallery, and a computer center.

A Master of Science in Nursing program is offered for students who have completed a four-year baccalaureate program.

A Master of Arts in Teaching (M.A.T.) degree program is available to qualified liberal arts graduates to prepare for teacher certification in elementary education or secondary education—biology (life science), computer science, English, and mathematics. A Master of Arts in Education (M.A.E.) degree program is available to certified teachers. Majors are offered in curriculum and instruction, reading, and teacher leadership and supervision.

Otterbein also offers an M.B.A. program.

Location

Otterbein is located in Westerville, Ohio, 20 minutes from downtown Columbus, one of the fastest-growing cities in the Midwest and Northeast. The College's proximity to Columbus means more than access to entertainment and recreation; as a thriving business center, the city provides many internship opportunities for students that often lead to full-time employment after graduation. The College is easily accessible from Interstates 71 and 270 and is close to the Port Columbus International Airport.

Majors and Degrees

The Bachelor of Arts degree is offered in accounting, broadcasting, business administration, chemistry, computer science, economics, English, equine science, French, health education, history, international studies, journalism, life science, mathematics, music, organizational communication, philosophy, physical education, physics, political science, psychology, public relations, religion, secondary education, sociology, Spanish, speech communication, sports medicine, sports wellness and management, theater, and visual arts. The Bachelor of Science degree is offered in accounting, business administration, chemistry, computer science, equine science, life science, mathematics, physics, psychology, and sports medicine. The Bachelor of Fine Arts is offered in theater with concentrations in acting-directing, design-technical, and musical theater programs. The Bachelor of Music Education prepares students for teaching careers in music. The Bachelor of Science in Education is awarded in early childhood education and middle childhood education. The Bachelor of Science in Nursing degree is also offered. The Bachelor of Music is offered for students interested in performance careers.

Preprofessional programs are offered in dentistry, law, medicine, optometry, and veterinary medicine.

A dual degree in engineering is offered in conjunction with Washington University in St. Louis and Case Western Reserve University in Cleveland.

Minors are offered in accounting, athletic training, black studies, broadcasting, business, chemistry, coaching, computer science, dance, economics, English, French, geology, health sciences, history, mathematics, music, philosophy, physical education, physics, political science, psychology, public relations, religion, sign language, sociology, Spanish, speech communication, visual art, and women's studies. In fall 2002 minors were added in sound production and arts administration.

Academic Program

Otterbein College offers a program of liberal arts education in the Christian tradition. The College encourages serious dialogue so that students will develop to serve within the community. The fulfillment of this purpose requires students to read well, write well, think clearly, and identify ideas; know how to discuss, listen, and seek data; and have the abilities of synthesis and creativity.

Graduation with a bachelor's degree from the College requires successful completion of 180 quarter hours, of which 50 quarter hours are in core requirements offered under the title of Integrative Studies in Human Nature. The College's quarter calendar lends itself to the wide variety of internships and other off-campus educational opportunities offered by the College. The academic year begins in mid-September and ends in early June.

Through other academic opportunities, students may design an individualized major as well as receive advanced placement by examination and credit through CLEP examinations in some academic areas.

Off-Campus Arrangements

A variety of off-campus programs are available, including foreign language study in Dijon, France. Semester at Sea, a shipboard-campus program offered in cooperation with the University of Pittsburgh, enables students to take a variety of liberal arts courses while cruising. Study opportunities also exist with the Washington Semester Plan, operated through the American University in Washington, D.C., and with the Philadelphia Center. The Roehampton Exchange, located in the Wimbledon area of London, England, consists of a federation of four institutions, providing the student with many cultural opportunities.

Academic Facilities

Roush Hall houses state-of-the-art computer labs, classrooms, a multimedia room, a two-story art gallery, and faculty and administrative offices. The Courtright Memorial Library houses 300,000 volumes and 1,015 periodical subscriptions and has an outstanding learning-resource center that includes the studios of the Otterbein-Westerville television station, WOCC. The McFadden-Schear Science Hall has modern laboratories and classrooms and a renovated planetarium and observatory. Cowan Hall houses modern facilities for speech and theater, including WOBN-FM, the campus radio station. The Battelle Fine Arts Center is the home for programs in music, art, and dance and also houses an electronic music laboratory. Historic Towers Hall, a campus landmark since 1870, had an $8.5-million renovation in 1999–2000 and houses classrooms, faculty offices, and updated math and computer science labs.

Costs

For 2002–03, Otterbein's tuition and fees were $18,993. Room and board cost $5727 per year. Books and supplies amount to approximately $600–$700 per year.

Financial Aid

Otterbein offers a wide variety of scholarships and grants, including Presidential Scholar Awards, Otterbein Scholar Awards, Endowed Scholarships, Dean's Scholarships, community service awards, talent awards, Federal Pell Grants, Ohio Instructional Grants, and Ammons-Thomas minority scholarships. In addition, Federal Perkins Loans, Federal Stafford Student Loans, and United Methodist Student Loans are available. To be considered for need-based College financial aid, students must file the Free Application for Federal Student Aid (FAFSA). Otterbein's financial aid policy is to attempt to meet the financial need of each full-time dependent and independent student offered admission who files financial aid forms by April 1.

Approximately 95 percent of Otterbein's students receive some form of financial aid. In addition to its need-based awards, the College offers scholarships to students on the basis of academic ability and proven talent.

Faculty

Otterbein has a faculty of 144 full-time and 105 part-time members (giving a student-faculty ratio of 13:1). Ninety-two percent of the full-time faculty members hold a doctorate or appropriate terminal degree. Faculty members are actively involved in campus governance, committees, and activities. The extensive sabbatical plan at Otterbein helps ensure that the faculty members constantly update and improve their classroom teaching.

Student Government

Otterbein's governance program gives students a voting voice along with faculty and administrators on all campus policymaking and decision-making bodies. Students are elected to the College Senate, to all governance committees, and to the College's Board of Trustees.

Admission Requirements

To be considered for admission to Otterbein College, students must complete and sign an admission application, submit an official copy of their high school transcript, and provide the College with their scores on either the ACT or SAT I. Applicants should have a solid high school academic record with at least 16 college-preparatory units. Otterbein does not discriminate on the basis of sex, race, gender, sexual orientation, age, political affiliation, national origin, or disabling condition in the admission of students, educational policies, financial aid and scholarships, housing, athletics, employment, and other activities. Inquiries regarding compliance with federal nondiscrimination regulations may be directed to the chairperson of the Affirmative Action Committee, the vice president for academic affairs, or the vice president for business affairs.

Students can gain a fuller understanding of student life at Otterbein by spending a day on campus. Prospective students are welcome to visit classes, eat in the Campus Center, and talk informally with Otterbein students and should simply notify the Office of Admission in advance so arrangements can be made.

Application and Information

Students are urged to begin the application process early in their senior year of high school. Applicants are notified of their admission status as soon as their application file is completed. Otterbein College's application is available on the Web at http://www.otterbein.edu.

For further information, students should contact:

Office of Admission
Otterbein College
Westerville, Ohio 43081
Telephone: 614-823-1500
800-488-8144 or 877-OTTERBEIN (toll-free)
E-mail: uotterb@otterbein.edu

Students on the campus of Otterbein College.

QUINCY UNIVERSITY

QUINCY, ILLINOIS

The University

Quincy University is a private Roman Catholic university of the liberal arts and sciences. It was founded in 1860 by the Franciscan Friars, who have influenced the world by caring about people as people and urging them to fulfill their potential. This spirit is still maintained at Quincy University today. The University prides itself on its personal approach to learning. Small classes, a dedicated faculty, close faculty-student relationships, and a comfortable atmosphere on campus all create an environment conducive to personal growth and development. The University offers courses on both its 52-acre main campus and the 23-acre North Campus, ten blocks away. Shuttle bus service moves students between these campuses regularly.

The 1,200 students come from diverse social and economic backgrounds. Although the majority are from the Midwest, twenty-four states and ten countries are represented in the student body. Quincy University is a residential campus with more than 70 percent of the students living on campus. Campus housing options are varied and include single-sex and coed residence halls, apartments, and houses. Numerous campus organizations offer unlimited opportunities for students to participate in both University and community activities. A National Public Radio station, music performance groups, publications, honor and service societies, a lecture series, and concerts are a few of the many extracurricular opportunities available to students. Eighty percent of the students participate in intramural sports. Quincy University also maintains membership in the NCAA and the Great Lakes Valley Conference. Intercollegiate sports for men are baseball, basketball, football, golf, soccer, tennis, and volleyball. Women's intercollegiate sports are basketball, golf, soccer, softball, tennis, and volleyball.

Career planning and placement counseling is available to students throughout their academic career. Quincy University has an outstanding placement record; more than 96 percent of graduates are placed in jobs or graduate schools within 180 days of graduation. Individual assistance with academic planning, study skills, and tutorial work, as well as personal and vocational counseling, is provided free of charge.

At the graduate level, Quincy University offers programs of study leading to the M.B.A. and M.S.Ed. degrees.

Location

The University is located in a residential section of Quincy, a city of 50,000 people, situated on the bluffs of the Mississippi River. It is within easy traveling time of St. Louis (2 hours), Kansas City (4 hours), and Chicago (4½ hours). Good highways and bus, train, and air service make the area easily accessible from any part of the nation. Quincy has a rich and distinguished tradition in the arts. It is noted for its fine architecture and extensive park system.

Majors and Degrees

Quincy University awards the Bachelor of Arts (B.A.), Bachelor of Fine Arts (B.F.A.), and Bachelor of Science (B.S.) degrees. Programs of study include accounting, art, aviation, aviation management, biology, biological sciences, biological sciences education, business administration, chemistry, clinical laboratory science, computer information systems, communication, computer science, criminal justice, elementary education, engineering, English, English education, finance, history, history education, humanities (interdisciplinary), human services, management, marketing, music, music education, nursing, physical education, political science, psychology, social work, special education–learning disabilities, sports management, theology, theology/Franciscan studies, and theology/pastoral ministry. A Bachelor of Science in Nursing (B.S.N.) is available through a cooperative program with Blessing-Riemann College of Nursing.

Minors are available in most programs; concentrations are offered in physics and reading. A certificate program in business and a coaching specialty in physical education are also available.

Preprofessional programs include dentistry, engineering, law, medicine, physical therapy, and veterinary medicine.

Academic Program

The academic program at Quincy University is based on the belief that liberal arts is the most functional and exciting tradition in education. The curriculum is designed to provide students with the fundamentals of a liberal arts education and at the same time prepare them for a rewarding professional and personal life. The flexible curriculum design allows for double majors or major-minor combinations, student-designed majors, and interdepartmental majors. An honors program, independent studies, special-topics courses, independent research, practicums, and internships are also available to meet the special needs of students.

To be eligible for a baccalaureate degree, a student must complete a minimum of 124 semester hours of university courses with at least a C average. The degree program requires 43 semester hours in general education and "tools" courses, 30–33 hours in a major, and at least 36 hours each in distributed electives and upper-level course work.

Quincy University accepts credit earned through the Advanced Placement Program, the College-Level Examination Program, challenge examinations, and, in some cases, academically related experience.

Off-Campus Arrangements

Arrangements are made with area schools, health facilities, businesses, and industries for such credit-bearing activities as student teaching, clinical training, internships, and practicums. The University also promotes the Early Exploratory Internship Program to its first- and second-year students, allowing them to gain preprofessional experience with area businesses and agencies. Study abroad is possible through many options, with the academic credit for this study preplanned and integrated into the degree program.

Academic Facilities

The Brenner Library, considered one of the top three private-college libraries in the state of Illinois, houses more than 240,000 volumes and 182,000 microtext items and subscribes to 725 periodicals. Among the outstanding holdings are a rare book collection, the 75,000-volume Bonaventure Collection of early Christian and medieval history and theology, and the 4,000-volume Fraborese Collection on Spanish-American history. Through the University's membership in the Online Computer Library Center, Quincy University students have access to millions of books in libraries throughout the Midwest and the nation. The library is also equipped with a computerized reference service.

A modern academic complex located at North Campus houses laboratories for chemistry, physics, biology, engineering, and psychology as well as lecture halls and faculty offices. Six computer labs and more than 200 workstations are available for student use. Students also have unlimited access to personal computers, various networks, Internet, and UNIX. Additional special facilities are a radio station; a fully equipped television studio; the Ameritech Center for Communication, a state-of-the-art computer writing lab and classroom; and a newly opened Student Health and Fitness Center.

Costs

The costs for the 2003–04 academic year are $16,400 for tuition (12–18 credit hours), $450 for the student activity/computer fee, $3265 for room (double occupancy), and $2215 for board.

Financial Aid

More than 95 percent of the students at Quincy University receive some form of financial assistance. The University participates in the Federal Pell Grant, Federal Supplemental Educational Opportunity Grant (FSEOG), Federal Perkins Loan, Federal Work-Study (FWS), and Federal Stafford Student Loan programs. Illinois State Grants are available for qualified Illinois residents. Quincy University awards academic scholarships ranging from $500 to full tuition. Need-based grants are also available. Students who wish to apply for aid must complete the Free Application for Federal Student Aid (FAFSA) as well as the brief QU Application for Financial Aid. Notification of financial aid awards is made on a rolling basis. Early application is recommended, and priority is given to students who apply before February 15. Transfer applicants are required to submit a transcript from each college or university attended.

Faculty

The Quincy University faculty is composed of 102 professionals, highly qualified in their respective fields. Although many are engaged in research, teaching is the top priority at Quincy University. The University's favorable student-faculty ratio of 11:1 and its experienced faculty members, many of whom have had actual work experience in their field, bring an added dimension to the classroom. Eighty-six percent of the faculty members have the highest degree possible in their field.

Student Government

Students participate in University governance through representation on most University committees, including the Academic Affairs Committee, Athletic Advisory Committee, Student Life Committee, and University Judicial Board. The Student Senate provides for effective student participation in all aspects of University life.

Admission Requirements

Quincy University encourages applications from students who are serious about enrolling in a coeducational university of the liberal arts and sciences and who have demonstrated through their previous academic work an ability to profit from and contribute to the University. Each applicant for admission is evaluated individually. Primary consideration is given to the student's previous academic record. Quincy University recommends that prospective students take a strong college-preparatory program in high school. The Office of Admissions evaluates the prospective freshman's high school record in the following areas: number of academic courses taken, level of difficulty of courses attempted, type of high school attended, grade point average, standardized test scores, class rank, and extracurricular activities. All freshmen are required to submit SAT I or ACT scores.

Transfer students who have earned fewer than 24 semester hours must submit a high school transcript in addition to their college transcripts and should have maintained an overall grade point average of at least 2.0 (C) during their collegiate years. Transfer students may enter at three times during the year: August, January, or June.

International students must submit a transcript from each secondary and collegiate institution they have attended. All non-English transcripts must be translated into English before submission to the Office of Admissions. All international students must also submit TOEFL scores or demonstrate proficiency in the English language.

Application and Information

All students seeking admission are encouraged to apply early. Applications are evaluated after all required application materials have been received. Notification of admission decisions is made on a rolling basis.

Parents, students, and student groups are always welcome to visit the University. The Office of Admissions welcomes visitors from 8 a.m. to 5 p.m., Monday through Friday. Saturday visitors are welcome by appointment. If possible, campus visits should be scheduled during the academic year, when classes are in session. Accepted students may stay overnight in residence halls during the academic year.

For more information about the University's 142-year tradition of excellence, students should contact:

Director of Admissions
Quincy University
1800 College Avenue
Quincy, Illinois 62301-2699
Telephone: 217-228-5210
800-688-HAWK (4295) (toll-free)
E-mail: admissions@quincy.edu
World Wide Web: http://www.quincy.edu

Quincy University's new $12-million Student Health and Fitness Center.

RIPON COLLEGE

RIPON, WISCONSIN

The College

One key reason why students choose Ripon College from among the more than 3,500 colleges and universities in the country is that Ripon offers an intensely personal undergraduate education. Since 1851, Ripon has provided a personal liberal arts education that makes a remarkable difference in the lives of students. *U.S. News & World Report* recently ranked Ripon among those national liberal arts colleges that offer "high quality education at a reasonable cost."

Companies look for college graduates who can adapt to change and who can write, use modern technology with confidence, communicate, and make a contribution to a team. These are the skills that a Ripon education offers students. In 2002, Ripon student Zach Morris became the College's third Rhodes Scholar.

Ripon's curricular emphasis focuses on Communicating Plus. This program aims to assist students in the development of superior written and oral communication, critical-thinking, and problem-solving skills.

Ripon is a residential college; 90 percent of students live on campus, and because students remain on campus after classes have ended, learning occurs around the clock. All students are encouraged to participate in Ripon's numerous extracurricular activities, including the campus radio station and the Student Senate.

Ripon College is fully accredited by the North Central Association of Colleges and Schools.

Location

Ripon College is situated on 250 tree-lined, rolling acres adjacent to downtown Ripon, Wisconsin, a charming turn-of-the-century community of 7,500 people. Ripon is a short drive from Green Bay, Madison, and Milwaukee. A variety of year-round recreational activities are available in Ripon and in Green Lake, a city just 6 miles from the campus.

Majors and Degrees

The Bachelor of Arts is offered in thirty majors: anthropology, art, biology, business administration, chemistry, chemistry-biology, computer science, economics, educational studies, English, environmental studies, exercise science, foreign languages, French, German, global studies, history, Latin American studies, mathematics, music, philosophy, physical science, politics and government, psychobiology, psychology, religion, sociology-anthropology, Spanish, communication, and theater. Self-designed majors and preprofessional programs are also available. Minors are available in most of the departments listed above and in leadership studies and women's studies. In addition, the educational studies department offers certification programs in elementary education, music, physical education, and secondary education.

Under a special program for engineers, a student may study for three years at Ripon and two at an engineering school, receiving a bachelor's degree from each institution. Ripon has formal cooperative engineering programs with Washington University in St. Louis and Rensselaer Polytechnic Institute. A student who desires to go into forestry may study for three years at Ripon and two years at Duke University, receiving both a bachelor's degree and a master's degree. In addition, Ripon College and Rush-Presbyterian-St. Luke's Medical Center in Chicago offer a cooperative program in nursing and allied health sciences in which students spend their first two years at Ripon and then transfer to Rush for their final two years.

Academic Program

Since its founding, Ripon has been a liberal arts college. Students have the opportunity to study all fields of human knowledge, including the social sciences, the natural sciences, the humanities, and the fine arts. While other colleges have become increasingly specialized, Ripon has remained steadfast in its belief that the liberal arts are the key for a life of both personal and professional success. Ripon operates on a schedule of two 15-week semesters and an optional 3-week "Maymester."

Off-Campus Arrangements

Ripon's off-campus studies program sends students to such places as Costa Rica, England, France, Germany, Italy, Japan, and Spain to study for a semester. In addition, students can select programs within the U.S., such as the Oak Ridge Laboratory Semester in Tennessee, the Newberry Library Seminar in the Humanities in Chicago, urban studies and urban teaching in Chicago, and study at the Marine Biological Laboratory at Wood's Hole Oceanographic Institution.

Academic Facilities

Ripon's campus combines the best of both historic and modern architecture. The College's three original buildings, constructed between 1851 and 1867, are still used for offices and classes. The Farr Hall of Science, which recently received a $4.4-million renovation and addition, holds a planetarium, a greenhouse, ample laboratory space, and state-of-the-art equipment. On the west side of campus, the C. J. Rodman Center for the Arts and the J. M. Storzer Physical Education Center house a recital hall, a theater, an art gallery, a sculpture garden, a multipurpose gymnasium, a pool, racquetball courts, free-weight and Nautilus rooms, and aerobics rooms. Adjacent to the Storzer Center is the Ceresco Prairie Conservancy, 3½ miles of recreational trails and 130 acres of restored native habitat. Ripon's student center, Harwood Memorial Union, holds a lecture hall, the Pub, a game room, the radio station, and student organization offices.

Costs

The costs for 2002–03 were as follows: tuition, $19,260; room, $2195; board, $2625; activity fee, $240; and additional fees, books, and miscellaneous personal expenses, $1000.

Financial Aid

Ninety percent of Ripon students receive financial assistance that meets 100 percent of their financial need. The average financial aid award equals 78 percent of a student's total costs. Ripon's extensive scholarship program is designed to recognize and reward applicants for their talents and abilities. Currently, seventeen types of scholarships that range from $1000 to full tuition annually are available.

Faculty

Ripon College's student-faculty ratio is 14:1, and the average class size is 17. Ninety-seven percent of the full-time faculty members have earned the highest degree in their fields, and, as a result of their hard work, Ripon has received ten National Science Foundation Grants since 1992 and six Fulbright Fellowships since 1989.

Student Government

The Student Senate, composed of representatives of all resident groups and campus organizations, is the main governing body and administers a budget of more than $100,000 for student organizations and activities. It is an active and influential means of bringing student opinion to bear on College affairs.

Admission Requirements

Important factors considered in the admission process include graduation from an accredited secondary school (or GED equivalent), the secondary school transcript, and results of standardized tests (SAT or ACT).

Application and Information

Prospective students who value a challenging liberal arts and sciences education in a small, caring community are invited to visit the campus, sit in on Ripon classes, and see firsthand how Ripon students and professors interact with one another.

Students who wish to apply to Ripon College should submit a completed application form, a secondary school transcript, results of standardized tests, and the $30 application fee. Ripon College application forms are available from the admission office and at the College's Web site (address below). Ripon participates in the Common Application Plan and accepts photocopies of the Common Application in place of the Ripon College application form. Common Application forms are available in many secondary school guidance offices. Ripon also accepts applications that are made through the Wisconsin Mentor site (http://www.wisconsinmentor.org/admissionapp).

Candidates for fall term consideration are encouraged to apply early. Notification of fall term admission occurs within two weeks of the completion of the student's application. Students applying for spring term consideration should submit applications by December 15. Notification occurs shortly thereafter.

For further information, students should contact:

Dean of Admission
Ripon College
300 Seward Street
P.O. Box 248
Ripon, Wisconsin 54971-0248
Telephone: 800-94-RIPON (toll-free)
E-mail: adminfo@ripon.edu
World Wide Web: http://www.ripon.edu

Ripon College students and their families celebrate commencement on the lawn of Harwood Memorial Union.

ROBERT MORRIS COLLEGE

CHICAGO, O'HARE, DUPAGE, ORLAND PARK, PEORIA, LAKE COUNTY, AND SPRINGFIELD, ILLINOIS

The College

Robert Morris College (RMC) is a private, not-for-profit, independent college dedicated to providing intensive career education and general education opportunities. Associate degrees, the Bachelor of Business Administration degree, the Bachelor of Applied Science degree in graphic design, and the Bachelor of Applied Science degree in computer studies are awarded. Robert Morris College is accredited by the Higher Learning Commission and is a member of the North Central Association of Colleges and Schools (30 North LaSalle Street, Suite 2400, Chicago, Illinois 60602; telephone: 312-263-0456; Web: http://www.ncahigherlearningcommission.org).

The history of Robert Morris College dates back to the founding of the Moser School, one of the outstanding independent business schools in Chicago, in 1913. Robert Morris College also has origins in Illinois at the site of the former Carthage College. Here, Robert Morris College was chartered and offered associate degrees in both liberal and vocational arts from 1965 to 1974. With the acquisition of the Moser School in 1975, RMC expanded to include business and allied health. The College now provides students with a choice of seven locations: Chicago, O'Hare, DuPage, Orland Park, Peoria, Lake County, and Springfield, Illinois.

RMC offers programs in the School of Business Administration, the School of Health Studies, the School of Computer Studies, the Institute of Culinary Arts, and the Institute of Art and Design. Each of these five divisions uses the most modern computer technology. Acquisition of such technology is imperative to providing real-world, educational experiences that are relevant to the evolving work place.

RMC's unique five-quarter system is designed for continuous learning. It enables students to accelerate their education, completing a bachelor's degreee in three years and an associate degreee in fifteen months.

The student body of approximately 6,000 is a cross-cultural, ethnic, and racial mix representative of the communities served. Each student works with a team of program directors, instructors, and placement specialists in an effort to achieve educational and career goals. The records of the College's students and graduates are the best indicators of what a prospective student can expect. Seventy percent of RMC students graduate from the programs they begin, compared to significantly lower percentages at other private and public colleges and universities.

The Placement Department, which has offices at each of the College's campuses, continuously cultivates employment opportunities for RMC graduates, with representatives in the business, allied health, art, and computer industries. Last year, 9 out of 10 RMC graduates who requested job placement assistance successfully secured employment in their chosen fields.

Robert Morris College is a member of the National Association of Intercollegiate Athletics (NAIA) and the Chicagoland Collegiate Athletic Conference (CCAC), Division II. The College offers men's and women's basketball, cross-country, golf, and soccer. It also offers men's baseball, men's and women's club hockey, and women's softball, volleyball, and tennis.

Location

Located in the heart of Chicago's bustling cultural and financial districts, the College's main campus is minutes from all that Chicago offers, including the Chicago Board of Trade, Art Institute, Field Museum, Merchandise Mart, lakefront, sports arenas, theaters, and all forms of public transportation. The Chicago campus is readily accessible from all parts of the city and suburbs by bus lines and trains. Parking is available in the immediate vicinity. Robert Morris Center is across the street from the renowned Harold Washington Public Library.

The O'Hare Campus opened to better serve the residents of western Cook and DuPage Counties and to meet the demands of employers in the area. The Springfield campus is located on Montvale Drive, just east of White Oaks Mall. The College is accessible by bus, and ample parking is also available. The recently expanded Orland Park campus now includes a technology center with the latest computer facilities available to industry and education. It is located adjacent to the Orland Square Mall, approximately 30 miles southwest of Chicago. It is accessible via public transportation and I-80 and I-55, which run parallel on the south and north ends of the campus, respectively. Orland Park is becoming a corporate center of the southwest Chicago suburbs, offering students ample opportunity for professional growth through internships and employment.

The DuPage campus opened on the border between Naperville and Aurora and serves students as well as employers along the East-West High Tech Corridor—the heart of rapid technological development and close to a wide range of employers. The Peoria campus in the busy downtown area of the city expands RMC's commitment to serving central Illinois. Beginning fall 2003, classes are available to Lake County area residents at a campus in Waukegan. Students in northern Illinois and southeastern Wisconsin can take advantage of RMC programs in this new setting.

All locations provide students with access to the unlimited variety of business services and enhance the students' understanding of the world of work and the employment process.

Majors and Degrees

The Bachelor of Business Administration degree at Robert Morris College offers concentrations in accounting, health-care management, hospitality management, and management. The Bachelor of Applied Science degree in graphic design offers concentrations in graphic arts and media arts. The Bachelor of Applied Science degree in computer studies offers concentrations in database management, networking, telecommunications management, and Web programming. RMC also awards associate degrees in accounting, business administration, CAD drafting (architectural/mechanical), computer networking, computer programming, culinary arts, fitness specialist, graphic arts, interior design, legal office assistant/paralegal studies, media arts, and medical assisting. More than twenty-six transfer agreements have been established between RMC and community colleges, allowing students who have earned associate degrees elsewhere to complete their bachelor's degrees at RMC by transferring in as a junior. Robert Morris College is the seventh-largest private college/university in Illinois; tuition is one of the lowest for Illinois private colleges/universities. RMC is the largest granter of baccalaureate degrees in business and awards more associate degrees (all disciplines combined) to members of minority groups than any institution in Illinois. RMC is the sixteenth-largest granter of Bachelor of Business Administration degrees to African Americans and the twenty-eighth to Hispanic Americans in the country.

Academic Program

The College's academic calendar consists of five quarters, each of which is ten weeks long. The program of study is designed so that students can complete their course work and enter their careers in the shortest time possible: in as little as three years for a bachelor's degree and fifteen months for an associate degree.

By concentrating on the specialized subjects related to the student's chosen career field, the College's curricula provide students with the skills and knowledge necessary to enter the job market. Each major consists of courses prescribed by the College to lead to this objective. An associate degree requires at least 92 quarter hours of credit with a minimum of 56 hours of credit in general education in the areas of communications, humanities, math and science, and social and behavioral science. A minimum of 52 quarter hours of credit are required in career courses, and the remaining hours are electives split between general education and career courses. A bachelor's degree requires a minimum of 188 quarter hours of credit. A minimum of 72 hours of credit are required in general education courses; 100 to 104 hours are required in major course work.

Robert Morris College offers students the opportunity to gain experience in their majors and improve their skills through internships and externships. Placement personnel work closely with students to secure positions related to their fields of study. Internships offer many educational and professional benefits and provide students with the opportunity to earn academic credit for participating in a career-specific work experience.

Off-Campus Arrangements

Robert Morris College offers students the opportunity to study abroad at the Institute of European Studies in Vienna, Austria; at Regent's College in London, England; and in Florence, Italy.

Academic Facilities

General purpose classrooms; high-tech equipment; specialized laboratories; study, practice, and leisure lounges; fitness centers; and cyber cafés are among the facilities the College provides at each campus. The technology-based library has online capabilities that connect the College's various campuses. Online Internet access offers students advanced research capabilities, sizable collections of reference and resource volumes, and periodical subscriptions. Vertical file information is available in addition to numerous computer and audio resources and a job search center.

Costs

Robert Morris College has one of the lowest tuition rates of any baccalaureate degree–granting private college in the state. Tuition for 2003–04 is $4500 per quarter. Book and supply costs vary by major from $300 to $500 per quarter.

Financial Aid

Robert Morris College participates in the following federal and state financial aid programs: the Federal Pell Grant, Illinois Monetary Award (SSIG/IMA), Federal Supplemental Educational Opportunity Grant (FSEOG), Federal Stafford Student Loan, Federal Perkins Loan, Federal PLUS Loan, and Federal Work-Study (FWS) programs. In addition, the College awards institutional grants on the basis of need, scholarship, residence, academic major, or a combination of these factors. All students must complete a financial planning interview with their admissions counselor, and all are urged to complete the Free Application for Federal Student Aid (FAFSA). Approximately 85 percent of the student body receive some financial assistance. In the 2001–02 academic year, the College awarded more than $12 million in institutional aid.

Faculty

The faculty members at Robert Morris College are selected on the basis of their academic credentials, career experiences in their field, and dedication to giving special attention to every student. All faculty members possess a master's degree in their chosen field, and many possess a Ph.D. in their area of specialization. In addition to teaching courses, faculty members promote the progress of their students through the individualized academic, employment, and personal development counseling they provide.

Student Government

Robert Morris College has no formal student government. Student representatives serve on committees that make recommendations about campus issues. Student organizations and activities are available.

Admission Requirements

All graduates of accredited high schools or the equivalent (GED) are eligible for admission to the College. All candidates are encouraged to have a personal interview with an admissions representative and to have a tour of the campus.

A variety of materials are considered for various applicants. Freshman applicants just graduating from high school must submit their high school record or GED score and test results from the ACT, SAT I, Applied Education Skills Assessment (AESA), Advanced Placement, and SAT II Subject Area tests.

Those enrolling as an adult (age 23 and above) must submit their high school record or GED score; test results from the ACT, SAT I, Applied Education Skills Assessment (AESA), College Level Examination Program (CLEP), and Dantes; and evidence of a successful employment experience.

Transfer students must present a minimum of 12 transferable credit hours from an accredited institution and their academic records from any high schools and colleges previously attended.

International students must forward their official education records, the results from either TOEFL or AESA, and an affidavit of financial support.

Home-schooled students must submit a complete transcript of all classes they have taken, curriculum documentation and its state certification, and results from any standardized examinations they have taken.

Application and Information

Applications can be obtained by contacting the Admissions Office at any of the College's campuses. The completed application and the $20 nonrefundable application fee ($100 nonrefundable application fee for international students) should be sent to the Admissions Office. The College operates on a rolling admissions basis, and students can enroll during any one of the five times offered during the year. For further information, prospective students should visit the Web site below or contact:

Admissions Office
Robert Morris College
401 South State Street
Chicago, Illinois 60605

Admissions Office
Robert Morris College
905 Meridian Lake Drive
Aurora, Illinois 60504

Admissions Office
Robert Morris College
43 Orland Square
Orland Park, Illinois 60462

Admissions Office
Robert Morris College
1000 Tower Lane
Bensenville, Illinois 60108

Admissions Office
Robert Morris College
211 Fulton Street
Peoria, Illinois 61602

Admissions Office
Robert Morris College
3101 Montvale Drive
Springfield, Illinois 62704

Admissions Office
Robert Morris College
Lake County
1507 South Waukegan Road
Lake County, Illinois 60085

Telephone: 800-RMC-5960 (toll-free)
World Wide Web: http://www.robertmorris.edu

ROCKFORD COLLEGE

ROCKFORD, ILLINOIS

The College

Rockford College, founded in 1847, is a fully accredited, private, independent, coeducational institution. The College offers undergraduate programs in more than forty fields of study and graduate programs in business and education. Academic programs are based on a foundation of learning in the liberal arts and sciences. The College emphasizes excellence in teaching and has a strong commitment to scholarly activity, creative expression, and community service. In 2002, Rockford College was again named by *U.S. News & World Report* as a top-tier Midwestern university. It is also one of only eleven colleges and universities in Illinois with a Phi Beta Kappa chapter.

Currently, 1,200 students attend Rockford College. Students come from more than twenty-five states and twenty countries. Residential students can choose from a variety of living arrangements. Rockford College strongly believes that campus life is vital to a well-rounded college education. Intramural programs, community service activities, departmental clubs, and honorary academic societies present opportunities for developing friendships and sharpening leadership skills. The Student Affairs Division provides career services, international student support services, recreational programming, and health and counseling services.

Approximately 25 percent of all full-time students participate in the intercollegiate athletic program. The Rockford College Regents are a member of the NCAA Division III and compete in the Northern Illinois and Iowa Conference (NIIC). Women compete in basketball, soccer, softball, tennis, and volleyball. Men compete in baseball, basketball, football, golf, soccer, and tennis.

Location

Rockford, the second-largest city in Illinois, is only 75 miles from both Chicago and Milwaukee and is easily accessible by car, bus, and plane. The College is located on a 130-acre wooded campus. The city of Rockford offers students all the advantages of a thriving community: off-campus entertainment includes more than 500 restaurants, concerts and attractions at the MetroCentre, the New American Theater, the Coronado Theater, the Rockford Dance Company, numerous malls and shopping centers, museums, riverside events, and an award-winning park district. Students benefit from volunteer, internship, and employment opportunities in the community. The involvement of students in the community provides unlimited experiences that enhance and complement their Rockford College education.

Majors and Degrees

The Bachelor of Arts degree is awarded in accounting, anthropology/sociology, art (with concentrations in ceramics, drawing, painting, photography, printmaking, and sculpture), art history, biology, business administration (with tracks in management and marketing), chemistry, classics, computer science (management information systems), criminal justice (program in anthropology/sociology), economics (with tracks in finance, international economics, and public policy), education, English, French, German, history, Latin, mathematics, music history and literature, philosophy, physical education (with tracks in business and teaching), political science, psychology, science and mathematics, social sciences, Spanish, theater arts, and urban studies.

The Bachelor of Fine Arts degree is awarded in art (with concentrations in ceramics, drawing, painting, photography, printmaking, and sculpture) and performing arts (musical theater performance).

The Bachelor of Science degree is awarded in accounting, anthropology/sociology, biochemistry, biology, business administration (with tracks in management and marketing), chemistry, computer science (management information systems), economics (with tracks in finance, international economics, and public policy), education, English, history, mathematics, physical education (with tracks in business and teaching), political science, pre–social work (program in anthropology/sociology), psychology, science and mathematics, social sciences, and urban studies.

A four-year NLNAC-accredited Bachelor of Science in Nursing program is offered. A B.S.N. completion program designed specifically for registered nurses is also available.

Preprofessional programs are carefully designed to meet the needs of students who plan to pursue careers in dentistry, engineering (3-2 program), health professions (optometry and physical therapy), law, medicine, pharmacy, and veterinary medicine.

In addition to the majors/programs/degrees listed above, Rockford College also offers minors in the following areas of study: British studies, communication, dance, Greek, human development, military science, peace and conflict studies, physics, and religious studies.

Academic Program

Education at Rockford College is intended to be both broad-based and preparatory. The liberal arts curriculum allows for a choice of course work with an emphasis on a major. To earn a degree from Rockford College, students must complete at least 124 credit hours. Courses are offered by semester; there are two semesters per year. Summer courses are also available. The Honors Program in Liberal Arts offers extensive study in the humanities, a challenging core curriculum, and rigorous distribution requirements. Entrance to this program is limited and available by application only. The Forum Series offers exposure to great scholars, artists, and ideas. Special features of the College's academic program include Phi Beta Kappa and other scholastic honor societies, the Archaeological Institute of America, faculty seminars, art exhibitions, independent study, academic internships, and an extensive study-abroad program. A freshman seminar program is required for new students.

Off-Campus Arrangements

Rockford College gives its students an opportunity to study for a semester or a year at Regent's College in London, England, for approximately the same cost as attending the Illinois campus. Regent's College, a residential campus located in Regent's Park, offers a wide variety of courses, including academic internships, in a fully accredited program. The campus is conveniently located close to museums, galleries, theaters, and other attractions. Residence at Regent's College makes travel throughout Britain and on the Continent possible.

Rockford College also participates in programs that allow students to study in Australia, France, Germany, Spain, and other countries.

In the United States, Rockford students may participate in the Washington and United Nations Semesters.

Academic Facilities

Among the major academic buildings on the Rockford College campus is the Howard Colman Library, which houses 170,000 volumes and more than 800 periodical subscriptions. CD-ROM computers provide easy access to library holdings and national indexes; the availability of resources is enhanced by the interlibrary loan system. Private study carrels are provided. The Starr Science Building houses the major science facilities, which include physics laboratories, chemistry teaching and research laboratories with a fully equipped instrumentation lab, biology and psychology teaching and research laboratories, and nursing laboratories. It also houses the student computer lab and language lab. Programs in fine and performing arts are housed in the Clark Arts Center, which has a 570-seat theater with computerized lighting and sound equipment; an experimental theater; an art gallery; a sculpture garden; studios for lithography/printmaking, drawing, painting, sculpting, and ceramics; a darkroom; and facilities for dance and music. The Seaver Physical Education Building is the campus sports complex. It includes locker rooms, a pool, a basketball court, a free-weight room, a fitness center, a training room, and classrooms. Dayton Hall houses the Learning Resources Center, which offers free tutoring. Scarborough Hall houses classrooms, faculty offices, and the writing center.

Costs

Costs for the 2003–04 academic year are $20,210 for tuition and $4034 for a double room. Several board plans are available, starting at $2547. Books are estimated to cost $900 per year. Miscellaneous expenses, including transportation, vary with individual needs but total approximately $2000 per year.

Financial Aid

Approximately 95 percent of students receive financial aid. Students may be considered for financial assistance if they are taking at least 6 credit hours per semester. Merit-based awards, including several full tuition scholarships, are available to full-time students. Need-based awards are determined by the results of the Free Application for Federal Student Aid (FAFSA). These awards include Rockford College grants and institutional loans as well as federal and state funds. Students are encouraged to file for financial aid by June 1. Rockford College students who attend Regent's College are eligible for the above awards.

Faculty

The student-faculty ratio at Rockford College is 12:1. The full-time faculty is composed of more than 80 men and women with outstanding academic backgrounds and varied international experience. Seventy percent hold terminal degrees in their respective fields. Some departments enlist part-time faculty members from the Rockford and Chicago professional communities to augment their programs. An extensive faculty development program helps ensure that the faculty members constantly update and improve their classroom teaching. Faculty members are involved in the lives of their students by serving as academic advisers, club and organization advisers, and mentors. A freshman advising program matches incoming freshmen with full-time faculty members who serve as advisers and mentors.

Student Government

The Rockford College Student Government serves its constituency in all areas of campus life. Students serve on College committees, judge their peers in student court, uphold the campus honor code, monitor campus media, and are consulted regarding changes in College policy. The Entertainment Council is responsible for organizing campus activities, including concerts, lectures, dances, and other social events.

Admission Requirements

Admission to Rockford College is based upon the applicant's potential for success as determined by prior academic preparation and personal achievement and is subject to satisfactory completion of academic work currently in progress. Students may apply upon completion of their junior year of high school. Admission is based on high school GPA, ACT or SAT test results, and class rank. Applicants must meet the following three criteria: a minimum 2.65 CGPA on a 4.0 scale; placement in the top 50 percent of their class; an ACT score of 19 or higher, with no subscore below 17; or an SAT score of 910 or higher. Applicants must provide official copies of these documents. Transfer applicants with more than 12 hours of college course work are evaluated on the cumulative GPA of all college course work attempted and must provide official transcripts from all colleges attended. Transfer students must have a CGPA of at least 2.3.

All applicants must submit an application and a nonrefundable $35 application fee. The fee is waived for students who visit the campus. On-campus interviews and personal statements are highly encouraged. Recommendations may be requested.

International students are welcome to apply; they should contact the Director of International Student Admission for specific application information. A TOEFL score of at least 550 is required of international applicants.

Students wishing to pursue a Rockford College degree are expected to have completed a college-preparatory program of 15 units at an accredited secondary school. A proper foundation for success at Rockford includes 4 years of English and at least three of the following four areas: 2 years of mathematics (algebra and geometry), 1 year of history, 1 year of foreign language, and 1 year of laboratory science. Freshmen who intend to pursue a Bachelor of Science in Nursing degree should take both biology and chemistry at the high school level.

Application and Information

Rockford College uses a rolling admission policy. Students can expect to be notified of decisions within two weeks of receipt of the completed application and all necessary documents.

For further information, students should contact:

Office of Admission
Nelson Hall
Rockford College
5050 East State Street
Rockford, Illinois 61108-2393
Telephone: 815-226-4050
800-892-2984 (toll-free in the U.S. and Canada)
Fax: 815-226-2822
E-mail: admission@rockford.edu
World Wide Web: http://www.rockford.edu

The accessibility of faculty members at Rockford College allows close interaction with students both in and out of the classroom.

SAINT MARY'S COLLEGE

NOTRE DAME, INDIANA

The College

One of the oldest Catholic colleges for women in the United States, Saint Mary's College was founded and continues to be sponsored by the Sisters of the Holy Cross in 1844. The College has long been recognized as a pioneer in exploring with integrity and imagination the roles of women in society. Today, Saint Mary's enjoys a national reputation for academic excellence and vitality of campus life.

With more than 1,600 students from forty-nine states and fifteen countries, Saint Mary's brings together women from a wide range of geographical areas, social backgrounds, and educational experiences. International and minority students comprise 8 percent of the student body.

Saint Mary's College's liberal arts emphasis enhances a comprehensive curriculum. Strong programs in the humanities and sciences are complemented by professional programs in business administration, education, nursing, and social work; majors in the fine and performing arts; and courses of preprofessional study that prepare students for law school, medical school, or advanced study in other health professions.

Small classes (median size: 16) and a low student-faculty ratio (12:1) encourage student participation in class discussions, collaboration with faculty members, and preparation for real-world challenges. The College enjoys a unique exchange program with the University of Notre Dame.

Approximately 80 percent of Saint Mary's students live on campus in four residence halls, each with its own distinctive character. Upperclass students may live off-campus. Residence halls offer a full calendar of activities, from twice-yearly dances to discussions with professors. The College has a college center, a dining hall, and a clubhouse for extracurricular activities. All residence halls have chapels, and the Church of Loretto is on campus.

As an NCAA Division III school and a member of the Michigan Intercollegiate Athletic Association, Saint Mary's sponsors varsity teams in basketball, cross-country, golf, soccer, softball, swimming and diving, tennis, and volleyball. Club sports, cosponsored with Notre Dame, include equestrian, gymnastics, sailing, skiing, and synchronized swimming. In addition, Saint Mary's offers many intramural sports.

The College's Angela Athletic Facility contains multipurpose courts for tennis, volleyball, and basketball; a training and fitness center; and racquetball courts. The campus has an indoor swimming pool, outdoor tennis courts, athletic fields, and a driving range for golf.

Location

Saint Mary's 275-acre campus, set alongside the Saint Joseph River, has great natural beauty. However, the College, located just across the street from the University of Notre Dame, just north of the city of South Bend, and just 90 miles from Chicago, is at the hub of much activity. Students from Saint Mary's and Notre Dame form a dynamic intercollegiate community. South Bend provides sites for internships and practicums and opportunities for volunteer service.

Majors and Degrees

Saint Mary's College offers programs leading to the Bachelor of Arts, Bachelor of Science, Bachelor of Fine Arts, Bachelor of Business Administration, and Bachelor of Music degrees.

For a Bachelor of Arts degree, students may choose majors in art, biology, chemistry, communication, economics, elementary education, English literature, English writing, French, history, humanistic studies, mathematics, music, philosophy, political science, psychology, religious studies, social work, sociology, Spanish, statistics and actuarial mathematics, and theater.

A Bachelor of Science degree may be obtained in biology, chemistry, computational mathematics, cytotechnology, mathematics, medical technology, nursing, and statistics and actuarial mathematics.

The Bachelor of Music degree program, which is a member of the National Association of Schools of Music, offers concentrations in applied music and music education. For talented art students, Saint Mary's offers a Bachelor of Fine Arts degree.

The Bachelor of Business Administration degree program offers a major in business administration (with concentrations in accounting, finance, international business, management, and marketing) and a major in management information systems.

Superior students who are candidates for either a Bachelor of Arts or a Bachelor of Science degree may design a program of study outside of the traditional department structure.

For women interested in engineering fields, a five-year dual-degree program offered in cooperation with the University of Notre Dame leads to a bachelor's degree from Saint Mary's College and a Bachelor of Science in Engineering degree from Notre Dame.

Saint Mary's education department, accredited by the National Council for Accreditation of Teacher Education, offers certification in elementary and secondary education.

In addition, the College offers more than forty minors in a variety of fields, including American studies, information science, justice studies, Latin American studies, urban studies, and women's studies.

Academic Program

Graduation from Saint Mary's College requires successful completion of at least 128 semester hours of credit with a minimum quality point average of 2.0. Every student must also complete a comprehensive examination in her major, which may take the form of a thesis, a research or creative project, or a written or oral examination, depending on the discipline. All students must demonstrate writing proficiency by satisfactorily completing a writing-intensive "W" course, usually in the first year, and an advanced portfolio of writings in the major discipline, usually as seniors.

Students spend approximately one third of their time in general education courses in humanities, fine arts, foreign language, natural and social sciences, theology, and philosophy. Remaining course hours are devoted to their major and electives or minors. The College assists those students interested in pursuing independent study or research and internships.

Off-Campus Arrangements

Through Saint Mary's international study programs, students can study with Irish students at the National University of Ireland Maynooth, just outside Dublin. They can absorb Italian art and culture on Saint Mary's campus in the center of Rome, or experience Southeast Asia and the Far East with the India-based Semester Around the World Program.

Students can spend a month during the summer based in London, earning credit hours while also traveling to other European countries.

Saint Mary's students may also enroll in the Spanish language programs of the Center for Cross-Cultural Study in Seville, Spain, or in the French language and culture study in Dijon, France. A new exchange program with the Australian University of Notre Dame has just begun.

Saint Mary's students may study in Austria, France, Japan, Mexico, and Toledo, Spain, as well as Jerusalem through a cooperative program with the University of Notre Dame.

A student majoring in political science has the opportunity to spend a semester at the American University in Washington, D.C. Saint Mary's also participates in student and faculty member exchange programs with the University of Notre Dame and members of the Northern Indiana Consortium for Education.

Academic Facilities

Students have abundant access to computers, the campus network, and the World Wide Web. Residence halls and classrooms are wired for network access. Computer labs for students are located in several campus buildings, and an expanding set of services and support is available. Many faculty members make use of information technology for teaching and research.

The modern Cushwa-Leighton Library houses a fine collection of 210,812 volumes. It includes offices, study areas, an after-hours study lounge, a media center, computer facilities, the College archives, and a rare book room.

In addition to extensive biology, chemistry, and physics lab facilities, laboratories for psychology research and for foreign language study and practice are available to students. Art studios, music practice rooms, the O'Laughlin Auditorium, and Moreau's Little Theatre provide ample space for arts creation, practice, and performance.

The professionally staffed Early Childhood Development Center on campus provides education and psychology majors with an unusual opportunity to work with young children. Other facilities include the Madeleva classroom building, Science Hall, Havican nursing facility, and Moreau Art Galleries.

Costs

The expenses for the 2002–03 academic year were tuition and fees, $20,550; room and board, $6942 (double occupancy); and miscellaneous expenses (books, transportation, and living costs), $2225.

Financial Aid

The College strives to make a Saint Mary's education available for every student by offering eligible students financial aid packages that may include grants, scholarships, work-study, and loans. Competitive scholarships, awarded solely on merit, as well as those determined by a combination of financial need and academic achievement are available. Last year, more than 87 percent of Saint Mary's students received more than $21 million in financial assistance, more than $9.7 million from the College alone.

All applicants for financial assistance must complete the Financial Aid PROFILE and the Free Application for Federal Student Aid (FAFSA) each year that they desire assistance. Applications for assistance must be received at the processing center by March 1 to be given priority consideration. Decisions concerning financial aid are made as soon as possible after a student has been accepted.

Faculty

Saint Mary's has 114 full-time and 75 part-time faculty members. About 96 percent of the faculty members hold earned doctorates or other terminal degrees; of these, most teach first-year students as well as upper-division students. Faculty members work with students in all phases of college life, including academic counseling.

Student Government

Students are active at every level of campus governance and share in community decision making. There are voting representatives on the president's two highest advisory boards, the Student Affairs Council and the Academic Affairs Council. A student is a voting member of the College Board of Trustees. Student government sponsors many extracurricular and cocurricular activities.

Admission Requirements

Applicants for admission to Saint Mary's College should be graduates of an accredited high school and should ordinarily have completed a four-year program of 16 or more academic units. They must include 4 units of English, 3 units of college-preparatory mathematics, 2 units of one foreign language, 2 units of social science, and 2 units of laboratory science. The remaining units should be in college-preparatory courses. An applicant's credentials should include an academic transcript showing current rank and senior-year subjects, a counselor/administrator recommendation, SAT I or ACT scores, and an essay.

Home-schooled students are encouraged to apply for admission and should contact the Admission Office for details.

An interview with an admission officer is recommended. Saint Mary's encourages students to visit the campus. The Admission Office can make arrangements for students who wish to attend classes or stay overnight.

Superior students who have studied for advanced placement may begin sophomore-level courses in their first year. Mature, well-qualified students who wish to enter college after three years of high school may apply for early admission. Saint Mary's College also grants deferred admission upon request to candidates who are accepted in the normal competition.

Application and Information

Saint Mary's has two application and notification programs: early decision and modified rolling admission. Highly qualified students who have selected Saint Mary's as their first choice for admission may apply under the early decision program. The application deadline is November 15, and the notification date is December 15. Students who apply for modified rolling admission and whose application files are complete on or before December 1 are notified of the admission decision in mid-January. Candidates are encouraged to apply by the end of their junior year of high school or in the fall of their senior year. Applications are accepted, however, as long as space is available.

Interested students are encouraged to contact:

Director of Admission
Saint Mary's College
Notre Dame, Indiana 46556-5001
Telephone: 574-284-4587
800-551-7621 (toll-free)
Fax: 574-284-4841
E-mail: admission@saintmarys.edu
World Wide Web: http://www.saintmarys.edu

SIMPSON COLLEGE

INDIANOLA, IOWA

The College

Simpson College was founded in 1860. The institution was named Simpson College to honor Bishop Matthew Simpson (1811–1884), one of the best-known and most influential religious leaders of his day. The College is coeducational; although it is affiliated with the United Methodist Church, it is nonsectarian in spirit and accepts students without regard to race, color, creed, national origin, religion, sex, age, or disability.

For more than a century, Simpson has played a vital role in the educational, cultural, intellectual, political, and religious life of the nation. The College has thirty-two buildings on 73 acres of beautiful campus and enrolls 1,900 students.

Extracurricular activities at Simpson are designed to supplement and reinforce the academic program and contribute toward a total learning experience. Students may participate in student government, publications, music, theater, and social groups. Simpson competes in eighteen intercollegiate sports and has an extensive intramural program for both men and women. Men's and women's athletics at Simpson are governed by the NCAA. Simpson also has chapters of three national fraternities, one local fraternity, and four national sororities.

Location

Simpson is located in the city of Indianola, a residential community of 13,000 people. Indianola is 12 miles south of Des Moines, Iowa's capital city; 12 miles east of Interstate 35; and 15 miles south of Interstates 80 and 235. The Des Moines International Airport is 20 minutes from campus. Five miles south of Indianola is Lake Ahquabi State Park, where swimming and other recreational facilities can be found. Every summer, Indianola is the home of the National Hot Air Balloon Classic and of the Des Moines Metropolitan Summer Opera Festival. The location of the residential campus provides the best of both metropolitan and suburban activities.

Majors and Degrees

Simpson College grants Bachelor of Arts and Bachelor of Music degrees in major and career programs, including accounting, art, athletic training, biochemistry, biology, chemistry, computer information systems, computer science, corporate communication, criminal justice, economics, education, English, environmental science, French, German, history, international management, international relations, journalism and mass communication, management, marketing, mathematics, music, music education, music performance, philosophy, physical education, physics, political science, psychology, religion, rhetoric and speech communication, sociology, Spanish, sports administration, and theater arts.

Simpson offers preprofessional programs in dentistry, engineering, law, medicine, optometry, physical therapy, theology, and veterinary medicine.

Academic Program

Simpson operates on a 4-4-1 academic calendar. The first semester starts in late August and ends in mid-December; the second semester starts in mid-January and ends in late April. A three-week session takes place during the month of May. During this period, students have the opportunity to take one class that focuses on a single subject, to study abroad, or to participate in a field experience or internship.

Students must participate in one May Term class or program for each year of full-time study at Simpson College. All students must complete the requirements of the Cornerstone Studies in liberal arts and competencies in foreign language, math, and writing. To earn the Bachelor of Arts degree, students may take no more than 42 hours in the major department, excluding May Term programs, and 84 hours in the division of the major, including May Term programs. Also, at least 128 semester hours of course work must be accumulated with a grade point average of C (2.0) or better.

For a Bachelor of Music degree, the same requirements apply, except that 84 hours must be earned in the major, excluding May Terms, and the candidate is limited to 12 additional hours in the division of fine arts. Also, at least 132 hours of course work must be completed with a cumulative grade point average of C (2.0) or better.

The First Year Program is a broadly inclusive program of orientation, group-building, mentoring, community service, advising, and classroom work structured to help new students adapt to their first year of college. The program begins with summer orientation and extends throughout the full year.

The academic component of the First Year Program is the Liberal Arts Seminar, a joint classroom and advising concept that is unique among first-year programs. The seminars are small in size—no more than 18 first-year students each—and all are taught by students' faculty advisers.

Off-Campus Arrangements

A variety of programs are offered for off-campus study. Simpson offers semester-long study-abroad programs in London, England; Schorndorf, Germany; and Managua, Nicaragua. During May Term and an optional summer session in June, qualified students may study in Mérida, Mexico, in the Yucatán Peninsula. Students also may study in Paris and other cities in France for a semester or a year or during May Term.

Simpson is an affiliate of the American Institute for Foreign Study, which provides access to carefully planned semester or academic-year study programs in Austria, Britain, China, France, Germany, Italy, and Spain. Additional international travel programs are offered on a regular basis during the May Term as well.

The Washington Semester, offered in conjunction with the American University in Washington, D.C., permits a qualified student to study the political process in the nation's capital. Also available is the United Nations Semester with Drew University in Madison, New Jersey. Students undertake a course of study at Drew and at the United Nations in New York City. With both programs, students maintain enrollment at Simpson. In addition, the Washington Center Internships and Symposia Program consists of semester-long, full-time, supervised work experiences in the nation's capital, supplemented by weekly academic seminars.

Academic Facilities

The George Washington Carver Science Center provides state-of-the-art research facilities, computer labs, and classrooms. The computer labs contain Macintosh and IBM-compatible microcomputers. For academic computing, Simpson has a Compaq DS20E Alpha server computer and a campuswide Ethernet fiber-optic network.

The Henry H. and Thomas H. McNeill Hall houses classrooms for management, accounting, economics, and communication studies. In addition, the hall houses a seminar room and the Pioneer Hi-Bred International Conference Center.

The Amy Robertson Music Center houses the music department and contains the Sven and Mildred Lekberg Recital Hall, ten studios, twenty-two practice rooms, a music computer lab, and the band rehearsal room. A new wing, completed in 1997, includes a choral rehearsal room, a classroom, and studios.

Dunn Library, a contemporary learning resource center, contains more than 151,359 volumes, 600 current periodicals, 1,859 DVDs and videotapes, 729 music CDs, and access to more than 4,594 e-books. Additional materials for research can be obtained through a national computer-based interlibrary loan network. The library also provides audiovisual equipment and services to the campus.

The A. H. and Theo Blank Performing Arts Center accommodates Simpson's well-known programs in theater arts and opera and includes the magnificent 500-seat Pote Theatre, with both proscenium and hydraulically controlled thrust stages; a studio theater; the Barborka Gallery; technical facilities and shops; and classrooms.

Wallace Hall reopened in 1996 after a complete internal renovation. Named to the National Register of Historic Places in 1991, Wallace Hall contains facilities for education, psychology, sociology, applied social science, and a biofeedback/psychology laboratory.

Costs

Tuition and fees for 2003–04 are $18,097, a room is $2669, and board is $2892. These figures do not include books, music fees, or personal expenses.

Financial Aid

Simpson College seeks to make it financially possible for qualified students to experience the advantages of a college education. Generous gifts from alumni, trustees, and friends of the College, in addition to state and federal student aid programs, make this opportunity possible. Simpson offers financial aid on both a need and non-need basis. Need is determined by filing the Free Application for Federal Student Aid.

Financial aid granted on a non-need basis includes academic scholarships, which are awarded on the basis of prior academic records, and talent scholarships, which are available in theater, music, and art. The talent scholarships are determined by audition/portfolio.

Faculty

Eighty-seven percent of Simpson's 84 full-time faculty members have earned their terminal degrees. At Simpson, faculty members serve as academic advisers as well as teachers and often attend College plays, operas, and athletic events, reinforcing their sincere interest in students. The student-faculty ratio is 14:1.

Student Government

Student involvement in College governance is an integral part of the organization of the College. Students annually elect a president and vice president of the Student Government. The members of each housing unit and the off-campus students elect representatives to the Student Senate. The Student Senate appoints student members to all College committees in which students hold membership. The senate also appoints 4 students-at-large who attend plenary sessions of the Board of Trustees as members on the Student Affairs Committee.

Admission Requirements

Admission to Simpson College is selective and competitive. A strong academic record is essential. Applications are acted upon by an admissions committee, which is elected by the faculty and represents the five academic divisions of the College. These faculty members consider the college-preparatory courses taken, the grades received in those courses, rank in class, and standardized test scores (ACT and/or SAT I), including test subscores. A short time after all required credentials are received, the application is reviewed by the admissions committee. Transfer applicants are accepted on the basis of successful completion of academic work at an accredited college or university. In addition, transfer applicants are required to submit official high school transcripts and ACT/SAT I results.

Application and Information

Simpson's rolling admission policy allows flexibility; however, early application is recommended. Transfer and foreign students are welcome. Students are strongly encouraged to visit the campus.

For additional information or to obtain application materials, students should contact:

Office of Admissions
Simpson College
701 North "C" Street
Indianola, Iowa 50125

Telephone: 515-961-1624
800-362-2454 (toll-free)
E-mail: admiss@simpson.edu
World Wide Web: http://www.simpson.edu

The George Washington Carver Science Center provides Simpson students with state-of-the-art labs and research facilities.

SOUTHERN ILLINOIS UNIVERSITY CARBONDALE

CARBONDALE, ILLINOIS

The University

Southern Illinois University Carbondale (SIUC), chartered in 1869, is a comprehensive state-supported institution with nationally and internationally recognized instructional, research, and service programs. SIUC is fully accredited by the North Central Association of Colleges and Schools.

SIUC offers more than 125 undergraduate majors, specializations, and minors; four associate degree programs; more than eighty baccalaureate degree programs; sixty master's degree programs; twenty-six doctoral programs; and professional degrees in law and medicine. SIUC is a multicampus university and includes the Carbondale campus as well as the SIUC School of Medicine at Springfield and a branch campus in Nakajo, Japan.

During the 2002–03 academic year, SIUC's enrollment reached 21,873, which included 16,863 undergraduate students, 4,360 graduate students, and 650 professional students. The average age of undergraduates is 23. Seven percent of SIUC's enrolled students are international students. Of U.S. students, 12 percent are African American, .37 percent are American Indian/Alaskan, 2 percent are Asian or Pacific Islander, and 3 percent are Hispanic.

Students who are ready to start college but not ready to commit to a specific major can enroll in SIUC's Pre-Major Program. Premajor advisers and career counselors help premajor students plan their education and careers. SIUC faculty members, staff members, and alumni help students arrange internships, cooperative education programs, and work-study programs.

Seventy-four percent of SIUC's on-campus freshmen live on campus. SIUC has three on-campus residential areas for single students. Each area includes a cafeteria, a post office, laundry facilities, and computer labs. SIUC residence hall dining services provide nineteen meals per week with no limit on quantity at each meal. Optional meal plans are available. Meal hours are long enough to accommodate most schedules, but students with conflicts can arrange for take-out lunches or late plates. Dining services provide a variety of menus and a full-time dietitian to help students who have special dietary needs. Off-campus housing includes many types of privately owned units, including residence halls, apartments, and houses; many are within easy walking distance of the campus.

SIUC intercollegiate sports teams compete at the NCAA Division I level (football is Division I-AA). Conference affiliations include the Missouri Valley and Gateway Conferences. Intercollegiate sports teams include men's and women's basketball, cross-country, diving, golf, swimming, tennis, and track and field; men's baseball and football; and women's softball and volleyball. The campus holds various playfields, several tennis courts, and a campus lake with a beach and a boat dock. SIUC's Student Recreation Center houses an Olympic-size pool; indoor tracks; handball/racquetball and squash courts; a climbing wall; weight rooms; and basketball, volleyball, and tennis courts. It also offers outdoor equipment rental, a aerobic area, walleyball, martial arts, dance and cardio studios.

The Student Center is one of the largest student centers in the U.S. without a hotel. It contains a bookstore, several restaurants, a craft shop, a bakery, and facilities for bowling and billiards. It is headquarters for 360 active student organizations and the student government office. It holds four ballrooms and an auditorium. On-campus events throughout the year include concerts, plays, festivals, guest speakers, and musicals.

Location

Carbondale is 6 hours south of Chicago, 2 hours southeast of St. Louis, and 3 hours north of Nashville. Four large recreational lakes, the two great rivers (the Mississippi and the Ohio), and the spectacular 270,000-acre Shawnee National Forest are within minutes of the campus. The mid-South climate is ideal for year-round outdoor activities.

Carbondale is a small city of 27,000 people that supports one large enclosed mall, several mini-malls, theaters, and restaurants. Students frequent the shops and restaurants that line Illinois and Grand Avenues.

Majors and Degrees

The University offers associate in applied science degree programs at the College of Applied Sciences and Arts in aviation flight, dental technology, physical therapist assistant studies, and respiratory therapy technology.

The College of Applied Sciences and Arts offers bachelor's degree programs in advanced technical studies, architectural studies, automotive technology, aviation management, aviation technologies, dental hygiene, electronics systems technologies, fire science management, health-care management, information systems technologies, interior design, mortuary science and funeral service, physician assistant studies, and radiologic sciences.

The College of Agriculture offers bachelor's degree programs in agribusiness economics, animal science, food and nutrition, forestry, general agriculture, and plant and soil science.

The College of Business and Administration offers bachelor's degree programs in accounting, business and administration, business economics, finance, management, and marketing.

The College of Education and Human Services offers bachelor's degree programs in communication disorders and sciences, early childhood education, elementary education, fashion design and merchandising, health education, physical education, recreation, rehabilitation services, social studies, social work, special education, and workforce education and development. Teacher preparation is available in art, biological sciences, English, French, German, health education, history, mathematics, music, physical education, secondary education, social studies, Spanish, and special education.

The College of Engineering offers bachelor's degree programs in civil engineering, computer engineering, electrical engineering, engineering technology, industrial technology, mechanical engineering, and mining engineering.

The College of Liberal Arts offers bachelor's degrees in administration of justice, anthropology, art, classics, design, economics, English, foreign language and international trade, French, geography, German, history, linguistics, mathematics, music, paralegal studies, philosophy, political science, psychology, Russian, sociology, Spanish, speech communication, theater, and university studies.

The College of Mass Communication and Media Arts offers bachelor's degrees in cinema and photography, journalism, and radio-television.

The College of Science offers bachelor's degree programs in biological sciences, chemistry, computer science, geology, mathematics, microbiology, physics, physiology, plant biology, zoology, and preprofessional programs in dentistry, medicine, nursing, optometry, osteopathy, pharmacy, physical therapy, physician assistant studies, podiatry, and veterinary medicine.

In addition to many majors offered at SIUC, specializations are offered in all colleges in many areas.

Academic Program

Each bachelor's degree candidate must earn a minimum of 120 semester hours of credit, including at least 60 at a senior-level institution and the last 30 at SIUC. Each student must maintain at least a C average in all course work at SIUC. Each student must fulfill the University core curriculum and the specific requirements of their degree programs. SIUC awards credit through qualifying extension and correspondence programs, military experience, the High School Advanced Placement Program, the College-Level Examination Program (CLEP), SIUC's proficiency examination program, and work experience.

SIUC offers honors course work and special recognition for students who demonstrate exceptional academic achievement. The Air

Force and Army offer ROTC programs at SIUC. SIUC offers three semesters: fall, spring, and summer.

Off-Campus Arrangements

At Southern Illinois University Carbondale, distance education courses are offered in interactive, print-based and Web-based formats. Print-based (correspondence) and Web-based courses are offered by the Individualized Learning Program (ILP). Web-based courses and Two-Way Interactive Video courses are offered through the Office of Distance Education. Many of the courses offered through the ILP and other distance education courses can be taken to complete the University Studies Degree (B.A.) in the College of Liberal Arts.

Off-campus credit programs are designed to meet the educational needs of adults wishing to pursue a degree but who are unable to travel to the Carbondale campus. Faculty members who teach off-campus courses travel to distant sites to teach SIUC courses.

Contractual services are provided and include specialized educational services to groups, organizations, governmental agencies, and businesses on a cost-recovery basis. These services are provided regionally, nationally, and internationally.

All credit courses offered through these programs carry full SIUC academic credit and are taught by faculty members appointed by the academic departments of the University. Additional information can be found on the Web (http://www.dce.siu.edu/siuconnected).

Academic Facilities

In addition to the 2.4 million volumes, 3.5 million microfilms, and more than 11,000 periodicals currently available in Morris Library, students and faculty members have access to more than 10,000 full-text electronic journals. SIUC students have access to several computer learning centers that are equipped, in all, with more than 1,600 microcomputers. Additional information can be found on the Web (http://www.lib.siu.edu).

Students learn and practice in the Southern Illinois Airport, outdoor laboratories, the student-run *Daily Egyptian* newspaper, WSIU-TV, WSIU-FM, art and natural history museums, a literary magazine, McCleod Theater, Memorial Hospital, a vivarium, the plant biology greenhouses, the University Farms, and the Touch of Nature Environmental Center.

Costs

Tuition and fee charges for the 2002–03 academic year (fall and spring) for students enrolled in 15 or more semester hours were $4865 for Illinois residents and $8525 for out-of-state residents, including international students. Room and board were $4627. All costs are subject to change. The cost of books and school supplies varies among programs. The average cost is $600 per academic year. Some courses require that students purchase special materials.

Financial Aid

More than $150 million in financial aid was distributed to 20,753 SIUC students in fiscal year 2002 through federal, state, and institutionally funded financial aid programs.

To apply for financial aid at SIUC, students should complete a Free Application for Federal Student Aid (FAFSA). Applications that are filed before April 1 receive priority consideration for campus-based aid. The FAFSA can be completed electronically at the U.S. Department of Education's Web site (http://www.fafsa.ed.gov). When completing the FAFSA, students should list Southern Illinois University Carbondale (Federal School Code 001758) as a school of choice.

SIUC has one of the largest student employment programs in the country, with approximately 6,000 students employed each year in a wide variety of job classifications. SIUC offers competitive scholarships based on talent and academic achievement.

Faculty

Faculty members are dedicated to excellence in teaching and to their advancement of knowledge in a wide variety of disciplines and professions. Many faculty members are well-known both nationally and internationally for their varied research contributions. The undergraduate student-faculty ratio is 17:1. There are 894 full-time and 218 part-time instructional faculty members.

Teaching assistants at SIUC are graduate students who assist faculty members in teaching. While some teach introductory undergraduate classes, others provide support to faculty members by assisting in laboratories, monitoring tests, and helping students.

Student Government

The undergraduate student government consists of a president, vice president, executive assistant, and chief of staff. Under the vice president, there are 58 senators: 1 senator per 300 students. Each student has at least 2 representatives: 1–6 for their residential area, and 1–6 for the college in which they are enrolled. Under the 6 commissioners are a list of committees on which a varying number of students sit to represent the student body. The student government writes and passes legislation on University policies, funding, student organizations, and other matters that affect the students and the University.

Admission Requirements

Freshman applicants whose ACT or SAT score is at or above the 50th percentile or whose ACT or SAT score is at or above the 33rd percentile and whose class rank is in the upper half are admitted. Admission standards are subject to change. Freshman applicants must meet course pattern requirements: 4 years of English, 3 years of mathematics, 3 years of laboratory science, 3 years of social science, and 2 years of electives.

Transfer applicants must have an overall grade point average of at least 2.0 on a 4.0 scale, based on work attempted at all institutions and calculated by SIUC grading policies. Transfer applicants must also be eligible to continue at the last institution attended.

Some programs have higher admission requirements or require additional screening for admission. Undergraduates can apply online (http://salukinet.siu.edu/admit/).

Application and Information

Admission is granted on a rolling basis. The application fee is $30.

Undergraduate Admissions
Southern Illinois University Carbondale
Carbondale, Illinois 62901-4710
Telephone: 618-536-4405
Fax: 618-453-3250
E-mail: admrec@siu.edu
World Wide Web: http://www.siuc.edu

SIUC's Pulliam Hall.

TRUMAN STATE UNIVERSITY

KIRKSVILLE, MISSOURI

The University

Truman State University is Missouri's premier liberal arts and sciences university and the only highly selective public institution in the state. Truman has forged a national reputation for offering an exceptionally high-quality undergraduate education at a competitive price. For the sixth consecutive year, *U.S. News & World Report* has ranked Truman State University as the number one master's-level public institution in the Midwest. In addition, Kaplan's 2003 National Survey of High School Guidance Counselors describes Truman as a "hidden treasure" and one of only forty-one universities that offer the best value when weighing the quality of education versus the cost. A commitment to student achievement and learning is at the core of everything the University does. This commitment is evidenced by faculty and staff members who recognize the importance of providing students with the opportunity to interact with their professors both in and out of the classroom. With class sizes averaging only 22 students and 95 percent of freshman courses being taught by full-time faculty members, students find ample opportunity to ask questions of professors as well as interact with their multitalented peers. Truman's academic environment is enhanced by a student body that achieves at remarkable levels. The 2002 freshman class had an ACT midrange of 25 to 30 and an average GPA of 3.75 on a 4.00 scale. In addition, numerous opportunities exist for students to engage in undergraduate research. Each year, approximately 1,000 students work side by side with professors on University research projects, gaining greater confidence, knowledge, and skill in their chosen disciplines. The University offers these students the opportunity to present the results of their research at the annual Undergraduate Research Symposium. In addition, selected students travel to the National Undergraduate Research Symposium to present their research findings. Undergraduate research stipends are also available.

The teaching degree at Truman is the Master of Arts in Education. Students wishing to pursue a teaching career first complete a bachelor's degree in an academic discipline and then apply for admission into professional study at the master's level. Master's programs in special education, elementary education, and secondary education are available.

With more than 200 University organizations available to students, encompassing service, Greek, honorary, professional, religious, social, political, and recreational influences, Truman students have tremendous opportunities to become involved while enrolled at the University. Truman's Student Activities Board provides popular culture entertainment such as current box office films like *The Bourne Identity, Scooby Doo, Murder by Numbers,* and *Changing Lanes;* special events like MTV's "Campus Invasion"; comedians such as Jimmy Fallon, David Chapelle, and Bill Bellamy; and musical artists like Alette Brooks and Lifehouse. In addition, admission to all varsity athletic events, Truman threater productions, and Lyceum Series events is free to Truman students. Recent theater productions have included *Hedda Gabler, A Midsummer Night's Dream,* and *Approaching Zanzibar.*

Location

Truman State University is located in Kirksville, a town of approximately 17,000, nestled in the northeast corner of Missouri. The town square, located within walking distance of the Truman campus, provides a connection to Kirksville's past. A multiplex movie theater opened on the town square in 2001. Local merchants operate specialized gift, book, and clothing stores, and several restaurants offer a wide selection of American and international cuisine.

The Kirksville Aquatic Center is a great place to have fun and get fit. An indoor/outdoor pool complex, the Aquatic Center, offers a variety of activities, classes, and programs designed to appeal to people of all ages. Inside the complex is a six-lane indoor swimming pool, perfect for swimming, relaxing, or playing a game of water-basketball. The outdoor pool is designed with a zero-depth entry, a 1-meter diving board, and four 25-yard outdoor lap lanes as well as a 20-foot water slide.

The northeast region of Missouri is also home to Thousand Hills State Park. A 3,252-acre state park and 573-acre lake for camping, hiking, biking, fishing, swimming, boating, and water skiing is located within 10 minutes of the Truman campus.

Majors and Degrees

Undergraduate degrees offered by Truman include the Bachelor of Arts (B.A.), Bachelor of Science (B.S.), Bachelor of Music: Performance (B.M.), Bachelor of Fine Arts (B.F.A.), and Bachelor of Science in Nursing (B.S.N.). Truman offers more than forty areas of study in the following disciplines: accounting, agricultural science, art, art history, biology, business administration, chemistry, classics, communication, communication disorders, computer science, economics, English, exercise science, French, German, health science, history, justice systems, mathematics, music, music: performance, nursing, philosophy and religion, physics, political science, psychology, Russian, sociology/anthropology, Spanish, and theater.

Professional paths include but are not limited to dentistry, engineering, law, medicine, optometry, pharmacy, physical therapy, and veterinary medicine.

Academic Program

The Liberal Studies Program is the heart of Truman's curriculum and is intended to serve as a foundation for all major programs of study offered by the University. Truman's mission is to "offer an exemplary undergraduate education, grounded in the liberal arts and sciences, in the context of a public institution of higher learning." Therefore, Truman is providing the kind of education in the liberal arts and sciences that has historically been offered only at private colleges. The program is a blend of two intellectual traditions in higher education, one that emphasizes the traditional thought and learning of the culture as reflected in the classical works produced by it, and the other that emphasizes personal investigation and freedom of discovery. The philosophy behind the Liberal Studies Program is based upon a commitment that Truman has made to provide students with essential skills needed for lifelong learning, breadth across the traditional liberal arts and sciences through exposure to various discipline-based modes of inquiry, and interconnecting perspectives that stress interdisciplinary thinking and integration as well as linkage to other cultures and experiences. All students graduating from Truman must complete 63 or more credit hours in liberal arts and sciences courses.

Truman's Residential College Program brings the University learning community inside the student residence halls. Historically, residential colleges have been places where faculty members and students join together as "friends of learning." At Truman, this living/learning tradition is honored as one means of furthering its specific goals as a public liberal arts university. The Residential College Program seeks to make liberal arts education personally vital and engaging to the whole person.

Truman also offers an especially challenging General Honors Program. This program provides students with the opportunity to select the most rigorous honors courses to satisfy the liberal arts component of their respective programs. Students who successfully complete this program not only benefit from an even richer academic experience at Truman but also receive special recognition at graduation. Departmental honors are also available in several disciplines.

Off-Campus Arrangements

Each year, more than 300 Truman students participate in enriching and life-changing study-abroad experiences. Truman's own study-abroad programs, combined with programs offered through Truman's membership in the College Consortium for International Studies, International Student Exchange Program, Australearn, and the Council on International Educational Exchange, provide students with study-abroad opportunities in more than thirty-five countries worldwide, including Australia, England, France, Hong Kong, Italy, Kenya, Russia, Spain, Thailand, and Wales.

In addition, there are several cooperative programs affiliated with biology. Students interested in medical technology may complete classes at one of several medical technology schools in Iowa, Illinois, or Missouri. Truman is also affiliated with the Gulf Coast Research Laboratory at Ocean Springs, Mississippi. Marine biology courses may be taken at the laboratory during the summer with credit awarded at Truman. In-depth study of the Ozark habitats is also available through Truman's affiliation with Reis Biological Station located near Steelville, Missouri.

In cooperation with the Washington Center for Internships and Academic Seminars, Truman offers a wide variety of experiential internships in Washington, D.C. Included are work-experience opportunities in such areas as public administration, the fine and performing arts, foreign affairs/diplomacy, government affairs, criminal justice, international relations, health and human services, environmental policy, business administration, and communications as well as other areas. Placement sites include non-profit groups, media organizations, Congress, museums, and much more.

Truman requires internships in education, health science, and exercise science and annually offers internship opportunities with the Missouri State Legislature. In recent years, students have completed internships with United States senators, the governor of Missouri, business and industry managers, zoos, broadcast and print media professionals, accountants, advertising agencies, physical therapists, musicians, artists, and the United States Supreme Court.

Academic Facilities

The Truman campus contains forty buildings in an expanse of 140 acres. Featured among these facilities is Pickler Memorial Library. This 441,431-volume facility provides a state-of-the-art library resource for students and faculty members alike. Materials not available in Pickler Memorial Library can be obtained through the Interlibrary Loan Office and MOBIUS.

Improvement to campus facilities have recently included the construction of a $750,000, eight-lane, all-weather track as well as construction of the $8-million Student Recreation Center complete with four athletic courts, an aerobic room, a weight room, an indoor track, and a lounge. In addition, the $7-million renovation to Violette Hall incorporated technologically advanced classrooms, two 100-seat auditoriums, and several student meeting rooms as well as faculty and division offices. The $20-million renovation and 80,000-square-foot addition to Ophelia Parrish Building was completed in summer 2002 and has transformed this facility into the new Fine Arts Center housing art studios, practice facilities, a performing arts center, and a black box theater. The $20-million renovation and expansion of Truman's science facility, Magruder Hall is under way.

Additional facilities include a student media center with a TV studio, a radio station, and print media production facilities, a biofeedback laboratory, an organic chemistry lab, an analytical chemistry lab, an independent learning center for nursing students, an observatory, a greenhouse, a 5,000-seat football stadium, a soccer field, tennis and racquetball courts, a softball diamond, a 3,000-seat arena with three basketball courts and an Olympic-size swimming pool, a multicultural affairs center, a writing center, and a career center.

Costs

Tuition for Missouri residents for the 2002–03 academic year was $4144; out-of-state tuition was $7544. Room and board totals for both Missouri residents and nonresidents were $4928. Additional fees included a $150 freshman orientation fee, an annual $56 activities fee, a $50 parking fee for those with a vehicle, and the costs of books and personal expenses.

Financial Aid

Truman offers automatic scholarships ranging from $1000 to $2000. Competitive scholarship awards vary from $500 up to full tuition, room, and board, plus a $4000 study-abroad stipend. The application for admission also serves as the application for the automatic and competitive scholarship programs.

Several scholarships are awarded to students for excellence in music, theater, or art. These scholarships are available for instrumental, strings, or vocal music; acting or dramatic production; and studio art or art history. Of special interest to piano students is the Truman Piano Fellowship Competition.

The National Collegiate Athletic Association and the University authorize a limited number of grants to outstanding athletes. The value of this aid may vary with each individual recipient.

Truman accepts the Free Application for Federal Student Aid (FAFSA) and participates in all Federal Title IV financial aid programs. Financial aid estimates are available upon request.

Faculty

Truman State University is committed to teaching the academically talented undergraduate student. The University has 366 full-time faculty members and 33 part-time faculty members. Of these, 97 percent teach undergraduates and 80 percent hold a doctoral degree or the highest terminal degree in their discipline. Most major graduate institutions are represented among the Truman faculty, including Harvard, Princeton, Yale, Berkeley, Oxford, and the Sorbonne. The student-faculty ratio at Truman is 15:1.

Student Government

Student Senate is the official elected governing body of the Student Association representing more than 6,000 students. Its mission is to represent the views of the Student Association in the formulation of the University policy through legislation and membership on all University committees; to facilitate communication and mutual understanding among the Student Association, faculty and staff members, and administration; to maintain a cohesive vision for the future of the University; and to actively participate in the fulfillment of the University's mission as an exemplary public liberal arts and sciences university.

Admission Requirements

Admission to Truman is competitive. Each applicant is evaluated for admission based upon academic and cocurricular record, ACT or SAT results, and the admission essay. Truman requires the following high school core: 4 units of English, 3 units of mathematics (4 recommended), 3 units of social studies/history, 3 units of natural science, 1 unit of fine arts, and 2 units of the same foreign language.

Application and Information

Students interested in early admission must submit an application by November 15. Notification of acceptance is mailed after December 15. Applications received after November 15 are processed on a rolling basis. The recommended final deadline to apply for the fall semester is March 1. There is no application fee. Students may apply online at the Web site listed below. For further information or to schedule a campus visit, students should contact:

Admission Office
Truman State University
205 McClain Hall
100 East Normal
Kirksville, Missouri 63501
Telephone: 660-785-4114
800-892-7792 (toll-free, Missouri only)
Fax: 660-785-7456
E-mail: admissions@truman.edu
World Wide Web: http://www.truman.edu

THE UNIVERSITY OF FINDLAY

FINDLAY, OHIO

The University

The University of Findlay is a private coeducational institution with 4,525 full- and part-time students. Founded in 1882 by the Churches of God, General Conference, it emphasizes preparation for careers and professions in an educational program that blends liberal arts and career education. Students of many denominations attend Findlay, and religious participation is a matter of personal choice.

Bachelor of Arts degree programs are available in forty different majors. The Associate of Arts degree is awarded in nearly twenty areas. Master's degrees are offered in business administration, education, environmental management, occupational therapy, physical therapy, and teaching English to speakers of other languages (TESOL).

The largest programs at Findlay are in natural sciences, business, and social sciences. Majors in the sciences include athletic training, equestrian studies (English, Western, and equine management), nuclear medicine, occupational therapy, physical therapy, physician assistant studies, and pre–veterinary medicine. Business degrees are founded in a three-year comprehensive core program with eight different majors, including an individualized major option.

Opportunities for internships and work-related experiences are available in most major fields through the Professional Experiences Program (PEP).

Most of Findlay's students come from Ohio and the surrounding states of Michigan, Indiana, and Pennsylvania. More than thirty other states are also represented. Because of the Intensive English Language Institute located on the campus, many international students are part of the total student body.

Resident students live in six modern residence halls. All students eat their meals in an attractive dining hall. Social life at Findlay centers on student organizations, fraternities, and sororities. Findlay has four officially recognized fraternities—Alpha Sigma Phi, Sigma Pi, Tau Kappa Epsilon, and Theta Chi—and two sororities. Each has its own house near campus. Organizations include department and special interest clubs, the newspaper, yearbook, musical groups, a radio station, Circle K, and Aristos Eklektos (honors).

Athletic programs are affiliated with NCAA Division II and the Great Lakes Intercollegiate Athletic Conference. Men's hockey, women's hockey, and men's volleyball are making a transition to Division I. Findlay offers fourteen intercollegiate sports for men: baseball, basketball, cross-country, equestrian, football, golf, hockey, indoor track and field, outdoor track and field, soccer, swimming and diving, tennis, volleyball, and wrestling. It has twelve varsity sports for women: basketball, cross-country, equestrian, golf, indoor track and field, outdoor track and field, soccer, softball, swimming and diving, tennis, track, and volleyball. Club sport teams include the equestrian and ice hockey teams. Athletic scholarships are available.

Croy Physical Education Center has a 25-meter swimming pool, exercise areas, a gymnasium, offices, and classrooms. The Gardner Fitness Center is a state-of-the-art facility. The 130,000-square-foot Koehler Recreation and Fitness Complex, opened in 1999, contains the Malcolm Athletic Center, with a six-lane, NCAA regulation track and four multipurpose courts; the Clauss Ice Arena; locker rooms; and offices for the athletic department.

Student services include career and placement counseling, the Cosiano Health Center, academic tutoring and personal counseling, and study skills assistance through the Academic Support Center.

Location

Findlay was voted the most livable micropolitan city in Ohio and scored among the top twelve in the United States. It is within easy driving distance of Toledo, Columbus, Detroit, and Fort Wayne. Interstate 75 and the Ohio Turnpike (Interstates 80 and 90) are major highways serving the area. Airports in Toledo, Columbus, and Detroit are convenient. The town of Findlay has 38,000 residents and is home to Marathon Oil Corporation and Cooper Tire and Rubber Company. The Findlay campus consists of more than 140 acres on several sites. A 70-acre campus-owned farm houses preveterinary and equine studies. A second 32-acre facility houses the English Hunt Seat Riding Program. Many opportunities exist for students who want business-related and social service agency experience. The University has established strong relationships with the community, which supports athletic and cultural events on the campus. Besides the full program of on-campus activities, off-campus trips to cultural and entertainment events are scheduled. The city of Findlay, which has an excellent business climate, offers part-time job opportunities, volunteer service organizations, and the chance to be involved with the larger civic community. Findlay's campus is attractive, safe, comfortable, and friendly.

Majors and Degrees

The Bachelor of Arts degree is awarded in the following majors: art; bilingual-multicultural education; communications (advertising emphasis); communications (broadcast journalism emphasis); communications (publications emphasis); communications (public relations emphasis); comprehensive religion, philosophy, and Christian education; comprehensive social science; criminal justice; English; English–speech education; history; Japanese; philosophy; political science; psychology; religion; social work; sociology; Spanish; Spanish bilingual-multicultural studies; Spanish-business; speech; speech-education; theater performance; theater production; technical writing; and writing.

Findlay has a dual-degree B.A./B.S.E. program with the engineering schools of Ohio Northern University, the University of Toledo, and Washington University in St. Louis. Minors are offered in gerontology, international business, international relations, and women's studies.

The Bachelor of Science degree is granted in accounting; athletic training; biology; business administration; comprehensive business education; computer science; economics; elementary education; environmental, safety, and occupational health management; equestrian studies (English and Western emphases); equine management; finance; hospitality management; marketing; mathematics; nature interpretation; nuclear medicine technology; occupational therapy; physical education; physical therapy; physician assistant studies; premedicine; prenursing; pre–veterinary medicine; science; systems analysis; and technology management.

The Associate of Arts degree is available in accounting, community social service, computer science, criminal justice (corrections or law enforcement emphasis), environmental and hazardous materials management, equestrian studies, financial management, general social studies, humanities, legal assisting, management information systems, nuclear medicine technology, office administration, religion, sales/retail management, small business/entrepreneurship, and technical communication.

Certificate programs are available in computer applications; environmental, safety, and occupational health management; gerontology; legal assisting; nuclear medicine technology; and the teaching of shorthand.

Academic Program

Findlay operates on the semester system. Students must complete at least 124 semester hours with a minimum overall grade point average of 2.0 to earn a bachelor's degree. General education requirements and competency requirements in English, reading, computer literacy, speech, and library use must be fulfilled. The Freshman Seminar introduces students to living and learning at Findlay and gives them the opportunity to work with the same teachers and student group in two related courses. The Foundations Program offers students the chance to develop those skills in writing, reading, and thinking needed for their success as college students. Study skills, time management, and academic advising are included. Students are selected for this program at the time of admission. The Honors Program provides additional challenge to those students who qualify on the basis of academic credentials. Study- and travel-abroad programs are offered by various departments. Credit and/or placement can be earned through Advanced Placement (AP) exams.

The Equestrian Program is a well-recognized program of its kind and serves approximately 250 students from throughout the United States and abroad. Majors in equine management and in English and Western riding are offered. The instruction, both in the classroom and on horseback, makes use of the expertise of recognized national equestrian champions. The pre–veterinary medicine program, using the farm facilities, offers the advantages of hands-on experience with livestock and an internship program in a distinctive curriculum. The pre–veterinary medicine program has a placement rate into veterinary schools that is much higher than the national average.

The Nuclear Medicine Institute provides the training necessary to qualify students for careers in nuclear medicine technology, a growing health-related career field.

Findlay's environmental science and hazardous materials management program is a bachelor's degree program that includes internships in the summer. Career opportunities for graduates in environmental sciences are excellent.

The Health Professions Program provides eleven majors, including athletic training, nuclear medicine, physical education (strength and conditioning or teaching emphasis), recreational therapy, occupational therapy, physical therapy, and physician assistant studies.

Academic Facilities

The focal point of the Findlay campus is Old Main, which houses classrooms, faculty and administrative offices, the Computer Center, facilities for various student activities, and the Ritz Auditorium. Shafer Library is a member of a sixteen-university consortium that provides extensive resources to the student. The Gardner Fine Arts Pavilion, dedicated in 1994, houses the Mazza Collection of original art from children's books. The University has three networked computer labs in Old Main and one computer lab in Shafer Library. Other academic buildings include the Frost Science Complex, with a greenhouse and the Newhard Planetarium, and the Egner Center for the Fine Arts, which houses ceramics and art facilities, a 200-seat theater, and the student-operated radio station. A 101,000-square-foot athletic complex was completed in January 1999. This facility houses a six-lane indoor track, sand pits for long jump, a state-of-the-art timing system, and a wrestling room. Also under the same roof is an ice arena with a seating capacity of 1,200. Approximately 450 horses are stabled and trained at the equestrian facilities, which offer barns and indoor and outdoor riding arenas.

Costs

Tuition for the 2003–04 academic year totals $19,052 for most programs, $22,402 for the equestrian programs, and $20,322 for the pre–veterinary medicine program. Room and board cost $7062. The estimated cost for transportation, books, and supplies is $1500.

Financial Aid

Ninety percent of Findlay students receive financial aid. Assistance is based on need as well as scholastic achievement. Factors used in determining aid are the Free Application for Federal Student Aid (FAFSA), grade point average, and ACT or SAT I results. Federal and state programs are used with institution grants and scholarships, including sibling grants. The FAFSA must be filed. Notification of aid awards is made on a rolling basis. Work-study jobs are available. Scholarships for high-achieving students and student athletes are offered.

Faculty

The 16:1 student-faculty ratio results in small classes—usually fewer than 30 students. Professors know their students, and every student has a faculty adviser.

Student Government

The Student Government Association (SGA) and the Campus Program Board are involved in planning and implementing student activities. SGA provides leadership experience for students and enhances cooperation between faculty, administration, and students. A representative from SGA sits on the Board of Trustees. The Campus Program Board plans activities for recreation and cultural enrichment, including free weekly movies and Homecoming and Family Weekend.

Admission Requirements

Applicants to Findlay should have a college-preparatory high school background, including 4 years of English, 2 to 3 years of mathematics, 2 to 3 years of social studies, and 2 years of sciences. A foreign language is recommended but not required. Results of the ACT or SAT I and high school transcripts should be submitted with the application for admission. Transfer students must be eligible to return to the institution last attended and must submit transcripts of all college work. Decisions are made on a rolling basis. Application deadlines are August 1 for fall semester and December 15 for spring semester. A campus visit is strongly recommended. For students not meeting regular minimum admission requirements, Findlay has a Foundations Program, which provides skill building and academic support during the first semester of the freshman year. Findlay is an equal opportunity institution in admission and employment.

Application and Information

For application forms and other information, students may contact:

Office of Undergraduate Admissions
The University of Findlay
1000 North Main Street
Findlay, Ohio 45840
Telephone: 419-434-4732
800-548-0932 (toll-free)
E-mail: admissions@findlay.edu
World Wide Web: http://www.findlay.edu

Old Main.

UNIVERSITY OF ILLINOIS AT SPRINGFIELD

SPRINGFIELD, ILLINOIS

The University

The University of Illinois at Springfield (UIS) is one of the three campuses of the world-class University of Illinois. Located near Lake Springfield on the southern edge of Illinois's capital city, UIS is situated on 746 beautiful acres planted with dozens of varieties of trees and flowers and anchored on its northern edge by a scenic pond. UIS is known as a premier liberal arts institution, offering small classes and affordable, high-quality degree programs in a personalized private college atmosphere. The student population hovers at about 4,500 freshman-level through senior-level undergraduates, graduate students, and non-degree-seeking students.

UIS was founded in 1969 as Sangamon State University, an institution that emphasized public affairs and nurtured the connection between degree programs and real-world experience. Sangamon State University became the University of Illinois at Springfield in 1996. The affiliation with Illinois's leading educator and world-renowned research university increased UIS's academic resources and enhanced its reputation. At the same time, UIS maintained its original commitment to practical learning and public service through community partnerships.

UIS stresses excellent teaching, and professors lead classes at the freshman level through the doctoral level. Real-world skills are taught in all programs, but at UIS the primary emphasis is firmly placed on imparting the basic skills of inquiry, analysis, and communication. UIS graduates leave, not poised to become the next generation's unemployed but prepared to participate in a rapidly changing marketplace and to invent and reinvent themselves over a lifetime in order to meet the world's new economic and social realities. UIS is committed to meeting the needs of both traditional and nontraditional students. Historically, UIS has been the institution of choice for junior and senior transfer students and adult students seeking a degree while working and raising a family. The campus's flexible hours and the accessible faculty accommodate the older student. At the same time, UIS attracts some of the Midwest's most academically talented high school seniors through its Capital Scholars honors freshmen program, and the growth of campus life reflects a new, more traditional college experience.

UIS undergraduates make up about 54 percent of the student population, which has an average age of 33 years old. Of the total student body, about 66 percent are women and 38 percent attend full-time. Approximately 12 percent are members of underrepresented groups, and 4 percent are international students. While most students commute to class, about 700 students live on campus in Lincoln Residence Hall (reserved for freshmen and sophomores) or in UIS's affordable apartments or town houses.

The Office of Minority Student Affairs addresses the concerns of minority students on the campus and in the community. The International Student Services Office helps international students become acclimated to their new surroundings and deal with various governmental regulations. The Women's Center provides a place where all UIS women can gather in a supportive environment to discuss common concerns. Students with special needs are encouraged to contact the Office of Disability Services.

The primary food service is a gourmet-quality Food Emporium open seven days a week for lunch and dinner and five days a week for breakfast. The LRH Café in Lincoln Residence Hall is open in the evenings and on weekends.

UIS students can enjoy a variety of lectures and cultural events on the campus, including discounted tickets to more than 100 music, theater, and dance performances presented annually in the 2,000-seat Sangamon Auditorium. More than fifty student clubs and organizations offer a variety of opportunities to become involved in student life at UIS. In varsity athletics, UIS fields nationally competitive teams in six National Association of Intercollegiate Athletics (NAIA) sports: men's basketball, men's soccer, men's tennis, women's basketball, women's tennis, and women's volleyball. The men's soccer team has participated in fourteen national tournaments in nineteen years and has won the NAIA national championship three times. Besides competitive athletics, UIS also offers students numerous intramural sports and campus recreational opportunities.

Location

Springfield (population 100,000) is the capital of Illinois and derives much of its character from its location in the state's heartland. However, since it is less than 100 miles northeast of St. Louis and less than 200 miles southwest of Chicago (easily accessible by interstate, rails, and air), Springfield residents can also enjoy the cultural and commercial resources of a major city.

UIS's academic programs are structured to make maximum use of the capital city's resources, particularly state and federal agencies that provide internship, research, or experiential opportunities. Politics at all levels and in all forms can be studied in Springfield. Local historic sites include Lincoln's home and tomb, Vachel Lindsay's home, and the Dana-Thomas House, designed by Frank Lloyd Wright. Resources such as the state archives and historical library are available for student research. Under construction less than 5 miles from UIS is the Abraham Lincoln Presidential Library and Museum, which is expected to attract historians and scholars from all over the world.

Majors and Degrees

UIS offers the Bachelor of Arts (B.A.) degree in the following programs: accountancy, communication, criminal justice, economics, English, history, legal studies, liberal studies, management, mathematical sciences, political studies, psychology, sociology/anthropology, and visual arts. The B.B.A. is offered in business administration; the Bachelor of Science (B.S.) is offered in biology, chemistry, clinical laboratory science, and computer science; and the B.S.W. is offered in social work. Undergraduate minors are offered in accountancy, African-American studies, anthropology, biology, business, chemistry, communication, computer science, criminal justice, economics, English, environmental studies, history, international studies, labor relations, management information systems, mathematical sciences, philosophy, political studies, psychology, sociology, teacher education (elementary and secondary), visual arts, and women's studies. Nondegree work is available in astronomy/physics and modern languages. Graduates of some programs, such as chemistry and legal studies, are eligible for national professional accreditation. Certifications are available in educational leadership (general administrative, instructional leadership, and master teacher), teacher education (elementary and secondary), public-sector labor relations, environmental risk assessment, and management of nonprofit organizations.

Academic Program

Individual programs set entrance and course requirements, but students who earn a bachelor's degree from UIS must meet the following basic criteria: earn 60 semester hours at the upper-division (junior and senior) levels; earn a minimum of 30 semester hours in residence at UIS; satisfy general education requirements; satisfy campus requirements of 12 hours in applied study, public affairs colloquia, or liberal studies colloquia (distribution determined by individual programs); complete an exit assessment by the midpoint of the final semester; meet program standards regarding adequacy in communication skills; earn a cumulative GPA of at least 2.0 (on a 4.0 scale); meet all requirements of the individual academic program; and complete a graduation contract. The fall semester runs from late August to mid-December; the spring semester begins in mid-January and ends in mid-May. There is an eight-week summer term in June and July.

Academic Facilities

Because of its location in the state capital, UIS honors a special mission through its Institute for Public Affairs, which directs the educational, research, and service efforts of the campus and houses its major public affairs units—the Center for Legal Studies, Illinois Legislative Studies Center, Survey Research Unit, Graduate Public Service Internship Program, Institute Publications, public radio station WUIS/WIPA, the UIS Television Office, and *Illinois Issues,* a monthly magazine of government and public affairs.

Brookens Library emphasizes instruction. A member of the library faculty is assigned to each academic program at UIS to act as a liaison in support of the program's particular information needs. The collection supports UIS's curricula with more than half a million volumes, nearly 2,500 journal subscriptions, and nearly 2,000 films and videos. Computer terminals provide information about the holdings and availability of materials at UIS and around the state. Also housed in the library are the Media Services, which provides a variety of educational production services, including multimedia workstations, and the Archives and Special Collections unit, offering students the chance to conduct research using primary sources.

The Computer Center consists of six labs and thirty-two technology-enhanced classrooms. Labs are open daily to students and faculty members for instruction and research. Users have access to a variety of Macintosh, Windows, and UNIX software and the Internet.

The Center for Teaching and Learning is a unit where all members of the campus community can find assistance with the UIS undergraduate assessment process and with developing their academic abilities to the highest level. Support specialists in reading, writing, mathematics, accounting, study skills, and English as a second language plus a corps of outstanding student tutors provide individual and group instruction in a variety of subjects or in general academic development.

Costs

In 2002–03, undergraduate students who were Illinois residents taking 1–16 hours paid $109.50 per credit hour. Nonresident undergraduate students paid $328.50 per credit hour. Full-time undergraduates also paid $172 in mandatory fees; part-time undergraduates paid $62 plus $4 per credit hour. Other fees may be assessed as applicable. Campus housing ranged from $707 to $3125 per semester in fall 2002, depending on the type of accommodations selected. Information on other projected expenses can be obtained from the Office of Admissions and Records.

Financial Aid

The UIS Office of Financial Assistance administers institutional, local, state, and federal grant, scholarship, and loan programs. Every attempt is made to meet the needs of eligible students by packaging funds. Total assistance in fiscal year 2002 was more than $14 million; approximately 67 percent of UIS students received some type of financial aid. Student employment is also administered through the financial assistance office.

Faculty

There are 253 full- and part-time faculty members, most of whom hold the doctorate. Although involved in professional and service pursuits, UIS faculty members consider excellence in teaching their primary mission. All faculty members teach and serve as student advisers and mentors; no classes are taught by graduate assistants.

Student Government

The Office of Student Life advises and counsels three components of extracurricular involvement that are operated by the Student Government Association: the Student Senate, Student Events, and the Inter-Club Council Board. The 15 members of the Student Senate are an integral part of campus governance and are actively involved in planning and implementing UIS codes and policies. Students are encouraged to seek office and play an active role in governing their academic programs and to serve on committees that oversee curricular and personnel matters. Each of the three University of Illinois campuses elects a student representative to the Board of Trustees.

Admission Requirements

Admission to the Capital Scholars Program (freshman class) is competitive and selective; students are encouraged to apply for admission in the fall of their senior year. Students admitted to the program are expected to have demonstrated high academic achievement, potential for creativity and leadership, and excellent written and oral communication skills. Students must have 15 units (1 unit is equal to one year of study) of high school work from among the following categories: 4 units of English, emphasizing written and oral communications and literature; 3 units of social studies emphasizing history and government; 3 units of mathematics that include introductory through advanced algebra, geometry, and trigonometry, or fundamentals of computer programming (4 units recommended); 3 units of laboratory science (4 units recommended); and 2 units of a foreign language (4 units recommended). In addition, students are selected based on an overall evaluation of college-preparatory course work, class rank, GPA, ACT or SAT scores, personal essay, letters of recommendation, and evidence of leadership potential.

Undergraduate transfer applicants holding an Associate in Arts or Associate in Science transfer degree from an Illinois-accredited community college are admissible as juniors and are considered to have met the general education requirements. Admission to UIS may also be granted to applicants who have completed 45 semester hours of credit with a cumulative GPA of 2.0 or better (on a 4.0 scale) from a regionally accredited college or university. Advanced standing as a senior is provided to students transferring with 30 semester hours of upper-division credit beyond the 60 hours required for junior status. Only transfer credit hours with a grade of C or better are acceptable for advanced standing. Although 39 semester hours of general education courses are preferred within the 45 hours for admission, the minimum general education requirement is a transferable 3-semester-hour English composition course that must be completed before enrolling at UIS. The other 36 hours of general education courses must be completed before graduation from UIS. A maximum of 12 hours of these general education courses may count toward upper-division (junior or senior) degree credits at the discretion of the academic programs. To avoid extending upper-division degree requirements, students are encouraged to complete the following before admission to UIS: English (two courses, one course in composition to be completed before entry to UIS; at least 6 semester hours), humanities (two courses; at least 6 semester hours), social science (two courses; at least 6 semester hours), math (one course; at least 3 semester hours), science (two courses, one with lab; at least 6 semester hours); and general education electives (any of the above areas; 12 semester hours).

Application and Information

The Office of Admissions and Records is open from 8:30 a.m. to 5 p.m. Monday through Friday. For further information, to arrange a campus tour or an interview with a counselor, or to request an admissions packet, students should contact:

Office of Admissions and Records
Student Affairs Building–Room 20
University of Illinois at Springfield
One University Plaza, MS SAB20
Springfield, Illinois 62703-5407
Telephone: 217-206-4UIS(4847)
888-977-4UIS(4847) (toll-free)
Fax: 217-206-6620
E-mail: admissions@uis.edu
World Wide Web: http://www.uis.edu

UNIVERSITY OF ST. FRANCIS
JOLIET, ILLINOIS

The University

Committed to the success of its students, the University of St. Francis (USF) provides a strong career preparation and liberal arts base, offering its students a global perspective and the self-confidence to take on the world. More than 90 percent of USF graduates find a job in their chosen field or placement in graduate school within six months of graduation.

The University of St. Francis offers an intimate, personalized college experience, and students—residents, commuters, adult learners, and graduate students—benefit from an innovative, student-centered approach. The University serves some 1,500 students at its Joliet campus. More than 3,000 students throughout the nation are served by programs offered at off-site locations, online, and through faculty-directed distance tutorials.

Some interesting facts about USF include the following: 60 percent of the University's science graduates are women; more than a third of all students are involved in volunteer programs; 50 percent of students are transfer students; the University has provided Illinois schools with more than 1,000 teachers; the average class size is 20; the University offers more than thirty student organizations; and prominent Chicago-based and national companies recruit on the campus each year.

More than sixty areas of undergraduate study are offered in the arts and sciences, business, computer science, education, and nursing. The University also offers undergraduate programs designed for adult learners, such as the Bachelor of Science in professional arts/applied organizational management, the RN-B.S.N. Fast Track program for registered nurses, and the health arts program.

Nine graduate programs are offered: the M.B.A., the M.Ed. in education with certification, and the M.S. in continuing education and training management, continuing education and training technology, education, health services administration, management, nursing, and physician assistant studies.

The University of St. Francis is committed to teaching and to providing students with the challenges and support essential to meeting their potential. Small class sizes ensure that students get the individual attention and focus they need. The University's writing and math centers and tutoring programs provide an important support network. Programs for scholars, such as the Biology Fellows Program and various honor societies, provide challenging and relevant educational experiences beyond classroom learning. USF is at the forefront of technology, providing a variety of online research work and experiences to its students.

USF is committed to educating the student as a whole. A variety of student clubs and organizations are available, as are volunteer activities. Student Affairs sponsors many entertainment events as well as the Student Government Association. Schola, the student choir, and *Loquitur*, the University's literary magazine, are popular activities. The University also hosts the annual Undergraduate Conference on English Language and Literature, which draws student presenters from prestigious colleges and universities throughout the nation. Cultural musical events, which bring internationally and nationally acclaimed performers to the University, are sponsored through the Featured Performances series. Exhibits that bring the works of regionally recognized artists to the campus are planned.

During the past twenty years, USF teams have won sixty conference championships, have had sixty-two national tournament appearances, and have won one national championship. USF has six sports programs for men and eight programs for women, as well as ten intramural programs.

Location

The University of St. Francis campus is on 16 acres in the midst of a historic residential area known as Joliet's Cathedral area. The University is 35 miles southwest of Chicago (about 45 minutes) and is easily accessible by major roadways and trains. USF is also conveniently located between Argonne National Laboratory and Midwein National Tallgrass Prairie. Both of these sites provide excellent opportunities for research, internships, and paid cooperative job programs with professionals in many disciplines, including math, natural sciences, education, computer science, and mass communication.

The University's St. Joseph College of Nursing and Allied Health is located adjacent to Provena Saint Joseph Medical Center, 5 minutes from the main Wilcox Street campus. The University also holds classes at a variety of health-care facilities throughout the nation and maintains a regional center in Albuquerque, New Mexico, where the M.S. in physician assistant studies and the Master of Science in Nursing with a family nurse practitioner track are offered.

The Regional Education Academy for Leadership (REAL), an initiative of the College of Education, is housed on Jefferson Street in the Twin Oaks office center, approximately 10 minutes from the campus. In partnership with area school districts, REAL offers educational opportunities for area educators at convenient locations throughout the region.

Majors and Degrees

Undergraduate programs of study include accounting, actuarial science, advertising/public relations, American politics, applied organizational management, art, arts–management, arts–marketing, biology, broadcasting/audio-video, commercial/public recreation, computer science, computer science/electronics, elementary education, English, environmental science, finance, general management, health arts, history, human resource management, management, marketing, mass communications, mathematics, media arts, medical technology, nuclear medicine technology, nursing, pastoral ministry, political science, predental, premedical, prepharmacy, pre–physical therapy, pre–veterinary medicine, professional arts/applied organizational management, psychology, public policy, radiation therapy, radiography, recreation administration, secondary education (science, language arts/English, social science, mathematics), social work, special education, studio art, teaching ministry, technology management, theology, therapeutic recreation, visual arts, and visual arts/graphic design.

Academic Program

The University of St. Francis offers a comprehensive education designed to introduce the student to various modes and areas of inquiry. The core curriculum includes interdisciplinary courses taken in the freshman through junior years. The relationship of the major to the liberal education courses is addressed in a senior capstone experience in the major. For a baccalaureate degree, a student must earn 128 semester hours. Thirty-two semester hours must be earned at USF. In addition to the overall requirement of at least a 2.0 GPA, a student must achieve a grade of C or better in every course required for the major program. The University also offers Prior Learning Assessment (PLAP), College-Level Examination Program (CLEP), and advanced placement opportunities. Various honors and internship programs are available.

Academic Facilities

The University's oldest building, Tower Hall, is the focal point of activities, housing interactive learning classrooms, state-of-the-art laboratories, offices, two residence wings, dining facilities, the chapel, the bookstore, and the radio and television stations. St. Albert Hall is home to the Natural Science Learning Center and the University's main computing lab. Marian Hall is a residence hall housing 225 students, a residence wing for science students, lounges, a game room, computing lab, and Information Services offices.

The main campus includes the three-story library, which offers Internet access and houses the distance learning classroom. Online and off-campus students may fully utilize USF library services through the University's Web site. The Admissions Office is also on campus. The recreation center, with seating for 1,500, is a three-level facility that includes basketball, volleyball, and racquetball courts; a Nautilus training and exercise room; a conference room; and a classroom. The Moser Performing Arts Center houses an auditorium, art gallery, studio theater, and music and choir practice rooms, as well as offices.

Costs

In 2002–03, tuition and fees for full-time undergraduate students were $16,030 per year; room and board were $5800 per year. Tuition for part-time students was $455 per credit hour; for RN-B.S.N. Fast Track, $325 per credit hour; for professional arts/applied organizational management, $440 per credit hour; and for health arts, $270 per credit hour.

Financial Aid

USF is committed to assisting students in obtaining a high-quality private education. The University spends nearly $4 million in institutional aid and scholarships (in addition to nearly $6 million in federal and state assistance) to enable students to attend USF. In order to apply for all forms of federal, state, and USF assistance, students must complete a financial aid application form. USF prefers that student complete the Free Application for Federal Student Aid (FAFSA).

Faculty

The University of St. Francis faculty is committed to teaching. The University has 76 full-time faculty members, more than half of whom have terminal degrees. Forty adjunct faculty members bring a variety of academic and professional experience to the classroom. Faculty advisers are an integral part of the USF experience.

The USF faculty is invested in the success of its students, both academically and personally. Nursing faculty members are strong clinicians. Their intense commitment to health care and to patients ensures that students are challenged academically and offered a personal, caring support system.

Admission Requirements

Although each applicant is considered individually, there are four general requirements for admission to the University of St. Francis as an incoming freshman: satisfactory ACT or SAT I scores; rank in the upper half of their graduating class; at least 16 high school units in academic subjects, or the equivalent of a high school diploma, including 4 units of English, 2 units of mathematics (algebra and geometry), 2 units of social studies, 2 units of science (one with lab), 3 units total with courses from two of three areas (foreign language, computer science, or music/art), and 3 units of electives; and satisfactory scores on the TOEFL from applicants for whom English is a second language.

A $100 registration deposit is required thirty days after acceptance. This deposit is credited to the applicant's bill and is fully refundable until May 1 for students entering in the fall semester or January 1 for students entering in the spring semester.

Students attending other colleges may transfer to the University of St. Francis at any time during their academic careers. A minimum 2.0 GPA and demonstration of college-ready proficiency in math and English are required of transfer students. Students attending community colleges are not required to earn an associate degree to enter. The University has outstanding services for transfer students. Articulation agreements with community colleges ensure a smooth transition to USF.

Application and Information

Freshmen are admitted in the fall and spring. Students should take the ACT or SAT I and visit the campus for an interview by April 1. Entrance exams should be taken in the spring of the junior year or the fall of the senior year in high school. Applications, including a high school transcript and an application fee, should be filed by July 15 for fall entry and December 1 for spring entry. Notification is on a rolling basis. Students transferring from a community college or another senior college or university may seek admission for either the fall or spring semester. Transfer students anticipating enrollment as nursing majors should submit an application for admission and have transcripts forwarded to the Admissions Office from one year to one semester before their projected entry date.

Registered nurses seeking admission to the RN-B.S.N. Fast Track degree completion program must submit the application for admission with the fee, official transcripts from each school attended, a copy of current licensure as an RN, and two letters of reference. Specific prerequisite and major supportive courses are also required.

Health-care professionals (dental hygienists, radiologic technologists, registered nurses, respiratory therapists, and other qualified health-care professionals) seeking admission as a health arts major must submit an application; transcripts of academic credit from all colleges, universities, or diploma programs; proof of current licensure; verification of work experience; and applicable fees.

For information about admissions:

Sheryl Paul, Executive Director of Admissions and Articulation
University of St. Francis
500 Wilcox Street
Joliet, Illinois 60435
Telephone: 815-740-3400
800-735-7500 (toll-free)
E-mail: admissions@stfrancis.edu
World Wide Web: http://www.stfrancis.edu

Tower Hall, on the campus of the University of St. Francis.

VANDERCOOK COLLEGE OF MUSIC

CHICAGO, ILLINOIS

The College

VanderCook College of Music traces it's roots back to the early 1900s when Hale A. VanderCook opened his downtown studio. By the late 1920s, the studio had developed into what would become one of the first three institutions to offer a degree in instrumental music education. The development of music education in the United States is closely linked to VanderCook's development as an institution.

VanderCook's hands-on curriculum is a practical and fundamental approach to learning. Having only one major, music education, VanderCook students are allowed a greater opportunity to focus on their education. The success of the College is determined by both the advancement of its students and the success of its graduates.

While students are taught all aspects of music, the main focus remains on music education. This is the point at which VanderCook students excel above all others. Their dedication to both education and performance helps make them aware of all areas of music. More than 95 percent of the graduates make their career in the field of music education. For the past six years, VanderCook has had a 100 percent job placement rate.

VanderCook College of Music is accredited by the National Association of Schools of Music, the North Central Association of Colleges and Schools, and the Illinois Board of Higher Education.

VanderCook also offers a Master of Music Education degree and a Master of Music Education degree with teaching certification.

Location

The College is in the South Loop area of Chicago on the campus of the Illinois Institute of Technology, close to the heart of the city's magnificent musical and cultural centers. VanderCook students have the opportunity to hear the world-renowned Chicago Symphony Orchestra, the Lyric Opera, and many other musical performers. Transportation to and from campus is readily accessible with public transportation stops located on campus and a shuttle bus, which runs between campus and the train stations. The city of Chicago is an important extension of the VanderCook campus.

Majors and Degrees

VanderCook College of Music offers one major at the undergraduate level, music education. Upon completing the appropriate course of study, vocal or instrumental, undergraduate students are awarded the Bachelor of Music Education degree.

Academic Program

VanderCook College of Music trains students in both a musical course of study and in general academic areas. The curriculum is practical, emphasizing the proven fundamentals of music education developed by founder H. A. VanderCook. In addition to studying voice, all students learn to perform and teach seventeen different types of instruments and up on graduation are prepared to teach both band and choir.

The academic year, which begins in the fall, is based on a semester system. Students may enter in either fall or spring. (Summer terms are for graduate students only.)

Academic Facilities

The College is housed in a two-story building located on the campus of the Illinois Institute of Technology. The building contains classrooms, an academic library, a music library, a listening laboratory, practice rooms, a recital hall, a conference room, an instrument repair laboratory, and various offices. VanderCook's newly renovated Electronic Music Center contains computer workstations and MIDI hardware that use the latest in computer technology and music software. In addition, VanderCook students have complete access to the student services provided by the Illinois Institute of Technology such as dormitories, the library, the gymnasium, and the recreation center.

Costs

Tuition in 2002–03 was $14,120. Room and board, provided by the Illinois Institute of Technology, totaled $5924, and fees were $370.

Financial Aid

Each student is considered on an individual basis for financial aid. Merit-based scholarships are given for musical talent and are based on competitive auditions. Academic scholarships are also available to qualified students. Scholarships are renewable based on musical growth and participation and also cumulative grade point average. Illinois residents may apply for the Monetary Award Program and Federal Stafford Student Loans are also available.

Faculty

At VanderCook College of Music, all undergraduate classes are taught by either full-time or part-time faculty members who have many years of in-depth, practical experience in the field of music education to share with their students. Faculty members are dedicated to giving individual instruction, made possible by a 6:1 student-teacher ratio.

Admission Requirements

VanderCook College of Music seeks musically proficient students who have demonstrated talent and who desire to become the finest music educators.

Candidates for admission must submit an application and essay along with high school transcripts, ACT or SAT I scores, and three letters of recommendation. Following the application, students should schedule and audition and interview with the Director of Admission.

Transfer students must submit both high school and college transcripts. International students must submit TOEFL scores and the I-20 form.

Application and Information

Applications are accepted up to four weeks prior to the beginning of a term, subject to the availability of space.

Information or an application may be obtained by contacting:

James P. Malley Jr.
Director of Undergraduate Admission
VanderCook College of Music
3140 South Federal Street
Chicago, Illinois 60616-3731
Telephone: 312-225-6288
800-448-2655 (toll-free)

WARTBURG COLLEGE

WAVERLY, IOWA

The College

Founded in 1852 by German Lutheran immigrants, Wartburg is a college of the Evangelical Lutheran Church in America. Wartburg challenges and nurtures students for lives of leadership and service as a spirited expression of their faith and learning. The College's name honors the Wartburg Castle, a landmark in Eisenach, Germany, where Martin Luther sought refuge during the stormy days of the Reformation. The College and the castle have close ties, and the communities of Waverly and Eisenach are sister cities.

Wartburg enrolls 1,695 students from twenty-four states and thirty-two countries. Eighty-seven percent of Wartburg's first-year students graduated in the top half of their high school class. The average ACT score for first-year students is 23.8. The campus is 82 percent residential. Living accommodations include traditional residence halls; small manor units; 4-, 6-, and 8-person suites; and town house–style apartments for senior students.

Wartburg students are active in more than 100 campus organizations, including honor societies, interest groups, and department-related clubs. The Wartburg Choir, Castle Singers, and Wind Ensemble make annual concert tours in the United States and travel abroad every fourth year during the College's one-month May Term. The annual Christmas with Wartburg production attracts more than 6,500 people to performances in Waverly, Cedar Falls, and Des Moines, Iowa. The Wartburg Community Symphony presents a five-concert season. Student publications include a weekly newspaper, a daily information bulletin, a yearbook, and a literary magazine. Students also manage a campus radio station, operate and produce programs for the College's local cable television access channel, and manage the city of Waverly's local channel. The Artist Series brings renowned performing artists to the campus, and a convocation series presents lectures by nationally and internationally recognized speakers. The Art Gallery features touring exhibitions and the work of prominent regional artists. Wartburg is a member of Division III of the National Collegiate Athletic Association. Its nineteen (10 men's, 9 women's) athletic teams compete in the Iowa Intercollegiate Athletic Conference and regularly earn conference championships and national rankings. The Physical Education Center provides recreational facilities that include an indoor track, handball and racquetball courts, a weight room, a sauna, a cardiovascular room, and an area that accommodates four basketball courts or five tennis courts. Walston-Hoover Stadium opened in 2001 with seating for 4,000 fans, a lighted FieldTurf football field, and an eight-lane all-weather track. Athletic facilities also include two new soccer fields and a throwing venue for track and field.

Wartburg welcomes students of all faiths and offers many avenues for worship, study, fellowship, service, and outreach. A chapel serves as a center for worship and a home for the College's active campus ministry program. Chapel services are scheduled three times a week, and a midweek Eucharist and Sunday morning service provide a variety of worship formats.

The College is accredited by the Commission on Institutions of Higher Education of the North Central Association of Colleges and Schools. Individual programs are accredited by the National Council for the Accreditation of Teacher Education, the Council on Social Work Education, the National Association of Schools of Music, and the American Music Therapy Association.

Location

Waverly, a northeast Iowa community of 10,000 residents, is recognized statewide for its progressive businesses and industries. Its quiet neighborhoods, low crime rate, clean air, and friendly atmosphere contribute to a high quality of life. Scenic parks along the Cedar River, shopping areas, restaurants, a hospital, medical clinics, dental offices, and many churches are within walking distance. Students find part-time jobs and internships in Waverly, and local residents attend campus events and support College programs. The Waterloo–Cedar Falls metropolitan area (population 128,000) is 20 minutes from Waverly.

Majors and Degrees

The heart of education at Wartburg College is a four-year liberal arts curriculum. The Bachelor of Arts degree signifies study in the liberal arts with a concentration of courses in a major. The Bachelor of Music degree adds an extended concentration of work in musical performance. The Bachelor of Music Education degree prepares students to teach music or major in music therapy.

Departmental majors are offered in accounting, applied music, art, biochemistry, biology, business administration (finance, international business, management, and marketing), chemistry, church music, communication arts (electronic media, print media, public relations), communication design, communication studies (speech and theater), computer information systems, computer science, economics, education (Christian day school, early childhood, elementary, and secondary), engineering science, English, fitness management, French, French studies, German, German studies, history, international relations, mathematics, music education (instrumental or vocal), music performance, music therapy, philosophy, physical education, physics, political science, psychology, religion (camping ministry, parish education, urban ministry, and youth and family ministry), social work, sociology, Spanish, Spanish studies, and writing.

Minors are offered in most academic departments and in four interdisciplinary programs: environmental studies, intercultural certification, leadership certification, and women's studies.

Wartburg offers cooperative programs and preprofessional advisement in dentistry, engineering, law, medical technology, medicine, nursing, occupational therapy, optometry, pharmacy, physical therapy, and veterinary medicine.

Wartburg is the only private college in Iowa offering a major in music therapy.

Academic Program

Academic studies are divided into three relatively equal parts. The Wartburg Plan of Essential Education comprises one third of the classwork and is designed to create liberally educated, ethically minded citizens for the twenty-first century. Essential Education courses emphasize thinking strategies, reasoning skills, fundamental literacies, faith and reflection, health and wellness, and a capstone course that addresses ethical issues in the student's academic major. The second third of work is devoted to a major field of study, consisting of a prescribed group of courses that offer depth of knowledge in a discipline. The final third consists of elective courses, which students may choose from any academic area.

The College's 4-4-1 calendar culminates in the one-month May Term, when students concentrate on one course. May Term classes travel within Iowa, across the country, and abroad.

The Pathways Center coordinates academic advising and support services, providing a one-stop resource for guiding students through college and beyond. Services include academic advising, career services, counseling services, first-year programming, senior-year experience, supplemental instruction, testing services, and the writing/reading/speaking laboratory. A special Exploring Majors program is available to students who have not settled on a major. Wartburg consistently places 90 percent or more of each year's graduating class in jobs or graduate school within seven months of graduation.

Wartburg encourages and fosters academic excellence through close faculty-student relationships and an integrated approach that combines the liberal arts with leadership education, global and multicultural studies, a focus on ethics, and opportunities for service and hands-on learning. The student-faculty ratio is 14:1.

The College recognizes credit through Advanced Placement examinations, the College-Level Examination Program, DANTES, Departmental Challenge Examinations, and work at other institutions. It also awards credit for experiential learning.

Off-Campus Arrangements

Wartburg West in Denver, Colorado, places students in internships or field experiences related to their majors or in community service organizations. They also take academic courses dealing with religion and urban issues. The Washington Center Program allows students to participate in an academic internship program in Washington, D.C. International exchange programs with Bonn University and Jena University in Germany and International Christian University in Japan enable students to study abroad. French, German, and Spanish majors spend significant time studying abroad. Through the Venture Education Program, cultural immersion experiences are available in Australia, China, England, France, Germany, Ghana, Guyana, Jamaica, Mexico, Palestine, Spain, and Tanzania. Academic travel and on-site course work are offered each May Term, and students may enroll in internships during any term.

Academic Facilities

The Vogel Library, opened in September 1999, is designed to accommodate all types of learning from individual research to group projects and faculty-student interaction. It houses books, periodicals, and reference materials as well as extensive electronic resources. Librarians teach courses in information literacy as part of the Wartburg Plan of Essential Education. The Classroom Technology Center is the home for the social sciences department and several technology-enhanced classrooms. Students have access to more than 400 Macintosh and PC-compatible microcomputers in open-access and departmental computing clusters throughout the campus. Classrooms and residence halls are connected to the campuswide computer network. The Fine Arts Center provides spacious rehearsal and recital halls, music studios, practice rooms, a music therapy suite, art studios, and an art gallery. Its 21-workstation Presser Music Technology Classroom is equipped with keyboard/synthesizers and Macintosh computers for music theory, composition, and ear training classes. McElroy Communication Arts Center includes a journalism laboratory with Macintosh computers, a television studio with video capabilities, and a television control room equipped with TV production and digital editing equipment. The College radio station has two on-air production studios, digital audio editing, and computer-controlled programming, and broadcasts over the Internet. Whitehouse Business Center has specially designed rooms for accounting, business, marketing, and economics classes. Current renovation and expansion projects are expected to double the College's science facilities and Student Union space and add a multipurpose performance space to the campus.

Costs

For the 2003–04 academic year, tuition is $17,150, room is $2300, board is $2500, and fees are $380, for a total cost of $22,330.

Financial Aid

Wartburg supports the concept of a socially, culturally, and economically diverse student body, believing that contact with others from various backgrounds better prepares students for contemporary life. The College admits applicants on the basis of academic and personal promise, not the ability to pay. More than 97 percent of students receive financial aid in the form of scholarships, grants, loans, and employment. Merit-based academic and music scholarships are awarded to qualified students. The College allocates more than $9 million annually from its own resources for student aid. The application deadline for financial aid is May 1.

Faculty

The 100 full-time and 66 part-time faculty members form a close living-learning community with students and serve as academic advisers. Seventy-four percent of the full-time faculty hold an earned doctoral degree, and 80 percent hold the highest degree in their discipline. Wartburg emphasizes good teaching and also provides faculty research and development opportunities. Many faculty members involve students in their research projects. A sabbatical program permits professors to spend a term or a year on a growth project. Endowments support academic chairs in banking and monetary economics, biology, chaplaincy, choral conducting, communication arts, ethics, global and multicultural studies, and leadership.

Student Government

The Student Senate provides a student voice on campus issues. Its 35 members are selected annually. The Senate selects students to serve on a number of faculty-student committees dealing with all aspects of campus life. Senate members represent student interests to the faculty, administration, and Board of Regents.

Admission Requirements

Applicants are considered according to their potential for academic success, based upon high school rank, breadth and depth of previous study, test scores on the ACT or SAT I, an academic recommendation, and a personal interview with an admission representative. The recommended high school background is 4 years of English, 3 years of mathematics (algebra I and advanced courses), 3 years of science, 2 years of social science, 2 years of foreign language, and 1 year of computer study. Transfer students and international students should contact the Admissions Office to determine any special admission requirements.

Application and Information

A rolling admission policy is used, and applicants may apply at any time. The Wartburg College application for admission, the $20 application fee, one academic recommendation from a teacher, ACT or SAT I scores, and official copies of high school and college transcripts should be sent to the Admissions Office. The application fee is waived for students who make an official campus visit.

Doug Bowman, Dean of Admissions and Financial Aid
Wartburg College
100 Wartburg Boulevard
P.O. Box 1003
Waverly, Iowa 50677-0903
Telephone: 319-352-8264
800-772-2085 (toll-free)
Fax: 319-352-8579

The Vogel Library, which opened in 1999, is designed as a learner's library. The library's espresso coffee shop is a popular gathering spot for students and faculty members.

WESTERN MICHIGAN UNIVERSITY

KALAMAZOO, MICHIGAN

The University

Western Michigan University (WMU), now nearly 100 years old, has emerged as one of the nation's top public universities and enjoys an international reputation in fields as varied as medieval studies, blind rehabilitation, jazz studies, aviation, paper science, graph theory, and evaluation.

The University is one of only 102 public universities in the nation placed by the Carnegie Foundation for the Advancement of Teaching in its top classification of Doctoral/Research–Universities–Extensive. It also is one of only ninety-four public universities in the United States to have its own chapter of Phi Beta Kappa, the nation's premier honor society. In addition, *U.S. News & World Report* has placed WMU in its list of the top 100 public universities for the past three years.

With 29,732 students, WMU is Michigan's fourth-largest university and is among the nation's fifty largest institutions of higher education. Despite its size, complexity, and variety of offerings, WMU is committed to its mission of being a student-centered research university and has worked to maintain a comfortable student-faculty ratio of 16:1. Only 129 of its more than 3,000 class offerings have more than 100 students. Because of its relatively low tuition and required fees, the University is often listed as one of the country's best buys in higher education.

Founded in 1903, WMU has seven degree-granting colleges: Arts and Sciences, Aviation, the Haworth College of Business, Education, Engineering and Applied Sciences, Fine Arts, and Health and Human Services as well as the Graduate College and Lee Honors College, which is one of the oldest such programs in the nation. The University offers 262 academic programs, with more than 160 of them at the undergraduate level. Because it has a vibrant graduate component that includes twenty-six doctoral degree programs, the University attracts faculty members who have been trained at the world's leading universities and who have well-established research and teaching careers.

Over the past decade, WMU has focused on enhancing its out-of-class learning opportunities by expanding its study-abroad programs, internships with organizations around the nation, and regional and national business partnerships. Its on-campus learning environment is bolstered by some of the best instructional, cultural, and recreational facilities. In recent years, more than half a billion dollars in new construction and equipment has transformed the campus, giving students access to acclaimed performance spaces; a state-of-the-art science pavilion; a world-class aviation college; a large, well-equipped student recreation center; and a cutting-edge engineering campus adjacent to a new Business Technology and Research Park.

The University is home to a diverse student body that includes students from all fifty states as well as an international enrollment of more than 1,900 students representing 102 nations. Minority students also are well represented and typically make up about 9 percent of the student body. The University's on-campus enrollment of more than 27,000 includes about 6,200 students who live in twenty-two campus residence halls that offer a variety of living arrangements.

There are more than 300 registered student organizations, including a wide range of Greek, academic honorary, and professional organizations. In addition, the University has nationally recognized arts programs, a lively cultural calendar, and NCAA Division I-A Mid-American and Central Collegiate Hockey Association sports teams. Nine men's and eleven women's varsity sports, intramural teams, and club sports add vitality to campus life.

Location

Kalamazoo, one of Michigan's larger cities, is at the center of a county whose population exceeds 280,000 residents. The campus is located midway between Detroit and Chicago, about 2 1/2 hours from each city. Commercial transportation includes train, bus, and airline services. The Kalamazoo community offers a wide array of lively entertainment: sports, such as professional baseball and hockey; music, from jazz to heavy metal; intimate comedy clubs; and dining, from fast food to international cuisine. West Michigan is also home to many thriving businesses, industries, and Fortune 500 companies, including Haworth Inc., the Whirlpool Corp., and the Kellogg Co.—many offering internship possibilities. Kalamazoo is just 45 minutes from Lake Michigan beaches and only 3 to 4 hours from northern Michigan's ski country. Excellent local skiing is only 30 minutes from the campus.

Majors and Degrees

WMU offers bachelor's degree programs in these fields: accountancy, administrative systems, advertising and promotion, aeronautical engineering, Africana studies, American studies, anthropology, art, art history, art teaching, Asian studies, aviation flight science, aviation maintenance and technology–advanced technology, aviation maintenance and technology–maintenance management, aviation science and administration, biochemistry, biology, biomedical sciences, broadcast and cable production, business-oriented chemistry, chemical engineering, chemistry, communication studies, community health (education), computer engineering, computer information systems, computer science, computer science–theory and analysis, construction engineering and management, criminal justice, dance, dietetics (education), earth science, economics, electrical engineering, elementary education, elementary education–music, engineering graphics and design technology, engineering management technology, English, environmental studies, European studies, exercise science (education), family studies (education), finance, food marketing, food service administration (education), French, general business, general engineering, geography, geology, geophysics, gerontology, German, graphic design, health education teaching, history, home economics education, human resource management, hydrogeology, industrial design, industrial engineering, industrial technology (education), integrated supply matrix management, interdisciplinary health services, interior design (education), interpersonal communication, journalism, Latin, Latin American Studies, management, manufacturing engineering, manufacturing engineering technology, marketing, materials engineering, mathematics, mechanical engineering, media studies, music, music composition, music education, music history, music–jazz studies, music performance, music theater performance, music theory, music therapy, nursing, occupational therapy, organizational communication, paper engineering, paper science, philosophy, physical education–teacher/coach, physics, political science, political science in public administration, prebusiness administration, predentistry, prelaw, premedicine, printing, psychology, public administration, public history, public relations, recreation (education), religion, Russian and East European studies, sales and business marketing, secondary education (biology, business, chemistry, earth science, English, French, geography, German, history, Latin, marketing, mathematics, physics, political science, and Spanish), social work, sociology, Spanish, special education–emotionally impaired, special education–visually impaired, speech pathology and audiology, statistics, student-planned major, technology and design (education), telecommunications management, textile and apparel studies (education), theater, theater education, tourism and travel, travel instruction, and women's studies.

Academic Program

WMU offers undergraduate students a rich blend of academic majors and minors, as well as its general education program and an honors college. These programs ensure that students graduate with the proficiencies and perspectives they need to succeed. The University Curriculum Program is available to students who are undecided about a major and wish to explore WMU's academic offerings. Last fall, more than 2,000 students enrolled in the program, which won a national award for outstanding academic advising. The Lee Honors College provides undergraduates with a unique living/learning environment, offering the intimacy of a small college with the resources of a major university.

Off-Campus Arrangements

A host of U.S. business-industry partnerships as well as exchange agreements with universities around the world provide numerous training and research opportunities for graduate and undergraduate students alike. The University provides assistance to students seeking internships in their chosen fields of study.

Academic Facilities

The University Libraries, with the fourth-largest holdings in Michigan, and the University Computing Center together provide campuswide access to worldwide information resources, comparable to other top universities in the Midwest. Computer labs are available across campus, many in residence halls. In addition, WMU is a completely wireless campus.

Costs

WMU is committed to keeping costs as low as possible to ensure that all qualified students have access to the University. WMU's tuition and fees are among the lowest in the state. Costs for 2002–03 were tuition and fees, $4924; room and board, $6128; and books and supplies, $804. Personal and travel expenses vary based on individual factors.

Financial Aid

Last year, nearly 21,300 students received financial assistance totaling over $160 million. There are three basic types of financial aid: merit-based programs, need-based programs, and student employment.

Merit-based programs include the Medallion Scholarships, which are valued at $32,000 over four years and are the University's most prestigious award for entering freshmen. Other financial aid includes the Army ROTC awards, Michigan National Guard awards, the National Merit Scholarships Award, and numerous sponsored and departmental scholarships for new and currently enrolled students. Merit-based scholarships also are available to community college transfer students, ranging in value from $2000 to $6000.

Need-based loans, grants, college work-study, and other aid options are provided for students who demonstrate particular financial need. To be considered, students should complete the Free Application for Federal Student Aid (FAFSA).

The student employment option reflects research indicating that students who work part time are more likely to graduate than students who do not work at all. About 40 percent of WMU's students work while in school, and more than 700 jobs are offered through the college work-study program.

WMU provides a tuition payment plan through Academic Management Services (AMS) and Tuition Management Systems (TMS). This allows parents and students to pay college costs in monthly installments. No interest is charged for these services, which may be renewed annually for $55. Students should contact AMS at 800-556-6684 or TMS at 800-722-4867 for more information.

Faculty

WMU's commitment to academic excellence means that many of its 985 full-time and 204 part-time faculty members conduct research. Tenured professors teach freshman-level courses, and full-time faculty members teach three quarters of all classes. Almost 93 percent of WMU faculty members have earned a doctorate or other terminal degree in their fields.

Student Government

Governance structures include the Western Student Association and its Student Senate and the Residence Hall Association. Each provides students with a wide variety of opportunities for leadership.

Admission Requirements

Admission to the University is based on a combination of factors, including grade point average, ACT scores, number and kinds of college-prep courses, and trend of grades. In addition, students must meet specific course requirements that include 4 years of English; 3 years of mathematics, including intermediate algebra; 3 years of social sciences; and 2 years of biological/physical sciences. Students who do not meet these requirements but are otherwise admissible may still be admitted to WMU and take the necessary courses as University-level work for credit during their first year.

Transfer students with a minimum of 26 transferable hours (39 quarter hours) at the time of application and a GPA of at least 2.0 (C average) are considered for admission. The trend of the most recent grades is also taken into account. Applicants with fewer than 26 transferable hours (39 quarter hours) at the time of application also must submit a high school transcript. In such cases, admission is based on both college and high school records. For more information, students can request a transfer brochure from the Office of Admissions and Orientation.

Application and Information

For an application or additional information, students should contact:

Office of Admissions and Orientation
Western Michigan University
1903 West Michigan Avenue
Kalamazoo, Michigan 49008-5720
Telephone: 269-387-2000
800-400-4WMU (toll-free)
World Wide Web: http://www.wmich.edu

This imposing clock tower joins Waldo Library, on the right, with the University Computing Center.

WILBERFORCE UNIVERSITY

WILBERFORCE, OHIO

The University

Currently, more than 800 students are enrolled at Wilberforce University, allowing for a 14:1 student-teacher ratio. The student body is diverse, with a number of students coming from Ohio, Michigan, Illinois, Indiana, New York, Pennsylvania, California, and Georgia. International students come from Africa, Canada, the Caribbean, and the British West Indies.

The experiences that students have outside the classroom are important elements of campus life. Wilberforce University is committed to the development of students. Social life and academic achievement are integral aspects of the educational experience. Activities include scholarly forums, service learning/volunteering, poetry readings, travel to nearby colleges and communities, plays, movies, and local sporting events.

Departmental clubs and social organizations enable students to concentrate on particular areas of study, career fields, and academic honors. Eight chapters of national Greek-letter fraternities and sororities offer service, social activities, and opportunities for lasting friendship. Other outlets include the Student Government Association, national honor societies, the campus newspaper, the yearbook staff, the campus radio station, the Debate Club, the Engineering and Computer Science Club, the Business and Economics Club, Students in Free Enterprise, the National Association of Black Accountants, the National Student Business League, the University Concert Choir, the Gospel Chorus, the Jazz Band, the Black Male Coalition, the International Student Club, the University Jazzers and Cheerleaders, and Black Women United.

Wilberforce University's athletic programs (NAIA Division I) include men's and women's basketball, cross-country, golf, and track and field. Wilberforce University is a member of the American MidEast Conference. The intramural program offers basketball, flag football, soccer, softball, and tennis.

The North Central Association of Colleges and Universities accredits Wilberforce University.

Location

The University is situated in southwestern Ohio in the city of Wilberforce, offering tranquility and proximity to major urban areas and their cultural opportunities. Dayton is just 20 miles away; Cincinnati and Columbus are within an hour's drive. Xenia, with a population of 25,000, is 3 miles from campus, and Springfield, a metropolitan area of 100,000, is 15 miles away. Southwestern Ohio is a region that has major cultural attractions, ballets, theaters, and museums. The National Afro-American Museum is located on the old campus of Wilberforce University. Near the campus are John Bryan State Park, the Clarence Brown Reservoir, and the Glen Helen wilderness area. The famed King's Island Amusement Park is less than an hour's drive from campus.

Majors and Degrees

Wilberforce University awards the Bachelor of Arts and Bachelor of Science degrees. Majors are offered in accounting, art, biology/premed, business economics, chemistry, communications, economics, finance, health-services administration, humanities, liberal studies, literature, management, marketing, mass media, mathematics, music (composition, piano, theory, and voice), philosophy and religion, political science/prelaw, psychology, rehabilitation services, social science, social work, sociology (applied and criminal justice), and sport management. Bachelor of Science degrees in engineering or computer science can be earned in computer engineering, computer information systems, computer information systems (graphic design), computer science, electrical engineering, engineering management, and mechanical engineering. Wilberforce University also offers dual-degree programs (3-2) in aerospace, architectural, and nuclear engineering in conjunction with the University of Cincinnati and in chemical, civil, electrical, and mechanical engineering in cooperation with the University of Dayton. Upon completion, students receive degrees in comprehensive science or mathematics and engineering or computer science. Additional courses are offered in Caribbean studies and the Black Heritage Series.

Academic Program

To receive a bachelor's degree, students must complete at least 128 semester hours with an overall grade point average of no less than 2.0. At least 30 semester hours must be completed in residence during the senior year. Graduation prerequisites also include the satisfactory completion of a program of core requirements. Advanced standing may be granted through successful scores on College-Level Examination Program (CLEP) general and subject tests and Advanced Placement (AP) examinations. All students must demonstrate competence in writing by passing the Junior Level Competency Test, become computer literate by enrolling in a required computer literacy course, and successfully complete two cooperative education experiences. Army and Air Force ROTC programs are offered through nearby Central State and Wright State universities.

Wilberforce follows a semester schedule. The fall semester begins in mid-August and ends in mid-December. The spring semester begins in mid-January and ends in mid-May. There are no summer sessions.

Off-Campus Arrangements

Wilberforce University is a member of the Southwestern Ohio Council of Higher Education (SOCHE), an eighteen-college consortium. Membership enables Wilberforce students to cross-register for courses and use the library facilities of any of the other seventeen institutions.

Academic Facilities

The University library, with more than 63,000 volumes, 350 periodicals, and 300 microfilm titles, operates seven days a week. The modern classroom building, like all of the facilities on the main campus, is air conditioned. It contains a radio station, a state-of-the-art computer center, numerous classrooms, and the reading, writing, math, and speech laboratories.

Costs

Wilberforce University is a competitively priced, private liberal arts university. Students are able to gain all the benefits of a high-quality liberal arts education at an affordable cost. Wilberforce University is affiliated and supported by grants the African Methodist Episcopal Church. The University is also a member institution of the United Negro College Fund (UNCF). Grants from the government, foundations, corporations, alumni, and other friends of the University help to keep the cost affordable. Student living on campus find each room equipped with a Pentium computer, which provides each student with online access, e-mail, research, and the Internet. Provisions for this service are included in the general fees.

Student dormitories and housing have been renovated and new buildings were built in 2000. Students who live on campus must apply for housing upon being admitted. Admitted students planning to attend the University must submit a $225 enrollment fee by June 1 for the fall semester and December 15 for the spring semester.

Financial Aid

Loans, grants, and scholarships are available and are awarded on the basis of need. Ninety-five percent of the enrolled students receive some form of financial assistance. Eligible students can receive federal funds, such as Federal Pell Grants, Federal Supplemental Educational Opportunity Grants, Federal Work-Study employment, Federal Perkins Loans, and Federal Stafford Student Loans. State grants are also available for residents of Ohio, Pennsylvania, and Washington, D.C.

The priority deadline to file for financial aid for the fall semester is April 30; the final deadline is June 1. The deadline for the spring semester is November 15. All students should use the Free Application for Federal Student Aid (FAFSA) in applying for aid. The University also requires the completion of its financial aid application. All students must provide proof of income through copies of income tax returns or related documents. All financial aid is awarded on a rolling basis.

Faculty

There are 55 full-time and 20 part-time faculty members at Wilberforce University. All have advanced degrees, and 53 percent have a Ph.D. or the terminal degree in their field. The student-faculty ratio is 14:1. Since the University has primarily a teaching faculty, each student is ensured personalized attention.

Student Government

Leadership opportunities are provided through the Student Government Association (SGA), class offices, committees, and residence halls. The SGA is the main voice and political force of the student body. The members are elected by students to serve as student representatives to the Board of Trustees or as officers in their respective classes. Student representation on faculty-staff committees ensures vital input regarding recommendations and changes in academic, student life, and University-wide policies.

Admission Requirements

Wilberforce University is a selective university that operates on a rolling admissions basis. Students applying for admission must have at least a 2.0 (C) grade point average with a strong showing in the college-preparatory areas and must have completed 15 acceptable units of study, including 4 units of English, 2 to 3 units of mathematics (including algebra), 2 to 3 units of science (including one laboratory science), and 2 units of social studies (including U.S. history). ACT or SAT scores are required for evaluation purposes. An interview is not required but is helpful, and it can be conducted either in person or by telephone. Early decision and early admission are also available.

Wilberforce actively recruits students from throughout the continental United States and other countries, as well as those who want to transfer from community and junior colleges or other four-year institutions. Wilberforce University has articulation agreements with several community colleges throughout the United States. Students are able to transfer credits from associate degree programs to the University and continue pursuing their bachelor's degree. Additional information can be requested from the Office of Admissions.

Applicants should arrange to have an official copy of their high school transcript or evidence of an equivalent level of academic attainment, such as the GED, sent to the admissions office. Ohio students must show proof of passing the Ninth Grade Proficiency Test. Applicants must also submit two recommendations (one from a counselor and one from a teacher) and an essay. In addition to high school transcripts, transfer students should provide copies of transcripts from any college or university attended.

Application and Information

New students are accepted for each semester. Applications for admission in the fall semester must be submitted by July 1. The application deadline for the spring semester is November 15. Applications are accepted anytime after the junior year is completed in high school.

For additional information or application materials, students should contact:

Office of Admissions
Wilberforce University
Wilberforce, Ohio 45384

Telephone: 937-376-2911
800-367-8568 (toll-free)
800-367-8565 (toll-free, Student Financial Services and Scholarships)
World Wide Web: http://www.wilberforce.edu

WILLIAM PENN UNIVERSITY

OSKALOOSA, IOWA

The University

A world of opportunities is available at William Penn University in Oskaloosa, Iowa. From excellent academic programs and a caring faculty to extracurricular activities and athletics to internships and exciting career prospects, William Penn University challenges students to explore all of these opportunities.

One hundred twenty-eight years ago, members of the Society of Friends (Quakers) had a vision for the future. The Quaker values of integrity, simplicity, compassion, ethical practice, acceptance, tolerance, and service continue to be the framework for the quality of education that William Penn University provides to students today. The recent change to university status reflects the rapid growth of the campus locations in Oskaloosa, Des Moines, and Ames, Iowa, and encompasses the two colleges—the College of Arts, Sciences, and Professional Studies and the College of Business and Management Science.

Opportunities abound for students to get involved at William Penn University, including student government, campus ministries, departmental clubs and organizations, intramural athletics, and fine arts activities. After-class activities include regular movie nights, organized dormitory events, performances by nationally recognized entertainers, late-night bowling, and snow-skiing outings. Special events like Christmas caroling, campus beautification, community-campus nights, and guest speakers provide students with study breaks.

William Penn University has a strong tradition of excellence in college athletics. William Penn has won a national championship, regional championships, and conference championships in both men's and women's athletics. Men compete in baseball, basketball, cross-country, football, golf, soccer, track, and wrestling. Women compete in basketball, cross-country, soccer, softball, track, and volleyball. William Penn is a member of the National Association of Intercollegiate Athletics (NAIA).

More than 1,500 students attend William Penn University on the Oskaloosa, Des Moines, and Ames campuses, with forty-one states and several countries represented. Seventeen undergraduate majors with twenty-four areas of emphasis are offered on a semester-system calendar. Twelve major buildings, including a women's residence hall, two coed residence halls, and a townhouse residence facility for upperclassmen are centered on the 40-acre campus. Also, one- and two-bedroom apartments are now open for upperclassmen and married students. Many student activities are held in the Atkins Memorial Union, gymnasium, and fitness center. The George Daily Auditorium, a community auditorium two blocks from the campus, is a 696-seat, state-of-the-art facility that is the site of many University functions.

Location

Located in the rolling hills of southeast Iowa, William Penn University lies on the north edge of Oskaloosa, Iowa. Oskaloosa was established as a small mining center in the early 1800s. It has since grown to more than 11,000 people but still retains a small-town atmosphere.

In the summer, the community band performs in the bandstand every Thursday night. At Christmas, thousands of tiny white lights brighten the city square and bandstand. A variety of city activities are planned—Sweet Corn Days in July, Oskyfest in October, a lighted Christmas parade in December, and Art on the Square in June.

The area also has parks and playgrounds, lighted ballparks, tennis courts, movie theaters, a bowling alley, a roller-skating rink, the YMCA-YWCA Center, and fitness centers. Hiking, boating, fishing, swimming, and camping are located nearby at Lake Keomah State Park, Red Rock Lake, and Lake Rathbun.

Majors and Degrees

The College of Arts, Sciences, and Professional Studies awards the Bachelor of Arts degree in applied computer science (computer information systems, engineering applications, communications applications); biology (general biology, environmental studies, preprofessional studies, bioprocess technology); communications (English, fine arts, journalism/electronic media, public relations); history/government (general history/government, American history, American government, prelaw); industrial technology (technical, industrial management, engineering technology); information technology; mathematics; mechanical engineering; physical education (sports administration, wellness and recreation); psychology (general psychology, human services); sociology (general sociology, criminology); elementary education, with endorsements in K–6 elementary education, health, reading, and special education; and secondary education, with endorsements in American government, American history, athletics coaching, biology, general business, driver and safety education, English as a second language, English/language arts, general science, health, industrial technology, journalism, math, multicategorical, natural science combinations, physical education, physical science, psychology, sociology, special education, and speech/theater.

Within the College of Business and Management Science, the School for Contemporary Business offers a degree in Business Administration, with majors in accounting (general and public), business management, contemporary business, information management, and marketing. The School for Working Adults offers programs in business (management, marketing, finance), information management (business applications, decision support systems), public administration (health services administration, nonprofit management, human resources management/organizational effectiveness), and an Associate of Arts degree in leadership studies.

Academic Program

William Penn University, accredited by the Commission on Institutions of Higher Education of the North Central Association of Colleges and Schools, offers two full semesters, a January term, and three 5-week summer sessions every academic year. The academic program is based on four foundational concepts: leadership, ethical practice, lifelong learning, and commitment to service. These concepts are emphasized throughout the University experience. The Leadership Core, William Penn University's general education requirement, has been named by the John Templeton Foundation to the Honor Roll for Character Building Colleges. It was one of thirty-five colleges in the nation cited for exemplary programming in leadership. Majors consist of at least 30 hours in the student's area of concentration and must be completed with a cumulative GPA of at least 2.0 (on a 4.0 scale).

William Penn's teacher-education program offers a major in elementary education and twenty secondary education endorsements. Penn is one of only a few universities in Iowa that offers the ESL endorsement and has just received a federal grant to expand the availability of the English as a Second Language K-12 endorsement. William Penn is one of only two institutions in the state to offer certification for industrial technology teachers and the only private institution in the state to offer the four-year major in industrial technology.

Academic Facilities

Wilcox Library currently holds nearly 75,000 volumes plus sound recordings, microforms, CD-ROM databases, and audio-visual materials. The library subscribes to more than 400 periodicals and to numerous online electronic databases. The Quaker Collection, an extensive holding of Quaker monographs, photographs, and other materials, is also part of Wilcox Library. In addition, the Academic Resource Center and the Jones Mid-East Collection are located in the library.

William Penn's computer facilities contain up-to-date equipment. Networked Macintosh and IBM-compatible microcomputers are available in the computer lab and connect students with e-mail and the Internet. Students also have access to the University's Hewlett-Packard 3000 superminicomputer through terminals located in the computer lab. Knowledgeable lab assistants are always on duty in the computer lab to answer questions and help students understand the computers and software. The dorms are part of the campus' local area network, and students with their own computers can access the Internet directly from their rooms for a small, one-time connection fee.

Ware Recital Hall, a 140-seat auditorium in McGrew Fine Arts Center, is the setting for many recitals, concerts, and lectures. Special speakers give talks in Penn 400, a 255-seat auditorium.

Most classes are held in Penn Hall, which was built in 1917. This building stands in the center of Penn's 40-acre campus.

Costs

Full-time tuition for 2002–03 was $13,284. The room fee was $1730. Board was $2700.

Financial Aid

To help admitted students meet their expenses, William Penn University has established a very strong financial aid program. Its goal is to provide assistance to students who have strong scholastic backgrounds, special abilities or talents, or financial need. Currently, more than 96 percent of the University's students receive financial assistance in some form.

Two types of financial assistance are available: merit-based academic and athletics scholarships and awards and need-based assistance. Merit-based scholarships and awards are based on academic achievement or on a student's special ability or talent, without consideration of financial need. William Penn University offers several merit-based scholarships and awards—academic scholarships, media awards, fine arts awards, athletic scholarships, and other institutional grants and scholarships. Need-based assistance is based on the financial help a student needs to attend William Penn University and is available in three forms: grants, campus employment, and loans.

Students must apply for financial assistance each year by completing the Free Application for Federal Student Aid (FAFSA).

Faculty

William Penn University's faculty is made up of 45 full-time and 22 part-time members. The emphasis at William Penn is on teaching, but students are often able to become involved and work with faculty members on individual research projects. Faculty members are encouraged to get to know students both in the classroom and through cocurricular activities. The faculty-student ratio is 1:14.

Student Government

The Student Government Association (SGA) serves as the governing organization for all students and student organizations. The SGA, led by the student body president, is very active in planning campus activities and events, including Homecoming and Parents' Weekend. The student body is represented by the student body president at all Board of Trustees meetings, and students are a part of many campus committees.

Admission Requirements

Students from accredited high schools and college transfers are considered for admission to William Penn University based on their grade point average, class rank, ACT or SAT I scores, and likelihood of academic success. William Penn University has a rolling admissions policy.

Application and Information

Applications are accepted on a rolling basis and are reviewed as soon as they are complete. Students should send a completed application, the $20 application fee, official copies of all high school and/or college transcripts or the GED score, and ACT or SAT I results to the Office of Admissions.

International students should submit TOEFL scores along with an international student application and a statement of financial support. An ESL program is available for students seeking to improve their English skills.

Campus tours and information sessions are available throughout the week.

To obtain additional information, students are encouraged to contact:

Mary Boyd
Director of Admissions
William Penn University
201 Trueblood Avenue
Oskaloosa, Iowa 52577
Telephone: 641-673-1012
800-779-7366 (toll-free)
E-mail: admissions@wmpenn.edu
World Wide Web: http://www.wmpenn.edu

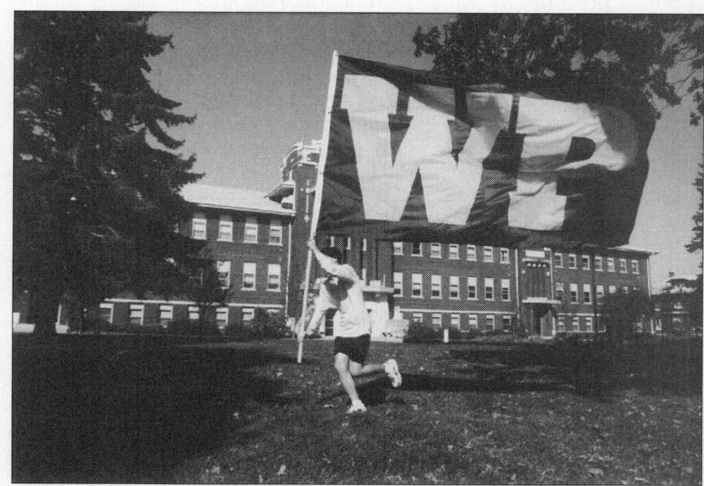

At William Penn University, students run toward a successful future.

YOUNGSTOWN STATE UNIVERSITY

YOUNGSTOWN, OHIO

The University

For almost a century, Youngstown State University (YSU) has prepared its graduates to become leaders in the region, the state, and the nation. Located on a beautiful 140-acre campus near downtown Youngstown, Ohio, YSU offers its students a comprehensive selection of major programs backed by a strong tradition of teaching and scholarship. YSU's diverse student body of 12,698 and a student-faculty ratio of 19:1 provide the personal contact associated with a smaller institution, and its connection to the Ohio state system of higher education enables it to draw on the vast resources of that system. The average undergraduate class size is 27 for lectures and 9 for labs.

Youngstown State seeks to offer its students a vital living and learning environment with a relatively small, cohesive campus and a wealth of curricular and cocurricular activities. Attractive residence halls house close to 1,000 students and include a special residential honors facility. Student activities abound, with more than 140 student organizations, including social sororities and fraternities and opportunities for participation in theater, performing groups, student publications, intramural and intercollegiate athletics, and activity planning.

Youngstown State University competes in NCAA athletics. In the past decade, it has captured four Division I-AA national football championships. During the same decade, the women's basketball team won five Mid-Continent Conference titles and played three years in the NCAA tournament. The University fields ten women's and eight men's intercollegiate Division I teams. Fitness and recreational facilities are free to all YSU students in the Beeghly Physical Education Center and the Stambaugh Sports Complex, including track, tennis, swimming, racquetball, basketball, handball, Nautilus, aerobic conditioning, and free weights.

Of the 12,698 students at YSU, 11,375 are undergraduates. Multicultural students make up 13 percent of the student body and international students hail from fifty-five countries. Students benefit from a wide range of student services: complete tutorial assistance in all subject areas, with special centers for writing, study skills, reading, and mathematics; counseling and health services; career testing, planning, and placement; special programs for multicultural, women, and adult students (those older than 25); and an orientation program that includes mentoring by faculty and staff members and upperclass students.

The University seeks a balance between teaching, service, and scholarly activity that serves both its students and the larger community of scholars. The University is committed to keeping its doors open to all who seek higher education and equally committed to giving students every opportunity to enrich their minds, develop their creativity and problem-solving abilities, and become informed, conscientious citizens of the world.

Location

Youngstown is at the center of a metropolitan area of 600,000, located 60 miles from both Pittsburgh and Cleveland. The campus is within easy driving or walking distance of restaurants, shopping centers, museums, and parks. The University is a major contributor to the city's cultural and recreational vitality, each year presenting hundreds of concerts, exhibits, lectures, performances, and athletic contests. The city offers an outstanding symphony orchestra, three community theaters, a vital arts community, and unlimited recreational options provided by 2,500-acre Mill Creek Park that is located 1 mile from the campus. YSU students can take advantage of close ties to area businesses for internships and work co-op programs, which provide valuable on-the-job experience.

Majors and Degrees

The College of Arts and Sciences offers majors in Africana studies, American studies, anthropology, biology, chemistry, computer information systems, computer science, earth science, economics, English, environmental studies, French, geography, geology, history, information technology, Italian, journalism, mathematics, philosophy, physics/astronomy, political science, professional writing and editing, psychology, religious studies, social studies, sociology, and Spanish.

The Beeghly College of Education offers majors in early and middle childhood education, gifted and talented educational specialist studies, multiage education (with specialized teaching fields), adolescent/young adult education (with specialized teaching fields), vocational education, and special education.

The Rayen College of Engineering and Technology offers majors in chemical engineering, civil engineering (structural and transportation option and environmental option), civil and construction engineering technology, drafting and design technology, electrical and computer engineering, electrical engineering technology, electric utility technology, industrial and systems engineering, mechanical engineering, and mechanical engineering technology.

The College of Fine and Performing Arts offers majors in studio art, art history, music/history and literature, music education, music/performance, music theory, music composition, communications studies, telecommunication studies, and theater.

The Bitonte College of Health and Human Services offers majors in allied health, Army and Air Force ROTC, clinical laboratory science, clinical laboratory technology, community health, criminal justice, dental hygiene, dietetic technology, emergency medical technology, family and consumer sciences education, exercise science, family and consumer studies, food and nutrition, health science, histotechnology , hospitality management, medical assisting technology, merchandising (fashion and interiors), nursing, nursing home administration, physical education, pre-kindergarten, pre–physical therapy, respiratory care, social service technology, and social work.

The Williamson College of Business Administration offers majors in accounting, advertising and public relations, business economics, finance, general administration, human resource management, management, management information systems, marketing, and marketing management. Associate degrees are offered with concentrations in accounting, finance, labor studies, management, and marketing.

Interdisciplinary minors are offered in gerontology, linguistics, peace and conflict studies, professional ethics, statistics, and women's studies.

Students may also enroll for a combined B.S./M.D. program with the Northeastern Ohio Universities College of Medicine. Each student successfully completing this program is awarded the Bachelor of Science degree from Youngstown State University and the M.D. degree from the College of Medicine.

Academic Program

Youngstown State University is one of a few comprehensive metropolitan institutions in Ohio that provide associate, baccalaureate, and graduate instruction and continuing education in one location. Currently, the University offers a broad curriculum in the School of Graduate Studies and six colleges: Arts and Sciences, Business Administration, Education, Engineering and Technology, Fine and Performing Arts, and Health and Human Services. The spirit of cooperation among departments and colleges permits students to pursue interdisciplinary majors and minors, to major in one department or college and minor in another, or to pursue double majors. Youngstown State University provides for a broad-based education through a core curriculum of 45 semester hours spread across five areas of concentration and emphasizing the development of writing, speaking, and critical-thinking skills. In addition to fulfilling this general education requirement, each student must complete the major and/or minor requirements and meet the semester hours required for the baccalaureate degree.

Application of associate degree credits to baccalaureate programs is possible within the University. Transfer and dual-admission agreements with two-year institutions and community colleges provide opportunities for transfer into baccalaureate programs at Youngstown State.

An individualized curriculum program is available to students whose needs are not met by existing conventional programs. Students may design curricula to suit their particular needs, allowing alternative paths for earning the undergraduate degrees currently offered.

Off-Campus Arrangements

YSU offers cooperative/internship education programs in which students participate in both classroom and experiential study via employment in a government, industry, or business setting. Opportunities for international studies for academic credit are available in several majors.

Academic Facilities

Maag Library houses more than a half-million books and more than 200,000 government documents and subscribes to more than 3,100 periodicals and scholarly journals. Online research services provide access to all state university libraries in Ohio and a wide range of other information sources. The library's resources are augmented by the Curriculum Resource Center in the College of Education. A Multimedia Center, housed in Maag Library, offers research materials in a variety of formats.

Comprehensive computing facilities are readily available to students throughout the campus. Scientific laboratories at YSU are fully outfitted with up-to-date instructional and research equipment. Studios and performance halls in the College of Fine and Performing Arts have been recently renovated for acoustic excellence, and the McDonough Museum of Art is an innovative exhibit space for student and faculty work.

Costs

Tuition and fees for an Ohio resident for the 2003 fall semester are $2736 for full-time (12–16 credits) attendance. For students residing in certain counties in New York, West Virginia, and western Pennsylvania, the out-of-state tuition surcharge is reduced, making the total semester cost $3887 for full-time attendance. The charge for University housing, including meals, is $5700 per year. The University estimates books and supplies at $860 per year, and on-campus parking is $68 per semester. Some laboratory and computer classes entail a lab/materials fee, ranging from $35 to $65. All fees and charges are subject to change.

Financial Aid

Financial aid is awarded in four basic forms: scholarships, grants, loans, and on-campus employment. Depending on the student's computed financial need, the award may include a package of any or all of these components in varying amounts. Financial aid applications should be submitted to the University by February 15 for fall-semester assistance and must be resubmitted each year. About 78 percent of Youngstown State's full-time students receive some form of financial aid through a comprehensive program that includes need-based and performance-based aid. Youngstown State prides itself on an exemplary scholarship program that rewards academic performance and promise. The University Scholars program provides full-cost scholarships for 160 high-achieving students, and numerous other scholarships are available under a wide range of criteria.

Faculty

Eighty percent of YSU's 360 full-time faculty members hold the highest degree in their field and most are engaged in active, cutting-edge research that they bring to their instruction. YSU classes are small—70 percent of undergraduate classes have fewer than 30 students—creating many opportunities for class discussion, projects, and interaction between faculty members and students.

Student Government

Student Government exercises the power to conduct student elections, to recommend student representatives to serve on joint faculty-student committees, and to supervise programs funded from its operating budget. Members are elected by the student body to executive positions and to the legislative branch in proportion to the enrollment in each college. Student Government nominates students for two gubernatorial appointments to the University Board of Trustees.

Admission Requirements

Ohio residents and residents of Mercer and Lawrence Counties in Pennsylvania must have graduated from high school with a state-approved diploma or passed the test of General Educational Development (GED). Nonresidents must have graduated in the upper two thirds of their high school class, have a minimum ACT composite score of 17, have a minimum combined recentered SAT I score of 820, or have passed the GED test. Transfer applicants must have earned at least a 2.0 accumulated point average and be in good standing at the last institution attended.

Application and Information

Application deadlines vary depending on the semester and the program for which a student is applying. Under the program, students who are admitted by February 15 become eligible for advance advisement and registration for fall classes. Applications must be accompanied by a nonrefundable fee. For more information and an application, students should contact:

Undergraduate Admissions
Youngstown State University
One University Plaza
Youngstown, Ohio 44555

Telephone: 330-941-2000
330-941-1564 (TTY/TDD)
877-468-6978 (toll-free)
Fax: 330-941-3674
E-mail: enroll@ysu.edu
World Wide Web: http://www.ysu.edu

YSU's beautiful, safe campus provides a pleasant backdrop for the students' college experience.

In-Depth Descriptions of Other Colleges to Consider

COLUMBIA UNIVERSITY, SCHOOL OF GENERAL STUDIES

NEW YORK, NEW YORK

The University and The School

One of the best kept secrets in American higher education, the School of General Studies at Columbia University is the nation's premier college for returning and nontraditional students. One of the four undergraduate colleges that grace Columbia, the School of General Studies is dedicated to those students who have interrupted or postponed their education by at least one academic year.

Unlike the division of the University dedicated to continuing education, the School of General Studies is a degree-granting liberal arts college. The School of General Studies is fully integrated into the Columbia undergraduate curriculum and provides an Ivy League education to the widest range of talented students with the demonstrated potential to succeed.

General Studies students come from all walks of life and from varied backgrounds, and for that reason may study full- or part-time. Many degree candidates hold jobs as well as study, and many have family responsibilities. Others attend full-time, experiencing Columbia's more traditional college life. The diversity in the student body makes attendance at Columbia highly attractive. The varied personal experience represented in each classroom allows for discussion and debate and, in turn, for the academic rigor and intellectual development that characterize a Columbia education. The School has more than 1,200 undergraduate degree candidates and about 300 postbaccalaureate premedical students. The average age of these students is 29. About half are full-time students. Between 80 percent and 85 percent of the School's students go on to graduate and professional schools after graduation. The acceptance rate for General Studies postbaccalaureate premedical students applying to U.S. medical schools is more than 85 percent.

In addition to its bachelor's degree program, the School of General Studies offers combined undergraduate/graduate degree programs with Columbia's Schools of Social Work, International and Public Affairs, Law, Business, and Dental and Oral Surgery, as well as with Teachers College, the College of Physicians and Surgeons, and the Juilliard School.

Location

Columbia University is located in Morningside Heights, on the Upper West Side of Manhattan. The University's neighbors include the Union Theological Seminary, the Jewish Theological Seminary, the Manhattan School of Music, St. Luke's Hospital, Women's Hospital, Riverside Church, and the Cathedral of St. John the Divine. The diversity of intellectual and social activities these institutions offer in the immediate vicinity is one of Columbia's great assets as a university; another is New York City itself, which offers students at Columbia an almost boundless and astonishingly rich variety of social, cultural, and recreational opportunities that are themselves an education.

Majors and Degrees

The School of General Studies grants the B.A. and B.S. degrees and offers the following majors: African-American studies, ancient studies, anthropology, applied mathematics, archaeology, architecture, art history, astronomy, biology, biology-psychology, chemistry, classics, comparative literature, computer science, dance, earth and environmental studies, East Asian studies, economics, English literature, film studies, French, German, history, Italian, Latino studies, literature-writing, mathematics, Middle East studies, music, philosophy, physics, Polish, political science, psychology, religion, Slavic language, sociology, Spanish, statistics, theater arts, urban studies, visual arts, and women's and gender studies. Individually designed majors are also available. In addition, the School offers two undergraduate dual-degree programs: one in conjunction with Columbia's School of Engineering and Applied Science and the other in conjunction with the Jewish Theological Seminary of America.

Academic Program

The School of General Studies offers a traditional liberal arts education designed to provide students with the broad knowledge and intellectual skills that make possible continued education and growth in the years after college and that constitute the soundest possible foundation on which to build competence for positions of responsibility in the professional world. Requirements for the bachelor's degree comprise three elements: (1) core requirements, intended to develop in students the ability to write and communicate clearly; to understand the modes of thought that characterize the humanities, the social sciences, and the sciences; to gain some familiarity with central cultural ideas through literature, fine arts, and music; and to acquire a working proficiency in a foreign language; (2) major requirements, designed to give students sustained and coherent exposure to a particular discipline in an area of strong intellectual interest; and (3) elective courses, in which students pursue particular interests and skills for their own personal growth or for their relationship to future professional or personal objectives. Students are required to complete a minimum of 124 credits for the bachelor's degree; 60 of these may be in transfer credit, but at least 64 credits (including the last 30 credits) must be completed at Columbia. In addition to the usual graduation honors (cum laude, magna cum laude, and summa cum laude), honors programs for superior students are available in a majority of the University's departments.

Off-Campus Arrangements

Columbia students may enhance their academic experiences through various study-abroad programs around the world. General Studies students may spend a term at the Reid Hall Program in the Montparnasse district of Paris; the Free University of Berlin; the Kyoto Center in Japan; the Biosphere 2 in Oracle, Arizona; or in Beijing, China.

Academic Facilities

The Columbia University libraries constitute the nation's sixth-largest academic library system, with a collection of more than 6 million volumes, more than 4 million microform pieces, and 26 million manuscript items in 850 separate collections. There are twenty-two libraries in the system; five are designated Distinctive Collections because of their unusual depth and nationally recognized excellence. All library divisions are available to General Studies students. The University's Computer Center is one of the largest and most powerful university installations in the world and has remote units and terminals in several parts of the campus to enhance its accessibility. The Fairchild Life Science Building houses research facilities, laboratories, electron microscopes, and a vast amount of biochemical equipment used for teaching and research. The University's physics building has been the scene of many important developments in the recent history of physics, including the invention of the laser and the first demonstration in this country of nuclear fission.

Costs

For the 2002–03 academic year, tuition was $878 per credit, monthly living expenses were about $1200 for single students and about $1800 for married students, fees were approximately $1200, and books cost about $900 to $1200.

Financial Aid

The School of General Studies awards financial aid based upon need and academic ability. Approximately 70 percent of General Studies degree candidates receive some form of financial aid, including Federal Pell Grants, New York State TAP Grants, Federal Stafford and unsubsidized Stafford Loans, Federal Perkins Loans, General Studies Scholarships, and Federal Work-Study Program awards. Priority application deadlines for new students are June 1 for the fall 2003 semester and November 1 for the spring 2004 semester.

Faculty

The faculty of the School of General Studies, which is shared with Columbia College, the Graduate School of Arts and Sciences, and the School of International and Public Affairs, includes distinguished scholars in virtually every discipline. Of the School's more than 600 faculty members, more than 99 percent hold a Ph.D. degree. Students, whether full-time or part-time, have many opportunities to work closely with this faculty, both in small classes and in research projects. Faculty members also serve as advisers to students majoring in their area of study and maintain regular office hours to see students.

Student Government

One student of the School represents General Studies students in the University Senate, a decision-making body composed of students and faculty and administrative staff members from each division of the University. In addition, 2 General Studies students sit as voting members on the Committee on Instruction, which oversees the curriculum of the School. The General Studies Student Council elects officers each year and sponsors activities for students. *The Observer,* the School's student-run magazine, is published several times each year. The Postbaccalaureate Premedical Program Student Organization sponsors events related to the medical school admissions process.

Admission Requirements

The admission policy of the School is geared to the maturity and varied backgrounds of its students. Aptitude and motivation are considered along with past academic performance, standardized test scores, and employment history. The School's admission decisions are based on a careful review of each application and reflect the Admissions Committee's considered judgment of the applicant's maturity, academic potential, and present ability to undertake course work at Columbia.

Admission requirements include a completed application form; a 1,000- to 1,500-word autobiographical statement relating the applicant's past educational history and work experience, present situation, and future plans; a personal statement of 500 to 700 words that describes why the applicant is a nontraditional student and would like to pursue their education at the School of General Studies; two letters of recommendation from an academic or professional evaluator; an official high school transcript; official transcripts from all colleges and universities attended; official SAT I or ACT scores or scores on the General Studies Admissions Examination; and a nonrefundable application fee of $50.

Students from outside the United States may apply to the School of General Studies to start or complete a baccalaureate degree. In addition to the materials described above, international applicants must submit official TOEFL scores.

Application and Information

Application deadlines are June 1 for the fall semester and November 1 for the spring semester. Applicants from countries outside the U.S. are urged to apply by August 15 for the spring semester and April 1 for the fall semester. Applications are reviewed as they are completed, and applicants are notified of decisions shortly thereafter.

For more information, students should contact:

Office of Admissions and Financial Aid
School of General Studies
408 Lewisohn Hall
2970 Broadway
Columbia University, Mail Code 4101
New York, New York 10027
Telephone: 212-854-2772
E-mail: gsdegree@columbia.edu
World Wide Web: http://www.gs.columbia.edu

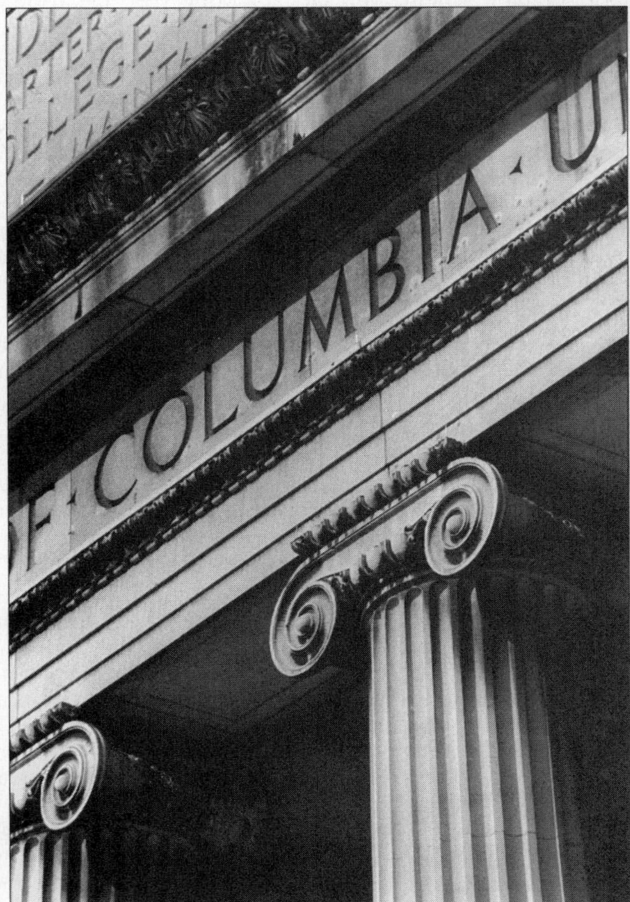

The Low Memorial Library/Visitors Center.

CUMBERLAND COLLEGE

WILLIAMSBURG, KENTUCKY

The College

For more than 100 years, Cumberland College has been committed to providing a superior education in an exceptional Christian atmosphere at an affordable cost. Emphasis is placed on the growth of the individual student. The College strives to instill in students the desire to be agents of change in the world and to use knowledge for the benefit of others as well as themselves.

Cumberland is a four-year, coed liberal arts college offering a broad curriculum with more than forty programs of undergraduate study from which to choose. A graduate program leading to the Master of Arts in Education is also offered.

The student body consists of 1,700 students representing thirty-eight states and fourteen countries. Most students live on campus in the College's ten residence halls. Each hall is supervised by a director assisted by student staff members.

Extracurricular activities abound, including debate team, theater, musical performance groups, academic societies, Baptist Student Union, Appalachian Ministries, departmental clubs, and intramural sports. Cumberland participates in intercollegiate competition in women's basketball, cross-country, golf, judo, soccer, softball, swimming, tennis, track, volleyball, and wrestling; men's baseball, basketball, cross-country, football, golf, judo, soccer, swimming, tennis, track, and wrestling; and coed cheerleading. The O. Wayne Rollins Convocation/Physical Education Center houses a 2,700-seat athletic arena, a swimming pool, an indoor walking/jogging track, and classrooms. The James H. Taylor II Stadium complex includes a football field, an eight-lane all-weather track, and soccer fields.

Students benefit from such special services as the Career Services Center, Center for Leadership Studies, Student Health Center, Academic Resource Center, and free tutorial assistance.

Cumberland College is accredited by the Commission on Colleges of the Southern Association of Colleges and Schools (1866 Southern Lane, Decatur, Georgia 30033-4097; telephone: 404-679-4501) to award Bachelor of Arts, Bachelor of General Studies, Bachelor of Music, Bachelor of Science, and Master of Arts in Education degrees.

Location

Williamsburg is located in southern Kentucky, 185 miles south of Cincinnati, Ohio, and 70 miles north of Knoxville, Tennessee. The campus is easily accessible from Interstate 75, about 1 mile from Exit 11. Williamsburg is one of Kentucky's older towns and is known for its beautiful homes and the hospitality of its people. The College is situated on three hills above the town and has a panoramic view of the surrounding mountains and Cumberland River Valley, an area known throughout the country for its lovely waterfalls, forests, and lakes. Famed Cumberland Falls State Resort Park is just 20 minutes from campus.

Majors and Degrees

Cumberland College confers the degrees of Bachelor of Arts, Bachelor of Science, Bachelor of General Studies, and Bachelor of Music. Major fields of study are accounting, art, biology, business administration, chemistry, church music, communications and theater arts, computer information systems, education, English, health, history, mathematics, medical technology, movement and leisure studies, music, office administration, philosophy, physics, political science, psychology, religion, social work, and special education.

Minor fields of study can be chosen from major fields or from athletic training (sports medicine), biblical languages, French, philosophy, and Spanish.

Preprofessional and special curricula are offered in medical technology, military science, predentistry, pre-engineering, prelaw, premedicine, prenursing, preoptometry, prepharmacy, pre–physical therapy, pre–veterinary medicine, and religious vocations.

Academic Program

Cumberland seeks to provide academic specialization within the broad framework of a liberal arts education. To supplement the in-depth knowledge acquired within each major, 47 semester hours of general studies from the areas of Christian faith and values, cultural and aesthetic values, the English language, humanities, leadership and community service, natural and mathematical sciences, physical education, and social sciences are required. Students must earn 128 semester hours to graduate with a bachelor's degree.

The academic year begins in late August, with the first semester ending in mid-December. The second semester runs from early January to early May. One 5-week undergraduate summer session and two 4-week graduate summer sessions are also offered. Orientation, preregistration, and academic advising by faculty members begin in the summer preceding entrance.

Students may receive credit for successful scores on the Advanced Placement examinations of the College Board, the College-Level Examination Program (CLEP), and special departmental tests. Through the honors program, highly qualified students have the opportunity to undertake advanced independent study.

Academic Facilities

Cumberland's campus contains thirty buildings, reflecting antebellum architectural style. The science building features well-equipped biology, chemistry, and physics labs providing graduate-level research opportunities.

The McGaw Music Building contains individual rehearsal and studio areas as well as a recital hall. The Norma Perkins Hagan Memorial Library houses more than 150,500 book titles, 1,630 periodical subscriptions, and 715,878 microform titles. Sophisticated computer equipment provides access to an additional 20 million or more items from many of the nation's outstanding libraries. The instructional media center includes a children's library, a computerized language lab, and a listening library.

Other special academic features include a computer center, an art gallery, a word processing center for English composition, a theater, the Career Services Center, a 600-seat chapel, two large lecture halls, and the Distance Learning Laboratory.

Costs

For 2002–03, the basic academic-year expenses were $10,958 for tuition and fees and $4676 for room and board, for a total of

$15,634. There are no additional fees for out-of-state students. The average cost for books and supplies is approximately $300 per semester.

Financial Aid

Cumberland sponsors a large financial aid program that coordinates money from federal, state, private, and College sources. Last year, 90 percent of Cumberland students shared more than $15 million in aid.

To apply for financial aid, it is necessary to complete the Free Application for Federal Student Aid (FAFSA). For further information about financial aid opportunities, students should contact the Director of Financial Aid at 800-532-0828 (toll-free). Applications made by March 15 are given priority for the fall semester.

Numerous scholarships and leadership grants are available.

Faculty

There are 95 full-time and 2 part-time faculty members who are respected scholars and whose primary responsibility is to teach. Courses are not taught by graduate assistants. The student-faculty ratio is 16:1, enabling students to receive ample attention and assistance from professors. Faculty members also serve as advisers to help students in planning their academic programs.

Student Government

The Student Government Association acts as a liaison between the students and the College administration. The organization also plans, implements, and governs various activities and special events each year to enhance the quality of campus social life. Members of the executive and legislative branches are elected by the student body.

Admission Requirements

In compliance with federal law, including provisions of Title IX of the Educational Amendments of 1972 and Section 504 of the Rehabilitation Act of 1973, Cumberland College does not illegally discriminate on the basis of race, sex, color, national or ethnic origin, age, disability, or military service in its administration of education policies, programs, or activities; admissions policies; or employment. Under federal law, the College may discriminate on the basis of religion in order to fulfill its purposes. The College reserves the right to discriminate on the basis of sex in its undergraduate admissions programs. Further, the College reserves the right to deny admission to any applicant whose academic preparation, character, or personal conduct is determined to be inconsistent with the purpose and objectives of the College. Where possible, the College will seek to reasonably accommodate a student's disability. However, the College's obligation to reasonably accommodate a student's disability ends where the accommodation would pose an undue hardship on the College or where the accommodation in question would fundamentally alter the academic program. Inquiries or complaints should be directed to the Vice President for Academic Affairs.

The purpose of the admission process is to identify applicants who are likely to succeed academically at Cumberland College and at the same time contribute positively to the campus community. The process considers such factors as high school records (including courses taken, grade trends, and rank in class), college records (if transferring from another institution), scores on the ACT or on the SAT I, application essay, letters of recommendation, extracurricular activities and honors, and personal contact.

Application and Information

Applicants for admission should contact the admissions office for an application form and return the completed form to the College, along with the appropriate application fee. Applicants should also have official transcripts of all high school and college work sent to the College, along with a copy of the ACT or SAT I scores. Each student is notified regarding official admission within ten working days after the application procedure has been completed.

Students accepted for admission must submit the required enrollment deposit.

Additional information may be obtained by contacting:

Office of Admissions
Cumberland College
Williamsburg, Kentucky 40769
Telephone: 606-539-4241
800-343-1609 (toll-free)
E-mail: admiss@cumberlandcollege.edu
World Wide Web: http://www.cumberlandcollege.edu

Students on the campus of Cumberland College.

LEHIGH UNIVERSITY

BETHLEHEM, PENNSYLVANIA

The University

Lehigh University is among the nation's most selective, highly ranked private research universities. It is rich in tradition, with an inspiring history that spans more than 135 years. Lehigh offers a comprehensive education that integrates courses from four colleges and dozens of fields of study to create a dynamic learning environment. Students choose from nationally recognized programs in the arts and sciences, humanities, business, engineering, and education. They can customize their college experience by tailoring their majors and academic programs from more than 2,000 courses, with opportunities to take courses outside their college or major field of study. At the graduate level, the M.B.A. program has a variety of concentrations, including the M.B.A. and Engineering and the M.B.A. and Educational Leadership programs.

Lehigh is the right size. It is small enough to be personal yet large enough to be powerful. The school combines learning opportunities found at larger research universities with the personal attention of a smaller, private college. At Lehigh, students have easy access to world-class faculty members who are renowned in their fields but also offer their time and personal attention to help students learn and succeed. With an 11:1 student-faculty ratio, a customized college experience, close mentoring by faculty members, hands-on projects, extensive industry internships, and innovative study, Lehigh students emerge as leaders in careers and life.

The University's 4,700 undergraduate students come from nearly every state and more than sixty-five countries. More than half ranked in the top 10 percent of their high school class. Women comprise 41 percent of the student body, and minorities, 13 percent. Seventy percent live on campus in residence halls, in fraternity or sorority houses, in apartments, or in specialty housing.

At Lehigh, students gain hands-on, real-world experience and take part in a variety of activities, in and out of the classroom. Twenty-four Division I varsity atheltic teams compete primarily in the Patriot League. Lehigh, consistently among the leaders in NCAA graduation rates, ranked first in the nation in 2001 with a 96 percent graduation rate. Its athletics program was in the top 20 of *U.S. News & World Report's* "America's Best College Sports Programs." There are more than 40 club and intramural sports, and more than 80 percent of Lehigh's students participate in them. Lehigh supports a vibrant campus life, offering many social and extracurricular activities outside the classroom. More than 130 different clubs and social organizations suit virtually any interest from politics and student government to music, drama, journalism, and religion.

Location

Lehigh's location in Pennsylvania's Lehigh Valley, the state's third-largest market, provides the best of all worlds. It combines the comfortable, secure setting of a suburban town with convenient access to the excitement of major cultural centers including Philadelphia (50 miles south) and New York (90 miles north). Lehigh is situated in Bethlehem, Pennsylvania, an ethnically diverse community of 78,000 that offers a variety of cultural events, ethnic restaurants, and entertainment to three quarters of a million people.

Lehigh offers a unique mixture of modern, state-of-the-art facilities and historic, ivy-covered stone buildings. Situated on the side and top of scenic South Mountain in the Saucon Valley, the University's three campuses rival the most beautiful parks. Tall trees, wooded hills, and colorful landscaping are spread over 1,600 acres. The classic college feel is evident on much of Lehigh's Asa Packer Campus. Newer buildings, such as the Rauch Business Center, are designed to complement the original stone ivy-covered buildings, some of which are on the historic register. The Mountaintop Campus provides additional teaching and research space for the biosciences and the graduate-level College of Education. The Murray H. Goodman Campus features the 16,000-seat Goodman Stadium for football; the 5,600-seat Stabler Arena for indoor athletics contests, concerts, and special events; Rauch Field House; Ulrich Sports Complex; and extensive outdoor athletic fields for intercollegiate and intramural sports.

Majors and Degrees

The College of Arts and Sciences, the largest college with just under half of the University's faculty members and undergraduates, offers flexible curricula, personal attention to students, and a problem-solving culture. Students explore seventy-seven majors and minors in forty disciplines in eighteen departments spanning the arts, humanities, social sciences, and natural sciences. Departments team on joint ventures in the new Humanities Center, where courses, lectures, and informal gatherings embrace literature, languages, religion studies, philosophy, the history of art, and architecture and music. Another example is the Lehigh Earth Observatory (LEO), in which teams of students work on real-world problems as they study environmental systems and their relationship with society. The modern Zoellner Arts Center is home to Lehigh's outstanding programs of music and theater. Cross-disciplinary programs like Africana studies, classical studies, computer science, economics, women's studies, and science, technology, and society provide a well-rounded education and a rich variety of career opportunities. The college offers a four-year curriculum in arts and sciences, a five-year curriculum in arts-engineering, double-degree programs, and a combined bachelor's/master's degree program in education.

With its interdisciplinary approach to learning, the College of Business and Economics is powerfully positioned to develop leaders. It provides strong programs at both the graduate and undergraduate levels. Traditional undergraduate business majors, as well as a variety of niche-based, market-driven programs such as supply chain management, computer science and business, and integrated business and engineering, are offered. The Bachelor of Science degree is offered with majors in accounting, business economics, business information systems, computer science and business, economics, finance, management, marketing, and supply chain management. The Bachelor of Science degree in business and engineering (BSBE) is offered to those completing the Integrated Business and Engineering (IBE) Honors Program. The business and accounting programs are accredited by AACSB International–The Association to Advance Collegiate Schools of Business.

In the College of Education, undergraduates discover new ways of learning with their world-renowned professors, fellow students, and the children and adults they serve. The College of Education has consistently climbed the ranks among U.S. graduate schools and offers some of the most competitive programs in the country. The college has a strong focus on the use of information technology in education, and faculty members are highly entrepreneurial in creating new learning experiences. The college offers a five-year combined-degree program leading to a B.S. or B.A. in a defined major and elementary or secondary education teaching certification.

The P.C. Rossin College of Engineering and Applied Science is internationally known for the quality of its professors and its research. Students receive a hands-on education and work on cutting-edge research projects with professors and with industry engineers. A co-op program allows students to work eight months for a company and still graduate in four years. The college offers the B.S. degree in biochemistry, bioengineering, chemical engineering, chemistry, civil engineering, computer engineering, computer science, electrical engineering, engineering mechanics, engineering physics, environmental engineering, fundamental sciences, industrial engineering, information and systems engineering, materials science and engineering, and mechanical engineering. The College of Engineering, with the College of Business and Economics, offers the demanding and popular Integrated Business and Engineering Honors Program and a computer science and business degree. With the College of Arts and Sciences, the engineering college offers an arts/engineering dual degree and a B.S. in bioengineering. The three colleges also offer an award-winning one-year course in integrated product development (IPD), in which student teams make and market products for corporate sponsors.

Academic Program

Students are expected to maintain regular progress toward the baccalaureate degree by carrying the normal course load of 12 to 18 credit hours each semester. They may, however, accelerate the pace by using Advanced Placement credits, summer-session study, and course overloads, and by gaining credit for courses through examination. Students in good academic standing earn their degrees by meeting the requirements of their specific degree curriculum as well as general University requirements. Students should confer with their advisers on curricular matters.

Off-Campus Arrangements

Semester and yearlong study-abroad programs are available in Australia, Austria, Belgium, China, Costa Rica, the Czech Republic, Denmark, Egypt, England, France, Germany, Ghana, Greece, Ireland, Israel, Italy, Japan, Kenya, Korea, Mexico, Russia, Scotland, Senegal, Spain, Sweden, Taiwan, and Wales. Lehigh summer-study programs are available in London and Paris and at other locations in Europe and China. All programs are approved for credit. Internships in other countries are available. Credit for off-campus study may be earned through Urban Semesters in Philadelphia and Washington, D.C., and by cross-registration with a consortium of five other Lehigh Valley colleges.

Academic Facilities

From technology to the arts, Lehigh students learn in outstanding facilities as partners with professors in research and scholarship. The Zoellner Arts Center provides a laboratory for learning, performing, and visual arts for the University and the Lehigh Valley community. Lehigh was one of America's first "wired" campuses, with information network links in every residence, classroom, and office and with large areas of wireless network access. Library and computing facilities provide access to more than 1 million print books and journals as well as a growing array of electronic databases and journals, computer software, and media collections.

Lehigh expects students to meet stringent academic demands, but the University provides support services to ensure each student ample opportunity to succeed. Lehigh's Dean of Students Office directs students toward help with academic or personal problems, legal issues, or general concerns. Lehigh offers a health center, fitness center, counseling service, drug and alcohol counseling service, testing service, and learning center. The University provides career planning and placement throughout students' undergraduate years and offers comprehensive support services for students who are members of minority groups.

Costs

Tuition in 2002–03 was $25,980; average room and board cost $7530.

Financial Aid

Lehigh offers nearly 140 merit scholarships each year based on academics, leadership, or talent in music or theater. Top Lehigh students who graduate and meet certain requirements can take a fifth year of courses, tuition-free, to earn a master's or second bachelor's degree through the President's Scholars program.

College selection should be based on educational growth opportunities, not on sticker price. Financial aid is designed to make college affordable for families unable to meets its costs. Lehigh is committed to providing need-based financial aid.

In 2002–03, Lehigh awarded more than $36 million in University grants and scholarships. Approximately 50 percent of freshmen receive financial aid awards. Financial aid packages are typically made up of a combination of scholarships/need-based grants, loans, and work-study. More than half of all incoming freshmen receive financial aid awards; the average freshman award for the 2002–03 school year was $19,156. Awards based on financial need ranged from $500 to $33,000.

In addition to providing students with extra cash to cover expenses, work-study jobs can also be a great opportunity to enhance a resume. At Lehigh, work-study positions can range from writing press releases in the Office of University Relations to working the front desk at the student health center.

Lehigh is a member of College Scholarship Service. To apply for need-based financial aid, the CSS/Profile and FAFSA are required. Financial aid application deadlines come early; the freshmen fall application deadline is January 15.

Faculty

Lehigh's 393 full-time professors, 99 percent of whom hold the terminal degree in their fields, are nationally and internationally known leaders in research and scholarship. They are committed first and foremost to undergraduate teaching and advising. It is common for a senior faculty member to teach a freshman course, and close student-faculty advising is the norm. Faculty members often meet with individual students and small groups outside of class, accompany students abroad, and participate in student governance and other activities. There are 100 part-time faculty members, and a relatively small number of graduate students are involved in laboratory assistance and review-session teaching.

Student Government

The Student Senate is an elected deliberative body that addresses student life and campus issues. Students are ensured access to the highest levels of decision making through two nonvoting representatives to the Board of Trustees.

Admission Requirements

Lehigh encourages men and women of all backgrounds to consider study at the University. All applicants should have completed 4 years of English, 3 or 4 years of mathematics, 2 to 4 years of history and social studies, 2 to 4 years of laboratory science, and 2 years of foreign language. An individual's potential cannot be fully reflected in the accumulation of units in a four-year college-preparatory program, so Lehigh considers a number of criteria in evaluating applicants, especially the strength of the high school record. The University requires either the SAT I or ACT, which must be taken by December of the senior year.

The middle 50 percent of students admitted to Lehigh score between 1210 and 1350 on the SAT I. However, the staff in Lehigh's admissions office works hard to move beyond the numbers and to look at a student's entire profile when making acceptance decisions. Admissions counselors review such factors as Advanced Placement or honors courses, evidence of special talent, and a student's leadership record. To provide prospective students with an opportunity to get to know the University and to determine if Lehigh is a good match, on-campus group or personal interviews are recommended.

Application and Information

Early-decision applications must be filed by November 15; regular applications must be submitted by January 1. Entrance exams should be taken by the January test date. Orientations for prospective students, consisting of general information sessions, campus tours, and personal interviews, are scheduled Monday through Friday. Interviews and tours are also available on some Saturdays. To schedule a visit, contact:

Bruce Gardiner, Dean of Admissions and Financial Aid
Office of Admissions
Lehigh University
27 Memorial Drive West
Bethlehem, Pennsylvania 18015

Telephone: 610-758-3100
Fax: 610-758-4361
E-mail: admissions@lehigh.edu
World Wide Web: http://www.lehigh.edu

NORTH CAROLINA AGRICULTURAL AND TECHNICAL STATE UNIVERSITY

GREENSBORO, NORTH CAROLINA

The University

North Carolina Agricultural and Technical State University was founded in 1891 as one of two land-grant institutions in the state. Originally, it was established to provide postsecondary education and training for black students. Today, the University is a comprehensive institution of higher education with an integrated faculty and student body, and it has been designated a constituent institution of the University of North Carolina, offering degrees at the baccalaureate, master's, and doctoral degree levels. Located on a 191-acre campus, the University has 110 buildings, including single-sex and coeducational residence halls. Of a total undergraduate population of 7,982, 3,853 students are men and 4,129 are women.

North Carolina Agricultural and Technical State University (A&T) provides outstanding academic programs through five undergraduate schools, two colleges, and a graduate school.

The mission of the University is to provide an intellectual setting in which students may find a sense of belonging, responsibility, and achievement that prepares them for roles of leadership and service in the communities where they will live and work. In this sense, the University serves as a laboratory for the development of excellence in teaching, research, and public service. As a result, A&T today stands as an example of well-directed higher education for all students.

Student life at the University is active and purposeful. The broad objective of the program provided by Student Development Services is to aid students in attaining the attitudes, understandings, insights, and skills that enable them to be socially competent. The program places special emphasis on campus relationships and experiences that complement formal instruction. Some of the services available are counseling, housing, health, and placement services. There is a University Student Union, and there are special services for international and minority students, veterans, and handicapped students. The University also provides a well-balanced program of activities to foster the moral, spiritual, cultural, and physical development of its students.

Location

Greensboro, North Carolina, is 300 miles south of Washington, D.C., and 349 miles north of Atlanta. It is readily accessible by air, bus, and automobile. The city offers a variety of cultural and recreational activities and facilities. These include sports events, concerts, bowling, boating, fishing, tennis, golf, and other popular forms of recreation. There are major shopping centers, churches, theaters, and medical facilities near the University. The heavy concentration of factories, service industries, government agencies, and shopping centers provides many job opportunities for students who desire part-time employment.

Majors and Degrees

North Carolina Agricultural and Technical State University grants the following degrees: Bachelor of Arts, Bachelor of Science, Bachelor of Fine Arts, Bachelor of Science in Nursing, and Bachelor of Social Work.

The School of Agriculture and Environmental Sciences offers programs in agricultural and biosystems engineering, agricultural economics, agricultural economics (agricultural business), agricultural education, agricultural education (agricultural extension), agricultural science–earth and environmental science (earth and environmental science, landscape horticulture design, plant science, soil science), agricultural science–natural resources (plant science), animal science, animal science (animal industry), child development, child development–early education and family studies B–K (teaching), family and consumer science (fashion merchandising and design), family and consumer science education, food and nutritional sciences, laboratory animal science, and landscape architecture.

In the College of Arts and Sciences, programs are available in applied mathematics, biology, biology–secondary education, broadcast production, chemistry, chemistry–secondary education, electronic/media journalism, English, English–secondary education, French, French–Romance languages and literatures, French–secondary education, history, history–secondary education, journalism and mass communications, mathematics, mathematics–secondary education, media management, music education, music–general, music–performance, physics, physics–secondary education, political science, print journalism, professional theater, psychology, public relations, sociology, social work, Spanish–Romance languages and literatures, Spanish–secondary education, speech, speech (speech pathology/audiology), visual arts–art education, and visual arts–design.

The School of Business and Economics offers programs in accounting, business education, business education (administrative systems, vocational business education, vocational business education–data processing), economics, finance, management, management (management information systems), marketing, and transportation.

In the School of Education, programs are available in elementary education, health and physical education (fitness/wellness management), health and physical education (teaching), recreation administration, and special education.

In the College of Engineering, programs are offered in architectural engineering, chemical engineering, civil engineering, computer science, electrical engineering, industrial engineering, and mechanical engineering.

The School of Nursing grants the Bachelor of Science in Nursing (B.S.N.) degree.

The School of Technology has programs in construction management, electronics technology, graphic communication systems, manufacturing systems, occupational safety and health, technology education, and vocational industrial education.

Academic Program

Students must complete a minimum of 124 semester hours to earn a bachelor's degree; the exact number varies with the program. Students are also required to demonstrate competence in English and mathematics.

As complements to the academic programs, the University's Army and Air Force ROTC programs and cooperative education program provide excellent opportunities for students to enrich their educational experiences. The ROTC programs are designed to prepare college graduates for military service careers. The cooperative education program provides an opportunity for qualified students to alternate periods of study on campus and meaningful employment off campus in private industrial or business firms or government agencies.

Academic Facilities

The University library has current holdings that include 507,036 book volumes and bound periodicals, as well as 5,446 current serials. As a select depository in North Carolina for U.S. government documents, the library contains a collection of more than 250,000 official publications. Among the library's other holdings are a collection of audiovisuals and 1,038,474 microforms, archives, and special collections in black studies and teacher-education materials. Special services are provided through formal and informal library instruction, interlibrary loans, and photocopying facilities.

The University's educational support centers are the Learning Assistance Center, the Audiovisual Center, the Closed Circuit Television Facility, a 1,000-watt student-operated educational radio station, the Computer Center, the Reading Center, the Language Laboratory, and the Center for Manpower Research and Training. The H. Clinton Taylor Art Gallery and the African Heritage Center are two exceptional art museums on campus. Throughout the year, these museums have on display a number of special exhibits of sculpture, paintings, graphics, and other media.

Costs

In 2002–03, tuition and fees for North Carolina residents were $2630 per year; for nonresidents of the state, they were $11,551. Board and lodging for the academic year were $4645.

Financial Aid

Through the student financial aid program, the University makes every effort to ensure that no qualified student is denied the opportunity to attend because of a lack of funds. Students who demonstrate financial need and have the potential to achieve academic success at the University may obtain assistance to meet their expenses in accordance with the funds available. Financial aid is awarded without regard to race, religion, color, national origin, or sex. The University provides financial aid for students from four basic sources: grants, scholarships, loans, and employment. To apply for aid, students must submit the Free Application for Federal Student Aid (FAFSA). The priority filing deadline is March 15 for fall semester. North Carolina residents may call 800-443-0835 (toll-free).

Faculty

The University's teaching faculty consists of 600 highly qualified members, of whom 88 percent hold the doctoral degree or the first professional degree in their discipline. Faculty members are recruited from many areas and backgrounds, thereby bringing together a diverse cadre of academic professionals from many nations.

Student Government

The Student Government Association (SGA), composed of senators elected from the student body, is primarily a policy-recommending group and represents the views and concerns of the students. The president of SGA reports directly to the vice-chancellor for student affairs. In addition, each student organization is represented by a senator, and these senators sit on the Faculty Senate.

Admission Requirements

Applicants for undergraduate admission are considered individually and in accordance with criteria applied flexibly to ensure that applicants with unusual qualifications are not denied admission. However, admission for out-of-state freshman students is competitive due to an 18 percent out-of-state enrollment cap. Students who are applying for admission as freshmen are expected to have completed a college-preparatory program in high school and taken the SAT I or the ACT. General requirements include graduation from an accredited high school with 16 units of credit, with no more than 4 units in vocational subjects and with at least 2 units in physical education; a satisfactory score on the SAT I or ACT; and a respectable GPA and/or class rank. The General Educational Development (GED) test score results or a high school equivalency certificate from the state department of education may be submitted in lieu of the high school transcript for applicants receiving equivalency before January 1988.

North Carolina A&T State University welcomes applications from graduates of accredited community, technical, and junior colleges and from students who wish to transfer from other senior colleges.

Application and Information

The suggested application deadline for students who expect to live on campus is February 1; for commuting students, it is June 1. Applications are processed upon the receipt of the completed application form with the application fee of $35, official transcripts, and SAT I or ACT scores. Out-of-state admission is limited; therefore, applications for admission should be filed by February 1.

To arrange an interview or a visit to the campus, students should contact:

Office of Admissions
B. C. Webb Hall
North Carolina Agricultural and Technical State University
Greensboro, North Carolina 27411

Telephone: 336-334-7946 or 7947
800-443-8964 (toll-free in North Carolina)
World Wide Web: http://www.ncat.edu

A professor and students in the chemical engineering lab.

THOMAS MORE COLLEGE

CRESTVIEW HILLS, KENTUCKY

The College

Thomas More College is a small, private, Catholic liberal arts college affiliated with the Diocese of Covington, Kentucky. The College was ranked in the top tier of Southern liberal arts colleges by *U.S. News & World Report* in their 2003 "America's Best Colleges" issue. Thomas More College fulfills its liberal arts commitment by maintaining an atmosphere and curriculum that give students the opportunity to grow academically, spiritually, and professionally.

Of the diverse student population of 1,446, there are 776 attending classes full-time; 240 are resident students. A new residence hall opened in fall 2002, adding 160 spaces to the College's expanding student life program. The student body is drawn primarily from the states of Kentucky, Ohio, and Indiana, but many other states and a number of countries are also represented. Students who choose to live on campus reside in one of three town-house-style residence halls. All residence halls offer comfortable, air-conditioned rooms; Internet and cable TV access; and free laundry facilities. The new 27,000-square-foot Holbrook Student Center contains a spacious bookstore, computer and study lounges, student activity offices, a TV and game room, food court, and dance rehearsal studio.

The students' college experience is enhanced through their participation in many academic, social, and sports organizations. Intercollegiate athletics are governed by NCAA Division III. Thomas More College competes in men's baseball, basketball, football, golf, soccer, and tennis and women's basketball, fast-pitch softball, soccer, tennis, and volleyball. Intramural sports offered include, among others, coed flag football, basketball, and volleyball. The campus contains a new on-campus football stadium; baseball, soccer, and softball fields; and volleyball and basketball courts as well as training and health facilities. Students can also enjoy world-class facilities for swimming, tennis, racquetball, basketball, and a complete fitness area at the Four Seasons Sports Club, adjacent to the campus.

Location

Thomas More College is located 10 minutes south of Cincinnati, Ohio, in Crestview Hills, Kentucky. The campus is convenient to major highways. The Greater Cincinnati/Northern Kentucky International Airport is just 10 minutes away. All students are permitted to have cars on campus.

The Greater Cincinnati area offers a wide array of cultural and sporting events. Local attractions include the Broadway Series, the Cincinnati Pops, the Riverbend Music Center, and the Cincinnati Reds and Bengals. Numerous shopping areas and restaurants are also available.

Majors and Degrees

Thomas More College offers bachelor's degrees in accounting, art, biology, business administration, chemistry, computer information systems, criminal justice, drama, economics, education, English, history, international studies, mathematics, medical technology, nursing, philosophy, physics, psychology, sociology, speech communication, and theology.

Preprofessional programs are available in dentistry, law, medicine, occupational therapy, optometry, pharmacy, physical therapy, and veterinary science. There is a 3-2 program in engineering.

The Associate of Arts degree is available in accounting, art, art history, biology, business administration, chemistry, computer information systems, criminal justice, drama, economics, English, exercise science, French, gerontology, history, international studies, math, philosophy, physics, political science, prelegal studies, psychology, sociology, Spanish, speech communication, and theology.

Academic Program

To earn the Bachelor of Arts, Bachelor of Science, or Bachelor of Science in Nursing degree, a student must complete 128 credit hours, including 61 credit hours in liberal arts courses. The Associate of Arts degree requires the completion of 64 credit hours, including a liberal arts component.

The academic calendar is composed of a fall and a spring semester and two summer sessions. The Office of Continuing Education offers a full schedule of evening and Saturday classes.

The Cooperative Education program enables students to gain hands-on professional experience in their field of interest. All students are eligible for this program after the completion of their freshman year. Cooperative Air Force and Army ROTC programs are available in conjunction with nearby universities.

Off-Campus Arrangements

Thirteen area colleges, including Thomas More College, form the Greater Cincinnati Consortium of Colleges and Universities through which all students at the local member colleges may take courses not available at their home institution. Thomas More encourages full-time students to take advantage of this opportunity for curriculum enrichment through cross-registration. In addition, students who wish to study abroad as part of their undergraduate education have a number of possibilities open to them.

Academic Facilities

The library has a collection of more than 130,000 volumes of books, periodicals, and audiovisual materials, and as a selective depository it houses more than 12,000 volumes of U.S. government documents. In addition, the library's membership in the Greater Cincinnati Library Consortium gives Thomas More students access to more than 10.6 million books and more than 50,000 periodicals held by forty-four other libraries in the region.

Thomas More's computer facilities include a PC classroom and three labs containing Pentium 350 PCs for student use. Student computers are also available in some academic departments and in the library. All PCs are connected to a campuswide Novell network, with access to e-mail, the Internet, and an on-campus Intranet server. There is a laser printer in each lab and a color laser printer and scanner in the PC lab in the main computer center. Software includes Microsoft Windows 98, Office 97 and Visual Studio; Adobe PageMaker and Illustrator; MicroFocus COBOL; and additional software used for departmental instruction.

Students in the science programs receive hands-on experience through the use of the advanced biology, chemistry, and physics laboratories. The facilities include an environmental chamber, an aquatic research station, research and measurement labs, a synthesis lab, a light-sensitive project room, and a machine and electronics shop.

The nursing and sociology departments have excellent working relationships with nearby hospitals and social service agencies.

Costs

The 2002–03 annual costs for Thomas More College were $14,200 for tuition and $5300 for room (double occupancy) and board. There was a differential fee of $30 per semester hour for all nursing courses. The Student Government fee was $50 per semester and the computer fee was $100 per semester for full-time students. The cost of books was estimated at $600 per year.

Financial Aid

Thomas More College assists approximately 90 percent of its full-time students in meeting college costs. Awards are determined on a rolling basis, with priority consideration given to applications filed by March 1. Financial aid awards are based on economic need, merit, scholastic achievement, and extracurricular activities. ROTC scholarships are also available. The filing of the Free Application for Federal Student Aid (FAFSA) and the Thomas More College Application for Financial Aid and Scholarship is required before any awards are determined. Other Thomas More College awards may require additional applications.

An extensive Federal Work-Study program is in place, and there are excellent opportunities for outside employment in the immediate area.

Faculty

The faculty is committed to the ideals of a Catholic liberal arts education with the main focus on teaching. The faculty has 174 members, of whom 30 percent hold tenure and 62 percent hold doctoral or other terminal degrees. Faculty members serve as academic advisers to students in their disciplines. The student-faculty ratio is 14:1.

Student Government

The purpose of the Student Government Association is to serve as the official representative organization of the Thomas More College student body; to serve as the liaison between the student body and the faculty, administration, and Board of Trustees; to promote student projects and activities and improve the quality of student life; to assist the Dean of Students in supervising student organizations and student activities on campus; to protect the rights of the individual; and to preserve the general welfare of the student body of Thomas More College.

Admission Requirements

The admission criteria are as follows: an applicant should have a high school grade point average (based on college-preparatory courses) of 80 percent or better; a high school rank in the top half of the graduating class; and a minimum composite score of 20 on the ACT Assessment, with a minimum of 20 in English, or a minimum combined score of 1010 on the SAT I, with a minimum of 530 on the verbal portion. If the applicant does not meet all the admission criteria, the file is forwarded to the Admissions Committee for individual consideration.

Transfer students with 24 or more semester hours of transferable credit and an overall grade point average of at least 2.0 on a 4.0 scale are automatically accepted. Transfer students with fewer than 24 transferable hours must meet the general admission criteria.

The applicant must provide a completed application with a nonrefundable $25 fee (waived for online applicants), high school transcripts, college transcripts (if applicable), and ACT or SAT I score reports.

Application and Information

Thomas More College operates under a rolling admission policy, with a final application deadline of August 15. Admission decisions are usually made within two weeks of receiving all application materials. Students can apply online at the Web site listed below. The $25 application fee is waived for online applications.

For further information or to schedule a campus visit, students should contact:

Bob McDermott
Director of Admissions
Thomas More College
333 Thomas More Parkway
Crestview Hills, Kentucky 41017
Telephone: 859-344-3332
800-825-4557 (toll-free)
E-mail: bob.mcdermott@thomasmore.edu
World Wide Web: http://www.thomasmore.edu

Residence life on the Thomas More College campus.

THE UNIVERSITY OF ALABAMA IN HUNTSVILLE

HUNTSVILLE, ALABAMA

UAH
The University of Alabama in Huntsville

The University

The University of Alabama in Huntsville (UAH) is a public, four-year, coeducational institution and is a member of the University of Alabama System. UAH was founded in 1950 as an extension center of the University of Alabama and became an autonomous campus in 1969. UAH has earned national recognition in engineering and the sciences, and its programs in the humanities, fine arts, social sciences, business, and nursing are outstanding. Students interact with some of the most productive researchers in their respective disciplines. Close ties with business, industry, and government give students real-world opportunities and experience. UAH is a partner with more than 100 high-tech industries as well as major federal laboratories such as NASA's Marshall Space Flight Center and the U.S. Army. Its unique location makes possible many co-op opportunities for students to earn much of their college costs and to maximize their employment potential. Students have many opportunities to work with some of the top scientists in the country. UAH is accredited by the Southern Association of Colleges and Schools' Commission on Colleges. In addition, UAH holds professional accreditation from the American Chemical Society; the Computing Sciences Accreditation Board; the Accreditation Board for Engineering and Technology, Inc.; the National League for Nursing Accrediting Commission; the National Association of Schools of Music; and AACSB–The International Association for Management Education.

The fall 2002 enrollment consisted of 5,598 undergraduate and 1,447 graduate students. Eighty percent are from Alabama, 8 percent are from other countries, 50 percent are men, and 50 percent are women. UAH students represent forty-nine states and more than one hundred countries. Of the total undergraduate enrollment, 22 percent are members of ethnic minority groups. The median ACT composite range for entering students was 22-27; the median GPA was 3.4.

UAH has more than 115 active student groups and organizations, including national fraternities and sororities, honor societies, special interest groups, religious organizations, the Student Government Association (SGA), the student-run newspaper, the student-run literary magazine, minority student organizations, international student organizations, the choir, the chorus, a film and lecture series, service organizations, professional interest groups, and intramural athletics. The University is a member of the NCAA Division II and the Gulf South Conference and competes in the following intercollegiate sports: men's baseball, basketball, cross-country, soccer, and tennis and women's basketball, cross-country, soccer, softball, tennis, and volleyball. In addition, UAH competes at the NCAA Division I level in men's ice hockey.

On-campus housing is available for undergraduate and graduate students. The new North Campus Residence Hall opened in fall 2002. The Central Campus Residence Hall is a seven-story residence hall that offers private bedrooms, is located in the center of campus, and is connected to the University Center by an enclosed walkway. Student apartments in Southeast Housing are reserved for upperclassmen and graduate students. Private apartments are available for married students and students with children. Handicapped-accessible apartments are available. Meals are available in the University Center cafeteria.

The Colleges of Administrative Science, Engineering, Liberal Arts, Nursing, and Science and the School of Graduate Studies administer the degree programs of the University. Through the School of Graduate Studies, students may earn the master's degree in accounting, atmospheric science, biological science, chemical engineering, chemistry, civil engineering, computer engineering, computer science, electrical engineering, English, history, industrial and systems engineering, management, management information systems, management of technology, materials science, mathematics, mechanical engineering, nursing, operations research, physics, psychology, and public affairs. The Ph.D. degree is awarded in applied mathematics, atmospheric science, biotechnology, computer engineering, computer science, electrical engineering, industrial and systems engineering, materials science, mechanical engineering, optical science and engineering, and physics.

Location

The University of Alabama in Huntsville is located in the Tennessee River Valley of north-central Alabama, 100 miles north of Birmingham and 100 miles south of Nashville, Tennessee. Huntsville is home to more than fifty Fortune 500 companies that specialize in high technology, including aerospace engineering, rocket propulsion, computer technology, weapons systems, telecommunications, software engineering, information systems design, and engineering services. Most of these companies are located in one of the top ten research parks in the world and the second-largest research park in the U.S., Cummings Research Park, which is adjacent to the UAH campus.

Majors and Degrees

The College of Administrative Science awards the Bachelor of Science in Business Administration (B.S.B.A.) degree in the fields of accounting, finance, management, management information systems, and marketing. The College of Engineering awards the Bachelor of Science in Engineering (B.S.E.) degree in the following engineering disciplines: chemical, civil, computer, electrical, industrial and systems, mechanical, and optical. The College of Nursing awards the Bachelor of Science in Nursing (B.S.N.) degree. The Bachelor of Arts (B.A.) degree is awarded by the College of Liberal Arts in the fields of art, communication arts, education, English, foreign languages and international trade, history, music, philosophy, political science, psychology, and sociology. In the College of Science, the Bachelor of Science (B.S.) degree is available in biological science, chemistry, computer science, mathematics, and physics. A Bachelor of Arts degree is available in biological science and mathematics.

Fifth-year certificates are available in accounting and education for individuals who already hold a bachelor's degree in another field. Undergraduate teacher certification programs are offered in the following areas: art education (N–12), elementary education (K–6), and music education (N–12) and in secondary/high school education (4–8 or 7–12), with majors in biology, chemistry, English, French, general science, German, history, language arts, mathematics, physics, social science, and Spanish.

Academic Program

The general education course work is designed to broaden intellectual awareness and enhance cultural literacy and analytical thinking. All undergraduates are required to complete course work in English composition, humanities and fine arts, history, social and behavioral sciences, natural and physical sciences, and mathematics. B.A., B.S., B.S.B.A., and

B.S.N. degrees require the completion of at least 128 total semester hours; B.S.E. degrees in electrical and industrial and systems engineering require 129; the B.S.E. in chemical engineering, 134; B.S.E. degrees in civil and mechanical engineering, 133; the B.S.E. in optical engineering, 137; and the B.A. in music, 134. A variety of special academic programs and options are available, including academic remediation, accelerated degree completion, cooperative education, cross-registration with other institutions, distance learning, double majors, dual enrollment, English as a second language, an honors program, independent study, internships, and learning disabilities services. Credit is awarded for appropriate scores on CLEP and AP examinations. UAH offers Army ROTC at a participating institution off campus. Special services are available for handicapped students, including note-taking services, readers, tape recorders, tutors, interpreters for the hearing impaired, special transportation, special housing, adaptive equipment, and Braille services. The fall 2003 semester begins August 25 and ends December 18; spring semester 2004 begins January 12 and ends May 4. Two summer sessions are offered and begin May 24 and June 28, 2003.

Academic Facilities

The 376-acre campus is in northwest Huntsville. All academic buildings have been constructed since 1960 and exemplify modern functional design. The UAH library houses more than 400,000 books, serial backfiles, and government documents; more than 2,000 current serials; and more than 420,000 microforms. The UAH Art Gallery hosts art exhibits by local, regional, and national artists as well as by students and faculty members. More than 300 personal computers are available across the campus for student use. Computer labs, one of which is open 24 hours a day, are located in several buildings and are staffed to provide assistance. Access to the University fiber-optic network is available in all buildings, including the Central Campus Residence Hall. Internet access and e-mail are available to all students. UAH has a number of state-of-the-art research labs that are accessible to undergraduates.

Costs

In 2002–03, tuition for undergraduate Alabama residents was $3764 (15 credits each semester) for the academic year. Out-of-state students paid $7940 (15 credits each semester) for the academic year. Undergraduates can expect to spend approximately $720 on books and supplies for the academic year. Undergraduate students pay an estimated $3200 for room, $1400 for board, $900 for transportation, and $1200 for personal and miscellaneous expenses per year.

Financial Aid

UAH awards more than $20 million annually in need-based and non-need-based financial aid in the form of scholarships, grants, loans, and campus jobs. The following financial aid programs are available: Federal Stafford Student Loans (subsidized and unsubsidized), Federal PLUS Loans, Consolidation Loans, Federal Pell Grants, Federal Supplemental Educational Opportunity Grants (FSEOG), state scholarships and grants, private scholarships, and institutional scholarships. Non-need-based scholarships are available for athletics, ROTC, academic merit, creative and performing arts, special achievement, leadership skills, and minority status. Students should submit the Free Application for Federal Student Aid (FAFSA) and the UAH financial aid form before April 1 for priority consideration and no later than the final closing date of July 31. Award notifications are made on a rolling basis. The priority date for scholarship application is February 1.

Faculty

Of the 284 full-time instructional faculty members, 91 percent hold the Ph.D. or other terminal degree in their field. The student-faculty ratio is 14:1. Graduate students teach 13 percent of introductory undergraduate courses. The average introductory lecture class size is 18.

Student Government

The primary purpose of the Student Government Association is to help improve the educational environment and promote the welfare of students in all areas of University life. The SGA is responsible for developing and sponsoring programs that enrich the students' cultural, intellectual, and social life. An executive branch, a 15-member legislature, and a 5-member arbitration board are responsible for carrying out the official business of the organization. The SGA sponsors more than 110 clubs and organizations in addition to providing many student services, such as health insurance, special rates for community cultural events, and a student directory.

Admission Requirements

High school graduates may be admitted as regular freshmen based on acceptable high school achievement and standardized test scores (SAT I or ACT), which are considered together. A higher result in one area offsets a lower performance in the other. For example, a minimum high school GPA of 3.0 is required if the ACT composite score is 18 or the combined SAT I score is 850. A high school GPA of 2.0 requires an ACT composite score of 23 or higher or a combined SAT I score of 1050 or higher. Applicants should present a minimum of 20 Carnegie high school units, including 4 units of English, 3 of social studies, 1 of algebra, 1 of geometry, 1 of biology (recommended), 1 of chemistry/physics (required by the Colleges of Engineering and Science and recommended by all other Colleges), 1 of algebra II/trigonometry (one each required by the College of Engineering and recommended by all other Colleges), and sufficient academic electives to meet the required 20 units. First-time freshmen and transfer students are admitted for every academic term. Transfer students with fewer than 18 hours of earned college credit are admitted based on high school transcripts, test scores, and college course work. Transfer students are required to submit transcripts of all university work and have at least a 2.0 average on all work attempted to qualify for regular admission.

Application and Information

Completed applications and a nonrefundable $20 application fee should be sent by August 1 for admission in the fall semester and by December 15 for admission in the spring semester. Admission notifications are sent on a rolling basis.

For an application form and more information, students should contact:

Office of Admissions
The University of Alabama in Huntsville
301 Sparkman Drive
Huntsville, Alabama 35899
Telephone: 256-824-6070
800-UAH-CALL (toll-free)
Fax: 256-824-6073
E-mail: admitme@email.uah.edu
World Wide Web: http://www.uah.edu

UNIVERSITY OF ARKANSAS

FAYETTEVILLE, ARKANSAS

The University

Established in 1871, the University of Arkansas (U of A) is the flagship campus of the University of Arkansas System. The University offers more than 215 undergraduate and graduate degrees in more than 150 fields of study in agricultural, food, and life sciences; architecture; the arts and sciences; business; education; education and health professions; engineering; and law. The University is also recognized as the only comprehensive doctoral degree–granting institution in the state. Fayetteville's 345-acre campus is home to students from all counties in Arkansas, every state in the U.S., and more than one hundred countries throughout the world. The enrollment for the 2002–03 school year was approximately 16,035 students (12,929 in undergraduate programs) and included a diverse student population, with 892 international students representing 107 countries.

Students choosing to live on campus may select from a diverse array of residential experiences. Many new students opt for a hall offering the First Year Experience program designed to support students academically, culturally, socially, and personally as they transition into the University. The Honors Hall is also among the more popular residences, along with specialized floors for specific academic fields and 24-hour quiet floors.

Among the 150 fields of study offered at the University, specialist and master's degrees are offered in ninety-six fields. The College of Education and Health Professions has recently added six degree programs, including a Master of Arts in Teaching and four Ph.D. programs. The School of Law offers a skilled and scholarly faculty of teaching and practicing lawyers. The National Center for Agricultural Law Research and Information has been praised for its research and publications and makes possible the law school's unique degree offering in agricultural law.

Location

The city of Fayetteville is a community of more than 60,000 people that was rated by *Money* magazine as one of the top ten most desirable places in the nation in which to live or work. Fayetteville is nestled in the Ozark Mountains near lakes and rivers but is accessible to major metropolitan amenities, making it an excellent place for a well-balanced college experience.

Majors and Degrees

Named for Senator J. William Fulbright, the Fulbright College of Arts and Sciences is the largest of the U of A colleges, with seventeen departments offering concentrations in advertising and public relations, anthropology, architectural studies, art, art history, biochemistry, biology, botany, broadcast journalism, chemistry, classical studies, communication, computer science, criminal justice, drama, earth science, economics, English, French, geography, geology, German, history, journalism, magazine journalism, mathematics, microbiology, music, philosophy, physics, political science, psychology, social work, sociology, Spanish, and zoology. The Dale Bumpers College of Agricultural, Food and Life Sciences offers more than twenty-five majors that give students the ability to improve agriculture and the family environment. The School of Architecture offers majors in architecture and landscape architecture.

The Sam M. Walton College of Business Administration offers programs in accounting, administrative management, business economics, computer information systems (with a concentration in accounting), finance (banking, insurance, and real estate), financial management, general business, human resource management, industrial management, industrial marketing, international economics and business, marketing management, public administration, quantitative analysis, retail marketing, small business/entrepreneurship, and transportation. Preparing professionals for research, teaching, and service-oriented positions, the College of Education and Health Professions offers majors in art education (K–12), athletic training, business education, commercial recreation, elementary education, exercise science, health sciences, industrial education, kinesiology (K–12), music education (K–12), outdoor recreation, public recreation, secondary education, speech pathology–audiology, teaching the mildly handicapped, and therapeutic recreation as well as a Bachelor of Science in Nursing degree. The College of Engineering offers programs in biological and agricultural engineering, chemical engineering, civil engineering, computer systems engineering, electrical engineering, industrial engineering, and mechanical engineering.

Academic Program

The U of A operates on a traditional two-semester academic year schedule, with two regular summer sessions and some special concurrent summer sessions. Requirements for graduation include a minimum University-wide core along with core requirements in each college. The majority of undergraduate degree offerings follow a four-year plan requiring from 124 to 136 course hours for graduation; there are some exceptions to this requirement, such as the five-year, design-oriented architecture program, which requires 163 hours.

A course in English as a second language is offered in five 9-week sessions throughout the year. Classes focus on all language skills: grammar, reading, writing, and listening/speaking.

Off-Campus Arrangements

The University conducts extensive cooperative education programs through several colleges that offer off-campus opportunities for work or learning in other cities and countries.

Academic Facilities

The University library contains nearly 1.5 million volumes, approximately 14,168 subscriptions to periodicals and journals, 3.2 million titles on microform, and more than 19,400 recordings. The University of Arkansas also provides computer labs with both IBM and Macintosh stations at locations across campus, some open around the clock. Recent renovations in the fine arts center provide stunning gallery and theater facilities. The state-of-the-art Bell Engineering Center is a recently built multimillion-dollar facility offering the optimum in computer capabilities and laboratory research. The Writing Center is a program offered to students to aid them in English grammar and style to further develop literacy skills and stimulate creativity. The Center of Excellence for Poultry Science is a $22-million facility offering the finest training for poultry scientists in the U.S.

Costs

For the 2002–03 school year, the average full-time tuition rate for in-state students (Arkansas residents) was $3573 per semester; nonresidents paid $8674. Students from neighboring states with an ACT score of 24 and a 3.0 GPA are eligible to pay in-state rates. Room and board costs for students on campus ranged from $2216 to $2328 per semester. Additional fees included a $6-per-hour student health fee, an $8-per-hour media fee, and a $10 student activity fee per semester. College miscellaneous fees, such as laboratory enhancement fees, ranged from $67 to $287. Students age 60 and older may have the fees waived for credit courses on a space-available basis. For international students, the annual nine-month academic year costs totaled $18,890 and included tuition, fees, housing, health insurance, books and supplies, equipment fees, and personal expenses. Summer living and full-time enrollment costs for a resident undergraduate totaled approximately $4754.58.

Financial Aid

A completed application for admission is required for students wishing to receive institutional, federal, or scholarship aid. Students are encouraged to visit U of A's scholarship Web site at http://www.uark.edu/scholarships to review the various scholarship programs available to new and returning students. A Free Application for Federal Student Aid (FAFSA) is required of all students requesting federal assistance such as student loans, Federal Pell Grants and Work Study. Some loans and campus employment do not require these forms and are also available to the students. To receive priority consideration for scholarships, a student enrolling for the fall semester must submit an application for admission by February 15. The fall scholarship deadline for international and transfer students is March 15.

Faculty

The University has 791 full-time faculty members, the majority of whom hold the highest degree in their field. There are 49 part-time faculty members, as well as 3,616 staff members, including 1,183 graduate assistants. For international students, an international student adviser and a fully staffed International Programs Office are available to assist with orientation sessions, immigration counseling, and activities programming.

Student Government

The University of Arkansas offers students the opportunity to participate in various forms of campus government. The Associated Student Government, the Off-Campus Student Government, Residents' Interhall Congress, the Interfraternity Council, and the Panhellenic Council are the main governing bodies that aid students in expressing their opinions or interests to the faculty, administration, and community.

Admission Requirements

Entering freshmen are advised to prepare for admission to the U of A while in high school by taking 4 years of English and 3 years each of math, social studies, natural sciences, and academic electives. For the best possible chance of being admitted to the University of Arkansas, students should have a minimum average of a B (3.0) and try to score a minimum of 20 on the ACT or 930 on the SAT I. The ACT code for the U of A is 0144, and the SAT I code is 6866. Transfer students must have an overall GPA of at least 2.0 on all college course work attempted. Any transfer student with fewer than 24 hours must also meet the requirements for entering freshmen.

International students must have above-average secondary school records, and those who are not native speakers of English must submit a minimum TOEFL score of 550 (paper) or 213 (computer). The University of Arkansas offers qualified applicants conditional admission to the Spring International Language Center, with academic admission granted upon reaching a satisfactory English language level.

Application and Information

To enroll in the University, students must submit a completed Application for Undergraduate Admission and an application fee of $30. An online admission form can be found at the University's Web site listed below. The priority application deadline for the fall semester is February 15 for freshman enrollment. Transfer students are advised to apply by March 15. The spring deadline is January 1. The student must also request that official transcripts be mailed to the Office of Admissions. A preliminary admission is provided for those high school seniors who have a transcript of six or seven semesters, but a final transcript is needed to certify high school graduation. ACT or SAT I scores no more than four years old must be submitted by all entering freshmen and transfer students with fewer than 24 transferable hours. These scores must be sent directly to the Office of Admissions from the testing agency or on an official high school transcript.

International students must submit an application for admission with a $50 application fee. A financial statement, a TOEFL score, and official secondary and postsecondary academic recorded are also required. For the fall term, the application deadline is May 1; the summer term deadline is March 1; and the spring term deadline is October 1. International students can download the undergraduate application at http://www.uark.edu.

For further information, students should contact:

Ed Schroeder
Office of Admissions
200 Silas H. Hunt Hall
University of Arkansas
Fayetteville, Arkansas 72701
Telephone: 479-575-5346
800-377-UOFA (toll-free)
479-575-6246 (international)
Fax: 479-575-7515
E-mail: uofadmis@uark.edu
uaiao@uark.edu (international)
World Wide Web: http://www.uark.edu

A friendly campus, the University of Arkansas offers a wide range of academic majors and campus activities for student involvement.

UNIVERSITY OF WEST FLORIDA

PENSACOLA, FLORIDA

The University

One of the eleven state universities of Florida, the University of West Florida (UWF) enrolls approximately 9,200 students in its Colleges of Arts and Sciences, Business, and Professional Studies. The University of West Florida, which opened in fall 1967, is located on a 1,600-acre nature preserve 10 miles north of downtown Pensacola. The University's facilities, valued at more than $81 million, have been designed to complement the natural beauty of the site.

The University currently enrolls students from forty-seven states and sixty countries. Students and professors enjoy a relationship that is more common at a small, private college. Approximately 865 freshmen began their studies at UWF last year. The middle 50 percent statistics for the class are as follows: high school grade point average ranged from 2.8 to 3.8; SAT I total score ranged from 980 to 1160; and ACT composite ranged from 20 to 26.

In addition to its undergraduate programs, UWF also offers the master's degree in twenty-nine areas of study and specialist and Ed.D. degrees in education.

UWF operates centers in downtown Pensacola and at Eglin Air Force Base, a branch campus in Fort Walton Beach (in conjunction with a local community college), and a Navy program office at Naval Air Station Pensacola. In addition, UWF owns 152 acres of beachfront property on nearby Santa Rosa Island, adjacent to the Gulf Islands National Seashore. Available for both recreation and research, this property provides special opportunities for students pursuing degrees in marine biology and coastal studies.

The University of West Florida is a member of the NCAA Division II. Men's sports include baseball, basketball, cross-country, golf, soccer, and tennis. Women's sports include basketball, cross-country, golf, soccer, softball, tennis, and volleyball. Students also participate in more than nineteen intramural sports and twenty club sports. The Program Council and the Residence Hall Advisory Council provide activities and events open to the entire campus community. The University serves as host to six national fraternities and five national sororities; 110 professional, academic, and religious organizations are open to UWF students.

A natatorium housing an Olympic-size pool adjoins the Field House, center for indoor sports and large-group activities and events. Varsity soccer fields, tennis courts, handball and racquetball courts, jogging trails, picnic areas, and sites for canoeing are available on campus. Varsity baseball and softball fields and a lighted track complete the UWF sports complex. Sailing and waterskiing facilities are nearby, and campus nature trails attract thousands of visitors annually.

Students may choose to live on or off campus. The Office of Housing oversees 1,250 total residence hall spaces that include low-rise residence halls, two- or four-bedroom residence hall apartments that are equipped with modern conveniences, and two new residence halls, one with 300 spaces and the other with 200 spaces.

There are also various apartment complexes conveniently located just beyond the campus.

Location

Students and visitors alike delight in the beauty of the campus, which is nestled in the rolling hills outside Pensacola, Florida. Wide verandas, massive moss-draped oaks, and spacious lawns capture the traditional charm and grace of the South, while modern architecture and state-of-the-art facilities blend in naturally among loblolly pines and meandering walkways.

Only minutes from the campus gate are the emerald waters and white beaches of the Gulf of Mexico and the Gulf Islands National Seashore, one of the nation's most beautiful beaches. The Pensacola area attracts vacationers from all around the country to its historic Seville Square, golf tournaments, sailing regattas, restaurants on the bay, and a variety of art and music festivals. WUWF, the University's public radio station, produces a monthly live program, Gulf Coast RadioLive. UWF is 3½ hours from New Orleans, 1 hour from Mobile, 3 hours from Tallahassee, and 5 hours from Atlanta.

Majors and Degrees

The University of West Florida awards the bachelor's degree in forty-four undergraduate programs with many areas of specialization. Undergraduate majors are available in the College of Arts and Sciences in anthropology, art, biology, chemistry, communication arts, computer information systems, computer science, English, environmental studies, fine arts, history, interdisciplinary humanities studies, interdisciplinary information technology, interdisciplinary science, international studies, leisure studies, marine biology, mathematics, medical technology, music, nursing, philosophy, physics, pre-engineering, preprofessional studies, psychology, social sciences (interdisciplinary), studio art, and theater as well as joint electrical engineering, computer engineering, and 7-year predental B.S./D.M.D. programs with the University of Florida.

Undergraduate majors in the College of Business include accounting, economics, finance, management, management information systems, and marketing. The College of Business is accredited by AACSB International–The Association to Advance Collegiate Schools of Business.

The College of Professional Studies, which includes education programs that are accredited by the National Council for Accreditation of Teacher Education (NCATE), offers professional training and majors leading to bachelor's degrees in the following areas: criminal justice; elementary education; engineering technology; health education; health, leisure, and science; legal administration; middle school education; political science; prekindergarten/primary education; prelaw; social work; special education (emotionally handicapped, mentally handicapped, learning disabled); sports science; and vocational education. There are specialist programs in educational leadership and in curriculum and instruction and a doctoral program in curriculum and instruction.

Academic Program

A general curriculum is required for entering freshmen and for transfer students without an Associate in Arts degree from a Florida public community college. General studies provide students with a broad foundation in the liberal arts, science, and career and life planning. The academic skills of reading, writing, discourse, critical inquiry, logical thinking, and mathematical reasoning are central elements of the general studies curriculum.

Students of high ability may enter an honors program offering intensive instruction in a more individualized setting. Cooperative education programs are available in nearly every field, allowing UWF students to get a head start on their careers while paying for their education. Army and Air Force ROTC programs and scholarships are also available.

Off-Campus Arrangements

The Office of International Education and Programs arranges more than twenty study-abroad and student exchange programs on every continent except Antarctica. Participants may study in Austria, Canada, England, Finland, France, Germany, Japan, Mexico, the Netherlands, and Portugal.

Academic Facilities

The main campus consists of more than 100 buildings. One of the most prominent of these is the five-floor John C. Pace Library, which houses a collection of more than 2.3 million bound volumes and micropieces. Interconnected through computer linkages with state and national libraries for research purposes, the UWF library contains one of the finest special collections about the Gulf Coast area. Some of the items in this collection date back to the fourteenth century, and there are also a manuscript letter signed by Thomas Jefferson, books autographed by Albert Einstein, and materials carried aboard the space shuttle by UWF alumni.

Excellent science and technology laboratories for preprofessional majors, extensive video and film equipment, desktop publishing labs, an AP wire service, and an impressive computer science facility also support students' scholarly endeavors. Microcomputers, minicomputers, a diverse inventory of software, a real-time laboratory, modem linkages to residence halls, and 24-hour-a-day access to the computer center all are available to students in every field of study. Other major facilities include a Center for Fine and Performing Arts, a College of Professional Studies Complex, a Student Services Complex, and a newly renovated Commons.

Expansion and renovation continue to enhance the main campus. Ongoing renovations of the Commons feature a new bookstore, post office, and snack bar. An archaeology building and museum opened in 1999. An expansion and renovation of the student sports and recreation facility is planned for the next few years.

Costs

For fall 2002, tuition is $87.94 per credit for Florida residents and $375.90 per credit for out-of-state students. Room and board costs total $6000. The cost of books is estimated at $800. Transportation and personal expenses vary according to students' individual needs.

Financial Aid

About 60 percent of UWF students receive some form of financial aid and scholarships. UWF is committed to meeting a student's financial need. Aid is awarded on a first-come, first-served basis.

The Scholarship Program for outstanding freshmen allows students to receive early scholarship commitments as soon as they have decided to enroll in UWF. The John C. Pace Jr. scholarships are awarded to meritorious freshmen, transfers with A.A. degrees from Florida's community colleges, and minority students who are Florida residents. Awards are $1000 per year. Special scholarships for members of minority groups, National Achievement Scholars, and students with talent in the arts are all awarded through this program. Non-Florida tuition grants are awarded to outstanding freshmen and transfer students. These awards reduce the amount of out-of-state fees.

Faculty

Faculty members at the University of West Florida include published authors, scientists engaged in a wide range of research projects, and journalists skilled in advertising and filmmaking. Eighty percent of the faculty members hold doctoral degrees from major institutions throughout the United States.

Student Government

The Student Government Association is authorized to represent the student body in all matters concerning student life. The basic purposes of the student government are to provide students with an opportunity to participate in the decision-making process of the University; to review, evaluate, and allocate all student activity and service fee monies as allowed by state law (annually, some $1 million is allocated by students); to consider and make recommendations on all phases of student life; and to serve as the principal forum for discussion of matters of broad concern to the students.

Admission Requirements

The University of West Florida admits freshman applicants based on high school GPA, completion of college-preparatory courses, and test scores (either the ACT or the SAT I is accepted). Special consideration is given to applicants with special talents. College-preparatory courses should include 4 years of English; 3 each of math, social science, and natural science; 2 of the same foreign language; and 4 academic electives.

Transfer applicants with fewer than 60 hours are required to submit SAT I or ACT test scores and official transcripts from both the college(s) and the high school attended. Students transferring with 60 hours or more must submit their college transcript(s) only.

Application and Information

Students are encouraged to apply early in order to allow time for receipt of transcripts and to receive full consideration for financial aid and scholarships. Admissions decisions are made on a rolling basis. The University encourages visits to its beautiful campus and offers riding tours Monday through Friday at 10 a.m. and 1 p.m. central standard time. Students can visit the University of West Florida's home page via the Internet at the World Wide Web address listed below. Among the available features are the catalog, Saturday Open House dates, applications for admission, and the course guide for the current term. The Lighthouse Information System allows applicants to view their admission and financial aid status via the Internet.

Additional information and application materials may be obtained by writing or calling:

Office of Admissions
University of West Florida
11000 University Parkway
Pensacola, Florida 32514-5750

Telephone: 850-474-2230
E-mail: admissions@uwf.edu
World Wide Web: http://uwf.edu

The UWF Sailing Club goes out for a day of sun and recreation on Pensacola Bay.

Indexes

Majors and Degrees

A—associate degree; B—bachelor's degree

ACCOUNTING

Academy Coll, MN A
Adrian Coll, MI B
AIB Coll of Business, IA A
Alma Coll, MI B
Anderson U, IN B
Andrews U, MI B
Aquinas Coll, MI B
Ashland U, OH B
Augsburg Coll, MN B
Augustana Coll, IL B
Augustana Coll, SD B
Aurora U, IL B
Avila U, MO B
Bacone Coll, OK A
Baker Coll of Auburn Hills, MI A,B
Baker Coll of Cadillac, MI A,B
Baker Coll of Clinton Township, MI A
Baker Coll of Flint, MI A,B
Baker Coll of Jackson, MI A,B
Baker Coll of Muskegon, MI A,B
Baker Coll of Owosso, MI A,B
Baker Coll of Port Huron, MI A,B
Baker U, KS B
Baldwin-Wallace Coll, OH B
Ball State U, IN B
Bellevue U, NE B
Bemidji State U, MN B
Benedictine Coll, KS A,B
Benedictine U, IL B
Bethany Coll, KS B
Bethel Coll, IN B
Bethel Coll, KS B
Bethel Coll, MN B
Black Hills State U, SD B
Bluffton Coll, OH B
Bowling Green State U, OH B
Bradley U, IL B
Briar Cliff U, IA B
Bryant and Stratton Coll, WI A
Buena Vista U, IA B
Butler U, IN B
Calumet Coll of Saint Joseph, IN A,B
Calvin Coll, MI B
Cameron U, OK B
Capital U, OH B
Cardinal Stritch U, WI B
Carroll Coll, WI B
Carthage Coll, WI B
Case Western Reserve U, OH B
Cedarville U, OH B
Central Christian Coll of Kansas, KS A,B
Central Coll, IA B
Central Methodist Coll, MO B
Central Michigan U, MI B
Central Missouri State U, MO B
Chicago State U, IL B
Clarke Coll, IA B
Cleary U, MI A,B
Cleveland State U, OH B
Coe Coll, IA B
Coll of Mount St. Joseph, OH A,B
Coll of Saint Benedict, MN B
Coll of St. Catherine, MN B
The Coll of St. Scholastica, MN B
Coll of the Ozarks, MO B
Colorado Tech U Sioux Falls Campus, SD A,B
Columbia Coll, MO B
Concordia Coll, MN B
Concordia U, IL B
Concordia U, MN B
Concordia U, NE B
Concordia U Wisconsin, WI B
Cornerstone U, MI B
Creighton U, NE B
Culver-Stockton Coll, MO B
Dakota State U, SD B
Dakota Wesleyan U, SD B
Davenport U, Grand Rapids, MI A,B
Davenport U, Kalamazoo, MI A,B
Davenport U, Lansing, MI A,B
Defiance Coll, OH B
DePaul U, IL B
Dickinson State U, ND B
Doane Coll, NE B
Dominican U, IL B
Donnelly Coll, KS A
Dordt Coll, IA B
Drake U, IA B
Drury U, MO B
East Central U, OK B
Eastern Illinois U, IL B
Eastern Michigan U, MI B
East-West U, IL B
Edgewood Coll, WI B
Elmhurst Coll, IL B
Emporia State U, KS B
Eureka Coll, IL B
Evangel U, MO A,B
Ferris State U, MI A,B
Fontbonne U, MO B
Fort Hays State U, KS B
The Franciscan U, IA B
Franciscan U of Steubenville, OH A,B
Franklin Coll, IN B
Franklin U, OH A,B
Gallipolis Career Coll, OH A
Goshen Coll, IN B
Governors State U, IL B
Grace Coll, IN B
Graceland U, IA B
Grace U, NE B
Grand Valley State U, MI B
Grand View Coll, IA B
Greenville Coll, IL B
Gustavus Adolphus Coll, MN B
Hamilton Coll, IA A
Hannibal-LaGrange Coll, MO A,B
Harris-Stowe State Coll, MO B
Haskell Indian Nations U, KS A
Hastings Coll, NE B
Heidelberg Coll, OH B
Hillsdale Coll, MI B
Hope Coll, MI B
Huntington Coll, IN B
Illinois Coll, IL B
Illinois State U, IL B
Illinois Wesleyan U, IL B
Indiana Inst of Technology, IN A,B
Indiana State U, IN B
Indiana U Bloomington, IN B
Indiana U Northwest, IN B
Indiana U–Purdue U Fort Wayne, IN B
Indiana Wesleyan U, IN A,B
International Business Coll, Fort Wayne, IN A,B
Iowa State U of Science and Technology, IA B
Iowa Wesleyan Coll, IA B
Jamestown Coll, ND B
John Carroll U, OH B
Judson Coll, IL B
Kansas State U, KS A,B
Kaplan Coll, IA A
Kent State U, OH B
Kent State U, Ashtabula Campus, OH A
Kent State U, Geauga Campus, OH A
Kent State U, Salem Campus, OH A
Kent State U, Tuscarawas Campus, OH A
Kettering U, MI B
Lake Erie Coll, OH B
Lakeland Coll, WI B
Langston U, OK B
Lewis Coll of Business, MI A
Lewis U, IL B
Lincoln Coll, Lincoln, IL A
Lincoln Coll, Normal, IL A
Lindenwood U, MO B
Loras Coll, IA B
Lourdes Coll, OH B
Loyola U Chicago, IL B
Luther Coll, IA B
MacMurray Coll, IL B
Madonna U, MI B
Malone Coll, OH B
Manchester Coll, IN A,B
Marian Coll, IN A,B
Marian Coll of Fond du Lac, WI B
Marietta Coll, OH B
Marquette U, WI B
Martin U, IN B
Marygrove Coll, MI A
Maryville U of Saint Louis, MO B
McKendree Coll, IL B
McPherson Coll, KS B
Metropolitan State U, MN B
Miami U, OH B
Miami U–Middletown Campus, OH A
Michigan State U, MI B
Michigan Technological U, MI B
MidAmerica Nazarene U, KS B
Midland Lutheran Coll, NE A,B
Midstate Coll, IL A
Millikin U, IL B
Minnesota School of Business-Richfield, MN A
Minnesota State U, Mankato, MN B
Minnesota State U, Moorhead, MN B
Minot State U, ND B
Missouri Southern State Coll, MO A,B
Missouri Valley Coll, MO B
Missouri Western State Coll, MO B
Monmouth Coll, IL B
Morningside Coll, IA B
Mount Marty Coll, SD A,B
Mount Mary Coll, WI B
Mount Mercy Coll, IA B
Mount Union Coll, OH B
Mount Vernon Nazarene U, OH B
Muskingum Coll, OH B
National American U, SD A,B
National American U–Sioux Falls Branch, SD A,B
National-Louis U, IL B
Newman U, KS B
North Central Coll, IL B
North Dakota State U, ND B
Northeastern Illinois U, IL B
Northeastern State U, OK B
Northern Illinois U, IL B
Northern Michigan U, MI B
Northern State U, SD B
North Park U, IL B
Northwestern Coll, IA B
Northwestern Coll, MN B
Northwestern Oklahoma State U, OK B
Northwest Missouri State U, MO B
Northwood U, MI A,B
Notre Dame Coll, OH B
Oakland City U, IN A,B
Oakland U, MI B
Ohio Dominican U, OH B
Ohio Northern U, OH B
The Ohio State U, OH B
Ohio U, OH B
Ohio U–Lancaster, OH A
Ohio Wesleyan U, OH B
Oklahoma Baptist U, OK B
Oklahoma Christian U, OK B
Oklahoma City U, OK B
Oklahoma Panhandle State U, OK B
Oklahoma State U, OK B
Oklahoma Wesleyan U, OK A,B
Olivet Coll, MI B
Olivet Nazarene U, IL B
Oral Roberts U, OK B
Otterbein Coll, OH B
Park U, MO B
Peru State Coll, NE B
Pittsburg State U, KS B
Presentation Coll, SD A
Purdue U, IN B
Purdue U Calumet, IN B
Purdue U North Central, IN A
Quincy U, IL B
Reformed Bible Coll, MI B
Rochester Coll, MI B
Rockford Business Coll, IL A

Rockford Coll, IL B
Rockhurst U, MO B
Rogers State U, OK A
Roosevelt U, IL B
Saginaw Valley State U, MI B
St. Ambrose U, IA B
St. Augustine Coll, IL A
St. Cloud State U, MN B
Saint John's U, MN B
Saint Joseph's Coll, IN B
Saint Louis U, MO B
Saint Mary-of-the-Woods Coll, IN B
Saint Mary's Coll, IN B
Saint Mary's Coll of Madonna U, MI B
Saint Mary's U of Minnesota, MN B
Saint Mary U, KS B
St. Norbert Coll, WI B
Saint Xavier U, IL B
Sanford-Brown Coll, Fenton, MO A
Shawnee State U, OH A
Siena Heights U, MI A,B
Silver Lake Coll, WI B
Simpson Coll, IA B
Si Tanka Huron U, SD A,B
Southeastern Oklahoma State U, OK B
Southeast Missouri State U, MO B
Southern Illinois U Carbondale, IL B
Southern Illinois U Edwardsville, IL B
Southern Nazarene U, OK B
Southwest Baptist U, MO A,B
Southwestern Oklahoma State U, OK B
Southwest Minnesota State U, MN A,B
Southwest Missouri State U, MO B
Spring Arbor U, MI B
Stephens Coll, MO B
Tabor Coll, KS B
Taylor U, IN B
Tiffin U, OH A,B
Trinity Christian Coll, IL B
Trinity International U, IL B
Tri-State U, IN A,B
Truman State U, MO B
Union Coll, NE B
The U of Akron, OH B
U of Central Oklahoma, OK B
U of Cincinnati, OH A,B
U of Dayton, OH B
U of Dubuque, IA A,B
U of Evansville, IN B
The U of Findlay, OH A,B
U of Illinois at Chicago, IL B
U of Illinois at Springfield, IL B
U of Illinois at Urbana–Champaign, IL B
U of Indianapolis, IN B
The U of Iowa, IA B
U of Kansas, KS B
U of Mary, ND A,B
U of Michigan, MI B
U of Michigan–Flint, MI B
U of Minnesota, Crookston, MN A,B
U of Minnesota, Duluth, MN B
U of Minnesota, Twin Cities Campus, MN B
U of Missouri–Columbia, MO B
U of Missouri–Kansas City, MO B
U of Missouri–St. Louis, MO B
U of Nebraska at Omaha, NE B
U of Nebraska–Lincoln, NE B
U of North Dakota, ND B
U of Northern Iowa, IA B
U of Northwestern Ohio, OH A,B
U of Notre Dame, IN B
U of Oklahoma, OK B
U of Phoenix–Metro Detroit Campus, MI B
U of Phoenix–Tulsa Campus, OK B
U of Phoenix-Wisconsin Campus, WI B
U of Rio Grande, OH A,B
U of St. Francis, IL B
U of Saint Francis, IN A,B
U of St. Thomas, MN B
U of Science and Arts of Oklahoma, OK B
U of Sioux Falls, SD B
The U of South Dakota, SD B
U of Southern Indiana, IN B
U of Toledo, OH A,B
U of Tulsa, OK B
U of Wisconsin–Eau Claire, WI B
U of Wisconsin–Green Bay, WI B
U of Wisconsin–La Crosse, WI B
U of Wisconsin–Madison, WI B
U of Wisconsin–Milwaukee, WI B
U of Wisconsin–Oshkosh, WI B
U of Wisconsin–Parkside, WI B
U of Wisconsin–Platteville, WI B
U of Wisconsin–River Falls, WI B
U of Wisconsin–Stevens Point, WI B
U of Wisconsin–Superior, WI B
U of Wisconsin–Whitewater, WI B
Upper Iowa U, IA B
Urbana U, OH A,B
Ursuline Coll, OH B
Valparaiso U, IN B
Viterbo U, WI B
Waldorf Coll, IA A
Walsh Coll of Accountancy and Business Administration, MI B
Walsh U, OH A,B
Wartburg Coll, IA B
Washington U in St. Louis, MO B
Wayne State Coll, NE B
Wayne State U, MI B
Webster U, MO B
Western Illinois U, IL B
Western Michigan U, MI B
Westminster Coll, MO B
Wichita State U, KS B
Wilberforce U, OH B
William Jewell Coll, MO B
William Penn U, IA B
William Woods U, MO B
Wilmington Coll, OH B
Winona State U, MN B
Wright State U, OH B
Xavier U, OH B
York Coll, NE B
Youngstown State U, OH A,B

ACCOUNTING RELATED

Maryville U of Saint Louis, MO B
Park U, MO A,B
Saint Mary-of-the-Woods Coll, IN B
The U of Akron, OH B

ACCOUNTING TECHNICIAN

Baker Coll of Flint, MI A
Kent State U, OH A
Miami U–Hamilton Campus, OH A
Ohio U, OH A
Robert Morris Coll, IL A
The U of Akron, OH A
U of Rio Grande, OH A
Youngstown State U, OH A

ACTING/DIRECTING

Central Christian Coll of Kansas, KS A
Columbia Coll Chicago, IL B
DePaul U, IL B
Maharishi U of Management, IA B
Ohio U, OH B
St. Cloud State U, MN B
The U of Akron, OH B
U of Northern Iowa, IA B
Youngstown State U, OH B

ACTUARIAL SCIENCE

Ball State U, IN B
Bradley U, IL B
Butler U, IN B
Carroll Coll, WI B
Central Michigan U, MI B
Central Missouri State U, MO B
Drake U, IA B
Eastern Michigan U, MI B
Elmhurst Coll, IL B
Indiana U Northwest, IN B
Jamestown Coll, ND B
Maryville U of Saint Louis, MO B
Missouri Valley Coll, MO B
North Central Coll, IL B
North Dakota State U, ND B
The Ohio State U, OH B
Ohio U, OH B
Roosevelt U, IL B
St. Cloud State U, MN B
Tabor Coll, KS B
U of Central Oklahoma, OK B
U of Illinois at Urbana–Champaign, IL B
The U of Iowa, IA B
U of Michigan–Flint, MI B
U of Minnesota, Duluth, MN B
U of Minnesota, Twin Cities Campus, MN B
U of Nebraska–Lincoln, NE B
U of Northern Iowa, IA B
U of St. Francis, IL B
U of St. Thomas, MN B
U of Wisconsin–Madison, WI B
U of Wisconsin–Stevens Point, WI B

ADAPTED PHYSICAL EDUCATION

Central Michigan U, MI B
Eastern Michigan U, MI B
Ohio U, OH B
St. Ambrose U, IA B
St. Cloud State U, MN B
U of Nebraska at Kearney, NE B
U of Toledo, OH B

ADMINISTRATIVE/ SECRETARIAL SERVICES

Ancilla Coll, IN A
The U of Akron, OH A

ADULT/CONTINUING EDUCATION

Andrews U, MI B
Bethel Coll, MN B
Cornerstone U, MI B
Dakota Wesleyan U, SD B
DePaul U, IL B
Iowa Wesleyan Coll, IA B
Martin U, IN B
Pittsburg State U, KS B
Tabor Coll, KS B
U of Central Oklahoma, OK B
U of Toledo, OH B
Urbana U, OH B

ADVERTISING

American Academy of Art, IL B
Ball State U, IN B
Bradley U, IL B
Brown Coll, MN A
Central Michigan U, MI B
Clarke Coll, IA B
Columbia Coll Chicago, IL B
Columbus Coll of Art and Design, OH B
Concordia Coll, MN B
DePaul U, IL B
Drake U, IA B
Ferris State U, MI B
Grand Valley State U, MI B
Hastings Coll, NE B
Iowa State U of Science and Technology, IA B
Kent State U, OH B
Marquette U, WI B
Metropolitan State U, MN B
Michigan State U, MI B
Minneapolis Coll of Art and Design, MN B
Minnesota State U, Moorhead, MN B
Northwest Missouri State U, MO B
Northwood U, MI A,B
Ohio U, OH B
Oklahoma Baptist U, OK B
Oklahoma Christian U, OK B
Oklahoma City U, OK B
Oklahoma State U, OK B
Pittsburg State U, KS B
St. Ambrose U, IA B
St. Cloud State U, MN B
Simpson Coll, IA B
Southeast Missouri State U, MO B
Stephens Coll, MO B
U of Central Oklahoma, OK B
U of Illinois at Urbana–Champaign, IL B
U of Kansas, KS B

Advertising (continued)
U of Missouri–Columbia, MO B
U of Nebraska at Omaha, NE B
U of Nebraska–Lincoln, NE B
U of Oklahoma, OK B
U of St. Thomas, MN B
The U of South Dakota, SD B
U of Southern Indiana, IN B
U of Wisconsin–Madison, WI B
Washington U in St. Louis, MO B
Wayne State Coll, NE B
Webster U, MO B
William Woods U, MO B
Winona State U, MN B
Xavier U, OH A,B
Youngstown State U, OH B

AEROSPACE ENGINEERING

Case Western Reserve U, OH B
Illinois Inst of Technology, IL B
Iowa State U of Science and Technology, IA B
Miami U, OH B
North Dakota State U, ND B
The Ohio State U, OH B
Oklahoma State U, OK B
Purdue U, IN B
Saint Louis U, MO B
U of Cincinnati, OH B
U of Illinois at Urbana–Champaign, IL B
U of Kansas, KS B
U of Michigan, MI B
U of Minnesota, Twin Cities Campus, MN B
U of Missouri–Rolla, MO B
U of North Dakota, ND B
U of Notre Dame, IN B
U of Oklahoma, OK B
Western Michigan U, MI B
Wichita State U, KS B

AEROSPACE ENGINEERING TECHNOLOGY

Central Missouri State U, MO A,B
Eastern Michigan U, MI B
Ohio U, OH B
Purdue U, IN A,B
Saint Louis U, MO A,B

AEROSPACE SCIENCE

Augsburg Coll, MN B
Spartan School of Aeronautics, OK A

AFRICAN-AMERICAN STUDIES

Antioch Coll, OH B
Coe Coll, IA B
The Coll of Wooster, OH B
Denison U, OH B
DePaul U, IL B
Earlham Coll, IN B
Eastern Illinois U, IL B
Eastern Michigan U, MI B
Grinnell Coll, IA B
Indiana State U, IN B
Indiana U Bloomington, IN B
Indiana U Northwest, IN B
Kent State U, OH B
Kenyon Coll, OH B
Knox Coll, IL B
Luther Coll, IA B
Marquette U, WI B
Martin U, IN B
Miami U, OH B
Northwestern U, IL B
Oberlin Coll, OH B
The Ohio State U, OH B
Ohio U, OH B
Ohio Wesleyan U, OH B
Purdue U, IN B
Roosevelt U, IL B
U of Chicago, IL B
U of Cincinnati, OH B
U of Illinois at Chicago, IL B
The U of Iowa, IA B
U of Kansas, KS B
U of Michigan, MI B
U of Michigan–Flint, MI B
U of Minnesota, Twin Cities Campus, MN B
U of Nebraska at Omaha, NE B
U of Oklahoma, OK B
U of Wisconsin–Madison, WI B
U of Wisconsin–Milwaukee, WI B
Washington U in St. Louis, MO B
Wayne State U, MI B
Western Michigan U, MI B
Youngstown State U, OH B

AFRICAN LANGUAGES

Ohio U, OH B
U of Wisconsin–Madison, WI B

AFRICAN STUDIES

Antioch Coll, OH B
Bowling Green State U, OH B
Carleton Coll, MN B
Chicago State U, IL B
The Coll of Wooster, OH B
DePaul U, IL B
Indiana U Bloomington, IN B
Lake Forest Coll, IL B
Luther Coll, IA B
Oakland U, MI B
The Ohio State U, OH B
Ohio U, OH B
U of Chicago, IL B
The U of Iowa, IA B
U of Kansas, KS B
U of Michigan, MI B
U of Minnesota, Twin Cities Campus, MN B
U of Wisconsin–Madison, WI B
Washington U in St. Louis, MO B
Youngstown State U, OH B

AGRIBUSINESS

Central Missouri State U, MO B
Coll of the Ozarks, MO B
Illinois State U, IL B
Michigan State U, MI B
North Dakota State U, ND B
Northwestern Coll, IA B
Sitting Bull Coll, ND A
South Dakota State U, SD B
Southwest Missouri State U, MO B

AGRICULTURAL ANIMAL HUSBANDRY/ PRODUCTION MANAGEMENT

Dordt Coll, IA B
North Dakota State U, ND B
Saint Mary-of-the-Woods Coll, IN A,B

AGRICULTURAL BUSINESS

Andrews U, MI A,B
Cameron U, OK B
Central Christian Coll of Kansas, KS A
Central Missouri State U, MO B
Concordia U Wisconsin, WI B
Dickinson State U, ND A,B
Dordt Coll, IA A,B
Fort Hays State U, KS B
Hannibal-LaGrange Coll, MO B
Iowa State U of Science and Technology, IA B
Kansas State U, KS B
McPherson Coll, KS B
Michigan State U, MI B
MidAmerica Nazarene U, KS A,B
Missouri Valley Coll, MO B
Northwestern Oklahoma State U, OK B
Northwest Missouri State U, MO B
The Ohio State U, OH B
Oklahoma Panhandle State U, OK B
Oklahoma State U, OK B
Rogers State U, OK A
Southeast Missouri State U, MO B
Southwest Minnesota State U, MN A,B
Tabor Coll, KS B
U of Minnesota, Crookston, MN A,B
U of Minnesota, Twin Cities Campus, MN B
U of Missouri–Columbia, MO B
U of Nebraska at Kearney, NE B
U of Nebraska–Lincoln, NE B
U of Northwestern Ohio, OH A
U of Wisconsin–Madison, WI B
U of Wisconsin–Platteville, WI B
U of Wisconsin–River Falls, WI B
Wayne State Coll, NE B
Wilmington Coll, OH B

AGRICULTURAL BUSINESS AND PRODUCTION RELATED

Michigan State U, MI B
U of Nebraska–Lincoln, NE B

AGRICULTURAL BUSINESS RELATED

U of Nebraska–Lincoln, NE B

AGRICULTURAL ECONOMICS

Central Missouri State U, MO B
Kansas State U, KS B
Langston U, OK B
McPherson Coll, KS B
Michigan State U, MI B
North Dakota State U, ND B
Northwest Missouri State U, MO B
The Ohio State U, OH B
Oklahoma State U, OK B
Purdue U, IN B
South Dakota State U, SD B
Southern Illinois U Carbondale, IL B
Truman State U, MO B
U of Illinois at Urbana–Champaign, IL B
U of Missouri–Columbia, MO B
U of Nebraska–Lincoln, NE B
U of Wisconsin–Madison, WI B

AGRICULTURAL EDUCATION

Andrews U, MI B
Central Missouri State U, MO B
Coll of the Ozarks, MO B
Iowa State U of Science and Technology, IA B
Langston U, OK B
North Dakota State U, ND B
Northwest Missouri State U, MO B
The Ohio State U, OH B
Oklahoma Panhandle State U, OK B
Oklahoma State U, OK B
Purdue U, IN B
South Dakota State U, SD B
Southwest Missouri State U, MO B
U of Illinois at Urbana–Champaign, IL B
U of Minnesota, Twin Cities Campus, MN B
U of Missouri–Columbia, MO B
U of Nebraska–Lincoln, NE B
U of Wisconsin–Madison, WI B
U of Wisconsin–River Falls, WI B
Wilmington Coll, OH B

AGRICULTURAL ENGINEERING

Iowa State U of Science and Technology, IA B
Kansas State U, KS B
Michigan State U, MI B
North Dakota State U, ND B
The Ohio State U, OH B
Purdue U, IN B
South Dakota State U, SD B
U of Illinois at Urbana–Champaign, IL B
U of Minnesota, Twin Cities Campus, MN B
U of Nebraska–Lincoln, NE B
U of Wisconsin–Madison, WI B

U of Wisconsin–River Falls, WI B

AGRICULTURAL/FOOD PRODUCTS PROCESSING

Kansas State U, KS B
Michigan State U, MI B
The Ohio State U, OH B
U of Illinois at Urbana–Champaign, IL B

AGRICULTURAL MECHANIZATION

Andrews U, MI A,B
Cameron U, OK B
Central Missouri State U, MO B
Coll of the Ozarks, MO B
Iowa State U of Science and Technology, IA B
Kansas State U, KS B
North Dakota State U, ND B
Northwest Missouri State U, MO B
Purdue U, IN B
South Dakota State U, SD B
U of Illinois at Urbana–Champaign, IL B
U of Missouri–Columbia, MO B
U of Nebraska–Lincoln, NE B

AGRICULTURAL PLANT PATHOLOGY

The Ohio State U, OH B

AGRICULTURAL PRODUCTION

North Dakota State U, ND B

AGRICULTURAL SCIENCES

Andrews U, MI A,B
Cameron U, OK B
Dordt Coll, IA B
Fort Hays State U, KS B
Illinois State U, IL B
Iowa State U of Science and Technology, IA B
Maharishi U of Management, IA B
North Dakota State U, ND B
Northwestern Oklahoma State U, OK B
Northwest Missouri State U, MO B
Oklahoma Panhandle State U, OK A
Oklahoma State U, OK B
Purdue U, IN B
South Dakota State U, SD A,B
Southeast Missouri State U, MO B
Southern Illinois U Carbondale, IL B
Southwest Missouri State U, MO B
Truman State U, MO B
U of Illinois at Urbana–Champaign, IL B
U of Minnesota, Crookston, MN A,B
U of Minnesota, Twin Cities Campus, MN B
U of Missouri–Columbia, MO B
U of Wisconsin–Madison, WI B
U of Wisconsin–River Falls, WI B
Western Illinois U, IL B
Wilmington Coll, OH B

AGRICULTURAL SCIENCES RELATED

Maharishi U of Management, IA B

AGRONOMY/CROP SCIENCE

Andrews U, MI A,B
Cameron U, OK B
Coll of the Ozarks, MO B
Fort Hays State U, KS B
Iowa State U of Science and Technology, IA B
Kansas State U, KS B
Michigan State U, MI B
North Dakota State U, ND B
Northwest Missouri State U, MO B
The Ohio State U, OH B
Oklahoma Panhandle State U, OK B
Purdue U, IN B
South Dakota State U, SD B
Southeast Missouri State U, MO B
Southwest Minnesota State U, MN B
Southwest Missouri State U, MO B
Truman State U, MO B
U of Illinois at Urbana–Champaign, IL B
U of Minnesota, Crookston, MN A,B
U of Minnesota, Twin Cities Campus, MN B
U of Nebraska–Lincoln, NE B
U of Wisconsin–Madison, WI B
U of Wisconsin–Platteville, WI B
U of Wisconsin–River Falls, WI B

AIRCRAFT MECHANIC/AIRFRAME

Kansas State U, KS A
Lewis U, IL A,B
Southern Illinois U Carbondale, IL A

AIRCRAFT MECHANIC/POWERPLANT

Kansas State U, KS A

AIRCRAFT PILOT (PRIVATE)

Central Christian Coll of Kansas, KS A

AIRCRAFT PILOT (PROFESSIONAL)

Academy Coll, MN A
Andrews U, MI A,B
Baker Coll of Flint, MI A
Baker Coll of Muskegon, MI A
Bowling Green State U, OH B
Central Christian Coll of Kansas, KS A
Concordia U, MI B
Concordia U Wisconsin, WI B
Cornerstone U, MI B
Grace U, NE B
Indiana State U, IN B
Kansas State U, KS A,B
Lewis U, IL B
Oklahoma State U, OK B
Purdue U, IN B
St. Cloud State U, MN B
Saint Louis U, MO B
Southeastern Oklahoma State U, OK B
Southern Illinois U Carbondale, IL A
Spartan School of Aeronautics, OK A
Springfield Coll in Illinois, IL A
U of Dubuque, IA A,B
U of Illinois at Urbana–Champaign, IL B
U of Minnesota, Crookston, MN A,B
U of North Dakota, ND B
U of Oklahoma, OK B
Western Michigan U, MI B
Winona State U, MN A

AIR FORCE R.O.T.C./AIR SCIENCE

Ohio U, OH B
The U of Iowa, IA B

AIR TRAFFIC CONTROL

St. Cloud State U, MN B
U of North Dakota, ND B

AIR TRANSPORTATION RELATED

Western Michigan U, MI B

ALCOHOL/DRUG ABUSE COUNSELING

Bacone Coll, OK A
Calumet Coll of Saint Joseph, IN A,B
Graceland U, IA B
Indiana Wesleyan U, IN A,B
Martin U, IN B
Metropolitan State U, MN B
Minot State U, ND B
National-Louis U, IL B
Nebraska Indian Comm Coll, NE A
Newman U, KS A,B
Rogers State U, OK A
St. Cloud State U, MN B
The U of Akron, OH A
U of Mary, ND B
U of St. Thomas, MN B
The U of South Dakota, SD B
U of Toledo, OH A

AMERICAN GOVERNMENT

Oklahoma Christian U, OK B

AMERICAN HISTORY

Calvin Coll, MI B
Central Christian Coll of Kansas, KS A
North Central Coll, IL B
The U of Iowa, IA B

AMERICAN LITERATURE

Michigan State U, MI B
Washington U in St. Louis, MO B

AMERICAN STUDIES

Albion Coll, MI B
Ashland U, OH B
Bowling Green State U, OH B
Carleton Coll, MN B
Case Western Reserve U, OH B
Cedarville U, OH B
Coe Coll, IA B
Creighton U, NE B
DePaul U, IL B
Dominican U, IL B
Elmhurst Coll, IL B
Franklin Coll, IN B
Grace U, NE B
Grinnell Coll, IA B
Hillsdale Coll, MI B
Kendall Coll, IL B
Kent State U, OH B
Kenyon Coll, OH B
Knox Coll, IL B
Lake Forest Coll, IL B
Lewis U, IL B
Miami U, OH B
Millikin U, IL B
Minnesota State U, Moorhead, MN B
Mount Union Coll, OH B
Muskingum Coll, OH B
Northwestern U, IL B
Oklahoma City U, OK B
Oklahoma State U, OK B
Roosevelt U, IL B
St. Cloud State U, MN B
Saint Louis U, MO B
St. Olaf Coll, MN B
Southern Nazarene U, OK B
U of Chicago, IL B
U of Dayton, OH B
The U of Iowa, IA B
U of Kansas, KS B
U of Michigan, MI B
U of Michigan–Dearborn, MI B
U of Minnesota, Twin Cities Campus, MN B
U of Missouri–Kansas City, MO B
U of Northern Iowa, IA B
U of Notre Dame, IN B
U of Rio Grande, OH B
U of Toledo, OH B
U of Wisconsin–Madison, WI B
Upper Iowa U, IA B
Ursuline Coll, OH B
Valparaiso U, IN B
Washington U in St. Louis, MO B
Wayne State U, MI B
Western Michigan U, MI B
Wittenberg U, OH B
Youngstown State U, OH B

ANATOMY

Andrews U, MI B
Minnesota State U, Mankato, MN B
U of Indianapolis, IN B

ANIMAL SCIENCES

Andrews U, MI A
Cameron U, OK B
Coll of the Ozarks, MO B
Dordt Coll, IA B

Animal Sciences (continued)

Fort Hays State U, KS B
Iowa State U of Science and Technology, IA B
Kansas State U, KS B
Langston U, OK B
Michigan State U, MI B
North Dakota State U, ND B
Northwest Missouri State U, MO B
The Ohio State U, OH B
Oklahoma Panhandle State U, OK B
Oklahoma State U, OK B
Purdue U, IN B
South Dakota State U, SD B
Southeast Missouri State U, MO B
Southern Illinois U Carbondale, IL B
Southwest Missouri State U, MO B
Truman State U, MO B
U of Illinois at Urbana–Champaign, IL B
U of Minnesota, Crookston, MN A,B
U of Minnesota, Twin Cities Campus, MN B
U of Missouri–Columbia, MO B
U of Nebraska–Lincoln, NE B
U of Wisconsin–Madison, WI B
U of Wisconsin–Platteville, WI B
U of Wisconsin–River Falls, WI B

ANTHROPOLOGY

Albion Coll, MI B
Antioch Coll, OH B
Augustana Coll, IL B
Ball State U, IN B
Beloit Coll, WI B
Butler U, IN B
Carleton Coll, MN B
Case Western Reserve U, OH B
Central Michigan U, MI B
Chicago State U, IL B
Cleveland State U, OH B
Cornell Coll, IA B
Denison U, OH B
DePaul U, IL B
DePauw U, IN B
Drake U, IA B
Eastern Michigan U, MI B
Franciscan U of Steubenville, OH B
Grand Valley State U, MI B
Grinnell Coll, IA B
Gustavus Adolphus Coll, MN B
Hamline U, MN B
Hanover Coll, IN B
Heidelberg Coll, OH B
Illinois State U, IL B
Indiana State U, IN B
Indiana U Bloomington, IN B
Indiana U–Purdue U Fort Wayne, IN B
Indiana U–Purdue U Indianapolis, IN B
Iowa State U of Science and Technology, IA B
Judson Coll, IL B
Kalamazoo Coll, MI B
Kansas State U, KS B
Kent State U, OH B
Kenyon Coll, OH B
Knox Coll, IL B
Lake Forest Coll, IL B
Lawrence U, WI B
Loyola U Chicago, IL B
Luther Coll, IA B
Macalester Coll, MN B
Marquette U, WI B
Miami U, OH B
Miami U–Middletown Campus, OH A
Michigan State U, MI B
Minnesota State U, Mankato, MN B
Minnesota State U, Moorhead, MN B
National-Louis U, IL B
North Central Coll, IL B
North Dakota State U, ND B
Northeastern Illinois U, IL B
Northern Illinois U, IL B
North Park U, IL B
Northwestern U, IL B
Oakland U, MI B
Oberlin Coll, OH B
The Ohio State U, OH B
Ohio U, OH B
Ohio Wesleyan U, OH B
Principia Coll, IL B
Ripon Coll, WI B
Rockford Coll, IL B
St. Cloud State U, MN B
Saint Mary's Coll, IN B
Southeast Missouri State U, MO B
Southern Illinois U Carbondale, IL B
Southern Illinois U Edwardsville, IL B
Southwest Missouri State U, MO B
U of Chicago, IL B
U of Cincinnati, OH B
U of Evansville, IN B
U of Illinois at Chicago, IL B
U of Illinois at Springfield, IL B
U of Illinois at Urbana–Champaign, IL B
U of Indianapolis, IN B
The U of Iowa, IA B
U of Kansas, KS B
U of Michigan, MI B
U of Michigan–Dearborn, MI B
U of Michigan–Flint, MI B
U of Minnesota, Duluth, MN B
U of Minnesota, Twin Cities Campus, MN B
U of Missouri–Columbia, MO B
U of Missouri–St. Louis, MO B
U of Nebraska–Lincoln, NE B
U of North Dakota, ND B
U of Northern Iowa, IA B
U of Notre Dame, IN B
U of Oklahoma, OK B
The U of South Dakota, SD B
U of Toledo, OH B
U of Tulsa, OK B
U of Wisconsin–Madison, WI B
U of Wisconsin–Milwaukee, WI B
U of Wisconsin–Oshkosh, WI B
Washington U in St. Louis, MO B
Wayne State U, MI B
Webster U, MO B
Western Michigan U, MI B
Westminster Coll, MO B
Wheaton Coll, IL B
Wichita State U, KS B
Wright State U, OH B
Youngstown State U, OH B

APPAREL MARKETING

Concordia Coll, MN B
Youngstown State U, OH B

APPLIED ART

American Academy of Art, IL B
Bemidji State U, MN B
Carthage Coll, WI B
Chicago State U, IL B
Cleveland State U, OH B
Coll for Creative Studies, MI B
Columbia Coll, MO B
Columbus Coll of Art and Design, OH B
DePaul U, IL B
Illinois Wesleyan U, IL B
Indiana U Bloomington, IN B
Iowa Wesleyan Coll, IA B
Lincoln Coll, Lincoln, IL A
Lincoln Coll, Normal, IL A
Lindenwood U, MO B
Marygrove Coll, MI B
Minnesota State U, Mankato, MN B
Minnesota State U, Moorhead, MN B
Mount Vernon Nazarene U, OH B
Muskingum Coll, OH B
Northern Michigan U, MI B
Oakland City U, IN B
Oklahoma Baptist U, OK B
Olivet Coll, MI B
Peru State Coll, NE B
St. Cloud State U, MN B
Truman State U, MO B
The U of Akron, OH B
U of Dayton, OH B
U of Michigan, MI B
U of Sioux Falls, SD B
The U of South Dakota, SD B
U of Toledo, OH B
U of Wisconsin–Madison, WI B
Viterbo U, WI B
Washington U in St. Louis, MO B
Winona State U, MN B

APPLIED ECONOMICS

Saint Joseph's Coll, IN B
U of Northern Iowa, IA B

APPLIED HISTORY

Western Michigan U, MI B

APPLIED MATHEMATICS

Case Western Reserve U, OH B
Central Methodist Coll, MO A
DePaul U, IL B
Ferris State U, MI B
Franklin Coll, IN B
Grand Valley State U, MI B
Grand View Coll, IA B
Illinois Inst of Technology, IL B
Indiana U South Bend, IN B
Kent State U, OH B
Kettering U, MI B
Lincoln Coll, Lincoln, IL A
Maryville U of Saint Louis, MO B
Metropolitan State U, MN B
Michigan State U, MI B
Michigan Technological U, MI B
North Central Coll, IL B
Northland Coll, WI B
Northwestern U, IL B
Oakland City U, IN B
Ohio U, OH B
Saint Joseph's Coll, IN B
Saint Louis U, MO B
Saint Mary's Coll, IN B
Shawnee State U, OH B
Southeast Missouri State U, MO B
The U of Akron, OH B
U of Central Oklahoma, OK B
U of Chicago, IL B
U of Michigan, MI B
U of Missouri–Rolla, MO B
U of Missouri–St. Louis, MO B
U of Sioux Falls, SD B
U of Tulsa, OK B
U of Wisconsin–Madison, WI B
U of Wisconsin–Milwaukee, WI B
U of Wisconsin–Stout, WI B
Washington U in St. Louis, MO B
Wayne State Coll, NE B
Western Michigan U, MI B
Winona State U, MN B

APPLIED MATHEMATICS RELATED

U of Dayton, OH B

AQUACULTURE OPERATIONS/ PRODUCTION MANAGEMENT

Lake Erie Coll, OH B
Purdue U, IN A,B

ARABIC

The Ohio State U, OH B
U of Chicago, IL B
U of Michigan, MI B
U of Notre Dame, IN B
Washington U in St. Louis, MO B

ARCHAEOLOGY

The Coll of Wooster, OH B
Kent State U, OH B
Minnesota State U, Moorhead, MN B
Oberlin Coll, OH B
U of Evansville, IN B
U of Indianapolis, IN B
U of Kansas, KS B
U of Michigan, MI B
U of Missouri–Columbia, MO B
U of Wisconsin–La Crosse, WI B
Washington U in St. Louis, MO B
Wheaton Coll, IL B

ARCHITECTURAL DRAFTING

Baker Coll of Flint, MI A
Baker Coll of Muskegon, MI A
Indiana State U, IN A
Indiana U–Purdue U Indianapolis, IN A
U of Toledo, OH A

ARCHITECTURAL ENGINEERING

Andrews U, MI B
Illinois Inst of Technology, IL B
Kansas State U, KS B
Milwaukee School of Engineering, WI B
Oklahoma State U, OK B
U of Cincinnati, OH B
U of Kansas, KS B
U of Missouri–Rolla, MO B
U of Nebraska–Lincoln, NE B

ARCHITECTURAL ENGINEERING TECHNOLOGY

Andrews U, MI B
Baker Coll of Cadillac, MI A
Baker Coll of Clinton Township, MI A
Baker Coll of Owosso, MI A
Baker Coll of Port Huron, MI A
Central Christian Coll of Kansas, KS A
Central Missouri State U, MO B
Ferris State U, MI A
Indiana State U, IN B
Indiana U–Purdue U Fort Wayne, IN A
Indiana U–Purdue U Indianapolis, IN B
Northern Michigan U, MI A
Purdue U, IN A,B
Purdue U Calumet, IN A
Purdue U North Central, IN A
Ranken Tech Coll, MO A
Southern Illinois U Carbondale, IL A
U of Cincinnati, OH A,B
Washington U in St. Louis, MO B

ARCHITECTURAL ENVIRONMENTAL DESIGN

Ball State U, IN B
Bowling Green State U, OH B
Coll for Creative Studies, MI B
Miami U, OH B
North Dakota State U, ND B
Northern Michigan U, MI A
U of Oklahoma, OK B

ARCHITECTURAL HISTORY

Ursuline Coll, OH B

ARCHITECTURE

Andrews U, MI B
Ball State U, IN B
Central Christian Coll of Kansas, KS A
Coe Coll, IA B
Concordia Coll, MN B
Cornell Coll, IA B
Drury U, MO B
Eastern Michigan U, MI B
Illinois Inst of Technology, IL B
Iowa State U of Science and Technology, IA B
Judson Coll, IL B
Kansas State U, KS B
Kent State U, OH B
Lawrence Technological U, MI B
Miami U, OH B
North Dakota State U, ND B
The Ohio State U, OH B
Oklahoma State U, OK B
Southern Illinois U Carbondale, IL B
U of Cincinnati, OH B
U of Illinois at Chicago, IL B
U of Kansas, KS B
U of Michigan, MI B
U of Minnesota, Twin Cities Campus, MN B
U of Nebraska–Lincoln, NE B
U of Notre Dame, IN B
U of Oklahoma, OK B
U of Wisconsin–Milwaukee, WI B
Washington U in St. Louis, MO B

ARCHITECTURE RELATED

U of Illinois at Urbana–Champaign, IL B
U of Kansas, KS B
Washington U in St. Louis, MO B

AREA, ETHNIC, AND CULTURAL STUDIES RELATED

Washington U in St. Louis, MO B

AREA STUDIES

Denison U, OH B
Eastern Michigan U, MI B
U of Oklahoma, OK B

AREA STUDIES RELATED

Lewis U, IL B
U of Illinois at Urbana–Champaign, IL B

ARMY R.O.T.C./MILITARY SCIENCE

Drake U, IA B
Minnesota State U, Mankato, MN B
Monmouth Coll, IL B
Northwest Missouri State U, MO B
Ohio U, OH B
Purdue U Calumet, IN B
The U of Iowa, IA B

ART

Adrian Coll, MI A,B
Albion Coll, MI B
Alma Coll, MI B
Alverno Coll, WI B
American Academy of Art, IL B
Andrews U, MI B
Aquinas Coll, MI B
Art Academy of Cincinnati, OH B
Ashland U, OH A,B
Augsburg Coll, MN B
Augustana Coll, IL B
Augustana Coll, SD B
Avila U, MO B
Bacone Coll, OK A
Baldwin-Wallace Coll, OH B
Ball State U, IN B
Bellevue U, NE B
Bemidji State U, MN B
Bethany Coll, KS B
Bethany Lutheran Coll, MN B
Bethel Coll, IN B
Bethel Coll, KS B
Bethel Coll, MN B
Blackburn Coll, IL B
Black Hills State U, SD B
Bluffton Coll, OH B
Bowling Green State U, OH B
Bradley U, IL B
Briar Cliff U, IA B
Buena Vista U, IA B
Calvin Coll, MI B
Cameron U, OK B
Capital U, OH B
Cardinal Stritch U, WI B
Carroll Coll, WI B
Central Christian Coll of Kansas, KS A
Central Coll, IA B
Central Michigan U, MI B
Chadron State Coll, NE B
Clarke Coll, IA B
Cleveland State U, OH B
Coe Coll, IA B
Coll for Creative Studies, MI B
Coll of Mount St. Joseph, OH A,B
Coll of Saint Benedict, MN B
Coll of St. Catherine, MN B
Coll of Visual Arts, MN B
The Coll of Wooster, OH B
Columbia Coll, MO B
Columbia Coll Chicago, IL B
Columbus Coll of Art and Design, OH B
Concordia Coll, MN B
Concordia U, IL B
Concordia U, MI B
Concordia U, NE B
Concordia U Wisconsin, WI B
Cornell Coll, IA B
Creighton U, NE B
Culver-Stockton Coll, MO B
Dakota Wesleyan U, SD B
Dana Coll, NE B
Defiance Coll, OH A,B
Denison U, OH B
DePaul U, IL B
Dickinson State U, ND B
Doane Coll, NE B
Dominican U, IL B
Dordt Coll, IA B
Drake U, IA B
Drury U, MO B
Earlham Coll, IN B
East Central U, OK B
Eastern Illinois U, IL B
Eastern Michigan U, MI B
Edgewood Coll, WI B
Elmhurst Coll, IL B
Emporia State U, KS B
Eureka Coll, IL B
Evangel U, MO B
Finlandia U, MI B
Fontbonne U, MO B
Fort Hays State U, KS B
Goshen Coll, IN B
Governors State U, IL B
Grace Coll, IN B
Graceland U, IA B
Grand Valley State U, MI B
Grand View Coll, IA B
Greenville Coll, IL B
Grinnell Coll, IA B
Gustavus Adolphus Coll, MN B
Hamline U, MN B
Hannibal-LaGrange Coll, MO B
Hanover Coll, IN B
Hastings Coll, NE B
Hillsdale Coll, MI B
Hiram Coll, OH B
Huntington Coll, IN B
Illinois Coll, IL B
Illinois State U, IL B
Illinois Wesleyan U, IL B
Indiana State U, IN B
Indiana U Bloomington, IN B
Indiana U Northwest, IN B
Indiana U South Bend, IN B
Indiana U Southeast, IN B
Indiana Wesleyan U, IN A,B
Iowa State U of Science and Technology, IA B
Iowa Wesleyan Coll, IA B
Jamestown Coll, ND B
Judson Coll, IL B
Kalamazoo Coll, MI B
Kansas State U, KS B
Kent State U, Stark Campus, OH A
Kenyon Coll, OH B
Knox Coll, IL B
Lake Erie Coll, OH B
Lakeland Coll, WI B
Langston U, OK B
Lewis U, IL B
Lindenwood U, MO B
Lourdes Coll, OH A,B
Loyola U Chicago, IL B
Luther Coll, IA B
MacMurray Coll, IL B
Madonna U, MI A,B
Maharishi U of Management, IA A,B
Malone Coll, OH B
Manchester Coll, IN A,B
Marian Coll, IN A,B
Marian Coll of Fond du Lac, WI B
Marietta Coll, OH B
Marygrove Coll, MI B
McKendree Coll, IL B
McPherson Coll, KS B
Miami U, OH B
Miami U–Middletown Campus, OH A
Michigan State U, MI B
Midland Lutheran Coll, NE B
Milwaukee Inst of Art and Design, WI B
Minnesota State U, Mankato, MN B
Minnesota State U, Moorhead, MN B
Minot State U, ND B
Missouri Valley Coll, MO B
Missouri Western State Coll, MO B
Monmouth Coll, IL B
Morningside Coll, IA B
Mount Mary Coll, WI B
Mount Mercy Coll, IA B
Mount Union Coll, OH B
Mount Vernon Nazarene U, OH B
Muskingum Coll, OH B

Art (continued)

National-Louis U, IL	B
Nebraska Wesleyan U, NE	B
North Central Coll, IL	B
North Dakota State U, ND	B
Northeastern Illinois U, IL	B
Northeastern State U, OK	B
Northern Illinois U, IL	B
Northern Michigan U, MI	B
Northern State U, SD	B
Northland Coll, WI	B
North Park U, IL	B
Northwestern Coll, IA	B
Northwestern U, IL	B
Northwest Missouri State U, MO	B
Notre Dame Coll, OH	B
Oakland City U, IN	B
Oberlin Coll, OH	B
Ohio Northern U, OH	B
The Ohio State U, OH	B
Ohio U, OH	B
Ohio U–Lancaster, OH	A
Oklahoma Baptist U, OK	B
Oklahoma Christian U, OK	B
Oklahoma City U, OK	B
Oklahoma State U, OK	B
Olivet Coll, MI	B
Olivet Nazarene U, IL	B
Ottawa U, KS	B
Otterbein Coll, OH	B
Peru State Coll, NE	B
Pittsburg State U, KS	B
Purdue U, IN	B
Quincy U, IL	B
Ripon Coll, WI	B
Rockford Coll, IL	B
Rogers State U, OK	A
Saginaw Valley State U, MI	B
St. Ambrose U, IA	B
St. Cloud State U, MN	B
Saint John's U, MN	B
Saint Mary-of-the-Woods Coll, IN	B
Saint Mary's Coll, IN	B
Saint Mary U, KS	B
St. Norbert Coll, WI	B
St. Olaf Coll, MN	B
Saint Xavier U, IL	B
School of the Art Inst of Chicago, IL	B
Shawnee State U, OH	A,B
Siena Heights U, MI	A,B
Silver Lake Coll, WI	B
Simpson Coll, IA	B
South Dakota State U, SD	B
Southeastern Oklahoma State U, OK	B
Southeast Missouri State U, MO	B
Southern Illinois U Carbondale, IL	B
Southern Illinois U Edwardsville, IL	B
Southwest Baptist U, MO	B
Southwest Minnesota State U, MN	B
Southwest Missouri State U, MO	B
Spring Arbor U, MI	B
Springfield Coll in Illinois, IL	A
Sterling Coll, KS	B
Taylor U, IN	B
Trinity Christian Coll, IL	B
Truman State U, MO	B
The U of Akron, OH	B
U of Central Oklahoma, OK	B
U of Chicago, IL	B
U of Cincinnati, OH	B
U of Dayton, OH	B
U of Evansville, IN	B
The U of Findlay, OH	B
U of Illinois at Springfield, IL	B
U of Indianapolis, IN	B
The U of Iowa, IA	B
U of Kansas, KS	B
U of Michigan–Flint, MI	B
U of Minnesota, Duluth, MN	B
U of Minnesota, Twin Cities Campus, MN	B
U of Missouri–Columbia, MO	B
U of Missouri–Kansas City, MO	B
U of Missouri–St. Louis, MO	B
U of Nebraska at Kearney, NE	B
U of Nebraska at Omaha, NE	B
U of North Dakota, ND	B
U of Northern Iowa, IA	B
U of Oklahoma, OK	B
U of Rio Grande, OH	A,B
U of Saint Francis, IN	B
U of Science and Arts of Oklahoma, OK	B
The U of South Dakota, SD	B
U of Southern Indiana, IN	B
U of Toledo, OH	A,B
U of Tulsa, OK	B
U of Wisconsin–Eau Claire, WI	B
U of Wisconsin–Green Bay, WI	A,B
U of Wisconsin–La Crosse, WI	B
U of Wisconsin–Madison, WI	B
U of Wisconsin–Milwaukee, WI	B
U of Wisconsin–Oshkosh, WI	B
U of Wisconsin–Parkside, WI	B
U of Wisconsin–Platteville, WI	B
U of Wisconsin–River Falls, WI	B
U of Wisconsin–Stevens Point, WI	B
U of Wisconsin–Whitewater, WI	B
Upper Iowa U, IA	B
Ursuline Coll, OH	B
Valley City State U, ND	B
Valparaiso U, IN	B
Viterbo U, WI	B
Wabash Coll, IN	B
Waldorf Coll, IA	A
Wartburg Coll, IA	B
Washington U in St. Louis, MO	B
Wayne State Coll, NE	B
Wayne State U, MI	B
Webster U, MO	B
Western Illinois U, IL	B
Western Michigan U, MI	B
Wheaton Coll, IL	B
Wichita State U, KS	B
William Jewell Coll, MO	B
William Woods U, MO	B
Winona State U, MN	B
Wisconsin Lutheran Coll, WI	B
Wittenberg U, OH	B
Wright State U, OH	B
Xavier U, OH	B
Youngstown State U, OH	B

ART EDUCATION

Adrian Coll, MI	B
Alma Coll, MI	B
Alverno Coll, WI	B
Anderson U, IN	B
Andrews U, MI	B
Aquinas Coll, MI	B
Ashland U, OH	B
Augsburg Coll, MN	B
Augustana Coll, IL	B
Augustana Coll, SD	B
Avila U, MO	B
Baker U, KS	B
Baldwin-Wallace Coll, OH	B
Ball State U, IN	B
Beloit Coll, WI	B
Bemidji State U, MN	B
Bethany Coll, KS	B
Bethel Coll, MN	B
Bluffton Coll, OH	B
Bowling Green State U, OH	B
Briar Cliff U, IA	B
Calumet Coll of Saint Joseph, IN	B
Calvin Coll, MI	B
Cameron U, OK	B
Capital U, OH	B
Cardinal Stritch U, WI	B
Carroll Coll, WI	B
Case Western Reserve U, OH	B
Central Christian Coll of Kansas, KS	A
Central Michigan U, MI	B
Central Missouri State U, MO	B
Chadron State Coll, NE	B
Chicago State U, IL	B
Clarke Coll, IA	B
Cleveland State U, OH	B
Coe Coll, IA	B
Coll of Mount St. Joseph, OH	B
Coll of Saint Benedict, MN	B
Coll of St. Catherine, MN	B
Coll of the Ozarks, MO	B
Columbia Coll, MO	B
Concordia Coll, MN	B
Concordia U, IL	B
Concordia U, NE	B
Concordia U Wisconsin, WI	B
Cornell Coll, IA	B
Creighton U, NE	B
Culver-Stockton Coll, MO	B
Dakota State U, SD	B
Dakota Wesleyan U, SD	B
Dana Coll, NE	B
Defiance Coll, OH	B
Dickinson State U, ND	B
Drury U, MO	B
East Central U, OK	B
Eastern Michigan U, MI	B
Edgewood Coll, WI	B
Elmhurst Coll, IL	B
Emporia State U, KS	B
Evangel U, MO	B
Fontbonne U, MO	B
Fort Hays State U, KS	B
Goshen Coll, IN	B
Grace Coll, IN	B
Graceland U, IA	B
Grand Valley State U, MI	B
Grand View Coll, IA	B
Greenville Coll, IL	B
Gustavus Adolphus Coll, MN	B
Hannibal-LaGrange Coll, MO	B
Hastings Coll, NE	B
Huntington Coll, IN	B
Indiana State U, IN	B
Indiana U Bloomington, IN	B
Indiana U–Purdue U Indianapolis, IN	B
Indiana Wesleyan U, IN	B
Iowa Wesleyan Coll, IA	B
Kent State U, OH	B
Langston U, OK	B
Lewis U, IL	B
Lincoln Coll, Lincoln, IL	A
Lincoln Coll, Normal, IL	A
Lindenwood U, MO	B
Loras Coll, IA	B
Luther Coll, IA	B
Madonna U, MI	B
Malone Coll, OH	B
Manchester Coll, IN	B
Marian Coll, IN	B
Marian Coll of Fond du Lac, WI	B
Maryville U of Saint Louis, MO	B
McKendree Coll, IL	B
McPherson Coll, KS	B
Miami U, OH	B
Michigan State U, MI	B
Midland Lutheran Coll, NE	B
Millikin U, IL	B
Minnesota State U, Mankato, MN	B
Minnesota State U, Moorhead, MN	B
Minot State U, ND	B
Missouri Western State Coll, MO	B
Morningside Coll, IA	B
Mount Mary Coll, WI	B
Mount Mercy Coll, IA	B
Mount Vernon Nazarene U, OH	B
Muskingum Coll, OH	B
North Central Coll, IL	B
Northeastern State U, OK	B
Northern Illinois U, IL	B
Northern Michigan U, MI	B
Northern State U, SD	B
Northland Coll, WI	B
North Park U, IL	B
Northwestern Coll, IA	B
Northwestern Coll, MN	B
Northwest Missouri State U, MO	B
Oakland City U, IN	B
Ohio Dominican U, OH	B
Ohio Northern U, OH	B
The Ohio State U, OH	B
Ohio U, OH	B
Ohio Wesleyan U, OH	B
Oklahoma Baptist U, OK	B
Oklahoma Christian U, OK	B
Oklahoma City U, OK	B
Olivet Coll, MI	B
Olivet Nazarene U, IL	B
Oral Roberts U, OK	B
Ottawa U, KS	B
Otterbein Coll, OH	B
Peru State Coll, NE	B
Pittsburg State U, KS	B
Quincy U, IL	B
Rockford Coll, IL	B
St. Ambrose U, IA	B
St. Cloud State U, MN	B
Saint John's U, MN	B

Saint Mary-of-the-Woods Coll, IN B
Saint Mary's Coll, IN B
Saint Xavier U, IL B
School of the Art Inst of Chicago, IL B
Siena Heights U, MI B
Silver Lake Coll, WI B
Simpson Coll, IA B
South Dakota State U, SD B
Southeastern Oklahoma State U, OK B
Southeast Missouri State U, MO B
Southern Nazarene U, OK B
Southwest Baptist U, MO B
Southwestern Oklahoma State U, OK B
Southwest Minnesota State U, MN B
Southwest Missouri State U, MO B
Tabor Coll, KS B
Taylor U, IN B
Trinity Christian Coll, IL B
Union Coll, NE B
The U of Akron, OH B
U of Central Oklahoma, OK B
U of Cincinnati, OH B
U of Dayton, OH B
U of Evansville, IN B
The U of Findlay, OH B
U of Illinois at Chicago, IL B
U of Illinois at Urbana–Champaign, IL B
U of Indianapolis, IN B
The U of Iowa, IA B
U of Kansas, KS B
U of Michigan, MI B
U of Michigan–Dearborn, MI B
U of Michigan–Flint, MI B
U of Minnesota, Duluth, MN B
U of Minnesota, Twin Cities Campus, MN B
U of Missouri–Columbia, MO B
U of Nebraska–Lincoln, NE B
U of Northern Iowa, IA B
U of Rio Grande, OH B
U of Saint Francis, IN B
U of Sioux Falls, SD B
The U of South Dakota, SD B
U of Toledo, OH B
U of Wisconsin–La Crosse, WI B
U of Wisconsin–Madison, WI B
U of Wisconsin–Milwaukee, WI B
U of Wisconsin–Oshkosh, WI B
U of Wisconsin–River Falls, WI B
U of Wisconsin–Stout, WI B
U of Wisconsin–Superior, WI B
U of Wisconsin–Whitewater, WI B
Upper Iowa U, IA B
Ursuline Coll, OH B
Valley City State U, ND B
Valparaiso U, IN B
Viterbo U, WI B
Waldorf Coll, IA A
Wartburg Coll, IA B
Washington U in St. Louis, MO B
Wayne State U, MI B
Western Michigan U, MI B
Wichita State U, KS B
William Woods U, MO B
Wilmington Coll, OH B
Winona State U, MN B
Wittenberg U, OH B
Wright State U, OH B
Youngstown State U, OH B

ART HISTORY

Andrews U, MI B
Aquinas Coll, MI B
Art Academy of Cincinnati, OH B
Augsburg Coll, MN B
Augustana Coll, IL B
Baker U, KS B
Baldwin-Wallace Coll, OH B
Beloit Coll, WI B
Bethel Coll, MN B
Blackburn Coll, IL B
Bowling Green State U, OH B
Bradley U, IL B
Calvin Coll, MI B
Carleton Coll, MN B
Case Western Reserve U, OH B
Chicago State U, IL B
Clarke Coll, IA B
Cleveland State U, OH B
Coll of Saint Benedict, MN B
Coll of St. Catherine, MN B
The Coll of Wooster, OH B
Concordia Coll, MN B
Concordia U, MN B
Cornell Coll, IA B
Creighton U, NE B
Denison U, OH B
DePaul U, IL B
DePauw U, IN B
Dominican U, IL B
Drake U, IA B
Drury U, MO B
Eastern Michigan U, MI B
Governors State U, IL B
Grand Valley State U, MI B
Gustavus Adolphus Coll, MN B
Hamline U, MN B
Hanover Coll, IN B
Hastings Coll, NE B
Hiram Coll, OH B
Hope Coll, MI B
Illinois Wesleyan U, IL B
Indiana State U, IN B
Indiana U Bloomington, IN B
Indiana U–Purdue U Indianapolis, IN B
John Carroll U, OH B
Kalamazoo Coll, MI B
Kansas City Art Inst, MO B
Kendall Coll of Art and Design of Ferris State U, MI B
Kent State U, OH B
Kenyon Coll, OH B
Knox Coll, IL B
Lake Forest Coll, IL B
Lawrence U, WI B
Lincoln Coll, Lincoln, IL A
Lindenwood U, MO B
Lourdes Coll, OH A,B
Loyola U Chicago, IL B
Macalester Coll, MN B
MacMurray Coll, IL B
Marian Coll, IN B
Miami U, OH B
Michigan State U, MI B
Minnesota State U, Mankato, MN B
Minnesota State U, Moorhead, MN B
Northern Illinois U, IL B
Northwestern U, IL B
Notre Dame Coll, OH B
Oakland U, MI B
Oberlin Coll, OH B
The Ohio State U, OH B
Ohio U, OH B
Ohio Wesleyan U, OH B
Oklahoma City U, OK B
Principia Coll, IL B
Rockford Coll, IL B
Roosevelt U, IL B
St. Cloud State U, MN B
Saint John's U, MN B
Saint Louis U, MO B
St. Olaf Coll, MN B
School of the Art Inst of Chicago, IL B
Truman State U, MO B
The U of Akron, OH B
U of Chicago, IL B
U of Cincinnati, OH B
U of Dayton, OH B
U of Evansville, IN B
U of Illinois at Chicago, IL B
U of Illinois at Urbana–Champaign, IL B
U of Indianapolis, IN B
The U of Iowa, IA B
U of Kansas, KS B
U of Michigan, MI B
U of Michigan–Dearborn, MI B
U of Minnesota, Duluth, MN B
U of Minnesota, Morris, MN B
U of Minnesota, Twin Cities Campus, MN B
U of Missouri–Kansas City, MO B
U of Missouri–St. Louis, MO B
U of Nebraska at Omaha, NE B
U of Nebraska–Lincoln, NE B
U of Northern Iowa, IA B
U of Notre Dame, IN B
U of Oklahoma, OK B
U of St. Thomas, MN B
U of Toledo, OH B
U of Tulsa, OK B
U of Wisconsin–Madison, WI B
U of Wisconsin–Milwaukee, WI B
U of Wisconsin–Superior, WI B
U of Wisconsin–Whitewater, WI B
Ursuline Coll, OH B
Valparaiso U, IN B
Washington U in St. Louis, MO B
Wayne State U, MI B
Webster U, MO B
Western Michigan U, MI B
Wichita State U, KS B
Wittenberg U, OH B
Wright State U, OH B
Youngstown State U, OH B

ARTS MANAGEMENT

Adrian Coll, MI B
Baldwin-Wallace Coll, OH B
Benedictine Coll, KS B
Benedictine U, IL B
Buena Vista U, IA B
Butler U, IN B
Columbia Coll Chicago, IL B
Culver-Stockton Coll, MO B
Dakota State U, SD B
DePaul U, IL B
Eastern Michigan U, MI B
Fontbonne U, MO B
Illinois Wesleyan U, IL B
Lakeland Coll, WI B
Luther Coll, IA B
Millikin U, IL B
Ohio U, OH B
Oklahoma City U, OK B
Quincy U, IL B
U of Evansville, IN B
The U of Iowa, IA B
U of Michigan–Dearborn, MI B
The U of South Dakota, SD B
U of Tulsa, OK B
U of Wisconsin–Stevens Point, WI B
Upper Iowa U, IA B
Viterbo U, WI B
Wartburg Coll, IA B

ART THERAPY

Alverno Coll, WI B
Avila U, MO B
Bowling Green State U, OH B
Capital U, OH B
Edgewood Coll, WI B
Goshen Coll, IN B
Marygrove Coll, MI B
Millikin U, IL B
Mount Mary Coll, WI B
Ohio U, OH B
Ohio Wesleyan U, OH B
Pittsburg State U, KS B
School of the Art Inst of Chicago, IL B
U of Indianapolis, IN B
U of Wisconsin–Superior, WI B
Webster U, MO B

ASIAN-AMERICAN STUDIES

The Ohio State U, OH B

ASIAN STUDIES

Augustana Coll, IL B
Beloit Coll, WI B
Bowling Green State U, OH B
Carleton Coll, MN B
Case Western Reserve U, OH B
Coe Coll, IA B
The Coll of Wooster, OH B
Earlham Coll, IN B
Hamline U, MN B
Indiana U Bloomington, IN B
John Carroll U, OH B
Kenyon Coll, OH B
Lake Forest Coll, IL B
Macalester Coll, MN B
Mount Union Coll, OH B
Northwestern U, IL B
Ohio U, OH B
St. Olaf Coll, MN B
U of Chicago, IL B
U of Cincinnati, OH B
U of Illinois at Urbana–Champaign, IL B
The U of Iowa, IA B
U of Michigan, MI B
U of Northern Iowa, IA B
U of Toledo, OH B

Asian Studies (continued)

U of Wisconsin–Madison, WI B
Washington U in St. Louis, MO B
Wayne State U, MI B
Western Michigan U, MI B
Wittenberg U, OH B

ASTRONOMY

Benedictine Coll, KS B
Case Western Reserve U, OH B
Central Michigan U, MI B
Drake U, IA B
Indiana U Bloomington, IN B
Minnesota State U, Mankato, MN B
Mount Union Coll, OH B
Northwestern U, IL B
The Ohio State U, OH B
Ohio Wesleyan U, OH B
U of Illinois at Urbana–Champaign, IL B
The U of Iowa, IA B
U of Kansas, KS B
U of Michigan, MI B
U of Minnesota, Twin Cities Campus, MN B
U of Oklahoma, OK B
U of Wisconsin–Madison, WI B
Valparaiso U, IN B
Youngstown State U, OH B

ASTROPHYSICS

Augsburg Coll, MN B
Indiana U Bloomington, IN B
Michigan State U, MI B
Ohio U, OH B
U of Minnesota, Twin Cities Campus, MN B
U of Missouri–St. Louis, MO B
U of Oklahoma, OK B

ATHLETIC TRAINING/SPORTS MEDICINE

Alma Coll, MI B
Anderson U, IN B
Aquinas Coll, MI B
Ashland U, OH B
Augsburg Coll, MN B
Augustana Coll, SD B
Baldwin-Wallace Coll, OH B
Ball State U, IN B
Bethany Coll, KS B
Bethel Coll, MN B
Bowling Green State U, OH B
Buena Vista U, IA B
Calvin Coll, MI B
Capital U, OH B
Carroll Coll, WI B
Carthage Coll, WI B
Cedarville U, OH B
Central Christian Coll of Kansas, KS A
Central Methodist Coll, MO B
Central Michigan U, MI B
Clarke Coll, IA B
Coe Coll, IA B
Concordia U, NE B
Concordia U Wisconsin, WI B
Culver-Stockton Coll, MO B
Dakota Wesleyan U, SD B
Defiance Coll, OH B
DePauw U, IN B
Eastern Michigan U, MI B
Eureka Coll, IL B
The Franciscan U, IA B
Franklin Coll, IN B
Graceland U, IA B
Grand Valley State U, MI B
Gustavus Adolphus Coll, MN B
Hamline U, MN B
Heidelberg Coll, OH B
Hope Coll, MI B
Indiana State U, IN B
Indiana U Bloomington, IN B
Indiana Wesleyan U, IN B
Kent State U, OH B
Lindenwood U, MO B
Loras Coll, IA B
Manchester Coll, IN B
Marietta Coll, OH B
Marquette U, WI B
McKendree Coll, IL B
Miami U, OH B
MidAmerica Nazarene U, KS B
Midland Lutheran Coll, NE B
Millikin U, IL B
Minnesota State U, Mankato, MN B
Mount Marty Coll, SD B
Mount Union Coll, OH B
Mount Vernon Nazarene U, OH B
National American U, SD B
Nebraska Wesleyan U, NE B
Newman U, KS B
North Central Coll, IL B
North Dakota State U, ND B
Northern Michigan U, MI B
North Park U, IL B
Northwestern Coll, MN B
Ohio Northern U, OH B
The Ohio State U, OH B
Ohio U, OH B
Oklahoma Baptist U, OK B
Oklahoma Wesleyan U, OK B
Olivet Coll, MI B
Olivet Nazarene U, IL B
Otterbein Coll, OH B
Park U, MO B
Quincy U, IL B
St. Ambrose U, IA B
Shawnee State U, OH B
Simpson Coll, IA B
South Dakota State U, SD B
Southeast Missouri State U, MO B
Southern Nazarene U, OK B
Southwest Baptist U, MO B
Southwestern Coll, KS B
Southwest Missouri State U, MO B
Sterling Coll, KS B
Tabor Coll, KS B
Taylor U, IN B
Trinity International U, IL B
The U of Akron, OH B
U of Evansville, IN B
The U of Findlay, OH B
U of Indianapolis, IN B
The U of Iowa, IA B
U of Mary, ND B
U of Michigan, MI B
U of Nebraska–Lincoln, NE B
U of North Dakota, ND B
U of Tulsa, OK B
U of Wisconsin–La Crosse, WI B
U of Wisconsin–Stevens Point, WI B
Upper Iowa U, IA B
Urbana U, OH B
Valparaiso U, IN B
Walsh U, OH B
Westminster Coll, MO B
William Woods U, MO B
Wilmington Coll, OH B
Winona State U, MN B
Xavier U, OH B
Youngstown State U, OH B

ATMOSPHERIC SCIENCES

Creighton U, NE B
Iowa State U of Science and Technology, IA B
Northern Illinois U, IL B
Northland Coll, WI B
Ohio U, OH B
St. Cloud State U, MN B
Saint Louis U, MO B
U of Kansas, KS B
U of Michigan, MI B
U of Missouri–Columbia, MO B
U of Nebraska–Lincoln, NE B
U of North Dakota, ND B
U of Oklahoma, OK B
U of Wisconsin–Milwaukee, WI B
Valparaiso U, IN B

AUDIO ENGINEERING

Cleveland Inst of Music, OH B
Mount Vernon Nazarene U, OH B
Webster U, MO B

AUTO BODY REPAIR

Ranken Tech Coll, MO A

AUTO MECHANIC/TECHNICIAN

Andrews U, MI A,B
Baker Coll of Flint, MI A
Central Missouri State U, MO A
Ferris State U, MI A,B
McPherson Coll, KS A
Northern Michigan U, MI A
Oakland City U, IN A
Pittsburg State U, KS A,B
Ranken Tech Coll, MO A
Southern Illinois U Carbondale, IL A
U of Northwestern Ohio, OH A

AUTOMOTIVE ENGINEERING TECHNOLOGY

Central Michigan U, MI B
Central Missouri State U, MO B
Indiana State U, IN B
Minnesota State U, Mankato, MN B
Southern Illinois U Carbondale, IL B
Western Michigan U, MI B

AVIATION/AIRWAY SCIENCE

Indiana State U, IN A
Kansas State U, KS B
Kent State U, OH B
Ohio U, OH B
Purdue U, IN B
Quincy U, IL B
U of North Dakota, ND B
Western Michigan U, MI B

AVIATION MANAGEMENT

Academy Coll, MN A
Baker Coll of Muskegon, MI B
Bowling Green State U, OH B
Indiana State U, IN B
Lewis U, IL B
Minnesota State U, Mankato, MN B
The Ohio State U, OH B
Ohio U, OH B
Oklahoma State U, OK B
Park U, MO A,B
Quincy U, IL B
St. Cloud State U, MN B
Saint Louis U, MO B
Southeastern Oklahoma State U, OK B
Southern Illinois U Carbondale, IL B
Southern Nazarene U, OK B
U of Dubuque, IA A,B
U of Nebraska at Kearney, NE B
U of Nebraska at Omaha, NE B
U of North Dakota, ND B
Western Michigan U, MI B
Winona State U, MN B

AVIATION TECHNOLOGY

Andrews U, MI A,B
Baker Coll of Flint, MI A
Coll of the Ozarks, MO B
Grace U, NE B
Hesston Coll, KS A
Lewis U, IL A,B
Moody Bible Inst, IL B
Northern Michigan U, MI A
The Ohio State U, OH B
Oklahoma State U, OK B
Southern Illinois U Carbondale, IL B
Spartan School of Aeronautics, OK A
U of Minnesota, Crookston, MN A
Western Michigan U, MI B

BANKING

Central Michigan U, MI B
Kent State U, OH A
Southeast Missouri State U, MO B
The U of Akron, OH A
U of Indianapolis, IN A,B
U of Nebraska at Omaha, NE B
Youngstown State U, OH B

BEHAVIORAL SCIENCES

Andrews U, MI B
Antioch Coll, OH B
Augsburg Coll, MN B
Avila U, MO B
Bemidji State U, MN B
Central Christian Coll of Kansas, KS A
Circleville Bible Coll, OH A,B
Columbia Coll, MO B
Concordia U, NE B
Dakota Wesleyan U, SD B
Drury U, MO B
East-West U, IL B
Evangel U, MO B

Grand Valley State U, MI B
Indiana U Kokomo, IN B
Lakeland Coll, WI B
Lincoln Coll, Lincoln, IL A
Lincoln Coll, Normal, IL A
McPherson Coll, KS B
Midland Lutheran Coll, NE B
Minnesota State U, Mankato, MN B
Mount Marty Coll, SD B
Mount Mary Coll, WI B
National-Louis U, IL B
Northwest Missouri State U, MO B
Oklahoma Wesleyan U, OK A,B
Purdue U Calumet, IN B
Rochester Coll, MI B
St. Cloud State U, MN B
Sterling Coll, KS B
The U of Akron, OH B
U of Chicago, IL B
U of Mary, ND B
U of Michigan–Dearborn, MI B
U of Missouri–St. Louis, MO B
U of St. Thomas, MN B
U of Sioux Falls, SD B
Waldorf Coll, IA A
Walsh U, OH B
Wittenberg U, OH B

BIBLICAL LANGUAGES/ LITERATURES

American Christian Coll and Seminary, OK B
Bethel Coll, IN A,B
Central Bible Coll, MO B
Concordia U, IL B
Concordia U, MI B
Concordia U Wisconsin, WI B
Cornerstone U, MI B
Indiana Wesleyan U, IN A,B
Laura and Alvin Siegal Coll of Judaic Studies, OH B
Luther Coll, IA B
Oklahoma Baptist U, OK B
Ozark Christian Coll, MO B
Taylor U, IN B
U of Chicago, IL B
York Coll, NE B

BIBLICAL STUDIES

Anderson U, IN B
Andrews U, MI B
Barclay Coll, KS A,B
Bethel Coll, IN A,B
Bethel Coll, MN B
Calvin Coll, MI B
Cedarville U, OH B
Central Bible Coll, MO A,B
Central Christian Coll of Kansas, KS A,B
Cincinnati Bible Coll and Seminary, OH A,B
Circleville Bible Coll, OH A,B
Cornerstone U, MI B
Crossroads Coll, MN B
Crown Coll, MN A,B
Emmaus Bible Coll, IA A,B
Evangel U, MO B
Faith Baptist Bible Coll and Theological Seminary, IA A,B
Global U of the Assemblies of God, MO B
God's Bible School and Coll, OH A,B
Goshen Coll, IN B
Grace Bible Coll, MI B
Grace Coll, IN A,B
Grace U, NE A,B
Great Lakes Christian Coll, MI B
Hannibal-LaGrange Coll, MO B
Hesston Coll, KS A
Hillsdale Free Will Baptist Coll, OK A
Huntington Coll, IN B
Indiana Wesleyan U, IN B
Judson Coll, IL B
Laura and Alvin Siegal Coll of Judaic Studies, OH B
Lincoln Christian Coll, IL A,B
Malone Coll, OH B
Manhattan Christian Coll, KS A,B
Maranatha Baptist Bible Coll, WI B
Messenger Coll, MO B
Moody Bible Inst, IL B
Mount Vernon Nazarene U, OH B
North Park U, IL B
Northwestern Coll, MN B
Oak Hills Christian Coll, MN A,B
Oakland City U, IN B
Oklahoma Baptist U, OK B
Oklahoma Christian U, OK B
Olivet Nazarene U, IL B
Oral Roberts U, OK B
Ozark Christian Coll, MO B
Pillsbury Baptist Bible Coll, MN B
Reformed Bible Coll, MI A,B
Rochester Coll, MI B
St. Louis Christian Coll, MO B
Southern Nazarene U, OK B
Southwest Baptist U, MO B
Tabor Coll, KS A,B
Taylor U, IN B
Taylor U, Fort Wayne Campus, IN B
Trinity Bible Coll, ND A,B
Trinity International U, IL B
U of Evansville, IN B
U of Michigan, MI B
Waldorf Coll, IA A
Wheaton Coll, IL B
York Coll, NE B

BILINGUAL/BICULTURAL EDUCATION

Adrian Coll, MI B
Calvin Coll, MI B
Chicago State U, IL B
Eastern Michigan U, MI B
Goshen Coll, IN B
Indiana U Bloomington, IN B
Marquette U, WI B
Mount Mary Coll, WI B
Northeastern Illinois U, IL B
The U of Findlay, OH B
U of Michigan–Dearborn, MI B
U of Wisconsin–Milwaukee, WI B
Western Illinois U, IL B

BIOCHEMISTRY

Alma Coll, MI B
Andrews U, MI B
Beloit Coll, WI B
Benedictine Coll, KS B
Benedictine U, IL B
Bethel Coll, MN B
Bowling Green State U, OH B
Bradley U, IL B
Calvin Coll, MI B
Carroll Coll, WI B
Case Western Reserve U, OH B
Coe Coll, IA B
Coll of Mount St. Joseph, OH B
Coll of Saint Benedict, MN B
Coll of St. Catherine, MN B
The Coll of St. Scholastica, MN B
The Coll of Wooster, OH B
Cornell Coll, IA B
Denison U, OH B
DePaul U, IL B
Dominican U, IL B
Eastern Michigan U, MI B
Grinnell Coll, IA B
Gustavus Adolphus Coll, MN B
Hope Coll, MI B
Indiana U Bloomington, IN B
Iowa State U of Science and Technology, IA B
Jamestown Coll, ND B
Kansas State U, KS B
Kenyon Coll, OH B
Knox Coll, IL B
Lewis U, IL B
Loras Coll, IA B
Loyola U Chicago, IL B
Madonna U, MI B
Maharishi U of Management, IA B
Marietta Coll, OH B
Marquette U, WI B
Miami U, OH B
Michigan State U, MI B
Michigan Technological U, MI B
Minnesota State U, Mankato, MN B
Nebraska Wesleyan U, NE B
North Central Coll, IL B
North Dakota State U, ND B
Northern Michigan U, MI B
Northwestern U, IL B
Notre Dame Coll, OH B
Oakland U, MI B
Oberlin Coll, OH B
Ohio Northern U, OH B
The Ohio State U, OH B
Ohio U, OH B
Oklahoma Christian U, OK B
Oklahoma City U, OK B
Oklahoma State U, OK B
Olivet Coll, MI B
Olivet Nazarene U, IL B
Oral Roberts U, OK B
Otterbein Coll, OH B
Purdue U, IN B
Ripon Coll, WI B
Rockford Coll, IL B
Saginaw Valley State U, MI B
Saint John's U, MN B
Saint Joseph's Coll, IN B
Simpson Coll, IA B
South Dakota State U, SD B
Southwestern Coll, KS B
Spring Arbor U, MI B
Union Coll, NE B
U of Chicago, IL B
U of Cincinnati, OH B
U of Dayton, OH B
U of Evansville, IN B
U of Illinois at Chicago, IL B
U of Illinois at Urbana–Champaign, IL B
The U of Iowa, IA B
U of Kansas, KS B
U of Michigan, MI B
U of Michigan–Dearborn, MI B
U of Minnesota, Duluth, MN B
U of Minnesota, Twin Cities Campus, MN B
U of Missouri–Columbia, MO B
U of Missouri–St. Louis, MO B
U of Nebraska–Lincoln, NE B
U of Northern Iowa, IA B
U of Notre Dame, IN B
U of Oklahoma, OK B
U of St. Thomas, MN B
U of Tulsa, OK B
U of Wisconsin–Eau Claire, WI B
U of Wisconsin–Madison, WI B
U of Wisconsin–Milwaukee, WI B
U of Wisconsin–River Falls, WI B
Viterbo U, WI B
Wartburg Coll, IA B
Washington U in St. Louis, MO B
Western Michigan U, MI B
William Jewell Coll, MO B
Wittenberg U, OH B

BIOENGINEERING

Case Western Reserve U, OH B
Illinois Inst of Technology, IL B
Indiana U–Purdue U Indianapolis, IN B
Marquette U, WI B
Michigan State U, MI B
Milwaukee School of Engineering, WI B
North Dakota State U, ND B
Northwestern U, IL B
Oklahoma State U, OK B
Oral Roberts U, OK B
Saint Louis U, MO B
The U of Akron, OH B
U of Central Oklahoma, OK B
U of Illinois at Chicago, IL B
U of Illinois at Urbana–Champaign, IL B
The U of Iowa, IA B
U of Missouri–Columbia, MO B
U of Nebraska–Lincoln, NE B
U of Toledo, OH B
U of Wisconsin–Madison, WI B
Washington U in St. Louis, MO B
Wright State U, OH B

BIOLOGICAL/PHYSICAL SCIENCES

Alma Coll, MI B
Antioch Coll, OH B
Aquinas Coll, MI A
Augsburg Coll, MN B
Bemidji State U, MN B
Benedictine Coll, KS B
Buena Vista U, IA B
Calvin Coll, MI B
Cameron U, OK B
Case Western Reserve U, OH B
Cedarville U, OH B

Biological/Physical Sciences (continued)

Central Christian Coll of Kansas, KS A
Coe Coll, IA B
Concordia U, IL B
Concordia U, MI B
Cottey Coll, MO A
Crown Coll, MN A
Donnelly Coll, KS A
Eastern Michigan U, MI B
Eureka Coll, IL B
Fort Hays State U, KS B
Grand Valley State U, MI B
Grand View Coll, IA B
Grinnell Coll, IA B
Huntington Coll, IN B
Indiana U East, IN A
Indiana U Kokomo, IN B
Iowa Wesleyan Coll, IA B
John Carroll U, OH B
Judson Coll, IL B
Kent State U, Stark Campus, OH A
Lincoln Coll, Lincoln, IL A
Madonna U, MI A,B
Marian Coll of Fond du Lac, WI B
Marygrove Coll, MI B
Maryville U of Saint Louis, MO B
Miami U–Middletown Campus, OH A
Michigan State U, MI B
Midland Lutheran Coll, NE B
Minnesota State U, Mankato, MN B
Mount Vernon Nazarene U, OH B
National-Louis U, IL B
Nebraska Wesleyan U, NE B
Northern State U, SD B
Northland Coll, WI B
North Park U, IL B
Northwestern U, IL B
Northwest Missouri State U, MO B
Oakland City U, IN B
Ohio U, OH A
Ohio U–Chillicothe, OH A
Ohio U–Lancaster, OH A
Ohio U–Southern Campus, OH A
Ohio U–Zanesville, OH A
Oklahoma Baptist U, OK B
Oklahoma Christian U, OK B
Oklahoma City U, OK B
Oklahoma Panhandle State U, OK B
Oklahoma Wesleyan U, OK B
Olivet Nazarene U, IL B
Palmer Coll of Chiropractic, IA B
Peru State Coll, NE B
Pillsbury Baptist Bible Coll, MN B
Purdue U, IN B
Purdue U Calumet, IN B
Rochester Coll, MI A,B
Rockford Coll, IL B
Saginaw Valley State U, MI B
Saint Mary-of-the-Woods Coll, IN B
St. Norbert Coll, WI B
Saint Xavier U, IL B
Shawnee State U, OH A,B
Simpson Coll, IA B
Southeast Missouri State U, MO B
Southern Nazarene U, OK B
Tabor Coll, KS B
Tri-State U, IN A
The U of Akron, OH B
U of Cincinnati, OH A
U of Dubuque, IA B
The U of Findlay, OH B
U of Kansas, KS B
U of Mary, ND B
U of Michigan–Dearborn, MI B
U of Nebraska at Omaha, NE B
U of Northern Iowa, IA B
U of Saint Francis, IN B
U of Southern Indiana, IN B
U of Toledo, OH B
U of Wisconsin–Platteville, WI B
U of Wisconsin–Superior, WI B
U of Wisconsin–Whitewater, WI B
Upper Iowa U, IA B
Valparaiso U, IN A
Waldorf Coll, IA A
Walsh U, OH B
Washington U in St. Louis, MO B
Wilmington Coll, OH B
Winona State U, MN B
Wittenberg U, OH B
Xavier U, OH B
York Coll, NE B
Youngstown State U, OH B

BIOLOGICAL SCIENCES/ LIFE SCIENCES RELATED

Kent State U, OH B
Loras Coll, IA B
Park U, MO B
U of Nebraska–Lincoln, NE B
U of Wisconsin–Parkside, WI B
Ursuline Coll, OH B
Washington U in St. Louis, MO B

BIOLOGICAL SPECIALIZATIONS RELATED

Kent State U, OH A
Saint Mary's U of Minnesota, MN B

BIOLOGICAL TECHNOLOGY

Ferris State U, MI A
Michigan Technological U, MI B
Minnesota State U, Mankato, MN B
Purdue U Calumet, IN B
St. Cloud State U, MN B
U of Missouri–St. Louis, MO B
U of Nebraska at Omaha, NE B

BIOLOGY

Adrian Coll, MI A,B
Albion Coll, MI B
Alma Coll, MI B
Alverno Coll, WI B
Ancilla Coll, IN A
Anderson U, IN B
Andrews U, MI B
Antioch Coll, OH B
Aquinas Coll, MI B
Ashland U, OH B
Augsburg Coll, MN B
Augustana Coll, IL B
Augustana Coll, SD B
Aurora U, IL B
Avila U, MO B
Baker U, KS B
Baldwin-Wallace Coll, OH B
Ball State U, IN B
Beloit Coll, WI B
Bemidji State U, MN B
Benedictine Coll, KS B
Benedictine U, IL B
Bethany Coll, KS B
Bethany Lutheran Coll, MN B
Bethel Coll, IN B
Bethel Coll, KS B
Bethel Coll, MN B
Blackburn Coll, IL B
Black Hills State U, SD B
Bluffton Coll, OH B
Bowling Green State U, OH B
Bradley U, IL B
Briar Cliff U, IA B
Buena Vista U, IA B
Butler U, IN B
Calvin Coll, MI B
Cameron U, OK B
Capital U, OH B
Cardinal Stritch U, WI B
Carleton Coll, MN B
Carroll Coll, WI B
Carthage Coll, WI B
Case Western Reserve U, OH B
Cedarville U, OH B
Central Christian Coll of Kansas, KS A
Central Coll, IA B
Central Methodist Coll, MO B
Central Michigan U, MI B
Central Missouri State U, MO B
Chadron State Coll, NE B
Chicago State U, IL B
Clarke Coll, IA B
Cleveland State U, OH B
Coe Coll, IA B
Coll of Mount St. Joseph, OH B
Coll of Saint Benedict, MN B
Coll of St. Catherine, MN B
Coll of Saint Mary, NE B
The Coll of St. Scholastica, MN B
Coll of the Ozarks, MO B
The Coll of Wooster, OH B
Columbia Coll, MO B
Concordia Coll, MN B
Concordia U, IL B
Concordia U, MI B
Concordia U, MN B
Concordia U, NE B
Concordia U Wisconsin, WI B
Cornell Coll, IA B
Cornerstone U, MI B
Creighton U, NE B
Crown Coll, MN A
Culver-Stockton Coll, MO B
Dakota State U, SD B
Dakota Wesleyan U, SD B
Dana Coll, NE B
Defiance Coll, OH B
Denison U, OH B
DePaul U, IL B
DePauw U, IN B
Dickinson State U, ND B
Doane Coll, NE B
Dominican U, IL B
Dordt Coll, IA B
Drake U, IA B
Drury U, MO B
Earlham Coll, IN B
East Central U, OK B
Eastern Illinois U, IL B
Eastern Michigan U, MI B
East-West U, IL B
Edgewood Coll, WI B
Elmhurst Coll, IL B
Emporia State U, KS B
Eureka Coll, IL B
Evangel U, MO B
Ferris State U, MI B
Fontbonne U, MO B
Fort Hays State U, KS B
The Franciscan U, IA B
Franciscan U of Steubenville, OH B
Franklin Coll, IN B
Goshen Coll, IN B
Governors State U, IL B
Grace Coll, IN B
Graceland U, IA B
Grand Valley State U, MI B
Grand View Coll, IA B
Greenville Coll, IL B
Grinnell Coll, IA B
Gustavus Adolphus Coll, MN B
Hamline U, MN B
Hannibal-LaGrange Coll, MO B
Hanover Coll, IN B
Hastings Coll, NE B
Heidelberg Coll, OH B
Hillsdale Coll, MI B
Hiram Coll, OH B
Hope Coll, MI B
Huntington Coll, IN B
Illinois Coll, IL B
Illinois Inst of Technology, IL B
Illinois State U, IL B
Illinois Wesleyan U, IL B
Indiana State U, IN B
Indiana U Bloomington, IN B
Indiana U East, IN B
Indiana U Kokomo, IN B
Indiana U Northwest, IN B
Indiana U–Purdue U Fort Wayne, IN A,B
Indiana U–Purdue U Indianapolis, IN B
Indiana U South Bend, IN A,B
Indiana U Southeast, IN B
Indiana Wesleyan U, IN A,B
Iowa State U of Science and Technology, IA B
Iowa Wesleyan Coll, IA B
Jamestown Coll, ND B
John Carroll U, OH B
Judson Coll, IL B
Kalamazoo Coll, MI B
Kansas State U, KS B
Kent State U, OH B
Kenyon Coll, OH B
Knox Coll, IL B
Lake Erie Coll, OH B
Lake Forest Coll, IL B
Lakeland Coll, WI B
Langston U, OK B
Lawrence U, WI B
Lewis U, IL B
Lincoln Coll, Lincoln, IL A
Lindenwood U, MO B
Logan U-Coll of Chiropractic, MO B

Loras Coll, IA	B
Lourdes Coll, OH	A,B
Loyola U Chicago, IL	B
Luther Coll, IA	B
Macalester Coll, MN	B
MacMurray Coll, IL	B
Madonna U, MI	A,B
Maharishi U of Management, IA	A,B
Malone Coll, OH	B
Manchester Coll, IN	B
Marian Coll, IN	B
Marian Coll of Fond du Lac, WI	B
Marietta Coll, OH	B
Marquette U, WI	B
Martin U, IN	B
Marygrove Coll, MI	B
Maryville U of Saint Louis, MO	B
Mayville State U, ND	B
McKendree Coll, IL	B
McPherson Coll, KS	B
Metropolitan State U, MN	B
Miami U, OH	B
Michigan State U, MI	B
Michigan Technological U, MI	B
MidAmerica Nazarene U, KS	B
Midland Lutheran Coll, NE	B
Millikin U, IL	B
Minnesota State U, Mankato, MN	B
Minnesota State U, Moorhead, MN	B
Minot State U, ND	B
Missouri Southern State Coll, MO	B
Missouri Valley Coll, MO	B
Missouri Western State Coll, MO	B
Monmouth Coll, IL	B
Morningside Coll, IA	B
Mount Marty Coll, SD	B
Mount Mary Coll, WI	B
Mount Mercy Coll, IA	B
Mount Union Coll, OH	B
Mount Vernon Nazarene U, OH	B
Muskingum Coll, OH	B
National-Louis U, IL	B
Nebraska Wesleyan U, NE	B
Newman U, KS	B
North Central Coll, IL	B
North Dakota State U, ND	B
Northeastern Illinois U, IL	B
Northeastern State U, OK	B
Northern Illinois U, IL	B
Northern Michigan U, MI	B
Northern State U, SD	B
Northland Coll, WI	B
North Park U, IL	B
Northwestern Coll, IA	B
Northwestern Coll, MN	B
Northwestern Oklahoma State U, OK	B
Northwestern U, IL	B
Northwest Missouri State U, MO	B
Notre Dame Coll, OH	B
Oakland City U, IN	B
Oakland U, MI	B
Oberlin Coll, OH	B
Ohio Dominican U, OH	B
Ohio Northern U, OH	B
The Ohio State U, OH	B
Ohio Wesleyan U, OH	B
Oklahoma Baptist U, OK	B
Oklahoma Christian U, OK	B
Oklahoma City U, OK	B
Oklahoma Panhandle State U, OK	B
Oklahoma State U, OK	B
Oklahoma Wesleyan U, OK	A,B
Olivet Coll, MI	B
Olivet Nazarene U, IL	B
Oral Roberts U, OK	B
Ottawa U, KS	B
Otterbein Coll, OH	B
Park U, MO	B
Peru State Coll, NE	B
Pittsburg State U, KS	B
Presentation Coll, SD	A
Principia Coll, IL	B
Purdue U, IN	B
Purdue U Calumet, IN	B
Purdue U North Central, IN	B
Quincy U, IL	B
Ripon Coll, WI	B
Rockford Coll, IL	B
Rockhurst U, MO	B
Rogers State U, OK	A,B
Roosevelt U, IL	B
Rose-Hulman Inst of Technology, IN	B
Saginaw Valley State U, MI	B
St. Ambrose U, IA	B
St. Cloud State U, MN	B
Saint John's U, MN	B
Saint Joseph's Coll, IN	B
Saint Louis U, MO	B
Saint Mary-of-the-Woods Coll, IN	B
Saint Mary's Coll, IN	B
Saint Mary's Coll of Madonna U, MI	B
Saint Mary's U of Minnesota, MN	B
Saint Mary U, KS	B
St. Norbert Coll, WI	B
St. Olaf Coll, MN	B
Saint Xavier U, IL	B
Shawnee State U, OH	A,B
Siena Heights U, MI	B
Silver Lake Coll, WI	B
Simpson Coll, IA	B
South Dakota State U, SD	B
Southeastern Oklahoma State U, OK	B
Southeast Missouri State U, MO	B
Southern Illinois U Carbondale, IL	B
Southern Illinois U Edwardsville, IL	B
Southern Nazarene U, OK	B
Southwest Baptist U, MO	B
Southwestern Coll, KS	B
Southwestern Oklahoma State U, OK	B
Southwest Minnesota State U, MN	B
Southwest Missouri State U, MO	B
Spring Arbor U, MI	B
Springfield Coll in Illinois, IL	A
Stephens Coll, MO	B
Sterling Coll, KS	B
Tabor Coll, KS	B
Taylor U, IN	B
Trinity Christian Coll, IL	B
Trinity International U, IL	B
Tri-State U, IN	B
Truman State U, MO	B
Union Coll, NE	B
The U of Akron, OH	B
U of Central Oklahoma, OK	B
U of Chicago, IL	B
U of Cincinnati, OH	B
U of Dayton, OH	B
U of Dubuque, IA	A,B
U of Evansville, IN	B
The U of Findlay, OH	B
U of Illinois at Chicago, IL	B
U of Illinois at Springfield, IL	B
U of Illinois at Urbana–Champaign, IL	B
U of Indianapolis, IN	B
The U of Iowa, IA	B
U of Kansas, KS	B
U of Mary, ND	B
U of Michigan, MI	B
U of Michigan–Dearborn, MI	B
U of Michigan–Flint, MI	B
U of Minnesota, Duluth, MN	B
U of Minnesota, Morris, MN	B
U of Minnesota, Twin Cities Campus, MN	B
U of Missouri–Columbia, MO	B
U of Missouri–Kansas City, MO	B
U of Missouri–Rolla, MO	B
U of Missouri–St. Louis, MO	B
U of Nebraska at Kearney, NE	B
U of Nebraska at Omaha, NE	B
U of North Dakota, ND	B
U of Northern Iowa, IA	B
U of Notre Dame, IN	B
U of Rio Grande, OH	A,B
U of St. Francis, IL	B
U of Saint Francis, IN	B
U of St. Thomas, MN	B
U of Science and Arts of Oklahoma, OK	B
U of Sioux Falls, SD	B
The U of South Dakota, SD	B
U of Southern Indiana, IN	B
U of Toledo, OH	A,B
U of Tulsa, OK	B
U of Wisconsin–Eau Claire, WI	B
U of Wisconsin–Green Bay, WI	A,B
U of Wisconsin–La Crosse, WI	B
U of Wisconsin–Madison, WI	B
U of Wisconsin–Milwaukee, WI	B
U of Wisconsin–Oshkosh, WI	B
U of Wisconsin–Platteville, WI	B
U of Wisconsin–River Falls, WI	B
U of Wisconsin–Stevens Point, WI	B
U of Wisconsin–Superior, WI	B
U of Wisconsin–Whitewater, WI	B
Upper Iowa U, IA	B
Urbana U, OH	B
Ursuline Coll, OH	B
Valley City State U, ND	B
Valparaiso U, IN	B
Viterbo U, WI	B
Wabash Coll, IN	B
Waldorf Coll, IA	A
Walsh U, OH	B
Wartburg Coll, IA	B
Washington U in St. Louis, MO	B
Wayne State Coll, NE	B
Wayne State U, MI	B
Webster U, MO	B
Western Illinois U, IL	B
Western Michigan U, MI	B
Westminster Coll, MO	B
Wheaton Coll, IL	B
Wichita State U, KS	B
Wilberforce U, OH	B
William Jewell Coll, MO	B
William Penn U, IA	B
William Woods U, MO	B
Wilmington Coll, OH	B
Winona State U, MN	B
Wisconsin Lutheran Coll, WI	B
Wittenberg U, OH	B
Wright State U, OH	A,B
Xavier U, OH	B
York Coll, NE	B
Youngstown State U, OH	B

BIOLOGY EDUCATION

Bethany Coll, KS	B
Bowling Green State U, OH	B
Cedarville U, OH	B
Central Methodist Coll, MO	B
Central Michigan U, MI	B
Central Missouri State U, MO	B
Chadron State Coll, NE	B
Coll of St. Catherine, MN	B
Coll of the Ozarks, MO	B
Concordia Coll, MN	B
Concordia U, IL	B
Concordia U, NE	B
Dakota Wesleyan U, SD	B
Eastern Michigan U, MI	B
Elmhurst Coll, IL	B
Franklin Coll, IN	B
Greenville Coll, IL	B
Gustavus Adolphus Coll, MN	B
Hastings Coll, NE	B
Indiana U Bloomington, IN	B
Indiana U Northwest, IN	B
Indiana U–Purdue U Fort Wayne, IN	B
Indiana U South Bend, IN	B
Indiana U Southeast, IN	B
Luther Coll, IA	B
Malone Coll, OH	B
Mayville State U, ND	B
McKendree Coll, IL	B
Miami U, OH	B
Minot State U, ND	B
North Dakota State U, ND	B
Ohio U, OH	B
Oklahoma Baptist U, OK	B
St. Ambrose U, IA	B
Saint Xavier U, IL	B
Southern Nazarene U, OK	B
Southwest Minnesota State U, MN	B
Southwest Missouri State U, MO	B
Trinity Christian Coll, IL	B
Union Coll, NE	B
U of Illinois at Chicago, IL	B
U of Mary, ND	B
U of Nebraska–Lincoln, NE	B
U of Rio Grande, OH	B
U of Wisconsin–River Falls, WI	B
U of Wisconsin–Superior, WI	B
Valley City State U, ND	B
Viterbo U, WI	B

Biology Education (continued)

Washington U in St. Louis, MO B
Xavier U, OH B
Youngstown State U, OH B

BIOMEDICAL ENGINEERING-RELATED TECHNOLOGY

Indiana State U, IN B
Indiana U–Purdue U Indianapolis, IN A
Oral Roberts U, OK B

BIOMEDICAL SCIENCE

Antioch Coll, OH B
Grand Valley State U, MI B
Marquette U, WI B
St. Cloud State U, MN B
Stephens Coll, MO B
U of Michigan, MI B
Western Michigan U, MI B

BIOMEDICAL TECHNOLOGY

Andrews U, MI B
Baker Coll of Flint, MI A
Cleveland State U, OH B
Northwest Missouri State U, MO B

BIOMETRICS

U of Michigan, MI B

BIOPHYSICS

Andrews U, MI B
Illinois Inst of Technology, IL B
Iowa State U of Science and Technology, IA B
Saint Mary's U of Minnesota, MN B
Southwestern Oklahoma State U, OK B
U of Illinois at Urbana–Champaign, IL B
U of Michigan, MI B
U of Southern Indiana, IN B
Washington U in St. Louis, MO B

BIOPSYCHOLOGY

Morningside Coll, IA B
Nebraska Wesleyan U, NE B
Washington U in St. Louis, MO B

BIOTECHNOLOGY RESEARCH

Calvin Coll, MI B
Cleveland State U, OH B
Missouri Southern State Coll, MO B
North Dakota State U, ND B
The Ohio State U, OH B
U of Nebraska at Omaha, NE B
U of Wisconsin–River Falls, WI B

BOTANY

Andrews U, MI B
Ball State U, IN B
Iowa State U of Science and Technology, IA B
Kent State U, OH B
Lincoln Coll, Lincoln, IL A
Miami U, OH B
Miami U–Middletown Campus, OH A
Michigan State U, MI B
Minnesota State U, Mankato, MN B
North Dakota State U, ND B
Northern Michigan U, MI B
Northwest Missouri State U, MO B
The Ohio State U, OH B
Ohio U, OH B
Ohio Wesleyan U, OH B
Oklahoma State U, OK B
Purdue U, IN B
Purdue U Calumet, IN B
St. Cloud State U, MN B
Saint Xavier U, IL B
Southeastern Oklahoma State U, OK B
Southern Illinois U Carbondale, IL B
The U of Akron, OH B
U of Illinois at Urbana–Champaign, IL B
U of Michigan, MI B
U of Minnesota, Twin Cities Campus, MN B
U of Oklahoma, OK B
U of Wisconsin–Madison, WI B
Wittenberg U, OH B

BRITISH LITERATURE

Maharishi U of Management, IA A,B
Oral Roberts U, OK B
Washington U in St. Louis, MO B

BROADCAST JOURNALISM

Adrian Coll, MI B
Baldwin-Wallace Coll, OH B
Bemidji State U, MN B
Bowling Green State U, OH B
Bradley U, IL B
Brown Coll, MN A
Cedarville U, OH B
Chicago State U, IL B
Coll of the Ozarks, MO B
Columbia Coll Chicago, IL B
Concordia Coll, MN B
Cornerstone U, MI A
Drake U, IA B
Eastern Michigan U, MI B
Evangel U, MO A,B
Fontbonne U, MO B
Franklin Coll, IN B
Goshen Coll, IN B
Grace U, NE B
Grand Valley State U, MI B
Huntington Coll, IN B
Indiana U Bloomington, IN B
Langston U, OK B
Lewis U, IL B
Lincoln Coll, Lincoln, IL A
Lindenwood U, MO B
Malone Coll, OH B
Manchester Coll, IN A
Marquette U, WI B
Midland Lutheran Coll, NE B
Minnesota State U, Moorhead, MN B
Mount Vernon Nazarene U, OH B
North Central Coll, IL B
Northern Michigan U, MI B
Northwest Missouri State U, MO B
Ohio Northern U, OH B
Ohio U, OH B
Ohio U–Zanesville, OH A
Ohio Wesleyan U, OH B
Oklahoma Baptist U, OK B
Oklahoma Christian U, OK B
Oklahoma City U, OK B
Oklahoma State U, OK B
Olivet Nazarene U, IL B
Pittsburg State U, KS B
Reformed Bible Coll, MI B
Rogers State U, OK A
St. Cloud State U, MN B
Southern Nazarene U, OK B
Stephens Coll, MO B
The U of Akron, OH B
U of Central Oklahoma, OK B
U of Cincinnati, OH B
U of Dayton, OH B
The U of Findlay, OH B
U of Illinois at Urbana–Champaign, IL B
The U of Iowa, IA B
U of Kansas, KS B
U of Missouri–Columbia, MO B
U of Nebraska at Omaha, NE B
U of Nebraska–Lincoln, NE B
U of Northern Iowa, IA B
U of Oklahoma, OK B
U of St. Francis, IL B
U of St. Thomas, MN B
The U of South Dakota, SD B
U of Tulsa, OK B
U of Wisconsin–Madison, WI B
U of Wisconsin–Milwaukee, WI B
U of Wisconsin–Oshkosh, WI B
U of Wisconsin–Platteville, WI B
U of Wisconsin–River Falls, WI B
U of Wisconsin–Superior, WI B
Waldorf Coll, IA A,B
Wartburg Coll, IA B
Webster U, MO B
William Woods U, MO B
Winona State U, MN B

BUILDING MAINTENANCE/ MANAGEMENT

Park U, MO A

BUSINESS

Anderson U, IN A
Aurora U, IL B
Baker Coll of Flint, MI A
Baker Coll of Jackson, MI B
Benedictine U, IL B
Bowling Green State U, OH B
Cameron U, OK A,B
Capella U, MN B
Central Michigan U, MI B
Circleville Bible Coll, OH B
Concordia Coll, MN B
Concordia U, NE B
Crown Coll, MN A
DePaul U, IL B
Drake U, IA B
Eastern Illinois U, IL B
Eastern Michigan U, MI B
Franklin Coll, IN B
Gallipolis Career Coll, OH A
Grace Coll, IN B
Hillsdale Free Will Baptist Coll, OK A,B
Indiana U Bloomington, IN B
Indiana U East, IN A,B
Indiana U Kokomo, IN A,B
Indiana U–Purdue U Indianapolis, IN B
Indiana U South Bend, IN A,B
Indiana U Southeast, IN A,B
Kent State U, OH A
Loras Coll, IA B
Luther Coll, IA B
Maharishi U of Management, IA B
Manchester Coll, IN B
Marygrove Coll, MI A,B
Maryville U of Saint Louis, MO B
Miami U, OH B
Miami U–Middletown Campus, OH A
Milwaukee School of Engineering, WI B
Northeastern Illinois U, IL B
Northern Illinois U, IL B
Ohio U, OH B
Oklahoma Christian U, OK B
Oklahoma City U, OK B
Oklahoma State U, OK B
Rockhurst U, MO B
Saginaw Valley State U, MI B
St. Ambrose U, IA B
Saint Mary's U of Minnesota, MN B
St. Norbert Coll, WI B
Saint Xavier U, IL B
Southern Illinois U Carbondale, IL B
Southern Illinois U Edwardsville, IL B
Southern Nazarene U, OK A
Southwest Baptist U, MO A
Southwest Missouri State U, MO B
Trinity Christian Coll, IL B
Union Inst & U, OH B
The U of Akron, OH B
U of Central Oklahoma, OK B
U of Illinois at Urbana–Champaign, IL B
U of Kansas, KS B
U of Missouri–Rolla, MO B
U of North Dakota, ND B
U of Notre Dame, IN B
U of Science and Arts of Oklahoma, OK B
U of Southern Indiana, IN A,B
U of Wisconsin–Whitewater, WI B
Washington U in St. Louis, MO B
Webster U, MO B
Western Illinois U, IL B
Western Michigan U, MI B
Xavier U, OH A,B
Youngstown State U, OH B

BUSINESS ADMINISTRATION

Academy Coll, MN B
Adrian Coll, MI A,B
AIB Coll of Business, IA A
Albion Coll, MI B
Alma Coll, MI B

Institution	Degree
Alverno Coll, WI	B
American Christian Coll and Seminary, OK	B
Ancilla Coll, IN	A
Anderson U, IN	B
Andrews U, MI	A,B
Antioch Coll, OH	B
Antioch U McGregor, OH	B
Aquinas Coll, MI	B
Ashland U, OH	B
Augsburg Coll, MN	B
Augustana Coll, IL	B
Augustana Coll, SD	B
Avila U, MO	B
Bacone Coll, OK	A
Baker Coll of Auburn Hills, MI	A,B
Baker Coll of Cadillac, MI	A,B
Baker Coll of Clinton Township, MI	A,B
Baker Coll of Flint, MI	A,B
Baker Coll of Jackson, MI	A,B
Baker Coll of Muskegon, MI	A,B
Baker Coll of Owosso, MI	A,B
Baker Coll of Port Huron, MI	A,B
Baker U, KS	B
Baldwin-Wallace Coll, OH	B
Ball State U, IN	A,B
Baptist Bible Coll, MO	A,B
Barclay Coll, KS	B
Bellevue U, NE	B
Beloit Coll, WI	B
Bemidji State U, MN	B
Benedictine Coll, KS	A,B
Benedictine U, IL	A
Bethany Coll, KS	B
Bethany Lutheran Coll, MN	B
Bethel Coll, IN	A,B
Bethel Coll, KS	B
Bethel Coll, MN	B
Blackburn Coll, IL	B
Black Hills State U, SD	B
Bluffton Coll, OH	B
Bowling Green State U, OH	B
Bradley U, IL	B
Briar Cliff U, IA	B
Bryant and Stratton Coll, WI	A
Buena Vista U, IA	B
Butler U, IN	B
Calumet Coll of Saint Joseph, IN	A,B
Calvin Coll, MI	B
Cameron U, OK	B
Capital U, OH	B
Cardinal Stritch U, WI	A,B
Carroll Coll, WI	B
Carthage Coll, WI	B
Case Western Reserve U, OH	B
Cedarville U, OH	B
Central Christian Coll of Kansas, KS	A,B
Central Coll, IA	B
Central Methodist Coll, MO	B
Central Michigan U, MI	B
Central Missouri State U, MO	B
Chadron State Coll, NE	B
Chatfield Coll, OH	A
Chicago State U, IL	B
Clarke Coll, IA	B
Clarkson Coll, NE	B
Cleary U, MI	A,B
Coe Coll, IA	B
Coll of Menominee Nation, WI	A
Coll of Mount St. Joseph, OH	A,B
Coll of Saint Benedict, MN	B
Coll of St. Catherine, MN	B
Coll of Saint Mary, NE	A,B
Coll of the Ozarks, MO	B
Colorado Tech U Sioux Falls Campus, SD	A,B
Columbia Coll, MO	A,B
Columbia Coll Chicago, IL	B
Concordia Coll, MN	B
Concordia U, IL	B
Concordia U, MI	B
Concordia U, MN	B
Concordia U, NE	B
Concordia U Wisconsin, WI	B
Cornerstone U, MI	B
Crown Coll, MN	A,B
Culver-Stockton Coll, MO	B
Dakota State U, SD	A,B
Dakota Wesleyan U, SD	A,B
Dana Coll, NE	B
Davenport U, Grand Rapids, MI	A,B
Davenport U, Kalamazoo, MI	A,B
Davenport U, Lansing, MI	A,B
Defiance Coll, OH	A,B
DePaul U, IL	B
Dickinson State U, ND	B
Doane Coll, NE	B
Dominican U, IL	B
Donnelly Coll, KS	A
Dordt Coll, IA	B
Drake U, IA	B
Drury U, MO	B
Earlham Coll, IN	B
East Central U, OK	B
Eastern Michigan U, MI	B
East-West U, IL	A,B
Edgewood Coll, WI	B
Elmhurst Coll, IL	B
Emporia State U, KS	B
Eureka Coll, IL	B
Evangel U, MO	B
Ferris State U, MI	B
Finlandia U, MI	B
Fontbonne U, MO	B
Fort Hays State U, KS	B
The Franciscan U, IA	B
Franciscan U of Steubenville, OH	A,B
Franklin Coll, IN	B
Gallipolis Career Coll, OH	A
Goshen Coll, IN	B
Governors State U, IL	B
Grace Bible Coll, MI	A,B
Grace Coll, IN	B
Graceland U, IA	B
Grace U, NE	B
Grand Valley State U, MI	B
Grand View Coll, IA	A,B
Greenville Coll, IL	B
Gustavus Adolphus Coll, MN	B
Hamilton Coll, IA	A
Hamline U, MN	B
Hannibal-LaGrange Coll, MO	B
Hanover Coll, IN	B
Harris-Stowe State Coll, MO	B
Haskell Indian Nations U, KS	A
Hastings Coll, NE	B
Heidelberg Coll, OH	B
Hesston Coll, KS	A
Hillsdale Coll, MI	B
Hiram Coll, OH	B
Hope Coll, MI	B
Huntington Coll, IN	B
Illinois Coll, IL	B
Illinois State U, IL	B
Illinois Wesleyan U, IL	B
Indiana Inst of Technology, IN	A,B
Indiana State U, IN	A,B
Indiana U Bloomington, IN	B
Indiana U Northwest, IN	A,B
Indiana U–Purdue U Fort Wayne, IN	A,B
Indiana Wesleyan U, IN	A,B
International Business Coll, Fort Wayne, IN	A,B
Iowa State U of Science and Technology, IA	B
Iowa Wesleyan Coll, IA	B
Jamestown Coll, ND	B
John Carroll U, OH	B
Judson Coll, IL	B
Kansas State U, KS	B
Kaplan Coll, IA	A,B
Kendall Coll, IL	B
Kent State U, OH	A,B
Kent State U, Ashtabula Campus, OH	A
Kent State U, Geauga Campus, OH	A,B
Kent State U, Salem Campus, OH	A
Kent State U, Stark Campus, OH	A
Kent State U, Tuscarawas Campus, OH	A,B
Kettering U, MI	B
Lake Erie Coll, OH	B
Lakeland Coll, WI	B
Langston U, OK	B
Lawrence Technological U, MI	B
Lewis Coll of Business, MI	A
Lewis U, IL	B
Lincoln Christian Coll, IL	B
Lincoln Coll, Lincoln, IL	A
Lincoln Coll, Normal, IL	A,B
Lindenwood U, MO	B
Loras Coll, IA	B
Lourdes Coll, OH	A,B
Loyola U Chicago, IL	B
Luther Coll, IA	B
MacMurray Coll, IL	A,B
Madonna U, MI	A,B
Maharishi U of Management, IA	A,B
Malone Coll, OH	B
Manchester Coll, IN	A,B
Manhattan Christian Coll, KS	B
Maranatha Baptist Bible Coll, WI	B
Marian Coll, IN	A,B
Marian Coll of Fond du Lac, WI	B
Marietta Coll, OH	A,B
Marquette U, WI	B
Martin U, IN	B
Marygrove Coll, MI	B
Maryville U of Saint Louis, MO	B
Mayville State U, ND	A,B
McKendree Coll, IL	B
McPherson Coll, KS	B
Metro Business Coll, MO	A
Metropolitan State U, MN	B
Miami U, OH	B
Miami U–Middletown Campus, OH	A
Michigan State U, MI	B
Michigan Technological U, MI	B
MidAmerica Nazarene U, KS	A,B
Midland Lutheran Coll, NE	B
Midstate Coll, IL	A,B
Millikin U, IL	B
Minnesota School of Business-Richfield, MN	A
Minnesota State U, Mankato, MN	B
Minnesota State U, Moorhead, MN	B
Minot State U, ND	B
Missouri Southern State Coll, MO	A,B
Missouri Valley Coll, MO	A,B
Missouri Western State Coll, MO	A,B
Monmouth Coll, IL	B
Morningside Coll, IA	B
Mount Marty Coll, SD	A,B
Mount Mary Coll, WI	B
Mount Mercy Coll, IA	B
Mount Union Coll, OH	B
Mount Vernon Nazarene U, OH	A,B
Muskingum Coll, OH	B
National American U, SD	A,B
National American U–Sioux Falls Branch, SD	A,B
National-Louis U, IL	B
Nebraska Indian Comm Coll, NE	A
Nebraska Wesleyan U, NE	B
Newman U, KS	B
North Central Coll, IL	B
North Dakota State U, ND	B
Northeastern State U, OK	B
Northern Illinois U, IL	B
Northern Michigan U, MI	A,B
Northern State U, SD	A,B
Northland Coll, WI	B
North Park U, IL	B
Northwestern Coll, IA	B
Northwestern Coll, MN	B
Northwestern Oklahoma State U, OK	B
Northwest Missouri State U, MO	B
Northwood U, MI	A,B
Notre Dame Coll, OH	A,B
Oak Hills Christian Coll, MN	B
Oakland City U, IN	A,B
Oakland U, MI	B
Ohio Dominican U, OH	B
Ohio Northern U, OH	B
The Ohio State U, OH	B
Ohio U, OH	A,B
Ohio U–Chillicothe, OH	A,B
Ohio U–Lancaster, OH	A,B
Ohio U–Southern Campus, OH	B
Ohio Wesleyan U, OH	B
Oklahoma Baptist U, OK	B
Oklahoma Christian U, OK	B
Oklahoma City U, OK	B
Oklahoma Panhandle State U, OK	A,B
Oklahoma Wesleyan U, OK	A,B
Olivet Coll, MI	B
Olivet Nazarene U, IL	B
Oral Roberts U, OK	B
Ottawa U, KS	B
Otterbein Coll, OH	B
Park U, MO	B
Peru State Coll, NE	B
Pillsbury Baptist Bible Coll, MN	B
Pittsburg State U, KS	B

Business Administration (continued)

Presentation Coll, SD	A,B
Principia Coll, IL	B
Purdue U, IN	B
Purdue U Calumet, IN	B
Purdue U North Central, IN	A,B
Quincy U, IL	B
Reformed Bible Coll, MI	B
Ripon Coll, WI	B
Robert Morris Coll, IL	A,B
Rochester Coll, MI	B
Rochester Comm and Tech Coll, MN	A
Rockford Business Coll, IL	A
Rockford Coll, IL	B
Rockhurst U, MO	B
Rogers State U, OK	A
Roosevelt U, IL	B
Saginaw Valley State U, MI	B
St. Ambrose U, IA	B
St. Augustine Coll, IL	A
St. Cloud State U, MN	B
St. Gregory's U, OK	A,B
Saint John's U, MN	B
Saint Joseph's Coll, IN	A,B
Saint Louis U, MO	B
Saint Mary-of-the-Woods Coll, IN	B
Saint Mary's Coll, IN	B
Saint Mary's Coll of Madonna U, MI	B
Saint Mary's U of Minnesota, MN	B
Saint Mary U, KS	B
Shawnee State U, OH	A,B
Siena Heights U, MI	A,B
Silver Lake Coll, WI	B
Simpson Coll, IA	B
Si Tanka Huron U, SD	A,B
Sitting Bull Coll, ND	A
Southeastern Oklahoma State U, OK	B
Southeast Missouri State U, MO	B
Southern Illinois U Carbondale, IL	B
Southern Nazarene U, OK	B
Southwest Baptist U, MO	A,B
Southwestern Coll, KS	B
Southwestern Oklahoma State U, OK	B
Southwest Minnesota State U, MN	A,B
Southwest Missouri State U, MO	B
Spring Arbor U, MI	B
Springfield Coll in Illinois, IL	A
Stephens Coll, MO	B
Sterling Coll, KS	B
Tabor Coll, KS	B
Taylor U, IN	A,B
Taylor U, Fort Wayne Campus, IN	A,B
Tiffin U, OH	A,B
Trinity Bible Coll, ND	A,B
Trinity Christian Coll, IL	B
Trinity International U, IL	B
Tri-State U, IN	A,B
Truman State U, MO	B
Union Coll, NE	A,B
The U of Akron, OH	A,B
U of Central Oklahoma, OK	B
U of Cincinnati, OH	A,B
U of Dayton, OH	B
U of Dubuque, IA	A,B
U of Evansville, IN	B
The U of Findlay, OH	A,B
U of Illinois at Chicago, IL	B
U of Illinois at Springfield, IL	B
U of Indianapolis, IN	A,B
The U of Iowa, IA	B
U of Mary, ND	A,B
U of Michigan, MI	B
U of Michigan–Dearborn, MI	B
U of Michigan–Flint, MI	B
U of Minnesota, Crookston, MN	A,B
U of Minnesota, Duluth, MN	B
U of Minnesota, Morris, MN	B
U of Missouri–Columbia, MO	B
U of Missouri–Kansas City, MO	B
U of Missouri–Rolla, MO	B
U of Missouri–St. Louis, MO	B
U of Nebraska at Kearney, NE	B
U of Nebraska–Lincoln, NE	B
U of Northern Iowa, IA	B
U of Northwestern Ohio, OH	A,B
U of Oklahoma, OK	B
U of Phoenix–Metro Detroit Campus, MI	B
U of Phoenix–Ohio Campus, OH	B
U of Phoenix–Oklahoma City Campus, OK	B
U of Phoenix–St. Louis Campus, MO	B
U of Phoenix–Tulsa Campus, OK	B
U of Phoenix–West Michigan Campus, MI	B
U of Phoenix–Wisconsin Campus, WI	B
U of Rio Grande, OH	A,B
U of St. Francis, IL	B
U of Saint Francis, IN	A,B
U of St. Thomas, MN	B
U of Science and Arts of Oklahoma, OK	B
U of Sioux Falls, SD	A,B
The U of South Dakota, SD	B
U of Southern Indiana, IN	B
U of Toledo, OH	A,B
U of Tulsa, OK	B
U of Wisconsin–Eau Claire, WI	B
U of Wisconsin–Green Bay, WI	A,B
U of Wisconsin–La Crosse, WI	B
U of Wisconsin–Madison, WI	B
U of Wisconsin–Milwaukee, WI	B
U of Wisconsin–Oshkosh, WI	B
U of Wisconsin–Parkside, WI	B
U of Wisconsin–Platteville, WI	B
U of Wisconsin–River Falls, WI	B
U of Wisconsin–Stevens Point, WI	B
U of Wisconsin–Stout, WI	B
U of Wisconsin–Superior, WI	B
U of Wisconsin–Whitewater, WI	B
Upper Iowa U, IA	A,B
Urbana U, OH	A,B
Ursuline Coll, OH	B
Valley City State U, ND	B
Valparaiso U, IN	B
Viterbo U, WI	B
Waldorf Coll, IA	A,B
Walsh Coll of Accountancy and Business Administration, MI	B
Walsh U, OH	A,B
Wartburg Coll, IA	B
Washington U in St. Louis, MO	B
Wayne State Coll, NE	B
Wayne State U, MI	B
Webster U, MO	B
Western Michigan U, MI	B
Westminster Coll, MO	B
Wichita State U, KS	B
Wilberforce U, OH	B
William Jewell Coll, MO	B
William Penn U, IA	B
William Woods U, MO	B
Wilmington Coll, OH	B
Winona State U, MN	B
Wittenberg U, OH	B
Wright State U, OH	B
Xavier U, OH	B
York Coll, NE	B
Youngstown State U, OH	A,B

BUSINESS ADMINISTRATION/ MANAGEMENT RELATED

DePaul U, IL	B
DeVry U, Addison, IL	B
DeVry U, Chicago, IL	B
DeVry U, Tinley Park, IL	B
DeVry U, MO	B
DeVry U, OH	B
Saint Mary-of-the-Woods Coll, IN	B
Trinity Christian Coll, IL	B
U of Notre Dame, IN	B
U of St. Thomas, MN	B
U of Wisconsin–Stout, WI	B

BUSINESS COMMUNICATIONS

Augustana Coll, SD	B
Calvin Coll, MI	B
Central Christian Coll of Kansas, KS	A
Coll of Saint Mary, NE	B
The Coll of St. Scholastica, MN	B
Marietta Coll, OH	B
Morningside Coll, IA	B
Ohio Dominican U, OH	B
Rochester Coll, MI	B
Rockhurst U, MO	B
Simpson Coll, IA	B
The U of Findlay, OH	B
U of Mary, ND	B
U of Rio Grande, OH	B
U of St. Thomas, MN	B

BUSINESS COMPUTER FACILITIES OPERATION

Eastern Illinois U, IL	B

BUSINESS COMPUTER PROGRAMMING

DePaul U, IL	B
Kent State U, OH	A,B
Luther Coll, IA	B
Oklahoma Baptist U, OK	B
Robert Morris Coll, IL	A
St. Norbert Coll, WI	B
Southern Illinois U Carbondale, IL	A
U of Toledo, OH	A
Western Michigan U, MI	B

BUSINESS ECONOMICS

Anderson U, IN	B
Andrews U, MI	B
Augsburg Coll, MN	B
Aurora U, IL	B
Ball State U, IN	B
Beloit Coll, WI	B
Benedictine U, IL	B
Bethany Coll, KS	B
Bluffton Coll, OH	B
Bradley U, IL	B
Buena Vista U, IA	B
Butler U, IN	B
Cameron U, OK	B
Cardinal Stritch U, WI	B
Central Christian Coll of Kansas, KS	A
Cleveland State U, OH	B
The Coll of Wooster, OH	B
Cornell Coll, IA	B
Creighton U, NE	B
DePaul U, IL	B
East Central U, OK	B
Eastern Michigan U, MI	B
Ferris State U, MI	B
Fort Hays State U, KS	B
Gustavus Adolphus Coll, MN	B
Huntington Coll, IN	B
Illinois Coll, IL	B
Indiana U Bloomington, IN	B
Indiana U–Purdue U Fort Wayne, IN	B
Indiana U Southeast, IN	B
Jamestown Coll, ND	B
Kalamazoo Coll, MI	B
Kent State U, OH	B
Lake Forest Coll, IL	B
Lakeland Coll, WI	B
Lewis U, IL	B
Lincoln Coll, Lincoln, IL	A
Loyola U Chicago, IL	B
Marian Coll of Fond du Lac, WI	B
Marquette U, WI	B
Miami U, OH	B
Miami U–Middletown Campus, OH	A
Michigan Technological U, MI	B
Northern State U, SD	B
Northland Coll, WI	B
Northwest Missouri State U, MO	B
Northwood U, MI	A,B
The Ohio State U, OH	B
Ohio Wesleyan U, OH	B
Oklahoma City U, OK	B
Oklahoma State U, OK	B
Olivet Nazarene U, IL	B
Otterbein Coll, OH	B
Park U, MO	B
Pittsburg State U, KS	B
Rockford Coll, IL	B
Roosevelt U, IL	B
Saginaw Valley State U, MI	B
Saint Louis U, MO	B
Southeastern Oklahoma State U, OK	B
Southeast Missouri State U, MO	B
Southern Illinois U Carbondale, IL	B

Southern Illinois U Edwardsville, IL B
U of Central Oklahoma, OK B
U of Dayton, OH B
U of Evansville, IN B
U of Indianapolis, IN B
The U of Iowa, IA B
U of Missouri–Columbia, MO B
U of Nebraska at Omaha, NE B
U of Nebraska–Lincoln, NE B
U of North Dakota, ND B
U of Oklahoma, OK B
The U of South Dakota, SD B
U of Toledo, OH B
U of Wisconsin–Platteville, WI B
U of Wisconsin–Superior, WI B
U of Wisconsin–Whitewater, WI B
Urbana U, OH A,B
Washington U in St. Louis, MO B
Wayne State Coll, NE B
Western Illinois U, IL B
Wheaton Coll, IL B
Wilberforce U, OH B
William Woods U, MO B
Wilmington Coll, OH B
Winona State U, MN B
Wisconsin Lutheran Coll, WI B
Wittenberg U, OH B
Wright State U, OH B
Xavier U, OH B
Youngstown State U, OH B

BUSINESS EDUCATION

Adrian Coll, MI B
Avila U, MO B
Bacone Coll, OK A
Baldwin-Wallace Coll, OH B
Ball State U, IN B
Bethany Coll, KS B
Bethel Coll, IN B
Black Hills State U, SD B
Bluffton Coll, OH B
Bowling Green State U, OH B
Buena Vista U, IA B
Central Christian Coll of Kansas, KS A
Central Michigan U, MI B
Central Missouri State U, MO B
Chadron State Coll, NE B
Chicago State U, IL B
Coll of the Ozarks, MO B
Columbia Coll, MO B
Concordia Coll, MN B
Concordia U, NE B
Concordia U Wisconsin, WI B
Cornell Coll, IA B
Cornerstone U, MI B
Dakota State U, SD B
Dakota Wesleyan U, SD B
Dana Coll, NE B
Defiance Coll, OH B
Dickinson State U, ND B
Doane Coll, NE B
Dordt Coll, IA B
Drake U, IA B
East Central U, OK B
Eastern Michigan U, MI B
Emporia State U, KS B
Evangel U, MO B
Ferris State U, MI B
Fort Hays State U, KS B
The Franciscan U, IA B
Goshen Coll, IN B
Grand View Coll, IA B
Hastings Coll, NE B
Huntington Coll, IN B
Illinois State U, IL B
Indiana State U, IN B
Kent State U, OH B
Lakeland Coll, WI B
Lincoln Coll, Lincoln, IL A
Lincoln Coll, Normal, IL A
Lindenwood U, MO B
Maranatha Baptist Bible Coll, WI B
Mayville State U, ND B
McKendree Coll, IL B
McPherson Coll, KS B
MidAmerica Nazarene U, KS B
Midland Lutheran Coll, NE B
Minot State U, ND B
Morningside Coll, IA B
Mount Mary Coll, WI B
Mount Vernon Nazarene U, OH B
Muskingum Coll, OH B
North Central Coll, IL B
Northeastern State U, OK B
Northern Michigan U, MI B
Northern State U, SD B
Northwestern Coll, IA B
Northwestern Oklahoma State U, OK B
Northwest Missouri State U, MO B
Oakland City U, IN B
Ohio U–Lancaster, OH B
Oklahoma Panhandle State U, OK B
Oklahoma Wesleyan U, OK B
Pillsbury Baptist Bible Coll, MN B
St. Ambrose U, IA B
Saint Joseph's Coll, IN B
Saint Mary's Coll, IN B
Siena Heights U, MI B
Southeastern Oklahoma State U, OK B
Southeast Missouri State U, MO B
Southern Nazarene U, OK B
Southwest Baptist U, MO B
Southwest Missouri State U, MO B
Tabor Coll, KS B
Trinity Christian Coll, IL B
Union Coll, NE B
The U of Akron, OH B
U of Central Oklahoma, OK B
The U of Findlay, OH B
U of Indianapolis, IN B
U of Minnesota, Twin Cities Campus, MN B
U of Missouri–St. Louis, MO B
U of Nebraska at Kearney, NE B
U of Nebraska–Lincoln, NE B
U of North Dakota, ND B
U of Northern Iowa, IA B
U of Rio Grande, OH B
U of Saint Francis, IN B
U of Southern Indiana, IN B
U of Toledo, OH B
U of Wisconsin–Superior, WI B
U of Wisconsin–Whitewater, WI B
Upper Iowa U, IA B
Valley City State U, ND B
Viterbo U, WI B
Walsh U, OH B
Wayne State Coll, NE B
Western Michigan U, MI B
William Penn U, IA B
Wilmington Coll, OH B
Winona State U, MN B
Wright State U, OH B
Youngstown State U, OH B

BUSINESS HOME ECONOMICS

The Ohio State U, OH B

BUSINESS INFORMATION/ DATA PROCESSING RELATED

Carroll Coll, WI B
Lewis U, IL B
Rogers State U, OK B

BUSINESS MANAGEMENT/ ADMINISTRATIVE SERVICES RELATED

Benedictine U, IL B
The Coll of St. Scholastica, MN B
Iowa State U of Science and Technology, IA B
Malone Coll, OH B
Nebraska Wesleyan U, NE B
Ohio U, OH B
Park U, MO B
Saint Mary's U of Minnesota, MN B
The U of Akron, OH A

BUSINESS MARKETING AND MARKETING MANAGEMENT

AIB Coll of Business, IA A
Alma Coll, MI B
Anderson U, IN B
Andrews U, MI B
Ashland U, OH B
Augsburg Coll, MN B
Augustana Coll, IL B
Aurora U, IL B
Avila U, MO B
Baker Coll of Auburn Hills, MI A,B
Baker Coll of Cadillac, MI A
Baker Coll of Clinton Township, MI A
Baker Coll of Flint, MI A,B
Baker Coll of Jackson, MI A,B
Baker Coll of Muskegon, MI A,B
Baker Coll of Owosso, MI A,B
Baker Coll of Port Huron, MI A,B
Baldwin-Wallace Coll, OH B
Ball State U, IN A,B
Bellevue U, NE B
Benedictine Coll, KS B
Benedictine U, IL B
Black Hills State U, SD B
Bowling Green State U, OH B
Bradley U, IL B
Buena Vista U, IA B
Butler U, IN B
Cameron U, OK B
Capital U, OH B
Carroll Coll, WI B
Cedarville U, OH B
Central Christian Coll of Kansas, KS A
Central Michigan U, MI B
Central Missouri State U, MO B
Chicago State U, IL B
Clarke Coll, IA B
Cleary U, MI A,B
Cleveland State U, OH B
Coll of St. Catherine, MN B
Coll of the Ozarks, MO B
Colorado Tech U Sioux Falls Campus, SD B
Columbia Coll, MO B
Columbia Coll Chicago, IL B
Concordia U Wisconsin, WI B
Cornerstone U, MI B
Creighton U, NE B
Dakota State U, SD B
Dakota Wesleyan U, SD B
Davenport U, Grand Rapids, MI A,B
Davenport U, Kalamazoo, MI A,B
Defiance Coll, OH B
DePaul U, IL B
Dickinson State U, ND B
Drake U, IA B
East Central U, OK B
Eastern Illinois U, IL B
Eastern Michigan U, MI B
Elmhurst Coll, IL B
Emporia State U, KS B
Evangel U, MO B
Ferris State U, MI B
Fontbonne U, MO B
Fort Hays State U, KS B
Franklin Coll, IN B
Franklin U, OH B
Governors State U, IL B
Grand Valley State U, MI B
Greenville Coll, IL B
Hannibal-LaGrange Coll, MO B
Hastings Coll, NE B
Hillsdale Coll, MI B
Illinois State U, IL B
Indiana Inst of Technology, IN B
Indiana State U, IN B
Indiana U Bloomington, IN B
Indiana U–Purdue U Fort Wayne, IN B
Indiana U South Bend, IN B
Indiana Wesleyan U, IN B
Iowa State U of Science and Technology, IA B
John Carroll U, OH B
Kansas State U, KS B
Kendall Coll, IL B
Kent State U, OH B
Kent State U, Ashtabula Campus, OH A
Kettering U, MI B
Lakeland Coll, WI B
Lewis U, IL B
Lincoln Coll, Lincoln, IL A
Lincoln Coll, Normal, IL A
Lindenwood U, MO B
Loras Coll, IA B
Loyola U Chicago, IL B
Luther Coll, IA B
MacMurray Coll, IL B
Madonna U, MI B
Manchester Coll, IN B
Marian Coll of Fond du Lac, WI B
Marietta Coll, OH B
Marquette U, WI B
Martin U, IN B
Marygrove Coll, MI B

Business Marketing And Marketing Management (continued)

Maryville U of Saint Louis, MO B
McKendree Coll, IL B
Metropolitan State U, MN B
Miami U, OH B
Miami U–Middletown Campus, OH A
Michigan State U, MI B
Michigan Technological U, MI B
Midland Lutheran Coll, NE B
Midstate Coll, IL A
Millikin U, IL B
Minnesota State U, Mankato, MN B
Minnesota State U, Moorhead, MN B
Minot State U, ND B
Missouri Southern State Coll, MO B
Missouri Valley Coll, MO B
Missouri Western State Coll, MO B
Morningside Coll, IA B
Mount Mercy Coll, IA B
Mount Vernon Nazarene U, OH B
Newman U, KS B
North Central Coll, IL B
Northeastern Illinois U, IL B
Northeastern State U, OK B
Northern Illinois U, IL B
Northern Michigan U, MI B
Northern State U, SD B
North Park U, IL B
Northwestern Coll, MN B
Northwest Missouri State U, MO B
Northwood U, MI A,B
Notre Dame Coll, OH B
Oakland U, MI B
The Ohio State U, OH B
Ohio U, OH B
Oklahoma Baptist U, OK B
Oklahoma Christian U, OK B
Oklahoma City U, OK B
Oklahoma State U, OK B
Olivet Coll, MI B
Olivet Nazarene U, IL B
Oral Roberts U, OK B
Otterbein Coll, OH B
Park U, MO B
Peru State Coll, NE B
Pittsburg State U, KS B
Purdue U Calumet, IN B
Purdue U North Central, IN A
Quincy U, IL B
Rochester Coll, MI B
Rockford Business Coll, IL A
Rockford Coll, IL B
Rockhurst U, MO B
Roosevelt U, IL B
St. Ambrose U, IA B
St. Cloud State U, MN B
Saint Joseph's Coll, IN B
Saint Louis U, MO B
Saint Mary-of-the-Woods Coll, IN B
Saint Mary's Coll, IN B
Saint Mary's Coll of Madonna U, MI B
Saint Mary's U of Minnesota, MN B
Siena Heights U, MI A,B
Sitting Bull Coll, ND A
Southeastern Oklahoma State U, OK B
Southeast Missouri State U, MO B
Southern Illinois U Carbondale, IL B
Southern Nazarene U, OK B
Southwestern Oklahoma State U, OK B
Southwest Minnesota State U, MN A,B
Southwest Missouri State U, MO B
Stephens Coll, MO B
Tabor Coll, KS B
Taylor U, IN B
Tiffin U, OH B
Trinity Christian Coll, IL B
Trinity International U, IL B
Tri-State U, IN B
The U of Akron, OH B
U of Central Oklahoma, OK B
U of Cincinnati, OH A,B
U of Dayton, OH B
U of Evansville, IN B
The U of Findlay, OH B
U of Illinois at Chicago, IL B
U of Indianapolis, IN B
The U of Iowa, IA B
U of Michigan–Dearborn, MI B
U of Minnesota, Duluth, MN B
U of Minnesota, Twin Cities Campus, MN B
U of Missouri–Columbia, MO B
U of Missouri–St. Louis, MO B
U of Nebraska at Omaha, NE B
U of Nebraska–Lincoln, NE B
U of North Dakota, ND B
U of Northern Iowa, IA B
U of Northwestern Ohio, OH A,B
U of Notre Dame, IN B
U of Oklahoma, OK B
U of Phoenix–Metro Detroit Campus, MI B
U of Phoenix–Ohio Campus, OH B
U of Rio Grande, OH B
U of St. Francis, IL B
U of Saint Francis, IN B
U of St. Thomas, MN B
U of Sioux Falls, SD A,B
The U of South Dakota, SD B
U of Southern Indiana, IN B
U of Toledo, OH A,B
U of Tulsa, OK B
U of Wisconsin–Eau Claire, WI B
U of Wisconsin–La Crosse, WI B
U of Wisconsin–Milwaukee, WI B
U of Wisconsin–Oshkosh, WI B
U of Wisconsin–River Falls, WI B
U of Wisconsin–Stout, WI B
U of Wisconsin–Superior, WI B
U of Wisconsin–Whitewater, WI B
Upper Iowa U, IA B
Urbana U, OH A,B
Ursuline Coll, OH B
Valparaiso U, IN B
Viterbo U, WI B
Walsh Coll of Accountancy and Business Administration, MI B
Walsh U, OH A,B
Wartburg Coll, IA B
Washington U in St. Louis, MO B
Wayne State U, MI B
Webster U, MO B
Western Illinois U, IL B
Western Michigan U, MI B
Westminster Coll, MO B
Wichita State U, KS B
Wilberforce U, OH B
Wilmington Coll, OH B
Winona State U, MN B
Wittenberg U, OH B
Wright State U, OH A,B
Xavier U, OH B
Youngstown State U, OH A,B

BUSINESS QUANTITATIVE METHODS/MANAGEMENT SCIENCE RELATED

Indiana State U, IN B
U of Nebraska–Lincoln, NE B

BUSINESS STATISTICS

Western Michigan U, MI B

BUSINESS SYSTEMS ANALYSIS/DESIGN

Cameron U, OK B
DeVry U, Addison, IL B
DeVry U, Chicago, IL B
DeVry U, Tinley Park, IL B
DeVry U, MO B
DeVry U, OH B
Kent State U, OH B
Metropolitan State U, MN B
Southern Illinois U Carbondale, IL B
U of Toledo, OH A

BUSINESS SYSTEMS NETWORKING/ TELECOMMUNICATIONS

Academy Coll, MN A
Aurora U, IL B
Baker Coll of Flint, MI A
Brown Coll, MN A
Crown Coll, MN A,B
DePaul U, IL B
DeVry U, Addison, IL B
DeVry U, Chicago, IL B
DeVry U, Tinley Park, IL B
DeVry U, MO B
Herzing Coll, Minneapolis Drafting School Campus, MN A
Illinois State U, IL B
Kaplan Coll, IA A
Northwestern Oklahoma State U, OK B
Robert Morris Coll, IL A
The U of Findlay, OH B
U of St. Francis, IL B
U of Wisconsin–Stout, WI B

BUYING OPERATIONS

Lake Erie Coll, OH B
The U of Akron, OH A
Youngstown State U, OH B

CANADIAN STUDIES

Franklin Coll, IN B

CARDIOVASCULAR TECHNOLOGY

Avila U, MO B
Nebraska Methodist Coll, NE A,B
U of Toledo, OH A

CARPENTRY

Andrews U, MI B
Central Christian Coll of Kansas, KS A
Nebraska Indian Comm Coll, NE A
Ranken Tech Coll, MO A
Sitting Bull Coll, ND A

CARTOGRAPHY

Ball State U, IN B
East Central U, OK B
Southwest Missouri State U, MO B
The U of Akron, OH B
U of Wisconsin–Madison, WI B
U of Wisconsin–Platteville, WI B
Wittenberg U, OH B

CELL AND MOLECULAR BIOLOGY RELATED

U of Illinois at Urbana–Champaign, IL B

CELL BIOLOGY

Ball State U, IN B
Beloit Coll, WI B
Lindenwood U, MO B
Northeastern State U, OK B
Northwestern U, IL B
Ohio U, OH B
Oklahoma State U, OK B
Southwest Missouri State U, MO B
U of Illinois at Urbana–Champaign, IL B
U of Michigan, MI B
U of Minnesota, Duluth, MN B
U of Minnesota, Twin Cities Campus, MN B
U of Wisconsin–Madison, WI B
U of Wisconsin–Superior, WI B
William Jewell Coll, MO B
Wittenberg U, OH B

CERAMIC ARTS

Ball State U, IN B
Bethany Coll, KS B
Bowling Green State U, OH B
Chicago State U, IL B
The Cleveland Inst of Art, OH B
Coll for Creative Studies, MI B
Columbus Coll of Art and Design, OH B
Finlandia U, MI B
Grand Valley State U, MI B
Indiana U Bloomington, IN B
Indiana Wesleyan U, IN B
Kansas City Art Inst, MO B
Lincoln Coll, Lincoln, IL A
Loyola U Chicago, IL B
Maharishi U of Management, IA B
Minnesota State U, Mankato, MN B

Minnesota State U, Moorhead, MN B
Northern Michigan U, MI B
Ohio Northern U, OH B
The Ohio State U, OH B
Ohio U, OH B
St. Cloud State U, MN B
Trinity Christian Coll, IL B
The U of Akron, OH B
U of Evansville, IN B
The U of Iowa, IA B
U of Michigan, MI B
U of Oklahoma, OK B
The U of South Dakota, SD B
U of Wisconsin–Milwaukee, WI B
Washington U in St. Louis, MO B
Webster U, MO B
Wittenberg U, OH B

CERAMIC SCIENCES/ ENGINEERING

Iowa State U of Science and Technology, IA B
The Ohio State U, OH B
U of Missouri–Rolla, MO B

CHEMICAL AND ATOMIC/ MOLECULAR PHYSICS

The Coll of Wooster, OH B
Ohio U, OH B
Saint Mary's U of Minnesota, MN B

CHEMICAL ENGINEERING

Calvin Coll, MI B
Case Western Reserve U, OH B
Cleveland State U, OH B
Illinois Inst of Technology, IL B
Iowa State U of Science and Technology, IA B
Kansas State U, KS B
Michigan State U, MI B
Michigan Technological U, MI B
Northwestern U, IL B
The Ohio State U, OH B
Ohio U, OH B
Oklahoma State U, OK B
Purdue U, IN B
Rose-Hulman Inst of Technology, IN B
South Dakota School of Mines and Technology, SD B
Tri-State U, IN B
The U of Akron, OH B
U of Cincinnati, OH B
U of Dayton, OH B
U of Illinois at Chicago, IL B
U of Illinois at Urbana–Champaign, IL B
The U of Iowa, IA B
U of Kansas, KS B
U of Michigan, MI B
U of Minnesota, Duluth, MN B
U of Minnesota, Twin Cities Campus, MN B
U of Missouri–Columbia, MO B
U of Missouri–Rolla, MO B
U of Nebraska–Lincoln, NE B
U of North Dakota, ND B
U of Notre Dame, IN B
U of Oklahoma, OK B
U of Toledo, OH B
U of Tulsa, OK B
U of Wisconsin–Madison, WI B
Washington U in St. Louis, MO B
Wayne State U, MI B
Western Michigan U, MI B
Winona State U, MN B
Xavier U, OH B
Youngstown State U, OH B

CHEMICAL ENGINEERING TECHNOLOGY

Ball State U, IN A
Ferris State U, MI A
Kansas State U, KS A
Lawrence Technological U, MI A
Miami U–Middletown Campus, OH A
Michigan Technological U, MI A
The U of Akron, OH B
U of Cincinnati, OH A
U of Toledo, OH A

CHEMICAL TECHNOLOGY

Indiana U–Purdue U Fort Wayne, IN A
U of Toledo, OH A

CHEMISTRY

Adrian Coll, MI A,B
Albion Coll, MI B
Alma Coll, MI B
Alverno Coll, WI B
Ancilla Coll, IN A
Anderson U, IN B
Andrews U, MI B
Antioch Coll, OH B
Aquinas Coll, MI B
Ashland U, OH B
Augsburg Coll, MN B
Augustana Coll, IL B
Augustana Coll, SD B
Aurora U, IL B
Avila U, MO B
Baker U, KS B
Baldwin-Wallace Coll, OH B
Ball State U, IN B
Beloit Coll, WI B
Bemidji State U, MN B
Benedictine Coll, KS B
Benedictine U, IL B
Bethany Coll, KS B
Bethany Lutheran Coll, MN B
Bethel Coll, IN A,B
Bethel Coll, KS B
Bethel Coll, MN B
Blackburn Coll, IL B
Black Hills State U, SD B
Bluffton Coll, OH B
Bowling Green State U, OH B
Bradley U, IL B
Briar Cliff U, IA B
Buena Vista U, IA B
Butler U, IN B
Calumet Coll of Saint Joseph, IN A
Calvin Coll, MI B
Cameron U, OK B
Cardinal Stritch U, WI B
Carleton Coll, MN B
Carroll Coll, WI B
Carthage Coll, WI B
Case Western Reserve U, OH B
Cedarville U, OH B
Central Christian Coll of Kansas, KS A
Central Coll, IA B
Central Methodist Coll, MO A,B
Central Michigan U, MI B
Central Missouri State U, MO B
Chadron State Coll, NE B
Chicago State U, IL B
Clarke Coll, IA B
Cleveland State U, OH B
Coe Coll, IA B
Coll of Mount St. Joseph, OH B
Coll of Saint Benedict, MN B
Coll of St. Catherine, MN B
Coll of Saint Mary, NE B
The Coll of St. Scholastica, MN B
Coll of the Ozarks, MO B
The Coll of Wooster, OH B
Columbia Coll, MO B
Concordia Coll, MN B
Concordia U, IL B
Concordia U, NE B
Cornell Coll, IA B
Creighton U, NE B
Culver-Stockton Coll, MO B
Dakota State U, SD B
Dana Coll, NE B
Defiance Coll, OH B
Denison U, OH B
DePaul U, IL B
DePauw U, IN B
Dickinson State U, ND B
Doane Coll, NE B
Dominican U, IL B
Dordt Coll, IA B
Drake U, IA B
Drury U, MO B
Earlham Coll, IN B
East Central U, OK B
Eastern Illinois U, IL B
Eastern Michigan U, MI B
Edgewood Coll, WI B
Elmhurst Coll, IL B
Emporia State U, KS B
Eureka Coll, IL B
Evangel U, MO B
Fort Hays State U, KS B
Franciscan U of Steubenville, OH B
Franklin Coll, IN B
Goshen Coll, IN B
Governors State U, IL B
Graceland U, IA B
Grand Valley State U, MI B
Greenville Coll, IL B
Grinnell Coll, IA B
Gustavus Adolphus Coll, MN B
Hamline U, MN B
Hanover Coll, IN B
Hastings Coll, NE B
Heidelberg Coll, OH B
Hillsdale Coll, MI B
Hiram Coll, OH B
Hope Coll, MI B
Huntington Coll, IN B
Illinois Coll, IL B
Illinois Inst of Technology, IL B
Illinois State U, IL B
Illinois Wesleyan U, IL B
Indiana State U, IN B
Indiana U Bloomington, IN B
Indiana U Northwest, IN B
Indiana U–Purdue U Fort Wayne, IN A,B
Indiana U–Purdue U Indianapolis, IN B
Indiana U South Bend, IN A,B
Indiana U Southeast, IN B
Indiana Wesleyan U, IN A,B
Iowa State U of Science and Technology, IA B
Iowa Wesleyan Coll, IA B
Jamestown Coll, ND B
John Carroll U, OH B
Judson Coll, IL B
Kalamazoo Coll, MI B
Kansas State U, KS B
Kent State U, OH B
Kenyon Coll, OH B
Kettering U, MI B
Knox Coll, IL B
Lake Erie Coll, OH B
Lake Forest Coll, IL B
Lakeland Coll, WI B
Langston U, OK B
Lawrence Technological U, MI B
Lawrence U, WI B
Lewis U, IL B
Lincoln Coll, Lincoln, IL A
Lindenwood U, MO B
Loras Coll, IA B
Lourdes Coll, OH A,B
Loyola U Chicago, IL B
Luther Coll, IA B
Macalester Coll, MN B
MacMurray Coll, IL B
Madonna U, MI A,B
Maharishi U of Management, IA A,B
Malone Coll, OH B
Manchester Coll, IN B
Marian Coll, IN B
Marian Coll of Fond du Lac, WI B
Marietta Coll, OH B
Marquette U, WI B
Martin U, IN B
Marygrove Coll, MI B
Maryville U of Saint Louis, MO B
Mayville State U, ND B
McKendree Coll, IL B
McPherson Coll, KS B
Miami U, OH B
Miami U–Middletown Campus, OH A
Michigan State U, MI B
Michigan Technological U, MI B
MidAmerica Nazarene U, KS B
Midland Lutheran Coll, NE B
Millikin U, IL B
Minnesota State U, Mankato, MN B
Minnesota State U, Moorhead, MN B
Minot State U, ND B
Missouri Southern State Coll, MO B
Missouri Western State Coll, MO B
Monmouth Coll, IL B
Morningside Coll, IA B
Mount Marty Coll, SD B
Mount Mary Coll, WI B
Mount Union Coll, OH B
Mount Vernon Nazarene U, OH B
Muskingum Coll, OH B
Nebraska Wesleyan U, NE B
Newman U, KS B

Chemistry (continued)
North Central Coll, IL B
North Dakota State U, ND B
Northeastern Illinois U, IL B
Northeastern State U, OK B
Northern Illinois U, IL B
Northern Michigan U, MI B
Northern State U, SD B
Northland Coll, WI B
North Park U, IL B
Northwestern Coll, IA B
Northwestern Oklahoma State U, OK B
Northwestern U, IL B
Northwest Missouri State U, MO B
Notre Dame Coll, OH B
Oakland City U, IN B
Oakland U, MI B
Oberlin Coll, OH B
Ohio Dominican U, OH A,B
Ohio Northern U, OH B
The Ohio State U, OH B
Ohio U, OH B
Ohio Wesleyan U, OH B
Oklahoma Baptist U, OK B
Oklahoma Christian U, OK B
Oklahoma City U, OK B
Oklahoma Panhandle State U, OK B
Oklahoma State U, OK B
Oklahoma Wesleyan U, OK A,B
Olivet Coll, MI B
Olivet Nazarene U, IL B
Oral Roberts U, OK B
Otterbein Coll, OH B
Park U, MO B
Peru State Coll, NE B
Pittsburg State U, KS B
Principia Coll, IL B
Purdue U, IN B
Purdue U Calumet, IN B
Quincy U, IL B
Ripon Coll, WI B
Rockford Coll, IL B
Rockhurst U, MO B
Rogers State U, OK A
Roosevelt U, IL B
Rose-Hulman Inst of Technology, IN B
Saginaw Valley State U, MI B
St. Ambrose U, IA B
St. Cloud State U, MN B
Saint John's U, MN B
Saint Joseph's Coll, IN B
Saint Louis U, MO B
Saint Mary's Coll, IN B
Saint Mary's Coll of Madonna U, MI B
Saint Mary's U of Minnesota, MN B
Saint Mary U, KS B
St. Norbert Coll, WI B
St. Olaf Coll, MN B
Saint Xavier U, IL B
Shawnee State U, OH B
Siena Heights U, MI A,B
Simpson Coll, IA B
South Dakota School of Mines and Technology, SD B
South Dakota State U, SD B
Southeastern Oklahoma State U, OK B
Southeast Missouri State U, MO B
Southern Illinois U Carbondale, IL B
Southern Illinois U Edwardsville, IL B
Southern Nazarene U, OK B
Southwest Baptist U, MO B
Southwestern Coll, KS B
Southwestern Oklahoma State U, OK B
Southwest Minnesota State U, MN B
Southwest Missouri State U, MO B
Spring Arbor U, MI B
Tabor Coll, KS B
Taylor U, IN B
Trinity Christian Coll, IL B
Trinity International U, IL B
Tri-State U, IN B
Truman State U, MO B
Union Coll, NE B
The U of Akron, OH B
U of Central Oklahoma, OK B
U of Chicago, IL B
U of Cincinnati, OH B
U of Dayton, OH B
U of Evansville, IN B
U of Illinois at Chicago, IL B
U of Illinois at Springfield, IL B
U of Illinois at Urbana–Champaign, IL B
U of Indianapolis, IN A,B
The U of Iowa, IA B
U of Kansas, KS B
U of Michigan, MI B
U of Michigan–Dearborn, MI B
U of Michigan–Flint, MI B
U of Minnesota, Duluth, MN B
U of Minnesota, Morris, MN B
U of Minnesota, Twin Cities Campus, MN B
U of Missouri–Columbia, MO B
U of Missouri–Kansas City, MO B
U of Missouri–Rolla, MO B
U of Missouri–St. Louis, MO B
U of Nebraska at Kearney, NE B
U of Nebraska at Omaha, NE B
U of Nebraska–Lincoln, NE B
U of North Dakota, ND B
U of Northern Iowa, IA B
U of Notre Dame, IN B
U of Oklahoma, OK B
U of Rio Grande, OH A,B
U of Saint Francis, IN B
U of St. Thomas, MN B
U of Science and Arts of Oklahoma, OK B
U of Sioux Falls, SD B
The U of South Dakota, SD B
U of Southern Indiana, IN B
U of Toledo, OH B
U of Tulsa, OK B
U of Wisconsin–Eau Claire, WI B
U of Wisconsin–Green Bay, WI A,B
U of Wisconsin–La Crosse, WI B
U of Wisconsin–Madison, WI B
U of Wisconsin–Milwaukee, WI B
U of Wisconsin–Oshkosh, WI B
U of Wisconsin–Parkside, WI B
U of Wisconsin–River Falls, WI B
U of Wisconsin–Stevens Point, WI B
U of Wisconsin–Superior, WI B
U of Wisconsin–Whitewater, WI B
Upper Iowa U, IA B
Urbana U, OH B
Valley City State U, ND B
Valparaiso U, IN B
Viterbo U, WI B
Wabash Coll, IN B
Waldorf Coll, IA A
Walsh U, OH B
Wartburg Coll, IA B
Washington U in St. Louis, MO B
Wayne State Coll, NE B
Wayne State U, MI B
Western Illinois U, IL B
Western Michigan U, MI B
Westminster Coll, MO B
Wheaton Coll, IL B
Wichita State U, KS B
Wilberforce U, OH B
William Jewell Coll, MO B
Wilmington Coll, OH B
Winona State U, MN B
Wisconsin Lutheran Coll, WI B
Wittenberg U, OH B
Wright State U, OH A,B
Xavier U, OH B
Youngstown State U, OH B

CHEMISTRY EDUCATION

Bethany Coll, KS B
Bowling Green State U, OH B
Central Methodist Coll, MO B
Central Michigan U, MI B
Central Missouri State U, MO B
Chadron State Coll, NE B
Coll of St. Catherine, MN B
Coll of the Ozarks, MO B
Concordia Coll, MN B
Concordia U, NE B
Eastern Michigan U, MI B
Elmhurst Coll, IL B
Franklin Coll, IN B
Greenville Coll, IL B
Gustavus Adolphus Coll, MN B
Hastings Coll, NE B
Indiana U Bloomington, IN B
Indiana U Northwest, IN B
Indiana U–Purdue U Fort Wayne, IN B
Indiana U South Bend, IN B
Luther Coll, IA B
Malone Coll, OH B
Mayville State U, ND B
Michigan State U, MI B
MidAmerica Nazarene U, KS B
Minot State U, ND B
Mount Marty Coll, SD B
North Dakota State U, ND B
Oklahoma Baptist U, OK B
St. Ambrose U, IA B
Saint Mary's U of Minnesota, MN B
Southern Nazarene U, OK B
Southwest Minnesota State U, MN B
Southwest Missouri State U, MO B
Trinity Christian Coll, IL B
Union Coll, NE B
U of Illinois at Chicago, IL B
The U of Iowa, IA B
U of Nebraska–Lincoln, NE B
U of Wisconsin–River Falls, WI B
U of Wisconsin–Superior, WI B
Valley City State U, ND B
Viterbo U, WI B
Washington U in St. Louis, MO B
Xavier U, OH B
Youngstown State U, OH B

CHEMISTRY RELATED

U of Notre Dame, IN B

CHILD CARE/ DEVELOPMENT

Alverno Coll, WI B
Ashland U, OH B
Bethel Coll, MN B
Bluffton Coll, OH B
Bowling Green State U, OH B
Cameron U, OK B
Coll of the Ozarks, MO B
Concordia Coll, MN B
Crown Coll, MN B
Evangel U, MO A
Ferris State U, MI A
Franciscan U of Steubenville, OH A
Goshen Coll, IN B
Indiana U Bloomington, IN B
Kansas State U, KS B
Lincoln Christian Coll, IL B
Madonna U, MI A,B
Miami U, OH B
Minnesota State U, Mankato, MN B
North Dakota State U, ND B
Northern Michigan U, MI A,B
Northwest Missouri State U, MO B
Ohio U, OH A,B
Ohio U–Lancaster, OH A
Oklahoma Baptist U, OK B
Oklahoma Christian U, OK B
Oklahoma State U, OK B
Olivet Nazarene U, IL B
Pittsburg State U, KS B
Purdue U Calumet, IN A
Reformed Bible Coll, MI A,B
St. Cloud State U, MN B
South Dakota State U, SD B
Southeast Missouri State U, MO A
Stephens Coll, MO B
The U of Akron, OH B
U of Central Oklahoma, OK B
U of Cincinnati, OH A
U of Illinois at Springfield, IL B
U of Michigan–Dearborn, MI B
U of Minnesota, Crookston, MN A
U of Missouri–St. Louis, MO B
U of Wisconsin–Madison, WI B
Waldorf Coll, IA A
Western Michigan U, MI B
Youngstown State U, OH A,B

CHILD CARE/GUIDANCE

Central Michigan U, MI B
Central Missouri State U, MO A
Sitting Bull Coll, ND A

Southeast Missouri State U, MO A
Youngstown State U, OH A

CHILD CARE PROVIDER

Mayville State U, ND A

CHILD CARE SERVICES MANAGEMENT

Mount Vernon Nazarene U, OH A
Saint Mary-of-the-Woods Coll, IN B

CHILD GUIDANCE

Coll of the Ozarks, MO B
Oklahoma Baptist U, OK B
Reformed Bible Coll, MI B
Rochester Coll, MI B
Rochester Comm and Tech Coll, MN A
Siena Heights U, MI A,B
U of Central Oklahoma, OK B

CHINESE

Grinnell Coll, IA B
Indiana U Bloomington, IN B
Michigan State U, MI B
The Ohio State U, OH B
U of Chicago, IL B
The U of Iowa, IA B
U of Kansas, KS B
U of Michigan, MI B
U of Minnesota, Twin Cities Campus, MN B
U of Notre Dame, IN B
U of Wisconsin–Madison, WI B
Washington U in St. Louis, MO B

CITY/COMMUNITY/ REGIONAL PLANNING

Ball State U, IN B
DePaul U, IL B
Eastern Michigan U, MI B
Indiana U Bloomington, IN B
Iowa State U of Science and Technology, IA B
Miami U, OH B
Michigan State U, MI B
Minnesota State U, Mankato, MN B
Northern Michigan U, MI B
The Ohio State U, OH B
St. Cloud State U, MN B
Southwest Missouri State U, MO B
U of Cincinnati, OH B
U of Illinois at Urbana–Champaign, IL B
U of Michigan–Flint, MI B
Winona State U, MN B
Wright State U, OH B

CIVIL ENGINEERING

Bradley U, IL B
Calvin Coll, MI B
Case Western Reserve U, OH B
Cleveland State U, OH B
Illinois Inst of Technology, IL B
Indiana Inst of Technology, IN B
Iowa State U of Science and Technology, IA B
Kansas State U, KS B
Lawrence Technological U, MI B
Marquette U, WI B
Michigan State U, MI B
Michigan Technological U, MI B
Minnesota State U, Mankato, MN B
North Dakota State U, ND B
Northwestern U, IL B
Ohio Northern U, OH B
The Ohio State U, OH B
Ohio U, OH B
Oklahoma State U, OK B
Purdue U, IN B
Rose-Hulman Inst of Technology, IN B
South Dakota School of Mines and Technology, SD B
South Dakota State U, SD B
Southern Illinois U Carbondale, IL B
Southern Illinois U Edwardsville, IL B
Tri-State U, IN B
The U of Akron, OH B
U of Cincinnati, OH B
U of Dayton, OH B
U of Evansville, IN B
U of Illinois at Chicago, IL B
U of Illinois at Urbana–Champaign, IL B
The U of Iowa, IA B
U of Kansas, KS B
U of Michigan, MI B
U of Minnesota, Twin Cities Campus, MN B
U of Missouri–Columbia, MO B
U of Missouri–Kansas City, MO B
U of Missouri–Rolla, MO B
U of Missouri–St. Louis, MO B
U of Nebraska–Lincoln, NE B
U of North Dakota, ND B
U of Notre Dame, IN B
U of Oklahoma, OK B
U of Toledo, OH B
U of Wisconsin–Madison, WI B
U of Wisconsin–Milwaukee, WI B
U of Wisconsin–Platteville, WI B
Valparaiso U, IN B
Washington U in St. Louis, MO B
Wayne State U, MI B
Youngstown State U, OH B

CIVIL ENGINEERING RELATED

Bradley U, IL B

CIVIL ENGINEERING TECHNOLOGY

Ferris State U, MI A
Fontbonne U, MO B
Indiana U–Purdue U Fort Wayne, IN A
Indiana U–Purdue U Indianapolis, IN A
Kansas State U, KS A
Lawrence Technological U, MI A
Michigan Technological U, MI A
Missouri Western State Coll, MO A,B
Purdue U Calumet, IN A,B
Purdue U North Central, IN A
Rochester Comm and Tech Coll, MN A
U of Cincinnati, OH A,B
U of Southern Indiana, IN A
U of Toledo, OH A,B
Washington U in St. Louis, MO B
Youngstown State U, OH A,B

CLASSICS

Augustana Coll, IL B
Ave Maria Coll, MI B
Ball State U, IN B
Beloit Coll, WI B
Bowling Green State U, OH B
Calvin Coll, MI B
Carleton Coll, MN B
Carthage Coll, WI B
Case Western Reserve U, OH B
Coe Coll, IA B
Coll of Saint Benedict, MN B
The Coll of Wooster, OH B
Concordia Coll, MN B
Cornell Coll, IA B
Creighton U, NE B
Denison U, OH B
DePauw U, IN B
Earlham Coll, IN B
Franciscan U of Steubenville, OH B
Grinnell Coll, IA B
Gustavus Adolphus Coll, MN B
Hanover Coll, IN B
Hillsdale Coll, MI B
Hiram Coll, OH B
Hope Coll, MI B
Indiana U Bloomington, IN B
John Carroll U, OH B
Kalamazoo Coll, MI B
Kent State U, OH B
Kenyon Coll, OH B
Knox Coll, IL B
Lawrence U, WI B
Loras Coll, IA B
Loyola U Chicago, IL B
Luther Coll, IA B
Macalester Coll, MN B
Marquette U, WI B
Miami U, OH B
Monmouth Coll, IL B
North Central Coll, IL B
Northwestern U, IL B
Oberlin Coll, OH B
The Ohio State U, OH B
Ohio U, OH B
Ohio Wesleyan U, OH B
Rockford Coll, IL B
Saint John's U, MN B
Saint Louis U, MO B
St. Olaf Coll, MN B
Southern Illinois U Carbondale, IL B
Truman State U, MO B
The U of Akron, OH B
U of Chicago, IL B
U of Cincinnati, OH B
U of Evansville, IN B
U of Illinois at Chicago, IL B
U of Illinois at Urbana–Champaign, IL B
The U of Iowa, IA B
U of Kansas, KS B
U of Michigan, MI B
U of Missouri–Columbia, MO B
U of Nebraska–Lincoln, NE B
U of Notre Dame, IN B
U of Oklahoma, OK B
U of St. Thomas, MN B
The U of South Dakota, SD B
U of Wisconsin–Madison, WI B
U of Wisconsin–Milwaukee, WI B
Valparaiso U, IN B
Wabash Coll, IN B
Washington U in St. Louis, MO B
Wayne State U, MI B
Westminster Coll, MO B
Wright State U, OH B
Xavier U, OH B

CLINICAL PSYCHOLOGY

Purdue U Calumet, IN B
U of Michigan–Flint, MI B
U of Missouri–St. Louis, MO B

CLOTHING/APPAREL/ TEXTILE

Concordia Coll, MN B
Wayne State U, MI B

CLOTHING/APPAREL/ TEXTILE STUDIES

Central Missouri State U, MO B
Coll of the Ozarks, MO B
Indiana State U, IN B
Indiana U Bloomington, IN B
Iowa State U of Science and Technology, IA B
Kansas State U, KS B
Michigan State U, MI B
North Dakota State U, ND B
Northern Illinois U, IL B
The Ohio State U, OH B
Ohio U, OH B
Purdue U, IN B
Southeast Missouri State U, MO B
Southern Illinois U Carbondale, IL B
Southwest Missouri State U, MO B
U of Missouri–Columbia, MO B
U of Nebraska–Lincoln, NE B
U of Northern Iowa, IA B
U of Wisconsin–Stout, WI B
Youngstown State U, OH B

CLOTHING/TEXTILES

Bluffton Coll, OH B
Bowling Green State U, OH B
Concordia Coll, MN B
Indiana U Bloomington, IN A,B
Minnesota State U, Mankato, MN B
North Dakota State U, ND B
Northwest Missouri State U, MO B
The Ohio State U, OH B
Oklahoma State U, OK B
Olivet Nazarene U, IL B
The U of Akron, OH B
U of Central Oklahoma, OK B
U of Minnesota, Twin Cities Campus, MN B

Clothing/Textiles (continued)
U of Wisconsin–Madison, WI B

COGNITIVE PSYCHOLOGY/ PSYCHOLINGUISTICS

Indiana U Bloomington, IN B
Lawrence U, WI B
Northwestern U, IL B
U of Kansas, KS B
Washington U in St. Louis, MO B

COLLEGE/ POSTSECONDARY STUDENT COUNSELING

Bowling Green State U, OH B

COMMERCIAL PHOTOGRAPHY

Minnesota State U, Moorhead, MN B
Ohio U, OH B

COMMUNICATION DISORDERS

Bowling Green State U, OH B
Case Western Reserve U, OH B
Eastern Illinois U, IL B
Kansas State U, KS B
Minnesota State U, Mankato, MN B
Minot State U, ND B
Northern Illinois U, IL B
Northwestern U, IL B
Oklahoma State U, OK B
Southern Illinois U Carbondale, IL B
Truman State U, MO B
The U of Akron, OH B
U of Kansas, KS B
U of Nebraska at Kearney, NE B
U of Wisconsin–Eau Claire, WI B
U of Wisconsin–River Falls, WI B
Western Illinois U, IL B

COMMUNICATION DISORDERS SCIENCES/ SERVICES RELATED

Ohio U, OH B

COMMUNICATION EQUIPMENT TECHNOLOGY

Cedarville U, OH B
Eastern Michigan U, MI B
Ferris State U, MI A,B
Hastings Coll, NE B
Saint Mary-of-the-Woods Coll, IN B
Spartan School of Aeronautics, OK A
U of Michigan–Dearborn, MI B

COMMUNICATIONS

Alverno Coll, WI B
Antioch Coll, OH B
Aquinas Coll, MI B
Aurora U, IL B
Avila U, MO B
Baker Coll of Jackson, MI A
Benedictine U, IL B
Bethany Coll, KS B
Bethany Lutheran Coll, MN B
Bethel Coll, IN B
Bethel Coll, KS B
Bowling Green State U, OH B
Bradley U, IL B
Buena Vista U, IA B
Cardinal Stritch U, WI B
Carroll Coll, WI B
Cedarville U, OH B
Central Coll, IA B
Central Methodist Coll, MO B
Coll of Mount St. Joseph, OH A,B
The Coll of St. Scholastica, MN B
The Coll of Wooster, OH B
Concordia Coll, MN B
Concordia U, IL B
Concordia U, MI B
Concordia U, NE B
Dana Coll, NE B
DePaul U, IL B
Doane Coll, NE B
Elmhurst Coll, IL B
Emporia State U, KS B
Franciscan U of Steubenville, OH B
Grace U, NE B
Hastings Coll, NE B
Hope Coll, MI B
Indiana State U, IN B
Indiana U Bloomington, IN B
Indiana U East, IN B
Indiana U Kokomo, IN B
Indiana U–Purdue U Indianapolis, IN B
Indiana U Southeast, IN B
Indiana Wesleyan U, IN A,B
Jamestown Coll, ND B
Kansas State U, KS B
Lake Forest Coll, IL B
Loyola U Chicago, IL B
Macalester Coll, MN B
Malone Coll, OH B
Marietta Coll, OH B
Marquette U, WI B
Martin U, IN B
Maryville U of Saint Louis, MO B
Metropolitan State U, MN B
Miami U–Middletown Campus, OH A
Michigan State U, MI B
Michigan Technological U, MI B
Millikin U, IL B
Moody Bible Inst, IL B
Mount Mary Coll, WI B
Mount Mercy Coll, IA B
Mount Union Coll, OH B
Mount Vernon Nazarene U, OH B
Nebraska Wesleyan U, NE B
Northern Illinois U, IL B
Northwestern Coll, MN B
Northwestern U, IL B
Notre Dame Coll, OH B
Oakland U, MI B
Ohio Dominican U, OH B
The Ohio State U, OH B
Ohio U, OH B
Oral Roberts U, OK B
Park U, MO B
Purdue U, IN B
Quincy U, IL B
Reformed Bible Coll, MI B
Rochester Coll, MI B
Rockhurst U, MO B
Saginaw Valley State U, MI B
Saint Joseph's Coll, IN B
Saint Louis U, MO B
Saint Mary's Coll, IN B
St. Norbert Coll, WI B
Saint Xavier U, IL B
Southeastern Oklahoma State U, OK B
Southern Nazarene U, OK A
Southwest Baptist U, MO B
Southwestern Coll, KS B
Southwest Minnesota State U, MN B
Southwest Missouri State U, MO B
Spring Arbor U, MI B
Tabor Coll, KS B
Tiffin U, OH B
Trinity Christian Coll, IL B
Tri-State U, IN A,B
Union Inst & U, OH B
U of Central Oklahoma, OK B
U of Indianapolis, IN B
U of Missouri–Columbia, MO B
U of Missouri–St. Louis, MO B
U of Nebraska at Omaha, NE B
U of Nebraska–Lincoln, NE B
U of North Dakota, ND B
U of Northern Iowa, IA B
U of Oklahoma, OK B
U of Rio Grande, OH A,B
U of Saint Francis, IN B
U of St. Thomas, MN B
U of Science and Arts of Oklahoma, OK B
U of Southern Indiana, IN A,B
U of Toledo, OH B
U of Tulsa, OK B
U of Wisconsin–Eau Claire, WI B
U of Wisconsin–Green Bay, WI B
U of Wisconsin–La Crosse, WI B
U of Wisconsin–Parkside, WI B
U of Wisconsin–Stevens Point, WI B
Valparaiso U, IN B
Washington U in St. Louis, MO B
Wayne State U, MI B
Western Illinois U, IL B
Western Michigan U, MI B
Wichita State U, KS B
William Penn U, IA B
William Woods U, MO B
Wisconsin Lutheran Coll, WI B
Wittenberg U, OH B
Youngstown State U, OH B

COMMUNICATIONS RELATED

Bradley U, IL B
The Franciscan U, IA B
Indiana State U, IN B
Loyola U Chicago, IL B
Milwaukee School of Engineering, WI B
The Ohio State U, OH B
Ohio U, OH B
Oklahoma State U, OK B
Saint Louis U, MO B
Sterling Coll, KS B
Taylor U, Fort Wayne Campus, IN B
The U of Akron, OH B
U of Nebraska–Lincoln, NE B
Wisconsin Lutheran Coll, WI B

COMMUNICATIONS TECHNOLOGIES RELATED

Alverno Coll, WI B
Columbia Coll Chicago, IL B
Saint Mary-of-the-Woods Coll, IN B
Saint Mary's U of Minnesota, MN B

COMMUNITY HEALTH LIAISON

Indiana State U, IN B
Minnesota State U, Moorhead, MN B
Northern Illinois U, IL B
Ohio U, OH B
U of Nebraska–Lincoln, NE B
U of Northern Iowa, IA B
Western Michigan U, MI B
Youngstown State U, OH B

COMMUNITY PSYCHOLOGY

Northwestern U, IL B
Saint Mary U, KS B

COMMUNITY SERVICES

Alverno Coll, WI B
Aquinas Coll, MI B
Bemidji State U, MN B
Central Michigan U, MI B
Iowa State U of Science and Technology, IA B
Midland Lutheran Coll, NE A
Northern State U, SD B
North Park U, IL B
Oklahoma Christian U, OK B
Rockhurst U, MO B
Roosevelt U, IL B
Saint Mary U, KS B
Siena Heights U, MI B
The U of Findlay, OH A
U of Toledo, OH B
Waldorf Coll, IA A

COMPARATIVE LITERATURE

Antioch Coll, OH B
Beloit Coll, WI B
Case Western Reserve U, OH B
The Coll of Wooster, OH B
DePaul U, IL B
Hillsdale Coll, MI B
Indiana U Bloomington, IN B
Northwestern U, IL B
Oberlin Coll, OH B
The Ohio State U, OH B
Roosevelt U, IL B
St. Cloud State U, MN B
U of Cincinnati, OH B
U of Illinois at Urbana–Champaign, IL B
The U of Iowa, IA B
U of Michigan, MI B
U of Michigan–Dearborn, MI B
U of Minnesota, Twin Cities Campus, MN B
U of St. Thomas, MN B

U of Wisconsin–Madison, WI B
U of Wisconsin–Milwaukee, WI B
Washington U in St. Louis, MO B
William Woods U, MO B
Wittenberg U, OH B

COMPUTER EDUCATION

Baker Coll of Flint, MI A
Bowling Green State U, OH B
Central Michigan U, MI B
Concordia U, IL B
Concordia U, NE B
Eastern Michigan U, MI B
South Dakota State U, SD B
Union Coll, NE B
The U of Akron, OH B
U of Illinois at Urbana–Champaign, IL B
U of Nebraska–Lincoln, NE B
U of Wisconsin–River Falls, WI B
Viterbo U, WI B
Youngstown State U, OH B

COMPUTER ENGINEERING

Case Western Reserve U, OH B
Dominican U, IL B
Eastern Michigan U, MI B
Illinois Inst of Technology, IL B
Indiana Inst of Technology, IN B
Indiana U–Purdue U Indianapolis, IN B
Iowa State U of Science and Technology, IA B
Kansas State U, KS B
Kettering U, MI B
Marquette U, WI B
Michigan State U, MI B
Michigan Technological U, MI B
Milwaukee School of Engineering, WI B
Minnesota State U, Mankato, MN B
Missouri Tech, MO B
North Dakota State U, ND B
Northwestern U, IL B
Oakland U, MI B
Ohio Northern U, OH B
The Ohio State U, OH B
Oklahoma Christian U, OK B
Oklahoma State U, OK B
Oral Roberts U, OK B
Purdue U, IN B
Purdue U Calumet, IN B
Rose-Hulman Inst of Technology, IN B
St. Cloud State U, MN B
South Dakota School of Mines and Technology, SD B
Southern Illinois U Carbondale, IL B
Southern Illinois U Edwardsville, IL B
Taylor U, IN B
The U of Akron, OH B
U of Cincinnati, OH B
U of Dayton, OH B
U of Evansville, IN B
U of Illinois at Chicago, IL B
U of Illinois at Urbana–Champaign, IL B
The U of Iowa, IA B
U of Kansas, KS B
U of Michigan, MI B
U of Minnesota, Duluth, MN B
U of Missouri–Columbia, MO B
U of Missouri–Rolla, MO B
U of Nebraska–Lincoln, NE B
U of Notre Dame, IN B
U of Oklahoma, OK B
U of Toledo, OH B
U of Wisconsin–Madison, WI B
Washington U in St. Louis, MO B
Western Michigan U, MI B
Wichita State U, KS B
Wilberforce U, OH B
Wright State U, OH B

COMPUTER ENGINEERING TECHNOLOGY

Andrews U, MI A,B
Baker Coll of Owosso, MI A
Bryant and Stratton Coll, Cleveland, OH A
Central Michigan U, MI B
DeVry U, Addison, IL B
DeVry U, Chicago, IL B
DeVry U, Tinley Park, IL B
DeVry U, MO B
DeVry U, OH B
East-West U, IL B
Haskell Indian Nations U, KS A
Indiana State U, IN B
International Business Coll, Fort Wayne, IN A,B
Kansas State U, KS A
Kent State U, Ashtabula Campus, OH A
Kent State U, Geauga Campus, OH A
Kent State U, Tuscarawas Campus, OH A
Madonna U, MI A
Martin U, IN B
Miami U–Hamilton Campus, OH A
Miami U–Middletown Campus, OH A
Minnesota State U, Mankato, MN B
Missouri Tech, MO A
National American U, SD A
Oakland City U, IN A
Ohio U–Lancaster, OH A
Purdue U Calumet, IN A,B
Purdue U North Central, IN A,B
Ranken Tech Coll, MO A
Rogers State U, OK A
Shawnee State U, OH B
U of Cincinnati, OH A
U of Dayton, OH B

COMPUTER GRAPHICS

Academy Coll, MN A
American Academy of Art, IL B
The Art Insts International Minnesota, MN B
Baker Coll of Cadillac, MI A
Baker Coll of Flint, MI B
Capella U, MN B
Coll for Creative Studies, MI B
Columbia Coll, MO B
Columbia Coll Chicago, IL B
Dakota State U, SD B
DePaul U, IL B
Dominican U, IL B
The Illinois Inst of Art, IL A,B
Indiana Wesleyan U, IN B
International Academy of Design & Technology, IL A
Judson Coll, IL B
Lincoln Coll, Normal, IL A
Maharishi U of Management, IA B
Minnesota School of Business-Richfield, MN A
Northern Michigan U, MI B
Oakland City U, IN B
School of the Art Inst of Chicago, IL B
South Dakota State U, SD B
U of Dubuque, IA B
Wittenberg U, OH B

COMPUTER/INFORMATION SCIENCES

Academy Coll, MN A
Andrews U, MI B
Aurora U, IL B
Baker Coll of Muskegon, MI B
Bethel Coll, IN B
Bowling Green State U, OH B
Bradley U, IL B
Cameron U, OK B
Carroll Coll, WI B
Central Michigan U, MI B
Central Missouri State U, MO B
Cleveland State U, OH B
Coll of St. Catherine, MN B
The Coll of St. Scholastica, MN B
Coll of the Ozarks, MO B
Concordia U, NE B
DePaul U, IL B
Doane Coll, NE B
Drury U, MO B
Eastern Michigan U, MI B
Emmaus Bible Coll, IA B
Emporia State U, KS B
The Franciscan U, IA B
Franciscan U of Steubenville, OH B
Franklin Coll, IN B
Grand Valley State U, MI B
Hastings Coll, NE B
Herzing Coll, WI A,B
Herzing Coll, Minneapolis Drafting School Campus, MN A
Indiana State U, IN B
Indiana U Bloomington, IN B
Indiana U–Purdue U Indianapolis, IN B
Indiana Wesleyan U, IN A,B
Kansas State U, KS B
Kaplan Coll, IA A
Kent State U, Salem Campus, OH A
Knox Coll, IL B
Luther Coll, IA B
Marygrove Coll, MI B
Mayville State U, ND B
Miami U, OH B
Miami U–Middletown Campus, OH A
Michigan State U, MI B
Midstate Coll, IL A
Millikin U, IL B
Minnesota State U, Moorhead, MN B
Missouri Southern State Coll, MO B
Missouri Western State Coll, MO B
Mount Mercy Coll, IA B
Northeastern Illinois U, IL B
Northwestern U, IL B
Oakland U, MI B
The Ohio State U, OH B
Oklahoma Baptist U, OK B
Oklahoma Panhandle State U, OK A
Oklahoma State U, OK B
Park U, MO B
Principia Coll, IL B
Purdue U, IN B
Purdue U Calumet, IN B
Reformed Bible Coll, MI B
Robert Morris Coll, IL B
Rockford Business Coll, IL A
Saginaw Valley State U, MI B
Saint Joseph's Coll, IN B
Saint Louis U, MO B
Saint Mary-of-the-Woods Coll, IN B
Saint Xavier U, IL B
Silver Lake Coll, WI B
South Dakota State U, SD B
Southeastern Oklahoma State U, OK B
Southeast Missouri State U, MO B
Southern Illinois U Carbondale, IL B
Southern Illinois U Edwardsville, IL B
Southwestern Coll, KS B
Southwestern Oklahoma State U, OK B
Sterling Coll, KS B
Tri-State U, IN A
U of Cincinnati, OH A,B
U of Illinois at Chicago, IL B
U of Illinois at Urbana–Champaign, IL B
U of Kansas, KS B
U of Michigan–Dearborn, MI B
U of Nebraska at Kearney, NE B
U of Nebraska at Omaha, NE B
U of North Dakota, ND B
U of Northern Iowa, IA B
U of Notre Dame, IN B
U of Phoenix–Ohio Campus, OH B
U of Phoenix–Tulsa Campus, OK B
U of Phoenix-Wisconsin Campus, WI B
U of St. Thomas, MN B
U of Southern Indiana, IN A,B
U of Wisconsin–Eau Claire, WI B
U of Wisconsin–River Falls, WI B
U of Wisconsin–Stevens Point, WI B
U of Wisconsin–Superior, WI B
Valley City State U, ND B
Walsh Coll of Accountancy and Business Administration, MI B
Washington U in St. Louis, MO B
Wayne State U, MI B
Western Illinois U, IL B
Western Michigan U, MI B

Computer/Information Sciences (continued)

Wichita State U, KS B
William Woods U, MO B
Winona State U, MN B
Youngstown State U, OH A,B

COMPUTER/INFORMATION SCIENCES RELATED

Columbia Coll Chicago, IL B
Park U, MO B
Saint Louis U, MO B
Saint Mary's U of Minnesota, MN B
Southwestern Coll, KS B
U of Missouri–Rolla, MO B
U of Notre Dame, IN B
Valley City State U, ND B
Washington U in St. Louis, MO B

COMPUTER/INFORMATION SYSTEMS SECURITY

Briar Cliff U, IA B
ITT Tech Inst, Mount Prospect, IL B
ITT Tech Inst, Fort Wayne, IN B
ITT Tech Inst, Indianapolis, IN B
ITT Tech Inst, Newburgh, IN B
ITT Tech Inst, Arnold, MO B
ITT Tech Inst, Earth City, MO B
ITT Tech Inst, Green Bay, WI B
ITT Tech Inst, Greenfield, WI B

COMPUTER/INFORMATION TECHNOLOGY SERVICES ADMINISTRATION AND MANAGEMENT RELATED

Bethel Coll, KS B
Capella U, MN B
Hesston Coll, KS A

COMPUTER MANAGEMENT

AIB Coll of Business, IA A
Coll of Saint Mary, NE B
Davenport U, Lansing, MI A
Lewis Coll of Business, MI A
Lincoln Coll, Normal, IL A
Luther Coll, IA B
National American U, SD B
National-Louis U, IL B
Northwest Missouri State U, MO B
Northwood U, MI A,B
Oakland City U, IN A,B
Oklahoma Baptist U, OK B
Oklahoma State U, OK B
Rochester Coll, MI B
Simpson Coll, IA B
Tiffin U, OH B
U of Cincinnati, OH B
Webster U, MO B

COMPUTER PROGRAMMING

Academy Coll, MN A
Ancilla Coll, IN A
Andrews U, MI B
Baker Coll of Flint, MI A,B
Baker Coll of Muskegon, MI A
Baker Coll of Owosso, MI A,B
Baker Coll of Port Huron, MI A
Brown Coll, MN A
Cleary U, MI A
Dakota State U, SD A
Davenport U, Grand Rapids, MI A,B
Davenport U, Kalamazoo, MI A,B
DePaul U, IL B
East-West U, IL B
Ferris State U, MI B
Fontbonne U, MO B
Grand Valley State U, MI B
Hamilton Coll, IA A
Hannibal-LaGrange Coll, MO B
Indiana U East, IN A
International Business Coll, Fort Wayne, IN A,B
Iowa Wesleyan Coll, IA B
ITT Tech Inst, Mount Prospect, IL A
ITT Tech Inst, Fort Wayne, IN A
ITT Tech Inst, Indianapolis, IN A
ITT Tech Inst, Newburgh, IN A
ITT Tech Inst, Arnold, MO A
ITT Tech Inst, Earth City, MO A
ITT Tech Inst, Green Bay, WI A
ITT Tech Inst, Greenfield, WI A
Kansas State U, KS A
Kaplan Coll, IA A
Kent State U, Geauga Campus, OH A
Lewis Coll of Business, MI A
Lincoln Coll, Lincoln, IL A
Lincoln Coll, Normal, IL A
Luther Coll, IA B
McPherson Coll, KS B
Michigan Technological U, MI B
Midland Lutheran Coll, NE A,B
Minnesota State U, Mankato, MN B
National American U, SD A,B
National American U–Sioux Falls Branch, SD A,B
Northern Michigan U, MI B
Northwest Missouri State U, MO B
Oakland City U, IN A
Pittsburg State U, KS B
Purdue U Calumet, IN A
Purdue U North Central, IN A
Rockhurst U, MO B
Rogers State U, OK A
Saint Joseph's Coll, IN A
Southeast Missouri State U, MO B
Taylor U, IN B
Tiffin U, OH A
U of Cincinnati, OH A,B
U of Indianapolis, IN A
U of Northwestern Ohio, OH A
U of St. Francis, IL B
U of Toledo, OH A,B
Vatterott Coll, St. Ann, MO A
Waldorf Coll, IA A
Westwood Coll of Technology–Chicago River Oaks, IL A
Winona State U, MN B
Youngstown State U, OH A,B

COMPUTER PROGRAMMING RELATED

Donnelly Coll, KS A
Herzing Coll, WI A

COMPUTER PROGRAMMING (SPECIFIC APPLICATIONS)

AIB Coll of Business, IA A
Sanford-Brown Coll, Fenton, MO A

COMPUTER PROGRAMMING, VENDOR/PRODUCT CERTIFICATION

Sanford-Brown Coll, Fenton, MO A

COMPUTER SCIENCE

Albion Coll, MI B
Alma Coll, MI B
Alverno Coll, WI B
Anderson U, IN B
Andrews U, MI B
Antioch Coll, OH B
Ashland U, OH B
Augsburg Coll, MN B
Augustana Coll, IL B
Augustana Coll, SD B
Avila U, MO B
Bacone Coll, OK A
Baker Coll of Muskegon, MI B
Baker Coll of Owosso, MI A,B
Baker U, KS B
Baldwin-Wallace Coll, OH B
Ball State U, IN B
Beloit Coll, WI B
Bemidji State U, MN B
Benedictine Coll, KS B
Benedictine U, IL B
Bethel Coll, IN A,B
Bethel Coll, KS B
Bethel Coll, MN B
Blackburn Coll, IL B
Black Hills State U, SD A
Bluffton Coll, OH B
Briar Cliff U, IA B
Buena Vista U, IA B
Butler U, IN B
Calvin Coll, MI B
Cameron U, OK B
Capital U, OH B
Cardinal Stritch U, WI B
Carleton Coll, MN B
Carroll Coll, WI B
Carthage Coll, WI B
Case Western Reserve U, OH B
Cedarville U, OH B
Central Christian Coll of Kansas, KS A
Central Coll, IA B
Central Methodist Coll, MO A,B
Chicago State U, IL B
Clarke Coll, IA B
Cleveland State U, OH B
Coe Coll, IA B
Coll of Menominee Nation, WI A
Coll of Mount St. Joseph, OH B
Coll of Saint Benedict, MN B
Coll of the Ozarks, MO B
The Coll of Wooster, OH B
Colorado Tech U Sioux Falls Campus, SD B
Concordia Coll, MN B
Concordia U, IL B
Concordia U, NE B
Concordia U Wisconsin, WI B
Cornell Coll, IA B
Creighton U, NE A,B
Dakota State U, SD B
Dana Coll, NE B
Defiance Coll, OH A,B
Denison U, OH B
DePaul U, IL B
DePauw U, IN B
Dickinson State U, ND B
Doane Coll, NE B
Dominican U, IL B
Donnelly Coll, KS A
Dordt Coll, IA B
Drake U, IA B
Drury U, MO B
Earlham Coll, IN B
East Central U, OK B
East-West U, IL A,B
Elmhurst Coll, IL B
Eureka Coll, IL B
Evangel U, MO B
Fontbonne U, MO B
Franciscan U of Steubenville, OH B
Franklin Coll, IN B
Gallipolis Career Coll, OH A
Goshen Coll, IN B
Governors State U, IL B
Graceland U, IA B
Grace U, NE B
Grand Valley State U, MI B
Grand View Coll, IA B
Greenville Coll, IL B
Grinnell Coll, IA B
Gustavus Adolphus Coll, MN B
Hanover Coll, IN B
Hastings Coll, NE B
Heidelberg Coll, OH B
Hillsdale Coll, MI B
Hiram Coll, OH B
Hope Coll, MI B
Huntington Coll, IN B
Illinois Coll, IL B
Illinois Inst of Technology, IL B
Illinois State U, IL B
Illinois Wesleyan U, IL B
Indiana Inst of Technology, IN B
Indiana U–Purdue U Fort Wayne, IN A,B
Indiana U South Bend, IN A,B
Indiana U Southeast, IN A,B
Iowa State U of Science and Technology, IA B
Iowa Wesleyan Coll, IA B
Jamestown Coll, ND B
John Carroll U, OH B
Judson Coll, IL B
Kalamazoo Coll, MI B
Kendall Coll, IL B
Kettering U, MI B
Lake Forest Coll, IL B
Lakeland Coll, WI B
Langston U, OK B
Lawrence Technological U, MI B
Lawrence U, WI B

Lewis Coll of Business, MI A
Lewis U, IL B
Lincoln Coll, Lincoln, IL A
Lincoln Coll, Normal, IL A
Lindenwood U, MO B
Loras Coll, IA B
Loyola U Chicago, IL B
Luther Coll, IA B
Macalester Coll, MN B
MacMurray Coll, IL B
Madonna U, MI A,B
Maharishi U of Management, IA A,B
Malone Coll, OH B
Manchester Coll, IN A,B
Marietta Coll, OH B
Marquette U, WI B
Maryville U of Saint Louis, MO B
McKendree Coll, IL B
McPherson Coll, KS B
Metropolitan State U, MN B
Miami U–Middletown Campus, OH A
Michigan Technological U, MI B
MidAmerica Nazarene U, KS B
Midland Lutheran Coll, NE B
Minnesota State U, Mankato, MN B
Minnesota State U, Moorhead, MN B
Minot State U, ND B
Missouri Southern State Coll, MO A,B
Missouri Valley Coll, MO B
Monmouth Coll, IL B
Morningside Coll, IA B
Mount Marty Coll, SD B
Mount Mary Coll, WI B
Mount Mercy Coll, IA B
Mount Union Coll, OH B
Mount Vernon Nazarene U, OH B
Muskingum Coll, OH B
Nebraska Indian Comm Coll, NE A
Nebraska Wesleyan U, NE B
North Central Coll, IL B
North Dakota State U, ND B
Northeastern State U, OK B
Northern Illinois U, IL B
Northern Michigan U, MI B
Northwestern Coll, IA B
Northwestern Oklahoma State U, OK B
Northwestern U, IL B
Northwest Missouri State U, MO B
Oakland City U, IN A
Oberlin Coll, OH B
Ohio Dominican U, OH B
Ohio Northern U, OH B
The Ohio State U, OH B
Ohio U, OH B
Ohio U–Lancaster, OH A
Ohio U–Southern Campus, OH A
Ohio Wesleyan U, OH B
Oklahoma Baptist U, OK B
Oklahoma Christian U, OK B
Oklahoma City U, OK B
Oklahoma State U, OK B
Olivet Coll, MI B
Olivet Nazarene U, IL B
Oral Roberts U, OK B
Otterbein Coll, OH B
Park U, MO B
Peru State Coll, NE B
Pittsburg State U, KS B
Purdue U Calumet, IN B
Quincy U, IL B
Ripon Coll, WI B
Rochester Comm and Tech Coll, MN A
Rockford Coll, IL B
Rockhurst U, MO B
Rogers State U, OK A
Roosevelt U, IL B
Rose-Hulman Inst of Technology, IN B
St. Ambrose U, IA B
St. Cloud State U, MN B
Saint John's U, MN B
Saint Joseph's Coll, IN A,B
Saint Mary's U of Minnesota, MN B
Saint Xavier U, IL B
Sanford-Brown Coll, Fenton, MO A
Simpson Coll, IA B
Si Tanka Huron U, SD B
South Dakota School of Mines and Technology, SD B
Southern Nazarene U, OK B
Southwest Baptist U, MO A,B
Southwestern Oklahoma State U, OK B
Southwest Minnesota State U, MN B
Southwest Missouri State U, MO B
Spring Arbor U, MI B
Springfield Coll in Illinois, IL A
Tabor Coll, KS A,B
Taylor U, IN B
Taylor U, Fort Wayne Campus, IN B
Trinity Christian Coll, IL B
Trinity International U, IL B
Tri-State U, IN B
Truman State U, MO B
Union Coll, NE B
The U of Akron, OH B
U of Central Oklahoma, OK B
U of Chicago, IL B
U of Cincinnati, OH B
U of Dayton, OH B
U of Dubuque, IA A,B
U of Evansville, IN B
The U of Findlay, OH A,B
U of Illinois at Springfield, IL B
U of Indianapolis, IN B
The U of Iowa, IA B
U of Michigan, MI B
U of Michigan–Dearborn, MI B
U of Michigan–Flint, MI B
U of Minnesota, Duluth, MN B
U of Minnesota, Morris, MN B
U of Minnesota, Twin Cities Campus, MN B
U of Missouri–Columbia, MO B
U of Missouri–Kansas City, MO B
U of Missouri–Rolla, MO B
U of Missouri–St. Louis, MO B
U of Nebraska at Omaha, NE B
U of Nebraska–Lincoln, NE B
U of Northern Iowa, IA B
U of Oklahoma, OK B
U of Rio Grande, OH A,B
U of St. Francis, IL B
U of Science and Arts of Oklahoma, OK B
U of Sioux Falls, SD B
The U of South Dakota, SD B
U of Toledo, OH B
U of Tulsa, OK B
U of Wisconsin–Green Bay, WI B
U of Wisconsin–La Crosse, WI B
U of Wisconsin–Madison, WI B
U of Wisconsin–Milwaukee, WI B
U of Wisconsin–Oshkosh, WI B
U of Wisconsin–Parkside, WI B
U of Wisconsin–Platteville, WI B
U of Wisconsin–River Falls, WI B
U of Wisconsin–Superior, WI B
U of Wisconsin–Whitewater, WI B
Valparaiso U, IN B
Waldorf Coll, IA A
Walsh U, OH B
Wartburg Coll, IA B
Washington U in St. Louis, MO B
Wayne State Coll, NE B
Webster U, MO B
Western Michigan U, MI B
Westminster Coll, MO B
Wheaton Coll, IL B
Wilberforce U, OH B
William Jewell Coll, MO B
William Penn U, IA B
Wilmington Coll, OH B
Winona State U, MN B
Wittenberg U, OH B
Wright State U, OH B
Xavier U, OH B
Youngstown State U, OH B

COMPUTER SCIENCE RELATED

Donnelly Coll, KS A
Indiana State U, IN B
Kenyon Coll, OH B

COMPUTER SOFTWARE AND MEDIA APPLICATIONS RELATED

AIB Coll of Business, IA A
Ancilla Coll, IN A
Carroll Coll, WI B
Dakota Wesleyan U, SD B
Gallipolis Career Coll, OH A
Grand View Coll, IA B

COMPUTER SOFTWARE ENGINEERING

Milwaukee School of Engineering, WI B
Saint Louis U, MO B

COMPUTER SYSTEMS ANALYSIS

Baker Coll of Flint, MI A,B
Kansas State U, KS A
Kent State U, OH B
Miami U, OH B
Oklahoma Baptist U, OK B
Rockhurst U, MO B
Saginaw Valley State U, MI B
St. Ambrose U, IA B

COMPUTER SYSTEMS NETWORKING/ TELECOMMUNICATIONS

AIB Coll of Business, IA A
Ancilla Coll, IN A
Capella U, MN B
Herzing Coll, WI A
Herzing Coll, Minneapolis Drafting School Campus, MN A
ITT Tech Inst, Fort Wayne, IN B
ITT Tech Inst, Newburgh, IN B
ITT Tech Inst, Arnold, MO B
ITT Tech Inst, Earth City, MO B
ITT Tech Inst, Green Bay, WI B
ITT Tech Inst, Greenfield, WI B
Westwood Coll of Technology-Chicago Du Page, IL A
Westwood Coll of Technology–Chicago River Oaks, IL A

COMPUTER/TECHNICAL SUPPORT

Gallipolis Career Coll, OH A

COMPUTER TYPOGRAPHY/ COMPOSITION

Baker Coll of Auburn Hills, MI A
Baker Coll of Cadillac, MI A
Baker Coll of Clinton Township, MI A
Baker Coll of Flint, MI A
Baker Coll of Jackson, MI A
Calumet Coll of Saint Joseph, IN A
Lincoln Coll, Lincoln, IL A
Lincoln Coll, Normal, IL A
Northern Michigan U, MI A
U of Toledo, OH A

CONSTRUCTION ENGINEERING

Andrews U, MI B
Bradley U, IL B
Lawrence Technological U, MI B
Michigan Technological U, MI B
North Dakota State U, ND B
U of Cincinnati, OH B
Western Michigan U, MI B

CONSTRUCTION MANAGEMENT

Andrews U, MI B
Baker Coll of Flint, MI A
Ferris State U, MI B
Minnesota State U, Mankato, MN B
North Dakota State U, ND B
Oklahoma State U, OK B
Pittsburg State U, KS B
U of Cincinnati, OH B
U of Minnesota, Twin Cities Campus, MN B

Construction Management (continued)

U of Wisconsin–Madison, WI B
U of Wisconsin–Platteville, WI B
Western Michigan U, MI B

CONSTRUCTION TECHNOLOGY

Andrews U, MI A,B
Baker Coll of Owosso, MI A
Bemidji State U, MN B
Bowling Green State U, OH B
Central Christian Coll of Kansas, KS A
Central Michigan U, MI B
Central Missouri State U, MO A,B
Ferris State U, MI A
Indiana U–Purdue U Fort Wayne, IN B
Lawrence Technological U, MI A
Minnesota State U, Moorhead, MN B
Morrison Inst of Technology, IL A
Northern Michigan U, MI A,B
Oklahoma State U, OK B
Pittsburg State U, KS B
Purdue U Calumet, IN A,B
Purdue U North Central, IN A
South Dakota State U, SD B
Southern Illinois U Carbondale, IL B
Southern Illinois U Edwardsville, IL B
Southwest Missouri State U, MO B
Tri-State U, IN A
The U of Akron, OH A
U of Cincinnati, OH A,B
U of Nebraska–Lincoln, NE B
U of Oklahoma, OK B
U of Toledo, OH A,B
U of Wisconsin–Stout, WI B

CONSUMER ECONOMICS

U of Illinois at Urbana–Champaign, IL B

CONSUMER SERVICES

Coll of the Ozarks, MO B
Iowa State U of Science and Technology, IA B
South Dakota State U, SD B
U of Wisconsin–Madison, WI B

CORRECTIONS

Baker Coll of Muskegon, MI A
Chicago State U, IL B
Coll of the Ozarks, MO B
Langston U, OK B
Lincoln Coll, Lincoln, IL A
Lincoln Coll, Normal, IL A
Marygrove Coll, MI A
Minnesota State U, Mankato, MN B
Oklahoma City U, OK B
St. Cloud State U, MN B
Saint Louis U, MO B
Southeast Missouri State U, MO B
Tiffin U, OH B
The U of Akron, OH B
U of Indianapolis, IN A,B
U of Toledo, OH A
Winona State U, MN B
Xavier U, OH A
Youngstown State U, OH A,B

COSMETOLOGY

Lincoln Coll, Lincoln, IL A

COUNSELING PSYCHOLOGY

Central Christian Coll of Kansas, KS A
Crossroads Coll, MN B
Grace Coll, IN B
Morningside Coll, IA B
Northwestern U, IL B
Rochester Coll, MI B
Saint Xavier U, IL B

COUNSELOR EDUCATION/ GUIDANCE

Bowling Green State U, OH B
Central Christian Coll of Kansas, KS A
Circleville Bible Coll, OH B
DePaul U, IL B
East Central U, OK B
Martin U, IN B
Northwest Missouri State U, MO B
Ohio U, OH B
Pittsburg State U, KS B
Purdue U Calumet, IN B
St. Cloud State U, MN B
U of Central Oklahoma, OK B
U of Wisconsin–Superior, WI B
Wayne State Coll, NE B

COURT REPORTING

AIB Coll of Business, IA A
Central Michigan U, MI B
Metro Business Coll, MO A
Metropolitan Coll, Tulsa, OK A,B
Midstate Coll, IL A
U of Cincinnati, OH A

CRAFT/FOLK ART

Bowling Green State U, OH B
The Cleveland Inst of Art, OH B
Kent State U, OH B
U of Illinois at Urbana–Champaign, IL B

CREATIVE WRITING

Antioch Coll, OH B
Ashland U, OH B
Augustana Coll, IL B
Beloit Coll, WI B
Bethel Coll, MN B
Bowling Green State U, OH B
Briar Cliff U, IA B
Cardinal Stritch U, WI B
Carroll Coll, WI B
Central Michigan U, MI B
Chicago State U, IL B
Coll of St. Catherine, MN B
Columbia Coll Chicago, IL B
Concordia Coll, MN B
Denison U, OH B
DePaul U, IL B
Grand Valley State U, MI B
Hastings Coll, NE B
Indiana Wesleyan U, IN B
Kenyon Coll, OH B
Knox Coll, IL B
Lakeland Coll, WI B
Lincoln Coll, Lincoln, IL A
Loras Coll, IA B
Maharishi U of Management, IA A
Manchester Coll, IN A
Marquette U, WI B
Miami U, OH B
Millikin U, IL B
Minnesota State U, Mankato, MN B
Northern Michigan U, MI B
Northland Coll, WI B
Northwestern Coll, MN B
Oberlin Coll, OH B
Ohio Northern U, OH B
The Ohio State U, OH B
Ohio U, OH B
Ohio Wesleyan U, OH B
Oklahoma Christian U, OK B
Rockhurst U, MO B
St. Cloud State U, MN B
Saint Joseph's Coll, IN B
Saint Mary's Coll, IN B
Southwest Minnesota State U, MN B
Stephens Coll, MO B
Taylor U, IN B
U of Chicago, IL B
U of Evansville, IN B
The U of Findlay, OH B
The U of Iowa, IA B
U of Michigan, MI B
U of Nebraska at Omaha, NE B
U of St. Thomas, MN B
The U of South Dakota, SD B
U of Wisconsin–Parkside, WI B
Washington U in St. Louis, MO B
Wayne State Coll, NE B
Webster U, MO B
Western Michigan U, MI B
Westminster Coll, MO B
Wittenberg U, OH B

CRIMINAL JUSTICE/ CORRECTIONS RELATED

Chadron State Coll, NE B
Mount Mary Coll, WI B

CRIMINAL JUSTICE/LAW ENFORCEMENT ADMINISTRATION

Adrian Coll, MI A,B
Ancilla Coll, IN A
Anderson U, IN A,B
Ashland U, OH A,B
Aurora U, IL B
Baldwin-Wallace Coll, OH B
Ball State U, IN A,B
Bellevue U, NE B
Bemidji State U, MN A,B
Benedictine Coll, KS B
Blackburn Coll, IL B
Bluffton Coll, OH B
Bradley U, IL B
Briar Cliff U, IA B
Buena Vista U, IA B
Calumet Coll of Saint Joseph, IN A,B
Calvin Coll, MI B
Cameron U, OK A,B
Carroll Coll, WI B
Carthage Coll, WI B
Cedarville U, OH B
Central Missouri State U, MO B
Chicago State U, IL B
Coll of the Ozarks, MO B
Columbia Coll, MO A,B
Concordia U, MI B
Concordia U Wisconsin, WI B
Culver-Stockton Coll, MO B
Dakota Wesleyan U, SD A,B
Defiance Coll, OH A,B
Dordt Coll, IA B
East Central U, OK B
Eastern Michigan U, MI B
Edgewood Coll, WI B
Evangel U, MO B
Ferris State U, MI B
Finlandia U, MI A
Governors State U, IL B
Grace Coll, IN B
Graceland U, IA B
Grand Valley State U, MI B
Grand View Coll, IA B
Gustavus Adolphus Coll, MN B
Hamline U, MN B
Hannibal-LaGrange Coll, MO A,B
Harris-Stowe State Coll, MO B
Indiana U Northwest, IN A,B
Indiana U South Bend, IN A,B
Iowa Wesleyan Coll, IA B
Langston U, OK B
Lewis U, IL B
Lincoln Coll, Lincoln, IL A
Lindenwood U, MO B
Lourdes Coll, OH A,B
MacMurray Coll, IL A,B
Madonna U, MI A,B
Marian Coll of Fond du Lac, WI B
Martin U, IN B
McKendree Coll, IL B
MidAmerica Nazarene U, KS B
Midland Lutheran Coll, NE B
Missouri Southern State Coll, MO B
Missouri Valley Coll, MO B
Mount Mercy Coll, IA B
Mount Vernon Nazarene U, OH B
Nebraska Indian Comm Coll, NE A
North Dakota State U, ND B
Northeastern State U, OK B
Northern Michigan U, MI A,B
Oakland City U, IN B
Oakland U, MI B
Ohio Dominican U, OH B
Ohio Northern U, OH B
Ohio U, OH B
Ohio U–Chillicothe, OH B
Ohio U–Lancaster, OH B
Ohio U–Southern Campus, OH A
Ohio U–Zanesville, OH B
Oklahoma City U, OK B
Olivet Nazarene U, IL B
Park U, MO B
Peru State Coll, NE B
Pittsburg State U, KS B
Purdue U Calumet, IN B
Quincy U, IL B
Rockford Coll, IL B
Rogers State U, OK A
St. Cloud State U, MN B
Saint Mary's U of Minnesota, MN B
Siena Heights U, MI A,B
Simpson Coll, IA B

Si Tanka Huron U, SD A,B
Southeast Missouri State U, MO B
Southern Illinois U Carbondale, IL B
Southwest Baptist U, MO B
Southwestern Oklahoma State U, OK B
Taylor U, Fort Wayne Campus, IN B
Tiffin U, OH B
Tri-State U, IN A,B
Truman State U, MO B
Union Inst & U, OH B
The U of Akron, OH B
U of Central Oklahoma, OK B
U of Cincinnati, OH A,B
U of Dayton, OH B
U of Dubuque, IA B
U of Evansville, IN B
The U of Findlay, OH A,B
U of Illinois at Springfield, IL B
U of Indianapolis, IN A,B
U of Michigan–Flint, MI B
U of Missouri–Kansas City, MO B
U of Missouri–St. Louis, MO B
U of Nebraska at Omaha, NE B
U of Phoenix–Tulsa Campus, OK B
The U of South Dakota, SD A,B
U of Wisconsin–Milwaukee, WI B
U of Wisconsin–Oshkosh, WI B
U of Wisconsin–Parkside, WI B
U of Wisconsin–Platteville, WI B
Urbana U, OH A,B
Viterbo U, WI B
Wayne State Coll, NE B
Western Illinois U, IL B
Wilmington Coll, OH B
Winona State U, MN B
Youngstown State U, OH A,B

CRIMINAL JUSTICE STUDIES

Augsburg Coll, MN B
Aurora U, IL B
Avila U, MO B
Bethany Coll, KS B
Bethel Coll, IN A,B
Bethel Coll, KS B
Butler U, IN B
Central Christian Coll of Kansas, KS A
Central Methodist Coll, MO B
Colorado Tech U Sioux Falls Campus, SD A,B
Concordia Coll, MN B
Fort Hays State U, KS B
The Franciscan U, IA B
Illinois State U, IL B
Indiana U Bloomington, IN B
Indiana U East, IN A
Indiana U Kokomo, IN A,B
Indiana U–Purdue U Fort Wayne, IN A,B
Indiana U–Purdue U Indianapolis, IN A,B
Indiana Wesleyan U, IN A,B
Jamestown Coll, ND B
Judson Coll, IL B
Kendall Coll, IL B
Kent State U, OH A,B
Loras Coll, IA B
Loyola U Chicago, IL B
Manchester Coll, IN A
Metropolitan State U, MN B
Michigan State U, MI B
Minnesota State U, Moorhead, MN B
Minot State U, ND B
Missouri Western State Coll, MO A,B
Mount Marty Coll, SD B
Northeastern Illinois U, IL B
Northwestern Coll, MN B
The Ohio State U, OH B
Ohio U, OH B
Olivet Coll, MI B
Pittsburg State U, KS B
Roosevelt U, IL B
Saginaw Valley State U, MI B
St. Ambrose U, IA B
St. Gregory's U, OK A
Saint Joseph's Coll, IN B
Saint Louis U, MO B
Saint Xavier U, IL B
Southeastern Oklahoma State U, OK B
Southeast Missouri State U, MO B
Southern Illinois U Edwardsville, IL B
Southern Nazarene U, OK B
Southwestern Coll, KS B
Southwest Minnesota State U, MN B
Southwest Missouri State U, MO B
Taylor U, Fort Wayne Campus, IN B
The U of Akron, OH B
U of Central Oklahoma, OK B
U of Illinois at Chicago, IL B
U of Nebraska at Kearney, NE B
U of Nebraska at Omaha, NE B
U of North Dakota, ND B
U of Toledo, OH B
U of Wisconsin–Eau Claire, WI B
U of Wisconsin–Superior, WI B
Wayne State U, MI B
Western Michigan U, MI B
Wichita State U, KS B
Xavier U, OH B
Youngstown State U, OH B

CRIMINOLOGY

Ball State U, IN A,B
Capital U, OH B
Central Michigan U, MI B
Coll of the Ozarks, MO B
Dominican U, IL B
Drury U, MO B
Eastern Michigan U, MI B
Indiana State U, IN A,B
Kent State U, OH B
Lincoln Coll, Lincoln, IL A
Lindenwood U, MO B
Marquette U, WI A,B
Maryville U of Saint Louis, MO B
Midland Lutheran Coll, NE B
The Ohio State U, OH B
Ohio U, OH B
St. Cloud State U, MN B
U of Minnesota, Duluth, MN B
U of Missouri–St. Louis, MO B
U of Northern Iowa, IA B
U of Oklahoma, OK B
U of St. Thomas, MN B
Upper Iowa U, IA B
Valparaiso U, IN B
Western Michigan U, MI B
William Penn U, IA B

CULINARY ARTS

The Art Insts International Minnesota, MN A
Baker Coll of Muskegon, MI A
Kendall Coll, IL A,B
Lexington Coll, IL A
Metropolitan State U, MN B
Northern Michigan U, MI B
Oakland City U, IN A
Purdue U Calumet, IN A
The U of Akron, OH A

CULTURAL STUDIES

Bethel Coll, MN B
Cornell Coll, IA B
Indiana Wesleyan U, IN A,B
Kent State U, OH B
Minnesota State U, Mankato, MN B
The Ohio State U, OH B
Ohio Wesleyan U, OH B
Reformed Bible Coll, MI B
Saint Mary-of-the-Woods Coll, IN B
St. Olaf Coll, MN B
U of Wisconsin–Milwaukee, WI B
Washington U in St. Louis, MO B

CURRICULUM AND INSTRUCTION

Ohio U, OH B

CYTOTECHNOLOGY

Eastern Michigan U, MI B
Edgewood Coll, WI B
Elmhurst Coll, IL B
The Franciscan U, IA B
Illinois Coll, IL B
Indiana U–Purdue U Indianapolis, IN A,B
Indiana U Southeast, IN A,B
Jewish Hospital Coll of Nursing and Allied Health, MO B
Luther Coll, IA B
Marian Coll of Fond du Lac, WI B
Mayo School of Health Sciences, MN B
Minnesota State U, Moorhead, MN B
Northern Michigan U, MI B
Oakland U, MI B
Roosevelt U, IL B
Saint Mary's Coll, IN B
Saint Mary's U of Minnesota, MN B
The U of Akron, OH B
U of Kansas, KS B
U of Missouri–St. Louis, MO B
U of North Dakota, ND B
Winona State U, MN B

DAIRY SCIENCE

Iowa State U of Science and Technology, IA B
South Dakota State U, SD B
U of Wisconsin–Madison, WI B
U of Wisconsin–River Falls, WI B

DANCE

Alma Coll, MI B
Antioch Coll, OH B
Baldwin-Wallace Coll, OH B
Ball State U, IN B
Bowling Green State U, OH B
Butler U, IN B
Columbia Coll Chicago, IL B
Denison U, OH B
Eastern Michigan U, MI B
Gustavus Adolphus Coll, MN B
Hope Coll, MI B
Indiana U Bloomington, IN B
Kent State U, OH B
Kenyon Coll, OH B
Lake Erie Coll, OH B
Lincoln Coll, Lincoln, IL A
Lindenwood U, MO B
Luther Coll, IA B
Marygrove Coll, MI B
Northwestern U, IL B
Oakland U, MI B
Oberlin Coll, OH B
The Ohio State U, OH B
Ohio U, OH B
Oklahoma City U, OK B
Otterbein Coll, OH B
St. Olaf Coll, MN B
Southern Illinois U Edwardsville, IL B
Southwest Missouri State U, MO B
Stephens Coll, MO B
The U of Akron, OH B
U of Central Oklahoma, OK B
U of Cincinnati, OH B
U of Illinois at Urbana–Champaign, IL B
The U of Iowa, IA B
U of Kansas, KS B
U of Michigan, MI B
U of Minnesota, Twin Cities Campus, MN B
U of Missouri–Kansas City, MO B
U of Nebraska–Lincoln, NE B
U of Oklahoma, OK B
U of Wisconsin–Milwaukee, WI B
U of Wisconsin–Stevens Point, WI B
Washington U in St. Louis, MO B
Wayne State U, MI B
Webster U, MO B
Western Michigan U, MI B
Wright State U, OH B

DATA ENTRY/ MICROCOMPUTER APPLICATIONS

Gallipolis Career Coll, OH A

DATA ENTRY/ MICROCOMPUTER APPLICATIONS RELATED

AIB Coll of Business, IA A
Donnelly Coll, KS A

DATA PROCESSING

Baker Coll of Clinton Township, MI A
Central Christian Coll of Kansas, KS A
Eastern Michigan U, MI B
Metro Business Coll, MO A
The U of Akron, OH A
U of Rio Grande, OH A
Youngstown State U, OH A

DATA PROCESSING TECHNOLOGY

Baker Coll of Auburn Hills, MI A
Baker Coll of Cadillac, MI A
Baker Coll of Clinton Township, MI A
Baker Coll of Flint, MI A
Baker Coll of Jackson, MI A
Baker Coll of Muskegon, MI A
Baker Coll of Owosso, MI A
Baker Coll of Port Huron, MI A
Bemidji State U, MN B
Cameron U, OK A
Chicago State U, IL B
Cleary U, MI B
Davenport U, Kalamazoo, MI A
Donnelly Coll, KS A
Dordt Coll, IA A
Hamilton Coll, IA A
Hannibal-LaGrange Coll, MO B
Indiana U Kokomo, IN B
Indiana U Northwest, IN B
Lewis Coll of Business, MI A
Lincoln Coll, Lincoln, IL A
Lincoln Coll, Normal, IL A
Miami U–Hamilton Campus, OH A
Minnesota State U, Mankato, MN B
Missouri Southern State Coll, MO A
Mount Vernon Nazarene U, OH B
Northern Michigan U, MI A,B
Northern State U, SD A
Northwest Missouri State U, MO B
Shawnee State U, OH A
U of Cincinnati, OH A
U of Southern Indiana, IN B
U of Toledo, OH A
Waldorf Coll, IA A
Wright State U, OH A
Youngstown State U, OH A

DENTAL ASSISTANT

Minnesota School of Business-Richfield, MN A
U of Southern Indiana, IN A

DENTAL HYGIENE

Baker Coll of Port Huron, MI A
Ferris State U, MI A
Indiana U Northwest, IN A
Indiana U–Purdue U Fort Wayne, IN A
Indiana U–Purdue U Indianapolis, IN A,B
Indiana U South Bend, IN A
Marquette U, WI B
Minnesota State U, Mankato, MN A,B
Missouri Southern State Coll, MO A
The Ohio State U, OH B
Rochester Comm and Tech Coll, MN A
Shawnee State U, OH A
Southern Illinois U Carbondale, IL B
U of Michigan, MI B
U of Minnesota, Twin Cities Campus, MN B
U of Missouri–Kansas City, MO B
U of Nebraska Medical Center, NE B
U of Oklahoma Health Sciences Center, OK B
The U of South Dakota, SD A,B
U of Southern Indiana, IN A
Wichita State U, KS A,B
Youngstown State U, OH A

DENTAL LABORATORY TECHNICIAN

Indiana U–Purdue U Fort Wayne, IN A
Southern Illinois U Carbondale, IL A

DESIGN/APPLIED ARTS RELATED

Ohio U, OH B
Robert Morris Coll, IL B
The U of Akron, OH B
U of Saint Francis, IN B
U of Wisconsin–Stout, WI B

DESIGN/VISUAL COMMUNICATIONS

American Academy of Art, IL B
Bethel Coll, IN B
Bowling Green State U, OH B
Calvin Coll, MI B
Carroll Coll, WI B
The Illinois Inst of Art-Schaumburg, IL B
International Academy of Design & Technology, IL B
Iowa State U of Science and Technology, IA B
Kendall Coll of Art and Design of Ferris State U, MI B
Maharishi U of Management, IA B
Mount Union Coll, OH B
Mount Vernon Nazarene U, OH B
Ohio Dominican U, OH B
The Ohio State U, OH B
Ohio U, OH B
Purdue U, IN B
Robert Morris Coll, IL A
Saginaw Valley State U, MI B
St. Ambrose U, IA B
Saint Mary-of-the-Woods Coll, IN B
Southern Illinois U Carbondale, IL B
Southwest Missouri State U, MO B
U of Kansas, KS B
U of Michigan, MI B
U of Notre Dame, IN B
Ursuline Coll, OH B
Washington U in St. Louis, MO B
William Woods U, MO B

DEVELOPMENTAL/CHILD PSYCHOLOGY

Bluffton Coll, OH B
Central Christian Coll of Kansas, KS A
Edgewood Coll, WI B
Iowa State U of Science and Technology, IA B
Langston U, OK B
Lincoln Coll, Lincoln, IL A
Madonna U, MI A,B
Metropolitan State U, MN B
Minnesota State U, Mankato, MN B
Northwest Missouri State U, MO B
Oklahoma Baptist U, OK B
Olivet Nazarene U, IL B
Rochester Comm and Tech Coll, MN A
Rockford Coll, IL B
The U of Akron, OH B
U of Kansas, KS B
U of Michigan–Dearborn, MI B
U of Minnesota, Twin Cities Campus, MN B
U of Missouri–Columbia, MO B
U of Sioux Falls, SD A
U of Toledo, OH B
U of Wisconsin–Green Bay, WI B
U of Wisconsin–Madison, WI B
Waldorf Coll, IA A
Wittenberg U, OH B

DEVELOPMENT ECONOMICS

The Ohio State U, OH B

DIAGNOSTIC MEDICAL SONOGRAPHY

Baker Coll of Owosso, MI A
Coll of St. Catherine, MN A
Coll of St. Catherine–Minneapolis, MN A
Nebraska Methodist Coll, NE A,B
U of Nebraska Medical Center, NE B
U of Toledo, OH A

DIESEL ENGINE MECHANIC

U of Northwestern Ohio, OH A

DIETETICS

Andrews U, MI B
Ashland U, OH B
Ball State U, IN A,B
Bluffton Coll, OH B
Bowling Green State U, OH B
Case Western Reserve U, OH B
Central Michigan U, MI B
Central Missouri State U, MO B
Coll of Saint Benedict, MN B
Coll of St. Catherine, MN B
Coll of the Ozarks, MO B
Concordia Coll, MN B
Dominican U, IL B
Eastern Michigan U, MI B
Fontbonne U, MO B
Indiana U Bloomington, IN B
Iowa State U of Science and Technology, IA B
Kansas State U, KS B
Langston U, OK B
Madonna U, MI B
Miami U, OH B
Michigan State U, MI B
Minnesota State U, Mankato, MN B
Mount Mary Coll, WI B
North Dakota State U, ND B
Northern Michigan U, MI B
Northwest Missouri State U, MO B
Notre Dame Coll, OH B
The Ohio State U, OH B
Ohio U, OH B
Olivet Nazarene U, IL B
Purdue U Calumet, IN A
Saint John's U, MN B
Saint Louis U, MO B
South Dakota State U, SD B
Southwest Missouri State U, MO B
The U of Akron, OH B
U of Central Oklahoma, OK B
U of Dayton, OH B
U of Minnesota, Crookston, MN A
U of Missouri–Columbia, MO B
U of Nebraska at Kearney, NE B
U of North Dakota, ND B
U of Northern Iowa, IA B
U of Oklahoma Health Sciences Center, OK B
U of Wisconsin–Madison, WI B
U of Wisconsin–Stevens Point, WI B
U of Wisconsin–Stout, WI B
Viterbo U, WI B
Wayne State U, MI B
Western Michigan U, MI B
Youngstown State U, OH A,B

DIETICIAN ASSISTANT

Youngstown State U, OH A

DISTRIBUTION OPERATIONS

McKendree Coll, IL B
U of Wisconsin–Superior, WI B
Youngstown State U, OH B

DIVINITY/MINISTRY

Baptist Bible Coll, MO B
Barclay Coll, KS B
Bethel Coll, IN B
Bluffton Coll, OH B
Cardinal Stritch U, WI B
Central Christian Coll of Kansas, KS A,B
Cincinnati Bible Coll and Seminary, OH B
Cornerstone U, MI B
Faith Baptist Bible Coll and Theological Seminary, IA A,B
Global U of the Assemblies of God, MO B
Grace Coll, IN B
Grace U, NE B

Great Lakes Christian Coll, MI B
Greenville Coll, IL B
Hannibal-LaGrange Coll, MO B
Huntington Coll, IN B
Lincoln Christian Coll, IL B
Manhattan Christian Coll, KS A,B
Messenger Coll, MO B
MidAmerica Nazarene U, KS A
Nebraska Christian Coll, NE A,B
North Park U, IL B
Oakland City U, IN B
Oklahoma Baptist U, OK B
Oklahoma Christian U, OK B
Oklahoma Wesleyan U, OK B
Pillsbury Baptist Bible Coll, MN B
Reformed Bible Coll, MI B
Sacred Heart Major Seminary, MI A
St. Louis Christian Coll, MO A,B
Tabor Coll, KS B
Taylor U, Fort Wayne Campus, IN B
Trinity International U, IL B
U of Mary, ND B
U of Saint Francis, IN B
Waldorf Coll, IA A

DRAFTING

Andrews U, MI A
Baker Coll of Auburn Hills, MI A
Baker Coll of Cadillac, MI A
Baker Coll of Clinton Township, MI A
Baker Coll of Flint, MI A,B
Baker Coll of Muskegon, MI A
Baker Coll of Owosso, MI A,B
Baker Coll of Port Huron, MI A
Black Hills State U, SD A
Bryant and Stratton Coll, Cleveland, OH A
Cameron U, OK A
Central Christian Coll of Kansas, KS A
Central Missouri State U, MO A,B
Columbus Coll of Art and Design, OH B
Donnelly Coll, KS A
East Central U, OK B
Ferris State U, MI A
Hamilton Tech Coll, IA A
Herzing Coll, WI A,B
Langston U, OK A
Missouri Southern State Coll, MO A
Northern Michigan U, MI A,B
Northern State U, SD A,B
Ohio U–Lancaster, OH A
Robert Morris Coll, IL A,B
Shawnee State U, OH A
Southwest Missouri State U, MO B
Tri-State U, IN A,B
The U of Akron, OH A
U of Cincinnati, OH A
U of Nebraska at Omaha, NE B
U of Rio Grande, OH A,B
U of Toledo, OH A
Western Michigan U, MI B
Wright State U, OH A
Youngstown State U, OH A

DRAFTING/DESIGN TECHNOLOGY

Hillsdale Coll, MI B
Tri-State U, IN A,B
Youngstown State U, OH A

DRAMA/DANCE EDUCATION

Bowling Green State U, OH B
Chadron State Coll, NE B
Coll of St. Catherine, MN B
Dana Coll, NE B
Eastern Michigan U, MI B
Greenville Coll, IL B
Hastings Coll, NE B
Indiana U–Purdue U Fort Wayne, IN B
Luther Coll, IA B
Minnesota State U, Moorhead, MN B
The Ohio State U, OH B
Oklahoma Baptist U, OK B
Southwestern Coll, KS B
Southwest Minnesota State U, MN B
The U of Akron, OH B
The U of Iowa, IA B
U of St. Thomas, MN B
Viterbo U, WI B
Washington U in St. Louis, MO B
William Jewell Coll, MO B
Youngstown State U, OH B

DRAMA/THEATER LITERATURE

DePaul U, IL B
Northwestern U, IL B
Ohio U, OH B
U of Northern Iowa, IA B
Washington U in St. Louis, MO B

DRAWING

Alma Coll, MI B
American Academy of Art, IL B
Antioch Coll, OH B
Aquinas Coll, MI B
Art Academy of Cincinnati, OH B
Ball State U, IN B
Bethany Coll, KS B
Bowling Green State U, OH B
Central Christian Coll of Kansas, KS A
Chicago State U, IL B
The Cleveland Inst of Art, OH B
Coll for Creative Studies, MI B
Coll of Visual Arts, MN B
Columbia Coll, MO B
Columbus Coll of Art and Design, OH B
DePaul U, IL B
Drake U, IA B
Governors State U, IL B
Grace Coll, IN B
Grand Valley State U, MI B
Illinois Wesleyan U, IL B
Indiana U Bloomington, IN B
Judson Coll, IL B
Lewis U, IL B
Lincoln Coll, Lincoln, IL A
Lincoln Coll, Normal, IL A
Lindenwood U, MO B
Maharishi U of Management, IA B
Milwaukee Inst of Art and Design, WI B
Minneapolis Coll of Art and Design, MN B
Minnesota State U, Mankato, MN B
Northern Michigan U, MI A,B
Northwest Missouri State U, MO B
The Ohio State U, OH B
Ohio U, OH B
St. Cloud State U, MN B
School of the Art Inst of Chicago, IL B
Shawnee State U, OH B
Trinity Christian Coll, IL B
The U of Akron, OH B
U of Evansville, IN B
The U of Iowa, IA B
U of Michigan, MI B
The U of South Dakota, SD B
U of Toledo, OH B
Washington U in St. Louis, MO B
Webster U, MO B
Winona State U, MN B
Wittenberg U, OH B
Wright State U, OH B

DRIVER/SAFETY EDUCATION

William Penn U, IA B

EARLY CHILDHOOD EDUCATION

Alma Coll, MI B
Ashland U, OH B
Augsburg Coll, MN B
Baker Coll of Clinton Township, MI A
Baker Coll of Muskegon, MI A
Baker Coll of Owosso, MI A
Ball State U, IN B
Bethel Coll, IN A
Bethel Coll, MN B
Black Hills State U, SD B
Bluffton Coll, OH B
Bowling Green State U, OH B
Bradley U, IL B
Cardinal Stritch U, WI B
Carroll Coll, WI B
Cedarville U, OH B
Central Christian Coll of Kansas, KS A
Central Methodist Coll, MO B
Chatfield Coll, OH A
Chicago State U, IL B
Cincinnati Bible Coll and Seminary, OH B
Clarke Coll, IA B
Cleveland State U, OH B
Coll of Mount St. Joseph, OH B
Coll of St. Catherine, MN B
Coll of Saint Mary, NE A,B
Columbia Coll Chicago, IL B
Concordia Coll, MN B
Concordia U, IL B
Concordia U, MN B
Concordia U, NE B
Concordia U Wisconsin, WI B
Cornerstone U, MI B
Crown Coll, MN A,B
DePaul U, IL B
Donnelly Coll, KS A
East Central U, OK B
Eastern Illinois U, IL B
Edgewood Coll, WI B
Elmhurst Coll, IL B
Evangel U, MO B
Fontbonne U, MO B
Fort Hays State U, KS B
The Franciscan U, IA B
Goshen Coll, IN B
Governors State U, IL B
Grace Bible Coll, MI B
Greenville Coll, IL B
Hannibal-LaGrange Coll, MO B
Harris-Stowe State Coll, MO B
Hesston Coll, KS A
Hillsdale Coll, MI B
Illinois State U, IL B
Indiana State U, IN A,B
Indiana U Bloomington, IN B
Indiana U–Purdue U Fort Wayne, IN A
Indiana U–Purdue U Indianapolis, IN A
Indiana U South Bend, IN A
Iowa State U of Science and Technology, IA B
Iowa Wesleyan Coll, IA B
John Carroll U, OH B
Judson Coll, IL B
Kendall Coll, IL A,B
Kent State U, OH B
Kent State U, Ashtabula Campus, OH A
Kent State U, Salem Campus, OH A
Lakeland Coll, WI B
Langston U, OK B
Lincoln Christian Coll, IL B
Lincoln Coll, Lincoln, IL A
Lindenwood U, MO B
Loras Coll, IA B
Lourdes Coll, OH A,B
Loyola U Chicago, IL B
Luther Coll, IA B
Malone Coll, OH B
Manchester Coll, IN A
Maranatha Baptist Bible Coll, WI A,B
Marian Coll, IN A,B
Marian Coll of Fond du Lac, WI B
Martin Luther Coll, MN B
Martin U, IN B
Marygrove Coll, MI A,B
Maryville U of Saint Louis, MO B
McPherson Coll, KS B
Miami U, OH B
Miami U–Hamilton Campus, OH A
Miami U–Middletown Campus, OH A
Midland Lutheran Coll, NE A,B
Minnesota State U, Mankato, MN B
Minnesota State U, Moorhead, MN B
Missouri Southern State Coll, MO B
Mount Mary Coll, WI B
Mount Union Coll, OH B
Mount Vernon Nazarene U, OH B
Muskingum Coll, OH B
National-Louis U, IL B
Nebraska Indian Comm Coll, NE A

Early Childhood Education (continued)

North Central Coll, IL B
Northeastern Illinois U, IL B
Northeastern State U, OK B
Northern Illinois U, IL B
North Park U, IL B
Northwestern Coll, MN B
Northwestern Oklahoma State U, OK B
Northwest Missouri State U, MO B
Notre Dame Coll, OH B
Ohio Northern U, OH B
Ohio U, OH B
Ohio U–Southern Campus, OH A
Oklahoma Baptist U, OK B
Oklahoma Christian U, OK B
Oklahoma City U, OK B
Olivet Nazarene U, IL B
Oral Roberts U, OK B
Park U, MO B
Peru State Coll, NE B
Pittsburg State U, KS B
Purdue U, IN B
Purdue U Calumet, IN A
Ripon Coll, WI B
Roosevelt U, IL B
St. Ambrose U, IA B
St. Augustine Coll, IL A
St. Cloud State U, MN B
Saint Joseph's Coll, IN A
Saint Mary-of-the-Woods Coll, IN B
Saint Mary's U of Minnesota, MN B
Saint Xavier U, IL B
Siena Heights U, MI B
Silver Lake Coll, WI B
Simpson Coll, IA B
South Dakota State U, SD B
Southeastern Oklahoma State U, OK B
Southeast Missouri State U, MO B
Southern Illinois U Carbondale, IL B
Southern Illinois U Edwardsville, IL B
Southern Nazarene U, OK B
Southwestern Coll, KS B
Southwest Minnesota State U, MN B
Southwest Missouri State U, MO B
Spring Arbor U, MI B
Stephens Coll, MO B
Tabor Coll, KS B
Taylor U, IN A
Taylor U, Fort Wayne Campus, IN A
The U of Akron, OH B
U of Central Oklahoma, OK B
U of Cincinnati, OH B
U of Dayton, OH B
U of Illinois at Urbana–Champaign, IL B
U of Mary, ND B
U of Michigan–Dearborn, MI B
U of Michigan–Flint, MI B
U of Minnesota, Crookston, MN A,B
U of Minnesota, Duluth, MN B
U of Minnesota, Twin Cities Campus, MN B
U of Missouri–Columbia, MO B
U of Missouri–Kansas City, MO B
U of Missouri–St. Louis, MO B
U of North Dakota, ND B
U of Northern Iowa, IA B
U of Oklahoma, OK B
U of Rio Grande, OH A
U of Science and Arts of Oklahoma, OK B
U of Sioux Falls, SD A
U of Toledo, OH B
U of Wisconsin–La Crosse, WI B
U of Wisconsin–Madison, WI B
U of Wisconsin–Milwaukee, WI B
U of Wisconsin–Oshkosh, WI B
U of Wisconsin–Platteville, WI B
U of Wisconsin–Stevens Point, WI B
U of Wisconsin–Stout, WI B
U of Wisconsin–Whitewater, WI B
Waldorf Coll, IA A,B
Walsh U, OH B
Wartburg Coll, IA B
Wayne State Coll, NE B
Webster U, MO B
Westminster Coll, MO B
Winona State U, MN B
Wright State U, OH B
Xavier U, OH A
Youngstown State U, OH B

EARTH SCIENCES

Adrian Coll, MI A,B
Antioch Coll, OH B
Augustana Coll, IL B
Bemidji State U, MN B
Central Michigan U, MI B
Central Missouri State U, MO B
DePauw U, IN B
Dickinson State U, ND B
Eastern Michigan U, MI B
Emporia State U, KS B
Grand Valley State U, MI B
Indiana U East, IN A
Iowa State U of Science and Technology, IA B
Kent State U, OH B
Lincoln Coll, Lincoln, IL A
Miami U, OH B
Michigan State U, MI B
Michigan Technological U, MI B
Minnesota State U, Mankato, MN B
Muskingum Coll, OH B
North Dakota State U, ND B
Northeastern Illinois U, IL B
Northern Michigan U, MI B
Northland Coll, WI B
Northwest Missouri State U, MO B
Ohio Wesleyan U, OH B
Olivet Nazarene U, IL B
St. Cloud State U, MN B
Southeast Missouri State U, MO B
U of Indianapolis, IN B
The U of Iowa, IA B
U of Michigan–Flint, MI B
U of Missouri–Kansas City, MO B
U of Nebraska at Omaha, NE B
The U of South Dakota, SD B
U of Wisconsin–Green Bay, WI A,B
U of Wisconsin–Madison, WI B
U of Wisconsin–Milwaukee, WI B
Washington U in St. Louis, MO B
Western Michigan U, MI B
Winona State U, MN B
Wittenberg U, OH B
Youngstown State U, OH B

EAST AND SOUTHEAST ASIAN LANGUAGES RELATED

Michigan State U, MI B
U of Kansas, KS B
Washington U in St. Louis, MO B

EAST ASIAN STUDIES

Augsburg Coll, MN B
Denison U, OH B
DePaul U, IL B
DePauw U, IN B
Hamline U, MN B
Indiana U Bloomington, IN B
John Carroll U, OH B
Lawrence U, WI B
Oakland U, MI B
Oberlin Coll, OH B
The Ohio State U, OH B
Ohio Wesleyan U, OH B
U of Chicago, IL B
U of Minnesota, Twin Cities Campus, MN B
U of St. Thomas, MN B
Valparaiso U, IN B
Washington U in St. Louis, MO B
Wayne State U, MI B
Wittenberg U, OH B

EASTERN EUROPEAN AREA STUDIES

Hamline U, MN B
Indiana U Bloomington, IN B
Kent State U, OH B
U of Chicago, IL B
The U of Iowa, IA B

ECOLOGY

Alma Coll, MI B
Ball State U, IN B
Bemidji State U, MN B
Bradley U, IL B
Defiance Coll, OH B
East Central U, OK B
Iowa State U of Science and Technology, IA B
Lawrence U, WI B
Maharishi U of Management, IA B
Manchester Coll, IN B
Michigan Technological U, MI B
Minnesota State U, Mankato, MN B
Missouri Southern State Coll, MO B
Northern Michigan U, MI B
Northland Coll, WI B
Northwestern U, IL B
Northwest Missouri State U, MO B
Oberlin Coll, OH B
St. Cloud State U, MN B
U of Illinois at Urbana–Champaign, IL B
U of Michigan, MI B
U of Minnesota, Twin Cities Campus, MN B
U of Missouri–St. Louis, MO B
U of Rio Grande, OH B
U of Wisconsin–Milwaukee, WI B
Winona State U, MN B

ECONOMICS

Adrian Coll, MI A,B
Albion Coll, MI B
Alma Coll, MI B
Andrews U, MI B
Antioch Coll, OH B
Aquinas Coll, MI B
Ashland U, OH B
Augsburg Coll, MN B
Augustana Coll, IL B
Augustana Coll, SD B
Aurora U, IL B
Ave Maria Coll, MI B
Baker U, KS B
Baldwin-Wallace Coll, OH B
Ball State U, IN B
Beloit Coll, WI B
Bemidji State U, MN B
Benedictine Coll, KS B
Benedictine U, IL B
Bethel Coll, MN B
Bluffton Coll, OH B
Bowling Green State U, OH B
Bradley U, IL B
Buena Vista U, IA B
Butler U, IN B
Calvin Coll, MI B
Capital U, OH B
Carleton Coll, MN B
Carthage Coll, WI B
Case Western Reserve U, OH B
Central Christian Coll of Kansas, KS A
Central Coll, IA B
Central Methodist Coll, MO B
Central Michigan U, MI B
Central Missouri State U, MO B
Chicago State U, IL B
Clarke Coll, IA B
Cleveland State U, OH B
Coe Coll, IA B
Coll of Saint Benedict, MN B
Coll of St. Catherine, MN B
The Coll of St. Scholastica, MN B
The Coll of Wooster, OH B
Concordia Coll, MN B
Concordia U, MN B
Concordia U Wisconsin, WI B
Cornell Coll, IA B
Creighton U, NE B
Denison U, OH B
DePaul U, IL B
DePauw U, IN B
Doane Coll, NE B
Dominican U, IL B
Drake U, IA B

Drury U, MO B
Earlham Coll, IN B
Eastern Illinois U, IL B
Eastern Michigan U, MI B
Edgewood Coll, WI B
Elmhurst Coll, IL B
Emporia State U, KS B
Eureka Coll, IL B
Fort Hays State U, KS B
Franciscan U of Steubenville, OH B
Franklin Coll, IN B
Goshen Coll, IN B
Graceland U, IA B
Grand Valley State U, MI B
Grinnell Coll, IA B
Gustavus Adolphus Coll, MN B
Hamline U, MN B
Hanover Coll, IN B
Hastings Coll, NE B
Heidelberg Coll, OH B
Hillsdale Coll, MI B
Hiram Coll, OH B
Hope Coll, MI B
Huntington Coll, IN B
Illinois Coll, IL B
Illinois State U, IL B
Illinois Wesleyan U, IL B
Indiana State U, IN B
Indiana U Bloomington, IN B
Indiana U Northwest, IN B
Indiana U–Purdue U Fort Wayne, IN B
Indiana U–Purdue U Indianapolis, IN B
Indiana U South Bend, IN B
Indiana U Southeast, IN B
Indiana Wesleyan U, IN B
Iowa State U of Science and Technology, IA B
John Carroll U, OH B
Kansas State U, KS B
Kent State U, OH B
Kenyon Coll, OH B
Knox Coll, IL B
Lake Forest Coll, IL B
Lakeland Coll, WI B
Langston U, OK B
Lawrence U, WI B
Lewis U, IL B
Lincoln Coll, Lincoln, IL A
Lincoln Coll, Normal, IL A
Lindenwood U, MO B
Loras Coll, IA B
Loyola U Chicago, IL B
Luther Coll, IA B
Macalester Coll, MN B
Manchester Coll, IN B
Marietta Coll, OH B
Marquette U, WI B
McKendree Coll, IL B
Metropolitan State U, MN B
Miami U, OH B
Miami U–Middletown Campus, OH A
Michigan State U, MI B
Midland Lutheran Coll, NE B
Minnesota State U, Mankato, MN B
Minnesota State U, Moorhead, MN B
Minot State U, ND B
Missouri Valley Coll, MO B
Missouri Western State Coll, MO B
Monmouth Coll, IL B
Mount Union Coll, OH B
Muskingum Coll, OH B
Nebraska Wesleyan U, NE B
North Central Coll, IL B
North Dakota State U, ND B
Northeastern Illinois U, IL B
Northern Illinois U, IL B
Northern Michigan U, MI B
Northern State U, SD B
Northland Coll, WI B
North Park U, IL B
Northwestern Coll, IA B
Northwestern U, IL B
Northwest Missouri State U, MO B
Northwood U, MI A,B
Oakland U, MI B
Oberlin Coll, OH B
Ohio Dominican U, OH B
The Ohio State U, OH B
Ohio U, OH B
Ohio Wesleyan U, OH B
Oklahoma State U, OK B
Olivet Coll, MI B
Olivet Nazarene U, IL B
Otterbein Coll, OH B
Park U, MO B
Pittsburg State U, KS B
Principia Coll, IL B
Purdue U, IN B
Purdue U Calumet, IN B
Ripon Coll, WI B
Rockford Coll, IL B
Rockhurst U, MO B
Roosevelt U, IL B
Rose-Hulman Inst of Technology, IN B
Saginaw Valley State U, MI B
St. Ambrose U, IA B
St. Cloud State U, MN B
Saint John's U, MN B
Saint Joseph's Coll, IN B
Saint Louis U, MO B
Saint Mary's Coll, IN B
St. Norbert Coll, WI B
St. Olaf Coll, MN B
Simpson Coll, IA B
South Dakota State U, SD B
Southeast Missouri State U, MO B
Southern Illinois U Carbondale, IL B
Southern Illinois U Edwardsville, IL B
Southwest Missouri State U, MO B
Taylor U, IN B
Tiffin U, OH B
Trinity International U, IL B
Truman State U, MO B
The U of Akron, OH B
U of Central Oklahoma, OK B
U of Chicago, IL B
U of Cincinnati, OH B
U of Dayton, OH B
U of Evansville, IN B
The U of Findlay, OH B
U of Illinois at Chicago, IL B
U of Illinois at Springfield, IL B
U of Illinois at Urbana–Champaign, IL B
The U of Iowa, IA B
U of Kansas, KS B
U of Michigan, MI B
U of Michigan–Dearborn, MI B
U of Michigan–Flint, MI B
U of Minnesota, Duluth, MN B
U of Minnesota, Morris, MN B
U of Minnesota, Twin Cities Campus, MN B
U of Missouri–Columbia, MO B
U of Missouri–Kansas City, MO B
U of Missouri–Rolla, MO B
U of Missouri–St. Louis, MO B
U of Nebraska at Kearney, NE B
U of Nebraska at Omaha, NE B
U of Nebraska–Lincoln, NE B
U of North Dakota, ND B
U of Northern Iowa, IA B
U of Notre Dame, IN B
U of Oklahoma, OK B
U of Rio Grande, OH B
U of Saint Francis, IN B
U of St. Thomas, MN B
U of Science and Arts of Oklahoma, OK B
U of Sioux Falls, SD A,B
The U of South Dakota, SD B
U of Southern Indiana, IN B
U of Toledo, OH B
U of Tulsa, OK B
U of Wisconsin–Eau Claire, WI B
U of Wisconsin–Green Bay, WI A,B
U of Wisconsin–La Crosse, WI B
U of Wisconsin–Madison, WI B
U of Wisconsin–Milwaukee, WI B
U of Wisconsin–Oshkosh, WI B
U of Wisconsin–Parkside, WI B
U of Wisconsin–Platteville, WI B
U of Wisconsin–River Falls, WI B
U of Wisconsin–Stevens Point, WI B
U of Wisconsin–Superior, WI B
U of Wisconsin–Whitewater, WI B
Valparaiso U, IN B
Wabash Coll, IN B
Wartburg Coll, IA B
Washington U in St. Louis, MO B
Wayne State U, MI B
Webster U, MO B
Western Illinois U, IL B
Western Michigan U, MI B
Westminster Coll, MO B
Wheaton Coll, IL B
Wichita State U, KS B
Wilberforce U, OH B
William Jewell Coll, MO B
Wilmington Coll, OH B
Winona State U, MN B
Wittenberg U, OH B
Wright State U, OH B
Xavier U, OH B
Youngstown State U, OH B

ECONOMICS RELATED

The U of Akron, OH B

EDUCATION

Adrian Coll, MI B
Albion Coll, MI B
Alma Coll, MI B
Alverno Coll, WI B
Anderson U, IN B
Andrews U, MI B
Antioch Coll, OH B
Ashland U, OH B
Augsburg Coll, MN B
Augustana Coll, IL B
Bacone Coll, OK A
Baldwin-Wallace Coll, OH B
Ball State U, IN B
Beloit Coll, WI B
Bemidji State U, MN B
Benedictine U, IL B
Bethany Coll, KS B
Bethel Coll, IN B
Bethel Coll, MN B
Bluffton Coll, OH B
Bowling Green State U, OH B
Briar Cliff U, IA B
Buena Vista U, IA B
Cameron U, OK B
Capital U, OH B
Cardinal Stritch U, WI B
Carroll Coll, WI B
Carthage Coll, WI B
Cedarville U, OH B
Central Christian Coll of Kansas, KS A
Central Methodist Coll, MO B
Central Missouri State U, MO B
Chicago State U, IL B
Cincinnati Bible Coll and Seminary, OH A,B
Circleville Bible Coll, OH A,B
Clarke Coll, IA B
Cleveland State U, OH B
Coe Coll, IA B
Coll of Menominee Nation, WI A
Coll of Saint Benedict, MN B
Coll of St. Catherine, MN B
Coll of Saint Mary, NE B
The Coll of St. Scholastica, MN B
Coll of the Ozarks, MO B
Columbia Coll, MO B
Concordia Coll, MN B
Concordia U, IL B
Concordia U, MN B
Concordia U, NE B
Concordia U Wisconsin, WI B
Cornell Coll, IA B
Cornerstone U, MI B
Creighton U, NE B
Dakota State U, SD B
Dana Coll, NE B
Defiance Coll, OH B
DePaul U, IL B
Dickinson State U, ND B
Donnelly Coll, KS A
Dordt Coll, IA B
Drury U, MO B
Earlham Coll, IN B
East Central U, OK B
Edgewood Coll, WI B
Elmhurst Coll, IL B
Eureka Coll, IL B
Evangel U, MO A,B
Ferris State U, MI B
Finlandia U, MI B
Fontbonne U, MO B
The Franciscan U, IA B
Goshen Coll, IN B
Graceland U, IA B
Grand Valley State U, MI B
Grand View Coll, IA B
Great Lakes Christian Coll, MI B
Greenville Coll, IL B

Education (continued)
Gustavus Adolphus Coll, MN B
Hamline U, MN B
Hannibal-LaGrange Coll, MO B
Hastings Coll, NE B
Heidelberg Coll, OH B
Hillsdale Coll, MI B
Huntington Coll, IN B
Illinois Coll, IL B
Illinois Wesleyan U, IL B
Indiana U Bloomington, IN B
Indiana U East, IN B
Indiana U Northwest, IN B
Indiana U–Purdue U Fort Wayne, IN B
Indiana U–Purdue U Indianapolis, IN B
Indiana U South Bend, IN B
Indiana U Southeast, IN B
Indiana Wesleyan U, IN B
Iowa State U of Science and Technology, IA B
Iowa Wesleyan Coll, IA B
John Carroll U, OH B
Judson Coll, IL B
Kent State U, OH B
Kent State U, Stark Campus, OH A
Knox Coll, IL B
Lake Forest Coll, IL B
Lakeland Coll, WI B
Langston U, OK B
Laura and Alvin Siegal Coll of Judaic Studies, OH B
Lewis U, IL B
Lincoln Coll, Lincoln, IL A
Lincoln Coll, Normal, IL A
Lindenwood U, MO B
Loras Coll, IA B
Luther Coll, IA B
Madonna U, MI B
Maharishi U of Management, IA A,B
Manchester Coll, IN B
Maranatha Baptist Bible Coll, WI B
Marian Coll, IN B
Marian Coll of Fond du Lac, WI B
Marietta Coll, OH B
Marquette U, WI B
Martin U, IN B
Mayville State U, ND B
McPherson Coll, KS B
Miami U–Middletown Campus, OH A
Midland Lutheran Coll, NE B
Minnesota State U, Mankato, MN B
Missouri Southern State Coll, MO B
Missouri Valley Coll, MO B
Monmouth Coll, IL B
Morningside Coll, IA B
Mount Marty Coll, SD B
Mount Mary Coll, WI B
Mount Mercy Coll, IA B
Mount Vernon Nazarene U, OH B
Muskingum Coll, OH B
Nebraska Indian Comm Coll, NE A
Newman U, KS B
North Central Coll, IL B
North Dakota State U, ND B
Northeastern State U, OK B
Northern Illinois U, IL B
Northern Michigan U, MI B
Northern State U, SD B
Northland Coll, WI B
North Park U, IL B
Northwestern Coll, IA B
Northwestern U, IL B
Northwest Missouri State U, MO B
Oakland City U, IN B
Ohio Dominican U, OH B
Ohio U, OH B
Ohio U–Lancaster, OH B
Ohio U–Southern Campus, OH B
Ohio Wesleyan U, OH B
Oklahoma Baptist U, OK B
Oklahoma City U, OK B
Oklahoma State U, OK B
Oklahoma Wesleyan U, OK B
Olivet Coll, MI B
Olivet Nazarene U, IL B
Oral Roberts U, OK B
Otterbein Coll, OH B
Peru State Coll, NE B
Pillsbury Baptist Bible Coll, MN B
Pittsburg State U, KS B
Purdue U, IN B
Purdue U Calumet, IN B
Ripon Coll, WI B
Rockford Coll, IL B
Rockhurst U, MO B
Roosevelt U, IL B
St. Ambrose U, IA B
St. Cloud State U, MN B
Saint John's U, MN B
Saint Mary-of-the-Woods Coll, IN B
Saint Mary's Coll, IN B
Shawnee State U, OH B
Simpson Coll, IA B
Sitting Bull Coll, ND A
South Dakota State U, SD B
Southeastern Oklahoma State U, OK B
Southern Nazarene U, OK B
Southwestern Oklahoma State U, OK B
Southwest Minnesota State U, MN B
Springfield Coll in Illinois, IL A
Tabor Coll, KS B
Taylor U, IN B
Trinity Christian Coll, IL B
Trinity International U, IL B
Tri-State U, IN B
Union Coll, NE B
Union Inst & U, OH B
The U of Akron, OH B
U of Cincinnati, OH B
U of Dayton, OH B
The U of Findlay, OH B
U of Indianapolis, IN B
The U of Iowa, IA B
U of Mary, ND B
U of Michigan, MI B
U of Michigan–Dearborn, MI B
U of Michigan–Flint, MI B
U of Minnesota, Duluth, MN B
U of Minnesota, Morris, MN B
U of Minnesota, Twin Cities Campus, MN B
U of Missouri–Columbia, MO B
U of Missouri–Kansas City, MO B
U of Missouri–St. Louis, MO B
U of Nebraska at Omaha, NE B
U of Rio Grande, OH B
U of Saint Francis, IN B
U of Sioux Falls, SD B
The U of South Dakota, SD B
U of Southern Indiana, IN A
U of Toledo, OH B
U of Tulsa, OK B
U of Wisconsin–La Crosse, WI B
U of Wisconsin–Milwaukee, WI B
U of Wisconsin–Oshkosh, WI B
U of Wisconsin–Platteville, WI B
U of Wisconsin–River Falls, WI B
U of Wisconsin–Stevens Point, WI B
U of Wisconsin–Superior, WI B
U of Wisconsin–Whitewater, WI B
Upper Iowa U, IA B
Urbana U, OH B
Ursuline Coll, OH B
Valley City State U, ND B
Valparaiso U, IN B
Waldorf Coll, IA A
Walsh U, OH B
Washington U in St. Louis, MO B
Wayne State Coll, NE B
Webster U, MO B
Westminster Coll, MO B
William Jewell Coll, MO B
William Penn U, IA B
William Woods U, MO B
Wilmington Coll, OH B
Winona State U, MN B
Wittenberg U, OH B
Wright State U, OH B
Xavier U, OH B
York Coll, NE B
Youngstown State U, OH B

EDUCATION ADMINISTRATION
Eureka Coll, IL B
Laura and Alvin Siegal Coll of Judaic Studies, OH B
Lindenwood U, MO B
Northwest Missouri State U, MO B
Ohio U, OH B
Oral Roberts U, OK B
Purdue U Calumet, IN B
St. Cloud State U, MN B
U of Central Oklahoma, OK B
U of Nebraska at Omaha, NE B
U of Wisconsin–Superior, WI B

EDUCATIONAL MEDIA DESIGN
Ball State U, IN B
The Coll of St. Scholastica, MN B
Ferris State U, MI A
Indiana State U, IN B
Ohio U, OH B
St. Cloud State U, MN B
U of Central Oklahoma, OK B
U of Nebraska at Omaha, NE B
U of Toledo, OH B
Western Illinois U, IL B

EDUCATIONAL MEDIA TECHNOLOGY
U of Wisconsin–Superior, WI A,B

EDUCATIONAL STATISTICS/RESEARCH METHODS
Ohio U, OH B

EDUCATION (K-12)
Adrian Coll, MI B
Augustana Coll, SD B
Briar Cliff U, IA B
Coll of Saint Mary, NE B
The Coll of St. Scholastica, MN B
Columbia Coll, MO B
Creighton U, NE B
Dickinson State U, ND B
Dominican U, IL B
Dordt Coll, IA B
Finlandia U, MI B
Franklin Coll, IN B
Graceland U, IA B
Grace U, NE B
Hamline U, MN B
Hastings Coll, NE B
Hillsdale Coll, MI B
Illinois Coll, IL B
Indiana Wesleyan U, IN B
Jamestown Coll, ND B
John Carroll U, OH B
Lake Erie Coll, OH B
Lewis U, IL B
Lindenwood U, MO B
McKendree Coll, IL B
McPherson Coll, KS B
Midland Lutheran Coll, NE B
Northwestern Oklahoma State U, OK B
Ohio Dominican U, OH B
Ohio Wesleyan U, OH B
Quincy U, IL B
St. Ambrose U, IA B
Saint Mary-of-the-Woods Coll, IN B
St. Norbert Coll, WI B
Southwest Baptist U, MO B
Tabor Coll, KS B
Trinity International U, IL B
U of Minnesota, Morris, MN B
U of St. Thomas, MN B
U of Wisconsin–Superior, WI B
Washington U in St. Louis, MO B

EDUCATION (MULTIPLE LEVELS)
Martin Luther Coll, MN B
Oral Roberts U, OK B
Saint Louis U, MO B
U of Nebraska–Lincoln, NE B
U of Rio Grande, OH B
York Coll, NE B
Youngstown State U, OH B

EDUCATION OF THE EMOTIONALLY HANDICAPPED
Bradley U, IL B
Central Michigan U, MI B
Eastern Michigan U, MI B
Hope Coll, MI B
Loras Coll, IA B

Marygrove Coll, MI	B
Minnesota State U, Moorhead, MN	B
Oklahoma Baptist U, OK	B
Trinity Christian Coll, IL	B
U of Nebraska at Omaha, NE	B
Western Michigan U, MI	B

EDUCATION OF THE HEARING IMPAIRED

Augustana Coll, SD	B
Bowling Green State U, OH	B
Eastern Michigan U, MI	B
Minot State U, ND	B
Ohio U–Chillicothe, OH	A
U of Nebraska at Omaha, NE	B
U of Nebraska–Lincoln, NE	B
U of Science and Arts of Oklahoma, OK	B

EDUCATION OF THE MENTALLY HANDICAPPED

Bowling Green State U, OH	B
Bradley U, IL	B
Central Michigan U, MI	B
Eastern Michigan U, MI	B
Loras Coll, IA	B
Minnesota State U, Moorhead, MN	B
Minot State U, ND	B
Oklahoma Baptist U, OK	B
Silver Lake Coll, WI	B
Trinity Christian Coll, IL	B
U of Northern Iowa, IA	B
U of Rio Grande, OH	B
Western Michigan U, MI	B
York Coll, NE	B

EDUCATION OF THE MULTIPLE HANDICAPPED

Bowling Green State U, OH	B
The U of Akron, OH	B
U of Northern Iowa, IA	B

EDUCATION OF THE PHYSICALLY HANDICAPPED

Eastern Michigan U, MI	B

EDUCATION OF THE SPECIFIC LEARNING DISABLED

Aquinas Coll, MI	B
Bowling Green State U, OH	B
Bradley U, IL	B
Hope Coll, MI	B
Malone Coll, OH	B
Minnesota State U, Moorhead, MN	B
Northwestern U, IL	B
Oklahoma Baptist U, OK	B
Silver Lake Coll, WI	B
Trinity Christian Coll, IL	B
The U of Akron, OH	B
U of Rio Grande, OH	B
Youngstown State U, OH	B

EDUCATION OF THE SPEECH IMPAIRED

Eastern Michigan U, MI	B
Minot State U, ND	B
The U of Akron, OH	B
U of Toledo, OH	B
Wayne State U, MI	B

EDUCATION OF THE VISUALLY HANDICAPPED

Eastern Michigan U, MI	B
Western Michigan U, MI	B

EDUCATION RELATED

Eastern Illinois U, IL	B
Kent State U, OH	A
Park U, MO	B
U of Missouri–St. Louis, MO	B

ELECTRICAL/ELECTRONIC ENGINEERING TECHNOLOGIES RELATED

Southern Illinois U Carbondale, IL	B
U of Southern Indiana, IN	A

ELECTRICAL/ELECTRONIC ENGINEERING TECHNOLOGY

Andrews U, MI	A,B
Baker Coll of Cadillac, MI	A
Baker Coll of Muskegon, MI	A,B
Baker Coll of Owosso, MI	A,B
Bowling Green State U, OH	B
Bradley U, IL	B
Brown Coll, MN	A
Bryant and Stratton Coll, Cleveland, OH	A,B
Cameron U, OK	B
Central Michigan U, MI	B
Central Missouri State U, MO	B
Cleveland State U, OH	B
DeVry U, Addison, IL	A,B
DeVry U, Chicago, IL	A,B
DeVry U, Tinley Park, IL	A,B
DeVry U, MO	A,B
DeVry U, OH	A,B
East Central U, OK	B
East-West U, IL	B
Ferris State U, MI	B
Hamilton Tech Coll, IA	A,B
Herzing Coll, WI	A,B
Indiana State U, IN	A,B
Indiana U–Purdue U Fort Wayne, IN	A,B
Indiana U–Purdue U Indianapolis, IN	A,B
ITT Tech Inst, Mount Prospect, IL	A,B
ITT Tech Inst, Fort Wayne, IN	A,B
ITT Tech Inst, Indianapolis, IN	A,B
ITT Tech Inst, Newburgh, IN	A,B
ITT Tech Inst, Arnold, MO	A,B
ITT Tech Inst, Earth City, MO	A,B
ITT Tech Inst, Green Bay, WI	A,B
ITT Tech Inst, Greenfield, WI	A,B
Kansas State U, KS	A,B
Kent State U, Ashtabula Campus, OH	A
Kent State U, Tuscarawas Campus, OH	A
Langston U, OK	A
Lawrence Technological U, MI	A
Maharishi U of Management, IA	B
Miami U–Hamilton Campus, OH	A
Miami U–Middletown Campus, OH	A
Michigan Technological U, MI	A,B
Milwaukee School of Engineering, WI	B
Minnesota State U, Mankato, MN	B
Missouri Tech, MO	A
Missouri Western State Coll, MO	A,B
Nebraska Indian Comm Coll, NE	A
Northeastern State U, OK	B
Northern Michigan U, MI	A,B
Northern State U, SD	A,B
Ohio U–Lancaster, OH	A
Oklahoma State U, OK	B
Pittsburg State U, KS	A,B
Purdue U, IN	A,B
Purdue U Calumet, IN	A,B
Purdue U North Central, IN	A
Ranken Tech Coll, MO	A
Rochester Comm and Tech Coll, MN	A
Roosevelt U, IL	B
St. Cloud State U, MN	B
South Dakota State U, SD	B
Southeastern Oklahoma State U, OK	B
Southeast Missouri State U, MO	B
Southern Illinois U Carbondale, IL	A
Southwest Missouri State U, MO	B
Spartan School of Aeronautics, OK	A
U of Cincinnati, OH	A,B
U of Dayton, OH	B
U of Southern Indiana, IN	A
U of Toledo, OH	A,B
Vatterott Coll, St. Ann, MO	A
Wayne State U, MI	B
Wichita State U, KS	A
Youngstown State U, OH	A,B

ELECTRICAL ENGINEERING

Bradley U, IL	B
Calvin Coll, MI	B
Case Western Reserve U, OH	B
Cedarville U, OH	B
Cleveland State U, OH	B
Dominican U, IL	B
Dordt Coll, IA	B
East-West U, IL	B
Grand Valley State U, MI	B
Illinois Inst of Technology, IL	B
Indiana Inst of Technology, IN	B
Indiana U–Purdue U Fort Wayne, IN	B
Indiana U–Purdue U Indianapolis, IN	B
Iowa State U of Science and Technology, IA	B
Kansas State U, KS	B
Kettering U, MI	B
Lawrence Technological U, MI	B
Maharishi U of Management, IA	B
Marquette U, WI	B
Michigan State U, MI	B
Michigan Technological U, MI	B
Milwaukee School of Engineering, WI	B
Minnesota State U, Mankato, MN	B
Missouri Tech, MO	A,B
North Dakota State U, ND	B
Northern Illinois U, IL	B
Northwestern U, IL	B
Oakland U, MI	B
Ohio Northern U, OH	B
The Ohio State U, OH	B
Ohio U, OH	B
Oklahoma Christian U, OK	B
Oklahoma State U, OK	B
Oral Roberts U, OK	B
Purdue U, IN	B
Purdue U Calumet, IN	B
Rose-Hulman Inst of Technology, IN	B
Saginaw Valley State U, MI	B
St. Cloud State U, MN	B
Saint Louis U, MO	B
South Dakota School of Mines and Technology, SD	B
South Dakota State U, SD	B
Southern Illinois U Carbondale, IL	B
Southern Illinois U Edwardsville, IL	B
Tri-State U, IN	B
The U of Akron, OH	B
U of Cincinnati, OH	B
U of Dayton, OH	B
U of Evansville, IN	B
U of Illinois at Chicago, IL	B
U of Illinois at Urbana–Champaign, IL	B
U of Indianapolis, IN	B
The U of Iowa, IA	B
U of Kansas, KS	B
U of Michigan, MI	B
U of Michigan–Dearborn, MI	B
U of Minnesota, Duluth, MN	B
U of Minnesota, Twin Cities Campus, MN	B
U of Missouri–Columbia, MO	B
U of Missouri–Kansas City, MO	B
U of Missouri–Rolla, MO	B
U of Missouri–St. Louis, MO	B
U of Nebraska–Lincoln, NE	B
U of North Dakota, ND	B
U of Notre Dame, IN	B
U of Oklahoma, OK	B
U of St. Thomas, MN	B
U of Toledo, OH	B
U of Tulsa, OK	B
U of Wisconsin–Madison, WI	B
U of Wisconsin–Milwaukee, WI	B
U of Wisconsin–Platteville, WI	B
Valparaiso U, IN	B
Washington U in St. Louis, MO	B
Wayne State U, MI	B
Western Michigan U, MI	B
Wichita State U, KS	B
Wilberforce U, OH	B
Wright State U, OH	B

Electrical Engineering (continued)
Youngstown State U, OH B

ELECTROMECHANICAL INSTRUMENTATION AND MAINTENANCE TECHNOLOGIES RELATED

Southeast Missouri State U, MO A

ELECTROMECHANICAL TECHNOLOGY

Miami U–Middletown Campus, OH A
Michigan Technological U, MI A
Northern Michigan U, MI A
Shawnee State U, OH A
U of Toledo, OH B
Wayne State U, MI B

ELEMENTARY EDUCATION

Adrian Coll, MI B
Albion Coll, MI B
Alma Coll, MI B
Alverno Coll, WI B
Ancilla Coll, IN A
Anderson U, IN B
Andrews U, MI B
Aquinas Coll, MI B
Ashland U, OH B
Augsburg Coll, MN B
Augustana Coll, IL B
Augustana Coll, SD B
Aurora U, IL B
Avila U, MO B
Baker U, KS B
Baldwin-Wallace Coll, OH B
Ball State U, IN B
Baptist Bible Coll, MO B
Barclay Coll, KS B
Beloit Coll, WI B
Bemidji State U, MN B
Benedictine Coll, KS B
Benedictine U, IL B
Bethany Coll, KS B
Bethel Coll, IN B
Bethel Coll, KS B
Bethel Coll, MN B
Blackburn Coll, IL B
Black Hills State U, SD B
Bluffton Coll, OH B
Bowling Green State U, OH B
Bradley U, IL B
Briar Cliff U, IA B
Buena Vista U, IA B
Butler U, IN B
Calumet Coll of Saint Joseph, IN B
Calvin Coll, MI B
Cameron U, OK B
Capital U, OH B
Cardinal Stritch U, WI B
Carroll Coll, WI B
Carthage Coll, WI B
Cedarville U, OH B
Central Christian Coll of Kansas, KS A
Central Coll, IA B
Central Methodist Coll, MO B
Central Michigan U, MI B
Central Missouri State U, MO B
Chadron State Coll, NE B
Chicago State U, IL B
Circleville Bible Coll, OH B
Clarke Coll, IA B
Cleveland State U, OH B
Coe Coll, IA B
Coll of Saint Benedict, MN B
Coll of St. Catherine, MN B
Coll of Saint Mary, NE B
Coll of the Ozarks, MO B
Columbia Coll, MO B
Concordia Coll, MN B
Concordia U, IL B
Concordia U, MI B
Concordia U, MN B
Concordia U, NE B
Concordia U Wisconsin, WI B
Cornell Coll, IA B
Cornerstone U, MI B
Creighton U, NE B
Crown Coll, MN B
Culver-Stockton Coll, MO B
Dakota State U, SD B
Dakota Wesleyan U, SD B
Dana Coll, NE B
Defiance Coll, OH B
DePaul U, IL B
DePauw U, IN B
Dickinson State U, ND B
Doane Coll, NE B
Dominican U, IL B
Dordt Coll, IA B
Drake U, IA B
Drury U, MO B
East Central U, OK B
Eastern Illinois U, IL B
Eastern Michigan U, MI B
Edgewood Coll, WI B
Elmhurst Coll, IL B
Emmaus Bible Coll, IA B
Emporia State U, KS B
Eureka Coll, IL B
Evangel U, MO B
Faith Baptist Bible Coll and Theological Seminary, IA B
Fontbonne U, MO B
Fort Hays State U, KS B
The Franciscan U, IA B
Franciscan U of Steubenville, OH B
Franklin Coll, IN B
Goshen Coll, IN B
Governors State U, IL B
Grace Bible Coll, MI B
Grace Coll, IN B
Graceland U, IA B
Grace U, NE B
Grand Valley State U, MI B
Grand View Coll, IA B
Greenville Coll, IL B
Gustavus Adolphus Coll, MN B
Hamline U, MN B
Hannibal-LaGrange Coll, MO B
Hanover Coll, IN B
Harris-Stowe State Coll, MO B
Haskell Indian Nations U, KS B
Hastings Coll, NE B
Heidelberg Coll, OH B
Hillsdale Coll, MI B
Hillsdale Free Will Baptist Coll, OK A
Hiram Coll, OH B
Hope Coll, MI B
Huntington Coll, IN B
Illinois Coll, IL B
Illinois State U, IL B
Illinois Wesleyan U, IL B
Indiana State U, IN B
Indiana U Bloomington, IN B
Indiana U East, IN B
Indiana U Kokomo, IN B
Indiana U Northwest, IN B
Indiana U–Purdue U Fort Wayne, IN B
Indiana U–Purdue U Indianapolis, IN B
Indiana U South Bend, IN B
Indiana U Southeast, IN B
Indiana Wesleyan U, IN B
Iowa State U of Science and Technology, IA B
Iowa Wesleyan Coll, IA B
Jamestown Coll, ND B
John Carroll U, OH B
Judson Coll, IL B
Kansas State U, KS B
Lake Erie Coll, OH B
Lake Forest Coll, IL B
Lakeland Coll, WI B
Langston U, OK B
Lewis U, IL B
Lincoln Christian Coll, IL B
Lincoln Coll, Lincoln, IL A
Lindenwood U, MO B
Loras Coll, IA B
Loyola U Chicago, IL B
Luther Coll, IA B
MacMurray Coll, IL B
Madonna U, MI B
Manchester Coll, IN B
Maranatha Baptist Bible Coll, WI B
Marian Coll, IN B
Marian Coll of Fond du Lac, WI B
Marietta Coll, OH B
Marquette U, WI B
Martin Luther Coll, MN B
Martin U, IN B
Maryville U of Saint Louis, MO B
Mayville State U, ND B
McKendree Coll, IL B
McPherson Coll, KS B
Miami U, OH B
Miami U–Middletown Campus, OH A
Michigan State U, MI B
MidAmerica Nazarene U, KS B
Midland Lutheran Coll, NE B
Millikin U, IL B
Minnesota State U, Mankato, MN B
Minnesota State U, Moorhead, MN B
Minot State U, ND B
Missouri Southern State Coll, MO B
Missouri Valley Coll, MO B
Missouri Western State Coll, MO B
Monmouth Coll, IL B
Morningside Coll, IA B
Mount Marty Coll, SD B
Mount Mary Coll, WI B
Mount Mercy Coll, IA B
Mount Vernon Nazarene U, OH B
Muskingum Coll, OH B
National-Louis U, IL B
Nebraska Christian Coll, NE B
Nebraska Wesleyan U, NE B
Newman U, KS B
North Central Coll, IL B
North Dakota State U, ND B
Northeastern Illinois U, IL B
Northeastern State U, OK B
Northern Illinois U, IL B
Northern Michigan U, MI B
Northern State U, SD B
Northland Coll, WI B
North Park U, IL B
Northwestern Coll, IA B
Northwestern Coll, MN B
Northwestern Oklahoma State U, OK B
Northwest Missouri State U, MO B
Notre Dame Coll, OH B
Oakland City U, IN B
Oakland U, MI B
Ohio Northern U, OH B
The Ohio State U at Lima, OH B
Ohio U, OH B
Ohio U–Chillicothe, OH B
Ohio U–Lancaster, OH B
Ohio U–Zanesville, OH B
Ohio Wesleyan U, OH B
Oklahoma Baptist U, OK B
Oklahoma Christian U, OK B
Oklahoma City U, OK B
Oklahoma Panhandle State U, OK B
Oklahoma State U, OK B
Oklahoma Wesleyan U, OK B
Olivet Coll, MI B
Olivet Nazarene U, IL B
Oral Roberts U, OK B
Ottawa U, KS B
Otterbein Coll, OH B
Ozark Christian Coll, MO A
Park U, MO B
Peru State Coll, NE B
Pillsbury Baptist Bible Coll, MN B
Pittsburg State U, KS B
Principia Coll, IL B
Purdue U, IN B
Purdue U Calumet, IN B
Purdue U North Central, IN B
Quincy U, IL B
Reformed Bible Coll, MI B
Ripon Coll, WI B
Rockford Coll, IL B
Rockhurst U, MO B
Rogers State U, OK A
Roosevelt U, IL B
Saginaw Valley State U, MI B
St. Ambrose U, IA B
St. Cloud State U, MN B
Saint John's U, MN B
Saint Joseph's Coll, IN B
Saint Mary-of-the-Woods Coll, IN B
Saint Mary's Coll, IN B
Saint Mary U, KS B
St. Norbert Coll, WI B
Saint Xavier U, IL B
Shawnee State U, OH B
Siena Heights U, MI B
Silver Lake Coll, WI B
Simpson Coll, IA B
Si Tanka Huron U, SD B
Southeastern Oklahoma State U, OK B
Southeast Missouri State U, MO B
Southern Illinois U Carbondale, IL B
Southern Illinois U Edwardsville, IL B
Southern Nazarene U, OK B
Southwest Baptist U, MO B

Southwestern Coll, KS B
Southwestern Oklahoma State U, OK B
Southwest Minnesota State U, MN B
Southwest Missouri State U, MO B
Spring Arbor U, MI B
Stephens Coll, MO B
Sterling Coll, KS B
Tabor Coll, KS B
Taylor U, IN B
Taylor U, Fort Wayne Campus, IN B
Trinity Bible Coll, ND B
Trinity Christian Coll, IL B
Trinity International U, IL B
Tri-State U, IN B
Union Coll, NE B
The U of Akron, OH B
U of Central Oklahoma, OK B
U of Cincinnati, OH B
U of Dayton, OH B
U of Dubuque, IA B
U of Evansville, IN B
The U of Findlay, OH B
U of Illinois at Chicago, IL B
U of Illinois at Springfield, IL B
U of Illinois at Urbana–Champaign, IL B
U of Indianapolis, IN B
The U of Iowa, IA B
U of Kansas, KS B
U of Mary, ND B
U of Michigan, MI B
U of Michigan–Dearborn, MI B
U of Michigan–Flint, MI B
U of Minnesota, Duluth, MN B
U of Minnesota, Morris, MN B
U of Minnesota, Twin Cities Campus, MN B
U of Missouri–Columbia, MO B
U of Missouri–Kansas City, MO B
U of Missouri–St. Louis, MO B
U of Nebraska at Kearney, NE B
U of Nebraska at Omaha, NE B
U of Nebraska–Lincoln, NE B
U of North Dakota, ND B
U of Northern Iowa, IA B
U of Oklahoma, OK B
U of Rio Grande, OH B
U of St. Francis, IL B
U of Saint Francis, IN B
U of St. Thomas, MN B
U of Science and Arts of Oklahoma, OK B
U of Sioux Falls, SD B
The U of South Dakota, SD B
U of Southern Indiana, IN B
U of Toledo, OH B
U of Tulsa, OK B
U of Wisconsin–Eau Claire, WI B
U of Wisconsin–Green Bay, WI B
U of Wisconsin–La Crosse, WI B
U of Wisconsin–Madison, WI B
U of Wisconsin–Milwaukee, WI B
U of Wisconsin–Oshkosh, WI B
U of Wisconsin–Platteville, WI B
U of Wisconsin–River Falls, WI B
U of Wisconsin–Stevens Point, WI B
U of Wisconsin–Superior, WI B
U of Wisconsin–Whitewater, WI B
Upper Iowa U, IA B
Urbana U, OH B
Valley City State U, ND B
Valparaiso U, IN B
Viterbo U, WI B
Walsh U, OH B
Wartburg Coll, IA B
Washington U in St. Louis, MO B
Wayne State Coll, NE B
Wayne State U, MI B
Webster U, MO B
Western Illinois U, IL B
Western Michigan U, MI B
Westminster Coll, MO B
Wheaton Coll, IL B
Wichita State U, KS B
William Jewell Coll, MO B
William Penn U, IA B
William Woods U, MO B
Wilmington Coll, OH B
Winona State U, MN B
Wisconsin Lutheran Coll, WI B
Wittenberg U, OH B
Wright State U, OH B
Xavier U, OH B
York Coll, NE B
Youngstown State U, OH B

ELEMENTARY/MIDDLE/SECONDARY EDUCATION ADMINISTRATION

Ohio U, OH B

EMERGENCY MEDICAL TECHNOLOGY

Baker Coll of Cadillac, MI A
Baker Coll of Clinton Township, MI A
Baker Coll of Muskegon, MI A
Ball State U, IN A
Creighton U, NE A,B
Davenport U, Grand Rapids, MI A
Hannibal-LaGrange Coll, MO A
Indiana U–Purdue U Indianapolis, IN A
Nebraska Methodist Coll, NE A,B
Rogers State U, OK A
Shawnee State U, OH A
Southern Illinois U Carbondale, IL A
Southwest Baptist U, MO A
U of Minnesota, Twin Cities Campus, MN B
U of Toledo, OH A
Youngstown State U, OH A

ENERGY MANAGEMENT TECHNOLOGY

Baker Coll of Flint, MI A
Eastern Michigan U, MI B
Ferris State U, MI B
U of Cincinnati, OH A
U of Oklahoma, OK B

ENGINEERING

Baker U, KS B
Beloit Coll, WI B
Bethel Coll, IN B
Calvin Coll, MI B
Carthage Coll, WI B
Case Western Reserve U, OH B
Central Christian Coll of Kansas, KS A
Donnelly Coll, KS A
Dordt Coll, IA B
Fontbonne U, MO B
Grand Valley State U, MI B
Hope Coll, MI B
Indiana U–Purdue U Fort Wayne, IN B
Indiana U–Purdue U Indianapolis, IN B
Iowa State U of Science and Technology, IA B
Marquette U, WI B
Miami U–Middletown Campus, OH A
Michigan State U, MI B
Michigan Technological U, MI B
North Dakota State U, ND B
Northwestern U, IL B
Ohio U, OH B
Oklahoma Christian U, OK B
Oklahoma State U, OK B
Olivet Nazarene U, IL B
Purdue U, IN B
Purdue U Calumet, IN B
St. Cloud State U, MN B
Union Coll, NE A
The U of Akron, OH B
U of Cincinnati, OH B
U of Illinois at Urbana–Champaign, IL B
The U of Iowa, IA B
U of Michigan, MI B
U of Michigan–Dearborn, MI B
U of Michigan–Flint, MI B
U of Oklahoma, OK B
U of Tulsa, OK B
U of Wisconsin–Madison, WI B
U of Wisconsin–Milwaukee, WI B
Valparaiso U, IN B
Waldorf Coll, IA A
Wartburg Coll, IA B
Washington U in St. Louis, MO B
Winona State U, MN B
Youngstown State U, OH A,B

ENGINEERING DESIGN

Cameron U, OK B
Lawrence Technological U, MI B

ENGINEERING/INDUSTRIAL MANAGEMENT

Grand Valley State U, MI B
Illinois Inst of Technology, IL B
International Business Coll, Fort Wayne, IN A,B
Kettering U, MI B
Miami U, OH B
Missouri Tech, MO B
North Dakota State U, ND B
Saint Louis U, MO B
Tri-State U, IN B
U of Evansville, IN B
U of Illinois at Chicago, IL B
The U of Iowa, IA B
U of Missouri–Rolla, MO B
U of Wisconsin–Stout, WI B
Western Michigan U, MI B

ENGINEERING MECHANICS

Dordt Coll, IA B
Michigan State U, MI B
Michigan Technological U, MI B
Oral Roberts U, OK B
U of Cincinnati, OH B
U of Illinois at Urbana–Champaign, IL B
U of Wisconsin–Madison, WI B

ENGINEERING PHYSICS

Augustana Coll, IL B
Augustana Coll, SD B
Aurora U, IL B
Bemidji State U, MN B
Bradley U, IL B
Case Western Reserve U, OH B
Hope Coll, MI B
John Carroll U, OH B
Loras Coll, IA B
Miami U, OH B
Michigan Technological U, MI B
Morningside Coll, IA B
North Dakota State U, ND B
Northeastern State U, OK B
Oakland U, MI B
The Ohio State U, OH B
Oklahoma Christian U, OK B
St. Ambrose U, IA B
Saint Mary's U of Minnesota, MN B
South Dakota State U, SD B
Southeast Missouri State U, MO B
Southwestern Oklahoma State U, OK B
Southwest Missouri State U, MO B
Taylor U, IN B
U of Illinois at Chicago, IL B
U of Illinois at Urbana–Champaign, IL B
U of Kansas, KS B
U of Michigan, MI B
U of Northern Iowa, IA B
U of Oklahoma, OK B
U of Tulsa, OK B
U of Wisconsin–Madison, WI B
Washington U in St. Louis, MO B
Wilberforce U, OH B
Wright State U, OH B

ENGINEERING RELATED

Eastern Illinois U, IL B
Iowa State U of Science and Technology, IA B
Northwestern U, IL B
Ohio U, OH B
Ohio Wesleyan U, OH B
Park U, MO B
Principia Coll, IL B
U of Nebraska–Lincoln, NE B
Western Michigan U, MI B

Engineering Related (continued)

Wheaton Coll, IL	B

ENGINEERING-RELATED TECHNOLOGY

Dordt Coll, IA	B
Missouri Tech, MO	A,B
Quincy U, IL	B
Southern Illinois U Carbondale, IL	B
Tri-State U, IN	A
The U of Akron, OH	B
Youngstown State U, OH	B

ENGINEERING SCIENCE

Baldwin-Wallace Coll, OH	B
Benedictine U, IL	B
Case Western Reserve U, OH	B
Franciscan U of Steubenville, OH	B
Iowa State U of Science and Technology, IA	B
Manchester Coll, IN	B
Northwestern U, IL	B
Ohio Wesleyan U, OH	B
U of Cincinnati, OH	A,B
U of Michigan, MI	B
U of Michigan–Flint, MI	B
Washington U in St. Louis, MO	B

ENGINEERING TECHNOLOGIES RELATED

Kent State U, OH	A
Ohio U, OH	B
Rogers State U, OK	A,B
Western Michigan U, MI	B

ENGINEERING TECHNOLOGY

Andrews U, MI	A,B
Kent State U, Ashtabula Campus, OH	A
Kent State U, Tuscarawas Campus, OH	A
Lawrence Technological U, MI	B
Miami U, OH	B
Miami U–Hamilton Campus, OH	A,B
Miami U–Middletown Campus, OH	A,B
Morrison Inst of Technology, IL	A
Northern Illinois U, IL	B
Oklahoma State U, OK	B
Pittsburg State U, KS	B
Purdue U Calumet, IN	B
Purdue U North Central, IN	A
St. Cloud State U, MN	B
Southern Illinois U Carbondale, IL	B
Southwestern Oklahoma State U, OK	B
U of Wisconsin–River Falls, WI	B
William Penn U, IA	B
Youngstown State U, OH	A,B

ENGLISH

Adrian Coll, MI	A,B
Albion Coll, MI	B
Alma Coll, MI	B
Alverno Coll, WI	B
American Christian Coll and Seminary, OK	B
Anderson U, IN	B
Andrews U, MI	B
Antioch Coll, OH	B
Aquinas Coll, MI	B
Ashland U, OH	B
Augsburg Coll, MN	B
Augustana Coll, IL	B
Augustana Coll, SD	B
Aurora U, IL	B
Avila U, MO	B
Baker U, KS	B
Baldwin-Wallace Coll, OH	B
Ball State U, IN	B
Bellevue U, NE	B
Beloit Coll, WI	B
Bemidji State U, MN	B
Benedictine Coll, KS	B
Benedictine U, IL	B
Bethany Coll, KS	B
Bethel Coll, IN	B
Bethel Coll, KS	B
Bethel Coll, MN	B
Blackburn Coll, IL	B
Black Hills State U, SD	B
Bluffton Coll, OH	B
Bowling Green State U, OH	B
Bradley U, IL	B
Briar Cliff U, IA	B
Buena Vista U, IA	B
Butler U, IN	B
Calumet Coll of Saint Joseph, IN	A,B
Calvin Coll, MI	B
Cameron U, OK	B
Capital U, OH	B
Cardinal Stritch U, WI	B
Carleton Coll, MN	B
Carroll Coll, WI	B
Carthage Coll, WI	B
Case Western Reserve U, OH	B
Cedarville U, OH	B
Central Christian Coll of Kansas, KS	A
Central Coll, IA	B
Central Methodist Coll, MO	A,B
Central Michigan U, MI	B
Central Missouri State U, MO	B
Chadron State Coll, NE	B
Chicago State U, IL	B
Clarke Coll, IA	B
Cleveland State U, OH	B
Coe Coll, IA	B
Coll of Mount St. Joseph, OH	B
Coll of Saint Benedict, MN	B
Coll of St. Catherine, MN	B
Coll of Saint Mary, NE	B
The Coll of St. Scholastica, MN	B
Coll of the Ozarks, MO	B
The Coll of Wooster, OH	B
Columbia Coll, MO	B
Concordia Coll, MN	B
Concordia U, IL	B
Concordia U, MI	B
Concordia U, MN	B
Concordia U, NE	B
Concordia U Wisconsin, WI	B
Cornell Coll, IA	B
Cornerstone U, MI	B
Creighton U, NE	B
Crown Coll, MN	B
Culver-Stockton Coll, MO	B
Dakota State U, SD	B
Dakota Wesleyan U, SD	B
Dana Coll, NE	B
Defiance Coll, OH	B
Denison U, OH	B
DePaul U, IL	B
DePauw U, IN	B
Dickinson State U, ND	B
Doane Coll, NE	B
Dominican U, IL	B
Donnelly Coll, KS	A
Dordt Coll, IA	B
Drake U, IA	B
Drury U, MO	B
Earlham Coll, IN	B
East Central U, OK	B
Eastern Illinois U, IL	B
Eastern Michigan U, MI	B
East-West U, IL	B
Edgewood Coll, WI	B
Elmhurst Coll, IL	B
Emporia State U, KS	B
Eureka Coll, IL	B
Evangel U, MO	B
Fontbonne U, MO	B
Fort Hays State U, KS	B
The Franciscan U, IA	B
Franciscan U of Steubenville, OH	B
Franklin Coll, IN	B
Goshen Coll, IN	B
Governors State U, IL	B
Grace Coll, IN	B
Graceland U, IA	B
Grand Valley State U, MI	B
Grand View Coll, IA	B
Greenville Coll, IL	B
Grinnell Coll, IA	B
Gustavus Adolphus Coll, MN	B
Hamline U, MN	B
Hannibal-LaGrange Coll, MO	A,B
Hanover Coll, IN	B
Hastings Coll, NE	B
Heidelberg Coll, OH	B
Hillsdale Coll, MI	B
Hillsdale Free Will Baptist Coll, OK	A
Hiram Coll, OH	B
Hope Coll, MI	B
Huntington Coll, IN	B
Illinois Coll, IL	B
Illinois State U, IL	B
Illinois Wesleyan U, IL	B
Indiana State U, IN	B
Indiana U Bloomington, IN	B
Indiana U East, IN	B
Indiana U Kokomo, IN	B
Indiana U Northwest, IN	B
Indiana U–Purdue U Fort Wayne, IN	A,B
Indiana U–Purdue U Indianapolis, IN	B
Indiana U South Bend, IN	B
Indiana U Southeast, IN	B
Indiana Wesleyan U, IN	A,B
Iowa State U of Science and Technology, IA	B
Iowa Wesleyan Coll, IA	B
Jamestown Coll, ND	B
John Carroll U, OH	B
Judson Coll, IL	B
Kalamazoo Coll, MI	B
Kansas State U, KS	B
Kent State U, OH	B
Kenyon Coll, OH	B
Knox Coll, IL	B
Lake Erie Coll, OH	B
Lake Forest Coll, IL	B
Lakeland Coll, WI	B
Langston U, OK	B
Lawrence U, WI	B
Lewis U, IL	B
Lincoln Coll, Lincoln, IL	A
Lindenwood U, MO	B
Loras Coll, IA	B
Lourdes Coll, OH	A,B
Loyola U Chicago, IL	B
Luther Coll, IA	B
Macalester Coll, MN	B
MacMurray Coll, IL	B
Madonna U, MI	A,B
Maharishi U of Management, IA	A,B
Malone Coll, OH	B
Manchester Coll, IN	A,B
Marian Coll, IN	B
Marian Coll of Fond du Lac, WI	B
Marietta Coll, OH	B
Marquette U, WI	B
Martin U, IN	B
Marygrove Coll, MI	B
Maryville U of Saint Louis, MO	B
Mayville State U, ND	B
McKendree Coll, IL	B
McPherson Coll, KS	B
Metropolitan State U, MN	B
Miami U, OH	B
Miami U–Middletown Campus, OH	A
Michigan State U, MI	B
Michigan Technological U, MI	B
MidAmerica Nazarene U, KS	B
Midland Lutheran Coll, NE	B
Millikin U, IL	B
Minnesota State U, Mankato, MN	B
Minnesota State U, Moorhead, MN	B
Minot State U, ND	B
Missouri Southern State Coll, MO	B
Missouri Valley Coll, MO	B
Missouri Western State Coll, MO	B
Monmouth Coll, IL	B
Morningside Coll, IA	B
Mount Marty Coll, SD	B
Mount Mary Coll, WI	B
Mount Mercy Coll, IA	B
Mount Union Coll, OH	B
Mount Vernon Nazarene U, OH	B
Muskingum Coll, OH	B
National-Louis U, IL	B
Nebraska Wesleyan U, NE	B
Newman U, KS	B
North Central Coll, IL	B
North Dakota State U, ND	B
Northeastern Illinois U, IL	B
Northeastern State U, OK	B
Northern Illinois U, IL	B
Northern Michigan U, MI	B
Northern State U, SD	B
Northland Coll, WI	B
North Park U, IL	B
Northwestern Coll, IA	B
Northwestern Coll, MN	B
Northwestern Oklahoma State U, OK	B
Northwestern U, IL	B
Northwest Missouri State U, MO	B
Notre Dame Coll, OH	B

Oakland City U, IN	B
Oakland U, MI	B
Oberlin Coll, OH	B
Ohio Dominican U, OH	B
Ohio Northern U, OH	B
The Ohio State U, OH	B
The Ohio State U at Lima, OH	B
Ohio U, OH	B
Ohio Wesleyan U, OH	B
Oklahoma Baptist U, OK	B
Oklahoma Christian U, OK	B
Oklahoma City U, OK	B
Oklahoma Panhandle State U, OK	B
Oklahoma State U, OK	B
Oklahoma Wesleyan U, OK	B
Olivet Coll, MI	B
Olivet Nazarene U, IL	B
Ottawa U, KS	B
Otterbein Coll, OH	B
Park U, MO	B
Peru State Coll, NE	B
Pillsbury Baptist Bible Coll, MN	B
Pittsburg State U, KS	B
Pontifical Coll Josephinum, OH	B
Presentation Coll, SD	A
Principia Coll, IL	B
Purdue U, IN	B
Purdue U Calumet, IN	B
Purdue U North Central, IN	B
Quincy U, IL	B
Ripon Coll, WI	B
Rochester Coll, MI	B
Rockford Coll, IL	B
Rockhurst U, MO	B
Roosevelt U, IL	B
Saginaw Valley State U, MI	B
St. Ambrose U, IA	B
St. Cloud State U, MN	B
Saint John's U, MN	B
Saint Joseph's Coll, IN	B
Saint Louis U, MO	B
Saint Mary-of-the-Woods Coll, IN	B
Saint Mary's Coll, IN	B
Saint Mary's Coll of Madonna U, MI	B
Saint Mary's U of Minnesota, MN	B
Saint Mary U, KS	B
St. Norbert Coll, WI	B
St. Olaf Coll, MN	B
Saint Xavier U, IL	B
Shawnee State U, OH	B
Siena Heights U, MI	A,B
Silver Lake Coll, WI	B
Simpson Coll, IA	B
South Dakota State U, SD	B
Southeastern Oklahoma State U, OK	B
Southeast Missouri State U, MO	B
Southern Illinois U Carbondale, IL	B
Southern Illinois U Edwardsville, IL	B
Southern Nazarene U, OK	B
Southwest Baptist U, MO	B
Southwestern Coll, KS	B
Southwestern Oklahoma State U, OK	B
Southwest Minnesota State U, MN	B
Southwest Missouri State U, MO	B
Spring Arbor U, MI	B
Stephens Coll, MO	B
Sterling Coll, KS	B
Tabor Coll, KS	B
Taylor U, IN	B
Taylor U, Fort Wayne Campus, IN	B
Trinity Christian Coll, IL	B
Trinity International U, IL	B
Truman State U, MO	B
Union Coll, NE	B
The U of Akron, OH	B
U of Central Oklahoma, OK	B
U of Chicago, IL	B
U of Cincinnati, OH	B
U of Dayton, OH	B
U of Dubuque, IA	A,B
U of Evansville, IN	B
The U of Findlay, OH	B
U of Illinois at Chicago, IL	B
U of Illinois at Springfield, IL	B
U of Illinois at Urbana–Champaign, IL	B
U of Indianapolis, IN	B
The U of Iowa, IA	B
U of Kansas, KS	B
U of Mary, ND	B
U of Michigan, MI	B
U of Michigan–Dearborn, MI	B
U of Michigan–Flint, MI	B
U of Minnesota, Duluth, MN	B
U of Minnesota, Morris, MN	B
U of Minnesota, Twin Cities Campus, MN	B
U of Missouri–Columbia, MO	B
U of Missouri–Kansas City, MO	B
U of Missouri–Rolla, MO	B
U of Missouri–St. Louis, MO	B
U of Nebraska at Kearney, NE	B
U of Nebraska at Omaha, NE	B
U of Nebraska–Lincoln, NE	B
U of North Dakota, ND	B
U of Northern Iowa, IA	B
U of Notre Dame, IN	B
U of Oklahoma, OK	B
U of Rio Grande, OH	A,B
U of St. Francis, IL	B
U of Saint Francis, IN	B
U of St. Thomas, MN	B
U of Science and Arts of Oklahoma, OK	B
U of Sioux Falls, SD	B
The U of South Dakota, SD	B
U of Southern Indiana, IN	B
U of Toledo, OH	B
U of Tulsa, OK	B
U of Wisconsin–Eau Claire, WI	B
U of Wisconsin–Green Bay, WI	A,B
U of Wisconsin–La Crosse, WI	B
U of Wisconsin–Madison, WI	B
U of Wisconsin–Milwaukee, WI	B
U of Wisconsin–Oshkosh, WI	B
U of Wisconsin–Parkside, WI	B
U of Wisconsin–Platteville, WI	B
U of Wisconsin–River Falls, WI	B
U of Wisconsin–Stevens Point, WI	B
U of Wisconsin–Superior, WI	B
U of Wisconsin–Whitewater, WI	B
Upper Iowa U, IA	B
Urbana U, OH	B
Ursuline Coll, OH	B
Valley City State U, ND	B
Valparaiso U, IN	B
Viterbo U, WI	B
Wabash Coll, IN	B
Waldorf Coll, IA	A,B
Walsh U, OH	B
Wartburg Coll, IA	B
Washington U in St. Louis, MO	B
Wayne State Coll, NE	B
Wayne State U, MI	B
Webster U, MO	B
Western Illinois U, IL	B
Western Michigan U, MI	B
Westminster Coll, MO	B
Wheaton Coll, IL	B
Wichita State U, KS	B
William Jewell Coll, MO	B
William Woods U, MO	B
Wilmington Coll, OH	B
Winona State U, MN	B
Wisconsin Lutheran Coll, WI	B
Wittenberg U, OH	B
Wright State U, OH	B
Xavier U, OH	A,B
York Coll, NE	B
Youngstown State U, OH	B

ENGLISH COMPOSITION

Aurora U, IL	B
Central Christian Coll of Kansas, KS	A
DePauw U, IN	B
Eastern Michigan U, MI	B
Graceland U, IA	B
Luther Coll, IA	B
Metropolitan State U, MN	B
Mount Union Coll, OH	B
Oklahoma Baptist U, OK	B
Rochester Coll, MI	B
U of Illinois at Urbana–Champaign, IL	B
Wartburg Coll, IA	B
William Woods U, MO	B

ENGLISH EDUCATION

Alverno Coll, WI	B
Anderson U, IN	B
Bethany Coll, KS	B
Bethel Coll, IN	B
Bowling Green State U, OH	B
Cedarville U, OH	B
Central Michigan U, MI	B
Central Missouri State U, MO	B
Chadron State Coll, NE	B
Coll of St. Catherine, MN	B
Coll of the Ozarks, MO	B
Concordia Coll, MN	B
Concordia U, IL	B
Concordia U, NE	B
Crown Coll, MN	B
Culver-Stockton Coll, MO	B
Dakota Wesleyan U, SD	B
Dana Coll, NE	B
Eastern Michigan U, MI	B
Elmhurst Coll, IL	B
Faith Baptist Bible Coll and Theological Seminary, IA	B
Franklin Coll, IN	B
Grace Coll, IN	B
Greenville Coll, IL	B
Hastings Coll, NE	B
Indiana U Bloomington, IN	B
Indiana U Northwest, IN	B
Indiana U–Purdue U Indianapolis, IN	B
Indiana U South Bend, IN	B
Indiana U Southeast, IN	B
Indiana Wesleyan U, IN	B
Luther Coll, IA	B
Malone Coll, OH	B
Mayville State U, ND	B
McKendree Coll, IL	B
Miami U, OH	B
MidAmerica Nazarene U, KS	B
Minnesota State U, Moorhead, MN	B
Minot State U, ND	B
Missouri Western State Coll, MO	B
Mount Marty Coll, SD	B
Mount Vernon Nazarene U, OH	B
North Dakota State U, ND	B
Northwestern Coll, MN	B
Oakland City U, IN	B
Oklahoma Baptist U, OK	B
Oklahoma Christian U, OK	B
Oral Roberts U, OK	B
St. Ambrose U, IA	B
Saint Mary's U of Minnesota, MN	B
Saint Xavier U, IL	B
Southeastern Oklahoma State U, OK	B
Southern Nazarene U, OK	B
Southwest Baptist U, MO	B
Southwestern Coll, KS	B
Southwestern Oklahoma State U, OK	B
Southwest Minnesota State U, MN	B
Southwest Missouri State U, MO	B
Trinity Christian Coll, IL	B
Tri-State U, IN	B
Union Coll, NE	B
U of Central Oklahoma, OK	B
U of Illinois at Chicago, IL	B
U of Illinois at Urbana–Champaign, IL	B
U of Indianapolis, IN	B
U of Mary, ND	B
U of Minnesota, Twin Cities Campus, MN	B
U of Nebraska–Lincoln, NE	B
U of Northern Iowa, IA	B
U of Oklahoma, OK	B
U of Rio Grande, OH	B
U of Toledo, OH	B
U of Wisconsin–River Falls, WI	B
U of Wisconsin–Superior, WI	B
Ursuline Coll, OH	B
Valley City State U, ND	B
Viterbo U, WI	B
Wayne State U, MI	B
William Penn U, IA	B
William Woods U, MO	B
Youngstown State U, OH	B

ENGLISH RELATED

Nebraska Wesleyan U, NE	B
Saint Mary-of-the-Woods Coll, IN	B

English Related (continued)

Washington U in St. Louis, MO B

ENTERPRISE MANAGEMENT

Baker Coll of Flint, MI A
Iowa State U of Science and Technology, IA B
Northwood U, MI A,B
Tri-State U, IN B
Union Coll, NE B
The U of Akron, OH A
U of Nebraska at Omaha, NE B
U of Phoenix–Metro Detroit Campus, MI B
U of Phoenix–Tulsa Campus, OK B
U of St. Thomas, MN B

ENTOMOLOGY

Iowa State U of Science and Technology, IA B
Michigan State U, MI B
The Ohio State U, OH B
Oklahoma State U, OK B
Purdue U, IN B
U of Illinois at Urbana–Champaign, IL B
U of Wisconsin–Madison, WI B

ENTREPRENEURSHIP

Baker Coll of Flint, MI A
Baker Coll of Jackson, MI A
Black Hills State U, SD B
Central Michigan U, MI B
Kendall Coll, IL B
Ohio U, OH B
Trinity Christian Coll, IL B
The U of Findlay, OH A,B
The U of Iowa, IA B
Wichita State U, KS B
Xavier U, OH B

ENVIRONMENTAL BIOLOGY

Antioch Coll, OH B
Beloit Coll, WI B
Bethel Coll, IN B
Cedarville U, OH B
Central Methodist Coll, MO B
Greenville Coll, IL B
Heidelberg Coll, OH B
Iowa Wesleyan Coll, IA B
Luther Coll, IA B
Maharishi U of Management, IA B
Minnesota State U, Mankato, MN B
Mount Union Coll, OH B
Northland Coll, WI B
Ohio U, OH B
Otterbein Coll, OH B
Pittsburg State U, KS B
St. Cloud State U, MN B
Simpson Coll, IA B
Tabor Coll, KS B
Taylor U, IN B
U of Dayton, OH B
U of Dubuque, IA B
U of Nebraska at Omaha, NE B
Ursuline Coll, OH B
William Penn U, IA B
Winona State U, MN B
Wittenberg U, OH B

ENVIRONMENTAL EDUCATION

Concordia U, MN B
Northland Coll, WI B
The Ohio State U, OH B

ENVIRONMENTAL ENGINEERING

Bradley U, IL B
Marquette U, WI B
Michigan Technological U, MI B
Northwestern U, IL B
Ohio U, OH A
Ohio U–Chillicothe, OH A
South Dakota School of Mines and Technology, SD B
South Dakota State U, SD B
The U of Iowa, IA B
U of Michigan, MI B
U of North Dakota, ND B
U of Notre Dame, IN B
U of Oklahoma, OK B
U of Wisconsin–Madison, WI B
Western Michigan U, MI B
Youngstown State U, OH B

ENVIRONMENTAL HEALTH

Bowling Green State U, OH B
East Central U, OK B
Ferris State U, MI B
Illinois State U, IL B
Indiana State U, IN B
Iowa Wesleyan Coll, IA B
Missouri Southern State Coll, MO A,B
Oakland U, MI B
Ohio U, OH B
The U of Akron, OH A
U of Michigan–Flint, MI B
U of Wisconsin–Eau Claire, WI B
Wright State U, OH B

ENVIRONMENTAL SCIENCE

Adrian Coll, MI B
Albion Coll, MI B
Alverno Coll, WI B
Antioch Coll, OH B
Aquinas Coll, MI B
Ashland U, OH B
Augustana Coll, IL B
Aurora U, IL B
Baldwin-Wallace Coll, OH B
Ball State U, IN B
Bellevue U, NE B
Beloit Coll, WI B
Bemidji State U, MN B
Benedictine U, IL B
Bethel Coll, MN B
Black Hills State U, SD B
Briar Cliff U, IA B
Calvin Coll, MI B
Cameron U, OK B
Capital U, OH B
Carroll Coll, WI B
Carthage Coll, WI B
Case Western Reserve U, OH B
Central Coll, IA B
Central Methodist Coll, MO B
Central Michigan U, MI B
Cleveland State U, OH B
Coe Coll, IA B
Concordia Coll, MN B
Concordia U, IL B
Concordia U, MN B
Cornell Coll, IA B
Creighton U, NE B
Dana Coll, NE B
Defiance Coll, OH A,B
Denison U, OH B
DePaul U, IL B
Dickinson State U, ND A,B
Doane Coll, NE B
Dominican U, IL B
Dordt Coll, IA B
Drake U, IA B
Drury U, MO B
Earlham Coll, IN B
East Central U, OK B
Elmhurst Coll, IL B
Goshen Coll, IN B
Grinnell Coll, IA B
Gustavus Adolphus Coll, MN B
Hamline U, MN B
Hiram Coll, OH B
Hope Coll, MI B
Illinois Coll, IL B
Indiana U Bloomington, IN B
Iowa State U of Science and Technology, IA B
John Carroll U, OH B
Kent State U, Ashtabula Campus, OH A
Kent State U, Salem Campus, OH A
Kent State U, Tuscarawas Campus, OH A
Kenyon Coll, OH B
Kettering U, MI B
Knox Coll, IL B
Lake Erie Coll, OH B
Lake Forest Coll, IL B
Lawrence U, WI B
Lewis U, IL B
Loyola U Chicago, IL B
Macalester Coll, MN B
Maharishi U of Management, IA A,B
Manchester Coll, IN B
Marian Coll of Fond du Lac, WI B
Marietta Coll, OH B
Marygrove Coll, MI B
Maryville U of Saint Louis, MO B
McPherson Coll, KS B
Midland Lutheran Coll, NE B
Minnesota State U, Mankato, MN B
Monmouth Coll, IL B
Mount Marty Coll, SD B
Muskingum Coll, OH B
Northeastern Illinois U, IL B
Northern Michigan U, MI B
Northern State U, SD B
Northland Coll, WI B
Northwestern Coll, IA B
Northwestern U, IL B
Notre Dame Coll, OH B
Oberlin Coll, OH B
Ohio Northern U, OH B
The Ohio State U, OH B
Ohio U–Chillicothe, OH A
Ohio Wesleyan U, OH B
Oklahoma State U, OK B
Olivet Coll, MI B
Olivet Nazarene U, IL B
Pittsburg State U, KS B
Principia Coll, IL B
Quincy U, IL B
Ripon Coll, WI B
Roosevelt U, IL B
Saint Joseph's Coll, IN B
Saint Louis U, MO B
Saint Mary's Coll of Madonna U, MI B
Sitting Bull Coll, ND A
Southeastern Oklahoma State U, OK B
Southeast Missouri State U, MO A,B
Southern Nazarene U, OK B
Southwest Minnesota State U, MN B
Stephens Coll, MO B
Taylor U, IN B
Tri-State U, IN B
U of Chicago, IL B
U of Cincinnati, OH A
U of Dayton, OH B
U of Dubuque, IA A,B
U of Evansville, IN B
The U of Findlay, OH A,B
U of Illinois at Urbana–Champaign, IL B
U of Indianapolis, IN B
The U of Iowa, IA B
U of Michigan, MI B
U of Michigan–Dearborn, MI B
U of Michigan–Flint, MI B
U of Minnesota, Crookston, MN B
U of Minnesota, Duluth, MN B
U of Minnesota, Twin Cities Campus, MN B
U of Nebraska–Lincoln, NE B
U of Northern Iowa, IA B
U of Notre Dame, IN B
U of Oklahoma, OK B
U of St. Francis, IL B
U of Saint Francis, IN A,B
U of St. Thomas, MN B
U of Toledo, OH A,B
U of Tulsa, OK B
U of Wisconsin–Green Bay, WI A,B
U of Wisconsin–River Falls, WI B
Valparaiso U, IN B
Washington U in St. Louis, MO B
Webster U, MO B
Western Michigan U, MI B
Westminster Coll, MO B
Wheaton Coll, IL B
Wittenberg U, OH B
Xavier U, OH B
Youngstown State U, OH B

ENVIRONMENTAL TECHNOLOGY

Baker Coll of Flint, MI A
Baker Coll of Owosso, MI A
Baker Coll of Port Huron, MI A
Kansas State U, KS A
Shawnee State U, OH B
U of Cincinnati, OH A
U of North Dakota, ND B
U of Toledo, OH A

EQUESTRIAN STUDIES

Lake Erie Coll, OH B
National American U, SD B
North Dakota State U, ND B
Ohio U, OH A

Otterbein Coll, OH	B
Rogers State U, OK	A
Saint Mary-of-the-Woods Coll, IN	A,B
Stephens Coll, MO	B
Truman State U, MO	B
The U of Findlay, OH	A,B
U of Minnesota, Crookston, MN	A,B
U of Wisconsin–River Falls, WI	B
William Woods U, MO	B

ETHNIC/CULTURAL STUDIES RELATED

Metropolitan State U, MN	B
St. Olaf Coll, MN	B
Washington U in St. Louis, MO	B

EUROPEAN HISTORY

Calvin Coll, MI	B

EUROPEAN STUDIES

Antioch Coll, OH	B
Beloit Coll, WI	B
Case Western Reserve U, OH	B
Central Michigan U, MI	B
The Coll of Wooster, OH	B
Grace U, NE	B
Hamline U, MN	B
Hillsdale Coll, MI	B
Illinois Wesleyan U, IL	B
Lake Forest Coll, IL	B
Ohio U, OH	B
U of Kansas, KS	B
U of Michigan, MI	B
U of Minnesota, Morris, MN	B
U of Minnesota, Twin Cities Campus, MN	B
U of Northern Iowa, IA	B
U of Toledo, OH	B
Valparaiso U, IN	B
Washington U in St. Louis, MO	B
Western Michigan U, MI	B

EVOLUTIONARY BIOLOGY

Case Western Reserve U, OH	B

EXECUTIVE ASSISTANT

Baker Coll of Flint, MI	A
Eastern Michigan U, MI	B
Rockford Business Coll, IL	A
The U of Akron, OH	A
Youngstown State U, OH	A,B

EXERCISE SCIENCES

Adrian Coll, MI	B
Alma Coll, MI	B
Andrews U, MI	B
Augustana Coll, SD	B
Avila U, MO	B
Ball State U, IN	B
Bethel Coll, IN	B
Bluffton Coll, OH	B
Bowling Green State U, OH	B
Calvin Coll, MI	B
Carroll Coll, WI	B
Central Coll, IA	B
The Coll of St. Scholastica, MN	B
Concordia Coll, MN	B
Concordia U, IL	B
Concordia U, NE	B
Cornell Coll, IA	B
Creighton U, NE	B
Dakota State U, SD	B
Defiance Coll, OH	B
Dordt Coll, IA	B
Drury U, MO	B
Elmhurst Coll, IL	B
Eureka Coll, IL	B
Hamline U, MN	B
Hope Coll, MI	B
Huntington Coll, IN	B
Indiana Wesleyan U, IN	B
Iowa Wesleyan Coll, IA	B
Kansas State U, KS	B
Kent State U, OH	B
Lakeland Coll, WI	B
Loras Coll, IA	B
Maharishi U of Management, IA	A
Malone Coll, OH	B
Manchester Coll, IN	A
Marquette U, WI	B
Miami U, OH	B
MidAmerica Nazarene U, KS	B
Minnesota School of Business-Richfield, MN	A
Missouri Southern State Coll, MO	B
Missouri Western State Coll, MO	B
Mount Union Coll, OH	B
Mount Vernon Nazarene U, OH	B
Nebraska Wesleyan U, NE	B
North Central Coll, IL	B
Northern Michigan U, MI	B
North Park U, IL	B
Northwestern Coll, IA	B
Oakland U, MI	B
The Ohio State U, OH	B
Ohio U, OH	B
Oklahoma Baptist U, OK	B
Oklahoma Wesleyan U, OK	B
Olivet Nazarene U, IL	B
Oral Roberts U, OK	B
St. Cloud State U, MN	B
Saint Louis U, MO	B
Southern Nazarene U, OK	B
Truman State U, MO	B
U of Dayton, OH	B
U of Evansville, IN	B
The U of Iowa, IA	B
U of Mary, ND	B
U of Michigan, MI	B
U of Minnesota, Duluth, MN	B
U of Nebraska–Lincoln, NE	B
U of Sioux Falls, SD	B
U of Southern Indiana, IN	B
U of Toledo, OH	B
U of Tulsa, OK	B
U of Wisconsin–Eau Claire, WI	B
U of Wisconsin–La Crosse, WI	B
Upper Iowa U, IA	B
Valparaiso U, IN	B
Wayne State Coll, NE	B
Western Michigan U, MI	B
Wheaton Coll, IL	B
Winona State U, MN	B
Youngstown State U, OH	B

EXPERIMENTAL PSYCHOLOGY

Millikin U, IL	B
U of Toledo, OH	B
U of Wisconsin–Madison, WI	B

FAMILY/COMMUNITY STUDIES

Andrews U, MI	B
Baker Coll of Flint, MI	A
Bowling Green State U, OH	B
Central Christian Coll of Kansas, KS	A
Eastern Illinois U, IL	B
Goshen Coll, IN	B
Iowa State U of Science and Technology, IA	B
Oklahoma Christian U, OK	B
Oklahoma State U, OK	B
Olivet Nazarene U, IL	B
Southern Nazarene U, OK	A
U of Minnesota, Twin Cities Campus, MN	B
U of Northern Iowa, IA	B
Ursuline Coll, OH	B
Youngstown State U, OH	B

FAMILY/CONSUMER RESOURCE MANAGEMENT RELATED

U of Nebraska–Lincoln, NE	B

FAMILY/CONSUMER STUDIES

Andrews U, MI	B
Ashland U, OH	B
Baldwin-Wallace Coll, OH	B
Ball State U, IN	B
Chadron State Coll, NE	B
Concordia Coll, MN	B
Illinois State U, IL	B
Indiana U Bloomington, IN	B
Iowa State U of Science and Technology, IA	B
Miami U, OH	B
Minnesota State U, Mankato, MN	B
North Dakota State U, ND	B
Northern Michigan U, MI	B
Northwest Missouri State U, MO	B
Oklahoma State U, OK	B
Southeast Missouri State U, MO	B
Southern Illinois U Carbondale, IL	B
The U of Akron, OH	B
U of Missouri–Columbia, MO	B
U of Nebraska at Kearney, NE	B
U of Northern Iowa, IA	B
U of Wisconsin–Madison, WI	B
U of Wisconsin–Stevens Point, WI	B
Wayne State Coll, NE	B

FAMILY RESOURCE MANAGEMENT STUDIES

Bradley U, IL	B
Central Michigan U, MI	B
Eastern Michigan U, MI	B
Iowa State U of Science and Technology, IA	B
Michigan State U, MI	B
The Ohio State U, OH	B
Ohio U, OH	B

FAMILY STUDIES

Anderson U, IN	B
Central Michigan U, MI	B
Michigan State U, MI	B
Southern Nazarene U, OK	A
Spring Arbor U, MI	B
The U of Akron, OH	B
Western Michigan U, MI	B

FARM/RANCH MANAGEMENT

Iowa State U of Science and Technology, IA	B
North Dakota State U, ND	B
Northwest Missouri State U, MO	B
Oklahoma Panhandle State U, OK	A
Rogers State U, OK	A
Sitting Bull Coll, ND	A
The U of Findlay, OH	B
U of Wisconsin–Madison, WI	B

FASHION DESIGN/ ILLUSTRATION

Bluffton Coll, OH	B
Bowling Green State U, OH	B
Columbia Coll Chicago, IL	B
Columbus Coll of Art and Design, OH	B
Dominican U, IL	B
The Illinois Inst of Art, IL	A,B
Indiana U Bloomington, IN	A,B
International Academy of Design & Technology, IL	A,B
Iowa State U of Science and Technology, IA	B
Kent State U, OH	B
Lindenwood U, MO	B
Minnesota State U, Mankato, MN	B
Mount Mary Coll, WI	B
North Dakota State U, ND	B
Northwest Missouri State U, MO	B
School of the Art Inst of Chicago, IL	B
Stephens Coll, MO	B
U of Cincinnati, OH	B
Ursuline Coll, OH	B
Washington U in St. Louis, MO	B

FASHION MERCHANDISING

Ashland U, OH	B
Ball State U, IN	B
Bluffton Coll, OH	B
Bowling Green State U, OH	B
Central Michigan U, MI	B
Central Missouri State U, MO	A
Coll of St. Catherine, MN	B
Dominican U, IL	B
East Central U, OK	B
Eastern Michigan U, MI	B
Fontbonne U, MO	B
The Illinois Inst of Art, IL	B
Indiana U Bloomington, IN	B
International Academy of Design & Technology, IL	A,B
Kent State U, OH	B
Lindenwood U, MO	B
Madonna U, MI	A,B
Marygrove Coll, MI	A,B

Fashion Merchandising (continued)

Mount Mary Coll, WI B
North Dakota State U, ND B
Northeastern State U, OK B
Northwest Missouri State U, MO B
Northwood U, MI A,B
Oklahoma State U, OK B
Olivet Nazarene U, IL B
Pittsburg State U, KS B
Rochester Comm and Tech Coll, MN A
South Dakota State U, SD B
Southeast Missouri State U, MO B
Stephens Coll, MO B
The U of Akron, OH A,B
U of Central Oklahoma, OK B
U of Nebraska at Omaha, NE B
U of Wisconsin–Madison, WI B
Ursuline Coll, OH B
Wayne State Coll, NE B
Youngstown State U, OH B

FILM STUDIES

Bowling Green State U, OH B
Calvin Coll, MI B
Columbia Coll Chicago, IL B
Denison U, OH B
Grand Valley State U, MI B
Indiana U South Bend, IN A
Northern Michigan U, MI B
Northwestern U, IL B
Olivet Nazarene U, IL B
St. Cloud State U, MN B
School of the Art Inst of Chicago, IL B
U of Chicago, IL B
The U of Iowa, IA B
U of Michigan, MI B
U of Minnesota, Twin Cities Campus, MN B
U of Nebraska–Lincoln, NE B
U of Toledo, OH B
U of Wisconsin–Milwaukee, WI B
Washington U in St. Louis, MO B
Wayne State U, MI B
Webster U, MO B
Wright State U, OH B

FILM/VIDEO AND PHOTOGRAPHIC ARTS RELATED

Coll for Creative Studies, MI B
Robert Morris Coll, IL A
Southern Illinois U Carbondale, IL B

FILM/VIDEO PRODUCTION

Antioch Coll, OH B
Columbia Coll Chicago, IL B
Grand Valley State U, MI B
The Illinois Inst of Art-Schaumburg, IL B
Iowa Wesleyan Coll, IA B
Maharishi U of Management, IA B
Minneapolis Coll of Art and Design, MN B
Northern Michigan U, MI B
Ohio U, OH B
Oklahoma City U, OK B
School of the Art Inst of Chicago, IL B
U of Illinois at Chicago, IL B
The U of Iowa, IA B
U of Oklahoma, OK B
The U of South Dakota, SD B
Waldorf Coll, IA A,B
Webster U, MO B

FINANCE

AIB Coll of Business, IA A
Anderson U, IN B
Ashland U, OH B
Augustana Coll, IL B
Aurora U, IL B
Avila U, MO B
Baldwin-Wallace Coll, OH B
Ball State U, IN B
Benedictine Coll, KS B
Benedictine U, IL B
Bethel Coll, MN B
Bowling Green State U, OH B
Bradley U, IL B
Buena Vista U, IA B
Butler U, IN B
Cameron U, OK B
Capital U, OH B
Carroll Coll, WI B
Cedarville U, OH B
Central Christian Coll of Kansas, KS A
Central Michigan U, MI B
Central Missouri State U, MO B
Chicago State U, IL B
Cleary U, MI B
Cleveland State U, OH B
Colorado Tech U Sioux Falls Campus, SD B
Columbia Coll, MO B
Concordia U, MN B
Creighton U, NE B
Culver-Stockton Coll, MO B
Dakota State U, SD B
Dakota Wesleyan U, SD B
Davenport U, Grand Rapids, MI B
Davenport U, Lansing, MI B
Defiance Coll, OH B
DePaul U, IL B
Dickinson State U, ND B
Drake U, IA B
East Central U, OK B
Eastern Illinois U, IL B
Eastern Michigan U, MI B
East-West U, IL B
Elmhurst Coll, IL B
Eureka Coll, IL B
Ferris State U, MI B
Fontbonne U, MO B
Fort Hays State U, KS B
Franklin Coll, IN B
Franklin U, OH B
Governors State U, IL B
Grand Valley State U, MI B
Hillsdale Coll, MI B
Illinois Coll, IL B
Illinois State U, IL B
Indiana Inst of Technology, IN B
Indiana State U, IN B
Indiana U Bloomington, IN B
Indiana U–Purdue U Fort Wayne, IN B
Indiana U South Bend, IN A
Indiana Wesleyan U, IN A,B
International Business Coll, Fort Wayne, IN A,B
Iowa State U of Science and Technology, IA B
John Carroll U, OH B
Kansas State U, KS B
Kent State U, OH B
Kent State U, Ashtabula Campus, OH A
Kettering U, MI B
Lake Forest Coll, IL B
Lakeland Coll, WI B
Lewis U, IL B
Lindenwood U, MO B
Loras Coll, IA B
Loyola U Chicago, IL B
Madonna U, MI B
Manchester Coll, IN B
Marian Coll, IN A,B
Marian Coll of Fond du Lac, WI B
Marquette U, WI B
McKendree Coll, IL B
McPherson Coll, KS B
Metropolitan State U, MN B
Miami U, OH B
Michigan State U, MI B
Michigan Technological U, MI B
Millikin U, IL B
Minnesota State U, Mankato, MN B
Minnesota State U, Moorhead, MN B
Minot State U, ND B
Missouri Southern State Coll, MO B
Missouri Western State Coll, MO B
North Central Coll, IL B
Northeastern Illinois U, IL B
Northeastern State U, OK B
Northern Illinois U, IL B
Northern Michigan U, MI B
Northern State U, SD B
North Park U, IL B
Northwestern Coll, MN B
Northwest Missouri State U, MO B
Northwood U, MI A,B
Notre Dame Coll, OH B
Oakland U, MI B
The Ohio State U, OH B
Ohio U, OH B
Oklahoma Baptist U, OK B
Oklahoma City U, OK B
Oklahoma State U, OK B
Olivet Coll, MI B
Olivet Nazarene U, IL B
Oral Roberts U, OK B
Otterbein Coll, OH B
Pittsburg State U, KS B
Quincy U, IL B
Rockford Coll, IL B
Rockhurst U, MO B
Roosevelt U, IL B
Saginaw Valley State U, MI B
St. Ambrose U, IA B
St. Cloud State U, MN B
Saint Joseph's Coll, IN B
Saint Louis U, MO B
Saint Mary's Coll, IN B
Si Tanka Huron U, SD B
Southeastern Oklahoma State U, OK B
Southeast Missouri State U, MO B
Southern Illinois U Carbondale, IL B
Southern Nazarene U, OK B
Southwestern Oklahoma State U, OK B
Southwest Missouri State U, MO B
Taylor U, IN B
Tiffin U, OH B
Truman State U, MO B
The U of Akron, OH B
U of Central Oklahoma, OK B
U of Cincinnati, OH A,B
U of Dayton, OH B
U of Evansville, IN B
U of Illinois at Chicago, IL B
U of Illinois at Urbana–Champaign, IL B
The U of Iowa, IA B
U of Michigan–Dearborn, MI B
U of Michigan–Flint, MI B
U of Minnesota, Duluth, MN B
U of Minnesota, Twin Cities Campus, MN B
U of Missouri–Columbia, MO B
U of Missouri–St. Louis, MO B
U of Nebraska at Omaha, NE B
U of Nebraska–Lincoln, NE B
U of North Dakota, ND B
U of Northern Iowa, IA B
U of Notre Dame, IN B
U of Oklahoma, OK B
U of St. Francis, IL B
U of Saint Francis, IN B
U of St. Thomas, MN B
The U of South Dakota, SD B
U of Southern Indiana, IN B
U of Toledo, OH B
U of Tulsa, OK B
U of Wisconsin–Eau Claire, WI B
U of Wisconsin–La Crosse, WI B
U of Wisconsin–Madison, WI B
U of Wisconsin–Milwaukee, WI B
U of Wisconsin–Oshkosh, WI B
U of Wisconsin–Parkside, WI B
U of Wisconsin–River Falls, WI B
U of Wisconsin–Whitewater, WI B
Valparaiso U, IN B
Waldorf Coll, IA A,B
Walsh Coll of Accountancy and Business Administration, MI B
Walsh U, OH A,B
Wartburg Coll, IA B
Washington U in St. Louis, MO B
Wayne State Coll, NE B
Wayne State U, MI B
Western Illinois U, IL B
Western Michigan U, MI B
Westminster Coll, MO B
Wichita State U, KS B
Wilberforce U, OH B
Winona State U, MN B
Wittenberg U, OH B
Wright State U, OH B
Xavier U, OH B
York Coll, NE B
Youngstown State U, OH A,B

FINANCIAL MANAGEMENT AND SERVICES RELATED

Park U, MO B
The U of Akron, OH B

FINANCIAL PLANNING

Bethany Coll, KS B
Central Michigan U, MI B
The Ohio State U at Lima, OH B
Trinity Christian Coll, IL B

FINE ARTS AND ART STUDIES RELATED

Ancilla Coll, IN A
Indiana State U, IN B
Loyola U Chicago, IL B
The U of Akron, OH B
U of Saint Francis, IN B

FINE/STUDIO ARTS

American Academy of Art, IL B
Anderson U, IN B
Aquinas Coll, MI B
Art Academy of Cincinnati, OH B
Ashland U, OH B
Augsburg Coll, MN B
Augustana Coll, IL B
Baker U, KS B
Baldwin-Wallace Coll, OH B
Ball State U, IN B
Beloit Coll, WI B
Bemidji State U, MN B
Benedictine U, IL B
Bethel Coll, MN B
Bradley U, IL B
Calvin Coll, MI B
Capital U, OH B
Cardinal Stritch U, WI B
Carleton Coll, MN B
Carroll Coll, WI B
Carthage Coll, WI B
Central Missouri State U, MO B
Chicago State U, IL B
Clarke Coll, IA B
Coe Coll, IA B
Coll for Creative Studies, MI B
Coll of Mount St. Joseph, OH B
Coll of Saint Benedict, MN B
Coll of St. Catherine, MN B
Coll of the Ozarks, MO B
The Coll of Wooster, OH B
Columbia Coll, MO B
Columbia Coll Chicago, IL B
Columbus Coll of Art and Design, OH B
Concordia Coll, MN B
Concordia U, NE B
Denison U, OH B
DePaul U, IL B
DePauw U, IN B
Dominican U, IL B
Drake U, IA B
Drury U, MO B
Ferris State U, MI B
Finlandia U, MI B
Fontbonne U, MO B
Governors State U, IL B
Graceland U, IA B
Grand Valley State U, MI B
Grand View Coll, IA B
Hamline U, MN B
Hiram Coll, OH B
Hope Coll, MI B
Illinois Wesleyan U, IL B
Indiana State U, IN B
Indiana U Bloomington, IN B
Indiana U–Purdue U Fort Wayne, IN B
Indiana U–Purdue U Indianapolis, IN B
Indiana U South Bend, IN B
Indiana U Southeast, IN B
Iowa Wesleyan Coll, IA B
Judson Coll, IL B
Kendall Coll of Art and Design of Ferris State U, MI B
Kent State U, OH B
Kenyon Coll, OH B
Lake Erie Coll, OH B
Lake Forest Coll, IL B
Lawrence U, WI B
Lewis U, IL B
Lincoln Coll, Lincoln, IL A
Lindenwood U, MO B
Loras Coll, IA B
Macalester Coll, MN B
MacMurray Coll, IL B
Manchester Coll, IN A,B
Marian Coll, IN B
Marietta Coll, OH B
Martin U, IN B
Marygrove Coll, MI B
Maryville U of Saint Louis, MO B
Miami U, OH B
Millikin U, IL B
Minneapolis Coll of Art and Design, MN B
Minnesota State U, Mankato, MN B
Minnesota State U, Moorhead, MN B
Morningside Coll, IA B
Northeastern State U, OK B
Northern Illinois U, IL B
Northern Michigan U, MI B
Northland Coll, WI B
North Park U, IL B
Northwestern Coll, MN B
Northwest Missouri State U, MO B
Notre Dame Coll, OH B
Oberlin Coll, OH B
Ohio Dominican U, OH B
The Ohio State U, OH B
Ohio U, OH B
Ohio Wesleyan U, OH B
Oklahoma Baptist U, OK B
Oklahoma City U, OK B
Oklahoma State U, OK B
Olivet Coll, MI B
Oral Roberts U, OK B
Park U, MO B
Pittsburg State U, KS B
Principia Coll, IL B
Quincy U, IL B
Rockford Coll, IL B
Saginaw Valley State U, MI B
St. Ambrose U, IA B
St. Cloud State U, MN B
Saint John's U, MN B
Saint Louis U, MO B
Saint Mary-of-the-Woods Coll, IN B
Saint Mary's U of Minnesota, MN B
School of the Art Inst of Chicago, IL B
Shawnee State U, OH B
Southern Illinois U Carbondale, IL B
Southern Illinois U Edwardsville, IL B
Southwest Minnesota State U, MN B
Truman State U, MO B
Union Coll, NE B
The U of Akron, OH B
U of Chicago, IL B
U of Dayton, OH B
U of Illinois at Chicago, IL B
U of Indianapolis, IN B
The U of Iowa, IA B
U of Kansas, KS B
U of Minnesota, Duluth, MN B
U of Minnesota, Morris, MN B
U of Missouri–Kansas City, MO B
U of Missouri–St. Louis, MO B
U of Nebraska at Omaha, NE B
U of Nebraska–Lincoln, NE B
U of Northern Iowa, IA B
U of Notre Dame, IN B
U of Oklahoma, OK B
The U of South Dakota, SD B
U of Toledo, OH B
U of Wisconsin–Milwaukee, WI B
U of Wisconsin–Oshkosh, WI B
U of Wisconsin–Stevens Point, WI B
U of Wisconsin–Superior, WI B
Valparaiso U, IN B
Washington U in St. Louis, MO B
Webster U, MO B
Western Illinois U, IL B
Wilberforce U, OH B
William Woods U, MO B
Winona State U, MN B
Wittenberg U, OH B
Xavier U, OH B
Youngstown State U, OH B

FIRE PROTECTION RELATED

The U of Akron, OH B

FIRE PROTECTION/ SAFETY TECHNOLOGY

Oklahoma State U, OK B
The U of Akron, OH A
U of Cincinnati, OH B
U of Nebraska–Lincoln, NE A
U of Toledo, OH A

FIRE SCIENCE

Madonna U, MI A,B
U of Cincinnati, OH A

FIRE SERVICES ADMINISTRATION

Southern Illinois U Carbondale, IL B

FISH/GAME MANAGEMENT

Iowa State U of Science and Technology, IA B
North Dakota State U, ND B
Northland Coll, WI B
Pittsburg State U, KS B
South Dakota State U, SD B
Southeastern Oklahoma State U, OK B
U of Minnesota, Duluth, MN B
U of Minnesota, Twin Cities Campus, MN B
U of Missouri–Columbia, MO B
The U of South Dakota, SD B
Winona State U, MN A

FISHING SCIENCES

The Ohio State U, OH B
U of Nebraska–Lincoln, NE B

FOLKLORE

Indiana U Bloomington, IN B
The Ohio State U, OH B

FOOD PRODUCTS RETAILING

Ball State U, IN A,B
Dominican U, IL B
Ferris State U, MI A
Iowa State U of Science and Technology, IA B
Lindenwood U, MO B
Madonna U, MI B
Northern Michigan U, MI A,B
Purdue U Calumet, IN A
U of Minnesota, Crookston, MN A
Wayne State Coll, NE B

FOOD SALES OPERATIONS

Northwest Missouri State U, MO B

FOOD SCIENCES

Dominican U, IL B
Kansas State U, KS B
Michigan State U, MI B
North Dakota State U, ND B
Northwest Missouri State U, MO B
The Ohio State U, OH B
Olivet Nazarene U, IL B
Purdue U, IN B
South Dakota State U, SD B
The U of Akron, OH B
U of Illinois at Urbana–Champaign, IL B
U of Missouri–Columbia, MO B
U of Nebraska–Lincoln, NE B
U of Wisconsin–Madison, WI B
U of Wisconsin–River Falls, WI B

FOOD SERVICES TECHNOLOGY

Iowa State U of Science and Technology, IA B
Madonna U, MI B
Purdue U Calumet, IN A

FOODS/NUTRITION STUDIES RELATED

U of Wisconsin–Stout, WI B

FOOD SYSTEMS ADMINISTRATION

Western Michigan U, MI B

FOREIGN LANGUAGES EDUCATION

Bowling Green State U, OH B
Central Methodist Coll, MO B
Dana Coll, NE B
Eastern Michigan U, MI B
Greenville Coll, IL B
Hastings Coll, NE B
Luther Coll, IA B
Southwestern Coll, KS B
Southwest Missouri State U, MO B
The U of Akron, OH B
U of Illinois at Chicago, IL B
U of Illinois at Urbana–Champaign, IL B
U of Minnesota, Twin Cities Campus, MN B
U of Nebraska–Lincoln, NE B
U of Northern Iowa, IA B
U of Oklahoma, OK B
Youngstown State U, OH B

FOREIGN LANGUAGES/ LITERATURES

Augustana Coll, SD B
Central Methodist Coll, MO B
Eastern Illinois U, IL B
Emporia State U, KS B
Graceland U, IA B
Hastings Coll, NE B
Indiana State U, IN B
Kansas State U, KS B
Knox Coll, IL B
Millikin U, IL B
Minnesota State U, Moorhead, MN B
Oakland U, MI B
Principia Coll, IL B
Purdue U, IN B
Southern Illinois U Edwardsville, IL B
Southwestern Coll, KS B
U of North Dakota, ND B
U of Northern Iowa, IA B
Wayne State U, MI B
Youngstown State U, OH B

FOREIGN LANGUAGES/ LITERATURES RELATED

Southern Illinois U Carbondale, IL B

FORENSIC TECHNOLOGY

Carroll Coll, WI B
Coll of the Ozarks, MO B
Columbia Coll, MO B
Indiana U Bloomington, IN B
U of Central Oklahoma, OK B

FOREST HARVESTING PRODUCTION TECHNOLOGY

Michigan Technological U, MI A

FOREST MANAGEMENT

U of Minnesota, Twin Cities Campus, MN B

FORESTRY

Coll of Saint Benedict, MN B
Iowa State U of Science and Technology, IA B
Michigan State U, MI B
Michigan Technological U, MI B
North Dakota State U, ND B
Northland Coll, WI B
Northwest Missouri State U, MO B
The Ohio State U, OH B
Oklahoma State U, OK B
Purdue U, IN B
Saint John's U, MN B
Southern Illinois U Carbondale, IL B
U of Illinois at Urbana–Champaign, IL B
U of Minnesota, Twin Cities Campus, MN B
U of Missouri–Columbia, MO B
U of Wisconsin–Madison, WI B
U of Wisconsin–Milwaukee, WI B
U of Wisconsin–Stevens Point, WI B
Winona State U, MN A

FRENCH

Adrian Coll, MI A,B
Albion Coll, MI B
Alma Coll, MI B
Anderson U, IN B
Andrews U, MI B
Antioch Coll, OH B
Aquinas Coll, MI B
Ashland U, OH B
Augsburg Coll, MN B
Augustana Coll, IL B
Augustana Coll, SD B
Baker U, KS B
Baldwin-Wallace Coll, OH B
Ball State U, IN B
Beloit Coll, WI B
Benedictine Coll, KS B
Bowling Green State U, OH B
Bradley U, IL B
Butler U, IN B
Calvin Coll, MI B
Capital U, OH B
Cardinal Stritch U, WI B
Carleton Coll, MN B
Carthage Coll, WI B
Case Western Reserve U, OH B
Central Coll, IA B
Central Methodist Coll, MO B
Central Michigan U, MI B
Central Missouri State U, MO B
Clarke Coll, IA B
Cleveland State U, OH B
Coe Coll, IA B
Coll of Saint Benedict, MN B
Coll of St. Catherine, MN B
Coll of the Ozarks, MO B
The Coll of Wooster, OH B
Concordia Coll, MN B
Cornell Coll, IA B
Creighton U, NE B
Denison U, OH B
DePaul U, IL B
DePauw U, IN B
Doane Coll, NE B
Dominican U, IL B
Drury U, MO B
Earlham Coll, IN B
Eastern Michigan U, MI B
Edgewood Coll, WI B
Elmhurst Coll, IL B
Fort Hays State U, KS B
Franciscan U of Steubenville, OH B
Franklin Coll, IN B
Grace Coll, IN B
Grand Valley State U, MI B
Grinnell Coll, IA B
Gustavus Adolphus Coll, MN B
Hamline U, MN B
Hanover Coll, IN B
Hillsdale Coll, MI B
Hiram Coll, OH B
Hope Coll, MI B
Illinois Coll, IL B
Illinois State U, IL B
Illinois Wesleyan U, IL B
Indiana State U, IN B
Indiana U Bloomington, IN B
Indiana U Northwest, IN B
Indiana U–Purdue U Fort Wayne, IN A,B
Indiana U–Purdue U Indianapolis, IN B
Indiana U South Bend, IN B
Indiana U Southeast, IN B
Iowa State U of Science and Technology, IA B
John Carroll U, OH B
Kalamazoo Coll, MI B
Kent State U, OH B
Kenyon Coll, OH B
Knox Coll, IL B
Lake Erie Coll, OH B
Lake Forest Coll, IL B
Lawrence U, WI B
Lindenwood U, MO B
Loras Coll, IA B
Loyola U Chicago, IL B
Luther Coll, IA B
Macalester Coll, MN B
Madonna U, MI B
Manchester Coll, IN B
Marian Coll, IN B
Marquette U, WI B
Miami U, OH B
Michigan State U, MI B
Millikin U, IL B
Minnesota State U, Mankato, MN B
Minot State U, ND B
Missouri Southern State Coll, MO B
Missouri Western State Coll, MO B
Monmouth Coll, IL B
Mount Mary Coll, WI B
Mount Union Coll, OH B
Muskingum Coll, OH B
Nebraska Wesleyan U, NE B
North Central Coll, IL B
North Dakota State U, ND B
Northeastern Illinois U, IL B
Northeastern State U, OK B
Northern Illinois U, IL B
Northern Michigan U, MI B
Northern State U, SD B
North Park U, IL B
Northwestern U, IL B
Northwest Missouri State U, MO B
Oakland U, MI B
Oberlin Coll, OH B
Ohio Northern U, OH B
The Ohio State U, OH B
Ohio U, OH B
Ohio Wesleyan U, OH B
Oklahoma Baptist U, OK B
Oklahoma City U, OK B
Oklahoma State U, OK B
Oral Roberts U, OK B
Otterbein Coll, OH B
Pittsburg State U, KS B
Principia Coll, IL B
Purdue U Calumet, IN B
Ripon Coll, WI B
Rockford Coll, IL B
Rockhurst U, MO B
Saginaw Valley State U, MI B
St. Ambrose U, IA B
St. Cloud State U, MN B
Saint John's U, MN B
Saint Louis U, MO B
Saint Mary-of-the-Woods Coll, IN B
Saint Mary's Coll, IN B
Saint Mary's U of Minnesota, MN B
St. Norbert Coll, WI B
St. Olaf Coll, MN B
Simpson Coll, IA B
South Dakota State U, SD B
Southeast Missouri State U, MO B
Southern Illinois U Carbondale, IL B
Southwest Missouri State U, MO B
Taylor U, IN B
Truman State U, MO B
Union Coll, NE B
The U of Akron, OH B
U of Central Oklahoma, OK B
U of Chicago, IL B
U of Cincinnati, OH B
U of Dayton, OH B
U of Evansville, IN B
U of Illinois at Chicago, IL B
U of Illinois at Urbana–Champaign, IL B
U of Indianapolis, IN B
The U of Iowa, IA B
U of Kansas, KS B
U of Michigan, MI B
U of Michigan–Dearborn, MI B
U of Michigan–Flint, MI B
U of Minnesota, Morris, MN B
U of Minnesota, Twin Cities Campus, MN B
U of Missouri–Columbia, MO B
U of Missouri–Kansas City, MO B
U of Missouri–St. Louis, MO B
U of Nebraska at Kearney, NE B
U of Nebraska at Omaha, NE B
U of Nebraska–Lincoln, NE B
U of North Dakota, ND B
U of Northern Iowa, IA B
U of Notre Dame, IN B
U of Oklahoma, OK B
U of St. Thomas, MN B
The U of South Dakota, SD B
U of Southern Indiana, IN B
U of Toledo, OH B
U of Tulsa, OK B
U of Wisconsin–Eau Claire, WI B
U of Wisconsin–Green Bay, WI A,B
U of Wisconsin–La Crosse, WI B
U of Wisconsin–Madison, WI B

U of Wisconsin–Milwaukee, WI B
U of Wisconsin–Oshkosh, WI B
U of Wisconsin–Parkside, WI B
U of Wisconsin–Platteville, WI B
U of Wisconsin–River Falls, WI B
U of Wisconsin–Stevens Point, WI B
U of Wisconsin–Whitewater, WI B
Valparaiso U, IN B
Wabash Coll, IN B
Walsh U, OH B
Wartburg Coll, IA B
Washington U in St. Louis, MO B
Wayne State Coll, NE B
Wayne State U, MI B
Webster U, MO B
Western Illinois U, IL B
Western Michigan U, MI B
Westminster Coll, MO B
Wheaton Coll, IL B
Wichita State U, KS B
William Jewell Coll, MO B
Winona State U, MN B
Wittenberg U, OH B
Wright State U, OH B
Xavier U, OH A,B
Youngstown State U, OH B

FRENCH LANGUAGE EDUCATION

Anderson U, IN B
Bowling Green State U, OH B
Central Michigan U, MI B
Central Missouri State U, MO B
Coll of St. Catherine, MN B
Concordia Coll, MN B
Eastern Michigan U, MI B
Elmhurst Coll, IL B
Franklin Coll, IN B
Grace Coll, IN B
Indiana U Bloomington, IN B
Indiana U Northwest, IN B
Indiana U–Purdue U Fort Wayne, IN B
Indiana U–Purdue U Indianapolis, IN B
Indiana U South Bend, IN B
Luther Coll, IA B
Minot State U, ND B
Missouri Western State Coll, MO B
North Dakota State U, ND B
Ohio U, OH B
Oklahoma Baptist U, OK B
Oral Roberts U, OK B
St. Ambrose U, IA B
Saint Mary's U of Minnesota, MN B
Southwest Missouri State U, MO B
U of Illinois at Chicago, IL B
U of Illinois at Urbana–Champaign, IL B
U of Indianapolis, IN B
The U of Iowa, IA B
U of Minnesota, Duluth, MN B
U of Nebraska–Lincoln, NE B
U of Toledo, OH B
U of Wisconsin–River Falls, WI B
Washington U in St. Louis, MO B
William Woods U, MO B
Youngstown State U, OH B

FURNITURE DESIGN

Ferris State U, MI B

GENERAL OFFICE/ CLERICAL

Sitting Bull Coll, ND A
Youngstown State U, OH A

GENERAL RETAILING/ WHOLESALING RELATED

The U of Akron, OH B

GENERAL STUDIES

Alverno Coll, WI B
Anderson U, IN A
Avila U, MO A,B
Bacone Coll, OK A
Black Hills State U, SD A
Calumet Coll of Saint Joseph, IN A,B
Central Christian Coll of Kansas, KS B
Central Coll, IA B
Coll of Mount St. Joseph, OH A,B
Crown Coll, MN A,B
DePaul U, IL B
Emporia State U, KS B
Finlandia U, MI A
The Franciscan U, IA B
Franciscan U of Steubenville, OH A
Hamilton Coll, IA A
Hillsdale Free Will Baptist Coll, OK A
Indiana State U, IN B
Indiana U Bloomington, IN A,B
Indiana U East, IN A,B
Indiana U Kokomo, IN A,B
Indiana U Northwest, IN A,B
Indiana U–Purdue U Fort Wayne, IN A,B
Indiana U–Purdue U Indianapolis, IN A,B
Indiana U South Bend, IN A,B
Indiana U Southeast, IN A,B
Indiana Wesleyan U, IN A,B
Kent State U, OH B
Kettering Coll of Medical Arts, OH A
Metropolitan State U, MN B
Michigan Technological U, MI B
Minot State U, ND B
Missouri Western State Coll, MO B
Mount Marty Coll, SD A,B
Ohio U, OH B
Ohio Wesleyan U, OH B
Oklahoma Panhandle State U, OK A
Rochester Comm and Tech Coll, MN A
Saginaw Valley State U, MI B
Siena Heights U, MI A,B
Silver Lake Coll, WI A
Si Tanka Huron U, SD A
South Dakota School of Mines and Technology, SD A
Southern Nazarene U, OK B
Southwest Baptist U, MO A
Southwestern Coll, KS B
U of Dayton, OH B
U of Michigan, MI B
U of Missouri–St. Louis, MO B
U of Nebraska at Kearney, NE B
U of Nebraska at Omaha, NE B
U of Rio Grande, OH A
U of Wisconsin–Green Bay, WI B
U of Wisconsin–Stevens Point, WI B
York Coll, NE B

GENETICS

Ball State U, IN B
Iowa State U of Science and Technology, IA B
Missouri Southern State Coll, MO B
North Dakota State U, ND B
The Ohio State U, OH B
Ohio Wesleyan U, OH B
St. Cloud State U, MN B
U of Minnesota, Twin Cities Campus, MN B
U of Wisconsin–Madison, WI B

GEOGRAPHY

Aquinas Coll, MI B
Augustana Coll, IL B
Ball State U, IN B
Bellevue U, NE B
Bemidji State U, MN B
Bowling Green State U, OH B
Calvin Coll, MI B
Carroll Coll, WI B
Carthage Coll, WI B
Central Michigan U, MI B
Central Missouri State U, MO B
Chicago State U, IL B
Concordia U, IL B
Concordia U, NE B
DePaul U, IL B
DePauw U, IN B
Dickinson State U, ND B
Eastern Illinois U, IL B
Eastern Michigan U, MI B
Elmhurst Coll, IL B
Gustavus Adolphus Coll, MN B
Illinois State U, IL B
Indiana State U, IN B
Indiana U Bloomington, IN B
Indiana U–Purdue U Indianapolis, IN B
Indiana U Southeast, IN B
Kansas State U, KS B
Kent State U, OH B
Lincoln Coll, Lincoln, IL A
Macalester Coll, MN B
Miami U, OH B
Miami U–Middletown Campus, OH A
Michigan State U, MI B
Minnesota State U, Mankato, MN B
Northeastern Illinois U, IL B
Northeastern State U, OK B
Northern Illinois U, IL B
Northern Michigan U, MI B
Northwestern U, IL B
Northwest Missouri State U, MO B
The Ohio State U, OH B
Ohio U, OH B
Ohio Wesleyan U, OH B
Oklahoma State U, OK B
Pittsburg State U, KS B
St. Cloud State U, MN B
South Dakota State U, SD B
Southeast Missouri State U, MO B
Southern Illinois U Carbondale, IL B
Southern Illinois U Edwardsville, IL B
Southwest Missouri State U, MO B
The U of Akron, OH B
U of Central Oklahoma, OK B
U of Chicago, IL B
U of Cincinnati, OH B
U of Illinois at Chicago, IL B
U of Illinois at Urbana–Champaign, IL B
The U of Iowa, IA B
U of Kansas, KS B
U of Michigan, MI B
U of Michigan–Flint, MI B
U of Minnesota, Duluth, MN B
U of Minnesota, Twin Cities Campus, MN B
U of Missouri–Columbia, MO B
U of Missouri–Kansas City, MO B
U of Nebraska at Kearney, NE B
U of Nebraska at Omaha, NE B
U of Nebraska–Lincoln, NE B
U of North Dakota, ND B
U of Northern Iowa, IA B
U of Oklahoma, OK B
U of St. Thomas, MN B
U of Toledo, OH B
U of Wisconsin–Eau Claire, WI B
U of Wisconsin–La Crosse, WI B
U of Wisconsin–Madison, WI B
U of Wisconsin–Milwaukee, WI B
U of Wisconsin–Oshkosh, WI B
U of Wisconsin–Parkside, WI B
U of Wisconsin–Platteville, WI B
U of Wisconsin–River Falls, WI B
U of Wisconsin–Stevens Point, WI B
U of Wisconsin–Whitewater, WI B
Valparaiso U, IN B
Wayne State Coll, NE B
Wayne State U, MI B
Western Illinois U, IL B
Western Michigan U, MI B
Wittenberg U, OH B
Wright State U, OH A,B
Youngstown State U, OH B

GEOLOGICAL ENGINEERING

Michigan Technological U, MI B
South Dakota School of Mines and Technology, SD B
The U of Akron, OH B

Geological Engineering (continued)

U of Minnesota, Twin Cities Campus, MN B
U of Missouri–Rolla, MO B
U of North Dakota, ND B
U of Oklahoma, OK B

GEOLOGICAL SCIENCES RELATED

Ohio U, OH B
The U of Akron, OH B
Western Michigan U, MI B

GEOLOGY

Albion Coll, MI B
Antioch Coll, OH B
Ashland U, OH B
Augustana Coll, IL B
Baldwin-Wallace Coll, OH B
Ball State U, IN B
Beloit Coll, WI B
Bemidji State U, MN B
Bowling Green State U, OH B
Bradley U, IL B
Calvin Coll, MI B
Carleton Coll, MN B
Case Western Reserve U, OH B
Central Michigan U, MI B
Central Missouri State U, MO B
Cleveland State U, OH B
The Coll of Wooster, OH B
Columbia Coll, MO B
Cornell Coll, IA B
Denison U, OH B
DePauw U, IN B
Earlham Coll, IN B
Eastern Illinois U, IL B
Eastern Michigan U, MI B
Fort Hays State U, KS B
Grand Valley State U, MI B
Gustavus Adolphus Coll, MN B
Hanover Coll, IN B
Hope Coll, MI B
Illinois State U, IL B
Indiana State U, IN B
Indiana U Bloomington, IN B
Indiana U Northwest, IN B
Indiana U–Purdue U Fort Wayne, IN B
Indiana U–Purdue U Indianapolis, IN B
Iowa State U of Science and Technology, IA B
Kansas State U, KS B
Kent State U, OH B
Lawrence U, WI B
Macalester Coll, MN B
Marietta Coll, OH B
Miami U, OH B
Michigan State U, MI B
Michigan Technological U, MI B
Minot State U, ND B
Mount Union Coll, OH B
Muskingum Coll, OH B
North Dakota State U, ND B
Northern Illinois U, IL B
Northland Coll, WI B
Northwestern U, IL B
Northwest Missouri State U, MO B
Oberlin Coll, OH B
The Ohio State U, OH B
Ohio U, OH B
Ohio Wesleyan U, OH B
Oklahoma State U, OK B
Olivet Nazarene U, IL B
Purdue U, IN B
Saint Louis U, MO B
St. Norbert Coll, WI B
South Dakota School of Mines and Technology, SD B
Southeast Missouri State U, MO B
Southern Illinois U Carbondale, IL B
Southwest Missouri State U, MO B
The U of Akron, OH B
U of Cincinnati, OH B
U of Dayton, OH B
U of Illinois at Chicago, IL B
U of Illinois at Urbana–Champaign, IL B
The U of Iowa, IA B
U of Kansas, KS B
U of Michigan, MI B
U of Minnesota, Duluth, MN B
U of Minnesota, Morris, MN B
U of Minnesota, Twin Cities Campus, MN B
U of Missouri–Columbia, MO B
U of Missouri–Kansas City, MO B
U of Missouri–Rolla, MO B
U of Nebraska at Omaha, NE B
U of Nebraska–Lincoln, NE B
U of North Dakota, ND B
U of Northern Iowa, IA B
U of Notre Dame, IN B
U of Oklahoma, OK B
U of St. Thomas, MN B
U of Southern Indiana, IN B
U of Toledo, OH B
U of Tulsa, OK B
U of Wisconsin–Eau Claire, WI B
U of Wisconsin–Madison, WI B
U of Wisconsin–Milwaukee, WI B
U of Wisconsin–Oshkosh, WI B
U of Wisconsin–Parkside, WI B
U of Wisconsin–Platteville, WI B
U of Wisconsin–River Falls, WI B
Valparaiso U, IN B
Wayne State U, MI B
Western Illinois U, IL B
Western Michigan U, MI B
Wheaton Coll, IL B
Wichita State U, KS B
Winona State U, MN B
Wittenberg U, OH B
Wright State U, OH B
Youngstown State U, OH B

GEOPHYSICS/ SEISMOLOGY

Bowling Green State U, OH B
Eastern Michigan U, MI B
Hope Coll, MI B
Kansas State U, KS B
Michigan Technological U, MI B
Saint Louis U, MO B
The U of Akron, OH B
U of Chicago, IL B
U of Minnesota, Twin Cities Campus, MN B
U of Missouri–Rolla, MO B
U of Oklahoma, OK B
U of Tulsa, OK B
U of Wisconsin–Madison, WI B
Western Michigan U, MI B

GERMAN

Adrian Coll, MI A,B
Albion Coll, MI B
Alma Coll, MI B
Anderson U, IN B
Antioch Coll, OH B
Aquinas Coll, MI B
Augsburg Coll, MN B
Augustana Coll, IL B
Augustana Coll, SD B
Baker U, KS B
Baldwin-Wallace Coll, OH B
Ball State U, IN B
Beloit Coll, WI B
Bemidji State U, MN B
Bethel Coll, KS B
Bowling Green State U, OH B
Bradley U, IL B
Butler U, IN B
Calvin Coll, MI B
Carleton Coll, MN B
Carthage Coll, WI B
Case Western Reserve U, OH B
Central Coll, IA B
Central Michigan U, MI B
Central Missouri State U, MO B
Cleveland State U, OH B
Coe Coll, IA B
Coll of Saint Benedict, MN B
Coll of the Ozarks, MO B
The Coll of Wooster, OH B
Concordia Coll, MN B
Concordia U, NE B
Concordia U Wisconsin, WI B
Cornell Coll, IA B
Creighton U, NE B
Dana Coll, NE B
Denison U, OH B
DePaul U, IL B
DePauw U, IN B
Doane Coll, NE B
Dordt Coll, IA B
Drury U, MO B
Earlham Coll, IN B
Eastern Michigan U, MI B
Elmhurst Coll, IL B
Fort Hays State U, KS B
Goshen Coll, IN B
Grace Coll, IN B
Graceland U, IA B
Grand Valley State U, MI B
Grinnell Coll, IA B
Gustavus Adolphus Coll, MN B
Hamline U, MN B
Hanover Coll, IN B
Hastings Coll, NE B
Heidelberg Coll, OH B
Hillsdale Coll, MI B
Hiram Coll, OH B
Hope Coll, MI B
Illinois Coll, IL B
Illinois State U, IL B
Illinois Wesleyan U, IL B
Indiana State U, IN B
Indiana U Bloomington, IN B
Indiana U–Purdue U Fort Wayne, IN A,B
Indiana U–Purdue U Indianapolis, IN B
Indiana U South Bend, IN B
Indiana U Southeast, IN B
Iowa State U of Science and Technology, IA B
John Carroll U, OH B
Kalamazoo Coll, MI B
Kent State U, OH B
Kenyon Coll, OH B
Knox Coll, IL B
Lake Erie Coll, OH B
Lake Forest Coll, IL B
Lakeland Coll, WI B
Lawrence U, WI B
Loyola U Chicago, IL B
Luther Coll, IA B
Manchester Coll, IN B
Marquette U, WI B
Miami U, OH B
Michigan State U, MI B
Millikin U, IL B
Minnesota State U, Mankato, MN B
Minot State U, ND B
Missouri Southern State Coll, MO B
Mount Union Coll, OH B
Muskingum Coll, OH B
Nebraska Wesleyan U, NE B
North Central Coll, IL B
Northeastern State U, OK B
Northern Illinois U, IL B
Northern State U, SD B
Northwestern U, IL B
Oakland U, MI B
Oberlin Coll, OH B
The Ohio State U, OH B
Ohio U, OH B
Ohio Wesleyan U, OH B
Oklahoma Baptist U, OK B
Oklahoma City U, OK B
Oklahoma State U, OK B
Oral Roberts U, OK B
Principia Coll, IL B
Purdue U Calumet, IN B
Ripon Coll, WI B
Rockford Coll, IL B
St. Ambrose U, IA B
St. Cloud State U, MN B
Saint John's U, MN B
Saint Louis U, MO B
St. Norbert Coll, WI B
St. Olaf Coll, MN B
Simpson Coll, IA B
South Dakota State U, SD B
Southeast Missouri State U, MO B
Southern Illinois U Carbondale, IL B
Southwest Missouri State U, MO B
Truman State U, MO B
Union Coll, NE B
The U of Akron, OH B
U of Central Oklahoma, OK B
U of Chicago, IL B
U of Cincinnati, OH B
U of Dayton, OH B
U of Evansville, IN B
U of Illinois at Chicago, IL B
U of Illinois at Urbana–Champaign, IL B
U of Indianapolis, IN B
The U of Iowa, IA B
U of Kansas, KS B

U of Michigan, MI B
U of Michigan–Dearborn, MI B
U of Michigan–Flint, MI B
U of Minnesota, Morris, MN B
U of Minnesota, Twin Cities Campus, MN B
U of Missouri–Columbia, MO B
U of Missouri–Kansas City, MO B
U of Missouri–St. Louis, MO B
U of Nebraska at Kearney, NE B
U of Nebraska at Omaha, NE B
U of Nebraska–Lincoln, NE B
U of North Dakota, ND B
U of Northern Iowa, IA B
U of Notre Dame, IN B
U of Oklahoma, OK B
U of St. Thomas, MN B
The U of South Dakota, SD B
U of Southern Indiana, IN B
U of Toledo, OH B
U of Tulsa, OK B
U of Wisconsin–Eau Claire, WI B
U of Wisconsin–Green Bay, WI A,B
U of Wisconsin–La Crosse, WI B
U of Wisconsin–Madison, WI B
U of Wisconsin–Milwaukee, WI B
U of Wisconsin–Oshkosh, WI B
U of Wisconsin–Parkside, WI B
U of Wisconsin–Platteville, WI B
U of Wisconsin–River Falls, WI B
U of Wisconsin–Stevens Point, WI B
U of Wisconsin–Whitewater, WI B
Valparaiso U, IN B
Wabash Coll, IN B
Waldorf Coll, IA A
Wartburg Coll, IA B
Washington U in St. Louis, MO B
Wayne State Coll, NE B
Wayne State U, MI B
Webster U, MO B
Western Michigan U, MI B
Wheaton Coll, IL B
Winona State U, MN B
Wittenberg U, OH B
Wright State U, OH B
Xavier U, OH A,B

GERMAN LANGUAGE EDUCATION

Anderson U, IN B
Central Michigan U, MI B
Central Missouri State U, MO B
Concordia Coll, MN B
Eastern Michigan U, MI B
Elmhurst Coll, IL B
Grace Coll, IN B
Indiana U Bloomington, IN B
Indiana U–Purdue U Fort Wayne, IN B
Indiana U–Purdue U Indianapolis, IN B
Indiana U South Bend, IN B
Luther Coll, IA B
Minot State U, ND B
Ohio U, OH B
Oklahoma Baptist U, OK B
Oral Roberts U, OK B
St. Ambrose U, IA B
Southwest Missouri State U, MO B
The U of Akron, OH B
U of Illinois at Chicago, IL B
U of Illinois at Urbana–Champaign, IL B
The U of Iowa, IA B
U of Minnesota, Duluth, MN B
U of Nebraska–Lincoln, NE B
U of Wisconsin–River Falls, WI B
Washington U in St. Louis, MO B
Youngstown State U, OH B

GERONTOLOGICAL SERVICES

Bowling Green State U, OH B
Ohio U, OH B
Saint Mary-of-the-Woods Coll, IN B
U of Toledo, OH A

GERONTOLOGY

Alma Coll, MI B
Avila U, MO B
Bowling Green State U, OH B
Case Western Reserve U, OH B
Coll of Mount St. Joseph, OH A,B
Coll of the Ozarks, MO B
Dominican U, IL B
John Carroll U, OH B
Langston U, OK B
Lindenwood U, MO B
Lourdes Coll, OH A,B
Madonna U, MI A,B
Manchester Coll, IN A
National-Louis U, IL B
Nebraska Indian Comm Coll, NE A
Ohio Dominican U, OH A
Roosevelt U, IL B
St. Cloud State U, MN B
Saint Mary-of-the-Woods Coll, IN B
Siena Heights U, MI A
Southeastern Oklahoma State U, OK B
Southwest Missouri State U, MO B
The U of Akron, OH B
U of Evansville, IN B
U of Missouri–St. Louis, MO B
U of Nebraska at Omaha, NE B
U of Toledo, OH A
Western Michigan U, MI B
Wichita State U, KS B
Winona State U, MN A

GRAPHIC DESIGN/ COMMERCIAL ART/ ILLUSTRATION

Academy Coll, MN A
American Academy of Art, IL B
Anderson U, IN B
Andrews U, MI A,B
Art Academy of Cincinnati, OH A,B
The Art Insts International Minnesota, MN A,B
Ashland U, OH B
Avila U, MO B
Baker Coll of Auburn Hills, MI A
Baker Coll of Clinton Township, MI A
Baker Coll of Flint, MI A,B
Baker Coll of Muskegon, MI A
Baker Coll of Owosso, MI A,B
Baker Coll of Port Huron, MI A
Ball State U, IN B
Bellevue U, NE B
Bemidji State U, MN B
Black Hills State U, SD B
Bluffton Coll, OH B
Briar Cliff U, IA B
Buena Vista U, IA B
Cardinal Stritch U, WI B
Carroll Coll, WI B
Carthage Coll, WI B
Central Michigan U, MI B
Central Missouri State U, MO B
Chicago State U, IL B
The Cleveland Inst of Art, OH B
Coll for Creative Studies, MI B
Coll of Mount St. Joseph, OH A,B
Coll of Visual Arts, MN B
Columbia Coll, MO B
Columbia Coll Chicago, IL B
Columbus Coll of Art and Design, OH B
Concordia U, IL B
Concordia U, NE B
Concordia U Wisconsin, WI B
Creighton U, NE B
DePaul U, IL B
Dominican U, IL B
Dordt Coll, IA B
Drake U, IA B
Edgewood Coll, WI B
Ferris State U, MI A
Fontbonne U, MO B
Fort Hays State U, KS B
Grace Coll, IN B
Graceland U, IA B
Grand Valley State U, MI B
Grand View Coll, IA B
Huntington Coll, IN B
The Illinois Inst of Art, IL A,B
Illinois Wesleyan U, IL B
Indiana U Bloomington, IN B
Indiana U–Purdue U Fort Wayne, IN A,B
International Business Coll, Fort Wayne, IN A,B
Iowa State U of Science and Technology, IA B
Iowa Wesleyan Coll, IA B
Judson Coll, IL B
Kansas City Art Inst, MO B
Kendall Coll of Art and Design of Ferris State U, MI B
Kent State U, OH B
Lewis U, IL B
Lincoln Coll, Lincoln, IL A
Lincoln Coll, Normal, IL A
Madonna U, MI A,B
Maharishi U of Management, IA B
Marietta Coll, OH B
Maryville U of Saint Louis, MO B
MidAmerica Nazarene U, KS B
Millikin U, IL B
Milwaukee Inst of Art and Design, WI B
Minneapolis Coll of Art and Design, MN B
Minnesota State U, Mankato, MN B
Minnesota State U, Moorhead, MN B
Missouri Southern State Coll, MO B
Missouri Western State Coll, MO B
Morningside Coll, IA B
Mount Mary Coll, WI B
Northeastern State U, OK B
Northern Michigan U, MI A,B
Northern State U, SD A
Northwestern Coll, MN B
Northwest Missouri State U, MO B
Ohio Northern U, OH B
The Ohio State U, OH B
Ohio U, OH B
Oklahoma Christian U, OK B
Oklahoma City U, OK B
Oklahoma State U, OK B
Olivet Coll, MI B
Olivet Nazarene U, IL B
Oral Roberts U, OK B
Park U, MO B
Peru State Coll, NE B
Pittsburg State U, KS B
Robert Morris Coll, IL A
Rogers State U, OK A
St. Cloud State U, MN B
Saint Mary's U of Minnesota, MN B
St. Norbert Coll, WI B
School of the Art Inst of Chicago, IL B
Silver Lake Coll, WI A
Simpson Coll, IA B
Southern Illinois U Carbondale, IL A
Southwest Baptist U, MO B
Southwestern Oklahoma State U, OK B
Taylor U, IN B
Trinity Christian Coll, IL B
Truman State U, MO B
Union Coll, NE B
The U of Akron, OH B
U of Central Oklahoma, OK B
U of Cincinnati, OH B
U of Dayton, OH B
U of Evansville, IN B
U of Illinois at Chicago, IL B
U of Illinois at Urbana–Champaign, IL B
U of Indianapolis, IN B
U of Michigan, MI B
U of Minnesota, Duluth, MN B
U of Minnesota, Twin Cities Campus, MN B
U of Missouri–St. Louis, MO B
U of Saint Francis, IN A,B
U of Sioux Falls, SD B
The U of South Dakota, SD B
U of Wisconsin–Platteville, WI B
U of Wisconsin–Stevens Point, WI B
Upper Iowa U, IA B

Graphic Design/Commercial Art/Illustration (continued)

Viterbo U, WI B
Waldorf Coll, IA A
Wartburg Coll, IA B
Washington U in St. Louis, MO B
Wayne State Coll, NE B
Webster U, MO B
Western Michigan U, MI B
Westwood Coll of Technology-Chicago Du Page, IL A
Westwood Coll of Technology–Chicago River Oaks, IL A
Wichita State U, KS B
William Woods U, MO B
Winona State U, MN B
Wittenberg U, OH B
Youngstown State U, OH B

GRAPHIC/PRINTING EQUIPMENT

Andrews U, MI A,B
Ball State U, IN A
Central Missouri State U, MO A,B
Ferris State U, MI A,B
Indiana State U, IN B
Pittsburg State U, KS B

GREEK (ANCIENT AND MEDIEVAL)

Carleton Coll, MN B
Indiana U Bloomington, IN B
Loyola U Chicago, IL B
Miami U, OH B
Ohio U, OH B
Saint Louis U, MO B
St. Olaf Coll, MN B
U of Chicago, IL B
U of Nebraska–Lincoln, NE B
U of Notre Dame, IN B
U of St. Thomas, MN B
Washington U in St. Louis, MO B

GREEK (MODERN)

Ball State U, IN B
Butler U, IN B
Calvin Coll, MI B
The Coll of Wooster, OH B
Concordia U Wisconsin, WI B
Cornell Coll, IA B
Creighton U, NE B
DePauw U, IN B
John Carroll U, OH B
Kenyon Coll, OH B
Luther Coll, IA B
Macalester Coll, MN B
Monmouth Coll, IL B
Oberlin Coll, OH B
The Ohio State U, OH B
Rockford Coll, IL B
The U of Iowa, IA B
U of Michigan, MI B
U of Minnesota, Twin Cities Campus, MN B
U of Wisconsin–Madison, WI B
U of Wisconsin–Milwaukee, WI B
Wabash Coll, IN B
Wright State U, OH B

GREENHOUSE MANAGEMENT

Rochester Comm and Tech Coll, MN A

HEALTH EDUCATION

Anderson U, IN B
Aquinas Coll, MI B
Ashland U, OH B
Augsburg Coll, MN B
Baldwin-Wallace Coll, OH B
Ball State U, IN B
Bemidji State U, MN B
Bethel Coll, MN B
Bluffton Coll, OH B
Bowling Green State U, OH B
Briar Cliff U, IA B
Capital U, OH B
Carroll Coll, WI B
Cedarville U, OH B
Central Christian Coll of Kansas, KS A
Central Michigan U, MI B
Chicago State U, IL B
Concordia Coll, MN B
Concordia U, MN B
Concordia U, NE B
Defiance Coll, OH B
Donnelly Coll, KS A
Eastern Illinois U, IL B
Emporia State U, KS B
Graceland U, IA B
Gustavus Adolphus Coll, MN B
Hamline U, MN B
Heidelberg Coll, OH B
Illinois State U, IL B
Indiana State U, IN B
Indiana U–Purdue U Indianapolis, IN B
Iowa State U of Science and Technology, IA B
Kent State U, OH B
Luther Coll, IA B
Malone Coll, OH B
Manchester Coll, IN B
Mayville State U, ND B
Miami U, OH B
MidAmerica Nazarene U, KS B
Minnesota State U, Mankato, MN B
Minnesota State U, Moorhead, MN B
Missouri Valley Coll, MO B
Mount Vernon Nazarene U, OH B
Muskingum Coll, OH B
North Central Coll, IL B
Northeastern State U, OK B
Northern Illinois U, IL B
Northern Michigan U, MI B
Northern State U, SD B
Northwestern Oklahoma State U, OK B
Northwest Missouri State U, MO B
Ohio Northern U, OH B
Ohio Wesleyan U, OH B
Otterbein Coll, OH B
Peru State Coll, NE B
Pittsburg State U, KS B
St. Ambrose U, IA B
St. Cloud State U, MN B
Southeastern Oklahoma State U, OK B
Southern Illinois U Carbondale, IL B
Southern Illinois U Edwardsville, IL B
Southern Nazarene U, OK B
Southwest Minnesota State U, MN B
Tabor Coll, KS B
The U of Akron, OH B
U of Cincinnati, OH B
U of Dayton, OH B
The U of Iowa, IA B
U of Kansas, KS B
U of Minnesota, Duluth, MN B
U of Nebraska at Omaha, NE B
U of Nebraska–Lincoln, NE B
U of Northern Iowa, IA B
U of Rio Grande, OH B
U of Saint Francis, IN B
U of St. Thomas, MN B
U of Sioux Falls, SD B
U of Toledo, OH B
U of Wisconsin–La Crosse, WI B
Upper Iowa U, IA B
Urbana U, OH B
Valley City State U, ND B
Waldorf Coll, IA A
Western Illinois U, IL B
Western Michigan U, MI B
William Penn U, IA B
Wilmington Coll, OH B
Winona State U, MN B
Wright State U, OH B
Youngstown State U, OH B

HEALTH FACILITIES ADMINISTRATION

Central Michigan U, MI B
Ohio U, OH B
Southern Illinois U Carbondale, IL B
U of Toledo, OH B

HEALTH/MEDICAL ADMINISTRATIVE SERVICES RELATED

Kent State U, OH A
Ursuline Coll, OH B

HEALTH/MEDICAL ASSISTANTS RELATED

Wayne State U, MI B

HEALTH/MEDICAL DIAGNOSTIC AND TREATMENT SERVICES RELATED

Kent State U, OH A
U of Toledo, OH B

HEALTH/MEDICAL LABORATORY TECHNOLOGIES RELATED

Saint Louis U, MO B
The U of Akron, OH A

HEALTH/MEDICAL PREPARATORY PROGRAMS RELATED

Ancilla Coll, IN A
Aurora U, IL B
Chadron State Coll, NE B
The U of Akron, OH B

HEALTH OCCUPATIONS EDUCATION

U of Central Oklahoma, OK B

HEALTH/PHYSICAL EDUCATION

Anderson U, IN B
Bethel Coll, KS B
Black Hills State U, SD B
Cameron U, OK B
Cedarville U, OH B
Central Christian Coll of Kansas, KS A
Central Michigan U, MI B
Coll of St. Catherine, MN B
Coll of the Ozarks, MO B
Concordia Coll, MN B
Concordia U, NE B
Dana Coll, NE B
Doane Coll, NE B
Eastern Michigan U, MI B
Elmhurst Coll, IL B
Hastings Coll, NE B
Iowa State U of Science and Technology, IA B
Luther Coll, IA B
Malone Coll, OH B
Mayville State U, ND B
Miami U, OH B
Minnesota State U, Moorhead, MN B
North Dakota State U, ND B
Ohio U, OH B
Oklahoma Baptist U, OK B
Oklahoma State U, OK B
Olivet Coll, MI B
Pillsbury Baptist Bible Coll, MN B
South Dakota State U, SD B
Southeast Missouri State U, MO B
Southern Illinois U Edwardsville, IL B
Southwestern Coll, KS B
Southwest Minnesota State U, MN B
Spring Arbor U, MI B
U of Illinois at Chicago, IL B
U of Illinois at Urbana–Champaign, IL B
U of Kansas, KS B
U of Missouri–Kansas City, MO B
U of Oklahoma, OK B
U of Rio Grande, OH B
U of St. Thomas, MN B
U of Science and Arts of Oklahoma, OK B
U of Wisconsin–Stevens Point, WI B
Valparaiso U, IN B
William Penn U, IA B
Youngstown State U, OH B

HEALTH/PHYSICAL EDUCATION/FITNESS RELATED

Briar Cliff U, IA B
Mayville State U, ND B
Robert Morris Coll, IL A
The U of Akron, OH B
U of Central Oklahoma, OK B

HEALTH PROFESSIONS AND RELATED SCIENCES

Bradley U, IL B

Maharishi U of Management, IA B
The Ohio State U, OH B
Ohio U, OH B
Washington U in St. Louis, MO B

HEALTH SCIENCE

Alma Coll, MI B
Ball State U, IN B
Benedictine U, IL B
Bradley U, IL B
The Coll of St. Scholastica, MN B
Coll of the Ozarks, MO B
Graceland U, IA B
Grand Valley State U, MI B
Hiram Coll, OH B
Kalamazoo Coll, MI B
Kansas State U, KS B
Kettering Coll of Medical Arts, OH B
Manchester Coll, IN B
Maryville U of Saint Louis, MO B
Minnesota State U, Mankato, MN B
Newman U, KS A,B
Northern Illinois U, IL B
Northwest Missouri State U, MO B
Oakland U, MI B
Ohio U, OH B
Oklahoma State U, OK B
Roosevelt U, IL B
Springfield Coll in Illinois, IL A
Truman State U, MO B
Union Coll, NE A
Union Inst & U, OH B
U of Missouri–St. Louis, MO B
U of St. Francis, IL B
U of Saint Francis, IN B
U of St. Thomas, MN B
U of Wisconsin–Milwaukee, WI B
Ursuline Coll, OH B
Waldorf Coll, IA A,B
Wayne State U, MI B
Winona State U, MN B
Youngstown State U, OH B

HEALTH SERVICES ADMINISTRATION

Augustana Coll, SD B
Baker Coll of Auburn Hills, MI A,B
Baker Coll of Flint, MI A,B
Baker Coll of Muskegon, MI A,B
Baker Coll of Owosso, MI B
Baker Coll of Port Huron, MI B
Bellevue U, NE B
Benedictine U, IL B
Black Hills State U, SD B
Bowling Green State U, OH B
Calumet Coll of Saint Joseph, IN B
Cleary U, MI B
Coll of Mount St. Joseph, OH B
The Coll of St. Scholastica, MN B
Concordia Coll, MN B
Concordia U, MI B
Concordia U, NE B
Concordia U Wisconsin, WI B
Creighton U, NE B
Davenport U, Grand Rapids, MI B
Davenport U, Kalamazoo, MI A,B
Eastern Michigan U, MI B
Ferris State U, MI B
The Franciscan U, IA B
Franklin U, OH B
Governors State U, IL B
Harris-Stowe State Coll, MO B
Hastings Coll, NE B
Heidelberg Coll, OH B
Indiana U Northwest, IN B
Indiana U–Purdue U Fort Wayne, IN B
Indiana U–Purdue U Indianapolis, IN B
Indiana U South Bend, IN B
Langston U, OK B
Lewis U, IL B
Lindenwood U, MO B
Maryville U of Saint Louis, MO B
Minnesota State U, Moorhead, MN B
National-Louis U, IL B
Northeastern State U, OK B
Ohio U, OH B
Presentation Coll, SD B
Purdue U North Central, IN A
Roosevelt U, IL B
Saint Louis U, MO B
Saint Mary's U of Minnesota, MN B
Southwestern Oklahoma State U, OK B
Spring Arbor U, MI B
U of Cincinnati, OH B
U of Evansville, IN B
U of Illinois at Springfield, IL B
U of Michigan–Dearborn, MI B
U of Michigan–Flint, MI B
U of Northwestern Ohio, OH B
The U of South Dakota, SD B
U of Southern Indiana, IN B
U of Wisconsin–Eau Claire, WI B
U of Wisconsin–Milwaukee, WI B
Ursuline Coll, OH B
Viterbo U, WI B
Webster U, MO B
Wichita State U, KS B
Wilberforce U, OH B
Winona State U, MN B

HEALTH UNIT MANAGEMENT

Ursuline Coll, OH B

HEARING SCIENCES

Indiana U Bloomington, IN B
Northwestern U, IL B
Ohio U, OH A

HEATING/AIR CONDITIONING/ REFRIGERATION

Ferris State U, MI A,B
Northern Michigan U, MI A
Oakland City U, IN A
Ranken Tech Coll, MO A
U of Cincinnati, OH A
U of Northwestern Ohio, OH A

HEATING/AIR CONDITIONING/ REFRIGERATION TECHNOLOGY

Central Missouri State U, MO A
Vatterott Coll, St. Ann, MO A

HEAVY EQUIPMENT MAINTENANCE

Ferris State U, MI A,B
Pittsburg State U, KS B

HEBREW

Concordia U Wisconsin, WI B
Laura and Alvin Siegal Coll of Judaic Studies, OH B
Luther Coll, IA B
The Ohio State U, OH B
U of Michigan, MI B
U of Minnesota, Twin Cities Campus, MN B
U of Wisconsin–Madison, WI B
U of Wisconsin–Milwaukee, WI B
Washington U in St. Louis, MO B

HIGHER EDUCATION ADMINISTRATION

Bowling Green State U, OH B

HISPANIC-AMERICAN STUDIES

Goshen Coll, IN B
St. Olaf Coll, MN B
U of Michigan, MI B
U of Michigan–Dearborn, MI B
U of Wisconsin–Madison, WI B
Wayne State U, MI B

HISTORY

Adrian Coll, MI A,B
Albion Coll, MI B
Alma Coll, MI B
Alverno Coll, WI B
Anderson U, IN B
Andrews U, MI B
Antioch Coll, OH B
Aquinas Coll, MI B
Ashland U, OH B
Augsburg Coll, MN B
Augustana Coll, IL B
Augustana Coll, SD B
Aurora U, IL B
Ave Maria Coll, MI B
Avila U, MO B
Bacone Coll, OK A
Baker U, KS B
Baldwin-Wallace Coll, OH B
Ball State U, IN B
Bellevue U, NE B
Beloit Coll, WI B
Bemidji State U, MN B
Benedictine Coll, KS B
Benedictine U, IL B
Bethany Coll, KS B
Bethel Coll, IN B
Bethel Coll, KS B
Bethel Coll, MN B
Blackburn Coll, IL B
Black Hills State U, SD B
Bluffton Coll, OH B
Bowling Green State U, OH B
Bradley U, IL B
Briar Cliff U, IA B
Buena Vista U, IA B
Butler U, IN B
Calvin Coll, MI B
Cameron U, OK B
Capital U, OH B
Cardinal Stritch U, WI B
Carleton Coll, MN B
Carroll Coll, WI B
Carthage Coll, WI B
Case Western Reserve U, OH B
Cedarville U, OH B
Central Christian Coll of Kansas, KS A
Central Coll, IA B
Central Methodist Coll, MO B
Central Michigan U, MI B
Central Missouri State U, MO B
Chadron State Coll, NE B
Chicago State U, IL B
Clarke Coll, IA B
Cleveland State U, OH B
Coe Coll, IA B
Coll of Mount St. Joseph, OH B
Coll of Saint Benedict, MN B
Coll of St. Catherine, MN B
The Coll of St. Scholastica, MN B
Coll of the Ozarks, MO B
The Coll of Wooster, OH B
Columbia Coll, MO B
Concordia Coll, MN B
Concordia U, IL B
Concordia U, MN B
Concordia U, NE B
Concordia U Wisconsin, WI B
Cornell Coll, IA B
Cornerstone U, MI B
Creighton U, NE B
Crown Coll, MN B
Culver-Stockton Coll, MO B
Dakota Wesleyan U, SD B
Dana Coll, NE B
Defiance Coll, OH B
Denison U, OH B
DePaul U, IL B
DePauw U, IN B
Dickinson State U, ND B
Doane Coll, NE B
Dominican U, IL B
Donnelly Coll, KS A
Dordt Coll, IA B
Drake U, IA B
Drury U, MO B
Earlham Coll, IN B
East Central U, OK B
Eastern Illinois U, IL B
Eastern Michigan U, MI B
Edgewood Coll, WI B
Elmhurst Coll, IL B
Emporia State U, KS B
Eureka Coll, IL B
Evangel U, MO B
Fontbonne U, MO B
Fort Hays State U, KS B
Franciscan U of Steubenville, OH B
Franklin Coll, IN B
Goshen Coll, IN B
Graceland U, IA B
Grand Valley State U, MI B
Grand View Coll, IA B
Greenville Coll, IL B
Grinnell Coll, IA B

History (continued)

Gustavus Adolphus Coll, MN B
Hamline U, MN B
Hannibal-LaGrange Coll, MO B
Hanover Coll, IN B
Hastings Coll, NE B
Heidelberg Coll, OH B
Hillsdale Coll, MI B
Hiram Coll, OH B
Hope Coll, MI B
Huntington Coll, IN B
Illinois Coll, IL B
Illinois State U, IL B
Illinois Wesleyan U, IL B
Indiana State U, IN B
Indiana U Bloomington, IN B
Indiana U East, IN A
Indiana U Northwest, IN B
Indiana U–Purdue U Fort Wayne, IN A,B
Indiana U–Purdue U Indianapolis, IN B
Indiana U South Bend, IN B
Indiana U Southeast, IN B
Indiana Wesleyan U, IN A,B
Iowa State U of Science and Technology, IA B
Iowa Wesleyan Coll, IA B
Jamestown Coll, ND B
John Carroll U, OH B
Judson Coll, IL B
Kalamazoo Coll, MI B
Kansas State U, KS B
Kent State U, OH B
Kenyon Coll, OH B
Knox Coll, IL B
Lake Forest Coll, IL B
Lakeland Coll, WI B
Langston U, OK B
Laura and Alvin Siegal Coll of Judaic Studies, OH B
Lawrence U, WI B
Lewis U, IL B
Lincoln Coll, Lincoln, IL A
Lindenwood U, MO B
Loras Coll, IA B
Lourdes Coll, OH A,B
Loyola U Chicago, IL B
Luther Coll, IA B
Macalester Coll, MN B
MacMurray Coll, IL B
Madonna U, MI B
Malone Coll, OH B
Manchester Coll, IN B
Marian Coll, IN A,B
Marian Coll of Fond du Lac, WI B
Marietta Coll, OH B
Marquette U, WI B
Martin U, IN B
Marygrove Coll, MI B
Maryville U of Saint Louis, MO B
McKendree Coll, IL B
McPherson Coll, KS B
Metropolitan State U, MN B
Miami U, OH B
Miami U–Middletown Campus, OH A
Michigan State U, MI B
Michigan Technological U, MI B
MidAmerica Nazarene U, KS B
Midland Lutheran Coll, NE B
Millikin U, IL B
Minnesota State U, Mankato, MN B
Minnesota State U, Moorhead, MN B
Minot State U, ND B
Missouri Southern State Coll, MO B
Missouri Valley Coll, MO B
Missouri Western State Coll, MO B
Monmouth Coll, IL B
Morningside Coll, IA B
Mount Marty Coll, SD B
Mount Mary Coll, WI B
Mount Mercy Coll, IA B
Mount Union Coll, OH B
Mount Vernon Nazarene U, OH B
Muskingum Coll, OH B
Nebraska Wesleyan U, NE B
Newman U, KS B
North Central Coll, IL B
North Dakota State U, ND B
Northeastern Illinois U, IL B
Northeastern State U, OK B
Northern Illinois U, IL B
Northern Michigan U, MI B
Northern State U, SD B
Northland Coll, WI B
North Park U, IL B
Northwestern Coll, IA B
Northwestern Coll, MN B
Northwestern Oklahoma State U, OK B
Northwestern U, IL B
Northwest Missouri State U, MO B
Notre Dame Coll, OH B
Oakland U, MI B
Oberlin Coll, OH B
Ohio Dominican U, OH B
Ohio Northern U, OH B
The Ohio State U, OH B
Ohio U, OH B
Ohio Wesleyan U, OH B
Oklahoma Baptist U, OK B
Oklahoma Christian U, OK B
Oklahoma City U, OK B
Oklahoma Panhandle State U, OK B
Oklahoma State U, OK B
Oklahoma Wesleyan U, OK B
Olivet Coll, MI B
Olivet Nazarene U, IL B
Oral Roberts U, OK B
Ottawa U, KS B
Otterbein Coll, OH B
Park U, MO B
Peru State Coll, NE B
Pillsbury Baptist Bible Coll, MN B
Pittsburg State U, KS B
Principia Coll, IL B
Purdue U, IN B
Purdue U Calumet, IN B
Quincy U, IL B
Ripon Coll, WI B
Rochester Coll, MI B
Rockford Coll, IL B
Rockhurst U, MO B
Rogers State U, OK A
Roosevelt U, IL B
Saginaw Valley State U, MI B
St. Ambrose U, IA B
St. Cloud State U, MN B
Saint John's U, MN B
Saint Joseph's Coll, IN B
Saint Louis U, MO B
Saint Mary-of-the-Woods Coll, IN B
Saint Mary's Coll, IN B
Saint Mary's U of Minnesota, MN B
Saint Mary U, KS B
St. Norbert Coll, WI B
St. Olaf Coll, MN B
Saint Xavier U, IL B
Shawnee State U, OH B
Siena Heights U, MI B
Silver Lake Coll, WI B
Simpson Coll, IA B
South Dakota State U, SD B
Southeastern Oklahoma State U, OK B
Southeast Missouri State U, MO B
Southern Illinois U Carbondale, IL B
Southern Illinois U Edwardsville, IL B
Southern Nazarene U, OK B
Southwest Baptist U, MO B
Southwestern Coll, KS B
Southwestern Oklahoma State U, OK B
Southwest Minnesota State U, MN B
Southwest Missouri State U, MO B
Spring Arbor U, MI B
Stephens Coll, MO B
Sterling Coll, KS B
Tabor Coll, KS B
Taylor U, IN B
Trinity Christian Coll, IL B
Trinity International U, IL B
Truman State U, MO B
Union Coll, NE B
Union Inst & U, OH B
The U of Akron, OH B
U of Central Oklahoma, OK B
U of Chicago, IL B
U of Cincinnati, OH B
U of Dayton, OH B
U of Evansville, IN B
The U of Findlay, OH B
U of Illinois at Chicago, IL B
U of Illinois at Springfield, IL B
U of Illinois at Urbana–Champaign, IL B
U of Indianapolis, IN B
The U of Iowa, IA B
U of Kansas, KS B
U of Michigan, MI B
U of Michigan–Dearborn, MI B
U of Michigan–Flint, MI B
U of Minnesota, Duluth, MN B
U of Minnesota, Morris, MN B
U of Minnesota, Twin Cities Campus, MN B
U of Missouri–Columbia, MO B
U of Missouri–Kansas City, MO B
U of Missouri–Rolla, MO B
U of Missouri–St. Louis, MO B
U of Nebraska at Kearney, NE B
U of Nebraska at Omaha, NE B
U of Nebraska–Lincoln, NE B
U of North Dakota, ND B
U of Northern Iowa, IA B
U of Notre Dame, IN B
U of Oklahoma, OK B
U of Rio Grande, OH A,B
U of St. Francis, IL B
U of Saint Francis, IN B
U of St. Thomas, MN B
U of Science and Arts of Oklahoma, OK B
U of Sioux Falls, SD B
The U of South Dakota, SD B
U of Southern Indiana, IN B
U of Toledo, OH B
U of Tulsa, OK B
U of Wisconsin–Eau Claire, WI B
U of Wisconsin–Green Bay, WI A,B
U of Wisconsin–La Crosse, WI B
U of Wisconsin–Madison, WI B
U of Wisconsin–Milwaukee, WI B
U of Wisconsin–Oshkosh, WI B
U of Wisconsin–Parkside, WI B
U of Wisconsin–Platteville, WI B
U of Wisconsin–River Falls, WI B
U of Wisconsin–Stevens Point, WI B
U of Wisconsin–Superior, WI B
U of Wisconsin–Whitewater, WI B
Urbana U, OH B
Ursuline Coll, OH B
Valley City State U, ND B
Valparaiso U, IN B
Wabash Coll, IN B
Waldorf Coll, IA A,B
Walsh U, OH B
Wartburg Coll, IA B
Washington U in St. Louis, MO B
Wayne State Coll, NE B
Wayne State U, MI B
Webster U, MO B
Western Illinois U, IL B
Western Michigan U, MI B
Westminster Coll, MO B
Wheaton Coll, IL B
Wichita State U, KS B
William Jewell Coll, MO B
William Penn U, IA B
William Woods U, MO B
Wilmington Coll, OH B
Winona State U, MN B
Wisconsin Lutheran Coll, WI B
Wittenberg U, OH B
Wright State U, OH A,B
Xavier U, OH A,B
York Coll, NE B
Youngstown State U, OH B

HISTORY EDUCATION

Bowling Green State U, OH B
Central Michigan U, MI B
Chadron State Coll, NE B
Coll of the Ozarks, MO B
Concordia Coll, MN B
Concordia U, IL B
Concordia U, NE B
Crown Coll, MN B
Culver-Stockton Coll, MO B
Dakota Wesleyan U, SD B
Dana Coll, NE B
Eastern Michigan U, MI B
Elmhurst Coll, IL B
Franklin Coll, IN B

Hastings Coll, NE B
Luther Coll, IA B
McKendree Coll, IL B
Minot State U, ND B
Mount Marty Coll, SD B
North Dakota State U, ND B
Oklahoma Baptist U, OK B
St. Ambrose U, IA B
Saint Xavier U, IL B
Si Tanka Huron U, SD B
Southwestern Oklahoma State U, OK B
Southwest Missouri State U, MO B
Trinity Christian Coll, IL B
Union Coll, NE B
The U of Akron, OH B
U of Central Oklahoma, OK B
U of Illinois at Chicago, IL B
The U of Iowa, IA B
U of Nebraska–Lincoln, NE B
U of Rio Grande, OH B
U of Wisconsin–River Falls, WI B
U of Wisconsin–Superior, WI B
Valley City State U, ND B
Wartburg Coll, IA B
Washington U in St. Louis, MO B
York Coll, NE B
Youngstown State U, OH B

HISTORY OF PHILOSOPHY

Marquette U, WI B
Spring Arbor U, MI B

HISTORY OF SCIENCE AND TECHNOLOGY

Case Western Reserve U, OH B
U of Chicago, IL B
U of Wisconsin–Madison, WI B

HISTORY RELATED

The Franciscan U, IA B
The Ohio State U, OH B
Ohio U, OH B
Saint Mary's U of Minnesota, MN B

HOME ECONOMICS

Ashland U, OH B
Bacone Coll, OK A
Baldwin-Wallace Coll, OH B
Ball State U, IN B
Bluffton Coll, OH B
Central Michigan U, MI B
Central Missouri State U, MO B
Coll of St. Catherine, MN B
Coll of the Ozarks, MO B
Concordia U, NE B
East Central U, OK B
Eastern Illinois U, IL B
Fontbonne U, MO B
Indiana State U, IN B
Iowa State U of Science and Technology, IA B
Kent State U, OH B
Langston U, OK B
Madonna U, MI B
Miami U, OH B
Michigan State U, MI B
Minnesota State U, Mankato, MN B
Mount Vernon Nazarene U, OH A,B
Northeastern State U, OK B
Northwest Missouri State U, MO B
Ohio U, OH B
Oklahoma State U, OK B
Olivet Nazarene U, IL B
Pittsburg State U, KS B
Purdue U, IN B
Southeast Missouri State U, MO B
The U of Akron, OH B
U of Central Oklahoma, OK B
U of Wisconsin–Madison, WI B
Waldorf Coll, IA A
Wayne State Coll, NE B
Western Illinois U, IL B
Youngstown State U, OH B

HOME ECONOMICS EDUCATION

Ashland U, OH B
Baldwin-Wallace Coll, OH B
Ball State U, IN B
Bluffton Coll, OH B
Bowling Green State U, OH B
Central Michigan U, MI B
Central Missouri State U, MO B
Chadron State Coll, NE B
Coll of St. Catherine, MN B
Coll of the Ozarks, MO B
Concordia U, NE B
Eastern Michigan U, MI B
Ferris State U, MI B
Fontbonne U, MO B
Iowa State U of Science and Technology, IA B
Langston U, OK B
Madonna U, MI B
Miami U, OH B
Michigan State U, MI B
Minnesota State U, Mankato, MN B
Mount Vernon Nazarene U, OH B
North Dakota State U, ND B
Northeastern State U, OK B
Northern Illinois U, IL B
Northwest Missouri State U, MO B
Olivet Nazarene U, IL B
Pittsburg State U, KS B
South Dakota State U, SD B
Southeast Missouri State U, MO B
Southwest Missouri State U, MO B
The U of Akron, OH B
U of Central Oklahoma, OK B
U of Illinois at Springfield, IL B
U of Minnesota, Twin Cities Campus, MN B
U of Wisconsin–Madison, WI B
U of Wisconsin–Stevens Point, WI B
U of Wisconsin–Stout, WI B
Wayne State Coll, NE B
Western Michigan U, MI B
Youngstown State U, OH B

HORTICULTURE SCIENCE

Andrews U, MI A
Bacone Coll, OK A
Cameron U, OK B
Coll of the Ozarks, MO B
Iowa State U of Science and Technology, IA B
Kansas State U, KS B
Kent State U, Salem Campus, OH A
Michigan State U, MI B
North Dakota State U, ND B
Northwest Missouri State U, MO B
The Ohio State U, OH B
Oklahoma State U, OK B
Purdue U, IN B
Southeast Missouri State U, MO B
Southwest Missouri State U, MO B
U of Illinois at Urbana–Champaign, IL B
U of Minnesota, Crookston, MN A,B
U of Nebraska–Lincoln, NE B
U of Wisconsin–Madison, WI B
U of Wisconsin–River Falls, WI B

HORTICULTURE SERVICES

Iowa State U of Science and Technology, IA B
Kent State U, OH A
Kent State U, Geauga Campus, OH A
South Dakota State U, SD B

HOSPITALITY MANAGEMENT

Baker Coll of Flint, MI A
Baker Coll of Owosso, MI A
Bowling Green State U, OH B
Central Michigan U, MI B
Eastern Michigan U, MI B
Ferris State U, MI B
Indiana U–Purdue U Fort Wayne, IN B
International Business Coll, Fort Wayne, IN A,B
Kendall Coll, IL A,B
Lakeland Coll, WI B
Lexington Coll, IL A
Madonna U, MI B
Metropolitan State U, MN B
Midstate Coll, IL A
The Ohio State U, OH B
The Ohio State U at Lima, OH B
Roosevelt U, IL B
Siena Heights U, MI A,B
Tiffin U, OH B
The U of Akron, OH A
U of Minnesota, Crookston, MN A
Youngstown State U, OH A,B

HOSPITALITY/ RECREATION MARKETING OPERATIONS

The U of Akron, OH A

HOSPITALITY SERVICES MANAGEMENT RELATED

Indiana U–Purdue U Indianapolis, IN B

HOTEL AND RESTAURANT MANAGEMENT

Ashland U, OH B
Baker Coll of Muskegon, MI A
Baker Coll of Owosso, MI A
Baker Coll of Port Huron, MI A
Central Michigan U, MI B
Central Missouri State U, MO B
Chicago State U, IL B
Coll of the Ozarks, MO B
Davenport U, Grand Rapids, MI A,B
Grand Valley State U, MI B
Indiana U–Purdue U Fort Wayne, IN A
Indiana U–Purdue U Indianapolis, IN A
Iowa State U of Science and Technology, IA B
Kansas State U, KS B
Kendall Coll, IL A,B
Langston U, OK B
Lexington Coll, IL A
Michigan State U, MI B
National American U–Sioux Falls Branch, SD A,B
North Dakota State U, ND B
Northwood U, MI A,B
Oklahoma State U, OK B
Presentation Coll, SD A
Purdue U, IN B
Purdue U Calumet, IN A,B
Purdue U North Central, IN A
South Dakota State U, SD B
Southwest Missouri State U, MO B
The U of Akron, OH A
U of Central Oklahoma, OK B
The U of Findlay, OH B
U of Minnesota, Crookston, MN A,B
U of Missouri–Columbia, MO B
U of Wisconsin–Stout, WI B
Youngstown State U, OH A,B

HOTEL/MOTEL SERVICES MARKETING OPERATIONS

AIB Coll of Business, IA A
Lake Erie Coll, OH B

HOUSING STUDIES

Iowa State U of Science and Technology, IA B
Ohio U, OH B
Southeast Missouri State U, MO B
Southwest Missouri State U, MO B
U of Missouri–Columbia, MO B
U of Northern Iowa, IA B

HUMAN ECOLOGY

Cameron U, OK B
Kansas State U, KS B

HUMANITIES

Alma Coll, MI B
Ancilla Coll, IN A
Antioch Coll, OH B
Antioch U McGregor, OH B
Augsburg Coll, MN B
Aurora U, IL B

Humanities (continued)

Avila U, MO B
Bacone Coll, OK A
Bemidji State U, MN B
Bluffton Coll, OH B
Bowling Green State U, OH B
Central Christian Coll of Kansas, KS A
Coll of Mount St. Joseph, OH B
Coll of Saint Benedict, MN B
Coll of Saint Mary, NE B
The Coll of St. Scholastica, MN B
Columbia Coll, MO B
Concordia Coll, MN B
Concordia U Wisconsin, WI B
The Franciscan U, IA B
Franciscan U of Steubenville, OH B
Grace U, NE B
Grand Valley State U, MI B
Hope Coll, MI B
Indiana State U, IN B
Indiana U Kokomo, IN B
John Carroll U, OH B
Kansas State U, KS B
Kenyon Coll, OH B
Lawrence Technological U, MI B
Lincoln Coll, Lincoln, IL A
Lincoln Coll, Normal, IL A
Loyola U Chicago, IL B
Macalester Coll, MN B
Maranatha Baptist Bible Coll, WI B
Martin U, IN B
Maryville U of Saint Louis, MO B
Michigan State U, MI B
Michigan Technological U, MI A
Midland Lutheran Coll, NE B
Minnesota State U, Mankato, MN B
Monmouth Coll, IL B
Muskingum Coll, OH B
North Central Coll, IL B
North Dakota State U, ND B
Northwestern Coll, IA B
Northwestern U, IL B
Northwest Missouri State U, MO B
Oakland City U, IN B
The Ohio State U, OH B
Ohio U, OH A
Ohio Wesleyan U, OH B
Oklahoma Baptist U, OK B
Oklahoma City U, OK B
Oklahoma Panhandle State U, OK B
Principia Coll, IL B
Purdue U, IN B
Purdue U Calumet, IN B
Quincy U, IL B
Rockford Coll, IL B
St. Gregory's U, OK A,B
Saint John's U, MN B
Saint Joseph's Coll, IN A
Saint Louis U, MO B
Saint Mary-of-the-Woods Coll, IN B
Saint Mary's Coll, IN B
St. Norbert Coll, WI B
Shawnee State U, OH A,B
Shimer Coll, IL B
Siena Heights U, MI B
Southwest Missouri State U, MO B
Tabor Coll, KS B
Tiffin U, OH B
Trinity International U, IL B
Union Inst & U, OH B
The U of Akron, OH B
U of Chicago, IL B
U of Cincinnati, OH A,B
The U of Findlay, OH A
U of Illinois at Urbana–Champaign, IL B
U of Kansas, KS B
U of Michigan, MI B
U of Michigan–Dearborn, MI B
U of Missouri–St. Louis, MO B
U of North Dakota, ND B
U of Northern Iowa, IA B
U of Rio Grande, OH B
U of Sioux Falls, SD A
U of Toledo, OH B
U of Wisconsin–Green Bay, WI A,B
U of Wisconsin–Parkside, WI B
Ursuline Coll, OH B
Viterbo U, WI B
Waldorf Coll, IA A,B
Wichita State U, KS A
Wittenberg U, OH B

HUMAN RESOURCES MANAGEMENT

Antioch U McGregor, OH B
Baker Coll of Owosso, MI A,B
Ball State U, IN B
Black Hills State U, SD B
Bowling Green State U, OH B
Briar Cliff U, IA B
Central Christian Coll of Kansas, KS A
Central Michigan U, MI B
Central Missouri State U, MO B
Cleary U, MI B
Colorado Tech U Sioux Falls Campus, SD B
Davenport U, Lansing, MI B
DePaul U, IL B
East Central U, OK B
Eastern Michigan U, MI B
Franklin U, OH B
Governors State U, IL B
Grace U, NE B
Grand Valley State U, MI B
Hastings Coll, NE B
Indiana Inst of Technology, IN B
Indiana State U, IN B
Judson Coll, IL B
Lewis U, IL B
Lindenwood U, MO B
Loras Coll, IA B
Loyola U Chicago, IL B
Marietta Coll, OH B
Marquette U, WI B
Martin U, IN B
Metropolitan State U, MN B
Miami U, OH B
Michigan State U, MI B
MidAmerica Nazarene U, KS B
Millikin U, IL B
Northeastern Illinois U, IL B
Northeastern State U, OK B
Notre Dame Coll, OH B
Oakland City U, IN B
Oakland U, MI B
The Ohio State U, OH B
Ohio U, OH B
Oklahoma Baptist U, OK B
Oklahoma State U, OK B
Olivet Nazarene U, IL B
Purdue U Calumet, IN B
Rockhurst U, MO B
Roosevelt U, IL B
St. Cloud State U, MN B
Saint Louis U, MO B
Saint Mary-of-the-Woods Coll, IN B
Saint Mary's Coll of Madonna U, MI B
Saint Mary's U of Minnesota, MN B
Silver Lake Coll, WI B
Southeast Missouri State U, MO B
Southwestern Coll, KS B
Spring Arbor U, MI B
Taylor U, IN B
Tiffin U, OH B
Trinity Christian Coll, IL B
Trinity International U, IL B
The U of Akron, OH B
U of Central Oklahoma, OK B
The U of Findlay, OH A,B
U of Indianapolis, IN B
The U of Iowa, IA B
U of Michigan–Flint, MI B
U of Minnesota, Duluth, MN B
U of Nebraska at Omaha, NE B
U of Saint Francis, IN B
U of St. Thomas, MN B
The U of South Dakota, SD B
U of Toledo, OH B
U of Wisconsin–Milwaukee, WI B
U of Wisconsin–Whitewater, WI B
Urbana U, OH A,B
Ursuline Coll, OH B
Valley City State U, ND B
Viterbo U, WI B
Washington U in St. Louis, MO B
Webster U, MO B
Western Illinois U, IL B
Western Michigan U, MI B
Wichita State U, KS B
Winona State U, MN B
Xavier U, OH B
York Coll, NE B

HUMAN RESOURCES MANAGEMENT RELATED

Capella U, MN B
Park U, MO A,B

HUMAN SERVICES

Adrian Coll, MI A,B
Albion Coll, MI B
Antioch U McGregor, OH B
Baker Coll of Clinton Township, MI A
Baker Coll of Flint, MI A
Baker Coll of Muskegon, MI A
Baldwin-Wallace Coll, OH B
Bethel Coll, IN B
Black Hills State U, SD B
Calumet Coll of Saint Joseph, IN B
Chatfield Coll, OH A
Coll of Saint Mary, NE B
Dakota Wesleyan U, SD B
Doane Coll, NE B
Finlandia U, MI B
Fontbonne U, MO B
The Franciscan U, IA B
Grace Bible Coll, MI A,B
Graceland U, IA B
Grand View Coll, IA B
Hannibal-LaGrange Coll, MO B
Hastings Coll, NE B
Indiana Inst of Technology, IN B
Indiana U East, IN A
Judson Coll, IL B
Kendall Coll, IL A,B
Kent State U, OH A
Kent State U, Ashtabula Campus, OH A
Kent State U, Salem Campus, OH A
Lake Erie Coll, OH B
Lindenwood U, MO B
Marian Coll of Fond du Lac, WI B
Metropolitan State U, MN B
Midland Lutheran Coll, NE B
Millikin U, IL B
Missouri Valley Coll, MO B
Mount Vernon Nazarene U, OH A
National-Louis U, IL B
Nebraska Indian Comm Coll, NE A
Ohio U, OH A
Ohio U–Chillicothe, OH A
Ottawa U, KS B
Park U, MO B
Quincy U, IL B
Rochester Comm and Tech Coll, MN A
Roosevelt U, IL B
Saint Mary-of-the-Woods Coll, IN B
Siena Heights U, MI B
Sitting Bull Coll, ND A
Southwest Baptist U, MO B
U of Cincinnati, OH A
U of Minnesota, Morris, MN B
U of Saint Francis, IN A
U of Wisconsin–Oshkosh, WI B
Upper Iowa U, IA B
Waldorf Coll, IA A
Walsh U, OH A,B
William Penn U, IA B

INDIVIDUAL/FAMILY DEVELOPMENT

Antioch Coll, OH B
Antioch U McGregor, OH B
Ashland U, OH B
Bowling Green State U, OH B
Cameron U, OK B
Concordia U, MI B
Crown Coll, MN B
Eastern Michigan U, MI B
Indiana State U, IN B
Indiana U Bloomington, IN B
Kansas State U, KS B
Kent State U, OH B
Lincoln Coll, Lincoln, IL A
Miami U, OH B
National-Louis U, IL B
Northern Illinois U, IL B
The Ohio State U, OH B
Ohio U, OH B
Purdue U, IN B
St. Olaf Coll, MN B

South Dakota State U, SD	B
Southeast Missouri State U, MO	B
Southwest Missouri State U, MO	B
U of Illinois at Urbana–Champaign, IL	B
U of Missouri–Columbia, MO	B
U of Wisconsin–Stout, WI	B
Youngstown State U, OH	B

INDIVIDUAL/FAMILY DEVELOPMENT RELATED

Saint Mary's U of Minnesota, MN	B
U of Toledo, OH	A

INDUSTRIAL ARTS

Andrews U, MI	B
Ball State U, IN	B
Bemidji State U, MN	B
Central Christian Coll of Kansas, KS	A
Chicago State U, IL	B
Coll of the Ozarks, MO	B
Fort Hays State U, KS	B
Langston U, OK	B
McPherson Coll, KS	B
Minnesota State U, Mankato, MN	B
Northeastern State U, OK	B
Northern State U, SD	B
Ohio Northern U, OH	B
Oklahoma Panhandle State U, OK	B
Oklahoma State U, OK	B
Pittsburg State U, KS	B
St. Cloud State U, MN	B
Southwestern Oklahoma State U, OK	B
U of Cincinnati, OH	A
U of Wisconsin–Platteville, WI	B
William Penn U, IA	B

INDUSTRIAL ARTS EDUCATION

Black Hills State U, SD	B
Central Michigan U, MI	B
Central Missouri State U, MO	B
Chadron State Coll, NE	B
Coll of the Ozarks, MO	B
Concordia U, NE	B
Eastern Michigan U, MI	B
Illinois State U, IL	B
Kent State U, OH	B
Northern Illinois U, IL	B
The Ohio State U, OH	B
Oklahoma Panhandle State U, OK	B
Purdue U, IN	B
Southeast Missouri State U, MO	B
Southwestern Oklahoma State U, OK	B
Southwest Missouri State U, MO	B
U of Nebraska–Lincoln, NE	B
U of Northern Iowa, IA	B
U of Wisconsin–Stout, WI	B
Valley City State U, ND	B
Viterbo U, WI	B

INDUSTRIAL DESIGN

The Cleveland Inst of Art, OH	B
Coll for Creative Studies, MI	B
Columbus Coll of Art and Design, OH	B
Ferris State U, MI	A
Finlandia U, MI	B
Kansas City Art Inst, MO	B
Kendall Coll of Art and Design of Ferris State U, MI	B
Milwaukee Inst of Art and Design, WI	B
Northern Michigan U, MI	A,B
Oakland City U, IN	A
The Ohio State U, OH	B
Ohio U–Lancaster, OH	A
Pittsburg State U, KS	B
U of Cincinnati, OH	B
U of Illinois at Chicago, IL	B
U of Illinois at Urbana–Champaign, IL	B
U of Michigan, MI	B
U of Wisconsin–Platteville, WI	B
Western Michigan U, MI	B

INDUSTRIAL/ MANUFACTURING ENGINEERING

Bradley U, IL	B
Central Michigan U, MI	B
Cleveland State U, OH	B
Ferris State U, MI	B
Grand Valley State U, MI	B
Iowa State U of Science and Technology, IA	B
Kansas State U, KS	B
Kent State U, OH	B
Kettering U, MI	B
Lawrence Technological U, MI	B
Marquette U, WI	B
Miami U, OH	B
Michigan Technological U, MI	B
Milwaukee School of Engineering, WI	B
North Dakota State U, ND	B
Northern Illinois U, IL	B
Northwestern U, IL	B
The Ohio State U, OH	B
Ohio U, OH	B
Oklahoma State U, OK	B
Purdue U, IN	B
Purdue U Calumet, IN	B
St. Ambrose U, IA	B
St. Cloud State U, MN	B
South Dakota School of Mines and Technology, SD	B
Southern Illinois U Edwardsville, IL	B
U of Cincinnati, OH	B
U of Illinois at Chicago, IL	B
U of Illinois at Urbana–Champaign, IL	B
The U of Iowa, IA	B
U of Michigan, MI	B
U of Michigan–Dearborn, MI	B
U of Minnesota, Duluth, MN	B
U of Minnesota, Twin Cities Campus, MN	B
U of Missouri–Columbia, MO	B
U of Nebraska–Lincoln, NE	B
U of Oklahoma, OK	B
U of Toledo, OH	A,B
U of Wisconsin–Madison, WI	B
U of Wisconsin–Milwaukee, WI	B
U of Wisconsin–Platteville, WI	B
U of Wisconsin–Stout, WI	B
Wayne State U, MI	B
Western Michigan U, MI	B
Wichita State U, KS	B
Youngstown State U, OH	B

INDUSTRIAL PRODUCTION TECHNOLOGIES RELATED

Chadron State Coll, NE	B
Indiana State U, IN	B
Kent State U, OH	A
Southwestern Coll, KS	B
The U of Akron, OH	B
U of Nebraska–Lincoln, NE	A,B
U of Wisconsin–Stout, WI	B
Wayne State U, MI	B

INDUSTRIAL RADIOLOGIC TECHNOLOGY

Andrews U, MI	B
Baker Coll of Owosso, MI	A,B
Ball State U, IN	A
Briar Cliff U, IA	B
Concordia U Wisconsin, WI	B
Ferris State U, MI	A
Fort Hays State U, KS	A
Jamestown Coll, ND	B
Madonna U, MI	B
Marian Coll of Fond du Lac, WI	B
National-Louis U, IL	B
Newman U, KS	A,B
Saint Mary's Coll of Madonna U, MI	B
Shawnee State U, OH	A
U of Cincinnati, OH	A
U of Oklahoma Health Sciences Center, OK	B
U of Sioux Falls, SD	B
Xavier U, OH	A

INDUSTRIAL TECHNOLOGY

Andrews U, MI	A,B
Baker Coll of Flint, MI	B
Baker Coll of Muskegon, MI	A
Ball State U, IN	A,B
Bemidji State U, MN	B
Black Hills State U, SD	B
Bowling Green State U, OH	B
Bradley U, IL	B
Central Missouri State U, MO	A,B
Eastern Illinois U, IL	B
Eastern Michigan U, MI	B
Ferris State U, MI	A,B
Illinois Inst of Technology, IL	B
Illinois State U, IL	B
Indiana State U, IN	B
Indiana U–Purdue U Fort Wayne, IN	A,B
Kansas State U, KS	A
Kent State U, OH	A,B
Kent State U, Ashtabula Campus, OH	A
Kent State U, Geauga Campus, OH	A
Kent State U, Salem Campus, OH	A
Kent State U, Tuscarawas Campus, OH	A,B
Langston U, OK	B
Lawrence Technological U, MI	A
Miami U–Middletown Campus, OH	A
Minnesota State U, Mankato, MN	B
Minnesota State U, Moorhead, MN	B
Missouri Western State Coll, MO	A
Northeastern State U, OK	B
Northern Illinois U, IL	B
Northern Michigan U, MI	A,B
Ohio Northern U, OH	B
Ohio U, OH	B
Ohio U–Lancaster, OH	A
Oklahoma Panhandle State U, OK	A,B
Oklahoma State U, OK	B
Pittsburg State U, KS	B
Purdue U, IN	B
Purdue U Calumet, IN	A,B
Purdue U North Central, IN	A
Saginaw Valley State U, MI	B
Saint Mary's U of Minnesota, MN	B
South Dakota State U, SD	B
Southeastern Oklahoma State U, OK	B
Southeast Missouri State U, MO	B
Southern Illinois U Carbondale, IL	B
Southwestern Coll, KS	B
Southwestern Oklahoma State U, OK	B
Tri-State U, IN	A
The U of Akron, OH	A,B
U of Cincinnati, OH	A
U of Dayton, OH	B
U of Nebraska–Lincoln, NE	B
U of North Dakota, ND	B
U of Northern Iowa, IA	B
U of Rio Grande, OH	A,B
U of Toledo, OH	A,B
U of Wisconsin–Platteville, WI	B
U of Wisconsin–Stout, WI	B
Wayne State U, MI	B
Western Illinois U, IL	B
Western Michigan U, MI	B
William Penn U, IA	B
Wright State U, OH	A

INFORMATION SCIENCES/ SYSTEMS

Alma Coll, MI	B
Anderson U, IN	B
Andrews U, MI	B
Aquinas Coll, MI	B
Ashland U, OH	B
Avila U, MO	B
Baker Coll of Cadillac, MI	A,B
Baker Coll of Clinton Township, MI	A
Baker Coll of Flint, MI	A,B
Baker Coll of Jackson, MI	A,B
Baker Coll of Muskegon, MI	A,B
Baker Coll of Owosso, MI	A,B
Baker Coll of Port Huron, MI	A,B
Baker U, KS	B
Baldwin-Wallace Coll, OH	B
Ball State U, IN	A,B

Information Sciences/Systems (continued)

Bemidji State U, MN	B
Benedictine U, IL	B
Bradley U, IL	B
Brown Coll, MN	A
Bryant and Stratton Coll, WI	A
Buena Vista U, IA	B
Calumet Coll of Saint Joseph, IN	A,B
Cameron U, OK	B
Carroll Coll, WI	B
Cedarville U, OH	B
Central Coll, IA	B
Chadron State Coll, NE	B
Chicago State U, IL	B
Clarke Coll, IA	B
Cleary U, MI	B
Cleveland State U, OH	B
Coll of Mount St. Joseph, OH	A,B
Coll of Saint Mary, NE	A,B
Colorado Tech U Sioux Falls Campus, SD	A,B
Columbia Coll, MO	A,B
Concordia U, IL	B
Concordia U, MI	B
Cornerstone U, MI	B
Culver-Stockton Coll, MO	B
Dakota State U, SD	A,B
Davenport U, Grand Rapids, MI	A,B
Davenport U, Kalamazoo, MI	A
Davenport U, Lansing, MI	A,B
DePaul U, IL	B
DeVry U, Addison, IL	B
DeVry U, Chicago, IL	B
DeVry U, Tinley Park, IL	B
DeVry U, MO	B
DeVry U, OH	B
Dominican U, IL	B
Drake U, IA	B
Eastern Michigan U, MI	B
Edgewood Coll, WI	B
Emporia State U, KS	B
Ferris State U, MI	B
Fontbonne U, MO	B
Fort Hays State U, KS	B
Goshen Coll, IN	B
Grand Valley State U, MI	B
Grand View Coll, IA	B
Hamilton Coll, IA	A
Hannibal-LaGrange Coll, MO	B
Harris-Stowe State Coll, MO	B
Heidelberg Coll, OH	B
Illinois Coll, IL	B
Illinois Inst of Technology, IL	B
Illinois State U, IL	B
Indiana Inst of Technology, IN	A,B
Indiana U–Purdue U Fort Wayne, IN	A,B
Iowa Wesleyan Coll, IA	B
Judson Coll, IL	B
Kansas State U, KS	B
Kendall Coll, IL	A,B
Kettering U, MI	B
Lawrence Technological U, MI	B
Lewis Coll of Business, MI	A
Lincoln Coll, Normal, IL	A
Loyola U Chicago, IL	B
MacMurray Coll, IL	B
Madonna U, MI	B
Marietta Coll, OH	B
Marquette U, WI	B
McKendree Coll, IL	B
Metropolitan State U, MN	B
Miami U–Middletown Campus, OH	A
Michigan Technological U, MI	B
Midstate Coll, IL	A
Minnesota School of Business-Richfield, MN	A
Minnesota State U, Mankato, MN	B
Missouri Southern State Coll, MO	A,B
Missouri Western State Coll, MO	B
Mount Union Coll, OH	B
National American U, SD	A,B
National American U–Sioux Falls Branch, SD	A,B
National-Louis U, IL	B
Nebraska Wesleyan U, NE	B
Newman U, KS	A,B
Northern Michigan U, MI	B
Northland Coll, WI	B
Northwestern Oklahoma State U, OK	B
Northwest Missouri State U, MO	B
Notre Dame Coll, OH	B
Oakland City U, IN	A,B
Ohio Dominican U, OH	B
The Ohio State U, OH	B
Oklahoma Baptist U, OK	B
Oklahoma Christian U, OK	B
Oklahoma Panhandle State U, OK	A,B
Oklahoma State U, OK	B
Oklahoma Wesleyan U, OK	A,B
Olivet Nazarene U, IL	B
Ottawa U, KS	B
Pittsburg State U, KS	B
Purdue U Calumet, IN	B
Purdue U North Central, IN	A
Quincy U, IL	B
Rockhurst U, MO	B
Rogers State U, OK	A
St. Ambrose U, IA	B
St. Cloud State U, MN	B
Saint Mary-of-the-Woods Coll, IN	B
Saint Mary's Coll of Madonna U, MI	B
Saint Mary's U of Minnesota, MN	B
Saint Mary U, KS	B
Shawnee State U, OH	A
Siena Heights U, MI	A,B
Simpson Coll, IA	B
Si Tanka Huron U, SD	A,B
South Dakota State U, SD	B
Southeastern Oklahoma State U, OK	B
Southeast Missouri State U, MO	B
Southern Nazarene U, OK	B
Southwest Baptist U, MO	B
Taylor U, IN	B
Tiffin U, OH	B
Trinity Christian Coll, IL	B
Union Coll, NE	A,B
U of Cincinnati, OH	A,B
U of Dayton, OH	B
U of Indianapolis, IN	A,B
The U of Iowa, IA	B
U of Mary, ND	B
U of Michigan–Dearborn, MI	B
U of Minnesota, Crookston, MN	A,B
U of Missouri–Kansas City, MO	B
U of Missouri–Rolla, MO	B
U of Nebraska at Omaha, NE	B
U of Northern Iowa, IA	B
U of Sioux Falls, SD	B
The U of South Dakota, SD	B
U of Toledo, OH	B
U of Tulsa, OK	B
U of Wisconsin–Green Bay, WI	A,B
U of Wisconsin–River Falls, WI	B
U of Wisconsin–Superior, WI	B
Viterbo U, WI	B
Waldorf Coll, IA	A,B
Wartburg Coll, IA	B
Washington U in St. Louis, MO	B
Wayne State Coll, NE	B
Wayne State U, MI	B
Webster U, MO	B
Wilberforce U, OH	B
William Jewell Coll, MO	B
Winona State U, MN	B
Youngstown State U, OH	A,B

INFORMATION TECHNOLOGY

Bryant and Stratton Coll, WI	A
Capella U, MN	B
ITT Tech Inst, Mount Prospect, IL	B
ITT Tech Inst, Fort Wayne, IN	B
ITT Tech Inst, Indianapolis, IN	B
ITT Tech Inst, Newburgh, IN	B
ITT Tech Inst, Arnold, MO	B
ITT Tech Inst, Earth City, MO	B
ITT Tech Inst, Green Bay, WI	B
ITT Tech Inst, Greenfield, WI	B
U of Phoenix–Metro Detroit Campus, MI	B
U of Phoenix–Oklahoma City Campus, OK	B
U of Phoenix–West Michigan Campus, MI	B

INSTITUTIONAL FOOD SERVICES

Dominican U, IL	B

INSTRUMENTATION TECHNOLOGY

Indiana State U, IN	B
Shawnee State U, OH	A
Spartan School of Aeronautics, OK	A

INSURANCE/RISK MANAGEMENT

Ball State U, IN	B
Bradley U, IL	B
Ferris State U, MI	B
Illinois State U, IL	B
Illinois Wesleyan U, IL	B
Indiana State U, IN	B
Martin U, IN	B
Minnesota State U, Mankato, MN	B
The Ohio State U, OH	B
Olivet Coll, MI	B
Roosevelt U, IL	B
St. Cloud State U, MN	B
Southwest Missouri State U, MO	B
U of Cincinnati, OH	A,B
U of Minnesota, Twin Cities Campus, MN	B
U of Wisconsin–Madison, WI	B

INTERDISCIPLINARY STUDIES

Antioch Coll, OH	B
Augsburg Coll, MN	B
Baldwin-Wallace Coll, OH	B
Beloit Coll, WI	B
Blackburn Coll, IL	B
Briar Cliff U, IA	B
Calvin Coll, MI	B
Cameron U, OK	A,B
Capital U, OH	B
Cardinal Stritch U, WI	A
Carleton Coll, MN	B
Central Coll, IA	B
Central Methodist Coll, MO	A,B
Central Michigan U, MI	B
Chadron State Coll, NE	B
Cleveland State U, OH	B
Coe Coll, IA	B
Coll of the Ozarks, MO	B
The Coll of Wooster, OH	B
Columbia Coll Chicago, IL	B
Concordia U, MN	B
Cornell Coll, IA	B
Cornerstone U, MI	B
Dana Coll, NE	B
DePaul U, IL	B
DePauw U, IN	B
Earlham Coll, IN	B
Eastern Michigan U, MI	B
Elmhurst Coll, IL	B
Franklin U, OH	B
Grand Valley State U, MI	B
Grand View Coll, IA	B
Grinnell Coll, IA	B
Gustavus Adolphus Coll, MN	B
Harris-Stowe State Coll, MO	B
Hastings Coll, NE	B
Hillsdale Coll, MI	B
Hillsdale Free Will Baptist Coll, OK	A,B
Hope Coll, MI	B
Illinois Coll, IL	B
Illinois Wesleyan U, IL	B
Iowa State U of Science and Technology, IA	B
John Carroll U, OH	B
Kalamazoo Coll, MI	B
Kansas State U, KS	A
Kendall Coll, IL	B
Kent State U, Stark Campus, OH	B
Kenyon Coll, OH	B
Luther Coll, IA	B
Macalester Coll, MN	B
Maharishi U of Management, IA	A,B
Manchester Coll, IN	B
Marquette U, WI	B
Martin Luther Coll, MN	B
Maryville U of Saint Louis, MO	B
McPherson Coll, KS	B
Miami U, OH	B

Miami U–Middletown Campus, OH	A
Millikin U, IL	B
Minneapolis Coll of Art and Design, MN	B
Minnesota State U, Moorhead, MN	B
Morningside Coll, IA	B
Mount Union Coll, OH	B
Muskingum Coll, OH	B
Nebraska Wesleyan U, NE	B
Northland Coll, WI	B
Northwestern U, IL	B
Oakland City U, IN	B
Oakland U, MI	B
Oberlin Coll, OH	B
Ohio Dominican U, OH	A,B
Ohio U, OH	B
Ohio U–Southern Campus, OH	A
Oklahoma Baptist U, OK	B
Olivet Nazarene U, IL	B
Purdue U, IN	B
Quincy U, IL	B
Reformed Bible Coll, MI	B
Ripon Coll, WI	B
Rochester Coll, MI	B
Saginaw Valley State U, MI	B
St. Cloud State U, MN	B
Saint Mary's Coll, IN	B
Saint Mary U, KS	B
St. Norbert Coll, WI	B
Silver Lake Coll, WI	B
South Dakota School of Mines and Technology, SD	B
Southeast Missouri State U, MO	B
Southern Nazarene U, OK	B
Southwest Minnesota State U, MN	B
Stephens Coll, MO	B
Sterling Coll, KS	B
Tabor Coll, KS	A,B
Taylor U, Fort Wayne Campus, IN	B
The U of Akron, OH	A,B
U of Chicago, IL	B
U of Illinois at Springfield, IL	B
The U of Iowa, IA	B
U of Mary, ND	B
U of Michigan, MI	B
U of Michigan–Dearborn, MI	B
U of Minnesota, Crookston, MN	B
U of Minnesota, Duluth, MN	B
U of Missouri–Columbia, MO	B
U of Missouri–Kansas City, MO	B
U of Missouri–St. Louis, MO	B
U of Nebraska at Omaha, NE	B
U of St. Thomas, MN	B
U of Sioux Falls, SD	A,B
U of Wisconsin–Green Bay, WI	A,B
U of Wisconsin–Milwaukee, WI	B
U of Wisconsin–Parkside, WI	B
Valparaiso U, IN	B
Washington U in St. Louis, MO	B
Wayne State Coll, NE	B
Wayne State U, MI	B
Webster U, MO	B
William Jewell Coll, MO	B
William Woods U, MO	B
Wisconsin Lutheran Coll, WI	B
Wittenberg U, OH	B

INTERIOR ARCHITECTURE

Central Michigan U, MI	B
Central Missouri State U, MO	B
Indiana State U, IN	B
Kansas State U, KS	B
Kent State U, OH	A
Lawrence Technological U, MI	B
Michigan State U, MI	B
Minneapolis Coll of Art and Design, MN	B
Ohio U, OH	B
U of Oklahoma, OK	B

INTERIOR DESIGN

Adrian Coll, MI	B
The Art Insts International Minnesota, MN	A
Baker Coll of Auburn Hills, MI	A
Baker Coll of Clinton Township, MI	A
Baker Coll of Flint, MI	A,B
Baker Coll of Muskegon, MI	A
Baker Coll of Owosso, MI	A
Baker Coll of Port Huron, MI	A
Bethel Coll, IN	B
Central Missouri State U, MO	B
The Cleveland Inst of Art, OH	B
Coll for Creative Studies, MI	B
Coll of Mount St. Joseph, OH	A,B
Columbia Coll Chicago, IL	B
Columbus Coll of Art and Design, OH	B
Concordia U Wisconsin, WI	B
Eastern Michigan U, MI	B
Ferris State U, MI	B
Harrington Inst of Interior Design, IL	A,B
The Illinois Inst of Art, IL	A,B
The Illinois Inst of Art-Schaumburg, IL	B
Indiana U Bloomington, IN	B
Indiana U–Purdue U Fort Wayne, IN	A
Indiana U–Purdue U Indianapolis, IN	B
International Academy of Design & Technology, IL	A,B
Iowa State U of Science and Technology, IA	B
Kansas State U, KS	B
Kendall Coll of Art and Design of Ferris State U, MI	B
Kent State U, OH	B
Marian Coll, IN	A
Maryville U of Saint Louis, MO	B
Miami U, OH	B
Milwaukee Inst of Art and Design, WI	B
Minnesota State U, Mankato, MN	B
Mount Mary Coll, WI	B
North Dakota State U, ND	B
Northwest Missouri State U, MO	B
The Ohio State U, OH	B
Oklahoma Christian U, OK	B
Oklahoma State U, OK	B
Park U, MO	B
Pittsburg State U, KS	B
Robert Morris Coll, IL	A
South Dakota State U, SD	B
Southern Illinois U Carbondale, IL	B
The U of Akron, OH	B
U of Central Oklahoma, OK	B
U of Cincinnati, OH	B
U of Michigan, MI	B
U of Minnesota, Twin Cities Campus, MN	B
U of Nebraska at Omaha, NE	B
U of Northern Iowa, IA	B
U of Wisconsin–Madison, WI	B
U of Wisconsin–Stevens Point, WI	B
Ursuline Coll, OH	B
Wayne State Coll, NE	B
Western Michigan U, MI	B
William Woods U, MO	B

INTERIOR ENVIRONMENTS

Ohio U, OH	B
The U of Akron, OH	B

INTERNATIONAL AGRICULTURE

Iowa State U of Science and Technology, IA	B
MidAmerica Nazarene U, KS	B

INTERNATIONAL BUSINESS

Adrian Coll, MI	B
Alma Coll, MI	B
Alverno Coll, WI	B
Aquinas Coll, MI	B
Augsburg Coll, MN	B
Avila U, MO	B
Baker U, KS	B
Benedictine U, IL	B
Bethany Coll, KS	B
Bethel Coll, IN	B
Bowling Green State U, OH	B
Bradley U, IL	B
Buena Vista U, IA	B
Butler U, IN	B
Cardinal Stritch U, WI	B
Cedarville U, OH	B
Central Coll, IA	B
Central Michigan U, MI	B
Clarke Coll, IA	B
Coll of St. Catherine, MN	B
The Coll of St. Scholastica, MN	B
Coll of the Ozarks, MO	B
Columbia Coll, MO	B
Concordia Coll, MN	B
Cornell Coll, IA	B
Creighton U, NE	B
Davenport U, Grand Rapids, MI	B
DePaul U, IL	B
Dickinson State U, ND	B
Dominican U, IL	B
Drake U, IA	B
Drury U, MO	B
Eastern Michigan U, MI	B
Elmhurst Coll, IL	B
Ferris State U, MI	B
Finlandia U, MI	B
Franklin Coll, IN	B
Grace Coll, IN	B
Graceland U, IA	B
Grand Valley State U, MI	B
Gustavus Adolphus Coll, MN	B
Hamline U, MN	B
Hiram Coll, OH	B
Illinois State U, IL	B
Illinois Wesleyan U, IL	B
Iowa State U of Science and Technology, IA	B
Judson Coll, IL	B
Lake Erie Coll, OH	B
Lakeland Coll, WI	B
Loras Coll, IA	B
Luther Coll, IA	B
Madonna U, MI	B
Marietta Coll, OH	B
Marquette U, WI	B
Marygrove Coll, MI	B
McPherson Coll, KS	B
Metropolitan State U, MN	B
Millikin U, IL	B
Milwaukee School of Engineering, WI	B
Minnesota State U, Mankato, MN	B
Minnesota State U, Moorhead, MN	B
Minot State U, ND	B
Missouri Southern State Coll, MO	B
Mount Union Coll, OH	B
Muskingum Coll, OH	B
National-Louis U, IL	B
Nebraska Wesleyan U, NE	B
North Central Coll, IL	B
Northern State U, SD	B
North Park U, IL	B
Northwestern Coll, MN	B
Northwest Missouri State U, MO	B
Northwood U, MI	A,B
Notre Dame Coll, OH	B
Ohio Dominican U, OH	B
Ohio Northern U, OH	B
The Ohio State U, OH	B
Ohio U, OH	B
Ohio Wesleyan U, OH	B
Oklahoma Baptist U, OK	B
Oklahoma City U, OK	B
Oklahoma State U, OK	B
Otterbein Coll, OH	B
Roosevelt U, IL	B
St. Ambrose U, IA	B
St. Cloud State U, MN	B
Saint Joseph's Coll, IN	B
Saint Louis U, MO	B
Saint Mary's Coll, IN	B
Saint Mary's U of Minnesota, MN	B
St. Norbert Coll, WI	B
Saint Xavier U, IL	B
Simpson Coll, IA	B
Taylor U, IN	B
Taylor U, Fort Wayne Campus, IN	B
Tiffin U, OH	B
The U of Akron, OH	B
U of Dayton, OH	B
U of Evansville, IN	B
The U of Findlay, OH	B
U of Indianapolis, IN	B
The U of Iowa, IA	B
U of Minnesota, Twin Cities Campus, MN	B
U of Missouri–Columbia, MO	B
U of Nebraska–Lincoln, NE	B
U of Oklahoma, OK	B

International Business (continued)

U of Rio Grande, OH B
U of Saint Francis, IN B
U of St. Thomas, MN B
U of Toledo, OH B
U of Tulsa, OK B
U of Wisconsin–La Crosse, WI B
Valparaiso U, IN B
Wartburg Coll, IA B
Washington U in St. Louis, MO B
Wayne State Coll, NE B
Webster U, MO B
Westminster Coll, MO B
Wichita State U, KS B
William Jewell Coll, MO B
William Woods U, MO B
Wittenberg U, OH B

INTERNATIONAL BUSINESS MARKETING

Eastern Michigan U, MI B
Oklahoma Baptist U, OK B

INTERNATIONAL ECONOMICS

Carthage Coll, WI B
Coll of St. Catherine, MN B
Hamline U, MN B
Hastings Coll, NE B
Hiram Coll, OH B
John Carroll U, OH B
Lawrence U, WI B
Ohio U, OH B
Rockford Coll, IL B
Taylor U, IN B
Valparaiso U, IN B
Washington U in St. Louis, MO B
Youngstown State U, OH B

INTERNATIONAL FINANCE

Washington U in St. Louis, MO B

INTERNATIONAL RELATIONS

Adrian Coll, MI B
Albion Coll, MI B
Alverno Coll, WI B
Antioch Coll, OH B
Aquinas Coll, MI B
Ashland U, OH B
Augsburg Coll, MN B
Augustana Coll, SD B
Baldwin-Wallace Coll, OH B
Beloit Coll, WI B
Benedictine U, IL B
Bethel Coll, MN B
Bowling Green State U, OH B
Bradley U, IL B
Butler U, IN B
Calvin Coll, MI B
Capital U, OH B
Carleton Coll, MN B
Carroll Coll, WI B
Case Western Reserve U, OH B
Cedarville U, OH B
Central Michigan U, MI B
Cleveland State U, OH B
Coll of St. Catherine, MN B
The Coll of St. Scholastica, MN B
The Coll of Wooster, OH B
Concordia Coll, MN B
Cornell Coll, IA B
Creighton U, NE B
Denison U, OH B
DePaul U, IL B
Doane Coll, NE B
Drake U, IA B
Earlham Coll, IN B
Edgewood Coll, WI B
Graceland U, IA B
Grand Valley State U, MI B
Hamline U, MN B
Hanover Coll, IN B
Hastings Coll, NE B
Heidelberg Coll, OH B
Hillsdale Coll, MI B
Illinois Coll, IL B
Illinois Wesleyan U, IL B
Iowa State U of Science and Technology, IA B
John Carroll U, OH B
Kent State U, OH B
Kenyon Coll, OH B
Knox Coll, IL B
Lawrence U, WI B
Lindenwood U, MO B
Loras Coll, IA B
Loyola U Chicago, IL B
Luther Coll, IA B
Macalester Coll, MN B
Marian Coll of Fond du Lac, WI B
Marquette U, WI B
McKendree Coll, IL B
Miami U, OH B
Michigan State U, MI B
Millikin U, IL B
Minnesota State U, Mankato, MN B
Missouri Southern State Coll, MO B
Mount Mary Coll, WI B
Mount Mercy Coll, IA B
Muskingum Coll, OH B
Nebraska Wesleyan U, NE B
North Central Coll, IL B
North Dakota State U, ND B
Northern Michigan U, MI B
North Park U, IL B
Northwestern U, IL B
Oakland U, MI B
Ohio Northern U, OH B
The Ohio State U, OH B
Ohio U, OH B
Ohio Wesleyan U, OH B
Olivet Coll, MI B
Oral Roberts U, OK B
Otterbein Coll, OH B
Rockford Coll, IL B
Rockhurst U, MO B
Roosevelt U, IL B
Saginaw Valley State U, MI B
St. Cloud State U, MN B
Saint Joseph's Coll, IN B
Saint Louis U, MO B
St. Norbert Coll, WI B
Saint Xavier U, IL B
Shawnee State U, OH B
Simpson Coll, IA B
Southern Nazarene U, OK B
Stephens Coll, MO B
Tabor Coll, KS B
Taylor U, IN B
Tiffin U, OH B
Union Coll, NE B
U of Cincinnati, OH B
U of Dayton, OH B
U of Evansville, IN B
U of Indianapolis, IN B
The U of Iowa, IA B
U of Kansas, KS B
U of Michigan, MI B
U of Michigan–Dearborn, MI B
U of Minnesota, Duluth, MN B
U of Minnesota, Twin Cities Campus, MN B
U of Missouri–St. Louis, MO B
U of Nebraska at Kearney, NE B
U of Nebraska at Omaha, NE B
U of Nebraska–Lincoln, NE B
U of St. Thomas, MN B
U of Toledo, OH B
U of Wisconsin–Madison, WI B
U of Wisconsin–Milwaukee, WI B
U of Wisconsin–Oshkosh, WI B
U of Wisconsin–Parkside, WI B
U of Wisconsin–Platteville, WI B
U of Wisconsin–Stevens Point, WI B
U of Wisconsin–Whitewater, WI B
Valparaiso U, IN B
Walsh U, OH B
Wartburg Coll, IA B
Washington U in St. Louis, MO B
Wayne State U, MI B
Webster U, MO B
Westminster Coll, MO B
Wheaton Coll, IL B
William Jewell Coll, MO B
William Woods U, MO B
Winona State U, MN B
Wittenberg U, OH B
Wright State U, OH B
Xavier U, OH B

INTERNET

Franklin U, OH B
ITT Tech Inst, Mount Prospect, IL A
ITT Tech Inst, Fort Wayne, IN A
ITT Tech Inst, Indianapolis, IN A
ITT Tech Inst, Newburgh, IN A
ITT Tech Inst, Arnold, MO A
ITT Tech Inst, Earth City, MO A
ITT Tech Inst, Green Bay, WI A
ITT Tech Inst, Greenfield, WI A

ISLAMIC STUDIES

East-West U, IL B
The Ohio State U, OH B
U of Michigan, MI B
Washington U in St. Louis, MO B

ITALIAN

DePaul U, IL B
Dominican U, IL B
Indiana U Bloomington, IN B
Lake Erie Coll, OH B
Loyola U Chicago, IL B
Northwestern U, IL B
The Ohio State U, OH B
U of Chicago, IL B
U of Illinois at Chicago, IL B
U of Illinois at Urbana–Champaign, IL B
The U of Iowa, IA B
U of Michigan, MI B
U of Minnesota, Twin Cities Campus, MN B
U of Notre Dame, IN B
U of Wisconsin–Madison, WI B
U of Wisconsin–Milwaukee, WI B
Washington U in St. Louis, MO B
Wayne State U, MI B
Youngstown State U, OH B

ITALIAN STUDIES

Dominican U, IL B
Lake Erie Coll, OH B

JAPANESE

Antioch Coll, OH B
Ball State U, IN B
DePaul U, IL B
Eastern Michigan U, MI B
Gustavus Adolphus Coll, MN B
Indiana U Bloomington, IN B
Mount Union Coll, OH B
North Central Coll, IL B
The Ohio State U, OH B
U of Chicago, IL B
The U of Findlay, OH B
The U of Iowa, IA B
U of Kansas, KS B
U of Michigan, MI B
U of Minnesota, Twin Cities Campus, MN B
U of Notre Dame, IN B
U of Wisconsin–Madison, WI B
Washington U in St. Louis, MO B
Winona State U, MN A

JAZZ

Aquinas Coll, MI B
Augustana Coll, IL B
Bowling Green State U, OH B
Capital U, OH B
Chicago State U, IL B
DePaul U, IL B
Indiana U Bloomington, IN B
Indiana U South Bend, IN A
Lincoln Coll, Lincoln, IL A
North Central Coll, IL B
Northwestern U, IL B
Oberlin Coll, OH B
The Ohio State U, OH B
Roosevelt U, IL B
U of Cincinnati, OH B
The U of Iowa, IA B
U of Michigan, MI B
U of Minnesota, Duluth, MN B
Webster U, MO B

JOURNALISM

Andrews U, MI B
Ashland U, OH B
Augustana Coll, SD B
Bacone Coll, OK A
Ball State U, IN A,B
Bemidji State U, MN B
Benedictine Coll, KS B

Bethel Coll, IN A
Bowling Green State U, OH B
Bradley U, IL B
Butler U, IN B
Cameron U, OK B
Carroll Coll, WI B
Central Christian Coll of Kansas, KS A
Central Michigan U, MI B
Central Missouri State U, MO B
Cincinnati Bible Coll and Seminary, OH B
Coll of St. Catherine, MN B
Coll of the Ozarks, MO B
Columbia Coll Chicago, IL B
Concordia Coll, MN B
Creighton U, NE A,B
Dordt Coll, IA B
Drake U, IA B
Eastern Illinois U, IL B
Eastern Michigan U, MI B
Evangel U, MO A,B
Fort Hays State U, KS B
The Franciscan U, IA B
Franklin Coll, IN B
Goshen Coll, IN B
Grace U, NE B
Grand Valley State U, MI B
Grand View Coll, IA B
Hastings Coll, NE B
Indiana State U, IN B
Indiana U Bloomington, IN B
Indiana U–Purdue U Indianapolis, IN B
Indiana U Southeast, IN A
Iowa State U of Science and Technology, IA B
Judson Coll, IL B
Kansas State U, KS B
Langston U, OK B
Lewis U, IL B
Lincoln Coll, Lincoln, IL A
Lindenwood U, MO B
Loras Coll, IA B
Loyola U Chicago, IL B
MacMurray Coll, IL B
Madonna U, MI A,B
Malone Coll, OH B
Manchester Coll, IN A
Marietta Coll, OH B
Marquette U, WI B
Miami U, OH B
Michigan State U, MI B
Midland Lutheran Coll, NE B
Minnesota State U, Mankato, MN B
Minnesota State U, Moorhead, MN B
Mount Vernon Nazarene U, OH B
Muskingum Coll, OH B
Northeastern State U, OK B
Northern Illinois U, IL B
Northwestern Coll, MN B
Northwestern U, IL B
Northwest Missouri State U, MO B
Oakland U, MI B
The Ohio State U, OH B
Ohio U, OH B
Ohio Wesleyan U, OH B
Oklahoma Baptist U, OK B
Oklahoma Christian U, OK B
Oklahoma City U, OK B
Oklahoma State U, OK B
Olivet Coll, MI B
Olivet Nazarene U, IL B
Oral Roberts U, OK B
Otterbein Coll, OH B
Pittsburg State U, KS B
Purdue U Calumet, IN B
Quincy U, IL B
Roosevelt U, IL B
St. Ambrose U, IA B
St. Cloud State U, MN B
Saint Mary-of-the-Woods Coll, IN B
Saint Mary's U of Minnesota, MN B
South Dakota State U, SD B
Southeast Missouri State U, MO B
Southern Illinois U Carbondale, IL B
Southern Nazarene U, OK B
Southwest Missouri State U, MO B
Spring Arbor U, MI B
Tabor Coll, KS B
Truman State U, MO B
Union Coll, NE B
U of Central Oklahoma, OK B
U of Dayton, OH B
The U of Findlay, OH B
U of Illinois at Urbana–Champaign, IL B
The U of Iowa, IA B
U of Kansas, KS B
U of Michigan, MI B
U of Minnesota, Twin Cities Campus, MN B
U of Missouri–Columbia, MO B
U of Nebraska at Kearney, NE B
U of Nebraska at Omaha, NE B
U of Oklahoma, OK B
U of St. Thomas, MN B
The U of South Dakota, SD B
U of Southern Indiana, IN B
U of Toledo, OH B
U of Wisconsin–Eau Claire, WI B
U of Wisconsin–Madison, WI B
U of Wisconsin–Milwaukee, WI B
U of Wisconsin–Oshkosh, WI B
U of Wisconsin–River Falls, WI B
U of Wisconsin–Superior, WI B
U of Wisconsin–Whitewater, WI B
Waldorf Coll, IA A,B
Wartburg Coll, IA B
Wayne State Coll, NE B
Wayne State U, MI B
Webster U, MO B
Western Illinois U, IL B
Western Michigan U, MI B
Winona State U, MN B
Youngstown State U, OH B

JOURNALISM AND MASS COMMUNICATION RELATED

Kent State U, OH B
Ohio U, OH B
Saint Mary's U of Minnesota, MN B
U of Nebraska–Lincoln, NE B
U of St. Thomas, MN B

JUDAIC STUDIES

DePaul U, IL B
Hamline U, MN B
Indiana U Bloomington, IN B
Laura and Alvin Siegal Coll of Judaic Studies, OH B
Oberlin Coll, OH B
The Ohio State U, OH B
U of Chicago, IL B
U of Cincinnati, OH B
U of Michigan, MI B
U of Minnesota, Twin Cities Campus, MN B
U of Missouri–Kansas City, MO B
Washington U in St. Louis, MO B

LABOR/PERSONNEL RELATIONS

Bowling Green State U, OH B
Cleveland State U, OH B
Ferris State U, MI B
Governors State U, IL B
Grand Valley State U, MI B
Indiana U Bloomington, IN A,B
Indiana U Kokomo, IN A,B
Indiana U Northwest, IN A,B
Indiana U–Purdue U Fort Wayne, IN A,B
Indiana U–Purdue U Indianapolis, IN A,B
Indiana U South Bend, IN A,B
Indiana U Southeast, IN A,B
Rockhurst U, MO B
The U of Iowa, IA B
U of Wisconsin–Madison, WI B
U of Wisconsin–Milwaukee, WI B
Wayne State U, MI B
Winona State U, MN B
Youngstown State U, OH A

LANDSCAPE ARCHITECTURE

Ball State U, IN B
Iowa State U of Science and Technology, IA B
Kansas State U, KS B
Kent State U, OH A
Michigan State U, MI B
North Dakota State U, ND B
Northwest Missouri State U, MO B
The Ohio State U, OH B
Oklahoma State U, OK B
Purdue U, IN B
U of Illinois at Urbana–Champaign, IL B
U of Michigan, MI B
U of Minnesota, Twin Cities Campus, MN B
U of Wisconsin–Madison, WI B

LANDSCAPING MANAGEMENT

Andrews U, MI B
Oklahoma State U, OK B
Rochester Comm and Tech Coll, MN A
South Dakota State U, SD B

LAND USE MANAGEMENT

Grand Valley State U, MI B
Northern Michigan U, MI B
Northland Coll, WI B
U of Wisconsin–Platteville, WI B
U of Wisconsin–River Falls, WI B

LASER/OPTICAL TECHNOLOGY

Indiana U Bloomington, IN A

LATIN AMERICAN STUDIES

Ball State U, IN B
Beloit Coll, WI B
Carleton Coll, MN B
Central Coll, IA B
The Coll of Wooster, OH B
Cornell Coll, IA B
Denison U, OH B
DePaul U, IL B
Earlham Coll, IN B
Grinnell Coll, IA B
Gustavus Adolphus Coll, MN B
Hamline U, MN B
Hanover Coll, IN B
Illinois Wesleyan U, IL B
Indiana U Bloomington, IN B
Kent State U, OH B
Lake Forest Coll, IL B
Luther Coll, IA B
Macalester Coll, MN B
Oakland U, MI B
Oberlin Coll, OH B
The Ohio State U, OH B
Ohio U, OH B
Pontifical Coll Josephinum, OH B
Ripon Coll, WI B
St. Cloud State U, MN B
U of Chicago, IL B
U of Cincinnati, OH B
U of Illinois at Chicago, IL B
U of Illinois at Urbana–Champaign, IL B
The U of Iowa, IA B
U of Kansas, KS B
U of Michigan, MI B
U of Minnesota, Morris, MN B
U of Minnesota, Twin Cities Campus, MN B
U of Nebraska–Lincoln, NE B
U of Northern Iowa, IA B
U of Toledo, OH B
U of Wisconsin–Eau Claire, WI B
U of Wisconsin–Madison, WI B
U of Wisconsin–Milwaukee, WI B
Walsh U, OH B
Washington U in St. Louis, MO B

LATIN (ANCIENT AND MEDIEVAL)

Augustana Coll, IL B
Ball State U, IN B
Bowling Green State U, OH B
Butler U, IN B
Calvin Coll, MI B
Carleton Coll, MN B
The Coll of Wooster, OH B
Concordia Coll, MN B
Cornell Coll, IA B
Creighton U, NE B
DePauw U, IN B

Latin (Ancient And Medieval) (continued)

Hope Coll, MI B
Indiana U Bloomington, IN B
John Carroll U, OH B
Kent State U, OH B
Kenyon Coll, OH B
Loyola U Chicago, IL B
Luther Coll, IA B
Macalester Coll, MN B
Miami U, OH B
Michigan State U, MI B
Monmouth Coll, IL B
Oberlin Coll, OH B
Ohio U, OH B
Rockford Coll, IL B
St. Olaf Coll, MN B
Southwest Missouri State U, MO B
U of Chicago, IL B
The U of Iowa, IA B
U of Michigan, MI B
U of Minnesota, Twin Cities Campus, MN B
U of Nebraska–Lincoln, NE B
U of Notre Dame, IN B
U of St. Thomas, MN B
The U of South Dakota, SD B
U of Wisconsin–Madison, WI B
U of Wisconsin–Milwaukee, WI B
Wabash Coll, IN B
Washington U in St. Louis, MO B
Western Michigan U, MI B
Wichita State U, KS B

LAW AND LEGAL STUDIES RELATED

Bethany Coll, KS B
U of Nebraska–Lincoln, NE B

LAW ENFORCEMENT/ POLICE SCIENCE

Bemidji State U, MN B
Chicago State U, IL B
Coll of the Ozarks, MO B
Defiance Coll, OH A,B
East Central U, OK B
Ferris State U, MI B
Grand Valley State U, MI B
Hannibal-LaGrange Coll, MO B
Kent State U, Ashtabula Campus, OH A
Kent State U, Tuscarawas Campus, OH A
Langston U, OK B
Lincoln Coll, Lincoln, IL A
MacMurray Coll, IL A,B
Madonna U, MI A,B
Metropolitan State U, MN B
Michigan State U, MI B
Minnesota State U, Mankato, MN B
Missouri Southern State Coll, MO A
Northeastern State U, OK B
Northern Michigan U, MI A,B
Northern State U, SD B
Northwestern Oklahoma State U, OK B
Ohio U, OH A
Ohio U–Chillicothe, OH A
Ohio U–Lancaster, OH A
Oklahoma City U, OK B
Purdue U Calumet, IN B
Rochester Comm and Tech Coll, MN A
Rogers State U, OK A
Saint Mary's U of Minnesota, MN B
Southeast Missouri State U, MO B
Southern Illinois U Carbondale, IL A
Tiffin U, OH A,B
Truman State U, MO B
The U of Akron, OH A
U of Cincinnati, OH A,B
U of Toledo, OH A
U of Wisconsin–Milwaukee, WI B
U of Wisconsin–Superior, WI A
Waldorf Coll, IA A
Wayne State Coll, NE B
Winona State U, MN B
Wright State U, OH B
Youngstown State U, OH A,B

LEGAL ADMINISTRATIVE ASSISTANT

AIB Coll of Business, IA A
Baker Coll of Auburn Hills, MI A
Baker Coll of Clinton Township, MI A
Baker Coll of Flint, MI A
Baker Coll of Jackson, MI A
Baker Coll of Muskegon, MI A
Baker Coll of Owosso, MI A
Baker Coll of Port Huron, MI A
Ball State U, IN A,B
Bryant and Stratton Coll, WI A
Central Missouri State U, MO A
Davenport U, Grand Rapids, MI A
Davenport U, Kalamazoo, MI A,B
Eastern Michigan U, MI B
Ferris State U, MI A
Hamilton Coll, IA A
Hannibal-LaGrange Coll, MO A
International Business Coll, Fort Wayne, IN A,B
Kent State U, Ashtabula Campus, OH A
Lewis Coll of Business, MI A
Lincoln Coll, Normal, IL A
Miami U–Middletown Campus, OH A
Midland Lutheran Coll, NE A
Midstate Coll, IL A
Northern Michigan U, MI A
Northwest Missouri State U, MO B
Ohio U–Lancaster, OH A
Presentation Coll, SD A
Robert Morris Coll, IL A
Rochester Comm and Tech Coll, MN A
Rockford Business Coll, IL A
Rogers State U, OK A
Shawnee State U, OH A
Tabor Coll, KS B
U of Cincinnati, OH A
U of Northwestern Ohio, OH A
U of Rio Grande, OH A
U of Toledo, OH A
Wright State U, OH A
Youngstown State U, OH A

LEGAL STUDIES

Central Christian Coll of Kansas, KS A
Concordia U, IL B
East Central U, OK B
Franciscan U of Steubenville, OH B
Grand Valley State U, MI B
Hamline U, MN B
Kenyon Coll, OH B
Oberlin Coll, OH B
Ohio Dominican U, OH A
Park U, MO B
Roosevelt U, IL B
U of Evansville, IN B
U of Illinois at Springfield, IL B
U of Tulsa, OK B
U of Wisconsin–Superior, WI B
Webster U, MO B
Winona State U, MN B

LIBERAL ARTS AND SCIENCES/LIBERAL STUDIES

Alma Coll, MI B
Alverno Coll, WI A
Ancilla Coll, IN A
Andrews U, MI A,B
Antioch U McGregor, OH B
Aquinas Coll, MI A,B
Ashland U, OH A,B
Augsburg Coll, MN B
Augustana Coll, IL B
Augustana Coll, SD B
Bacone Coll, OK A
Ball State U, IN A,B
Bemidji State U, MN A,B
Benedictine Coll, KS B
Bethany Lutheran Coll, MN A,B
Bethel Coll, IN A,B
Bethel Coll, MN A
Blackburn Coll, IL B
Bluffton Coll, OH B
Bowling Green State U, OH B
Bradley U, IL B
Briar Cliff U, IA A
Buena Vista U, IA B
Butler U, IN A
Calumet Coll of Saint Joseph, IN A,B
Capital U, OH B
Cardinal Stritch U, WI A,B
Central Christian Coll of Kansas, KS B
Chatfield Coll, OH A
Clarke Coll, IA A
Cleveland State U, OH B
Coe Coll, IA B
Coll of Menominee Nation, WI A
Coll of Mount St. Joseph, OH B
Coll of Saint Benedict, MN B
Coll of St. Catherine, MN A
Coll of St. Catherine–Minneapolis, MN A
Coll of Saint Mary, NE A,B
The Coll of St. Scholastica, MN B
Columbia Coll, MO A,B
Columbia Coll Chicago, IL B
Conception Seminary Coll, MO B
Concordia U, MI A
Concordia U, MN A,B
Concordia U Wisconsin, WI B
Cornell Coll, IA B
Cottey Coll, MO A
Crossroads Coll, MN A,B
Crown Coll, MN A,B
Dakota State U, SD A
Dakota Wesleyan U, SD A
Defiance Coll, OH B
Dickinson State U, ND A,B
Donnelly Coll, KS A
Eastern Illinois U, IL B
East-West U, IL A
Edgewood Coll, WI A,B
Eureka Coll, IL B
Ferris State U, MI A
Finlandia U, MI B
Fontbonne U, MO B
Fort Hays State U, KS B
The Franciscan U, IA A,B
Goshen Coll, IN B
Governors State U, IL B
Grace Bible Coll, MI A
Graceland U, IA B
Grace U, NE A,B
Grand Valley State U, MI B
Grand View Coll, IA A,B
Greenville Coll, IL B
Hannibal-LaGrange Coll, MO A,B
Haskell Indian Nations U, KS A
Hastings Coll, NE B
Hesston Coll, KS A
Hillsdale Free Will Baptist Coll, OK A
Holy Cross Coll, IN A
Illinois Coll, IL B
Illinois State U, IL B
Illinois Wesleyan U, IL B
Indiana State U, IN A
Iowa State U of Science and Technology, IA B
Iowa Wesleyan Coll, IA B
Kendall Coll, IL B
Kent State U, OH A,B
Kent State U, Ashtabula Campus, OH A
Kent State U, Geauga Campus, OH A
Kent State U, Salem Campus, OH A
Kent State U, Stark Campus, OH A
Kent State U, Tuscarawas Campus, OH A
Langston U, OK B
Lewis Coll of Business, MI A
Lewis U, IL B
Lincoln Coll, Lincoln, IL A
Lincoln Coll, Normal, IL A,B
Lindenwood U, MO B
Loras Coll, IA A,B
Lourdes Coll, OH A,B
MacMurray Coll, IL B
Malone Coll, OH B
Maranatha Baptist Bible Coll, WI B
Marian Coll, IN A
Marian Coll of Fond du Lac, WI B
Marietta Coll, OH A,B
Marygrove Coll, MI A
Maryville U of Saint Louis, MO B
Mayville State U, ND B
Messenger Coll, MO A
Metropolitan State U, MN B

Miami U–Hamilton Campus, OH A
Miami U–Middletown Campus, OH A
Michigan State U, MI B
MidAmerica Nazarene U, KS A
Midland Lutheran Coll, NE B
Minnesota State U, Mankato, MN A,B
Minnesota State U, Moorhead, MN A
Missouri Valley Coll, MO A,B
Monmouth Coll, IL B
Mount Marty Coll, SD A,B
Mount Mercy Coll, IA B
Mount Vernon Nazarene U, OH A
National American U, SD A
National-Louis U, IL B
Nebraska Indian Comm Coll, NE A
Newman U, KS A,B
North Central Coll, IL B
Northeastern Illinois U, IL B
Northern Illinois U, IL B
Northern Michigan U, MI A,B
Northern State U, SD A
Northwestern Coll, MN A
Northwestern U, IL B
Oak Hills Christian Coll, MN A
Oakland City U, IN A
Oakland U, MI B
The Ohio State U at Lima, OH A
Ohio U, OH A,B
Ohio U–Chillicothe, OH A,B
Ohio U–Lancaster, OH A,B
Ohio U–Southern Campus, OH A
Ohio U–Zanesville, OH A,B
Oklahoma Christian U, OK B
Oklahoma City U, OK B
Oklahoma Wesleyan U, OK A
Olivet Coll, MI B
Olivet Nazarene U, IL B
Oral Roberts U, OK B
Park U, MO B
Pittsburg State U, KS B
Presentation Coll, SD A
Principia Coll, IL B
Purdue U Calumet, IN B
Purdue U North Central, IN B
Reformed Bible Coll, MI A
Rochester Coll, MI A
Rochester Comm and Tech Coll, MN A
Rogers State U, OK A,B
Roosevelt U, IL B
St. Augustine Coll, IL A
St. Cloud State U, MN A,B
St. Gregory's U, OK A,B
St. Louis Christian Coll, MO A
Saint Mary-of-the-Woods Coll, IN A,B
Saint Mary U, KS A,B
St. Olaf Coll, MN B
Saint Xavier U, IL B
Shimer Coll, IL B
Sitting Bull Coll, ND A
Southeast Missouri State U, MO B
Southern Illinois U Carbondale, IL B
Southern Illinois U Edwardsville, IL B
Southwestern Coll, KS B
Spring Arbor U, MI A
Springfield Coll in Illinois, IL A
Stephens Coll, MO A,B
Taylor U, Fort Wayne Campus, IN A
Tiffin U, OH B
Trinity Bible Coll, ND A
Trinity International U, IL B
Tri-State U, IN A
Union Inst & U, OH B
The U of Akron, OH A,B
U of Central Oklahoma, OK B
U of Chicago, IL B
U of Cincinnati, OH A,B
U of Evansville, IN B
U of Illinois at Springfield, IL B
U of Illinois at Urbana–Champaign, IL B
U of Indianapolis, IN A,B
U of Kansas, KS B
U of Mary, ND B
U of Michigan, MI B
U of Michigan–Dearborn, MI B
U of Michigan–Flint, MI B
U of Minnesota, Crookston, MN A
U of Minnesota, Morris, MN B
U of Missouri–Columbia, MO B
U of Missouri–Kansas City, MO B
U of Missouri–St. Louis, MO B
U of Nebraska–Lincoln, NE B
U of Northern Iowa, IA B
U of Notre Dame, IN B
U of St. Francis, IL B
U of Saint Francis, IN B
U of Sioux Falls, SD B
The U of South Dakota, SD B
U of Southern Indiana, IN B
U of Toledo, OH A,B
U of Wisconsin–Eau Claire, WI A
U of Wisconsin–La Crosse, WI A
U of Wisconsin–Oshkosh, WI A,B
U of Wisconsin–Platteville, WI A,B
U of Wisconsin–River Falls, WI B
U of Wisconsin–Stevens Point, WI A
U of Wisconsin–Superior, WI A
U of Wisconsin–Whitewater, WI A
Upper Iowa U, IA A
Urbana U, OH A,B
Valparaiso U, IN B
Viterbo U, WI B
Waldorf Coll, IA A
Walsh U, OH A,B
Washington U in St. Louis, MO B
Webster U, MO B
Wentworth Military Academy and Jr Coll, MO A
Western Illinois U, IL B
Wichita State U, KS A,B
Wilberforce U, OH B
Wilmington Coll, OH B
Winona State U, MN A,B
Wittenberg U, OH B
Xavier U, OH A,B
York Coll, NE A,B

LIBERAL ARTS AND STUDIES RELATED

Ohio U, OH B
The U of Akron, OH A,B
U of Nebraska–Lincoln, NE B
U of Oklahoma, OK B

LIBRARY SCIENCE

Chadron State Coll, NE B
Northeastern State U, OK B
Ohio Dominican U, OH A,B
St. Cloud State U, MN B
U of Nebraska at Omaha, NE B
U of Oklahoma, OK B

LINGUISTICS

Central Coll, IA B
Cleveland State U, OH B
Crown Coll, MN B
Eastern Michigan U, MI B
Grinnell Coll, IA B
Indiana U Bloomington, IN B
Iowa State U of Science and Technology, IA B
Judson Coll, IL B
Lawrence U, WI B
Macalester Coll, MN B
Miami U, OH B
Michigan State U, MI B
Moody Bible Inst, IL B
Northeastern Illinois U, IL B
Northwestern U, IL B
Oakland U, MI B
The Ohio State U, OH B
Ohio U, OH B
Oklahoma Wesleyan U, OK A,B
St. Cloud State U, MN B
Southern Illinois U Carbondale, IL B
U of Chicago, IL B
U of Cincinnati, OH B
U of Illinois at Urbana–Champaign, IL B
The U of Iowa, IA B
U of Kansas, KS B
U of Michigan, MI B
U of Minnesota, Twin Cities Campus, MN B
U of Missouri–Columbia, MO B
U of Missouri–St. Louis, MO B
U of Northern Iowa, IA B
U of Oklahoma, OK B
U of Toledo, OH B
U of Wisconsin–Madison, WI B
U of Wisconsin–Milwaukee, WI B
Wayne State U, MI B

LITERATURE

Alma Coll, MI B
Antioch Coll, OH B
Augustana Coll, IL B
Ave Maria Coll, MI B
Beloit Coll, WI B
Bethel Coll, MN B
Blackburn Coll, IL B
Capital U, OH B
Chicago State U, IL B
Coe Coll, IA B
Coll of St. Catherine, MN B
Concordia U, MN B
Concordia U, NE B
Defiance Coll, OH B
DePaul U, IL B
East Central U, OK B
Eureka Coll, IL B
Graceland U, IA B
Grand Valley State U, MI B
Hastings Coll, NE B
Indiana U Bloomington, IN B
John Carroll U, OH B
Judson Coll, IL B
Kenyon Coll, OH B
Maharishi U of Management, IA A,B
Manchester Coll, IN A
Minnesota State U, Mankato, MN B
Morningside Coll, IA B
Mount Vernon Nazarene U, OH B
North Central Coll, IL B
North Park U, IL B
Northwest Missouri State U, MO B
Ohio Wesleyan U, OH B
Olivet Nazarene U, IL B
Otterbein Coll, OH B
Purdue U Calumet, IN B
Rochester Coll, MI B
Rockford Coll, IL B
Roosevelt U, IL B
Shimer Coll, IL B
Southern Nazarene U, OK B
Southwest Minnesota State U, MN B
Taylor U, IN B
The U of Akron, OH B
U of Cincinnati, OH B
U of Evansville, IN B
The U of Iowa, IA B
U of Michigan, MI B
U of Missouri–St. Louis, MO B
U of Toledo, OH B
U of Wisconsin–Milwaukee, WI B
Washington U in St. Louis, MO B
Wayne State Coll, NE B
Webster U, MO B
Westminster Coll, MO B
Wilberforce U, OH B
Wittenberg U, OH B

LOGISTICS/MATERIALS MANAGEMENT

Bowling Green State U, OH B
Central Michigan U, MI B
Elmhurst Coll, IL B
Iowa State U of Science and Technology, IA B
Michigan State U, MI B
The Ohio State U, OH B
Park U, MO A,B
The U of Akron, OH A
The U of Findlay, OH B
Wayne State U, MI B
Western Michigan U, MI B

MACHINE TECHNOLOGY

Ferris State U, MI A
Missouri Southern State Coll, MO A
Ranken Tech Coll, MO A

MANAGEMENT INFORMATION SYSTEMS/ BUSINESS DATA PROCESSING

Augsburg Coll, MN B
Augustana Coll, SD B

Management Information Systems/Business Data Processing (continued)

Aurora U, IL B
Baker Coll of Flint, MI B
Ball State U, IN B
Bellevue U, NE B
Bethel Coll, MN B
Bowling Green State U, OH B
Bradley U, IL B
Briar Cliff U, IA B
Buena Vista U, IA B
Central Michigan U, MI B
Central Missouri State U, MO B
Chicago State U, IL B
Clarke Coll, IA B
Cleary U, MI B
Coll of St. Catherine, MN B
Colorado Tech U Sioux Falls Campus, SD A,B
Concordia U, MN B
Concordia U, NE B
Creighton U, NE B
DePaul U, IL B
Dordt Coll, IA B
Eastern Illinois U, IL B
Eastern Michigan U, MI B
Elmhurst Coll, IL B
Eureka Coll, IL B
Ferris State U, MI B
Fontbonne U, MO B
Franklin U, OH B
Governors State U, IL B
Grace Coll, IN B
Graceland U, IA B
Grand Valley State U, MI B
Grand View Coll, IA B
Greenville Coll, IL B
Illinois Coll, IL B
Indiana State U, IN B
Indiana U Bloomington, IN B
Iowa State U of Science and Technology, IA B
Jamestown Coll, ND B
Judson Coll, IL B
Lewis U, IL B
Lindenwood U, MO B
Loras Coll, IA B
Loyola U Chicago, IL B
Luther Coll, IA B
MacMurray Coll, IL B
Marquette U, WI B
Maryville U of Saint Louis, MO B
Metropolitan State U, MN B
Miami U, OH B
Miami U–Middletown Campus, OH A
Michigan Technological U, MI B
Midland Lutheran Coll, NE B
Millikin U, IL B
Milwaukee School of Engineering, WI B
Minnesota State U, Moorhead, MN B
Minot State U, ND B
Morningside Coll, IA B
National American U, SD B
National American U–Sioux Falls Branch, SD A,B
North Central Coll, IL B
North Dakota State U, ND B
Northern Michigan U, MI A,B
Northern State U, SD B
Northwestern Coll, MN B
Northwest Missouri State U, MO B
Oakland U, MI B
The Ohio State U, OH B
Ohio U, OH B
Oklahoma Baptist U, OK B
Oklahoma City U, OK B
Oklahoma State U, OK B
Oral Roberts U, OK B
Park U, MO B
Peru State Coll, NE B
Robert Morris Coll, IL A
Rockford Coll, IL B
St. Augustine Coll, IL A
Saint Joseph's Coll, IN B
Saint Louis U, MO B
Saint Mary's Coll, IN B
St. Norbert Coll, WI B
Shawnee State U, OH B
Southeast Missouri State U, MO B
Southern Illinois U Edwardsville, IL B
Southern Nazarene U, OK B
Southwestern Coll, KS B
Southwest Missouri State U, MO B
Spring Arbor U, MI B
Taylor U, IN A
Tiffin U, OH B
Trinity Christian Coll, IL B
Tri-State U, IN B
The U of Akron, OH A
U of Cincinnati, OH B
U of Dayton, OH B
U of Illinois at Chicago, IL B
The U of Iowa, IA B
U of Minnesota, Twin Cities Campus, MN B
U of Missouri–St. Louis, MO B
U of Nebraska at Omaha, NE B
U of Northern Iowa, IA B
U of Notre Dame, IN B
U of Oklahoma, OK B
U of Phoenix–Metro Detroit Campus, MI B
U of Phoenix–Ohio Campus, OH B
U of Phoenix–Oklahoma City Campus, OK B
U of Phoenix–St. Louis Campus, MO B
U of Phoenix–Tulsa Campus, OK B
U of Phoenix–West Michigan Campus, MI B
U of Sioux Falls, SD B
U of Tulsa, OK B
U of Wisconsin–Eau Claire, WI B
U of Wisconsin–La Crosse, WI B
U of Wisconsin–Milwaukee, WI B
U of Wisconsin–Oshkosh, WI B
U of Wisconsin–River Falls, WI B
U of Wisconsin–Whitewater, WI B
Upper Iowa U, IA B
Ursuline Coll, OH B
Wayne State U, MI B
Webster U, MO B
Western Illinois U, IL B
Western Michigan U, MI B
Westminster Coll, MO B
Wichita State U, KS B
William Woods U, MO B
Winona State U, MN B
Wright State U, OH A,B
Xavier U, OH B
Youngstown State U, OH B

MANAGEMENT SCIENCE

Capella U, MN B
Central Methodist Coll, MO B
The Coll of St. Scholastica, MN B
Franklin U, OH B
Hamilton Coll, IA A
Lourdes Coll, OH B
Maharishi U of Management, IA B
Miami U, OH B
Minnesota State U, Mankato, MN B
Oakland City U, IN B
Oklahoma State U, OK B
Oral Roberts U, OK B
Rockhurst U, MO B
Saint Louis U, MO B
Southeastern Oklahoma State U, OK B
Southern Nazarene U, OK B
Southwestern Coll, KS B
The U of Iowa, IA B
U of Minnesota, Morris, MN B
U of North Dakota, ND B
U of Phoenix–Metro Detroit Campus, MI B
U of Phoenix–Oklahoma City Campus, OK B
U of Phoenix–Tulsa Campus, OK B

MARINE BIOLOGY

Ball State U, IN B
Bemidji State U, MN B
Lincoln Coll, Lincoln, IL A
Missouri Southern State Coll, MO B
Southwestern Coll, KS B
U of Wisconsin–Superior, WI B
Wittenberg U, OH B

MARKETING/ DISTRIBUTION EDUCATION

Bowling Green State U, OH B
Central Michigan U, MI B
Eastern Michigan U, MI B
Kent State U, OH B
U of Nebraska–Lincoln, NE B
U of North Dakota, ND B
U of Wisconsin–Stout, WI B
Western Michigan U, MI B

MARKETING MANAGEMENT AND RESEARCH RELATED

Capella U, MN B
Maryville U of Saint Louis, MO B
Washington U in St. Louis, MO B
Western Michigan U, MI B

MARKETING OPERATIONS

Avila U, MO B
Colorado Tech U Sioux Falls Campus, SD B
Lake Erie Coll, OH B
McKendree Coll, IL B
Purdue U North Central, IN A,B
Robert Morris Coll, IL A
U of Illinois at Urbana–Champaign, IL B
U of Wisconsin–Superior, WI B
Youngstown State U, OH B

MARKETING OPERATIONS/MARKETING AND DISTRIBUTION RELATED

Southeast Missouri State U, MO B
Washington U in St. Louis, MO B

MARKETING RESEARCH

Ashland U, OH B
Baker Coll of Jackson, MI B
Bowling Green State U, OH B
Carthage Coll, WI B
Saginaw Valley State U, MI B
U of Nebraska at Omaha, NE B

MARRIAGE/FAMILY COUNSELING

Central Christian Coll of Kansas, KS A
Grace U, NE B
Oklahoma Baptist U, OK B

MASS COMMUNICATIONS

Adrian Coll, MI A,B
Albion Coll, MI B
Alma Coll, MI B
Anderson U, IN B
Andrews U, MI B
Antioch Coll, OH B
Ashland U, OH B
Augsburg Coll, MN B
Augustana Coll, IL B
Augustana Coll, SD B
Bacone Coll, OK A
Baker U, KS B
Baldwin-Wallace Coll, OH B
Beloit Coll, WI B
Bemidji State U, MN B
Bethel Coll, MN B
Black Hills State U, SD A,B
Bluffton Coll, OH B
Bowling Green State U, OH B
Briar Cliff U, IA B
Buena Vista U, IA B
Calvin Coll, MI B
Cameron U, OK B
Central Christian Coll of Kansas, KS A
Central Missouri State U, MO B
Clarke Coll, IA B
Cleveland State U, OH B
Coll of St. Catherine, MN B
Coll of the Ozarks, MO B
The Coll of Wooster, OH B
Concordia Coll, MN B
Concordia U, MN B
Concordia U, NE B
Concordia U Wisconsin, WI B
Cornerstone U, MI A,B
Creighton U, NE A,B
Culver-Stockton Coll, MO B
Defiance Coll, OH B
Denison U, OH B
DePaul U, IL B

DePauw U, IN B
Doane Coll, NE B
Dominican U, IL B
Dordt Coll, IA B
Drake U, IA B
Drury U, MO B
East Central U, OK B
Edgewood Coll, WI B
Eureka Coll, IL B
Evangel U, MO A,B
Ferris State U, MI B
Fort Hays State U, KS B
Goshen Coll, IN B
Governors State U, IL B
Grace Coll, IN B
Grace U, NE B
Grand Valley State U, MI B
Grand View Coll, IA B
Greenville Coll, IL B
Gustavus Adolphus Coll, MN B
Hamline U, MN B
Hannibal-LaGrange Coll, MO B
Hanover Coll, IN B
Hastings Coll, NE B
Heidelberg Coll, OH B
Hiram Coll, OH B
Huntington Coll, IN B
Illinois Coll, IL B
Illinois State U, IL B
Indiana U Bloomington, IN B
Indiana U Northwest, IN B
Indiana U South Bend, IN B
Iowa State U of Science and Technology, IA B
Iowa Wesleyan Coll, IA B
John Carroll U, OH B
Judson Coll, IL B
Lake Erie Coll, OH B
Langston U, OK B
Lewis U, IL B
Lincoln Coll, Lincoln, IL A
Lindenwood U, MO B
Loras Coll, IA B
Luther Coll, IA B
Madonna U, MI A,B
Manchester Coll, IN B
Marian Coll, IN B
Marian Coll of Fond du Lac, WI B
Marquette U, WI B
McKendree Coll, IL B
Miami U, OH B
Miami U–Middletown Campus, OH A
MidAmerica Nazarene U, KS B
Midland Lutheran Coll, NE B
Minnesota State U, Mankato, MN B
Minnesota State U, Moorhead, MN B
Missouri Southern State Coll, MO B
Missouri Valley Coll, MO B
Monmouth Coll, IL B
Morningside Coll, IA B
Mount Union Coll, OH B
Mount Vernon Nazarene U, OH B
Muskingum Coll, OH B
Newman U, KS B
North Central Coll, IL B
North Dakota State U, ND B
Northern Michigan U, MI B
North Park U, IL B
Northwestern Coll, IA B
Northwestern Oklahoma State U, OK B
Northwest Missouri State U, MO B
Ohio Northern U, OH B
Oklahoma Baptist U, OK B
Oklahoma Christian U, OK B
Oklahoma City U, OK B
Oklahoma Wesleyan U, OK B
Olivet Coll, MI B
Olivet Nazarene U, IL B
Ottawa U, KS B
Pittsburg State U, KS B
Presentation Coll, SD B
Principia Coll, IL B
Purdue U Calumet, IN B
Roosevelt U, IL B
St. Ambrose U, IA B
St. Cloud State U, MN B
Saint Joseph's Coll, IN B
Saint Mary-of-the-Woods Coll, IN B
Saint Mary's Coll of Madonna U, MI B
Saint Mary U, KS B
Simpson Coll, IA B
South Dakota State U, SD B
Southeast Missouri State U, MO B
Southern Illinois U Edwardsville, IL B
Southern Nazarene U, OK B
Southwestern Oklahoma State U, OK B
Southwest Missouri State U, MO B
Stephens Coll, MO B
Tabor Coll, KS B
Taylor U, IN B
Truman State U, MO B
The U of Akron, OH B
U of Cincinnati, OH B
U of Dayton, OH B
U of Dubuque, IA A,B
U of Evansville, IN B
U of Illinois at Springfield, IL B
U of Illinois at Urbana–Champaign, IL B
The U of Iowa, IA B
U of Mary, ND B
U of Michigan, MI B
U of Michigan–Flint, MI B
U of Minnesota, Morris, MN B
U of Minnesota, Twin Cities Campus, MN B
U of Missouri–Columbia, MO B
U of Missouri–Kansas City, MO B
U of Missouri–St. Louis, MO B
U of Nebraska at Kearney, NE B
U of Nebraska at Omaha, NE B
U of Rio Grande, OH A,B
U of St. Francis, IL B
U of Saint Francis, IN B
U of St. Thomas, MN B
U of Sioux Falls, SD B
The U of South Dakota, SD B
U of Toledo, OH B
U of Wisconsin–Eau Claire, WI B
U of Wisconsin–Madison, WI B
U of Wisconsin–Milwaukee, WI B
U of Wisconsin–Oshkosh, WI B
U of Wisconsin–Platteville, WI B
U of Wisconsin–Superior, WI B
U of Wisconsin–Whitewater, WI B
Upper Iowa U, IA B
Urbana U, OH B
Waldorf Coll, IA A,B
Walsh U, OH B
Wartburg Coll, IA B
Wayne State Coll, NE B
Wilberforce U, OH B
Wilmington Coll, OH B
Winona State U, MN B
Wright State U, OH B

MATERIALS ENGINEERING

Case Western Reserve U, OH B
Illinois Inst of Technology, IL B
Michigan Technological U, MI B
Northwestern U, IL B
The Ohio State U, OH B
Purdue U, IN B
The U of Iowa, IA B
U of Michigan, MI B
U of Minnesota, Twin Cities Campus, MN B
U of Wisconsin–Milwaukee, WI B
Western Michigan U, MI B
Winona State U, MN B
Wright State U, OH B

MATERIALS SCIENCE

Case Western Reserve U, OH B
Kent State U, Ashtabula Campus, OH A
Michigan State U, MI B
Northwestern U, IL B
The Ohio State U, OH B
U of Illinois at Urbana–Champaign, IL B
U of Michigan, MI B
U of Minnesota, Twin Cities Campus, MN B

MATHEMATICAL STATISTICS

Bowling Green State U, OH B
Case Western Reserve U, OH B
Central Michigan U, MI B
Cleveland State U, OH B
DePaul U, IL B
Eastern Michigan U, MI B
Grand Valley State U, MI B
Iowa State U of Science and Technology, IA B
Kansas State U, KS B
Kettering U, MI B
Lincoln Coll, Lincoln, IL A
Loyola U Chicago, IL B
Luther Coll, IA B
Marquette U, WI B
Miami U, OH B
Michigan State U, MI B
Michigan Technological U, MI B
Northwestern U, IL B
Oakland U, MI B
Ohio Northern U, OH B
Ohio Wesleyan U, OH B
Oklahoma State U, OK B
Purdue U, IN B
St. Cloud State U, MN B
The U of Akron, OH B
U of Chicago, IL B
U of Illinois at Chicago, IL B
U of Illinois at Urbana–Champaign, IL B
The U of Iowa, IA B
U of Michigan, MI B
U of Minnesota, Morris, MN B
U of Missouri–Columbia, MO B
U of Missouri–Kansas City, MO B
U of Nebraska at Kearney, NE B
The U of South Dakota, SD B
U of Wisconsin–Madison, WI B
U of Wisconsin–Milwaukee, WI B
Washington U in St. Louis, MO B
Western Michigan U, MI B
Winona State U, MN B

MATHEMATICS

Adrian Coll, MI B
Albion Coll, MI B
Alma Coll, MI B
Alverno Coll, WI B
Ancilla Coll, IN A
Anderson U, IN B
Andrews U, MI B
Antioch Coll, OH B
Aquinas Coll, MI B
Ashland U, OH B
Augsburg Coll, MN B
Augustana Coll, IL B
Augustana Coll, SD B
Aurora U, IL B
Ave Maria Coll, MI B
Avila U, MO B
Bacone Coll, OK A
Baker U, KS B
Baldwin-Wallace Coll, OH B
Ball State U, IN B
Bellevue U, NE B
Beloit Coll, WI B
Bemidji State U, MN B
Benedictine Coll, KS B
Benedictine U, IL B
Bethany Coll, KS B
Bethel Coll, IN B
Bethel Coll, KS B
Bethel Coll, MN B
Blackburn Coll, IL B
Black Hills State U, SD B
Bluffton Coll, OH B
Bowling Green State U, OH B
Bradley U, IL B
Briar Cliff U, IA B
Buena Vista U, IA B
Butler U, IN B
Calvin Coll, MI B
Cameron U, OK B
Capital U, OH B
Cardinal Stritch U, WI B
Carleton Coll, MN B
Carroll Coll, WI B
Carthage Coll, WI B
Case Western Reserve U, OH B
Cedarville U, OH B
Central Christian Coll of Kansas, KS A
Central Coll, IA B
Central Methodist Coll, MO B

Mathematics (continued)

Institution	Degree
Central Michigan U, MI	B
Central Missouri State U, MO	B
Chadron State Coll, NE	B
Chicago State U, IL	B
Clarke Coll, IA	B
Cleveland State U, OH	B
Coe Coll, IA	B
Coll of Mount St. Joseph, OH	B
Coll of Saint Benedict, MN	B
Coll of St. Catherine, MN	B
Coll of Saint Mary, NE	B
The Coll of St. Scholastica, MN	B
Coll of the Ozarks, MO	B
The Coll of Wooster, OH	B
Columbia Coll, MO	B
Concordia Coll, MN	B
Concordia U, IL	B
Concordia U, MI	B
Concordia U, NE	B
Concordia U Wisconsin, WI	B
Cornell Coll, IA	B
Cornerstone U, MI	B
Creighton U, NE	A,B
Culver-Stockton Coll, MO	B
Dakota State U, SD	B
Dakota Wesleyan U, SD	B
Dana Coll, NE	B
Defiance Coll, OH	B
Denison U, OH	B
DePaul U, IL	B
DePauw U, IN	B
Dickinson State U, ND	B
Doane Coll, NE	B
Dominican U, IL	B
Donnelly Coll, KS	A
Dordt Coll, IA	B
Drake U, IA	B
Drury U, MO	B
Earlham Coll, IN	B
East Central U, OK	B
Eastern Illinois U, IL	B
Eastern Michigan U, MI	B
East-West U, IL	B
Edgewood Coll, WI	B
Elmhurst Coll, IL	B
Emporia State U, KS	B
Eureka Coll, IL	B
Evangel U, MO	B
Ferris State U, MI	B
Fontbonne U, MO	B
Fort Hays State U, KS	B
Franciscan U of Steubenville, OH	B
Franklin Coll, IN	B
Goshen Coll, IN	B
Grace Coll, IN	B
Graceland U, IA	B
Grace U, NE	B
Grand Valley State U, MI	B
Greenville Coll, IL	B
Grinnell Coll, IA	B
Gustavus Adolphus Coll, MN	B
Hamline U, MN	B
Hannibal-LaGrange Coll, MO	B
Hanover Coll, IN	B
Hastings Coll, NE	B
Heidelberg Coll, OH	B
Hillsdale Coll, MI	B
Hillsdale Free Will Baptist Coll, OK	A
Hiram Coll, OH	B
Hope Coll, MI	B
Huntington Coll, IN	B
Illinois Coll, IL	B
Illinois State U, IL	B
Illinois Wesleyan U, IL	B
Indiana State U, IN	B
Indiana U Bloomington, IN	B
Indiana U East, IN	A
Indiana U Kokomo, IN	B
Indiana U Northwest, IN	B
Indiana U–Purdue U Fort Wayne, IN	A,B
Indiana U–Purdue U Indianapolis, IN	B
Indiana U South Bend, IN	B
Indiana U Southeast, IN	B
Indiana Wesleyan U, IN	A,B
Iowa State U of Science and Technology, IA	B
Iowa Wesleyan Coll, IA	B
Jamestown Coll, ND	B
John Carroll U, OH	B
Judson Coll, IL	B
Kalamazoo Coll, MI	B
Kansas State U, KS	B
Kent State U, OH	B
Kenyon Coll, OH	B
Knox Coll, IL	B
Lake Erie Coll, OH	B
Lake Forest Coll, IL	B
Lakeland Coll, WI	B
Langston U, OK	B
Lawrence Technological U, MI	B
Lawrence U, WI	B
Lewis U, IL	B
Lincoln Coll, Lincoln, IL	A
Lindenwood U, MO	B
Loras Coll, IA	B
Loyola U Chicago, IL	B
Luther Coll, IA	B
Macalester Coll, MN	B
MacMurray Coll, IL	B
Madonna U, MI	A,B
Maharishi U of Management, IA	A,B
Malone Coll, OH	B
Manchester Coll, IN	B
Marian Coll, IN	B
Marian Coll of Fond du Lac, WI	B
Marietta Coll, OH	B
Marquette U, WI	B
Martin U, IN	B
Marygrove Coll, MI	B
Maryville U of Saint Louis, MO	B
Mayville State U, ND	B
McKendree Coll, IL	B
McPherson Coll, KS	B
Miami U, OH	B
Miami U–Middletown Campus, OH	A
Michigan State U, MI	B
Michigan Technological U, MI	B
MidAmerica Nazarene U, KS	B
Midland Lutheran Coll, NE	B
Millikin U, IL	B
Minnesota State U, Mankato, MN	B
Minnesota State U, Moorhead, MN	B
Minot State U, ND	B
Missouri Southern State Coll, MO	B
Missouri Valley Coll, MO	B
Missouri Western State Coll, MO	B
Monmouth Coll, IL	B
Morningside Coll, IA	B
Mount Marty Coll, SD	B
Mount Mary Coll, WI	B
Mount Mercy Coll, IA	B
Mount Union Coll, OH	B
Mount Vernon Nazarene U, OH	B
Muskingum Coll, OH	B
National-Louis U, IL	B
Nebraska Wesleyan U, NE	B
Newman U, KS	B
North Central Coll, IL	B
North Dakota State U, ND	B
Northeastern Illinois U, IL	B
Northeastern State U, OK	B
Northern Illinois U, IL	B
Northern Michigan U, MI	B
Northern State U, SD	B
Northland Coll, WI	B
North Park U, IL	B
Northwestern Coll, IA	B
Northwestern Coll, MN	B
Northwestern Oklahoma State U, OK	B
Northwestern U, IL	B
Northwest Missouri State U, MO	B
Notre Dame Coll, OH	B
Oakland City U, IN	B
Oakland U, MI	B
Oberlin Coll, OH	B
Ohio Dominican U, OH	B
Ohio Northern U, OH	B
The Ohio State U, OH	B
Ohio U, OH	B
Ohio Wesleyan U, OH	B
Oklahoma Baptist U, OK	B
Oklahoma Christian U, OK	B
Oklahoma City U, OK	B
Oklahoma Panhandle State U, OK	B
Oklahoma State U, OK	B
Oklahoma Wesleyan U, OK	B
Olivet Coll, MI	B
Olivet Nazarene U, IL	B
Oral Roberts U, OK	B
Ottawa U, KS	B
Otterbein Coll, OH	B
Park U, MO	B
Peru State Coll, NE	B
Pittsburg State U, KS	B
Principia Coll, IL	B
Purdue U, IN	B
Purdue U Calumet, IN	B
Quincy U, IL	B
Ripon Coll, WI	B
Rochester Coll, MI	B
Rockford Coll, IL	B
Rockhurst U, MO	B
Rogers State U, OK	A
Roosevelt U, IL	B
Rose-Hulman Inst of Technology, IN	B
Saginaw Valley State U, MI	B
St. Ambrose U, IA	B
St. Cloud State U, MN	B
Saint John's U, MN	B
Saint Joseph's Coll, IN	B
Saint Louis U, MO	B
Saint Mary-of-the-Woods Coll, IN	B
Saint Mary's Coll, IN	B
Saint Mary's U of Minnesota, MN	B
Saint Mary U, KS	B
St. Norbert Coll, WI	B
St. Olaf Coll, MN	B
Saint Xavier U, IL	B
Shawnee State U, OH	B
Siena Heights U, MI	B
Silver Lake Coll, WI	B
Simpson Coll, IA	B
South Dakota School of Mines and Technology, SD	B
South Dakota State U, SD	B
Southeastern Oklahoma State U, OK	B
Southeast Missouri State U, MO	B
Southern Illinois U Carbondale, IL	B
Southern Illinois U Edwardsville, IL	B
Southern Nazarene U, OK	B
Southwest Baptist U, MO	B
Southwestern Coll, KS	B
Southwestern Oklahoma State U, OK	B
Southwest Minnesota State U, MN	B
Southwest Missouri State U, MO	B
Spring Arbor U, MI	B
Stephens Coll, MO	B
Sterling Coll, KS	B
Tabor Coll, KS	B
Taylor U, IN	B
Trinity Christian Coll, IL	B
Trinity International U, IL	B
Tri-State U, IN	A,B
Truman State U, MO	B
Union Coll, NE	B
The U of Akron, OH	B
U of Central Oklahoma, OK	B
U of Chicago, IL	B
U of Cincinnati, OH	B
U of Dayton, OH	B
U of Evansville, IN	B
The U of Findlay, OH	B
U of Illinois at Chicago, IL	B
U of Illinois at Springfield, IL	B
U of Illinois at Urbana–Champaign, IL	B
U of Indianapolis, IN	B
The U of Iowa, IA	B
U of Kansas, KS	B
U of Mary, ND	B
U of Michigan, MI	B
U of Michigan–Dearborn, MI	B
U of Michigan–Flint, MI	B
U of Minnesota, Duluth, MN	B
U of Minnesota, Morris, MN	B
U of Minnesota, Twin Cities Campus, MN	B
U of Missouri–Columbia, MO	B
U of Missouri–Kansas City, MO	B
U of Missouri–St. Louis, MO	B
U of Nebraska at Kearney, NE	B
U of Nebraska at Omaha, NE	B
U of Nebraska–Lincoln, NE	B
U of North Dakota, ND	B
U of Northern Iowa, IA	B
U of Notre Dame, IN	B
U of Oklahoma, OK	B
U of Rio Grande, OH	A,B
U of St. Francis, IL	B
U of St. Thomas, MN	B
U of Science and Arts of Oklahoma, OK	B
U of Sioux Falls, SD	B
The U of South Dakota, SD	B

- U of Southern Indiana, IN B
- U of Toledo, OH B
- U of Tulsa, OK B
- U of Wisconsin–Eau Claire, WI B
- U of Wisconsin–Green Bay, WI A,B
- U of Wisconsin–La Crosse, WI B
- U of Wisconsin–Madison, WI B
- U of Wisconsin–Milwaukee, WI B
- U of Wisconsin–Oshkosh, WI B
- U of Wisconsin–Parkside, WI B
- U of Wisconsin–Platteville, WI B
- U of Wisconsin–River Falls, WI B
- U of Wisconsin–Stevens Point, WI B
- U of Wisconsin–Superior, WI B
- U of Wisconsin–Whitewater, WI B
- Upper Iowa U, IA B
- Ursuline Coll, OH B
- Valley City State U, ND B
- Valparaiso U, IN B
- Viterbo U, WI B
- Wabash Coll, IN B
- Waldorf Coll, IA A
- Walsh U, OH B
- Wartburg Coll, IA B
- Washington U in St. Louis, MO B
- Wayne State Coll, NE B
- Wayne State U, MI B
- Webster U, MO B
- Western Illinois U, IL B
- Western Michigan U, MI B
- Westminster Coll, MO B
- Wheaton Coll, IL B
- Wichita State U, KS B
- Wilberforce U, OH B
- William Jewell Coll, MO B
- William Woods U, MO B
- Wilmington Coll, OH B
- Winona State U, MN B
- Wisconsin Lutheran Coll, WI B
- Wittenberg U, OH B
- Wright State U, OH B
- Xavier U, OH B
- Youngstown State U, OH B

MATHEMATICS/ COMPUTER SCIENCE

- Anderson U, IN B
- Bethel Coll, IN B
- Cardinal Stritch U, WI B
- Central Coll, IA B
- Coll of Saint Benedict, MN B
- Eastern Illinois U, IL B
- Loyola U Chicago, IL B
- Saginaw Valley State U, MI B
- Saint John's U, MN B
- Saint Joseph's Coll, IN B
- Saint Mary's Coll, IN B
- Saint Mary's U of Minnesota, MN B
- St. Norbert Coll, WI B
- The U of Akron, OH B
- U of Illinois at Chicago, IL B
- U of Illinois at Urbana–Champaign, IL B
- Washington U in St. Louis, MO B

MATHEMATICS EDUCATION

- Anderson U, IN B
- Bethany Coll, KS B
- Bethel Coll, IN B
- Cedarville U, OH B
- Central Michigan U, MI B
- Central Missouri State U, MO B
- Chadron State Coll, NE B
- Coll of St. Catherine, MN B
- Coll of the Ozarks, MO B
- Concordia Coll, MN B
- Concordia U, IL B
- Concordia U, NE B
- Culver-Stockton Coll, MO B
- Dakota Wesleyan U, SD B
- Dana Coll, NE B
- Eastern Michigan U, MI B
- Elmhurst Coll, IL B
- Franklin Coll, IN B
- Grace Coll, IN B
- Greenville Coll, IL B
- Gustavus Adolphus Coll, MN B
- Hastings Coll, NE B
- Indiana U Bloomington, IN B
- Indiana U Northwest, IN B
- Indiana U–Purdue U Fort Wayne, IN B
- Indiana U South Bend, IN B
- Indiana U Southeast, IN B
- Indiana Wesleyan U, IN B
- Luther Coll, IA B
- Mayville State U, ND B
- McKendree Coll, IL B
- MidAmerica Nazarene U, KS B
- Minnesota State U, Moorhead, MN B
- Minot State U, ND B
- Mount Marty Coll, SD B
- Mount Vernon Nazarene U, OH B
- North Dakota State U, ND B
- Northwestern Coll, MN B
- Northwestern U, IL B
- Oakland City U, IN B
- Ohio U, OH B
- Oklahoma Baptist U, OK B
- Oklahoma Christian U, OK B
- Oral Roberts U, OK B
- St. Ambrose U, IA B
- Saint Mary's U of Minnesota, MN B
- Saint Xavier U, IL B
- Southeastern Oklahoma State U, OK B
- Southeast Missouri State U, MO B
- Southern Nazarene U, OK B
- Southwestern Coll, KS B
- Southwest Minnesota State U, MN B
- Southwest Missouri State U, MO B
- Trinity Christian Coll, IL B
- Tri-State U, IN B
- Union Coll, NE B
- U of Central Oklahoma, OK B
- U of Illinois at Chicago, IL B
- U of Indianapolis, IN B
- The U of Iowa, IA B
- U of Mary, ND B
- U of Minnesota, Duluth, MN B
- U of Minnesota, Twin Cities Campus, MN B
- U of Nebraska–Lincoln, NE B
- U of Northern Iowa, IA B
- U of Oklahoma, OK B
- U of Rio Grande, OH B
- U of St. Thomas, MN B
- U of Toledo, OH B
- U of Wisconsin–River Falls, WI B
- U of Wisconsin–Superior, WI B
- Ursuline Coll, OH B
- Valley City State U, ND B
- Viterbo U, WI B
- Wartburg Coll, IA B
- Washington U in St. Louis, MO B
- Wayne State U, MI B
- William Penn U, IA B
- William Woods U, MO B
- York Coll, NE B
- Youngstown State U, OH B

MATHEMATICS RELATED

- Anderson U, IN B
- Bradley U, IL B
- The Ohio State U, OH B
- Ohio U, OH B
- The U of Akron, OH B

MECHANICAL DESIGN TECHNOLOGY

- Bowling Green State U, OH B
- Ferris State U, MI A
- Pittsburg State U, KS B

MECHANICAL DRAFTING

- Baker Coll of Flint, MI A
- Indiana U–Purdue U Indianapolis, IN A
- Morrison Inst of Technology, IL A
- Purdue U, IN A,B

MECHANICAL ENGINEERING

- Andrews U, MI B
- Baker Coll of Flint, MI B
- Bradley U, IL B
- Calvin Coll, MI B
- Case Western Reserve U, OH B
- Cedarville U, OH B
- Cleveland State U, OH B
- Grand Valley State U, MI B
- Illinois Inst of Technology, IL B
- Indiana Inst of Technology, IN B
- Indiana U–Purdue U Fort Wayne, IN B
- Indiana U–Purdue U Indianapolis, IN B
- Iowa State U of Science and Technology, IA B
- Kansas State U, KS B
- Kettering U, MI B
- Lawrence Technological U, MI B
- Marquette U, WI B
- Miami U, OH B
- Michigan State U, MI B
- Michigan Technological U, MI B
- Milwaukee School of Engineering, WI B
- Minnesota State U, Mankato, MN B
- North Dakota State U, ND B
- Northern Illinois U, IL B
- Northwestern U, IL B
- Oakland U, MI B
- Ohio Northern U, OH B
- The Ohio State U, OH B
- Ohio U, OH B
- Oklahoma Christian U, OK B
- Oklahoma State U, OK B
- Oral Roberts U, OK B
- Purdue U, IN B
- Purdue U Calumet, IN B
- Rose-Hulman Inst of Technology, IN B
- Saginaw Valley State U, MI B
- St. Cloud State U, MN B
- Saint Louis U, MO B
- South Dakota School of Mines and Technology, SD B
- South Dakota State U, SD B
- Southern Illinois U Carbondale, IL B
- Southern Illinois U Edwardsville, IL B
- Tri-State U, IN B
- The U of Akron, OH B
- U of Cincinnati, OH B
- U of Dayton, OH B
- U of Evansville, IN B
- U of Illinois at Chicago, IL B
- U of Illinois at Urbana–Champaign, IL B
- The U of Iowa, IA B
- U of Kansas, KS B
- U of Michigan, MI B
- U of Michigan–Dearborn, MI B
- U of Minnesota, Twin Cities Campus, MN B
- U of Missouri–Columbia, MO B
- U of Missouri–Kansas City, MO B
- U of Missouri–Rolla, MO B
- U of Missouri–St. Louis, MO B
- U of Nebraska–Lincoln, NE B
- U of North Dakota, ND B
- U of Notre Dame, IN B
- U of Oklahoma, OK B
- U of St. Thomas, MN B
- U of Toledo, OH B
- U of Tulsa, OK B
- U of Wisconsin–Madison, WI B
- U of Wisconsin–Milwaukee, WI B
- U of Wisconsin–Platteville, WI B
- Valparaiso U, IN B
- Washington U in St. Louis, MO B
- Wayne State U, MI B
- Western Michigan U, MI B
- Wichita State U, KS B
- William Penn U, IA B
- Winona State U, MN B
- Wright State U, OH B
- Youngstown State U, OH B

MECHANICAL ENGINEERING TECHNOLOGIES RELATED

- Indiana State U, IN B
- U of Southern Indiana, IN A

MECHANICAL ENGINEERING TECHNOLOGY

- Andrews U, MI A,B
- Baker Coll of Flint, MI A
- Central Michigan U, MI B
- Cleveland State U, OH B

Mechanical Engineering Technology (continued)

Ferris State U, MI A
Indiana U–Purdue U Fort Wayne, IN A,B
Indiana U–Purdue U Indianapolis, IN A,B
Kansas State U, KS A,B
Kent State U, OH A
Kent State U, Ashtabula Campus, OH A
Kent State U, Tuscarawas Campus, OH A
Lawrence Technological U, MI A
Miami U–Hamilton Campus, OH A
Miami U–Middletown Campus, OH A
Michigan Technological U, MI A,B
Milwaukee School of Engineering, WI B
Oklahoma State U, OK B
Pittsburg State U, KS B
Purdue U Calumet, IN A,B
Purdue U North Central, IN A,B
Rochester Comm and Tech Coll, MN A
Southwest Missouri State U, MO B
The U of Akron, OH A,B
U of Cincinnati, OH A,B
U of Dayton, OH B
U of Rio Grande, OH A,B
U of Southern Indiana, IN A
U of Toledo, OH A,B
Wayne State U, MI B
Youngstown State U, OH A,B

MEDICAL ADMINISTRATIVE ASSISTANT

AIB Coll of Business, IA A
Baker Coll of Auburn Hills, MI A,B
Baker Coll of Cadillac, MI A
Baker Coll of Clinton Township, MI A
Baker Coll of Flint, MI A
Baker Coll of Jackson, MI A
Baker Coll of Muskegon, MI A
Baker Coll of Owosso, MI A
Baker Coll of Port Huron, MI A
Bryant and Stratton Coll, WI A
Davenport U, Grand Rapids, MI A
Davenport U, Kalamazoo, MI A
Davenport U, Lansing, MI A
Dickinson State U, ND A
Gallipolis Career Coll, OH A
Hamilton Coll, IA A
Hannibal-LaGrange Coll, MO A
Lewis Coll of Business, MI A
Lincoln Coll, Normal, IL A
Metro Business Coll, MO A
Miami U–Middletown Campus, OH A
Midland Lutheran Coll, NE A
Midstate Coll, IL A
Northern Michigan U, MI A
Ohio U, OH B
Ohio U–Lancaster, OH A
Presentation Coll, SD A
Rochester Comm and Tech Coll, MN A
Tabor Coll, KS B
The U of Akron, OH A
U of Cincinnati, OH A
U of Northwestern Ohio, OH A
U of Rio Grande, OH A
Wright State U, OH A
Youngstown State U, OH A

MEDICAL ASSISTANT

Baker Coll of Auburn Hills, MI A
Baker Coll of Cadillac, MI A
Baker Coll of Clinton Township, MI A
Baker Coll of Flint, MI A
Baker Coll of Jackson, MI A
Baker Coll of Muskegon, MI A
Baker Coll of Owosso, MI A
Baker Coll of Port Huron, MI A
Bryant and Stratton Coll, WI A
Colorado Tech U Sioux Falls Campus, SD A
Davenport U, Grand Rapids, MI A
Davenport U, Kalamazoo, MI A
Davenport U, Lansing, MI A
Hamilton Coll, IA A
International Business Coll, Fort Wayne, IN A,B
Kaplan Coll, IA A
Midstate Coll, IL A
Minnesota School of Business-Richfield, MN A
National American U–Sioux Falls Branch, SD A
Ohio U, OH A
Palmer Coll of Chiropractic, IA A
Presentation Coll, SD A
Robert Morris Coll, IL A
Rockford Business Coll, IL A
The U of Akron, OH A
U of Northwestern Ohio, OH A
U of Toledo, OH A
Waldorf Coll, IA A
Youngstown State U, OH A

MEDICAL DIETICIAN

The Ohio State U, OH B
U of Illinois at Chicago, IL B

MEDICAL ILLUSTRATING

Alma Coll, MI B
The Cleveland Inst of Art, OH B
Iowa State U of Science and Technology, IA B
Olivet Coll, MI B

MEDICAL LABORATORY ASSISTANT

Youngstown State U, OH A

MEDICAL LABORATORY TECHNICIAN

Andrews U, MI B
Baker Coll of Owosso, MI A
Concordia U, NE B
Dakota State U, SD A
DePaul U, IL B
East Central U, OK B
Ferris State U, MI A,B
Indiana U Northwest, IN A
Madonna U, MI A
Marquette U, WI B
Mercy Coll of Northwest Ohio, OH A
Northern Michigan U, MI A,B
Northern State U, SD B
Northwestern Oklahoma State U, OK B
Northwest Missouri State U, MO B
Presentation Coll, SD A
Purdue U Calumet, IN B
Rochester Comm and Tech Coll, MN A
Shawnee State U, OH A,B
U of Cincinnati, OH A
U of Mary, ND B
U of Missouri–Kansas City, MO B
U of Rio Grande, OH A
U of Science and Arts of Oklahoma, OK B
Winona State U, MN B
Youngstown State U, OH A

MEDICAL LABORATORY TECHNOLOGY

The Coll of St. Scholastica, MN B
Concordia Coll, MN B
Evangel U, MO A
Ferris State U, MI A
Oakland U, MI B
Purdue U North Central, IN A
Rockhurst U, MO B
Roosevelt U, IL B
Southeastern Oklahoma State U, OK B
U of Cincinnati, OH B
U of Illinois at Springfield, IL B
U of Oklahoma, OK B

MEDICAL MICROBIOLOGY

U of Wisconsin–La Crosse, WI B

MEDICAL NUTRITION

Elmhurst Coll, IL B

MEDICAL OFFICE MANAGEMENT

Minnesota School of Business-Richfield, MN A
The U of Akron, OH A
Youngstown State U, OH A

MEDICAL RADIOLOGIC TECHNOLOGY

Avila U, MO B
Bacone Coll, OK A
Coll of St. Catherine, MN A
Coll of St. Catherine–Minneapolis, MN A
Indiana U Northwest, IN A,B
Indiana U–Purdue U Indianapolis, IN A,B
Indiana U South Bend, IN A
Kent State U, OH A
Kent State U, Salem Campus, OH A
Marygrove Coll, MI A,B
Mercy Coll of Northwest Ohio, OH A
Minot State U, ND B
Missouri Southern State Coll, MO A
Mount Marty Coll, SD B
The Ohio State U, OH B
Presentation Coll, SD B
Shawnee State U, OH A
Southern Illinois U Carbondale, IL B
Southwest Missouri State U, MO B
The U of Akron, OH A
U of Nebraska Medical Center, NE B
U of St. Francis, IL B
U of Southern Indiana, IN A
Wayne State U, MI B

MEDICAL RECORDS ADMINISTRATION

Baker Coll of Auburn Hills, MI A,B
Baker Coll of Cadillac, MI A
Baker Coll of Clinton Township, MI A
Baker Coll of Flint, MI A,B
Baker Coll of Jackson, MI A
Baker Coll of Port Huron, MI A
Chicago State U, IL B
Coll of St. Catherine–Minneapolis, MN A
Coll of Saint Mary, NE A,B
Dakota State U, SD A,B
Davenport U, Kalamazoo, MI A
East Central U, OK B
Ferris State U, MI A,B
Illinois State U, IL B
Indiana U Northwest, IN A,B
Indiana U–Purdue U Indianapolis, IN B
The Ohio State U, OH B
Park U, MO A
Presentation Coll, SD A
Southwestern Oklahoma State U, OK B
U of Illinois at Chicago, IL B
U of Kansas, KS B
U of Wisconsin–Milwaukee, WI B

MEDICAL RECORDS TECHNOLOGY

Baker Coll of Flint, MI A
Baker Coll of Jackson, MI A
Coll of St. Catherine, MN A
Mercy Coll of Northwest Ohio, OH A
Missouri Western State Coll, MO A
Robert Morris Coll, IL A,B

MEDICAL TECHNOLOGY

Anderson U, IN B
Andrews U, MI B
Aquinas Coll, MI B
Augustana Coll, SD B
Aurora U, IL B
Avila U, MO B
Baldwin-Wallace Coll, OH B
Ball State U, IN B
Bemidji State U, MN B
Benedictine U, IL B
Blackburn Coll, IL B
Bluffton Coll, OH B
Bowling Green State U, OH B
Bradley U, IL B
Briar Cliff U, IA B

Cameron U, OK B
Carroll Coll, WI B
Cedarville U, OH B
Central Michigan U, MI B
Central Missouri State U, MO B
Coll of Mount St. Joseph, OH B
Coll of St. Catherine, MN B
Coll of St. Catherine–Minneapolis, MN A
Coll of Saint Mary, NE B
Coll of the Ozarks, MO B
Concordia Coll, MN B
Culver-Stockton Coll, MO B
Defiance Coll, OH B
DePaul U, IL B
DePauw U, IN B
Dominican U, IL B
Dordt Coll, IA B
Eastern Illinois U, IL B
Eastern Michigan U, MI B
Edgewood Coll, WI B
Elmhurst Coll, IL B
Eureka Coll, IL B
Evangel U, MO B
Ferris State U, MI B
Fort Hays State U, KS B
Graceland U, IA B
Grand Valley State U, MI B
Illinois Coll, IL B
Illinois State U, IL B
Illinois Wesleyan U, IL B
Indiana State U, IN B
Indiana U East, IN A,B
Indiana U Kokomo, IN B
Indiana U–Purdue U Fort Wayne, IN B
Indiana U–Purdue U Indianapolis, IN B
Indiana U Southeast, IN B
Indiana Wesleyan U, IN B
Jamestown Coll, ND B
Jewish Hospital Coll of Nursing and Allied Health, MO B
Kansas State U, KS B
Kent State U, OH B
Langston U, OK B
Lewis U, IL B
Lindenwood U, MO B
Luther Coll, IA B
Madonna U, MI B
Malone Coll, OH B
Manchester Coll, IN B
Marian Coll of Fond du Lac, WI B
Maryville U of Saint Louis, MO B
Mayo School of Health Sciences, MN A
McKendree Coll, IL B
Miami U, OH B
Michigan State U, MI B
Michigan Technological U, MI B
Minnesota State U, Mankato, MN B
Minnesota State U, Moorhead, MN B
Minot State U, ND B
Missouri Southern State Coll, MO B
Missouri Western State Coll, MO B
Morningside Coll, IA B
Mount Marty Coll, SD B
Mount Mercy Coll, IA B
Mount Vernon Nazarene U, OH B
Muskingum Coll, OH B
National-Louis U, IL B
North Dakota State U, ND B
Northeastern State U, OK B
Northern Illinois U, IL B
Northern Michigan U, MI A,B
Northern State U, SD B
North Park U, IL B
Northwestern Coll, IA B
Northwest Missouri State U, MO B
Notre Dame Coll, OH B
Oakland U, MI B
Ohio Northern U, OH B
The Ohio State U, OH B
Oklahoma Christian U, OK B
Oklahoma Panhandle State U, OK B
Oklahoma State U, OK B
Olivet Nazarene U, IL B
Peru State Coll, NE B
Pittsburg State U, KS B
Purdue U, IN B
Purdue U Calumet, IN B
Purdue U North Central, IN A
Quincy U, IL B
Roosevelt U, IL B
Rush U, IL B
Saginaw Valley State U, MI B
St. Cloud State U, MN B
Saint Joseph's Coll, IN B
Saint Mary-of-the-Woods Coll, IN B
Saint Mary's Coll, IN B
Saint Mary's U of Minnesota, MN B
St. Norbert Coll, WI B
Simpson Coll, IA B
South Dakota State U, SD B
Southeastern Oklahoma State U, OK B
Southeast Missouri State U, MO B
Southwest Baptist U, MO B
Southwestern Oklahoma State U, OK B
Southwest Missouri State U, MO B
Springfield Coll in Illinois, IL A
Tabor Coll, KS B
Taylor U, IN B
Union Coll, NE B
The U of Akron, OH B
U of Central Oklahoma, OK B
U of Cincinnati, OH B
U of Evansville, IN B
The U of Findlay, OH B
U of Illinois at Chicago, IL B
U of Indianapolis, IN B
The U of Iowa, IA B
U of Kansas, KS B
U of Mary, ND B
U of Michigan, MI B
U of Michigan–Flint, MI B
U of Minnesota, Twin Cities Campus, MN B
U of Missouri–St. Louis, MO B
U of Nebraska Medical Center, NE B
U of North Dakota, ND B
U of Rio Grande, OH B
U of St. Francis, IL B
U of Saint Francis, IN B
U of Sioux Falls, SD B
The U of South Dakota, SD B
U of Toledo, OH B
U of Wisconsin–La Crosse, WI B
U of Wisconsin–Madison, WI B
U of Wisconsin–Milwaukee, WI B
U of Wisconsin–Oshkosh, WI B
U of Wisconsin–Stevens Point, WI B
Wartburg Coll, IA B
Wayne State Coll, NE B
Western Illinois U, IL B
Wichita State U, KS B
William Jewell Coll, MO B
Winona State U, MN B
Wright State U, OH B
Xavier U, OH B
Youngstown State U, OH B

MEDICAL TRANSCRIPTION

Baker Coll of Flint, MI A
Baker Coll of Jackson, MI A
Kaplan Coll, IA A
Rockford Business Coll, IL A

MEDICINAL/ PHARMACEUTICAL CHEMISTRY

Butler U, IN B
Ohio Northern U, OH B

MEDIEVAL/RENAISSANCE STUDIES

Cleveland State U, OH B
Cornell Coll, IA B
Hanover Coll, IN B
Ohio Wesleyan U, OH B
U of Chicago, IL B
The U of Iowa, IA B
U of Michigan, MI B
U of Michigan–Dearborn, MI B
U of Nebraska–Lincoln, NE B
U of Notre Dame, IN B
U of Toledo, OH B
Washington U in St. Louis, MO B

MENTAL HEALTH/ REHABILITATION

Evangel U, MO A,B
Governors State U, IL B
Newman U, KS B
Pittsburg State U, KS B
St. Augustine Coll, IL A
St. Cloud State U, MN B
U of Toledo, OH A
Wright State U, OH B

METAL/JEWELRY ARTS

Bowling Green State U, OH B
The Cleveland Inst of Art, OH B
Coll for Creative Studies, MI B
Grand Valley State U, MI B
Indiana U Bloomington, IN B
Loyola U Chicago, IL B
Northern Michigan U, MI B
Northwest Missouri State U, MO B
The U of Akron, OH B
The U of Iowa, IA B
U of Michigan, MI B
U of Wisconsin–Milwaukee, WI B

METALLURGICAL ENGINEERING

Illinois Inst of Technology, IL B
Iowa State U of Science and Technology, IA B
Michigan Technological U, MI B
The Ohio State U, OH B
South Dakota School of Mines and Technology, SD B
U of Cincinnati, OH B
U of Michigan, MI B
U of Missouri–Rolla, MO B
U of Wisconsin–Madison, WI B

METALLURGICAL TECHNOLOGY

Purdue U Calumet, IN A
U of Cincinnati, OH B

METALLURGY

Eastern Michigan U, MI B

MEXICAN-AMERICAN STUDIES

U of Michigan, MI B
U of Minnesota, Twin Cities Campus, MN B

MICROBIOLOGY/ BACTERIOLOGY

Ball State U, IN B
Bowling Green State U, OH B
Central Michigan U, MI B
Indiana U Bloomington, IN B
Iowa State U of Science and Technology, IA B
Kansas State U, KS B
Miami U, OH B
Michigan State U, MI B
Michigan Technological U, MI B
Minnesota State U, Mankato, MN B
Missouri Southern State Coll, MO B
North Dakota State U, ND B
Northeastern State U, OK B
Northern Michigan U, MI B
The Ohio State U, OH B
Ohio U, OH B
Ohio Wesleyan U, OH B
Oklahoma State U, OK B
Purdue U Calumet, IN B
St. Cloud State U, MN B
South Dakota State U, SD B
Southern Illinois U Carbondale, IL B
The U of Akron, OH B
U of Cincinnati, OH B
U of Illinois at Urbana–Champaign, IL B
The U of Iowa, IA B
U of Kansas, KS B
U of Michigan, MI B
U of Michigan–Dearborn, MI B
U of Minnesota, Twin Cities Campus, MN B
U of Missouri–Columbia, MO B
U of Oklahoma, OK B
U of Wisconsin–La Crosse, WI B
U of Wisconsin–Madison, WI B

Microbiology/Bacteriology (continued)

U of Wisconsin–Oshkosh, WI B
Wittenberg U, OH B

MIDDLE EASTERN STUDIES

Indiana U Bloomington, IN B
Oberlin Coll, OH B
The Ohio State U, OH B
U of Chicago, IL B
U of Michigan, MI B
U of Minnesota, Twin Cities Campus, MN B
U of Toledo, OH B
Washington U in St. Louis, MO B

MIDDLE SCHOOL EDUCATION

Alverno Coll, WI B
Antioch Coll, OH B
Ashland U, OH B
Avila U, MO B
Baldwin-Wallace Coll, OH B
Bethel Coll, IN B
Black Hills State U, SD B
Bowling Green State U, OH B
Carthage Coll, WI B
Central Methodist Coll, MO B
Central Missouri State U, MO B
Chadron State Coll, NE B
Clarke Coll, IA B
Coll of Mount St. Joseph, OH B
Coll of the Ozarks, MO B
Columbia Coll, MO B
Concordia U, MN B
Concordia U, NE B
Concordia U Wisconsin, WI B
Eastern Illinois U, IL B
Fontbonne U, MO B
The Franciscan U, IA B
Governors State U, IL B
Grace U, NE B
Grand View Coll, IA B
Harris-Stowe State Coll, MO B
Illinois State U, IL B
Indiana Wesleyan U, IN B
Kent State U, OH B
Lakeland Coll, WI B
Lincoln Coll, Lincoln, IL A
Lindenwood U, MO B
Lourdes Coll, OH B
Luther Coll, IA B
Malone Coll, OH B
Marian Coll of Fond du Lac, WI B
Marquette U, WI B
Maryville U of Saint Louis, MO B
Miami U, OH B
MidAmerica Nazarene U, KS B
Midland Lutheran Coll, NE B
Minnesota State U, Moorhead, MN B
Missouri Southern State Coll, MO B
Mount Mercy Coll, IA B
Mount Union Coll, OH B
Mount Vernon Nazarene U, OH B
Nebraska Wesleyan U, NE B
Northland Coll, WI B
Northwest Missouri State U, MO B
Oakland City U, IN B
Ohio Dominican U, OH B
Ohio Northern U, OH B
Otterbein Coll, OH B
Peru State Coll, NE B
St. Cloud State U, MN B
Southwest Baptist U, MO B
Southwest Missouri State U, MO B
Taylor U, IN B
Trinity Christian Coll, IL B
The U of Akron, OH B
U of Kansas, KS B
U of Michigan–Dearborn, MI B
U of Minnesota, Duluth, MN B
U of Missouri–Columbia, MO B
U of Missouri–St. Louis, MO B
U of Nebraska–Lincoln, NE B
U of North Dakota, ND B
U of Northern Iowa, IA B
U of Sioux Falls, SD B
The U of South Dakota, SD B
U of Wisconsin–Platteville, WI B
Upper Iowa U, IA B
Urbana U, OH B
Ursuline Coll, OH B
Viterbo U, WI B
Washington U in St. Louis, MO B
Webster U, MO B
Westminster Coll, MO B
William Woods U, MO B
Winona State U, MN B
Wittenberg U, OH B
Xavier U, OH B
York Coll, NE B
Youngstown State U, OH B

MINING/MINERAL ENGINEERING

Michigan Technological U, MI B
South Dakota School of Mines and Technology, SD B
Southern Illinois U Carbondale, IL B
U of Missouri–Rolla, MO B
U of Wisconsin–Madison, WI B

MISSIONARY STUDIES

Bethel Coll, IN B
Cedarville U, OH B
Central Christian Coll of Kansas, KS A,B
Circleville Bible Coll, OH A,B
Crown Coll, MN B
Emmaus Bible Coll, IA B
Faith Baptist Bible Coll and Theological Seminary, IA A,B
Global U of the Assemblies of God, MO B
God's Bible School and Coll, OH B
Grace U, NE B
Hillsdale Free Will Baptist Coll, OK A,B
Manhattan Christian Coll, KS A,B
MidAmerica Nazarene U, KS B
Moody Bible Inst, IL B
Northwestern Coll, MN B
Oak Hills Christian Coll, MN B
Oklahoma Baptist U, OK B
Oklahoma Christian U, OK B
Oral Roberts U, OK B
Reformed Bible Coll, MI B
Southern Nazarene U, OK B

MODERN LANGUAGES

Albion Coll, MI B
Alma Coll, MI B
Ball State U, IN B
Beloit Coll, WI B
Bemidji State U, MN B
Benedictine Coll, KS B
Buena Vista U, IA B
Carthage Coll, WI B
Chicago State U, IL B
Cornell Coll, IA B
Creighton U, NE B
DePaul U, IL B
Greenville Coll, IL B
Hastings Coll, NE B
Kenyon Coll, OH B
Lake Erie Coll, OH B
Luther Coll, IA B
Marian Coll of Fond du Lac, WI B
MidAmerica Nazarene U, KS B
Minnesota State U, Mankato, MN B
Monmouth Coll, IL B
North Central Coll, IL B
North Park U, IL B
Oakland U, MI B
Olivet Nazarene U, IL B
Stephens Coll, MO B
U of Chicago, IL B
U of Missouri–St. Louis, MO B
Walsh U, OH B
Washington U in St. Louis, MO B
Wayne State Coll, NE B
Wilmington Coll, OH B
Wittenberg U, OH B
Wright State U, OH B

MOLECULAR BIOLOGY

Ball State U, IN B
Beloit Coll, WI B
Benedictine U, IL B
Bethel Coll, MN B
Bradley U, IL B
Coe Coll, IA B
Kenyon Coll, OH B
Marquette U, WI B
Muskingum Coll, OH B
Northwestern U, IL B
Ohio Northern U, OH B
Otterbein Coll, OH B
Southwest Missouri State U, MO B
U of Michigan, MI B
U of Minnesota, Duluth, MN B
U of Wisconsin–Madison, WI B
U of Wisconsin–Parkside, WI B
U of Wisconsin–Superior, WI B
William Jewell Coll, MO B

MORTUARY SCIENCE

Cincinnati Coll of Mortuary Science, OH A,B
Lindenwood U, MO B
Mid-America Coll of Funeral Service, IN A
Southern Illinois U Carbondale, IL B
U of Central Oklahoma, OK B
U of Minnesota, Twin Cities Campus, MN B
Wayne State U, MI B
Worsham Coll of Mortuary Science, IL A

MULTI/ INTERDISCIPLINARY STUDIES RELATED

Eastern Illinois U, IL B
The Franciscan U, IA B
Grace Bible Coll, MI B
Kent State U, OH B
Ohio U, OH A
Ohio Wesleyan U, OH B
Otterbein Coll, OH B
St. Olaf Coll, MN B
The U of Akron, OH A
U of Toledo, OH A,B
Ursuline Coll, OH B
Washington U in St. Louis, MO B
Wheaton Coll, IL B

MULTIMEDIA

The Art Insts International Minnesota, MN A,B
Calumet Coll of Saint Joseph, IN B
Columbia Coll Chicago, IL B
Columbus Coll of Art and Design, OH B
International Academy of Design & Technology, IL A
Maharishi U of Management, IA B
Minneapolis Coll of Art and Design, MN B
U of Michigan, MI B
Westwood Coll of Technology-Chicago Du Page, IL A
Westwood Coll of Technology–Chicago River Oaks, IL A

MUSEUM STUDIES

Beloit Coll, WI B
Luther Coll, IA B
Oklahoma Baptist U, OK B
The U of Iowa, IA B

MUSIC

Adrian Coll, MI B
Albion Coll, MI B
Alma Coll, MI B
Alverno Coll, WI B
Andrews U, MI B
Antioch Coll, OH B
Aquinas Coll, MI B
Ashland U, OH B
Augsburg Coll, MN B
Augustana Coll, IL B
Augustana Coll, SD B
Avila U, MO B
Baker U, KS B
Baldwin-Wallace Coll, OH B
Ball State U, IN B
Baptist Bible Coll, MO B
Beloit Coll, WI B
Bemidji State U, MN B
Benedictine Coll, KS B
Benedictine U, IL B
Bethany Coll, KS B
Bethany Lutheran Coll, MN B
Bethel Coll, IN A,B
Bethel Coll, KS B

Institution	Degree
Bethel Coll, MN	B
Blackburn Coll, IL	B
Black Hills State U, SD	B
Bluffton Coll, OH	B
Bowling Green State U, OH	B
Bradley U, IL	B
Briar Cliff U, IA	B
Buena Vista U, IA	B
Butler U, IN	B
Calvin Coll, MI	B
Cameron U, OK	B
Capital U, OH	B
Cardinal Stritch U, WI	B
Carleton Coll, MN	B
Carroll Coll, WI	B
Carthage Coll, WI	B
Case Western Reserve U, OH	B
Cedarville U, OH	B
Central Christian Coll of Kansas, KS	A
Central Coll, IA	B
Central Methodist Coll, MO	B
Central Michigan U, MI	B
Central Missouri State U, MO	B
Chadron State Coll, NE	B
Chicago State U, IL	B
Clarke Coll, IA	B
Cleveland Inst of Music, OH	B
Cleveland State U, OH	B
Coe Coll, IA	B
Coll of Mount St. Joseph, OH	B
Coll of Saint Benedict, MN	B
Coll of St. Catherine, MN	B
The Coll of St. Scholastica, MN	B
Coll of the Ozarks, MO	B
The Coll of Wooster, OH	B
Columbia Coll Chicago, IL	B
Concordia Coll, MN	B
Concordia U, IL	B
Concordia U, MI	B
Concordia U, MN	B
Concordia U, NE	B
Concordia U Wisconsin, WI	B
Cornell Coll, IA	B
Cornerstone U, MI	B
Creighton U, NE	B
Crown Coll, MN	A,B
Culver-Stockton Coll, MO	B
Dana Coll, NE	B
Denison U, OH	B
DePaul U, IL	B
DePauw U, IN	B
Dickinson State U, ND	B
Doane Coll, NE	B
Dordt Coll, IA	B
Drake U, IA	B
Drury U, MO	B
Earlham Coll, IN	B
East Central U, OK	B
Eastern Illinois U, IL	B
Eastern Michigan U, MI	B
Edgewood Coll, WI	B
Elmhurst Coll, IL	B
Emporia State U, KS	B
Eureka Coll, IL	B
Evangel U, MO	B
Fort Hays State U, KS	B
The Franciscan U, IA	B
Goshen Coll, IN	B
Grace Bible Coll, MI	A,B
Graceland U, IA	B
Grace U, NE	A,B
Grand Valley State U, MI	B
Grand View Coll, IA	A
Great Lakes Christian Coll, MI	B
Greenville Coll, IL	B
Grinnell Coll, IA	B
Gustavus Adolphus Coll, MN	B
Hamline U, MN	B
Hannibal-LaGrange Coll, MO	B
Hanover Coll, IN	B
Hastings Coll, NE	B
Heidelberg Coll, OH	B
Hillsdale Coll, MI	B
Hillsdale Free Will Baptist Coll, OK	A
Hiram Coll, OH	B
Hope Coll, MI	B
Huntington Coll, IN	B
Illinois Coll, IL	B
Illinois State U, IL	B
Illinois Wesleyan U, IL	B
Indiana State U, IN	B
Indiana U Bloomington, IN	B
Indiana U–Purdue U Fort Wayne, IN	B
Indiana U Southeast, IN	B
Indiana Wesleyan U, IN	A,B
Iowa State U of Science and Technology, IA	B
Iowa Wesleyan Coll, IA	B
Jamestown Coll, ND	B
Judson Coll, IL	B
Kalamazoo Coll, MI	B
Kansas State U, KS	B
Kent State U, OH	B
Kenyon Coll, OH	B
Knox Coll, IL	B
Lake Erie Coll, OH	B
Lake Forest Coll, IL	B
Lakeland Coll, WI	B
Langston U, OK	B
Lawrence U, WI	B
Lewis U, IL	B
Lincoln Coll, Lincoln, IL	A
Lindenwood U, MO	B
Loras Coll, IA	B
Lourdes Coll, OH	A
Loyola U Chicago, IL	B
Luther Coll, IA	B
Macalester Coll, MN	B
MacMurray Coll, IL	B
Madonna U, MI	B
Malone Coll, OH	B
Manchester Coll, IN	B
Maranatha Baptist Bible Coll, WI	B
Marian Coll, IN	A,B
Marian Coll of Fond du Lac, WI	B
Marietta Coll, OH	B
Martin U, IN	B
Marygrove Coll, MI	B
Maryville U of Saint Louis, MO	B
McKendree Coll, IL	B
McPherson Coll, KS	B
Messenger Coll, MO	B
Miami U, OH	B
MidAmerica Nazarene U, KS	B
Midland Lutheran Coll, NE	B
Millikin U, IL	B
Minnesota State U, Mankato, MN	B
Minnesota State U, Moorhead, MN	B
Minot State U, ND	B
Missouri Southern State Coll, MO	B
Missouri Western State Coll, MO	B
Monmouth Coll, IL	B
Morningside Coll, IA	B
Mount Marty Coll, SD	B
Mount Mary Coll, WI	B
Mount Mercy Coll, IA	B
Mount Union Coll, OH	B
Mount Vernon Nazarene U, OH	B
Muskingum Coll, OH	B
Nebraska Wesleyan U, NE	B
North Central Coll, IL	B
North Dakota State U, ND	B
Northeastern Illinois U, IL	B
Northeastern State U, OK	B
Northern Illinois U, IL	B
Northern Michigan U, MI	B
Northern State U, SD	B
Northland Coll, WI	B
North Park U, IL	B
Northwestern Coll, IA	B
Northwestern Coll, MN	B
Northwestern Oklahoma State U, OK	B
Northwestern U, IL	B
Northwest Missouri State U, MO	B
Oak Hills Christian Coll, MN	B
Oakland City U, IN	B
Oakland U, MI	B
Oberlin Coll, OH	B
Ohio Northern U, OH	B
The Ohio State U, OH	B
Ohio U, OH	B
Ohio Wesleyan U, OH	B
Oklahoma Baptist U, OK	B
Oklahoma Christian U, OK	B
Oklahoma City U, OK	B
Oklahoma State U, OK	B
Oklahoma Wesleyan U, OK	B
Olivet Nazarene U, IL	B
Oral Roberts U, OK	B
Ottawa U, KS	B
Otterbein Coll, OH	B
Peru State Coll, NE	B
Pillsbury Baptist Bible Coll, MN	B
Pittsburg State U, KS	B
Principia Coll, IL	B
Quincy U, IL	B
Ripon Coll, WI	B
Rochester Coll, MI	B
Roosevelt U, IL	B
Saginaw Valley State U, MI	B
St. Ambrose U, IA	B
St. Cloud State U, MN	B
Saint John's U, MN	B
Saint Joseph's Coll, IN	A,B
Saint Louis U, MO	B
Saint Mary-of-the-Woods Coll, IN	B
Saint Mary's Coll, IN	B
Saint Mary's U of Minnesota, MN	B
St. Norbert Coll, WI	B
St. Olaf Coll, MN	B
Saint Xavier U, IL	B
Siena Heights U, MI	B
Silver Lake Coll, WI	B
Simpson Coll, IA	B
South Dakota State U, SD	B
Southeastern Oklahoma State U, OK	B
Southeast Missouri State U, MO	B
Southern Illinois U Carbondale, IL	B
Southern Illinois U Edwardsville, IL	B
Southwest Baptist U, MO	B
Southwestern Coll, KS	B
Southwestern Oklahoma State U, OK	B
Southwest Minnesota State U, MN	B
Southwest Missouri State U, MO	B
Spring Arbor U, MI	B
Springfield Coll in Illinois, IL	A
Sterling Coll, KS	B
Tabor Coll, KS	B
Taylor U, IN	B
Taylor U, Fort Wayne Campus, IN	B
Trinity Bible Coll, ND	A,B
Trinity Christian Coll, IL	B
Trinity International U, IL	B
Truman State U, MO	B
Union Coll, NE	B
The U of Akron, OH	B
U of Central Oklahoma, OK	B
U of Chicago, IL	B
U of Cincinnati, OH	B
U of Dayton, OH	B
U of Evansville, IN	B
U of Illinois at Chicago, IL	B
U of Illinois at Urbana–Champaign, IL	B
U of Indianapolis, IN	B
The U of Iowa, IA	B
U of Kansas, KS	B
U of Mary, ND	B
U of Michigan, MI	B
U of Michigan–Dearborn, MI	B
U of Michigan–Flint, MI	B
U of Minnesota, Duluth, MN	B
U of Minnesota, Morris, MN	B
U of Minnesota, Twin Cities Campus, MN	B
U of Missouri–Columbia, MO	B
U of Missouri–Kansas City, MO	B
U of Missouri–St. Louis, MO	B
U of Nebraska at Kearney, NE	B
U of Nebraska at Omaha, NE	B
U of Nebraska–Lincoln, NE	B
U of North Dakota, ND	B
U of Northern Iowa, IA	B
U of Notre Dame, IN	B
U of Oklahoma, OK	B
U of Rio Grande, OH	A,B
U of St. Thomas, MN	B
U of Science and Arts of Oklahoma, OK	B
U of Sioux Falls, SD	B
The U of South Dakota, SD	B
U of Toledo, OH	B
U of Tulsa, OK	B
U of Wisconsin–Eau Claire, WI	B
U of Wisconsin–Green Bay, WI	B
U of Wisconsin–La Crosse, WI	B
U of Wisconsin–Madison, WI	B
U of Wisconsin–Milwaukee, WI	B
U of Wisconsin–Oshkosh, WI	B

Music (continued)

U of Wisconsin–Parkside, WI B
U of Wisconsin–Platteville, WI B
U of Wisconsin–River Falls, WI B
U of Wisconsin–Stevens Point, WI B
U of Wisconsin–Superior, WI B
U of Wisconsin–Whitewater, WI B
Upper Iowa U, IA B
Valley City State U, ND B
Valparaiso U, IN B
Viterbo U, WI B
Wabash Coll, IN B
Waldorf Coll, IA A
Wartburg Coll, IA B
Washington U in St. Louis, MO B
Wayne State Coll, NE B
Wayne State U, MI B
Webster U, MO B
Western Illinois U, IL B
Western Michigan U, MI B
Wheaton Coll, IL B
Wichita State U, KS B
William Jewell Coll, MO B
Winona State U, MN B
Wisconsin Lutheran Coll, WI B
Wittenberg U, OH B
Wright State U, OH B
Xavier U, OH B
York Coll, NE B
Youngstown State U, OH B

MUSICAL INSTRUMENT TECHNOLOGY

Ball State U, IN B
Central Christian Coll of Kansas, KS A
Indiana U Bloomington, IN A
Malone Coll, OH B

MUSIC BUSINESS MANAGEMENT/ MERCHANDISING

Anderson U, IN B
Baldwin-Wallace Coll, OH B
Benedictine Coll, KS B
Butler U, IN B
Capital U, OH B
Central Christian Coll of Kansas, KS A
Coll of the Ozarks, MO B
Columbia Coll Chicago, IL B
DePaul U, IL B
DePauw U, IN B
Drake U, IA B
Elmhurst Coll, IL B
Ferris State U, MI B
Grace Bible Coll, MI B
Heidelberg Coll, OH B
Illinois Wesleyan U, IL B
Lewis U, IL B
Lincoln Coll, Lincoln, IL A
Luther Coll, IA B
Madonna U, MI B
Marian Coll of Fond du Lac, WI B
Millikin U, IL B
Minnesota State U, Mankato, MN B
Minnesota State U, Moorhead, MN B
North Park U, IL B
Northwest Missouri State U, MO B
Ohio Northern U, OH B
Ohio U, OH B
Oklahoma City U, OK B
Oklahoma State U, OK B
Otterbein Coll, OH B
Peru State Coll, NE B
Quincy U, IL B
Saint Mary's U of Minnesota, MN B
South Dakota State U, SD B
Southern Nazarene U, OK B
Southwestern Oklahoma State U, OK B
Tabor Coll, KS B
Taylor U, IN B
U of Evansville, IN B
U of St. Thomas, MN B
U of Sioux Falls, SD B
Valparaiso U, IN B
Wheaton Coll, IL B
Winona State U, MN B

MUSIC CONDUCTING

Bowling Green State U, OH B
Calvin Coll, MI B
Central Christian Coll of Kansas, KS A
Luther Coll, IA B
Ohio U, OH B

MUSIC (GENERAL PERFORMANCE)

Anderson U, IN B
Bethel Coll, IN B
Black Hills State U, SD B
Bowling Green State U, OH B
Bradley U, IL B
Calvin Coll, MI B
Cameron U, OK B
Capital U, OH B
Central Christian Coll of Kansas, KS A
Central Methodist Coll, MO B
Columbia Coll Chicago, IL B
Concordia Coll, MN B
DePaul U, IL B
DePauw U, IN B
Eastern Michigan U, MI B
Hope Coll, MI B
Illinois State U, IL B
Indiana U South Bend, IN B
Luther Coll, IA B
Marygrove Coll, MI B
Miami U, OH B
Millikin U, IL B
Mount Union Coll, OH B
Nebraska Wesleyan U, NE B
Northwestern Coll, MN B
Northwestern U, IL B
The Ohio State U, OH B
Ohio U, OH B
Oklahoma Wesleyan U, OK B
Oral Roberts U, OK B
Otterbein Coll, OH B
Saint Mary's U of Minnesota, MN B
St. Olaf Coll, MN B
Saint Xavier U, IL B
Simpson Coll, IA B
Southeastern Oklahoma State U, OK B
Southeast Missouri State U, MO B
Southern Nazarene U, OK B
Southwest Missouri State U, MO B
Trinity Christian Coll, IL B
Union Coll, NE B
The U of Akron, OH B
U of Illinois at Urbana–Champaign, IL B
U of Indianapolis, IN B
U of North Dakota, ND B
U of Northern Iowa, IA B
Valparaiso U, IN B
Viterbo U, WI B
Wartburg Coll, IA B
Webster U, MO B
Western Michigan U, MI B
Wheaton Coll, IL B
William Jewell Coll, MO B
Youngstown State U, OH B

MUSIC HISTORY

Aquinas Coll, MI B
Baldwin-Wallace Coll, OH B
Bowling Green State U, OH B
Butler U, IN B
Calvin Coll, MI B
Central Christian Coll of Kansas, KS A
Central Michigan U, MI B
The Coll of Wooster, OH B
Hastings Coll, NE B
Hope Coll, MI B
Indiana U Bloomington, IN B
Lincoln Coll, Lincoln, IL A
Luther Coll, IA B
Northwestern U, IL B
Oberlin Coll, OH B
The Ohio State U, OH B
Ohio U, OH B
Otterbein Coll, OH B
Rockford Coll, IL B
Roosevelt U, IL B
St. Cloud State U, MN B
Saint Joseph's Coll, IN B
The U of Akron, OH B
U of Chicago, IL B
U of Cincinnati, OH B
U of Illinois at Urbana–Champaign, IL B
The U of Iowa, IA B
U of Kansas, KS B
U of Michigan, MI B
U of Michigan–Dearborn, MI B
U of Missouri–St. Louis, MO B
U of Wisconsin–Milwaukee, WI B
Washington U in St. Louis, MO B
Western Michigan U, MI B
Wheaton Coll, IL B
Wright State U, OH B
Youngstown State U, OH B

MUSICOLOGY

St. Olaf Coll, MN B
The U of Akron, OH B

MUSIC (PIANO AND ORGAN PERFORMANCE)

Andrews U, MI B
Aquinas Coll, MI B
Augustana Coll, IL B
Baldwin-Wallace Coll, OH B
Ball State U, IN B
Benedictine Coll, KS B
Bethel Coll, IN A,B
Bowling Green State U, OH B
Butler U, IN B
Calvin Coll, MI B
Cameron U, OK B
Capital U, OH B
Cedarville U, OH B
Central Christian Coll of Kansas, KS A
Cincinnati Bible Coll and Seminary, OH B
Cleveland Inst of Music, OH B
Concordia Coll, MN B
Concordia U, IL B
Concordia U, MI B
Concordia U, NE B
DePaul U, IL B
Drake U, IA B
Grace Coll, IN B
Grand Valley State U, MI B
Hannibal-LaGrange Coll, MO B
Hastings Coll, NE B
Heidelberg Coll, OH B
Huntington Coll, IN B
Illinois Wesleyan U, IL B
Indiana U Bloomington, IN B
Indiana U–Purdue U Fort Wayne, IN B
Lawrence U, WI B
Lincoln Christian Coll, IL B
Lincoln Coll, Lincoln, IL A
Luther Coll, IA B
Minnesota State U, Mankato, MN B
Minnesota State U, Moorhead, MN B
Mount Vernon Nazarene U, OH B
North Central Coll, IL B
Northeastern State U, OK B
Northern Michigan U, MI B
Northwestern Coll, MN B
Northwestern U, IL B
Northwest Missouri State U, MO B
Oakland U, MI B
Oberlin Coll, OH B
The Ohio State U, OH B
Ohio U, OH B
Oklahoma Baptist U, OK B
Oklahoma City U, OK B
Olivet Nazarene U, IL B
Otterbein Coll, OH B
Pittsburg State U, KS B
Roosevelt U, IL B
Saint Mary-of-the-Woods Coll, IN B
Saint Mary's Coll, IN B
Southern Nazarene U, OK B
Southwestern Oklahoma State U, OK B
Spring Arbor U, MI B
Tabor Coll, KS B
Taylor U, IN B
Trinity Christian Coll, IL B
Truman State U, MO B
The U of Akron, OH B
U of Central Oklahoma, OK B
U of Cincinnati, OH B
The U of Iowa, IA B
U of Kansas, KS B
U of Michigan, MI B
U of Minnesota, Duluth, MN B
U of Missouri–Kansas City, MO B
U of Oklahoma, OK B
U of Sioux Falls, SD B
The U of South Dakota, SD B
U of Tulsa, OK B
Viterbo U, WI B

Waldorf Coll, IA A
Webster U, MO B
Wittenberg U, OH B
Youngstown State U, OH B

MUSIC RELATED

Indiana State U, IN B
Northwestern U, IL B
Saint Mary's U of Minnesota, MN B
St. Olaf Coll, MN B
U of St. Thomas, MN B
Wheaton Coll, IL B

MUSIC TEACHER EDUCATION

Adrian Coll, MI B
Alma Coll, MI B
Alverno Coll, WI B
Anderson U, IN B
Andrews U, MI B
Aquinas Coll, MI B
Ashland U, OH B
Augsburg Coll, MN B
Augustana Coll, IL B
Augustana Coll, SD B
Baker U, KS B
Baldwin-Wallace Coll, OH B
Ball State U, IN B
Baptist Bible Coll, MO B
Beloit Coll, WI B
Bemidji State U, MN B
Benedictine Coll, KS B
Benedictine U, IL B
Bethany Coll, KS B
Bethel Coll, IN B
Bethel Coll, MN B
Bluffton Coll, OH B
Bowling Green State U, OH B
Bradley U, IL B
Buena Vista U, IA B
Butler U, IN B
Calvin Coll, MI B
Cameron U, OK B
Capital U, OH B
Carroll Coll, WI B
Carthage Coll, WI B
Case Western Reserve U, OH B
Cedarville U, OH B
Central Christian Coll of Kansas, KS A
Central Coll, IA B
Central Methodist Coll, MO B
Central Michigan U, MI B
Central Missouri State U, MO B
Chadron State Coll, NE B
Chicago State U, IL B
Clarke Coll, IA B
Cleveland Inst of Music, OH B
Coe Coll, IA B
Coll of Saint Benedict, MN B
Coll of St. Catherine, MN B
Coll of the Ozarks, MO B
The Coll of Wooster, OH B
Concordia Coll, MN B
Concordia U, IL B
Concordia U, MN B
Concordia U, NE B
Concordia U Wisconsin, WI B
Cornell Coll, IA B
Cornerstone U, MI B
Crown Coll, MN B
Culver-Stockton Coll, MO B
Dakota State U, SD B
Dakota Wesleyan U, SD B
Dana Coll, NE B
DePaul U, IL B
DePauw U, IN B
Dickinson State U, ND B
Dordt Coll, IA B
Drake U, IA B
Drury U, MO B
East Central U, OK B
Eastern Michigan U, MI B
Elmhurst Coll, IL B
Emporia State U, KS B
Eureka Coll, IL B
Evangel U, MO B
Faith Baptist Bible Coll and Theological Seminary, IA B
Fort Hays State U, KS B
The Franciscan U, IA B
God's Bible School and Coll, OH B
Goshen Coll, IN B
Grace Bible Coll, MI B
Grace Coll, IN B
Graceland U, IA B
Grace U, NE B
Grand Valley State U, MI B
Greenville Coll, IL B
Gustavus Adolphus Coll, MN B
Hamline U, MN B
Hannibal-LaGrange Coll, MO B
Hastings Coll, NE B
Heidelberg Coll, OH B
Hope Coll, MI B
Huntington Coll, IN B
Illinois State U, IL B
Illinois Wesleyan U, IL B
Indiana U Bloomington, IN B
Indiana U–Purdue U Fort Wayne, IN B
Indiana U South Bend, IN B
Indiana Wesleyan U, IN B
Iowa State U of Science and Technology, IA B
Iowa Wesleyan Coll, IA B
Judson Coll, IL B
Kansas State U, KS B
Kent State U, OH B
Lakeland Coll, WI B
Langston U, OK B
Lawrence U, WI B
Lindenwood U, MO B
Luther Coll, IA B
MacMurray Coll, IL B
Madonna U, MI B
Malone Coll, OH B
Manchester Coll, IN B
Maranatha Baptist Bible Coll, WI B
Marian Coll, IN B
Marian Coll of Fond du Lac, WI B
McPherson Coll, KS B
Miami U, OH B
Michigan State U, MI B
MidAmerica Nazarene U, KS B
Midland Lutheran Coll, NE B
Millikin U, IL B
Minnesota State U, Mankato, MN B
Minnesota State U, Moorhead, MN B
Minot State U, ND B
Missouri Southern State Coll, MO B
Missouri Western State Coll, MO B
Morningside Coll, IA B
Mount Marty Coll, SD B
Mount Mary Coll, WI B
Mount Mercy Coll, IA B
Mount Union Coll, OH B
Mount Vernon Nazarene U, OH B
Muskingum Coll, OH B
Nebraska Wesleyan U, NE B
North Dakota State U, ND B
Northeastern State U, OK B
Northern Illinois U, IL B
Northern Michigan U, MI B
Northern State U, SD B
Northland Coll, WI B
North Park U, IL B
Northwestern Coll, IA B
Northwestern Coll, MN B
Northwestern Oklahoma State U, OK B
Northwestern U, IL B
Northwest Missouri State U, MO B
Oakland City U, IN B
Oakland U, MI B
Oberlin Coll, OH B
Ohio Northern U, OH B
The Ohio State U, OH B
Ohio U, OH B
Ohio Wesleyan U, OH B
Oklahoma Baptist U, OK B
Oklahoma Christian U, OK B
Oklahoma City U, OK B
Oklahoma State U, OK B
Olivet Nazarene U, IL B
Oral Roberts U, OK B
Ottawa U, KS B
Otterbein Coll, OH B
Peru State Coll, NE B
Pillsbury Baptist Bible Coll, MN B
Pittsburg State U, KS B
Quincy U, IL B
Reformed Bible Coll, MI B
Ripon Coll, WI B
Rochester Coll, MI B
Roosevelt U, IL B
St. Ambrose U, IA B
St. Cloud State U, MN B
Saint John's U, MN B
Saint Joseph's Coll, IN B
Saint Mary-of-the-Woods Coll, IN B
Saint Mary's Coll, IN B
Saint Mary's U of Minnesota, MN B
St. Norbert Coll, WI B
St. Olaf Coll, MN B
Saint Xavier U, IL B
Siena Heights U, MI B
Silver Lake Coll, WI B
Simpson Coll, IA B
South Dakota State U, SD B
Southeastern Oklahoma State U, OK B
Southeast Missouri State U, MO B
Southern Nazarene U, OK B
Southwest Baptist U, MO B
Southwestern Coll, KS B
Southwestern Oklahoma State U, OK B
Southwest Minnesota State U, MN B
Southwest Missouri State U, MO B
Spring Arbor U, MI B
Sterling Coll, KS B
Tabor Coll, KS B
Taylor U, IN B
Trinity Christian Coll, IL B
Trinity International U, IL B
Union Coll, NE A,B
The U of Akron, OH B
U of Central Oklahoma, OK B
U of Cincinnati, OH B
U of Dayton, OH B
U of Evansville, IN B
U of Illinois at Urbana–Champaign, IL B
U of Indianapolis, IN B
The U of Iowa, IA B
U of Kansas, KS B
U of Mary, ND B
U of Michigan, MI B
U of Michigan–Flint, MI B
U of Minnesota, Duluth, MN B
U of Minnesota, Twin Cities Campus, MN B
U of Missouri–Columbia, MO B
U of Missouri–Kansas City, MO B
U of Missouri–St. Louis, MO B
U of Nebraska at Omaha, NE B
U of Nebraska–Lincoln, NE B
U of North Dakota, ND B
U of Northern Iowa, IA B
U of Oklahoma, OK B
U of Rio Grande, OH B
U of St. Thomas, MN B
U of Sioux Falls, SD B
The U of South Dakota, SD B
U of Toledo, OH B
U of Tulsa, OK B
U of Wisconsin–La Crosse, WI B
U of Wisconsin–Madison, WI B
U of Wisconsin–Milwaukee, WI B
U of Wisconsin–Oshkosh, WI B
U of Wisconsin–River Falls, WI B
U of Wisconsin–Stevens Point, WI B
U of Wisconsin–Superior, WI B
U of Wisconsin–Whitewater, WI B
Upper Iowa U, IA B
Valley City State U, ND B
Valparaiso U, IN B
VanderCook Coll of Music, IL B
Viterbo U, WI B
Waldorf Coll, IA A
Wartburg Coll, IA B
Wayne State Coll, NE B
Webster U, MO B
Western Michigan U, MI B
Wheaton Coll, IL B
Wichita State U, KS B
William Jewell Coll, MO B
Wilmington Coll, OH B
Winona State U, MN B
Wittenberg U, OH B
Wright State U, OH B
Xavier U, OH B
York Coll, NE B
Youngstown State U, OH B

MUSIC THEORY AND COMPOSITION

Bowling Green State U, OH B
Bradley U, IL B

Music Theory And Composition (continued)

Calvin Coll, MI B
Cameron U, OK B
Central Christian Coll of Kansas, KS A
Central Michigan U, MI B
Central Missouri State U, MO B
Concordia Coll, MN B
DePaul U, IL B
DePauw U, IN B
Hope Coll, MI B
Indiana Wesleyan U, IN B
Luther Coll, IA B
Michigan State U, MI B
Minnesota State U, Moorhead, MN B
Northwestern U, IL B
Oakland U, MI B
The Ohio State U, OH B
Ohio U, OH B
Oklahoma Baptist U, OK B
Oklahoma City U, OK B
Oral Roberts U, OK B
Southeast Missouri State U, MO B
The U of Akron, OH B
U of Illinois at Urbana–Champaign, IL B
U of Kansas, KS B
U of Michigan, MI B
U of Northern Iowa, IA B
U of Oklahoma, OK B
Valparaiso U, IN B
Viterbo U, WI B
Wartburg Coll, IA B
Washington U in St. Louis, MO B
Webster U, MO B
Western Michigan U, MI B
Wheaton Coll, IL B
Wilberforce U, OH B
William Jewell Coll, MO B
Youngstown State U, OH B

MUSIC THERAPY

Alverno Coll, WI B
Augsburg Coll, MN B
Baldwin-Wallace Coll, OH B
The Coll of Wooster, OH B
Eastern Michigan U, MI B
Indiana U–Purdue U Fort Wayne, IN B
Maryville U of Saint Louis, MO B
Michigan State U, MI B
Saint Mary-of-the-Woods Coll, IN B
Southwestern Oklahoma State U, OK B
U of Dayton, OH B
U of Evansville, IN B
The U of Iowa, IA B
U of Kansas, KS B
U of Minnesota, Twin Cities Campus, MN B
U of Missouri–Kansas City, MO B
U of Wisconsin–Eau Claire, WI B
U of Wisconsin–Milwaukee, WI B
U of Wisconsin–Oshkosh, WI B
Wartburg Coll, IA B
Western Michigan U, MI B

MUSIC (VOICE AND CHORAL/OPERA PERFORMANCE)

Alma Coll, MI B
Andrews U, MI B
Aquinas Coll, MI B
Augustana Coll, IL B
Baldwin-Wallace Coll, OH B
Ball State U, IN B
Benedictine Coll, KS B
Bethel Coll, IN B
Black Hills State U, SD B
Bowling Green State U, OH B
Butler U, IN B
Calvin Coll, MI B
Cameron U, OK B
Capital U, OH B
Carroll Coll, WI B
Cedarville U, OH B
Central Christian Coll of Kansas, KS A
Cincinnati Bible Coll and Seminary, OH B
Clarke Coll, IA B
Cleveland Inst of Music, OH B
The Coll of Wooster, OH B
Concordia Coll, MN B
Concordia U, IL B
Concordia U, NE B
DePaul U, IL B
Drake U, IA B
Eureka Coll, IL B
God's Bible School and Coll, OH B
Grand Valley State U, MI B
Hannibal-LaGrange Coll, MO B
Hastings Coll, NE B
Heidelberg Coll, OH B
Huntington Coll, IN B
Illinois Wesleyan U, IL B
Indiana U Bloomington, IN B
Indiana U–Purdue U Fort Wayne, IN B
Judson Coll, IL B
Langston U, OK B
Lawrence U, WI B
Lincoln Christian Coll, IL B
Lincoln Coll, Lincoln, IL A
Lindenwood U, MO B
Luther Coll, IA B
MidAmerica Nazarene U, KS B
Millikin U, IL B
Minnesota State U, Mankato, MN B
Minnesota State U, Moorhead, MN B
Mount Mercy Coll, IA B
Mount Vernon Nazarene U, OH B
North Central Coll, IL B
Northeastern State U, OK B
Northern Michigan U, MI B
Northern State U, SD B
North Park U, IL B
Northwestern Coll, MN B
Northwestern U, IL B
Northwest Missouri State U, MO B
Oakland U, MI B
Oberlin Coll, OH B
The Ohio State U, OH B
Ohio U, OH B
Oklahoma Baptist U, OK B
Oklahoma Christian U, OK B
Oklahoma City U, OK B
Olivet Nazarene U, IL B
Otterbein Coll, OH B
Peru State Coll, NE B
Pittsburg State U, KS B
Rochester Coll, MI B
Roosevelt U, IL B
St. Cloud State U, MN B
Saint Mary-of-the-Woods Coll, IN B
Saint Mary's Coll, IN B
Southern Nazarene U, OK B
Southwestern Oklahoma State U, OK B
Tabor Coll, KS B
Taylor U, IN B
Trinity Christian Coll, IL B
Truman State U, MO B
The U of Akron, OH B
U of Central Oklahoma, OK B
U of Cincinnati, OH B
U of Illinois at Urbana–Champaign, IL B
The U of Iowa, IA B
U of Kansas, KS B
U of Michigan, MI B
U of Missouri–Kansas City, MO B
U of Nebraska at Omaha, NE B
U of Oklahoma, OK B
U of Sioux Falls, SD B
The U of South Dakota, SD B
U of Tulsa, OK B
U of Wisconsin–Milwaukee, WI B
Viterbo U, WI B
Waldorf Coll, IA A
Washington U in St. Louis, MO B
Webster U, MO B
Western Michigan U, MI B
Wilberforce U, OH B
Winona State U, MN B
Wittenberg U, OH B
Youngstown State U, OH B

NATIVE AMERICAN LANGUAGES

Bemidji State U, MN B

NATIVE AMERICAN STUDIES

Bacone Coll, OK A
Bemidji State U, MN B
Black Hills State U, SD B
Nebraska Indian Comm Coll, NE A
Northeastern State U, OK B
Northland Coll, WI B
Rogers State U, OK A
Sitting Bull Coll, ND A
The U of Iowa, IA B
U of Minnesota, Duluth, MN B
U of Minnesota, Twin Cities Campus, MN B
U of North Dakota, ND B
U of Oklahoma, OK B
U of Science and Arts of Oklahoma, OK B
U of Wisconsin–Eau Claire, WI B
U of Wisconsin–Milwaukee, WI B

NATURAL RESOURCES CONSERVATION

Central Michigan U, MI B
Coll of Menominee Nation, WI A
Iowa Wesleyan Coll, IA B
Kent State U, OH B
Michigan State U, MI B
Mount Vernon Nazarene U, OH B
Muskingum Coll, OH B
Northern Michigan U, MI B
Northland Coll, WI B
Northwest Missouri State U, MO B
Peru State Coll, NE B
Purdue U, IN B
Rochester Comm and Tech Coll, MN A
Southeastern Oklahoma State U, OK B
U of Minnesota, Crookston, MN A
U of Nebraska–Lincoln, NE B
U of Wisconsin–Milwaukee, WI B
U of Wisconsin–River Falls, WI B
U of Wisconsin–Stevens Point, WI B
Upper Iowa U, IA B
Washington U in St. Louis, MO B
Winona State U, MN B

NATURAL RESOURCES MANAGEMENT

Bacone Coll, OK A
Ball State U, IN B
Bowling Green State U, OH B
Fort Hays State U, KS B
Grand Valley State U, MI B
Haskell Indian Nations U, KS A
Huntington Coll, IN B
Iowa State U of Science and Technology, IA B
Nebraska Indian Comm Coll, NE A
North Dakota State U, ND B
Northland Coll, WI B
The Ohio State U, OH B
U of Michigan, MI B
U of Michigan–Flint, MI B
U of Minnesota, Crookston, MN A,B
U of Minnesota, Twin Cities Campus, MN B
U of Nebraska–Lincoln, NE B
U of Wisconsin–Madison, WI B
U of Wisconsin–Stevens Point, WI B

NATURAL RESOURCES PROTECTIVE SERVICES

The Ohio State U, OH B

NATURAL SCIENCES

Antioch Coll, OH B
Augsburg Coll, MN B
Avila U, MO B
Bemidji State U, MN B
Benedictine Coll, KS B
Bethel Coll, KS B
Buena Vista U, IA B
Calvin Coll, MI B
Cameron U, OK B
Carthage Coll, WI B

Central Christian Coll of Kansas, KS A
Coll of Mount St. Joseph, OH B
Coll of Saint Benedict, MN B
Coll of Saint Mary, NE B
The Coll of St. Scholastica, MN B
Concordia U, IL B
Concordia U, MN B
Concordia U, NE B
Defiance Coll, OH B
Doane Coll, NE B
Dordt Coll, IA B
Edgewood Coll, WI B
Eureka Coll, IL B
Goshen Coll, IN B
Grand Valley State U, MI B
Iowa Wesleyan Coll, IA B
Kenyon Coll, OH B
Lourdes Coll, OH A
Loyola U Chicago, IL B
Madonna U, MI A,B
Midland Lutheran Coll, NE B
Minnesota State U, Mankato, MN B
Monmouth Coll, IL B
North Central Coll, IL B
Northland Coll, WI B
North Park U, IL B
Oklahoma Baptist U, OK B
Oklahoma Panhandle State U, OK B
Oklahoma Wesleyan U, OK B
Olivet Nazarene U, IL B
Park U, MO B
Peru State Coll, NE B
St. Cloud State U, MN B
St. Gregory's U, OK B
Saint John's U, MN B
Shawnee State U, OH B
Shimer Coll, IL B
Siena Heights U, MI B
Southern Nazarene U, OK B
Stephens Coll, MO B
Tabor Coll, KS B
Taylor U, IN B
The U of Akron, OH B
U of Cincinnati, OH A,B
The U of Findlay, OH B
U of Mary, ND B
U of Michigan–Dearborn, MI B
U of Science and Arts of Oklahoma, OK B
U of Toledo, OH A,B
U of Wisconsin–River Falls, WI B
U of Wisconsin–Stevens Point, WI B
Waldorf Coll, IA A
Walsh U, OH B
Washington U in St. Louis, MO B
Wayne State Coll, NE B
Winona State U, MN B
Wittenberg U, OH B
York Coll, NE B

NAVAL ARCHITECTURE/ MARINE ENGINEERING

U of Michigan, MI B

NEUROSCIENCE

Baldwin-Wallace Coll, OH B
Bowling Green State U, OH B
Carthage Coll, WI B
Central Michigan U, MI B
John Carroll U, OH B
Kenyon Coll, OH B
Lawrence U, WI B
Macalester Coll, MN B
Muskingum Coll, OH B
Northwestern U, IL B
Oberlin Coll, OH B
Ohio Wesleyan U, OH B
U of Minnesota, Twin Cities Campus, MN B
Washington U in St. Louis, MO B

NONPROFIT/PUBLIC MANAGEMENT

Manchester Coll, IN B
Saint Mary-of-the-Woods Coll, IN B

NUCLEAR ENGINEERING

Kansas State U, KS B
Purdue U, IN B
U of Cincinnati, OH B
U of Illinois at Urbana–Champaign, IL B
U of Michigan, MI B
U of Missouri–Rolla, MO B
U of Wisconsin–Madison, WI B

NUCLEAR MEDICAL TECHNOLOGY

Alverno Coll, WI B
Aquinas Coll, MI B
Ball State U, IN A
Benedictine U, IL B
Ferris State U, MI A,B
Indiana U–Purdue U Indianapolis, IN B
Kent State U, OH A
Kettering Coll of Medical Arts, OH A
Oakland U, MI B
Peru State Coll, NE B
St. Cloud State U, MN B
Saint Louis U, MO B
Saint Mary's U of Minnesota, MN B
U of Cincinnati, OH B
The U of Findlay, OH A,B
The U of Iowa, IA B
U of Missouri–Columbia, MO B
U of Nebraska Medical Center, NE B
U of Oklahoma Health Sciences Center, OK B
U of St. Francis, IL B
U of Wisconsin–La Crosse, WI B

NURSE ASSISTANT/AIDE

Central Christian Coll of Kansas, KS A

NURSING

Allen Coll, IA B
Alverno Coll, WI B
Anderson U, IN B
Andrews U, MI B
Augsburg Coll, MN B
Augustana Coll, SD B
Aurora U, IL B
Avila U, MO B
Bacone Coll, OK A
Baker U, KS B
Ball State U, IN A,B
Bellin Coll of Nursing, WI B
Bemidji State U, MN B
Bethel Coll, IN A,B
Bethel Coll, KS B
Bethel Coll, MN B
Blessing-Rieman Coll of Nursing, IL B
Bowling Green State U, OH B
Bradley U, IL B
Briar Cliff U, IA B
Calvin Coll, MI B
Capital U, OH B
Cardinal Stritch U, WI A,B
Carroll Coll, WI B
Case Western Reserve U, OH B
Cedarville U, OH B
Central Christian Coll of Kansas, KS A
Central Methodist Coll, MO B
Central Missouri State U, MO B
Chicago State U, IL B
Clarkson Coll, NE B
Cleveland State U, OH B
Coe Coll, IA B
Coll of Mount St. Joseph, OH B
Coll of Saint Benedict, MN B
Coll of St. Catherine, MN B
Coll of St. Catherine–Minneapolis, MN A
Coll of Saint Mary, NE A,B
The Coll of St. Scholastica, MN B
Columbia Coll, MO A
Columbia Coll of Nursing, WI B
Concordia Coll, MN B
Concordia U, IL B
Concordia U Wisconsin, WI B
Creighton U, NE B
Culver-Stockton Coll, MO B
Dakota Wesleyan U, SD A
Deaconess Coll of Nursing, MO A,B
DePaul U, IL B
Dickinson State U, ND B
Donnelly Coll, KS A
Dordt Coll, IA B
Drury U, MO B
East Central U, OK B
Eastern Michigan U, MI B
Edgewood Coll, WI B
Elmhurst Coll, IL B
Eureka Coll, IL B
Ferris State U, MI A,B
Finlandia U, MI A
Fort Hays State U, KS B
Franciscan U of Steubenville, OH B
Goshen Coll, IN B
Governors State U, IL B
Graceland U, IA B
Grace U, NE B
Grand Valley State U, MI B
Grand View Coll, IA B
Gustavus Adolphus Coll, MN B
Hannibal-LaGrange Coll, MO A,B
Hesston Coll, KS A
Hillsdale Free Will Baptist Coll, OK A
Hope Coll, MI B
Illinois State U, IL B
Illinois Wesleyan U, IL B
Indiana State U, IN A,B
Indiana U East, IN A,B
Indiana U Kokomo, IN A,B
Indiana U Northwest, IN A,B
Indiana U–Purdue U Fort Wayne, IN A,B
Indiana U–Purdue U Indianapolis, IN A,B
Indiana U South Bend, IN A,B
Indiana U Southeast, IN B
Indiana Wesleyan U, IN B
Iowa Wesleyan Coll, IA B
Jamestown Coll, ND B
Jewish Hospital Coll of Nursing and Allied Health, MO A,B
Judson Coll, IL B
Kent State U, OH A,B
Kent State U, Ashtabula Campus, OH A
Kent State U, Tuscarawas Campus, OH A
Kettering Coll of Medical Arts, OH A
Lakeview Coll of Nursing, IL B
Langston U, OK B
Lester L. Cox Coll of Nursing and Health Sciences, MO A,B
Lewis U, IL B
Lincoln Coll, Lincoln, IL A
Lincoln Coll, Normal, IL A
Lourdes Coll, OH B
Loyola U Chicago, IL B
Luther Coll, IA B
MacMurray Coll, IL B
Madonna U, MI B
Maranatha Baptist Bible Coll, WI B
Marian Coll, IN B
Marian Coll of Fond du Lac, WI B
Marquette U, WI B
Maryville U of Saint Louis, MO B
McKendree Coll, IL B
Medcenter One Coll of Nursing, ND B
Mercy Coll of Northwest Ohio, OH A
Miami U, OH B
Miami U–Hamilton Campus, OH A,B
Miami U–Middletown Campus, OH A,B
Michigan State U, MI B
MidAmerica Nazarene U, KS B
Midland Lutheran Coll, NE B
Millikin U, IL B
Milwaukee School of Engineering, WI B
Minnesota State U, Mankato, MN B
Minnesota State U, Moorhead, MN B
Minot State U, ND B
Missouri Southern State Coll, MO B
Missouri Western State Coll, MO B
Morningside Coll, IA B
Mount Marty Coll, SD B
Mount Mercy Coll, IA B
Nebraska Methodist Coll, NE A,B
Newman U, KS A,B
North Dakota State U, ND B
Northeastern State U, OK B
Northern Illinois U, IL B
Northern Michigan U, MI B

Nursing (continued)
North Park U, IL B
Northwestern Oklahoma State U, OK B
Oakland U, MI B
The Ohio State U, OH B
Ohio U, OH A,B
Ohio U–Chillicothe, OH A,B
Ohio U–Zanesville, OH A,B
Oklahoma Baptist U, OK B
Oklahoma City U, OK B
Oklahoma Panhandle State U, OK A,B
Oklahoma Wesleyan U, OK B
Olivet Nazarene U, IL B
Oral Roberts U, OK B
Otterbein Coll, OH B
Park U, MO A
Pittsburg State U, KS B
Presentation Coll, SD A,B
Purdue U, IN A,B
Purdue U Calumet, IN A,B
Purdue U North Central, IN A,B
Quincy U, IL B
Research Coll of Nursing, MO B
Rochester Comm and Tech Coll, MN A
Rockford Coll, IL B
Rockhurst U, MO B
Rogers State U, OK A
Rush U, IL B
Saginaw Valley State U, MI B
St. Ambrose U, IA B
Saint Anthony Coll of Nursing, IL B
St. Cloud State U, MN B
Saint Francis Medical Center Coll of Nursing, IL B
St. John's Coll, IL B
Saint John's U, MN B
Saint Louis U, MO B
Saint Luke's Coll, MO B
St. Luke's Coll of Nursing and Health Sciences, IA A
Saint Mary's Coll, IN B
St. Olaf Coll, MN B
Saint Xavier U, IL B
Shawnee State U, OH A
Si Tanka Huron U, SD A,B
South Dakota State U, SD B
Southeast Missouri State U, MO B
Southern Illinois U Edwardsville, IL B
Southern Nazarene U, OK B
Southwest Baptist U, MO A,B
Southwestern Coll, KS B
Southwestern Oklahoma State U, OK B
Southwest Missouri State U, MO B
Springfield Coll in Illinois, IL A
Trinity Christian Coll, IL B
Trinity Coll of Nursing and Health Sciences Schools, IL A,B
Truman State U, MO B
Union Coll, NE B
The U of Akron, OH B
U of Central Oklahoma, OK B
U of Cincinnati, OH A,B
U of Evansville, IN B
U of Illinois at Chicago, IL B
U of Illinois at Springfield, IL B
U of Indianapolis, IN A,B
The U of Iowa, IA B
U of Mary, ND B
U of Michigan, MI B
U of Michigan–Flint, MI B
U of Minnesota, Twin Cities Campus, MN B
U of Missouri–Columbia, MO B
U of Missouri–Kansas City, MO B
U of Missouri–St. Louis, MO B
U of Nebraska Medical Center, NE B
U of North Dakota, ND B
U of Oklahoma Health Sciences Center, OK B
U of Phoenix–Tulsa Campus, OK B
U of Rio Grande, OH A
U of St. Francis, IL B
U of Saint Francis, IN B
The U of South Dakota, SD A
U of Southern Indiana, IN A,B
U of Toledo, OH A,B
U of Tulsa, OK B
U of Wisconsin–Eau Claire, WI B
U of Wisconsin–Madison, WI B
U of Wisconsin–Milwaukee, WI B
U of Wisconsin–Oshkosh, WI B
U of Wisconsin–Parkside, WI B
Ursuline Coll, OH B
Valparaiso U, IN B
Viterbo U, WI B
Waldorf Coll, IA A
Walsh U, OH A,B
Wayne State U, MI B
Webster U, MO B
Western Michigan U, MI B
West Suburban Coll of Nursing, IL B
William Jewell Coll, MO B
Winona State U, MN B
Wright State U, OH B
Youngstown State U, OH B

NURSING ADMINISTRATION
Central Methodist Coll, MO B
Clarkson Coll, NE B
Nebraska Wesleyan U, NE B

NURSING (ANESTHETIST)
Webster U, MO B

NURSING (MIDWIFERY)
Marquette U, WI B

NURSING RELATED
Alverno Coll, WI B
Malone Coll, OH B
Metropolitan State U, MN B
Rogers State U, OK A
The U of Akron, OH B
Wheaton Coll, IL B

NURSING SCIENCE
Benedictine U, IL B
Clarke Coll, IA B
Clarkson Coll, NE B
Emporia State U, KS B
The Ohio State U, OH B
Saint Joseph's Coll, IN B
Trinity Coll of Nursing and Health Sciences Schools, IL A,B
The U of Akron, OH B
U of Kansas, KS B
U of Phoenix–Metro Detroit Campus, MI B
U of Phoenix–Tulsa Campus, OK B
U of Phoenix–West Michigan Campus, MI B
U of Wisconsin–Green Bay, WI B
Wichita State U, KS B
Xavier U, OH B

NUTRITIONAL SCIENCES
Benedictine U, IL B
U of Wisconsin–Green Bay, WI B

NUTRITION SCIENCE
Andrews U, MI B
Ashland U, OH B
Bluffton Coll, OH B
Bowling Green State U, OH B
Case Western Reserve U, OH B
Coll of Saint Benedict, MN B
Coll of St. Catherine, MN B
Coll of the Ozarks, MO B
Concordia Coll, MN B
Dominican U, IL B
Indiana U Bloomington, IN B
Iowa State U of Science and Technology, IA B
Langston U, OK B
Lincoln Coll, Lincoln, IL A
Madonna U, MI A,B
Michigan State U, MI B
Minnesota State U, Mankato, MN B
Mount Marty Coll, SD B
North Dakota State U, ND B
Northeastern State U, OK B
Northwest Missouri State U, MO B
Notre Dame Coll, OH B
Oklahoma State U, OK B
Saint John's U, MN B
South Dakota State U, SD B
Southeast Missouri State U, MO B
U of Central Oklahoma, OK B
U of Cincinnati, OH B
U of Dayton, OH B
U of Michigan, MI B
U of Minnesota, Twin Cities Campus, MN B
U of Missouri–Columbia, MO B
U of Northern Iowa, IA B
U of Oklahoma Health Sciences Center, OK B
U of Wisconsin–Madison, WI B

NUTRITION STUDIES
Eastern Michigan U, MI B
Indiana State U, IN B
Kansas State U, KS B
Kent State U, OH B
Loyola U Chicago, IL B
Marygrove Coll, MI B
Northern Illinois U, IL B
The Ohio State U, OH B
Ohio U, OH B
Purdue U, IN B
Southern Illinois U Carbondale, IL B
The U of Akron, OH B
U of Nebraska–Lincoln, NE B
U of Northern Iowa, IA B
U of Wisconsin–Stout, WI B
Wayne State U, MI B
Western Michigan U, MI B
Youngstown State U, OH B

OCCUPATIONAL HEALTH/ INDUSTRIAL HYGIENE
Illinois State U, IL B
Oakland U, MI B

OCCUPATIONAL SAFETY/ HEALTH TECHNOLOGY
Ball State U, IN B
Central Missouri State U, MO B
Ferris State U, MI A,B
Grand Valley State U, MI B
Indiana State U, IN B
Indiana U Bloomington, IN A
Madonna U, MI B
Southeastern Oklahoma State U, OK B
Southwest Baptist U, MO A,B
U of Central Oklahoma, OK B
U of Cincinnati, OH A
U of North Dakota, ND B

OCCUPATIONAL THERAPY
Alma Coll, MI B
Augustana Coll, IL B
Avila U, MO B
Baker Coll of Flint, MI B
Calvin Coll, MI B
Carthage Coll, WI B
Chicago State U, IL B
Clarkson Coll, NE A
Cleveland State U, OH B
Coll of Saint Benedict, MN B
Coll of St. Catherine, MN B
Coll of Saint Mary, NE B
The Coll of St. Scholastica, MN B
Concordia Coll, MN B
Concordia U Wisconsin, WI B
Eastern Michigan U, MI B
Elmhurst Coll, IL B
Gustavus Adolphus Coll, MN B
Hamline U, MN B
Illinois Coll, IL B
Indiana U–Purdue U Indianapolis, IN B
Lourdes Coll, OH A
Mount Mary Coll, WI B
Newman U, KS B
The Ohio State U, OH B
Saginaw Valley State U, MI B
Saint John's U, MN B
Saint Louis U, MO B
Shawnee State U, OH A,B
Stephens Coll, MO B
The U of Findlay, OH B
U of Minnesota, Twin Cities Campus, MN B
U of Missouri–Columbia, MO B
U of North Dakota, ND B
U of Southern Indiana, IN B
U of Wisconsin–La Crosse, WI B
U of Wisconsin–Madison, WI B
U of Wisconsin–Milwaukee, WI B
Wartburg Coll, IA B
Wayne State U, MI B

Western Michigan U, MI B
Xavier U, OH B

OCCUPATIONAL THERAPY ASSISTANT

Baker Coll of Muskegon, MI A
Coll of St. Catherine, MN A
Coll of St. Catherine–Minneapolis, MN A
Grand Valley State U, MI B
Kent State U, OH A
U of Southern Indiana, IN A
Wichita State U, KS A

OCEANOGRAPHY

Central Michigan U, MI B
U of Michigan, MI B

OFFICE MANAGEMENT

Baker Coll of Flint, MI A,B
Baker Coll of Jackson, MI A
Bowling Green State U, OH B
Central Michigan U, MI B
Central Missouri State U, MO B
Concordia Coll, MN B
Indiana State U, IN B
Mayville State U, ND B
Miami U–Middletown Campus, OH A
Minnesota School of Business-Richfield, MN A
Park U, MO A
Southeastern Oklahoma State U, OK B
Southeast Missouri State U, MO B
Union Coll, NE A
U of Nebraska–Lincoln, NE B
U of North Dakota, ND B
Valley City State U, ND B
Youngstown State U, OH A,B

OPERATING ROOM TECHNICIAN

Baker Coll of Clinton Township, MI A
Baker Coll of Flint, MI A
Baker Coll of Jackson, MI A
Baker Coll of Muskegon, MI A
Presentation Coll, SD A
Rochester Comm and Tech Coll, MN A
The U of Akron, OH A

OPERATIONS MANAGEMENT

Aurora U, IL B
Baker Coll of Flint, MI A,B
Bowling Green State U, OH B
Central Michigan U, MI B
Concordia U, NE B
DeVry U, Addison, IL B
DeVry U, Chicago, IL B
DeVry U, Tinley Park, IL B
DeVry U, MO B
DeVry U, OH B
Franklin U, OH B
Indiana State U, IN A
Indiana U–Purdue U Fort Wayne, IN A,B
Indiana U–Purdue U Indianapolis, IN A,B
Kettering U, MI B
Loyola U Chicago, IL B
Metropolitan State U, MN B
Miami U, OH B
Michigan State U, MI B
Michigan Technological U, MI B
Northern Illinois U, IL B
The Ohio State U, OH B
Purdue U, IN A,B
Saginaw Valley State U, MI B
Southeast Missouri State U, MO B
Tri-State U, IN B
U of Indianapolis, IN B
U of Nebraska at Kearney, NE B
U of Nebraska at Omaha, NE B
U of St. Francis, IL B
U of St. Thomas, MN B
Washington U in St. Louis, MO B
Youngstown State U, OH B

OPERATIONS RESEARCH

DePaul U, IL B
Miami U, OH B
U of Cincinnati, OH B
U of Michigan–Flint, MI B

OPHTHALMIC/ OPTOMETRIC SERVICES

Ferris State U, MI B
Indiana U Bloomington, IN B
Northeastern State U, OK B

OPHTHALMIC/ OPTOMETRIC SERVICES RELATED

Concordia Coll, MN B

OPTICAL TECHNICIAN

Indiana U Bloomington, IN A

OPTICIANRY

The U of Akron, OH A

OPTICS

Rose-Hulman Inst of Technology, IN B
Saginaw Valley State U, MI B

OPTOMETRIC/ OPHTHALMIC LABORATORY TECHNICIAN

Indiana U Bloomington, IN A
Viterbo U, WI B

ORGANIZATIONAL BEHAVIOR

Anderson U, IN B
Benedictine U, IL B
Carroll Coll, WI B
Denison U, OH B
Miami U, OH B
Northwestern Coll, MN B
Northwestern U, IL B
Oakland City U, IN B
St. Ambrose U, IA B
Wayne State U, MI B

ORGANIZATIONAL PSYCHOLOGY

Maryville U of Saint Louis, MO B
Nebraska Wesleyan U, NE B
Saint Xavier U, IL B

ORNAMENTAL HORTICULTURE

Ferris State U, MI A
Iowa State U of Science and Technology, IA B
U of Illinois at Urbana–Champaign, IL B

PAINTING

American Academy of Art, IL B
Bethany Coll, KS B
Bowling Green State U, OH B
Central Christian Coll of Kansas, KS A
The Cleveland Inst of Art, OH B
Coll of Visual Arts, MN B
Columbus Coll of Art and Design, OH B
Grace Coll, IN B
Indiana Wesleyan U, IN B
Kansas City Art Inst, MO B
Lewis U, IL B
Lincoln Coll, Lincoln, IL A
Maharishi U of Management, IA B
Milwaukee Inst of Art and Design, WI B
Minneapolis Coll of Art and Design, MN B
Minnesota State U, Moorhead, MN B
The Ohio State U, OH B
Ohio U, OH B
Shawnee State U, OH B
Trinity Christian Coll, IL B
U of Illinois at Urbana–Champaign, IL B
The U of Iowa, IA B
U of Kansas, KS B
U of Michigan, MI B
Washington U in St. Louis, MO B
Webster U, MO B
Youngstown State U, OH B

PALEONTOLOGY

Bowling Green State U, OH B
Southeast Missouri State U, MO B

PARALEGAL/LEGAL ASSISTANT

Avila U, MO B
Ball State U, IN A,B
Calumet Coll of Saint Joseph, IN B
Coll of Mount St. Joseph, OH A,B
Coll of Saint Mary, NE A,B
Concordia U Wisconsin, WI B
Davenport U, Grand Rapids, MI A,B
Davenport U, Kalamazoo, MI A,B
Ferris State U, MI A
Grand Valley State U, MI B
Hamline U, MN B
Indiana U South Bend, IN A
International Business Coll, Fort Wayne, IN A,B
Kent State U, OH A
Lake Erie Coll, OH B
Lincoln Coll, Normal, IL A
Madonna U, MI A,B
Maryville U of Saint Louis, MO B
Metro Business Coll, MO A
Metropolitan Coll, Tulsa, OK A
Midstate Coll, IL A
Minnesota School of Business-Richfield, MN A
Minnesota State U, Moorhead, MN B
Missouri Western State Coll, MO A
National American U, SD A,B
National American U–Sioux Falls Branch, SD A,B
Notre Dame Coll, OH B
Ohio U–Chillicothe, OH A
Robert Morris Coll, IL A,B
Rockford Business Coll, IL A
Rogers State U, OK A
Roosevelt U, IL B
Saint Mary-of-the-Woods Coll, IN A,B
Sanford-Brown Coll, Fenton, MO A
Shawnee State U, OH A
Southern Illinois U Carbondale, IL B
The U of Akron, OH A
U of Cincinnati, OH A
U of Indianapolis, IN A
U of Nebraska at Omaha, NE B
U of Northwestern Ohio, OH A
U of Toledo, OH A
U of Wisconsin–Superior, WI B
Wichita State U, KS A
William Woods U, MO A,B
Winona State U, MN B

PARKS, RECREATION, LEISURE AND FITNESS STUDIES RELATED

Chadron State Coll, NE B
Culver-Stockton Coll, MO B

PASTORAL COUNSELING

American Christian Coll and Seminary, OK B
Baptist Bible Coll, MO B
Barclay Coll, KS B
Cedarville U, OH B
Central Bible Coll, MO B
Central Christian Coll of Kansas, KS A,B
Coll of Mount St. Joseph, OH B
Concordia U, IL B
Concordia U, MN B
Concordia U, NE B
Concordia U Wisconsin, WI B
Cornerstone U, MI B
Crown Coll, MN B
Dordt Coll, IA B
Faith Baptist Bible Coll and Theological Seminary, IA B
Global U of the Assemblies of God, MO B
God's Bible School and Coll, OH B
Grace Bible Coll, MI B
Grace Coll, IN B
Grace U, NE B
Greenville Coll, IL B
Hannibal-LaGrange Coll, MO B
Hesston Coll, KS A

Pastoral Counseling (continued)

Indiana Wesleyan U, IN A,B
Madonna U, MI B
Malone Coll, OH B
Manhattan Christian Coll, KS B
Nebraska Christian Coll, NE A,B
Newman U, KS B
Northwestern Coll, MN B
Notre Dame Coll, OH A,B
Oklahoma Baptist U, OK B
Oklahoma Christian U, OK B
Olivet Nazarene U, IL B
Oral Roberts U, OK B
Pillsbury Baptist Bible Coll, MN B
Reformed Bible Coll, MI B
Rochester Coll, MI B
Saint Mary-of-the-Woods Coll, IN B
Saint Mary's Coll of Madonna U, MI B
Saint Mary's U of Minnesota, MN B
Tabor Coll, KS B
Taylor U, Fort Wayne Campus, IN B
Trinity Bible Coll, ND B
Union Coll, NE B
U of Sioux Falls, SD B
Walsh U, OH B

PEACE/CONFLICT STUDIES

Antioch Coll, OH B
Bethel Coll, KS B
Bluffton Coll, OH B
Coll of Saint Benedict, MN B
DePauw U, IN B
Earlham Coll, IN B
Goshen Coll, IN B
Kent State U, OH B
Manchester Coll, IN B
Nebraska Wesleyan U, NE B
Northland Coll, WI B
Ohio Dominican U, OH B
The Ohio State U, OH B
Saint John's U, MN B
U of St. Thomas, MN B
U of Wisconsin–Milwaukee, WI B
Wayne State U, MI B

PERFUSION TECHNOLOGY

Rush U, IL B

PERSONAL SERVICES MARKETING OPERATIONS

Lake Erie Coll, OH B

PETROLEUM ENGINEERING

Marietta Coll, OH B
U of Kansas, KS B
U of Missouri–Rolla, MO B
U of Oklahoma, OK B
U of Tulsa, OK B

PHARMACOLOGY

U of Cincinnati, OH B
U of Wisconsin–Madison, WI B

PHARMACY

Briar Cliff U, IA B
Butler U, IN B
Drake U, IA B
Ferris State U, MI B
North Dakota State U, ND B
Ohio Northern U, OH B
The Ohio State U, OH B
Purdue U, IN B
St. Louis Coll of Pharmacy, MO B
South Dakota State U, SD B
Southwestern Oklahoma State U, OK B
U of Cincinnati, OH B
The U of Iowa, IA B
U of Michigan, MI B
U of Missouri–Kansas City, MO B
U of Toledo, OH B
U of Wisconsin–Madison, WI B
Wayne State U, MI B

PHARMACY ADMINISTRATION/ PHARMACEUTICS

Drake U, IA B

PHARMACY TECHNICIAN/ ASSISTANT

Baker Coll of Flint, MI A
Baker Coll of Jackson, MI A
Baker Coll of Muskegon, MI A
Mercy Coll of Northwest Ohio, OH A
U of Northwestern Ohio, OH A

PHILOSOPHY

Albion Coll, MI B
Alma Coll, MI B
Alverno Coll, WI B
Anderson U, IN B
Antioch Coll, OH B
Aquinas Coll, MI B
Ashland U, OH B
Augsburg Coll, MN B
Augustana Coll, IL B
Augustana Coll, SD B
Aurora U, IL B
Ave Maria Coll, MI B
Baker U, KS B
Baldwin-Wallace Coll, OH B
Ball State U, IN B
Bellevue U, NE B
Beloit Coll, WI B
Bemidji State U, MN B
Benedictine Coll, KS B
Benedictine U, IL B
Bethany Coll, KS B
Bethel Coll, IN B
Bethel Coll, MN B
Bluffton Coll, OH B
Bowling Green State U, OH B
Bradley U, IL B
Buena Vista U, IA B
Butler U, IN B
Calvin Coll, MI B
Capital U, OH B
Carleton Coll, MN B
Carthage Coll, WI B
Case Western Reserve U, OH B
Cedarville U, OH B
Central Coll, IA B
Central Methodist Coll, MO B
Central Michigan U, MI B
Clarke Coll, IA B
Cleveland State U, OH B
Coe Coll, IA B
Coll of Saint Benedict, MN B
Coll of St. Catherine, MN B
Coll of the Ozarks, MO B
The Coll of Wooster, OH B
Concordia Coll, MN B
Concordia U, IL B
Cornell Coll, IA B
Creighton U, NE B
Dakota Wesleyan U, SD B
Denison U, OH B
DePaul U, IL B
DePauw U, IN B
Doane Coll, NE B
Dominican U, IL B
Donnelly Coll, KS A
Dordt Coll, IA B
Drake U, IA B
Drury U, MO B
Earlham Coll, IN B
Eastern Illinois U, IL B
Eastern Michigan U, MI B
Elmhurst Coll, IL B
Eureka Coll, IL B
Fort Hays State U, KS B
Franciscan U of Steubenville, OH B
Franklin Coll, IN B
Grand Valley State U, MI B
Greenville Coll, IL B
Grinnell Coll, IA B
Gustavus Adolphus Coll, MN B
Hamline U, MN B
Hanover Coll, IN B
Hastings Coll, NE B
Heidelberg Coll, OH B
Hillsdale Coll, MI B
Hiram Coll, OH B
Hope Coll, MI B
Huntington Coll, IN B
Illinois Coll, IL B
Illinois State U, IL B
Illinois Wesleyan U, IL B
Indiana State U, IN B
Indiana U Bloomington, IN B
Indiana U Northwest, IN B
Indiana U–Purdue U Fort Wayne, IN B
Indiana U–Purdue U Indianapolis, IN B
Indiana U South Bend, IN B
Indiana U Southeast, IN B
Indiana Wesleyan U, IN B
Iowa State U of Science and Technology, IA B
Jamestown Coll, ND B
John Carroll U, OH B
Judson Coll, IL B
Kalamazoo Coll, MI B
Kansas State U, KS B
Kent State U, OH B
Kenyon Coll, OH B
Knox Coll, IL B
Lake Forest Coll, IL B
Lakeland Coll, WI B
Lawrence U, WI B
Lewis U, IL B
Lincoln Coll, Lincoln, IL A
Lincoln Coll, Normal, IL A
Loras Coll, IA B
Loyola U Chicago, IL B
Luther Coll, IA B
Macalester Coll, MN B
MacMurray Coll, IL B
Manchester Coll, IN B
Marian Coll, IN B
Marietta Coll, OH B
Marquette U, WI B
Maryville U of Saint Louis, MO B
McKendree Coll, IL B
McPherson Coll, KS B
Metropolitan State U, MN B
Miami U, OH B
Miami U–Middletown Campus, OH A
Michigan State U, MI B
Millikin U, IL B
Minnesota State U, Mankato, MN B
Minnesota State U, Moorhead, MN B
Missouri Valley Coll, MO B
Monmouth Coll, IL B
Morningside Coll, IA B
Mount Mary Coll, WI B
Mount Union Coll, OH B
Mount Vernon Nazarene U, OH B
Muskingum Coll, OH B
Nebraska Wesleyan U, NE B
North Central Coll, IL B
Northeastern Illinois U, IL B
Northern Illinois U, IL B
Northern Michigan U, MI B
Northland Coll, WI B
North Park U, IL B
Northwestern Coll, IA B
Northwestern U, IL B
Northwest Missouri State U, MO B
Oakland U, MI B
Oberlin Coll, OH B
Ohio Dominican U, OH B
Ohio Northern U, OH B
The Ohio State U, OH B
Ohio U, OH B
Ohio Wesleyan U, OH B
Oklahoma Baptist U, OK B
Oklahoma City U, OK B
Oklahoma State U, OK B
Olivet Nazarene U, IL B
Oral Roberts U, OK B
Otterbein Coll, OH B
Pontifical Coll Josephinum, OH B
Principia Coll, IL B
Purdue U, IN B
Purdue U Calumet, IN B
Quincy U, IL B
Ripon Coll, WI B
Rockford Coll, IL B
Rockhurst U, MO B
Roosevelt U, IL B
Sacred Heart Major Seminary, MI B
St. Ambrose U, IA B
St. Cloud State U, MN B
Saint John's U, MN B
Saint Joseph's Coll, IN B
Saint Louis U, MO B
Saint Mary's Coll, IN B
Saint Mary's Coll of Madonna U, MI B
Saint Mary's U of Minnesota, MN B
St. Norbert Coll, WI B
St. Olaf Coll, MN B
Saint Xavier U, IL B
Siena Heights U, MI B
Simpson Coll, IA B
Southeast Missouri State U, MO B
Southern Illinois U Carbondale, IL B

Southern Illinois U Edwardsville, IL B
Southern Nazarene U, OK B
Southwest Minnesota State U, MN B
Southwest Missouri State U, MO B
Spring Arbor U, MI B
Stephens Coll, MO B
Tabor Coll, KS B
Taylor U, IN B
Trinity Christian Coll, IL B
Trinity International U, IL B
Truman State U, MO B
The U of Akron, OH B
U of Central Oklahoma, OK B
U of Chicago, IL B
U of Cincinnati, OH B
U of Dayton, OH B
U of Dubuque, IA B
U of Evansville, IN B
The U of Findlay, OH B
U of Illinois at Chicago, IL B
U of Illinois at Urbana–Champaign, IL B
U of Indianapolis, IN B
The U of Iowa, IA B
U of Kansas, KS B
U of Michigan, MI B
U of Michigan–Dearborn, MI B
U of Michigan–Flint, MI B
U of Minnesota, Duluth, MN B
U of Minnesota, Morris, MN B
U of Minnesota, Twin Cities Campus, MN B
U of Missouri–Columbia, MO B
U of Missouri–Kansas City, MO B
U of Missouri–Rolla, MO B
U of Missouri–St. Louis, MO B
U of Nebraska at Omaha, NE B
U of Nebraska–Lincoln, NE B
U of North Dakota, ND B
U of Northern Iowa, IA B
U of Notre Dame, IN B
U of Oklahoma, OK B
U of St. Thomas, MN B
U of Sioux Falls, SD B
The U of South Dakota, SD B
U of Southern Indiana, IN B
U of Toledo, OH B
U of Tulsa, OK B
U of Wisconsin–Eau Claire, WI B
U of Wisconsin–Green Bay, WI A,B
U of Wisconsin–La Crosse, WI B
U of Wisconsin–Madison, WI B
U of Wisconsin–Milwaukee, WI B
U of Wisconsin–Oshkosh, WI B
U of Wisconsin–Parkside, WI B
U of Wisconsin–Platteville, WI B
U of Wisconsin–Stevens Point, WI B
Urbana U, OH B
Ursuline Coll, OH B
Valparaiso U, IN B
Wabash Coll, IN B
Walsh U, OH B
Wartburg Coll, IA B
Washington U in St. Louis, MO B
Wayne State U, MI B
Webster U, MO B
Western Illinois U, IL B
Western Michigan U, MI B
Westminster Coll, MO B
Wheaton Coll, IL B
Wichita State U, KS B
William Jewell Coll, MO B
Wilmington Coll, OH B
Wittenberg U, OH B
Wright State U, OH B
Xavier U, OH B
Youngstown State U, OH B

PHILOSOPHY AND RELIGION RELATED

Graceland U, IA B
Southwestern Coll, KS B
Sterling Coll, KS B
U of Notre Dame, IN B
U of Oklahoma, OK B
Washington U in St. Louis, MO B

PHOTOGRAPHIC TECHNOLOGY

Kent State U, OH B
Ohio U, OH B
Southern Illinois U Carbondale, IL A

PHOTOGRAPHY

Andrews U, MI A,B
Art Academy of Cincinnati, OH B
Ball State U, IN B
Bowling Green State U, OH B
Central Christian Coll of Kansas, KS A
Central Missouri State U, MO B
The Cleveland Inst of Art, OH B
Coll for Creative Studies, MI B
Coll of Visual Arts, MN B
Columbia Coll, MO B
Columbia Coll Chicago, IL B
Columbus Coll of Art and Design, OH B
Dominican U, IL B
Governors State U, IL B
Grand Valley State U, MI B
Indiana U Bloomington, IN B
Indiana Wesleyan U, IN B
Kansas City Art Inst, MO B
Lincoln Coll, Lincoln, IL A
Loyola U Chicago, IL B
Milwaukee Inst of Art and Design, WI B
Minneapolis Coll of Art and Design, MN B
Morningside Coll, IA B
Northern Michigan U, MI B
Ohio U, OH B
Saint Mary-of-the-Woods Coll, IN B
Trinity Christian Coll, IL B
The U of Akron, OH B
U of Central Oklahoma, OK B
U of Dayton, OH B
U of Illinois at Chicago, IL B
U of Illinois at Urbana–Champaign, IL B
The U of Iowa, IA B
U of Michigan, MI B
U of Missouri–St. Louis, MO B
The U of South Dakota, SD B
Washington U in St. Louis, MO B
Webster U, MO B
Wright State U, OH B
Youngstown State U, OH B

PHYSICAL EDUCATION

Adrian Coll, MI A,B
Albion Coll, MI B
Anderson U, IN B
Andrews U, MI B
Aquinas Coll, MI B
Ashland U, OH B
Augsburg Coll, MN B
Augustana Coll, IL B
Augustana Coll, SD B
Aurora U, IL B
Baker U, KS B
Baldwin-Wallace Coll, OH B
Ball State U, IN B
Bellevue U, NE B
Bemidji State U, MN B
Benedictine Coll, KS B
Bethany Coll, KS B
Bethel Coll, IN B
Bethel Coll, MN B
Blackburn Coll, IL B
Bluffton Coll, OH B
Bowling Green State U, OH B
Briar Cliff U, IA B
Buena Vista U, IA B
Calvin Coll, MI B
Cameron U, OK B
Capital U, OH B
Carroll Coll, WI B
Carthage Coll, WI B
Cedarville U, OH B
Central Christian Coll of Kansas, KS A
Central Methodist Coll, MO B
Central Michigan U, MI B
Central Missouri State U, MO B
Chadron State Coll, NE B
Chicago State U, IL B
Clarke Coll, IA B
Cleveland State U, OH B
Coe Coll, IA B
Coll of Mount St. Joseph, OH B
Coll of St. Catherine, MN B
Coll of the Ozarks, MO B
Concordia Coll, MN B
Concordia U, IL B
Concordia U, MI B
Concordia U, MN B
Concordia U, NE B
Concordia U Wisconsin, WI B
Cornell Coll, IA B
Cornerstone U, MI B
Crown Coll, MN B
Culver-Stockton Coll, MO B
Dakota State U, SD B
Dakota Wesleyan U, SD B
Dana Coll, NE B
Defiance Coll, OH B
Denison U, OH B
DePaul U, IL B
Dickinson State U, ND B
Doane Coll, NE B
Dordt Coll, IA B
Drury U, MO B
East Central U, OK B
Eastern Illinois U, IL B
Eastern Michigan U, MI B
Elmhurst Coll, IL B
Emporia State U, KS B
Eureka Coll, IL B
Evangel U, MO B
Fort Hays State U, KS B
Franklin Coll, IN B
Goshen Coll, IN B
Grace Coll, IN B
Graceland U, IA B
Grand Valley State U, MI B
Greenville Coll, IL B
Gustavus Adolphus Coll, MN B
Hamline U, MN B
Hannibal-LaGrange Coll, MO B
Hanover Coll, IN B
Haskell Indian Nations U, KS A
Hastings Coll, NE B
Heidelberg Coll, OH B
Hillsdale Coll, MI B
Hillsdale Free Will Baptist Coll, OK A
Hope Coll, MI B
Huntington Coll, IN B
Illinois Coll, IL B
Illinois State U, IL B
Indiana State U, IN B
Indiana U Bloomington, IN B
Indiana U–Purdue U Indianapolis, IN B
Indiana Wesleyan U, IN B
Iowa Wesleyan Coll, IA B
Jamestown Coll, ND B
John Carroll U, OH B
Judson Coll, IL B
Kent State U, OH B
Langston U, OK B
Lewis U, IL B
Lincoln Coll, Lincoln, IL A
Lincoln Coll, Normal, IL A
Lindenwood U, MO B
Loras Coll, IA B
Luther Coll, IA B
MacMurray Coll, IL B
Malone Coll, OH B
Manchester Coll, IN B
Maranatha Baptist Bible Coll, WI B
Marian Coll, IN B
Mayville State U, ND B
McKendree Coll, IL B
McPherson Coll, KS B
Miami U, OH B
Michigan State U, MI B
MidAmerica Nazarene U, KS B
Midland Lutheran Coll, NE B
Millikin U, IL B
Minnesota State U, Mankato, MN B
Minnesota State U, Moorhead, MN B
Minot State U, ND B
Missouri Southern State Coll, MO B
Missouri Valley Coll, MO B
Monmouth Coll, IL B
Mount Marty Coll, SD B
Mount Union Coll, OH B
Mount Vernon Nazarene U, OH B
Muskingum Coll, OH B
Nebraska Wesleyan U, NE B
North Central Coll, IL B
North Dakota State U, ND B
Northeastern Illinois U, IL B
Northeastern State U, OK B
Northern Illinois U, IL B

Physical Education (continued)
Northern Michigan U, MI B
Northern State U, SD B
North Park U, IL B
Northwestern Coll, IA B
Northwestern Coll, MN B
Northwestern Oklahoma State U, OK B
Northwest Missouri State U, MO B
Oakland City U, IN B
Ohio Northern U, OH B
The Ohio State U, OH B
Ohio U, OH B
Ohio Wesleyan U, OH B
Oklahoma Baptist U, OK B
Oklahoma Christian U, OK B
Oklahoma City U, OK B
Oklahoma Panhandle State U, OK B
Oklahoma State U, OK B
Oklahoma Wesleyan U, OK B
Olivet Coll, MI B
Olivet Nazarene U, IL B
Oral Roberts U, OK B
Ottawa U, KS B
Otterbein Coll, OH B
Peru State Coll, NE B
Pittsburg State U, KS B
Purdue U, IN B
Quincy U, IL B
Ripon Coll, WI B
Rockford Coll, IL B
Saginaw Valley State U, MI B
St. Ambrose U, IA B
St. Cloud State U, MN B
Saint Joseph's Coll, IN B
Simpson Coll, IA B
Si Tanka Huron U, SD B
South Dakota State U, SD B
Southeastern Oklahoma State U, OK B
Southeast Missouri State U, MO B
Southern Illinois U Carbondale, IL B
Southern Nazarene U, OK B
Southwest Baptist U, MO B
Southwestern Coll, KS B
Southwestern Oklahoma State U, OK B
Southwest Minnesota State U, MN B
Southwest Missouri State U, MO B
Spring Arbor U, MI B
Sterling Coll, KS B
Tabor Coll, KS B
Taylor U, IN B
Trinity Christian Coll, IL B
Trinity International U, IL B
Tri-State U, IN B
Union Coll, NE B
The U of Akron, OH B
U of Central Oklahoma, OK B
U of Cincinnati, OH B
U of Dayton, OH B
U of Evansville, IN B
The U of Findlay, OH B
U of Indianapolis, IN B
U of Kansas, KS B
U of Mary, ND B
U of Michigan, MI B
U of Minnesota, Duluth, MN B
U of Minnesota, Twin Cities Campus, MN B
U of Missouri–Kansas City, MO B
U of Missouri–St. Louis, MO B
U of Nebraska at Kearney, NE B
U of Nebraska at Omaha, NE B
U of Nebraska–Lincoln, NE B
U of North Dakota, ND B
U of Northern Iowa, IA B
U of Rio Grande, OH A,B
U of St. Thomas, MN B
U of Sioux Falls, SD B
The U of South Dakota, SD B
U of Southern Indiana, IN B
U of Toledo, OH B
U of Wisconsin–La Crosse, WI B
U of Wisconsin–Madison, WI B
U of Wisconsin–Oshkosh, WI B
U of Wisconsin–River Falls, WI B
U of Wisconsin–Stevens Point, WI B
U of Wisconsin–Superior, WI B
U of Wisconsin–Whitewater, WI B
Upper Iowa U, IA B
Valley City State U, ND B
Valparaiso U, IN B
Waldorf Coll, IA A
Walsh U, OH B
Wartburg Coll, IA B
Wayne State Coll, NE B
Wayne State U, MI B
Western Illinois U, IL B
Western Michigan U, MI B
Westminster Coll, MO B
Wichita State U, KS B
William Penn U, IA B
William Woods U, MO B
Wilmington Coll, OH B
Winona State U, MN B
Wright State U, OH B
York Coll, NE B
Youngstown State U, OH B

PHYSICAL SCIENCES

Antioch Coll, OH B
Bemidji State U, MN B
Black Hills State U, SD B
Calvin Coll, MI B
Central Christian Coll of Kansas, KS A
Central Michigan U, MI B
Coe Coll, IA B
Concordia U, IL B
Concordia U, MN B
Concordia U, NE B
Defiance Coll, OH B
Doane Coll, NE B
Eastern Michigan U, MI B
Emporia State U, KS B
Eureka Coll, IL B
Fort Hays State U, KS B
Goshen Coll, IN B
Graceland U, IA B
Grand Valley State U, MI B
Judson Coll, IL B
Kansas State U, KS B
Lincoln Coll, Lincoln, IL A
Loras Coll, IA B
Mayville State U, ND B
McPherson Coll, KS B
Michigan State U, MI B
Michigan Technological U, MI B
Midland Lutheran Coll, NE B
Minnesota State U, Mankato, MN B
Minot State U, ND B
Northwest Missouri State U, MO B
Oklahoma Baptist U, OK B
Olivet Nazarene U, IL B
Otterbein Coll, OH B
Peru State Coll, NE B
Pittsburg State U, KS B
Purdue U, IN A
Rogers State U, OK A
St. Cloud State U, MN B
Shawnee State U, OH B
Southwest Minnesota State U, MN B
Tri-State U, IN B
U of Dayton, OH B
U of Michigan–Dearborn, MI B
U of Michigan–Flint, MI B
U of Missouri–St. Louis, MO B
U of Rio Grande, OH B
U of Toledo, OH B
U of Wisconsin–River Falls, WI B
U of Wisconsin–Superior, WI B
Waldorf Coll, IA A
Walsh U, OH B
Washington U in St. Louis, MO B
Wayne State Coll, NE B
Wheaton Coll, IL B
Winona State U, MN B
Wittenberg U, OH B

PHYSICAL SCIENCES RELATED

Grand View Coll, IA B
Ohio U, OH B

PHYSICAL SCIENCE TECHNOLOGIES RELATED

The U of Akron, OH A

PHYSICAL/THEORETICAL CHEMISTRY

Michigan State U, MI B

PHYSICAL THERAPY

Andrews U, MI B
Avila U, MO B
Baldwin-Wallace Coll, OH B
Bowling Green State U, OH B
Bradley U, IL B
Central Christian Coll of Kansas, KS A
Clarke Coll, IA B
Clarkson Coll, NE A
Cleveland State U, OH B
Coll of Mount St. Joseph, OH B
Coll of Saint Benedict, MN B
The Coll of St. Scholastica, MN B
Concordia Coll, MN B
Concordia U Wisconsin, WI B
Davenport U, Lansing, MI A
Donnelly Coll, KS A
Elmhurst Coll, IL B
Grand Valley State U, MI B
Gustavus Adolphus Coll, MN B
Hamline U, MN B
Indiana U–Purdue U Indianapolis, IN B
Kent State U, Ashtabula Campus, OH A
Langston U, OK B
Marquette U, WI B
Mount Vernon Nazarene U, OH B
Northern Illinois U, IL B
Oakland U, MI B
The Ohio State U, OH B
Oklahoma Wesleyan U, OK B
Pittsburg State U, KS B
St. Cloud State U, MN B
Saint John's U, MN B
Saint Mary's U of Minnesota, MN B
Shawnee State U, OH A
Simpson Coll, IA B
Springfield Coll in Illinois, IL A
U of Cincinnati, OH A
U of Evansville, IN A,B
The U of Findlay, OH B
U of Illinois at Chicago, IL B
U of Minnesota, Morris, MN B
U of Minnesota, Twin Cities Campus, MN B
U of Missouri–Columbia, MO B
U of North Dakota, ND B
U of Toledo, OH B
U of Wisconsin–Milwaukee, WI B
Winona State U, MN B

PHYSICAL THERAPY ASSISTANT

Baker Coll of Flint, MI A
Baker Coll of Muskegon, MI A
Central Christian Coll of Kansas, KS A
Coll of St. Catherine, MN A
Coll of St. Catherine–Minneapolis, MN A
Finlandia U, MI A
Kent State U, OH A
Missouri Western State Coll, MO A
Southern Illinois U Carbondale, IL A
U of Evansville, IN A
U of Indianapolis, IN A
Wichita State U, KS A

PHYSICIAN ASSISTANT

Augsburg Coll, MN B
Butler U, IN B
Central Christian Coll of Kansas, KS A
Elmhurst Coll, IL B
Grand Valley State U, MI B
Kettering Coll of Medical Arts, OH A,B
Marquette U, WI B
Peru State Coll, NE B
Saint Louis U, MO B
Southern Illinois U Carbondale, IL B
Union Coll, NE B
The U of Findlay, OH B
The U of South Dakota, SD B
U of Wisconsin–La Crosse, WI B
U of Wisconsin–Madison, WI B
Wichita State U, KS B

PHYSICS

Adrian Coll, MI A,B

Albion Coll, MI B
Alma Coll, MI B
Anderson U, IN B
Andrews U, MI B
Antioch Coll, OH B
Ashland U, OH B
Augsburg Coll, MN B
Augustana Coll, IL B
Augustana Coll, SD B
Baker U, KS B
Baldwin-Wallace Coll, OH B
Ball State U, IN B
Beloit Coll, WI B
Bemidji State U, MN B
Benedictine Coll, KS B
Benedictine U, IL B
Bethel Coll, IN B
Bethel Coll, KS B
Bethel Coll, MN B
Bluffton Coll, OH B
Bowling Green State U, OH B
Bradley U, IL B
Buena Vista U, IA B
Butler U, IN B
Calvin Coll, MI B
Cameron U, OK B
Carleton Coll, MN B
Carthage Coll, WI B
Case Western Reserve U, OH B
Central Coll, IA B
Central Methodist Coll, MO B
Central Michigan U, MI B
Central Missouri State U, MO B
Chadron State Coll, NE B
Cleveland State U, OH B
Coe Coll, IA B
Coll of Saint Benedict, MN B
Coll of St. Catherine, MN B
The Coll of Wooster, OH B
Columbia Coll, MO B
Concordia Coll, MN B
Cornell Coll, IA B
Creighton U, NE B
Dakota State U, SD B
Denison U, OH B
DePaul U, IL B
DePauw U, IN B
Doane Coll, NE B
Dordt Coll, IA B
Drake U, IA B
Drury U, MO B
Earlham Coll, IN B
East Central U, OK B
Eastern Illinois U, IL B
Eastern Michigan U, MI B
Elmhurst Coll, IL B
Emporia State U, KS B
Fort Hays State U, KS B
Franklin Coll, IN B
Goshen Coll, IN B
Grand Valley State U, MI B
Greenville Coll, IL B
Grinnell Coll, IA B
Gustavus Adolphus Coll, MN B
Hamline U, MN B
Hanover Coll, IN B
Hastings Coll, NE B
Heidelberg Coll, OH B
Hillsdale Coll, MI B
Hiram Coll, OH B
Hope Coll, MI B
Illinois Coll, IL B
Illinois Inst of Technology, IL B
Illinois State U, IL B
Illinois Wesleyan U, IL B
Indiana State U, IN B
Indiana U Bloomington, IN B
Indiana U–Purdue U Fort Wayne, IN B
Indiana U–Purdue U Indianapolis, IN B
Indiana U South Bend, IN B
Iowa State U of Science and Technology, IA B
John Carroll U, OH B
Kalamazoo Coll, MI B
Kansas State U, KS B
Kent State U, OH B
Kenyon Coll, OH B
Kettering U, MI B
Knox Coll, IL B
Lake Forest Coll, IL B
Lawrence Technological U, MI B
Lawrence U, WI B
Lewis U, IL B
Loras Coll, IA B
Loyola U Chicago, IL B
Luther Coll, IA B
Macalester Coll, MN B
MacMurray Coll, IL B
Manchester Coll, IN B
Marietta Coll, OH B
Marquette U, WI B
Miami U, OH B
Miami U–Middletown Campus, OH A
Michigan State U, MI B
Michigan Technological U, MI B
MidAmerica Nazarene U, KS B
Millikin U, IL B
Minnesota State U, Mankato, MN B
Minnesota State U, Moorhead, MN B
Minot State U, ND B
Missouri Southern State Coll, MO B
Monmouth Coll, IL B
Morningside Coll, IA B
Mount Union Coll, OH B
Muskingum Coll, OH B
Nebraska Wesleyan U, NE B
North Central Coll, IL B
North Dakota State U, ND B
Northeastern Illinois U, IL B
Northeastern State U, OK B
Northern Illinois U, IL B
Northern Michigan U, MI B
North Park U, IL B
Northwestern U, IL B
Northwest Missouri State U, MO B
Oakland U, MI B
Oberlin Coll, OH B
Ohio Northern U, OH B
The Ohio State U, OH B
Ohio U, OH B
Ohio Wesleyan U, OH B
Oklahoma Baptist U, OK B
Oklahoma City U, OK B
Oklahoma State U, OK B
Oral Roberts U, OK B
Otterbein Coll, OH B
Pittsburg State U, KS B
Principia Coll, IL B
Purdue U, IN B
Purdue U Calumet, IN B
Ripon Coll, WI B
Rockhurst U, MO B
Rose-Hulman Inst of Technology, IN B
Saginaw Valley State U, MI B
St. Ambrose U, IA B
St. Cloud State U, MN B
Saint John's U, MN B
Saint Louis U, MO B
St. Norbert Coll, WI B
St. Olaf Coll, MN B
South Dakota School of Mines and Technology, SD B
South Dakota State U, SD B
Southeastern Oklahoma State U, OK B
Southeast Missouri State U, MO B
Southern Illinois U Carbondale, IL B
Southern Illinois U Edwardsville, IL B
Southern Nazarene U, OK B
Southwestern Coll, KS B
Southwestern Oklahoma State U, OK B
Southwest Missouri State U, MO B
Taylor U, IN B
Truman State U, MO B
Union Coll, NE B
The U of Akron, OH B
U of Central Oklahoma, OK B
U of Chicago, IL B
U of Cincinnati, OH B
U of Dayton, OH B
U of Evansville, IN B
U of Illinois at Chicago, IL B
U of Illinois at Urbana–Champaign, IL B
U of Indianapolis, IN B
The U of Iowa, IA B
U of Kansas, KS B
U of Michigan, MI B
U of Michigan–Dearborn, MI B
U of Michigan–Flint, MI B
U of Minnesota, Duluth, MN B
U of Minnesota, Morris, MN B
U of Minnesota, Twin Cities Campus, MN B
U of Missouri–Columbia, MO B
U of Missouri–Kansas City, MO B
U of Missouri–Rolla, MO B
U of Missouri–St. Louis, MO B
U of Nebraska at Kearney, NE B
U of Nebraska at Omaha, NE B
U of Nebraska–Lincoln, NE B
U of North Dakota, ND B
U of Northern Iowa, IA B
U of Notre Dame, IN B
U of Oklahoma, OK B
U of St. Thomas, MN B
U of Science and Arts of Oklahoma, OK B
The U of South Dakota, SD B
U of Toledo, OH B
U of Tulsa, OK B
U of Wisconsin–Eau Claire, WI B
U of Wisconsin–La Crosse, WI B
U of Wisconsin–Madison, WI B
U of Wisconsin–Milwaukee, WI B
U of Wisconsin–Oshkosh, WI B
U of Wisconsin–Parkside, WI B
U of Wisconsin–River Falls, WI B
U of Wisconsin–Stevens Point, WI B
U of Wisconsin–Whitewater, WI B
Valparaiso U, IN B
Wabash Coll, IN B
Waldorf Coll, IA A
Wartburg Coll, IA B
Washington U in St. Louis, MO B
Wayne State U, MI B
Western Illinois U, IL B
Western Michigan U, MI B
Westminster Coll, MO B
Wheaton Coll, IL B
Wichita State U, KS B
William Jewell Coll, MO B
Winona State U, MN B
Wittenberg U, OH B
Wright State U, OH B
Xavier U, OH B
Youngstown State U, OH B

PHYSICS EDUCATION

Bowling Green State U, OH B
Central Methodist Coll, MO B
Central Michigan U, MI B
Central Missouri State U, MO B
Chadron State Coll, NE B
Concordia Coll, MN B
Concordia U, NE B
Eastern Michigan U, MI B
Elmhurst Coll, IL B
Greenville Coll, IL B
Gustavus Adolphus Coll, MN B
Hastings Coll, NE B
Indiana U Bloomington, IN B
Indiana U–Purdue U Fort Wayne, IN B
Indiana U South Bend, IN B
Luther Coll, IA B
Malone Coll, OH B
Minot State U, ND B
North Dakota State U, ND B
St. Ambrose U, IA B
Saint Mary's U of Minnesota, MN B
Southwest Missouri State U, MO B
Union Coll, NE B
U of Illinois at Chicago, IL B
U of Nebraska–Lincoln, NE B
U of Rio Grande, OH B
U of Wisconsin–River Falls, WI B
Washington U in St. Louis, MO B
Xavier U, OH B
Youngstown State U, OH B

PHYSICS RELATED

Ohio U, OH B
U of Notre Dame, IN B

PHYSIOLOGICAL PSYCHOLOGY/ PSYCHOBIOLOGY

Grand Valley State U, MI B
Hiram Coll, OH B
Luther Coll, IA B
Oberlin Coll, OH B
Ripon Coll, WI B
U of Evansville, IN B
Wittenberg U, OH B

Physiological Psychology/Psychobiology (continued)
York Coll, NE B

PHYSIOLOGY
Michigan State U, MI B
Minnesota State U, Mankato, MN B
Northern Michigan U, MI B
St. Cloud State U, MN B
Southern Illinois U Carbondale, IL B
The U of Akron, OH B
U of Illinois at Urbana–Champaign, IL B
U of Minnesota, Twin Cities Campus, MN B

PLANT BREEDING
North Dakota State U, ND B

PLANT PATHOLOGY
Michigan State U, MI B

PLANT PROTECTION
Iowa State U of Science and Technology, IA B
North Dakota State U, ND B
U of Nebraska–Lincoln, NE B

PLANT SCIENCES
The Ohio State U, OH B
Oklahoma State U, OK B
Southern Illinois U Carbondale, IL B
U of Minnesota, Twin Cities Campus, MN B
U of Missouri–Columbia, MO B

PLASTICS ENGINEERING
Ball State U, IN B
Case Western Reserve U, OH B
Eastern Michigan U, MI B
Ferris State U, MI B
Kent State U, OH A
Kettering U, MI B
North Dakota State U, ND B
The U of Akron, OH B
Winona State U, MN B

PLASTICS TECHNOLOGY
Ball State U, IN B
Eastern Michigan U, MI B
Ferris State U, MI A,B
Kent State U, OH A
Pittsburg State U, KS B
Shawnee State U, OH A,B

PLAY/SCREENWRITING
Columbia Coll Chicago, IL B
DePaul U, IL B
Metropolitan State U, MN B
Ohio U, OH B
U of Michigan, MI B

PLUMBING
Nebraska Indian Comm Coll, NE A
Ranken Tech Coll, MO A

POLITICAL SCIENCE
Adrian Coll, MI A,B
Albion Coll, MI B
Alma Coll, MI B
Anderson U, IN B
Andrews U, MI B
Antioch Coll, OH B
Aquinas Coll, MI B
Ashland U, OH B
Augsburg Coll, MN B
Augustana Coll, IL B
Augustana Coll, SD B
Aurora U, IL B
Ave Maria Coll, MI B
Avila U, MO B
Bacone Coll, OK A
Baker U, KS B
Baldwin-Wallace Coll, OH B
Ball State U, IN B
Bellevue U, NE B
Beloit Coll, WI B
Bemidji State U, MN B
Benedictine Coll, KS B
Benedictine U, IL B
Bethany Coll, KS B
Bethel Coll, MN B
Blackburn Coll, IL B
Black Hills State U, SD B
Bluffton Coll, OH B
Bowling Green State U, OH B
Bradley U, IL B
Briar Cliff U, IA B
Buena Vista U, IA B
Butler U, IN B
Calumet Coll of Saint Joseph, IN B
Calvin Coll, MI B
Cameron U, OK B
Capital U, OH B
Cardinal Stritch U, WI B
Carleton Coll, MN B
Carroll Coll, WI B
Carthage Coll, WI B
Case Western Reserve U, OH B
Cedarville U, OH B
Central Coll, IA B
Central Methodist Coll, MO B
Central Michigan U, MI B
Central Missouri State U, MO B
Chicago State U, IL B
Cleveland State U, OH B
Coe Coll, IA B
Coll of Menominee Nation, WI A
Coll of Saint Benedict, MN B
Coll of St. Catherine, MN B
Coll of the Ozarks, MO B
The Coll of Wooster, OH B
Columbia Coll, MO B
Concordia Coll, MN B
Concordia U, IL B
Cornell Coll, IA B
Creighton U, NE B
Denison U, OH B
DePaul U, IL B
DePauw U, IN B
Dickinson State U, ND B
Doane Coll, NE B
Dominican U, IL B
Donnelly Coll, KS A
Dordt Coll, IA B
Drake U, IA B
Drury U, MO B
Earlham Coll, IN B
East Central U, OK B
Eastern Illinois U, IL B
Eastern Michigan U, MI B
Edgewood Coll, WI B
Elmhurst Coll, IL B
Emporia State U, KS B
Eureka Coll, IL B
Evangel U, MO B
Fort Hays State U, KS B
Franciscan U of Steubenville, OH B
Franklin Coll, IN B
Goshen Coll, IN B
Grand Valley State U, MI B
Grand View Coll, IA B
Greenville Coll, IL B
Grinnell Coll, IA B
Gustavus Adolphus Coll, MN B
Hamline U, MN B
Hanover Coll, IN B
Hastings Coll, NE B
Heidelberg Coll, OH B
Hillsdale Coll, MI B
Hiram Coll, OH B
Hope Coll, MI B
Illinois Coll, IL B
Illinois Inst of Technology, IL B
Illinois State U, IL B
Illinois Wesleyan U, IL B
Indiana State U, IN B
Indiana U Bloomington, IN B
Indiana U Northwest, IN B
Indiana U–Purdue U Fort Wayne, IN A,B
Indiana U–Purdue U Indianapolis, IN B
Indiana U South Bend, IN B
Indiana U Southeast, IN B
Indiana Wesleyan U, IN A,B
Iowa State U of Science and Technology, IA B
Jamestown Coll, ND B
John Carroll U, OH B
Kalamazoo Coll, MI B
Kansas State U, KS B
Kent State U, OH B
Kenyon Coll, OH B
Knox Coll, IL B
Lake Forest Coll, IL B
Lawrence U, WI B
Lewis U, IL B
Lincoln Coll, Lincoln, IL A
Lindenwood U, MO B
Loras Coll, IA B
Loyola U Chicago, IL B
Luther Coll, IA B
Macalester Coll, MN B
MacMurray Coll, IL B
Malone Coll, OH B
Manchester Coll, IN B
Marian Coll of Fond du Lac, WI B
Marietta Coll, OH B
Marquette U, WI B
Martin U, IN B
Marygrove Coll, MI B
Maryville U of Saint Louis, MO B
McKendree Coll, IL B
Miami U, OH B
Miami U–Middletown Campus, OH A
Michigan State U, MI B
Millikin U, IL B
Minnesota State U, Mankato, MN B
Minnesota State U, Moorhead, MN B
Missouri Southern State Coll, MO B
Missouri Valley Coll, MO B
Missouri Western State Coll, MO B
Monmouth Coll, IL B
Morningside Coll, IA B
Mount Mercy Coll, IA B
Mount Union Coll, OH B
Muskingum Coll, OH B
Nebraska Wesleyan U, NE B
North Central Coll, IL B
North Dakota State U, ND B
Northeastern Illinois U, IL B
Northeastern State U, OK B
Northern Illinois U, IL B
Northern Michigan U, MI B
Northern State U, SD B
North Park U, IL B
Northwestern Coll, IA B
Northwestern Oklahoma State U, OK B
Northwestern U, IL B
Northwest Missouri State U, MO B
Notre Dame Coll, OH B
Oakland U, MI B
Oberlin Coll, OH B
Ohio Dominican U, OH B
Ohio Northern U, OH B
The Ohio State U, OH B
Ohio U, OH B
Ohio Wesleyan U, OH B
Oklahoma Baptist U, OK B
Oklahoma City U, OK B
Oklahoma State U, OK B
Oklahoma Wesleyan U, OK B
Oral Roberts U, OK B
Ottawa U, KS B
Otterbein Coll, OH B
Park U, MO B
Pittsburg State U, KS B
Principia Coll, IL B
Purdue U, IN B
Purdue U Calumet, IN B
Quincy U, IL B
Ripon Coll, WI B
Rockford Coll, IL B
Rockhurst U, MO B
Rogers State U, OK A
Roosevelt U, IL B
Saginaw Valley State U, MI B
St. Ambrose U, IA B
St. Cloud State U, MN B
Saint John's U, MN B
Saint Joseph's Coll, IN B
Saint Louis U, MO B
Saint Mary's Coll, IN B
Saint Mary's U of Minnesota, MN B
Saint Mary U, KS B
St. Norbert Coll, WI B
St. Olaf Coll, MN B
Saint Xavier U, IL B
Simpson Coll, IA B
South Dakota State U, SD B
Southeastern Oklahoma State U, OK B
Southeast Missouri State U, MO B
Southern Illinois U Carbondale, IL B
Southern Illinois U Edwardsville, IL B
Southern Nazarene U, OK B
Southwest Baptist U, MO B
Southwestern Oklahoma State U, OK B
Southwest Minnesota State U, MN B
Southwest Missouri State U, MO B
Stephens Coll, MO B

Taylor U, IN B
Truman State U, MO B
The U of Akron, OH B
U of Central Oklahoma, OK B
U of Chicago, IL B
U of Cincinnati, OH B
U of Dayton, OH B
U of Evansville, IN B
The U of Findlay, OH B
U of Illinois at Chicago, IL B
U of Illinois at Springfield, IL B
U of Illinois at Urbana–Champaign, IL B
U of Indianapolis, IN B
The U of Iowa, IA B
U of Kansas, KS B
U of Michigan, MI B
U of Michigan–Dearborn, MI B
U of Michigan–Flint, MI B
U of Minnesota, Duluth, MN B
U of Minnesota, Morris, MN B
U of Minnesota, Twin Cities Campus, MN B
U of Missouri–Columbia, MO B
U of Missouri–Kansas City, MO B
U of Missouri–St. Louis, MO B
U of Nebraska at Kearney, NE B
U of Nebraska at Omaha, NE B
U of Nebraska–Lincoln, NE B
U of North Dakota, ND B
U of Northern Iowa, IA B
U of Notre Dame, IN B
U of Oklahoma, OK B
U of Rio Grande, OH B
U of St. Francis, IL B
U of St. Thomas, MN B
U of Science and Arts of Oklahoma, OK B
U of Sioux Falls, SD B
The U of South Dakota, SD B
U of Southern Indiana, IN B
U of Toledo, OH A,B
U of Tulsa, OK B
U of Wisconsin–Eau Claire, WI B
U of Wisconsin–Green Bay, WI A,B
U of Wisconsin–La Crosse, WI B
U of Wisconsin–Madison, WI B
U of Wisconsin–Milwaukee, WI B
U of Wisconsin–Oshkosh, WI B
U of Wisconsin–Parkside, WI B
U of Wisconsin–Platteville, WI B
U of Wisconsin–River Falls, WI B
U of Wisconsin–Stevens Point, WI B
U of Wisconsin–Superior, WI B
U of Wisconsin–Whitewater, WI B
Valparaiso U, IN B
Wabash Coll, IN B
Walsh U, OH B
Wartburg Coll, IA B
Washington U in St. Louis, MO B
Wayne State Coll, NE B
Wayne State U, MI B
Webster U, MO B
Western Illinois U, IL B
Western Michigan U, MI B
Westminster Coll, MO B
Wheaton Coll, IL B
Wichita State U, KS B
Wilberforce U, OH B
William Jewell Coll, MO B
William Penn U, IA B
William Woods U, MO B
Wilmington Coll, OH B
Winona State U, MN B
Wisconsin Lutheran Coll, WI B
Wittenberg U, OH B
Wright State U, OH B
Xavier U, OH A,B
Youngstown State U, OH B

POLITICAL SCIENCE/ GOVERNMENT RELATED

Nebraska Wesleyan U, NE B
The U of Akron, OH B

POLYMER CHEMISTRY

Loras Coll, IA B
North Dakota State U, ND B
The U of Akron, OH B
U of Wisconsin–Stevens Point, WI B
Winona State U, MN B

PORTUGUESE

Indiana U Bloomington, IN B
The Ohio State U, OH B
U of Illinois at Urbana–Champaign, IL B
The U of Iowa, IA B
U of Minnesota, Twin Cities Campus, MN B
U of Wisconsin–Madison, WI B

POULTRY SCIENCE

Coll of the Ozarks, MO B
U of Wisconsin–Madison, WI B

PRACTICAL NURSE

Central Christian Coll of Kansas, KS A
Coll of Menominee Nation, WI A
Dickinson State U, ND A
Lincoln Coll, Lincoln, IL A
Lincoln Coll, Normal, IL A

PRE-DENTISTRY

Alma Coll, MI B
Anderson U, IN B
Aquinas Coll, MI B
Ashland U, OH B
Augsburg Coll, MN B
Augustana Coll, IL B
Augustana Coll, SD B
Baker U, KS B
Baldwin-Wallace Coll, OH B
Ball State U, IN B
Beloit Coll, WI B
Benedictine U, IL B
Bethel Coll, IN B
Bethel Coll, MN B
Blackburn Coll, IL B
Briar Cliff U, IA B
Buena Vista U, IA B
Calvin Coll, MI B
Capital U, OH B
Cardinal Stritch U, WI B
Carthage Coll, WI B
Cedarville U, OH B
Central Christian Coll of Kansas, KS A
Central Missouri State U, MO B
Chicago State U, IL B
Coe Coll, IA B
Coll of Saint Benedict, MN B
Coll of St. Catherine, MN B
Coll of Saint Mary, NE B
The Coll of Wooster, OH B
Columbia Coll, MO B
Concordia Coll, MN B
Concordia U, IL B
Concordia U Wisconsin, WI B
Cornerstone U, MI B
Dakota State U, SD B
Defiance Coll, OH B
Dickinson State U, ND B
Dominican U, IL B
Dordt Coll, IA B
Drake U, IA B
Drury U, MO B
East Central U, OK B
Edgewood Coll, WI B
Elmhurst Coll, IL B
Eureka Coll, IL B
Evangel U, MO B
Goshen Coll, IN B
Graceland U, IA B
Grand Valley State U, MI B
Greenville Coll, IL B
Gustavus Adolphus Coll, MN B
Hamline U, MN B
Hastings Coll, NE B
Heidelberg Coll, OH B
Hillsdale Coll, MI B
Hiram Coll, OH B
Huntington Coll, IN B
Illinois Coll, IL B
Illinois Wesleyan U, IL B
Indiana U Bloomington, IN B
Indiana U–Purdue U Fort Wayne, IN B
Indiana U–Purdue U Indianapolis, IN B
Indiana Wesleyan U, IN B
Iowa State U of Science and Technology, IA B
Iowa Wesleyan Coll, IA B
John Carroll U, OH B
Kansas State U, KS B
Kent State U, OH B
Lake Erie Coll, OH B
Lake Forest Coll, IL B
Langston U, OK B
Lawrence U, WI B
Lewis U, IL B
Lindenwood U, MO B
Loyola U Chicago, IL B
Luther Coll, IA B
MacMurray Coll, IL B
Manchester Coll, IN B
Marian Coll, IN B
Marian Coll of Fond du Lac, WI B
Marquette U, WI B
Mayville State U, ND B
McKendree Coll, IL B
McPherson Coll, KS B
Miami U, OH B
Michigan Technological U, MI B
Midland Lutheran Coll, NE B
Millikin U, IL B
Minnesota State U, Mankato, MN B
Minnesota State U, Moorhead, MN B
Missouri Southern State Coll, MO B
Morningside Coll, IA B
Mount Mary Coll, WI B
Mount Mercy Coll, IA B
Mount Vernon Nazarene U, OH B
Muskingum Coll, OH B
Newman U, KS B
North Central Coll, IL B
North Dakota State U, ND B
Northeastern State U, OK B
Northern Michigan U, MI B
Northern State U, SD B
Northland Coll, WI B
North Park U, IL B
Northwestern Oklahoma State U, OK B
Northwest Missouri State U, MO B
Notre Dame Coll, OH B
Oakland U, MI B
Ohio U, OH B
Ohio Wesleyan U, OH B
Oklahoma Baptist U, OK B
Oklahoma City U, OK B
Oklahoma State U, OK B
Oklahoma Wesleyan U, OK B
Olivet Coll, MI B
Olivet Nazarene U, IL B
Oral Roberts U, OK B
Otterbein Coll, OH B
Peru State Coll, NE B
Pittsburg State U, KS B
Purdue U Calumet, IN B
Quincy U, IL B
Ripon Coll, WI B
Rockford Coll, IL B
Roosevelt U, IL B
Saint John's U, MN B
Saint Mary-of-the-Woods Coll, IN B
St. Norbert Coll, WI B
Simpson Coll, IA B
South Dakota State U, SD B
Southern Nazarene U, OK B
Southwestern Oklahoma State U, OK B
Southwest Minnesota State U, MN B
Tabor Coll, KS B
Taylor U, IN B
Trinity Christian Coll, IL B
Truman State U, MO B
The U of Akron, OH B
U of Dayton, OH B
U of Evansville, IN B
U of Illinois at Chicago, IL B
U of Indianapolis, IN B
The U of Iowa, IA B
U of Minnesota, Duluth, MN B
U of Minnesota, Morris, MN B
U of Minnesota, Twin Cities Campus, MN B
U of Missouri–Rolla, MO B
U of Missouri–St. Louis, MO B
U of Nebraska–Lincoln, NE B
U of Oklahoma, OK B
U of Rio Grande, OH B
U of St. Francis, IL B
U of Saint Francis, IN B
U of Sioux Falls, SD B
The U of South Dakota, SD B
U of Toledo, OH B
U of Wisconsin–Green Bay, WI B

Pre-Dentistry (continued)
U of Wisconsin–Milwaukee, WI B
U of Wisconsin–Oshkosh, WI B
U of Wisconsin–Parkside, WI B
U of Wisconsin–River Falls, WI B
Upper Iowa U, IA B
Urbana U, OH B
Valley City State U, ND B
Viterbo U, WI B
Walsh U, OH B
Washington U in St. Louis, MO B
Westminster Coll, MO B
William Jewell Coll, MO B
William Penn U, IA B
Wilmington Coll, OH B
Winona State U, MN B
Wittenberg U, OH B
Youngstown State U, OH B

PRE-ENGINEERING

Anderson U, IN A
Briar Cliff U, IA A
Columbia Coll, MO B
Concordia Coll, MN B
Edgewood Coll, WI A
Ferris State U, MI A
Grand View Coll, IA B
Hannibal-LaGrange Coll, MO A
Marian Coll, IN A
McPherson Coll, KS B
Miami U–Middletown Campus, OH A
Minnesota State U, Mankato, MN A
Missouri Southern State Coll, MO A
Newman U, KS A
Northern State U, SD A
Purdue U North Central, IN A
Rochester Comm and Tech Coll, MN A
St. Gregory's U, OK A
St. Norbert Coll, WI B
Shawnee State U, OH A
Siena Heights U, MI A
Springfield Coll in Illinois, IL A
U of Sioux Falls, SD A
The U of South Dakota, SD A
Valley City State U, ND B
Waldorf Coll, IA A
Winona State U, MN A

PRE-LAW

Albion Coll, MI B
Alma Coll, MI B
Anderson U, IN B
Andrews U, MI B
Antioch Coll, OH B
Aquinas Coll, MI B
Ashland U, OH B
Augsburg Coll, MN B
Augustana Coll, IL B
Augustana Coll, SD B
Baker U, KS B
Baldwin-Wallace Coll, OH B
Ball State U, IN B
Beloit Coll, WI B
Bemidji State U, MN B
Benedictine Coll, KS B
Benedictine U, IL B
Bethel Coll, IN B
Bethel Coll, MN B
Blackburn Coll, IL B
Bluffton Coll, OH B
Bowling Green State U, OH B
Briar Cliff U, IA B
Buena Vista U, IA B
Calumet Coll of Saint Joseph, IN A,B
Calvin Coll, MI B
Cardinal Stritch U, WI B
Carthage Coll, WI B
Cedarville U, OH B
Central Christian Coll of Kansas, KS B
Chicago State U, IL B
Coe Coll, IA B
Coll of Saint Benedict, MN B
Coll of St. Catherine, MN B
Coll of Saint Mary, NE B
The Coll of Wooster, OH B
Columbia Coll, MO B
Concordia Coll, MN B
Concordia U, IL B
Concordia U, MI B
Concordia U Wisconsin, WI B
Cornerstone U, MI B
Dakota State U, SD B
Defiance Coll, OH B
DePaul U, IL B
Dickinson State U, ND B
Dominican U, IL B
Drake U, IA B
Drury U, MO B
Earlham Coll, IN B
East Central U, OK B
Edgewood Coll, WI B
Elmhurst Coll, IL B
Eureka Coll, IL B
Evangel U, MO B
Fontbonne U, MO B
Fort Hays State U, KS B
The Franciscan U, IA B
Goshen Coll, IN B
Graceland U, IA B
Grand Valley State U, MI B
Grand View Coll, IA B
Greenville Coll, IL B
Gustavus Adolphus Coll, MN B
Hamline U, MN B
Hastings Coll, NE B
Heidelberg Coll, OH B
Hiram Coll, OH B
Huntington Coll, IN B
Illinois Coll, IL B
Illinois Wesleyan U, IL B
Indiana U Bloomington, IN B
Indiana U–Purdue U Indianapolis, IN B
Indiana Wesleyan U, IN B
Iowa State U of Science and Technology, IA B
Iowa Wesleyan Coll, IA B
John Carroll U, OH B
Judson Coll, IL B
Lake Erie Coll, OH B
Lake Forest Coll, IL B
Lakeland Coll, WI B
Langston U, OK B
Lawrence U, WI B
Lewis U, IL B
Lindenwood U, MO B
Loyola U Chicago, IL B
Luther Coll, IA B
MacMurray Coll, IL B
Madonna U, MI B
Maharishi U of Management, IA B
Manchester Coll, IN B
Marian Coll, IN B
Marian Coll of Fond du Lac, WI B
Marquette U, WI B
Mayville State U, ND B
McKendree Coll, IL B
Miami U, OH B
Midland Lutheran Coll, NE B
Millikin U, IL B
Minnesota State U, Mankato, MN B
Minnesota State U, Moorhead, MN B
Missouri Valley Coll, MO B
Morningside Coll, IA B
Mount Mary Coll, WI B
Mount Mercy Coll, IA B
Mount Vernon Nazarene U, OH B
Muskingum Coll, OH B
Newman U, KS B
North Central Coll, IL B
North Dakota State U, ND B
Northeastern State U, OK B
Northern Michigan U, MI B
Northern State U, SD B
Northland Coll, WI B
North Park U, IL B
Northwestern Oklahoma State U, OK B
Northwest Missouri State U, MO B
Notre Dame Coll, OH B
Oakland City U, IN B
Oakland U, MI B
Ohio U, OH B
Ohio Wesleyan U, OH B
Oklahoma Baptist U, OK B
Oklahoma Christian U, OK B
Oklahoma City U, OK B
Oklahoma State U, OK B
Oklahoma Wesleyan U, OK B
Olivet Coll, MI B
Olivet Nazarene U, IL B
Otterbein Coll, OH B
Peru State Coll, NE B
Pittsburg State U, KS B
Purdue U Calumet, IN B
Ripon Coll, WI B
Rockford Coll, IL B
Roosevelt U, IL B
St. Cloud State U, MN B
Saint John's U, MN B
Saint Mary-of-the-Woods Coll, IN B
St. Norbert Coll, WI B
Shawnee State U, OH B
Siena Heights U, MI B
Simpson Coll, IA B
South Dakota State U, SD B
Southern Nazarene U, OK B
Southwestern Oklahoma State U, OK B
Southwest Minnesota State U, MN B
Stephens Coll, MO B
Taylor U, IN B
Taylor U, Fort Wayne Campus, IN B
Tri-State U, IN B
Truman State U, MO B
The U of Akron, OH B
U of Cincinnati, OH B
U of Dayton, OH B
U of Evansville, IN B
The U of Findlay, OH B
U of Illinois at Chicago, IL B
U of Indianapolis, IN B
The U of Iowa, IA B
U of Minnesota, Duluth, MN B
U of Minnesota, Morris, MN B
U of Minnesota, Twin Cities Campus, MN B
U of Missouri–Rolla, MO B
U of Missouri–St. Louis, MO B
U of Nebraska at Omaha, NE B
U of Rio Grande, OH B
U of Saint Francis, IN B
U of Sioux Falls, SD B
The U of South Dakota, SD B
U of Toledo, OH B
U of Wisconsin–Milwaukee, WI B
U of Wisconsin–Oshkosh, WI B
U of Wisconsin–Parkside, WI B
U of Wisconsin–River Falls, WI B
U of Wisconsin–Superior, WI B
U of Wisconsin–Whitewater, WI B
Urbana U, OH B
Ursuline Coll, OH B
Valley City State U, ND B
Viterbo U, WI B
Wabash Coll, IN B
Walsh U, OH B
Westminster Coll, MO B
William Jewell Coll, MO B
William Penn U, IA B
Wilmington Coll, OH B
Winona State U, MN B
Wittenberg U, OH B
Youngstown State U, OH B

PRE-MEDICINE

Adrian Coll, MI B
Albion Coll, MI B
Alma Coll, MI B
Anderson U, IN B
Andrews U, MI B
Antioch Coll, OH B
Aquinas Coll, MI B
Ashland U, OH B
Augsburg Coll, MN B
Augustana Coll, IL B
Augustana Coll, SD B
Avila U, MO B
Baker U, KS B
Baldwin-Wallace Coll, OH B
Ball State U, IN B
Beloit Coll, WI B
Bemidji State U, MN B
Benedictine U, IL B
Bethel Coll, IN B
Bethel Coll, MN B
Blackburn Coll, IL B
Bluffton Coll, OH B
Briar Cliff U, IA B
Buena Vista U, IA B
Calvin Coll, MI B
Capital U, OH B
Cardinal Stritch U, WI B
Carroll Coll, WI B
Carthage Coll, WI B
Cedarville U, OH B
Central Christian Coll of Kansas, KS A
Central Missouri State U, MO B
Chicago State U, IL B
Cleveland State U, OH B
Coe Coll, IA B
Coll of Saint Benedict, MN B
Coll of St. Catherine, MN B

Coll of Saint Mary, NE B
Coll of the Ozarks, MO B
The Coll of Wooster, OH B
Columbia Coll, MO B
Concordia Coll, MN B
Concordia U, IL B
Concordia U, MI B
Concordia U Wisconsin, WI B
Cornerstone U, MI B
Dakota State U, SD B
Defiance Coll, OH B
Dickinson State U, ND B
Dominican U, IL B
Dordt Coll, IA B
Drake U, IA B
Drury U, MO B
Earlham Coll, IN B
East Central U, OK B
Eastern Michigan U, MI B
Edgewood Coll, WI B
Elmhurst Coll, IL B
Eureka Coll, IL B
Evangel U, MO B
Fontbonne U, MO B
The Franciscan U, IA B
Goshen Coll, IN B
Graceland U, IA B
Grand Valley State U, MI B
Greenville Coll, IL B
Gustavus Adolphus Coll, MN B
Hamline U, MN B
Hastings Coll, NE B
Heidelberg Coll, OH B
Hillsdale Coll, MI B
Hiram Coll, OH B
Huntington Coll, IN B
Illinois Coll, IL B
Illinois Wesleyan U, IL B
Indiana U Bloomington, IN B
Indiana U–Purdue U Fort Wayne, IN B
Indiana U–Purdue U Indianapolis, IN B
Indiana Wesleyan U, IN B
Iowa State U of Science and Technology, IA B
Iowa Wesleyan Coll, IA B
John Carroll U, OH B
Judson Coll, IL B
Kansas State U, KS B
Lake Erie Coll, OH B
Lake Forest Coll, IL B
Langston U, OK B
Lawrence U, WI B
Lewis U, IL B
Lindenwood U, MO B
Lourdes Coll, OH B
Loyola U Chicago, IL B
Luther Coll, IA B
MacMurray Coll, IL B
Madonna U, MI B
Maharishi U of Management, IA B
Manchester Coll, IN B
Marian Coll, IN B
Marian Coll of Fond du Lac, WI B
Marquette U, WI B
Mayville State U, ND B
McKendree Coll, IL B
McPherson Coll, KS B
Miami U, OH B
Michigan Technological U, MI B
Midland Lutheran Coll, NE B
Millikin U, IL B
Minnesota State U, Mankato, MN B
Minnesota State U, Moorhead, MN B
Missouri Southern State Coll, MO B
Missouri Valley Coll, MO B
Morningside Coll, IA B
Mount Mary Coll, WI B
Mount Mercy Coll, IA B
Mount Vernon Nazarene U, OH B
Muskingum Coll, OH B
Newman U, KS B
North Central Coll, IL B
North Dakota State U, ND B
Northeastern State U, OK B
Northern Michigan U, MI B
Northern State U, SD B
Northland Coll, WI B
North Park U, IL B
Northwestern Oklahoma State U, OK B
Northwestern U, IL B
Northwest Missouri State U, MO B
Notre Dame Coll, OH B
Oakland City U, IN B
Oakland U, MI B
Ohio U, OH B
Ohio Wesleyan U, OH B
Oklahoma Baptist U, OK B
Oklahoma City U, OK B
Oklahoma State U, OK B
Oklahoma Wesleyan U, OK B
Olivet Coll, MI B
Olivet Nazarene U, IL B
Oral Roberts U, OK B
Otterbein Coll, OH B
Peru State Coll, NE B
Pittsburg State U, KS B
Purdue U, IN B
Purdue U Calumet, IN B
Quincy U, IL B
Ripon Coll, WI B
Rockford Coll, IL B
Roosevelt U, IL B
St. Cloud State U, MN B
Saint John's U, MN B
Saint Mary-of-the-Woods Coll, IN B
St. Norbert Coll, WI B
Shawnee State U, OH B
Simpson Coll, IA B
South Dakota State U, SD B
Southern Nazarene U, OK B
Southwestern Oklahoma State U, OK B
Southwest Minnesota State U, MN B
Stephens Coll, MO B
Tabor Coll, KS B
Taylor U, IN B
Trinity Christian Coll, IL B
Trinity International U, IL B
Tri-State U, IN B
Truman State U, MO B
The U of Akron, OH B
U of Cincinnati, OH B
U of Dayton, OH B
U of Evansville, IN B
The U of Findlay, OH B
U of Indianapolis, IN B
The U of Iowa, IA B
U of Minnesota, Duluth, MN B
U of Minnesota, Morris, MN B
U of Minnesota, Twin Cities Campus, MN B
U of Missouri–Rolla, MO B
U of Missouri–St. Louis, MO B
U of Nebraska at Omaha, NE B
U of Nebraska–Lincoln, NE B
U of Notre Dame, IN B
U of Oklahoma, OK B
U of Rio Grande, OH B
U of St. Francis, IL B
U of Saint Francis, IN B
U of Sioux Falls, SD B
The U of South Dakota, SD B
U of Toledo, OH B
U of Wisconsin–Milwaukee, WI B
U of Wisconsin–Oshkosh, WI B
U of Wisconsin–Parkside, WI B
U of Wisconsin–River Falls, WI B
Upper Iowa U, IA B
Urbana U, OH B
Ursuline Coll, OH B
Valley City State U, ND B
Viterbo U, WI B
Wabash Coll, IN B
Walsh U, OH B
Washington U in St. Louis, MO B
Wayne State Coll, NE B
Westminster Coll, MO B
William Jewell Coll, MO B
William Penn U, IA B
Wilmington Coll, OH B
Winona State U, MN B
Wittenberg U, OH B
Youngstown State U, OH B

PRE-PHARMACY STUDIES

Ashland U, OH B
Central Christian Coll of Kansas, KS A
Central Missouri State U, MO B
Coll of Saint Benedict, MN B
Coll of the Ozarks, MO B
Elmhurst Coll, IL B
Mayville State U, ND B
McPherson Coll, KS B
Missouri Southern State Coll, MO B
Mount Vernon Nazarene U, OH B
Ohio U, OH B
Oklahoma Baptist U, OK B
Saint John's U, MN B
Saint Mary-of-the-Woods Coll, IN B
Southern Nazarene U, OK B
The U of Akron, OH B
The U of Iowa, IA B
U of Minnesota, Duluth, MN B
U of Minnesota, Morris, MN B
U of Nebraska–Lincoln, NE B
U of Wisconsin–Parkside, WI B
U of Wisconsin–River Falls, WI B
Valley City State U, ND B
Viterbo U, WI B
Washington U in St. Louis, MO B
Youngstown State U, OH B

PRE-THEOLOGY

Alma Coll, MI B
Ashland U, OH B
Bacone Coll, OK A
Central Christian Coll of Kansas, KS B
Circleville Bible Coll, OH B
Coll of Saint Benedict, MN B
Concordia Coll, MN B
Concordia U, IL B
Emmaus Bible Coll, IA B
Grace U, NE B
Loras Coll, IA B
Loyola U Chicago, IL B
Luther Coll, IA B
Manchester Coll, IN A
Martin Luther Coll, MN B
Minnesota State U, Mankato, MN B
Moody Bible Inst, IL B
Northwestern Coll, MN B
Ohio Wesleyan U, OH B
Reformed Bible Coll, MI B
Saint John's U, MN B
Southwestern Coll, KS B
Trinity Christian Coll, IL B
U of Indianapolis, IN B
U of Rio Grande, OH B
Valparaiso U, IN B

PRE-VETERINARY STUDIES

Adrian Coll, MI B
Albion Coll, MI B
Alma Coll, MI B
Anderson U, IN B
Andrews U, MI B
Antioch Coll, OH B
Aquinas Coll, MI B
Ashland U, OH B
Augsburg Coll, MN B
Augustana Coll, IL B
Augustana Coll, SD B
Baker U, KS B
Baldwin-Wallace Coll, OH B
Bemidji State U, MN B
Benedictine U, IL B
Bethel Coll, MN B
Blackburn Coll, IL B
Briar Cliff U, IA B
Buena Vista U, IA B
Calvin Coll, MI B
Capital U, OH B
Cardinal Stritch U, WI B
Carthage Coll, WI B
Cedarville U, OH B
Central Christian Coll of Kansas, KS A
Central Missouri State U, MO B
Chicago State U, IL B
Cleveland State U, OH B
Coe Coll, IA B
Coll of Saint Benedict, MN B
Coll of St. Catherine, MN B
Coll of Saint Mary, NE B
Coll of the Ozarks, MO B
The Coll of Wooster, OH B
Columbia Coll, MO B
Concordia Coll, MN B
Cornerstone U, MI B
Dakota State U, SD B
Defiance Coll, OH B
Dickinson State U, ND B
Dominican U, IL B
Dordt Coll, IA B
Drake U, IA B
Drury U, MO B
East Central U, OK B
Edgewood Coll, WI B
Elmhurst Coll, IL B
Eureka Coll, IL B
Evangel U, MO B

Pre-Veterinary Studies (continued)

Goshen Coll, IN B
Grand Valley State U, MI B
Greenville Coll, IL B
Gustavus Adolphus Coll, MN B
Hamline U, MN B
Hastings Coll, NE B
Heidelberg Coll, OH B
Hillsdale Coll, MI B
Hiram Coll, OH B
Huntington Coll, IN B
Illinois Coll, IL B
Illinois Wesleyan U, IL B
Indiana U–Purdue U Indianapolis, IN B
Indiana Wesleyan U, IN B
Iowa State U of Science and Technology, IA B
Iowa Wesleyan Coll, IA B
John Carroll U, OH B
Kansas State U, KS B
Lake Erie Coll, OH B
Lake Forest Coll, IL B
Langston U, OK B
Lawrence U, WI B
Lewis U, IL B
Lindenwood U, MO B
Loyola U Chicago, IL B
Luther Coll, IA B
MacMurray Coll, IL B
Madonna U, MI B
Manchester Coll, IN B
Marian Coll, IN B
Marian Coll of Fond du Lac, WI B
Mayville State U, ND B
McKendree Coll, IL B
McPherson Coll, KS B
Miami U, OH B
Michigan Technological U, MI B
Midland Lutheran Coll, NE B
Millikin U, IL B
Minnesota State U, Mankato, MN B
Minnesota State U, Moorhead, MN B
Missouri Southern State Coll, MO B
Missouri Valley Coll, MO B
Morningside Coll, IA B
Mount Mary Coll, WI B
Mount Mercy Coll, IA B
Mount Vernon Nazarene U, OH B
Muskingum Coll, OH B
Newman U, KS B
North Central Coll, IL B
North Dakota State U, ND B
Northeastern State U, OK B
Northern Michigan U, MI B
Northland Coll, WI B
North Park U, IL B
Northwest Missouri State U, MO B
Oakland City U, IN B
Oakland U, MI B
Ohio U, OH B
Ohio Wesleyan U, OH B
Oklahoma Baptist U, OK B
Oklahoma City U, OK B
Oklahoma State U, OK B
Oklahoma Wesleyan U, OK B
Olivet Coll, MI B
Olivet Nazarene U, IL B
Otterbein Coll, OH B
Peru State Coll, NE B
Pittsburg State U, KS B
Purdue U, IN B
Purdue U Calumet, IN B
Quincy U, IL B
Ripon Coll, WI B
Rockford Coll, IL B
St. Cloud State U, MN B
Saint John's U, MN B
Saint Mary-of-the-Woods Coll, IN B
St. Norbert Coll, WI B
Shawnee State U, OH B
Simpson Coll, IA B
South Dakota State U, SD B
Southwestern Oklahoma State U, OK B
Southwest Minnesota State U, MN B
Stephens Coll, MO B
Taylor U, IN B
Trinity Christian Coll, IL B
Tri-State U, IN B
Truman State U, MO B
The U of Akron, OH B
U of Cincinnati, OH B
U of Evansville, IN B
The U of Findlay, OH B
U of Illinois at Urbana–Champaign, IL B
U of Indianapolis, IN B
The U of Iowa, IA B
U of Minnesota, Duluth, MN B
U of Minnesota, Morris, MN B
U of Minnesota, Twin Cities Campus, MN B
U of Missouri–St. Louis, MO B
U of Nebraska–Lincoln, NE B
U of Oklahoma, OK B
U of Rio Grande, OH B
U of St. Francis, IL B
U of Saint Francis, IN B
U of Sioux Falls, SD B
The U of South Dakota, SD B
U of Wisconsin–Oshkosh, WI B
U of Wisconsin–Parkside, WI B
U of Wisconsin–River Falls, WI B
Upper Iowa U, IA B
Urbana U, OH B
Valley City State U, ND B
Viterbo U, WI B
Wabash Coll, IN B
Walsh U, OH B
Washington U in St. Louis, MO B
Wayne State Coll, NE B
Westminster Coll, MO B
William Jewell Coll, MO B
Wilmington Coll, OH B
Winona State U, MN B
Wittenberg U, OH B
Youngstown State U, OH B

PRINTMAKING

Ball State U, IN B
Bowling Green State U, OH B
The Cleveland Inst of Art, OH B
Coll of Visual Arts, MN B
Columbus Coll of Art and Design, OH B
Grand Valley State U, MI B
Indiana Wesleyan U, IN B
Kansas City Art Inst, MO B
Milwaukee Inst of Art and Design, WI B
Minneapolis Coll of Art and Design, MN B
Minnesota State U, Moorhead, MN B
Northern Michigan U, MI B
The Ohio State U, OH B
Ohio U, OH B
School of the Art Inst of Chicago, IL B
Trinity Christian Coll, IL B
The U of Akron, OH B
The U of Iowa, IA B
U of Kansas, KS B
U of Michigan, MI B
U of Missouri–St. Louis, MO B
U of Oklahoma, OK B
The U of South Dakota, SD B
Washington U in St. Louis, MO B
Webster U, MO B
Youngstown State U, OH B

PROFESSIONAL STUDIES

Bemidji State U, MN B
Briar Cliff U, IA B
Grand View Coll, IA B
Kent State U, OH B
Lake Erie Coll, OH B
Missouri Southern State Coll, MO B
Saint Mary-of-the-Woods Coll, IN B
U of Dubuque, IA B
U of Oklahoma, OK B

PROTECTIVE SERVICES RELATED

Franklin U, OH B
Lewis U, IL B
Northwestern Oklahoma State U, OK B
Ohio U, OH B

PSYCHIATRIC/MENTAL HEALTH SERVICES

Franciscan U of Steubenville, OH B
U of Toledo, OH A

PSYCHOLOGY

Adrian Coll, MI A,B
Albion Coll, MI B
Alma Coll, MI B
Alverno Coll, WI B
Anderson U, IN B
Andrews U, MI B
Antioch Coll, OH B
Aquinas Coll, MI B
Ashland U, OH B
Augsburg Coll, MN B
Augustana Coll, IL B
Augustana Coll, SD B
Aurora U, IL B
Avila U, MO B
Baker U, KS B
Baldwin-Wallace Coll, OH B
Ball State U, IN B
Barclay Coll, KS B
Bellevue U, NE B
Beloit Coll, WI B
Bemidji State U, MN B
Benedictine Coll, KS B
Benedictine U, IL B
Bethany Coll, KS B
Bethel Coll, IN B
Bethel Coll, KS B
Bethel Coll, MN B
Blackburn Coll, IL B
Black Hills State U, SD B
Bluffton Coll, OH B
Bowling Green State U, OH B
Bradley U, IL B
Briar Cliff U, IA B
Buena Vista U, IA B
Butler U, IN B
Calumet Coll of Saint Joseph, IN A,B
Calvin Coll, MI B
Cameron U, OK B
Cardinal Stritch U, WI B
Carleton Coll, MN B
Carroll Coll, WI B
Carthage Coll, WI B
Case Western Reserve U, OH B
Cedarville U, OH B
Central Christian Coll of Kansas, KS A
Central Coll, IA B
Central Methodist Coll, MO A,B
Central Michigan U, MI B
Central Missouri State U, MO B
Chadron State Coll, NE B
Chicago State U, IL B
Cincinnati Bible Coll and Seminary, OH B
Clarke Coll, IA B
Cleveland State U, OH B
Coe Coll, IA B
Coll of Mount St. Joseph, OH B
Coll of Saint Benedict, MN B
Coll of St. Catherine, MN B
Coll of Saint Mary, NE B
The Coll of St. Scholastica, MN B
Coll of the Ozarks, MO B
The Coll of Wooster, OH B
Columbia Coll, MO B
Concordia Coll, MN B
Concordia U, IL B
Concordia U, MI B
Concordia U, MN B
Concordia U, NE B
Concordia U Wisconsin, WI B
Cornell Coll, IA B
Cornerstone U, MI B
Creighton U, NE B
Crown Coll, MN A,B
Culver-Stockton Coll, MO B
Dakota Wesleyan U, SD B
Dana Coll, NE B
Defiance Coll, OH B
Denison U, OH B
DePaul U, IL B
DePauw U, IN B
Dickinson State U, ND B
Doane Coll, NE B
Dominican U, IL B
Donnelly Coll, KS A
Dordt Coll, IA B
Drake U, IA B
Drury U, MO B
Earlham Coll, IN B
East Central U, OK B
Eastern Illinois U, IL B
Eastern Michigan U, MI B
Edgewood Coll, WI B
Elmhurst Coll, IL B
Emporia State U, KS B
Eureka Coll, IL B
Evangel U, MO B

Institution	Degree
Fontbonne U, MO	B
Fort Hays State U, KS	B
The Franciscan U, IA	B
Franciscan U of Steubenville, OH	B
Franklin Coll, IN	B
Goshen Coll, IN	B
Governors State U, IL	B
Grace Coll, IN	B
Graceland U, IA	B
Grace U, NE	B
Grand Valley State U, MI	B
Grand View Coll, IA	B
Greenville Coll, IL	B
Grinnell Coll, IA	B
Gustavus Adolphus Coll, MN	B
Hamline U, MN	B
Hannibal-LaGrange Coll, MO	B
Hanover Coll, IN	B
Hastings Coll, NE	B
Heidelberg Coll, OH	B
Hillsdale Coll, MI	B
Hillsdale Free Will Baptist Coll, OK	A
Hiram Coll, OH	B
Hope Coll, MI	B
Huntington Coll, IN	B
Illinois Coll, IL	B
Illinois Inst of Technology, IL	B
Illinois State U, IL	B
Illinois Wesleyan U, IL	B
Indiana State U, IN	B
Indiana U Bloomington, IN	B
Indiana U East, IN	B
Indiana U Kokomo, IN	B
Indiana U Northwest, IN	B
Indiana U–Purdue U Fort Wayne, IN	A,B
Indiana U–Purdue U Indianapolis, IN	B
Indiana U South Bend, IN	B
Indiana U Southeast, IN	B
Indiana Wesleyan U, IN	B
Iowa State U of Science and Technology, IA	B
Iowa Wesleyan Coll, IA	B
Jamestown Coll, ND	B
John Carroll U, OH	B
Judson Coll, IL	B
Kalamazoo Coll, MI	B
Kansas State U, KS	B
Kendall Coll, IL	B
Kent State U, OH	B
Kenyon Coll, OH	B
Knox Coll, IL	B
Lake Erie Coll, OH	B
Lake Forest Coll, IL	B
Lakeland Coll, WI	B
Langston U, OK	B
Lawrence U, WI	B
Lewis U, IL	B
Lincoln Coll, Lincoln, IL	A
Lincoln Coll, Normal, IL	A
Lindenwood U, MO	B
Loras Coll, IA	B
Lourdes Coll, OH	A,B
Loyola U Chicago, IL	B
Luther Coll, IA	B
Macalester Coll, MN	B
MacMurray Coll, IL	B
Madonna U, MI	B
Maharishi U of Management, IA	A,B
Malone Coll, OH	B
Manchester Coll, IN	B
Marian Coll, IN	A,B
Marian Coll of Fond du Lac, WI	B
Marietta Coll, OH	B
Marquette U, WI	B
Martin U, IN	B
Marygrove Coll, MI	B
Maryville U of Saint Louis, MO	B
McKendree Coll, IL	B
McPherson Coll, KS	B
Metropolitan State U, MN	B
Miami U, OH	B
Miami U–Middletown Campus, OH	A
Michigan State U, MI	B
MidAmerica Nazarene U, KS	B
Midland Lutheran Coll, NE	B
Millikin U, IL	B
Minnesota State U, Mankato, MN	B
Minnesota State U, Moorhead, MN	B
Minot State U, ND	B
Missouri Southern State Coll, MO	B
Missouri Valley Coll, MO	B
Missouri Western State Coll, MO	B
Monmouth Coll, IL	B
Morningside Coll, IA	B
Mount Mercy Coll, IA	B
Mount Union Coll, OH	B
Mount Vernon Nazarene U, OH	B
Muskingum Coll, OH	B
National-Louis U, IL	B
Nebraska Wesleyan U, NE	B
Newman U, KS	B
North Central Coll, IL	B
North Dakota State U, ND	B
Northeastern Illinois U, IL	B
Northeastern State U, OK	B
Northern Illinois U, IL	B
Northern Michigan U, MI	B
Northern State U, SD	B
Northland Coll, WI	B
North Park U, IL	B
Northwestern Coll, IA	B
Northwestern Coll, MN	B
Northwestern Oklahoma State U, OK	B
Northwestern U, IL	B
Northwest Missouri State U, MO	B
Notre Dame Coll, OH	B
Oak Hills Christian Coll, MN	B
Oakland U, MI	B
Oberlin Coll, OH	B
Ohio Dominican U, OH	B
Ohio Northern U, OH	B
The Ohio State U, OH	B
The Ohio State U at Lima, OH	B
Ohio U, OH	B
Ohio Wesleyan U, OH	B
Oklahoma Baptist U, OK	B
Oklahoma Christian U, OK	B
Oklahoma City U, OK	B
Oklahoma Panhandle State U, OK	B
Oklahoma State U, OK	B
Olivet Coll, MI	B
Olivet Nazarene U, IL	B
Oral Roberts U, OK	B
Ottawa U, KS	B
Otterbein Coll, OH	B
Park U, MO	B
Peru State Coll, NE	B
Pittsburg State U, KS	B
Purdue U, IN	B
Purdue U Calumet, IN	B
Quincy U, IL	B
Ripon Coll, WI	B
Rochester Coll, MI	B
Rockford Coll, IL	B
Rockhurst U, MO	B
Roosevelt U, IL	B
Saginaw Valley State U, MI	B
St. Ambrose U, IA	B
St. Cloud State U, MN	B
Saint John's U, MN	B
Saint Joseph's Coll, IN	B
Saint Louis U, MO	B
Saint Mary-of-the-Woods Coll, IN	B
Saint Mary's Coll, IN	B
Saint Mary's Coll of Madonna U, MI	B
Saint Mary's U of Minnesota, MN	B
Saint Mary U, KS	B
St. Norbert Coll, WI	B
St. Olaf Coll, MN	B
Saint Xavier U, IL	B
Siena Heights U, MI	A,B
Silver Lake Coll, WI	B
Simpson Coll, IA	B
South Dakota State U, SD	B
Southeastern Oklahoma State U, OK	B
Southeast Missouri State U, MO	B
Southern Illinois U Carbondale, IL	B
Southern Illinois U Edwardsville, IL	B
Southern Nazarene U, OK	B
Southwest Baptist U, MO	B
Southwestern Coll, KS	B
Southwestern Oklahoma State U, OK	B
Southwest Minnesota State U, MN	B
Southwest Missouri State U, MO	B
Spring Arbor U, MI	B
Stephens Coll, MO	B
Tabor Coll, KS	B
Taylor U, IN	B
Taylor U, Fort Wayne Campus, IN	B
Tiffin U, OH	B
Trinity Bible Coll, ND	B
Trinity Christian Coll, IL	B
Trinity International U, IL	B
Tri-State U, IN	B
Truman State U, MO	B
Union Coll, NE	B
Union Inst & U, OH	B
The U of Akron, OH	B
U of Central Oklahoma, OK	B
U of Chicago, IL	B
U of Cincinnati, OH	B
U of Dayton, OH	B
U of Dubuque, IA	B
U of Evansville, IN	B
The U of Findlay, OH	B
U of Illinois at Chicago, IL	B
U of Illinois at Springfield, IL	B
U of Illinois at Urbana–Champaign, IL	B
U of Indianapolis, IN	B
The U of Iowa, IA	B
U of Kansas, KS	B
U of Mary, ND	B
U of Michigan, MI	B
U of Michigan–Dearborn, MI	B
U of Michigan–Flint, MI	B
U of Minnesota, Duluth, MN	B
U of Minnesota, Morris, MN	B
U of Minnesota, Twin Cities Campus, MN	B
U of Missouri–Columbia, MO	B
U of Missouri–Kansas City, MO	B
U of Missouri–Rolla, MO	B
U of Missouri–St. Louis, MO	B
U of Nebraska at Kearney, NE	B
U of Nebraska at Omaha, NE	B
U of Nebraska–Lincoln, NE	B
U of North Dakota, ND	B
U of Northern Iowa, IA	B
U of Notre Dame, IN	B
U of Oklahoma, OK	B
U of Rio Grande, OH	A
U of St. Francis, IL	B
U of Saint Francis, IN	B
U of St. Thomas, MN	B
U of Science and Arts of Oklahoma, OK	B
U of Sioux Falls, SD	B
The U of South Dakota, SD	B
U of Southern Indiana, IN	B
U of Toledo, OH	B
U of Tulsa, OK	B
U of Wisconsin–Eau Claire, WI	B
U of Wisconsin–Green Bay, WI	A,B
U of Wisconsin–La Crosse, WI	B
U of Wisconsin–Madison, WI	B
U of Wisconsin–Milwaukee, WI	B
U of Wisconsin–Oshkosh, WI	B
U of Wisconsin–Parkside, WI	B
U of Wisconsin–Platteville, WI	B
U of Wisconsin–River Falls, WI	B
U of Wisconsin–Stevens Point, WI	B
U of Wisconsin–Stout, WI	B
U of Wisconsin–Superior, WI	B
U of Wisconsin–Whitewater, WI	B
Upper Iowa U, IA	B
Urbana U, OH	B
Ursuline Coll, OH	B
Valparaiso U, IN	B
Viterbo U, WI	B
Wabash Coll, IN	B
Waldorf Coll, IA	A
Walsh U, OH	B
Wartburg Coll, IA	B
Washington U in St. Louis, MO	B
Wayne State Coll, NE	B
Wayne State U, MI	B
Webster U, MO	B
Western Illinois U, IL	B
Western Michigan U, MI	B
Westminster Coll, MO	B
Wheaton Coll, IL	B
Wichita State U, KS	B
Wilberforce U, OH	B
William Jewell Coll, MO	B
William Penn U, IA	B

Psychology (continued)

William Woods U, MO B
Wilmington Coll, OH B
Winona State U, MN B
Wisconsin Lutheran Coll, WI B
Wittenberg U, OH B
Wright State U, OH A,B
Xavier U, OH A,B
York Coll, NE B
Youngstown State U, OH B

PSYCHOLOGY RELATED

Loyola U Chicago, IL B

PUBLIC ADMINISTRATION

Augustana Coll, IL B
Blackburn Coll, IL B
Bowling Green State U, OH B
Buena Vista U, IA B
Calvin Coll, MI B
Cedarville U, OH B
Central Methodist Coll, MO A,B
Doane Coll, NE B
Eastern Michigan U, MI B
Edgewood Coll, WI B
Evangel U, MO B
Ferris State U, MI B
Governors State U, IL B
Grand Valley State U, MI B
Hamline U, MN B
Heidelberg Coll, OH B
Indiana U Bloomington, IN A,B
Indiana U Northwest, IN A,B
Indiana U–Purdue U Fort Wayne, IN A,B
Indiana U–Purdue U Indianapolis, IN A,B
Indiana U South Bend, IN A,B
Iowa State U of Science and Technology, IA B
John Carroll U, OH B
Lakeland Coll, WI B
Lewis U, IL B
Lindenwood U, MO B
Madonna U, MI A,B
Metropolitan State U, MN B
Miami U, OH B
Michigan State U, MI B
Minnesota State U, Mankato, MN B
Missouri Valley Coll, MO B
Nebraska Indian Comm Coll, NE A
Northern Michigan U, MI B
Northern State U, SD B
Northwest Missouri State U, MO B
Oakland U, MI B
Ohio Wesleyan U, OH B
Park U, MO B
Roosevelt U, IL B
Saginaw Valley State U, MI B
St. Ambrose U, IA B
St. Cloud State U, MN B
Saint Mary's U of Minnesota, MN B
Siena Heights U, MI B
Southwest Minnesota State U, MN B
Southwest Missouri State U, MO B
Union Inst & U, OH B
U of Michigan–Dearborn, MI B
U of Michigan–Flint, MI B
U of Missouri–St. Louis, MO B
U of Nebraska at Omaha, NE B
U of North Dakota, ND B
U of Northern Iowa, IA B
U of Oklahoma, OK B
U of Wisconsin–Green Bay, WI A,B
U of Wisconsin–La Crosse, WI B
U of Wisconsin–Stevens Point, WI B
U of Wisconsin–Whitewater, WI B
Upper Iowa U, IA B
Wayne State Coll, NE B
Wayne State U, MI B
Western Michigan U, MI B
Westminster Coll, MO B
Winona State U, MN B
Youngstown State U, OH B

PUBLIC ADMINISTRATION AND SERVICES RELATED

Ohio U, OH B
The U of Akron, OH A
U of Phoenix–West Michigan Campus, MI B

PUBLIC HEALTH

Alma Coll, MI B
Central Michigan U, MI B
Grand Valley State U, MI B
Indiana U Bloomington, IN B
Indiana U–Purdue U Indianapolis, IN B
Maryville U of Saint Louis, MO B
Minnesota State U, Mankato, MN B
Truman State U, MO B
U of Cincinnati, OH B
U of Minnesota, Twin Cities Campus, MN B
U of Wisconsin–Eau Claire, WI B
Winona State U, MN B

PUBLIC HEALTH EDUCATION/PROMOTION

Malone Coll, OH B
U of St. Thomas, MN B
U of Toledo, OH B
U of Wisconsin–La Crosse, WI B

PUBLIC HEALTH RELATED

U of Illinois at Urbana–Champaign, IL B

PUBLIC POLICY ANALYSIS

Albion Coll, MI B
DePaul U, IL B
Edgewood Coll, WI B
Grand Valley State U, MI B
Indiana U Bloomington, IN A,B
Kenyon Coll, OH B
Muskingum Coll, OH B
Northwestern U, IL B
St. Cloud State U, MN B
U of Chicago, IL B
U of Cincinnati, OH B
U of Missouri–St. Louis, MO B
U of Toledo, OH B
U of Wisconsin–Whitewater, WI B

PUBLIC RELATIONS

Andrews U, MI B
Ball State U, IN B
Bowling Green State U, OH B
Bradley U, IL B
Buena Vista U, IA B
Butler U, IN B
Cameron U, OK B
Capital U, OH B
Cardinal Stritch U, WI B
Carroll Coll, WI B
Central Michigan U, MI B
Central Missouri State U, MO B
Clarke Coll, IA B
Cleveland State U, OH B
Coe Coll, IA B
Coll of the Ozarks, MO B
Columbia Coll Chicago, IL B
Concordia Coll, MN B
Defiance Coll, OH B
Doane Coll, NE B
Drake U, IA B
Eastern Michigan U, MI B
Ferris State U, MI B
Fontbonne U, MO B
Fort Hays State U, KS B
Grand Valley State U, MI B
Greenville Coll, IL B
Hastings Coll, NE B
Heidelberg Coll, OH B
Illinois State U, IL B
Indiana U Northwest, IN B
Indiana U–Purdue U Fort Wayne, IN B
Kent State U, OH B
Lewis U, IL B
Lindenwood U, MO B
Loras Coll, IA B
Madonna U, MI A,B
Malone Coll, OH B
Marietta Coll, OH B
Marquette U, WI B
McKendree Coll, IL B
MidAmerica Nazarene U, KS B
Minnesota State U, Mankato, MN B
Minnesota State U, Moorhead, MN B
Monmouth Coll, IL B
Mount Mary Coll, WI B
North Central Coll, IL B
Northern Michigan U, MI B
Northwestern Coll, MN B
Northwestern Oklahoma State U, OK B
Northwest Missouri State U, MO B
Ohio Dominican U, OH B
Ohio Northern U, OH B
Ohio U, OH B
Ohio U–Zanesville, OH B
Oklahoma Baptist U, OK B
Oklahoma Christian U, OK B
Oklahoma City U, OK B
Oral Roberts U, OK B
Otterbein Coll, OH B
Pittsburg State U, KS B
Purdue U Calumet, IN B
Quincy U, IL B
Rockhurst U, MO B
Roosevelt U, IL B
St. Ambrose U, IA B
St. Cloud State U, MN B
Saint Louis U, MO B
Saint Mary-of-the-Woods Coll, IN B
Saint Mary's U of Minnesota, MN B
Southeast Missouri State U, MO B
Stephens Coll, MO B
Tabor Coll, KS B
Taylor U, Fort Wayne Campus, IN B
Trinity Christian Coll, IL B
Union Coll, NE B
U of Central Oklahoma, OK B
U of Dayton, OH B
The U of Findlay, OH B
The U of Iowa, IA B
U of Nebraska at Omaha, NE B
U of Northern Iowa, IA B
U of Oklahoma, OK B
U of Rio Grande, OH B
U of St. Thomas, MN B
U of Sioux Falls, SD B
The U of South Dakota, SD B
U of Southern Indiana, IN B
U of Wisconsin–Madison, WI B
U of Wisconsin–River Falls, WI B
Ursuline Coll, OH B
Wartburg Coll, IA B
Wayne State U, MI B
Webster U, MO B
Western Michigan U, MI B
William Woods U, MO B
Winona State U, MN B
Xavier U, OH A,B
Youngstown State U, OH B

PUBLISHING

Benedictine U, IL B
Graceland U, IA B
U of Missouri–Columbia, MO B
U of St. Thomas, MN B

PURCHASING/ CONTRACTS MANAGEMENT

Eastern Michigan U, MI B
Miami U, OH B
Michigan State U, MI B

QUALITY CONTROL TECHNOLOGY

Baker Coll of Cadillac, MI A
Baker Coll of Flint, MI A
Baker Coll of Muskegon, MI A
Ferris State U, MI B
Spartan School of Aeronautics, OK A
U of Cincinnati, OH A
Winona State U, MN B

QUANTITATIVE ECONOMICS

U of Northern Iowa, IA B
Youngstown State U, OH B

RADIOLOGICAL SCIENCE

Allen Coll, IA A
Clarkson Coll, NE A,B
Indiana U Northwest, IN A,B
Kettering Coll of Medical Arts, OH A,B
Mayo School of Health Sciences, MN A
The Ohio State U, OH B
Sanford-Brown Coll, Fenton, MO A
Springfield Coll in Illinois, IL A
The U of Findlay, OH B

U of Mary, ND B
U of Michigan, MI B
U of Missouri–Columbia, MO B
U of St. Francis, IL B
U of Southern Indiana, IN B

RADIO/TELEVISION BROADCASTING

Ashland U, OH A,B
Bemidji State U, MN B
Bowling Green State U, OH B
Bradley U, IL B
Buena Vista U, IA B
Cameron U, OK B
Cedarville U, OH B
Central Michigan U, MI B
Central Missouri State U, MO B
Chicago State U, IL B
Columbia Coll Chicago, IL B
Concordia Coll, MN B
Drake U, IA B
East Central U, OK B
Evangel U, MO B
Fort Hays State U, KS B
Grace U, NE B
Grand Valley State U, MI B
Grand View Coll, IA B
Hastings Coll, NE B
Indiana State U, IN B
Indiana U Bloomington, IN B
Kent State U, OH B
Langston U, OK B
Lincoln Coll, Lincoln, IL A
Lindenwood U, MO B
Marietta Coll, OH B
Minot State U, ND B
Muskingum Coll, OH B
Northwestern Coll, MN A,B
Northwestern U, IL B
Northwest Missouri State U, MO B
Ohio U, OH A,B
Ohio U–Zanesville, OH A
Oklahoma Baptist U, OK B
Oklahoma Christian U, OK B
Oklahoma City U, OK B
Olivet Coll, MI B
Olivet Nazarene U, IL B
Oral Roberts U, OK B
Otterbein Coll, OH B
Pittsburg State U, KS B
Purdue U Calumet, IN B
Quincy U, IL B
Rogers State U, OK A
St. Ambrose U, IA B
St. Cloud State U, MN B
Southeast Missouri State U, MO B
Southern Illinois U Carbondale, IL B
Southwest Minnesota State U, MN B
Spring Arbor U, MI B
Stephens Coll, MO B
U of Central Oklahoma, OK B
U of Cincinnati, OH B
U of Dayton, OH B
The U of Iowa, IA B
U of Kansas, KS B
U of Missouri–Columbia, MO B
U of Nebraska at Omaha, NE B
U of Northern Iowa, IA B
U of Oklahoma, OK B
U of Sioux Falls, SD B
The U of South Dakota, SD B
U of Southern Indiana, IN B
U of Wisconsin–Madison, WI B
U of Wisconsin–Oshkosh, WI B
U of Wisconsin–River Falls, WI B
U of Wisconsin–Superior, WI B
Wayne State U, MI B
Webster U, MO B
Western Michigan U, MI B
William Woods U, MO B
Winona State U, MN B
Xavier U, OH A,B
Youngstown State U, OH B

RADIO/TELEVISION BROADCASTING TECHNOLOGY

Eastern Michigan U, MI B
Lewis U, IL B
Ohio U, OH B

RANGE MANAGEMENT

Chadron State Coll, NE B
Fort Hays State U, KS B
North Dakota State U, ND B
South Dakota State U, SD B
U of Nebraska–Lincoln, NE B

READING EDUCATION

Aquinas Coll, MI B
Bowling Green State U, OH B
Central Missouri State U, MO B
Chicago State U, IL B
Grand Valley State U, MI B
Luther Coll, IA B
Northeastern State U, OK B
Northwest Missouri State U, MO B
Ohio U, OH B
St. Cloud State U, MN B
U of Central Oklahoma, OK B
U of Missouri–St. Louis, MO B
U of Northern Iowa, IA B
U of Wisconsin–Superior, WI B
Upper Iowa U, IA B
Walsh U, OH B
Winona State U, MN B
Wright State U, OH B
York Coll, NE B

REAL ESTATE

Ball State U, IN B
Eastern Michigan U, MI B
Ferris State U, MI A
Indiana U Bloomington, IN B
Kent State U, OH A
Kent State U, Ashtabula Campus, OH A
Miami U–Middletown Campus, OH A
Minnesota State U, Mankato, MN B
The Ohio State U, OH B
St. Cloud State U, MN B
U of Central Oklahoma, OK B
U of Cincinnati, OH A,B
U of Missouri–Columbia, MO B
U of Nebraska at Omaha, NE B
U of Northern Iowa, IA B
U of Oklahoma, OK B
U of St. Thomas, MN B
U of Toledo, OH A
U of Wisconsin–Madison, WI B
U of Wisconsin–Milwaukee, WI B
Webster U, MO B

RECREATIONAL THERAPY

Ashland U, OH B
Coll of Mount St. Joseph, OH B
Grand Valley State U, MI B
Indiana Inst of Technology, IN A,B
Indiana U Bloomington, IN B
Minnesota State U, Mankato, MN B
Northland Coll, WI B
Northwest Missouri State U, MO B
Ohio U, OH B
Pittsburg State U, KS B
Southwestern Oklahoma State U, OK B
The U of Findlay, OH B
The U of Iowa, IA B
U of St. Francis, IL B
U of Toledo, OH B
U of Wisconsin–La Crosse, WI B
U of Wisconsin–Milwaukee, WI B
Winona State U, MN B

RECREATION/LEISURE FACILITIES MANAGEMENT

Ball State U, IN B
Central Michigan U, MI B
Coll of the Ozarks, MO B
Eastern Illinois U, IL B
Eastern Michigan U, MI B
Grand Valley State U, MI B
Hannibal-LaGrange Coll, MO B
Illinois State U, IL B
Indiana Inst of Technology, IN A,B
Indiana State U, IN B
Indiana U Bloomington, IN B
Indiana U Southeast, IN B
Indiana Wesleyan U, IN B
Kansas State U, KS B
Kent State U, OH B
Michigan State U, MI B
Minnesota State U, Mankato, MN B
Missouri Valley Coll, MO B
Missouri Western State Coll, MO B
Mount Marty Coll, SD B
Northland Coll, WI B
Oak Hills Christian Coll, MN B
Ohio U, OH B
South Dakota State U, SD B
Southeast Missouri State U, MO B
Tri-State U, IN B
U of Minnesota, Twin Cities Campus, MN B
U of Wisconsin–La Crosse, WI B
Western Illinois U, IL B
Winona State U, MN B

RECREATION/LEISURE STUDIES

Ashland U, OH B
Bemidji State U, MN B
Bethany Coll, KS B
Black Hills State U, SD B
Bluffton Coll, OH B
Bowling Green State U, OH B
Calvin Coll, MI B
Carthage Coll, WI B
Central Christian Coll of Kansas, KS A,B
Central Michigan U, MI B
Central Missouri State U, MO B
Chicago State U, IL B
Dordt Coll, IA B
Emporia State U, KS B
Evangel U, MO B
Ferris State U, MI B
Franklin Coll, IN B
Graceland U, IA B
Greenville Coll, IL B
Hannibal-LaGrange Coll, MO B
Huntington Coll, IN B
Indiana U Bloomington, IN B
Kansas State U, KS B
Malone Coll, OH B
Midland Lutheran Coll, NE B
Minnesota State U, Mankato, MN B
Missouri Valley Coll, MO B
North Dakota State U, ND B
Northern Michigan U, MI B
Northland Coll, WI B
Northwest Missouri State U, MO B
Ohio U, OH B
Oklahoma Baptist U, OK B
Oklahoma Panhandle State U, OK A,B
Pittsburg State U, KS B
South Dakota State U, SD B
Southeastern Oklahoma State U, OK B
Southeast Missouri State U, MO B
Southern Illinois U Carbondale, IL B
Southwest Baptist U, MO B
Southwestern Oklahoma State U, OK B
Southwest Missouri State U, MO B
Taylor U, IN B
U of Illinois at Urbana–Champaign, IL B
The U of Iowa, IA B
U of Michigan, MI B
U of Minnesota, Duluth, MN B
U of Missouri–Columbia, MO B
U of Nebraska at Kearney, NE B
U of Nebraska at Omaha, NE B
U of North Dakota, ND B
U of Northern Iowa, IA B
U of St. Francis, IL B
The U of South Dakota, SD B
U of Toledo, OH B
U of Wisconsin–Madison, WI B
U of Wisconsin–Milwaukee, WI B
Upper Iowa U, IA B

Recreation/Leisure Studies (continued)

Wayne State Coll, NE B
Wayne State U, MI B
Western Michigan U, MI B
William Penn U, IA B
Winona State U, MN B

REHABILITATION/ THERAPEUTIC SERVICES RELATED

Central Michigan U, MI B
Southern Illinois U Carbondale, IL B

REHABILITATION THERAPY

Baker Coll of Muskegon, MI B
Wilberforce U, OH B

RELIGIOUS EDUCATION

Andrews U, MI B
Aquinas Coll, MI B
Ashland U, OH B
Baptist Bible Coll, MO B
Barclay Coll, KS B
Cardinal Stritch U, WI B
Central Bible Coll, MO A,B
Cincinnati Bible Coll and Seminary, OH A,B
Circleville Bible Coll, OH A,B
Coll of Mount St. Joseph, OH B
Coll of Saint Benedict, MN B
Concordia U, IL B
Concordia U, MN B
Concordia U, NE B
Cornerstone U, MI A,B
Crossroads Coll, MN B
Crown Coll, MN B
Defiance Coll, OH B
Faith Baptist Bible Coll and Theological Seminary, IA B
Global U of the Assemblies of God, MO B
God's Bible School and Coll, OH B
Grace Bible Coll, MI A,B
Grace U, NE B
Great Lakes Christian Coll, MI A
Hannibal-LaGrange Coll, MO B
Hillsdale Free Will Baptist Coll, OK A,B
Indiana Wesleyan U, IN A,B
John Carroll U, OH B
Laura and Alvin Siegal Coll of Judaic Studies, OH B
Lincoln Christian Coll, IL B
Lincoln Coll, Lincoln, IL A
Manhattan Christian Coll, KS A,B
Maranatha Baptist Bible Coll, WI B
Marian Coll, IN B
MidAmerica Nazarene U, KS A,B
Moody Bible Inst, IL B
Mount Mary Coll, WI B
Mount Vernon Nazarene U, OH B
Nebraska Christian Coll, NE A,B
Northwestern Coll, IA B
Northwestern Coll, MN B
Oakland City U, IN B
Oklahoma Baptist U, OK B
Oklahoma Christian U, OK B
Oklahoma City U, OK B
Olivet Nazarene U, IL B
Ozark Christian Coll, MO B
Pillsbury Baptist Bible Coll, MN B
Reformed Bible Coll, MI A,B
Saint John's U, MN B
St. Louis Christian Coll, MO B
Saint Mary-of-the-Woods Coll, IN B
Southern Nazarene U, OK B
Sterling Coll, KS B
Taylor U, IN B
Taylor U, Fort Wayne Campus, IN B
Trinity Bible Coll, ND B
Trinity Christian Coll, IL B
Union Coll, NE B
U of Dayton, OH B
Viterbo U, WI B
Waldorf Coll, IA A
Wheaton Coll, IL B
York Coll, NE B

RELIGIOUS MUSIC

Anderson U, IN B
Aquinas Coll, MI A,B
Augustana Coll, IL B
Barclay Coll, KS B
Bethany Lutheran Coll, MN B
Bethel Coll, IN B
Bethel Coll, MN B
Calvin Coll, MI B
Cedarville U, OH B
Central Bible Coll, MO A,B
Cincinnati Bible Coll and Seminary, OH A,B
Circleville Bible Coll, OH A,B
Coll of the Ozarks, MO B
Concordia U, IL B
Concordia U, MI B
Concordia U, MN B
Concordia U, NE B
Crossroads Coll, MN B
Drake U, IA B
Evangel U, MO B
Faith Baptist Bible Coll and Theological Seminary, IA B
God's Bible School and Coll, OH B
Grace U, NE B
Greenville Coll, IL B
Gustavus Adolphus Coll, MN B
Hannibal-LaGrange Coll, MO B
Hillsdale Free Will Baptist Coll, OK A,B
Indiana Wesleyan U, IN A,B
Lincoln Christian Coll, IL B
Malone Coll, OH B
Manhattan Christian Coll, KS A,B
Maranatha Baptist Bible Coll, WI B
MidAmerica Nazarene U, KS A,B
Millikin U, IL B
Moody Bible Inst, IL B
Mount Vernon Nazarene U, OH A,B
Nebraska Christian Coll, NE A,B
Northeastern State U, OK B
North Park U, IL B
Oak Hills Christian Coll, MN B
Oklahoma Baptist U, OK B
Oklahoma City U, OK B
Olivet Nazarene U, IL B
Oral Roberts U, OK B
Ozark Christian Coll, MO B
Pillsbury Baptist Bible Coll, MN B
Saint Joseph's Coll, IN A,B
St. Louis Christian Coll, MO B
Southern Nazarene U, OK B
Southwestern Oklahoma State U, OK B
Taylor U, IN B
Trinity International U, IL B
Valparaiso U, IN B
Wartburg Coll, IA B
William Jewell Coll, MO B

RELIGIOUS STUDIES

Adrian Coll, MI A,B
Albion Coll, MI B
Alma Coll, MI B
Alverno Coll, WI B
Anderson U, IN B
Andrews U, MI B
Antioch Coll, OH B
Aquinas Coll, MI A,B
Ashland U, OH B
Augsburg Coll, MN B
Augustana Coll, IL B
Augustana Coll, SD B
Baldwin-Wallace Coll, OH B
Ball State U, IN B
Beloit Coll, WI B
Bemidji State U, MN B
Benedictine Coll, KS B
Bethany Coll, KS B
Bethel Coll, KS B
Bluffton Coll, OH B
Bradley U, IL B
Buena Vista U, IA B
Butler U, IN B
Calumet Coll of Saint Joseph, IN A,B
Calvin Coll, MI B
Capital U, OH B
Cardinal Stritch U, WI B
Carleton Coll, MN B
Carroll Coll, WI B
Carthage Coll, WI B
Case Western Reserve U, OH B
Central Bible Coll, MO B
Central Christian Coll of Kansas, KS A,B
Central Coll, IA B
Central Methodist Coll, MO B
Central Michigan U, MI B
Circleville Bible Coll, OH A,B
Clarke Coll, IA B
Cleveland State U, OH B
Coe Coll, IA B
Coll of Mount St. Joseph, OH B
The Coll of St. Scholastica, MN B
Coll of the Ozarks, MO B
The Coll of Wooster, OH B
Concordia Coll, MN B
Concordia U, MI B
Concordia U, MN B
Concordia U Wisconsin, WI B
Cornell Coll, IA B
Cornerstone U, MI B
Culver-Stockton Coll, MO B
Dakota Wesleyan U, SD B
Dana Coll, NE B
Defiance Coll, OH B
Denison U, OH B
DePaul U, IL B
DePauw U, IN B
Doane Coll, NE B
Dominican U, IL B
Dordt Coll, IA B
Drake U, IA B
Drury U, MO B
Earlham Coll, IN B
Eastern Michigan U, MI B
Edgewood Coll, WI B
Eureka Coll, IL B
The Franciscan U, IA B
Franklin Coll, IN B
Global U of the Assemblies of God, MO A
Goshen Coll, IN B
Grace Bible Coll, MI A
Graceland U, IA B
Grand View Coll, IA B
Greenville Coll, IL B
Grinnell Coll, IA B
Gustavus Adolphus Coll, MN B
Hamline U, MN B
Hannibal-LaGrange Coll, MO B
Hastings Coll, NE B
Heidelberg Coll, OH B
Hillsdale Coll, MI B
Hiram Coll, OH B
Hope Coll, MI B
Huntington Coll, IN B
Illinois Coll, IL B
Illinois Wesleyan U, IL B
Indiana U Bloomington, IN B
Indiana U–Purdue U Indianapolis, IN B
Iowa State U of Science and Technology, IA B
Jamestown Coll, ND B
John Carroll U, OH B
Judson Coll, IL B
Kalamazoo Coll, MI B
Kenyon Coll, OH B
Lakeland Coll, WI B
Laura and Alvin Siegal Coll of Judaic Studies, OH B
Lawrence U, WI B
Lewis U, IL B
Lindenwood U, MO B
Loras Coll, IA B
Lourdes Coll, OH A,B
Luther Coll, IA B
Macalester Coll, MN B
MacMurray Coll, IL B
Madonna U, MI A,B
Manchester Coll, IN A,B
Manhattan Christian Coll, KS B
Maranatha Baptist Bible Coll, WI A,B
Martin U, IN B
Marygrove Coll, MI B
Maryville U of Saint Louis, MO B
McKendree Coll, IL B
McPherson Coll, KS B
Miami U, OH B
Michigan State U, MI B
MidAmerica Nazarene U, KS A,B
Midland Lutheran Coll, NE B
Missouri Valley Coll, MO B
Monmouth Coll, IL B
Morningside Coll, IA B
Mount Marty Coll, SD A,B
Mount Mary Coll, WI B
Mount Mercy Coll, IA B
Mount Union Coll, OH B
Mount Vernon Nazarene U, OH B
Muskingum Coll, OH B
Nebraska Christian Coll, NE B

Nebraska Wesleyan U, NE B
North Central Coll, IL B
Northland Coll, WI B
North Park U, IL B
Northwestern Coll, IA B
Northwestern U, IL B
Oakland City U, IN B
Oberlin Coll, OH B
Ohio Northern U, OH B
The Ohio State U, OH B
Ohio Wesleyan U, OH B
Oklahoma Baptist U, OK B
Oklahoma Christian U, OK B
Oklahoma City U, OK B
Oklahoma Wesleyan U, OK B
Olivet Nazarene U, IL B
Oral Roberts U, OK B
Ottawa U, KS B
Otterbein Coll, OH B
Presentation Coll, SD A
Principia Coll, IL B
Ripon Coll, WI B
Saint Joseph's Coll, IN B
Saint Mary-of-the-Woods Coll, IN B
Saint Mary's Coll, IN B
St. Norbert Coll, WI B
St. Olaf Coll, MN B
Saint Xavier U, IL B
Siena Heights U, MI B
Simpson Coll, IA B
Southern Nazarene U, OK B
Southwest Baptist U, MO B
Southwest Missouri State U, MO B
Spring Arbor U, MI B
Tabor Coll, KS A,B
Taylor U, IN B
Trinity Christian Coll, IL B
Truman State U, MO B
Union Coll, NE B
U of Chicago, IL B
U of Dayton, OH B
U of Dubuque, IA B
U of Evansville, IN B
The U of Findlay, OH A,B
U of Illinois at Urbana–Champaign, IL B
U of Indianapolis, IN B
The U of Iowa, IA B
U of Kansas, KS B
U of Mary, ND B
U of Michigan, MI B
U of Minnesota, Twin Cities Campus, MN B
U of Missouri–Columbia, MO B
U of Nebraska at Omaha, NE B
U of North Dakota, ND B
U of Northern Iowa, IA B
U of Notre Dame, IN B
U of Oklahoma, OK B
U of Saint Francis, IN B
U of St. Thomas, MN B
U of Sioux Falls, SD A,B
U of Tulsa, OK B
U of Wisconsin–Eau Claire, WI B
U of Wisconsin–Milwaukee, WI B
U of Wisconsin–Oshkosh, WI B
Urbana U, OH B
Ursuline Coll, OH B
Viterbo U, WI B
Wabash Coll, IN B
Waldorf Coll, IA A
Walsh U, OH B
Wartburg Coll, IA B
Washington U in St. Louis, MO B
Webster U, MO B
Western Michigan U, MI B
Westminster Coll, MO B
Wheaton Coll, IL B
William Jewell Coll, MO B
Wilmington Coll, OH B
Wittenberg U, OH B
Wright State U, OH B
York Coll, NE B
Youngstown State U, OH B

RESPIRATORY THERAPY

Ball State U, IN A
Coll of St. Catherine, MN A
Coll of St. Catherine–Minneapolis, MN A
Concordia Coll, MN B
Dakota State U, SD A,B
Ferris State U, MI A
Indiana U Northwest, IN A
Indiana U–Purdue U Indianapolis, IN A,B
Kettering Coll of Medical Arts, OH A,B
Marygrove Coll, MI A,B
Mayo School of Health Sciences, MN A
Midland Lutheran Coll, NE A,B
Missouri Southern State Coll, MO A
National-Louis U, IL B
Nebraska Methodist Coll, NE A,B
Newman U, KS A
North Dakota State U, ND B
The Ohio State U, OH B
Rochester Comm and Tech Coll, MN A
St. Augustine Coll, IL A
Sanford-Brown Coll, Fenton, MO A
Shawnee State U, OH A
Southern Illinois U Carbondale, IL A
Southwest Missouri State U, MO B
The U of Akron, OH A
U of Kansas, KS B
U of Mary, ND B
U of Missouri–Columbia, MO B
U of Southern Indiana, IN A
U of Toledo, OH A,B
Youngstown State U, OH A,B

RETAILING OPERATIONS

Lake Erie Coll, OH B
Robert Morris Coll, IL A
The U of Akron, OH B
Youngstown State U, OH B

RETAIL MANAGEMENT

Baker Coll of Owosso, MI A
Bluffton Coll, OH B
Chicago State U, IL B
Ferris State U, MI B
Fontbonne U, MO B
Governors State U, IL B
Indiana U Bloomington, IN B
International Business Coll, Fort Wayne, IN A,B
Lindenwood U, MO B
Northern Michigan U, MI B
Northwest Missouri State U, MO B
U of Central Oklahoma, OK B
U of Minnesota, Crookston, MN A
U of Nebraska at Omaha, NE B
U of Toledo, OH A
Winona State U, MN B
Youngstown State U, OH B

ROBOTICS

U of Cincinnati, OH A

ROBOTICS TECHNOLOGY

Indiana State U, IN B
Indiana U–Purdue U Indianapolis, IN A,B
ITT Tech Inst, Fort Wayne, IN B
ITT Tech Inst, Indianapolis, IN B
ITT Tech Inst, Newburgh, IN B
Purdue U, IN A,B
U of Rio Grande, OH A,B

ROMANCE LANGUAGES

Beloit Coll, WI B
Cameron U, OK B
Carleton Coll, MN B
DePauw U, IN B
Kenyon Coll, OH B
Northwest Missouri State U, MO B
Oberlin Coll, OH B
Olivet Nazarene U, IL B
Ripon Coll, WI B
U of Chicago, IL B
U of Cincinnati, OH B
U of Michigan, MI B
Walsh U, OH B
Washington U in St. Louis, MO B

RUSSIAN

Beloit Coll, WI B
Bowling Green State U, OH B
Carleton Coll, MN B
The Coll of Wooster, OH B
Cornell Coll, IA B
Grinnell Coll, IA B
Gustavus Adolphus Coll, MN B
Indiana U Bloomington, IN B
Iowa State U of Science and Technology, IA B
Kent State U, OH B
Knox Coll, IL B
Lawrence U, WI B
Macalester Coll, MN B
Miami U, OH B
Michigan State U, MI B
Northern Illinois U, IL B
Oakland U, MI B
Oberlin Coll, OH B
The Ohio State U, OH B
Ohio U, OH B
Oklahoma State U, OK B
Principia Coll, IL B
Saint Louis U, MO B
St. Olaf Coll, MN B
Southern Illinois U Carbondale, IL B
Truman State U, MO B
U of Chicago, IL B
U of Illinois at Chicago, IL B
U of Illinois at Urbana–Champaign, IL B
The U of Iowa, IA B
U of Kansas, KS B
U of Michigan, MI B
U of Minnesota, Twin Cities Campus, MN B
U of Missouri–Columbia, MO B
U of Nebraska–Lincoln, NE B
U of Northern Iowa, IA B
U of Notre Dame, IN B
U of Oklahoma, OK B
U of St. Thomas, MN B
U of Wisconsin–Madison, WI B
U of Wisconsin–Milwaukee, WI B
Washington U in St. Louis, MO B
Wayne State U, MI B

RUSSIAN/SLAVIC STUDIES

Beloit Coll, WI B
Concordia Coll, MN B
Cornell Coll, IA B
DePauw U, IN B
Grand Valley State U, MI B
Gustavus Adolphus Coll, MN B
Hamline U, MN B
Indiana U Bloomington, IN B
Kent State U, OH B
Knox Coll, IL B
Lawrence U, WI B
Macalester Coll, MN B
Oakland U, MI B
Oberlin Coll, OH B
The Ohio State U, OH B
St. Olaf Coll, MN B
U of Chicago, IL B
U of Illinois at Urbana–Champaign, IL B
U of Kansas, KS B
U of Michigan, MI B
U of Minnesota, Twin Cities Campus, MN B
U of Missouri–Columbia, MO B
U of Northern Iowa, IA B
U of St. Thomas, MN B
U of Wisconsin–Milwaukee, WI B
Washington U in St. Louis, MO B
Western Michigan U, MI B
Wittenberg U, OH B

SAFETY/SECURITY TECHNOLOGY

Madonna U, MI A,B
Ohio U, OH A
Ohio U–Chillicothe, OH A
U of Central Oklahoma, OK B
U of Cincinnati, OH A
U of Wisconsin–Whitewater, WI B

SALES OPERATIONS

Lake Erie Coll, OH B
The U of Akron, OH A,B
U of Toledo, OH A
Youngstown State U, OH B

SANITATION TECHNOLOGY

Grand Valley State U, MI B

SCANDINAVIAN LANGUAGES

Augsburg Coll, MN B
Augustana Coll, IL B
Concordia Coll, MN B
Gustavus Adolphus Coll, MN B
Luther Coll, IA B
North Park U, IL B
St. Olaf Coll, MN B
U of Minnesota, Twin Cities Campus, MN B
U of North Dakota, ND B
U of Wisconsin–Madison, WI B

SCANDINAVIAN STUDIES

Luther Coll, IA B
U of Michigan, MI B

SCHOOL PSYCHOLOGY

Bowling Green State U, OH B
Fort Hays State U, KS B

SCIENCE EDUCATION

Adrian Coll, MI B
Alverno Coll, WI B
Anderson U, IN B
Andrews U, MI B
Antioch Coll, OH B
Ashland U, OH B
Baldwin-Wallace Coll, OH B
Ball State U, IN B
Beloit Coll, WI B
Bemidji State U, MN B
Benedictine Coll, KS B
Benedictine U, IL B
Bethel Coll, IN B
Bethel Coll, MN B
Bowling Green State U, OH B
Buena Vista U, IA B
Calvin Coll, MI B
Capital U, OH B
Cardinal Stritch U, WI B
Carroll Coll, WI B
Carthage Coll, WI B
Cedarville U, OH B
Central Christian Coll of Kansas, KS A
Central Methodist Coll, MO B
Central Michigan U, MI B
Central Missouri State U, MO B
Chadron State Coll, NE B
Chicago State U, IL B
Coe Coll, IA B
Coll of Saint Mary, NE B
Coll of the Ozarks, MO B
Columbia Coll, MO B
Concordia Coll, MN B
Concordia U, IL B
Concordia U, MN B
Concordia U, NE B
Concordia U Wisconsin, WI B
Cornerstone U, MI B
Culver-Stockton Coll, MO B
Dana Coll, NE B
Defiance Coll, OH B
Dickinson State U, ND B
Drake U, IA B
Eastern Michigan U, MI B
Emporia State U, KS B
Eureka Coll, IL B
Evangel U, MO B
Ferris State U, MI B
Fort Hays State U, KS B
The Franciscan U, IA B
Goshen Coll, IN B
Governors State U, IL B
Grace Coll, IN B
Graceland U, IA B
Grand Valley State U, MI B
Grand View Coll, IA B
Greenville Coll, IL B
Hamline U, MN B
Hastings Coll, NE B
Heidelberg Coll, OH B
Huntington Coll, IN B
Illinois Wesleyan U, IL B
Indiana State U, IN B
Indiana U Bloomington, IN B
Indiana U–Purdue U Fort Wayne, IN B
Indiana U South Bend, IN B
Indiana U Southeast, IN B
Indiana Wesleyan U, IN B
Judson Coll, IL B
Kent State U, OH B
Lakeland Coll, WI B
Luther Coll, IA B
Malone Coll, OH B
Manchester Coll, IN B
Maranatha Baptist Bible Coll, WI B
Marian Coll of Fond du Lac, WI B
Mayville State U, ND B
Miami U, OH B
Michigan Technological U, MI B
MidAmerica Nazarene U, KS B
Midland Lutheran Coll, NE B
Minnesota State U, Mankato, MN B
Minnesota State U, Moorhead, MN B
Minot State U, ND B
Missouri Valley Coll, MO B
Morningside Coll, IA B
Mount Mercy Coll, IA B
Mount Vernon Nazarene U, OH B
Muskingum Coll, OH B
Nebraska Wesleyan U, NE B
North Central Coll, IL B
North Dakota State U, ND B
Northern Michigan U, MI B
Northland Coll, WI B
Northwestern Oklahoma State U, OK B
Northwest Missouri State U, MO B
Oakland City U, IN B
Ohio Dominican U, OH B
Ohio U, OH B
Oklahoma Baptist U, OK B
Oklahoma Christian U, OK B
Oklahoma City U, OK B
Oklahoma Panhandle State U, OK B
Oklahoma Wesleyan U, OK B
Olivet Nazarene U, IL B
Oral Roberts U, OK B
Otterbein Coll, OH B
Peru State Coll, NE B
Pillsbury Baptist Bible Coll, MN B
Pittsburg State U, KS B
Purdue U Calumet, IN B
Rockford Coll, IL B
Saginaw Valley State U, MI B
St. Ambrose U, IA B
St. Cloud State U, MN B
Saint Mary's U of Minnesota, MN B
Shawnee State U, OH B
Si Tanka Huron U, SD B
Southeastern Oklahoma State U, OK B
Southeast Missouri State U, MO B
Southern Illinois U Edwardsville, IL B
Southwestern Coll, KS B
Southwestern Oklahoma State U, OK B
Southwest Missouri State U, MO B
Tabor Coll, KS B
Taylor U, IN B
Trinity Christian Coll, IL B
Tri-State U, IN B
The U of Akron, OH B
U of Central Oklahoma, OK B
U of Cincinnati, OH A
U of Dayton, OH B
U of Evansville, IN B
The U of Findlay, OH B
U of Illinois at Chicago, IL B
U of Indianapolis, IN B
The U of Iowa, IA B
U of Michigan–Dearborn, MI B
U of Minnesota, Duluth, MN B
U of Minnesota, Twin Cities Campus, MN B
U of Missouri–Columbia, MO B
U of Missouri–St. Louis, MO B
U of Nebraska–Lincoln, NE B
U of North Dakota, ND B
U of Northern Iowa, IA B
U of Notre Dame, IN B
U of Oklahoma, OK B
U of Rio Grande, OH B
U of Saint Francis, IN B
U of St. Thomas, MN B
U of Sioux Falls, SD B
The U of South Dakota, SD B
U of Toledo, OH B
U of Wisconsin–Eau Claire, WI B
U of Wisconsin–La Crosse, WI B
U of Wisconsin–Madison, WI B
U of Wisconsin–Platteville, WI B
U of Wisconsin–River Falls, WI B
U of Wisconsin–Superior, WI B
Upper Iowa U, IA B
Urbana U, OH B
Ursuline Coll, OH B
Valley City State U, ND B
Viterbo U, WI B
Walsh U, OH B
Washington U in St. Louis, MO B
Wayne State Coll, NE B
Wayne State U, MI B
Wichita State U, KS B
William Penn U, IA B
William Woods U, MO B
Wilmington Coll, OH B
Winona State U, MN B
Wittenberg U, OH B
Wright State U, OH B
Xavier U, OH B
York Coll, NE B
Youngstown State U, OH B

SCIENCE TECHNOLOGIES RELATED

U of Wisconsin–Stout, WI B

SCIENCE/TECHNOLOGY AND SOCIETY

Grinnell Coll, IA B
Washington U in St. Louis, MO B

SCULPTURE

Antioch Coll, OH B
Aquinas Coll, MI B
Art Academy of Cincinnati, OH B
Ball State U, IN B
Bethany Coll, KS B
Bowling Green State U, OH B
The Cleveland Inst of Art, OH B
Coll for Creative Studies, MI B
Coll of Visual Arts, MN B
Columbus Coll of Art and Design, OH B
DePaul U, IL B
Drake U, IA B
Grand Valley State U, MI B
Indiana U Bloomington, IN B
Kansas City Art Inst, MO B
Maharishi U of Management, IA B
Milwaukee Inst of Art and Design, WI B
Minneapolis Coll of Art and Design, MN B
Minnesota State U, Mankato, MN B
Minnesota State U, Moorhead, MN B
Northern Michigan U, MI B
Northwest Missouri State U, MO B
The Ohio State U, OH B
Ohio U, OH B
School of the Art Inst of Chicago, IL B
Trinity Christian Coll, IL B
The U of Akron, OH B
U of Evansville, IN B
U of Illinois at Urbana–Champaign, IL B
The U of Iowa, IA B
U of Kansas, KS B
U of Michigan, MI B
U of Oklahoma, OK B
The U of South Dakota, SD B
U of Wisconsin–Milwaukee, WI B
Washington U in St. Louis, MO B
Webster U, MO B
Western Michigan U, MI B
Wittenberg U, OH B

SECONDARY EDUCATION

Adrian Coll, MI B
Albion Coll, MI B
Alma Coll, MI B
Alverno Coll, WI B
Andrews U, MI B
Antioch Coll, OH B
Aquinas Coll, MI B
Ashland U, OH B
Augsburg Coll, MN B
Augustana Coll, IL B
Augustana Coll, SD B

Baldwin-Wallace Coll, OH B
Ball State U, IN B
Beloit Coll, WI B
Bemidji State U, MN B
Benedictine Coll, KS B
Benedictine U, IL B
Bethel Coll, MN B
Blackburn Coll, IL B
Bluffton Coll, OH B
Bowling Green State U, OH B
Briar Cliff U, IA B
Buena Vista U, IA B
Butler U, IN B
Calumet Coll of Saint Joseph, IN B
Calvin Coll, MI B
Capital U, OH B
Cardinal Stritch U, WI B
Carthage Coll, WI B
Cedarville U, OH B
Central Coll, IA B
Central Methodist Coll, MO B
Central Missouri State U, MO B
Chadron State Coll, NE B
Chicago State U, IL B
Clarke Coll, IA B
Coe Coll, IA B
Coll of Saint Benedict, MN B
Coll of St. Catherine, MN B
Coll of Saint Mary, NE B
Coll of the Ozarks, MO B
Columbia Coll, MO B
Concordia Coll, MN B
Concordia U, IL B
Concordia U, MI B
Concordia U, MN B
Concordia U, NE B
Concordia U Wisconsin, WI B
Cornell Coll, IA B
Cornerstone U, MI B
Dakota State U, SD B
Dana Coll, NE B
Defiance Coll, OH B
DePaul U, IL B
Dickinson State U, ND B
Doane Coll, NE B
Dordt Coll, IA B
Drake U, IA B
Drury U, MO B
East Central U, OK B
Eastern Michigan U, MI B
Elmhurst Coll, IL B
Emporia State U, KS B
Eureka Coll, IL B
Evangel U, MO B
Ferris State U, MI B
Fontbonne U, MO B
The Franciscan U, IA B
Goshen Coll, IN B
Grace Bible Coll, MI B
Graceland U, IA B
Grace U, NE B
Grand Valley State U, MI B
Grand View Coll, IA B
Greenville Coll, IL B
Gustavus Adolphus Coll, MN B
Hamline U, MN B
Hannibal-LaGrange Coll, MO B
Harris-Stowe State Coll, MO B
Hastings Coll, NE B
Heidelberg Coll, OH B
Hillsdale Coll, MI B
Hiram Coll, OH B
Hope Coll, MI B
Huntington Coll, IN B
Illinois Coll, IL B
Illinois Wesleyan U, IL B
Indiana U Bloomington, IN B
Indiana U East, IN B
Indiana U Northwest, IN B
Indiana U–Purdue U Fort Wayne, IN B
Indiana U–Purdue U Indianapolis, IN B
Indiana U South Bend, IN B
Indiana U Southeast, IN B
Indiana Wesleyan U, IN B
Iowa State U of Science and Technology, IA B
Iowa Wesleyan Coll, IA B
John Carroll U, OH B
Judson Coll, IL B
Kansas State U, KS B
Lake Forest Coll, IL B
Lakeland Coll, WI B
Langston U, OK B
Lawrence U, WI B
Lewis U, IL B
Lincoln Christian Coll, IL B
Lindenwood U, MO B
Loras Coll, IA B
Luther Coll, IA B
MacMurray Coll, IL B
Madonna U, MI B
Manchester Coll, IN B
Maranatha Baptist Bible Coll, WI B
Marian Coll, IN B
Marian Coll of Fond du Lac, WI B
Marietta Coll, OH B
Marquette U, WI B
Martin U, IN B
Maryville U of Saint Louis, MO B
McKendree Coll, IL B
McPherson Coll, KS B
Miami U, OH B
Michigan Technological U, MI B
MidAmerica Nazarene U, KS B
Midland Lutheran Coll, NE B
Minnesota State U, Mankato, MN B
Minnesota State U, Moorhead, MN B
Missouri Southern State Coll, MO B
Missouri Valley Coll, MO B
Monmouth Coll, IL B
Morningside Coll, IA B
Mount Marty Coll, SD B
Mount Mary Coll, WI B
Mount Mercy Coll, IA B
Mount Vernon Nazarene U, OH B
Muskingum Coll, OH B
Nebraska Christian Coll, NE B
Newman U, KS B
North Central Coll, IL B
North Dakota State U, ND B
Northeastern State U, OK B
Northern Michigan U, MI B
Northern State U, SD B
Northland Coll, WI B
North Park U, IL B
Northwestern Coll, IA B
Northwestern Oklahoma State U, OK B
Northwestern U, IL B
Northwest Missouri State U, MO B
Notre Dame Coll, OH B
Oakland City U, IN B
Oakland U, MI B
Ohio Dominican U, OH B
Ohio U, OH B
Ohio Wesleyan U, OH B
Oklahoma Baptist U, OK B
Oklahoma Christian U, OK B
Oklahoma City U, OK B
Oklahoma Panhandle State U, OK B
Oklahoma State U, OK B
Oklahoma Wesleyan U, OK B
Olivet Coll, MI B
Olivet Nazarene U, IL B
Otterbein Coll, OH B
Peru State Coll, NE B
Pillsbury Baptist Bible Coll, MN B
Pittsburg State U, KS B
Principia Coll, IL B
Purdue U Calumet, IN B
Reformed Bible Coll, MI B
Ripon Coll, WI B
Rockhurst U, MO B
Rogers State U, OK A
Roosevelt U, IL B
St. Ambrose U, IA B
St. Cloud State U, MN B
Saint John's U, MN B
Saint Joseph's Coll, IN B
Saint Mary-of-the-Woods Coll, IN B
Shawnee State U, OH B
Siena Heights U, MI B
Simpson Coll, IA B
Si Tanka Huron U, SD B
South Dakota State U, SD B
Southeastern Oklahoma State U, OK B
Southeast Missouri State U, MO B
Southern Nazarene U, OK B
Southwest Baptist U, MO B
Southwestern Oklahoma State U, OK B
Southwest Minnesota State U, MN B
Spring Arbor U, MI B
Tabor Coll, KS B
Taylor U, IN B
Trinity Christian Coll, IL B
Trinity International U, IL B
Tri-State U, IN B
Union Coll, NE B
The U of Akron, OH B
U of Central Oklahoma, OK B
U of Cincinnati, OH B
U of Dayton, OH B
U of Evansville, IN B
The U of Findlay, OH B
U of Illinois at Chicago, IL B
U of Illinois at Springfield, IL B
U of Indianapolis, IN B
The U of Iowa, IA B
U of Kansas, KS B
U of Michigan, MI B
U of Michigan–Dearborn, MI B
U of Michigan–Flint, MI B
U of Minnesota, Morris, MN B
U of Missouri–Kansas City, MO B
U of Missouri–Rolla, MO B
U of Missouri–St. Louis, MO B
U of Nebraska at Omaha, NE B
U of Rio Grande, OH B
U of Saint Francis, IN B
U of St. Thomas, MN B
U of Sioux Falls, SD B
The U of South Dakota, SD B
U of Toledo, OH B
U of Wisconsin–La Crosse, WI B
U of Wisconsin–Madison, WI B
U of Wisconsin–Milwaukee, WI B
U of Wisconsin–Oshkosh, WI B
U of Wisconsin–Platteville, WI B
U of Wisconsin–River Falls, WI B
U of Wisconsin–Stevens Point, WI B
U of Wisconsin–Whitewater, WI B
Upper Iowa U, IA B
Urbana U, OH B
Valley City State U, ND B
Valparaiso U, IN B
Walsh U, OH B
Wartburg Coll, IA B
Washington U in St. Louis, MO B
Webster U, MO B
Westminster Coll, MO B
Wichita State U, KS B
William Jewell Coll, MO B
William Penn U, IA B
William Woods U, MO B
Wilmington Coll, OH B
Winona State U, MN B
Wittenberg U, OH B
Wright State U, OH B
York Coll, NE B
Youngstown State U, OH B

SECRETARIAL SCIENCE

AIB Coll of Business, IA A
Bacone Coll, OK A
Baker Coll of Auburn Hills, MI A
Baker Coll of Cadillac, MI A
Baker Coll of Clinton Township, MI A
Baker Coll of Flint, MI A,B
Baker Coll of Jackson, MI A
Baker Coll of Muskegon, MI A,B
Baker Coll of Owosso, MI A,B
Baker Coll of Port Huron, MI A,B
Ball State U, IN A
Baptist Bible Coll, MO A,B
Black Hills State U, SD A
Bryant and Stratton Coll, WI A
Cedarville U, OH A,B
Central Missouri State U, MO A
Dakota State U, SD A
Davenport U, Grand Rapids, MI A
Davenport U, Kalamazoo, MI A,B
Davenport U, Lansing, MI A,B
Dickinson State U, ND A
Dordt Coll, IA A
East Central U, OK B
East-West U, IL B
Evangel U, MO A,B
Faith Baptist Bible Coll and Theological Seminary, IA A
Fort Hays State U, KS A,B
Gallipolis Career Coll, OH A
God's Bible School and Coll, OH A
Grace Coll, IN A

Secretarial Science (continued)

Hamilton Coll, IA	A
Hannibal-LaGrange Coll, MO	A
Haskell Indian Nations U, KS	A
Indiana State U, IN	A
International Business Coll, Fort Wayne, IN	A,B
Kent State U, OH	A
Kent State U, Ashtabula Campus, OH	A
Kent State U, Salem Campus, OH	A
Kent State U, Tuscarawas Campus, OH	A
Langston U, OK	B
Lewis Coll of Business, MI	A
Lincoln Christian Coll, IL	A,B
Maranatha Baptist Bible Coll, WI	A,B
Mayville State U, ND	A,B
Miami U–Middletown Campus, OH	A
Midland Lutheran Coll, NE	B
Midstate Coll, IL	A
Mount Vernon Nazarene U, OH	A,B
Nebraska Christian Coll, NE	A
Nebraska Indian Comm Coll, NE	A
Northern State U, SD	A,B
Northwestern Coll, IA	A
Northwest Missouri State U, MO	B
Oakland City U, IN	A
Ohio U, OH	A
Ohio U–Chillicothe, OH	A
Ohio U–Lancaster, OH	A
Oklahoma Wesleyan U, OK	A
Pillsbury Baptist Bible Coll, MN	A,B
Presentation Coll, SD	A
Reformed Bible Coll, MI	A
Robert Morris Coll, IL	A
Rochester Comm and Tech Coll, MN	A
Rogers State U, OK	A
St. Augustine Coll, IL	A
Shawnee State U, OH	A
Sitting Bull Coll, ND	A
Southeast Missouri State U, MO	B
Southwest Baptist U, MO	A
Tabor Coll, KS	A,B
Trinity Bible Coll, ND	A,B
U of Cincinnati, OH	A
The U of Findlay, OH	A
U of Northwestern Ohio, OH	A
U of Rio Grande, OH	A
U of Sioux Falls, SD	A,B
U of Southern Indiana, IN	A
U of Toledo, OH	A
U of Wisconsin–Superior, WI	B
Winona State U, MN	A,B
Wright State U, OH	A
Youngstown State U, OH	A,B

SECURITY

Ohio U, OH	B
Youngstown State U, OH	A,B

SIGN LANGUAGE INTERPRETATION

Bethel Coll, IN	A,B
Cincinnati Bible Coll and Seminary, OH	A
Coll of St. Catherine, MN	A
Columbia Coll Chicago, IL	B
Goshen Coll, IN	B
Indiana U–Purdue U Indianapolis, IN	B
MacMurray Coll, IL	B
Madonna U, MI	A,B
Nebraska Christian Coll, NE	A
Ozark Christian Coll, MO	B
William Woods U, MO	B

SLAVIC LANGUAGES

Indiana U Bloomington, IN	B
Northwestern U, IL	B
Saint Mary's Coll of Madonna U, MI	B
U of Chicago, IL	B
U of Illinois at Chicago, IL	B
U of Wisconsin–Madison, WI	B
U of Wisconsin–Milwaukee, WI	B
Wayne State U, MI	B

SOCIAL/PHILOSOPHICAL FOUNDATIONS OF EDUCATION

Northwestern U, IL	B
Ohio U, OH	B
Washington U in St. Louis, MO	B

SOCIAL PSYCHOLOGY

Central Christian Coll of Kansas, KS	A
Loyola U Chicago, IL	B
Maryville U of Saint Louis, MO	B
Park U, MO	A,B
U of Wisconsin–Superior, WI	B

SOCIAL SCIENCE EDUCATION

Alverno Coll, WI	B
Bowling Green State U, OH	B
Central Methodist Coll, MO	B
Central Michigan U, MI	B
Chadron State Coll, NE	B
The Coll of St. Scholastica, MN	B
Concordia U, IL	B
Concordia U, NE	B
Dana Coll, NE	B
Eastern Illinois U, IL	B
Eastern Michigan U, MI	B
Hastings Coll, NE	B
Luther Coll, IA	B
Mayville State U, ND	B
McKendree Coll, IL	B
Michigan State U, MI	B
Millikin U, IL	B
Minot State U, ND	B
North Dakota State U, ND	B
Oklahoma Baptist U, OK	B
St. Ambrose U, IA	B
Saint Mary's U of Minnesota, MN	B
Southern Nazarene U, OK	B
Southwestern Oklahoma State U, OK	B
Union Coll, NE	B
The U of Akron, OH	B
U of Illinois at Chicago, IL	B
U of Mary, ND	B
U of Minnesota, Twin Cities Campus, MN	B
U of Nebraska–Lincoln, NE	B
U of Northern Iowa, IA	B
U of Rio Grande, OH	B
U of Wisconsin–River Falls, WI	B
U of Wisconsin–Superior, WI	B
Valley City State U, ND	B
Wartburg Coll, IA	B
Washington U in St. Louis, MO	B
William Penn U, IA	B
Youngstown State U, OH	B

SOCIAL SCIENCES

Adrian Coll, MI	A,B
Alma Coll, MI	B
Alverno Coll, WI	B
Ancilla Coll, IN	A
Andrews U, MI	B
Antioch Coll, OH	B
Aquinas Coll, MI	B
Ashland U, OH	B
Augsburg Coll, MN	B
Ball State U, IN	B
Bellevue U, NE	B
Bemidji State U, MN	B
Benedictine Coll, KS	B
Benedictine U, IL	B
Bethel Coll, IN	B
Bethel Coll, KS	B
Black Hills State U, SD	B
Bluffton Coll, OH	B
Bowling Green State U, OH	B
Buena Vista U, IA	B
Calvin Coll, MI	B
Cardinal Stritch U, WI	B
Carthage Coll, WI	B
Cedarville U, OH	B
Central Christian Coll of Kansas, KS	A
Central Coll, IA	B
Central Michigan U, MI	B
Cleveland State U, OH	B
Coll of Saint Benedict, MN	B
Coll of St. Catherine, MN	B
Coll of Saint Mary, NE	B
Concordia U, MI	B
Concordia U, MN	B
Concordia U, NE	B
Crown Coll, MN	A
Dana Coll, NE	B
Defiance Coll, OH	B
DePaul U, IL	B
Dickinson State U, ND	B
Doane Coll, NE	B
Dominican U, IL	B
Dordt Coll, IA	B
Eastern Michigan U, MI	B
East-West U, IL	B
Edgewood Coll, WI	B
Emporia State U, KS	B
Eureka Coll, IL	B
Evangel U, MO	A,B
Fontbonne U, MO	B
The Franciscan U, IA	B
Governors State U, IL	B
Graceland U, IA	B
Grand Valley State U, MI	B
Gustavus Adolphus Coll, MN	B
Hamline U, MN	B
Indiana Wesleyan U, IN	A,B
Judson Coll, IL	B
Kansas State U, KS	B
Kendall Coll, IL	B
Kent State U, OH	B
Lake Erie Coll, OH	B
Lakeland Coll, WI	B
Lincoln Coll, Normal, IL	A
Madonna U, MI	A,B
Marygrove Coll, MI	B
Mayville State U, ND	B
McKendree Coll, IL	B
McPherson Coll, KS	B
Metropolitan State U, MN	B
Miami U–Middletown Campus, OH	A
Michigan State U, MI	B
Michigan Technological U, MI	B
Midland Lutheran Coll, NE	B
Minnesota State U, Mankato, MN	B
Minot State U, ND	B
Mount Vernon Nazarene U, OH	B
Muskingum Coll, OH	B
National-Louis U, IL	B
North Central Coll, IL	B
North Dakota State U, ND	B
Northern Illinois U, IL	B
Northern Michigan U, MI	B
Northland Coll, WI	B
North Park U, IL	B
Northwestern Coll, MN	B
Northwestern Oklahoma State U, OK	B
Northwest Missouri State U, MO	B
Oakland City U, IN	B
Ohio Dominican U, OH	B
The Ohio State U, OH	B
Ohio U, OH	A,B
Ohio U–Zanesville, OH	A
Oklahoma Baptist U, OK	B
Oklahoma Panhandle State U, OK	B
Oklahoma Wesleyan U, OK	B
Olivet Coll, MI	B
Olivet Nazarene U, IL	B
Peru State Coll, NE	B
Pittsburg State U, KS	B
Purdue U, IN	B
Rockford Coll, IL	B
Rockhurst U, MO	B
Rogers State U, OK	A,B
Roosevelt U, IL	B
St. Cloud State U, MN	B
St. Gregory's U, OK	B
Saint John's U, MN	B
Saint Joseph's Coll, IN	B
Saint Louis U, MO	B
Saint Mary-of-the-Woods Coll, IN	B
Saint Mary's Coll of Madonna U, MI	B
Saint Mary's U of Minnesota, MN	B
Saint Xavier U, IL	B
Shawnee State U, OH	A,B
Shimer Coll, IL	B
Siena Heights U, MI	B
Silver Lake Coll, WI	B
Simpson Coll, IA	B
Southern Illinois U Carbondale, IL	B
Southwest Baptist U, MO	B
Spring Arbor U, MI	B
Stephens Coll, MO	B
Tabor Coll, KS	B
Taylor U, IN	B
Tiffin U, OH	B
Trinity International U, IL	B
Tri-State U, IN	A,B

Union Coll, NE	B
Union Inst & U, OH	B
The U of Akron, OH	B
U of Chicago, IL	B
U of Cincinnati, OH	A,B
The U of Findlay, OH	A,B
The U of Iowa, IA	B
U of Mary, ND	B
U of Michigan, MI	B
U of Michigan–Dearborn, MI	B
U of Michigan–Flint, MI	B
U of Minnesota, Morris, MN	B
U of Missouri–St. Louis, MO	B
U of North Dakota, ND	B
U of Rio Grande, OH	B
U of St. Thomas, MN	B
U of Sioux Falls, SD	A,B
U of Southern Indiana, IN	A,B
U of Toledo, OH	A
U of Wisconsin–Madison, WI	B
U of Wisconsin–Platteville, WI	B
U of Wisconsin–River Falls, WI	B
U of Wisconsin–Stevens Point, WI	B
U of Wisconsin–Superior, WI	B
Upper Iowa U, IA	B
Valley City State U, ND	B
Valparaiso U, IN	A
Waldorf Coll, IA	A
Washington U in St. Louis, MO	B
Wayne State Coll, NE	B
Webster U, MO	B
Wilmington Coll, OH	B
Winona State U, MN	B
Wisconsin Lutheran Coll, WI	B
Wittenberg U, OH	B
Youngstown State U, OH	B

SOCIAL SCIENCES AND HISTORY RELATED

Bethel Coll, KS	B
Nebraska Wesleyan U, NE	B
Northwestern U, IL	B
Saint Mary's U of Minnesota, MN	B

SOCIAL STUDIES EDUCATION

Alverno Coll, WI	B
Anderson U, IN	B
Augustana Coll, SD	B
Bethany Coll, KS	B
Bethel Coll, IN	B
Bowling Green State U, OH	B
Cedarville U, OH	B
Central Michigan U, MI	B
Central Missouri State U, MO	B
Coll of St. Catherine, MN	B
Concordia Coll, MN	B
Crown Coll, MN	B
Dakota Wesleyan U, SD	B
Eastern Michigan U, MI	B
Franklin Coll, IN	B
Greenville Coll, IL	B
Gustavus Adolphus Coll, MN	B
Hastings Coll, NE	B
Illinois State U, IL	B
Indiana State U, IN	B
Indiana U Bloomington, IN	B
Indiana U Northwest, IN	B
Indiana U–Purdue U Fort Wayne, IN	B
Indiana U–Purdue U Indianapolis, IN	B
Indiana U South Bend, IN	B
Indiana U Southeast, IN	B
Indiana Wesleyan U, IN	B
Kent State U, OH	B
Malone Coll, OH	B
Miami U, OH	B
MidAmerica Nazarene U, KS	B
Minnesota State U, Mankato, MN	B
Minnesota State U, Moorhead, MN	B
Mount Vernon Nazarene U, OH	B
Northwestern Coll, MN	B
Oakland City U, IN	B
Ohio U, OH	B
Oklahoma Baptist U, OK	B
Oklahoma Christian U, OK	B
Oral Roberts U, OK	B
St. Olaf Coll, MN	B
Southeastern Oklahoma State U, OK	B
Southeast Missouri State U, MO	B
Tri-State U, IN	B
The U of Akron, OH	B
U of Central Oklahoma, OK	B
U of Indianapolis, IN	B
The U of Iowa, IA	B
U of Minnesota, Duluth, MN	B
U of Oklahoma, OK	B
U of St. Francis, IL	B
U of St. Thomas, MN	B
U of Toledo, OH	B
U of Wisconsin–Eau Claire, WI	B
U of Wisconsin–La Crosse, WI	B
U of Wisconsin–River Falls, WI	B
U of Wisconsin–Superior, WI	B
Ursuline Coll, OH	B
Viterbo U, WI	B
Washington U in St. Louis, MO	B
Wayne State U, MI	B
Wheaton Coll, IL	B
Youngstown State U, OH	B

SOCIAL WORK

Adrian Coll, MI	B
Anderson U, IN	B
Andrews U, MI	B
Ashland U, OH	B
Augsburg Coll, MN	B
Augustana Coll, SD	B
Aurora U, IL	B
Avila U, MO	B
Baldwin-Wallace Coll, OH	B
Ball State U, IN	B
Bemidji State U, MN	B
Bethany Coll, KS	B
Bethel Coll, KS	B
Bethel Coll, MN	B
Bluffton Coll, OH	B
Bowling Green State U, OH	B
Bradley U, IL	B
Briar Cliff U, IA	B
Buena Vista U, IA	B
Calvin Coll, MI	B
Capital U, OH	B
Carroll Coll, WI	B
Carthage Coll, WI	B
Cedarville U, OH	B
Central Christian Coll of Kansas, KS	A
Central Michigan U, MI	B
Central Missouri State U, MO	B
Chadron State Coll, NE	B
Clarke Coll, IA	B
Cleveland State U, OH	B
Coll of Menominee Nation, WI	A
Coll of Mount St. Joseph, OH	B
Coll of Saint Benedict, MN	B
Coll of St. Catherine, MN	B
The Coll of St. Scholastica, MN	B
Coll of the Ozarks, MO	B
Columbia Coll, MO	B
Concordia Coll, MN	B
Concordia U, IL	B
Concordia U Wisconsin, WI	B
Cornerstone U, MI	B
Creighton U, NE	B
Dana Coll, NE	B
Defiance Coll, OH	B
Dickinson State U, ND	B
Dordt Coll, IA	B
East Central U, OK	B
Eastern Michigan U, MI	B
Evangel U, MO	B
Ferris State U, MI	B
Fort Hays State U, KS	B
Franciscan U of Steubenville, OH	B
Goshen Coll, IN	B
Governors State U, IL	B
Grace Coll, IN	B
Graceland U, IA	B
Grand Valley State U, MI	B
Greenville Coll, IL	B
Hope Coll, MI	B
Illinois State U, IL	B
Indiana State U, IN	B
Indiana U Bloomington, IN	B
Indiana U East, IN	A,B
Indiana U–Purdue U Indianapolis, IN	B
Indiana Wesleyan U, IN	B
Iowa Wesleyan Coll, IA	B
Kansas State U, KS	B
Lewis U, IL	B
Lindenwood U, MO	B
Loras Coll, IA	B
Lourdes Coll, OH	B
Loyola U Chicago, IL	B
Luther Coll, IA	B
MacMurray Coll, IL	B
Madonna U, MI	B
Malone Coll, OH	B
Manchester Coll, IN	B
Marian Coll of Fond du Lac, WI	B
Marquette U, WI	B
Marygrove Coll, MI	B
McKendree Coll, IL	B
Metropolitan State U, MN	B
Miami U, OH	B
Miami U–Middletown Campus, OH	A
Michigan State U, MI	B
Minnesota State U, Mankato, MN	B
Minnesota State U, Moorhead, MN	B
Minot State U, ND	B
Missouri Western State Coll, MO	B
Mount Mary Coll, WI	B
Mount Mercy Coll, IA	B
Mount Vernon Nazarene U, OH	A,B
Nebraska Wesleyan U, NE	B
Northeastern Illinois U, IL	B
Northeastern State U, OK	B
Northern Michigan U, MI	B
Northern State U, SD	A
Northwestern Coll, IA	B
Northwestern Oklahoma State U, OK	B
Ohio Dominican U, OH	B
The Ohio State U, OH	B
Ohio U, OH	B
Oklahoma Baptist U, OK	B
Oral Roberts U, OK	B
Pittsburg State U, KS	B
Presentation Coll, SD	B
Purdue U Calumet, IN	B
Quincy U, IL	B
Reformed Bible Coll, MI	B
Rockford Coll, IL	B
Saginaw Valley State U, MI	B
St. Augustine Coll, IL	B
St. Cloud State U, MN	B
Saint John's U, MN	B
Saint Louis U, MO	B
Saint Mary's Coll, IN	B
St. Olaf Coll, MN	B
Siena Heights U, MI	A,B
Sitting Bull Coll, ND	A
Southeast Missouri State U, MO	B
Southern Illinois U Carbondale, IL	B
Southern Illinois U Edwardsville, IL	B
Southern Nazarene U, OK	B
Southwestern Oklahoma State U, OK	B
Southwest Minnesota State U, MN	B
Southwest Missouri State U, MO	B
Spring Arbor U, MI	B
Taylor U, IN	B
Taylor U, Fort Wayne Campus, IN	B
Union Coll, NE	B
Union Inst & U, OH	B
The U of Akron, OH	B
U of Cincinnati, OH	A,B
The U of Findlay, OH	B
U of Illinois at Chicago, IL	B
U of Illinois at Springfield, IL	B
U of Indianapolis, IN	B
The U of Iowa, IA	B
U of Kansas, KS	B
U of Mary, ND	B
U of Michigan–Flint, MI	B
U of Missouri–Columbia, MO	B
U of Missouri–St. Louis, MO	B
U of Nebraska at Kearney, NE	B
U of Nebraska at Omaha, NE	B
U of North Dakota, ND	B
U of Northern Iowa, IA	B
U of Oklahoma, OK	B
U of Rio Grande, OH	A,B
U of St. Francis, IL	B
U of Saint Francis, IN	B
U of St. Thomas, MN	B
U of Sioux Falls, SD	B
The U of South Dakota, SD	B
U of Southern Indiana, IN	B
U of Toledo, OH	A,B

Social Work (continued)

U of Wisconsin–Eau Claire, WI B
U of Wisconsin–Green Bay, WI A,B
U of Wisconsin–Madison, WI B
U of Wisconsin–Milwaukee, WI B
U of Wisconsin–Oshkosh, WI B
U of Wisconsin–River Falls, WI B
U of Wisconsin–Superior, WI B
U of Wisconsin–Whitewater, WI B
Ursuline Coll, OH B
Valparaiso U, IN B
Viterbo U, WI B
Waldorf Coll, IA A
Wartburg Coll, IA B
Wayne State U, MI B
Western Illinois U, IL B
Western Michigan U, MI B
Wichita State U, KS B
William Woods U, MO B
Wilmington Coll, OH B
Winona State U, MN B
Wright State U, OH A,B
Xavier U, OH B
Youngstown State U, OH A,B

SOCIOBIOLOGY

Beloit Coll, WI B

SOCIOLOGY

Adrian Coll, MI A,B
Albion Coll, MI B
Alma Coll, MI B
Anderson U, IN B
Andrews U, MI B
Antioch Coll, OH B
Aquinas Coll, MI B
Ashland U, OH B
Augsburg Coll, MN B
Augustana Coll, IL B
Augustana Coll, SD B
Aurora U, IL B
Avila U, MO B
Bacone Coll, OK A
Baker U, KS B
Baldwin-Wallace Coll, OH B
Ball State U, IN B
Bellevue U, NE B
Beloit Coll, WI B
Bemidji State U, MN B
Benedictine Coll, KS B
Benedictine U, IL B
Bethany Coll, KS B
Bethel Coll, IN B
Black Hills State U, SD B
Bluffton Coll, OH B
Bowling Green State U, OH B
Bradley U, IL B
Briar Cliff U, IA B
Butler U, IN B
Calumet Coll of Saint Joseph, IN B
Calvin Coll, MI B
Cameron U, OK B
Capital U, OH B
Cardinal Stritch U, WI B
Carleton Coll, MN B
Carroll Coll, WI B
Carthage Coll, WI B
Case Western Reserve U, OH B
Cedarville U, OH B
Central Christian Coll of Kansas, KS A
Central Coll, IA B
Central Methodist Coll, MO B
Central Michigan U, MI B
Central Missouri State U, MO B
Chadron State Coll, NE B
Chicago State U, IL B
Clarke Coll, IA B
Cleveland State U, OH B
Coe Coll, IA B
Coll of Mount St. Joseph, OH B
Coll of Saint Benedict, MN B
Coll of St. Catherine, MN B
Coll of the Ozarks, MO B
The Coll of Wooster, OH B
Columbia Coll, MO B
Concordia Coll, MN B
Concordia U, IL B
Concordia U, MI B
Concordia U, MN B
Concordia U, NE B
Cornell Coll, IA B
Cornerstone U, MI B
Creighton U, NE B
Culver-Stockton Coll, MO B
Dakota Wesleyan U, SD B
Dana Coll, NE B
Denison U, OH B
DePaul U, IL B
DePauw U, IN B
Doane Coll, NE B
Dominican U, IL B
Dordt Coll, IA B
Drake U, IA B
Drury U, MO B
Earlham Coll, IN B
East Central U, OK B
Eastern Illinois U, IL B
Eastern Michigan U, MI B
East-West U, IL B
Edgewood Coll, WI B
Elmhurst Coll, IL B
Emporia State U, KS B
Eureka Coll, IL B
Evangel U, MO B
Fort Hays State U, KS B
Franciscan U of Steubenville, OH B
Franklin Coll, IN B
Goshen Coll, IN B
Grace Coll, IN B
Graceland U, IA B
Grand Valley State U, MI B
Grand View Coll, IA A
Greenville Coll, IL B
Grinnell Coll, IA B
Gustavus Adolphus Coll, MN B
Hamline U, MN B
Hanover Coll, IN B
Hastings Coll, NE B
Hillsdale Coll, MI B
Hiram Coll, OH B
Hope Coll, MI B
Huntington Coll, IN B
Illinois Coll, IL B
Illinois State U, IL B
Illinois Wesleyan U, IL B
Indiana State U, IN B
Indiana U Bloomington, IN B
Indiana U East, IN B
Indiana U Kokomo, IN B
Indiana U Northwest, IN B
Indiana U–Purdue U Fort Wayne, IN B
Indiana U–Purdue U Indianapolis, IN B
Indiana U South Bend, IN B
Indiana U Southeast, IN B
Indiana Wesleyan U, IN B
Iowa State U of Science and Technology, IA B
John Carroll U, OH B
Judson Coll, IL B
Kalamazoo Coll, MI B
Kansas State U, KS B
Kent State U, OH B
Kenyon Coll, OH B
Knox Coll, IL B
Lake Erie Coll, OH B
Lake Forest Coll, IL B
Lakeland Coll, WI B
Langston U, OK B
Lewis U, IL B
Lincoln Coll, Lincoln, IL A
Lindenwood U, MO B
Loras Coll, IA B
Lourdes Coll, OH A,B
Loyola U Chicago, IL B
Luther Coll, IA B
Macalester Coll, MN B
Madonna U, MI B
Manchester Coll, IN B
Marian Coll, IN B
Marquette U, WI B
Martin U, IN B
Maryville U of Saint Louis, MO B
McKendree Coll, IL B
McPherson Coll, KS B
Miami U, OH B
Miami U–Middletown Campus, OH A
Michigan State U, MI B
MidAmerica Nazarene U, KS B
Midland Lutheran Coll, NE B
Millikin U, IL B
Minnesota State U, Mankato, MN B
Minnesota State U, Moorhead, MN B
Minot State U, ND B
Missouri Southern State Coll, MO B
Missouri Valley Coll, MO B
Monmouth Coll, IL B
Mount Mercy Coll, IA B
Mount Union Coll, OH B
Mount Vernon Nazarene U, OH B
Muskingum Coll, OH B
Nebraska Wesleyan U, NE B
Newman U, KS B
North Central Coll, IL B
North Dakota State U, ND B
Northeastern Illinois U, IL B
Northeastern State U, OK B
Northern Illinois U, IL B
Northern Michigan U, MI B
Northern State U, SD B
Northland Coll, WI B
North Park U, IL B
Northwestern Coll, IA B
Northwestern Oklahoma State U, OK B
Northwestern U, IL B
Northwest Missouri State U, MO B
Oakland U, MI B
Oberlin Coll, OH B
Ohio Dominican U, OH B
Ohio Northern U, OH B
The Ohio State U, OH B
Ohio U, OH B
Ohio Wesleyan U, OH B
Oklahoma Baptist U, OK B
Oklahoma City U, OK B
Oklahoma State U, OK B
Olivet Coll, MI B
Ottawa U, KS B
Otterbein Coll, OH B
Park U, MO B
Peru State Coll, NE B
Pittsburg State U, KS B
Principia Coll, IL B
Purdue U, IN B
Purdue U Calumet, IN B
Quincy U, IL B
Ripon Coll, WI B
Rockford Coll, IL B
Rockhurst U, MO B
Roosevelt U, IL B
Saginaw Valley State U, MI B
St. Ambrose U, IA B
St. Cloud State U, MN B
Saint John's U, MN B
Saint Joseph's Coll, IN B
Saint Louis U, MO B
Saint Mary's Coll, IN B
Saint Mary's Coll of Madonna U, MI B
Saint Mary's U of Minnesota, MN B
Saint Mary U, KS B
St. Norbert Coll, WI B
St. Olaf Coll, MN B
Saint Xavier U, IL B
Simpson Coll, IA B
South Dakota State U, SD B
Southeastern Oklahoma State U, OK B
Southeast Missouri State U, MO B
Southern Illinois U Carbondale, IL B
Southern Illinois U Edwardsville, IL B
Southern Nazarene U, OK B
Southwest Baptist U, MO B
Southwest Minnesota State U, MN B
Southwest Missouri State U, MO B
Spring Arbor U, MI B
Tabor Coll, KS B
Taylor U, IN B
Trinity Christian Coll, IL B
Trinity International U, IL B
Truman State U, MO B
The U of Akron, OH B
U of Central Oklahoma, OK B
U of Chicago, IL B
U of Cincinnati, OH B
U of Dayton, OH B
U of Dubuque, IA A,B
U of Evansville, IN B
The U of Findlay, OH B
U of Illinois at Chicago, IL B
U of Illinois at Springfield, IL B
U of Illinois at Urbana–Champaign, IL B
U of Indianapolis, IN B
The U of Iowa, IA B
U of Kansas, KS B
U of Michigan, MI B
U of Michigan–Dearborn, MI B
U of Michigan–Flint, MI B
U of Minnesota, Duluth, MN B
U of Minnesota, Morris, MN B
U of Minnesota, Twin Cities Campus, MN B

U of Missouri–Columbia, MO B
U of Missouri–Kansas City, MO B
U of Missouri–St. Louis, MO B
U of Nebraska at Kearney, NE B
U of Nebraska at Omaha, NE B
U of Nebraska–Lincoln, NE B
U of North Dakota, ND B
U of Northern Iowa, IA B
U of Notre Dame, IN B
U of Oklahoma, OK B
U of Rio Grande, OH A,B
U of St. Thomas, MN B
U of Science and Arts of Oklahoma, OK B
U of Sioux Falls, SD B
The U of South Dakota, SD B
U of Southern Indiana, IN B
U of Toledo, OH B
U of Tulsa, OK B
U of Wisconsin–Eau Claire, WI B
U of Wisconsin–La Crosse, WI B
U of Wisconsin–Madison, WI B
U of Wisconsin–Milwaukee, WI B
U of Wisconsin–Oshkosh, WI B
U of Wisconsin–Parkside, WI B
U of Wisconsin–River Falls, WI B
U of Wisconsin–Stevens Point, WI B
U of Wisconsin–Superior, WI B
U of Wisconsin–Whitewater, WI B
Upper Iowa U, IA B
Urbana U, OH B
Ursuline Coll, OH B
Valparaiso U, IN B
Viterbo U, WI B
Waldorf Coll, IA A
Walsh U, OH B
Wartburg Coll, IA B
Wayne State Coll, NE B
Wayne State U, MI B
Webster U, MO B
Western Illinois U, IL B
Western Michigan U, MI B
Westminster Coll, MO B
Wheaton Coll, IL B
Wichita State U, KS B
Wilberforce U, OH B
William Penn U, IA B
Winona State U, MN B
Wittenberg U, OH B
Wright State U, OH A,B
Xavier U, OH A,B
Youngstown State U, OH B

SOCIO-PSYCHOLOGICAL SPORTS STUDIES

U of Minnesota, Twin Cities Campus, MN B

SOIL CONSERVATION

Ball State U, IN B
The Ohio State U, OH B
U of Minnesota, Crookston, MN A
U of Wisconsin–Stevens Point, WI B

SOIL SCIENCES

Michigan State U, MI B
North Dakota State U, ND B
U of Minnesota, Twin Cities Campus, MN B
U of Nebraska–Lincoln, NE B
U of Wisconsin–River Falls, WI B

SOUTH ASIAN LANGUAGES

Northwestern U, IL B

SOUTH ASIAN STUDIES

The Coll of Wooster, OH B
Oakland U, MI B
U of Chicago, IL B
U of Michigan, MI B
U of Minnesota, Twin Cities Campus, MN B
U of Missouri–Columbia, MO B

SOUTHEAST ASIAN STUDIES

U of Chicago, IL B
U of Michigan, MI B
U of Wisconsin–Madison, WI B

SPANISH

Adrian Coll, MI A,B
Albion Coll, MI B
Alma Coll, MI B
Anderson U, IN B
Andrews U, MI B
Antioch Coll, OH B
Aquinas Coll, MI B
Ashland U, OH B
Augsburg Coll, MN B
Augustana Coll, IL B
Augustana Coll, SD B
Baker U, KS B
Baldwin-Wallace Coll, OH B
Ball State U, IN B
Bellevue U, NE B
Beloit Coll, WI B
Bemidji State U, MN B
Benedictine Coll, KS B
Benedictine U, IL B
Bethel Coll, KS B
Bethel Coll, MN B
Blackburn Coll, IL B
Black Hills State U, SD B
Bluffton Coll, OH B
Bowling Green State U, OH B
Bradley U, IL B
Briar Cliff U, IA B
Buena Vista U, IA B
Butler U, IN B
Calvin Coll, MI B
Capital U, OH B
Cardinal Stritch U, WI B
Carleton Coll, MN B
Carroll Coll, WI B
Carthage Coll, WI B
Case Western Reserve U, OH B
Cedarville U, OH B
Central Christian Coll of Kansas, KS A
Central Coll, IA B
Central Methodist Coll, MO B
Central Michigan U, MI B
Central Missouri State U, MO B
Chadron State Coll, NE B
Chicago State U, IL B
Clarke Coll, IA B
Cleveland State U, OH B
Coe Coll, IA B
Coll of Saint Benedict, MN B
Coll of St. Catherine, MN B
Coll of the Ozarks, MO B
The Coll of Wooster, OH B
Concordia Coll, MN B
Concordia U, NE B
Concordia U Wisconsin, WI B
Cornell Coll, IA B
Cornerstone U, MI B
Creighton U, NE B
Dana Coll, NE B
Denison U, OH B
DePaul U, IL B
DePauw U, IN B
Dickinson State U, ND B
Doane Coll, NE B
Dominican U, IL B
Dordt Coll, IA B
Drury U, MO B
Earlham Coll, IN B
Eastern Michigan U, MI B
Edgewood Coll, WI B
Elmhurst Coll, IL B
Evangel U, MO B
Fort Hays State U, KS B
Franciscan U of Steubenville, OH B
Franklin Coll, IN B
Goshen Coll, IN B
Grace Coll, IN B
Graceland U, IA B
Grand Valley State U, MI B
Greenville Coll, IL B
Grinnell Coll, IA B
Gustavus Adolphus Coll, MN B
Hamline U, MN B
Hanover Coll, IN B
Hastings Coll, NE B
Heidelberg Coll, OH B
Hillsdale Coll, MI B
Hiram Coll, OH B
Hope Coll, MI B
Illinois Coll, IL B
Illinois State U, IL B
Illinois Wesleyan U, IL B
Indiana State U, IN B
Indiana U Bloomington, IN B
Indiana U Northwest, IN B
Indiana U–Purdue U Fort Wayne, IN A,B
Indiana U–Purdue U Indianapolis, IN B
Indiana U South Bend, IN B
Indiana U Southeast, IN B
Indiana Wesleyan U, IN B
Iowa State U of Science and Technology, IA B
John Carroll U, OH B
Kalamazoo Coll, MI B
Kent State U, OH B
Kenyon Coll, OH B
Knox Coll, IL B
Lake Erie Coll, OH B
Lake Forest Coll, IL B
Lakeland Coll, WI B
Lawrence U, WI B
Lincoln Coll, Lincoln, IL A
Lindenwood U, MO B
Loras Coll, IA B
Loyola U Chicago, IL B
Luther Coll, IA B
Macalester Coll, MN B
MacMurray Coll, IL B
Madonna U, MI B
Malone Coll, OH B
Manchester Coll, IN B
Marian Coll, IN B
Marian Coll of Fond du Lac, WI B
Marietta Coll, OH B
Marquette U, WI B
McPherson Coll, KS B
Miami U, OH B
Miami U–Middletown Campus, OH A
Michigan State U, MI B
MidAmerica Nazarene U, KS B
Millikin U, IL B
Minnesota State U, Mankato, MN B
Minnesota State U, Moorhead, MN B
Minot State U, ND B
Missouri Southern State Coll, MO B
Missouri Western State Coll, MO B
Monmouth Coll, IL B
Morningside Coll, IA B
Mount Mary Coll, WI B
Mount Union Coll, OH B
Mount Vernon Nazarene U, OH B
Muskingum Coll, OH B
Nebraska Wesleyan U, NE B
North Central Coll, IL B
North Dakota State U, ND B
Northeastern Illinois U, IL B
Northeastern State U, OK B
Northern Illinois U, IL B
Northern Michigan U, MI B
Northern State U, SD B
North Park U, IL B
Northwestern Coll, IA B
Northwestern Coll, MN B
Northwestern Oklahoma State U, OK B
Northwestern U, IL B
Northwest Missouri State U, MO B
Notre Dame Coll, OH B
Oakland U, MI B
Oberlin Coll, OH B
Ohio Northern U, OH B
The Ohio State U, OH B
Ohio U, OH B
Ohio Wesleyan U, OH B
Oklahoma Baptist U, OK B
Oklahoma Christian U, OK B
Oklahoma City U, OK B
Oklahoma State U, OK B
Olivet Nazarene U, IL B
Oral Roberts U, OK B
Otterbein Coll, OH B
Park U, MO B
Pittsburg State U, KS B
Principia Coll, IL B
Purdue U Calumet, IN B
Ripon Coll, WI B
Rockford Coll, IL B
Rockhurst U, MO B
Roosevelt U, IL B
Saginaw Valley State U, MI B
St. Ambrose U, IA B
St. Cloud State U, MN B
Saint John's U, MN B
Saint Louis U, MO B
Saint Mary-of-the-Woods Coll, IN B
Saint Mary's Coll, IN B

Spanish (continued)

Saint Mary's U of Minnesota, MN	B
Saint Mary U, KS	B
St. Norbert Coll, WI	B
St. Olaf Coll, MN	B
Saint Xavier U, IL	B
Siena Heights U, MI	B
Simpson Coll, IA	B
South Dakota State U, SD	B
Southeast Missouri State U, MO	B
Southern Illinois U Carbondale, IL	B
Southern Nazarene U, OK	B
Southwest Baptist U, MO	B
Southwest Minnesota State U, MN	B
Southwest Missouri State U, MO	B
Spring Arbor U, MI	B
Taylor U, IN	B
Trinity Christian Coll, IL	B
Truman State U, MO	B
Union Coll, NE	B
The U of Akron, OH	B
U of Central Oklahoma, OK	B
U of Chicago, IL	B
U of Cincinnati, OH	B
U of Dayton, OH	B
U of Evansville, IN	B
The U of Findlay, OH	B
U of Illinois at Chicago, IL	B
U of Illinois at Urbana–Champaign, IL	B
U of Indianapolis, IN	B
The U of Iowa, IA	B
U of Kansas, KS	B
U of Michigan, MI	B
U of Michigan–Dearborn, MI	B
U of Michigan–Flint, MI	B
U of Minnesota, Duluth, MN	B
U of Minnesota, Morris, MN	B
U of Minnesota, Twin Cities Campus, MN	B
U of Missouri–Columbia, MO	B
U of Missouri–Kansas City, MO	B
U of Missouri–St. Louis, MO	B
U of Nebraska at Kearney, NE	B
U of Nebraska at Omaha, NE	B
U of Nebraska–Lincoln, NE	B
U of North Dakota, ND	B
U of Northern Iowa, IA	B
U of Notre Dame, IN	B
U of Oklahoma, OK	B
U of St. Thomas, MN	B
The U of South Dakota, SD	B
U of Southern Indiana, IN	B
U of Toledo, OH	B
U of Tulsa, OK	B
U of Wisconsin–Eau Claire, WI	B
U of Wisconsin–Green Bay, WI	A,B
U of Wisconsin–La Crosse, WI	B
U of Wisconsin–Madison, WI	B
U of Wisconsin–Milwaukee, WI	B
U of Wisconsin–Oshkosh, WI	B
U of Wisconsin–Parkside, WI	B
U of Wisconsin–Platteville, WI	B
U of Wisconsin–River Falls, WI	B
U of Wisconsin–Stevens Point, WI	B
U of Wisconsin–Whitewater, WI	B
Valley City State U, ND	B
Valparaiso U, IN	B
Viterbo U, WI	B
Wabash Coll, IN	B
Waldorf Coll, IA	A
Walsh U, OH	B
Wartburg Coll, IA	B
Washington U in St. Louis, MO	B
Wayne State Coll, NE	B
Wayne State U, MI	B
Webster U, MO	B
Western Illinois U, IL	B
Western Michigan U, MI	B
Westminster Coll, MO	B
Wheaton Coll, IL	B
Wichita State U, KS	B
William Jewell Coll, MO	B
William Woods U, MO	B
Wilmington Coll, OH	B
Winona State U, MN	B
Wisconsin Lutheran Coll, WI	B
Wittenberg U, OH	B
Wright State U, OH	B
Xavier U, OH	A,B
Youngstown State U, OH	B

SPANISH LANGUAGE EDUCATION

Anderson U, IN	B
Bowling Green State U, OH	B
Cedarville U, OH	B
Central Michigan U, MI	B
Central Missouri State U, MO	B
Chadron State Coll, NE	B
Coll of St. Catherine, MN	B
Concordia Coll, MN	B
Concordia U, NE	B
Eastern Michigan U, MI	B
Elmhurst Coll, IL	B
Franklin Coll, IN	B
Grace Coll, IN	B
Greenville Coll, IL	B
Indiana U Bloomington, IN	B
Indiana U Northwest, IN	B
Indiana U–Purdue U Fort Wayne, IN	B
Indiana U–Purdue U Indianapolis, IN	B
Indiana U South Bend, IN	B
Luther Coll, IA	B
Malone Coll, OH	B
MidAmerica Nazarene U, KS	B
Minnesota State U, Moorhead, MN	B
Minot State U, ND	B
Missouri Western State Coll, MO	B
North Dakota State U, ND	B
Ohio U, OH	B
Oklahoma Baptist U, OK	B
Oral Roberts U, OK	B
St. Ambrose U, IA	B
Saint Mary's U of Minnesota, MN	B
Saint Xavier U, IL	B
Southeastern Oklahoma State U, OK	B
Southern Nazarene U, OK	B
Southwest Missouri State U, MO	B
U of Illinois at Chicago, IL	B
U of Illinois at Urbana–Champaign, IL	B
U of Indianapolis, IN	B
The U of Iowa, IA	B
U of Minnesota, Duluth, MN	B
U of Nebraska–Lincoln, NE	B
U of Toledo, OH	B
U of Wisconsin–River Falls, WI	B
Valley City State U, ND	B
Viterbo U, WI	B
Washington U in St. Louis, MO	B
Youngstown State U, OH	B

SPECIAL EDUCATION

Aquinas Coll, MI	B
Ashland U, OH	B
Augustana Coll, SD	B
Avila U, MO	B
Baldwin-Wallace Coll, OH	B
Ball State U, IN	B
Benedictine Coll, KS	B
Benedictine U, IL	B
Black Hills State U, SD	B
Bluffton Coll, OH	B
Bowling Green State U, OH	B
Buena Vista U, IA	B
Calvin Coll, MI	B
Cardinal Stritch U, WI	B
Carthage Coll, WI	B
Cedarville U, OH	B
Central Missouri State U, MO	B
Chadron State Coll, NE	B
Chicago State U, IL	B
Clarke Coll, IA	B
Cleveland State U, OH	B
Coll of Mount St. Joseph, OH	B
Coll of Saint Mary, NE	B
Concordia U, NE	B
Creighton U, NE	B
Culver-Stockton Coll, MO	B
Dakota State U, SD	B
Dakota Wesleyan U, SD	B
Dana Coll, NE	B
Defiance Coll, OH	B
Doane Coll, NE	B
East Central U, OK	B
Eastern Illinois U, IL	B
Eastern Michigan U, MI	B
Elmhurst Coll, IL	B
Evangel U, MO	B
Fontbonne U, MO	B
Grand Valley State U, MI	B
Grand View Coll, IA	B
Greenville Coll, IL	B
Hastings Coll, NE	B
Heidelberg Coll, OH	B
Huntington Coll, IN	B
Illinois State U, IL	B
Indiana State U, IN	B
Indiana U Bloomington, IN	B
Indiana U South Bend, IN	B
Indiana U Southeast, IN	B
Indiana Wesleyan U, IN	B
John Carroll U, OH	B
Kent State U, OH	B
Langston U, OK	B
Lewis U, IL	B
Lindenwood U, MO	B
Loyola U Chicago, IL	B
Luther Coll, IA	B
MacMurray Coll, IL	B
Madonna U, MI	B
Manchester Coll, IN	B
Marian Coll, IN	B
McPherson Coll, KS	B
Miami U, OH	B
Michigan State U, MI	B
Minnesota State U, Moorhead, MN	B
Missouri Southern State Coll, MO	B
Missouri Valley Coll, MO	B
Monmouth Coll, IL	B
Morningside Coll, IA	B
Mount Marty Coll, SD	B
Mount Vernon Nazarene U, OH	B
Muskingum Coll, OH	B
Nebraska Wesleyan U, NE	B
Northeastern Illinois U, IL	B
Northeastern State U, OK	B
Northern Illinois U, IL	B
Northern Michigan U, MI	B
Northern State U, SD	B
Northwestern Oklahoma State U, OK	B
Northwest Missouri State U, MO	B
Ohio Dominican U, OH	B
The Ohio State U, OH	B
Ohio U, OH	B
Oklahoma Baptist U, OK	B
Oklahoma Christian U, OK	B
Oral Roberts U, OK	B
Peru State Coll, NE	B
Purdue U Calumet, IN	B
Quincy U, IL	B
Saginaw Valley State U, MI	B
St. Cloud State U, MN	B
Saint Mary-of-the-Woods Coll, IN	B
Southeastern Oklahoma State U, OK	B
Southeast Missouri State U, MO	B
Southern Illinois U Carbondale, IL	B
Southern Illinois U Edwardsville, IL	B
Southwestern Oklahoma State U, OK	B
Southwest Missouri State U, MO	B
Tabor Coll, KS	B
Trinity Christian Coll, IL	B
U of Central Oklahoma, OK	B
U of Cincinnati, OH	B
U of Dayton, OH	B
U of Evansville, IN	B
The U of Findlay, OH	B
U of Illinois at Urbana–Champaign, IL	B
U of Mary, ND	B
U of Minnesota, Duluth, MN	B
U of Missouri–St. Louis, MO	B
U of Nebraska at Kearney, NE	B
U of Nebraska at Omaha, NE	B
U of Northern Iowa, IA	B
U of Oklahoma, OK	B
U of St. Francis, IL	B
U of Saint Francis, IN	B
The U of South Dakota, SD	B
U of Toledo, OH	B
U of Tulsa, OK	B

U of Wisconsin–Eau Claire, WI B
U of Wisconsin–Madison, WI B
U of Wisconsin–Milwaukee, WI B
U of Wisconsin–Oshkosh, WI B
U of Wisconsin–Superior, WI B
U of Wisconsin–Whitewater, WI B
Upper Iowa U, IA B
Ursuline Coll, OH B
Walsh U, OH B
Wayne State Coll, NE B
Wayne State U, MI B
Webster U, MO B
Western Illinois U, IL B
William Penn U, IA B
William Woods U, MO B
Winona State U, MN B
Wittenberg U, OH B
Xavier U, OH B
Youngstown State U, OH B

SPECIAL EDUCATION RELATED

Briar Cliff U, IA B
Minot State U, ND A,B
The U of Akron, OH B
U of Nebraska–Lincoln, NE B

SPEECH EDUCATION

Anderson U, IN B
Bowling Green State U, OH B
Cedarville U, OH B
Central Michigan U, MI B
Central Missouri State U, MO B
Chadron State Coll, NE B
Coll of St. Catherine, MN B
Concordia U, IL B
Concordia U, NE B
Dana Coll, NE B
Emporia State U, KS B
Greenville Coll, IL B
Hastings Coll, NE B
Indiana U Bloomington, IN B
Indiana U–Purdue U Fort Wayne, IN B
Indiana U–Purdue U Indianapolis, IN B
Malone Coll, OH B
Minnesota State U, Moorhead, MN B
North Dakota State U, ND B
Oklahoma Baptist U, OK B
Southeastern Oklahoma State U, OK B
Southeast Missouri State U, MO B
Southern Nazarene U, OK B
Southwest Minnesota State U, MN B
Southwest Missouri State U, MO B
The U of Akron, OH B
U of Indianapolis, IN B
The U of Iowa, IA B
U of Rio Grande, OH B
William Jewell Coll, MO B
Youngstown State U, OH B

SPEECH-LANGUAGE PATHOLOGY

Baker Coll of Muskegon, MI A
Central Missouri State U, MO B
Indiana State U, IN A
Miami U, OH B
Northwestern U, IL B
Rockhurst U, MO B
Saint Xavier U, IL B
Southeast Missouri State U, MO B
U of Nebraska at Omaha, NE B
U of Nebraska–Lincoln, NE B
U of Northern Iowa, IA B
U of Science and Arts of Oklahoma, OK B
U of Toledo, OH B
Wayne State U, MI B

SPEECH-LANGUAGE PATHOLOGY/AUDIOLOGY

Andrews U, MI B
Augustana Coll, IL B
Augustana Coll, SD B
Baldwin-Wallace Coll, OH B
Ball State U, IN B
Butler U, IN B
Calvin Coll, MI B
Central Michigan U, MI B
Cleveland State U, OH B
The Coll of Wooster, OH B
Elmhurst Coll, IL B
Fontbonne U, MO B
Fort Hays State U, KS B
Governors State U, IL B
Illinois State U, IL B
Indiana State U, IN B
Indiana U Bloomington, IN B
Indiana U–Purdue U Fort Wayne, IN B
Kent State U, OH B
Marquette U, WI B
Miami U, OH B
Michigan State U, MI B
Minnesota State U, Mankato, MN B
Minnesota State U, Moorhead, MN B
Northeastern State U, OK B
Northern Michigan U, MI B
Northern State U, SD B
Northwestern U, IL B
The Ohio State U, OH B
Ohio U, OH B
Otterbein Coll, OH B
Purdue U, IN B
St. Cloud State U, MN B
Southern Illinois U Edwardsville, IL B
Southwest Missouri State U, MO B
The U of Akron, OH B
U of Central Oklahoma, OK B
U of Cincinnati, OH B
U of Illinois at Urbana–Champaign, IL B
The U of Iowa, IA B
U of Minnesota, Duluth, MN B
U of Minnesota, Twin Cities Campus, MN B
U of Nebraska at Omaha, NE B
U of North Dakota, ND B
U of Oklahoma Health Sciences Center, OK B
The U of South Dakota, SD B
U of Tulsa, OK B
U of Wisconsin–Milwaukee, WI B
U of Wisconsin–Oshkosh, WI B
U of Wisconsin–Stevens Point, WI B
Western Michigan U, MI B
Wichita State U, KS B

SPEECH/RHETORICAL STUDIES

Ashland U, OH B
Augsburg Coll, MN B
Augustana Coll, IL B
Baker U, KS B
Ball State U, IN B
Bemidji State U, MN B
Bethel Coll, MN B
Blackburn Coll, IL B
Black Hills State U, SD B
Bluffton Coll, OH B
Bowling Green State U, OH B
Bradley U, IL B
Buena Vista U, IA B
Butler U, IN B
Calvin Coll, MI B
Cameron U, OK B
Capital U, OH B
Carthage Coll, WI B
Cedarville U, OH B
Central Michigan U, MI B
Central Missouri State U, MO B
Chadron State Coll, NE B
Coe Coll, IA B
Coll of Saint Benedict, MN B
Coll of St. Catherine, MN B
Coll of the Ozarks, MO B
The Coll of Wooster, OH B
Concordia Coll, MN B
Concordia U, NE B
Cornell Coll, IA B
Cornerstone U, MI B
Creighton U, NE B
Defiance Coll, OH B
Denison U, OH B
Dickinson State U, ND B
Doane Coll, NE B
Drake U, IA B
East Central U, OK B
Eastern Illinois U, IL B
Eastern Michigan U, MI B
Evangel U, MO B
Ferris State U, MI A
Governors State U, IL B
Graceland U, IA B
Greenville Coll, IL B
Gustavus Adolphus Coll, MN B
Hannibal-LaGrange Coll, MO B
Hastings Coll, NE B
Hillsdale Coll, MI B
Illinois Coll, IL B
Illinois State U, IL B
Indiana U Bloomington, IN B
Indiana U South Bend, IN B
Iowa State U of Science and Technology, IA B
Judson Coll, IL B
Kent State U, OH B
Lewis U, IL B
Manchester Coll, IN B
Maranatha Baptist Bible Coll, WI B
Marietta Coll, OH B
Marquette U, WI B
McKendree Coll, IL B
Miami U, OH B
Minnesota State U, Mankato, MN B
Minnesota State U, Moorhead, MN B
Minot State U, ND B
Missouri Valley Coll, MO B
Missouri Western State Coll, MO B
Monmouth Coll, IL B
Mount Mercy Coll, IA B
Nebraska Wesleyan U, NE B
North Central Coll, IL B
North Dakota State U, ND B
Northeastern Illinois U, IL B
Northern Michigan U, MI B
Northern State U, SD B
North Park U, IL B
Northwestern Coll, IA B
Northwestern Oklahoma State U, OK B
Northwestern U, IL B
Northwest Missouri State U, MO B
Ohio Northern U, OH B
Ohio U, OH B
Oklahoma Baptist U, OK B
Oklahoma Christian U, OK B
Oklahoma City U, OK B
Oklahoma State U, OK B
Olivet Nazarene U, IL B
Pillsbury Baptist Bible Coll, MN B
Pittsburg State U, KS B
Ripon Coll, WI B
St. Cloud State U, MN B
Saint John's U, MN B
Simpson Coll, IA B
South Dakota State U, SD B
Southeast Missouri State U, MO B
Southern Illinois U Carbondale, IL B
Southern Illinois U Edwardsville, IL B
Southern Nazarene U, OK B
Truman State U, MO B
The U of Akron, OH B
U of Dubuque, IA B
U of Illinois at Chicago, IL B
U of Illinois at Urbana–Champaign, IL B
The U of Iowa, IA B
U of Kansas, KS B
U of Michigan, MI B
U of Michigan–Dearborn, MI B
U of Minnesota, Morris, MN B
U of Nebraska at Kearney, NE B
U of Nebraska at Omaha, NE B
U of Sioux Falls, SD B
The U of South Dakota, SD B
U of Wisconsin–La Crosse, WI B
U of Wisconsin–Platteville, WI B
U of Wisconsin–River Falls, WI B
U of Wisconsin–Superior, WI B
U of Wisconsin–Whitewater, WI B
Wabash Coll, IN B
Waldorf Coll, IA A
Wayne State Coll, NE B
Wheaton Coll, IL B
William Jewell Coll, MO B
Winona State U, MN B

Speech/Rhetorical Studies (continued)

Youngstown State U, OH B

SPEECH/THEATER EDUCATION

Augustana Coll, SD B
Bemidji State U, MN B
Briar Cliff U, IA B
Culver-Stockton Coll, MO B
Dickinson State U, ND B
Graceland U, IA B
Hamline U, MN B
Hastings Coll, NE B
Lewis U, IL B
McKendree Coll, IL B
McPherson Coll, KS B
Midland Lutheran Coll, NE B
Missouri Western State Coll, MO B
Northwestern Oklahoma State U, OK B
Oklahoma City U, OK B
St. Ambrose U, IA B
Southwest Baptist U, MO B
Southwest Minnesota State U, MN B
U of Minnesota, Morris, MN B
U of St. Thomas, MN B
Viterbo U, WI B
Wartburg Coll, IA B
William Woods U, MO B
York Coll, NE B

SPEECH THERAPY

Augustana Coll, IL B
Fontbonne U, MO B
Indiana U Bloomington, IN B
Northeastern State U, OK B
Northwestern U, IL B
Ohio U, OH B
St. Cloud State U, MN B
Southeast Missouri State U, MO B
The U of Iowa, IA B
U of Oklahoma Health Sciences Center, OK B
U of Toledo, OH B
U of Wisconsin–Madison, WI B
U of Wisconsin–River Falls, WI B

SPORT/FITNESS ADMINISTRATION

Augustana Coll, SD B
Baldwin-Wallace Coll, OH B
Ball State U, IN B
Bemidji State U, MN B
Benedictine Coll, KS B
Bethel Coll, IN B
Black Hills State U, SD B
Bluffton Coll, OH B
Bowling Green State U, OH B
Central Christian Coll of Kansas, KS A
Central Methodist Coll, MO B
Concordia U, MI B
Concordia U, NE B
Cornerstone U, MI B
Crown Coll, MN B
Defiance Coll, OH B
Elmhurst Coll, IL B
Graceland U, IA B
Hastings Coll, NE B
Indiana U Bloomington, IN B
Indiana Wesleyan U, IN B
Iowa Wesleyan Coll, IA B
Judson Coll, IL B
Loras Coll, IA B
Luther Coll, IA B
MacMurray Coll, IL B
Malone Coll, OH B
Marian Coll of Fond du Lac, WI B
Miami U, OH B
MidAmerica Nazarene U, KS B
Millikin U, IL B
Minnesota State U, Mankato, MN B
Minnesota State U, Moorhead, MN B
Minot State U, ND B
Mount Union Coll, OH B
Mount Vernon Nazarene U, OH B
National American U, SD B
Nebraska Wesleyan U, NE B
Northwestern Coll, MN B
Northwest Missouri State U, MO B
Ohio Northern U, OH B
Ohio U, OH B
Olivet Coll, MI B
Olivet Nazarene U, IL B
Otterbein Coll, OH B
Principia Coll, IL B
Quincy U, IL B
Rochester Coll, MI B
St. Ambrose U, IA B
Shawnee State U, OH B
Simpson Coll, IA B
Southeast Missouri State U, MO B
Southern Nazarene U, OK B
Southwest Baptist U, MO B
Southwestern Coll, KS B
Spring Arbor U, MI B
Taylor U, IN B
Tiffin U, OH B
Tri-State U, IN B
Union Coll, NE B
U of Dayton, OH B
The U of Iowa, IA B
U of Michigan, MI B
U of Nebraska at Kearney, NE B
U of Tulsa, OK B
U of Wisconsin–La Crosse, WI B
U of Wisconsin–Parkside, WI B
Valparaiso U, IN B
Wartburg Coll, IA B
Wayne State Coll, NE B
William Penn U, IA B
Wilmington Coll, OH B
Winona State U, MN B
Xavier U, OH B
Youngstown State U, OH B

STRINGED INSTRUMENTS

Alma Coll, MI B
Aquinas Coll, MI B
Augustana Coll, IL B
Baldwin-Wallace Coll, OH B
Ball State U, IN B
Benedictine Coll, KS B
Butler U, IN B
Capital U, OH B
Cleveland Inst of Music, OH B
DePaul U, IL B
Grand Valley State U, MI B
Hastings Coll, NE B
Heidelberg Coll, OH B
Illinois Wesleyan U, IL B
Lawrence U, WI B
Lindenwood U, MO B
Luther Coll, IA B
Northern Michigan U, MI B
Northwest Missouri State U, MO B
Oberlin Coll, OH B
Oklahoma City U, OK B
Olivet Nazarene U, IL B
Otterbein Coll, OH B
Pittsburg State U, KS B
Roosevelt U, IL B
The U of Akron, OH B
U of Central Oklahoma, OK B
U of Cincinnati, OH B
The U of Iowa, IA B
U of Kansas, KS B
U of Michigan, MI B
U of Missouri–Kansas City, MO B
U of Oklahoma, OK B
The U of South Dakota, SD B
U of Wisconsin–Milwaukee, WI B
Youngstown State U, OH B

SURVEYING

Ferris State U, MI A,B
Kansas State U, KS A
Michigan Technological U, MI B
The Ohio State U, OH B
Purdue U, IN B
The U of Akron, OH A,B
U of Wisconsin–Madison, WI B

SYSTEM/NETWORKING/ LAN/WAN MANAGEMENT

AIB Coll of Business, IA A
ITT Tech Inst, Mount Prospect, IL A
ITT Tech Inst, Fort Wayne, IN A
ITT Tech Inst, Indianapolis, IN A
ITT Tech Inst, Newburgh, IN A
ITT Tech Inst, Arnold, MO A
ITT Tech Inst, Earth City, MO A
ITT Tech Inst, Green Bay, WI A
ITT Tech Inst, Greenfield, WI A

SYSTEMS ENGINEERING

Case Western Reserve U, OH B
Minnesota School of Business-Richfield, MN A
Missouri Tech, MO A,B
Oakland U, MI B
The Ohio State U, OH B
Ohio U, OH B
Washington U in St. Louis, MO B

SYSTEMS SCIENCE/ THEORY

Indiana U Bloomington, IN B
Miami U, OH B
Miami U–Middletown Campus, OH A
U of Kansas, KS B
Washington U in St. Louis, MO B

TEACHER ASSISTANT/ AIDE

Alverno Coll, WI A
Concordia U, MN A
Dordt Coll, IA A
Sitting Bull Coll, ND A

TEACHER EDUCATION RELATED

Xavier U, OH B

TEACHER EDUCATION, SPECIFIC PROGRAMS RELATED

Bradley U, IL B
Chadron State Coll, NE B
Franklin Coll, IN B
Minot State U, ND B
Ohio U, OH B
The U of Akron, OH B
U of Central Oklahoma, OK B
U of Nebraska–Lincoln, NE B
U of St. Thomas, MN B
U of Toledo, OH B

TEACHING ENGLISH AS A SECOND LANGUAGE

Bethel Coll, MN B
Calvin Coll, MI B
Concordia U Wisconsin, WI B
Doane Coll, NE B
Goshen Coll, IN B
Langston U, OK B
Moody Bible Inst, IL B
Northwestern Coll, MN B
Ohio Dominican U, OH B
Ohio U, OH B
Oklahoma Christian U, OK B
Oklahoma Wesleyan U, OK B
Oral Roberts U, OK B
The U of Findlay, OH B
U of Nebraska–Lincoln, NE B
U of Northern Iowa, IA B
U of Wisconsin–Oshkosh, WI B
U of Wisconsin–River Falls, WI B

TECHNICAL/BUSINESS WRITING

Bowling Green State U, OH B
Cedarville U, OH B
Central Michigan U, MI B
Chicago State U, IL B
Ferris State U, MI A,B
Grand Valley State U, MI B
Iowa State U of Science and Technology, IA B
Lawrence Technological U, MI B
Madonna U, MI B
Metropolitan State U, MN B
Miami U, OH B
Michigan Technological U, MI B
Mount Mary Coll, WI B
Northwestern Coll, MN B
Oklahoma State U, OK B
Southwest Missouri State U, MO B
U of Wisconsin–Stout, WI B
Wittenberg U, OH B
Youngstown State U, OH B

TECHNICAL EDUCATION

Bowling Green State U, OH B
The Ohio State U, OH B
The U of Akron, OH B
U of Nebraska at Kearney, NE B
U of Wisconsin–Stout, WI B
Valley City State U, ND B
Wayne State U, MI B

TELECOMMUNICATIONS

Ball State U, IN B
Bowling Green State U, OH B
Butler U, IN B
Cameron U, OK A,B
Coll of Saint Mary, NE A
Ferris State U, MI A,B
Grand Valley State U, MI B
Indiana U Bloomington, IN B
Michigan State U, MI B
Ohio U, OH B
Oklahoma Baptist U, OK B
Roosevelt U, IL B
U of Wisconsin–Platteville, WI B
Waldorf Coll, IA A
Western Michigan U, MI B
Winona State U, MN B
Youngstown State U, OH B

TEXTILE ARTS

Bowling Green State U, OH B
The Cleveland Inst of Art, OH B
Coll for Creative Studies, MI B
Finlandia U, MI B
Kansas City Art Inst, MO B
Northern Michigan U, MI B
Northwest Missouri State U, MO B
School of the Art Inst of Chicago, IL B
U of Michigan, MI B
U of Wisconsin–Milwaukee, WI B

THEATER ARTS/DRAMA

Adrian Coll, MI A,B
Albion Coll, MI B
Alma Coll, MI B
Anderson U, IN B
Antioch Coll, OH B
Ashland U, OH B
Augsburg Coll, MN B
Augustana Coll, IL B
Augustana Coll, SD B
Avila U, MO B
Bacone Coll, OK A
Baker U, KS B
Baldwin-Wallace Coll, OH B
Ball State U, IN B
Beloit Coll, WI B
Bemidji State U, MN B
Benedictine Coll, KS B
Bethel Coll, IN B
Bethel Coll, MN B
Bowling Green State U, OH B
Bradley U, IL B
Briar Cliff U, IA B
Buena Vista U, IA B
Butler U, IN B
Calvin Coll, MI B
Cameron U, OK B
Cardinal Stritch U, WI B
Carroll Coll, WI B
Carthage Coll, WI B
Case Western Reserve U, OH B
Cedarville U, OH B
Central Christian Coll of Kansas, KS A
Central Coll, IA B
Central Methodist Coll, MO B
Central Michigan U, MI B
Central Missouri State U, MO B
Chadron State Coll, NE B
Clarke Coll, IA B
Cleveland State U, OH B
Coe Coll, IA B
Coll of Saint Benedict, MN B
Coll of St. Catherine, MN B
Coll of the Ozarks, MO B
The Coll of Wooster, OH B
Columbia Coll Chicago, IL B
Concordia Coll, MN B
Concordia U, IL B
Concordia U, MN B
Concordia U, NE B
Concordia U Wisconsin, WI B
Cornell Coll, IA B
Creighton U, NE B
Culver-Stockton Coll, MO B
Dakota Wesleyan U, SD B
Denison U, OH B
DePaul U, IL B
Dickinson State U, ND B
Doane Coll, NE B
Dominican U, IL B
Dordt Coll, IA B
Drake U, IA B
Drury U, MO B
Earlham Coll, IN B
Eastern Illinois U, IL B
Eastern Michigan U, MI B
Edgewood Coll, WI B
Elmhurst Coll, IL B
Emporia State U, KS B
Eureka Coll, IL B
Fontbonne U, MO B
Franklin Coll, IN B
Goshen Coll, IN B
Graceland U, IA B
Grand Valley State U, MI B
Grand View Coll, IA B
Greenville Coll, IL B
Grinnell Coll, IA B
Gustavus Adolphus Coll, MN B
Hamline U, MN B
Hannibal-LaGrange Coll, MO B
Hanover Coll, IN B
Hastings Coll, NE B
Heidelberg Coll, OH B
Hillsdale Coll, MI B
Hiram Coll, OH B
Hope Coll, MI B
Huntington Coll, IN B
Illinois Coll, IL B
Illinois State U, IL B
Illinois Wesleyan U, IL B
Indiana State U, IN B
Indiana U Bloomington, IN A,B
Indiana U Northwest, IN B
Indiana U–Purdue U Fort Wayne, IN B
Indiana U South Bend, IN B
Iowa State U of Science and Technology, IA B
Jamestown Coll, ND B
Judson Coll, IL B
Kalamazoo Coll, MI B
Kansas State U, KS B
Kent State U, OH B
Kenyon Coll, OH B
Knox Coll, IL B
Lake Erie Coll, OH B
Lakeland Coll, WI B
Langston U, OK B
Lawrence U, WI B
Lewis U, IL B
Lincoln Coll, Lincoln, IL A
Lindenwood U, MO B
Loyola U Chicago, IL B
Luther Coll, IA B
Macalester Coll, MN B
MacMurray Coll, IL B
Maharishi U of Management, IA B
Malone Coll, OH B
Manchester Coll, IN B
Marietta Coll, OH B
Marquette U, WI B
McPherson Coll, KS B
Metropolitan State U, MN B
Miami U, OH B
Michigan State U, MI B
Midland Lutheran Coll, NE B
Millikin U, IL B
Minnesota State U, Mankato, MN B
Minnesota State U, Moorhead, MN B
Missouri Southern State Coll, MO B
Missouri Valley Coll, MO B
Monmouth Coll, IL B
Morningside Coll, IA B
Mount Mercy Coll, IA B
Mount Union Coll, OH B
Mount Vernon Nazarene U, OH B
Muskingum Coll, OH B
National-Louis U, IL B
Nebraska Wesleyan U, NE B
North Central Coll, IL B
North Dakota State U, ND B
Northeastern State U, OK B
Northern Illinois U, IL B
Northern Michigan U, MI B
Northern State U, SD B
North Park U, IL B
Northwestern Coll, IA B
Northwestern Coll, MN B
Northwestern U, IL B
Northwest Missouri State U, MO B
Oakland U, MI B
Oberlin Coll, OH B
Ohio Northern U, OH B
The Ohio State U, OH B
Ohio U, OH B
Ohio Wesleyan U, OH B
Oklahoma Baptist U, OK B
Oklahoma Christian U, OK B
Oklahoma City U, OK B
Oklahoma State U, OK B
Oral Roberts U, OK B
Ottawa U, KS B
Otterbein Coll, OH B
Principia Coll, IL B
Purdue U, IN B
Ripon Coll, WI B
Rockford Coll, IL B
Rockhurst U, MO B
Roosevelt U, IL B
Saginaw Valley State U, MI B
St. Ambrose U, IA B
St. Cloud State U, MN B
Saint John's U, MN B
Saint Louis U, MO B
Saint Mary-of-the-Woods Coll, IN B
Saint Mary's Coll, IN B
Saint Mary's U of Minnesota, MN B
Saint Mary U, KS B
St. Olaf Coll, MN B
Siena Heights U, MI B
Simpson Coll, IA B
South Dakota State U, SD B
Southeastern Oklahoma State U, OK B
Southeast Missouri State U, MO B
Southern Illinois U Carbondale, IL B
Southern Illinois U Edwardsville, IL B
Southwest Baptist U, MO B
Southwestern Coll, KS B
Southwest Minnesota State U, MN B
Southwest Missouri State U, MO B
Stephens Coll, MO B
Sterling Coll, KS B
Taylor U, IN B
Trinity Bible Coll, ND B
Truman State U, MO B
The U of Akron, OH B
U of Central Oklahoma, OK B
U of Cincinnati, OH B
U of Dayton, OH B
U of Evansville, IN B
The U of Findlay, OH B
U of Illinois at Chicago, IL B
U of Illinois at Urbana–Champaign, IL B
U of Indianapolis, IN B
The U of Iowa, IA B
U of Kansas, KS B
U of Michigan, MI B
U of Michigan–Flint, MI B
U of Minnesota, Duluth, MN B
U of Minnesota, Morris, MN B
U of Minnesota, Twin Cities Campus, MN B
U of Missouri–Columbia, MO B
U of Missouri–Kansas City, MO B
U of Nebraska at Kearney, NE B
U of Nebraska at Omaha, NE B
U of Nebraska–Lincoln, NE B
U of North Dakota, ND B
U of Northern Iowa, IA B
U of Notre Dame, IN B
U of Oklahoma, OK B
U of St. Thomas, MN B
U of Science and Arts of Oklahoma, OK B
U of Sioux Falls, SD A,B
The U of South Dakota, SD B
U of Southern Indiana, IN B
U of Toledo, OH B
U of Wisconsin–Eau Claire, WI B
U of Wisconsin–Green Bay, WI A,B
U of Wisconsin–La Crosse, WI B
U of Wisconsin–Madison, WI B
U of Wisconsin–Milwaukee, WI B

Theater Arts/Drama (continued)

U of Wisconsin–Oshkosh, WI B
U of Wisconsin–Parkside, WI B
U of Wisconsin–River Falls, WI B
U of Wisconsin–Stevens Point, WI B
U of Wisconsin–Superior, WI B
U of Wisconsin–Whitewater, WI B
Valparaiso U, IN B
Viterbo U, WI B
Wabash Coll, IN B
Waldorf Coll, IA A,B
Washington U in St. Louis, MO B
Wayne State Coll, NE B
Wayne State U, MI B
Webster U, MO B
Western Illinois U, IL B
Western Michigan U, MI B
Wichita State U, KS B
William Jewell Coll, MO B
William Woods U, MO B
Wilmington Coll, OH B
Winona State U, MN B
Wittenberg U, OH B
Wright State U, OH B
Youngstown State U, OH B

THEATER ARTS/DRAMA AND STAGECRAFT RELATED

DePaul U, IL B
Nebraska Wesleyan U, NE B
Ohio U, OH B
The U of Akron, OH B

THEATER DESIGN

Columbia Coll Chicago, IL B
DePaul U, IL B
Indiana U Bloomington, IN A
Maharishi U of Management, IA B
Ohio U, OH B
Oklahoma City U, OK B
U of Kansas, KS B
U of Michigan, MI B
U of Northern Iowa, IA B
U of Rio Grande, OH A
Webster U, MO B
Western Michigan U, MI B
William Woods U, MO B
Youngstown State U, OH B

THEOLOGY

Anderson U, IN B
Andrews U, MI B
Augsburg Coll, MN B
Ave Maria Coll, MI B
Avila U, MO B
Baker U, KS B
Benedictine Coll, KS B
Briar Cliff U, IA A,B
Calumet Coll of Saint Joseph, IN B
Calvin Coll, MI B
Cedarville U, OH B
Central Bible Coll, MO B
Central Christian Coll of Kansas, KS A,B
Circleville Bible Coll, OH A,B
Coll of Saint Benedict, MN B
Coll of St. Catherine, MN B
Concordia U, IL B
Concordia U, MN B
Concordia U, NE B
Concordia U Wisconsin, WI B
Creighton U, NE A,B
Crossroads Coll, MN B
Crown Coll, MN B
Dakota Wesleyan U, SD B
Dordt Coll, IA B
Elmhurst Coll, IL B
Franciscan U of Steubenville, OH A,B
Global U of the Assemblies of God, MO B
Grace Bible Coll, MI B
Great Lakes Christian Coll, MI B
Greenville Coll, IL B
Hannibal-LaGrange Coll, MO B
Hanover Coll, IN B
Hillsdale Free Will Baptist Coll, OK B
Huntington Coll, IN B
Indiana Wesleyan U, IN B
Laura and Alvin Siegal Coll of Judaic Studies, OH B
Lincoln Christian Coll, IL B
Loyola U Chicago, IL B
Luther Coll, IA B
Manhattan Christian Coll, KS B
Marian Coll, IN A,B
Marquette U, WI B
Martin Luther Coll, MN B
Mount Vernon Nazarene U, OH B
Nebraska Christian Coll, NE B
Newman U, KS B
North Park U, IL B
Northwestern Coll, IA B
Notre Dame Coll, OH A,B
Oakland City U, IN B
Ohio Dominican U, OH A,B
Oklahoma Baptist U, OK B
Oklahoma Wesleyan U, OK B
Olivet Nazarene U, IL B
Oral Roberts U, OK B
Ozark Christian Coll, MO A,B
Quincy U, IL B
Reformed Bible Coll, MI B
Rockhurst U, MO B
St. Ambrose U, IA B
St. Gregory's U, OK B
Saint John's U, MN B
St. Louis Christian Coll, MO B
Saint Louis U, MO B
Saint Mary-of-the-Woods Coll, IN B
Saint Mary's Coll of Madonna U, MI B
Saint Mary's U of Minnesota, MN B
Saint Mary U, KS B
Silver Lake Coll, WI B
Taylor U, IN B
Trinity Bible Coll, ND B
Trinity Christian Coll, IL B
Union Coll, NE B
U of Dubuque, IA B
U of Notre Dame, IN B
U of St. Francis, IL B
U of St. Thomas, MN B
Valparaiso U, IN B
Viterbo U, WI B
Waldorf Coll, IA A
Walsh U, OH B
Wisconsin Lutheran Coll, WI B
Wittenberg U, OH B
Xavier U, OH A,B

THEOLOGY/MINISTRY RELATED

Malone Coll, OH B
Northwestern Coll, MN B
Wheaton Coll, IL B

TOOL/DIE MAKING

Southern Illinois U Carbondale, IL A

TOURISM PROMOTION OPERATIONS

AIB Coll of Business, IA A
Eastern Michigan U, MI B

TOURISM/TRAVEL MARKETING

Central Missouri State U, MO B
Eastern Michigan U, MI B
Ohio U, OH B

TOXICOLOGY

Ashland U, OH B
Eastern Michigan U, MI B
Minnesota State U, Mankato, MN B
U of Wisconsin–Madison, WI B

TRADE/INDUSTRIAL EDUCATION

Ball State U, IN B
Bemidji State U, MN B
Cincinnati Bible Coll and Seminary, OH A
Dakota State U, SD B
Gustavus Adolphus Coll, MN B
Indiana State U, IN B
Iowa State U of Science and Technology, IA B
Kent State U, OH B
Madonna U, MI B
Northeastern State U, OK B
Oklahoma State U, OK B
Pittsburg State U, KS B
Purdue U, IN A
Southern Illinois U Carbondale, IL B
U of Central Oklahoma, OK B
U of Nebraska at Omaha, NE B
U of Nebraska–Lincoln, NE B
U of North Dakota, ND B
U of Northern Iowa, IA B
U of Toledo, OH B
Western Illinois U, IL B

TRANSPORTATION TECHNOLOGY

Baker Coll of Flint, MI A
Iowa State U of Science and Technology, IA B
U of Cincinnati, OH A,B
U of Toledo, OH A

TRAVEL SERVICES MARKETING OPERATIONS

AIB Coll of Business, IA A

TRAVEL/TOURISM MANAGEMENT

AIB Coll of Business, IA A
Baker Coll of Flint, MI A
Baker Coll of Muskegon, MI A
Ball State U, IN B
Black Hills State U, SD A,B
Grand Valley State U, MI B
Hamilton Coll, IA A
International Business Coll, Fort Wayne, IN A,B
Kaplan Coll, IA A
Lincoln Coll, Lincoln, IL A
Lincoln Coll, Normal, IL A
Midland Lutheran Coll, NE A
Midstate Coll, IL A
National American U–Sioux Falls Branch, SD A
Northeastern State U, OK B
Ohio U, OH A
Robert Morris Coll, IL A
St. Cloud State U, MN B
U of Northwestern Ohio, OH A
Western Michigan U, MI B
Youngstown State U, OH B

TURF MANAGEMENT

The Ohio State U, OH B
Rochester Comm and Tech Coll, MN A

URBAN STUDIES

Aquinas Coll, MI B
Augsburg Coll, MN B
Bellevue U, NE B
Cleveland State U, OH B
The Coll of Wooster, OH B
DePaul U, IL B
Elmhurst Coll, IL B
Hamline U, MN B
Harris-Stowe State Coll, MO B
Indiana U Bloomington, IN B
Langston U, OK B
Macalester Coll, MN B
Minnesota State U, Mankato, MN B
Mount Mercy Coll, IA B
Northeastern Illinois U, IL B
North Park U, IL B
Northwestern U, IL B
Ohio Wesleyan U, OH B
Rockford Coll, IL B
Roosevelt U, IL B
St. Cloud State U, MN B
Saint Louis U, MO B
Taylor U, Fort Wayne Campus, IN B
U of Cincinnati, OH B
U of Michigan–Flint, MI B
U of Minnesota, Duluth, MN B
U of Minnesota, Twin Cities Campus, MN B
U of Missouri–Kansas City, MO B
U of Missouri–St. Louis, MO B
U of Nebraska at Omaha, NE B
U of Toledo, OH B
U of Wisconsin–Green Bay, WI A,B
U of Wisconsin–Madison, WI B
U of Wisconsin–Milwaukee, WI B
U of Wisconsin–Oshkosh, WI B
Washington U in St. Louis, MO B
Wayne State U, MI B
Wittenberg U, OH B
Wright State U, OH B

VEHICLE/EQUIPMENT OPERATION
Baker Coll of Flint, MI A

VETERINARIAN ASSISTANT
Michigan State U, MI B
Minnesota School of Business-Richfield, MN A
Purdue U, IN A
U of Nebraska–Lincoln, NE B

VETERINARY SCIENCES
Northland Coll, WI B
Springfield Coll in Illinois, IL A
Waldorf Coll, IA A

VETERINARY TECHNOLOGY
Michigan State U, MI B
National American U, SD A
North Dakota State U, ND B

VISUAL AND PERFORMING ARTS RELATED
Illinois State U, IL B
The U of Akron, OH B
U of Oklahoma, OK B

VISUAL/PERFORMING ARTS
American Academy of Art, IL B
Antioch Coll, OH B
Bethel Coll, KS B
The Franciscan U, IA B
Indiana U East, IN A
Iowa State U of Science and Technology, IA B
Maharishi U of Management, IA A,B
Northwestern U, IL B
Oakland U, MI B
Ohio U, OH B
Saint Mary U, KS B
St. Olaf Coll, MN B
South Dakota State U, SD B
Southwest Missouri State U, MO B
U of Michigan, MI B
U of Rio Grande, OH B
U of St. Francis, IL B
Wichita State U, KS B

VOCATIONAL REHABILITATION COUNSELING
Emporia State U, KS B
U of Wisconsin–Stout, WI B

WATER RESOURCES
East Central U, OK B
Grand Valley State U, MI B
Heidelberg Coll, OH B
Northern Michigan U, MI B
Northland Coll, WI B
U of Wisconsin–Madison, WI B
U of Wisconsin–Stevens Point, WI B
Wright State U, OH B

WEB/MULTIMEDIA MANAGEMENT/ WEBMASTER
Nebraska Wesleyan U, NE B

WEB PAGE, DIGITAL/ MULTIMEDIA AND INFORMATION RESOURCES DESIGN
Academy Coll, MN A
Capella U, MN B
The Cleveland Inst of Art, OH B
Dakota State U, SD B
Greenville Coll, IL B
Maharishi U of Management, IA B

WELDING TECHNOLOGY
Ferris State U, MI A,B
Oakland City U, IN A
U of Toledo, OH A

WESTERN CIVILIZATION
Central Christian Coll of Kansas, KS A
Grand Valley State U, MI B
Lincoln Coll, Lincoln, IL A

WESTERN EUROPEAN STUDIES
Central Coll, IA B
Grinnell Coll, IA B
Knox Coll, IL B
The Ohio State U, OH B
U of Nebraska–Lincoln, NE B

WILDLIFE BIOLOGY
Baker U, KS B
Ball State U, IN B
Central Christian Coll of Kansas, KS A
Grand Valley State U, MI B
Iowa State U of Science and Technology, IA B
Kansas State U, KS B
Northeastern State U, OK B
Northern Michigan U, MI B
Northland Coll, WI B
Northwest Missouri State U, MO B
Ohio U, OH B
St. Cloud State U, MN B
U of Michigan, MI B
Waldorf Coll, IA A
Winona State U, MN B

WILDLIFE MANAGEMENT
Fort Hays State U, KS B
Grand Valley State U, MI B
Michigan State U, MI B
Northland Coll, WI B
Northwest Missouri State U, MO B
The Ohio State U, OH B
Oklahoma State U, OK B
Peru State Coll, NE B
Pittsburg State U, KS B
Purdue U, IN B
Purdue U Calumet, IN B
South Dakota State U, SD B
Southeastern Oklahoma State U, OK B
Southwest Missouri State U, MO B
U of Minnesota, Crookston, MN A
U of Wisconsin–Madison, WI B
U of Wisconsin–Stevens Point, WI B
Waldorf Coll, IA A
Winona State U, MN A,B

WIND/PERCUSSION INSTRUMENTS
Alma Coll, MI B
Augustana Coll, IL B
Baldwin-Wallace Coll, OH B
Ball State U, IN B
Bowling Green State U, OH B
Butler U, IN B
Capital U, OH B
Chicago State U, IL B
Cleveland Inst of Music, OH B
Concordia U, IL B
DePaul U, IL B
Grand Valley State U, MI B
Illinois Wesleyan U, IL B
Indiana U Bloomington, IN B
Lawrence U, WI B
Luther Coll, IA B
Minnesota State U, Mankato, MN B
Minnesota State U, Moorhead, MN B
Mount Vernon Nazarene U, OH B
Northern Michigan U, MI B
Northwestern U, IL B
Northwest Missouri State U, MO B
Oberlin Coll, OH B
Oklahoma Baptist U, OK B
Oklahoma Christian U, OK B
Oklahoma City U, OK B
Olivet Nazarene U, IL B
Otterbein Coll, OH B
Peru State Coll, NE B
Pittsburg State U, KS B
Roosevelt U, IL B
Southwestern Oklahoma State U, OK B
The U of Akron, OH B
U of Central Oklahoma, OK B
U of Cincinnati, OH B
The U of Iowa, IA B
U of Kansas, KS B
U of Michigan, MI B
U of Missouri–Kansas City, MO B
U of Oklahoma, OK B
U of Sioux Falls, SD B
The U of South Dakota, SD B
U of Wisconsin–Milwaukee, WI B

WOMEN'S STUDIES
Albion Coll, MI B
Antioch Coll, OH B
Augsburg Coll, MN B
Augustana Coll, IL B
Beloit Coll, WI B
Bowling Green State U, OH B
Carleton Coll, MN B
Case Western Reserve U, OH B
Coll of St. Catherine, MN B
The Coll of Wooster, OH B
Cornell Coll, IA B
Denison U, OH B
DePaul U, IL B
DePauw U, IN B
Earlham Coll, IN B
Eastern Michigan U, MI B
Grand Valley State U, MI B
Grinnell Coll, IA B
Hamline U, MN B
Indiana U Bloomington, IN B
Indiana U–Purdue U Fort Wayne, IN A,B
Indiana U South Bend, IN B
Iowa State U of Science and Technology, IA B
Kansas State U, KS B
Kenyon Coll, OH B
Knox Coll, IL B
Lake Forest Coll, IL B
Macalester Coll, MN B
Marquette U, WI B
Metropolitan State U, MN B
Michigan State U, MI B
Minnesota State U, Mankato, MN B
Nebraska Wesleyan U, NE B
Northeastern Illinois U, IL B
Northwestern U, IL B
Oakland U, MI B
Oberlin Coll, OH B
The Ohio State U, OH B
Ohio U, OH B
Ohio Wesleyan U, OH B
Purdue U Calumet, IN B
Roosevelt U, IL B
St. Olaf Coll, MN B
The U of Iowa, IA B
U of Kansas, KS B
U of Michigan, MI B
U of Michigan–Dearborn, MI B
U of Minnesota, Duluth, MN B
U of Minnesota, Morris, MN B
U of Minnesota, Twin Cities Campus, MN B
U of Nebraska–Lincoln, NE B
U of Oklahoma, OK B
U of St. Thomas, MN B
U of Toledo, OH B
U of Wisconsin–Madison, WI B
U of Wisconsin–Milwaukee, WI B
U of Wisconsin–Whitewater, WI B
Washington U in St. Louis, MO B
Wayne State U, MI B
Western Illinois U, IL B
Western Michigan U, MI B
Wichita State U, KS B

WOOD SCIENCE/PAPER TECHNOLOGY
Miami U, OH B
Pittsburg State U, KS B
U of Minnesota, Twin Cities Campus, MN B
U of Wisconsin–Stevens Point, WI B

ZOOLOGY
Andrews U, MI B
Ball State U, IN B
Central Christian Coll of Kansas, KS A
Iowa State U of Science and Technology, IA B
Kent State U, OH B
Lincoln Coll, Lincoln, IL A
Miami U, OH B
Miami U–Middletown Campus, OH A
Michigan State U, MI B
North Dakota State U, ND B
Northeastern State U, OK B
Northern Michigan U, MI B

Zoology (continued)
Northland Coll, WI B
Northwest Missouri State U, MO B
The Ohio State U, OH B
Ohio U, OH B
Ohio Wesleyan U, OH B
Oklahoma State U, OK B
Olivet Nazarene U, IL B
St. Cloud State U, MN B
Southeastern Oklahoma State U, OK B
Southern Illinois U Carbondale, IL B
The U of Akron, OH B
U of Michigan, MI B
U of Oklahoma, OK B
The U of South Dakota, SD B
U of Wisconsin–Madison, WI B
U of Wisconsin–Milwaukee, WI B
Winona State U, MN B

Athletic Programs and Scholarships

M—for men; W—for women; (s)—scholarship offered

ARCHERY

Case Western Reserve U, OH M, W
Miami U, OH M, W
North Dakota State U, ND M, W
Purdue U, IN M, W

BADMINTON

The Coll of Wooster, OH M, W
Dickinson State U, ND M, W
Purdue U, IN M, W
Washington U in St. Louis, MO M, W

BASEBALL

Adrian Coll, MI M
Albion Coll, MI M
Alma Coll, MI M
Ancilla Coll, IN M(s)
Anderson U, IN M
Aquinas Coll, MI M(s)
Ashland U, OH M(s)
Augsburg Coll, MN M
Augustana Coll, IL M
Augustana Coll, SD M
Aurora U, IL M
Avila U, MO M(s)
Bacone Coll, OK M(s)
Baker U, KS M(s)
Baldwin-Wallace Coll, OH M
Ball State U, IN M(s)
Barclay Coll, KS M
Bellevue U, NE M(s)
Beloit Coll, WI M
Bemidji State U, MN M(s)
Benedictine Coll, KS M(s)
Benedictine U, IL M
Bethany Coll, KS M(s)
Bethany Lutheran Coll, MN M(s)
Bethel Coll, IN M(s)
Bethel Coll, MN M
Blackburn Coll, IL M
Blessing-Rieman Coll of Nursing, IL M(s), W(s)
Bluffton Coll, OH M
Bowling Green State U, OH M(s)
Bradley U, IL M(s)
Briar Cliff U, IA M(s)
Buena Vista U, IA M
Butler U, IN M(s)
Calumet Coll of Saint Joseph, IN M
Calvin Coll, MI M
Cameron U, OK M(s)
Capital U, OH M
Cardinal Stritch U, WI M
Carleton Coll, MN M
Carroll Coll, WI M
Carthage Coll, WI M
Case Western Reserve U, OH M
Cedarville U, OH M(s)
Central Christian Coll of Kansas, KS M(s)
Central Coll, IA M
Central Methodist Coll, MO M(s)
Central Michigan U, MI M(s)
Central Missouri State U, MO M(s)
Chicago State U, IL M
Circleville Bible Coll, OH M
Clarke Coll, IA M
Cleveland State U, OH M(s)
Coe Coll, IA M
Coll of Mount St. Joseph, OH M
The Coll of St. Scholastica, MN M
Coll of the Ozarks, MO M(s)
The Coll of Wooster, OH M
Concordia Coll, MN M
Concordia U, IL M
Concordia U, MI M(s)
Concordia U, MN M(s)
Concordia U, NE M(s)
Concordia U Wisconsin, WI M
Cornell Coll, IA M
Creighton U, NE M(s)
Crossroads Coll, MN M
Crown Coll, MN M
Culver-Stockton Coll, MO M(s)
Dakota State U, SD M
Dakota Wesleyan U, SD M(s)
Dana Coll, NE M(s)
Defiance Coll, OH M
Denison U, OH M
DePauw U, IN M
Dickinson State U, ND M(s)
Doane Coll, NE M(s)
Dominican U, IL M
Earlham Coll, IN M
East Central U, OK M(s)
Eastern Illinois U, IL M(s)
Eastern Michigan U, MI M(s)
Edgewood Coll, WI M
Elmhurst Coll, IL M
Emporia State U, KS M(s)
Eureka Coll, IL M
Evangel U, MO M(s)
Finlandia U, MI M
Fontbonne U, MO M
Fort Hays State U, KS M(s)
The Franciscan U, IA M(s)
Franklin Coll, IN M
Goshen Coll, IN M(s)
Grace Coll, IN M(s)
Graceland U, IA M(s)
Grand Valley State U, MI M(s)
Grand View Coll, IA M(s)
Greenville Coll, IL M
Grinnell Coll, IA M
Gustavus Adolphus Coll, MN M
Hamline U, MN M
Hannibal-LaGrange Coll, MO M(s)
Hanover Coll, IN M
Harris-Stowe State Coll, MO M(s)
Hastings Coll, NE M(s)
Heidelberg Coll, OH M
Hesston Coll, KS M(s)
Hillsdale Coll, MI M(s)
Hillsdale Free Will Baptist Coll, OK M
Hiram Coll, OH M
Hope Coll, MI M
Huntington Coll, IN M(s)
Illinois Coll, IL M
Illinois Inst of Technology, IL M(s)
Illinois State U, IL M(s)
Illinois Wesleyan U, IL M
Indiana Inst of Technology, IN M(s)
Indiana State U, IN M(s)
Indiana U Bloomington, IN M(s)
Indiana U Northwest, IN M
Indiana U–Purdue U Fort Wayne, IN M(s)
Indiana U–Purdue U Indianapolis, IN M(s)
Indiana Wesleyan U, IN M(s)
Iowa Wesleyan Coll, IA M(s)
Jamestown Coll, ND M(s)
John Carroll U, OH M
Judson Coll, IL M(s)
Kalamazoo Coll, MI M
Kansas State U, KS M(s)
Kent State U, OH M(s)
Kenyon Coll, OH M
Knox Coll, IL M
Lake Erie Coll, OH M
Lake Forest Coll, IL M
Lakeland Coll, WI M
Lawrence U, WI M
Lewis U, IL M(s)
Lincoln Christian Coll, IL M
Lincoln Coll, Lincoln, IL M(s)
Lincoln Coll, Normal, IL M
Lindenwood U, MO M(s)
Loras Coll, IA M
Luther Coll, IA M
Macalester Coll, MN M
MacMurray Coll, IL M
Madonna U, MI M(s)
Malone Coll, OH M(s)
Manchester Coll, IN M
Maranatha Baptist Bible Coll, WI M
Marian Coll, IN M(s)
Marian Coll of Fond du Lac, WI M
Marietta Coll, OH M
Marquette U, WI M
Martin Luther Coll, MN M
Maryville U of Saint Louis, MO M
Mayville State U, ND M(s)
McKendree Coll, IL M(s)
Miami U, OH M(s)
Miami U–Hamilton Campus, OH M
Miami U–Middletown Campus, OH M
Michigan State U, MI M
MidAmerica Nazarene U, KS M(s)
Midland Lutheran Coll, NE M(s)
Millikin U, IL M
Milwaukee School of Engineering, WI M
Minnesota State U, Mankato, MN M(s)
Minot State U, ND M(s)
Missouri Southern State Coll, MO M(s)
Missouri Valley Coll, MO M(s)
Missouri Western State Coll, MO M(s)
Monmouth Coll, IL M
Mount Marty Coll, SD M(s)
Mount Mercy Coll, IA M
Mount Union Coll, OH M
Mount Vernon Nazarene U, OH M(s)
Muskingum Coll, OH M
Nebraska Wesleyan U, NE M
Newman U, KS M(s)
North Central Coll, IL M
North Dakota State U, ND M(s)
Northeastern State U, OK M(s)
Northern Illinois U, IL M(s)
Northern State U, SD M
Northland Coll, WI M
North Park U, IL M
Northwestern Coll, IA M(s)
Northwestern Coll, MN M
Northwestern Oklahoma State U, OK M(s)
Northwestern U, IL M(s)
Northwest Missouri State U, MO M(s)
Northwood U, MI M(s)
Oakland City U, IN M(s)
Oakland U, MI M(s)

Baseball (continued)

Oberlin Coll, OH	M
Ohio Dominican U, OH	M(s)
Ohio Northern U, OH	M
The Ohio State U, OH	M(s)
Ohio U, OH	M(s)
Ohio U–Chillicothe, OH	M
Ohio U–Zanesville, OH	M
Ohio Wesleyan U, OH	M
Oklahoma Baptist U, OK	M(s)
Oklahoma City U, OK	M(s)
Oklahoma Panhandle State U, OK	M(s)
Oklahoma State U, OK	M(s)
Oklahoma Wesleyan U, OK	M(s)
Olivet Coll, MI	M
Olivet Nazarene U, IL	M(s)
Oral Roberts U, OK	M(s)
Ottawa U, KS	M(s)
Otterbein Coll, OH	M
Park U, MO	M(s)
Peru State Coll, NE	M(s)
Pillsbury Baptist Bible Coll, MN	M
Pittsburg State U, KS	M(s)
Principia Coll, IL	M
Purdue U, IN	M(s)
Quincy U, IL	M(s)
Research Coll of Nursing, MO	M(s)
Ripon Coll, WI	M
Robert Morris Coll, IL	M(s)
Rochester Coll, MI	M(s)
Rochester Comm and Tech Coll, MN	M
Rockford Coll, IL	M
Rockhurst U, MO	M(s)
Rose-Hulman Inst of Technology, IN	M
Saginaw Valley State U, MI	M(s)
St. Ambrose U, IA	M(s)
St. Cloud State U, MN	M(s)
St. Gregory's U, OK	M(s)
Saint John's U, MN	M
Saint Joseph's Coll, IN	M(s)
St. Louis Christian Coll, MO	M
Saint Louis U, MO	M(s)
Saint Mary's Coll of Madonna U, MI	M
Saint Mary's U of Minnesota, MN	M
Saint Mary U, KS	M(s)
St. Norbert Coll, WI	M
St. Olaf Coll, MN	M
Saint Xavier U, IL	M(s)
Shawnee State U, OH	M
Siena Heights U, MI	M(s)
Simpson Coll, IA	M
Si Tanka Huron U, SD	M(s)
South Dakota State U, SD	M(s)
Southeastern Oklahoma State U, OK	M(s)
Southeast Missouri State U, MO	M(s)
Southern Illinois U Carbondale, IL	M(s)
Southern Illinois U Edwardsville, IL	M(s)
Southern Nazarene U, OK	M(s)
Southwest Baptist U, MO	M(s)
Southwestern Oklahoma State U, OK	M(s)
Southwest Minnesota State U, MN	M(s)
Southwest Missouri State U, MO	M(s)
Spring Arbor U, MI	M(s)
Springfield Coll in Illinois, IL	M(s)
Sterling Coll, KS	M(s)
Tabor Coll, KS	M(s)
Taylor U, IN	M(s)
Tiffin U, OH	M(s)
Trinity Bible Coll, ND	M
Trinity Christian Coll, IL	M(s)
Trinity International U, IL	M(s)
Tri-State U, IN	M
Truman State U, MO	M(s)
The U of Akron, OH	M(s)
U of Central Oklahoma, OK	M(s)
U of Chicago, IL	M
U of Dayton, OH	M(s)
U of Dubuque, IA	M
U of Evansville, IN	M(s)
The U of Findlay, OH	M(s)
U of Illinois at Chicago, IL	M(s)
U of Illinois at Urbana–Champaign, IL	M(s)
U of Indianapolis, IN	M(s)
The U of Iowa, IA	M(s)
U of Kansas, KS	M(s)
U of Mary, ND	M(s)
U of Michigan, MI	M(s)
U of Minnesota, Crookston, MN	M(s)
U of Minnesota, Duluth, MN	M(s)
U of Minnesota, Morris, MN	M
U of Minnesota, Twin Cities Campus, MN	M(s)
U of Missouri–Columbia, MO	M(s)
U of Missouri–Rolla, MO	M(s)
U of Missouri–St. Louis, MO	M(s)
U of Nebraska at Kearney, NE	M(s)
U of Nebraska at Omaha, NE	M(s)
U of Nebraska–Lincoln, NE	M(s)
U of North Dakota, ND	M(s)
U of Northern Iowa, IA	M(s)
U of Notre Dame, IN	M(s)
U of Oklahoma, OK	M(s)
U of Rio Grande, OH	M(s)
U of St. Francis, IL	M(s)
U of Saint Francis, IN	M(s)
U of St. Thomas, MN	M
U of Science and Arts of Oklahoma, OK	M(s)
U of Sioux Falls, SD	M(s)
The U of South Dakota, SD	M(s)
U of Southern Indiana, IN	M(s)
U of Toledo, OH	M(s)
U of Wisconsin–La Crosse, WI	M
U of Wisconsin–Milwaukee, WI	M
U of Wisconsin–Oshkosh, WI	M
U of Wisconsin–Parkside, WI	M(s)
U of Wisconsin–Platteville, WI	M
U of Wisconsin–Stevens Point, WI	M
U of Wisconsin–Stout, WI	M
U of Wisconsin–Superior, WI	M
U of Wisconsin–Whitewater, WI	M
Upper Iowa U, IA	M
Urbana U, OH	M(s)
Valley City State U, ND	M(s)
Valparaiso U, IN	M(s)
Viterbo U, WI	M(s)
Wabash Coll, IN	M
Waldorf Coll, IA	M(s)
Walsh U, OH	M(s)
Wartburg Coll, IA	M
Washington U in St. Louis, MO	M
Wayne State Coll, NE	M(s)
Wayne State U, MI	M
Webster U, MO	M
Western Illinois U, IL	M(s)
Western Michigan U, MI	M(s)
Westminster Coll, MO	M
Wheaton Coll, IL	M
Wichita State U, KS	M(s)
William Jewell Coll, MO	M(s)
William Penn U, IA	M(s)
William Woods U, MO	M(s)
Wilmington Coll, OH	M
Winona State U, MN	M(s)
Wisconsin Lutheran Coll, WI	M
Wittenberg U, OH	M
Wright State U, OH	M(s)
Xavier U, OH	M(s)
York Coll, NE	M(s)
Youngstown State U, OH	M(s)

BASKETBALL

Adrian Coll, MI	M, W
Albion Coll, MI	M, W
Alma Coll, MI	M, W
Alverno Coll, WI	W
Ancilla Coll, IN	M(s), W(s)
Anderson U, IN	M, W
Aquinas Coll, MI	M(s), W(s)
Ashland U, OH	M(s), W(s)
Augsburg Coll, MN	M, W
Augustana Coll, IL	M, W
Augustana Coll, SD	M(s), W(s)
Aurora U, IL	M, W
Avila U, MO	M(s), W(s)
Bacone Coll, OK	M(s), W(s)
Baker U, KS	M(s), W(s)
Baldwin-Wallace Coll, OH	M, W
Ball State U, IN	M(s), W(s)
Baptist Bible Coll, MO	M, W
Barclay Coll, KS	M, W
Bellevue U, NE	M(s)
Beloit Coll, WI	M, W
Bemidji State U, MN	M(s), W(s)
Benedictine Coll, KS	M(s), W(s)
Benedictine U, IL	M, W
Bethany Coll, KS	M(s), W(s)
Bethany Lutheran Coll, MN	M(s), W(s)
Bethel Coll, IN	M(s), W(s)
Bethel Coll, KS	M(s), W(s)
Bethel Coll, MN	M, W
Blackburn Coll, IL	M, W
Black Hills State U, SD	M(s), W(s)
Blessing-Rieman Coll of Nursing, IL	M(s), W(s)
Bluffton Coll, OH	M, W
Bowling Green State U, OH	M(s), W(s)
Bradley U, IL	M(s), W(s)
Briar Cliff U, IA	M(s), W(s)
Buena Vista U, IA	M, W
Butler U, IN	M(s), W(s)
Calumet Coll of Saint Joseph, IN	M, W
Calvin Coll, MI	M, W
Cameron U, OK	M(s), W(s)
Capital U, OH	M, W
Cardinal Stritch U, WI	M, W
Carleton Coll, MN	M, W
Carroll Coll, WI	M, W
Carthage Coll, WI	M, W
Case Western Reserve U, OH	M, W
Cedarville U, OH	M(s), W(s)
Central Bible Coll, MO	M, W
Central Christian Coll of Kansas, KS	M(s), W(s)
Central Coll, IA	M, W
Central Methodist Coll, MO	M(s), W(s)
Central Michigan U, MI	M(s), W(s)
Central Missouri State U, MO	M(s), W(s)
Chadron State Coll, NE	M(s), W(s)
Chicago State U, IL	M(s), W(s)
Cincinnati Bible Coll and Seminary, OH	M, W
Circleville Bible Coll, OH	M, W
Clarke Coll, IA	M, W
Cleveland State U, OH	M(s), W(s)
Coe Coll, IA	M, W
Coll of Mount St. Joseph, OH	M, W
Coll of Saint Benedict, MN	W
Coll of St. Catherine, MN	W
Coll of Saint Mary, NE	W(s)
The Coll of St. Scholastica, MN	M, W
Coll of the Ozarks, MO	M(s), W(s)
The Coll of Wooster, OH	M, W
Columbia Coll, MO	M(s), W(s)
Concordia Coll, MN	M, W
Concordia U, IL	M, W
Concordia U, MI	M(s), W(s)
Concordia U, MN	M(s), W(s)
Concordia U, NE	M(s), W(s)
Concordia U Wisconsin, WI	M, W

College	Programs
Cornell Coll, IA	M, W
Cornerstone U, MI	M(s), W(s)
Cottey Coll, MO	W
Creighton U, NE	M(s), W(s)
Crossroads Coll, MN	M, W
Crown Coll, MN	M, W
Culver-Stockton Coll, MO	M(s), W(s)
Dakota State U, SD	M(s), W(s)
Dakota Wesleyan U, SD	M(s), W(s)
Dana Coll, NE	M(s), W(s)
Davenport U, Grand Rapids, MI	W
Defiance Coll, OH	M, W
Denison U, OH	M, W
DePaul U, IL	M(s), W(s)
DePauw U, IN	M, W
Dickinson State U, ND	M(s), W(s)
Doane Coll, NE	M(s), W(s)
Dominican U, IL	M, W
Dordt Coll, IA	M(s), W(s)
Drake U, IA	M(s), W(s)
Drury U, MO	M(s)
Earlham Coll, IN	M, W
East Central U, OK	M(s), W(s)
Eastern Illinois U, IL	M(s), W(s)
Eastern Michigan U, MI	M(s), W(s)
Edgewood Coll, WI	M, W
Elmhurst Coll, IL	M, W
Emmaus Bible Coll, IA	M, W
Emporia State U, KS	M(s), W(s)
Eureka Coll, IL	M, W
Evangel U, MO	M(s), W(s)
Faith Baptist Bible Coll and Theological Seminary, IA	M, W
Ferris State U, MI	M(s), W(s)
Finlandia U, MI	M, W
Fontbonne U, MO	M, W
Fort Hays State U, KS	M(s), W(s)
The Franciscan U, IA	M(s), W(s)
Franklin Coll, IN	M, W
Goshen Coll, IN	M(s), W(s)
Grace Bible Coll, MI	M, W
Grace Coll, IN	M(s), W(s)
Graceland U, IA	M(s), W(s)
Grace U, NE	M, W
Grand Valley State U, MI	M(s), W(s)
Grand View Coll, IA	M(s), W(s)
Great Lakes Christian Coll, MI	M, W
Greenville Coll, IL	M, W
Grinnell Coll, IA	M, W
Gustavus Adolphus Coll, MN	M, W
Hamline U, MN	M, W
Hannibal-LaGrange Coll, MO	M(s), W(s)
Hanover Coll, IN	M, W
Harris-Stowe State Coll, MO	M(s), W(s)
Haskell Indian Nations U, KS	M, W
Hastings Coll, NE	M(s), W(s)
Heidelberg Coll, OH	M, W
Hesston Coll, KS	M(s), W(s)
Hillsdale Coll, MI	M(s), W(s)
Hillsdale Free Will Baptist Coll, OK	M, W
Hiram Coll, OH	M, W
Hope Coll, MI	M, W
Huntington Coll, IN	M(s), W(s)
Illinois Inst of Technology, IL	M(s), W(s)
Illinois State U, IL	M(s), W(s)
Illinois Wesleyan U, IL	M, W
Indiana Inst of Technology, IN	M(s), W(s)
Indiana State U, IN	M(s), W(s)
Indiana U Bloomington, IN	M(s), W(s)
Indiana U Northwest, IN	M
Indiana U–Purdue U Fort Wayne, IN	M(s), W(s)
Indiana U–Purdue U Indianapolis, IN	M(s), W(s)
Indiana U South Bend, IN	M(s), W(s)
Indiana U Southeast, IN	M(s), W(s)
Indiana Wesleyan U, IN	M(s), W(s)
Iowa State U of Science and Technology, IA	M(s), W(s)
Iowa Wesleyan Coll, IA	M(s), W(s)
Jamestown Coll, ND	M(s), W(s)
John Carroll U, OH	M, W
Judson Coll, IL	M(s), W(s)
Kalamazoo Coll, MI	M, W
Kansas State U, KS	M(s), W(s)
Kendall Coll, IL	M, W
Kent State U, OH	M(s), W(s)
Kenyon Coll, OH	M, W
Knox Coll, IL	M, W
Lake Erie Coll, OH	M, W
Lake Forest Coll, IL	M, W
Lakeland Coll, WI	M, W
Langston U, OK	M(s), W(s)
Lawrence U, WI	M, W
Lewis Coll of Business, MI	M
Lewis U, IL	M(s), W(s)
Lincoln Christian Coll, IL	M, W
Lincoln Coll, Lincoln, IL	M(s), W(s)
Lincoln Coll, Normal, IL	M, W
Lindenwood U, MO	M(s), W(s)
Loras Coll, IA	M, W
Loyola U Chicago, IL	M(s), W(s)
Luther Coll, IA	M, W
Macalester Coll, MN	M, W
MacMurray Coll, IL	M, W
Madonna U, MI	M(s), W(s)
Maharishi U of Management, IA	M
Malone Coll, OH	M(s), W(s)
Manchester Coll, IN	M, W
Manhattan Christian Coll, KS	M, W
Maranatha Baptist Bible Coll, WI	M, W
Marian Coll, IN	M(s), W(s)
Marian Coll of Fond du Lac, WI	M, W
Marietta Coll, OH	M, W
Marquette U, WI	M(s), W(s)
Martin Luther Coll, MN	M, W
Marygrove Coll, MI	M, W
Maryville U of Saint Louis, MO	M, W
Mayville State U, ND	M(s), W(s)
McKendree Coll, IL	M(s), W(s)
McPherson Coll, KS	M, W
Messenger Coll, MO	M, W
Miami U, OH	M(s), W(s)
Miami U–Hamilton Campus, OH	M, W
Miami U–Middletown Campus, OH	M, W
Michigan State U, MI	M(s), W(s)
Michigan Technological U, MI	M(s), W(s)
MidAmerica Nazarene U, KS	M(s), W(s)
Midland Lutheran Coll, NE	M(s), W(s)
Millikin U, IL	M, W
Milwaukee School of Engineering, WI	M, W
Minnesota State U, Mankato, MN	M(s), W(s)
Minnesota State U, Moorhead, MN	M(s), W(s)
Minot State U, ND	M(s), W(s)
Missouri Southern State Coll, MO	M(s), W(s)
Missouri Valley Coll, MO	M(s), W(s)
Missouri Western State Coll, MO	M(s), W(s)
Monmouth Coll, IL	M, W
Moody Bible Inst, IL	M, W
Mount Marty Coll, SD	M(s), W(s)
Mount Mary Coll, WI	W
Mount Mercy Coll, IA	M, W
Mount Union Coll, OH	M, W
Mount Vernon Nazarene U, OH	M(s), W(s)
Muskingum Coll, OH	M, W
Nebraska Christian Coll, NE	M, W
Nebraska Wesleyan U, NE	M, W
Newman U, KS	M(s), W(s)
North Central Coll, IL	M, W
North Dakota State U, ND	M(s), W(s)
Northeastern State U, OK	M(s), W(s)
Northern Illinois U, IL	M(s), W(s)
Northern Michigan U, MI	M(s), W(s)
Northern State U, SD	M(s), W(s)
Northland Coll, WI	M, W
North Park U, IL	M, W
Northwestern Coll, IA	M(s), W(s)
Northwestern Coll, MN	M, W
Northwestern Oklahoma State U, OK	M(s), W(s)
Northwestern U, IL	M(s), W(s)
Northwest Missouri State U, MO	M(s), W(s)
Northwood U, MI	M(s), W(s)
Notre Dame Coll, OH	W
Oak Hills Christian Coll, MN	M
Oakland City U, IN	M(s), W(s)
Oakland U, MI	M(s), W(s)
Oberlin Coll, OH	M, W
Ohio Dominican U, OH	M(s), W(s)
Ohio Northern U, OH	M, W
The Ohio State U, OH	M(s), W(s)
The Ohio State U at Lima, OH	M, W
Ohio U, OH	M(s), W(s)
Ohio U–Chillicothe, OH	M, W
Ohio U–Lancaster, OH	M, W
Ohio U–Southern Campus, OH	M, W
Ohio U–Zanesville, OH	M, W
Ohio Wesleyan U, OH	M, W
Oklahoma Baptist U, OK	M(s), W(s)
Oklahoma Christian U, OK	M(s), W(s)
Oklahoma City U, OK	M(s), W(s)
Oklahoma Panhandle State U, OK	M(s), W(s)
Oklahoma State U, OK	M(s), W(s)
Oklahoma Wesleyan U, OK	M(s), W(s)
Olivet Coll, MI	M, W
Olivet Nazarene U, IL	M(s), W(s)
Oral Roberts U, OK	M(s), W(s)
Ottawa U, KS	M(s), W(s)
Otterbein Coll, OH	M, W
Ozark Christian Coll, MO	M, W
Park U, MO	M(s), W(s)
Peru State Coll, NE	M(s), W(s)
Pillsbury Baptist Bible Coll, MN	M, W
Pittsburg State U, KS	M(s), W(s)
Presentation Coll, SD	M, W
Principia Coll, IL	M, W
Purdue U, IN	M(s), W(s)
Purdue U Calumet, IN	M(s), W(s)
Quincy U, IL	M(s), W(s)
Research Coll of Nursing, MO	M(s), W(s)
Ripon Coll, WI	M, W
Robert Morris Coll, IL	M(s), W(s)
Rochester Coll, MI	M(s), W(s)
Rochester Comm and Tech Coll, MN	M, W
Rockford Coll, IL	M, W
Rockhurst U, MO	M(s), W(s)
Rose-Hulman Inst of Technology, IN	M, W
Saginaw Valley State U, MI	M(s), W(s)
St. Ambrose U, IA	M(s), W(s)
St. Cloud State U, MN	M(s), W(s)
St. Gregory's U, OK	M(s), W(s)
Saint John's U, MN	M
Saint Joseph's Coll, IN	M(s), W(s)
St. Louis Christian Coll, MO	M
St. Louis Coll of Pharmacy, MO	M, W
Saint Louis U, MO	M(s), W(s)
Saint Mary-of-the-Woods Coll, IN	W(s)
Saint Mary's Coll, IN	W
Saint Mary's Coll of Madonna U, MI	M
Saint Mary's U of Minnesota, MN	M, W
Saint Mary U, KS	M(s), W(s)
St. Norbert Coll, WI	M, W
St. Olaf Coll, MN	M, W
Saint Xavier U, IL	M(s)
Sanford-Brown Coll, Fenton, MO	M
Shawnee State U, OH	M, W
Siena Heights U, MI	M(s), W(s)
Silver Lake Coll, WI	W
Simpson Coll, IA	M, W
Si Tanka Huron U, SD	M(s), W(s)
Sitting Bull Coll, ND	M, W

Basketball (continued)

South Dakota School of Mines and Technology, SD	M(s), W(s)
South Dakota State U, SD	M(s), W(s)
Southeastern Oklahoma State U, OK	M(s), W(s)
Southeast Missouri State U, MO	M(s), W(s)
Southern Illinois U Carbondale, IL	M(s), W(s)
Southern Illinois U Edwardsville, IL	M(s), W(s)
Southern Nazarene U, OK	M(s), W(s)
Southwest Baptist U, MO	M(s), W(s)
Southwestern Coll, KS	M(s), W(s)
Southwestern Oklahoma State U, OK	M(s), W(s)
Southwest Minnesota State U, MN	M(s), W(s)
Southwest Missouri State U, MO	M(s), W(s)
Spring Arbor U, MI	M(s), W(s)
Springfield Coll in Illinois, IL	M(s)
Stephens Coll, MO	W
Sterling Coll, KS	M(s), W(s)
Tabor Coll, KS	M(s), W(s)
Taylor U, IN	M(s), W(s)
Taylor U, Fort Wayne Campus, IN	M, W
Tiffin U, OH	M(s), W(s)
Trinity Bible Coll, ND	M, W
Trinity Christian Coll, IL	M(s), W(s)
Trinity International U, IL	M(s), W(s)
Tri-State U, IN	M, W
Truman State U, MO	M(s), W(s)
Union Coll, NE	M, W
The U of Akron, OH	M(s), W(s)
U of Central Oklahoma, OK	M(s), W(s)
U of Chicago, IL	M, W
U of Cincinnati, OH	M(s), W(s)
U of Dayton, OH	M(s), W(s)
U of Dubuque, IA	M, W
U of Evansville, IN	M(s), W(s)
The U of Findlay, OH	M(s), W(s)
U of Illinois at Chicago, IL	M(s), W(s)
U of Illinois at Springfield, IL	W(s)
U of Illinois at Urbana–Champaign, IL	M(s), W(s)
U of Indianapolis, IN	M(s), W(s)
The U of Iowa, IA	M(s), W(s)
U of Kansas, KS	M(s), W(s)
U of Mary, ND	M(s), W(s)
U of Michigan, MI	M(s), W(s)
U of Michigan–Dearborn, MI	M(s), W(s)
U of Minnesota, Crookston, MN	M(s), W(s)
U of Minnesota, Duluth, MN	M(s), W(s)
U of Minnesota, Morris, MN	M(s), W(s)
U of Minnesota, Twin Cities Campus, MN	M(s), W(s)
U of Missouri–Columbia, MO	M(s), W(s)
U of Missouri–Kansas City, MO	M(s), W(s)
U of Missouri–Rolla, MO	M(s), W(s)
U of Missouri–St. Louis, MO	M(s), W(s)
U of Nebraska at Kearney, NE	M(s), W(s)
U of Nebraska at Omaha, NE	M(s), W(s)
U of Nebraska–Lincoln, NE	M(s), W(s)
U of North Dakota, ND	M(s), W(s)
U of Northern Iowa, IA	M(s), W(s)
U of Notre Dame, IN	M(s), W(s)
U of Oklahoma, OK	M(s), W(s)
U of Rio Grande, OH	M(s), W(s)
U of St. Francis, IL	M(s), W(s)
U of Saint Francis, IN	M(s), W(s)
U of St. Thomas, MN	M, W
U of Science and Arts of Oklahoma, OK	M(s), W(s)
U of Sioux Falls, SD	M(s), W(s)
The U of South Dakota, SD	M(s), W(s)
U of Southern Indiana, IN	M(s), W(s)
U of Toledo, OH	M(s), W(s)
U of Tulsa, OK	M(s), W(s)
U of Wisconsin–Eau Claire, WI	M, W
U of Wisconsin–Green Bay, WI	M(s), W(s)
U of Wisconsin–La Crosse, WI	M, W
U of Wisconsin–Madison, WI	M(s), W(s)
U of Wisconsin–Milwaukee, WI	M(s), W(s)
U of Wisconsin–Oshkosh, WI	M, W
U of Wisconsin–Parkside, WI	M(s), W(s)
U of Wisconsin–Platteville, WI	M, W
U of Wisconsin–River Falls, WI	M, W
U of Wisconsin–Stevens Point, WI	M, W
U of Wisconsin–Stout, WI	M, W
U of Wisconsin–Superior, WI	M, W
U of Wisconsin–Whitewater, WI	M, W
Upper Iowa U, IA	M, W
Urbana U, OH	M(s), W(s)
Ursuline Coll, OH	W(s)
Valley City State U, ND	M(s), W(s)
Valparaiso U, IN	M(s), W(s)
Vennard Coll, IA	M, W
Viterbo U, WI	M(s), W(s)
Wabash Coll, IN	M
Waldorf Coll, IA	M(s), W(s)
Walsh U, OH	M(s), W(s)
Wartburg Coll, IA	M, W
Washington U in St. Louis, MO	M, W
Wayne State Coll, NE	M(s), W(s)
Wayne State U, MI	M(s), W(s)
Webster U, MO	M, W
Western Illinois U, IL	M(s), W(s)
Western Michigan U, MI	M(s), W(s)
Westminster Coll, MO	M, W
Wheaton Coll, IL	M, W
Wichita State U, KS	M(s), W(s)
Wilberforce U, OH	M, W
William Jewell Coll, MO	M(s), W(s)
William Penn U, IA	M(s), W(s)
William Woods U, MO	W(s)
Wilmington Coll, OH	M, W
Winona State U, MN	M(s), W(s)
Wisconsin Lutheran Coll, WI	M, W
Wittenberg U, OH	M, W
Wright State U, OH	M(s), W(s)
Xavier U, OH	M(s), W(s)
York Coll, NE	M(s), W(s)
Youngstown State U, OH	M(s), W(s)

BOWLING

Central Missouri State U, MO	M, W
Indiana State U, IN	M, W
Lindenwood U, MO	M(s), W(s)
McKendree Coll, IL	M(s), W(s)
North Dakota State U, ND	M, W
Saginaw Valley State U, MI	M(s)
St. Cloud State U, MN	M, W
Southwest Missouri State U, MO	M, W
U of Minnesota, Duluth, MN	M, W
U of Nebraska–Lincoln, NE	M
U of Wisconsin–Whitewater, WI	M, W
Wichita State U, KS	M, W
Winona State U, MN	M, W
Wittenberg U, OH	W

CHEERLEADING

Albion Coll, MI	M, W
Augustana Coll, SD	W
Avila U, MO	W(s)
Bacone Coll, OK	M(s), W(s)
Barclay Coll, KS	M, W
Benedictine Coll, KS	M(s), W(s)
Bethel Coll, IN	M(s), W(s)
Bradley U, IL	M, W
Calvin Coll, MI	M, W
Cedarville U, OH	M, W
Central Christian Coll of Kansas, KS	M, W
Coe Coll, IA	W
The Coll of Wooster, OH	W
Columbia Coll, MO	W
Concordia Coll, MN	W
Concordia U, IL	M, W
Dakota State U, SD	M, W
Dakota Wesleyan U, SD	M(s), W(s)
DePauw U, IN	M, W
Drake U, IA	M(s), W(s)
Emporia State U, KS	M(s), W(s)
Ferris State U, MI	M, W
Fontbonne U, MO	W
Grace Coll, IN	M(s), W(s)
Harris-Stowe State Coll, MO	W(s)
Haskell Indian Nations U, KS	M, W
Hillsdale Coll, MI	M, W
Hope Coll, MI	M, W
Illinois Coll, IL	W
Indiana Inst of Technology, IN	M(s), W(s)
Iowa Wesleyan Coll, IA	W
Lake Erie Coll, OH	W
Lewis U, IL	M, W
Lincoln Christian Coll, IL	M, W
Lindenwood U, MO	M(s), W(s)
Malone Coll, OH	M, W
Manchester Coll, IN	M, W
Marian Coll, IN	M(s), W(s)
Marquette U, WI	M, W
McKendree Coll, IL	M(s), W(s)
Miami U–Hamilton Campus, OH	W
Michigan State U, MI	M, W
MidAmerica Nazarene U, KS	M(s), W(s)
Minnesota State U, Mankato, MN	M, W
Minot State U, ND	W
Missouri Valley Coll, MO	M(s), W(s)
Monmouth Coll, IL	M, W
Mount Mercy Coll, IA	W
Mount Union Coll, OH	W
North Central Coll, IL	W
North Dakota State U, ND	M, W
Northeastern State U, OK	M, W
Northern Michigan U, MI	M, W
Northwestern Coll, MN	W
Northwestern Oklahoma State U, OK	M(s), W(s)
Northwest Missouri State U, MO	M(s), W(s)
Ohio U, OH	M, W
Ohio U–Lancaster, OH	W
Oklahoma City U, OK	M(s), W(s)
Olivet Nazarene U, IL	M(s), W(s)
Ottawa U, KS	M(s), W(s)
Otterbein Coll, OH	M, W
Ozark Christian Coll, MO	M, W
Purdue U North Central, IN	M, W
Ripon Coll, WI	W
Rose-Hulman Inst of Technology, IN	M, W
Saginaw Valley State U, MI	M, W
Saint Joseph's Coll, IN	M, W
Saint Louis U, MO	M(s), W(s)
Simpson Coll, IA	M, W
Southwestern Coll, KS	M(s), W(s)
Southwestern Oklahoma State U, OK	M, W
Tabor Coll, KS	M, W(s)
Taylor U, Fort Wayne Campus, IN	M, W
Tiffin U, OH	M(s), W(s)
The U of Akron, OH	M, W
U of Cincinnati, OH	M, W
U of Illinois at Urbana–Champaign, IL	M, W
U of Minnesota, Duluth, MN	W
U of Missouri–Kansas City, MO	W
U of St. Francis, IL	W(s)
U of Saint Francis, IN	M(s), W(s)
U of Science and Arts of Oklahoma, OK	M(s), W(s)
U of Sioux Falls, SD	W(s)
U of Southern Indiana, IN	M, W
U of Wisconsin–Superior, WI	M, W
U of Wisconsin–Whitewater, WI	M, W
Walsh U, OH	W
Wartburg Coll, IA	W
Wichita State U, KS	M, W

William Penn U, IA	M(s), W(s)
Wittenberg U, OH	M, W

CREW

Beloit Coll, WI	M, W
Bowling Green State U, OH	M
Butler U, IN	M, W
Calvin Coll, MI	M, W
Carleton Coll, MN	M, W
Case Western Reserve U, OH	M, W
Coll of Saint Benedict, MN	W
Creighton U, NE	W(s)
Denison U, OH	M
DePauw U, IN	M, W
Drake U, IA	W
Eastern Michigan U, MI	W(s)
Grand Valley State U, MI	M, W
Indiana U Bloomington, IN	W(s)
John Carroll U, OH	M, W
Kansas State U, KS	W(s)
Lawrence U, WI	M, W
Macalester Coll, MN	M, W
Marietta Coll, OH	M, W
Marquette U, WI	M, W
Michigan State U, MI	W(s)
Northern Michigan U, MI	M, W
Purdue U, IN	M, W
St. Cloud State U, MN	M, W
Saint John's U, MN	M
Saint Louis U, MO	M, W
Saint Mary's Coll, IN	W
U of Cincinnati, OH	M, W
U of Dayton, OH	W
The U of Iowa, IA	M, W(s)
U of Kansas, KS	M, W(s)
U of Michigan, MI	W
U of Nebraska–Lincoln, NE	M, W
U of Notre Dame, IN	W(s)
U of St. Thomas, MN	M, W
U of Tulsa, OK	W(s)
U of Wisconsin–Madison, WI	M(s), W(s)
Wabash Coll, IN	M
Washington U in St. Louis, MO	M, W
Wheaton Coll, IL	M, W
Wichita State U, KS	M, W
Wittenberg U, OH	M, W
Xavier U, OH	M, W

CROSS-COUNTRY RUNNING

Adrian Coll, MI	M, W
Albion Coll, MI	M, W
Alma Coll, MI	M, W
Alverno Coll, WI	W
Anderson U, IN	M, W
Aquinas Coll, MI	M(s), W(s)
Ashland U, OH	M(s), W(s)
Augsburg Coll, MN	M, W
Augustana Coll, IL	M, W
Augustana Coll, SD	M(s), W(s)
Bacone Coll, OK	M(s), W(s)
Baker U, KS	M(s), W(s)
Baldwin-Wallace Coll, OH	M, W
Ball State U, IN	M(s), W(s)
Beloit Coll, WI	M, W
Bemidji State U, MN	W
Benedictine Coll, KS	M(s), W(s)
Benedictine U, IL	M, W
Bethany Coll, KS	M(s), W(s)
Bethany Lutheran Coll, MN	M(s), W(s)
Bethel Coll, IN	M(s), W(s)
Bethel Coll, MN	M, W
Blackburn Coll, IL	M, W
Black Hills State U, SD	M(s), W(s)
Bluffton Coll, OH	M, W
Bowling Green State U, OH	M(s), W(s)
Bradley U, IL	M(s), W(s)
Briar Cliff U, IA	M(s), W(s)
Buena Vista U, IA	M, W
Butler U, IN	M(s), W(s)
Calvin Coll, MI	M, W
Capital U, OH	M, W
Cardinal Stritch U, WI	M, W
Carleton Coll, MN	M, W
Carroll Coll, WI	M, W
Carthage Coll, WI	M, W
Case Western Reserve U, OH	M, W
Cedarville U, OH	M(s), W(s)
Central Christian Coll of Kansas, KS	M(s), W(s)
Central Coll, IA	M, W
Central Methodist Coll, MO	M(s), W(s)
Central Michigan U, MI	M(s), W(s)
Central Missouri State U, MO	M(s), W(s)
Chicago State U, IL	M(s), W(s)
Clarke Coll, IA	M, W
Cleveland State U, OH	W(s)
Coe Coll, IA	M, W
Coll of Mount St. Joseph, OH	M, W
Coll of Saint Benedict, MN	W
Coll of St. Catherine, MN	W
Coll of Saint Mary, NE	W(s)
The Coll of St. Scholastica, MN	M, W
The Coll of Wooster, OH	M, W
Concordia Coll, MN	M, W
Concordia U, IL	M, W
Concordia U, MN	M(s), W(s)
Concordia U, NE	M(s), W(s)
Concordia U Wisconsin, WI	M, W
Cornell Coll, IA	M, W
Cornerstone U, MI	M(s), W(s)
Creighton U, NE	M(s), W(s)
Crown Coll, MN	M, W
Dakota State U, SD	M(s), W(s)
Dakota Wesleyan U, SD	M(s), W(s)
Dana Coll, NE	M(s), W(s)
Defiance Coll, OH	M, W
Denison U, OH	M, W
DePaul U, IL	M(s), W(s)
DePauw U, IN	M, W
Dickinson State U, ND	M(s), W(s)
Doane Coll, NE	M(s), W(s)
Dominican U, IL	M, W
Dordt Coll, IA	M(s), W(s)
Drake U, IA	M(s), W(s)
Drury U, MO	M(s), W(s)
Earlham Coll, IN	M, W
East Central U, OK	M(s), W(s)
Eastern Illinois U, IL	M(s), W(s)
Eastern Michigan U, MI	M(s), W(s)
Edgewood Coll, WI	M, W
Elmhurst Coll, IL	M, W
Emporia State U, KS	M(s), W(s)
Evangel U, MO	M(s), W(s)
Ferris State U, MI	W(s)
Finlandia U, MI	M, W
Fontbonne U, MO	M, W
Fort Hays State U, KS	M(s), W(s)
The Franciscan U, IA	M(s), W(s)
Franklin Coll, IN	M, W
Goshen Coll, IN	M(s), W(s)
Grace Coll, IN	M(s), W(s)
Graceland U, IA	M(s), W(s)
Grand Valley State U, MI	M(s), W(s)
Grand View Coll, IA	M, W
Greenville Coll, IL	M, W
Grinnell Coll, IA	M, W
Gustavus Adolphus Coll, MN	M, W
Hamline U, MN	M, W
Hanover Coll, IN	M, W
Haskell Indian Nations U, KS	M, W
Hastings Coll, NE	M(s), W(s)
Heidelberg Coll, OH	M, W
Hillsdale Coll, MI	M(s), W(s)
Hiram Coll, OH	M, W
Hope Coll, MI	M, W
Huntington Coll, IN	M(s), W(s)
Illinois Coll, IL	M, W
Illinois Inst of Technology, IL	M(s), W(s)
Illinois State U, IL	M(s), W(s)
Illinois Wesleyan U, IL	M, W
Indiana State U, IN	M(s), W(s)
Indiana U Bloomington, IN	M(s), W(s)
Indiana U–Purdue U Fort Wayne, IN	M(s), W(s)
Indiana U–Purdue U Indianapolis, IN	M(s), W(s)
Indiana Wesleyan U, IN	M(s), W(s)
Iowa State U of Science and Technology, IA	M(s), W(s)
Jamestown Coll, ND	M(s), W(s)
John Carroll U, OH	M, W
Judson Coll, IL	M(s), W(s)
Kalamazoo Coll, MI	M, W
Kansas State U, KS	M(s), W(s)
Kent State U, OH	M(s), W(s)
Kenyon Coll, OH	M, W
Knox Coll, IL	M, W
Lake Erie Coll, OH	M, W
Lake Forest Coll, IL	M, W
Lakeland Coll, WI	M, W
Lawrence U, WI	M, W
Lewis U, IL	M(s), W(s)
Lindenwood U, MO	M(s), W(s)
Loras Coll, IA	M, W
Loyola U Chicago, IL	M(s), W(s)
Luther Coll, IA	M, W
Macalester Coll, MN	M, W
MacMurray Coll, IL	M, W
Malone Coll, OH	M(s), W(s)
Manchester Coll, IN	M, W
Maranatha Baptist Bible Coll, WI	M, W
Marian Coll, IN	M(s), W(s)
Marietta Coll, OH	M, W
Marquette U, WI	M(s), W(s)
Martin Luther Coll, MN	M, W
Maryville U of Saint Louis, MO	M, W
McKendree Coll, IL	M(s), W(s)
McPherson Coll, KS	M, W
Miami U, OH	M(s), W(s)
Michigan State U, MI	M(s), W(s)
Michigan Technological U, MI	M, W
MidAmerica Nazarene U, KS	M(s), W(s)
Midland Lutheran Coll, NE	M(s), W(s)
Millikin U, IL	M, W
Milwaukee School of Engineering, WI	M, W
Minnesota State U, Mankato, MN	M(s), W(s)
Minnesota State U, Moorhead, MN	M, W
Minot State U, ND	M(s), W(s)
Missouri Southern State Coll, MO	M(s), W(s)
Missouri Valley Coll, MO	M(s), W(s)
Monmouth Coll, IL	M, W
Mount Marty Coll, SD	M(s), W(s)
Mount Mercy Coll, IA	M, W
Mount Union Coll, OH	M, W
Muskingum Coll, OH	M, W
Nebraska Wesleyan U, NE	M, W
Newman U, KS	M(s), W(s)
North Central Coll, IL	M, W
North Dakota State U, ND	M(s), W(s)
Northern Illinois U, IL	W
Northern Michigan U, MI	W(s)
Northern State U, SD	M(s), W(s)
Northland Coll, WI	M, W
North Park U, IL	M, W
Northwestern Coll, IA	M(s), W(s)
Northwestern Coll, MN	M, W
Northwestern Oklahoma State U, OK	M(s), W(s)
Northwestern U, IL	W(s)
Northwest Missouri State U, MO	M(s), W(s)
Northwood U, MI	M(s), W(s)
Notre Dame Coll, OH	W
Oakland City U, IN	M(s), W(s)

Cross-country running (continued)

Oakland U, MI	M(s), W(s)
Oberlin Coll, OH	M, W
Ohio Northern U, OH	M, W
The Ohio State U, OH	M(s), W(s)
Ohio U, OH	M(s), W(s)
Ohio Wesleyan U, OH	M, W
Oklahoma Baptist U, OK	M(s), W(s)
Oklahoma Christian U, OK	M(s), W(s)
Oklahoma Panhandle State U, OK	W(s)
Oklahoma State U, OK	M(s), W(s)
Olivet Coll, MI	M, W
Olivet Nazarene U, IL	M(s), W(s)
Oral Roberts U, OK	M(s), W(s)
Ottawa U, KS	M(s), W(s)
Otterbein Coll, OH	M, W
Park U, MO	M(s), W(s)
Pittsburg State U, KS	M(s), W
Principia Coll, IL	M, W
Purdue U, IN	M(s), W(s)
Ripon Coll, WI	M, W
Robert Morris Coll, IL	M(s), W(s)
Rochester Coll, MI	M(s), W(s)
Rose-Hulman Inst of Technology, IN	M, W
Saginaw Valley State U, MI	M(s), W(s)
St. Ambrose U, IA	M(s), W(s)
St. Cloud State U, MN	M(s), W
St. Gregory's U, OK	M(s), W(s)
Saint John's U, MN	M
Saint Joseph's Coll, IN	M(s), W(s)
St. Louis Coll of Pharmacy, MO	M, W
Saint Louis U, MO	M(s), W(s)
Saint Mary's Coll, IN	W
Saint Mary's U of Minnesota, MN	M, W
St. Norbert Coll, WI	M, W
St. Olaf Coll, MN	M, W
Saint Xavier U, IL	W(s)
Shawnee State U, OH	M, W
Siena Heights U, MI	M(s), W(s)
Simpson Coll, IA	M, W
South Dakota School of Mines and Technology, SD	M(s), W(s)
South Dakota State U, SD	M(s), W(s)
Southeastern Oklahoma State U, OK	W(s)
Southeast Missouri State U, MO	M(s), W(s)
Southern Illinois U Carbondale, IL	M(s), W(s)
Southern Illinois U Edwardsville, IL	M(s), W(s)
Southern Nazarene U, OK	M(s), W(s)
Southwest Baptist U, MO	M(s), W(s)
Southwestern Coll, KS	M(s), W(s)
Southwestern Oklahoma State U, OK	W(s)
Southwest Missouri State U, MO	M(s), W(s)
Spring Arbor U, MI	M(s), W(s)
Sterling Coll, KS	M(s), W(s)
Tabor Coll, KS	M(s), W(s)
Taylor U, IN	M(s), W(s)
Tiffin U, OH	M(s), W(s)
Trinity Christian Coll, IL	M(s), W(s)
Trinity International U, IL	M, W
Tri-State U, IN	M, W
Truman State U, MO	M(s), W(s)
The U of Akron, OH	M(s), W(s)
U of Central Oklahoma, OK	M(s), W(s)
U of Chicago, IL	M, W
U of Cincinnati, OH	M(s), W(s)
U of Dayton, OH	M(s), W(s)
U of Dubuque, IA	M, W
U of Evansville, IN	M(s), W(s)
The U of Findlay, OH	M(s), W(s)
U of Illinois at Chicago, IL	M(s), W(s)
U of Illinois at Urbana–Champaign, IL	M(s), W(s)
U of Indianapolis, IN	M(s), W(s)
The U of Iowa, IA	M(s), W(s)
U of Kansas, KS	M(s), W(s)
U of Mary, ND	M(s), W(s)
U of Michigan, MI	M(s), W(s)
U of Minnesota, Duluth, MN	M(s), W(s)
U of Minnesota, Morris, MN	W
U of Minnesota, Twin Cities Campus, MN	M(s), W(s)
U of Missouri–Columbia, MO	M(s), W(s)
U of Missouri–Kansas City, MO	M(s), W(s)
U of Missouri–Rolla, MO	M(s), W(s)
U of Nebraska at Kearney, NE	M(s), W(s)
U of Nebraska at Omaha, NE	W(s)
U of Nebraska–Lincoln, NE	M(s), W(s)
U of North Dakota, ND	M, W
U of Northern Iowa, IA	M(s), W(s)
U of Notre Dame, IN	M(s), W(s)
U of Oklahoma, OK	M(s), W(s)
U of Rio Grande, OH	M(s), W(s)
U of St. Francis, IL	W(s)
U of Saint Francis, IN	M(s), W(s)
U of St. Thomas, MN	M, W
U of Sioux Falls, SD	M(s), W(s)
The U of South Dakota, SD	M(s), W(s)
U of Southern Indiana, IN	M(s), W(s)
U of Toledo, OH	M(s), W(s)
U of Tulsa, OK	M(s), W(s)
U of Wisconsin–Eau Claire, WI	M, W
U of Wisconsin–Green Bay, WI	M(s), W(s)
U of Wisconsin–La Crosse, WI	M, W
U of Wisconsin–Madison, WI	M(s), W(s)
U of Wisconsin–Milwaukee, WI	M(s), W(s)
U of Wisconsin–Oshkosh, WI	M, W
U of Wisconsin–Parkside, WI	M(s), W(s)
U of Wisconsin–Platteville, WI	M, W
U of Wisconsin–River Falls, WI	M, W
U of Wisconsin–Stevens Point, WI	M, W
U of Wisconsin–Stout, WI	M, W
U of Wisconsin–Superior, WI	M, W
U of Wisconsin–Whitewater, WI	M, W
Upper Iowa U, IA	M, W
Valley City State U, ND	M(s), W(s)
Valparaiso U, IN	M(s), W(s)
Wabash Coll, IN	M
Walsh U, OH	M(s), W(s)
Wartburg Coll, IA	M, W
Washington U in St. Louis, MO	M, W
Wayne State Coll, NE	M(s), W(s)
Wayne State U, MI	M(s), W(s)
Webster U, MO	W
Wentworth Military Academy and Jr Coll, MO	M
Western Illinois U, IL	M(s), W(s)
Western Michigan U, MI	M(s), W(s)
Wheaton Coll, IL	M, W
Wichita State U, KS	M(s), W(s)
Wilberforce U, OH	M, W
William Jewell Coll, MO	M(s), W(s)
William Penn U, IA	M(s), W(s)
Wilmington Coll, OH	M, W
Winona State U, MN	M, W(s)
Wisconsin Lutheran Coll, WI	M, W
Wittenberg U, OH	M, W
Wright State U, OH	M(s), W(s)
Xavier U, OH	M(s), W(s)
York Coll, NE	M(s), W(s)
Youngstown State U, OH	M(s), W(s)

EQUESTRIAN SPORTS

Ball State U, IN	M, W
Chadron State Coll, NE	M, W
Denison U, OH	M, W
Earlham Coll, IN	M, W
Hillsdale Coll, MI	W
Hiram Coll, OH	M, W
Kenyon Coll, OH	M, W
Lake Erie Coll, OH	M, W
Miami U, OH	M, W
Michigan State U, MI	M, W
National American U, SD	M(s), W(s)
Northern Michigan U, MI	M, W
Oberlin Coll, OH	M, W
Ohio U, OH	M, W
Ohio Wesleyan U, OH	M, W
Oklahoma Panhandle State U, OK	M(s), W(s)
Oklahoma State U, OK	W(s)
Otterbein Coll, OH	M, W
Purdue U, IN	M, W
Saint Mary-of-the-Woods Coll, IN	W(s)
Saint Mary's Coll, IN	W
Southwestern Oklahoma State U, OK	M(s), W(s)
Southwest Missouri State U, MO	M, W
Taylor U, IN	M, W
Truman State U, MO	M, W
U of Wisconsin–River Falls, WI	M, W
Wittenberg U, OH	W

FENCING

Beloit Coll, WI	M, W
Bradley U, IL	M, W
Carleton Coll, MN	M, W
Case Western Reserve U, OH	M, W
Cleveland State U, OH	M(s), W(s)
Kenyon Coll, OH	M, W
Lake Forest Coll, IL	M, W
Lawrence U, WI	M, W
Macalester Coll, MN	M, W
Marquette U, WI	M, W
Miami U, OH	M, W
Michigan Technological U, MI	M, W
Northwestern U, IL	W(s)
Oberlin Coll, OH	M, W
The Ohio State U, OH	M(s), W(s)
Purdue U, IN	M, W
St. Cloud State U, MN	M, W
Saint Louis U, MO	M, W
U of Kansas, KS	M, W
U of Nebraska–Lincoln, NE	M, W
U of Notre Dame, IN	M(s), W(s)
Washington U in St. Louis, MO	M, W
Wayne State U, MI	M(s), W(s)
Winona State U, MN	M, W
Xavier U, OH	M, W

FIELD HOCKEY

Ball State U, IN	W(s)
Carleton Coll, MN	W
Central Michigan U, MI	W(s)
The Coll of Wooster, OH	W
Denison U, OH	W
DePauw U, IN	W
Earlham Coll, IN	W
Hanover Coll, IN	W
Kent State U, OH	W(s)
Kenyon Coll, OH	W
Lindenwood U, MO	W(s)
Miami U, OH	W(s)
Michigan State U, MI	W(s)
Northwestern U, IL	W(s)
Oberlin Coll, OH	W
The Ohio State U, OH	W(s)
Ohio U, OH	W(s)
Ohio Wesleyan U, OH	W
Saint Louis U, MO	W(s)
Saint Mary's Coll, IN	W
Southwest Missouri State U, MO	W(s)
The U of Iowa, IA	W(s)
U of Michigan, MI	W(s)
Washington U in St. Louis, MO	W
Wheaton Coll, IL	W
Wittenberg U, OH	W

FOOTBALL

Adrian Coll, MI	M
Albion Coll, MI	M
Alma Coll, MI	M

Anderson U, IN	M
Ashland U, OH	M(s)
Augsburg Coll, MN	M
Augustana Coll, IL	M
Augustana Coll, SD	M(s)
Aurora U, IL	M
Avila U, MO	M(s)
Bacone Coll, OK	M(s)
Baker U, KS	M(s)
Baldwin-Wallace Coll, OH	M
Ball State U, IN	M(s)
Beloit Coll, WI	M
Bemidji State U, MN	M(s)
Benedictine Coll, KS	M(s)
Benedictine U, IL	M
Bethany Coll, KS	M(s)
Bethel Coll, KS	M(s)
Bethel Coll, MN	M
Blackburn Coll, IL	M
Black Hills State U, SD	M(s)
Blessing-Rieman Coll of Nursing, IL	M(s)
Bluffton Coll, OH	M
Bowling Green State U, OH	M(s)
Briar Cliff U, IA	M(s)
Buena Vista U, IA	M
Butler U, IN	M
Capital U, OH	M
Carleton Coll, MN	M
Carroll Coll, WI	M
Carthage Coll, WI	M
Case Western Reserve U, OH	M
Central Coll, IA	M
Central Methodist Coll, MO	M(s)
Central Michigan U, MI	M(s)
Central Missouri State U, MO	M(s)
Chadron State Coll, NE	M(s)
Coe Coll, IA	M
Coll of Mount St. Joseph, OH	M
The Coll of Wooster, OH	M
Concordia Coll, MN	M
Concordia U, IL	M
Concordia U, MN	M(s)
Concordia U, NE	M(s)
Concordia U Wisconsin, WI	M
Cornell Coll, IA	M
Crown Coll, MN	M
Culver-Stockton Coll, MO	M(s)
Dakota State U, SD	M(s)
Dakota Wesleyan U, SD	M(s)
Dana Coll, NE	M(s)
Defiance Coll, OH	M
Denison U, OH	M
DePauw U, IN	M
Dickinson State U, ND	M(s)
Doane Coll, NE	M(s)
Drake U, IA	M
Earlham Coll, IN	M
East Central U, OK	M(s)
Eastern Illinois U, IL	M(s)
Eastern Michigan U, MI	M(s)
Elmhurst Coll, IL	M
Emporia State U, KS	M(s)
Eureka Coll, IL	M
Evangel U, MO	M(s)
Ferris State U, MI	M(s)
Fort Hays State U, KS	M(s)
Franklin Coll, IN	M
Graceland U, IA	M(s)
Grand Valley State U, MI	M(s)
Greenville Coll, IL	M
Grinnell Coll, IA	M
Gustavus Adolphus Coll, MN	M
Hamline U, MN	M
Hanover Coll, IN	M
Haskell Indian Nations U, KS	M
Hastings Coll, NE	M(s)
Heidelberg Coll, OH	M
Hillsdale Coll, MI	M(s)

Hiram Coll, OH	M
Hope Coll, MI	M
Illinois Coll, IL	M
Illinois State U, IL	M(s)
Illinois Wesleyan U, IL	M
Indiana State U, IN	M(s)
Indiana U Bloomington, IN	M(s)
Iowa State U of Science and Technology, IA	M(s)
Iowa Wesleyan Coll, IA	M(s)
Jamestown Coll, ND	M(s)
John Carroll U, OH	M
Kalamazoo Coll, MI	M
Kansas State U, KS	M(s)
Kent State U, OH	M(s)
Kenyon Coll, OH	M
Knox Coll, IL	M
Lake Forest Coll, IL	M
Lakeland Coll, WI	M
Langston U, OK	M(s)
Lawrence U, WI	M
Lindenwood U, MO	M(s)
Loras Coll, IA	M
Luther Coll, IA	M
Macalester Coll, MN	M
MacMurray Coll, IL	M
Malone Coll, OH	M(s)
Manchester Coll, IN	M
Maranatha Baptist Bible Coll, WI	M
Marietta Coll, OH	M
Marquette U, WI	M
Martin Luther Coll, MN	M
Mayville State U, ND	M(s)
McKendree Coll, IL	M(s)
McPherson Coll, KS	M
Miami U, OH	M(s)
Michigan State U, MI	M(s)
Michigan Technological U, MI	M(s)
MidAmerica Nazarene U, KS	M(s)
Midland Lutheran Coll, NE	M(s)
Millikin U, IL	M
Minnesota State U, Mankato, MN	M(s)
Minnesota State U, Moorhead, MN	M(s)
Minot State U, ND	M(s)
Missouri Southern State Coll, MO	M(s)
Missouri Valley Coll, MO	M(s)
Missouri Western State Coll, MO	M(s)
Monmouth Coll, IL	M
Mount Union Coll, OH	M
Muskingum Coll, OH	M, W
Nebraska Wesleyan U, NE	M
North Central Coll, IL	M
North Dakota State U, ND	M(s)
Northeastern State U, OK	M(s)
Northern Illinois U, IL	M(s)
Northern Michigan U, MI	M(s)
Northern State U, SD	M(s)
North Park U, IL	M
Northwestern Coll, IA	M(s)
Northwestern Coll, MN	M
Northwestern Oklahoma State U, OK	M(s)
Northwestern U, IL	M(s)
Northwest Missouri State U, MO	M(s)
Northwood U, MI	M(s)
Oberlin Coll, OH	M
Ohio Northern U, OH	M
The Ohio State U, OH	M(s)
Ohio U, OH	M(s)
Ohio Wesleyan U, OH	M
Oklahoma Panhandle State U, OK	M(s)
Oklahoma State U, OK	M(s)
Olivet Coll, MI	M
Olivet Nazarene U, IL	M(s)
Ottawa U, KS	M(s)
Otterbein Coll, OH	M
Peru State Coll, NE	M(s)
Pittsburg State U, KS	M(s)

Principia Coll, IL	M
Purdue U, IN	M(s)
Ripon Coll, WI	M
Rochester Comm and Tech Coll, MN	M
Rockford Coll, IL	M
Rose-Hulman Inst of Technology, IN	M
Saginaw Valley State U, MI	M(s)
St. Ambrose U, IA	M(s)
St. Cloud State U, MN	M(s)
Saint John's U, MN	M
Saint Joseph's Coll, IN	M(s)
Saint Mary U, KS	M(s)
St. Norbert Coll, WI	M
St. Olaf Coll, MN	M
Saint Xavier U, IL	M(s)
Simpson Coll, IA	M
Si Tanka Huron U, SD	M(s)
South Dakota School of Mines and Technology, SD	M(s)
South Dakota State U, SD	M(s)
Southeastern Oklahoma State U, OK	M(s)
Southeast Missouri State U, MO	M(s)
Southern Illinois U Carbondale, IL	M(s)
Southern Nazarene U, OK	M(s)
Southwest Baptist U, MO	M(s)
Southwestern Coll, KS	M(s)
Southwestern Oklahoma State U, OK	M(s)
Southwest Minnesota State U, MN	M(s)
Southwest Missouri State U, MO	M(s)
Sterling Coll, KS	M(s)
Tabor Coll, KS	M(s)
Taylor U, IN	M(s)
Tiffin U, OH	M(s)
Trinity Bible Coll, ND	M
Trinity International U, IL	M(s)
Tri-State U, IN	M
Truman State U, MO	M(s)
The U of Akron, OH	M(s)
U of Central Oklahoma, OK	M(s)
U of Chicago, IL	M
U of Cincinnati, OH	M(s)
U of Dayton, OH	M
U of Dubuque, IA	M
The U of Findlay, OH	M(s)
U of Illinois at Urbana–Champaign, IL	M(s)
U of Indianapolis, IN	M(s)
The U of Iowa, IA	M(s)
U of Kansas, KS	M(s)
U of Mary, ND	M(s)
U of Michigan, MI	M(s)
U of Minnesota, Crookston, MN	M(s)
U of Minnesota, Duluth, MN	M(s)
U of Minnesota, Morris, MN	M(s)
U of Minnesota, Twin Cities Campus, MN	M(s)
U of Missouri–Columbia, MO	M(s)
U of Missouri–Rolla, MO	M(s)
U of Nebraska at Kearney, NE	M(s)
U of Nebraska at Omaha, NE	M(s)
U of Nebraska–Lincoln, NE	M(s)
U of North Dakota, ND	M(s)
U of Northern Iowa, IA	M(s)
U of Notre Dame, IN	M(s)
U of Oklahoma, OK	M(s)
U of St. Francis, IL	M(s)
U of Saint Francis, IN	M(s)
U of St. Thomas, MN	M
U of Sioux Falls, SD	M(s)
The U of South Dakota, SD	M(s)
U of Toledo, OH	M(s)
U of Tulsa, OK	M(s)
U of Wisconsin–Eau Claire, WI	M
U of Wisconsin–La Crosse, WI	M
U of Wisconsin–Madison, WI	M(s)
U of Wisconsin–Oshkosh, WI	M

Football (continued)

U of Wisconsin–Platteville, WI	M
U of Wisconsin–River Falls, WI	M
U of Wisconsin–Stevens Point, WI	M
U of Wisconsin–Stout, WI	M
U of Wisconsin–Whitewater, WI	M
Upper Iowa U, IA	M
Urbana U, OH	M(s)
Valley City State U, ND	M(s)
Valparaiso U, IN	M
Wabash Coll, IN	M
Waldorf Coll, IA	M(s)
Walsh U, OH	M(s)
Wartburg Coll, IA	M
Washington U in St. Louis, MO	M
Wayne State Coll, NE	M(s)
Wayne State U, MI	M(s)
Western Illinois U, IL	M(s)
Western Michigan U, MI	M(s)
Westminster Coll, MO	M
Wheaton Coll, IL	M
William Jewell Coll, MO	M(s)
William Penn U, IA	M(s)
Wilmington Coll, OH	M
Winona State U, MN	M(s)
Wisconsin Lutheran Coll, WI	M
Wittenberg U, OH	M
Youngstown State U, OH	M(s)

GOLF

Adrian Coll, MI	M, W
Albion Coll, MI	M, W
Alma Coll, MI	M, W
Ancilla Coll, IN	M(s)
Anderson U, IN	M, W
Aquinas Coll, MI	M(s), W(s)
Ashland U, OH	M(s), W(s)
Augsburg Coll, MN	M, W
Augustana Coll, IL	M, W
Augustana Coll, SD	M, W
Aurora U, IL	M
Avila U, MO	W(s)
Bacone Coll, OK	M(s), W(s)
Baker U, KS	M(s), W(s)
Baldwin-Wallace Coll, OH	M, W
Ball State U, IN	M(s)
Beloit Coll, WI	M, W
Bemidji State U, MN	M, W
Benedictine Coll, KS	M(s), W(s)
Benedictine U, IL	M
Bethany Coll, KS	M(s)
Bethany Lutheran Coll, MN	M(s), W(s)
Bethel Coll, IN	M(s), W
Bethel Coll, MN	M
Blackburn Coll, IL	M
Bluffton Coll, OH	M
Bowling Green State U, OH	M(s), W(s)
Bradley U, IL	M(s), W(s)
Briar Cliff U, IA	M(s), W(s)
Buena Vista U, IA	M, W
Butler U, IN	M(s), W(s)
Calvin Coll, MI	M, W
Cameron U, OK	M(s)
Capital U, OH	M, W
Carleton Coll, MN	M, W
Carroll Coll, WI	M, W
Carthage Coll, WI	M, W
Case Western Reserve U, OH	M
Cedarville U, OH	M(s)
Central Christian Coll of Kansas, KS	M(s), W(s)
Central Coll, IA	M, W
Central Methodist Coll, MO	M(s), W(s)
Central Missouri State U, MO	M(s)
Chadron State Coll, NE	W(s)
Chicago State U, IL	M, W
Cincinnati Bible Coll and Seminary, OH	M
Clarke Coll, IA	M, W
Cleveland State U, OH	M(s)
Coe Coll, IA	M, W
Coll of Saint Benedict, MN	W
Coll of Saint Mary, NE	W(s)
The Coll of Wooster, OH	M
Concordia Coll, MN	M, W
Concordia U, IL	M
Concordia U, MN	W(s)
Concordia U, NE	M(s), W(s)
Concordia U Wisconsin, WI	M, W
Cornell Coll, IA	M, W
Cornerstone U, MI	M(s)
Creighton U, NE	M(s), W(s)
Crossroads Coll, MN	M, W
Crown Coll, MN	M, W
Culver-Stockton Coll, MO	M(s), W(s)
Dakota State U, SD	M, W
Dakota Wesleyan U, SD	M(s), W(s)
Davenport U, Grand Rapids, MI	M
Defiance Coll, OH	M, W
Denison U, OH	M
DePaul U, IL	M(s), W
DePauw U, IN	M, W
Dickinson State U, ND	M(s), W(s)
Doane Coll, NE	M(s), W(s)
Dordt Coll, IA	M(s)
Drake U, IA	M(s)
Drury U, MO	M(s), W(s)
East Central U, OK	M(s)
Eastern Illinois U, IL	M(s), W(s)
Eastern Michigan U, MI	M(s), W(s)
Edgewood Coll, WI	M, W
Elmhurst Coll, IL	M, W
Eureka Coll, IL	M, W
Evangel U, MO	M(s), W(s)
Ferris State U, MI	M(s), W(s)
Fontbonne U, MO	M, W
Fort Hays State U, KS	M(s)
The Franciscan U, IA	M(s)
Franklin Coll, IN	M, W
Goshen Coll, IN	M(s)
Grace Coll, IN	M(s)
Graceland U, IA	M(s), W(s)
Grand Valley State U, MI	M(s), W(s)
Grinnell Coll, IA	M, W
Gustavus Adolphus Coll, MN	M, W
Hannibal-LaGrange Coll, MO	M(s)
Hanover Coll, IN	M, W
Haskell Indian Nations U, KS	M
Hastings Coll, NE	M(s), W(s)
Heidelberg Coll, OH	M, W
Hillsdale Coll, MI	M(s)
Hiram Coll, OH	M, W
Hope Coll, MI	M, W
Huntington Coll, IN	M(s), W(s)
Illinois Coll, IL	M, W
Illinois State U, IL	M(s), W(s)
Illinois Wesleyan U, IL	M, W
Indiana U Bloomington, IN	M(s), W(s)
Indiana U Northwest, IN	M
Indiana U–Purdue U Indianapolis, IN	M(s)
Indiana Wesleyan U, IN	M(s)
Iowa State U of Science and Technology, IA	M(s), W(s)
Jamestown Coll, ND	M(s), W(s)
John Carroll U, OH	M, W
Kalamazoo Coll, MI	M, W
Kansas State U, KS	M(s), W(s)
Kent State U, OH	M(s), W(s)
Kenyon Coll, OH	M, W
Knox Coll, IL	M, W
Lake Erie Coll, OH	M
Lakeland Coll, WI	M, W
Lawrence U, WI	M
Lewis U, IL	M(s), W(s)
Lincoln Coll, Lincoln, IL	M(s), W(s)
Lincoln Coll, Normal, IL	M, W
Lindenwood U, MO	M(s), W(s)
Loras Coll, IA	M, W
Loyola U Chicago, IL	M(s), W(s)
Luther Coll, IA	M, W
Macalester Coll, MN	M, W
MacMurray Coll, IL	M, W
Maharishi U of Management, IA	M
Malone Coll, OH	M(s), W(s)
Manchester Coll, IN	M, W
Marian Coll, IN	M(s), W(s)
Marian Coll of Fond du Lac, WI	M, W
Marquette U, WI	M(s)
Martin Luther Coll, MN	M
Maryville U of Saint Louis, MO	M
McKendree Coll, IL	M(s), W(s)
Miami U, OH	M(s)
Miami U–Hamilton Campus, OH	M
Miami U–Middletown Campus, OH	M, W
Michigan State U, MI	M(s), W(s)
Midland Lutheran Coll, NE	M(s), W(s)
Millikin U, IL	M, W
Milwaukee School of Engineering, WI	M, W
Minnesota State U, Mankato, MN	M(s), W(s)
Minnesota State U, Moorhead, MN	M, W
Minot State U, ND	M, W
Missouri Southern State Coll, MO	M(s)
Missouri Valley Coll, MO	M(s), W(s)
Missouri Western State Coll, MO	M(s)
Monmouth Coll, IL	M, W
Mount Marty Coll, SD	M(s), W(s)
Mount Mercy Coll, IA	M, W
Mount Union Coll, OH	M, W
Mount Vernon Nazarene U, OH	M(s)
Muskingum Coll, OH	M, W
Nebraska Wesleyan U, NE	M, W
Newman U, KS	M(s), W(s)
North Central Coll, IL	M, W
North Dakota State U, ND	M, W(s)
Northeastern State U, OK	M(s), W(s)
Northern Illinois U, IL	M(s), W(s)
Northern Michigan U, MI	M(s)
Northern State U, SD	M, W(s)
North Park U, IL	M
Northwestern Coll, IA	M(s), W(s)
Northwestern Coll, MN	M, W
Northwestern U, IL	M(s), W(s)
Northwest Missouri State U, MO	M(s)
Northwood U, MI	M(s), W(s)
Oakland City U, IN	M, W
Oakland U, MI	M(s), W(s)
Oberlin Coll, OH	M, W
Ohio Northern U, OH	M, W
The Ohio State U, OH	M(s), W(s)
The Ohio State U at Lima, OH	M
Ohio U, OH	M(s), W(s)
Ohio U–Chillicothe, OH	M, W
Ohio U–Lancaster, OH	M, W
Ohio U–Zanesville, OH	M, W
Ohio Wesleyan U, OH	M
Oklahoma Baptist U, OK	M(s), W(s)
Oklahoma Christian U, OK	M(s)
Oklahoma City U, OK	M(s), W(s)
Oklahoma Panhandle State U, OK	M(s)
Oklahoma State U, OK	M(s), W(s)
Oklahoma Wesleyan U, OK	M(s)
Olivet Coll, MI	M, W
Olivet Nazarene U, IL	M(s)
Oral Roberts U, OK	M(s), W(s)
Ottawa U, KS	M(s)
Otterbein Coll, OH	M, W
Park U, MO	W
Pillsbury Baptist Bible Coll, MN	M, W
Pittsburg State U, KS	M(s)
Presentation Coll, SD	M
Principia Coll, IL	M
Purdue U, IN	M(s), W(s)

Quincy U, IL	M(s), W(s)
Research Coll of Nursing, MO	M(s), W(s)
Ripon Coll, WI	M, W
Rochester Comm and Tech Coll, MN	M, W
Rockford Coll, IL	M
Rockhurst U, MO	M(s), W(s)
Rose-Hulman Inst of Technology, IN	M, W
Saginaw Valley State U, MI	M(s)
St. Ambrose U, IA	M(s), W(s)
St. Cloud State U, MN	M, W(s)
St. Gregory's U, OK	M(s), W(s)
Saint John's U, MN	M
Saint Joseph's Coll, IN	M(s), W(s)
Saint Louis U, MO	M
Saint Mary's U of Minnesota, MN	M, W
St. Norbert Coll, WI	M, W
St. Olaf Coll, MN	M, W
Saint Xavier U, IL	M(s)
Shawnee State U, OH	M
Siena Heights U, MI	M(s)
Simpson Coll, IA	M, W
South Dakota School of Mines and Technology, SD	M, W
South Dakota State U, SD	M, W
Southeast Missouri State U, MO	M(s)
Southern Illinois U Carbondale, IL	M(s), W(s)
Southern Illinois U Edwardsville, IL	W(s)
Southern Nazarene U, OK	M(s), W(s)
Southwest Baptist U, MO	M(s)
Southwestern Coll, KS	M(s), W(s)
Southwestern Oklahoma State U, OK	M(s), W(s)
Southwest Minnesota State U, MN	W(s)
Southwest Missouri State U, MO	M(s), W(s)
Spring Arbor U, MI	M(s)
Springfield Coll in Illinois, IL	M, W
Tabor Coll, KS	M(s), W(s)
Taylor U, IN	M(s)
Tiffin U, OH	M(s), W(s)
Tri-State U, IN	M, W
Truman State U, MO	M(s), W(s)
The U of Akron, OH	M(s)
U of Central Oklahoma, OK	M(s)
U of Cincinnati, OH	M(s)
U of Dayton, OH	M(s), W(s)
U of Dubuque, IA	M, W
U of Evansville, IN	M(s)
The U of Findlay, OH	M(s), W(s)
U of Illinois at Urbana–Champaign, IL	M(s), W(s)
U of Indianapolis, IN	M(s), W(s)
The U of Iowa, IA	M(s), W(s)
U of Kansas, KS	M(s), W(s)
U of Mary, ND	M(s), W(s)
U of Michigan, MI	M(s), W(s)
U of Minnesota, Crookston, MN	M(s), W
U of Minnesota, Morris, MN	M, W
U of Minnesota, Twin Cities Campus, MN	M(s), W(s)
U of Missouri–Columbia, MO	M(s), W(s)
U of Missouri–Kansas City, MO	M(s), W(s)
U of Missouri–Rolla, MO	M(s)
U of Missouri–St. Louis, MO	M(s), W(s)
U of Nebraska at Kearney, NE	M(s), W(s)
U of Nebraska at Omaha, NE	W
U of Nebraska–Lincoln, NE	M(s), W(s)
U of North Dakota, ND	M, W
U of Northern Iowa, IA	M(s), W(s)
U of Notre Dame, IN	M(s), W(s)
U of Oklahoma, OK	M(s), W(s)
U of St. Francis, IL	M(s), W(s)
U of Saint Francis, IN	M(s)
U of St. Thomas, MN	M, W
U of Sioux Falls, SD	M(s), W(s)
U of Southern Indiana, IN	M(s), W(s)
U of Toledo, OH	M(s), W(s)
U of Tulsa, OK	M(s), W(s)
U of Wisconsin–Eau Claire, WI	M, W
U of Wisconsin–Madison, WI	M(s), W(s)
U of Wisconsin–Oshkosh, WI	W
U of Wisconsin–Parkside, WI	M(s)
U of Wisconsin–Platteville, WI	M
U of Wisconsin–Stevens Point, WI	W
U of Wisconsin–Superior, WI	W
U of Wisconsin–Whitewater, WI	W
Upper Iowa U, IA	M, W
Urbana U, OH	M(s)
Ursuline Coll, OH	W(s)
Wabash Coll, IN	M
Waldorf Coll, IA	M(s), W(s)
Walsh U, OH	M(s), W(s)
Wartburg Coll, IA	M, W
Wayne State Coll, NE	M(s), W(s)
Wayne State U, MI	M(s)
Webster U, MO	M
Western Illinois U, IL	M(s), W
Western Michigan U, MI	W(s)
Westminster Coll, MO	M, W
Wheaton Coll, IL	M, W
Wichita State U, KS	M(s), W(s)
Wilberforce U, OH	M, W
William Jewell Coll, MO	M(s), W(s)
William Penn U, IA	M(s), W(s)
William Woods U, MO	M(s), W(s)
Wilmington Coll, OH	M, W
Winona State U, MN	M(s), W(s)
Wisconsin Lutheran Coll, WI	M, W
Wittenberg U, OH	M, W
Wright State U, OH	M(s)
Xavier U, OH	M(s), W(s)
York Coll, NE	M(s), W(s)
Youngstown State U, OH	M(s), W

GYMNASTICS

Ball State U, IN	W(s)
Bowling Green State U, OH	W(s)
Central Michigan U, MI	W(s)
Eastern Michigan U, MI	W(s)
Gustavus Adolphus Coll, MN	W
Hamline U, MN	W
Illinois State U, IL	W(s)
Iowa State U of Science and Technology, IA	W(s)
Kent State U, OH	W(s)
Miami U, OH	M, W
Michigan State U, MI	M(s), W(s)
Northern Illinois U, IL	W(s)
The Ohio State U, OH	M(s), W(s)
Purdue U, IN	M, W
Saint Mary's Coll, IN	W
Southeast Missouri State U, MO	W(s)
U of Illinois at Chicago, IL	M(s), W(s)
U of Illinois at Urbana–Champaign, IL	M(s), W(s)
The U of Iowa, IA	M(s), W(s)
U of Michigan, MI	M(s), W(s)
U of Minnesota, Twin Cities Campus, MN	M(s), W(s)
U of Missouri–Columbia, MO	W(s)
U of Nebraska–Lincoln, NE	M(s), W(s)
U of Oklahoma, OK	M(s), W(s)
U of Wisconsin–Eau Claire, WI	W
U of Wisconsin–La Crosse, WI	W
U of Wisconsin–Oshkosh, WI	W
U of Wisconsin–Stout, WI	W
U of Wisconsin–Whitewater, WI	W
Washington U in St. Louis, MO	M, W
Western Michigan U, MI	W(s)
Winona State U, MN	W(s)

ICE HOCKEY

Augsburg Coll, MN	M, W
Ball State U, IN	M
Beloit Coll, WI	M, W
Bemidji State U, MN	M(s), W(s)
Bethel Coll, MN	M, W
Bowling Green State U, OH	M(s)
Bradley U, IL	M
Butler U, IN	M
Calvin Coll, MI	M
Carleton Coll, MN	M, W
Carthage Coll, WI	M
Case Western Reserve U, OH	M, W
Coll of Saint Benedict, MN	W
Coll of St. Catherine, MN	W
The Coll of St. Scholastica, MN	M
The Coll of Wooster, OH	M
Concordia Coll, MN	M, W
Davenport U, Grand Rapids, MI	M
Denison U, OH	M
Dordt Coll, IA	M(s)
Ferris State U, MI	M(s)
Finlandia U, MI	M
Grand Valley State U, MI	M
Gustavus Adolphus Coll, MN	M, W
Hamline U, MN	M
Hillsdale Coll, MI	M
Hope Coll, MI	M
John Carroll U, OH	M
Kenyon Coll, OH	M, W
Kettering U, MI	M
Lake Forest Coll, IL	M, W
Lawrence U, WI	M, W
Loras Coll, IA	M
Macalester Coll, MN	M, W
Marian Coll of Fond du Lac, WI	M
Miami U, OH	M(s)
Michigan State U, MI	M(s)
Michigan Technological U, MI	M(s), W
Milwaukee School of Engineering, WI	M
Minnesota State U, Mankato, MN	M(s), W(s)
Minot State U, ND	M
North Dakota State U, ND	M
Northern Michigan U, MI	M(s), W
Northland Coll, WI	M
Northwestern Coll, MN	M
Northwood U, MI	M
Oakland U, MI	M, W
Oberlin Coll, OH	M, W
The Ohio State U, OH	M(s), W(s)
Ohio U, OH	M
Ohio Wesleyan U, OH	M
Purdue U, IN	M
Ripon Coll, WI	M, W
St. Cloud State U, MN	M(s), W(s)
Saint John's U, MN	M
Saint Louis U, MO	M
Saint Mary's U of Minnesota, MN	M, W
St. Norbert Coll, WI	M
St. Olaf Coll, MN	M, W
Southwest Missouri State U, MO	M
The U of Findlay, OH	M(s), W(s)
The U of Iowa, IA	M, W
U of Michigan, MI	M(s)
U of Minnesota, Crookston, MN	M(s)
U of Minnesota, Duluth, MN	M(s), W
U of Minnesota, Twin Cities Campus, MN	M(s), W(s)
U of Missouri–St. Louis, MO	M
U of Nebraska at Omaha, NE	M(s)
U of North Dakota, ND	M(s), W(s)
U of Notre Dame, IN	M(s)
U of St. Thomas, MN	M, W
U of Southern Indiana, IN	M
U of Wisconsin–Eau Claire, WI	M, W
U of Wisconsin–Madison, WI	M(s), W(s)
U of Wisconsin–Platteville, WI	M
U of Wisconsin–River Falls, WI	M, W
U of Wisconsin–Stevens Point, WI	M, W
U of Wisconsin–Stout, WI	M, W
U of Wisconsin–Superior, WI	M, W

Ice hockey (continued)

U of Wisconsin–Whitewater, WI M, W
Washington U in St. Louis, MO M
Wayne State U, MI M, W
Western Michigan U, MI M(s)
Wheaton Coll, IL M
Wichita State U, KS M, W
Winona State U, MN M
Wittenberg U, OH M

LACROSSE

Beloit Coll, WI M, W
Butler U, IN M(s)
Calvin Coll, MI M, W
Carleton Coll, MN M, W
Coll of Saint Benedict, MN W
The Coll of Wooster, OH M, W
Denison U, OH M, W
Dordt Coll, IA M
Earlham Coll, IN M, W
Gustavus Adolphus Coll, MN M
Hope Coll, MI M
John Carroll U, OH M, W
Kenyon Coll, OH M, W
Kettering U, MI M
Lake Forest Coll, IL M, W
Lawrence U, WI M, W
Lindenwood U, MO M(s), W(s)
Marietta Coll, OH M
Marquette U, WI M
Miami U, OH M
Michigan State U, MI M
Northern Michigan U, MI M
Northwestern U, IL W(s)
Oberlin Coll, OH M, W
The Ohio State U, OH M(s), W(s)
Ohio U, OH M, W
Ohio Wesleyan U, OH M, W
Purdue U, IN M, W
Saint John's U, MN M
Southwest Missouri State U, MO M
Taylor U, IN M, W
Truman State U, MO M, W
The U of Iowa, IA M, W
U of Minnesota, Duluth, MN M, W
U of Notre Dame, IN M(s), W(s)
U of St. Thomas, MN M, W
U of Wisconsin–Madison, WI W(s)
U of Wisconsin–Whitewater, WI M
Wabash Coll, IN M
Washington U in St. Louis, MO M, W
Wheaton Coll, IL M, W
Wittenberg U, OH M, W
Xavier U, OH M, W

RACQUETBALL

Miami U, OH M, W
Michigan Technological U, MI M, W
Purdue U, IN M, W
Southwest Missouri State U, MO M, W
Wichita State U, KS M, W

RIFLERY

Denison U, OH M, W
Lindenwood U, MO M(s), W(s)
Michigan Technological U, MI M, W
North Dakota State U, ND M, W
The Ohio State U, OH M, W
Purdue U, IN M, W
Rose-Hulman Inst of Technology, IN M, W
Saint John's U, MN M
Saint Louis U, MO M, W
Southwest Missouri State U, MO M, W
The U of Akron, OH M, W
U of Missouri–Kansas City, MO M(s), W(s)
U of Nebraska–Lincoln, NE W(s)
U of Wisconsin–Oshkosh, WI M, W
Xavier U, OH M(s), W(s)

ROCK CLIMBING

St. Ambrose U, IA M(s), W(s)

RUGBY

Ball State U, IN M, W
Butler U, IN M
Carleton Coll, MN M, W
Central Missouri State U, MO M, W
Coll of Saint Benedict, MN W
The Coll of Wooster, OH M, W
Denison U, OH M, W
DePauw U, IN M
Drake U, IA M
Earlham Coll, IN M
Eastern Illinois U, IL W(s)
Gustavus Adolphus Coll, MN M, W
Hiram Coll, OH M, W
John Carroll U, OH M, W
Kenyon Coll, OH M, W
Lake Forest Coll, IL M
Lawrence U, WI W
Loras Coll, IA M
Macalester Coll, MN M, W
Marquette U, WI M, W
Miami U, OH M
North Dakota State U, ND M, W
Northern Michigan U, MI M, W
Oberlin Coll, OH M, W
Ohio U, OH M, W
Ohio Wesleyan U, OH M, W
Purdue U, IN M, W
Ripon Coll, WI M
St. Cloud State U, MN M, W
Saint John's U, MN M
Simpson Coll, IA M, W
Tabor Coll, KS M
Truman State U, MO M, W
U of Cincinnati, OH M
The U of Iowa, IA M, W
U of Kansas, KS M, W
U of Minnesota, Duluth, MN M, W
U of Wisconsin–Madison, WI M
U of Wisconsin–Platteville, WI M
U of Wisconsin–River Falls, WI M, W
U of Wisconsin–Whitewater, WI M, W
Wabash Coll, IN M
Washington U in St. Louis, MO M, W
Wichita State U, KS M
Winona State U, MN M, W
Wittenberg U, OH M, W
Xavier U, OH M, W

SAILING

Ball State U, IN M, W
Denison U, OH M, W
Hiram Coll, OH M, W
Illinois Wesleyan U, IL M, W
John Carroll U, OH M, W
Marquette U, WI M, W
Miami U, OH M, W
Ohio Wesleyan U, OH M, W
Purdue U, IN M, W
Saint Mary's Coll, IN W
The U of Iowa, IA M, W
U of Wisconsin–Madison, WI M, W
Wabash Coll, IN M
Washington U in St. Louis, MO M, W
Xavier U, OH M, W

SKIING (CROSS-COUNTRY)

Carleton Coll, MN M, W
Coll of Saint Benedict, MN W
Concordia Coll, MN M, W
Finlandia U, MI M, W
Gustavus Adolphus Coll, MN M, W
Macalester Coll, MN M, W
Michigan Technological U, MI M, W
Northern Michigan U, MI M(s), W(s)
St. Cloud State U, MN M, W(s)
Saint John's U, MN M
Saint Mary's U of Minnesota, MN M, W
St. Olaf Coll, MN M, W
U of Wisconsin–Green Bay, WI M(s), W(s)

SKIING (DOWNHILL)

Carleton Coll, MN M, W
Denison U, OH M, W
Grand Valley State U, MI M, W
John Carroll U, OH M, W
Loras Coll, IA M
Marquette U, WI M, W
Michigan Technological U, MI M, W
Northern Michigan U, MI M, W(s)
Purdue U, IN M, W
St. Cloud State U, MN M, W
Saint Mary's Coll, IN W
St. Olaf Coll, MN M, W
U of Minnesota, Duluth, MN M, W
U of St. Thomas, MN M, W
Winona State U, MN M, W
Xavier U, OH M, W

SOCCER

Adrian Coll, MI M, W
Albion Coll, MI M, W
Alma Coll, MI M, W
Alverno Coll, WI W
Anderson U, IN M, W
Aquinas Coll, MI M(s), W(s)
Ashland U, OH M(s), W(s)
Augsburg Coll, MN M, W
Augustana Coll, IL M, W
Augustana Coll, SD W(s)
Aurora U, IL M, W
Avila U, MO M(s), W(s)
Bacone Coll, OK M(s), W(s)
Baker U, KS M(s), W(s)
Baldwin-Wallace Coll, OH M, W
Ball State U, IN M, W
Baptist Bible Coll, MO M
Barclay Coll, KS M
Bellevue U, NE M(s), W
Beloit Coll, WI M, W
Bemidji State U, MN W(s)
Benedictine Coll, KS M(s), W(s)
Benedictine U, IL M, W
Bethany Coll, KS M(s), W(s)
Bethany Lutheran Coll, MN M(s), W(s)
Bethel Coll, IN M(s), W(s)
Bethel Coll, KS M(s), W(s)
Bethel Coll, MN M, W
Blackburn Coll, IL M, W
Blessing-Rieman Coll of Nursing, IL M(s), W(s)
Bluffton Coll, OH M, W
Bowling Green State U, OH M(s)
Bradley U, IL M(s), W
Briar Cliff U, IA M(s), W(s)
Buena Vista U, IA M, W
Butler U, IN M(s), W(s)
Calumet Coll of Saint Joseph, IN M
Calvin Coll, MI M, W
Capital U, OH M, W
Cardinal Stritch U, WI M, W
Carleton Coll, MN M, W
Carroll Coll, WI M, W
Carthage Coll, WI M, W
Case Western Reserve U, OH M, W
Cedarville U, OH M(s), W(s)
Central Bible Coll, MO M
Central Christian Coll of Kansas, KS M(s), W(s)
Central Coll, IA M, W

Central Methodist Coll, MO	M(s), W(s)
Central Michigan U, MI	W(s)
Central Missouri State U, MO	M, W(s)
Cincinnati Bible Coll and Seminary, OH	M, W
Clarke Coll, IA	M, W
Cleveland State U, OH	M(s)
Coe Coll, IA	M, W
Coll of Mount St. Joseph, OH	W
Coll of Saint Benedict, MN	W
Coll of St. Catherine, MN	W
Coll of Saint Mary, NE	W(s)
The Coll of St. Scholastica, MN	M, W
The Coll of Wooster, OH	M, W
Columbia Coll, MO	M(s)
Concordia Coll, MN	M, W
Concordia U, IL	M, W
Concordia U, MI	M(s), W(s)
Concordia U, MN	M, W(s)
Concordia U, NE	M(s), W(s)
Concordia U Wisconsin, WI	M, W
Cornell Coll, IA	M, W
Cornerstone U, MI	M(s), W(s)
Creighton U, NE	M(s), W(s)
Crown Coll, MN	M, W
Culver-Stockton Coll, MO	M(s), W(s)
Dana Coll, NE	M(s), W(s)
Defiance Coll, OH	M, W
Denison U, OH	M, W
DePaul U, IL	M(s), W(s)
DePauw U, IN	M, W
Doane Coll, NE	M(s), W(s)
Dominican U, IL	M, W
Dordt Coll, IA	M(s), W(s)
Drake U, IA	M(s), W(s)
Drury U, MO	M(s), W(s)
Earlham Coll, IN	M, W
East Central U, OK	W(s)
Eastern Illinois U, IL	M(s), W(s)
Eastern Michigan U, MI	W(s)
Edgewood Coll, WI	M, W
Elmhurst Coll, IL	W
Emporia State U, KS	W(s)
Faith Baptist Bible Coll and Theological Seminary, IA	M, W
Finlandia U, MI	M, W
Fontbonne U, MO	M, W
The Franciscan U, IA	M(s), W(s)
Franklin Coll, IN	M, W
Goshen Coll, IN	M(s), W(s)
Grace Bible Coll, MI	M
Grace Coll, IN	M(s), W(s)
Graceland U, IA	M(s), W(s)
Grace U, NE	M
Grand Valley State U, MI	M, W(s)
Grand View Coll, IA	M(s), W(s)
Great Lakes Christian Coll, MI	M, W
Greenville Coll, IL	M, W
Grinnell Coll, IA	M, W
Gustavus Adolphus Coll, MN	M, W
Hamline U, MN	M, W
Hanover Coll, IN	M, W
Harris-Stowe State Coll, MO	M(s), W(s)
Hastings Coll, NE	M(s), W(s)
Heidelberg Coll, OH	M, W
Hesston Coll, KS	M(s)
Hiram Coll, OH	M, W
Hope Coll, MI	M, W
Huntington Coll, IN	M(s), W(s)
Illinois Coll, IL	M, W
Illinois Inst of Technology, IL	M(s), W(s)
Illinois State U, IL	W(s)
Illinois Wesleyan U, IL	M, W
Indiana Inst of Technology, IN	M(s), W(s)
Indiana State U, IN	M, W
Indiana U Bloomington, IN	M(s), W(s)
Indiana U–Purdue U Fort Wayne, IN	M(s), W(s)
Indiana U–Purdue U Indianapolis, IN	M(s), W(s)
Indiana U South Bend, IN	M
Indiana Wesleyan U, IN	M(s), W(s)
Iowa State U of Science and Technology, IA	W(s)
Iowa Wesleyan Coll, IA	M(s), W(s)
Jamestown Coll, ND	W(s)
John Carroll U, OH	M, W
Judson Coll, IL	M(s), W(s)
Kalamazoo Coll, MI	M, W
Kendall Coll, IL	M, W
Kent State U, OH	W(s)
Kenyon Coll, OH	M, W
Kettering U, MI	M
Knox Coll, IL	M, W
Lake Erie Coll, OH	M, W
Lake Forest Coll, IL	M, W
Lakeland Coll, WI	M, W
Lawrence U, WI	M, W
Lewis U, IL	M(s), W(s)
Lincoln Christian Coll, IL	M, W
Lincoln Coll, Lincoln, IL	M(s), W(s)
Lincoln Coll, Normal, IL	M, W
Lindenwood U, MO	M(s), W(s)
Loras Coll, IA	M, W
Loyola U Chicago, IL	M(s), W(s)
Luther Coll, IA	M, W
Macalester Coll, MN	M, W
MacMurray Coll, IL	M, W
Madonna U, MI	M(s)
Maharishi U of Management, IA	M, W
Malone Coll, OH	M(s), W(s)
Manchester Coll, IN	M, W
Manhattan Christian Coll, KS	M, W
Maranatha Baptist Bible Coll, WI	M, W
Marian Coll, IN	M(s), W(s)
Marian Coll of Fond du Lac, WI	M, W
Marietta Coll, OH	M, W
Marquette U, WI	M(s), W(s)
Martin Luther Coll, MN	M, W
Maryville U of Saint Louis, MO	M, W
McKendree Coll, IL	M(s), W(s)
Miami U, OH	M, W(s)
Michigan State U, MI	M(s)
Michigan Technological U, MI	M, W
MidAmerica Nazarene U, KS	M(s), W(s)
Midland Lutheran Coll, NE	M(s), W(s)
Millikin U, IL	M, W
Milwaukee School of Engineering, WI	M, W
Minnesota State U, Mankato, MN	W(s)
Minnesota State U, Moorhead, MN	W(s)
Missouri Southern State Coll, MO	M(s), W(s)
Missouri Valley Coll, MO	M(s), W(s)
Monmouth Coll, IL	M, W
Moody Bible Inst, IL	M
Mount Marty Coll, SD	M(s)
Mount Mary Coll, WI	W
Mount Mercy Coll, IA	M, W
Mount Union Coll, OH	M, W
Mount Vernon Nazarene U, OH	M(s), W(s)
Muskingum Coll, OH	M, W
Nebraska Christian Coll, NE	M
Nebraska Wesleyan U, NE	M, W
Newman U, KS	M(s), W(s)
North Central Coll, IL	M, W
North Dakota State U, ND	M, W(s)
Northeastern State U, OK	M(s), W(s)
Northern Illinois U, IL	M(s), W(s)
Northern Michigan U, MI	W(s)
Northern State U, SD	W(s)
Northland Coll, WI	M, W
North Park U, IL	M, W
Northwestern Coll, IA	M(s), W(s)
Northwestern Coll, MN	M, W
Northwestern Oklahoma State U, OK	W(s)
Northwestern U, IL	M(s), W(s)
Northwest Missouri State U, MO	W(s)
Northwood U, MI	M(s), W(s)
Notre Dame Coll, OH	M, W
Oakland City U, IN	M, W
Oakland U, MI	M(s), W(s)
Oberlin Coll, OH	M, W
Ohio Dominican U, OH	M(s), W
Ohio Northern U, OH	M, W
The Ohio State U, OH	M(s), W(s)
Ohio U, OH	M, W(s)
Ohio Wesleyan U, OH	M, W
Oklahoma Christian U, OK	M(s), W(s)
Oklahoma City U, OK	M(s), W(s)
Oklahoma State U, OK	W
Oklahoma Wesleyan U, OK	M(s), W(s)
Olivet Coll, MI	M, W
Olivet Nazarene U, IL	M(s), W(s)
Oral Roberts U, OK	M(s), W(s)
Ottawa U, KS	M(s), W(s)
Otterbein Coll, OH	M, W
Ozark Christian Coll, MO	M
Park U, MO	M(s), W(s)
Pillsbury Baptist Bible Coll, MN	M
Presentation Coll, SD	M, W
Principia Coll, IL	M, W
Purdue U, IN	M, W(s)
Quincy U, IL	M(s), W(s)
Research Coll of Nursing, MO	M(s), W(s)
Ripon Coll, WI	M, W
Robert Morris Coll, IL	M(s), W(s)
Rochester Coll, MI	M(s), W(s)
Rochester Comm and Tech Coll, MN	W
Rockford Coll, IL	M, W
Rockhurst U, MO	M(s), W(s)
Rose-Hulman Inst of Technology, IN	M, W
Saginaw Valley State U, MI	M(s), W(s)
St. Ambrose U, IA	M(s), W(s)
St. Cloud State U, MN	M, W(s)
St. Gregory's U, OK	M(s), W(s)
Saint John's U, MN	M
Saint Joseph's Coll, IN	M(s), W(s)
Saint Louis U, MO	M(s), W(s)
Saint Mary-of-the-Woods Coll, IN	W(s)
Saint Mary's Coll, IN	W
Saint Mary's Coll of Madonna U, MI	M, W
Saint Mary's U of Minnesota, MN	M, W
Saint Mary U, KS	M(s), W(s)
St. Norbert Coll, WI	M, W
St. Olaf Coll, MN	M, W
Saint Xavier U, IL	M(s), W(s)
Shawnee State U, OH	M, W
Siena Heights U, MI	M(s), W(s)
Simpson Coll, IA	M, W
Si Tanka Huron U, SD	M(s), W(s)
South Dakota State U, SD	W(s)
Southeast Missouri State U, MO	W(s)
Southern Illinois U Edwardsville, IL	M(s), W(s)
Southern Nazarene U, OK	M(s), W(s)
Southwest Baptist U, MO	M(s), W(s)
Southwestern Coll, KS	M(s), W(s)
Southwestern Oklahoma State U, OK	W(s)
Southwest Minnesota State U, MN	W(s)
Southwest Missouri State U, MO	M(s), W(s)
Spring Arbor U, MI	M(s), W(s)
Springfield Coll in Illinois, IL	M(s), W(s)
Stephens Coll, MO	W
Sterling Coll, KS	M(s), W(s)
Tabor Coll, KS	M(s), W(s)
Taylor U, IN	M(s), W(s)
Taylor U, Fort Wayne Campus, IN	M
Tiffin U, OH	M(s), W(s)
Trinity Christian Coll, IL	M(s), W(s)
Trinity International U, IL	M(s), W(s)
Tri-State U, IN	M, W
Truman State U, MO	M(s), W(s)

Soccer (continued)

The U of Akron, OH	M(s), W
U of Central Oklahoma, OK	W
U of Chicago, IL	M, W
U of Cincinnati, OH	M(s), W(s)
U of Dayton, OH	M(s), W(s)
U of Dubuque, IA	M, W
U of Evansville, IN	M(s), W
The U of Findlay, OH	M(s), W(s)
U of Illinois at Chicago, IL	M(s)
U of Illinois at Springfield, IL	M(s)
U of Illinois at Urbana–Champaign, IL	W(s)
U of Indianapolis, IN	M(s), W(s)
The U of Iowa, IA	M, W(s)
U of Kansas, KS	M, W(s)
U of Mary, ND	M(s), W(s)
U of Michigan, MI	W(s)
U of Minnesota, Crookston, MN	W(s)
U of Minnesota, Duluth, MN	M, W(s)
U of Minnesota, Morris, MN	W(s)
U of Minnesota, Twin Cities Campus, MN	W(s)
U of Missouri–Columbia, MO	W(s)
U of Missouri–Kansas City, MO	M(s)
U of Missouri–Rolla, MO	M(s), W(s)
U of Missouri–St. Louis, MO	M(s), W(s)
U of Nebraska at Omaha, NE	W
U of Nebraska–Lincoln, NE	W(s)
U of North Dakota, ND	W
U of Northern Iowa, IA	W(s)
U of Notre Dame, IN	M(s), W(s)
U of Oklahoma, OK	W(s)
U of Rio Grande, OH	M(s)
U of St. Francis, IL	M(s), W(s)
U of Saint Francis, IN	M(s), W(s)
U of St. Thomas, MN	M, W
U of Science and Arts of Oklahoma, OK	M(s), W(s)
U of Sioux Falls, SD	M(s), W(s)
U of Southern Indiana, IN	M(s), W(s)
U of Toledo, OH	W(s)
U of Tulsa, OK	M(s), W(s)
U of Wisconsin–Eau Claire, WI	W
U of Wisconsin–Green Bay, WI	M(s), W(s)
U of Wisconsin–La Crosse, WI	W
U of Wisconsin–Madison, WI	M(s), W(s)
U of Wisconsin–Milwaukee, WI	M(s), W(s)
U of Wisconsin–Oshkosh, WI	M, W
U of Wisconsin–Parkside, WI	M(s), W(s)
U of Wisconsin–Platteville, WI	M, W
U of Wisconsin–River Falls, WI	M, W
U of Wisconsin–Stevens Point, WI	W
U of Wisconsin–Stout, WI	M, W
U of Wisconsin–Superior, WI	M, W
U of Wisconsin–Whitewater, WI	M, W
Upper Iowa U, IA	M, W
Urbana U, OH	M(s), W(s)
Ursuline Coll, OH	W(s)
Valparaiso U, IN	M(s), W(s)
Vennard Coll, IA	M
Viterbo U, WI	M(s), W(s)
Wabash Coll, IN	M
Waldorf Coll, IA	M(s), W(s)
Walsh U, OH	M(s), W(s)
Wartburg Coll, IA	M, W
Washington U in St. Louis, MO	M, W
Wayne State Coll, NE	M, W(s)
Webster U, MO	M, W
Western Illinois U, IL	M(s), W(s)
Western Michigan U, MI	M(s), W(s)
Westminster Coll, MO	M, W
Wheaton Coll, IL	M, W
Wichita State U, KS	M, W
William Jewell Coll, MO	M(s), W(s)
William Penn U, IA	M(s), W(s)
William Woods U, MO	M(s), W(s)
Wilmington Coll, OH	M, W
Winona State U, MN	M, W(s)
Wisconsin Lutheran Coll, WI	M, W
Wittenberg U, OH	M, W
Wright State U, OH	M(s), W(s)
Xavier U, OH	M(s), W(s)
York Coll, NE	M(s), W(s)
Youngstown State U, OH	W

SOFTBALL

Adrian Coll, MI	W
Albion Coll, MI	W
Alma Coll, MI	W
Alverno Coll, WI	W
Ancilla Coll, IN	W(s)
Anderson U, IN	W
Aquinas Coll, MI	W(s)
Ashland U, OH	M, W(s)
Augsburg Coll, MN	W
Augustana Coll, IL	W
Augustana Coll, SD	W(s)
Aurora U, IL	W
Avila U, MO	W(s)
Bacone Coll, OK	W(s)
Baker U, KS	W(s)
Baldwin-Wallace Coll, OH	W
Ball State U, IN	W(s)
Bellevue U, NE	W(s)
Beloit Coll, WI	W
Bemidji State U, MN	W(s)
Benedictine Coll, KS	W(s)
Benedictine U, IL	W
Bethany Coll, KS	W(s)
Bethany Lutheran Coll, MN	W(s)
Bethel Coll, IN	W(s)
Bethel Coll, MN	W
Blackburn Coll, IL	W
Bluffton Coll, OH	W
Bowling Green State U, OH	W(s)
Bradley U, IL	W(s)
Briar Cliff U, IA	W(s)
Buena Vista U, IA	W
Butler U, IN	W(s)
Calumet Coll of Saint Joseph, IN	W
Calvin Coll, MI	W
Cameron U, OK	W(s)
Capital U, OH	W
Cardinal Stritch U, WI	W
Carleton Coll, MN	W
Carroll Coll, WI	W
Carthage Coll, WI	W
Case Western Reserve U, OH	W
Cedarville U, OH	W(s)
Central Christian Coll of Kansas, KS	W(s)
Central Coll, IA	W
Central Methodist Coll, MO	W(s)
Central Michigan U, MI	W(s)
Central Missouri State U, MO	W(s)
Clarke Coll, IA	W
Cleveland State U, OH	W(s)
Coe Coll, IA	W
Coll of Mount St. Joseph, OH	W
Coll of Saint Benedict, MN	W
Coll of St. Catherine, MN	W
Coll of Saint Mary, NE	W(s)
The Coll of St. Scholastica, MN	W
The Coll of Wooster, OH	W
Columbia Coll, MO	W(s)
Concordia Coll, MN	W
Concordia U, IL	W
Concordia U, MI	W(s)
Concordia U, MN	W(s)
Concordia U, NE	W(s)
Concordia U Wisconsin, WI	W
Cornell Coll, IA	W
Cornerstone U, MI	W(s)
Creighton U, NE	W(s)
Crossroads Coll, MN	W
Crown Coll, MN	W
Culver-Stockton Coll, MO	W(s)
Dakota State U, SD	W
Dakota Wesleyan U, SD	W(s)
Dana Coll, NE	W(s)
Defiance Coll, OH	W
Denison U, OH	W
DePaul U, IL	W(s)
DePauw U, IN	W
Dickinson State U, ND	W(s)
Doane Coll, NE	W(s)
Dominican U, IL	W
Dordt Coll, IA	W(s)
Drake U, IA	W(s)
East Central U, OK	W(s)
Eastern Illinois U, IL	W(s)
Eastern Michigan U, MI	W(s)
Edgewood Coll, WI	W
Elmhurst Coll, IL	W
Emporia State U, KS	W(s)
Eureka Coll, IL	W
Evangel U, MO	W(s)
Ferris State U, MI	W(s)
Finlandia U, MI	W
Fontbonne U, MO	W
Fort Hays State U, KS	W
The Franciscan U, IA	W(s)
Franklin Coll, IN	W
Goshen Coll, IN	W(s)
Grace Coll, IN	W(s)
Graceland U, IA	W(s)
Grand Valley State U, MI	W(s)
Grand View Coll, IA	W(s)
Greenville Coll, IL	W
Grinnell Coll, IA	W
Gustavus Adolphus Coll, MN	W
Hamline U, MN	W
Hannibal-LaGrange Coll, MO	W(s)
Hanover Coll, IN	W
Haskell Indian Nations U, KS	W
Hastings Coll, NE	W(s)
Heidelberg Coll, OH	W
Hesston Coll, KS	W(s)
Hillsdale Coll, MI	W(s)
Hillsdale Free Will Baptist Coll, OK	W
Hiram Coll, OH	W
Hope Coll, MI	W
Huntington Coll, IN	W(s)
Illinois Coll, IL	W
Illinois State U, IL	W(s)
Illinois Wesleyan U, IL	W
Indiana Inst of Technology, IN	W(s)
Indiana State U, IN	W(s)
Indiana U Bloomington, IN	W(s)
Indiana U Northwest, IN	W
Indiana U–Purdue U Fort Wayne, IN	W(s)
Indiana U–Purdue U Indianapolis, IN	W(s)
Indiana Wesleyan U, IN	W(s)
Iowa State U of Science and Technology, IA	W(s)
Iowa Wesleyan Coll, IA	W(s)
Jamestown Coll, ND	W(s)
John Carroll U, OH	W
Judson Coll, IL	W(s)
Kalamazoo Coll, MI	W
Kent State U, OH	W(s)
Kenyon Coll, OH	W
Knox Coll, IL	W
Lake Erie Coll, OH	W
Lake Forest Coll, IL	W
Lakeland Coll, WI	W
Lawrence U, WI	W
Lewis U, IL	W(s)
Lincoln Coll, Lincoln, IL	W(s)
Lincoln Coll, Normal, IL	W

Lindenwood U, MO	W(s)
Loras Coll, IA	W
Loyola U Chicago, IL	W(s)
Luther Coll, IA	W
Macalester Coll, MN	W
MacMurray Coll, IL	W
Madonna U, MI	W(s)
Malone Coll, OH	W(s)
Manchester Coll, IN	W
Maranatha Baptist Bible Coll, WI	W
Marian Coll, IN	W(s)
Marian Coll of Fond du Lac, WI	W
Marietta Coll, OH	W
Marquette U, WI	W
Martin Luther Coll, MN	W
Maryville U of Saint Louis, MO	W
Mayville State U, ND	W(s)
McKendree Coll, IL	W(s)
McPherson Coll, KS	W
Miami U, OH	W(s)
Miami U–Middletown Campus, OH	W
Michigan State U, MI	W
Mid-America Coll of Funeral Service, IN	M, W
MidAmerica Nazarene U, KS	W(s)
Midland Lutheran Coll, NE	W(s)
Millikin U, IL	W
Milwaukee School of Engineering, WI	W
Minnesota State U, Mankato, MN	W(s)
Minnesota State U, Moorhead, MN	W(s)
Minot State U, ND	W(s)
Missouri Southern State Coll, MO	W(s)
Missouri Valley Coll, MO	W(s)
Missouri Western State Coll, MO	W(s)
Monmouth Coll, IL	W
Mount Marty Coll, SD	W(s)
Mount Mary Coll, WI	W
Mount Mercy Coll, IA	W
Mount Union Coll, OH	W
Mount Vernon Nazarene U, OH	W(s)
Muskingum Coll, OH	W
Nebraska Wesleyan U, NE	W
Newman U, KS	W(s)
North Central Coll, IL	W
North Dakota State U, ND	W(s)
Northeastern State U, OK	W(s)
Northern Illinois U, IL	W(s)
Northern Michigan U, MI	W
Northern State U, SD	W(s)
Northland Coll, WI	W
North Park U, IL	W
Northwestern Coll, IA	W(s)
Northwestern Coll, MN	W
Northwestern Oklahoma State U, OK	W(s)
Northwestern U, IL	W(s)
Northwest Missouri State U, MO	W(s)
Northwood U, MI	W(s)
Notre Dame Coll, OH	W
Oakland City U, IN	W(s)
Oakland U, MI	W(s)
Oberlin Coll, OH	W
Ohio Dominican U, OH	W(s)
Ohio Northern U, OH	W
The Ohio State U, OH	W(s)
Ohio U, OH	W(s)
Ohio U–Lancaster, OH	W
Ohio U–Zanesville, OH	W
Ohio Wesleyan U, OH	W
Oklahoma Baptist U, OK	W(s)
Oklahoma Christian U, OK	W(s)
Oklahoma City U, OK	W(s)
Oklahoma Panhandle State U, OK	W(s)
Oklahoma State U, OK	W(s)
Oklahoma Wesleyan U, OK	W(s)
Olivet Coll, MI	W
Olivet Nazarene U, IL	W(s)
Ottawa U, KS	W(s)
Otterbein Coll, OH	W
Park U, MO	W(s)
Peru State Coll, NE	W(s)
Pillsbury Baptist Bible Coll, MN	W
Pittsburg State U, KS	W(s)
Presentation Coll, SD	W
Purdue U, IN	W(s)
Purdue U North Central, IN	W
Quincy U, IL	W(s)
Ripon Coll, WI	W
Robert Morris Coll, IL	W(s)
Rochester Coll, MI	W(s)
Rochester Comm and Tech Coll, MN	W
Rockford Coll, IL	W
Rose-Hulman Inst of Technology, IN	W
Saginaw Valley State U, MI	W(s)
St. Ambrose U, IA	W(s)
St. Cloud State U, MN	W(s)
St. Gregory's U, OK	W(s)
Saint Joseph's Coll, IN	W(s)
Saint Louis U, MO	W(s)
Saint Mary-of-the-Woods Coll, IN	W(s)
Saint Mary's Coll, IN	W
Saint Mary's U of Minnesota, MN	W
Saint Mary U, KS	W(s)
St. Norbert Coll, WI	W
St. Olaf Coll, MN	W
Saint Xavier U, IL	W(s)
Shawnee State U, OH	W
Siena Heights U, MI	W(s)
Simpson Coll, IA	W
Si Tanka Huron U, SD	W(s)
South Dakota State U, SD	W(s)
Southeastern Oklahoma State U, OK	W(s)
Southeast Missouri State U, MO	W(s)
Southern Illinois U Carbondale, IL	W(s)
Southern Illinois U Edwardsville, IL	W(s)
Southern Nazarene U, OK	W(s)
Southwest Baptist U, MO	W(s)
Southwestern Coll, KS	W(s)
Southwestern Oklahoma State U, OK	W(s)
Southwest Minnesota State U, MN	W(s)
Southwest Missouri State U, MO	W(s)
Spartan School of Aeronautics, OK	W
Spring Arbor U, MI	W(s)
Springfield Coll in Illinois, IL	W(s)
Sterling Coll, KS	W(s)
Tabor Coll, KS	W(s)
Taylor U, IN	W(s)
Taylor U, Fort Wayne Campus, IN	W
Tiffin U, OH	W(s)
Trinity Christian Coll, IL	W(s)
Trinity International U, IL	W(s)
Tri-State U, IN	W
Truman State U, MO	W(s)
The U of Akron, OH	W(s)
U of Central Oklahoma, OK	W(s)
U of Chicago, IL	W
U of Dayton, OH	W(s)
U of Dubuque, IA	W
U of Evansville, IN	W
The U of Findlay, OH	W(s)
U of Illinois at Chicago, IL	W(s)
U of Illinois at Springfield, IL	W(s)
U of Indianapolis, IN	W(s)
The U of Iowa, IA	W(s)
U of Kansas, KS	W(s)
U of Mary, ND	W(s)
U of Michigan, MI	W(s)
U of Minnesota, Crookston, MN	W(s)
U of Minnesota, Duluth, MN	W(s)
U of Minnesota, Morris, MN	W
U of Minnesota, Twin Cities Campus, MN	W(s)
U of Missouri–Columbia, MO	W(s)
U of Missouri–Kansas City, MO	W(s)
U of Missouri–Rolla, MO	W(s)
U of Missouri–St. Louis, MO	W(s)
U of Nebraska at Kearney, NE	W(s)
U of Nebraska at Omaha, NE	W(s)
U of Nebraska–Lincoln, NE	W(s)
U of North Dakota, ND	W(s)
U of Northern Iowa, IA	W(s)
U of Notre Dame, IN	W(s)
U of Oklahoma, OK	W(s)
U of Rio Grande, OH	W(s)
U of St. Francis, IL	W(s)
U of Saint Francis, IN	W(s)
U of St. Thomas, MN	W
U of Science and Arts of Oklahoma, OK	W(s)
U of Sioux Falls, SD	W(s)
The U of South Dakota, SD	W(s)
U of Southern Indiana, IN	W(s)
U of Toledo, OH	W(s)
U of Tulsa, OK	W(s)
U of Wisconsin–Eau Claire, WI	W
U of Wisconsin–Green Bay, WI	W(s)
U of Wisconsin–La Crosse, WI	W
U of Wisconsin–Madison, WI	W(s)
U of Wisconsin–Oshkosh, WI	W
U of Wisconsin–Parkside, WI	W(s)
U of Wisconsin–Platteville, WI	W
U of Wisconsin–River Falls, WI	W
U of Wisconsin–Stevens Point, WI	W
U of Wisconsin–Stout, WI	W
U of Wisconsin–Superior, WI	W
U of Wisconsin–Whitewater, WI	W
Upper Iowa U, IA	W
Urbana U, OH	W(s)
Ursuline Coll, OH	W(s)
Valley City State U, ND	W(s)
Valparaiso U, IN	W(s)
Viterbo U, WI	W(s)
Waldorf Coll, IA	W(s)
Walsh U, OH	W(s)
Wartburg Coll, IA	W
Washington U in St. Louis, MO	W
Wayne State Coll, NE	W(s)
Wayne State U, MI	W(s)
Webster U, MO	W
Western Illinois U, IL	W(s)
Western Michigan U, MI	W(s)
Westminster Coll, MO	W
Wheaton Coll, IL	W
Wichita State U, KS	W(s)
William Jewell Coll, MO	W(s)
William Penn U, IA	W(s)
William Woods U, MO	W(s)
Wilmington Coll, OH	W
Winona State U, MN	W(s)
Wisconsin Lutheran Coll, WI	W
Wittenberg U, OH	W
Wright State U, OH	W(s)
York Coll, NE	W(s)
Youngstown State U, OH	W(s)

SQUASH

Denison U, OH	M, W
Michigan Technological U, MI	M, W
Purdue U, IN	M, W

SWIMMING

Albion Coll, MI	M, W
Alma Coll, MI	M, W
Ashland U, OH	M(s), W(s)
Augustana Coll, IL	M, W
Baldwin-Wallace Coll, OH	M, W
Ball State U, IN	M(s), W(s)
Beloit Coll, WI	M, W
Benedictine U, IL	M, W
Bowling Green State U, OH	M(s), W(s)

Swimming (continued)

Buena Vista U, IA	M, W
Butler U, IN	M, W
Calvin Coll, MI	M, W
Carleton Coll, MN	M, W
Carroll Coll, WI	M, W
Carthage Coll, WI	M, W
Case Western Reserve U, OH	M, W
Cleveland State U, OH	M(s), W(s)
Coe Coll, IA	M, W
Coll of Saint Benedict, MN	W
Coll of St. Catherine, MN	W
The Coll of Wooster, OH	M, W
Concordia Coll, MN	W
Denison U, OH	M, W
DePauw U, IN	M, W
Drury U, MO	M(s), W(s)
Eastern Illinois U, IL	M(s), W(s)
Eastern Michigan U, MI	M(s), W(s)
Eureka Coll, IL	M, W
Grand Valley State U, MI	M(s), W(s)
Grinnell Coll, IA	M, W
Gustavus Adolphus Coll, MN	M, W
Hamline U, MN	M, W
Hillsdale Coll, MI	W(s)
Hiram Coll, OH	M, W
Hope Coll, MI	M, W
Illinois Inst of Technology, IL	M(s), W(s)
Illinois State U, IL	W(s)
Illinois Wesleyan U, IL	M, W
Indiana State U, IN	M, W
Indiana U Bloomington, IN	M(s), W(s)
Indiana U–Purdue U Indianapolis, IN	M(s), W(s)
Iowa State U of Science and Technology, IA	M(s), W(s)
John Carroll U, OH	M, W
Kalamazoo Coll, MI	M, W
Kenyon Coll, OH	M, W
Knox Coll, IL	M, W
Lake Forest Coll, IL	M, W
Lawrence U, WI	M, W
Lewis U, IL	M(s), W(s)
Lincoln Coll, Lincoln, IL	M(s), W(s)
Lincoln Coll, Normal, IL	M, W
Lindenwood U, MO	M(s), W(s)
Loras Coll, IA	M, W
Luther Coll, IA	M, W
Macalester Coll, MN	M, W
MacMurray Coll, IL	M, W
Marquette U, WI	M, W
Miami U, OH	M(s), W(s)
Michigan State U, MI	M(s), W(s)
Michigan Technological U, MI	M, W
Millikin U, IL	M, W
Minnesota State U, Mankato, MN	M(s), W(s)
Mount Union Coll, OH	M, W
North Central Coll, IL	M, W
Northern Illinois U, IL	M(s), W(s)
Northern Michigan U, MI	W(s)
Northwestern U, IL	M(s), W(s)
Oakland U, MI	M(s), W(s)
Oberlin Coll, OH	M, W
Ohio Northern U, OH	M, W
The Ohio State U, OH	M(s), W(s)
Ohio U, OH	M(s), W(s)
Ohio Wesleyan U, OH	M, W
Olivet Coll, MI	W
Principia Coll, IL	M, W
Purdue U, IN	M(s), W(s)
Ripon Coll, WI	M, W
Rose-Hulman Inst of Technology, IN	M, W
St. Cloud State U, MN	M(s), W(s)
Saint John's U, MN	M
Saint Louis U, MO	M(s), W(s)
Saint Mary's Coll, IN	W
Saint Mary's U of Minnesota, MN	M, W
St. Norbert Coll, WI	W
St. Olaf Coll, MN	M, W
Simpson Coll, IA	M, W
South Dakota State U, SD	M(s), W(s)
Southern Illinois U Carbondale, IL	M(s), W(s)
Southwest Missouri State U, MO	M(s), W(s)
Stephens Coll, MO	W
Tri-State U, IN	M, W
Truman State U, MO	M(s), W(s)
U of Chicago, IL	M, W
U of Cincinnati, OH	M(s), W(s)
U of Evansville, IN	M(s), W(s)
The U of Findlay, OH	M(s), W(s)
U of Illinois at Chicago, IL	M(s), W(s)
U of Illinois at Urbana–Champaign, IL	W(s)
U of Indianapolis, IN	M(s), W(s)
The U of Iowa, IA	M(s), W(s)
U of Kansas, KS	W(s)
U of Michigan, MI	M(s), W(s)
U of Minnesota, Twin Cities Campus, MN	M(s), W(s)
U of Missouri–Columbia, MO	M(s), W(s)
U of Missouri–Rolla, MO	M(s)
U of Nebraska at Kearney, NE	W(s)
U of Nebraska at Omaha, NE	W
U of Nebraska–Lincoln, NE	W(s)
U of North Dakota, ND	M, W(s)
U of Northern Iowa, IA	W(s)
U of Notre Dame, IN	M(s), W(s)
U of St. Thomas, MN	M, W
The U of South Dakota, SD	M(s), W
U of Toledo, OH	M(s), W(s)
U of Wisconsin–Eau Claire, WI	M, W
U of Wisconsin–Green Bay, WI	M(s), W(s)
U of Wisconsin–La Crosse, WI	M, W
U of Wisconsin–Madison, WI	M(s), W(s)
U of Wisconsin–Milwaukee, WI	M(s), W(s)
U of Wisconsin–Oshkosh, WI	M, W
U of Wisconsin–River Falls, WI	M, W
U of Wisconsin–Stevens Point, WI	M, W
U of Wisconsin–Whitewater, WI	M, W
Valparaiso U, IN	M(s), W(s)
Wabash Coll, IN	M
Walsh U, OH	W(s)
Washington U in St. Louis, MO	M, W
Wayne State U, MI	M(s), W(s)
Webster U, MO	W
Western Illinois U, IL	M(s), W(s)
Wheaton Coll, IL	M, W
Wichita State U, KS	M, W
Wilmington Coll, OH	M, W
Wittenberg U, OH	M, W
Wright State U, OH	M(s), W(s)
Xavier U, OH	M(s), W(s)
Youngstown State U, OH	W

TABLE TENNIS

Bradley U, IL	M, W
Hiram Coll, OH	M, W
Indiana U South Bend, IN	M, W
Michigan Technological U, MI	M, W
Purdue U, IN	M, W
The U of Iowa, IA	M, W
Washington U in St. Louis, MO	M, W

TENNIS

Adrian Coll, MI	M, W
Albion Coll, MI	M, W
Alma Coll, MI	M, W
Ancilla Coll, IN	M(s), W(s)
Anderson U, IN	M, W
Aquinas Coll, MI	M(s), W(s)
Ashland U, OH	M, W
Augustana Coll, IL	M, W
Augustana Coll, SD	M, W
Aurora U, IL	M, W
Baker U, KS	M(s), W(s)
Baldwin-Wallace Coll, OH	M, W
Ball State U, IN	M(s), W(s)
Barclay Coll, KS	M, W
Beloit Coll, WI	M, W
Bemidji State U, MN	W(s)
Benedictine Coll, KS	M(s), W(s)
Benedictine U, IL	W
Bethany Coll, KS	M(s), W(s)
Bethany Lutheran Coll, MN	M(s), W(s)
Bethel Coll, IN	M(s), W(s)
Bethel Coll, KS	M(s), W(s)
Bethel Coll, MN	M, W
Blackburn Coll, IL	W
Bluffton Coll, OH	M, W
Bowling Green State U, OH	M(s), W(s)
Bradley U, IL	M(s), W(s)
Buena Vista U, IA	M, W
Butler U, IN	M(s), W(s)
Calvin Coll, MI	M, W
Cameron U, OK	M(s), W(s)
Capital U, OH	M, W
Carleton Coll, MN	M, W
Carroll Coll, WI	M, W
Carthage Coll, WI	M, W
Case Western Reserve U, OH	M, W
Cedarville U, OH	M(s), W(s)
Central Christian Coll of Kansas, KS	M(s), W(s)
Central Coll, IA	M, W
Chicago State U, IL	M, W
Clarke Coll, IA	M, W
Cleveland State U, OH	W(s)
Coe Coll, IA	M, W
Coll of Mount St. Joseph, OH	M, W
Coll of Saint Benedict, MN	W
Coll of St. Catherine, MN	W
The Coll of St. Scholastica, MN	M, W
The Coll of Wooster, OH	M, W
Concordia Coll, MN	M, W
Concordia U, IL	M, W
Concordia U, NE	M(s), W(s)
Concordia U Wisconsin, WI	M, W
Cornell Coll, IA	M, W
Cornerstone U, MI	M(s)
Creighton U, NE	M(s), W(s)
Crossroads Coll, MN	M, W
Defiance Coll, OH	M, W
Denison U, OH	M, W
DePaul U, IL	M(s), W(s)
DePauw U, IN	M, W
Doane Coll, NE	M, W
Dominican U, IL	M, W
Dordt Coll, IA	M(s), W(s)
Drake U, IA	M(s), W(s)
Drury U, MO	M(s), W(s)
Earlham Coll, IN	M, W
East Central U, OK	M(s), W(s)
Eastern Illinois U, IL	M(s), W(s)
Eastern Michigan U, MI	W(s)
Edgewood Coll, WI	M, W
Elmhurst Coll, IL	M, W
Emporia State U, KS	M(s), W(s)
Eureka Coll, IL	M, W
Evangel U, MO	M(s), W(s)
Ferris State U, MI	M(s), W(s)
Fontbonne U, MO	M, W
Fort Hays State U, KS	W(s)
Franklin Coll, IN	M, W
Goshen Coll, IN	M(s), W(s)
Grace Coll, IN	M(s), W(s)
Graceland U, IA	M(s), W(s)
Grand Valley State U, MI	M(s), W(s)
Greenville Coll, IL	M, W
Grinnell Coll, IA	M, W
Gustavus Adolphus Coll, MN	M, W
Hamline U, MN	M, W
Hanover Coll, IN	M, W
Hastings Coll, NE	M(s), W(s)

Heidelberg Coll, OH	M, W
Hesston Coll, KS	M, W
Hillsdale Coll, MI	W(s)
Hiram Coll, OH	M, W
Hope Coll, MI	M, W
Huntington Coll, IN	M(s), W(s)
Illinois Coll, IL	M, W
Illinois State U, IL	M(s), W(s)
Illinois Wesleyan U, IL	M, W
Indiana State U, IN	M(s), W(s)
Indiana U Bloomington, IN	M(s), W(s)
Indiana U–Purdue U Fort Wayne, IN	M(s), W(s)
Indiana U–Purdue U Indianapolis, IN	M(s), W(s)
Indiana Wesleyan U, IN	M(s), W(s)
Iowa State U of Science and Technology, IA	W(s)
John Carroll U, OH	M, W
Judson Coll, IL	M(s), W(s)
Kalamazoo Coll, MI	M, W
Kansas State U, KS	W(s)
Kenyon Coll, OH	M, W
Knox Coll, IL	M, W
Lake Erie Coll, OH	W
Lake Forest Coll, IL	M, W
Lakeland Coll, WI	M, W
Lawrence U, WI	M, W
Lewis U, IL	M(s), W(s)
Lincoln Coll, Lincoln, IL	M, W
Lindenwood U, MO	M(s), W(s)
Loras Coll, IA	M, W
Luther Coll, IA	M, W
Macalester Coll, MN	M, W
MacMurray Coll, IL	M, W
Maharishi U of Management, IA	M
Malone Coll, OH	M(s), W(s)
Manchester Coll, IN	M, W
Manhattan Christian Coll, KS	M, W
Marian Coll, IN	M(s), W(s)
Marian Coll of Fond du Lac, WI	M, W
Marietta Coll, OH	M, W
Marquette U, WI	M(s), W(s)
Martin Luther Coll, MN	M, W
Maryville U of Saint Louis, MO	M, W
McKendree Coll, IL	M(s), W(s)
Miami U, OH	M, W(s)
Miami U–Hamilton Campus, OH	M, W
Miami U–Middletown Campus, OH	M, W
Michigan State U, MI	M(s), W(s)
Michigan Technological U, MI	M, W(s)
Midland Lutheran Coll, NE	M(s), W(s)
Millikin U, IL	M, W
Milwaukee School of Engineering, WI	M, W
Minnesota State U, Mankato, MN	M(s), W(s)
Minnesota State U, Moorhead, MN	W
Missouri Southern State Coll, MO	W(s)
Missouri Valley Coll, MO	M(s), W(s)
Missouri Western State Coll, MO	W(s)
Monmouth Coll, IL	M, W
Mount Mary Coll, WI	W
Mount Union Coll, OH	M, W
Muskingum Coll, OH	M, W
Nebraska Wesleyan U, NE	M, W
North Central Coll, IL	M, W
Northeastern State U, OK	W(s)
Northern Illinois U, IL	M(s), W(s)
Northern Michigan U, MI	W(s)
Northern State U, SD	M, W(s)
North Park U, IL	W
Northwestern Coll, IA	M(s), W(s)
Northwestern Coll, MN	M, W
Northwestern U, IL	M(s), W(s)
Northwest Missouri State U, MO	M(s), W(s)
Northwood U, MI	M(s), W(s)
Oakland U, MI	W(s)
Oberlin Coll, OH	M, W
Ohio Dominican U, OH	M, W
Ohio Northern U, OH	M, W
The Ohio State U, OH	M(s), W(s)
Ohio U–Lancaster, OH	M, W
Ohio U–Zanesville, OH	M, W
Ohio Wesleyan U, OH	M, W
Oklahoma Baptist U, OK	M(s), W(s)
Oklahoma Christian U, OK	M(s), W(s)
Oklahoma City U, OK	M(s), W(s)
Oklahoma State U, OK	M(s), W(s)
Olivet Coll, MI	M, W
Olivet Nazarene U, IL	M(s), W(s)
Oral Roberts U, OK	M(s), W(s)
Otterbein Coll, OH	M, W
Principia Coll, IL	M, W
Purdue U, IN	M(s), W(s)
Quincy U, IL	M(s), W(s)
Research Coll of Nursing, MO	M(s), W(s)
Ripon Coll, WI	M, W
Robert Morris Coll, IL	W(s)
Rockford Coll, IL	M, W
Rockhurst U, MO	M(s), W(s)
Rose-Hulman Inst of Technology, IN	M, W
Saginaw Valley State U, MI	W(s)
St. Ambrose U, IA	M(s), W(s)
St. Cloud State U, MN	M(s), W(s)
Saint John's U, MN	M
Saint Joseph's Coll, IN	M(s), W(s)
Saint Louis U, MO	M(s), W(s)
Saint Mary's Coll, IN	W
Saint Mary's U of Minnesota, MN	M, W
St. Norbert Coll, WI	M, W
St. Olaf Coll, MN	M, W
Shawnee State U, OH	W
Simpson Coll, IA	M, W
South Dakota School of Mines and Technology, SD	M
South Dakota State U, SD	M, W
Southeastern Oklahoma State U, OK	M(s), W(s)
Southeast Missouri State U, MO	W(s)
Southern Illinois U Carbondale, IL	M(s), W(s)
Southern Illinois U Edwardsville, IL	M(s), W(s)
Southern Nazarene U, OK	M(s), W(s)
Southwest Baptist U, MO	M(s), W(s)
Southwestern Coll, KS	M(s), W(s)
Southwest Minnesota State U, MN	W(s)
Southwest Missouri State U, MO	M(s), W(s)
Spring Arbor U, MI	M(s), W(s)
Springfield Coll in Illinois, IL	W(s)
Stephens Coll, MO	W
Tabor Coll, KS	M(s), W(s)
Taylor U, IN	M(s), W(s)
Tiffin U, OH	M(s), W(s)
Tri-State U, IN	M, W
Truman State U, MO	M(s), W(s)
The U of Akron, OH	M(s), W(s)
U of Central Oklahoma, OK	M(s), W(s)
U of Chicago, IL	M, W
U of Cincinnati, OH	M(s), W(s)
U of Dayton, OH	M(s), W(s)
U of Dubuque, IA	M, W
U of Evansville, IN	M(s), W(s)
The U of Findlay, OH	M(s), W(s)
U of Illinois at Chicago, IL	M(s), W(s)
U of Illinois at Springfield, IL	M(s), W(s)
U of Illinois at Urbana–Champaign, IL	M(s), W(s)
U of Indianapolis, IN	M(s), W(s)
The U of Iowa, IA	M(s), W(s)
U of Kansas, KS	W(s)
U of Mary, ND	M(s), W(s)
U of Michigan, MI	M(s), W(s)
U of Minnesota, Crookston, MN	W(s)
U of Minnesota, Duluth, MN	M(s), W(s)
U of Minnesota, Morris, MN	M, W
U of Minnesota, Twin Cities Campus, MN	M(s), W(s)
U of Missouri–Columbia, MO	W(s)
U of Missouri–Kansas City, MO	M(s), W(s)
U of Missouri–Rolla, MO	M(s)
U of Missouri–St. Louis, MO	M(s), W(s)
U of Nebraska at Kearney, NE	M(s), W(s)
U of Nebraska at Omaha, NE	W
U of Nebraska–Lincoln, NE	M(s), W(s)
U of North Dakota, ND	W
U of Northern Iowa, IA	M, W(s)
U of Notre Dame, IN	M(s), W(s)
U of Oklahoma, OK	M(s), W(s)
U of St. Francis, IL	M(s), W(s)
U of Saint Francis, IN	W(s)
U of St. Thomas, MN	M, W
U of Sioux Falls, SD	M(s), W(s)
The U of South Dakota, SD	M(s), W(s)
U of Southern Indiana, IN	M(s), W(s)
U of Toledo, OH	M(s), W(s)
U of Tulsa, OK	M(s), W(s)
U of Wisconsin–Eau Claire, WI	M, W
U of Wisconsin–Green Bay, WI	M(s), W(s)
U of Wisconsin–La Crosse, WI	M, W
U of Wisconsin–Madison, WI	M(s), W(s)
U of Wisconsin–Milwaukee, WI	M(s), W(s)
U of Wisconsin–Oshkosh, WI	M, W
U of Wisconsin–River Falls, WI	W
U of Wisconsin–Stevens Point, WI	W
U of Wisconsin–Stout, WI	W
U of Wisconsin–Whitewater, WI	M, W
Upper Iowa U, IA	M, W
Valparaiso U, IN	M(s), W(s)
Wabash Coll, IN	M
Walsh U, OH	M(s), W(s)
Wartburg Coll, IA	M, W
Washington U in St. Louis, MO	M, W
Wayne State U, MI	M(s), W(s)
Webster U, MO	M, W
Western Illinois U, IL	M(s), W(s)
Western Michigan U, MI	M(s), W(s)
Westminster Coll, MO	M, W
Wheaton Coll, IL	M, W
Wichita State U, KS	M(s), W(s)
William Jewell Coll, MO	M(s), W(s)
Wilmington Coll, OH	M, W
Winona State U, MN	M(s), W(s)
Wisconsin Lutheran Coll, WI	W
Wittenberg U, OH	M, W
Wright State U, OH	M(s), W(s)
Xavier U, OH	M(s), W(s)
Youngstown State U, OH	M(s), W(s)

TRACK AND FIELD

Adrian Coll, MI	M, W
Albion Coll, MI	M, W
Alma Coll, MI	M, W
Anderson U, IN	M, W
Aquinas Coll, MI	M(s), W(s)
Ashland U, OH	M(s), W(s)
Augsburg Coll, MN	M, W
Augustana Coll, IL	M, W
Augustana Coll, SD	M(s), W(s)
Bacone Coll, OK	M(s), W(s)
Baker U, KS	M(s), W(s)
Baldwin-Wallace Coll, OH	M, W
Ball State U, IN	M(s), W(s)
Beloit Coll, WI	M, W
Bemidji State U, MN	M(s), W(s)
Benedictine Coll, KS	M(s), W(s)
Benedictine U, IL	M, W
Bethany Coll, KS	M(s), W(s)
Bethel Coll, IN	M(s), W(s)
Bethel Coll, KS	M(s), W(s)
Bethel Coll, MN	M, W
Black Hills State U, SD	M(s), W(s)
Bluffton Coll, OH	M, W
Bowling Green State U, OH	M(s), W(s)
Bradley U, IL	W(s)
Briar Cliff U, IA	M(s), W(s)

Track and field (continued)

Buena Vista U, IA	M, W
Butler U, IN	M, W
Calvin Coll, MI	M, W
Capital U, OH	M, W
Carleton Coll, MN	M, W
Carroll Coll, WI	M, W
Carthage Coll, WI	M, W
Case Western Reserve U, OH	M, W
Cedarville U, OH	M(s), W(s)
Central Coll, IA	M, W
Central Methodist Coll, MO	M(s), W(s)
Central Michigan U, MI	M(s), W(s)
Central Missouri State U, MO	M(s), W(s)
Chadron State Coll, NE	M(s), W(s)
Chicago State U, IL	M(s), W(s)
Cleveland State U, OH	W(s)
Coe Coll, IA	M, W
Coll of Saint Benedict, MN	W
Coll of St. Catherine, MN	W
The Coll of Wooster, OH	M, W
Concordia Coll, MN	M, W
Concordia U, IL	M, W
Concordia U, MN	M(s), W(s)
Concordia U, NE	M(s), W(s)
Concordia U Wisconsin, WI	M, W
Cornell Coll, IA	M, W
Dakota State U, SD	M(s), W(s)
Dakota Wesleyan U, SD	M(s), W(s)
Dana Coll, NE	M(s), W(s)
Defiance Coll, OH	M, W
Denison U, OH	M, W
DePaul U, IL	M(s), W(s)
DePauw U, IN	M, W
Dickinson State U, ND	M(s), W(s)
Doane Coll, NE	M(s), W(s)
Dordt Coll, IA	M(s), W(s)
Drake U, IA	M(s), W(s)
Earlham Coll, IN	M, W
Eastern Illinois U, IL	M(s), W(s)
Eastern Michigan U, MI	M(s), W(s)
Elmhurst Coll, IL	M, W
Emporia State U, KS	M(s), W(s)
Eureka Coll, IL	M, W
Evangel U, MO	M(s), W(s)
Ferris State U, MI	M(s), W(s)
Fort Hays State U, KS	M(s), W(s)
The Franciscan U, IA	M(s), W(s)
Franklin Coll, IN	M, W
Goshen Coll, IN	M(s), W(s)
Grace Coll, IN	M(s), W(s)
Graceland U, IA	M(s), W(s)
Grand Valley State U, MI	M(s), W(s)
Greenville Coll, IL	M, W
Grinnell Coll, IA	M, W
Gustavus Adolphus Coll, MN	M, W
Hamline U, MN	M, W
Hanover Coll, IN	M, W
Harris-Stowe State Coll, MO	W(s)
Haskell Indian Nations U, KS	M, W
Hastings Coll, NE	M(s), W(s)
Heidelberg Coll, OH	M, W
Hillsdale Coll, MI	M(s), W(s)
Hiram Coll, OH	M, W
Hope Coll, MI	M, W
Huntington Coll, IN	M(s), W(s)
Illinois Coll, IL	M, W
Illinois State U, IL	M(s), W(s)
Illinois Wesleyan U, IL	M, W
Indiana State U, IN	M(s), W(s)
Indiana U Bloomington, IN	M(s), W(s)
Indiana U–Purdue U Fort Wayne, IN	M(s), W(s)
Indiana Wesleyan U, IN	M(s), W(s)
Iowa State U of Science and Technology, IA	M(s), W(s)
Iowa Wesleyan Coll, IA	M(s), W(s)
Jamestown Coll, ND	M(s), W(s)
John Carroll U, OH	M, W
Kansas State U, KS	M(s), W(s)
Kent State U, OH	M(s), W(s)
Kenyon Coll, OH	M, W
Knox Coll, IL	M, W
Langston U, OK	M(s), W(s)
Lawrence U, WI	M, W
Lewis U, IL	M(s), W(s)
Lindenwood U, MO	M(s), W(s)
Loras Coll, IA	M, W
Loyola U Chicago, IL	M(s), W(s)
Luther Coll, IA	M, W
Macalester Coll, MN	M, W
Malone Coll, OH	M(s), W(s)
Manchester Coll, IN	M, W
Marian Coll, IN	M(s), W(s)
Marietta Coll, OH	M, W
Marquette U, WI	M(s), W(s)
Martin Luther Coll, MN	M, W
McKendree Coll, IL	M(s), W(s)
McPherson Coll, KS	M, W
Miami U, OH	M(s), W(s)
Michigan State U, MI	M(s), W(s)
Michigan Technological U, MI	M, W
MidAmerica Nazarene U, KS	M(s), W(s)
Midland Lutheran Coll, NE	M(s), W(s)
Millikin U, IL	M, W
Milwaukee School of Engineering, WI	M, W
Minnesota State U, Mankato, MN	M(s), W(s)
Minnesota State U, Moorhead, MN	M(s), W(s)
Minot State U, ND	M(s), W(s)
Missouri Southern State Coll, MO	M(s), W(s)
Missouri Valley Coll, MO	M(s), W(s)
Monmouth Coll, IL	M, W
Mount Marty Coll, SD	M(s), W(s)
Mount Mercy Coll, IA	M, W
Mount Union Coll, OH	M, W
Muskingum Coll, OH	M, W
Nebraska Wesleyan U, NE	M, W
North Central Coll, IL	M, W
North Dakota State U, ND	M(s), W(s)
Northern State U, SD	M(s), W(s)
North Park U, IL	M, W
Northwestern Coll, IA	M(s), W(s)
Northwestern Coll, MN	M, W
Northwest Missouri State U, MO	M(s), W(s)
Northwood U, MI	M(s), W(s)
Oberlin Coll, OH	M, W
Ohio Northern U, OH	M, W
The Ohio State U, OH	M(s), W(s)
Ohio U, OH	M(s), W(s)
Ohio Wesleyan U, OH	M, W
Oklahoma Baptist U, OK	M(s), W(s)
Oklahoma Christian U, OK	M(s), W(s)
Oklahoma State U, OK	M(s), W(s)
Olivet Coll, MI	M, W
Olivet Nazarene U, IL	M(s), W(s)
Oral Roberts U, OK	M(s), W(s)
Ottawa U, KS	M(s), W(s)
Otterbein Coll, OH	M, W
Park U, MO	M(s), W(s)
Pittsburg State U, KS	M(s), W(s)
Principia Coll, IL	M, W
Purdue U, IN	M(s), W(s)
Ripon Coll, WI	M, W
Robert Morris Coll, IL	W(s)
Rochester Coll, MI	M(s), W(s)
Rose-Hulman Inst of Technology, IN	M, W
Saginaw Valley State U, MI	M(s), W(s)
St. Ambrose U, IA	M(s), W(s)
St. Cloud State U, MN	M(s), W(s)
St. Gregory's U, OK	W
Saint John's U, MN	M
Saint Joseph's Coll, IN	M(s), W(s)
Saint Mary's U of Minnesota, MN	M, W
St. Norbert Coll, WI	M, W
St. Olaf Coll, MN	M, W
Siena Heights U, MI	M(s), W(s)
Simpson Coll, IA	M, W
Si Tanka Huron U, SD	M(s), W(s)
South Dakota School of Mines and Technology, SD	M(s), W(s)
South Dakota State U, SD	M(s), W(s)
Southeast Missouri State U, MO	M(s), W(s)
Southern Illinois U Carbondale, IL	M(s), W(s)
Southern Illinois U Edwardsville, IL	M(s), W(s)
Southern Nazarene U, OK	M(s), W(s)
Southwestern Coll, KS	M(s), W(s)
Southwest Missouri State U, MO	M(s), W(s)
Spring Arbor U, MI	M(s), W(s)
Sterling Coll, KS	M(s), W(s)
Tabor Coll, KS	M(s), W(s)
Taylor U, IN	M(s), W(s)
Tiffin U, OH	M(s), W(s)
Trinity Christian Coll, IL	M(s), W(s)
Trinity International U, IL	M, W
Tri-State U, IN	M, W
Truman State U, MO	M(s), W(s)
The U of Akron, OH	M(s), W(s)
U of Chicago, IL	M, W
U of Cincinnati, OH	M(s), W
U of Dayton, OH	W(s)
U of Dubuque, IA	M, W
The U of Findlay, OH	M(s), W(s)
U of Illinois at Chicago, IL	M(s), W(s)
U of Illinois at Urbana–Champaign, IL	M(s), W(s)
U of Indianapolis, IN	M(s), W(s)
The U of Iowa, IA	M(s), W(s)
U of Kansas, KS	M(s), W(s)
U of Mary, ND	M(s), W(s)
U of Michigan, MI	M(s), W(s)
U of Minnesota, Duluth, MN	M(s), W(s)
U of Minnesota, Morris, MN	M, W
U of Minnesota, Twin Cities Campus, MN	M(s), W(s)
U of Missouri–Columbia, MO	M(s), W(s)
U of Missouri–Kansas City, MO	M(s), W(s)
U of Missouri–Rolla, MO	M(s), W(s)
U of Nebraska at Kearney, NE	M(s), W(s)
U of Nebraska–Lincoln, NE	M(s), W(s)
U of North Dakota, ND	M(s), W(s)
U of Northern Iowa, IA	M(s), W(s)
U of Notre Dame, IN	M(s), W(s)
U of Oklahoma, OK	M(s), W(s)
U of Rio Grande, OH	M(s), W(s)
U of St. Francis, IL	W(s)
U of Saint Francis, IN	M(s), W(s)
U of St. Thomas, MN	M, W
U of Sioux Falls, SD	M(s), W(s)
The U of South Dakota, SD	M(s), W(s)
U of Toledo, OH	M(s), W(s)
U of Tulsa, OK	M(s), W(s)
U of Wisconsin–Eau Claire, WI	M, W
U of Wisconsin–La Crosse, WI	M, W
U of Wisconsin–Madison, WI	M(s), W(s)
U of Wisconsin–Milwaukee, WI	M(s), W(s)
U of Wisconsin–Oshkosh, WI	M, W
U of Wisconsin–Parkside, WI	M(s), W(s)
U of Wisconsin–Platteville, WI	M, W
U of Wisconsin–River Falls, WI	M, W
U of Wisconsin–Stevens Point, WI	M, W
U of Wisconsin–Stout, WI	M, W
U of Wisconsin–Superior, WI	M, W
U of Wisconsin–Whitewater, WI	M, W
Upper Iowa U, IA	M, W
Valley City State U, ND	M(s), W(s)
Wabash Coll, IN	M
Walsh U, OH	M(s), W(s)
Wartburg Coll, IA	M, W
Washington U in St. Louis, MO	M, W
Wayne State Coll, NE	M(s), W(s)
Wentworth Military Academy and Jr Coll, MO	M, W

Western Illinois U, IL M(s), W(s)
Western Michigan U, MI M(s), W(s)
Wheaton Coll, IL M, W
Wichita State U, KS M(s), W(s)
Wilberforce U, OH M, W
William Jewell Coll, MO M(s), W(s)
William Penn U, IA M(s), W(s)
Wilmington Coll, OH M, W
Winona State U, MN W(s)
Wisconsin Lutheran Coll, WI M, W
Wittenberg U, OH M, W
Wright State U, OH W(s)
York Coll, NE M(s), W(s)
Youngstown State U, OH M(s), W(s)

ULTIMATE FRISBEE

Augustana Coll, IL M, W
Calvin Coll, MI M, W
Carleton Coll, MN M, W
Case Western Reserve U, OH M, W
Gustavus Adolphus Coll, MN M, W
Kenyon Coll, OH M, W
Lake Forest Coll, IL M, W
Lawrence U, WI M, W
Oberlin Coll, OH M, W
Ohio Wesleyan U, OH M, W
Saint Mary's Coll, IN W
Southwest Missouri State U, MO M, W
The U of Iowa, IA M, W
Washington U in St. Louis, MO M, W

VOLLEYBALL

Adrian Coll, MI W
Albion Coll, MI M, W
Alma Coll, MI W
Alverno Coll, WI W
Anderson U, IN W
Aquinas Coll, MI W(s)
Ashland U, OH W(s)
Augsburg Coll, MN W
Augustana Coll, IL M, W
Augustana Coll, SD W(s)
Aurora U, IL W
Avila U, MO M(s), W(s)
Bacone Coll, OK M(s), W(s)
Baker U, KS W(s)
Baldwin-Wallace Coll, OH W
Ball State U, IN M(s), W(s)
Baptist Bible Coll, MO W
Barclay Coll, KS W
Bellevue U, NE W(s)
Beloit Coll, WI W
Bemidji State U, MN W(s)
Benedictine Coll, KS W(s)
Benedictine U, IL W
Bethany Coll, KS W(s)
Bethany Lutheran Coll, MN W(s)
Bethel Coll, IN W(s)
Bethel Coll, KS W(s)
Bethel Coll, MN M, W
Blackburn Coll, IL W
Black Hills State U, SD W(s)
Blessing-Rieman Coll of Nursing, IL M(s), W(s)
Bluffton Coll, OH W
Bowling Green State U, OH M, W(s)
Bradley U, IL W(s)
Briar Cliff U, IA W(s)
Buena Vista U, IA W
Butler U, IN W(s)
Calumet Coll of Saint Joseph, IN M, W
Calvin Coll, MI M, W
Cameron U, OK W(s)
Capital U, OH W
Cardinal Stritch U, WI M, W
Carleton Coll, MN M, W
Carroll Coll, WI W
Carthage Coll, WI W
Case Western Reserve U, OH M, W
Cedarville U, OH W(s)
Central Bible Coll, MO W
Central Christian Coll of Kansas, KS W(s)
Central Coll, IA W
Central Methodist Coll, MO W(s)
Central Michigan U, MI W(s)
Central Missouri State U, MO W(s)
Chadron State Coll, NE W(s)
Chicago State U, IL W(s)
Cincinnati Bible Coll and Seminary, OH W
Circleville Bible Coll, OH W
Clarke Coll, IA M, W
Cleveland State U, OH W(s)
Coe Coll, IA W
Coll of Mount St. Joseph, OH W
Coll of Saint Benedict, MN W
Coll of St. Catherine, MN W
Coll of Saint Mary, NE W(s)
The Coll of St. Scholastica, MN W
Coll of the Ozarks, MO W(s)
The Coll of Wooster, OH M, W
Columbia Coll, MO W(s)
Concordia Coll, MN M, W
Concordia U, IL W
Concordia U, MI W(s)
Concordia U, MN W(s)
Concordia U, NE W(s)
Concordia U Wisconsin, WI W
Cornell Coll, IA M, W
Cornerstone U, MI W(s)
Cottey Coll, MO W
Creighton U, NE W(s)
Crossroads Coll, MN M, W
Crown Coll, MN W
Culver-Stockton Coll, MO W(s)
Dakota State U, SD W(s)
Dakota Wesleyan U, SD W(s)
Dana Coll, NE W(s)
Defiance Coll, OH W
Denison U, OH W
DePaul U, IL W(s)
DePauw U, IN W
Dickinson State U, ND W(s)
Doane Coll, NE W(s)
Dominican U, IL W
Dordt Coll, IA W(s)
Drake U, IA W(s)
Drury U, MO W(s)
Earlham Coll, IN M, W
Eastern Illinois U, IL W(s)
Eastern Michigan U, MI W(s)
Edgewood Coll, WI W
Elmhurst Coll, IL W
Emporia State U, KS W(s)
Eureka Coll, IL W
Evangel U, MO W(s)
Faith Baptist Bible Coll and Theological Seminary, IA W
Ferris State U, MI W(s)
Finlandia U, MI W
Fontbonne U, MO W
Fort Hays State U, KS W(s)
The Franciscan U, IA W(s)
Franklin Coll, IN W
Goshen Coll, IN W(s)
Grace Bible Coll, MI W
Grace Coll, IN W(s)
Graceland U, IA M(s), W(s)
Grace U, NE W
Grand Valley State U, MI M, W(s)
Grand View Coll, IA W(s)
Great Lakes Christian Coll, MI W
Greenville Coll, IL M, W
Grinnell Coll, IA W
Gustavus Adolphus Coll, MN M, W
Hamline U, MN W
Hannibal-LaGrange Coll, MO W(s)
Hanover Coll, IN W
Harris-Stowe State Coll, MO W(s)
Haskell Indian Nations U, KS W
Hastings Coll, NE W(s)
Heidelberg Coll, OH W
Hesston Coll, KS W(s)
Hillsdale Coll, MI W(s)
Hiram Coll, OH W
Hope Coll, MI M, W
Huntington Coll, IN W(s)
Illinois Coll, IL W
Illinois Inst of Technology, IL W(s)
Illinois State U, IL W(s)
Illinois Wesleyan U, IL W
Indiana State U, IN M, W(s)
Indiana U Bloomington, IN W(s)
Indiana U–Purdue U Fort Wayne, IN M(s), W(s)
Indiana U–Purdue U Indianapolis, IN W(s)
Indiana U South Bend, IN M, W
Indiana U Southeast, IN W(s)
Indiana Wesleyan U, IN W(s)
Iowa State U of Science and Technology, IA W(s)
Iowa Wesleyan Coll, IA W(s)
Jamestown Coll, ND W(s)
John Carroll U, OH M, W
Judson Coll, IL W(s)
Kalamazoo Coll, MI W
Kansas State U, KS W(s)
Kendall Coll, IL M, W
Kent State U, OH W(s)
Kenyon Coll, OH W
Kettering U, MI M
Knox Coll, IL W
Lake Erie Coll, OH W
Lake Forest Coll, IL M, W
Lakeland Coll, WI M, W
Lawrence U, WI M, W
Lewis U, IL M(s), W(s)
Lincoln Christian Coll, IL W
Lincoln Coll, Lincoln, IL W(s)
Lincoln Coll, Normal, IL W
Lindenwood U, MO M(s), W(s)
Loras Coll, IA M, W
Loyola U Chicago, IL M(s), W(s)
Luther Coll, IA W
Macalester Coll, MN M, W
MacMurray Coll, IL W
Madonna U, MI W(s)
Malone Coll, OH W(s)
Manchester Coll, IN W
Manhattan Christian Coll, KS W
Maranatha Baptist Bible Coll, WI W
Marian Coll, IN W(s)
Marian Coll of Fond du Lac, WI W
Marietta Coll, OH W
Marquette U, WI M, W(s)
Martin Luther Coll, MN W
Maryville U of Saint Louis, MO W
Mayville State U, ND W(s)
McKendree Coll, IL W(s)
McPherson Coll, KS W
Messenger Coll, MO W
Miami U, OH M, W(s)
Miami U–Hamilton Campus, OH W
Miami U–Middletown Campus, OH W
Michigan State U, MI W(s)
Michigan Technological U, MI W(s)
MidAmerica Nazarene U, KS W(s)
Midland Lutheran Coll, NE W(s)
Millikin U, IL W
Milwaukee School of Engineering, WI M, W
Minnesota State U, Mankato, MN W(s)
Minnesota State U, Moorhead, MN W(s)

Volleyball (continued)

Minot State U, ND	W(s)
Missouri Southern State Coll, MO	W(s)
Missouri Valley Coll, MO	M(s), W(s)
Missouri Western State Coll, MO	W(s)
Monmouth Coll, IL	W
Moody Bible Inst, IL	M, W
Mount Marty Coll, SD	W(s)
Mount Mary Coll, WI	W
Mount Mercy Coll, IA	W
Mount Union Coll, OH	W
Mount Vernon Nazarene U, OH	W(s)
Muskingum Coll, OH	W
National American U, SD	W(s)
Nebraska Christian Coll, NE	W
Nebraska Wesleyan U, NE	W
Newman U, KS	M(s), W(s)
North Central Coll, IL	W
North Dakota State U, ND	M, W(s)
Northern Illinois U, IL	W(s)
Northern Michigan U, MI	W(s)
Northern State U, SD	W(s)
Northland Coll, WI	W
North Park U, IL	M, W
Northwestern Coll, IA	W(s)
Northwestern Coll, MN	W
Northwestern U, IL	W(s)
Northwest Missouri State U, MO	W(s)
Northwood U, MI	W(s)
Notre Dame Coll, OH	W
Oak Hills Christian Coll, MN	W
Oakland City U, IN	W(s)
Oakland U, MI	W(s)
Oberlin Coll, OH	M, W
Ohio Dominican U, OH	W(s)
Ohio Northern U, OH	W
The Ohio State U, OH	M(s), W(s)
Ohio U, OH	M, W(s)
Ohio U–Chillicothe, OH	W
Ohio U–Lancaster, OH	W
Ohio U–Zanesville, OH	W
Ohio Wesleyan U, OH	M, W
Oklahoma Wesleyan U, OK	W(s)
Olivet Coll, MI	W
Olivet Nazarene U, IL	W(s)
Oral Roberts U, OK	W(s)
Ottawa U, KS	W(s)
Otterbein Coll, OH	W
Ozark Christian Coll, MO	W
Park U, MO	M(s), W(s)
Peru State Coll, NE	W(s)
Pillsbury Baptist Bible Coll, MN	W
Pittsburg State U, KS	W(s)
Presentation Coll, SD	W
Principia Coll, IL	W
Purdue U, IN	M, W(s)
Quincy U, IL	M(s), W(s)
Research Coll of Nursing, MO	W(s)
Ripon Coll, WI	W
Robert Morris Coll, IL	W(s)
Rochester Coll, MI	W(s)
Rochester Comm and Tech Coll, MN	W
Rockford Coll, IL	M, W
Rockhurst U, MO	W(s)
Rose-Hulman Inst of Technology, IN	W
Saginaw Valley State U, MI	W(s)
St. Ambrose U, IA	M(s), W(s)
St. Cloud State U, MN	M, W(s)
Saint John's U, MN	M
Saint Joseph's Coll, IN	W(s)
St. Louis Christian Coll, MO	W
St. Louis Coll of Pharmacy, MO	W
Saint Louis U, MO	M, W(s)
Saint Mary's Coll, IN	W
Saint Mary's U of Minnesota, MN	W
Saint Mary U, KS	W(s)
St. Norbert Coll, WI	W
St. Olaf Coll, MN	W
Saint Xavier U, IL	W(s)
Shawnee State U, OH	W
Siena Heights U, MI	W(s)
Simpson Coll, IA	W
Si Tanka Huron U, SD	W(s)
South Dakota School of Mines and Technology, SD	W(s)
South Dakota State U, SD	W(s)
Southeastern Oklahoma State U, OK	W(s)
Southeast Missouri State U, MO	W(s)
Southern Illinois U Carbondale, IL	W(s)
Southern Illinois U Edwardsville, IL	W(s)
Southern Nazarene U, OK	W(s)
Southwest Baptist U, MO	W(s)
Southwestern Coll, KS	W(s)
Southwest Minnesota State U, MN	W(s)
Southwest Missouri State U, MO	M, W(s)
Spring Arbor U, MI	W(s)
Springfield Coll in Illinois, IL	W(s)
Stephens Coll, MO	W
Sterling Coll, KS	W(s)
Tabor Coll, KS	W(s)
Taylor U, IN	M, W(s)
Taylor U, Fort Wayne Campus, IN	W
Tiffin U, OH	W(s)
Trinity Bible Coll, ND	W
Trinity Christian Coll, IL	M(s), W(s)
Trinity International U, IL	M(s), W(s)
Tri-State U, IN	W
Truman State U, MO	M, W(s)
The U of Akron, OH	W(s)
U of Central Oklahoma, OK	W(s)
U of Chicago, IL	W
U of Cincinnati, OH	W(s)
U of Dayton, OH	W(s)
U of Dubuque, IA	W
U of Evansville, IN	W(s)
The U of Findlay, OH	M(s), W(s)
U of Illinois at Chicago, IL	W(s)
U of Illinois at Springfield, IL	W(s)
U of Illinois at Urbana–Champaign, IL	W(s)
U of Indianapolis, IN	W(s)
The U of Iowa, IA	M, W(s)
U of Kansas, KS	W(s)
U of Mary, ND	W(s)
U of Michigan, MI	W(s)
U of Michigan–Dearborn, MI	W(s)
U of Minnesota, Crookston, MN	W(s)
U of Minnesota, Duluth, MN	M, W(s)
U of Minnesota, Morris, MN	W(s)
U of Minnesota, Twin Cities Campus, MN	W(s)
U of Missouri–Columbia, MO	W(s)
U of Missouri–Kansas City, MO	W(s)
U of Missouri–St. Louis, MO	W(s)
U of Nebraska at Kearney, NE	W(s)
U of Nebraska at Omaha, NE	W(s)
U of Nebraska–Lincoln, NE	W(s)
U of North Dakota, ND	W(s)
U of Northern Iowa, IA	W(s)
U of Notre Dame, IN	W(s)
U of Oklahoma, OK	W(s)
U of Rio Grande, OH	W(s)
U of St. Francis, IL	W(s)
U of Saint Francis, IN	W(s)
U of St. Thomas, MN	W
U of Sioux Falls, SD	W(s)
The U of South Dakota, SD	W(s)
U of Southern Indiana, IN	W(s)
U of Toledo, OH	W(s)
U of Tulsa, OK	W(s)
U of Wisconsin–Eau Claire, WI	W
U of Wisconsin–Green Bay, WI	W(s)
U of Wisconsin–La Crosse, WI	W
U of Wisconsin–Madison, WI	W(s)
U of Wisconsin–Milwaukee, WI	M, W(s)
U of Wisconsin–Oshkosh, WI	W
U of Wisconsin–Parkside, WI	W(s)
U of Wisconsin–Platteville, WI	M, W
U of Wisconsin–River Falls, WI	M, W
U of Wisconsin–Stevens Point, WI	W
U of Wisconsin–Stout, WI	M, W
U of Wisconsin–Superior, WI	W
U of Wisconsin–Whitewater, WI	M, W
Upper Iowa U, IA	W
Urbana U, OH	W(s)
Ursuline Coll, OH	W(s)
Valley City State U, ND	W(s)
Valparaiso U, IN	W(s)
Vennard Coll, IA	W
Viterbo U, WI	W(s)
Waldorf Coll, IA	W(s)
Walsh U, OH	W(s)
Wartburg Coll, IA	W
Washington U in St. Louis, MO	M, W
Wayne State Coll, NE	W(s)
Wayne State U, MI	W(s)
Webster U, MO	W
Western Illinois U, IL	W(s)
Western Michigan U, MI	W(s)
Westminster Coll, MO	W
Wheaton Coll, IL	M, W
Wichita State U, KS	M, W(s)
Wilberforce U, OH	W
William Jewell Coll, MO	W(s)
William Penn U, IA	W(s)
William Woods U, MO	M(s), W(s)
Wilmington Coll, OH	W
Winona State U, MN	M, W(s)
Wisconsin Lutheran Coll, WI	M, W
Wittenberg U, OH	M, W
Wright State U, OH	W(s)
Xavier U, OH	M, W(s)
Youngstown State U, OH	W(s)

WATER POLO

Ball State U, IN	M
Bowling Green State U, OH	M, W
Carleton Coll, MN	M, W
Hope Coll, MI	M, W
Indiana U Bloomington, IN	W(s)
Lake Forest Coll, IL	M
Macalester Coll, MN	M, W
Michigan Technological U, MI	M, W
Oberlin Coll, OH	M, W
Ohio U, OH	M, W
Purdue U, IN	M, W
Saint John's U, MN	M
Saint Mary's Coll, IN	W
The U of Findlay, OH	M, W
U of Michigan, MI	W
Wabash Coll, IN	M
Washington U in St. Louis, MO	M, W

WEIGHT LIFTING

Bowling Green State U, OH	M, W
Ohio U, OH	M
Purdue U, IN	M, W
U of Minnesota, Duluth, MN	M, W
U of Wisconsin–River Falls, WI	M, W
U of Wisconsin–Whitewater, WI	M

WRESTLING

Ashland U, OH	M(s)
Augsburg Coll, MN	M
Augustana Coll, IL	M
Augustana Coll, SD	M(s)
Bacone Coll, OK	M(s)
Baldwin-Wallace Coll, OH	M
Ball State U, IN	M
Bethel Coll, IN	M(s)
Briar Cliff U, IA	M(s)

Buena Vista U, IA M
Capital U, OH M
Carleton Coll, MN M
Case Western Reserve U, OH M
Central Coll, IA M
Central Michigan U, MI M(s)
Central Missouri State U, MO M(s)
Chadron State Coll, NE M(s)
Cleveland State U, OH M(s)
Coe Coll, IA M
Coll of Mount St. Joseph, OH M
Concordia Coll, MN M
Concordia U Wisconsin, WI M
Cornell Coll, IA M
Dakota Wesleyan U, SD M(s)
Dana Coll, NE M(s)
Dickinson State U, ND M(s)
Eastern Illinois U, IL M(s)
Eastern Michigan U, MI M(s)
Elmhurst Coll, IL M
Fort Hays State U, KS M(s)
Grand Valley State U, MI M
Heidelberg Coll, OH M
Illinois Coll, IL M
Indiana U Bloomington, IN M(s)
Iowa State U of Science and Technology, IA M(s)
Jamestown Coll, ND M(s)
John Carroll U, OH M
Kent State U, OH M(s)
Knox Coll, IL M
Lakeland Coll, WI M
Lawrence U, WI M
Lincoln Coll, Lincoln, IL M(s)
Lincoln Coll, Normal, IL M
Lindenwood U, MO M(s)
Loras Coll, IA M
Luther Coll, IA M
MacMurray Coll, IL M
Manchester Coll, IN M
Maranatha Baptist Bible Coll, WI M
McKendree Coll, IL M(s)
Miami U, OH M
Michigan State U, MI M(s)
Millikin U, IL M
Milwaukee School of Engineering, WI M
Minnesota State U, Mankato, MN M(s)
Minnesota State U, Moorhead, MN M(s)
Missouri Valley Coll, MO M(s), W(s)
Mount Union Coll, OH M
Muskingum Coll, OH M
North Central Coll, IL M
North Dakota State U, ND M(s)
Northern Illinois U, IL M(s)
Northern State U, SD M(s)
Northwestern Coll, IA M(s)
Northwestern U, IL M(s)
Ohio Northern U, OH M
The Ohio State U, OH M(s)
Ohio U, OH M(s)
Oklahoma State U, OK M(s)
Olivet Coll, MI M
Purdue U, IN M(s)
Ripon Coll, WI M, W
Rochester Comm and Tech Coll, MN M
Rose-Hulman Inst of Technology, IN M
St. Cloud State U, MN M(s)
Saint John's U, MN M
St. Olaf Coll, MN M
Simpson Coll, IA M
Si Tanka Huron U, SD M(s)
South Dakota State U, SD M(s)
Southern Illinois U Edwardsville, IL M(s)
Southwest Minnesota State U, MN M(s)
Southwest Missouri State U, MO M
Trinity Bible Coll, ND M
Truman State U, MO M(s)
U of Central Oklahoma, OK M(s)
U of Chicago, IL M
U of Dubuque, IA M
The U of Findlay, OH M(s)
U of Illinois at Urbana–Champaign, IL M(s)
U of Indianapolis, IN M(s)
The U of Iowa, IA M(s)
U of Mary, ND M(s)
U of Michigan, MI M(s)
U of Minnesota, Morris, MN M(s), W
U of Minnesota, Twin Cities Campus, MN M(s)
U of Missouri–Columbia, MO M(s)
U of Nebraska at Kearney, NE M(s)
U of Nebraska at Omaha, NE M(s)
U of Nebraska–Lincoln, NE M(s)
U of Northern Iowa, IA M(s)
U of Oklahoma, OK M(s)
U of Wisconsin–Eau Claire, WI M
U of Wisconsin–La Crosse, WI M
U of Wisconsin–Madison, WI M(s)
U of Wisconsin–Oshkosh, WI M
U of Wisconsin–Parkside, WI M(s)
U of Wisconsin–Platteville, WI M
U of Wisconsin–Stevens Point, WI M
U of Wisconsin–Whitewater, WI M, W
Upper Iowa U, IA M
Wabash Coll, IN M
Waldorf Coll, IA M(s)
Wartburg Coll, IA M
Wentworth Military Academy and Jr Coll, MO M
Wheaton Coll, IL M
Wichita State U, KS M
William Penn U, IA M(s)
Wilmington Coll, OH M
Winona State U, MN M
Xavier U, OH M

ROTC Programs

A—Army; N—Navy; AF—Air Force; (c)—available through a cooperating host institution

Allen Coll, IA	A(c)
Alma Coll, MI	A(c)
Alverno Coll, WI	A(c), AF(c)
Augsburg Coll, MN	A(c), N(c), AF(c)
Aurora U, IL	A(c)
Avila U, MO	A(c)
Baker U, KS	A(c), AF(c)
Baldwin-Wallace Coll, OH	A(c), AF(c)
Ball State U, IN	A
Baptist Bible Coll, MO	A(c)
Bellevue U, NE	A(c), AF(c)
Bellin Coll of Nursing, WI	A(c)
Benedictine Coll, KS	A
Benedictine U, IL	A(c)
Bethany Lutheran Coll, MN	A(c)
Bethel Coll, IN	A(c), AF(c)
Bethel Coll, MN	A(c), AF(c)
Black Hills State U, SD	A
Bowling Green State U, OH	A, AF
Bradley U, IL	A
Butler U, IN	A(c), AF(c)
Calvin Coll, MI	A(c)
Cameron U, OK	A
Capital U, OH	A, AF(c)
Carroll Coll, WI	AF(c)
Carthage Coll, WI	A(c), AF(c)
Case Western Reserve U, OH	A(c), AF(c)
Cedarville U, OH	A(c), AF(c)
Central Methodist Coll, MO	A(c), AF(c)
Central Michigan U, MI	A
Central Missouri State U, MO	A, AF(c)
Chicago State U, IL	A, N(c), AF(c)
Clarkson Coll, NE	A(c), AF(c)
Cleveland Inst of Music, OH	A(c), AF(c)
Cleveland State U, OH	A(c), AF(c)
Coe Coll, IA	A(c), AF(c)
Coll of Mount St. Joseph, OH	A(c), AF(c)
Coll of Saint Benedict, MN	A(c)
Coll of St. Catherine, MN	AF(c)
Coll of Saint Mary, NE	A(c), AF(c)
The Coll of St. Scholastica, MN	AF(c)
Coll of the Ozarks, MO	A
Colorado Tech U Sioux Falls Campus, SD	A(c)
Columbia Coll, MO	A(c), N(c), AF(c)
Concordia Coll, MN	A(c), AF(c)
Concordia U, MI	A(c), AF(c)
Concordia U, MN	A(c), AF(c)
Concordia U, NE	A(c), AF(c)
Cornerstone U, MI	A(c)
Creighton U, NE	A, AF(c)
Dakota State U, SD	AF(c)
Dana Coll, NE	A(c), AF(c)
Davenport U, Lansing, MI	A(c)
Deaconess Coll of Nursing, MO	A(c)
Denison U, OH	A(c)
DePaul U, IL	A
DePauw U, IN	A(c), AF(c)
DeVry U, OH	A(c)
Doane Coll, NE	A(c), AF(c)
Drake U, IA	A, AF(c)
Drury U, MO	A(c)
Eastern Illinois U, IL	A
Eastern Michigan U, MI	A, N(c), AF(c)
Elmhurst Coll, IL	A(c), AF(c)
[illegible]ngel U, MO	A
[illegible] State U, MI	A(c)
[illegible]a U, MI	A(c), AF(c)
[illegible] U, MO	A(c)
[illegible], IN	A(c)
Franklin U, OH	A(c), AF(c)
Governors State U, IL	A(c), AF(c)
Grace U, NE	A(c), AF(c)
Grand View Coll, IA	A(c), AF(c)
Gustavus Adolphus Coll, MN	A(c)
Hamline U, MN	AF(c)
Harris-Stowe State Coll, MO	AF(c)
Haskell Indian Nations U, KS	AF(c)
Heidelberg Coll, OH	A(c), AF(c)
Holy Cross Coll, IN	A(c), AF(c)
Illinois Inst of Technology, IL	A, N, AF
Illinois State U, IL	A
Illinois Wesleyan U, IL	A(c)
Indiana State U, IN	A, AF
Indiana U Bloomington, IN	A, AF
Indiana U Kokomo, IN	A(c)
Indiana U Northwest, IN	A
Indiana U–Purdue U Indianapolis, IN	A, N(c), AF(c)
Indiana U South Bend, IN	A(c), N(c), AF(c)
Indiana U Southeast, IN	A(c), AF(c)
Iowa State U of Science and Technology, IA	A, N, AF
John Carroll U, OH	A
Kalamazoo Coll, MI	A(c)
Kansas State U, KS	A, AF
Kent State U, OH	A, AF
Kent State U, Ashtabula Campus, OH	A(c)
Kent State U, Geauga Campus, OH	A(c), AF(c)
Kent State U, Salem Campus, OH	A(c), AF(c)
Kent State U, Stark Campus, OH	A(c), AF(c)
Kent State U, Tuscarawas Campus, OH	A(c), AF(c)
Langston U, OK	A(c)
Lawrence Technological U, MI	A(c), AF(c)
Lewis U, IL	A(c), AF(c)
Lindenwood U, MO	A, AF(c)
Lourdes Coll, OH	A(c)
Loyola U Chicago, IL	A(c), N(c)
Macalester Coll, MN	N(c), AF(c)
Malone Coll, OH	A(c), AF(c)
Manhattan Christian Coll, KS	A(c), AF(c)
Maranatha Baptist Bible Coll, WI	AF(c)
Marian Coll, IN	A(c)
Marian Coll of Fond du Lac, WI	A
Marquette U, WI	A, N, AF
Maryville U of Saint Louis, MO	A(c)
Mayville State U, ND	AF(c)
McKendree Coll, IL	A(c), AF(c)
Miami U, OH	A(c), N, AF
Miami U–Hamilton Campus, OH	N(c), AF(c)
Miami U–Middletown Campus, OH	AF(c)
Michigan State U, MI	A, AF
Michigan Technological U, MI	A, AF
MidAmerica Nazarene U, KS	A(c), AF(c)
Milwaukee School of Engineering, WI	A(c), N(c), AF(c)
Minnesota State U, Mankato, MN	A
Minnesota State U, Moorhead, MN	A(c), AF(c)
Missouri Valley Coll, MO	A(c)
Missouri Western State Coll, MO	A
Monmouth Coll, IL	A(c)
Mount Marty Coll, SD	A(c)
Mount Mary Coll, WI	A(c)
Mount Union Coll, OH	A(c), AF(c)
National American U, SD	A(c)
Nebraska Methodist Coll, NE	A(c)
Nebraska Wesleyan U, NE	A(c), AF(c)
North Central Coll, IL	A(c), AF(c)
North Dakota State U, ND	A, AF
Northeastern Illinois U, IL	A(c), AF(c)
Northeastern State U, OK	A
Northern Illinois U, IL	A, AF(c)
Northern Michigan U, MI	A
Northwestern Coll, MN	A(c), AF(c)
Northwestern U, IL	A(c), N, AF(c)
Northwest Missouri State U, MO	A
Oakland U, MI	AF(c)
Ohio Dominican U, OH	A(c)
Ohio Northern U, OH	A(c), AF(c)
The Ohio State U, OH	A, AF
The Ohio State U at Lima, OH	A(c), N(c), AF(c)
Ohio U, OH	A, AF
Ohio U–Chillicothe, OH	A(c), AF(c)
Ohio U–Lancaster, OH	A(c), AF(c)
Ohio Wesleyan U, OH	A(c)
Oklahoma Baptist U, OK	AF(c)
Oklahoma Christian U, OK	A(c), AF(c)
Oklahoma City U, OK	A(c), AF(c)
Oklahoma State U, OK	A, AF
Olivet Nazarene U, IL	A
Oral Roberts U, OK	AF(c)
Otterbein Coll, OH	A(c), AF(c)
Park U, MO	A
Pittsburg State U, KS	A
Purdue U, IN	A, N, AF
Purdue U Calumet, IN	A(c)
Research Coll of Nursing, MO	A(c)
Ripon Coll, WI	A
Rockford Coll, IL	A(c)
Rockhurst U, MO	A(c)
Rogers State U, OK	AF(c)
Rose-Hulman Inst of Technology, IN	A, AF
St. Cloud State U, MN	A
St. Gregory's U, OK	A(c), N(c), AF(c)
Saint John's U, MN	A
St. Louis Coll of Pharmacy, MO	A(c), AF(c)
Saint Louis U, MO	A(c), AF
Saint Mary-of-the-Woods Coll, IN	A(c), AF(c)
Saint Mary's Coll, IN	A(c), N(c), AF(c)
Saint Mary U, KS	A(c)
St. Norbert Coll, WI	A(c)
Saint Xavier U, IL	AF(c)
South Dakota School of Mines and Technology, SD	A
South Dakota State U, SD	A, AF
Southeast Missouri State U, MO	AF
Southern Illinois U Carbondale, IL	A, AF
Southern Illinois U Edwardsville, IL	A, AF
Southern Nazarene U, OK	A(c), AF(c)
Southwest Baptist U, MO	A(c)
Southwest Missouri State U, MO	A
Stephens Coll, MO	A(c), AF(c)

Institution	Programs
Tiffin U, OH	A(c), AF(c)
Truman State U, MO	A
The U of Akron, OH	A, AF
U of Central Oklahoma, OK	A
U of Chicago, IL	A(c), AF(c)
U of Cincinnati, OH	A, AF
U of Dayton, OH	A, AF(c)
U of Dubuque, IA	A
The U of Findlay, OH	A(c), AF(c)
U of Illinois at Chicago, IL	A, N(c), AF(c)
U of Illinois at Urbana–Champaign, IL	A, AF
U of Indianapolis, IN	A(c)
The U of Iowa, IA	A, AF
U of Kansas, KS	A, N, AF
U of Michigan, MI	A, AF
U of Michigan–Dearborn, MI	A(c), N(c), AF(c)
U of Minnesota, Crookston, MN	AF(c)
U of Minnesota, Duluth, MN	AF
U of Minnesota, Twin Cities Campus, MN	A, N, AF
U of Missouri–Columbia, MO	A, N, AF
U of Missouri–Kansas City, MO	A
U of Missouri–Rolla, MO	A, AF
U of Missouri–St. Louis, MO	A(c), AF(c)
U of Nebraska at Omaha, NE	A(c), AF
U of Nebraska–Lincoln, NE	A, N, AF
U of Nebraska Medical Center, NE	A(c), AF(c)
U of North Dakota, ND	A, AF
U of Northern Iowa, IA	A
U of Notre Dame, IN	A, N, AF
U of Oklahoma, OK	A, AF
U of Oklahoma Health Sciences Center, OK	A(c), AF(c)
U of Rio Grande, OH	A(c)
U of St. Thomas, MN	A(c), N(c), AF
The U of South Dakota, SD	A
U of Southern Indiana, IN	A
U of Toledo, OH	A, AF(c)
U of Tulsa, OK	AF(c)
U of Wisconsin–Green Bay, WI	A
U of Wisconsin–La Crosse, WI	A
U of Wisconsin–Madison, WI	A
U of Wisconsin–Oshkosh, WI	A
U of Wisconsin–Parkside, WI	A(c)
U of Wisconsin–Stevens Point, WI	A
U of Wisconsin–Superior, WI	AF(c)
U of Wisconsin–Whitewater, WI	A, AF
Valparaiso U, IN	AF
Viterbo U, WI	A(c)
Wabash Coll, IN	A(c)
Washington U in St. Louis, MO	A, AF(c)
Wayne State Coll, NE	A(c)
Wayne State U, MI	AF(c)
Webster U, MO	A(c), AF(c)
Wentworth Military Academy and Jr Coll, MO	A
Western Illinois U, IL	A
Western Michigan U, MI	A
Westminster Coll, MO	A(c), AF(c)
Wheaton Coll, IL	A, AF(c)
Wilberforce U, OH	A(c), AF(c)
William Woods U, MO	A(c), N(c), AF(c)
Winona State U, MN	A(c)
Wisconsin Lutheran Coll, WI	A(c), N(c), AF(c)
Wittenberg U, OH	A(c), AF(c)
Wright State U, OH	A, AF
Xavier U, OH	A, AF(c)
York Coll, NE	A(c), N(c), AF(c)
Youngstown State U, OH	A, AF(c)

Alphabetical Listing of Colleges and Universities

The page numbers for the college profiles are printed in regular type, italic if there is a special message, and bold for in-depth descriptions.

Alphabetical Listing of Colleges and Universities

Alphabetical Listing of Colleges and Universities

Alphabetical Listing of Colleges and Universities

Notes

THOMSON
PETERSON'S

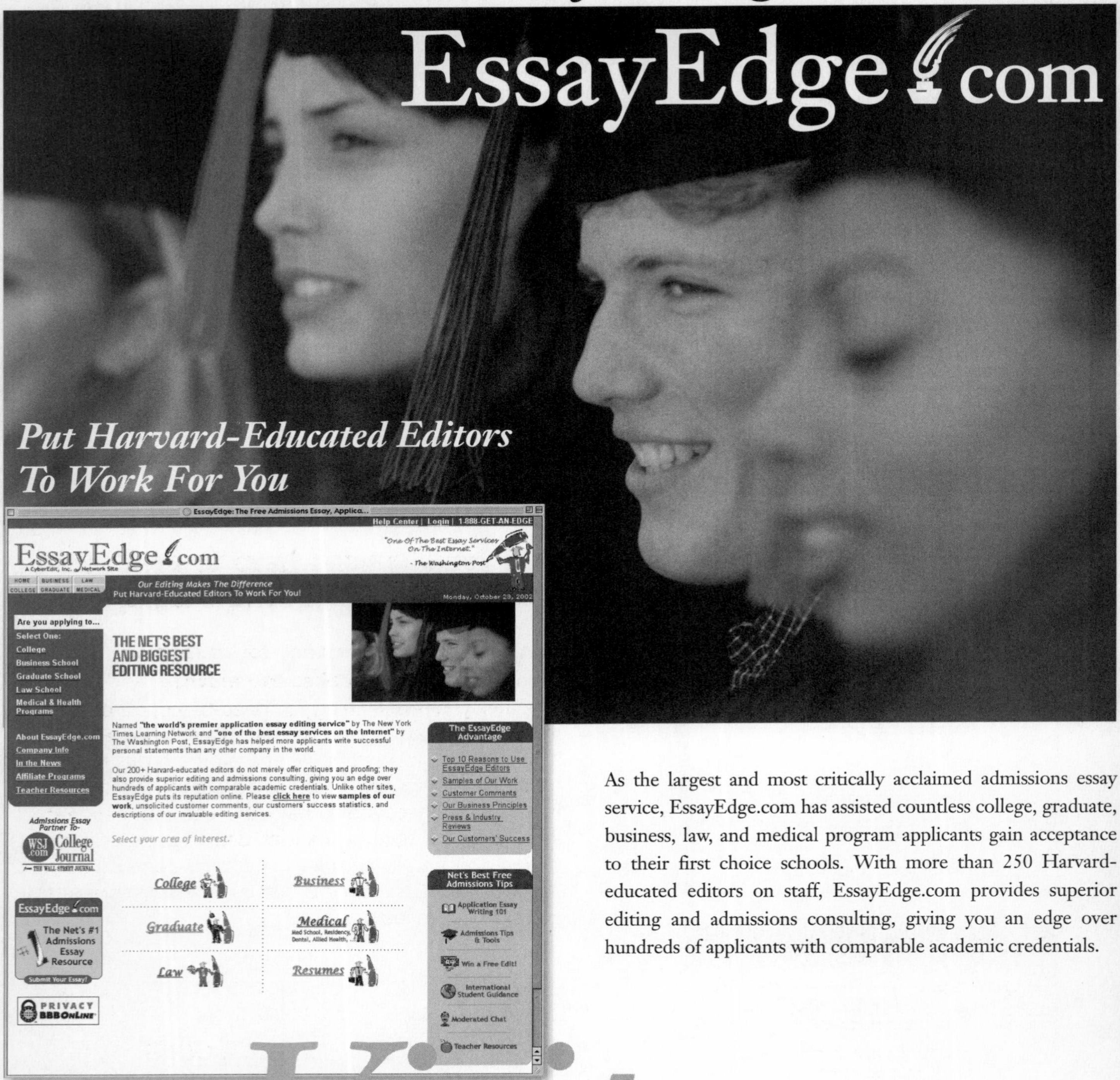